Keeping the Republic

Power and Citizenship in American Politics

Keeping the Republic

Power and Citizenship in American Politics

5th Edition

Christine Barbour, Indiana University

Gerald C. Wright, Indiana University

CQ PRESS

A Division of SAGE
Washington, D.C.

CQ Press
2300 N Street, NW, Suite 800
Washington, DC 20037

Phone: 202-729-1900; toll-free, 1-866-4CQ-PRESS (1-866-427-7737)

Web: www.cqpress.com

Cover and interior design: TODA The Office of Design and Architecture
Photos: Illustration credits can be found on page C-1.
Composition: C&M Digitals (P) Ltd.

♾ The paper used in this publication exceeds the requirements of the American National Standard for Information Sciences—Permanence of Paper for Printed Library Materials, ANSI Z39.48-1992.

Printed and bound in Canada

15   14   13   12   11   1   2   3   4   5

Library of Congress Cataloging-in-Publication Data

Barbour, Christine
    Keeping the republic : power and citizenship in American politics / Christine Barbour, Gerald C. Wright. — 5th ed.
        p. cm.
    Includes bibliographical references and index.
    ISBN 978-1-60871-272-4 (alk. paper)
    1. United States—Politics and government. I. Wright, Gerald C. II. Title.

JK276.B37 2012
320.473—dc22   2010052220

We dedicate this book with love to our parents, Patti Barbour and John Barbour and

Doris and Gerry Wright,

To our kids, Andrea and Darrin, Monica and Michael,

To our grandkids, Amelia, Elena, Paloma, and Asher

And to each other.

About the Authors

Authors Christine Barbour (center) and Gerald Wright (right) and *KTR* contributor Patrick Haney (second left) meet with Vice President Joe Biden for a *Profiles in Citizenship* interview. *Official White House Photo by David Lienemann.*

Christine Barbour

Christine Barbour teaches in the Political Science Department and the Honors College at Indiana University, where she has become increasingly interested in how teachers of large classes can maximize what their students learn. At Indiana, Professor Barbour has been a Lilly Fellow, working on a project to increase student retention in large introductory courses, and a member of the Freshman Learning Project, a university-wide effort to improve the first-year undergraduate experience. She has served on the *New York Times* College Advisory Board, working with other educators to develop ways to integrate newspaper reading into the undergraduate curriculum. She has won several teaching honors, but the two awarded by her students mean the most to her: the Indiana University Student Alumni Association Award for Outstanding Faculty (1995–1996) and the Indiana University Chapter of the Society of Professional Journalists Brown Derby Award (1997). When not teaching or writing textbooks, Professor Barbour enjoys playing with her dogs, traveling with her coauthor, and writing about food. She is the food editor for *Bloom Magazine* of Bloomington and is a coauthor of *Indiana Cooks!* (2005) and *Home Grown Indiana* (2008). She is currently working on another cookbook and a book about local politics, development, and the fishing industry in Apalachicola, Florida.

Gerald C. Wright

Gerald C. Wright has taught political science at Indiana University since 1981. An accomplished scholar of American politics, his books include *Statehouse Democracy: Public Opinion and Policy in the American States* (1993), coauthored with Robert S. Erikson and John P. McIver, and he has published more than fifty articles on elections, public opinion, and state politics. Professor Wright has long studied the relationship among citizens, their preferences, and public policy. He is currently conducting research with grants from the National Science Foundation and the Russell Sage Foundation on the factors that influence the equality of policy representation in the states and in Congress. He is also writing a book about representation in U.S. legislatures. He has been a consultant for Project Vote Smart in the last several elections. Professor Wright is a member of Indiana University's Freshman Learning Project, a university-wide effort to improve the first-year undergraduate experience by focusing on how today's college students learn and how teachers can adapt their pedagogical methods to best teach them. In his nonworking hours, Professor Wright also likes to spend time with his dogs, travel, eat good food, and play golf.

Brief Contents

Contents

Ch 3 — Politics of the American Founding 65

Federalism and the U.S. Constitution   97

 Ch 6

The Struggle for Equal Rights   187

Ch 10   The American Legal System and the Courts   367

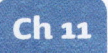 **Ch 11**   Public Opinion   405

Ch 14

Voting, Campaigns, and Elections   515

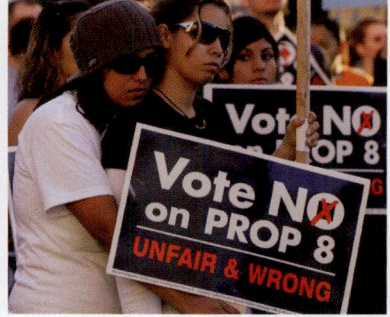

Ch 15 — The Media — 555

When one of us was a freshman journalism major in college, more years ago now than she cares to remember, she took an introduction to American politics course—mostly because the other courses she wanted were already full. But the class was a revelation. The teacher was terrific, the textbook provocative, and the final paper assignment an eye opener. "As Benjamin Franklin was leaving Independence Hall," the assignment read, "he was stopped by a woman who asked, 'What have you created?' Franklin replied, 'A Republic, Madam, if you can keep it.'" Have we succeeded in keeping our republic? Had we been given a democracy in the first place? These questions sparked the imagination, the writing of an impassioned freshman essay about the limits and possibilities of American democracy, and a lifetime love affair with politics. If we have one goal in writing this textbook, it is to share the excitement of discovering humankind's capacity to find innovative solutions to those problems that arise from our efforts to live together on a planet too small, with resources too scarce, and with saintliness in too short a supply. In this book we honor the human capacity to manage our collective lives with peace and even, at times, dignity. And, in particular, we celebrate the American political system and the founders' extraordinary contribution to the possibilities of human governance.

Where We Are Going

Between the two of us, we have been teaching American politics for way more than half a century. We have used a lot of textbooks in that time. Some of them have been too difficult for introductory students (although we have enjoyed them as political scientists!), and others have tried excessively to accommodate the beginning student and have ended up being too light in their coverage of basic information. When we had to scramble to find enough details to write reasonable exam questions, we knew that the effort to write an accessible textbook had gone too far. We wanted our students to have the best and most complete treatment of the American political system we could find, presented in a way that would catch their imagination, be easy to understand, and engage them in the system about which they were learning.

This book is the result of that desire. It covers essential topics with clear explanations, but it is also a thematic book, intended to guide students through a wealth of material and to help them make sense of the content both academically and personally. To that end we develop two themes that run throughout every chapter: an analytic theme to assist students in organizing the details and connect them to the larger ideas and concepts of American politics and an evaluative theme to help them find personal meaning in the American political system and develop standards for making judgments about how well the system works. Taken together, these themes provide students a framework on which to hang the myriad complexities of American politics.

The analytic theme we chose is a classic in political science: politics is a struggle over limited power and resources, as gripping as a sporting event in its final minutes, but much more vital. The rules guiding that struggle influence who will win and who will lose, so that often the struggles with the most at stake are over the rule making itself. In short, and in the words of a very famous political scientist, *politics is about who gets what and how they get it.* To illustrate this theme, we begin and end every chapter with a feature called *What's at Stake?* that poses a question about what people want from politics—what they are struggling to get and how the rules affect who gets it. At the end of every major chapter section, we stop to revisit Harold Laswell's definition in context and ask *Who, What, How?* This periodic analytic summary helps solidify the conceptual work of the book and gives students a sturdy framework within which to organize the facts and other empirical information we want them to learn. In addition, there is a timeline feature—*Who, What, How, and WHEN*—to show students how dramatically the winners and losers in the struggle for power can change over time.

For the evaluative theme, we focus on the "who" in the formulation of "who gets what and how." Who are the country's citizens? What are the ways they engage in political life? To "keep" a republic, citizens must shoulder responsibilities as well as exercise their rights. We challenge students to view democratic participation among the diverse population as the price of maintaining liberty.

Our citizenship theme has three dimensions. First, in our *Profiles in Citizenship* feature, present in every chapter, we introduce students to important figures in American politics and ask the subjects why they are involved in public service or some aspect of political life. Based on personal interviews with these people, the profiles model republic-keeping behavior for students, helping them to see what is expected of them as members of a democratic polity. We unabashedly feel that a primary goal of teaching introductory politics is not only to create good scholars but also to create good citizens. Second, at the end of nearly every chapter, the feature *The Citizens and . . .* provides a critical view of what citizens can or cannot do in American politics, evaluating how democratic various aspects of the American system actually are and what possibilities exist for change. Third, we premise this book on the belief that the skills that make good students and good academics are the same skills that make good citizens: the ability to think critically about and process new information and the ability to be actively engaged in one's subject. Accordingly, in our *Consider the Source* feature, we help students critically examine all the various kinds of political information they are bombarded with—from information in textbooks like this one, to information from the media or the Internet, to information from their congressional representative or political party.

How We Get There

In many ways this book follows the path of most American politics texts: there are chapters on all the subjects that instructors scramble to cover in a short amount of time. But in keeping with our goal of making the enormous amount of material here more accessible to our students, we have made some changes to the typical format. After our introductory chapter, we have included a chapter not found in every book: "American Citizens and Political Culture." Given our emphasis on citizens, this chapter is key. It covers the history and legal status of citizens and immigrants in America and the ideas and beliefs that unite us as Americans as well as the ideas that divide us politically. This chapter introduces an innovative feature called *Who Are We?* that describes through graphs and charts just who we Americans are and where we come from, what we believe, how educated we are, and how much money we make. This recurring feature aims at exploding stereotypes and providing questions to lead students to think critically about the political consequences of America's demographic profile. To guide students in understanding just what the numbers and figures mean, the *Consider the Source* feature in Chapter 2 teaches some basic skills for statistical analysis.

Another chapter that breaks with tradition is Chapter 4, "Federalism and the U.S. Constitution," which provides an analytic and comparative study of the basic rules governing this country—highlighted up front because of our emphasis on the *how* of American politics. This chapter covers the essential elements of the Constitution: federalism, the three branches, separation of powers and checks and balances, and amendability. In each case we examine the rules the founders provided, look at the alternatives they might have chosen, and ask what difference the rules make to who wins and who loses in America. This chapter is explicitly comparative. For each rule change considered, we look at a country that does things differently. We drive home early the idea that understanding the rules is crucial to understanding how and to whose advantage the system works. Throughout the text we look carefully at alternatives to our system of government as manifested in other countries—and among the fifty states.

Because of the prominence we give to rules—and to institutions—this book covers Congress, the presidency, the bureaucracy, and the courts before looking at public opinion, parties, interest groups, voting, and the media—the inputs or processes of politics that are shaped by those rules. While this approach may seem counterintuitive to instructors who have logged many miles teaching it the other way around, we have found that it is not counterintuitive to students, who have an easier time grasping the notion that the rules make a difference when they are presented with those rules in the first half of the course. We have, however, taken care to write the chapters so that they will fit into any organizational framework.

We have long believed that teaching is a two-way street, and we welcome comments, criticisms, or just a pleasant chat about politics or pedagogy. You can email us directly at barbour@indiana.edu and wright1@indiana.edu, or write to us at the Department of Political Science, Indiana University, Bloomington, IN 47405.

What's New in the Fifth Edition

Elections are almost as rough on American government textbook authors as they are on the candidates—to get books in the bookstores for the new semester we get less than a week to pull all the new information together and update our texts. In the case of 2010, that means that as we write, a couple of House races are still up in the air (which is still better than 2000, when we wrote the election update without knowing who had won the presidency). All considered, this fifth edition of *Keeping the Republic* is as current as we can make it.

The 2008 election turned some of the conventional wisdom about who gets what in American politics upside down. Americans elected an African American to the presidency and seriously entertained the idea of a woman president or vice president. Young people, traditionally nonvoters, turned out for the primaries and caucuses, and for the second time in a row they turned out in large numbers for the general election. Changing demographics and the passing of time had blurred the distinction between red states and blue states. In 2010, however, amidst a painfully slow economic recovery, politics looked more like business as usual. The president's party took a midterm beating (President Obama called it a "shellacking"—larger than but similar to what President George W. Bush described in 2006 as a "thumping"). Young people stayed home, and the electoral map was blue at the coasts and red in the center. We have updated the text throughout to reflect the current balance of power in the House and Senate and tried to put the election results into historical perspective.

And that's not all. Writing the fifth edition also gave us an opportunity to revise, improve, and update graphics and features to make them more useful and pertinent to both instructors and students. Graphs in every chapter reflect the newest data available, and the book now features nearly 360 images and cartoons, the majority of them brand new. New *What's at Stake?* vignettes examine such topics as the rise of the Tea Party, a state attorney general's effort to prosecute a professor for what he saw as fraudulent scientific research, the use of the filibuster in the Senate to stymie Obama's presidential ambitions, the role of interest groups in the passage of health care reform, the implications for elections of the *Citizens United v. Federal Election Commission* decision by the Supreme Court, the slow demise of print media in favor of electronic forms of information distribution, the conflict between Arizona's new immigration law and the federal government's responsibility for such legislation, and the implications of BP's 2010 oil spill in the Gulf for the future of domestic oil drilling (the latter two appear only in the Full edition of KTR). Two other *What's at Stakes?* have been updated to reflect the differences between the Obama and Bush administrations with respect to enforcing federal drug laws over state laws permitting the sale of medical marijuana and the use of presidential signing statements.

We also had the opportunity to add to our *Profiles in Citizenship*, interviewing Vice President Joe Biden, Sen. Jon Tester, former OMB director Peter Orszag (in Full edition only), former Bush speech writer David Frum, blogger Andrew Sullivan, data guru Nate Silver, and young Republican Meagan Szydlowski.

Supplements

We know how important good resources can be in the teaching of American government. Our goal has been to create resources that not only support but also enhance the text's themes and features. As well, the book's companion site at http://republic.cqpress.com helps students master each chapter's learning objectives, vocabulary, and conceptual information. We greatly appreciate the efforts of adopters and instructors Frank Codspoti of Lone Star College and Heidi Getchell-Bastien of Northern Essex Community College, who have updated and improved the resources that accompany our text.

For instructors:

- Our **KTRblog** will provide news postings, connecting current events to the book's themes and topics.

- Our **Test Bank** has more than 1,400 test questions, separated into factual and conceptual multiple-choice, short-answer, fill-in-the-blank, and short-essay questions to help you create exams. The test bank is available in *Respondus*—a flexible and easy-to-use test-generation software that allows you to build and customize exams or load them into course management systems.

- **PowerPoint Lecture Slides** provide an outline for each chapter, highlighting key concepts and leaving plenty of room for adaptation.

- The online **Instructor's Manual** includes chapter overviews, lecture starters, class activities, and discussion questions, all of which point to ways the power and citizenship themes can be developed further.

- All of the book's **Figures, Tables, and Maps**, in full color, are available both as PowerPoint slides and as PDFs, so that you can easily teach with them in the classroom.

- All features from the Full edition are available in PDF form for instructors to assign to students, including the critical thinking boxes **Consider the Source** and a full set of **Profiles in Citizenship** interviews.

- **A free six-month subscription to CQ Weekly** is available through CQ Press to instructors who adopt *Keeping the Republic* (subject to minimum quantities). We use *CQ Weekly* to stay up to date on current developments, and we know many of our colleagues do as well. This is a useful source to animate your lectures with topical and insightful analysis from the same magazine that informs politicians and policymakers in Washington.

Instructors should go to **http://cqpress.college.com/ instructors-resources/republic** to register and download these materials.

For students:

- A **Study** section offers summaries and learning objectives that encapsulate the most important facts and concepts of each chapter.

- Interactive **Quizzes** allow students to work through approximately twenty multiple-choice questions per chapter and receive immediate results, both by question type (for example, conceptual, factual, and vocabulary) and by chapter section, so that they can effectively gauge their comprehension. If you would like to track your students' online work, you can have them email their quiz results directly to you.

- **Flashcards and crosswords** are a handy way for students to review the book's key terms. Students can also mark terms they would like to return to as well as shuffle and reset their cards.

- Web-based **Exercises** provide activities that encourage students to apply information, concepts, and principles from the text in a series of interactive questions.

- An **Explore** section has annotated web links to facilitate further research.

- Our **Take a Position** feature builds on particular issues or controversies covered in the text, leading students through the critical thinking process so that they can build a balanced, well-argued position on current events.

Acknowledgments

The Africans say that it takes a village to raise a child—it is certainly true that it takes one to write a textbook! We could not have done it without a community of family, friends, colleagues, students, reviewers, and editors who supported us, nagged us, maddened us, and kept us on our toes. Not only is this a better book because of their help and support, but it would not have been a book at all without them.

On the home front, we thank our families, who have hung in there with us even when they thought we were nuts (and even when they were right). Our friends, old and new, have all listened to endless progress reports (and reports of no progress at all) and cheered the small victories with us. Sharing slow food with fast friends has kept us sane, and we especially thank Bob and Kathleen, as always, and Pat and Julia, Fenton and Rich, Dave and Krissy, David and Scott, Ronnie and Evan, Malcolm and Jenny, and Russ and Connie. Thanks also to John Bond for his long friendship and good book advice. We are forever grateful for the unconditional love and support, not to mention occasional intellectual revelation (Hobbes was wrong: it is not a dog-eat-dog world after all!), offered up gladly by Bandon, Ollie, Gracie, and Maggie. (Though we lost Max, Clio, Daphne, Gina, Zoë, Ginger, and Spook along the way, they were among our earliest and strongest supporters and we miss them still.) And we are so very thankful to Pam Stogsdill and Tammy Blunck for looking after us and keeping the whole lot in order.

Colleagues now or once in the Political Science Department at Indiana University have given us invaluable help on details beyond our ken: Yvette Alex Assensoh, Bill Bianco, Jack Bielasiak, Doris Burton, Ted Carmines, Dana Chabot, Mike Ensley, Chuck Epp, Judy Failer, Russ Hanson, Margie Hershey, Bobbi Herzberg, Virginia Hettinger, Jeff Isaac, Fenton Martin, Burt Monroe, Lin Ostrom, Rich Pacelle, Karen Rasler, Leroy Rieselbach, Jean Robinson, Steve Sanders, Pat Sellers, and the late John Williams. IU colleagues from other schools and departments have been terrific: Trevor Brown, Dave Weaver, and Cleve Wilhoit from the Journalism School; Bill McGregor and Roger Parks from the School of Public and Environmental Affairs; John Patrick from the School of Education; and Julia Lamber and Pat Baude from the Law School have all helped out on substantive matters. Many IU folks have made an immeasurable contribution by raising our consciousness about teaching to new levels: Joan Middendorf and David Pace, as well as all the Freshman Learning Project people. James Russell and Bob Goelhert, and all the librarians in the Government Publications section of our library have done yeoman service for us. We are also grateful to colleagues from other institutions: Joe Aistrup, Shaun Bowler, Bob Brown, Tom Carsey, Kisuk Cho, E. J. Dionne, Todd Donovan, Bob Erikson, David Hobbs, Kathleen Knight, David Lee, David McCuan, John McIver, Dick Merriman, Glenn Parker, Denise Scheberle, John Sislin, Donald Stoltz, and Linda Streb. Rich Pacelle and Robert Sahr were particularly helpful.

Special thanks to all our students—undergraduate and graduate, past and present—who inspired us to write this book in the first place. Many students helped us in more concrete ways, working tirelessly as research assistants, writing boxed features, and putting together the material at the end of the chapters. On previous editions these former students, now colleagues at other universities, helped enormously: Tom Carsey, Jessica Gerrity, Dave Holian, Tracy Osborn, Brian Schaffner, Mike Wagner, and Jon Winburn. Nate Birkhead, still at IU, has been super helpful in the creation of the last two editions. We are also grateful to Hugh Aprile, Liz Bevers, Christopher McCollough, Rachel Shelton, Jim Trilling, and Kevin Willhite for their help early in the project.

Thanks also to Mike Stull, for taking us seriously in the first place; to Jean Woy, for the vision that helped shape the book; and to our early development editors, Ann West and Ann Kirby-Payne. Ann West in particular was a friend, a support, and a fabulous editor. We will love her forever.

We have also benefited tremendously from the help of the folks at Project Vote Smart and the many outstanding political scientists across the country who have provided critical reviews of the manuscript at every step of the way. We'd like to thank the following people who took time away from their own work to critique and make suggestions for the improvement of ours. They include all the candy reviewers—Sheldon Appleton, Paul Babbitt, Harry Bralley, Scott Brown, Peter Carlson, David Holian, Carol Humphrey, Glen Hunt, Marilyn Mote-Yale, and Craig Ortsey—and also:

Yishaiya Abosch, California State University, Fresno
Amy Acord, Lone Star College, Cy-Fair
Danny M. Adkison, Oklahoma State University
Ellen Andersen, Indiana University–Purdue University, Indianapolis
Don Arnold, Laney College
Kevin Bailey, Texas House of Representatives, District 140
David C. Benford, Tarrant County College
Jeffrey A. Bosworth, Mansfield University
Ralph Edward Bradford, University of Central Florida
James Bromeland, Winona State University
Scott E. Buchanan, Columbus State University
John F. Burke, University of St. Thomas
Charity Butcher, Kennesaw State University
Anne Marie Cammisa, Saint Anselm College
David Campbell, University of Notre Dame

Francis Carleton, University of Nevada, Las Vegas
Jennifer B. Clark, South Texas Community College
Frank Codispoti, Lone Star College, Cy-Fair
Albert Craig, Augusta State University
Renee Cramer, Drake University
Paul Davis, Truckee Meadows Community College
Christine L. Day, University of New Orleans
Mary C. Deason, University of Mississippi
Robert E. DiClerico, West Virginia University
Robert L. Dion, University of Evansville
Price Dooley, University of Central Arkansas
Lois Duke-Whitaker, Georgia Southern University
Victoria Farrar-Myers, University of Texas at Arlington
Femi Ferreira, Hutchinson Community College
Heidi Getchell-Bastien, Northern Essex Community College
Dana K. Glencross, Oklahoma City Community College
Abe Goldberg, University of South Carolina Upstate
Eugene Goss, Long Beach City College
Victoria Hammond, Austin Community College—Northridge
Patrick J. Haney, Miami University
Charles A. Hantz, Danville Area Community College
Ronald J. Hrebenar, University of Utah
Tseggai Isaac, Missouri University of Science and Technology
William G. Jacoby, Michigan State University
W. Lee Johnston, University of North Carolina Wilmington
Kelechi A. Kalu, Ohio State University
Joshua Kaplan, University of Notre Dame
John D. Kay, Santa Barbara City College
Elizabeth Klages, Augsburg College
Kendra A. King, Oglethorpe University
Tyson King-Meadows, University of Maryland–Baltimore County
Bernard D. Kolasa, University of Nebraska at Omaha
John F. Kozlowicz, University of Wisconsin–Whitewater
Lisa Langenbach, Middle Tennessee State University
Jeff Lee, Blinn College—Bryan
Ted Lewis, Naval Postgraduate School
Brad Lockerbie, East Carolina University
Paul M. Lucko, Angelina College
Vincent N. Mancini, Delaware County Community College
Ursula G. McGraw, Coastal Bend College
Tom McInnis, University of Central Arkansas
Amy McKay, Georgia State University
Tim McKeown, University of North Carolina at Chapel Hill

Sam Wescoat McKinstry, East Tennessee State University

Utz Lars McKnight, University of Alabama

Lauri McNown, University of Colorado at Boulder

Bryan McQuide, University of Idaho

Lawrence Miller, Collin County Community College–
Spring Creek

Maureen F. Moakley, University of Rhode Island

Sarah Moats, West Virginia University

Theodore R. Mosch, University of Tennessee at Martin

T. Sophia Mrouri, Lone Star College, Fairbanks Center

Melinda A. Mueller, Eastern Illinois University

Steven Neiheisel, St. Mary's University

David Nice, Washington State University

James A. Norris, Texas A&M International University

George E. Pippin, Jones County Junior College

David Robinson, University of Houston–Downtown

Dario Albert Rozas, Milwaukee Area Technical College

Thomas A. Schmeling, Rhode Island College

Paul Scracic, Youngstown State University

Todd Shaw, University of South Carolina

Daniel M. Shea, Allegheny College

Neil Snortland, University of Arkansas at Little Rock

Michael W. Sonnleitner, Portland Community
College–Sylvania

Robert E. Sterken Jr., University of Texas at Tyler

Ruth Ann Strickland, Appalachian State University

Tom Sweeney, North Central College

Richard S. Unruh, Fresno Pacific University

Lynn Vacca, Lambuth University

Jan P. Vermeer, Nebraska Wesleyan University

Elizabeth A Wabindato, Northern Arizona University

Molly Waite, Rainey College

Julian Westerhout, Illinois State University

Matt Wetstein, San Joaquin Delta College

Cheryl Wilf, Kutztown University

David C. Wilson, University of Delaware

David E. Woodard, Concordia University

David J. Zimny, Los Medanos College

In this edition we are also incredibly indebted to the busy public servants who made the *Profiles in Citizenship* possible. We are gratified and humbled that they believed in the project enough to give us their valuable time. Deep appreciation to Meagan Szydlowski, Esmeralda Santiago, Newt Gingrich, Mitch Daniels, Bill Maher, Ward Connerly, Jon Tester, Rahm Emanuel, Coleen Rowley, Sandra Day O'Connor, Nate Silver,

David Frum, Wayne Pacelle, James Carville, Andrew Sullivan, Bill Richardson, Christine Todd Whitman, Peter Orszag, and Joe Biden. Thanks, also, to Naomi Cohenour for her quick and careful transcriptions of the interviews.

There are several people in particular without whom this edition would never have seen the light of day. Pat Haney has provided the nuts and bolts of the foreign policy chapter since the first edition. Pat has been a cheerful, tireless collaborator for more than ten years now, and we are so grateful to him. Tracy Osborn helped conceptualize the *Who, What, How, and WHEN* feature, and then executed it beautifully, as well as helped keep our coverage of women and politics up to date, and Elizabeth Rigby lent her expertise to the social policy chapter. We thank them both. Matthew Streb and Michael Wolf have also been involved with this book since its inception, first serving as research assistants while they were in grad school and then stepping up to the bat to help us get the third edition out quickly. Though they were too busy with other projects to take on a continuing role, their impact is still felt. We thank them from the bottom of our hearts for everything they contributed.

Finally, it is our great privilege to acknowledge and thank all the people at CQ Press who believed in this book and made this edition possible. In this day and age of huge publishing conglomerates, it has been such a pleasure to work with a small, committed team who is dedicated to top-quality work. Brenda Carter's vision of the Press and our place in it is inspiring and exciting; Charisse Kiino earned our instant gratitude for so thoroughly and immediately "getting" what this book is about. They have both worked tirelessly with us on decisions big and small, and we have relied heavily on their good sense, their wisdom, and their patience. Thanks to Linda Trygar and her team of field reps across the country. For putting this beautiful book together and drawing your attention to it, we thank the folks on the production, editorial, and marketing teams: Chloe Favilene, Christopher O'Brien, Steve Pazdan, Paul Pressau, Dwain Smith, Erin Snow, and Laura Stewart. We are indebted to everyone who made such a heroic effort to get this book out under a tight deadline, including Emily Bakely, Talia Greenberg, and Enid Zafran, but special mention goes to Nancy Matusak, our development editor, whose patience and unflagging spirits never wavered, Joan Gossett, our production editor who held the whole thing together so well, and Amy Marks for her always gentle but thorough copyediting.

Christine Barbour
Gerald C. Wright

To the Student

Suggestions on How to Read This Textbook

1. As they say in Chicago about voting, do it **early and often.** If you open the book for the first time the night before the exam, you will not learn much from it and it won't help your grade. Start reading the chapters in conjunction with the lectures, and reread them all at least once before the exam.

2. Read the **chapter outlines.** They tell you what we think is important, what our basic argument is, and how all the material fits together. Often, chapter subheadings list elements of an argument that may show up on a quiz. Be alert to these clues.

3. **Read actively.** Constantly ask yourself: What does this mean? Why is this important? How do these different facts fit together? What are the broad arguments here? How does this material relate to class lectures? How does it relate to the broad themes of the class? When you stop asking these questions you are merely moving your eyes over the page, and that is a waste of time.

4. **Highlight or take notes.** Some people prefer highlighting because it's quicker than taking notes, but others think that writing down the most important points helps in remembering them later on. Whichever method you choose (and you can do both), be sure you're doing it properly.

   Highlighting. Highlight with a pen or marker that enables you to read what's on the page. Do not highlight too much. An entirely yellow page will not give you any clues about what is important. Read each paragraph and ask yourself: What is the basic idea of this paragraph? Highlight that. Avoid highlighting all the examples and illustrations. You should be able to recall them on your own when you see the main idea.

   Beware of highlighting too little. If whole pages go by with no marking, you are probably not highlighting enough.

   Outlining. Again, the key is to write down enough, but not too much. Recopying a chapter written by someone else is deadly boring—and a waste of time. Go for key ideas, terms, and arguments.

5. Read and reread the *Who, What, How summaries* at the end of each chapter section. These will help you digest the material just covered and get you ready to go on to the next section.

6. Note all **key terms,** including those that appear in chapter headings. Be sure you understand the definition and significance, and write the significance in the margin of your book!

7. Do not skip **charts, graphs, pictures, or other illustrations.** These things are there for a purpose, because they convey crucial information or illustrate a point in the text. Pay special attention to the *Who Are We?* features. These graphs and tables will enhance your understanding of how demographic changes are likely to affect policy in the future.

8. Do not skip the **boxes** in the book. They are not filler! The *Consider the Source* boxes provide advice on becoming a critical consumer of political information. They list questions to ask yourself about the articles you read, the campaign ads and movies you see, and the graphs you study, among other things. The *Profiles in Citizenship* boxes highlight the achievements of a political actor pertinent to that chapter's focus. They model citizen participation and can serve as a beacon for your own political power long after you've completed your American government course.

9. Make use of the book's web site at **http://republic .cqpress.com.** There are chapter summaries, flashcards, and interactive quizzes that will help prepare you for exams.

Chapter 1

Politics: Who Gets What, and How?

▶ What's at Stake?

Barack Obama was rocking the vote, big time, but still the talking heads were skeptical. Would younger voters turn out at the polls, giving Obama the electoral edge he needed to win? The conventional wisdom said no.

"Are they going to show up?" asked ABC News's Cokie Roberts back in February. "Probably not. They never have before. By the time November comes, they'll be tired," she added, authoritatively.[1]

But they did show up. They showed up in force on the cold January night in 2008 when Iowans caucused to choose their Democratic nominee for president. They showed up throughout the spring, as state after state racked up delegate totals for Obama. They showed up for rallies and speeches and volunteer efforts throughout the summer in the days after the nomination was clinched but before the general election campaign was launched on Labor Day. They gave money and signed up on the Internet, and they organized on campuses across the country, registering their peers and preparing to get them to the polls on Election Day. And they showed up on November 4.

Tired? Looks like Roberts had her facts wrong.

Young and Involved
Young voters defied the expectations of political analysts during the 2008 election, when they not only turned out in greater numbers but also played a key role in Barack Obama's election.

Obama was banking on it. Speaking of his campaign in his victory speech after his election as the first African American president in our nation's history, he said, "It drew strength from the young people who rejected the myth of their generation's apathy; who left their homes and their families for jobs that offered little pay and less sleep."

And when the exit poll data came rolling in, it was clear: young voters had played a huge, if uncharacteristic, part in his election. More than half, 51 percent, of young voters showed up to vote in 2008, an 11 percent increase over 2000 and almost 2 percent over 2004. They made up 17 percent of the electorate, a 2.2 million voter increase over 2004, with turnout especially high in the battleground states where campaigning was fiercest.[2]

Most important for Obama was the fact that the 23 million voters under age thirty broke decisively for him over his Republican opponent, John McCain. Obama carried the youth vote by 66 to 39—a more than two-to-one margin—much higher than the 53-to-46 split among the population as a whole. For an age cohort that politicians usually write off as apathetic, uninformed, and uninvolved, young people came through for Obama in a big way.

These statistics would surely have given considerable peace of mind to Benjamin Franklin, who was keenly aware of the importance of popular attention to the political process. In 1787, when asked by a woman what he and other founders of the Constitution had created, he answered: "A Republic, Madam, if you can keep it." But ever since eighteen year olds had been given the vote in 1972, their voting turnout had been low, their efforts to keep the republic distinctly lackluster.

Young people have generally been less interested in politics than their elders, and less informed. In one 2002 survey, only 51 percent of those aged eighteen to twenty-five could name Dick Cheney as vice president of the United States and only 45 percent said they were interested in local politics, fewer than any other age group.[3] One writer, noting that Americans of all ages expressed increasingly high levels of distrust in government and dislike for politics, sounded the dire warning that "a nation that hates politics will not long thrive as a democracy."[4]

For those who believe that political engagement is essential to the prosperity of democracy, a critical question is whether 2008 constitutes a lasting change in young people's political attitudes. Perhaps it was a fluke, a one-time thing, tied to vague rumors about the Iraqi war, or to an unusually close election, or to extraordinary get-out-the-vote efforts made by the political parties and other activist groups. Is young people's political involvement really such a big deal, or is concern about keeping the republic just an idiosyncrasy of long-deceased founders and hyperactive political science professors? What is really at stake for American democracy in the issue of youthful engagement in the political system? We will be able to address this question better after we explore the meaning of politics and the difference it makes in our lives. ■

Politics can best be understood as the struggle over who gets the power and resources in society.

Have you got grand ambitions for your life? Do you want a powerful position in business, influence in high places, money to make things happen? Perhaps you would like to make a difference in the world, heal the sick, fight for peace, feed the poor. Or maybe all you want from life is a good education; a well-paying job; a comfortable home; and a safe, prosperous, contented existence. Think politics has nothing to do with any of those things? Think again.

The things that make those goals attainable—a strong national defense, education loans or tax deductions for tuition money, economic prosperity, full employment, favorable mortgage rates, policies that let us take time off from work to have kids, secure streets and neighborhoods, cheap and efficient public transportation—are all influenced by or are the products of politics.

Yet, if you listen to the news, politics may seem like one long campaign commercial: eternal bickering and finger-pointing by people who are feathering their nests and those of their cronies at the expense of the voters and who publicly proclaimly themselves to be morally upstanding while keeping the tabloids busy with the tawdry details of their private lives. Politics, which we would like to think of as a noble and even morally elevated activity, takes on all the worst characteristics of the business world, where we expect people to take advantage of each other and pursue their own private interests. Can this really be the heritage of Thomas Jefferson and Abraham Lincoln? Can this be the "world's greatest democracy" at work?

In this chapter we get to the heart of what politics is, how it relates to other concepts such as power, government, rules, economics, and citizenship. We propose that politics can best be understood as the struggle over who gets power and resources in society. Politics produces winners and losers, and much of the reason it can look so ugly is that people fight desperately not to be losers.

Contrary to their depictions in the media, and maybe even in our own minds, the people who are doing that desperate fighting are not some special breed who are different—more corrupt or self-interested or greedy—from the rest of us. They *are* us—whether they are officials in Washington or mayors of small towns, corporate CEOs or representatives of labor unions, local cops or soldiers in the Middle East, churchgoers or atheists, doctors or lawyers, shopkeepers or consumers, professors or students, they are the people that in a democracy we call *citizens*.

As we will see, it is the beauty of a democracy that all the people, including the everyday people like us, get to fight for what they want. Not everyone can win, of course, and many never come close. There is no denying that some people bring resources to the process that give them an edge, and that the rules give advantages to some groups of people over others. But the people who pay attention and who learn how the rules work can begin to use those rules to increase their chances of getting what they want, whether it is a lower personal tax bill, greater pollution controls, a more aggressive foreign policy, safer streets, a better-educated population, or more public parks. If they become very skilled citizens, they can even begin to change the rules so that they can fight more easily for the kind of society they think is important, and so that people like them are more likely to end up winners in the high-stakes game we call politics.

The government our founders created for us gives us a remarkable playing field on which to engage in that game. Like any other politicians, the designers of the American system were caught up in the struggle for power and resources, and in the desire to write laws that would maximize the chances that they, and people like them, would be winners in the new system. Nonetheless, they crafted a government remarkable for its ability to generate compromise and stability, and also for its potential to realize freedom and prosperity for its citizens.

To help you better understand the system they gave us and our place in it, in this chapter you will learn

- *the meaning of "politics"*
- *the varieties of political systems and the roles they endorse for the individuals who live in them*
- *the historical origins of American democracy*
- *the goals and concerns of the founders as they created the American system*
- *the components of critical thinking and how the themes of power and citizenship will serve as our framework for understanding American politics*

politics who gets what, when, and how; a process of determining how power and resources are distributed in a society without recourse to violence

power the ability to get other people to do what you want

social order the way we organize and live our collective lives

legitimate accepted as "right" or proper

government a system or organization for exercising authority over a body of people

What Is Politics?

A peaceful means of determining who gets power and influence in society

Over two thousand years ago, the Greek philosopher Aristotle said that we are political animals, and political animals we seem destined to remain. The truth is that politics is a fundamental and complex human activity. In some ways it is our capacity to be political—to cooperate, bargain, and compromise—that helps distinguish us from all the other animals out there. Politics may have its baser moments—Watergate and White House interns come to mind—but it also allows us to reach more exalted heights than we could ever achieve alone, from the dedication of a new public library, to the building of a national highway system, to the stabilization of a crashing economy, to the guarantee of health care to all U.S. citizens.

Since this book is about politics, in all its glory as well as its shame, we need to begin with a clear definition. One of the most famous definitions, put forth by the well-known political scientist Harold Lasswell, is still one of the best, and we use it to frame our discussion throughout this book. Lasswell defined *politics* as "who gets what when and how."[5]

Politics is a way of determining, without recourse to violence, who gets power and resources in society, and how they get them. **Power** is the ability to get other people to do what you want them to do. The resources in question here might be governmental jobs, tax revenues, laws that help you get your way, or public policies that work to your advantage.

The tools of politics are compromise and cooperation; discussion and debate; even, sometimes, bribery and deceit. Politics is the process through which we try to arrange our collective lives in some kind of *social order* so that we can live without crashing into each other at every turn, and to provide ourselves with goods and services we could not obtain alone. But politics is also about getting our own way. Our way may be a noble goal for society or pure self-interest, but the struggle we engage in is a political struggle. Because politics is about power and other scarce resources, there will always be winners and losers in politics. If we could always get our own way, politics would disappear. It is because we cannot always get what we want that politics exists.

What would a world without politics be like? There would be no resolution or compromise between conflicting interests, because those are certainly political activities. There would be no agreements struck, bargains made, or alliances formed. Unless there were enough of every valued resource to go around, or unless the world were big enough that we could live our lives without coming into contact with other human beings, life would be constant conflict—what the philosopher Thomas Hobbes (1588–1679) called a "war of all against all." Individuals, unable to cooperate with one another (because cooperation is essentially political), would have no option but to resort to brute force to settle disputes and allocate resources.

Our capacity to be political saves us from that fate. We do have the ability to persuade, cajole, bargain, promise, compromise, and cooperate. We do have the ability to agree on what principles should guide our handling of power and other scarce resources and to live our collective lives according to those principles. Because there are many potential theories about how to manage power—who should have it, how it should be used, how it should be transferred—agreement on which principles are *legitimate*, or accepted as "right," can break down. When agreement on what is legitimate fails, violence often takes its place. Indeed, the human history of warfare attests to the fragility of political life.

Although one characteristic of government is that it has a monopoly on the legitimate use of force, politics means that we have alternatives, that bloodshed is not the only way of dealing with human conflict. Interestingly, the word *politics* comes from the Greek word *polis*, meaning "city-state." Similarly, the word *civilization* comes from the Latin word *civitas*, meaning "city" or "state." Thus our Western notions of politics and civilization share similar roots, all tied up with what it means to live a shared public life.

Politics and Government

Although the words *politics* and *government* are sometimes used interchangeably, they refer to different things. Politics is a process or an activity through which power and resources are gained and lost. *Government*, on the other hand, is a system or organization for exercising authority over a body of people.

American *politics* is what happens in the halls of Congress, on the campaign trail, at Washington cocktail parties, and in neighborhood association meetings. It is the making of promises, deals, and laws. American *government* is the Constitution and the institutions set up by the Constitution for the exercise of authority by the American people, over the American people.

authority power that is recognized as legitimate

rules directives that specify how resources will be distributed or what procedures govern collective activity

institutions organizations in which governmental power is exercised

Authority is power that citizens view as legitimate, or "right"—power to which we have given our implicit consent. You can think of it this way: as children, we probably did as our parents told us, or submitted to their punishment if we didn't, because we recognized their authority over us. As we became adults, we started to claim that our parents had less authority over us, that we could do what we wanted. We no longer saw their power as wholly legitimate or appropriate. Governments exercise authority because people recognize them as legitimate even if they often do not like doing what they are told (paying taxes, for instance). When governments cease to be regarded as legitimate, the result may be revolution or civil war, unless the state is powerful enough to suppress all opposition.

Rules and Institutions

Government is shaped by the process of politics, but it in turn provides the rules and institutions that shape the way politics continues to operate. The rules and institutions of government have a profound effect on how power is distributed and who wins and loses in the political arena. Life is different for people in other countries not only because they speak different languages and eat different foods but also because their governments establish rules that cause life to be lived in different ways.

Rules can be thought of as the *how* in the definition "who gets what . . . and *how*." They are directives that determine how resources are allocated and how collective action takes place—that is, they determine how we try to get the things we want. We can do it violently, or we can do it politically, according to the rules. Those rules can provide for a single dictator, for a king, for rule by God's representative on earth or by the rich, for rule by a majority of the people, or for any other arrangement. The point of the rules is to provide some framework for us to solve without violence the problems that are generated by our collective lives.

Because the rules we choose can influence which people will get what they want most often, understanding the rules is crucial to understanding politics. Consider for a moment the impact a change of rules would have on the outcome of the sport of basketball, for instance. What if the average height of the players could be no more than 5'10"? What if the baskets were lowered? What if foul shots counted for two points rather than one? Basketball would be a very different game, and the teams recruited would look quite unlike the

Managing Conflict
The political parties and their candidates are frequently opposed on issues and ideology. Norms of courtesy have evolved so that competing elites continue to work together to reach the compromises that make democratic politics possible. Here, then–Republican presidential candidate Senator John McCain (bottom right) and others laugh at Democratic candidate Senator Barack Obama's satirical commentary at the 2008 Alfred E. Smith Dinner.

teams we now cheer for. So it is with governments and politics: change the people who are allowed to vote or the length of time a person can serve in office, and the political process and the potential winners and losers change drastically.

We can think of **institutions** as the *where* of the political struggle, though Lasswell didn't include a "where" component in his definition. They are the organizations where governmental power is exercised. In the United States, our rules provide for the institutions of a representative democracy—that is, rule by the elected representatives of the people, and for a federal political system. Our Constitution lays the foundation for the institutions of Congress, the presidency, the courts, and the bureaucracy as a stage on which the drama of politics plays itself out. Other systems might call for different institutions—perhaps an all-powerful parliament, or a monarch, or even a committee of rulers.

These complicated systems of rules and institutions do not appear out of thin air. They are carefully designed by the founders of different systems to create the kinds of society they think will be stable and prosperous, but also where people like themselves are likely to be winners. Remember that not only the rules but also the institutions we

> **economics**   production and distribution of a society's material resources and services

> **capitalist economy**   an economic system in which the market determines production, distribution, and price decisions, and property is privately owned

choose influence who most easily and most often get their own way.

Politics and Economics

Whereas politics is concerned with the distribution of power and resources in society, **economics** is concerned specifically with the production and distribution of society's wealth—material goods like bread, toothpaste, and housing, and services like medical care, education, and entertainment. Because both politics and economics focus on the distribution of society's resources, political and economic questions often get confused in contemporary life. Questions about how to pay for government, about government's role in the economy, and about whether government or the private sector should provide certain services have political and economic dimensions. Because there are no clear-cut distinctions here, it can be difficult to keep these terms straight.

The sources of the words *politics* and *economics* suggest that their meanings were once more distinct than they are today.

We already saw that the Greek source of the word *political* was *polis*, or "city-state," the basic political unit of ancient Greece. For the free male citizens of the city-state of Athens (by no means the majority of the inhabitants), politics was a prestigious and jealously restricted activity. However, the public, political world of Athens was possible only because a whole class of people (slaves and women) existed to support the private world, the *oikonomia*, or "household." This early division of the world into the political and the economic clearly separated the two realms. Political life was public, and economic life was private. Today, that distinction is not nearly so simple. What is public and private now depends on what is controlled by government. The various forms of economic systems are shown in Figure 1.1.

Capitalism

In a pure **capitalist economy**, all the means used to produce material resources (industry, business, and land, for instance) are owned privately, and decisions about production and distribution are left to individuals operating through the

---

Figure 1.1

A Comparison of Economic Systems

Economic systems are defined largely by the degree to which government owns the means by which material resources are produced (for example, factories and industry) and controls economic decision making. On a scale ranging from socialism—complete government ownership and control of the economy (on the left)—to laissez-faire capitalism—complete individual ownership and control of the economy (on the right)—social democracies would be located in the center. These hybrid systems are characterized by mostly private ownership of the means of production but considerable government control over economic decisions.

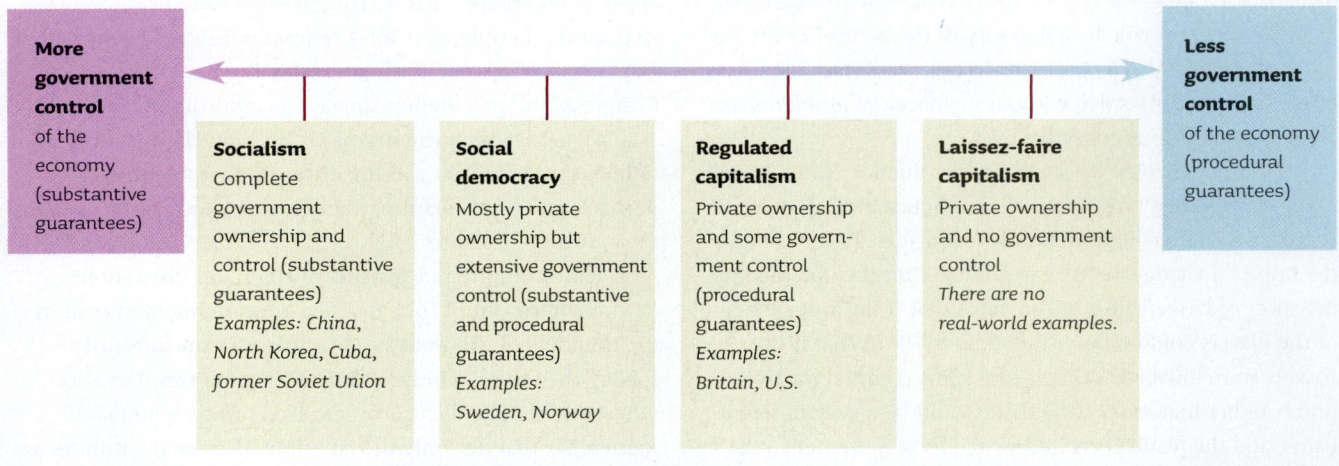

| **More government control** of the economy (substantive guarantees) | **Socialism** Complete government ownership and control (substantive guarantees) *Examples: China, North Korea, Cuba, former Soviet Union* | **Social democracy** Mostly private ownership but extensive government control (substantive and procedural guarantees) *Examples: Sweden, Norway* | **Regulated capitalism** Private ownership and some government control (procedural guarantees) *Examples: Britain, U.S.* | **Laissez-faire capitalism** Private ownership and no government control *There are no real-world examples.* | **Less government control** of the economy (procedural guarantees) |

laissez-faire capitalism an economic system in which the market makes all decisions and the government plays no role

regulated capitalism a market system in which the government intervenes to protect rights and make procedural guarantees

procedural guarantees government assurance that the rules will work smoothly and treat everyone fairly, with no promise of particular outcomes

socialist economy an economic system in which the state determines production, distribution, and price decisions, and property is government owned

substantive guarantees government assurance of particular outcomes or results

free-market process. Capitalist economies rely on the market—the process of supply and demand—to decide how much of a given item to produce or how much to charge for it. In capitalist countries, people do not believe that the government is capable of making such judgments (like how much toothpaste to produce), and they want to keep such decisions out of the hands of government and in the hands of individuals who they believe know best about what they want. The philosophy that corresponds with this belief is called **laissez-faire capitalism**, from a French term that, loosely translated, means "let people do as they wish." The government has no economic role at all in such a system. However, no economic system today maintains a purely unregulated form of capitalism, with the government completely uninvolved.

Like most other countries today, the United States has a system of **regulated capitalism**. It maintains a capitalist economy and individual freedom from government interference remains the norm, but it allows government to step in and regulate the economy to guarantee individual rights and to provide **procedural guarantees** that the rules will work smoothly and fairly. Although in theory the market ought to provide everything that people need and want, and should regulate itself as well, sometimes the market breaks down, or fails. In regulated capitalism, the government steps in to try to fix it.

Markets have cycles, with periods of growth often followed by periods of slowdown or recession. Individuals and businesses look to government for protection from these cyclical effects. For example, President Franklin D. Roosevelt created the Works Progress Administration to get Americans back to work during the Great Depression and, more recently, Congress acted to stabilize the economy in the wake of the financial collapse caused by the subprime mortgage crisis in the fall of 2008. Government may also act to ensure the safety of the consumer public and of working people, or to encourage fair business practices (like prevention of monopolies), or to provide goods and services that people have no incentive to produce themselves.

Highways, streetlights, libraries, museums, schools, Social Security, national defense, and a clean environment are some examples of the goods and services that many people are unable or unwilling to produce privately. Consequently, government undertakes to provide these things (with money provided by taxpayers) and, in doing so, becomes not only a political but an economic actor as well. To the extent that government gets involved in a capitalist economy, we move away from laissez-faire to regulated capitalism.

Capitalizing on Entrepreneurship
Private entrepreneurs like billionaire Richard Branson may invest in unique endeavors such as the VSS *Enterprise*, the first of five SpaceShipTwo model crafts built for Branson's Virgin Galatic company. The spaceship took its maiden flight in March 2010 and reached an altitude of 45,000 feet. The ultimate plan is for such a ship to carry paying passengers into outer space. In contrast to such private investments, government-funded space exploration and research must compete with numerous budgetary concerns for limited tax dollars and is constrained by swings in public opinion.

Socialism

In a **socialist economy** like that of the former Soviet Union (based loosely on the ideas of German economist Karl Marx), economic decisions are made not by individuals through the market but rather by politicians, based on their judgment of what society needs. Rather than allowing the market to determine the proper distribution of material resources, politicians decide what the distribution ought to be and then create economic policy to bring about that outcome. In other words, they emphasize not procedural guarantees of fair rules and process, but rather **substantive guarantees** of what they believe to be fair outcomes.

According to the basic values of a socialist or communist system (although the two systems have some theoretical differences, they are similar for our purposes here), it is unjust for some people to own more property than others and to have power over them because of it. Consequently, the theory goes, the state or society—not corporations or individuals—should own the property (like land, factories,

Too Small?
If the U.S. Postal Service is forced to make a profit, small rural sites like this one in Bradley, Michigan, would probably be shut down. As a public corporation, the Postal Service has to be accessible and deliver mail everywhere, from the icy slopes of Alaska to the swamps of Florida, for the cost of one first class stamp.

> *social democracy* a hybrid system combining a capitalist economy and a government that supports equality

hybrid economic systems. As noted in Figure 1.1, these systems represent something of a middle ground between socialist and capitalist systems. Primarily capitalist, in that they believe most property can be held privately, proponents of *social democracy* argue nonetheless that the values of equality promoted by socialism are attractive and can be brought about by democratic reform rather than revolution. Believing that the economy does not have to be owned by the state for its effects to be controlled by the state, social democratic countries attempt to strike a difficult balance between providing substantive guarantees of fair outcomes and procedural guarantees of fair rules.

Since World War II, the citizens of many Western European nations have elected social democrats to office, where they have enacted policies to bring about more equality—for instance, the elimination of poverty and unemployment, better housing, and adequate health care for all. Even where social democratic governments are voted out of office, such programs have proved so popular that it is often difficult for new leaders to alter them.

and corporations). In such systems, the public and private spheres overlap, and politics controls the distribution of all resources. The societies that have tried to put these theories into practice have ended up with very repressive political systems, but Marx hoped that eventually socialism would evolve to a point where each individual had control over his or her own life—a radical form of democracy.

Many theories hold that socialism is possible only after a revolution that thoroughly overthrows the old system to make way for new values and institutions. This is what happened in Russia in 1917 and in China in the 1940s. Since the socialist economies of the former Soviet Union and Eastern Europe have fallen apart, socialism has been left with few supporters, although some nations, such as China, North Korea, and Cuba, still claim allegiance to it.

Social Democracy

Some countries in Western Europe, especially the Scandinavian nations of Norway, Denmark, and Sweden, have developed

Political Systems and the Concept of Citizenship
Different ideas about power and the social order, different models of governing

Just as there are different kinds of economic systems, there are different sorts of political systems, based on different ideas about who should have power and what the social order should be—that is, how much public regulation there should be over individual behavior. For our purposes, we can divide political systems into two types: those in which the government has the power to impose a particular social order, deciding how individuals ought to behave, and those in which individuals exercise personal power over most of their own behavior and ultimately over government as well. These two types of systems are not just different in a theoretical sense. The differences have very real implications for the people who live in them. Thus the notion of citizenship (or the lack of it) is closely tied to the kind of political system a nation has.

Figure 1.2 offers a comparison of these systems. One type of system, called authoritarian government, potentially has total power over its subjects; the other type, nonauthoritarian government, permits citizens to limit the state's power by claiming rights that the government must protect. Another way to think about the distinction is that in authoritarian

totalitarian a system in which absolute power is exercised over every aspect of life

authoritarian capitalism a system in which the state allows people economic freedom but maintains stringent social regulations to limit noneconomic behavior

authoritarian governments systems in which the state holds all power over the social order

Figure 1.2

A Comparison of Political Systems

Political systems are defined by the extent to which individual citizens or governments decide what the social order should look like—that is, how people should live their collective, noneconomic lives. Except for anarchies, every system allots a role to government to regulate individual behavior—for example, to prohibit murder, rape, and theft. But beyond such basic regulation, they differ radically on who gets to determine how individuals live their lives, and whether government's role is simply to provide procedural guarantees that protect individuals' rights to make their own decisions or to provide a much more substantive view of how individuals should behave.

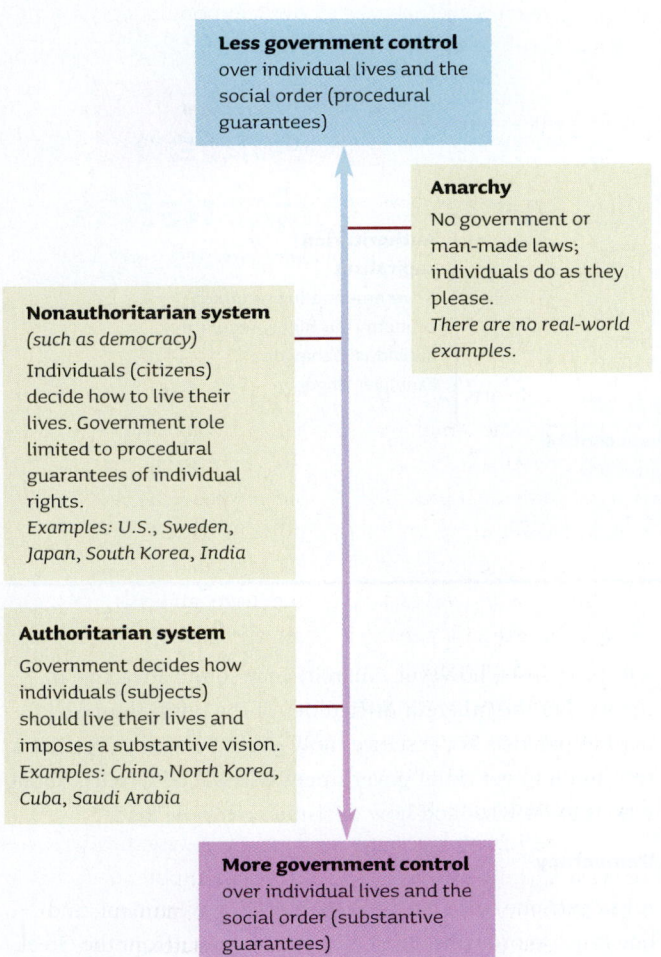

Less government control over individual lives and the social order (procedural guarantees)

Anarchy
No government or man-made laws; individuals do as they please.
There are no real-world examples.

Nonauthoritarian system
(such as democracy)
Individuals (citizens) decide how to live their lives. Government role limited to procedural guarantees of individual rights.
Examples: U.S., Sweden, Japan, South Korea, India

Authoritarian system
Government decides how individuals (subjects) should live their lives and imposes a substantive vision.
Examples: China, North Korea, Cuba, Saudi Arabia

More government control over individual lives and the social order (substantive guarantees)

systems, government makes substantive decisions about how people ought to live their lives; in nonauthoritarian systems, government merely guarantees that there are fair rules and leaves the rest to individual control. Sometimes governments that exercise substantive decision making in the economic realm also do so with respect to the social order. But, as Figure 1.3 shows, there are several possible combinations of economic and political systems.

Authoritarian Systems

Authoritarian governments give ultimate power to the state rather than to the people to decide how they ought to live their lives. By "authoritarian governments," we usually mean those in which the people cannot effectively claim rights against the state; where the state chooses to exercise its power, the people have no choice but to submit to its will.

Authoritarian governments can take various forms: sovereignty can be vested in an individual (dictatorship or monarchy), in God (theocracy), in the state itself (fascism), or in a ruling class (oligarchy). When a system combines an authoritarian government with a socialist economy, we say that the system is ***totalitarian***. As in the earlier example of the former Soviet Union, a totalitarian system exercises its power over every part of society—economic, social, political, and moral—leaving little or no private realm for individuals.

But an authoritarian state may also limit its own power. In such cases, it may deny individuals rights in those spheres where it chooses to act, but it may leave large areas of society, such as a capitalist economy, free from governmental interference. Singapore is an example of this type of ***authoritarian capitalism***, where people have considerable economic freedom but stringent social regulations limit their noneconomic behavior. When American teenager Michael Fay was caught vandalizing cars in Singapore in 1994, the government there sentenced him to be caned. In the United States, people have rights that prevent cruel and unusual punishment like caning, but in Singapore, Fay had no such rights and had to submit to the government's will.

Authoritarian governments often pay lip service to the people, but when push comes to shove, as it usually does in such states, the people have no effective power against the government. Again, to use the terminology we introduced earlier, government does not provide guarantees of fair processes for individuals; it guarantees a substantive vision of what life will be like—what individuals will believe, how they will act, what they will choose.

Figure 1.3

Political and Economic Systems

Political systems work in conjunction with economic systems, but government control over the economy does not necessarily translate into tight control over the social order. We have identified four possible combinations of these systems, signified by the labeled points in each quadrant. These points are approximate, however, and some nations cannot be classified so easily. Sweden is an advanced industrial democracy by most measures, for instance, but because of its commitment to substantive economic values, it would be located much closer to the vertical axis.

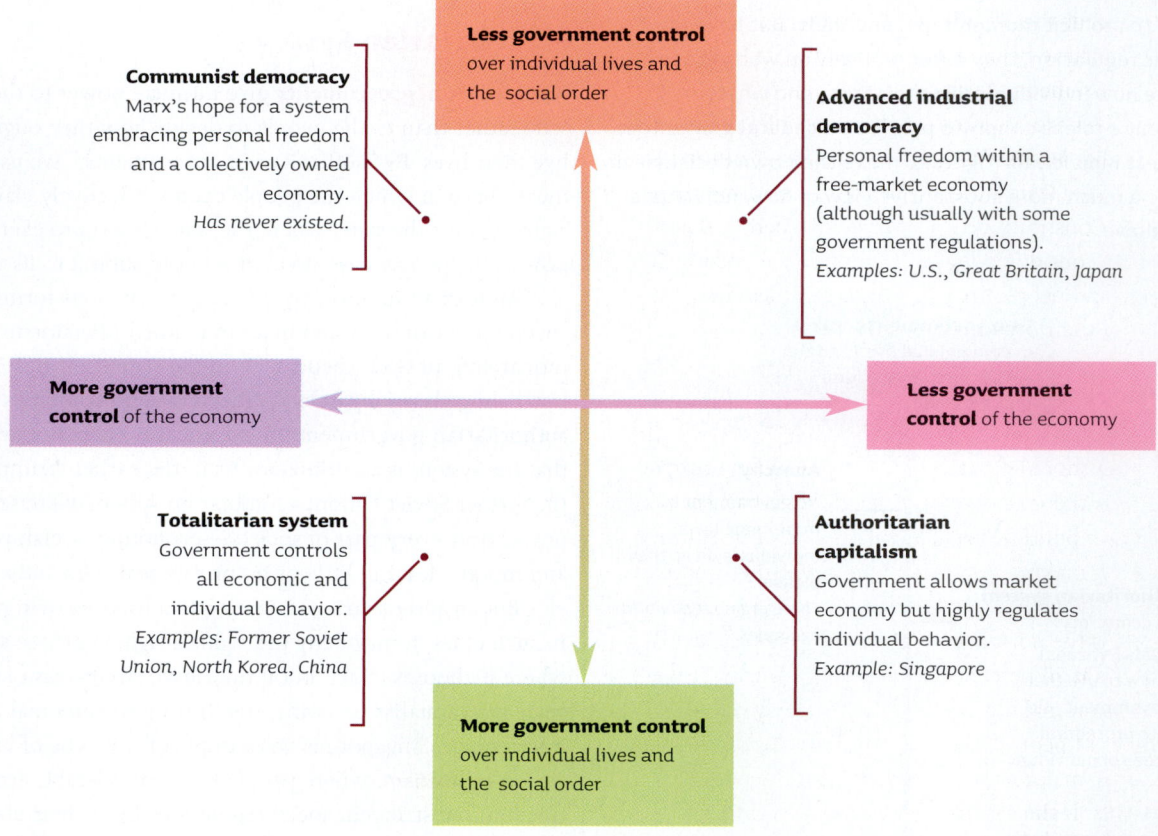

Less government control over individual lives and the social order

Communist democracy
Marx's hope for a system embracing personal freedom and a collectively owned economy.
Has never existed.

Advanced industrial democracy
Personal freedom within a free-market economy (although usually with some government regulations).
Examples: U.S., Great Britain, Japan

More government control of the economy

Less government control of the economy

Totalitarian system
Government controls all economic and individual behavior.
Examples: Former Soviet Union, North Korea, China

Authoritarian capitalism
Government allows market economy but highly regulates individual behavior.
Example: Singapore

More government control over individual lives and the social order

Nonauthoritarian Systems

In nonauthoritarian systems, ultimate power rests with the individuals to make decisions concerning their lives. The most extreme form of nonauthoritarianism is called *anarchy*. Anarchists would do away with government and laws altogether. People advocate anarchy because they value the freedom to do whatever they want more than they value the order and security that governments provide by forbidding or regulating certain kinds of behavior. Few people are true anarchists, however. Anarchy may sound attractive in theory, but the inherent difficulties of the position make it hard to practice. For instance, how could you even organize a revolution to get rid of government without some rules about who is to do what and how decisions are to be made?

Democracy

A less extreme form of nonauthoritarian government, and one much more familiar to us, is *democracy* (from the Greek *demos*, meaning "people"). In democracies, government is not

> **popular sovereignty** the concept that the citizens are the ultimate source of political power
>
> **elite democracy** a theory of democracy that limits the citizens' role to choosing among competing leaders

> **pluralist democracy** a theory of democracy that holds that citizen membership in groups is the key to political power
>
> **participatory democracy** a theory of democracy that holds that citizens should actively and directly control all aspects of their lives

external to the people, as it is in authoritarian systems; in a fundamental sense, government is the people. Recognizing that collective life usually calls for some restrictions on what individuals may do (laws forbidding murder, for instance, or theft), democracies nevertheless try to maximize freedom for the individuals who live under them. Although they generally make decisions through some sort of majority rule, democracies still provide procedural guarantees to preserve individual rights—usually protections of due process and minority rights. This means that if individuals living in a democracy feel their rights have been violated, they have the right to ask government to remedy the situation.

Democracies are based on the principle of **popular sovereignty**; that is, there is no power higher than the people and, in the United States, the document establishing their authority, the Constitution. The central idea here is that no government is considered legitimate unless the governed consent to it, and people are not truly free unless they live under a law of their own making.

Theories of Democracy

Generally, as we indicated, democracies hold that the will of the majority should prevail. This is misleadingly simple, however. Some theories of democracy hold that all the people should agree on political decisions. This rule of unanimity makes decision making very slow, and sometimes impossible, since everyone has to be persuaded to agree. Even when majority rule is the norm, there are many ways of calculating the majority. Is it 50 percent plus one? Two-thirds? Three-fourths? Decision making becomes increasingly difficult as the number of people who are required to agree grows. And, of course, majority rule brings with it the problem of minority rights. If the majority gets its way, what happens to the rights of those who disagree? Democratic theorists have tried to grapple with these problems in various ways, none of them entirely satisfactory to all people:

- Theorists of **elite democracy** propose that democracy is merely a system of choosing among competing leaders; for the average citizen, input ends after the leader is chosen.[6] Some proponents of this view believe that political decisions are made not by elected officials but by the elite in business, the military, the media, and education. In this view, elections are merely symbolic—to perpetuate the illusion that citizens have consented to their government. Elite

theorists may claim that participation is important, if not for self-rule, then because people should at least feel as if they are making a difference. Otherwise they have no stake in the political system.

- Advocates of **pluralist democracy** argue that what is important is not so much individual participation but membership in groups that participate in government decision making on their members' behalf.[7] As a way of trying to influence a system that gives them a limited voice, citizens join groups of people with whom they share an interest, such as labor unions, professional associations, and environmental or business groups. These groups represent their members' interests and try to influence government to enact policy that carries out the group's will. Some pluralists argue that individual citizens have little effective power and that only when they are organized into groups are they truly a force for government to reckon with.

- Supporters of **participatory democracy** claim that more than consent or majority rule in making governmental decisions is needed. Individuals have the right to control all the circumstances of their lives, and direct democratic participation should take place not only in government but in industry, education, and community affairs as well.[8] For advocates of this view, democracy is more than a way to make decisions: it is a way of life, an end in itself.

These theories about how democracy should (or does) work locate the focus of power in individuals, groups, and elites. Real-world examples of democracy probably include elements of more than one of these theories; they are not mutually exclusive.

The people of many Western countries have found the idea of democracy persuasive enough to found their governments on it. In recent years, especially since the mid-1980s, democracy has been spreading rapidly through the rest of the world as the preferred form of government. No longer the primary province of industrialized Western nations, attempts at democratic governance now extend into Asia, Latin America, Africa, Eastern Europe, and the republics of the former Soviet Union. There are many varieties of democracy other than our own. Some democracies make the legislature (the representatives of the people) the most important authority; some retain a monarch with limited powers; some

advanced industrial democracy a system in which a democratic government allows citizens a considerable amount of personal freedom and maintains a free-market (though still usually regulated) economy

communist democracy a utopian system in which property is communally owned and all decisions are made democratically

subjects individuals who are obliged to submit to a government authority against which they have no rights

citizens members of a political community with both rights and responsibilities

Dangerous Protests
A supporter of Iranian opposition leader Mir Hossein Mousavi holds up his photo during a demonstration in Tehran, Iran, in June 2009. Following disputed election results in which front-runner Mousavi lost, demonstrators met with violence and imprisonment as the Iranian government suppressed opposition.

hold referenda at the national level to get direct feedback on how the people want them to act on specific issues.

Most democratic forms of government, because of their commitment to procedural values, practice a capitalist form of economics. Fledgling democracies may rely on a high degree of government economic regulation, but ***advanced industrial democracies*** combine a considerable amount of personal freedom with a free-market (though still usually regulated) economy. It is rare to find a country that is truly committed to individual political freedom that also tries to

regulate the economy heavily. The philosopher Karl Marx believed that radical democracy would coexist with communally owned property, in a form of ***communist democracy***, but such a system has never existed, and most real-world systems fall somewhere along the horizontal continuum shown in Figure 1.3.

The Role of the People

What is important about the political and economic systems we have been sorting out here is that they have direct impact on the lives of the people who live in them. So far we have given a good deal of attention to the latter parts of Lasswell's definition of politics. But easily as important as the *what* and the *how* in Lasswell's formulation is the *who*. Underlying the different political theories we have looked at are fundamental differences in the powers and opportunities possessed by everyday people.

The People as Subjects

In authoritarian systems, the people are ***subjects*** of their government. They possess no rights that protect them from that government; they must do whatever the government says or face the consequences, without any other recourse. They have obligations to the state but no rights or privileges to offset those obligations. They may be winners or losers in government decisions, but they have very little control over which it may be.

The People as Citizens

Everyday people in democratic systems have a potentially powerful role to play. They are more than mere subjects; they are ***citizens***, or members of a political community with rights as well as obligations. Democratic theory says that power is drawn from the people, that the people are sovereign, that they must consent to be governed, and that their government must respond to their will. In practical terms, this may not seem to mean much, since not consenting doesn't necessarily give us the right to disobey government. It does give us the option of leaving, however, and seeking a more congenial set of rules elsewhere. Subjects of authoritarian governments rarely have this freedom.

In democratic systems, the rules of government can provide for all sorts of different roles for citizens. At a minimum, citizens can usually vote in periodic and free elections. They may be able to run for office, subject to certain

▶ **Profiles in Citizenship: Meagan Szydlowski**

"Don't be afraid to get involved right away—don't think you are too young or your voice doesn't matter. During campaigns they love young people and their energy and excitement, and you will be welcomed. . . ."

You don't hear college students say this every day, but Meagan Szydlowski loves politics. Her imagination was captured by her father's election to the city council. "I went to everything I could with him, like meetings, talking to newspapers and stuff, and I loved it! It was so exciting," she says of her dad's campaign.

She calls that election her "jump start"—she has been hooked on politics ever since. A term as the chair of the Illinois College Republicans followed, and internships in her local state representative's office as well as in her congressman's office—a congressman who just happened to be Dennis Hastert, Speaker of the House of Representatives. When we caught up with her, she was spending a summer in Washington, D.C., having been selected as one of five participants in Northern Illinois's Congressional Internship Program, working on Capitol Hill, and loving it.

Szydlowski says she always knew she was a Republican. "My dad and I talked about these things," she says. "Our conversations were always political." So once she got to college at NIU and saw

a sign that said, "Join the NIU College Republicans," she knew it was for her.

"I went to the first meeting, and it was perfect," she says. "It was a great way to meet people. . . . So I volunteered for everything they had and went to all the meetings." And, then the chairman at the time asked her to run for chair for next year. "And I was like, I've only been here a year, there's people that's been here longer than me, he's like—no, you are active, you are involved in things and I want you to do this." So she ran and she won, and spent her sophomore year running the NIU College Republicans.

Within the year she was being approached to run as chair of the statewide organization. She did some research and decided to take it on, contacting all the different campus chairs around the state and developing relationships with them. It all paid off: "We had a big convention in downtown Chicago and had a campaign and I got elected to chairman of the statewide convention." She served from January 2008 to April 2009, also getting to sit on the national College Republican's Executive Committee and serving as a member of the Illinois Republican Party's State Central Committee as a result.

That position involved her in Republican Party politics around the state, but maybe the best part of the job included attending the 2008 Republican National Convention in Minneapolis that September as an alternate. She had a blast. The most exciting event was the night of Sarah Palin's speech. Rudy Giuliani spoke first, and Meagan had been a big supporter of his, working on his primary campaign, so she was already fired up, and then Palin's speech electrified the crowd. While disappointed in the outcome of that election, she's philosophical, knowing that in American politics no party stays on top forever.

Meagan managed to fit a few more activities into her college career before she graduated—she studied in Oxford, England, and held a variety of student government posts, and was a student research assistant for one of her professors. She is thinking graduate school might lie in her future. "I got a great education at NIU, and I want to have that influence on other people," she says.

What? No running for office herself? At least right now, Meagan is pretty sure that's not for her. The scrutiny of public officials turns her off. But whatever she ends up doing, she's confident that it will involve politics.

Here's some of her advice for fellow students:

On majoring in political science:

I'm just really, really happy that I found something I love so much, and that I've been able to turn it into my area of study and hopefully a career. I love this— political science is not just my major, it is my life—I read all the newspapers every day, check the web sites, and watch the news every day. It's pretty rewarding.

On keeping the republic:

Keeping the republic is all about involvement and interest. Don't be afraid to get involved right away—don't think you are too young or your voice doesn't matter. During campaigns they love young people and their energy and excitement, and you will be welcomed. . . . Alexander Hamilton in the *Federalist Papers* said, "The ingredients which constitute safety in the republican sense are a due dependence on the people, and a due responsibility." That basically sums up how important I think it is for people to be active and engaged. ■

conditions, like age or residence. They can support candidates for office, organize political groups or parties, attend meetings, write letters to officials or the press, march in protest or support of various causes, even speak out on street corners.

Theoretically, democracies are ruled by "the people," but different democracies have at times been very selective about whom they count as citizens. Beginning with our days as colonists, Americans have excluded many groups of people from citizenship: people of the "wrong" religion, income bracket, race, ethnic group, lifestyle, and gender have all been excluded from enjoying the full rights of colonial or U.S. citizenship at different times. In fact, American history is the story of those various groups fighting to be included as citizens. Just because a system is called a democracy is no guarantee that all or even most of the residents under that system possess the status of citizen.

Citizen Rights and Responsibilities

Citizens in democratic systems are said to possess certain rights, or powers to act, that government cannot limit. Just what these rights are varies in different democracies, but they usually include freedoms of speech and the press, the right to assemble, and certain legal protections guaranteeing fair treatment in the criminal justice system. Almost all of these rights are designed to allow citizens to criticize their government openly without threat of retribution by that government.

Citizens of democracies also possess obligations or responsibilities to the public realm. They have the obligation to obey the law, for instance, once they have consented to the government (even if that consent amounts only to not leaving); they may also have the obligation to pay taxes, serve in the military, or sit on juries. Some theorists argue that virtuous citizens should put community interests ahead of personal interests. A less extreme version of this view holds that while citizens may go about their own business and pursue their own interests, they must continue to pay attention to their government. Participating in its decision-making process is the price of maintaining their own liberty and, by extension, the liberty of the whole. Should citizens abdicate this role by tuning out of public life, the safeguards of democracy can disappear, to be replaced with the trappings of authoritarian government. There is nothing automatic about democracy. If left unattended by nonvigilant citizens, the freedoms of democracy can be lost to an all-powerful state, and citizens can become transformed into subjects of the government they failed to keep in check.

Origins of Democracy in America
From divine right to social contract

Government in the United States is the product of particular decisions the founders made about the who, what, and how of American politics. There was nothing inevitable about those decisions, and had the founders decided otherwise, our system would look very different indeed.

Given the world in which the founders lived, democracy was not an obvious choice for them, and many scholars argue that in some respects the system they created is not really very democratic. We can see this more clearly if we understand the intellectual heritage of the early Americans, the historical experience, and the theories about government that informed them.

The Ancient Greek Experience

The heyday of democracy, of course, was ancient Athens, from about 500 to 300 BCE. Even Athenian democracy, as we have already indicated, was a pretty selective business. To be sure, it was rule by "the people," but "the people" was defined narrowly to exclude women, slaves, youth, and resident aliens. Athenian democracy was not built on values of equality, even of opportunity, except for the 10 percent of the population defined as citizens. With its limited number of citizens and its small area of only one thousand square miles, Athens was a participatory democracy in which all citizens could gather in one place to vote on political matters. While this privileged group indulged its passion for public activity, the vast majority of residents were required to do all the work to support them. We can see parallels to early American democracy, which restricted participation in political affairs to a relatively small number of white men.

Politics in the Middle Ages

Limited as Athenian democracy was, it was positively wide open compared to most of the forms of government that existed during the Middle Ages, from roughly AD 600 to 1500. During this period, monarchs gradually consolidated their power over their subjects, and some even challenged the greatest political power of the time,

divine right of kings the principle that earthly rulers receive their authority from God

Protestant Reformation the break from the Roman Catholic Church in the 1500s by those who believed in direct access to God and salvation by faith

Enlightenment a philosophical movement (1600s–1700s) that emphasized human reason, scientific examination, and industrial progress

social contract the notion that society is based on an agreement between government and the governed in which people agree to give up some rights in exchange for the protection of others

the Catholic Church. Some earthly rulers claimed to take their authority from God, in a principle called the *divine right of kings*. Privileged groups in society, like the clergy or the nobles, had some rights, but ordinary individuals were quite powerless politically. Subjects of authoritarian governments and an authoritarian church, they had obligations to their rulers but no rights they could claim as their own. If a ruler is installed by divine mandate, who, after all, has any rights against God? Education was restricted, and most people in the Middle Ages were dependent on political and ecclesiastical leaders for protection and information, as well as salvation.

The Protestant Reformation and the Enlightenment

Between 1500 and 1700, important changes took place in the ways that people thought about politics and their political leaders. The *Protestant Reformation* led the way in the 1500s, claiming essentially that individuals could pray directly to God and receive salvation on faith alone, without the church's involvement. In fact, Martin Luther, the German priest who spearheaded the Reformation, argued that the whole complex structure of the medieval church could be dispensed with. His ideas spread and were embraced by a number of European monarchs, leading to a split between Catholic and Protestant countries. Where the church was seen as unnecessary, it lost political as well as religious clout, and its decline paved the way for new ideas about the world.

Those new ideas came with the *Enlightenment* period of the late 1600s and 1700s, when ideas about science and the possibilities of knowledge began to blow away the shadows and cobwebs of medieval superstition. A new and refreshing understanding of human beings and their place in the natural world, based on human reasoning, took hold. Enlightenment philosophy said that human beings were not at the mercy of a world they could not understand, but rather they could learn the secrets of nature and, with education as their tool, harness the world to do their bidding.

Not only did scientific and economic development take off, but philosophers applied the intoxicating new theories about the potential of knowledge to the political world. Thomas Hobbes (who slightly preceded the Enlightenment) and John Locke, two English philosophers, came up with theories about how government should be established that discredited divine right. Governments are born not because

God ordains them, but because life without government is "solitary, poor, nasty, brutish, and short" in Hobbes's words, and "inconvenient" in Locke's. The foundation of government is reason, not faith, and reason leads people to consent to being governed because they are better off that way.

The idea of citizenship that was born in the Enlightenment constituted another break with the past. People have freedom and rights before government exists, declared Locke. When they decide they are better off with government than without it, they enter into a *social contract*, giving up a few of those rights in exchange for the protection of the rest of their rights by a government established by the majority. If that government fails to protect their rights, then it has broken the contract and the people are free to form a new government, or not, as they please. But the key element here is that for authority to be legitimate, citizens must *consent* to it. Note, however, that nowhere did Locke suggest that all people ought to participate in politics, or that people are necessarily equal. In fact, he was concerned mostly with the preservation of private property, suggesting that only property owners would have cause to be bothered with government because only they have something concrete to lose.

Sources of Democracy Closer to Home

While philosophers in Europe were beginning to explore the idea of individual rights and democratic governance, there had long been democratic stirrings on the founders' home continent. The Iroquois Confederacy was an alliance of five (and eventually six) East Coast Native American nations whose constitution, the "Great Law of Peace," impressed American leaders such as Benjamin Franklin with its suggestions of federalism, separation of powers, checks and balances, and consensus building. While historians are not sure that these ideas had any direct influence on the founders' thinking about American governance, they were clearly part of the stew of ideas that the founders could dip into, and some scholars make the case that their influence was significant.[9]

Do subjects enjoy any advantages that citizens don't have?

Thinking Outside **the Box**

> **republic** a government in which decisions are made through representatives of the people

Citizenship in America
The tension between a self-interested nature and a public-interested ideal

For our purposes, the most important thing about these ideas about politics is that they were prevalent at the same time the American founders were thinking about how to build a new government. Locke particularly influenced the writings of James Madison, a major author of our Constitution. The founders wanted to base their new government on popular consent, but they did not want to go too far. Madison, as we will see, was particularly worried about a system that was too democratic.

The Dangers of Democracy

Enthusiastic popular participation under the government established by the Articles of Confederation—the document that tied the colonies together before the Constitution was drafted—almost ended the new government before it began. Like Locke, Madison thought government had a duty to protect property, and if people who didn't have property could get involved in politics, they might not care about protecting the property of others. Worse, they might form "factions," groups pursuing their own self-interests rather than the public interest, and even try to get some of that property for themselves. So Madison rejected notions of "pure democracy," in which all citizens would have direct power to control government, and opted instead for what he called a "republic."

A **republic**, according to Madison, differs from a democracy mainly in that it employs representation and can work in a large state. Most theorists agree that democracy is impossible in practice if there are a lot of citizens and all have to be

heard from. But we do not march to Washington or phone our legislator every time we want to register a political preference. Instead, we choose representatives—members of the House of Representatives, senators, and the president—to represent our views for us. Madison thought this would be a safer system than direct participation (all of us crowding into town halls or the Capitol) because public passions would be cooled off by the process. You might be furious about health care costs when you vote for your senator, but he or she will represent your views with less anger. The founders hoped that the representatives would be older, wealthier, and wiser than the average American, and that they would be better able to make cool and rational decisions.

Madison's Vision of Citizenship

The notion of citizenship that emerges from Madison's writings is not a very flattering one for the average American, and it is important to note that it is not the only ideal of citizenship in the American political tradition. Madison's low expectations of the American public were a reaction to an earlier tradition that had put great faith in the ability of democratic man to put the interests of the community ahead of his own, to act with what scholars call "republican virtue." According to this idea, a virtuous citizen could be trusted with the most serious of political decisions because if he (women were not citizens at that time, of course) were properly educated and kept from the influence of scandal and corruption, he would be willing to sacrifice his own advancement for the sake of the whole. His decisions would be guided not by his self-interest but by his public-interested spirit. At the time of the founding, hope was strong that, although the court of the British monarch had become corrupt beyond redemption, America was still a land where virtue could triumph over greed. In fact, for many people this was a crucial argument for American independence: severing the ties would prevent that corruption from creeping across the Atlantic and would allow the new country to keep its virtuous political nature free from the British taint.[10]

When democratic rules that relied on the virtue, or public interestedness, of the American citizen were put into effect, however, especially in the days immediately after independence, these expectations seemed to be doomed. Instead of acting for the good of the community, Americans

Thinking Outside the Box

When, if ever, should individuals be asked to sacrifice their own good for that of their country?

seemed to be just as self-interested as the British had been. When given nearly free rein to rule themselves, they had no trouble remembering the rights of citizenship but ignored the responsibilities that come with it. They passed laws in state legislatures that canceled debts and contracts and otherwise worked to the advantage of the poor majority of farmers and debtors—and that seriously threatened the economic and political stability of the more well-to-do. It was in this context of national disappointment that Madison devised his notion of the republic. Since people had proved, so he thought, not to be activated by virtue, then a government must be designed that would produce virtuous results, regardless of the character of the citizens who participated in it.

American Citizenship Today

Today two competing views of citizenship still exist in the United States. One, echoing Madison, sees human nature as self-interested and holds that individual participation in government should be limited, that "too much" democracy is a bad thing. The second view continues to put its faith in the citizen's ability to act virtuously, not just for his or her own good but for the common good. President John F. Kennedy movingly evoked such a view in his inaugural address in 1960, when he urged Americans to "ask not what your country can do for you—ask what you can do for your country." These views of citizenship have coexisted throughout our history. Especially in times of crisis such as war or national tragedy, the second view of individual sacrifice for the public good has seemed more prominent. In the wake of September 11, 2001, citizens freely gave their time and money to help their fellow countrypeople and were more willing to join the military and volunteer for community service. At other times, and particularly at the national level of politics, the dominant view of citizenship has appeared to be one of self-interested actors going about their own business with little regard for the public good. When observers claim, as they often do today, that there is a crisis of American citizenship, they usually mean that civic virtue is taking second place to self-interest as a guiding principle of citizenship.

These two notions of citizenship do not necessarily have to be at loggerheads, however. Where self-interest and public

Involved Citizenship
While Americans emphasize the individual, they don't always shun collective action. Americans contribute to the public interest through volunteer efforts, particularly in times of crisis. Such involvement is a prominent sign of civic virtue, which usually comes second to self-interest in the American view of citizenship.

spirit meet in democratic practice is in the process of deliberation, collectively considering and evaluating goals and ideals for communal life and action. Individuals bring their own agendas and interests, but in the process of discussing them with others holding different views, parties can find common ground and turn it into a base for collective action. Conflict can erupt too, of course, but the process of deliberation at least creates a forum from which the possibility of consensus might emerge. Scholar and journalist E. J. Dionne reflects on this possibility: "At the heart of republicanism [remember that this is not a reference to our modern parties] is the belief that self-government is not a drab necessity but a joy to be treasured. It is the view that politics is not simply a grubby confrontation of competing interests but an arena in which citizens can learn from each other and discover an 'enlightened self-interest' in common." Despite evidence of a growing American disaffection for politics, Dionne hopes that Americans will find again the "joy" in self-governance because, he warns, "A nation that hates politics will not long thrive as a democracy."[11]

This book is an introduction to American politics, and in a way it is also an introduction to political science. Political science is not exactly the same kind of science as biology or geology. Not only is it difficult to put our subjects (people and political systems) under a microscope to observe their behavior, but we are somewhat limited in our ability to test our theories. We cannot replay World War II to test our ideas about what caused it, for example. A further problem is our subjectivity; we are the phenomena under investigation, and so we may have stronger feelings about our research and our findings than we would, say, about cells and rocks.

These difficulties do not make a science of politics impossible, but they do mean we must proceed with caution. Even among political scientists there is disagreement about whether a rigorous science of the political world is a reasonable goal. What we can agree on is that it is possible to advance our understanding of politics beyond mere guessing or debates about political preferences. Although we use many methods in our work (statistical analysis, mathematical modeling, case studies, and philosophical reasoning, to name only a few), what political scientists have in common is an emphasis on *critical thinking* about politics.

Critical thinking means challenging the conclusions of others, asking why or why not, turning the accepted wisdom upside down, and exploring alternative interpretations. It means considering the sources of information— not accepting an explanation just because someone in authority offers it, or because you have always been told that it is the true explanation, but because you have independently discovered that there are good reasons for accepting it. You may emerge from reading this textbook with the same ideas about politics that you have always had; it is not our goal to change your mind. But as a critical thinker, you will be able to back up your old ideas with new and persuasive arguments of your own, or to move beyond your current ideas to see politics in a new light.

Becoming adept at critical thinking has a number of benefits:

- We learn to be good democratic citizens. Critical thinking helps us sort through the barrage of information that regularly assails us, and it teaches us to process this information thoughtfully. Critical awareness of what our leaders are doing and the ability to understand and evaluate what they tell us is the lifeblood of democratic government.

- We are better able to hold our own in political (or other) arguments: we think more logically and clearly, we are more persuasive, and we impress people with our grasp of reason and fact. There is not a career in the world that is not enhanced by critical thinking skills.

- We become much better students. The skills of the critical thinker are not just the skills of the good citizen; they are the skills of the scholar. When we read critically we figure out what is important quickly and easily, we know what questions to ask to tease out more meaning, we can decide whether what we are reading is worth our time, and we know what to take with us and what to discard.

Although it may sound a little dull and dusty, critical thinking can be a vital and enjoyable activity. When we are good at it, it empowers and liberates us. We are not at the mercy of others' conclusions and decisions. We can evaluate facts and arguments for ourselves, turning conventional wisdom upside down and exploring the world of ideas with confidence.

How does one learn to think critically?

The trick to learning how to think critically is to do it. It helps to have a model to follow, however, and we provide one below. The focus of critical thinking here is on understanding political argument. Argument in this case refers not to a confrontation or a fight, but rather to a political contention, based on a set of assumptions, supported by evidence, leading to a clear, well-developed conclusion with consequences for how we understand the world.

Critical thinking involves constantly asking questions about the arguments we read: who has created it, what is the basic case and what values underlie it, what evidence is used to back it up, what conclusions are drawn, and what difference does the whole thing make. To help you remember the questions to ask, we have used a mnemonic device that creates an acronym from the five major steps of critical thinking. Until asking these questions becomes second nature, thinking of them as CLUES to critical thinking about American politics will help you keep them in mind as you read.

This is what CLUES stands for:

- **C**onsider the source and the audience
- **L**ay out the argument and the underlying values and assumptions

- **U**ncover the evidence
- **E**valuate the conclusion
- **S**ort out the political implications

We'll investigate each of these steps in a little more depth.

Consider the source and the audience

Who wrote the argument in question? Where did the item appear? What audience is it directed toward? What does the author or publisher need to do to attract and keep the audience? How might that affect content?

If the person is a mainstream journalist, he or she probably has a reputation as an objective reporter to preserve, and will at least make an honest attempt to provide unbiased information. Even so, knowing the actual news source will help you nail that down. Even in a reputable national paper like the *New York Times* or the *Wall Street Journal*, if the item comes from the editorial pages, you can count on it having an ideological point of view—usually (but not exclusively) liberal in the case of the *Times*, conservative in the case of the *Wall Street Journal*. Opinion magazines will have even more blatant points of view. Readers go to those sources looking for a particular perspective, and that may affect the reliability of the information you find.

Lay out the argument and the underlying values and assumptions

What basic argument does the author want to make? What assumptions about the world does he or she make? What values does he or she hold about what is important and what government should do? Are all the important terms clearly defined?

If these things aren't clear to you, the author may be unclear about them, too. There is a lot of sloppy thinking out there, and being able to identify it and discard it is very valuable. You may be intimidated by a smart-sounding argument, only to discover on closer examination that it just doesn't hold up. A more insidious situation occurs when the author is trying to obscure the point to get you to sign on to something that you might not otherwise accept. If the argument, values, and assumptions are not perfectly clear and up front, there may be a hidden agenda you should know about. You don't want to be persuaded by someone who claims to be an advocate for democracy, only to

find out that democracy means something completely different to him or her than it does to you.

Uncover the evidence

Has the author done basic research to back up his or her argument with facts and evidence?

Good arguments cannot be based on gut feelings, rumor, or wishful thinking. They should be based on hard evidence, either empirical, verifiable observations about the world or solid, logical reasoning. If the argument is worth being held, it should stand up to rigorous examination, and the author should be able to defend it on these grounds. If the evidence or logic is missing, the argument can usually be dismissed.

Evaluate the conclusion

Is the argument successful? Does it convince you? Why or why not? Does it change your mind about any beliefs you held previously? Does accepting this argument require you to rethink any of your other beliefs?

Conclusions should follow logically from the assumptions and values of an argument, if solid evidence and reasoning support it. What is the conclusion here? What is the author asking you to accept as the product of his or her argument? Does it make sense to you? Do you "buy it"? If you do, does it fit with your other ideas, or do you need to refine what you previously thought? Have you learned from this argument, or have you merely had your own beliefs reinforced?

Sort out the political implications

What is the political significance of this argument? What difference does it make to your understanding of the way the political world works? How does it affect who gets what scarce resources and how they get them? How does it affect who wins in the political process and who loses?

Political news is valuable if it means something. If it doesn't, it may entertain you, but essentially it wastes your time if it claims to be something more than entertainment. Make the information you get prove its importance, and if it doesn't, find a different news source to rely on.

Source: Adapted from the authors' "Preface to the Student," in Christine Barbour and Matthew J. Streb, eds., *Clued in to Politics: A Critical Thinking Reader in American Government*, 2nd ed. (Washington, D.C.: CQ Press, 2006).

> *critical thinking* analysis and evaluation of ideas and arguments based on reason and evidence
>
> *analysis* understanding how something works by breaking it down into its component parts

> *evaluation* assessing how well something works or performs according to a particular standard or yardstick

How to Use the Themes and Features in This Book

Our primary goal in this book is to get you thinking critically about American politics. Critical thinking is a crucial skill to learn no matter what training your major or career plans call for. As we discuss in the *Consider the Source* box in this chapter, *critical thinking* is the analysis and evaluation of ideas and arguments based on reason and evidence—it means digging deep into what you read and what you hear and asking tough questions. Critical thinking is what all good scholars do, and it is also what savvy citizens do.

As Figure 1.4 illustrates, our analytic and evaluative tasks in this book focus on the twin themes of power and citizenship. We have adopted the classic definition of politics proposed by the late political scientist Harold Lasswell that politics is "who gets what when and how." We simplify his understanding by dropping the *when* and focusing on politics as the struggle by citizens over who gets power and resources in society and how they get them, although we do occasionally use timelines to illustrate how the struggle for power and resources can change dramatically over time. (Look for the *Who, What, How, and WHEN* feature in many chapters, as well as other timelines that help to highlight the role of time in determining who gets what and how in American politics.)

Lasswell's definition of politics gives us a framework of *analysis* for this book; that is, it outlines how we break down politics into its component parts in order to understand it. Analysis helps us understand how something works, much like taking apart a car and putting it back together again helps us understand how it runs. Lasswell's definition provides a strong analytic framework because it focuses our attention on questions we can ask to figure out what is going on in politics.

Accordingly, in this book, we analyze American politics in terms of three sets of questions:

- **Who** are the parties involved? What resources, powers, and rights do they bring to the struggle?

- **What** do they have at stake? What do they stand to win or lose? Is it power, influence, position, policy, or values?

- **How** do the rules shape the outcome? Where do the rules come from? What strategies or tactics do the political actors employ to use the rules to get what they want?

If you know who is involved in a political situation, what is at stake, and how (under what rules) the conflict over resources will eventually be resolved, you will have a pretty good grasp of what is going on, and you will probably be able to figure out new situations, even when your days of taking a course in American government are far behind you. To get you in the habit of asking those questions, we have designed several features in this text explicitly to reinforce them.

As you found at the start of your reading, each chapter opens with a *What's at Stake?* feature that analyzes a political situation in terms of what various groups of citizens stand to win or lose. Each chapter ends with a *What's at Stake Revisited* feature, where we return to the issues raised in the introduction, once you have the substantive material of the chapter under your belt. We also focus our analysis along the way by closing each major chapter section with a *Who, What, How* feature that explicitly addresses these questions and concisely summarizes what you have learned. We reinforce the task of analysis with a *Consider the Source* feature in each chapter that discusses ways you can improve your critical thinking skills by analyzing (that is, taking apart) different kinds of sources of information about politics. Finally, *Thinking Outside the Box* questions, found throughout each chapter, help you take the analysis one step further: What if the rules or the actors or the stakes were different? What would be the impact on American politics? How would it work differently?

As political scientists, however, we not only want to understand *how* the system works, we also want to assess *how well* it works. A second task of critical thinking is *evaluation*, or seeing how well something measures up according to a standard or principle. We could choose any number of standards by which to evaluate American politics, but the most relevant, for most of us, is the principle of democracy and the role of citizens.

We can draw on the two traditions of self-interested and public-interested citizenship we have discussed to evaluate the powers, opportunities, and challenges presented to

Figure 1.4

Themes and Goal of This Book

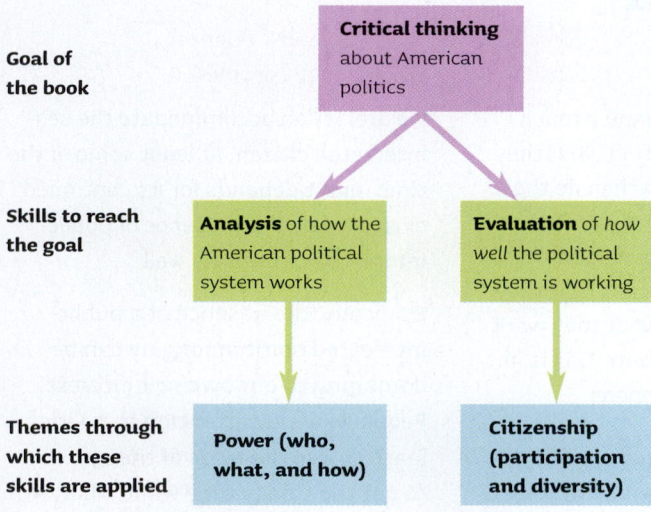

Goal of the book — Critical thinking about American politics

Skills to reach the goal — **Analysis** of how the American political system works · **Evaluation** of *how well* the political system is working

Themes through which these skills are applied — **Power (who, what, and how)** · **Citizenship (participation and diversity)**

American citizens by the system of government under which they live. In addition to the two competing threads of citizenship in America, we can also look at the kinds of action that citizens engage in and whether they take advantage of the options available to them. For instance, citizen action might be restricted by the rules, or by popular interest, to merely choosing between competing candidates for office, as in the model of *elite democracy* described earlier. Alternatively, the rules of the system might encourage citizens to band together in groups to get what they want, as they do in *pluralist democracy*. Or the system might be open and offer highly motivated citizens a variety of opportunities to get involved, as they do in *participatory democracy*. American democracy has elements of all three of these models, and one way to evaluate citizenship in America is to look at what opportunities for each type of participation exist and whether citizens take advantage of them.

To evaluate how democratic the United States is, we look at the changing concept and practice of citizenship in this country with respect to the subject matter of most chapters in a section called *The Citizens and. . . .* That feature looks at

citizenship from many angles, considering the following types of questions: What role do "the people" have in American politics? How has that role expanded or diminished over time? What kinds of political participation do the rules of American politics (formal and informal) allow, encourage, or require citizens to take? What kinds of political participation are discouraged, limited, or forbidden? Do citizens take advantage of the opportunities for political action that the rules provide them? How do they react to the rules that limit their participation? How do citizens in different times exercise their rights and responsibilities? What do citizens need to do to "keep" the republic? How democratic is the United States?

To put all this in perspective, the book includes two other features that give you a more concrete idea of what citizen participation might mean on a personal level. In each chapter, *Profiles in Citizenship* introduce you to individuals who have committed a good part of their lives to public service and focus on what citizenship means to those people and what inspired them to take on a public role. *Who Are We?* provides some demographic data to bring the diversity of the American citizenry front and center and highlight the difficulties inherent in uniting into a single nation individuals and groups with such different and often conflicting interests.

We have outlined nine features that recur throughout this book. Remember that each is designed to help you to think critically about American politics either by analyzing power in terms of who gets what, and how, or by evaluating citizenship to determine how well we are keeping Benjamin Franklin's mandate to keep the republic. And remember that further exploration of the book's themes is always available on the companion web site at http://republic.cqpress.com.

Thinking Outside the Box

Why does critical thinking feel like so much more work than "regular thinking"?

▶ What's at Stake Revisited

We began this chapter by asking whether youthful engagement in politics is really a matter of great importance, and what might be at stake in the question of whether the gains in the youth vote we saw in 2008 turn out to be permanent. Since then we have covered a lot of ground, arguing that politics is fundamental to human life and, in fact, makes life easier for us by giving us a nonviolent way to resolve disputes. We pointed out that politics is a method by which power and resources get distributed in society: politics is who gets what, and how they get it. Citizens who are aware and involved stand a much greater chance of getting what they want from the system than do those who check out or turn away. One clear consequence when young people disregard politics, then, is that they are less likely to get what they want from the political system. This is, in fact, exactly what happens.

There are also consequences for the system as a whole. Democracy is neither inevitable nor self-sustaining. As we will see in this book, the American system is a work of political genius that in many ways takes us as we are. It can accommodate the self-interested citizen, at least some of the time, but it depends for its continued existence on the presence of public-interested citizens as well.

Ironically, the absence of a public-interested spirit among us can be damaging to our own self-interest. People who pay attention to politics learn to use the rules of the system to get the things they want. Many college students complained that the 2000 election, with its focus on prescription drug coverage for the elderly and the financial solvency of Social Security, was "not about them" or the issues they cared about. A glance at voter turnout statistics tells us why: older people vote in far greater numbers than do young people. By not participating, young people ensure that they are not a force that politicians have to reckon with.

The increased youth vote in 2004 and 2008, however, makes it likely that politicians will not soon risk ignoring the areas of government action that matter to young people. "Young voters are back, and politicians will ignore them at their peril," one political science professor told the *Boston Globe*. "I'm convinced that we've turned the corner and that young Americans will continue to be important players in the electoral process."[12]

GENERATION GAP

We always rely on government to provide some things—good schools, safe neighborhoods, well-maintained roads, a stable economy—but in times of war or other national crises, government looms even larger in our lives. We depend on it to protect us, our families, our homes, and our livelihoods. At that point, our failure to be able to use the system to get the things we value becomes far more critical. Consider one issue that has affected many generations of young people during wartime: the draft. From 1948 to 1973, young American men were drafted into compulsory military service. Although the draft ended in 1973, President Jimmy Carter made it mandatory for men aged eighteen to twenty-five to register with the Selective Service. Failure to do so can be punished with a $250,000 fine and five years in jail, and offenders cannot get student loans or government jobs. Although there are no current plans to reinstate the draft, officials moved fast after September 11, 2001, to fill vacancies on Selective Service or draft boards around the country.[13] Before the 2004 election, rumors flew fast and furiously that the Iraq war, almost universally believed to need more manpower, would require a draft.[14] Young people could hardly claim that issue is "not about them."

But it is not just young people who have a stake in their own indifference to politics. All American citizens are at risk, for in a very real sense, the future of the American republic is in the hands of those who are just today learning to keep it. As we have argued in this chapter, keeping the republic requires constant vigilance and critical citizenship. As we proceed through this introduction to American politics, remember what you have at stake in becoming an educated citizen of the U.S. government.

To Sum Up

Key terms, chapter summaries, practice quizzes, Internet links, and other study aids are available on the companion web site at http://republic.cqpress.com.

Define | **Understand** | **Practice** | **Read** | **Click** | **Watch**

advanced industrial democracy (p. 14)

analysis (p. 22)

anarchy (p. 12)

authoritarian capitalism (p. 11)

authoritarian governments (p. 11)

authority (p. 7)

capitalist economy (p. 8)

citizens (p. 14)

communist democracy (p. 14)

critical thinking (p. 22)

democracy (p. 12)

divine right of kings (p. 17)

economics (p. 8)

elite democracy (p. 13)

Enlightenment (p. 17)

evaluation (p. 22)

government (p. 6)

institutions (p. 7)

laissez-faire capitalism (p. 9)

legitimate (p. 6)

participatory democracy (p. 13)

pluralist democracy (p. 13)

politics (p. 6)

popular sovereignty (p. 13)

power (p. 6)

procedural guarantees (p. 9)

Protestant Reformation (p. 17)

regulated capitalism (p. 9)

republic (p. 18)

rules (p. 7)

social contract (p. 17)

social democracy (p. 10)

social order (p. 6)

socialist economy (p. 9)

subjects (p. 14)

substantive guarantees (p. 9)

totalitarian (p. 11)

Define | **Understand** | **Practice** | **Read** | **Click** | **Watch**

- Politics may appear to be a grubby, greedy pursuit, filled with scandal and backroom dealing. In fact, despite its shortcomings and sometimes shabby reputation, politics is an essential means for resolving differences and determining how power and resources are distributed in society. Politics is about who gets power and resources in society—and how they get them.

- Government, a product of the political process, is the system established for exercising authority over a group of people. In America, the government is embodied in the Constitution and the institutions set up by the Constitution. The Constitution represents the compromises and deals made by the founders on a number of fundamental issues, including how best to divide governing power.

- Politics establishes the rules and institutions that shape how power is distributed in political interactions. The most fundamental rules of our political system are those that define and empower our political institutions and the way these institutions interact with each other and with individual citizens.

- Government is shaped not only by politics but also by economics, which is concerned specifically with the distribution of wealth and society's resources. The United States has a regulated capitalist economy, which means that property is owned privately and decisions about the production of goods and the distribution of wealth are left to marketplace forces with some governmental control.

- Political systems dictate how power is distributed among leaders and citizens, and these systems take many forms. Authoritarian systems give ultimate power to the state; non-authoritarian systems, like democracy, place power largely in the hands of the people. Democracy is based on the principle of popular sovereignty, giving the people the ultimate power to govern. The meaning of citizenship is key to the definition of democracy, and citizens are believed to have rights protecting them from government as well as responsibilities to the public realm.

- The meaning of American democracy can be traced to the time of the nation's founding. During that period, two competing views of citizenship emerged. The first view, articulated by James Madison, sees the citizen as fundamentally self-interested; this view led the founders to fear too much citizen participation in government. The second view puts faith in citizens' ability to act for the common good, to put their obligation to the public ahead of their own self-interest. Both views are still alive and well today, and we can see evidence of both sentiments at work in political life.

- In this book we look at two ways of thinking critically about American politics: analyzing how our American political system works and evaluating how well it works. We rely on two underlying themes to pursue this course. The first is the assumption that all political events and situations can be examined by looking at who the actors are, what they have to win or lose, and how the rules shape the way these actors engage in their struggle. This analytic framework should provide us with a clear understanding of how power functions in our system. Examining who gets what they want and how they achieve it in political outcomes highlights the second theme of this text: how diverse citizens participate in political life to improve their own individual situations and to promote the interests of the community at large. We evaluate citizenship carefully as a means to determine how well the American system is working.

Define | **Understand** | **Practice** | **Read** | **Click** | **Watch**

1. **In the definition of politics we have discussed, rules can be thought of as the**
   a. who.
   b. what.
   c. how.
   d. where.
   e. when.

2. **Which of the following systems is based on substantive guarantees?**
   a. Regulated capitalism
   b. Laissez-faire
   c. Socialism
   d. Anarchy
   e. Democracy

3. **The two competing views of U.S. citizenship incorporate**
   a. authority and subjecthood.
   b. public interest and private interest.
   c. virtue and vice.
   d. tolerance and bigotry.
   e. democracy and republicanism.

4. **Which of the following is true regarding ancient Greek (Athenian) democracy?**
   a. It became the model copied in its entirety in the Articles of Confederation.
   b. It established a republic in which representatives were chosen to voice the people's wishes.
   c. It was a participatory democracy, but only a small percentage of the people were citizens.
   d. It was the first system in which slaves were given the right to vote.
   e. It became the model copied in its entirety in the Constitution.

5. **Which of the following is NOT associated with Locke's argument about a social contract?**
   a. For governmental authority to be legitimate, citizens must consent to it.
   b. People give government legitimacy by deciding it is better to be governed than not.
   c. People enter into a social contract, agreeing to give up certain rights for the protection of others.
   d. If government fails to protect citizens' rights, then people are free to form a new government.
   e. The divine right of kings should provide the legitimacy of any government.

Define | **Understand** | **Practice** | **Read** | **Click** | **Watch**

Dalton, Russell J. 2008. *The Good Citizen: How a Younger Generation Is Reshaping American Politics*. Washington, D.C.: CQ Press. Dalton shows that trends in participation and policy priorities reflect a younger generation that is more engaged, more tolerant, and more supportive of social justice, leading, he claims, to new norms of citizenship and a renaissance of democratic participation.

Dionne, E. J., Jr. 1991. *Why Americans Hate Politics*. New York: Simon & Schuster. Why do Americans "hate" politics? Dionne argues that partisan politics make it impossible for politicians to solve the very problems they promise the voters they'll address.

Hobbes, Thomas. 1996. *Leviathan*. Edited by Richard Tuck. Cambridge Texts in the History of Political Thought. New York: Cambridge University Press. Writing in 1651, English philosopher Thomas Hobbes described a state of nature in which life is "solitary, poor, nasty, brutish, and short." His analysis of society and power explains why citizens agree to be ruled by a powerful state: to preserve peace and security.

Jamieson, Kathleen Hall. 2000. *Everything You Think You Know About Politics . . . and Why You're Wrong*. New York: Basic Books. In a collection of essays, Jamieson uses political fact rather than personal opinions to dispel a variety of myths regarding American politics.

Lasswell, Harold. 1936. *Politics: Who Gets What, When, and How*. New York: McGraw-Hill. Lasswell's classic work on politics, originally published in 1911, lays out the definition of politics that is used throughout this textbook.

Locke, John. 1952. *Second Treatise on Government*. With Introduction by Thomas P. Peardon. Indianapolis, Ind.: Bobbs-Merrill. Here you'll find Locke's influential ideas about natural rights, consent, the social contract, and the legitimacy of revolting against a government that breaks the contract.

Putnam, Robert D. 2000. *Bowling Alone: The Collapse and Revival of American Community*. New York: Simon & Schuster. In this influential book, Putnam argues that Americans have become increasingly disconnected from the societal bonds that hold their culture together.

Tocqueville, Alexis de. 1945. *Democracy in America*. Edited by Phillips Bradley. New York: Vintage Books. An intricate and extremely interesting report on American politics and culture as described by a visiting Frenchman during the nineteenth century.

Define   **Understand**   **Practice**   **Read**   **Click**   **Watch**

American Political Science Association   *www.apsanet.org. This web site of the leading professional organization for the study of political science offers excellent information on the study of political science, careers in the field, and its many publications.*

FirstGov.com   *Official information resource for the U.S. federal government, providing easy access to all online government resources.*

Internet Public Library   *www.ipl.org. The Internet Public Library, hosted by the University of Michigan, is a gateway to countless online sources. Look for the government and political science categories.*

Rock the Vote   *www.rockthevote.com. With endorsements from celebrities such as Christina Aguilera, Leonardo DiCaprio, and Bono, this campaign uses music and popular culture to incite young people to "step up, claim their voice in the political process, and change the way politics is done."*

SpeakOut.com   *This site, managed by an online opinion research company, provides a way for visitors to participate in online polls, send messages to public officials, and sign petitions on issues they care about.*

Define   **Understand**   **Practice**   **Read**   **Click**   **Watch**

Erin Brockovich   *2000. A woman down on her luck manages to find a job as a legal assistant and by connecting with others works toward the good of the community by exposing a power company that has been dumping toxic waste and poisoning a community. This popular film exposes what's at stake when an everyday citizen takes an interest and gets involved.*

Lord of the Flies   *1963. A group of schoolboys are shipwrecked on an uninhabited island and turn into savages for their own survival. While the movie (based on William Golding's 1954 novel) is chilling, it provides an excellent illustration of what life would be like without a ruling government.*

Nineteen Eighty-Four   *1984. This adaptation of George Orwell's classic novel depicts a totalitarian society in which the government controls all aspects of life.*

V for Vendetta   *2005. Heralded as a modern-day 1984, this movie imagines Britain under the yoke of a repressive and totalitarian regime in 2020. Inspired by Guy Fawkes's failed bombing of the British parliament in 1605, V, the mask-wearing antihero, must take drastic action to shake the citizenry from its indifference and effect revolutionary change.*

Chapter 2

American Citizens and Political Culture

▶ What's at Stake?

Let's test your knowledge of some basic American trivia. Is our national bird the eagle, or the turkey? (It's the eagle, adopted by Congress in 1782.) How about the national flower: the daffodil, or the rose? (The rose was declared our "national floral emblem" in 1986.) What's our official song: "America, the Beautiful" or "The Star Spangled Banner"? ("The Star Spangled Banner" became our national anthem in 1931.) Doing okay so far? Try this one: Is the official language of the United States of America called American or English? Stumped? Don't worry, it's a trick question. The United States has no official language at all.

No official language? Such a fact seems jarring on its face. Don't nations need an official language to hold them together and to provide for a common culture? Isn't language at least as important a symbol of national unity and pride as a bird, a flower, or a song?

Say What?

Though the United States has no official language, some people advocate for an "English Only" policy, which critics say would limit the rights of immigrants.

Supporters of a movement called "Official English" answer with an emphatic "yes," and they are working hard to make it happen. To them Official English means that, except in matters of public safety, English should be the only language sanctioned and used by the government—not only for official business in Congress, the courts, and the executive branch, but also on driver's license applications, ballots, applications for federal aid, and tax forms.

They argue that immigrants are better off when they learn English, so they should be forced to do so as fast as they can by being immersed in it—an approach their opponents call "sink or swim." They say bilingual education merely postpones the moment that immigrant children are assimilated into American culture, and that printing paperwork in multiple languages is costly to taxpayers and sends a signal to immigrants that it is not important that they learn English. Accordingly, they actively support legislation, or even an amendment to the Constitution, that would make English the official tongue of the United States.

Their opponents advocate a concept they call "English Plus." They hold that while English is and should remain the primary language in the United States, the languages that immigrants bring with them are a valuable resource that should be preserved. They say further that the guarantee of equal rights in the Constitution means that until people do learn English, they have a right to language assistance to give them equal access to American society.

National policy today comes closest to the English Plus model. Public schools must teach students in a language that they can understand while they are learning English, and official documents are printed in a variety of languages (for example, driver's license exams are given in forty-three languages, voting ballots are printed in twenty-eight, and instructions for the 2010 census were printed in fifty-nine). In 2000 President Bill Clinton gave the movement some teeth when he signed Executive Order 13166, which requires that federally funded programs be accessible to those with limited proficiency in English.

Supporters of English Plus say that, while not perfect, the system works. Although well over three hundred different languages are spoken in the United States, census figures say that 92 percent of the country's residents claim to speak English very well. Meanwhile, the ethnic diversity and traditions that immigrants cherish are preserved and honored, and the civil rights of all are protected. They say that their opponents, whom they call "English Only" advocates, are anti-immigrant and even racist.

Official English supporters, on the other hand, contend that the system is very broken indeed, and that English is in danger of losing its status as the primary national language, as more and more immigrants hold on to their own languages and cultures. They say that their opponents take political correctness too far or that they are un-American.

What is it about the idea of a national language that elicits such vigorous fighting and name-calling? Why is it so much more controversial than the effort to name our favored flora, fauna, or music? What is really at stake in the debate over whether English ought to be named the official language of the United States? ■

Our politics—what we want from government and how we try to get it— stems from who we are.

Over the years, American schoolchildren have grown up hearing two conflicting stories about who we are as a nation. The first, that we are a melting pot, implies that the United States is a vast cauldron into which go many cultures and ethnicities, all of which are boiled down into some sort of homogenized American stew. The other story, that we are a multicultural nation, tells us that each cultural, ethnic, and religious identity should be preserved and celebrated, lest its distinctive nature be lost. Reality, as is often the case, falls somewhere between these two competing images of the American people.

The rich diversity of the American people is one of the United States' greatest strengths, combining talents, tradition, culture, and custom from every corner of the world. But our diversity, far from being uniformly celebrated, has also contributed to some of the nation's deepest conflicts. We cannot possibly understand the drama that is American politics without an in-depth look at who the actors are: the *who* in many ways shapes the *what* and *how* of politics.

Our politics—what we want from government and how we try to get it—stems from who we are. Who Americans are—where they have come from and what they have brought with them, what their lives look like and how they spend their time and money, what they believe and how they act on those beliefs—helps determine what they choose to fight for politically and how they elect to carry out the fight. It is critically important, as we approach the study of American politics, that we understand who American citizens are: where their roots lie, what their lives are like, and what sorts of things they need and value.

Since we cannot, of course, meet all the Americans who are out there, we settle for the next best thing: we use statistics to provide us with relevant details about a large and unwieldy population. Throughout this book we use statistics, in the form of charts and graphs, to examine the demographic trends that shape our national culture—political and otherwise—in a feature called *Who Are We?* We'll use this information not only to understand better who we are but also to consider how the characteristics, habits, and lives of real people relate to the political issues that shape our society. (Be sure to read "*Consider the Source:* Don't Be Fooled by Charts and Graphs" on page 40, for a discussion of the uses and limits of statistics in politics. It will serve you well as you read this book.)

In "*Who Are We?* The American People," you will see that our population is aging gradually; older people demand more money for pensions and nursing home care, and they compete for scarce resources with younger families, who want better schools and health care for children. You will see that the white population in the United States will soon be outnumbered by ethnic and racial minority populations that traditionally support affirmative action and other policies (less popular with whites) designed to raise them up from the lower end of the socioeconomic scale. Our population is in constant flux, and every change in the make-up of the people brings a change in what we try to get from government and how we try to get it.

As you look at these depictions of the American people and American life, try to imagine the political problems that arise from such incredible diversity. How can a government represent the interests of people with such varied backgrounds, needs, and preferences? How does who we are affect what we want and how we go about getting it?

To help you better understand the *who* in American politics, in this chapter you will learn about

- **our roots as immigrants and the role of immigration in American politics**
- **demographic trends that help us see what Americans are like in terms of crucial variables like age, race, income level, and education, and the ways these trends affect American political life**
- **American political beliefs—those that pull us together as a nation and those that drive us into partisan divisions**

Who Is an American?
Native-born and naturalized citizens

In Chapter 1 we said that citizenship exacts obligations from individuals and also confers rights on them, and that the American concept of citizenship contains both self-interested and public-spirited elements. But citizenship is not only a normative concept—that is, a prescription for how governments ought to treat residents and how those residents ought to act; it is also a very precise legal status. A fundamental element of democracy is not just the careful specification of the rights and obligations of citizenship but also an equally careful legal description of just who is a citizen and how that status can be acquired by immigrants who choose to switch their allegiance to a new country. In this section we look at the legal definition

▶ Who Are We?

The American people

Who we are, as Americans, and who we will be in the future influences the types of demands we make on government, how much attention these demands will receive, and the government's ability to meet them. Over the next fifty years, the American population will become older; the most economically productive groups will decline as a percentage of the population. What do fewer workers and more dependents mean for the government's ability to get the revenues necessary to pay for the benefits and services citizens want? In addition, the racial and ethnic balance in the population will change as the white majority shrinks. Whose concerns are likely to get more attention from public officials in the future?

The Aging of America, 2000 to 2050: More dependents, fewer working Americans.

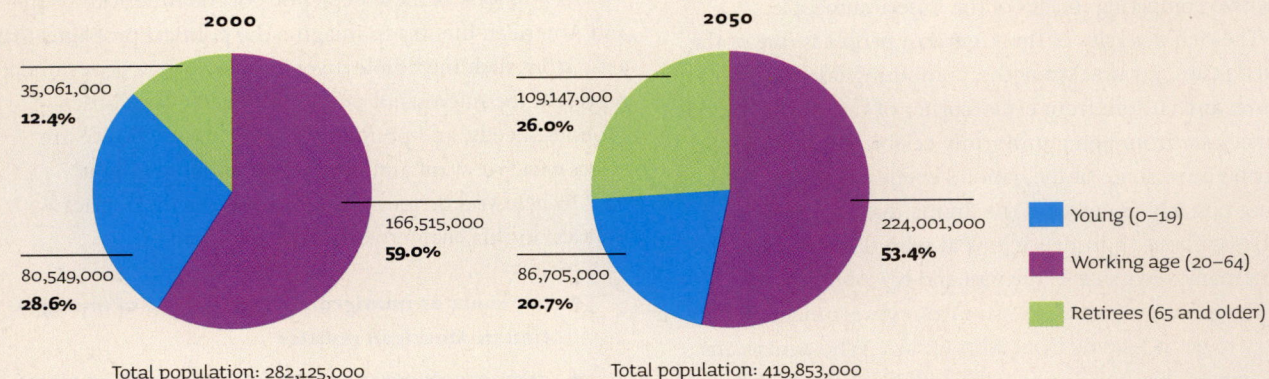

2000

35,061,000
12.4%

166,515,000
59.0%

80,549,000
28.6%

Total population: 282,125,000

2050

109,147,000
26.0%

224,001,000
53.4%

86,705,000
20.7%

Total population: 419,853,000

■ Young (0–19)

■ Working age (20–64)

■ Retirees (65 and older)

Source: U.S. Census Bureau, "U.S. Interim Projections by Age, Sex, Race, and Hispanic Origin," March 18, 2004, www.census.gov/ipc/www/usinterimproj/.

The U.S. Population by Race and Hispanic Origin, 2000 to 2050: The white majority is shrinking.

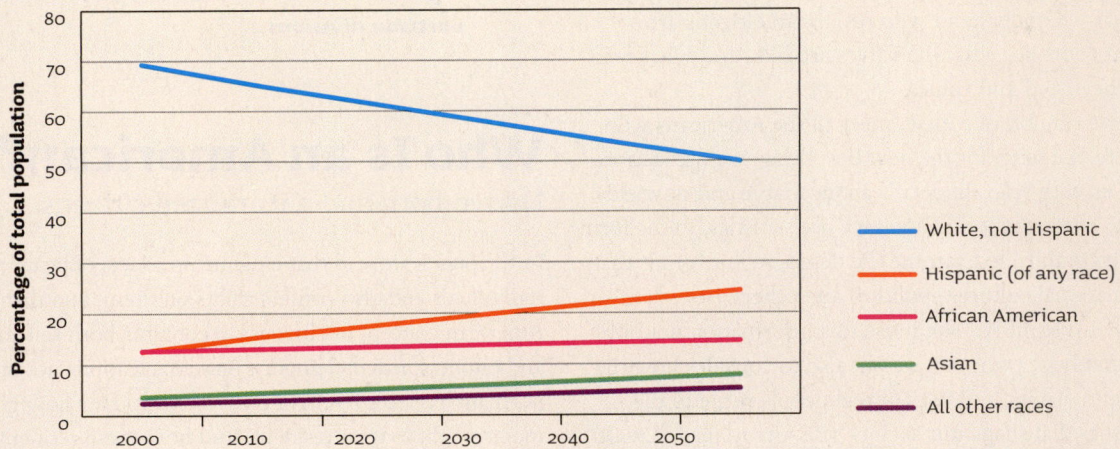

Percentage of total population

80 70 60 50 40 30 20 10 0

2000 2010 2020 2030 2040 2050

— White, not Hispanic

— Hispanic (of any race)

— African American

— Asian

— All other races

Source: U.S. Census Bureau, "U.S. Interim Projections by Age, Sex, Race, and Hispanic Origin," March 14, 2004, www.census.gov/ipc/www/usinterimproj.

Note: "All other races" includes those identified as "American Indian and Alaska Native" alone, "Native Hawaiian and Other Pacific Islander" alone, and "Two or More Races." Race and Hispanic origin are two separate concepts; people who identify their origin as Hispanic may be of any race.

> **immigrants** citizens or subjects of one country who move to another country to live or work
>
> **naturalization** the legal process of acquiring citizenship for someone who has not acquired it by birth

> **asylum** protection or sanctuary, especially from political persecution
>
> **refugees** individuals who flee an area or a country because of persecution on the basis of race, nationality, religion, group membership, or political opinion

of American citizenship and at the long history of immigration that has shaped our body politic.

American Citizenship

American citizens are usually born, not made. If you are born in any of the fifty states or in most of America's overseas territories, such as Puerto Rico or Guam, you are an American citizen, whether your parents are Americans or not. This follows the principle of international law called *jus soli*, which means literally "the right of the soil." The exceptions to this rule in the United States are children born to foreign diplomats serving in the United States and children born on foreign ships in U.S. waters. These children would not be considered U.S. citizens. According to another legal principle, *jus sanguinis* ("the right by blood"), if you are born outside the United States to American parents, you are also an American citizen (or you can become one if you are adopted by American parents). Interestingly, if you are born in the United States but one of your parents holds citizenship in another country, depending on that country's laws, you may be able to hold dual citizenship. Most countries, including the United States, require that a child with dual citizenship declare allegiance to one country on turning age eighteen. It is worth noting that requirements for U.S. citizenship, particularly as they affect people born outside the country, have changed frequently over time.

So far, citizenship seems relatively straightforward. But as we know, the United States since before its birth has been attractive to **immigrants**, people who are citizens or subjects of another country who come here to live and work. The feature *"Who Are We? Where We Come From"* helps us to understand some characteristics of the foreign-born population of the United States. Today there are strict limitations on the numbers of immigrants who may legally enter the country. There are also strict rules governing the criteria for entry. If immigrants come here legally on permanent resident visas—that is, if they follow the rules and regulations of the U.S. Citizenship and Immigration Services (USCIS)—they may be eligible to apply for citizenship through a process called **naturalization**.

Nonimmigrants

Many people who come to the United States do not come as legal permanent residents. The USCIS refers to these

people as nonimmigrants. Some arrive seeking **asylum**, or protection. These are political **refugees**, who are allowed into the United States if they face or are threatened with persecution because of their race, religion, nationality, membership in a particular social group, or political opinions. Not everyone who feels threatened is given legal refugee status, however. The USCIS requires that the fear of persecution be "well founded," and it is itself the final judge of a well-founded fear. Refugees may become legal permanent residents after they have lived here continuously for one year (although there are annual limits on the number who may do so), at which time they can begin accumulating the in-residence time required to become a citizen, if they wish to.

Other people who may come to the United States legally but without official permanent resident status include visitors, foreign government officials, students, international

>
> **Thinking Outside the Box**
>
> **Should it be possible to lose one's citizenship under any circumstances?**

Who Are We?

Where we come from

America has always been a land of immigrants. In recent years the number of immigrants has surged so that about one in eight people residing in the United States was born somewhere else. Of these, most come from Latin America and Asia, in contrast to earlier waves of immigration, which brought predominately white Europeans to America. What challenges does immigration make on a democratic system? What role does a common language play in forming a national identity and in enabling new arrivals to reach the American Dream?

Size of the Foreign-Born Population and Foreign Born as a Percentage of the Total Population, for the United States, 1850 to 2006: Major loosening of immigration policy in 1965 and 1986 has increased the immigrant population.

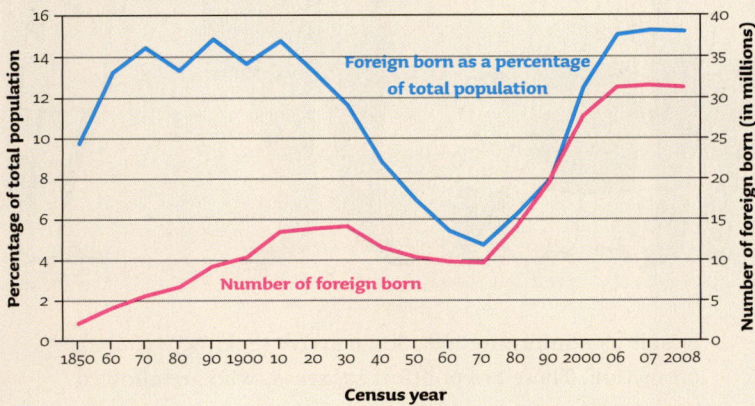

Source: Data from 2006–2008 are from the 2006, 2007, and 2008 American Community Surveys; 2000 data are from Census 2000 (see www.census.gov). All other data are from Campbell Gibson and Emily Lennon, U.S. Census Bureau, Working Paper No. 29, Historical Census Statistics on the Foreign-Born Population of the United States: 1850 to 1990 (Washington, D.C.: U.S. Government Printing Office, 1999), www.migrationinformation.org/datahub/charts/final.fb.shtml.

The Languages We Speak

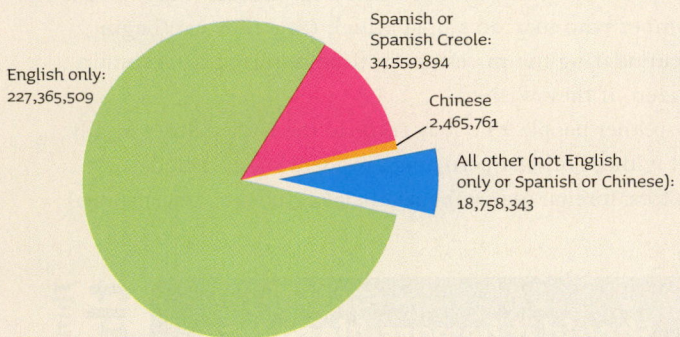

English only: 227,365,509

Spanish or Spanish Creole: 34,559,894

Chinese 2,465,761

All other (not English only or Spanish or Chinese): 18,758,343

Source: U.S. Census Bureau, 2008 American Community Survey, www.migration information.org/DataHub/state2.cfm?ID=US#table5.

Note: Data are for languages spoken at home by persons aged five years old and over.

Country of Origin for Today's Foreign-Born Americans:

More than 37,960,773 Americans were born outside the United States in 2008.

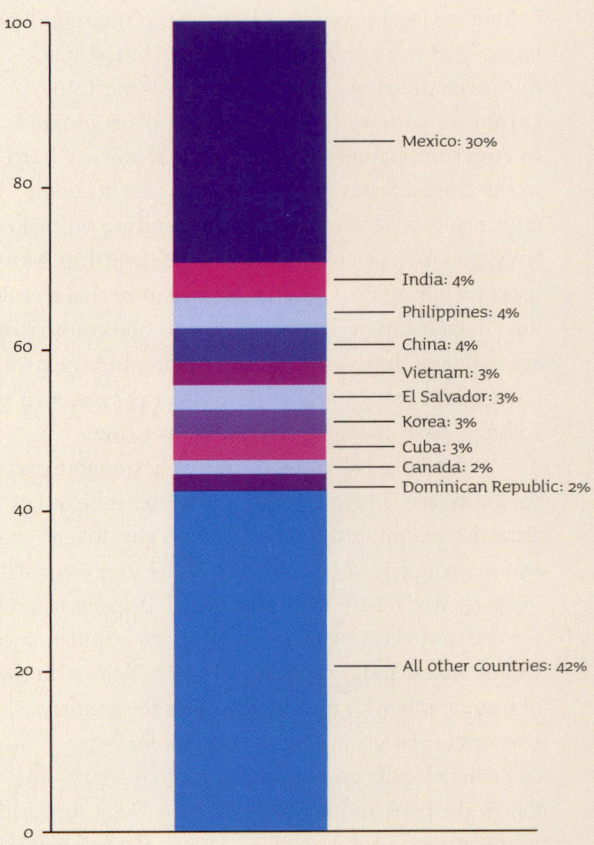

Mexico: 30%

India: 4%
Philippines: 4%
China: 4%
Vietnam: 3%
El Salvador: 3%
Korea: 3%
Cuba: 3%
Canada: 2%
Dominican Republic: 2%

All other countries: 42%

Source: U.S. Census Bureau, 2006, 2007, and 2008 American Community Surveys, "Table B05006: Place of Birth for the Foreign-Born Population"; Decennial Census 2000, Summary File 3, "Table QT-P15: Region and Country or Area of Birth of the Foreign-Born Population: 2000," www.migrationinformation.org/datahub/charts/10.2008.shtml.

representatives, temporary workers, members of foreign media, and exchange visitors. These people are expected to return to their home countries and not take up permanent residence in the United States.

Illegal immigrants have arrived here by avoiding the USCIS regulations, usually because they would not qualify for one reason or another. American laws have become increasingly harsh with respect to illegal immigrants, but people continue to come anyway. Many illegal immigrants act like "citizens," obeying the laws, paying taxes, and sending their children to school. Nonetheless, some areas of the country, particularly those near the Mexican-American border, like Texas and California, often have serious problems brought on by illegal immigration. Even with border controls to regulate the number of new arrivals, communities can find themselves swamped with new residents, often poor and unskilled, looking for a better life. Because their children must be educated and they themselves may be entitled to receive social services, they can pose a significant financial burden on those communities without necessarily increasing the available funds. Although many illegals pay taxes, many also work off the books, meaning they do not contribute to the tax base. Furthermore, most income taxes are federal, and federal money is distributed back to states and localities to fund social services based on the population count in the census. Since illegal immigrants are understandably reluctant to come forward to be counted, their communities are typically underfunded in that respect as well.

Just because a person is not a legal permanent resident of the United States does not mean that he or she has no rights and responsibilities here, any more than our traveling in another country means that we have no rights and obligations there. Immigrants enjoy some rights, primarily legal protections. Not only are they entitled to due process in the courts (guarantee of a fair trial, right to a lawyer, and so on), but the U.S. Supreme Court has ruled that it is illegal to discriminate against immigrants in the United States.[1] Nevertheless, their rights are limited. They cannot, for instance, vote in our national elections (although some localities, in the hopes of integrating immigrants into their communities, allow them to vote in local elections[2]) or decide to live here permanently without permission (which may or may not be granted). In addition, immigrants, even legal ones, are subject to the decisions of the USCIS, which is empowered by Congress to exercise authority in immigration matters.

Pledging Allegiance

Immigrants may serve in the U.S. military regardless of their citizenship. When becoming naturalized, they renounce their former home and vow to "support and defend" the United States "against all enemies." Shown here are some of the eighty-eight military personnel taking the oath of allegiance during a naturalization ceremony aboard the aircraft carrier USS *Ronald Reagan*.

U.S. Immigration Policy

Immigration law is made by Congress (with the approval of the president) and implemented by the federal agency we discussed in the previous section, the U.S. Citizenship and Immigration Services. The 1996 Illegal Immigration Reform and Immigrant Responsibility Act had granted the agency, then known as the Immigration and Naturalization Service (INS), considerable power to make nonappealable decisions at the border that can result in the deportation of an immigrant who may have quite innocently violated an immigration rule and then cannot reenter the country for five years. In the wake of September 11, 2001, security issues have come

▶ **Profiles in Citizenship: Esmeralda Santiago**

"The minute that I realized that I would not be silenced, then I knew I had to speak."

The weird thing about meeting a person whose memoirs you have read is that you know the intimate details of her life, and yet you don't know her at all. She's an old friend and a stranger, at once familiar and unknown.

But Esmeralda Santiago's voice is as warm as her writing, lilting with the echoes of her Puerto Rican childhood, curling around you, drawing you in. Welcomed into her home, offered a cup of tea, you don't stay a stranger for long. Santiago's fast grin dissolves into a rich, delicious chuckle, her huge brown eyes crinkle up, her soft dark hair, laced with silver, waves back from a face gently lined with a life generously lived.

It's an amazing journey she has made from the metal shack in Macun with the rude privy out back, where ripe, luscious guavas hang from the trees, free for the picking, to the tony hills of suburban New York, where the houses look like mansions and the indoor plumbing is elegant but the imported guavas in the grocery store are hard and expensive. It's an immigrant's journey that has taken every bit of strength and pluck and intelligence she could muster, and it has left her suspended between two cultures, at home in both, but belonging entirely to neither.

Sitting in her bright, light dining room, she describes how this cultural odyssey has shaped her allegiances. "When I talk about my community—depending on who's listening—they respond to different things. And so if I say 'my community' in a roomful of Latinos they think I'm speaking about Puerto Ricans, and if I'm in a roomful of women they think I'm talking about women, and of course in Westchester County they think I'm talking about Westchester."

Like all Puerto Ricans, she is an American citizen, but her faint accent and exotic beauty make it clear she is not "from here." But when she goes back to Puerto Rico, a place that means home even though she left when she was thirteen, she is not from there either. On the island she has been told that she is too American—that her accent is not right, her personality too assertive.

And so, in a voice that belongs to all immigrants, she says, "It's a constant flux of—Where is my culture? Which culture do I belong to? Which is my community? Who am I representing now? And is there a point at which I represent just me? And who is that person? That's why I write memoirs. To answer those questions."

---

to play a central role in deciding who may enter the country, and new legislation took the INS out of the Department of Justice, where it was formerly located, renamed it the U.S. Citizenship and Immigration Services, and placed it under the jurisdiction of the newly formed Department of Homeland Security.

Whom to Admit

No country, not even the huge United States, can manage to absorb every impoverished or threatened global resident who wants a better or safer life. Deciding whom to admit is a political decision—like all political decisions, one that results in winner and losers. Every job given to an immigrant means one less job for an American citizen, and jobs are just the sort of scarce resource over which political battles are fought. If times are good and unemployment is low, newcomers, who are often willing to do jobs Americans reject in prosperous times, may be welcomed with open arms, but when the economy hits hard times, immigration can become a bitter issue among jobless Americans. Immigrants, especially the very young and the very old, are also large consumers of social services and community resources. Immigrants do contribute to the economy through their labor and their taxes, but because they are distributed disproportionately throughout the population, some areas

And it is why her memoirs resonate so thoroughly with so many people who themselves have launched a new life in a new place, while not entirely releasing their grip on the old.

In all her communities, Santiago has become a voice for those who cannot speak for themselves. She says, "I think it comes from having to accompany my mother to the welfare office where I saw that somebody had to help these people, you know. And I would go there with my mother, but we would frequently spend the whole day because there were no translators for the other women and men there and so I would be the translator. I would be this little fifteen year old with really broken English, but I was the only one who could be an intermediary, and I think that that experience is one that I still live. I really feel like I'm out there speaking for people who, for whatever reasons, are not able to do that."

So today she is actively involved in issues she cares about, ranging from the protection of battered women, to the artistic development of adolescents, to the support of public libraries. Of the latter, she says, it is essential for the survival of democracy in an information age that there be places where people can go to get "the knowledge of the world" without having to spend the grocery money to get it. "That, to me," she says, "is democracy."

On why she speaks out:

With gifts comes responsibility. If you have a gift, it's not just a gift. If you're a painter, then it's not just a talent that you have. You have the responsibility to then express the soul of a people—of your community, whatever that community is. And for me, the minute that I realized that I would not be silenced, then I knew I had to speak. It was really that simple. I couldn't sleep, I couldn't look at myself in the mirror if I didn't speak about these things. . . . No matter what the personal cost and no matter what other people think. . . . I want to let them lose sleep over it [laughs]. I would like that better. I love it when I get calls the next day, saying, "I was up all night thinking about what you said yesterday," and I'm going, "Oh, good!" [laughs].

On the American founders and the job of keeping the republic:

Well, we forget about them. They're these old guys in funny costumes. We don't think of them as great thinkers and people who had a passion. . . . I mean they were humanists. They were not [just] creating a government, they were creating a community. We go back to that word . . . and they saw this as a community of people, of human beings, and that to me is what a country is. It's not the institutions; it's the people living there.

[Students] have to stop thinking about patriotism in terms of the country, the nation. . . . They have to think of it in terms of the guy sitting next to them. *Patria* is the people who make up a country. When it all changed for me was when I had to help somebody. . . . That's when I became patriotic. Because that human being needed help. And I could give it. ■

find their social service systems more burdened than others, and immigration can be a much more controversial issue in places where immigrants settle.

Nations typically want to admit immigrants who can do things the country's citizens are unable or unwilling to do. During and after World War II, when the United States wanted to develop a rocket program, German scientists with the necessary expertise were desirable immigrants. When the Soviet Union fell in 1991, we became concerned that former Soviets familiar with Moscow's weapons of mass destruction and other defense technology might be lured to work in countries we considered to be our enemies, so in 1992 Congress passed a special law making it easier for such scientists and their families to immigrate to the United States.

At times in our history when our labor force was insufficient for the demands of industrialization and railroad building and when western states wanted larger populations, immigrants were welcomed. Today, immigration law allows for temporary workers to come to work in agriculture when our own labor force falls short or is unwilling to work for low wages. President George W. Bush worked with Congress, although without success, to try to establish a formal guest worker program that would have allowed unskilled workers to work in the United States for a limited time. As a rule, however, our official immigration policy expects immigrants

When we talk about American politics, we frequently talk about large numbers—of people, of votes, of incomes, of ages, of policy preferences or opinions. Thinking about thousands, millions, even billions of things can boggle the mind, but charts, graphs, and other visual depictions can help us think about numbers and numerical relationships without getting tangled up in the sheer size of the quantities involved. As savvy consumers of American politics, we need to be able to sort through the barrage of numbers that are thrown at us daily.

Data and statistics

Political scientists, in fact all scientists, are focused on the empirical results of their research. When those data are in numerical or quantitative terms, like how many people say they voted for Democrats or Republicans, or how much of the federal budget is devoted to various programs like welfare and education, the result can look like one gigantic, unorganized mass of numbers.

To help bring order to the chaos, scientists use statistical analysis. Whereas a statistic, such as the population of the United States, is a numerical fact, statistics is the science of collecting, organizing, and interpreting numerical data. At its simplest, statistics allows us to calculate the mean, or average, of a bunch of numbers, and to see how far individual datapoints fall away from, or deviate from, the mean. For instance, instead of having to deal with income figures for all Americans, we can talk about the average income, and we can compare averages for different groups, and make intelligent observations about the distribution of income in the United States. When we do this, the numbers start to take on shape and organization, and we can talk about them in a useful way.

Statistical techniques allow us to compare groups and characteristics of groups with one another and over time, to discern relationships among characteristics that we might not otherwise be able to see, to look at the distribution of characteristics across a population, and to see how a part relates to the whole group. Although statistics can be used in almost any discipline, from economics to medicine, it is interesting to note that the word comes from the Latin for "state" or "government." Statistics might have been tailor-made for investigating political puzzles.

Displaying the data

Scientists need a way to show other people the data they have gathered and analyzed. It is here that a picture can often be worth a thousand words. Here are a few of the most common ways to display numerical data graphically:

- Tables are perhaps the simplest way to display data, and many tables appear in this book. In a table, information is arranged in columns (going down) and in rows (going across). To read information presented in this way, look carefully at the title or caption to see what the table is about. Read the column headings, and then follow the information along the rows.

- Bar charts are designed to allow you to compare two categories of things with each other: for example, groups of people (ages, gender, races), states, regions, or units of time. One set is plotted along the horizontal axis, the other on the vertical axis. The first graph on page 45 is a bar chart. To get the maximum amount of information from a bar chart, read the title carefully, and be sure you understand what is being

to be skilled and financially stable so that they do not become a burden on the American social services system. Remember that politics is about how power and resources are distributed in society; who gets to consume government services is a hotly contested issue.

Whether motivated by cultural stereotypes, global events, or domestic economic circumstances, Americans have decided at times that we have allowed "enough" immigrants to settle here, or that we are admitting too many of the "wrong" kind of immigrants, and we have encouraged politicians to enact restrictions. As the *Who, What, How, and WHEN* feature on pages 42 and 43 illustrates, all too often immigrants are scapegoated for the nation's problems and demonized as a threat to American culture. From 1882 to 1943, legislation outlawed Chinese immigration because westerners saw it as an economic and a cultural threat. Similarly, reacting to the large numbers of southern and eastern Europeans who began flooding into the country in the very late 1800s and early 1900s, legislation in the 1920s limited immigration by individual nationalities to a small percentage of the total number of immigrants already in residence from each country. This quota system favored the northern and western

measured on each axis and that you note the relationship between the two.

- Line graphs are related to bar charts, except that points are plotted to show up as a continuous line instead of a series of steps. In a line graph you can find a value on the vertical axis for every value on the horizontal axis. In a bar chart you want to make individual comparisons of the columns to each other, but in a line graph, you want your eye to sweep from one end of the graph to the other, to note broad trends and patterns. Frequently the variable on the horizontal axis is time, and the graph traces some other variable, perhaps age or number of immigrants or average income, across time. The upper left-hand graph on page 36, marking changes in the foreign-born population over time, is a line graph.

- Pie charts are a way of showing how some parts fit into the whole. In a pie chart, each wedge is a certain percentage (or so many hundredths) of the whole pie (which is 100 percent). For example, the top pie charts on page 34 allow us to see the population of the United States, broken down by age group—young (19 and under), working age (20–64), or retirees (65 and older). Seeing this information graphically gives us a clearer idea of the relationship of the parts and their relative sizes than we would get simply from reading the information in words. Another way to convey the same information in multiple pie charts is with a stacked bar chart, which is much like a pie chart except that the space is a rectangle instead of a circle, and it is divided into sections instead of wedges.

What to watch out for

Charts and graphs are a boon to our ability to communicate information about large numbers, but they can also be easily manipulated. Some common distortions include the following:

- Altering the baseline. Normally, the numbers that go up the vertical axis begin at zero and move up at regularly scheduled intervals. The real relationship between the numbers on each axis can be disguised, however, if the baseline is not zero—especially if it is below zero. Do not take for granted that you know what the baseline is until you check.

- Using misleading averages or means. The mean, calculated by adding up a series of values and dividing by the number of values, generally gives us a good mid-range estimate. However, sometimes the outlying values, the ones at the top or bottom, are so far from the middle that the mean is too high or too low to represent the middle. When this happens, we often prefer to use the median, calculated by arranging all the values numerically and then finding the one in the physical middle.

- Not using constant dollars. Dollar values cannot be compared over time because inflation means that a dollar today buys far less than it did, say, fifty years ago. For an accurate comparison, constant dollars—that is, dollars that have been adjusted for changing price levels over time—should be used.

- Not showing populations as a percentage of the base. Often charts and graphs will show a growth in the numbers of a group without relating the group to the population as a whole. Always ask yourself if a graph removes data from some context that would help you understand it better.

- Implying causality where none exists. The fact that two variables shift at the same time does not mean that one has caused the other. Causality is very difficult to show, and generally the best we can do is to show that two things are correlated. Beware of cause-and-effect claims.

nationalities, seen as more desirable immigrants, who had arrived in larger numbers earlier, allowing Great Britain and Ireland to send 65,721 immigrants yearly, for instance, but Italy only 5,802.[3] As we will see, today's debate over illegal immigration taps into some of the same emotions and passions as earlier efforts to limit legal immigration.

Immigration Law Today

Congress abolished the existing immigration quota system in 1965 with the Immigration and Nationality Act. This act doubled the number of people allowed to enter the country, set limits on immigration from the Western Hemisphere, and made it easier for families to join members who had already immigrated. More open borders meant immigration was increasingly harder to control. Reacting to the waves of illegal immigrants who entered the country in the 1970s and 1980s, Congress passed the Immigration Reform and Control Act in 1986, granting amnesty to illegals who had entered before 1982 and attempting to tighten controls on those who came after. Although this law included sanctions for those who hired illegal immigrants, people continued to cross the

▶ Who, What, How, and WHEN: Immigration

Visitors to New York City often stop by the famous icon of immigration, the Statue of Liberty. Though Lady Liberty welcomes the tired, hungry, huddled masses, Americans have not always been so hospitable. As waves of newcomers stepped onto U.S. soil in the 1800s and 1900s, they were often greeted with resistance, even though today the members of these groups seem like ordinary Americans. Consider the following groups of immigrants over time:

1845 — "Potato Blight" in Ireland

The Irish Potato Famine, caused by a fungus that attacked the mainstay of the Irish diet, created a wave of immigration in the 1840s. In this decade nearly half of all immigrants to the United States were Irish. The American Party began as a secret organization opposing these waves of Irish Catholic immigrants. Dubbed the "Know-Nothing Party" because of its members' response to questions about the organization ("I know nothing"), the American Party won local elections in Massachusetts, California, and Pennsylvania; incited riots; and, with Millard Fillmore as its presidential candidate, won 22 percent of the popular vote in the 1856 election, all on a platform of nativism.

1882 — Chinese Exclusion Act Passed

In 1848 the California gold rush started mass immigration of Chinese to California. In response, the Chinese Exclusion Act passed in 1882. The first major law in the United States limiting immigration, it stopped Chinese immigration unless the immigrants had documentation proving they were skilled laborers, stopped naturalization of Chinese immigrants (meaning they could never become citizens), and forced Chinese immigrants to register and carry papers. The law was not repealed fully until 1965.

1891 — Sicilian Prisoners Lynched in New Orleans

By the late 1800s Italian immigration began. More than four million Italian immigrants would come to the United States by 1920. Many of them came through Ellis Island, which opened in 1892. Most of these immigrants worked as laborers; almost 90 percent of the laborers working for the New York City Department of Public Works in 1890 were Italian. Backlash was widespread, including the lynching of eleven Sicilian prisoners in New Orleans in 1891.

border illegally from Mexico looking for work. In the 1990s, legislation under President Clinton strengthened the power of the INS.

Despite the trend of tightening immigration laws, President George W. Bush indicated early in his first administration that he was considering giving amnesty—freedom from punishment, including deportation—to Mexicans living illegally in the United States. Confronted with opposition from the president's own party, the White House soon reported that its real interest was in an expanded guest worker program, in which workers could enter the country from Mexico to work temporarily in industries that needed low-wage labor. Some of these guest workers would be able to "earn" the right to become permanent residents and citizens by working and paying taxes. In addition, illegal immigrants already here might be able to earn their own legalization through similar means. These plans were put on hold in the aftermath of the tougher enforcement of immigration laws and heightened scrutiny of immigrants that followed September 11, 2001, but Bush revived his call for a guest worker program immediately after the 2004 election. He claimed it would

1942 **U.S.-Mexican Bracero Program** It is hard to date the beginning of Mexican immigration to the United States. People who lived in parts of Mexico that became U.S. territory (states like California, New Mexico, Texas, Arizona, and Nevada) became Americans in the 1800s. Because labor was badly needed while American men were at war, the United States and Mexico created the Bracero program during World War II. Through this program, Mexican citizens could enter the United States, work on a contract basis, and then return home. This program established the use of Mexican labor in the United States and left a vacuum when the program ended.

In the 1990s another wave of Mexican immigration to the United States began. While some of this immigration has been legal, in 2003 U.S. immigration services determined that about seven million illegal Mexican immigrants had come to the country, and the number of illegal immigrants was growing by about 500,000 people each year.

1959 **Castro's Takeover in Cuba** Cuban immigration to the United States doubled after Fidel Castro's takeover of Cuba in 1959. Many of these immigrants were given special immigration status, such as quick permanent residency, because they were seen as political refugees. Cuban immigration continues, but in 1994 it was limited to 20,000 immigrant visas per year. Many Cubans still attempt to immigrate to the United States by crossing from Cuba to Florida in makeshift boats. The "wet foot dry foot" policy allows Cubans who reach U.S. soil to stay, but those who are intercepted by the Coast Guard must return to Cuba.

help fill jobs Americans were unwilling to take and bolster homeland security by providing a record of who was in the United States. Democrats and moderate Republican legislators such as Arizona senator John McCain hailed the proposals, but conservatives again vowed to block passage of any such legislation, demanding instead new laws to crack down on illegal immigrants.

The tension between, on the one hand, those who sought to grapple with the issue of what was by now an estimated 12 million illegal immigrants already in this country and the demands of American business for the cheap labor that immigration provides and, on the other, those who were determined to send undocumented immigrants home and tighten the borders against the arrival of any more, has come to define efforts to pass immigration reform in recent years. In Bush's last term in office, Congress tried repeatedly to pass reform that emphasized border security and more stringent enforcement of legislation on the books. Immigrants pushed back. Between March and May 2006, several million immigrants protested anti-immigrant sentiment in Congress, marching in 120 American cities under banners proclaiming, "We Are

▶ **Who Are We?**

How we fit in once we arrive

Immigrants and Native-Born Americans are not dispersed evenly across the states, and their incomes and educational attainment are not the same on average. Do these differences have consequences for the kinds of jobs immigrants might compete for? Do states with the highest immigration rates face different policy problems than those with lower rates? What kinds of needs might those not born in the United States have that states might try to meet?

Foreign-Born as Percentage of Total Population: The Southwest contains the heaviest concentration of foreign-born populations.

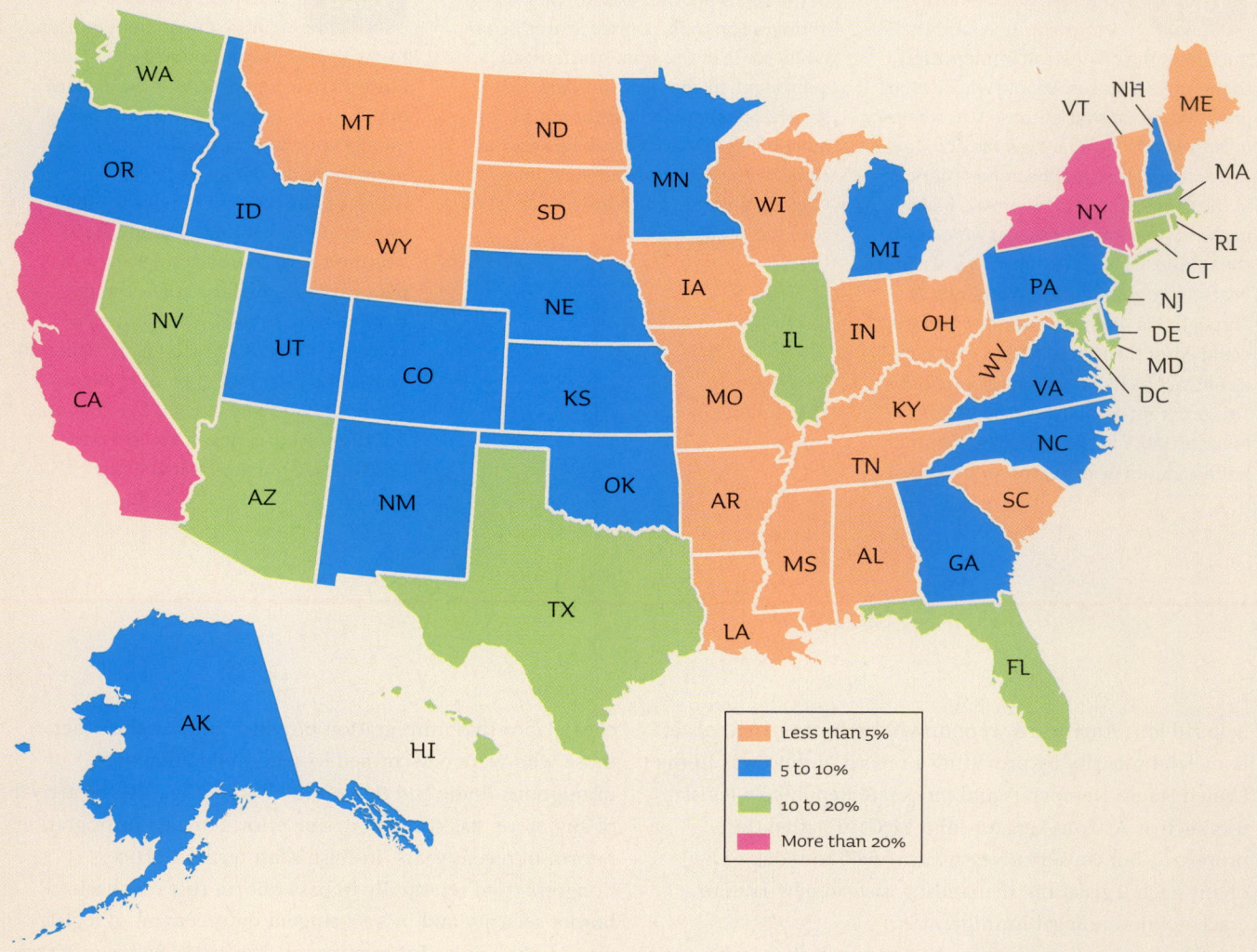

Legend:
- Less than 5%
- 5 to 10%
- 10 to 20%
- More than 20%

Source: U.S. Census Bureau, *Statistical Abstract of the United States*, 2010, Table 40.

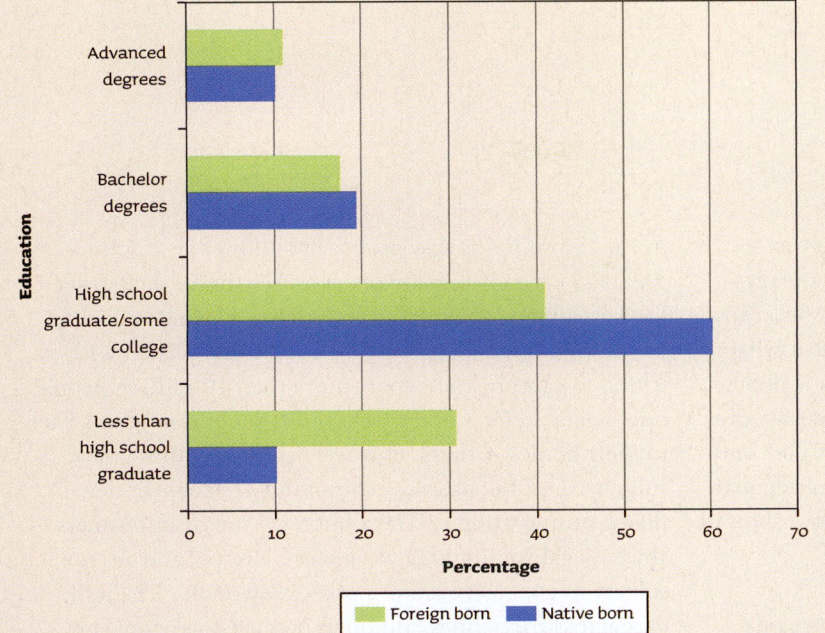

Native-Born and Immigrant Education:
Native-born residents are in general much more likely than those who are foreign born to graduate from high school and attend college, but there is a small cohort of highly educated immigrants in this country.

Source: U.S. Census Bureau, *Statistical Abstract of the United States, 2010.*

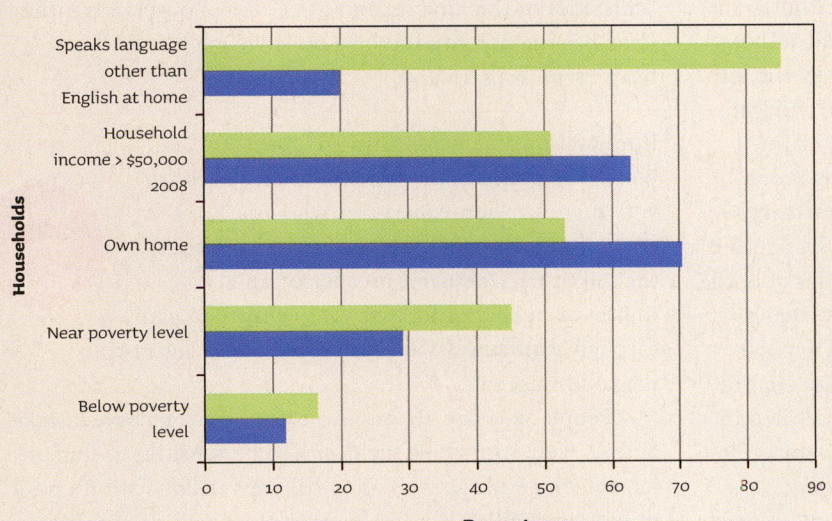

Native-Born and Immigrant Households:
Compared with native-born households, approximately 30 percent more foreign-born households live in or near poverty.

Source: U.S. Census Bureau, *Statistical Abstract of the United States, 2010,* Table 42; Eric Newburger and Thomas Gryn, "The Foreign-Born Labor Force in the United States: 2007," www.census.gov/prod/2009pubs/acs-10.pdf.

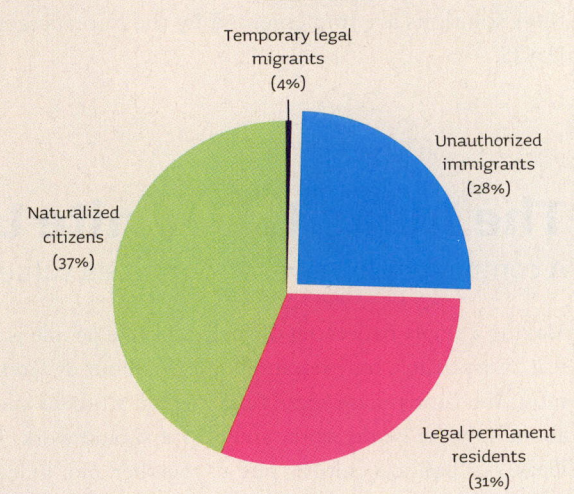

Status of Foreign Born: Foreign-born legal residents and citizens outnumber unauthorized immigrants.

Source: Jeffrey S. Passel and D'Vera Cohn, "U.S. Unauthorized Immigration Flows Are Down Sharply Since Mid-Decade," Pew Hispanic Center Report, September 1, 2010, Table 3, http://pewhispanic.org/files/reports/126.pdf.

America." Another proposal, in 2007, to create a guest worker program and to allow illegal immigrants already here to remain and eventually earn citizenship status, also failed to pass, and Bush had to confront the fact that what he had hoped to make a signature piece of domestic policy in his administration was not to be. The furious debate over immigration during the Republican primaries in 2008, and the eagerness of Senator McCain's rivals for the presidential nomination to brand him as a supporter of amnesty, showed that immigration remained a hot-potato issue for conservatives.

The issue exploded again in 2010, when the Arizona legislature passed a law that made it a crime for immigrants to fail to carry their documentation on them, and authorized police to demand that documentation if they had any reason to suspect that a person was in the country illegally. (*See What's at Stake*, page 597.) Critics immediately claimed that the law would lead to racial profiling, but its proponents, including Senator McCain who, facing a primary challenge in Arizona, had swung hard right on the issue, said that Arizona was only trying to deal with a leaky border that the federal government had failed to police.[4] Democrats, eager to use the issue as a wedge to divide Republicans, were anxious to get immigration reform back on the national agenda so that it would continue to be debated in the run-up to the 2010 midterm elections in November, but in light of the heightened anxiety over the economy, immigration reform did not pick up the traction it needed.

After the election was over, Democrats hoped to get a chance to pass the Development, Relief and Education for Alien Minor (DREAM) Act, a piece of legislation that would have allowed illegal immigrants who had arrived in this country as minors to earn legal residency through higher education or military service. The House had passed the bill in 2009, but conservative Republicans had blocked it in the Senate. When the Senate attempted to vote on it one last time in December 2010, Republicans (with the help of a few more conservative Democrats) blocked the vote. With Republicans set to take the House majority in 2011, the bill was essentially dead for the foreseeable future.

Illegal immigration is controversial today not only for all the economic and cultural reasons that make immigration a sensitive topic at any time but also because of anger among some Americans that those who cross the border illegally are breaking the law and getting away with it.

Amnesty programs that propose to allow illegal immigrants to earn citizenship, even as they make the border harder to cross, are seen as condoning a crime and, undeterred by the logistical difficulties associated with trying to capture and deport more than 10 million people, opponents prefer a policy that sends such immigrants back to their homes. Others, however, especially those in or supportive of the business community, recognize that illegal immigration can be a boon to American business since illegal immigrants work more cheaply and are not subject to expensive labor market protections. The issue cuts across party lines, although because the people on both sides of this divide tend to be more conservative, the issue has the potential to be a divisive one for the Republican Party in particular.

Immigration and citizenship are issues in which the political and humanitarian stakes are very high. For non-Americans who are threatened or impoverished in their native countries, the stakes are sanctuary, prosperity, and improved quality of life, which they seek to gain through acquiring asylum or by becoming legal or illegal immigrants.

Who What How

People who are already American citizens have a stake here as well. At issue is the desire to be sensitive to humanitarian concerns, as well as to fill gaps in the nation's pool of workers and skills, and to meet the needs of current citizens. These often conflicting goals are turned into law by policymakers in Congress and the White House, and their solutions are implemented by the bureaucracy of the USCIS.

The Ideas That Unite Us
A common culture based on shared values

Making a single nation out of such a diverse people is no easy feat. It is possible only because, despite all our differences, most Americans share some fundamental attitudes and beliefs about how the world works and how it should work. These ideas, our political culture, pull us together and, indeed, provide a framework in which we can also disagree politically without resorting to violence and civil war.

political culture the broad pattern of ideas, beliefs, and values about citizens and government held by a population

values central ideas, principles, or standards that most people agree are important

normative describes beliefs or values about how things should be or what people ought to do rather than what actually is

procedural guarantees government assurance that the rules will work smoothly and treat everyone fairly, with no promise of particular outcomes

individualism belief that what is good for society is based on what is good for individuals

Political culture refers to the general political orientation or disposition of a nation—the shared values and beliefs about the nature of the political world that give us a common language in which to discuss and debate political ideas. *Values* are ideals or principles that most people agree are important, even though they may disagree on exactly how the value—such as "equality" or "freedom"—ought to be defined. Political culture is shared, although certainly some individuals find themselves at odds with it. When we say, "Americans think . . . ," we mean that most Americans hold those views, not that there is unanimous agreement on them. Political culture is handed down from generation to generation, through families, schools, communities, literature, churches and synagogues, and so on, helping to provide stability for the nation by ensuring that a majority of citizens are well grounded in and committed to the basic values that sustain it. We will talk about the process through which values are transferred in Chapter 11, "Public Opinion."

Note that statements about values and beliefs are not descriptive of how the world actually *is*, but rather are prescriptive, or *normative*, statements about how the value-holders believe the world *ought* to be. Our culture consists of deep-seated, collectively held ideas about how life *should* be lived. Normative statements aren't true or false but depend for their worth on the arguments that are made to back them up. Often we take our own culture (that is, our common beliefs about how the world should work) so much for granted that we aren't even aware of it. We don't think we have a culture or a normative view of the world; we just think we have the right outlook and those who differ from us are simply mistaken. Just as anyone who has traveled in another country has probably noticed that that country's citizens have different ideas about how the world should work and define their core values differently than we do, visitors to the United States can sometimes see our culture more clearly than we can. For that reason, it is often easier to see our own political culture by contrasting it to another, and we will engage in some comparisons in the rest of this chapter.

Faith in Rules and Individuals

In American political culture, our expectations of government focus on rules and processes rather than on results. For example, we think government should guarantee a fair playing field but not guarantee equal outcomes for all the players. In addition, we believe that individuals are responsible for their own welfare and that what is good for them is good for society as a whole. Our insistence on fair rules, as we saw in Chapter 1, is an emphasis on *procedural guarantees*, while the belief in the primacy of the individual citizen is called *individualism*. American culture is not wholly procedural and individualistic—indeed, differences on these matters constitute some of the major partisan divisions in American politics—but these characteristics are more prominent in the United States than they are in most other nations.

To illustrate this point, we can compare American culture to the more social democratic cultures of Scandinavia, such as Sweden, Denmark, and Norway. In many ways, the United States and the countries in Scandinavia are more similar than they are different: they are all capitalist democracies, and they essentially agree that individuals ought to make most of the decisions about their own lives. Recall our comparison of political and economic systems from Chapter 1; the United States and Scandinavia, which reject substantial governmental control of both the social order and the economy, would all fit into the upper-right quadrant of Figure 1.3, along with other advanced industrial democracies like Japan and Great Britain.

They do differ in some important ways, however. While all advanced industrial democracies repudiate the whole-hearted substantive guarantees of communism, the Scandinavian countries have a greater tolerance for some substantive economic policy than does the more procedural United States. We explore these differences here in more detail so that we can better understand what American culture supports and what it does not.

Procedural Guarantees

As we have noted, when we say that American political culture is procedural, we mean that Americans generally think government should guarantee fair processes—such as a free market to distribute goods, majority rule to make decisions, due process to determine guilt and innocence—rather than specific outcomes. The social democratic countries of Sweden, Denmark, and Norway, however, as we saw in Chapter 1, believe that government should actively seek to realize the values of equality—perhaps to guarantee a certain quality of life to all citizens or to increase equality of income. Government can then be evaluated by how well it produces those substantive outcomes, not just on how well it guarantees fair processes.

While American politics does set some substantive goals for public policy, Americans are generally more comfortable ensuring that things are done in a fair and proper way, and trusting that the outcomes will be good ones because the rules are fair. Although the American government is involved in social programs and welfare, it aims more at helping individuals get on their feet so that they can participate in the market (fair procedures) than at cleaning up slums or eliminating poverty (substantive goals).

Individualism

The individualistic nature of American political culture means that individuals are seen as responsible for their own well-being. This contrasts with a collectivist point of view, which gives government or society some responsibility for individual welfare, and holds that what is good for society may not be the same as what is in the interest of individuals.

Thus our politics revolves around the belief that individuals are usually the best judges of what is good for them; we assume that what is good for society will follow automatically. For contrast, let's look again at Sweden, a democratic capitalist country like the United States, but one with a more collectivist political culture. At one time, Sweden had a policy that held down the wages of workers so that more profitable and less profitable industries would be more equal, and society, according to the Swedish view, would be better off. Americans would reject this policy as violating their belief in individualism (and proceduralism as well). American government rarely asks citizens to make major economic sacrifices for the public good, although individuals often do so privately and voluntarily. Where Americans are asked to make economic sacrifices, like paying taxes, such requests are unpopular and more modest than in most other countries. A collective interest that supersedes individual interests is generally invoked in the United States only in times of war or national crisis. This echoes the two American notions of self-interested and public-interested citizenship we discussed in Chapter 1.

Core American Values: Democracy, Freedom, and Equality

We can see our American procedural and individualistic perspective when we examine the different meanings of three core American values: democracy, freedom, and equality.

Democracy

Democracy in America, as we have seen, means representative democracy, based on consent and majority rule. Basically, Americans believe democracy should be a procedure to make political decisions, to choose political leaders, and to select policies for the nation. It is seen as a fundamentally just or fair way of making decisions because every individual who cares to participate is heard in the process, and all interests are considered. We don't reject a democratically made decision because it is not fair; it is fair precisely *because* it is democratically made. Democracy is valued primarily not for the way it makes citizens feel, or the effects it has on them, but for the decisions it produces. Americans see democracy as the appropriate procedure for making public decisions—that is, decisions about government—but generally not for decisions in the private realm. Rarely do employees have a binding vote on company policy, for example, as they do in some Scandinavian countries.

Freedom

Americans also put a very high premium on the value of freedom, defined as freedom for the individual from restraint by the state. This view of freedom is procedural in the sense that it holds that no unfair restrictions should be put in the way of your pursuit of what you want, but it does not guarantee you any help in achieving those things. For instance, when Americans say, "We are all free to get a job," we mean that no discriminatory laws or other legal barriers are stopping us from applying for any particular position; a substantive view of freedom would ensure us the training to get a job so that our freedom meant a positive opportunity, not just the absence of restraint.

Americans have an extraordinary commitment to procedural freedom, perhaps because our values were forged during the Enlightenment, when liberty was a guiding principle. This commitment can be seen nowhere so clearly as in the Bill of Rights, the first ten amendments to the U.S. Constitution, which guarantee our basic civil liberties, the areas where government cannot interfere with individual action. Those civil liberties include freedom of speech and expression, freedom of belief, freedom of the press, and the right to assemble, just to name a few. (See Chapter 5,

"Fundamental American Liberties," for a complete discussion of these rights.)

But Americans also believe in economic freedom, the freedom to participate in the marketplace, to acquire money and property, and to do with those resources pretty much as we please. Americans believe that government should protect our property, not take it away or regulate our use of it too heavily. Our commitment to individualism is apparent here, too. Even if society as a whole would benefit if we paid off the federal debt (the amount our government owes from spending more than it brings in), our individualistic view of economic freedom means that Americans have one of the lowest tax rates in the industrialized world (see Figure 2.1). This reflects our national tendency in normal times to emphasize the rights of citizenship over its obligations.

Figure 2.1

U.S. Tax Burden Compared to Other Countries

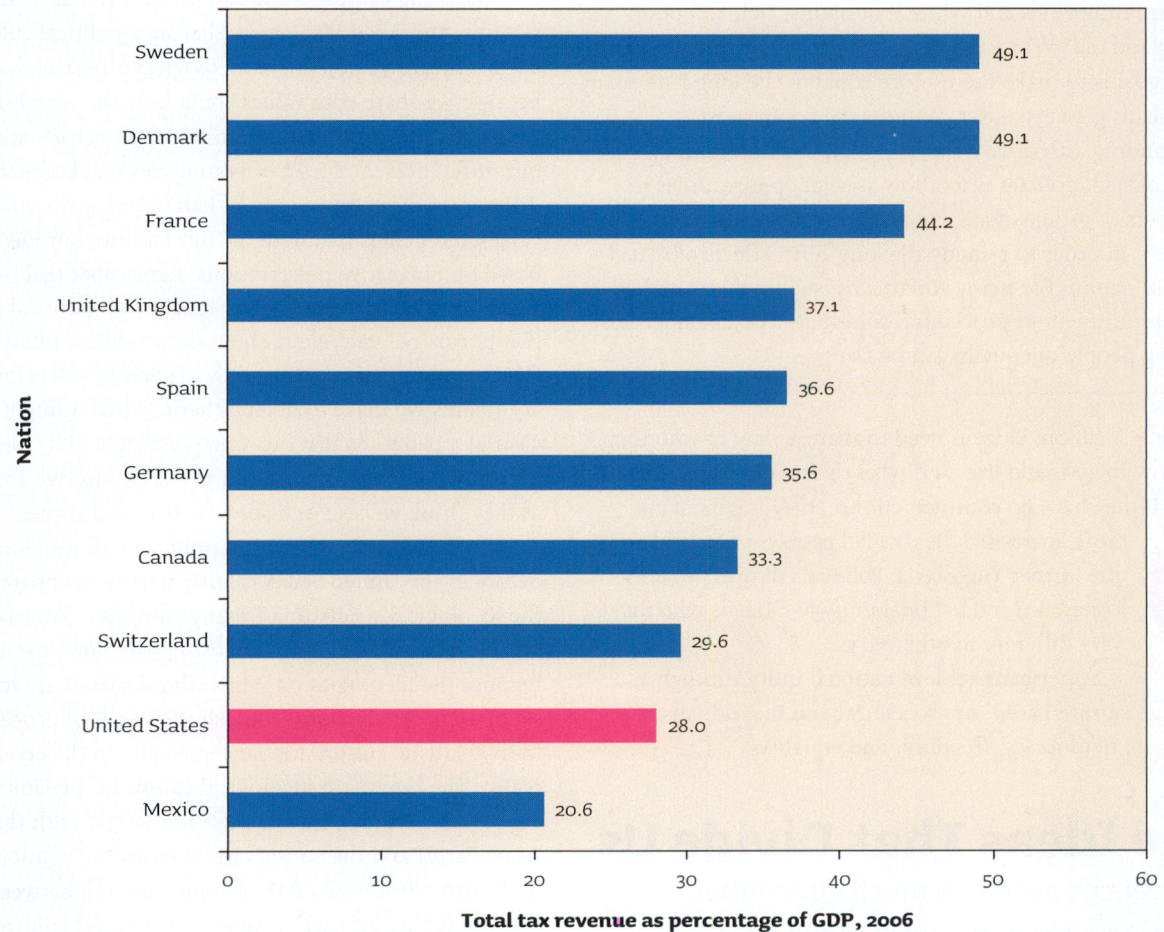

Source: Table A, p. 19 in OECD (2008), Revenue Statistics 2008, OECD Publishing, http://dx.doi.org/10.1787/rev_stats-2008-en-fr.

ideologies sets of beliefs about politics and society that help people make sense of their world

Equality

Another central value in American political culture is equality. Of all the values we hold dear, equality is probably the one we cast most clearly in procedural versus substantive terms. Equality in America means government should guarantee equality of treatment, of access, of opportunity, not equality of result. People should have equal access to run the race, but we don't expect everyone to finish in the same place. Thus we believe in political equality (one person, one vote) and equality before the law—that the law shouldn't make unreasonable distinctions among people the basis for treating them differently, and that all people should have equal access to the legal system.

One problem the courts have faced is deciding what counts as a reasonable distinction. Can the law justifiably discriminate between—that is, treat differently—men and women, minorities and white Protestants, rich and poor, young and old? When the rules treat people differently, even if the goal is to make them more equal in the long run, many Americans get very upset. Witness the controversy surrounding affirmative action policies in this country. The point of such policies is to allow special opportunities to members of groups that have been discriminated against in the past, in order to remedy the long-term effects of that discrimination. For many Americans, such policies violate our commitment to procedural solutions. They wonder how treating people unequally can be fair.

Who What How

To live as a nation, citizens need to share a view of who they are, how they should live, and what their world should be like. If they have no common culture, they fragment and break apart, like the divided peoples of Ireland and the former Yugoslavia. Political cultures provide coherence and national unity to citizens who may be very different in other ways.

Americans achieve national unity through a political culture based on procedural and individualistic visions of democracy, freedom, and equality.

The Ideas That Divide Us

Differences over how much government control there should be in our lives

Most Americans are united in their commitment at some level to a political culture based on proceduralism and individualism

and to the key values of democracy, freedom, and equality. This shared political culture gives us a common political language, a way to talk about politics that keeps us united even though we may disagree about many specific ideas and issues.

That's a good thing since, human nature being what it is, we are likely to disagree about politics, and disagree often. Although Americans have much in common, there are over 250 million of us, and the *Who Are We?* features demonstrate graphically how dramatically different we are in terms of our religious, educational, geographic, and professional backgrounds. We have different interests, different beliefs, different prejudices, different hopes and dreams.

With all that diversity, we are bound to have a variety of beliefs and opinions about politics, the economy, and society that help us make sense of our world but that can divide us into opposing camps. These camps, or different belief systems, are called *ideologies*. Sharing a political culture doesn't mean we don't have ideological differences, but because we share core values about how the world should be, we have a common language in which to debate, and resolve our differences, and a set of boundaries that keeps those differences from getting out of hand. And again, like the values and beliefs that underlie our culture, our ideologies are based on normative prescriptions. Remember that one of the reasons we can disagree so passionately on political issues is that normative statements about the world are not true or false, good or bad—instead they depend for their force on the arguments we make to defend them. While it might seem clear as a bell to us that our values are right and true, to a person who disagrees with our prescriptions, we are as wrong as they think we are. And so we debate and argue.

But because we share that political culture, our range of debate in the United States is fairly narrow compared with the ideological spectrum of many countries. We have no successful communist or socialist parties here, for instance, because the ideologies on which those parties are founded seem to most Americans to push the limits of procedural and individualistic culture too far, especially in the economic realm. The two main ideological camps in the United States are the liberals (associated, since the 1930s, with the Democratic Party) and the conservatives (with the Republicans), with many Americans falling somewhere in between. But because we are all part of American political culture, we are still procedural and individualistic; we still believe in democracy, freedom, and equality, even if we are also liberals or conservatives.

conservatives people who generally favor limited government and are cautious about change

liberals people who generally favor government action and view change as progress

There are lots of different ways of characterizing American ideologies. In general terms, we can say that **conservatives** tend to be in favor of traditional social values, distrust government action except in matters of national security, are slow to advocate change, and place a priority on the maintenance of social order. **Liberals**, in contrast, value the possibilities of progress and change, trust government, look for innovations as answers to social problems, and focus on the expansion of individual rights and expression. For a more rigorous understanding of ideology in America we can focus on the two main ideological dimensions of economics and social order issues.

The Economic Dimension

Traditionally, we have understood ideology to be centered on differences in economic views, much like those located on our economic continuum in Chapter 1 (see Figure 1.1). Based on these economic ideological dimensions, we often say that the liberals who advocate a large role for government in regulating the economy are on the far left, and those conservatives who think government control should be minimal are on the far right. Because we lack any widespread radical socialist traditions in the United States, both American liberals and conservatives are found on the right side of the broader economic continuum we discussed in Chapter 1.

Since the Great Depression in the 1930s and Franklin Roosevelt's New Deal (a set of government policies designed to get the economy moving and to protect citizens from the worst effects of the Depression), American conservatives and liberals have taken the following positions with respect to government and the economy. Conservatives, reflecting a belief that government is not to be trusted with too much power and is, in any case, not a competent economic actor, and that private property is sacrosanct and should remain wholly private, have reacted against the increasing role of the government in the American economy. Liberals, in contrast, arguing that the economic market cannot regulate itself and, left alone, is susceptible to such ailments as depressions and recessions, have a much more positive view of government and the good it can do in addressing economic and social problems. Typically, conservatives have tended to be wealthier, upper-class Americans, whereas liberals have been more likely to be lower-paid, blue collar workers. See *"Who Are We? Who Is Getting How Much?"* to see how much American incomes vary.

Thou Shalt Not . . .
The U.S. Constitution says there will be no establishment of religion, but many conservative Christians support the display of religious symbols in and outside of public buildings. Despite several high-profile court cases and such government actions as the removal of a monument of the Ten Commandments from outside a school in Ohio (above), the public continues to debate government's role when it comes to religion and its display.

The Social Order Dimension

In the 1980s and 1990s, another ideological dimension became prominent in the United States. Perhaps because, as some researchers have argued, most people are able to meet their basic economic needs and more people than ever before are identifying themselves as middle class, many Americans began to focus less on economic questions and more on issues of morality and quality of life. The new ideological dimension, which is analogous to the social order dimension we discussed in Chapter 1, divides

▶ Who Are We?

Who is getting how much?

Almost everyone would like more money. These figures tell us who is earning it and who is not. While men make more than women on average, and non-Hispanic whites earn more than Hispanics and African Americans, the biggest differences emerge among education levels. Since higher education is so clearly linked to economic success, should access to higher education be more open? How large should the gap between America's richest and poorest people be?

Work Time versus Leisure Time: Where does the day go?

The Rich Get Richer: The income gap is getting wider.

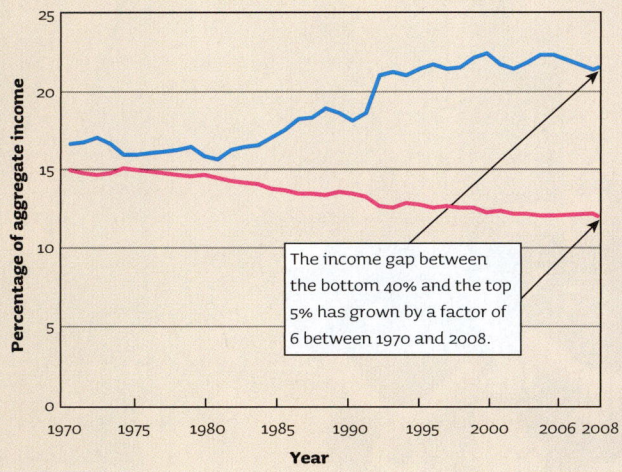

The income gap between the bottom 40% and the top 5% has grown by a factor of 6 between 1970 and 2008.

Source: U.S. Census Bureau, Current Population Survey, Annual Social and Economic Supplements, "Table H-2: Share of Aggregate Income Received by Each Fifth and Top 5 Percent of Households, All Races: 1967 to 2008," www.census.gov/hhes/www/income/histinc/inchhtoc.html.

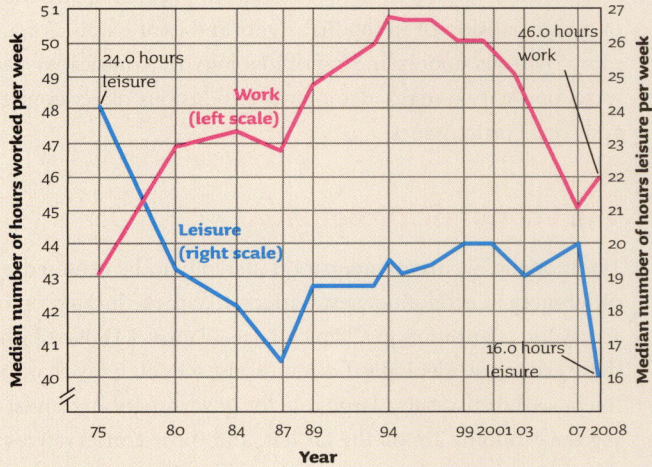

Source: *The Harris Poll*, Harris Interactive.

Note: Work includes working for pay, keeping house, and going to school. For work hours, survey participants were asked, "First, we would like to know approximately how many hours a week you spend at your job or occupation, and that includes keeping house or going to school as well as working for pay or profit. How many hours would you estimate you spend at work, housekeeping or studies, including any travel time to and from the job or school?" For leisure hours, participants were asked, "And about how many hours each week do you estimate you have available to relax, watch TV, take part in sports or hobbies, go swimming or skiing, go to the movies, theater, concerts, or other forms of entertainment, get together with friends, and so forth?"

people on the question of how much government control there should be over the moral and social order—whether government's role should be limited to protecting individual rights and providing procedural guarantees of equality and due process, or whether the government should be involved in making more substantive judgments about how people should live their lives.

While few people in the United States want to go so far as to create a social order that makes all moral and political decisions for its subjects, some people hold that it is the government's job to create and protect a preferred social order, although visions of what that preferred order should be may differ. A conservative view of the preferred social order usually includes an emphasis on religion in public life (prayer in school, public posting of religious documents like the Ten Commandments), a rejection of abortion and physician-assisted suicide, promotion of traditional family values (including a rejection of gay marriage and other gay rights), emphasis on the "American Way" (rejecting the value of diversity for conformity and restricting immigration), and censorship of materials that promote alternative visions of the social order. Conservatives are not the only ones who seek to

The Size of Our Paychecks: Income level by gender, race, and education level

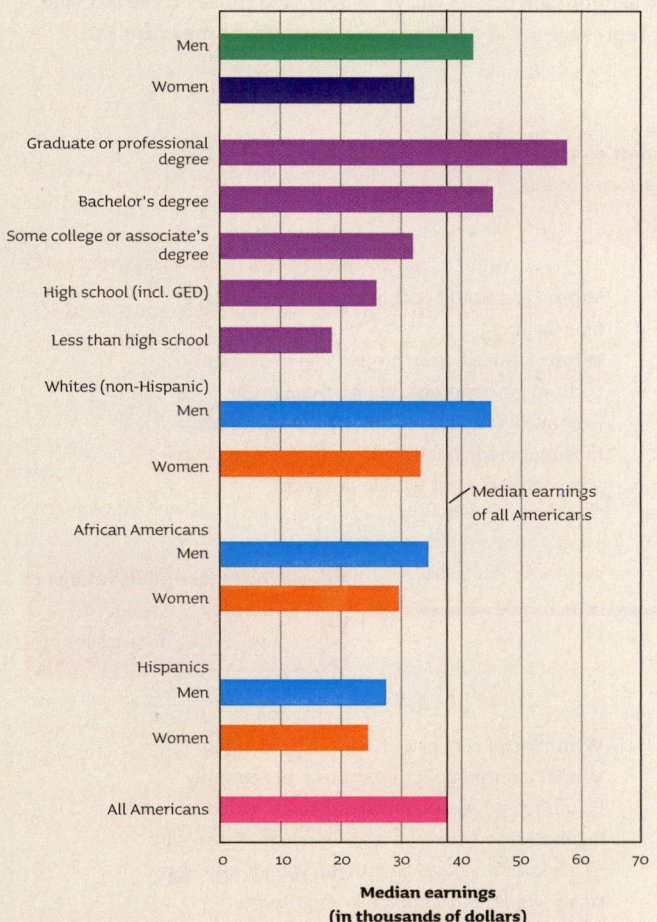

Median earnings (in thousands of dollars)

Source: U.S. Census Bureau, 2005 American Community Survey, "Median Earnings in the Past 12 months (in 2005 Inflation-Adjusted Dollars) of Workers," http://factfinder.census.gov.

Note: Full-time, year-round workers aged sixteen or older with earnings. Educational attainment: population twenty five years and over with earnings.

Enrollment in Higher Education: More and more Americans are going to college.

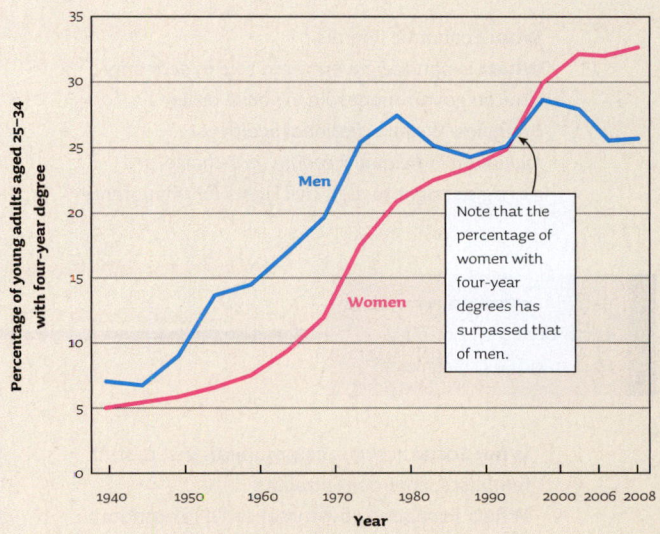

Source: U.S. Census Bureau, 2008 American Community Survey, "S1501 .Educational Attainment," http://factfinder.census.gov.

tell individuals how to live their lives, however. There is also a newer, more liberal vision of the social order that prescribes an expanded government role to regulate individual lives to achieve different substantive ends—the preservation of the environment, for instance (laws that require individuals to recycle or that tax gasoline to encourage conservation), or the creation of a sense of community based on equality and protection of minorities (rules that urge political correctness and censorship of pornography), or even the promotion of individual safety (laws promoting gun control, seat belts, and motorcycle helmets).

The Relationship Between the Two Ideological Dimensions

Clearly this social order ideological dimension does not dovetail neatly with the more traditional liberal and conservative orientations toward government action. Figure 2.2 shows some of the ideological positions yielded by these two dimensions. Note that what this figure shows is a detail of the broader political spectrum we saw in Chapter 1 and is focused on the narrower spectrum commonly found in an advanced industrial democracy. For instance,

Figure 2.2

Ideological Beliefs in the United States

Although committed generally to a procedural and individualistic political culture (this entire figure would fit in the upper-right quadrant of Figure 1.3), Americans still find plenty of room for political disagreement. This figure outlines the two main dimensions of that conflict: beliefs about government's role in the economy and beliefs about government's role in establishing a preferred social order. Those ideological beliefs on the right side of the figure are conservative beliefs, and those on the left side are more liberal. The axes in these figures are continuums and do not represent all-or-nothing positions; most Americans fall somewhere in between.

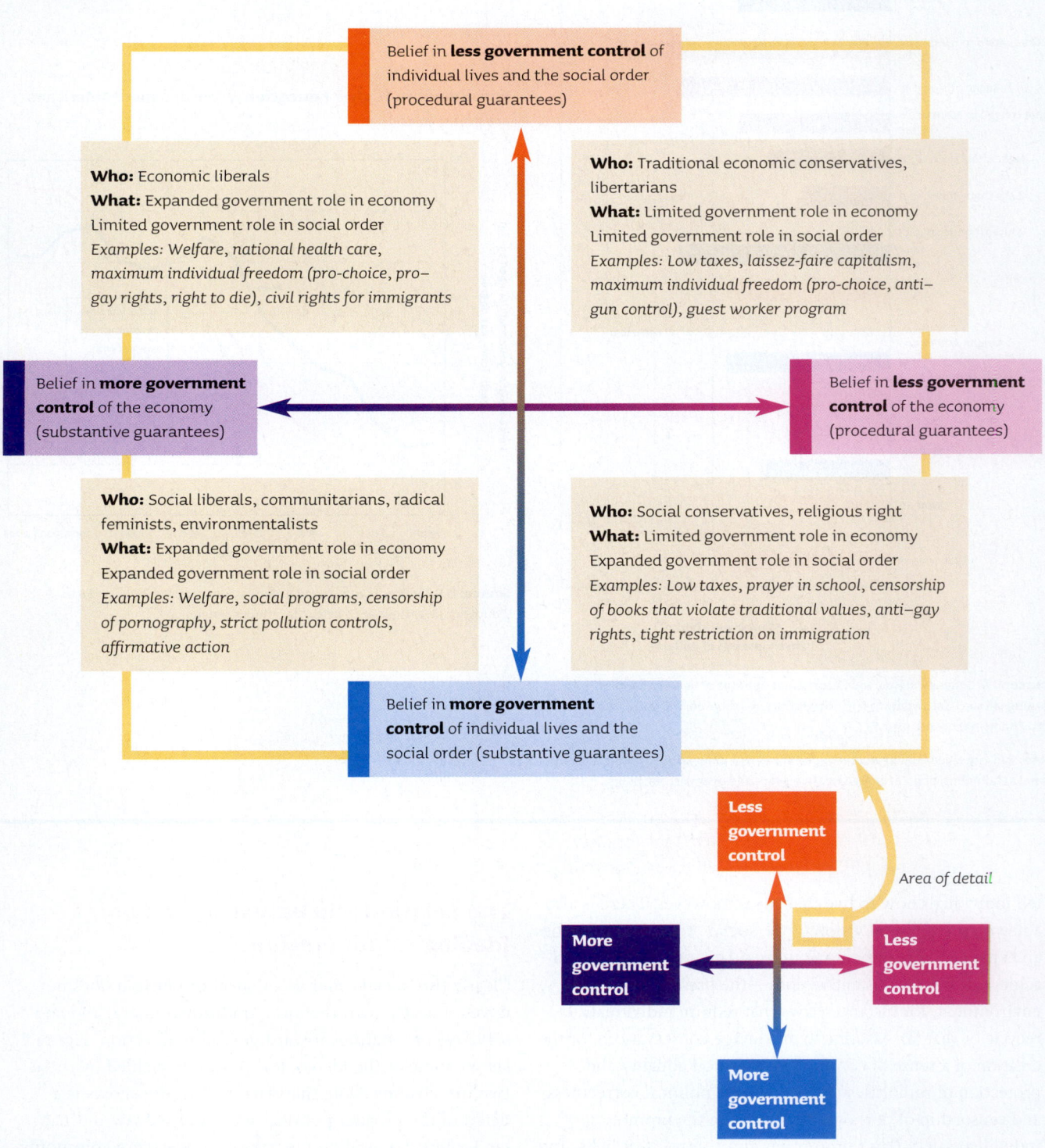

economic liberals those who favor an expanded government role in the economy but a limited role in the social order

economic conservatives those who favor a strictly procedural government role in the economy and the social order

libertarians those who favor a minimal government role in any sphere

social liberals those who favor greater control of the economy and the social order to bring about greater equality and to regulate the effects of progress

communitarians those who favor a strong, substantive government role in the economy and the social order in order to realize their vision of a community of equals

economic liberals, who are willing to allow government to make substantive decisions about the economy, tend to embrace the top procedural individualistic position on the social order dimension, and so they fall into the upper-left quadrant of the figure. Some economic policies they favor are job training and housing subsidies for the poor, taxation to support social programs, and affirmative action to ensure that opportunities for economic success are truly equal. As far as government regulation of individuals' private lives, however, these liberals favor a hands-off stance, preferring individuals to have maximum freedom over their noneconomic affairs. While they are willing to let government regulate such behaviors as murder, rape, and theft, they believe that most moral issues (such as abortion and the right to die) are questions of individual responsibility. They have an expansive vision of individual rights, valuing diversity and including in the system people who historically have been left out—women, minorities, gays, and immigrants. Their love for their country is tempered by the view that the government should be held to the same strict procedural standard to which individuals are held—laws must be followed, checks and balances adhered to in order to limit government power, and individual rights protected, even when the individuals are citizens of another country.

Economic conservatives share their liberal counterparts' reluctance to allow government interference in people's private lives, but they combine this with a conviction that government should limit involvement in the economy as well. In the upper-right quadrant of the figure, these economic conservatives prefer government to limit its role in economic decision making to regulation of the market (like changing interest rates and cutting taxes to end recessions), elimination of "unfair" trade practices (like monopolies), and provision of some public goods (like highways and national defense). When it comes to immigration they favor more open policies since immigrants often work more cheaply and help keep the labor market competitive for business. The most extreme holders of economic conservative views are called *libertarians*, people who believe that only minimal government action in any sphere is acceptable. Consequently, economic conservatives also hold the government accountable for sticking to the constitutional checks and balances that limit its own power.

In the lower-left quadrant of the figure, people tend to favor a substantive government role in achieving a more equal distribution of material resources (such as welfare programs and health care for the poor) but want that equality carried into the social order as well. They are willing, at least to some extent, to allow government to regulate individual behavior to create what they see as a better society. While they continue to want the freedom to make individual moral choices that economic liberals want, *social liberals* are happy to see some government action to realize a substantive vision of what society should be like. This liberal vision is forward looking and adaptive to changing social roles and technological progress. It seeks to regulate the effects of that progress, protecting the physical environment and individual well-being from the hazards of modern life. Government is valued for how well it realizes this vision of substantive fairness, and it is criticized when it falls short.

The most extreme adherents of social liberalism are sometimes called *communitarians* for their strong commitment to a community based on radical equality of all people. It is a collectivist, community-based vision that holds that individuals should be expected to make some sacrifices for the betterment of society. Because collectivism is not very popular in the American individualist culture, strong adherents to this view are relatively few in number. Many economic liberals, however, pick up some of the policy prescriptions of social liberals, like environmentalism and gun control.

To the right of them, and below economic conservatives on the figure, are *social conservatives*. These people share economic conservatives' views on limited government involvement in the economy, but with less force and perhaps for different reasons (in fact, many social conservatives, as members of the working class, were once New Deal liberals). Their primary concern is with their vision of the moral tone of life, not economics, and it does not seem incongruous to them that they should want a limited economic role for government while requiring that politicians enact a fairly substantive set of laws to create a particular moral order. Their vision of that order includes an emphasis on fundamentalist religious values and traditional family roles, and a rejection of change or diversity that it sees as destructive to the preferred social order. Immigration is threatening because it brings into the system people who are different and threatens to dilute the majority that keeps the social order in place. Social conservatives seek to protect people's moral character rather than their physical or economic well-being, and embrace a notion of community that emphasizes a hierarchical order

social conservatives those who endorse limited government control of the economy but considerable government intervention to realize a traditional social order; based on religious values and hierarchy rather than equality

Do ideological differences strengthen or weaken a political culture?

(everyone in his or her proper place) rather than equality for all. Since limited political power is not valued here, a large and powerful state is appreciated as being a sign of strength on the international stage. Patriotism for social conservatives is not a matter of holding the government to the highest procedural standards, as it is for those at the top half of Figure 2.2. Less worried about limiting government power over individual lives, they adopt more of a "my country right or wrong," "America First" view that sees criticism of the United States as unpatriotic.

Who Fits Where?

Many people, indeed most of us, might find it difficult to identify ourselves as simply "liberal" or "conservative," because we consider ourselves liberal on some issues, conservative on others. The framework in Figure 2.3 allows us to see ourselves and major groups in society as we might line up if we distinguish between economic and social-moral values. We can see, for instance, the real spatial distances that lie among (1) *the religious right* (as social conservatives are known), who are very conservative on political and moral issues but who were once part of the coalition of southern blue-collar workers who supported Roosevelt on the New Deal; (2) *traditional Republicans*, who are very conservative on economic issues but often more libertarian on political and moral issues, wanting government to guarantee procedural fairness and keep the peace, but otherwise to leave them alone; and (3) *moderate Republicans*, who are far less conservative economically and morally. In 2008 Republican presidential candidate John McCain had difficulty holding this coalition together. A moderate Republican himself, he was viewed with suspicion by the social conservatives in his party, and he struggled to find the levels of support that were enjoyed by George W. Bush when he ran in 2000 and 2004.

In the summer of 2009, as debate over health care reform dragged on in Washington and unemployment continued to rise, a wave of populist anger swept the nation. The so-called

Tea Party movement (named after the Boston Tea Party rebellion against taxation in 1773) was antigovernment (except for programs like Medicare that benefit the Tea Partiers), anticorporation, and pro-American. Mostly it was angry, fed by emotional appeals of conservative talk show hosts and others, whose rhetoric took political debate out of the range of logic and analysis and into the world of emotional drama and angry invective.

While many of the Tea Partiers are social conservatives, many are also libertarians. They are largely conservative, wanting to return to what they remember as a more gloried past. A *New York Times* poll found that 18 percent of Americans identified themselves as Tea Party supporters—a group of people who were more likely to be Republican, white, married, male, and over forty-five, and whose views were more conservative than Republicans generally.[5] In fact, they succeeded in shaking up the Republican Party in mid-2010, as they supported primary challenges to officeholders who did not share their antigovernment ideology. For instance, conservative Republican senator Bob Bennett of Utah lost a primary race in May of that year, and Republican Florida governor Charlie Crist decided to run for the Senate as an independent when it became clear that he would lose the primary to Tea Party–supported candidate Marco Rubio. The Tea Partiers are tough to fit neatly on to the scheme depicted in Figure 2.3 precisely because their appeal is largely emotionally based and not internally consistent. What is clear is that they are outside the circle that defines mainstream American beliefs, posing a challenge to Republicans who run statewide or nationally as they need to satisfy two divergent constituencies.

Similarly, the Democrats must try to respond to the *economic liberals* in the party, very procedural on most political and moral issues (barring affirmative action) but relatively (for Americans) substantive on economic concerns; to *social liberals*, substantive on both economic and social issues; and to newer groups, like the *Democratic Leadership Conference* (DLC), that are fairly procedural on political and moral issues but not very substantive on economic matters at all. It was President Clinton, as a DLC founder, who helped move his party closer to the mainstream from a position that, we can see in Figure 2.3, is clearly out of alignment with the position taken by most Americans. Ironically, in the 2000 election, Al Gore's commitment to the DLC position left him vulnerable to attack from Ralph Nader, who, as a representative of the Green Party, came from the lower-left quadrant. This position does not draw huge numbers of supporters, but in an election as

Figure 2.3

Approximate Ideological Placement of Parties and Groups in U.S. Politics

Within the confines of American political culture (remember that this entire figure still fits in the upper-right quadrant of Figure 1.3), American political groups take very divisive positions—many of them outside the mainstream where most Americans are located. The job of a political party—to capture the support of those groups without losing the Americans in the middle—can be a tough one.

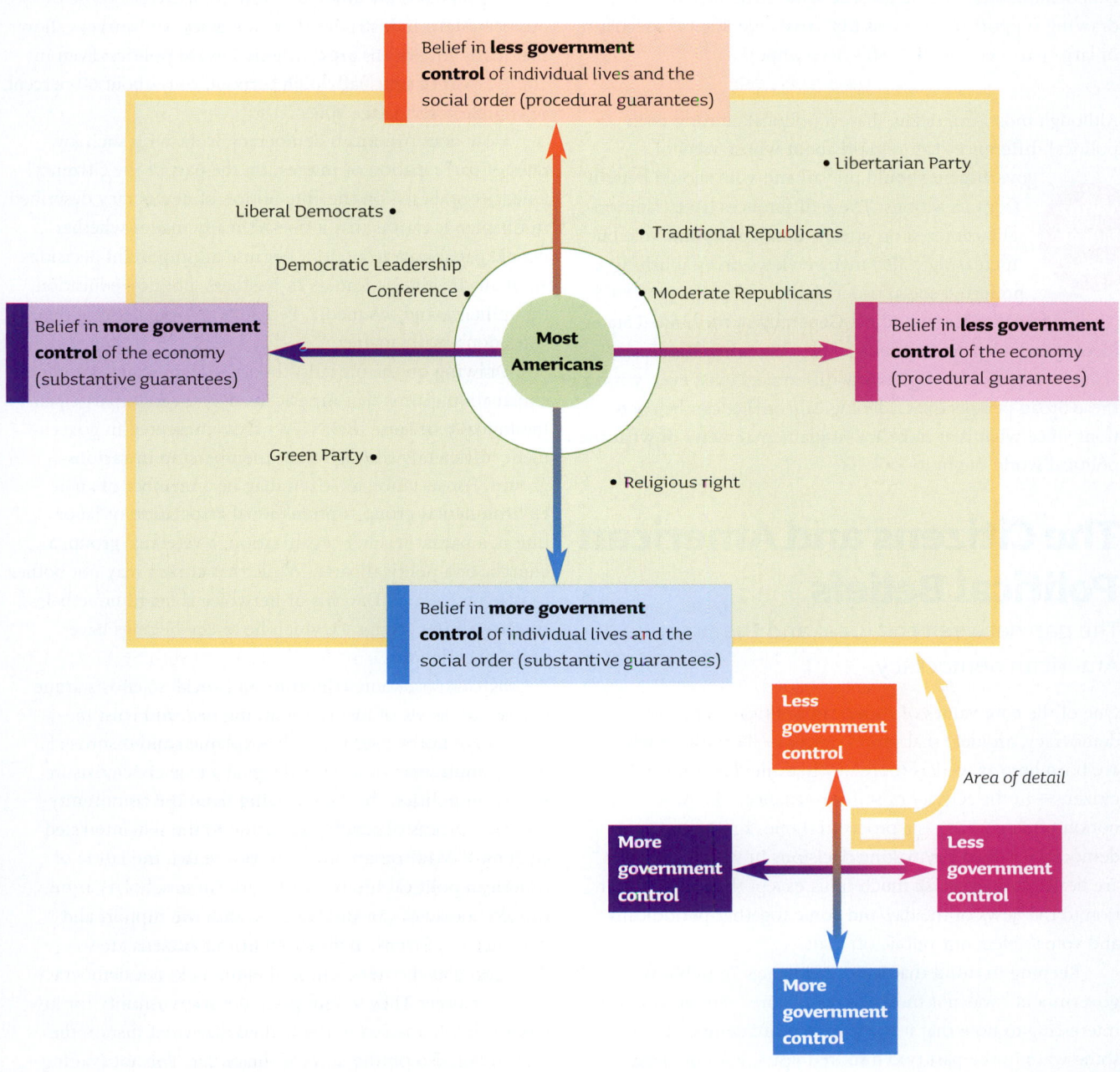

close as the one in 2000, it probably drew sufficient support from Gore to cost him the election. In 2004 Democratic candidate John Kerry did not have to worry as much about appealing to voters in that lower-left quadrant since many of them disliked George W. Bush so much that they were willing to vote for a candidate with whom they did not completely agree in order to try to oust Bush from office. Democrat Barack Obama had the same advantage in 2008, drawing support from across his party's ideological spectrum in large part because of Bush's deep unpopularity.

Although most Americans share a political culture, deep political differences can remain about whose view of government should prevail and who should benefit

Who What How

from its actions. These differences have traditionally centered on government's economic role but increasingly also involve views on establishing a preferred social order, and on what the preferred social order should be. Generally in the United States, ideologies go by the umbrella labels "liberalism" and "conservatism," although many differences exist even within these broad perspectives. Ideological conflict can be contentious since what is at stake are fundamental views of what the political world ought to look like.

The Citizens and American Political Beliefs

The gap between the ideal and the practice of American democracy

One of the core values of American political culture is democracy, an ideal that unites citizens—both those who are born here as well as more newly minted naturalized citizens—in the activity of self-governance. The American notion of democracy is a procedural one, a representative democracy valued for making decisions in which all voices are heard. It doesn't ask much of us except that we pay attention to the news of the day and come together periodically and vote to elect our public officials.

Keeping in mind that James Madison's "republican government" was not meant to be a "pure" democracy, it is interesting to note that it has grown more democratic in some ways in the past two hundred years. For one thing, more people can participate now—such as women and

African Americans—and, since eighteen year olds won the right to vote, the electorate is younger than ever before. But in many ways government remains removed from "the people," even if the definition of "the people" has expanded over time. While more people *can* participate in American politics, the truth is that not very many *do*. American turnout rates (the percentages of people who go to the polls and vote on election days) are abysmally low compared to those of other Western industrialized democracies, and surveys show that many Americans are apathetic toward politics. Even in 2008, a year of unusually high turnout, only about 60 percent of eligible voters cast a vote.

How does American democracy work with such low rates of participation or interest on the part of the citizenry? One theory, based on the elite notion of democracy described in Chapter 1, claims that it doesn't really matter whether people participate in politics because all important decisions are made by elites—leaders in business, politics, education, the military, and the media. People don't vote because their votes don't really matter.

Drawing on the pluralist theory of democracy, another explanation claims that Americans don't need to participate individually because their views are represented in government sufficiently through their membership in various groups. For instance, a citizen may be a member of an environmental group, a professional association or labor union, a parent-teacher organization, a veterans' group, a church, or a political party. While that citizen may not bother to vote on Election Day, his or her voice is heard nonetheless because all the groups to which he or she belongs have political influence.

By contrast, some educators and social scientists argue that falling levels of involvement, interest, and trust in politics are not something to be explained and dismissed with complacency, but instead signal a true civic crisis in American politics. They see a swing from the community-minded citizens of republican virtue to the self-interested citizens of Madisonian theory so severe that the fabric of American political life is threatened. These scholars argue that democracies can survive only with the support and vigilance of citizens, and that American citizens are so disengaged as the new century begins as to put democracy itself in danger. They would place the responsibility for low levels of participation in the United States not just on the system but also on the citizens themselves for not availing themselves of the opportunities for engagement that exist.

For instance, Benjamin Barber, discussing the tendency of Americans to take their freedoms for granted and to assume that since they were born free they will naturally remain free, says that citizenship is the "price of liberty."[6] For all the importance of presidents and senators and justices in the American political system, it is the people, the citizens, who are entrusted with "keeping the republic." The founders did not have great expectations of the citizens of the new country, and they feared the ravages of mob rule if there were "too much" democracy, but they knew well that the ultimate safeguards of free government are free citizens. Government whose citizens abdicate their role is government whose freedom, fragile at the best of times, is in jeopardy. We live in an age of overwhelming cynicism about and distrust in government. One manifestation of that cynicism and distrust is that citizens are opting out of government participation, not only not voting but not even paying attention.

While the question of how democratic the United States is may seem to be largely an academic one—that is, one that has little or no relevance to your personal life—it is really a question of who has the power, who is likely to be a winner in the political process. Looked at this way, the question has quite a lot to do with your life, especially as government starts to make more demands on you and you on it. Are you likely to be a winner or a loser? Are you going to get what you want from the political system? How much power do people like you have to get their way in government?

Thinking Outside the Box

Does it matter to the success of a democracy if relatively few people take an active political role (by paying attention, voting, exchanging political views, and the like)?

▶ What's at Stake Revisited

America has been a polyglot country since its founding (as early as 1664 there were eighteen languages spoken on the island of Manhattan alone), but although some states passed "English-only" laws, especially in the 1800s, there has been little national enthusiasm for endorsing an "official" language until recently. Since it has been obvious to all that, despite the influx of immigrants, it is necessary to speak English to succeed in the United States, the goal of most language policy in the United States has traditionally been to accommodate those who are less than proficient.

But according to groups like ProEnglish, U.S. English, Inc., and English First, the efforts at accommodation have gotten out of hand. They argue that the goal of language policy should not be the promotion or celebration of diversity but rather assimilation of immigrants into the mainstream, and their motives range from the desire to "protect English" to the belief that immigrants will be better off if less assistance in their native tongues is provided.

Since 1981, members of Congress have regularly introduced legislation to make English the country's official language, most recently in the 108th Congress (2002–2004). Although the bills have not yet passed into law, advocates remain hopeful. State-level efforts have been successful in more than half the states. Backing those efforts, a 2008 poll found that 67 percent of Americans believe that official documents should be printed in English only.[7] On its surface, the debate between Official English and English Plus supporters seems to be about issues such as whether bilingual education "works" or how much it costs to print ballots in many languages. A casual observer could be forgiven for thinking that the issue is just about which means to use to pursue an agreed-upon end—a cost-effective improvement in the quality of life of immigrants.

But what is really at stake here is something much deeper than pedagogy or fiscal discipline as means to an end. Truthfully, there is no agreed-upon end, and for many the welfare of immigrants is really secondary to the primary conflict with which we opened this chapter—a conflict between a vision of the United States as a melting pot in which all cultures are boiled into a homogenized "American culture," or as a crazy salad, where all the ingredients keep their own separate and distinct identities. What is at stake in the debate over an official language is a view of an America based on assimilation versus one based on multiculturalism.

These two competing visions can be located on either end of the social order ideological dimension that we discussed earlier in this chapter

(see Figure 2.3). Many English Plus advocates tend to be at the top of the social order axis on this issue, believing in less government control over individual lives and more procedural guarantees to allow individuals to decide how to live their own lives. These people see the issue as one of equal rights and access, a fundamentally procedural issue. Both moderate liberals and traditional conservatives fit into this group, which is why the Official English movement is opposed by such strange bedfellows as former president George W. Bush, former president Clinton, and the libertarian American Civil Liberties Union.

It is at the substantive end of the social order dimension that the debate gets more complex and interesting from a political point of view, since there are supporters of English Plus in the lower-left quadrant of Figure 2.3 and supporters of Official English in the lower-right quadrant. These two groups are not just arguing about rights for immigrants but rather are debating the very nature of the America they want to live in.

On the left is a view of America as multicultural, a thriving marketplace of cultures, beliefs, languages, traditions, all recognizably American, but retaining some of the distinctive immigrant heritage they brought to this country. Such an America is eclectic and diverse, tolerant and open. By its nature it is always changing and evolving. It views the other side's vision as being hidebound and stagnant, and fundamentally unjust to the cultures

whose distinguishing characteristics it would see subsumed into a homogenized white European Christian "Americanism."

On the right is a vision of America that is more resistant to change, where traditional values from the nation's predominantly Christian heritage form the backbone of the country, and immigrants, no matter what their origins, are expected to assimilate to those values as they become part of American culture. Such a vision sees a multicultural America as a threat to American life. This is a substantive vision of America bound by the values of stability, order, and conformity.

Given the fundamental differences in how they view America, the two lower quadrants in American culture are bound to clash on the subject of English as an official language. Each side would like to convince the public that they differ only on approaches to solving a particular problem, when in fact many of them disagree on what the problem is to be solved. And, of course, the issue is complicated by the fact that for many Americans in the upper ideological quadrants the debate really is about different means to the end of improving immigrants' lives.

With so many deeply held convictions at stake, this issue is unlikely to be resolved any time soon, but it illustrates how ideologically complicated some issues can be in American political culture. Such complexity is difficult to sort out, but unless we take the time to do so, we may never be clear on what is really at stake in American politics.

To Sum Up

Key terms, chapter summaries, practice quizzes, Internet links, and other study aids are available on the companion web site at http://republic.cqpress.com.

Define | Understand | Practice | Read | Click | Watch

asylum (p. 35)
communitarians (p. 55)
conservatives (p. 51)
economic conservatives (p. 55)
economic liberals (p. 55)
ideologies (p. 50)
immigrants (p. 35)
individualism (p. 47)
liberals (p. 51)

libertarians (p. 55)
naturalization (p. 35)
normative (p. 47)
political culture (p. 47)
procedural guarantees (p. 47)
refugees (p. 35)
social conservatives (p. 55)
social liberals (p. 55)
values (p. 47)

Define | **Understand** | Practice | Read | Click | Watch

- U.S. immigrants are citizens or subjects of another country who come here to live and work. To become full citizens, they must undergo naturalization by fulfilling requirements designated by the U.S. Citizenship and Immigration Services.

- In recent years the influx of illegal immigrants, particularly in the southwestern states, has occupied national debate. Advocates of strict immigration policy complain that illegal aliens consume government services without paying taxes. Opponents of these policies support the provision of basic services for people who, like our ancestors, are escaping hardship and hoping for a better future. Congress, with the president's approval, makes immigration law, but these rules change frequently.

- Americans share common values and beliefs about how the world should work that allow us to be a nation despite our diversity.

- The American political culture is described as both procedural and individualistic. Because we focus more on fair rules than on the outcomes of those rules, our culture has a procedural nature. In addition, our individualistic nature means that we assume that individuals know what is best for them and that individuals, not government or society, are responsible for their own well-being.

- Democracy, freedom, and equality are three central American values. Generally, Americans acknowledge democracy as the most appropriate way to make public decisions. We value freedom for the individual from government restraint, and we value equality of opportunity rather than equality of result.

- While the range of ideological debate is fairly narrow in America when compared to other countries, there exists an ideological division among economic liberals, social liberals, economic conservatives, and social conservatives based largely on attitudes toward government control of the economy and of the social order.

- America's growing political apathy is well documented. Yet despite abysmal voting rates, the country continues to function, a fact that may be explained by several theories. However, many people claim that such apathy may indeed signal a crisis of democracy.

Define   Understand   Practice   Read   Click   Watch

1. **If immigrants follow the rules and regulations of the U.S. Citizenship and Immigration Services, they may apply for citizenship through the process of**
   a. immigration substantiation.
   b. initiation.
   c. initialization.
   d. dual citizenship.
   e. naturalization.

2. **According to the first *Who Are We?* feature in this chapter, which of the following statements is correct concerning projections of the American population between now and 2050?**
   a. As a percentage of the total population, whites continue to grow at a faster pace than do ethnic or racial majorities.
   b. By 2050, the number of retirees will diminish by half.
   c. By 2050, African Americans are projected to comprise twice the number of Hispanics in the U.S. population.
   d. By 2050, white Americans will make up only slightly more than half of the total U.S. population.
   e. Hispanics remain the slowest-growing-ethnic group in the United States.

3. **Which of the following is NOT one of the core values that make up American political culture?**
   a. Democracy
   b. Freedom

   c. Libertarianism
   d. Equality
   e. All of the above are core values in American political culture.

4. **Which of the following terms refers to the sets of beliefs about politics and society that help people make sense of their world?**
   a. Political culture
   b. Political ideology
   c. Democracy
   d. Liberalism
   e. Social conservatism

5. **The phrase "we want government to guarantee a fair playing field but not to guarantee equal outcomes for all the players" best reflects**
   a. the importance Americans place on individualism and procedural guarantees in their political culture.
   b. the enduring idea that immigration to the United States is completely open to all immigrants, no matter their country of origin.
   c. the main contention between conservatives and liberals in American ideological debates.
   d. the reason we are not a very diverse nation.
   e. issues we believe in but that divide us.

Define   Understand   Practice   Read   Click   Watch

DeLaet, Debra L. 2000. *U.S. Immigration Policy in an Age of Rights.* Westport, Conn.: Praeger. *A historical discussion of the development of immigration policy.*

Mills, Nicolaus. 2007. *Arguing Immigration: The Debate Over the Changing Face of America.* Austin, Texas: Touchstone. *This collection of short essays examines immigration from all sides and all viewpoints to both inform and let readers form their own opinions.*

Schlesinger, Arthur, Jr. 1991. *The Disuniting of America.* Knoxville, Tenn.: Whittle. *One of America's greatest characteristics is its multicultural make-up. Schlesinger, one of America's most prominent historians, warns us about the problems also associated with multiculturalism.*

Schreuder, Sally Abel. 2001. *How to Become a United States Citizen: A Step-by-Step Guidebook for Self-Instruction,* 6th ed. Occidental, Calif.: Nolo Press-Occidental. *Ever wonder what it would take to become a U.S. citizen if you were not born one? This book provides all of the interesting details.*

Schudson, Michael. 1998. *The Good Citizen: A History of American Civil Life.* New York: Martin Kessler Books. *A provocative analysis of how this country's definition of what makes "a good citizen" has changed over time. Schudson believes we expect too much from our citizens.*

Smith, Rogers M. 1997. *Civic Ideals: Conflicting Visions of Citizenship in U.S. History.* New Haven: Yale University Press. *A comprehensive and troubling look at the ways in which citizens have been denied basic citizenship rights from the colonial period to the Progressive Era.*

White, John Kenneth. 2003. *The Values Divide: American Politics and Culture in Transition.* New York: Chatham House. *A study of the role that values play in American public and private life. White argues that the values divide in America was responsible for the close 2000 presidential election.*

Two excellent sources for statistics on just about every facet of American life are The New York Times Almanac and The Wall Street Journal Almanac.

Define | **Understand** | **Practice** | **Read** | **Click** | **Watch**

Craig Ferguson Takes Citizenship Test *www.youtube.com/watch?v=YvV6V3IJLX8. Irish native Craig Ferguson, host of The Late Late Show on CBS, goes through the U.S. citizenship process to see just what it takes to become a citizen. America, known as the land of immigrants, now turns away more and more foreigners seeking to gain full membership benefits.*

Ellis Island *www.ellisisland.org. Information about what was once America's main immigrant entry facility is posted here, including passenger searches, immigrant experiences, timelines, photos, and other useful information on the history of immigration in the United States.*

FedStats *www.fedstats.gov. This portal to all statistics produced by the federal government is searchable by agency or topic.*

MTV's True Life: I Live on the Border *www.mtv.com/overdrive/?id=1570607&vid=178514. This MTV series follows individuals whose lives are affected by certain issues. This particular episode documents "three young people overwhelmed by the problems caused by illegal immigration, who are doing everything they can to handle a situation with no easy solutions."*

SuperNews!—The Immigration Debate *www.youtube.com/watch?v=YhE16HdfqWM. "The immigration debate blows up when the Pilgrims protest limitations to their rights in America."*

U.S. Census Bureau *www.census.gov. This extremely valuable site contains vast amounts of data—current, historical, and future projections—on the American people and businesses.*

U.S. Citizenship and Immigration Services *www.uscis.gov. A rich resource, this page contains immigration statistics, reports, and information on immigration and naturalization law.*

Define | **Understand** | **Practice** | **Read** | **Click** | **Watch**

In America *2002. A moving portrait of an Irish immigrant family in New York struggling to make ends meet and find their place in a chaotic new city.*

Crossing Arizona *2006. This film follows the influx of migrants across the Arizona desert, detailing the frustrations from all sides: the farmers who hire the laborers, humanitarian groups who help them, ranchers who must repair broken fences and other resultant problems that endanger their livestock, and the Minutemen who've taken up border patrol duty as citizen activists.*

A Day Without A Mexican *2004. With a thick fog surrounding the border between California and Mexico, Hispanic mothers, fathers, and children disappear. Fruit is left unpicked, trash is building up on the streets, and even the border patrols mourn the loss as the state's economy slows to a standstill. This film explores the role Hispanics play in American society and examines ethnicity and racial identification.*

De Nadie *2005. A documentary that highlights the journey immigrants make to enter the United States illegally from Mexico, this film explores the questions of why people take the risks they do and the challenges they face along the way.*

Ellis Island *2000. Produced for the History Channel, this thorough and moving documentary chronicles the experiences endured by the more than 12 million immigrants who passed through New York's Ellis Island en route to their new lives in America.*

The Terminal *2004. A man traveling from his Eastern European country to New York finds that his home country disintegrated, and as a man without a country, he becomes trapped in a loophole in the Department of Homeland Security's immigration policies.*

Chapter 3

Politics of the American Founding

▶ What's at Stake?

It might have been 1773 all over again. Antitax and antigovernment, the 2010 Tea Partiers were angry, and if they didn't go as far as to empty shiploads of tea into Boston Harbor, they made their displeasure known in other ways. Though their ire was directed at government in general, they found specific targets in the Bush administration's Troubled Asset Relief Program (TARP) bailouts of big financial institutions in 2008 and other measures taken in response to the economic crisis that began that year, including the mortgage assistance for people facing foreclosure, the stimulus bill, and the health reform act, all passed by Congress in 2009 and 2010 with the strong backing of President Barack Obama.

Many of the Tea Partiers were simply focused on airing their aversion to the agenda of President Obama and the Democrats who had swept into office after the 2008 election, and they signaled their intention to vote for more conservative replacements in 2010 and 2012. Other messages were more ominous, rejecting the very legitimacy of the U.S. government—by doubting the citizenship of the president, by claiming that the election that brought him to power had been rigged by groups like ACORN, or by arguing that the government in Washington was tyrannical and it was the job of patriotic citizens to resist it.

A New Revolution
A member of the Tea Party demonstrates against government policies during the Obama administration. His sign refers to a quotation by Thomas Jefferson about the occasional necessity for revolution to maintain freedom.

The Tea Party movement is a decentralized mix of many groups—most simply frustrated Republicans (the major party that most Tea Partiers identify with or lean toward) but others more extreme. David Barstow of the *New York Times* wrote in early 2010 that a "significant undercurrent within the Tea Party movement" was less like a part of the Republican Party than it was like "the Patriot movement, a brand of politics historically associated with libertarians, militia groups, anti-immigration advocates and those who

argue for the abolition of the Federal Reserve."[1] He quotes a Tea Party leader so worried about the impending tyranny threatening her country that she can imagine being called to violence in its defense: "I don't see us being the ones to start it, but I would give up my life for my country. . . . Peaceful means are the best way of going about it. But sometimes you are not given a choice."

Reflecting these same feelings, Tea Party members in Oklahoma City in April 2010 declared their intention to pass a state law to create a militia to defend their state against the federal government.[2] Their announcement came just days before the fifteenth anniversary of the day Timothy McVeigh, holding many similar views about the illegitimacy of the federal government, attacked the federal building in Oklahoma City, killing 168 people, including 19 children.

Like the extreme Tea Partiers quoted above and even McVeigh and his associates, Patriot and militia group members are everyday men and women who say they are the ideological heirs of the American Revolution. They liken themselves to the colonial Sons of Liberty who rejected the authority of the British government and took it upon themselves to enforce the laws they thought were just. The Sons of Liberty instigated the Boston Massacre and the Boston Tea Party, historical events that we celebrate as patriotic but that would be considered treason or terrorism if they took place today—and were considered as such by the British back when they occurred.

Today's so-called Patriot groups claim that the federal government has become as tyrannical as the British government ever was, that

it deprives citizens of their liberty and over-regulates their everyday lives. They go so far as to claim that federal authority is illegitimate. Militia members reject federal laws that do everything from limiting the weapons that individual citizens can own, to imposing taxes on income, to requiring the registration of motor vehicles, to creating the Federal Reserve Bank, to reforming the health care system. They maintain that government should stay out of individual lives, providing security at the national level, perhaps, but allowing citizens to regulate and protect their own lives.

Some militias go even further. Many militia members, for instance, are convinced that the United Nations is seeking to take over the United States (and that top U.S. officials are letting this happen). Others blend their quests for individual liberty with rigid requirements about who should enjoy that liberty. White supremacist or anti-Semitic groups aim at achieving an all-white continent or see Jewish collaboration behind ominous plots to destroy America.

Although there are some indications that militia membership was down in the wake of the negative publicity surrounding the 1995 Oklahoma City bombing, membership in such groups has surged since Obama's election. Currently there are 127 militias in the United States, among 512 Patriot groups.[3] The groups base their claim to legitimate existence on the Constitution's Second Amendment, which reads, "A well regulated Militia, being necessary to the security of a free State, the right of the people to keep and bear Arms, shall not be infringed." Members of state militias, and other groups like them, take this amendment literally and absolutely, as did Timothy

McVeigh and members of a Michigan militia group, Hutaree, who were arrested by police in March 2010, after their plan to use roadside bombs was discovered. They face charges of sedition and intent to use weapons of mass destruction.[4]

The federal government has reacted strongly to limit the threat presented by state militias and others who believe that its authority is not legitimate. Partly in response to the Oklahoma City bombing, Congress passed an antiterrorism bill signed by President Bill Clinton in 1996 that would make it easier for federal agencies to monitor the activities of such groups. Those powers were broadened in the wake of the September 11, 2001, attacks on the United States by foreign terrorists. President George W. Bush gave the Department of Homeland Security a broad mandate to combat terrorism, including the homegrown variety.

Is the federal government responding appropriately to these threats? Are these groups, as they claim, the embodiment of revolutionary patriotism? Do they support the Constitution, or sabotage it? And where do we draw the line between a Tea Party member who wants to sound off against elected officials and policies she doesn't like, and one who advocates resorting to violence to protect her particular reading of the Constitution? Think about these questions as you read this chapter on the founding of the United States. Think about the consequences and implications of revolutionary activity then and now. We return to the question of what's at stake for American politics in the militia movement at the end of the chapter. ∎

[T]he founding of the United States is central not because it inspires warm feelings of patriotism but because it can teach us about American politics, the struggles for power that forged the political system that continues to shape our collective struggles today.

From the moment students start coloring in pictures of grateful **Pilgrims and cutting out construction paper turkeys in grade school**, the founding of the United States is a recurring focus of American education, and with good reason. Democratic societies, as we saw in Chapter 1, rely on the consent of their citizens to maintain lawful behavior and public order. To be committed to the rules and the goals of the American system requires that we feel good about that system. What better way to stir up good feelings and patriotism than by recounting thrilling stories of bravery and derring-do on the part of selfless heroes dedicated to the cause of American liberty? We celebrate the Fourth of July with fireworks and parades, displaying publicly our commitment to American values and our belief that our country is special, in the same way that other nations celebrate their origins all over the world. Bastille Day (July 14) in France, May 17 in Norway, October 1 in China, July 6 in Malawi, Africa—all are days on which people rally together to celebrate their common past and their hopes for the future.

Of course people feel real pride in their countries and of course many nations, not only our own, do have amazing stories to tell about their earliest days. But as political scientists, we must separate myth from reality. For us, the founding of the United States is central not because it inspires warm feelings of patriotism but because it can teach us about American politics, the struggles for power that forged the political system that continues to shape our collective struggles today.

The history of the American founding has been told from many points of view. You are probably most familiar with this account: The early colonists escaped to America to avoid religious persecution in Europe. Having arrived on the shores of the New World, they built communities that allowed them to practice their religions in peace and to govern themselves as free people. When the tyrannical British king made unreasonable demands on the colonists, they had no choice but to protect their liberty by going to war and by establishing a new government of their own.

But sound historical evidence suggests that the story is more complicated, and more interesting, than that. A closer look shows that the early Americans were complex beings with economic and political agendas as well as religious

Consider these two passages describing the same familiar event: Christopher Columbus's arrival in the Americas.[1]

From a 1947 textbook:

At last the rulers of Spain gave Columbus three small ships, and he sailed away to the west across the Atlantic Ocean. His sailors became frightened. They were sure the ships would come to the edge of the world and just fall off into space. The sailors were ready to throw their captain into the ocean and turn around and go back. Then, at last they all saw the land ahead. They saw low green shores with tall palm trees swaying in the wind. Columbus had found the New World. This happened on October 12, 1492. It was a great day for Christopher Columbus—and for the whole world as well.

And from a 1991 text:

When Columbus stepped ashore on Guanahani Island in October 1492, he planted the Spanish flag in the sand and claimed the land as a possession of Ferdinand and Isabella. He did so despite the obvious fact that the island already belonged to someone else—the "Indians" who gathered on the beach to gaze with wonder at the strangers who had suddenly arrived in three great, white-winged canoes. He gave no thought to the rights of the local inhabitants. Nearly every later explorer—French, English, Dutch and all the others as well as the Spanish—thoughtlessly dismissed the people they encountered. What we like to think of as the discovery of America was actually the invasion and conquest of America.

Which one of these passages is "true"? The first was the conventional textbook wisdom through the 1950s and 1960s in America. The latter reflects a growing criticism that traditional American history has been told from the perspective of history's "winners," largely white middle-class males of European background. Together they highlight the point that history does vary depending on who is telling it, and when they are telling it, and even to whom they are telling it. The telling of history is a potent political act, as one recent study explains, citing George Orwell's *1984* that "who controls the past controls the future."[2] What this means to you is that the critical vigilance we urge you to apply to all the information that regularly bombards you should be applied to your textbooks as well. And yes, that means this textbook, too.

There is some truth to the idea that history is written by the winners, but it is also true that the winners change over time. If history was once securely in the hands of the white European male, it is now the battleground of a cultural war between those who believe the old way of telling (and teaching) history was accurate, and those who believe it left out the considerable achievements of women and minorities and masked some of the less admirable episodes of our past in order to glorify our heritage.[3] For instance, one author in the 1990s studied twelve high school history textbooks and documented areas where he felt the "history" was inaccurate or misleading. His criticism includes claims that history textbooks create heroic figures by emphasizing the positive aspects of their lives and ignoring their less admirable traits; that they create myths about the American founding that glorify Anglo-European settlers at the expense of the Native Americans and Spanish settlers who were already here; that they virtually ignore racism and its opponents, minimizing its deep and lasting effects on our culture; that they neglect the recent past; and that they idealize progress and the exceptional role America plays in the world, skipping over very real problems and issues of concern.[4]

The battle over textbook content had reached a peak with the publication of the National History Standards, written under a bipartisan effort initiated by President George H. W. Bush in 1989. The objective was to ensure that all high school students would be exposed to a common core of scholarship in a variety of subjects. Bipartisanship quickly dissolved when the standards were published. Emphasizing a view of American history that went beyond the usual European orientation, the standards focused less on traditional historical personalities and achievements and more on issues, conflicts, and the effort to get students to question traditional assumptions about our past. They were quickly accused of undervaluing white male historical figures in favor of minorities and women; of engaging in "quota history," in which people were discussed because of their demographic fit rather than their substantive contribution; of celebrating non-Western players in American history but ignoring their atrocities; and of pushing a liberal ideological agenda that favored the interests of feminists and multiculturalists.[5] Counting mentions of various topics in the index of the standards, a critic pointed out that the Seneca Indians' constitution was mentioned nine times, but Paul Revere's ride not at all. The U.S. Senate resolved 99–1 to denounce the standards for showing too little respect for the contributions of Western civilization. Ultimately revised to recapture some of the traditional themes of American history and to be less prescriptive, the standards are now influencing the writing of new high school history textbooks. That the battle to restore the traditional view of American history in textbooks is not over, however, was evident in 2010, when the Texas Board of Education voted along party lines to create a social studies curriculum that emphasizes conservative principles and viewpoints (for instance, questioning the founders' commitment to the separation of church and state and including the claim that the McCarthyism of the 1950s was vindicated by later events).[6]

The question of bias in textbooks is not reserved for history books. We state in Chapters 1 and 3 that this textbook itself has

a point of view, an interest in highlighting the issues of power and citizenship, and in focusing on the impact of the rules in American politics. In addition, we take a multicultural approach. While we do not ignore or disparage the achievements of the traditional heroes of American history, we do not think that their outstanding political accomplishments warrant ignoring the contributions, also substantial, of people who have not traditionally been politically powerful.

The fact that all textbooks have some sort of bias means you must be as critically careful in what you accept from textbook authors as you are (or should be) in what you accept from any other scholars or newspaper writers or other media commentators. Apply the rules of critical thinking discussed in Chapter 1. In addition, here are some specific questions you can ask yourself about your textbooks:

1. **Who are the authors?** Do they have a particular point of view (that is, do they promote particular values or ideas)? What is it? Are any points of view left out of the story they tell? Whose? How might this influence the book's content? (Clues to an author's orientation can often be found in the preface or the introduction, where the author tells you what has motivated him or her to write the book. Ironically, this is the section most readers skip.)

2. **Who is the audience of the book?** If it is a big, colorful book, it is probably aimed at a wide market. If so, what is that likely to say about its content? If it is a smaller book with a tighter focus, what sorts of people is it trying to appeal to? Why did your teacher or school select this book?

3. **What kinds of evidence does the book provide?** If it backs up an argument with plenty of facts from reputable sources, then perhaps its claims are true, even if they are surprising or unfamiliar to you. On the other hand, if the book is telling you things that you have always assumed to be true but does not offer factual support, what might that say to you? What kinds of counterevidence could be provided? Do the authors make an effort to cover both sides of an issue or controversy? Read the footnotes, and if something troubles you, locate the primary source (the one the authors relied on) and read it yourself.

4. **What are the book's conclusions?** Do they cause you to look at a subject in a new way? Are they surprising? Exciting? Troublesome? What is the source of your reaction? Is it intellectual, or emotional? What caused you to react this way?

5. **How would your friends or classmates react to your book's arguments?** What does your professor have to say about them? As you analyze your textbook, asking the questions we have listed here, discuss some of the issues that arise with your colleagues. Their perspective might strengthen your convictions, or they might even change your mind. Coworkers can prove to be one of your chief assets in life. Take advantage of what they have to offer.

1. These two passages were cited in a chart accompanying Sam Dillon, "Schools Growing Harsher in Scrutiny of Columbus," *New York Times*, October 12, 1992, 4, web version. The first paragraph is from Merlin M. Ames, *My Country* (Sacramento: California State Department of Education, 1947); the second is from John A. Garraty, *The Story of America* (New York: Holt Rinehart Winston, Harcourt Brace Jovanovich, 1991).

2. Laura Hein and Mark Seldon, eds., *Censoring History: Citizenship and Memory in Japan, Germany, and the United States* (Armonk, N.Y.: M. E. Sharpe, 2000).

3. Frances Fitzgerald, *America Revised* (New York: Vintage Books, 1979).

4. James W. Loewen, *Lies My Teacher Told Me* (New York: New Press, 1995).

5. John Fonte, "History on Trial: Culture and the Teaching of the Past" (book reviews), *National Review*, November 10, 1997.

6. James C. McKinley Jr., "Texas Conservatives Win Curriculum Change," *New York Times*, March 12, 2010, www.nytimes.com/2010/03/13/education/13texas.html.

and philosophical motives. After much struggle among themselves, the majority of Americans decided that those agendas could be better and more profitably carried out if they broke their ties with England.[5]

Just because a controversial event like the founding is recounted by historians or political scientists one or two hundred years after it happens does not guarantee that there is common agreement on what actually took place. People write history not from a position of absolute truth but from particular points of view. When we read a historical account, as critical thinkers we need to ask probing questions: Who is telling the story? What point of view is being represented? What values and priorities lie behind it? If I accept this interpretation, what else will I have to accept? (See "*Consider the Source: Don't Be Fooled by Your Textbook.*")

In this chapter we talk a lot about history—the history of the American founding and the creation of the Constitution. Like all other authors, we have a particular point of view that affects how we tell the story. True to the first basic theme of this book, we are interested in power and politics. We want to understand American government in terms of who the winners and losers are likely to be. It makes sense for us to begin by looking at the founding to see who the winners and losers were then. We are also interested in how rules and institutions make it more likely that some people will win and others lose. Certainly an examination of the early debates about rules and institutions will help us understand that. Finally, because we are interested in winners and losers, we are interested in understanding how people come to be defined as players in the system in the first place, the focus of the second theme of this book—citizenship. It was during the founding that many of the initial decisions were made about who "We the People" would actually be. Specifically, in this chapter, you will learn about

- **the battle of colonial powers for control of America and the process of settlement by the English**

- **the break with England and the Revolution**

- **the initial attempt at American government: the Articles of Confederation**

- **the Constitutional Convention**

- **the ratification of the Constitution**

- **the role of everyday citizens in the founding**

Politics in the English Colonies
Power struggles in the new world

America was a battlefield—both political and military—long before the war for independence from Britain was fought. Not only did the English settlers have to struggle with brutal winters, harsh droughts, disease, and other unanticipated natural disasters, but they quickly came into conflict with the people who already inhabited the New World when they arrived—Native Americans and Spanish and French colonists.

Declaring that they had a legitimate right to colonize unoccupied territory, the British set about populating the eastern coast of America. Many Native Americans initially helped the British overcome the rigors of life in the New World. But cultural differences between the Indians and the British, and the latter's conviction that their beliefs and practices were superior to Indian ways, made the relationship between the two unpredictable. Some Indians engaged in political dealings with the Europeans, forming military coalitions (partnerships), trade alliances, and other arrangements. Others were more hostile, particularly in the face of the European assumption that the New World was theirs to subdue and exploit.

The Spanish, too, were an obstacle to English domination. Spain in the sixteenth century seemed to be well on its way to owning the New World. Spanish explorers had laid claim to both eastern and western North America as well as key parts of Central and South America. The ancestors of many of the 21 million Spanish-speaking people in America today were living in what is now New Mexico, California, Colorado, and Texas, for instance, before many people were speaking English in America at all. But the monarchs of England liked the idea of getting a piece of the treasure that was being exported regularly from the Americas. Spain and England were already in conflict in Europe, and Spain was vulnerable. Despite treaties, Spanish spies, intrigue with Native Americans, and occasional military action, Britain edged Spain out of the colonial picture in eastern America. Had Spain been able to enforce the treaties Britain had signed, or had it been able to form a more constant and productive alliance with France, it might have been able to reverse its fortunes. In due time the English would have to fend off the Dutch and the French as well, but by the late 1700s the eastern seaboard colonies were heavily English. Though Spain maintained its presence in the West and the Southwest, those territories did not figure in American politics until much later.

> *feudalism* a social system based on a rigid social and political hierarchy based on the ownership of land

Reasons for Leaving England

Many British subjects were eager and willing to try their luck across the Atlantic. They came to America to make their fortunes, to practice their religions without interference, to become landowners—to take advantage of a host of opportunities that England, still struggling out of the straightjacket of feudalism, could not offer. **Feudalism** was a social system in which a rigid social and political hierarchy was based on the ownership of land, but land ownership was restricted to the very few. Individuals lived out their lives in the class to which they were born; it was unheard of to work one's way up from peasant to landowner.

Although the colonists did not know it, life in England in the 1600s was on the brink of major change. Within the century, political thinkers would begin to reject the idea that monarchs ruled through divine right, would favor increasing the power of Parliament at the expense of the king, and would promote the idea that individuals were not merely subjects but citizens, with rights that government could not violate. Civil war and revolution in England would give teeth to these fresh ideas. The new philosophy, a product of the Enlightenment, was open to religious tolerance, giving rise to more reformist and separatist sects. Commerce and trade would create the beginnings of a new middle class with financial power independent of the landed class of feudalism, a class that would blossom with the rise of industry in the 1700s.

But in the early 1600s, settlers came to America in part because England seemed resistant to change. It would be a mistake to think, however, that the colonists, having been repressed in England, came to America hoping to achieve liberty for all people. The colonists emigrated in order to practice their religions freely (but not necessarily to let others practice theirs), to own land, to engage in trade, to avoid debtors' prison. England also had a national interest in sending colonists to America. Under the economic system of mercantilism, nations competed for the world's resources through trade, and colonies were a primary source of raw materials for manufacturing. Entrepreneurs often supported colonization as an investment, and the government issued charters to companies, giving them the right to settle land as English colonies.

Political Participation in the Colonies

It shouldn't surprise us, therefore, to find that the settlers often created communities that were in some ways as restrictive and repressive as the ones they had left behind in England. The difference, of course, was that they were now the ones doing the repressing rather than the ones being repressed. In other ways, life in America was more open than life in Britain. Land was widely available. Although much of it was inhabited by Native Americans, the Indians believed in communal or shared use of property. The Europeans arrived with notions of private property and the sophisticated weaponry to defend the land they claimed. Some colonies set up systems of self-rule, with representative assemblies such as Virginia's House of Burgesses, Maryland's House of Delegates, and the town meetings of the northern colonies. Though they had governors, often appointed by the king, at least until the late 1600s the colonies were left largely, though not exclusively, to their own devices.

Clearly, while the colonies offered more opportunities than did life in Britain, they also continued many of the injustices that some colonists had hoped to escape. A useful way to understand who had power in the colonies is to look at the rules regulating political participation—that is, who was allowed to vote in colonial lawmaking bodies, who wasn't, and why. Each colony set its own voting rules, based on such factors as property, religion, gender, and race.

- *Property.* Although voting laws varied in England by locality as well, there they had in common an emphasis on property-holding requirements. Very simply, conventional British wisdom held that if you didn't own property, you were unlikely to take a serious interest in government (whose job was largely to protect property, after all), and you were equally unlikely to share the values and virtues attached to rural life, which formed the core of British upper-class culture. Gradually the colonies too began to require of voters some degree of property ownership or, later, tax-paying status. This requirement did not exclude as many people from voting in America as in England since property owning was so much more widespread among the settlers.

- *Religion.* More pervasive than property-owning or tax-paying requirements, at least in the earliest days of colonial government, were moral or religious qualifications. The northern colonies especially were concerned about keeping the ungodly out of government. By 1640, for instance, religious tests for voting prevented three-fourths of the Massachusetts population from having any political power. By 1691, however, Massachusetts

A Political Divide

Under English rule, some women in the American colonies were able to participate in politics. Once the United States was formed, however, the states crafted a strict political divide that restricted voting primarily to wealthy, land-owning men.

had moved into line with Virginia and the other colonies that based an individual's political rights on his wealth rather than his character.

- *Gender.* Women weren't officially excluded from political participation in America until the Revolution. Until then, as in England, they occasionally could exercise the vote when they satisfied the property requirement and when there were no voting males in their households. In some localities, widows particularly, or daughters who had inherited a parent's property, could vote or participate in church meetings (which sometimes amounted to the same thing). Some colonies allowed women to vote, whereas others, notably Pennsylvania, Delaware, Virginia, Georgia, New York, and South Carolina, excluded them, at least for some period of time.[6]

- *Race.* Before **slavery** took hold as an American institution at the end of the 1600s, Africans were subjected to the same laws and codes of behavior as Europeans living in America.[7] The colonies required tremendous amounts of cheap labor to produce the raw materials and goods needed for trade with England under the mercantilist system, and when English people from the Caribbean island of Barbados settled in South Carolina in 1670, they brought with them the institution of slavery. Slavery proved economically profitable even in the more commercial areas of New England, but it utterly transformed the tobacco plantations of Maryland and Virginia.[8]

Not surprisingly, as slavery became accepted in the colonies, the rights of blacks were gradually stripped away. In the 1640s, Maryland denied blacks the right to bear arms. A 1669 Virginia law declared that if a slave "should chance to die" when resisting his or her master or the master's agent, it would not be a felony—a crime that legally required malice—because no one would destroy his own property with malice. Most politically damaging, by the 1680s free blacks were forbidden to own property, the only access to political power that colonial society recognized.[9] Reasons for these legal changes are not hard to find. Slavery can work only if slaves are dependent, defenseless, and afraid to escape. Also, an institution as dehumanizing as slavery requires some justification that enables slaveholders to live with themselves, especially in the Enlightenment era, when words like "natural rights" and "liberty" were on everyone's tongue. It was said that the Africans were childlike, lazy, and undisciplined, and that they needed the supervision of slaveowners. The worse slaves were treated, the more their humanity was denied. Racism, the belief that one race is superior to another, undoubtedly existed before slavery was well established in America, but the institution of slavery made it a part of American political culture. We discuss the issue of race in American politics in more detail in Chapter 6.

The English colonists wanted, first and foremost, to find new opportunities in America. But those opportunities were not available to all. Religious and property qualifications for the vote, and the exclusion of women and blacks from political life, meant that the colonial leaders did not feel that simply living in a place or obeying the laws or even paying taxes carried with it the right to participate in government. Following the rigid British social hierarchy, they wanted rules to ensure that the "right kind" of people could participate, people who could be depended on to make the kind of rules that would ensure their status and maintain the established order. The danger of expanding the vote, of course, is that the new majority might want something very different from what the old majority wanted.

Who What How

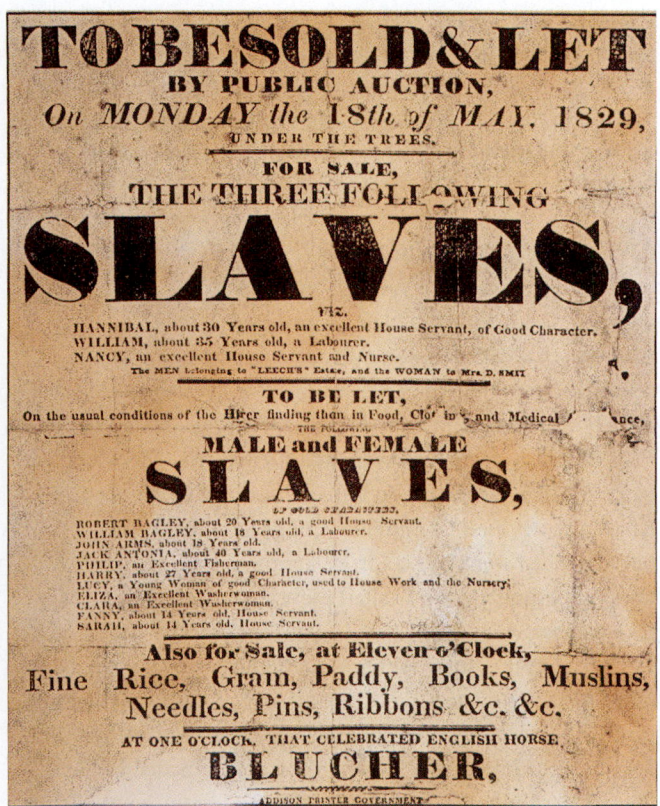

Human Trade

Slaves were used to meet the needs of the South's burgeoning economy in tobacco and cotton, which required plentiful, cheap labor. They were shipped from Africa and sold to farmers alongside rice, books, and other goods. In the eighteenth century, approximately 275,000 slaves were shipped to the American colonies. Many did not survive the harsh conditions of the passage.

The Split From England

Making the transition from British subjects to American citizens

Both England and America accepted as perfectly normal the relationships of colonial power that initially bound them together. Americans, as colonists, were obliged to make England their primary trading partner, and all goods they traded to other countries had to pass through Britain, where a tax was collected on them. The benefits of being a colony, however, including financial support by British corporations, military defense by the British army and navy, and a secure market for their agricultural products, usually outweighed any burdens of colonial obligation. Eventually the relationship started to sour as the colonists developed an identity as Americans rather than as transplanted English people, and as the British became a more intrusive political presence. Even then, they searched painstakingly for a way to fix the relationship before they decided to eliminate it altogether. Revolution was not an idea that occurred readily to either side.

slavery the ownership, for forced labor, of one people by another

French and Indian War a war fought between France and England, and allied Indians, from 1754 to 1763; resulted in France's expulsion from the New World

British Attempts to Gain Control of the Colonies

Whether the British government had actually become oppressive in the years before 1776 is open to interpretation. Certainly the colonists thought so. Britain was deeply in debt, having won the **French and Indian War**, which effectively forced the French out of North America and the Spanish to vacate Florida and retreat west of the Mississippi. The war, fought to defend the British colonies and colonists in America, turned into a major and expensive conflict across the Atlantic as well. Britain, having done its protective duty as a colonial power and having taxed British citizens heavily to finance the war, turned to its colonies to help pay for their defense. It chose to do that by levying taxes on the colonies and by attempting to enforce more strictly the trade laws that would increase British profits from American resources.

The irony is that, with the British victory in the war, the colonies were largely free of Spanish, French, and Indian threat. No longer in need of British protection, they could afford to resist British efforts to make them help pay for it.[10] The series of acts the British passed infuriated the colonists. The Sugar Act of 1764, which imposed customs taxes, or duties, on sugar, was seen as unfair and unduly burdensome in a depressed postwar economy, and the Stamp Act of 1765 incited protests and demonstrations throughout the colonies. Similar to a tax in effect in Great Britain for nearly a century, it required that a tax be paid, in scarce British currency, on every piece of printed matter in the colonies, including newspapers, legal documents, and even playing cards. The colonists claimed that the law was an infringement on their liberty and a violation of their rights not to be taxed without their consent. Continued protests and political changes in England resulted in the repeal of the Stamp Act in 1766. The Townshend Acts of 1767, taxing goods imported from England such as paper, glass, and tea, followed by the Tea Act of 1773, were seen by the colonists as intolerable violations of their rights. To show their displeasure they hurled 342 chests of tea into Boston Harbor in the infamous Boston Tea Party. Britain responded by passing the Coercive Acts of 1774, designed to punish the citizens of Massachusetts. In the process, Parliament sowed the seeds that would blossom into revolution in just a few years.

Changing Ideas About Politics

The American reluctance to cooperate with Britain was reinforced by the colonists' changing worldview. Philosophical ideas that were fermenting in England and the European

> **popular sovereignty** the concept that the citizens are the ultimate source of political power

> **Common Sense** 1776 pamphlet by Thomas Paine that persuaded many Americans to support the Revolutionary cause

Enlightenment as a whole, especially those of John Locke, were finding a natural home in America. Bernard Bailyn, a scholar of early American history, says that American thinking challenged and broke with British ideology on the interpretation of three major concepts: representation, constitution, and sovereignty.[11]

With respect to representation, Americans came to believe that elected representatives should do precisely what the people who elected them told them to do. This was very different from the British notion of "virtual representation," in which the representative followed his conscience, acting in the best interests of the country as a whole and thus, by definition, of the citizens who lived there. The colonists also began to understand the notion of a constitution as a specific grant of powers to and limitations on government, including Parliament itself. This idea was in turn directly connected to the notion of sovereignty. For the British, the sovereign authority was Parliament, which established the rule of law and constitutional principles. But the colonists held fast to the principle of *popular sovereignty*; that is, the ultimate authority, the power to govern, belonged in the hands of the people.

These philosophical changes meant that any British colonial authority had begun to seem illegitimate to many of the colonists. Much has been made in American schoolbooks about the colonists' defiant rejection of British taxation without representation. The British had offered Americans representation in Parliament, however, and they had rejected it in the assemblies of South Carolina and Virginia.[12] It wasn't just taxation the colonists objected to; it was the British parliament itself.

Some loyalists to the Crown continued to support British authority because they were involved in British administration of the colonies, because they had commercial ties to Britain, because they believed that America still needed British military protection, or because they were committed to the notion of monarchy. For the rest of the colonists, however, it became harder and harder to recognize British power over them as legitimate authority.

Revolution

From the moment that the unpopularly taxed tea plunged into Boston Harbor in December 1773, it became apparent that the Americans were not going to settle down and behave like proper and orthodox colonists. Even before the Tea Party, mobs in many towns were demonstrating and rioting against British control. Calling themselves the Sons of Liberty, and under the guidance of the eccentric Samuel Adams, cousin to

the future president John Adams, rebellious colonists routinely caused extensive damage and, in early 1770, provoked the so-called Boston Massacre, an attack by British soldiers that left six civilians dead and further inflamed popular sentiments.

By the time of the Boston Tea Party, also incited by the Sons of Liberty, passions were at a fever pitch. The American patriots called a meeting in Philadelphia in September 1774. Known as the First Continental Congress, the meeting declared the Coercive Acts void, announced a plan to stop trade with England, and called for a second meeting in May 1775. Before they could meet again, in the early spring of 1775, the king's army went marching to arrest Samuel Adams and another patriot, John Hancock, and to discover the hiding place of the colonists' weapons. Roused by the silversmith Paul Revere, Americans in Lexington and Concord fired the first shots of rebellion at the British, and revolution was truly under way.

The Declaration of Independence

Even in the midst of war, the colonists did not at first clearly articulate a desire for independence from England. But publication of the pamphlet *Common Sense*, written by the English-born Thomas Paine, turned their old ideas upside-down. Paine called for the rejection of the king, for independence, and for republican government, and his passionate writing crystallized the thinking of the colonial leaders.[13]

In 1776, at the direction of a committee of the Continental Congress, thirty-four-year-old Thomas Jefferson sat down to write a declaration of independence from England. His training as a lawyer at the College of William and Mary, and his service as a representative in the Virginia House of Burgesses, helped prepare him for his task, but he had an impressive intellect in any case. President John Kennedy once announced to a group of Nobel Prize winners he was entertaining that they were "the

Thinking Outside **the Box**

Are there any circumstances in which it would be justifiable for groups in the United States to rebel against the federal government today?

most extraordinary collection of talents that has ever gathered at the White House, with the possible exception of when Thomas Jefferson dined alone."[14] A testimony to Jefferson's capabilities is the strategically brilliant document that he produced.

The **Declaration of Independence** is first and foremost a political document. Having decided to make the break from England, the American founders had to convince themselves, their fellow colonists, and the rest of the world that they were doing the right thing. Revolutions are generally frowned on politically, unless the revolutionaries can convince the world that they have particularly good and legitimate reasons for their actions. Other national leaders don't like them because they upset the status quo and give ideas to the politically discontent in their own countries. In addition, revolutionaries face the problem of justifying *their* revolution, but no other ones. After all, they presumably intend to set up a new government after the revolution, and they don't want people revolting against it. The story told to justify a revolution has to guard against setting off a chain reaction. The Declaration of Independence admirably performs all these tasks.

Jefferson did not have to hunt farther than the writing of John Locke for a good reason for his revolution. Recall from Chapter 1 that Locke said that government is based on a contract between the rulers and the ruled. The ruled agree to obey the laws as long as the rulers protect their basic rights to life, liberty, and property. If the rulers fail to do that, they break the contract and the ruled are free to set up another government. This is exactly what the second paragraph of the Declaration of Independence says, except that Jefferson changed "property" to "the pursuit of happiness," perhaps to garner the support of those Americans who didn't own enough property to worry about. Having established that the breaking of the social contract was a good reason for revolution, Jefferson could justify the American Revolution if he could show that Britain had broken such a contract by violating the colonists' rights.

Consequently, he spelled out all the things that King George III had allegedly done to breach the social contract. Turn to the Declaration in the Appendix of this book and notice the extensive list of grievances against the king. For twenty-seven paragraphs, Jefferson documented just how badly the monarch had treated the colonists. Note, however, that many of the things the colonists complained of were the normal acts of a colonial power. No one had told the king that he was a party to a Lockean contract, so it isn't surprising that he violated it at every turn. Furthermore, some of the things he was blamed for

were the acts of Parliament, not of the king at all. Perhaps because the colonists intended to have some sort of parliament of their own, or perhaps, as some scholars have argued, because they simply did not recognize Parliament's authority over them, George III was the sole focus of their wrath and resentment. But the clear goal of the document was to so thoroughly discredit George III that this revolution became inevitable in the eyes of every American, and the world.

". . . That All Men Are Created Equal"

The Declaration of Independence begins with a statement of the equality of all men. Since so much of this document relies heavily on Locke, and since clearly the colonists did *not* mean that all men are created equal, it is worth turning to Locke for some help in seeing exactly what they did mean. In his most famous work, *A Second Treatise on Government*, Locke wrote,

> Though I have said above that all men are by nature equal, I cannot be supposed to understand all sorts of equality. Age or virtue may give men a just precedency. Excellency of parts and merit may place others above the common level. Birth may subject some, and alliance or benefits others, to pay an observance to those whom nature, gratitude, or other respects may have made it due.[15]

Men are equal in a natural sense, said Locke, but society quickly establishes many dimensions on which they may be unequal. A particularly sticky point for Locke's ideas on equality is his treatment of slavery, which he did not endorse but ultimately failed to condemn. Here too our founders would have been in agreement with him.

The founders' ambivalence about slavery and equality can be seen in a passage that Jefferson included in the original draft of the Declaration, as part of the political indictment of George III. He wrote:

> He [George III] has waged cruel war against human nature itself, violating its most sacred rights of life and liberty in the persons of a distant people who never offended him, captivating and carrying them into slavery in another hemisphere or to incur miserable death in their transportation thither.[16]

Blaming King George for the institution of slavery, and including it on a list of behaviors so horrible that they justify revolution, was an amazing act on the part of a man who not only owned slaves himself, but was writing on behalf of

▶ Who, What, How, and WHEN: Revolutions

Americans know all about their own revolution—tea dumped in a harbor, freezing winters at Valley Forge, and the Declaration of Independence. But what goes on in other countries when governments lose their legitimacy and the people decide it is time for a change? Here are a few examples of revolutions over time.

1775   American Revolution

Thirteen British colonies banded together to separate from the British empire due to their frustration with heavy-handed British policy. The American Revolution was the first in a series of breaks between colonies and European empires around the world, though many of these colonies, such as Canada and Australia, broke away from their parent empires peacefully. It also acted as a test of republican theories of government.

1789   French Revolution

The French Revolution grew out of French subjects' dissatisfaction with high taxes and their resentment of the monarchy's absolute rule. The Revolution made popular the concepts of individual rights and constitutional government in a country long controlled by kings. Even though France went through several other forms of government after the Revolution before arriving at the democratic government it has today, the French Revolution marked the beginning of the loss of monarchical power in many European countries, such as Sweden and Belgium.

1917   Russian Revolution

The Russian Revolution was actually several revolutions, following each other like toppling dominoes, all in the space of one year. First, Czar Nicolas II abdicated the throne after protests about the economy and Russian losses in World War I. A few months later, Vladimir Ilyich Lenin led a takeover of the temporary government and tried to establish a communist government. This led to civil war over the type of new government and, eventually, to the establishment of the Soviet Union and the spread of communist government.

---

many other slave owners. His action shows just how politically confusing and morally ambiguous the issue was at that time. Reflecting the political realities of the time, the passage was eventually deleted.

African Americans and the Revolution

The Revolution was a mixed blessing for American slaves. On the one hand, many slaves won their freedom as a result of the war; slavery was outlawed north of Maryland, and many slaves in the Upper South also were freed. The British offered freedom in exchange for service in the British army, although the conditions they provided were not always a great improvement over enslavement. The abolitionist, or antislavery, movement gathered steam in some northern cities, expressing moral and constitutional objections to the institution of slavery. Whereas before the Revolution only about 5 percent of American blacks were free, the number grew tremendously with the coming of war.[17]

Many African Americans served in the war. There were probably about twelve blacks in the first battle at Lexington and Concord, in Massachusetts. The South feared the idea of arming slaves, for obvious reasons, but by the time Congress began to fix troop quotas for each state, southerners were drafting slaves to serve in their masters' places.

1966 **Chinese Cultural Revolution**

After Mao Zedong took control of China in 1949, bad policy decisions led to economic problems, famine, and a loss of power for Mao. The Cultural Revolution was an attempt by Mao to regain power by ridding China of pre-communist traditions, using the student "Red Army" to circulate Mao's views of government, and purging the ruling communist party of Mao's detractors. Varying estimates say more than one million people died as a result of the Cultural Revolution.

1979 **Iranian Islamic Revolution**

The Islamic Revolution in Iran took place when the Ayatollah Khomeini, an exiled cleric, overthrew the monarch, the Shah of Iran. Khomeini set up a constitutional theocracy, in which Islamic clerics hold much of the power in government and civil laws must be reconciled with Islamic religious law, or Shari'a. The Islamic Revolution was unusual because, unlike many other revolutions, it did not involve war, and because it created a government closely tied with religion.

In the aftermath of war, however, African Americans did not find their lot greatly improved, despite the ringing rhetoric of equality that fed the Revolution. The economic profitability of slave labor still existed in the South, and slaves continued to be imported from Africa in large numbers. The explanatory myth—that all men were created equal but that blacks weren't quite men and thus could be treated unequally—spread throughout the new country, making even free blacks unwelcome in many communities. By 1786 New Jersey prohibited free blacks from entering the state, and within twenty years northern states had started passing laws specifically denying free blacks the right to vote.[18] No wonder the well-known black abolitionist Frederick Douglass said, in 1852: "This Fourth of July is yours, not mine. You may rejoice, I must mourn."

Native Americans and the Revolution

Native Americans were another group the founders did not consider to be prospective citizens. Not only were they already considered members of their own sovereign nations, but their communal property holding, their nonmonarchical political systems, and their divisions of labor between women working in the fields and men hunting for game were not compatible with European political notions. Pushed farther and farther

Determined Fighters
Deborah Sampson and a few other women disguised themselves as males and served in the colonial army. Sampson served under George Washington's command but was dishonorably discharged after the war when it became known she was a woman. Ten years later, after Washington's intervention, she became the first woman in the U.S. Army to receive a soldier's pension.

west by land-hungry colonists, the Indians were actively hostile to the American cause in the Revolution. Knowing this, the British hoped to gain their allegiance in the war. But the colonists, having asked in vain for the Indians to stay out of what they called a "family quarrel," were able to suppress early on the Indians' attempts to get revenge for their treatment at the hands of the settlers.[19] There was certainly no suggestion that the claim of equality at the beginning of the Declaration of Independence might include the peoples who had lived on the continent for centuries before the white man arrived.

Women and the Revolution

Neither was there any question that "all men" might somehow be a generic term for human beings that would include women. Politically the Revolution proved to be a step backward for women. It was after the war that states began specifically to prohibit women, even those with property, from voting.[20] That doesn't mean, however, that women did not get involved in the war effort. Within the constraints of society, they contributed what they could to the American cause. They boycotted tea and other British imports, sewed flags, made bandages and clothing, nursed and housed soldiers, and collected money to support the Continental Army. Under the name Daughters of Liberty, women in many towns met

publicly to discuss the events of the day, spinning and weaving to make the colonies less dependent on imported cotton and woolens from England, and drinking herbal tea instead of tea that was taxed by the British. Some women moved beyond such mild patriotic activities to outright political behavior, writing pamphlets urging independence, spying on enemy troops, carrying messages, and even, in isolated instances, fighting on the battlefields.[21]

Men's understanding of women's place in early American politics is nicely put by Thomas Jefferson, writing from Europe to a woman in America in 1788:

> But our good ladies, I trust, have been too wise to wrinkle their foreheads with politics. They are contented to soothe & calm the minds of their husbands returning ruffled from political debate. They have the good sense to value domestic happiness above all others. There is no part of the earth where so much of this is enjoyed as in America.[22]

Women's role with respect to politics is plain: they may be wise and prudent, but their proper sphere is the domestic, not the political, world. They are almost "too good" for politics, representing peace and serenity, moral happiness rather than political dissension, the values of the home over the values of the state. This explanation provides a flattering reason for keeping women in "their place," while allowing men to reign in the world of politics.

Who What How

By the mid-1700s the interests of the British and the colonists were clearly beginning to separate. If the colonists had played by the rules of imperial politics, England would have been content. It would have taxed the colonies to pay its war debts, but it also would have continued to protect them and rule benignly from across the sea.

The colonial leaders, however, changed the rules. Rejecting British authority, they established new rules based on Enlightenment thought. Then they used impassioned rhetoric and inspiring theory to engage the rest of the colonists in their rebellion. Finally, they used revolution to sever their ties with England.

While the Revolution dramatically changed American fortunes, not everyone's life was altered for the good by political independence. Many of those who were not enfranchised before the war—slaves and free blacks, American Indians, and women—remained powerless afterward, and in some cases voting rules became even more restrictive.

> **constitution**   the rules that establish a government
>
> **Articles of Confederation**   the first constitution of the United States (1777) creating an association of states with weak central government

> **confederation**   a government in which independent states unite for common purpose, but retain their own sovereignty

The Articles of Confederation

Political and economic instability under the nation's first constitution

In 1777 the Continental Congress met to try to come up with a framework or constitution for the new government. We use the word *constitution* in this country almost as if it could refer only to one specific document. In truth, a **constitution** is any establishment of rules that "constitutes"—that is, makes up—a government. It may be written, as in our case, or unwritten, as in Great Britain's. One constitution can endure for over two hundred years, as ours has, or it can change quite frequently, as the French constitution has. What's important about a constitution is that it sets up a government, the rules and institutions for running a nation. As we have said before, those rules have direct consequences for how politics works in a given country, who the winners are and who the losers will be.

The **Articles of Confederation**, our first constitution, created the kind of government the founders, fresh from their colonial experience, preferred. The rules set up by the Articles of Confederation show the states' jealousy of their own power. Having just won their independence from one large national power, the last thing they wanted to do was create another. They were also extremely wary of one another, and much of the debate over the Articles of Confederation reflected wide concern that the rules not give any states preferential treatment. (See the Appendix for the text of the Articles of Confederation.)

The Articles established a "firm league of friendship" among the thirteen American states, but they did not empower a central government to act effectively on behalf of those states. The Articles were ultimately replaced because, without a strong central government, they were unable to provide the economic and political stability that the founders wanted. Even so, under this set of rules, some people were better off, and some problems, namely the resolution of boundary disputes and the political organization of new territories, were handled extremely well.

The Provisions of the Articles

The government set up by the Articles was called a **confederation** because it established a system in which each state would retain almost all of its own power to do what it wanted. In other words, in a confederation, each state is sovereign, and the central government has only the job of running the collective business of the states. It has no independent source of power and resources for its operations. Another characteristic of a confederation is that, because it is founded on state sovereignty (authority), it says nothing about individuals. It creates neither rights nor obligations for individual citizens, leaving such matters to be handled by state constitutions.

Under the Articles of Confederation, Congress had many formal powers, including the power to establish and direct the armed forces, to decide matters of war and peace, to coin money, and to enter into treaties. Its powers, however, were quite limited. For example, while Congress controlled the armed forces, it had no power to draft soldiers or to tax citizens to pay for its military needs. Its inability to tax put Congress—and the central government as a whole—at the mercy of the states. The government could ask, but it was up to the states to contribute or not as they chose. Furthermore, Congress lacked the ability to regulate commerce between states, and between states and foreign powers. It could not establish a common and stable monetary system. In essence, the Articles allowed the states to be thirteen independent units, printing their own currencies, setting their own tariffs, and establishing their own laws with regard to financial and political matters. In every critical case—national security, national economic prosperity, and the general welfare—the United States government had to rely on the voluntary goodwill and cooperation of the state governments. That meant that the success of the new nation depended on what went on in state legislatures around the country.

Some Winners, Some Losers

The era of American history following the Revolution was dubbed "this critical period" by John Quincy Adams, nephew of patriot Samuel Adams, son of John Adams, and himself a future president of the country. During this time, while the states were under the weak union of the Articles, the future of the United States was very much up in the air. The lack of an effective central government meant that the country had difficulty conducting business with other countries and enforcing harmonious trade relations and treaties. Domestic politics was equally difficult. Economic conditions following the war were poor. Many people owed money and could not pay their

popular tyranny   the unrestrained power of the people

Shays's Rebellion   a grassroots uprising (1787) by armed Massachusetts farmers protesting foreclosures

Thinking Outside the Box

How would American politics be different today if we had retained the Articles of Confederation instead of adopting the Constitution?

debts. State taxes were high and the economy was depressed, offering farmers few opportunities to sell their produce, for example, and hindering those with commercial interests from conducting business as they had before the war.

The radical poverty of some Americans seemed particularly unjust to those hardest hit, especially in light of the rhetoric of the Revolution about equality for all. Having used "equality" as a rallying cry during the war, the founders were afterward faced with a population that wanted to take equality seriously and eliminate the differences that existed between men.[23]

One of the ways this passion for equality manifested itself was in some of the state legislatures, where laws were passed to ease the burden of debtors and farmers. Often the focus of the laws was property, but rather than preserving property, as Lockean theory said laws should do, these laws frequently were designed to confiscate or redistribute property instead. The have-nots in society, and the people acting on their behalf, were using the law to redress what they saw as injustices in early American life. To relieve postwar suffering, they printed paper money, seized property, and suspended "the ordinary means for the recovery of debts."[24] In other words, in those states, people with debts and mortgages could legally escape or postpone paying the money they owed. With so much economic insecurity, naturally those who owned property would not continue to invest and lend money. The Articles of Confederation, in their effort to preserve power for the states, had provided for no checks or limitations on state legislatures. In fact, such action would have been seen under the Articles as infringing on the sovereignty of the states.

The political elite in the new country started to grumble about *popular tyranny*. In a monarchy, one feared the unrestrained power of the king, but perhaps in a republican government one had to fear the unrestrained power of the

people. The final straw was *Shays's Rebellion*. Massachusetts was a state whose legislature, dominated by wealthy and secure citizens, had not taken measures to aid the debt-ridden population. In an effort to keep their land from foreclosure (seizure by those to whom they owed money), a mob of angry musket-wielding farmers from western Massachusetts, led by a former officer of the Continental Army, Daniel Shays, stormed a federal armory in Springfield that housed 450 tons of military supplies in January 1787. The mob was turned back after a violent clash with state militia, but the attack frightened and embarrassed the leaders of the United States, who feared that the rebellion fore-shadowed the failure of their grand experiment in self-governance. In their minds, it underscored the importance of discovering what James Madison would call "a republican remedy for those diseases most incident to republican government."[25] In other words, the leaders had to find a way to contain and limit the will of the people in a government that was to be based on the will of the people. If the rules of government were not producing the "right" winners and losers, then the rules would have to be changed before the elite lost the power to change them.

Who What How

The fledgling states had an enormous amount at stake as they forged their new government after the Revolution. Perceiving that alarming abuses of power by the British king had come from a strong national government, they were determined to limit the central power of the new nation. The solution was to form a "firm league of friendship" among the several states but to keep the power of any central institutions as weak as possible.

With widespread land ownership possible and with the need for popular support, most farmers and artisans enjoyed the status of citizenship. Given easy access to the state legislatures under the Articles of Confederation, they were able to use the rules of the new political system to take the edge off the economic hardships they were facing.

But the same rules that made it so easy for the new citizens to influence their state governments made it more difficult for the political and economic leaders of the former colonies to protect their own economic security. In their eyes, new rules were needed that would remove government from the rough-and-ready hands of the farmers and protect it from what they saw as unreasonable demands.

> **Constitutional Convention** the assembly of fifty-five delegates in the summer of 1787 to recast the Articles of Confederation; the result was the U.S. Constitution

The Constitutional Convention

Division and compromise over state power and representation

Even before Shays and his men attacked the Springfield armory, delegates from key states had met in Annapolis, Maryland, to discuss the nation's commercial weaknesses. There they adopted a proposal to have each state send delegates to a national convention to be held in Philadelphia in May 1787. The purpose of the meeting would be to make the national government strong enough to handle the demands of united action.

The Philadelphia Convention was authorized to try to fix the Articles of Confederation, but it was clear that many of the fifty-five state delegates who gathered in May were not interested in saving the existing framework at all. Many of the delegates represented the elite of American society, and thus they were among those being most injured under the terms of the Articles. When it became apparent that the **Constitutional Convention** was replacing, not revising, the Articles, some delegates refused to attend, declaring that such a convention was outside the Articles of Confederation and therefore illegal—in fact, it was treason. The convention was in essence overthrowing the government.

"An Assembly of Demigods"

When Thomas Jefferson, unable to attend the convention because he was on a diplomatic mission to Europe, heard about the Philadelphia meeting, he called it "an assembly of demigods."[26] Certainly the delegates were among the most educated, powerful, and wealthy citizens of the new country. Some leading figures were absent. Not only was Jefferson in Paris, but John Adams was also in Europe. Samuel Adams had not been elected but had declared his general disapproval of the "unconstitutional" undertaking, as had Patrick Henry, another hotheaded revolutionary patriot and advocate of states' rights. But there was George Washington, from Virginia, the general who had led American troops to victory in the Revolution. Also from Virginia were George Mason, Edmund Randolph, and James Madison, the sickly and diminutive but brilliant politician who would make a greater imprint on the final Constitution than all the other delegates combined. Other delegates were also impressive:

eighty-one-year-old Benjamin Franklin, as mentally astute as ever, if increasingly feeble in body; Gouverneur Morris from Pennsylvania; and Alexander Hamilton among the New Yorkers.

These delegates represented the very cream of American society. They were well educated in an age when most of the population was not, about 50 percent having gone to schools like Harvard, William and Mary, Columbia (called King's College until 1784), and other institutions that are still at the top of the educational hierarchy. They were also wealthy; they were lawyers, land speculators, merchants, planters, and investors. Even though they were, on the whole, a young group (over half were under forty, and James Madison just thirty-six), they were politically experienced. Many had been active in Revolutionary politics, and they were well read in the political theories of the day, like the ideas of Enlightenment thinker John Locke.

Members of the delegations met through a sweltering Philadelphia summer to reconstruct the foundations of American government. The heat and humidity were heightened because the windows of Convention Hall were kept closed against listening ears and, consequently, the possibility of a cooling breeze. So serious was the convention about secrecy that when a delegate found a copy of one of the major proposals, apparently dropped by another delegate, he turned it over to presiding officer George Washington. Washington took the entire convention to task for its carelessness and threw the document on the table, saying, "Let him who owns it take it." No one dared.[27] We owe most of what we know about the convention today to the notes of James Madison, which he insisted not be published until after the deaths of all the convention delegates.[28]

How Strong a Central Government?

As the delegates had hoped, the debates at the Constitutional Convention produced a very different system of rules than that established by the Articles of Confederation. Many of these rules were compromises to resolve the conflicting interests brought by delegates to the convention.

Imagine that you face the delegates' challenge—to construct a new government from scratch. You can create all the rules, arrange all the institutions, just to your liking. The only hitch is that you have other delegates to work with. Delegate A, for instance, is a merchant with a lot of property; he has big plans for a strong government that can ensure

Founders of a Nation
Delegates to the Constitutional Convention gathered in Philadelphia in 1787 to determine the course of the new nation's government. The fifty-five men represented the colonies' elite, and the Constitution they provided has endured for more than two hundred years.

secure conditions for conducting business and can adequately protect property. Delegate B is a planter. In Delegate B's experience, big governments are dangerous. Big governments are removed from the people, and it is easy for corruption to take root when people can't keep a close eye on what their officials are doing. People like Delegate B think that they do better when power is broken up and localized and there is no strong central government. In fact, Delegate B would prefer a government like that provided by the Articles of Confederation. How do you reconcile these two very different agendas?

The solution adopted under the Articles of Confederation had basically favored Delegate B's position. The new Constitution, given the profiles of the delegates in attendance, was moving strongly in favor of Delegate A's position. Naturally the agreement of all those who followed Delegate B would be important in ratifying, or getting approval for, the final Constitution, so their concerns could not be ignored. The compromise chosen by the founders at the Constitutional Convention was called *federalism*. Unlike a confederation, in which the states retain the ultimate power over the whole, federalism gives the central government its own source of power, in this case the Constitution of the people of the United States. But unlike a unitary system, which we discuss in Chapter 4, federalism also gives independent power to the states.

Compared to how they fared under the Articles of Confederation, the advocates of states' rights were losers under the new Constitution, but they were better off than they might have been. The states could have had *all* their power stripped away. The economic elite, people like Delegate A, were clear winners under the new rules. This proved to be one of the central issues during the ratification debates. Those who sided with the federalism alternative, who mostly resembled Delegate A, came to be known as *Federalists*. The people like Delegate B, who continued to hold onto the strong state–weak central government option, were called *Anti-Federalists*. We will return to them shortly.

Large States, Small States

Once the convention delegates agreed that federalism would provide the framework of the new government, they had to decide how to allot power among the states. Should all states count the same in decision making, or should the larger states have more power than the smaller ones? The rules chosen here could have a crucial impact on the politics of the country. If small states and large states had equal amounts of power in national government, residents of large states such as Virginia, Massachusetts, and New York would effectively have less voice in the government than would residents of small states, like New Jersey and Rhode Island, since they would have proportionately less influence on how their power was wielded. If power were allocated on the basis of size, however, the importance of the small states would be reduced.

Two plans were offered by convention delegates to resolve this issue. The first, the *Virginia Plan*, was created by James Madison and presented at the convention by Edmund Randolph. The Virginia Plan represented the preference of the large, more populous states. This plan proposed that the country would have a strong national government, run by a bicameral (two-house) legislature. One house would be

federalism a political system in which power is divided between the central and regional units

Federalists supporters of the Constitution who favored a strong central government

Anti-Federalists advocates of states' rights who opposed the Constitution

Virginia Plan a proposal at the Constitutional Convention that congressional representation be based on population, thus favoring the large states

New Jersey Plan a proposal at the Constitutional Convention that congressional representation be equal, thus favoring the small states

Great Compromise the constitutional solution to congressional representation: equal votes in the Senate, votes by population in the House

elected directly by the people, one indirectly by a combination of the state legislatures and the popularly elected national house. But the numbers of representatives would be determined by the taxes paid by the residents of the state, which would reflect the free population in the state. In other words, large states would have more representatives in both houses of the legislature, and national law and policy would be weighted heavily in their favor. Just three large states, Virginia, Massachusetts, and Pennsylvania, would be able to form a majority and carry national legislation their way. The Virginia Plan also called for a single executive, to see that the laws were carried out, and a national judiciary, both appointed by the legislature, and it gave the national government power to override state laws.

A different plan, presented by William Paterson of New Jersey, was designed by the smaller states to offer the convention an alternative that would better protect their interests. The **New Jersey Plan** amounted to a reinforcement, not a replacement, of the Articles of Confederation. It provided for a multiperson executive, so that no one person could possess too much power, and for congressional acts to be the "supreme law of the land." Most significantly, however, the Congress was much like the one that had existed under the Articles. In a unicameral (one-house) legislature, each state got only one vote. The delegates would be chosen by state legislatures. The powers of Congress were stronger than under the Articles, but the national government was still dependent on the states for some of its funding. The large states disliked this plan because small states together could block what the larger states wanted, even though the larger states had more people and contributed more revenue.

The prospects for a new government could have foundered on this issue. The stuffy heat of the closed Convention Hall shortened the tempers of the weary delegates, and frustration made compromise difficult. Each side had too much to lose by yielding to the other's plan. The solution finally arrived at was politics at its best. The **Great Compromise** kept much of the framework of the Virginia Plan. It was a strong federal structure headed by a central government with sufficient power to tax its citizens, regulate commerce, conduct foreign affairs, organize the military, and exercise other central powers. It called for a single executive and a national judicial system. The compromise that allowed the smaller states to live with it involved the composition of the legislature. Like the Virginia Plan, it provided for two houses. The House of Representatives would be based on state

population, giving the large states the extra clout they felt they deserved, but in the Senate each state had two votes. This gave the smaller states relatively much more power in the Senate than in the House of Representatives. Members of the House of Representatives would be elected directly by the people, members of the Senate by the state legislatures. Thus the government would be directly binding on the people as well as on the states. A key to the compromise was that most legislation would need the approval of both houses, so that neither large states nor small states could hold the entire government hostage to their wishes. The smaller states were sufficiently happy with this plan that most of them voted to approve, or ratify, the Constitution quickly and easily. See Table 3.1 for a comparison of the Constitution with the Articles of Confederation and the different plans for reform.

North and South

The compromise reconciling the large and small states was not the only one crafted by the delegates. The northern and the southern states, which is to say the non-slave-owning and the slave-owning states, were at odds over how population was to be determined for purposes of representation in the House of Representatives. The southern states wanted to count slaves as part of their populations when determining how many representatives they got, even though they had no intention of letting the slaves vote. Including slaves would give them more representatives and, thus, more power in the House. For exactly that reason, the northern states said that if slaves could not vote, they should not be counted. The compromise, also a triumph of politics if not humanity, is known as the **Three-fifths Compromise**. It was based on a formula developed by the Confederation Congress in 1763 to allocate tax assessments among the states. According to this compromise, for representation purposes, each slave would count as three-fifths of a person, every five slaves counting as three people. Interestingly, the actual language in the Constitution is a good deal cagier than this. It says that representatives and taxes shall be determined according to population, figured "by adding to the whole Number of free Persons, including those bound to Service for a Term of Years, and excluding Indians not taxed, three fifths of *all other persons*."

The issue of slavery was divisive enough for the early Americans that the most politically safe approach was not to mention it explicitly at all and thus to avoid having to

> ***Three-fifths Compromise*** the formula for counting five slaves as three people for purposes of representation that reconciled northern and southern factions at the Constitutional Convention

Table 3.1

Distribution of Powers Under the Articles of Confederation, the New Jersey and Virginia Plans, and the U.S. Constitution

Key questions	Articles of Confederation	New Jersey Plan	Virginia Plan	The Constitution
Who is sovereign?	States	States	People	People
What law is supreme?	State law	State law	National law	National law
What kind of legislature; what is the basis for representation?	Unicameral legislature; equal votes for all states	Unicameral legislature; one vote per state	Bicameral legislature; representation in both houses based on population	Bicameral legislature; equal votes in Senate, representation by population in House
How are laws passed?	Two-thirds vote to pass important measures	Extraordinary majority to pass measures	Majority decision making	Simple majority vote in Congress, presidential veto
What powers are given to Congress?	No congressional power to levy taxes, regulate commerce	Congressional power to regulate commerce and tax	Congressional power to regulate commerce and tax	Congressional power to regulate commerce and tax
What kind of executive is there?	No executive branch; laws executed by congressional committee	Multiple executive	No restriction on strong single executive	Strong executive
What kind of judiciary is there?	No federal court system	No federal court system	National judiciary	Federal court system
How can the document be changed?	All states required to approve amendments	Unanimous approval of amendments by states	Popular ratification	Amendment process less difficult

endorse or condemn it. Implicitly, of course, their silence had the effect of letting slavery continue. Article I, Section 9, of the Constitution, in similarly vague language, allows that "The Migration or Importation of such Persons as any of the States now existing shall think proper to admit, shall not be prohibited by Congress prior to the Year one thousand eight hundred and eight, but a Tax or duty may be imposed on such Importation, not exceeding ten dollars for each Person." Even more damning, Article IV, Section 2, obliquely provides for the return of runaway slaves: "No Person held to Service or Labour in one State under the Laws thereof, escaping into another, shall, in Consequence of any Law or Regulation therein, be discharged from such Service or Labour, but shall be delivered up on Claim of the Party to whom such Service or Labour may be due." The word *slavery* does not appear in the Constitution until it is expressly outlawed in the Thirteenth Amendment, passed in December 1865, over eighty years after the writing of the Constitution.

Not only the political and economic elite but also the everyday citizens who did not attend the Constitutional Convention stood to gain or lose dramatically from the proceedings. At stake that summer were the very rules that would provide the framework for so many political battles in the future.

Who What How

Differences clearly existed among the founding elites. Those representing large states, of course, wanted rules that would give their states more power, based on their larger population, tax base, and size. Representatives of small states, on the other hand, wanted rules that would give the states equal power, so that they would not be squashed by the large states. North and South also differed on the rules. The North wanted representation to be based on the population of free citizens, while the South wanted to include slaves in the population count. The Great Compromise and the Three-fifths Compromise solved both disagreements.

Finally, the people at the convention were divided along another dimension as well. The Federalists sought to create a

The Federalist Papers a series of essays written in support of the Constitution to build support for its ratification

factions groups of citizens united by some common passion or interest and opposed to the rights of other citizens or to the interests of the whole community

ratification the process through which a proposal is formally approved and adopted by vote

strong central government more resistant to the whims of popular opinion. Opposing them, the Anti-Federalists wanted a decentralized government, closer to the control of the people. It was the Federalists who controlled the agenda at the convention and who ultimately determined the structure of the new government.

Ratification
Selling the Constitution to Americans

For the Constitution to become the law of the land, it had to go through the process of **ratification**—being voted on and approved by state conventions in at least nine of the states. As it happens, the Constitution was eventually ratified by all thirteen states, but not until some major political battles had been fought.

Federalists Versus Anti-Federalists

So strongly partisan were the supporters and opponents of the Constitution, that if the battle were taking place today we would probably find them sniping at each other on shows like *Hannity & Colmes* and *Hardball with Chris Matthews*, and Stephen Colbert would be busy mocking both sides. It was a fierce, lively battle that produced, instead of high television ratings, some of the finest writings for and against the American system.

Those in favor of ratification called themselves the Federalists. The Federalists, like Delegate A in our hypothetical constitution-building scenario, were mostly men with a considerable economic stake in the new nation. Having fared poorly under the Articles, they were certain that if America were to grow as an economic and world power, it needed to be the kind of country people with property would want to invest in. Security and order were key values, as was popular control. The Federalists thought people like themselves should be in charge of the government, although some of them did not object to an expanded suffrage if government had enough built-in protections. Mostly, these students of the Enlightenment were convinced that a good government could be designed if the underlying principles of human behavior were known. If people were ambitious and tended toward corruption, then government should make use of those characteristics to produce good outcomes.

The Anti-Federalists, on the other hand, rejected the notion that ambition and corruption were inevitable parts of human nature. If government could be kept small and local,

and popular scrutiny truly vigilant, then Americans could live happy and contented lives without getting involved in the seamier side of politics. If America did not stray from its rural roots and values, it could permanently avoid the creeping corruption that they believed threatened it. The Articles of Confederation were more attractive to the Anti-Federalists than was the Constitution because they did not call for a strong central government that, tucked away from the voters' eyes, could become a hotbed of political intrigue. Instead, the Articles vested power in the state governments, which could be more easily watched and controlled.

Writing under various aliases as well as their own names, the Federalists and Anti-Federalists fired arguments back and forth in pamphlets and newspaper editorials, aimed at persuading undecided Americans to come out for or against the Constitution. The Federalists were far more aggressive and organized in their "media blitz," hitting New York newspapers with a series of eloquent editorials published under the pen name Publius, but really written by Alexander Hamilton, James Madison, and John Jay. These essays were bound and distributed in other states where the ratification struggle was close. Known as *The Federalist Papers*, they are one of the main texts on early American politics today. In response, the Anti-Federalists published essays written under such names as Cato, Brutus, and The Federal Farmer.[29]

The Federalist Papers

There were eighty-five essays written by Publius. These essays are clever, they are well thought out and logical, but they are also tricky and persuasive examples of the hard sell. Two of the most important of the essays, numbers 10 and 51, are reprinted in the Appendix of this book. Their archaic language makes *The Federalist Papers* generally difficult reading for contemporary students. However, the arguments in support of the Constitution are laid out so beautifully that taking the trouble to read them is worthwhile. It would be a good idea to turn to them and read them carefully now.

In *Federalist* No. 10, Madison tried to convince Americans that a large country was no more likely to succumb to the effects of special interests than a small one (preferred by the Anti-Federalists). He explained that the greatest danger to a republic came from **factions**—what we might call interest groups. Factions are groups of people motivated by a common interest, but one different from the interest of the country as a whole. Farmers, for instance, have an interest in keeping food prices high, even though that would make most

Americans worse off. Businesspeople prefer high import duties on foreign goods, even though they make both foreign and domestic goods more expensive for the rest of us. Factions are not a particular problem when they constitute a minority of the population because they are offset by majority rule. They become problematic, however, when they are a majority. Factions usually have economic roots, the most basic being between the haves and have-nots in society. One of the majority factions that worried Madison was the mass of propertyless people whose behavior was so threatening to property holders under the Articles of Confederation.

To control the *causes* of factions would be to infringe on individual liberty. But Madison believed that the *effects* of factions were easily managed in a large republic. First of all, representation would dilute the effects of factions, and it was in this essay that Madison made his famous distinction between "pure democracy" and a "republic." In addition, if the territory were sufficiently large, factions would be neutralized because there would be so many of them that no one would be likely to become a majority. Furthermore, it would be difficult for people who shared common interests to find one another if some lived in South Carolina, for instance, and others lived in New Hampshire. Clearly Madison never anticipated the invention of the fax machine or the Internet. We discuss Madison's argument about factions again in Chapter 13, when we take up the topic of interest groups. In the meantime, however, notice how Madison relied on mechanical elements of politics (size and representation) to remedy a flaw in human nature (the tendency to form divisive factions). This is typical of the Federalists' approach to government, and it reflects the importance of institutions as well as rules in bringing about desired outcomes in politics.

We see the same emphasis on mechanical solutions to political problems in *Federalist No. 51*. Madison argued here that the institutions proposed in the Constitution would lead to neither corruption nor tyranny. The solution was the principles of checks and balances and separation of powers. We discuss these at length in Chapter 4, but it is worth looking at Madison's interesting explanation of why such checks work. Again building his case on a potential defect of human character, he said, "Ambition must be made to counteract ambition."[30] If men tend to be ambitious, give two ambitious men the job of watching over each other, and neither will let the other have an advantage.

The eighty-fourth *Federalist Paper* was written by Hamilton. It doesn't reflect great principles, but it is interesting politically because it failed dismally. The Constitution was ratified in spite of it, not because of it. In this essay, Hamilton argued that a **Bill of Rights**—a listing of the protections against government infringement of individual rights guaranteed to citizens by government itself—was not necessary in a constitution.

The original draft of the Constitution contained no Bill of Rights. Some state constitutions had them, and so the Federalists argued that a federal Bill of Rights would be redundant. Moreover, the limited government set up by the federal Constitution didn't have the power to infringe on individual rights anyway, and many of the rights that would be included in a Bill of Rights were already in the body of the text. To the Anti-Federalists, already afraid of the invasive power of the national government, this omission was more appalling than any other aspect of the Constitution.

Hamilton argued that a Bill of Rights was unnecessary, even dangerous. As it stood, Hamilton said, the national government didn't have the power to interfere with citizens' lives in many ways, and any interference at all would be suspect. But if the Constitution were prefaced with a list of things government could *not* do to individuals, then government would assume it had the power to do anything that wasn't expressly forbidden. Therefore, government, instead of being unlikely to trespass on its citizens' rights, would be more likely to do so with a Bill of Rights than without. This argument was so unpersuasive to Americans at that time that the Federalists were forced to give in to Anti-Federalist pressure during the ratification process. The price of ratification exacted by several states was the Bill of Rights, really a Bill of "Limits" on the federal government, added to the Constitution as the first ten amendments. We look at those limits in detail in Chapter 5, on fundamental American liberties.

The Final Vote

The smaller states, gratified by the compromise that gave them equal representation in the Senate, and believing they would be better off as part of a strong nation, ratified the Constitution quickly. The vote was unanimous in Delaware, New Jersey, and Georgia. In Connecticut (128–40) and Pennsylvania (46–23), the convention votes, though not unanimous, were strongly in favor of the Constitution. This may have helped to tip the balance for Massachusetts, voting much more closely to ratify (187–168). Maryland (63–11)

Figure 3.1

Ratification of the Constitution

State	Date of ratification	Vote in convention	Rank in population
1. Delaware	Dec. 7, 1787	30 to 0	13
2. Pennsylvania	Dec. 12, 1787	46 to 23	3
3. New Jersey	Dec. 18, 1787	38 to 0	9
4. Georgia	Jan. 2, 1788	26 to 0	11
5. Connecticut	Jan. 9, 1788	128 to 40	8
6. Massachusetts (including Maine)	Feb. 7, 1788	187 to 168	2
7. Maryland	Apr. 28, 1788	63 to 11	6
8. South Carolina	May 23, 1788	149 to 73	7
9. New Hampshire	June 21, 1788	57 to 47	10
10. Virginia	June 26, 1788	89 to 79	1
11. New York	July 26, 1788	30 to 27	5
12. North Carolina	Nov. 21, 1789	194 to 77	4
13. Rhode Island	May 29, 1790	34 to 32	12

and South Carolina (149–73) voted in favor of ratification in the spring of 1788, leaving only one more state to supply the requisite nine to make the Constitution law.

The battles in the remaining states were much tighter. When the Virginia convention met in June 1788, the Federalists felt that it could provide the decisive vote and threw much of their effort into securing passage. Madison and his Federalist colleagues debated with such Anti-Federalist advocates as George Mason and Patrick Henry, promising as they had in Massachusetts to support a Bill of Rights. Virginia ratified the Constitution by the narrow margin of 89 to 79, preceded by a few days by New Hampshire, voting 57 to 47. Establishment of the Constitution as the law of the land was ensured with approval of ten states. New York also narrowly passed the Constitution, 30 to 27, but North Carolina defeated it (193–75) and Rhode Island, which had not sent delegates to the Constitutional Convention, refused to call a state convention to put it to the vote. Later both North Carolina and Rhode Island voted to ratify and join the union, in November 1789 and May 1790, respectively.[31] Figure 3.1 summarizes the voting on the Constitution.

Again we can see how important rules are in determining outcomes. The Articles of Confederation had required the approval of all the states. Had the Constitutional Convention chosen a similar rule of unanimity, the Constitution may very well have been defeated. Recognizing that unanimous approval was not probable, however, the Federalists decided to require ratification by only nine of the thirteen, making adoption of the Constitution far more likely.

The fight over ratification of the Constitution not only had the actual form of government at stake but also represented a deep philosophical difference about the nature of human beings and the possibilities of republican government. The Federalists favored the new Constitution. For the Anti-Federalists, the Constitution seemed to present innumerable opportunities for corruption to fester. Knowing they had lost the battle for public opinion and for votes, they made the attachment of a Bill of Rights a condition of their acquiescence.

Who What How

Thinking Outside **the Box**

Would we have more freedoms today, or fewer, without the Bill of Rights?

▶ **Profiles in Citizenship: Newt Gingrich**

"The primary breakthroughs have all been historic. It was the Greeks discovering the concept of self-governance, it was the Romans creating the objective sense of law. . . ."

History is anything but dull when it comes from the mouth of the man who has made so much of it. Newt Gingrich is the architect of the Contract With America, a document that helped propel the Republicans into the majority in Congress in 1994 for the first time in forty years, and made him Speaker of the U.S. House of Representatives from 1995 to 1998. As you will see in Chapter 7, his ideas and the

policies they generated still inform the terms of political debate in this country a decade later.

But sitting at his desk at the American Enterprise Institute, with his distinguished gray head tilted slightly as he listens to a question, his fingertips pressed lightly together as he thinks over the answer, it is hard to forget that long before he revolutionized American politics in the 1990s, Newt Gingrich was a history professor at Western Georgia College. For the last six years he has resumed the work of a scholar in the rarified atmosphere of the American Enterprise Institute, a conservative Washington think tank where, in addition to being a media commentator and adviser to his party, he can play with ideas and talk to other smart people to his heart's content.

Clearly life as an intellectual suits him. Does it mean Gingrich has given up politics for good? Maybe, but maybe not. The media had a field day speculating on the possibility that he'd run for president in 2008, and he is on many pundits' lists as a possible candidate in 2012. It's hard to imagine that all that energy and

creativity and leadership potential aren't going to run for something. His 2010 book, *To Save America: Stopping Obama's Secular-Socialist Machine*, certainly hints at his intention to stay active in public life.

It seems to be part of who he is. When he was as young as ten years old, he was flexing his civic muscles by petitioning the Harrisburg (Pennsylvania) City Council to build a zoo. They didn't, but only, he claims with a smile, because his military family moved away before he could persuade them. Given his extraordinary record of public achievement since, it is a good bet he'd have gotten his zoo if the Gingrich family had stayed put.

But they did not. Throughout his junior high years the Gingriches lived in a number of post–World War II European cities—gracious, civilized cities-turned-battlefields that still bore the scars of combat. There was no pretending that the atrocities of war "couldn't happen there"; they had happened, and it was apparent to Gingrich that they could happen at home, too, if serious steps weren't taken. He says, "Out of all that experience I concluded that citizenship was central

The Citizens and the Founding
New rights bring obligations

As we said at the beginning of this chapter, there are different stories to be told about the American founding. We did not want to fall into the oversimplification trap, portraying the founding as a headlong rush to liberty on the

part of an oppressed people. Politics is always a good deal more complicated than that, and this is a book about politics. We also wanted to avoid telling a story that errs on the other end of onesidedness, depicting the American founding as an elite-driven period of history, in which the political, economic, and religious leaders decided they were better off without English rule, inspired the masses to revolt, and then created a Constitution that established rules that benefited people like themselves. Neither of these stories is entirely untrue, but they obscure two very important points.

to our freedom and our safety, and that having civilian leaders who thought about it every day was central to our survival. I spent the summer of 1958 praying about it, and then in August of 1958 [when he was 15] I decided to do what I've been doing ever since."

What he does—the short answer—is to study history and glean from it insights about human motivation and behavior, and then use those historical insights to make things happen today. He is committed to crafting new ideas out of old lessons, leading his fellow citizens on a mission he believes will restore the country to fundamental principles.

Ask him to explain just why it's important to study history and he pauses so long you wonder if he's forgotten the question or perhaps thinks it's so obvious that he won't deign to give it an answer. But no, he's just assembling his thoughts; you can almost hear the clicks and whirls of the processors. He opens his mouth and gracefully constructed sentences tumble out, fully formed. No umms, no stumbles; just perfect, elegant prose. Here's what he says:

If you've never run out of gas, you may not understand why filling your gas tank matters. And if you've never had your brakes fail, you may not care about having your brakes checked. And if you've never slid on an icy road, you may not understand why learning to drive on ice really matters. For citizens, if you haven't lived in a bombed-out city like Beirut or Baghdad, if you haven't seen a genocidal massacre like Rwanda, if you haven't been in a situation where people were starving to death, like Calcutta, you may not understand why you ought to study history. Because your life is good and it's easy and it's soft.

But for most of the history of the human race, most people, most of the time, have lived as slaves or as subjects to other people. And they lived lives that were short and desperate and where they had very little hope. And the primary breakthroughs have all been historic. It was the Greeks discovering the concept of self-governance, it was the Romans creating the objective sense of law, it was the Jewish tradition of being endowed by God—those came together and fused in Britain with the Magna Carta, and created a sense of rights that we take for granted every day. Because we have several hundred years of history protecting us. And the morning that history disappears, there's no reason to believe we'll be any better than Beirut or Baghdad.

Be responsible, live out your responsibilities as a citizen, dedicate some amount of your time every day or every week to knowing what is going on in the world, be active in campaigns, and if nobody is worthy of your support, run yourself. . . . The whole notion of civil society [is] doing something as a volunteer, doing something, helping your fellow American, being involved with human beings. America only works as an organic society. . . . We're the most stunningly voluntaristic society in the world. And so if voluntarism dries up, in some ways America dries up. ◼

Competing Elites

The first point is that there was not just one "elite" group at work during the founding period. Although political and economic leaders might have acted together over the matter of the break with England (and even then, important elites remained loyal to Britain), once the business of independence was settled, it was clear that competing elite groups existed: leaders of big states and small states, leaders of the northern and southern states, merchant elites and agricultural elites, elites who found their security in a strong national government and those who found it in decentralized power. The power struggle between all those adversaries resulted in the compromises that form the framework of our government today.

The Rise of the "Ordinary" Citizen

The second point is that not all the actors during the founding period were among the top tier of political, economic, and religious leadership. Just because the Revolution and the

the product of a contractual agreement between rulers and ruled that makes obeying the law contingent on having one's rights protected by the state.

These new ideas were not all equally easy to put into practice. The notion of citizenship based on consent was relatively straightforward. In a way, the Declaration of Independence constituted a withdrawal of colonial consent to be ruled by George III, and the ratification of the Constitution was a collective consent to the new government. It was more difficult for Americans to work out how to avoid different levels of citizenship and to confer equal rights on all citizens.

In the European tradition, people born into different orders of society (based largely on their families' ownership of land) had, if not different levels of citizenship, then different social and political status. In America, the abundance of land meant that people who in Europe would have been at the bottom of the social and political order were catapulted into the landowner class and were thus eligible to be citizens in the new republic. Under the Articles of Confederation especially, Americans embraced this new definition of mass citizenship, but their experience during the critical period led the founders to mistrust it profoundly. To some extent, the writing of the Constitution was about reining in the power of the citizens, checking and balancing the power of the people as well as the power of the government.

The final element of the new definition of citizenship was the notion that citizenship conferred equal rights. Here principle clashed with profound prejudice. We saw throughout this chapter that the rights of citizenship were systematically denied to Native Americans, to African Americans, and to women. The ideals of citizenship that were born during the founding are truly innovative and inspiring, but they were unavailable in practice to a major portion of the population for well over a hundred years. While it is conventional today to be appalled at the failure of the founders to practice the principles of equality they preached, and certainly that failure is appalling in light of today's values, we should remember that the whole project of citizenship was new to the founders and that in many ways they were far more democratic than any who had come before them. One of our tasks in this book will be to trace the evolving concept and practice of American citizenship, as the conferral of equal rights so majestically proclaimed in the Declaration slowly becomes reality for all Americans.

government-building that followed it were not the product of ordinary citizens zealous for liberty does not mean that ordinary citizens had nothing to do with it.

Citizenship as we know it today was a fledgling creation at the time of the founding. The British had not been citizens of the English government but subjects of the English Crown. There is a world of difference between a subject and a citizen, as we pointed out in Chapter 1. The subject has a personal tie to the monarch; the citizen has a legal tie to a national territory. The subject has obligations; the citizen has both obligations and rights. One writer identifies three elements of American citizenship that were accepted in principle (though hard to put into practice) after the Revolution: (1) Citizenship should rest on consent, (2) there should not be grades or levels of citizenship, and (3) citizenship should confer equal rights on all citizens.[32] The source for these new ideas about citizenship was Enlightenment thinking. We have seen in the ideas of John Locke the concept of the social contract—that citizenship is

▶ What's at Stake Revisited

Having read the history of Revolutionary America, what would you say is at stake in the modern militia movement? The existence of state militias and similar groups poses a troubling dilemma for the federal government and groups, like the Tea Partiers, whose members are mostly benign, are even trickier for the government to deal with. Bill Clinton, who was president when Timothy McVeigh bombed the federal building in Oklahoma City, warned at the time of the fifteenth anniversary of those attacks that "There can be real consequences when what you say animates people who do things you would never do." There are those out there, like Timothy McVeigh, who "were profoundly alienated, disconnected people who bought into this militant antigovernment line."[33]

The dilemma is that, on the one hand, the purpose of government is to protect our rights, and the Constitution surely guarantees Americans freedom of speech and assembly. On the other hand, government must hold the monopoly on the legitimate use of force in society or it will fall, just as the British government fell to the American colonies. If groups are allowed to amass weapons and forcibly resist or even attack U.S. law enforcers, then they constitute "mini-governments," or competing centers of authority, and life for citizens becomes chaotic and dangerous.

The American system was designed to be relatively responsive to the wishes of the American public. Citizens can get involved, they can vote, run for office, change the laws, and amend the Constitution. By permitting these legitimate ways of affecting American politics, the founders hoped to prevent the rise of groups, like the Hutaree, that would promote and act toward violence. The founders intended to create a society characterized by political stability, not by revolution, which is why Jefferson's Declaration of Independence is so careful to point out that revolutions should occur only when there is no alternative course of action.

Some militia members reject the idea of working through the system; they say, as did Timothy McVeigh, that they consider themselves at war with the federal government. We call disregard for the law at the individual level "crime," at the group level "terrorism" or "insurrection," and at the majority level "revolution." It is the job of any government worth its salt to prevent all three kinds of activities. Thus it is not the existence or the beliefs but the *activities* of the militia groups that government seeks to control.

What's at stake in the challenges to the legitimacy of government are the very issues of government authority and the rights of individual citizens. It is very difficult to draw the line between the protection of individual rights and the exercise of government authority. In a democracy, we want to respect the rights of all citizens, but this respect can be thwarted when a small number of individuals reject the rules of the game agreed on by the vast majority.

To Sum Up

Key terms, chapter summaries, practice quizzes, Internet links, and other study aids are available on the companion web site at http:// republic.cqpress.com.

Define | **Understand** | **Practice** | **Read** | **Click** | **Watch**

Anti-Federalists (p. 82)

Articles of Confederation (p. 79)

Bill of Rights (p. 86)

Common Sense (p. 74)

confederation (p. 79)

constitution (p. 79)

Constitutional Convention (p. 81)

Declaration of Independence (p. 75)

factions (p. 85)

federalism (p. 82)

The Federalist Papers (p. 85)

Federalists (p. 82)

feudalism (p. 71)

French and Indian War (p. 73)

Great Compromise (p. 83)

New Jersey Plan (p. 83)

popular sovereignty (p. 74)

popular tyranny (p. 80)

ratification (p. 85)

Shays's Rebellion (p. 80)

slavery (p. 72)

Three-fifths Compromise (p. 83)

Virginia Plan (p. 82)

Define | **Understand** | **Practice** | **Read** | **Click** | **Watch**

- The politics of the American founding shaped the political compromises embodied in the Constitution. This in turn defined the institutions and many of the rules that do much to determine the winners and losers in political struggles today.

- The battle for America involved a number of different groups, including American Indians, the Spanish, the French, and the British colonists. The English settlers came for many reasons, including religious and economic, but then duplicated many of the politically restrictive practices in the colonies that they had sought to escape in England. These included restrictions on political participation and a narrow definition of citizenship.

- The Revolution was caused by many factors, including British attempts to get the colonies to pay for the costs of the wars fought to protect them.

- The pressures from the Crown for additional taxes coincided with new ideas about the proper role of government among colonial elites. These ideas are embodied in Jefferson's politically masterful writing of the Declaration of Independence.

- The government under the Articles of Confederation granted too much power to the states, which in a number of cases came to serve the interests of farmers and debtors. The Constitutional Convention was called to design a government with stronger centralized powers that would overcome the weaknesses elites perceived in the Articles.

- The new Constitution was derived from a number of key compromises: federalism was set as a principle to allocate power to both the central government and the states; the Great Compromise allocated power in the new national legislature; and the Three-fifths Compromise provided a political solution to the problem of counting slaves in the southern states for purposes of representation in the House of Representatives.

- The politics of ratification of the Constitution provides a lesson in the marriage between practical politics and political principle. *The Federalist Papers* served as political propaganda to convince citizens to favor ratification, and they serve today as a record of the reasoning behind many of the elements of our Constitution.

Define **Understand** **Practice** **Read** **Click** **Watch**

1. **Britain established its dominance over the colonies by**
   a. winning the French and Indian War.
   b. winning the War of the Roses.
   c. winning the Spanish-American War.
   d. legal agreements such as the Mayflower Compact.
   e. constant intimidation of the colonists.

2. **The significance of *Common Sense* was that it**
   a. provided a persuasive argument for taxation without representation.
   b. convinced the founders to eliminate property rights for voting.
   c. articulated the idea that the British monarch was the legitimate ruler of the colonies.
   d. convinced many people that revolution was necessary.
   e. was the first document to argue that slavery had no place in the colonies.

3. **The government created by the Articles of Confederation is described in this chapter as**
   a. the first grant of national power in the United States.
   b. an association of states with a weak central government.
   c. presidential government.
   d. the "great American Parliament."

   e. no more democratic than when the colonies were under British rule.

4. **Which of the following was missing from the original draft of the Constitution?**
   a. A listing of the protections against government infringement of individual rights
   b. National treaty power
   c. A provision for the return of fugitive slaves
   d. Power of the national government to coin money or levy taxes
   e. Presidential veto power

5. **According to this chapter, the politics of the American founding was**
   a. dominated solely by elites.
   b. quite contentious, and the founders were rarely able to compromise.
   c. influenced by both the views of competing elites and a new notion of citizenship.
   d. unique because ordinary citizens played a leading role in creating the Constitution.
   e. surprisingly not contentious, and little disagreement existed over the development of the new government.

Define **Understand** **Practice** **Read** **Click** **Watch**

Bailyn, Bernard. 1967. *The Ideological Origins of the American Revolution*. Cambridge, Mass.: Belknap Press. *An exceptionally detailed account of the pamphlets and other writings that convinced the thirteen colonies to revolt from Mother England.*

Beard, Charles A. 1913. *An Economic Interpretation of the Constitution of the United States*. New York: Free Press. *Beard argues that the framers of the Constitution were really more concerned about protecting their own interests than about guarding the strength of the nation.*

Berkin, Carol. 2005. *Revolutionary Mothers: Women in the Struggle for America's Independence*. New York: Knopf. *A thorough historical account of the many roles women played during the struggle for independence, from boycotting household goods produced by the British and managing farms to fundraising and inciting sentiments through propaganda.*

Ellis, Joseph J. 2002. *Founding Brothers: The Revolutionary Generation*. New York: Vintage. *Ellis takes a close look at six crucial moments in early American history and examines the differences between Republicans and Federalists to reveal just how self-evident those unalienable rights really were at the time the Declaration of Independence was written.*

Loewen, James W. 1995. *Lies My Teacher Told Me: Everything Your American History Textbook Got Wrong*. New York: New Press. *A stimulating book even for those who find history boring; Loewen explains why some of what you read in your high school history class may have been just plain wrong!*

McCullough, David. 2005. *1776*. New York: Simon & Schuster. *The human story of those who marched with General George Washington in the year of the Declaration of Independence.*

Paine, Thomas. 1953. *Common Sense and Other Political Writings*. Indianapolis, Ind.: Bobbs-Merrill. *Paine's writing may have been the most influential document in persuading the colonists to revolt against the English monarchy.*

West, Thomas G. 1997. *Vindicating the Founders: Race, Sex, Class, and Justice in the Origins of America*. Lanham, Md.: Rowman & Littlefield. *A provocative account of the beliefs of our founding fathers that refutes those who argue that our founders were really hypocrites who did not live by the words "all men are created equal."*

Wood, Gordon S. 1998. *The Creation of the American Republic, 1776–1787*. Chapel Hill: University of North Carolina Press. *The most comprehensive and respected source available on political thought during the early development of the United States.*

Define   Understand   Practice   Read   Click   Watch

American Memory *http://memory.loc.gov. The Library of Congress' American Memory collection is a gateway to numerous historical topics—such as African American, American Indian, and women's history; immigration; religion; maps; and more.*

The Federalist Papers Online *www.foundingfathers.info/federalistpapers/. A guide to all of The Federalist Papers, with links to other important constitutional documents.*

National Archives and Records Administration *www.archives.gov. See the original Declaration of Independence, the U.S. Constitution, the Bill of Rights, and countless other historical documents and records on this site.*

National Constitution Center *www.constitutioncenter.org. The web site for this center has educational resources, an interactive Constitution, a constitutional timeline, and other information on the historical context of this founding document.*

Define   Understand   Practice   Read   Click   Watch

1776 *1972. A musical comedy about the signing of the Declaration of Independence.*

Benedict Arnold: A Question of Honor *2003. This film attempts to set the record straight on the most famous traitor in U.S. history. While explaining the reasons and circumstances of the treason, the film also demonstrates Arnold's influence on the creation of the United States.*

The Crossing *2000. This made-for-TV movie chronicles "Washington's desperate and audacious decision in December 1776 to cross the icy Delaware River and attack the fearsome Hessian mercenaries in Trenton." This was a turning point both for America's first president and in the Revolutionary War against the Crown.*

The History Channel Presents the Revolution *2006. This four-disc set comprehensively examines the American Revolution through interviews with historians, letters from the day, and reenactments that illustrate the real people involved, with all their virtues and faults.*

John Adams *2008. This made-for-TV miniseries traces John Adams's life and his crucial role in the establishment of the United States. The seven-part film covers Adams's early start as the lawyer for the British soldiers standing trial for the Boston Massacre, and his rise from the Continental Congresses to the White House.*

Liberty! The American Revolution *1998. The acclaimed PBS documentary covers the political maneuverings of the American War for Independence in six episodes. Dramatic readings of historical letters and documents breathe life into this compelling series.*

The Patriot *2000. Mel Gibson plays a veteran of the French and Indian War who reluctantly joins the fight for independence against the British in the Revolution after one son is killed and another is captured by the enemy.*

Chapter 4

Federalism and the U.S. Constitution

▶ What's at Stake?

When is an illegal drug not an illegal drug? When a doctor prescribes it for you to cure or alleviate an illness, injury, or pain. Simple, right?

Not very, as it turns out.

Everyone knows that smoking marijuana is against the law. Among other things, the United States federal Controlled Substances Act says so. Under that law, passed in 1970, marijuana is a "schedule one drug," equivalent, in legal terms, to heroin and LSD.

But some scientists and doctors, as well as their patients, argue that marijuana is a drug, like morphine or codeine, that is beneficial for people who are sick, even though it can be abused by those who are not.

Joseph Kintzel, a Colorado dad who works as a respiratory therapist, is a case in point. After having several back surgeries for herniated disks, Kintzel was out of work for two years due to the severe pain that he tried to control with morphine, Percocet, and Vicodin.

In 2002, with his doctor's authorization, he began treating the pain with regular use of marijuana. He says that in a few months he was off all the narcotic pain killers and was back at work, where he has taken only one sick day in the past four years.[1]

Kintzel can do that because he lives in Colorado, one of twelve states that have passed medical marijuana laws that in different ways protect from prosecution those patients who have documented need for the drug.

Be Careful Where You Smoke

Laws in fourteen states allow doctors to prescribe marijuana to treat their patients' conditions; however, the federal government considers it to be an illegal substance. The U.S. system distributes power across its levels of government, which can result in such contradictory positions.

clause, the part of Article I, Section 8, of the Constitution that gives Congress the power to regulate commerce among the states. In 2005 the Supreme Court, voting six to three in *Gonzales v. Raich*, a case concerning a California medical marijuana law, backed that view.[2] Occasionally, federal agents raided local distribution centers, seizing and confiscating quantities of the drug.[3]

Defenders of the laws responded that growing, selling, or smoking marijuana for personal medical use within a single state has nothing to do with interstate commerce. Fourteen states passed laws decriminalizing the use of marijuana for medical purposes by prescription, and slowly, federal law swung in their direction. In May 2009 the Supreme Court refused to hear a case challenging the California law, essentially handing a victory to medical marijuana proponents, and in October, the Justice Department, now under the Obama administration, signaled that, as long as use was consistent with state laws, marijuana use by those holding a prescription for it would not be prosecuted.[4]

Why is this issue so controversial that it twice made its way to the highest court in the land? Why did states continue to defy federal law to allow this practice? And why would the national government change its stance on the issue? Just what is at stake in the use of marijuana to treat medical conditions? ■

But while Kintzel's use of marijuana for medical reasons may be legal in Colorado, it is illegal in the United States. That strange combination is possible because of our federal system, which gives some powers to the state, some to the national government, and some to be shared between them. In the case of medical marijuana laws, the federal government under the George W. Bush administration claimed that its law trumped state laws because of the commerce

[R]ules set up the institutions and the procedures that are the heart of the political system, and these institutions and procedures help determine who will be the winners and losers in politics. . . .

Imagine that you are playing Monopoly but you've lost the rule book. You and your friends decide to play anyway and make up the rules as you go along. Even though the game still looks like Monopoly, and you're using the Monopoly board, and the money, and the game pieces, and the little houses and hotels, if you aren't following the official Monopoly rules, you aren't really playing Monopoly.

In the same way, imagine that America becomes afflicted with a sort of collective amnesia so that all the provisions of the Constitution are forgotten. Or perhaps the whole country gets fed up with politics as usual in America and votes to replace our Constitution with, say, the French Constitution. Even if we kept all our old politicians, and the White House and the Capitol, and the streets of Washington, what went on there would no longer be recognizable as American politics. What is distinctive about any political system is not just the people or the buildings, but also the rules and the ideas that lie behind them and give them life and meaning.

Thinking Outside the Box

Are there any advantages to living under Calvinball rules?

In politics, as in games, rules are crucial. The rules set up the institutions and the procedures that are the heart of the political system, and these institutions and procedures help determine who will be the winners and losers in politics, what outcomes will result, and how resources will be distributed. Political rules are themselves the product of a political process, as we saw in Chapter 3. Rules do not drop from the sky, all written and ready to be implemented. Instead they are created by human beings, determined to establish procedures that will help them, and people like them, get what they want from the system. If you change the rules, you change the people who will be advantaged and disadvantaged by those rules.

The founders were not in agreement about the sorts of rules that should be the base of American government. Instead they were feeling their way, weighing historical experience against contemporary reality. They had to craft new rules to achieve their goal of a government whose authority comes from the people but whose power was limited so as to preserve the liberty of those people. The questions that consumed them may surprise us. We know about the debate over how much power should belong to the national government and how much to the states. But discussions ranged far beyond issues of federalism versus states' rights. How should laws be made, and by whom? Should the British parliament be a model for the new legislature, with the "lords" represented in one house and the "common people" in the other? Or should there even be two houses at all? What about the executive? Should it be a king, as in England? Should it be just one person, or should several people serve as executive at the same time? How much power should the executive have, and how should he or they be chosen? And what role would the courts play? How could all these institutions be designed so that no one could become powerful enough to destroy the others? How could the system change with the times and yet still provide for stable governance?

Their answers to those questions are contained in the official rule book for who gets what, and how, in America, which is of course the Constitution. In Chapter 3 we talked about the political forces that produced the Constitution, the preferences of various groups for certain rules, and the compromises these groups evolved to get the document passed. In this chapter we look at the Constitution from the inside. Since rules are so important in producing certain kinds of outcomes in the political system, it is essential that we understand not only what the rules provide for, but also what the choice of those rules means, what other kinds of rules exist that the founders did *not* choose, and what outcomes the founders rejected by not choosing those alternative rules.

Scholars spend whole lifetimes studying the Constitution. We can't achieve their level of detail here, but fortunately we don't need to. To familiarize you with some key issues that all constitution builders have to deal with, in this chapter you will learn about

- *what institutions the founders created to perform the three main tasks of governing: making the laws, executing the laws, and adjudicating the laws*
- *the constitutional relationship among those institutions*
- *how the founders resolved constitutionally the issue of relations between regional units (states, in our case) and national government*
- *the flexibility the founders built into the Constitution to change with the times*

The best way to understand these issues is to look at the founders' concerns, the constitutional provisions they established, the alternatives they might have chosen, and how their choices affect who gets what, and how, in American politics.

The Three Branches of Government
Making, executing, and interpreting the laws

All governments must have the power to do three things: (1) legislate, or make the laws; (2) administer, or execute the laws; and (3) adjudicate, or interpret the laws. The kinds of institutions they create to manage those powers vary widely. Because of our system of separation of powers, which we discuss later in this chapter, separate branches of government handle the legislative, executive, and judicial powers. Article I of the Constitution sets up Congress, our legislature; Article II establishes the presidency, our executive; and Article III outlines the federal court system, our judiciary.

> **legislature**   the body of government that makes laws
>
> **bicameral legislature**   legislature with two chambers

> **republic**   a government in which decisions are made through representatives of the people
>
> **unicameral legislature**   a legislature with one chamber

The Legislative Branch

Legislative power is lawmaking power. Laws can be created by a single ruler or by a political party, they can be divined from natural or religious principles, or they can be made by the citizens who will have to obey the laws or by representatives working on their behalf. Most countries that claim to be democratic choose the last method of lawmaking. The body of government that makes laws is called the **legislature**. Legislatures themselves can be set up in different ways: they can have one or two chambers, or houses; members can be elected, appointed, or hereditary; and if elected, they can be chosen by the people directly or by some other body. A variety of electoral rules can apply. The U.S. Congress is a **bicameral legislature**, meaning there are two chambers, and the legislators are elected directly by the people for terms of two or six years, depending on the house.

The Case for Representation

In *Federalist* No. 10, James Madison argued that American laws should be made by representatives of the people rather than by the people themselves. He rejected what he called "pure democracies," small political systems in which the citizens make and administer their own laws. Instead Madison recommended a **republic**, a system in which a larger number of citizens delegate, or assign, the tasks of governing to a smaller body. A republic claims two advantages: the dangers of factions are reduced, and the people running the government are presumably the best equipped to do so. Representation, said Madison, helps to "refine and enlarge the public views by passing them through the medium of a chosen body of citizens," distinguished by their wisdom, patriotism, and love of justice.[5]

Of course, Americans were already long accustomed to the idea of representation. All the states had legislatures. The Articles of Confederation had provided for representation as well, and even Britain had representation of a sort in Parliament.

What Does the Constitution Say?

Article I sets out the framework of the legislative branch of government. Since the founders expected the legislature to be the most important part of the new government, they spent the most time specifying its composition, the qualifications for membership, its powers, and its limitations.

The best known part of Article I is the famous Section 8, which spells out the specific powers of Congress. This list is followed by the provision that Congress can do anything "necessary and proper" to carry out its duties. The Supreme Court has interpreted this clause so broadly that there are few effective restrictions on what Congress can do.

The House of Representatives, where representation is based on population, was intended to be truly the representative of all the people, the "voice of the common man," as it were. To be elected to the House, a candidate need be only twenty-five years old and a citizen for seven years. Since House terms last two years, members run for reelection often and can be ousted fairly easily, according to public whim. The founders intended this office to be accessible to and easily influenced by citizens and to reflect frequent changes in public opinion.

The Senate is another matter. Candidates have to be at least thirty years old and citizens for nine years—older, wiser, and, the founders hoped, more stable than the representatives in the House. Because senatorial terms last for six years, senators are not so easily swayed by changes in public sentiment. In addition, senators were originally elected not directly by the people, but by members of their state legislatures. Election by state legislators, themselves already a "refinement" of the general public, would ensure that senators were a higher caliber of citizen: more in tune with "the commercial and monied interest," as Massachusetts delegate Elbridge Gerry put it at the Constitutional Convention.[6] The Senate would thus be a more aristocratic body; that is, it would look more like the British House of Lords, where members are admitted on the basis of their birth or achievement, not by election.

Possible Alternatives: A Unicameral Legislature?

The Congress we have is not the only Congress the founders could have given us. Instead of establishing the House of Representatives and the Senate, for instance, they could have established one legislative chamber only, what we call a **unicameral legislature**. Many countries today have unicameral legislatures—Malta, New Zealand, Denmark, Sweden, Spain, Israel, North Korea, Kuwait, Syria, Malawi, and Cameroon, to name a few. And while most of the fifty United States have followed the national example with bicameral state legislatures, Nebraska has chosen a unicameral, nonpartisan legislature.

Proponents of such institutions claim that lawmaking is faster and more efficient when laws are debated and voted on in only one chamber. They say such laws are also more

An Enduring Institution
Then–House Speaker Nancy Pelosi receives the gavel from House Minority Leader John Boehner only to reverse the exchange in 2011, when Boehner became Speaker, and Pelosi was once again the minority leader. The U.S. Congress is the oldest democratic legislative body in the world, still fulfilling the functions originally detailed in the Constitution.

responsive to changes in public opinion, which at least theoretically is a good thing in a democracy.

On the national level, a unicameral system can help encourage citizens to feel a sense of identity with their government, since it implies that the whole country shares the same fundamental interests and can thus be represented by a single body. Originally in Europe, governments had different legislative chambers to represent different social classes or estates in society. We can see the remnants of this system in the British parliament, whose upper chamber is called the House of Lords, and lower, the House of Commons, or the common people. The French once had five houses in their legislature, and the Swedish four. As countries become more democratic—that is, as their governments become more representative of the people as a whole and not of social classes—the legislatures become more streamlined. Sweden eventually moved to two legislative houses, and in 1971 it adopted a unicameral legislature. France now has two. Britain still has the Lords and the Commons, but increasing democratization has meant less legislative power for the House of Lords, which now can only delay, not block, laws made by the House of Commons.[7] In that sense, the fewer chambers a legislature has, the more representative it is of the people as a whole.

A unicameral system has several clear disadvantages, however. For one thing, such a system makes it difficult for the legislature to represent more than one set of interests. Although the United States did not have the feudal history of Europe, with its remnants of nobility and commons, it was still a country with frequently conflicting economic interests, as politics under the Articles of Confederation had made

painfully evident. Our founders preferred bicameralism in part because the two houses could represent different interests in society—the people's interests in the House and the more elite interests in the Senate.

In addition to providing for representation of different interests, another advantage of a bicameral legislature was its ability to represent the different levels of the federal government in the legislative process. Typically, federal governments that preserve a bicameral structure do so with the intention of having the "people" represented in one house and the individual regions, in our case the states, in another. In the United States, representation in the House is based on the state's population, and representation in the Senate is based simply on statehood, with each state getting two votes. The fact that the senators used to be elected by the state legislatures reinforces the *federal* aspect of this arrangement. In the German *Bundesrat*, the members are chosen by the governments of each state.

A final reason the founders were convinced that bicameralism was better for the young republic than unicameralism is that they believed the more they divided the power of government into smaller units, the safer the government would be from those who would abuse its power. Two legislative chambers would keep a watch over each other and check their tendencies to get out of hand. The quick legislative responsiveness of a unicameral legislature can have some drawbacks. Changes in public opinion are often only temporary, and perhaps a society in a calmer moment would not want the laws to be changed so hastily. Rapid-response lawmaking can also result in excessive amounts of legislation, creating a legal system that confuses and baffles the citizenry.

executive the branch of government responsible for putting laws into effect

Electoral College an intermediary body that elects the president

When asked by Thomas Jefferson, who had been in France during the Constitutional Convention, why the delegates had adopted a bicameral legislature, George Washington explained that just as one would pour one's coffee into the saucer to cool it off (a common practice of the day), "we pour legislation into the senatorial saucer to cool it." As Professor Richard Fenno points out, legislation has as often been cooled by pouring it into the House of Representatives. Each chamber has served to cool the passions of the other; this requirement that laws be passed twice has helped keep the American legislature in check.[8]

The Executive Branch

The **executive** is the part of government that "executes" the laws, or sees they are carried out. Although technically executives serve in an administrative role, many end up with some decision-making or legislative power as well. National executives are the leaders of their countries, and they participate, with varying amounts of power, in making laws and policies. That role can range from the U.S. president, who, while not a part of the legislature itself, can propose, encourage, and veto legislation, to European prime ministers, who are part of the legislature and may have, as in the British case, the power to dissolve the entire legislature and call a new election.

Fears of the Founders

That the Articles of Confederation provided for no executive power at all was a testimony to the founders' conviction that such a power threatened their liberty. The chaos that resulted under the Articles, however, made it clear that a stronger government was called for—not only a stronger legislature but a stronger executive as well. The constitutional debates reveal that many of the founders were haunted by the idea that they might inadvertently reestablish that same tyrannical power over themselves that they had escaped only recently with the Revolution. The central controversies focused on whether the executive should be more than one person, whether he should be able to seek reelection as many times as he wanted, and whether he should be elected directly by the people or indirectly by the legislature.

The founders were divided. On one side were those like Alexander Hamilton, who insisted that only a vigorous executive could provide the stability necessary to preserve liberty. Hamilton recommended an executive appointed for life so that he would be independent of the political process.

Others, like Edmund Randolph of Virginia, were unwilling to entertain the notion of a single executive, let alone one chosen for life. Randolph proposed instead three executives, representing various regions of the country, as a safer repository of power.[9]

Those fearing a strong executive believed its power could be limited by dividing it among several officeholders, but they eventually lost to those who believed there should be a single president. The issue of whether the executive should be allowed to run for reelection for an unlimited number of terms got tangled up with the question of just how the president was to be elected. If, as some founders argued, he were chosen by Congress rather than by the people, then he should be limited to one term. Since he would be dependent on Congress for his power, he might fail to provide an adequate check on that body, perhaps currying favor with Congress in order to be chosen for additional terms.

On the other hand, the founders had no great trust in "the people," as we have seen, so popular election of the president was considered highly suspect, even though it would free the executive from dependence on Congress and allow him to be elected for multiple terms. Alexander Hamilton wanted to go so far as to have the president serve for life, thereby eliminating the problem of being dependent on Congress *or* on the popular will.

That these diverse ideas were resolved and consensus was achieved is one of the marvels of the American founding. The final provision of presidential authority was neither as powerful as Hamilton's kinglike lifetime executive nor as constrained as Randolph's multiple executive. Still, it was a much stronger office than many of the founders, particularly the Anti-Federalists, wanted.

What Does the Constitution Say?

The solution chosen by the founders was a complicated one, but it satisfied all the concerns raised at the convention. The president, a single executive, would serve an unlimited number of four-year terms. (A constitutional amendment in 1951 limited the president to two elected terms.) But in addition, the president would be chosen neither by Congress nor directly by the people. Instead the Constitution provides for his selection by an intermediary body called the **Electoral College**. Citizens vote not for the presidential candidates, but for a slate of electors, who cast their votes for the candidates about six weeks after the general election. The founders believed that this procedure would ensure a president elected

> **presidential system**   government in which the executive is chosen independently of the legislature and the two branches are separate

> **parliamentary system**   government in which the executive is chosen by the legislature from among its members and the two branches are merged

by well-informed delegates who, having no other lawmaking power, could not be bribed or otherwise influenced by candidates. We will say more about how this process works in Chapter 14, on elections.

Article II of the Constitution establishes the executive. The four sections of that article make the following provisions:

- Section 1 sets out the four-year term and the manner of election (that is, the details of the Electoral College). It also provides for the qualifications for office: that the president must be a natural-born citizen of the United States, at least thirty-five years old, and a resident of the United States for at least fourteen years. The vice president serves if the president cannot, and Congress can make laws about the succession if the vice president is incapacitated.

- Section 2 establishes the powers of the chief executive. He is commander-in-chief of the armed forces and of the state militias when they are serving the nation, and he has the power to grant pardons for offenses against the United States. With the advice and consent of two-thirds of the Senate, the president can make treaties, and with a simple majority vote of the Senate the president can appoint ambassadors, ministers, consuls, Supreme Court justices, and other U.S. officials whose appointments are not otherwise provided for.

- Section 3 says that the president will periodically tell Congress how the country is doing (the State of the Union address given every January) and will propose to the members those measures he thinks appropriate and necessary. Under extraordinary circumstances the president calls Congress into session or, if the two houses of Congress cannot agree on when to end their sessions, may adjourn them. The president also receives ambassadors and public officials, executes the laws, and commissions all officers of the United States.

- Section 4 specifies that the president, vice president, and other civil officers of the United States (such as Supreme Court justices) can be impeached, tried, and convicted for "treason, bribery, or other high crimes and misdemeanors."

Possible Alternatives: A Parliamentary System?

As the debates over the American executive clearly show, many options were open to the founders as they designed the executive office. They chose what is referred to today as a **presidential system**, in which a leader is chosen independently of the legislature to serve a fixed term of office that is unaffected by the success or failure of the legislature. The principal alternative to a presidential system among contemporary democracies is called a **parliamentary system**, in which the executive is a member of the legislature, chosen by the legislators themselves, not by a separate national election. When the founders briefly considered the consequences of having a president chosen by Congress, they were discussing something like a parliamentary system. The fundamental difference between a parliamentary system and a presidential system is that in the former the legislature and the executive are merged, but in the latter they are separate. In parliamentary systems the executive is accountable to the legislature, but in a presidential system he or she is independent.

Generally speaking, the executive or prime minister in a parliamentary system is the chosen leader of the majority party in the legislature. This would be roughly equivalent to allowing the majority party in the House of Representatives to install its leader, the Speaker of the House, as the national executive. What is striking about the parliamentary system is that most of the citizens of the country never vote for the national leader. Only members of the prime minister's legislative district actually cast a vote for him or her. If the parliament does not think the prime minister is doing a good job, it can replace him or her without consulting the voters of the country.

This process is very different from the American provision for impeachment of the president for criminal activity. Parliaments can remove executives for reasons of political or ideological disagreement. Although there may be political disagreement over the grounds for impeachment in the American case, as there was in the impeachment of President Bill Clinton, there must be at least an allegation of criminal activity, which need not exist for removal in a parliamentary system. (If the United States had a parliamentary system, then a legislative vote of "no confidence" could have ousted the president at the beginning of the process.) Consequently the executive in a parliamentary system is dependent on the legislature and cannot provide any effective check if the legislature abuses its power. In Germany's parliamentary government, an independent court can restrain the legislature and keep it within the bounds of the constitution, but the British system has no check at all. The upper house of Parliament, the House of Lords, is the highest court and even

Parliamentary Practice
Britain's prime minister is also the head of the majority party, and if party members in Parliament become unhappy with his performance, they can force the prime minister to step down. While parliamentary systems may be more efficient than ours in some respects, they lack the separation of powers and checks and balances that are hallmarks of the American system.

it cannot declare an act of the House of Commons unconstitutional. The French system is a curious hybrid. It is parliamentary since the prime minister is chosen from the majority party in the legislature, but there is *also* a strong president who is independent of the legislature. Because the French split the executive functions, there is an executive check on the legislature, even though it is a parliamentary system.

Politics is very different in a parliamentary system than it is in a presidential system. Leadership is clearly more concentrated in the former case. Because the prime minister usually chooses his or her cabinet from the legislature, the executive and legislative truly overlap. It is much easier for a prime minister to get his or her programs and laws passed by the legislature because, under normal circumstances, he or she already has the party votes to pass them. If the party has a serious loss of faith or "confidence" in the prime minister, it can force the prime minister out of office. Thus the prime minister has a strong incentive to cooperate with the legislature. In some cases, like the British, the prime minister has some countervailing clout of his or her own. The British prime minister has the power to call parliamentary elections

at will within a five-year period and consequently can jeopardize the jobs of members of parliament, or at least threaten to do so. This does not necessarily result in more frequent elections in Britain than in the United States with its fixed elections (from 1900 to 2004 Britain held twenty-seven general elections to the United States' twenty-four), but it does mean the prime minister can time the elections to take place when the party's fortunes are high. One result of this close relationship between executive and legislative is that the ties of political party membership seem to be stronger in a parliamentary system, in which a party's domination of national politics depends on block voting along party lines. As we will see in Chapter 12, party discipline, as this is called, is much reduced in the U.S. system.

The Judicial Branch

Judicial power is the power to interpret the laws and to judge whether the laws have been broken. Naturally, by establishing how a given law is to be understood, the courts (the agents of judicial power) end up making law as well. Our constitutional

judicial power   the power to interpret laws and judge whether a law has been broken

judicial review   the power of the Supreme Court to rule on the constitutionality of laws

provisions for the establishment of the judiciary are brief and vague; much of the American federal judiciary under the Supreme Court is left to Congress to arrange. But the founders left plenty of clues as to how they felt about judicial power in their debates and their writings, particularly in *The Federalist Papers*.

The "Least Dangerous" Branch

In *Federalist No. 78*, Hamilton made clear his view that the judiciary was the least threatening branch of power. The executive and the legislature might endanger liberty, but not so the judiciary. Hamilton said that as long as government functions are separate from one another (that is, as long as the judiciary is not part of the executive or the legislature) then the judiciary "will always be the least dangerous to the political rights of the Constitution; because it has the least capacity to annoy or injure them." The executive "holds the sword," and the legislature "commands the purse." The judiciary, controlling neither sword nor purse, neither "strength nor wealth of the society," has neither "FORCE nor WILL but merely judgment."[10]

Although the founders were not particularly worried, then, that the judiciary would be too powerful, they did want to be sure it would not be too political—that is, caught up in the fray of competing interests and influence. The only federal court they discussed in much detail was the Supreme Court, but the justices of that Court were to be appointed for life, provided they maintain "good behavior," in part to preserve them from politics. Once appointed they need not be concerned with seeking the favor of the legislature, the executive, or the people. Instead of trying to do what is popular, they can concentrate on doing what is just, or constitutional.

Even though the founders wanted to keep the Court out of politics, they did make it possible for the justices to get involved when they considered it necessary. The practice of judicial review is introduced through the back door, first mentioned by Hamilton in *Federalist No. 78* and then institutionalized by the Supreme Court itself, with Chief Justice John Marshall's 1803 ruling in *Marbury v. Madison*, a dispute over presidential appointments. **Judicial review** allows the Supreme Court to rule that an act of Congress or the executive branch (or of a state or local government) is unconstitutional, that it runs afoul of constitutional principles. This review process is not an automatic part of lawmaking; the Court does not examine every law that Congress passes or every executive order to be sure that it does not violate the Constitution. Rather, if a law is challenged as unconstitutional by an individual or a group, and

Define Danger
Although the judiciary was touted by Hamilton as the least dangerous branch, its decisions can have huge political impact. The Supreme Court ruled in *Citizens United v. Federal Election Commission* (2010) that corporate funding of political advertisements cannot be limited under the First Amendment's protection of free speech. The decision overrode legislation limiting contributions and has led to concerns about the likelihood of increasing corporate and special interest spending on political advertisements.

if it is appealed all the way to the Supreme Court, then the justices may decide to rule on it.

This remarkable grant of power to the "least dangerous" branch to nullify legislation is *not* itself in the Constitution. In *Federalist No. 78*, Hamilton argued that it was consistent with the Constitution, however. In response to critics who objected that such a practice would place the unelected Court in a position superior to that of the elected representatives of the people, Hamilton wrote that, on the contrary, it raised the people, as authors of the Constitution, over the government as a whole. Thus judicial review enhanced democracy rather than diminished it.

In 1803 Marshall agreed. As the nation's highest law, the Constitution sets the limits on what is acceptable legislation. As the interpreter of the Constitution, the Supreme Court has a duty to determine when laws fall outside those limits. Interestingly, this gigantic grant of power to the Court was made by the Court itself and remains unchallenged by the other branches. The irony is that the sort of empire-building the founders hoped to avoid appears in the branch they took the least care to safeguard. We return to *Marbury v. Madison* and judicial review in Chapter 10, on the court system.

What Does the Constitution Say?

Article III of the Constitution is very short. It says that the judicial power of the United States is to be "vested in one Supreme Court, and in such inferior courts as the Congress may from time to time ordain and establish," and that judges serve as long as they demonstrate "good behavior." It also explains that the Supreme Court has original jurisdiction in some types of cases and appellate jurisdiction in others. That is, in some cases the Supreme Court is the only court that can rule; much more often, inferior courts try cases, but their rulings can be appealed to the Supreme Court. Article III provides for jury trials in all criminal cases except impeachment, and it defines the practice of and punishment for acts of treason. Because the Constitution is so silent on the role of the courts in America, that role has been left to be defined by Congress and, in some cases, by the courts themselves.

Possible Alternatives: Legislative Supremacy?

Clearly one alternative to judicial review is to allow the legislature's laws to stand unchallenged. This system of

legislative supremacy underlies British politics. The British have no written constitution. Acts of Parliament are the final law of the land and cannot be reviewed or struck down by the courts. They become part of the general collection of acts, laws, traditions, and court cases that make up the British "unwritten constitution." Our Court is thus more powerful, and our legislature correspondingly less powerful, than the same institutions in the British system. We are accustomed to believing that judicial review is an important limitation on Congress and a protection of individual liberty. Britain is not remarkably behind the United States, however, in terms of either legislative tyranny or human rights. Think about how much difference judicial review really makes, especially if you consider the experience of a country like Japan, where judicial review usually results in upholding government behavior over individual rights and liberties.[11]

Yet another alternative to our system would be to give judicial review *more* teeth. The German Constitutional Court also reviews legislation to determine if it fits with the German Basic Law, but it does not need to wait for cases to come to it on appeal. National and state executives, the lower house of the legislature (the *Bundestag*), or even citizens can ask the German high court to determine whether a law is constitutional. Like the U.S. Supreme Court, the Constitutional Court is flooded with far more cases than it can accept and must pick and choose the issues on which it will rule.

The founders' goal was to devise a legislature, an executive, and a judiciary that would correct the flaws of the Articles of Confederation while balancing the rights and powers of citizens against the need for the government to be secure from abuse and corruption. The means they employed were unusual—they had the unique opportunity to write the rule book, the Constitution, from scratch, constrained only by the necessity of gaining the approval of sufficient states to allow the Constitution to be ratified and thus seen as legitimate.

Who What How

Which really is the least dangerous branch of the federal government?

Thinking Outside **the Box**

> **separation of powers** the institutional arrangement that assigns judicial, executive, and legislative powers to different persons or groups, thereby limiting the powers of each

> **checks and balances** the principle that allows each branch of government to exercise some form of control over the others

Separation of Powers and Checks and Balances

Mechanical arrangements to limit abuses of power

Separation of powers means that the legislature, the executive, and the judicial powers are not exercised by the same person or group of people, lest they abuse the considerable amount of power they hold. We are indebted to the French Enlightenment philosopher the Baron de Montesquieu for explaining this notion. In his massive book *The Spirit of the Laws,* Montesquieu wrote that liberty could be threatened only if the same group that enacted tyrannical laws also executed them. He said, "There would be an end of everything, were the same man or the same body, whether of nobles or of the people, to exercise those three powers, that of enacting laws, that of executing the public resolutions, and of trying the causes of individuals."[12] Putting all political power into one set of hands is like putting all our eggs in one basket. If the person or body of people entrusted with all the power becomes corrupt or dictatorial, the whole system will go bad. If, on the other hand, power is divided so that each branch is in separate hands, one may go bad while leaving the other two intact. The principle of separation of powers gives each of the branches authority over its own domain.

A complementary principle, **checks and balances**, allows each of the branches to police the others, checking any abuses and balancing the powers of government. The purpose of this additional authority is to ensure that no branch can exercise power tyrannically. In our case, the president can veto an act of Congress, Congress can override a veto, the Supreme Court can declare a law of Congress unconstitutional, Congress can—with the help of the states—amend the Constitution itself, and so on. Figure 4.1 illustrates these relationships.

Republican Remedies

In *Federalist* No. 51, James Madison wrote, "If men were angels, no government would be necessary. If angels were to govern men, neither external nor internal controls on government would be necessary."[13] Alas, we are not angels, nor are we governed by angels. Since human nature is flawed and humans are sometimes ambitious, greedy, and corruptible, precautions must be taken to create a government that will make use of

human nature, not be destroyed by it. A republic, which offers so many opportunities to so many people to take advantage of political power, requires special controls. The job, according to Madison, was to find a "republican remedy for those diseases most incident to republican government."[14] He said, "In framing a government which is to be administered by men over men, the great difficulty is this: you must first enable the government to control the governed; and in the next place oblige it to control itself."[15] The founders used separation of powers and checks and balances to oblige government to control itself, to impose internal limitations on government power in order to safeguard the liberty of the people.

The founders were generally supportive of separation of powers, some form of which appeared in all the state governments. Not so readily accepted was the notion of checks and balances, that once power was separated, it should be somehow shared. Having carefully kept the executive from taking on a legislative role, the founders were reluctant, for example, to give the president veto power.

In *Federalist* No. 47, Madison explained the relationship of separation of powers to checks and balances. Rather than damaging the protection offered by separation of powers, sharing some control over each branch reinforced security because no branch could wield its power without some check. The trick was to give people in each branch an interest in controlling the behavior of the others. This is how human nature, flawed though it might be, could be used to limit the abuses of power. As Madison put it, in *Federalist* No. 51: "Ambition must be made to counteract ambition."[16] Thus there was no danger in sharing some control over the branches because jealous humans would always be looking over their shoulders for potential abuses.

What Does the Constitution Say?

The Constitution establishes separation of powers with articles setting up a different institution for each branch of government. We have already examined Article I, establishing Congress as the legislature; Article II, establishing the president as the executive; and Article III, outlining the court system. Checks and balances are provided by clauses within each of those articles.

- Article I sets up a bicameral legislature. Because both houses must agree on all legislation, each can check the other. Article I also describes the presidential veto, with which the president can check Congress, and the override provision, by which two-thirds of

Figure 4.1

Separation of Powers and Checks and Balances

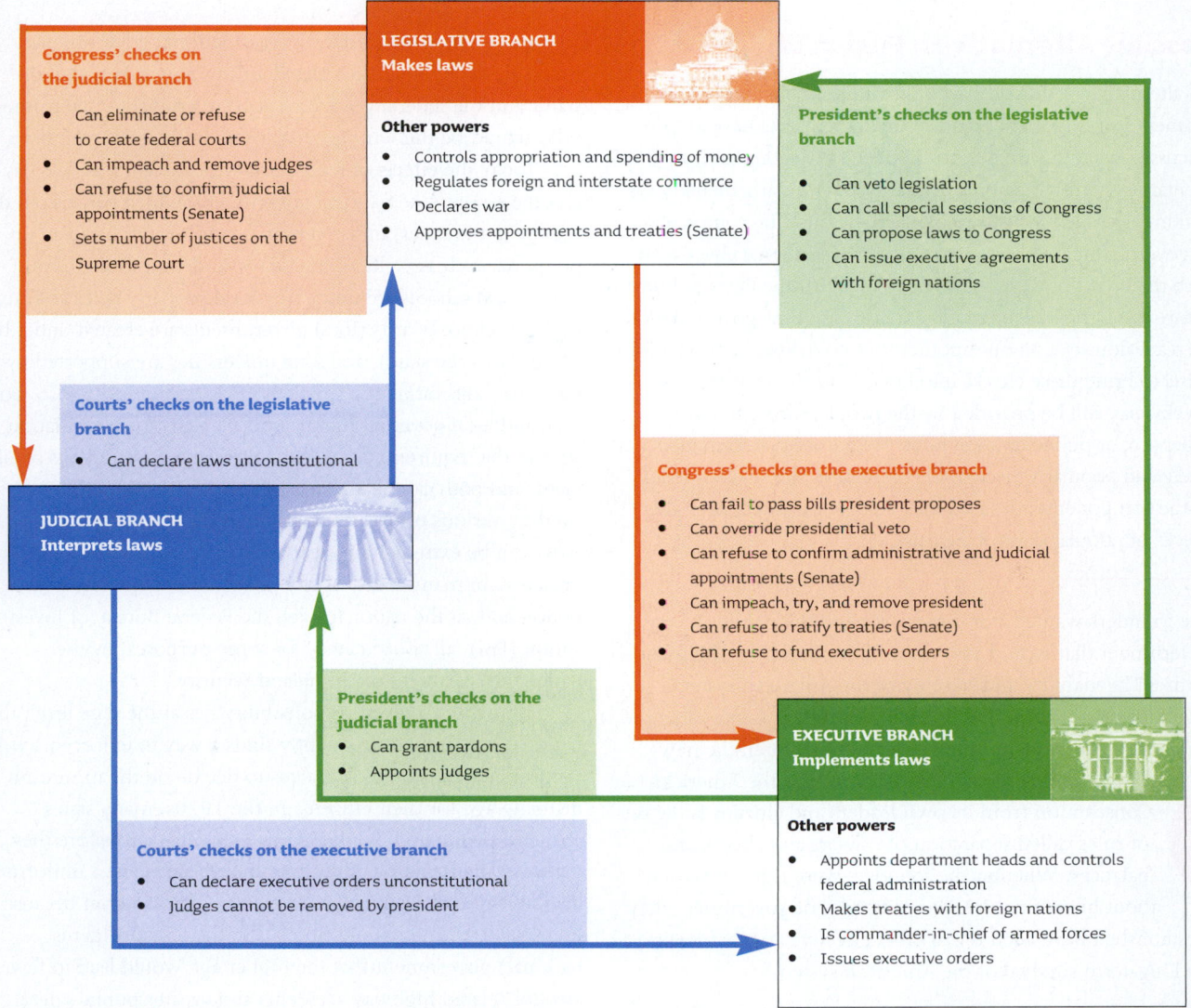

LEGISLATIVE BRANCH
Makes laws

Other powers
- Controls appropriation and spending of money
- Regulates foreign and interstate commerce
- Declares war
- Approves appointments and treaties (Senate)

Congress' checks on the judicial branch
- Can eliminate or refuse to create federal courts
- Can impeach and remove judges
- Can refuse to confirm judicial appointments (Senate)
- Sets number of justices on the Supreme Court

President's checks on the legislative branch
- Can veto legislation
- Can call special sessions of Congress
- Can propose laws to Congress
- Can issue executive agreements with foreign nations

Courts' checks on the legislative branch
- Can declare laws unconstitutional

Congress' checks on the executive branch
- Can fail to pass bills president proposes
- Can override presidential veto
- Can refuse to confirm administrative and judicial appointments (Senate)
- Can impeach, try, and remove president
- Can refuse to ratify treaties (Senate)
- Can refuse to fund executive orders

JUDICIAL BRANCH
Interprets laws

President's checks on the judicial branch
- Can grant pardons
- Appoints judges

EXECUTIVE BRANCH
Implements laws

Courts' checks on the executive branch
- Can declare executive orders unconstitutional
- Judges cannot be removed by president

Other powers
- Appoints department heads and controls federal administration
- Makes treaties with foreign nations
- Is commander-in-chief of armed forces
- Issues executive orders

Congress can check the president. Congress can also use impeachment to check abuses of the executive or judicial branch.

- Article II empowers the president to execute the laws and to share some legislative function by "recommending laws." He has some checks on the judiciary through his power to appoint judges, but his appointment power is checked by the requirement that a majority of the Senate must confirm his choices. The president can also check the judiciary by granting pardons. The president is commander-in-chief of the armed forces, but his ability to exercise his authority is checked by the Article I provision that only Congress can declare war.

- Article III creates the Supreme Court. The Court's ruling in the case of *Marbury v. Madison* fills in some of the gaps in this vague article by establishing judicial review, a true check on the legislative and executive branches. Congress can countercheck judicial review by amending the Constitution (with the help of the states).

The Constitution wisely ensures that no branch of the government can act independently of the others, yet none is wholly dependent on the others, either. This approach results in a structure of separation of powers and checks and balances that is distinctly American.

> **fusion of powers** an alternative to separation of powers, combining or blending branches of government

Possible Alternatives: Fusion of Powers?

An alternative way to deal with the different branches of government is to fuse rather than separate them. We have already discussed what this might look like when we compared a parliamentary system with a presidential system. A parliamentary system involves a clear *fusion of powers*. Because the components of government are not separate, no formal internal checks can curb the use of power. That is not to say that the flaws in human nature might not still encourage members of the government to keep a jealous eye on one another, but no deliberate mechanism exists to bring these checks into being. In a democracy, external checks may still be provided by the people, through either the ballet box or public opinion polls. Where the government is not freely and popularly elected, or, more rarely these days, when all the components are fused into a single monarch, even the checks of popular control are missing.

Who What How

The founders wanted, for themselves and the public, a government that would not succumb to the worst of human nature. The viability and stability of the American system would be jeopardized if they could not find a way to tame the jealousy, greed, and ambition that might threaten the new republic. The remedy they chose to save the American Constitution from its own leaders and citizens is the set of rules called separation of powers and checks and balances. Whether the founders were right or wrong about human nature, the principles of government they established have been remarkably effective at guaranteeing the long-term survival of the American system.

Federalism

Balancing power between national and state governments

Federalism, as we said in Chapter 3, is a political system in which authority is divided between different levels of government. In the United States, federalism refers to the relationship between the national government (also frequently, but confusingly, called the *federal* government) and the states. Each level has some power independent of the other levels so that no level is entirely dependent on another for its existence. For the founders, federalism was a compromise in the bitter dispute between those who wanted stronger state governments

and those who preferred a stronger national government. Both sides knew that the rules dividing power between the states and the federal government were crucial to determining who would be the winners and losers in the new country.

Today the effects of federalism are all around us. We pay income taxes to the national government, which parcels out the money to the states, under certain conditions, to be spent on programs such as welfare, highways, and education. In most states, local schools are funded by local property taxes and run by local school boards (local governments are created under the authority of the state), and state universities are supported by state taxes and influenced by the state legislatures. Even so, both state and local governments are subject to national legislation, such as the requirement that schools be open to students of all races, and both can be affected by national decisions about funding various programs. Sometimes the lines of responsibility can be extremely unclear. Witness the simultaneous presence, in many areas, of city police, county police, state police, and, at the national level, the Federal Bureau of Investigation (FBI), all coordinated, for some purposes, by the national Department of Homeland Security.

Even when a given responsibility lies at the state level, the national government frequently finds a way to enforce its will. For instance, it is up to the states to decide on the minimum drinking age for their citizens. In the 1970s, many states required people to be only eighteen or nineteen before they could legally buy alcohol; today all the states have a uniform drinking age of twenty-one. The change came about because interest groups persuaded officials in the federal (that is, national) government that the higher age would lead to fewer alcohol-related highway accidents and greater public safety. The federal government couldn't pass a law setting a nationwide drinking age of twenty-one, but it could control the flow of highway money to the states. By withholding 5 percent of federal highway funds, which every state wants and needs, until a state raised the drinking age to twenty-one, Congress prevailed. Similar congressional pressure led states to lower the legal standard for drunk driving to a 0.08 percent blood alcohol level by the fall of 2003.[17] These examples show how the relations between levels of government work when neither level can directly force the other to do what it wants.

What Does the Constitution Say?

No single section of the Constitution deals with federalism. Instead the provisions dividing up power between the states

enumerated powers of Congress congressional powers specifically named in the Constitution (Article I, Section 8)

necessary and proper clause constitutional authorization for Congress to make any law required to carry out its powers

supremacy clause constitutional declaration (Article VI) that the Constitution and laws made under its provisions are the supreme law of the land

concurrent powers powers that are shared by both the federal and state governments

and the national government appear throughout the Constitution. Local government is not mentioned in the Constitution at all, because it is completely under the jurisdiction of the states. Most of the Constitution is concerned with establishing the powers of the national government. Since Congress is the main lawmaking arm of the national government, many of the powers of the national government are the powers of Congress. The strongest statement of national power is a list of the **enumerated powers of Congress** (Article I, Section 8). This list is followed by a clause that gives Congress the power to make all laws that are "necessary and proper" to carry out its powers. The **necessary and proper clause** (also called the "elastic clause" because the Supreme Court has interpreted it broadly) has been used to justify giving Congress many powers never mentioned in the Constitution. National power is also based on the **supremacy clause** of Article VI, which says that the Constitution and laws made in accordance with it are "the supreme law of the land." This means that when national and state laws conflict, the national laws will be followed. The Constitution also sets some limitations on the national government. Article I, Section 9, lists some specific powers not granted to Congress, and the Bill of Rights (the first ten

amendments to the Constitution) limits the power of the national government over individuals.

The Constitution says considerably less about the powers granted to the states. The Tenth Amendment says that all powers not given to the national government are reserved for the states, although, as we will soon see, the Court's interpretation of the necessary and proper clause as elastic makes it difficult to see which powers are withheld from the national government. The states are given the power to approve the Constitution itself and any amendments to it. The Constitution also limits state powers. Article I, Section 10, denies the states certain powers, mostly the kinds they possessed under the Articles of Confederation. The Fourteenth Amendment limits the power of the states over individual liberties, essentially a Bill of Rights that protects individuals from state action, since the first ten amendments apply only to the national government.

What these constitutional provisions mean is that the line between the national government and the state governments is not clearly drawn. We can see from Figure 4.2 that the Constitution designates specific powers as national, state, or concurrent. **Concurrent powers** are those that both levels of

Figure 4.2

The Constitutional Division of Powers Between the National Government and the States

NATIONAL POWERS	CONCURRENT POWERS	STATE POWERS
• Admit new states into the Union • Coin money • Conduct foreign affairs • Declare war • Establish courts inferior to the Supreme Court • Make laws that are necessary for carrying out the powers vested by the Constitution • Raise and maintain armies, navies • Regulate commerce with foreign nations and among the states	• Borrow and spend money for the general welfare • Charter and regulate banks; charter corporations • Collect taxes • Establish courts • Establish highways • Pass and enforce laws • Take private property for public purposes, with just compensation	**Powers reserved to the states:** • Conduct elections and determine voter qualifications • Establish local governments • Maintain militia (National Guard) • Provide for public health, safety, and morals • Ratify amendments to the federal Constitution • Regulate intrastate commerce **States expressly prohibited from:** • Abridging the privileges or immunities of citizens or denying due process and equal protection of the laws (14th Amendment) • Coining money • Entering into treaties • Keeping troops or navies • Levying import or export taxes on goods • Making war

> ***dual federalism*** the federal system under which the national and state governments are responsible for separate policy areas
>
> ***cooperative federalism*** the federal system under which the national and state governments share responsibilities for most domestic policy areas

> ***unitary system*** government in which all power is centralized
>
> ***confederal systems*** governments in which local units hold all the power

government may exercise. But the federal relationship is a good deal more complex than this figure would lead us to believe. The Supreme Court has become crucial to establishing the exact limits of such provisions as the necessary and proper clause, the supremacy clause, the Tenth Amendment, and the Fourteenth Amendment. Its interpretation has changed over time, especially as historical demands have forced the Court to think about federalism in new ways.

Two Views of Federalism

Political scientists have also changed the way they think about federalism. For many years the prevailing theory was known as *dual federalism,* basically arguing that the relationship between the two levels of government was like a layer cake. That is, the national and state governments were to be understood as two self-contained layers, each essentially separate from the other and carrying out its functions independently. In its own area of power, each level was supreme. Dual federalism reflects the formal distribution of powers in the Constitution, and perhaps it was an accurate portrayal of the judicial interpretation of the federal system for our first hundred years or so.

But this theory was criticized for not realistically describing the way the federal relationship was evolving in the twentieth century. It certainly did not take into account the changes brought about by the New Deal. The layer cake image was replaced by a new bakery metaphor. According to the new theory of *cooperative federalism*, rather than being two distinct layers, the national and state levels were swirled together like the chocolate and vanilla batter in a marble cake.[18] National and state powers were interdependent, and each level required the cooperation of the other to get things done. In fact, federalism came to be seen by political scientists as a partnership, but one in which the dominant partner was, more often than not, the national government.

Possible Alternatives to Federalism

The federal system was not the only alternative available to our founders for organizing the relationship between the central government and the states. In fact, as we know, it wasn't even their first choice as a framework for government. The Articles of Confederation, which preceded the Constitution, handled the relationship quite differently. We can look at federalism as a compromise system that borrows some attributes from a unitary system and some from a confederal system, as shown in Figure 4.3. Had the founders chosen either of these alternatives, American government would look very different today.

Unitary Systems

In a *unitary system* the central government ultimately has all the power. Local units (states or counties) may have some power at some times, but basically they are dependent on the central unit, which can alter or even abolish them. Many contemporary countries have unitary systems, among them Britain, France, Japan, Denmark, Norway, Sweden, Hungary, and the Philippines.

Politics in Britain, for example, works very differently from politics in the United States, partly due to the different rules that organize central and local government. Most important decisions are made in London, from foreign policy to housing policy—even the details of what ought to be included in the school curriculum. Even local taxes are determined centrally. When Margaret Thatcher, the former British prime minister, believed that some municipal units in London were not supportive of her government's policies, she simply dissolved the administrative units. Similarly, in 1972, when the legislature in Northern Ireland (a part of Great Britain) could not resolve its religious conflicts, the central government suspended the local lawmaking body and ruled Northern Ireland from London. These actions are tantamount to a Republican president's dissolving a Democratic state that disagreed with his policies, or the national government's deciding to suspend the state legislature in Alabama and run the state from Washington during the days of segregation. Such an arrangement has been impossible in the United States except during the chaotic state of emergency following the Civil War. What is commonplace under a unitary system is unimaginable under our federal rules.

Confederal Systems

Confederal systems provide an equally sharp contrast to federal systems, even though the names sound quite similar. In *confederal systems* the local units hold all the power, and the central government is dependent on them for its existence. The local units remain sovereign, and the central government has only as much power as those units allow it to have. Examples of confederal systems include America under the Articles of Confederation and associations such as the United Nations and the European Union, twenty-seven European

Figure 4.3

The Division and Flow of Power in Confederal, Federal, and Unitary Systems of Government

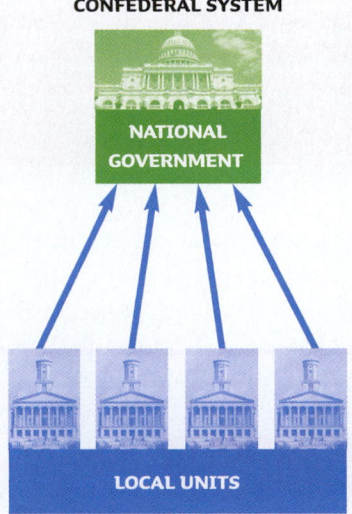
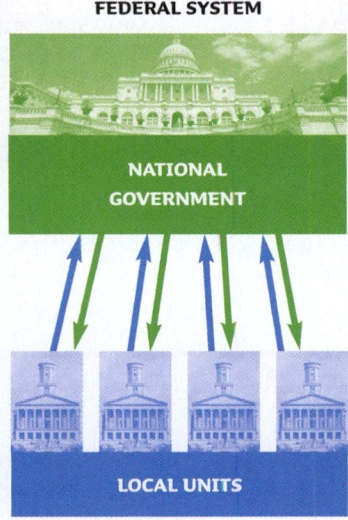
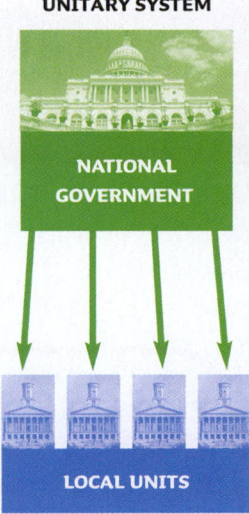

In a confederal system the local units hold all the powers, and the central government is dependent on those units for its existence. In a federal system the flow of power goes in both directions: power is shared, with both the central and local governments holding some powers independent of the other. In a unitary system the central government ultimately has all the power, and the local units are dependent on it.

nations that have joined economic and political forces. The European Union has been experiencing problems much like ours after the Revolutionary War, debating whether it ought to move in a federal direction. Some of the nations involved, jealous of their sovereignty, have been reluctant.

What Difference Does Federalism Make?

That our founders settled on federalism, rather than a unitary or a confederal system, makes a great deal of difference to American politics. Federalism gave the founders a government that could take effective action, restore economic stability, and regulate disputes among the states, while still allowing the states considerable autonomy. Several specific consequences of that autonomy deserve discussion.

Creating Competition Among the States

The federal relationship has an impact on state politics by placing the states in competition with one another for scarce resources. For example, consider the so-called race to the bottom that some observers and academics fear results when states have discretion over benefit levels and eligibility requirements for social programs such as welfare. The concern is that the states will cut benefits because they worry that

being more generous than neighboring states will cause poor people to move into their states. That is, some policymakers fear that if they don't cut payments, their states will become "welfare magnets." When benefits and program requirements are set by the national government, states have fewer incentives to cut benefits in the race to the bottom.[19]

A second consequence of competition among the states is their competition for industry. "Smokestack chasing" happens as states bid against one another to get industries to locate within their borders by providing them with property and corporate income tax breaks, loan financing, and educational training for workers, and by assuming the costs of roads, sewers, and other infrastructure that new industries would otherwise have to pay for themselves. For instance, in the early 1980s, Tennessee outbid other states for a Nissan automobile plant by paying roughly $11,000 per job. After that, the stakes became increasingly higher so that, in 1993, Alabama "won" a thirty-five-state race to grab the Mercedes-Benz sport utility vehicle plant with an incentive plan that cost the state around $200,000 for each of the expected 1,500 jobs.[20]

More recently, as economic experts have concluded that these bidding wars benefit the industries much more than they do the states, the states have developed other strategies for economic development.[21] Nevertheless, the states don't seem able to kick the smokestack-chasing habit entirely.

▶ Who, What, How, and WHEN: Constitutions

Every year, Americans line up at the National Archives to view one of the few original copies of the U.S. Constitution. The Constitution lays out the basics of American government: the three branches, balance of powers, and a little later on, the Bill of Rights. Even though Americans may not know exactly what the Constitution says, they know it's an important part of U.S. government. But there have been many important constitutions besides the document Americans consider "The One." Consider the following examples:

1795–1750 BCE — Code of Hammurabi

Hammurabi was a king of Babylon and the first known leader to create and distribute a constitution—in this case, a list of written laws—for the society over which he ruled. Examples of these laws include the rule that a witness who gave false testimony should be killed. The code was carved on an eight-foot black stone on public display and was found in 1901 in the Persian mountains.

604 — The Seventeen-Article Constitution of Prince Shotoku

The Seventeen-Article Constitution was an attempt by the Yamato rulers of Japan to gain control over problems in their government. It used Confucian and Buddhist principles to create a set of moral guidelines for government officials, such as harmony and refraining from angry looks.

Circa 1100 — Gayanashagowa

The Gayanashagowa, or the Great Law of Peace, was an oral constitution established by the Iroquois Confederation of Native American tribes to hold the tribes together peacefully. It required unanimity among the tribes for decision making, provided instructions for who could serve as a leader, and created an amendment process. The constitution was passed down by oral recitation over generations.

Consider, for example, Florida's 2004 use of federal money intended to relieve the state's fiscal burdens to lure a large biotech firm to Palm Beach County.[22]

Providing Increased Access to Government

Federalism also makes a difference in the lives of citizens. It provides real power at levels of government that are close to the citizens. Citizens can thus have access to officials and processes of government that they could not have if there were just one distant, effective unit. Federalism also enhances the power of interest groups in that it provides a variety of government levels at which different groups can try to gain political advantage. Often a group that is not successful at one level can try again at another and "shop" for institutions or agencies that are more receptive to its requests. The states vary considerably in their political ideologies and thus in the policies they are likely to adopt. (See *Who Are We? How We Differ From State to State.*) For example, African Americans were unable to achieve significant political influence in the South as long as the southern states, with their segregationist traditions, were allowed to control access to the voting booths. When the national government stepped in to stop segregation with the Civil Rights Act of 1964, the balance of power began to become less lopsided. Conversely, when women were unable to get the vote at the national level, they turned their attention to the states, and won their suffrage there first. Today we

'EURO 2008'

PARESH

1688 — **British Constitution**

The British Constitution is unusual in that it is not one written document, as are many other national constitutions. Rather, it is said to be the laws and acts of Parliament, accumulated over time, that established government operations. A major piece of the constitution developed in 1688–1689, when William and Mary ascended the throne and Parliament's powers, in relation to those of the monarchs, were established. The British Constitution continues to change; as recently as 2005 the House of Lords' powers changed.

1787 — **U.S. Constitution**

The U.S. Constitution replaced the Articles of Confederation, the document designed to unite the colonies during the Revolution that left too much power in the hands of the states for the new country to succeed. The Constitution created a strong national government, and a Bill of Rights was added in 1791. The U.S. Constitution is still in effect today and has been amended only twenty-seven times, though its interpretation changes over time through constitutional law.

1958 — **French Constitution of the Fifth Republic**

Unlike the United States, France has adopted numerous constitutions since the French Revolution began in 1789. The 1958 constitution replaced the previous one from 1946. One major change was an increase in presidential power; the constitution also provided for amendments through national referenda.

2005 — **European Union Constitution**

In 2005 the European Union tried to create a constitution to establish clearer rules for the EU's government. For the constitution to pass, all twenty-five countries of the EU had to ratify it. However, France and the Netherlands voted it down. In 2007 the Treaty of Lisbon was created to establish rules similar to those of the rejected constitution, but the treaty was voted down by Ireland in 2008. For now, the prior treaties, rather than a constitution, remain the basis for the EU's government.

can see the effects of group power in the area of the environment. Without the action of the federal government, many of the states in the American West would adopt much more lenient rules for use of federal lands for grazing, farming, and oil exploration, all of which can be quite profitable for them. Although environmentalists have little clout in places like Utah or Alaska, they are far more influential in Washington, D.C., where policy is currently made.

Allowing Flexibility at the Local Level

Federalism gives government considerable flexibility to preserve local standards and to respond to local needs—that is, to solve problems at the levels at which they occur. Examples include local traffic laws, community school policies, and city and county housing codes. Federalism also allows experimentation with public policy. If all laws and policies need not be uniform across the country, then different states may try different solutions to common problems and share the results of their experiments. For instance, in 1993, policymakers in Georgia, hoping to stem the loss of their brightest young people to out-of-state colleges and universities, developed a way to fund higher education that would make going to school in Georgia more attractive. Using funds from the state lottery, Georgia's Hope Scholarships pay for tuition, mandatory fees, and a book allowance for any Georgia resident who completes high school with a "B" average, a program that

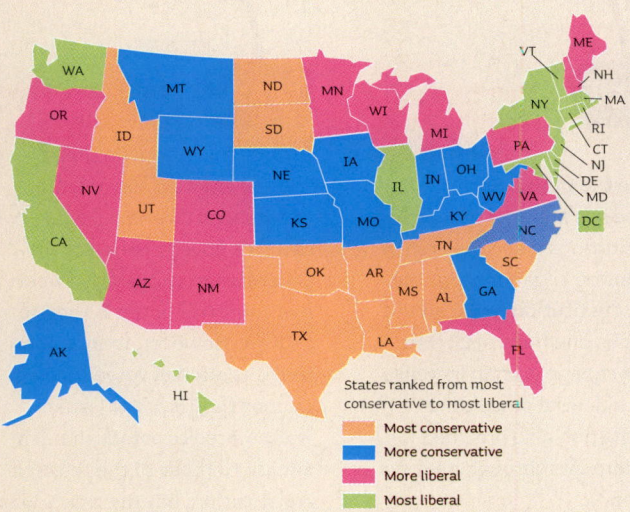
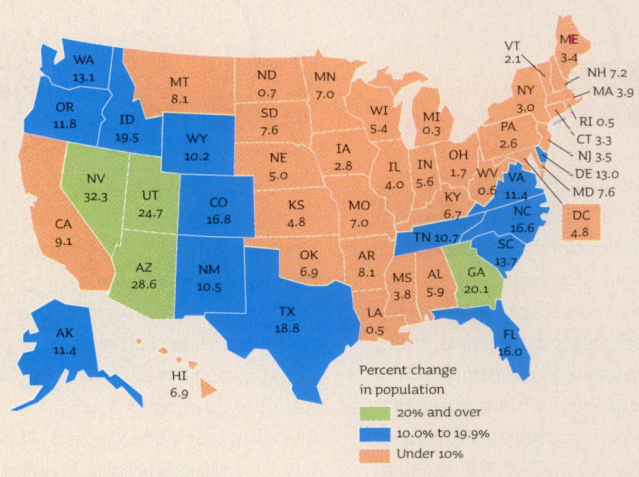
one close observer calls "probably the most successful public initiative in Georgia history." The program has been so successful that other states, including Florida, Kentucky, Nevada, Maryland, and Texas, have adopted versions tailored to meet their own particular needs.[23]

The flexibility that federalism offers states has disadvantages as well. Where policies are made and enforced locally, all economies of scale are lost. Many functions are also repeated across the country as states locally administer national programs. Making and enforcing laws can be troublesome as well under federalism. Different penalties for the same crime can make it difficult to gauge the consequences of one's behavior across states. For example, being caught with an ounce of marijuana will get an offender a $5,000 fine and up to five years in jail in Florida, but in California it draws only a $100 fine, and in Massachusetts a first-time offender gets probation.[24] Most problematic is the fact that federalism permits, even encourages, local prejudices to find their way into law. To the degree that states have more rather than less power, the uniform enforcement of civil rights cannot be guaranteed. Gay Americans, for example, do not have the same rights in all localities of the United States today.

Even though federalism is not a perfect system, overall it has proved to be a flexible and effective compromise for American government. The United States is not the only nation with a federal system, although other countries may distribute power among their various units differently than we do. Germany, Canada, Mexico, Australia, and Switzerland are all examples of federal systems.

The Changing Balance: American Federalism Over Time

Although the Constitution provides for both national and state powers (as well as some shared powers), several factors have caused the balance between the two to change considerably since it was written. First, because of the founders' disagreement over how power should be distributed in the new country, the final wording about national and state powers was kept vague intentionally, which probably helped the Constitution get ratified. Because it wasn't clear how much power the different levels held, it has been possible ever since for both ardent Federalists and states' rights advocates to find support for their positions in the document.

Another factor that has caused the balance of national and state powers to shift over time has to do with the role given to the Supreme Court to step in and interpret what it thinks the Constitution really means when conflict exists over which level of government should have the final say on a given issue. Those interpretations have varied along with the people sitting on the Court and with historical circumstances.

The circumstances themselves have helped to alter the balance of state and national powers over time. The context of American life is transformed periodically through major events such as the end of slavery and the Civil War, the process of industrialization and the growth of big business, the economic collapse of the Great Depression in the 1930s, world wars (both hot and cold) followed by the fall of communism in the 1980s, and the devastating terrorist attacks of September 11, 2001. The most recent of these events was the huge economic recession that began in 2008 with the mortgage crisis and that has resulted in massive federal government economic stimulus programs to stem the economy's downward spiral. With these events come shifts in the demands made on the different levels of government. When we talk about federalism in the United States, we are talking about specific constitutional rules and provisions, but we are also talking about a continuously changing context in which those rules are understood.

Two trends are apparent when we examine American federalism throughout our history. One is that American government in general is growing in size, at both the state and national levels. We make many more demands than did, say, the citizens of George Washington's time, or Abraham Lincoln's, and the apparatus to satisfy those demands has grown accordingly. But within that overall growth, a second trend has been the gradual strengthening of the national government at the expense of the states.

The increase in the size of government shouldn't surprise us. One indisputable truth about the United States is that, over the years, it has gotten bigger, more industrialized, more urban, and more technical. As the country has grown, so have our expectations of what the government will do for us. We want to be protected from the fluctuations of the market, from natural disasters, from terrorists, from unfair business practices, and from unsafe foods and drugs. We want government to protect our "rights," but our concept of those rights has expanded beyond the first ten amendments to the Constitution to include things like economic security in old age, a minimum standard of living for all citizens, a safe interstate highway system, and crime-free neighborhoods. These new demands and expectations create larger government at all levels but particularly at the national level, where the resources and will to accomplish such broad policy goals are more likely to exist.

Traditionally, liberals have preferred to rely on a strong central government to solve many social problems that the states have not solved, such as discrimination and poverty. Conservatives have tended to believe that "big government" causes more problems than it solves. Like the Anti-Federalists at the founding, they have preferred to see power and government services located at the state or local level, closer to the people being governed. From 2000 to 2006, however, with Republicans holding the reins of power in both the legislative and executive branches, the conservative distaste for big government waned somewhat as they were the ones dictating the actions of that government. President Bush's No Child Left Behind Act, for instance, took away many of the prerogatives of local school districts to decide whether to engage in regular testing of students, and yet it enjoyed the support of many conservatives. Some Republicans themselves noted that, once they come to Washington, conservatives can be "as bad as liberals" about enforcing the national will on states.[25] Once President Obama was elected and the Democrats passed the economic stimulus bill and health care reform, however, Republicans quickly returned to their traditional views and decried the return of "big government." Both Democrats and Republicans are more willing to entertain the possibility of national government action when they are the ones controlling the national government.

The growth of the national government's power over the states can be traced by looking at four moments in our

"All the news that's fit to print," proclaims the banner of the *New York Times.* But news isn't the only thing you'll find in what readers fondly refer to as "the old gray lady." Some of the most informative, entertaining, and, frequently, infuriating "news" printed in the *New York Times*—and most other newspapers today—can be found in the op-ed pages, where opinion pieces, editorials, and letters to the editor reign supreme. Often the last two inside pages of the first section, the op-ed pages need to be read differently from the rest of the paper. Writers of the standard news pages try to be objective, and while their values and beliefs may sneak in, they attempt to minimize the influence of their opinions on their work.

Writers on the op-ed pages, in contrast, flaunt their opinions, proudly display their biases, and make value-laden claims with abandon. This can make for fascinating reading, and can help you to formulate your own opinions, if you know what you are reading. Op-ed writers include:

- The newspaper's editorial board—editors employed by the paper who take stands on public matters, recommend courses of action to officials, and endorse candidates for office. On the whole, editorial boards are more conservative than liberal (for example, they have endorsed Republican presidential candidates far more often than they have endorsed Democrats)—but they often reflect the ideological tendencies of their reader base. The editors of the *New York Times*, which is read by a liberal urban population, take stances that are on the more liberal side, while the *Wall Street Journal*, subscribed to by the national business community, is more conservative. *USA Today*, which aspires to a broad national circulation, attempts to be more moderate in its outlook.

- Columnists—writers employed by the paper or by a news syndicate (whose work is distributed to many newspapers) who analyze current events from their personal ideological point of view. Columnists can be liberal, like Ellen Goodman (*Boston Globe*) and Molly Ivins (*Fort Worth Star-Telegram*), or conservative, like David Brooks and Ross Douthat (*New York Times*), and George Will (*Washington Post*). The *Washington Post*'s E. J. Dionne and David Broder, and the *New York Times*'s Maureen Dowd, are all cogent observers and critics of the political scene who defy precise placement on an ideological scale. While their values tend toward the liberal, they are equally hard on both parties.

- Guest columnists—ranging from the country's elite in the *New York Times* to everyday Americans in *USA Today*—who expound their views on a wide range of issues.

- Readers of the newspaper—who write letters to the editor, responding either to points of news coverage in the newspaper or to other items on the op-ed pages.

Here are some questions to ask yourself as you read the op-ed section of the newspaper:

- Who is the author? What do you know about him or her? As you get used to reading certain newspaper editorial pages and columnists you will know what to expect from them. Guest columnists are harder to gauge. The paper should tell you who they are, but you can always do further research on the web or elsewhere. Figure out how the author's job or achievements might influence his or her views.

- What are the values underlying the piece you are reading? Does the author make his or her values clear? If not, can you figure them out based on what the person writes? Unless you know the values that motivate an author, it is difficult to judge fairly what he or she has to say, and it can be difficult not to be hoodwinked as well.

- Is the author building an argument? If so, are the premises or assumptions that the author makes clear? Does the author cite adequate evidence to back up his or her points? Does the argument make sense? Notice that these are versions of the same questions we set out as guides to critical thinking in Chapter 1. Always think critically when you are reading an op-ed piece, or you are in danger of taking someone's opinions and preferences as fact!

- What kinds of literary devices does the author use that you might not find in a straight news story? Opinion writers, especially columnists, might use sarcasm or irony to expose what they see as the absurdities of politics or political figures, and they might even invent fictional characters. What is the point of these literary devices? Are they effective?

- Has the author persuaded you? Why or why not? Has the author shown you how to look at a familiar situation in a new light, or has he or she merely reinforced your own opinions? Do you feel inspired to write a letter to the editor on the subject? If so, do it!

national history: the early judicial decisions of Chief Justice John Marshall, the Civil War, the New Deal, and the civil rights movement and the expanded use of the Fourteenth Amendment from the 1950s through the 1970s. Since the late 1970s, we have seen increasing opposition to the growth of what is called "big government" on the part of citizens and officials alike, but most of the efforts to cut it back in size and to restore power to the states have been mixed.

McCulloch v. Maryland Supreme Court ruling (1819) confirming the supremacy of national over state government

Gibbons v. Ogden Supreme Court ruling (1824) establishing national authority over interstate business

nullification declaration by a state that a federal law is void within its borders

John Marshall: Strengthening the Constitutional Powers of the National Government

John Marshall, the third chief justice of the United States (1801–1835), was a man of decidedly Federalist views. His rulings did much to strengthen the power of the national government both during his lifetime and after. The 1819 case of *McCulloch v. Maryland* set the tone. In resolving this dispute about whether Congress had the power to charter a bank and whether the state of Maryland had the power to tax that bank, Marshall had plenty of scope for exercising his preference for a strong national government. Congress did have the power, he ruled, even though the Constitution didn't spell it out, because Congress was empowered to do whatever was necessary and proper to fulfill its constitutional obligations.

Marshall did not interpret the word *necessary* to mean "absolutely essential," but rather he took a looser view, holding that Congress could do whatever was "appropriate" to execute its powers. If that meant chartering a bank, then the necessary and proper clause could be stretched to include chartering a bank. Furthermore, Maryland could not tax the federal bank because "the power to tax involves the power to destroy."[26] If Maryland could tax the federal bank, that would imply the state had the power to destroy the bank, making Maryland supreme over the national government and violating the Constitution's supremacy clause, which makes the national government supreme.

Marshall continued this theme in *Gibbons v. Ogden* in 1824.[27] In deciding that New York did not have the right to create a steamboat monopoly on the Hudson River, Marshall focused on the part of Article I, Section 8, that allows Congress to regulate commerce "among the several states." He interpreted commerce very broadly to include almost any kind of business, creating a justification for a national government that could freely regulate business and that was dominant over the states.

Gibbons v. Ogden did not immediately establish national authority over business. Business interests were far too strong to meekly accept government authority, and subsequent Court decisions recognized that strength and a prevailing public philosophy of laissez-faire. The national government's power in general was limited by cases such as *Cooley v. Board of Wardens of Port of Philadelphia* (1851),[28] which gave the states greater power to regulate commerce if local interests outweigh national interests, and *Dred Scott v. Sanford* (1857),[29] which held that Congress did not have the power to outlaw slavery in the territories.

The Civil War: National Domination of the States

The Civil War represented a giant step in the direction of a stronger national government. The war itself was fought for a variety of reasons. Besides the issue of slavery and the conflicting economic and cultural interests of the North and South, the war was fought to resolve the question of national versus state supremacy. When the national government, dominated by the northern states, passed legislation that would have furthered northern interests, the southern states tried to invoke the doctrine of nullification. **Nullification** was the idea that states could render national laws null if they disagreed with them, but the national government never recognized this doctrine. The southern states also seceded, or withdrew from the United States, as a way of rejecting national authority, but the Union's victory in the ensuing war showed decisively that states did not retain their sovereignty under the Constitution.

The New Deal: National Power Over Business

The Civil War did not settle the question of the proper balance of power between national government and business interests. In the years following the war, the courts struck down both state and national laws regulating business. For example, *Pollock v. Farmer's Loan and Trust Company* (1895) held that the federal income tax was unconstitutional[30] (until it was legalized by the Sixteenth Amendment in 1913). *Lochner v. New York* (1905) said that states could not regulate working hours for bakers.[31] This ruling was used as the basis for rejecting state and national regulation of business until the middle of the New Deal in the 1930s. *Hammer v. Dagenhart* (1918) said that national laws prohibiting child labor were outside Congress' power to regulate commerce and therefore were unconstitutional.[32]

Throughout the early years of Franklin Roosevelt's New Deal, designed amid the devastation of the Great Depression of the 1930s to recapture economic stability through economic regulations, the Supreme Court maintained its antiregulation stance. But the president berated the Court for

What would the U.S. government be like today if states had the power of nullification?

Thinking Outside the Box

Redefining American Government

This highly partisan contemporary cartoon shows President Franklin Roosevelt cheerfully steering the American ship of state toward economic recovery, despite detractors in big business. New Deal policies redefined the scope of both national and state powers.

striking down his programs, and public opinion backed the New Deal and Roosevelt himself against the interests of big business. Eventually the Court had a change of heart. Once established as constitutional, New Deal policies redefined the purpose of American government and thus the scope of both national and state powers. The relationship between the nation and the states became more cooperative as the government became employer, provider, and insurer of millions of Americans in times of hardship. Our Social Security system was born during the New Deal, as were many other national programs designed to get America back to work and back on its feet. A sharper contrast to the laissez-faire policies of the turn of the century can hardly be imagined.

Civil Rights: National Protection Against State Abuse

The national government picked up a host of new roles as American society became more complex, including that of guarantor of individual rights against state abuse. The Fourteenth Amendment to the Constitution was passed after the Civil War to make sure southern states extended all the protections of the Constitution to the newly freed slaves. In the 1950s and 1960s the Supreme Court used the amendment to strike down a variety of state laws that maintained segregated, or separate, facilities for whites and African Americans, from railway cars to classrooms. By the 1970s the Court's interpretation of the Fourteenth Amendment had expanded, allowing it to declare unconstitutional many state laws that it said deprived state citizens of their rights as U.S. citizens. For instance, the Court ruled that states had to guarantee those accused of state crimes the same protections that the Bill of

Rights guaranteed those accused of federal crimes. As we will see in more detail in Chapter 5, the Fourteenth Amendment has come to be a means for severely limiting the states' powers over their own citizens.

The trend toward increased national power has not put an end to the debate over federalism, however. In the 1970s and 1980s, Presidents Richard Nixon and Ronald Reagan tried hard to return some responsibilities to the states, mainly by giving them more control over how they spend federal money. In the next section, we look at recent efforts to alter the balance of federal power in favor of the states.

The Politics of Contemporary Federalism

Clearly federalism is a continually renegotiated compromise between advocates of strong national government on the one hand and advocates of state power on the other. Making the job of compromise more complex, however, is that, as we have suggested, federalism is not a purely ideological issue, but also reflects pragmatic politics. If a party dominates the federal government for a long time, its members become accustomed to looking to that government to accomplish their aims. Those whose party persists in the minority on the federal level tend to look to the states. As one expert put it, "Fundamentally, though, neither federal officials nor most state and local officials values federalism as a constitutional end rather than a political means to partisan ends."[33] In short, most of the time people will fight to have decisions made in the arena (national or state) where they are most likely to prevail, or where the opposition will have the greatest difficulty achieving their policy goals.

> **devolution** the transfer of powers and responsibilities from the federal government to the states

Although the Supreme Court, since the days of *Marbury v. Madison,* had endorsed an extension of the range of the national government, the conservative Supreme Court under Chief Justice William Rehnquist passed down a set of decisions beginning in 1991 that signaled a rejection of congressional encroachment on the prerogatives of the states—a power shift that was dubbed **devolution**. However, that movement came to an abrupt stop in 2002 following the attacks of September 11, 2001. The Court continues to have a conservative majority under Chief Justice John Roberts, but its inclinations have been more toward favoring business than resurrecting federalism.[34]

Whether or not the Supreme Court's decisions give the federal government greater latitude in exercising its powers, the states are still responsible for the policies that most affect our lives. For instance, the states retain primary responsibility for everything from education to regulation of funeral parlors, from licensing physicians to building roads and telling us how fast we can drive on them. Most questions of contemporary federalism involve the national government trying to influence how the states and localities go about providing the goods and services and regulating the behaviors that have traditionally been within their jurisdictions.

Why should the national government care so much about what the states do? There are several reasons. First, from a Congress member's perspective, it is easier to solve many social and economic problems at the national level. Pervasive problems such as race discrimination or air and water pollution do not affect just the populations of individual states. When a political problem does not stop at the state border, it can be easier to conceive of solutions that cross the border as well; such solutions require national coordination. In some instances, national problem solving involves redistributing resources from one state or region to another, which individual states, on their own, would be unwilling or unable to do.

Second, members of Congress gain electoral favor by passing laws and regulations that force the states to do things that their supporters prefer. Incumbents have embraced their roles as representatives who can deliver highways; parks; welfare benefits; urban renewal; and assistance to farmers, ranchers, miners, educators, and just about everyone else. Doing well by constituents gets incumbents reelected, even if it means getting state and local officials to change how they do their business.[35]

Third, sometimes members of Congress prefer to adopt national legislation to preempt what states may be doing or planning to do. In some cases they might object to state laws, as Congress did when it passed civil rights legislation against the strong preferences of the southern states. In other cases they might enact legislation to prevent states from making fifty different regulatory laws for the same product. Here they are being sensitive to the wishes of corporations and businesses—generally large contributors to politicians—to have a single set of laws governing their activities. If Congress makes a set of nationally binding regulations, a business does not have to incur the expense of altering its product or service to meet different state standards.

To deliver on their promises, national politicians must have the cooperation of the states. Although some policies, such as Social Security, can be administered easily at the national level, others, such as changing educational policy or altering the drinking age, remain under state authority and cannot be legislated in Washington. Federal policymakers face one of their biggest challenges in this regard: how to get the states to do what federal officials have decided they should do.

Let's take the question of mathematics education as an example. Assume that members of Congress have decided that we face a "math crisis" and that more math training needs to take place in our high schools for the nation to remain competitive in the world economy of the twenty-first century. How will they get the education policymakers—that is, the states—to go along with them? One sure way to influence math education would be for the federal government to build and staff a system of "federal schools." Then it could have any kind of a curriculum it wanted. But doing so would be enormously expensive and wasteful, because the states and localities already have schools and already teach math in them. The more efficient alternative would be to try to influence how the states and localities teach math. Here Congress would face the same challenges it does with respect to other policy areas such as health, occupational safety, transportation, and welfare. When Congress wants to act in these areas, it has to find ways to work with the states and localities.

Congressional Strategies for Influencing State Policy

Congress makes two key decisions when it attempts to influence what the states are doing. One is about the character of the rules and regulations that are issued: Will they be broad and allow the states flexibility, or narrow and specific to guarantee that policy is executed as Washington wishes? The other is about whether the cost of the new programs will be paid for by the national government and, if so, by how much. The combination of these two decisions yields the four general congressional strategies for influencing the states we see in Table 4.1.

> **categorical grant** federal funds provided for a specific purpose, restricted by detailed instructions, regulations, and compliance standards

Table 4.1

How the National Government Influences the States

		Provide Federal Funds?	
		Yes, Federal grants as incentives	No Federal funding
How strict are the rules?	Strict and specific requirements	**Categorical Grants:** • Good for congressional credit taking. • Ensures state compliance and policy uniformity. • Heavy federal regulatory burden ("red tape"). • National policy requirements may not be appropriate for local conditions.	**Unfunded Mandates:** • Very cheap for the federal government. • Easy way for members of Congress to garner favor. • States complain about unfairness and burdensome regulations. • Undermines state cooperation.
	No rules, or broad grants of power within program areas	**Block Grants:** • Greater state flexibility, program economy. • State politicians love money without "strings." • Greater program innovation. Undermines congressional credit taking. • Grants become highly vulnerable to federal budget cuts. • Leads to policy diversity and inequality, meeting state rather than national goals.	**No Federal Influence:** • States have autonomy and pay for their own programs. • Results in high diversity of policies, including inequality. Promotes state competition and its outcomes. • Calls for congressional and presidential restraint in exercising their powers

• *Option One: No National Government Influence.* In the period of dual federalism, the federal government left most domestic policy decisions to the states. Precollege education is a good example: the federal government did not provide instructions to the states about curriculum goals (let alone math training), nor did it provide the funds for education. The combination of no instructions and no funding (bottom row in Table 4.1) yields the outcome of no national government influence. This means the states organized education as they wished. To follow our math example, the outcome of no national government influence would be that some states might concentrate on math, whereas others might emphasize a different educational issue. Such policy differences are a natural outcome of a situation in which the states, rather than the federal government, have more power in a given policy area.

• *Option Two: Categorical Grants.* In our example, Congress might decide that the nation's long-run economic health depends on massive improvements in high school mathematics education. "No national government influence" is clearly not an option here.

Congress could pass a resolution declaring its desire for better math education in high school, but if it wants results, it would have to put some teeth in its "request." If Congress really wants to effect a change, it would have to provide instructions and an incentive for the states to improve math education.

The most popular tool Congress has devised for this purpose is the **categorical grant** (see upper left Table 4.1), which provides very detailed instructions, regulations, and compliance requirements for the states (and sometimes for local governments, as well) in specific policy areas. If a state complies with the requirements, federal money is released for those specified purposes. If a state doesn't comply with the detailed provisions of the categorical grant, it doesn't get the money. In many cases the states have to provide some funding themselves. They might, for instance, have to match the amount contributed by the federal government.

In our example, the federal government could pass a math education act that would provide funds on a per-pupil basis for math education in the high schools. The bill might set standards for certain performance or testing levels, requirements for teacher certification in advanced math

> **block grant** federal funds provided for a broad purpose, unrestricted by detailed requirements and regulations

education training, and perhaps specific goals for decreasing the gender and racial gaps in math performance. School districts and state school boards would have to document their compliance in order to receive their funds.

The states, like most governments, never have enough money to meet all their citizens' demands, so categorical grants can look very attractive, at least on the surface. The grants can be refused, but most of the time they are welcomed. In fact, state and local governments have become so dependent on federal grants that these subsidies now make up 27 percent of all state and local spending.[36] Thus the categorical grant has become a powerful tool of the federal government in getting the states to do what it wants.

Use of categorical grants, which are responsible for the large growth in federal influence on the states, blossomed in the 1960s and 1970s. Members of Congress receive credit for sponsoring specific grant programs, which in turn help establish members as national policy leaders, building their reputations with their constituents for bringing "home" federal money. Also, because senators and House members are backed by coalitions of various interest groups, specific program requirements help to ensure that a policy does what

members (and their backers) want—even in states where local political leaders prefer a different course. By contrast, state politicians hate the requirements and all the paperwork that go with reporting compliance with federal regulations. States and localities also frequently argue that federal regulations prevent them from doing a good job. They want the money, but they also want more flexibility.

- *Option Three: Block Grants.* Conservatives have long chafed at the detailed, Washington-centered nature of categorical grants. State politicians understandably want the maximum amount of freedom possible. They want to control their own destinies, not just carry out political deals made in Washington, and they want to please the coalitions of interests and voters that put them in power in the states. Thus they argue for maintaining federal funding but with fewer regulations. Their preferred policy tool, the **block grant** (seen in the lower left of Table 4.1), combines broad (rather than detailed) program requirements and regulations with funding from the federal treasury. Block grants give the states considerable freedom in using the funds in broad policy areas.

Funding Recovery
A sign at a Kentucky construction site credits the expansion work to funds received from the American Recovery and Reinvestment Act. The act included grants to states and industries to stimulate growth in an economy hard hit by recession.

> *unfunded mandate* a federal order mandating that states operate and pay for a program created at the national level

To continue our math education example, the federal government might provide the states with a lump-sum block grant and instructions to spend it on education as each state sees fit. If Congress demanded that the money be spent on math education and insisted on other conditions, then the grant would start to look more like a categorical grant and less like a block grant. With an education block grant, members of Congress could not count on their math education problem being solved on a national basis unless it coincidentally resulted from the individual decisions in fifty states and innumerable localities.

One extreme and short-lived form of the block grant in the 1970s was President Richard Nixon's proposal to give money to the states and localities with no strings attached in the form of General Revenue Sharing (GRS)—not in place of categorical grants, but largely in addition to existing programs. GRS was immensely popular with the governors and mayors, but it never had great congressional backing because members of Congress could neither take credit for nor control how lower governments were spending these federal funds. Congress did not object when, in 1986, President Ronald Reagan suggested abolishing GRS as a way of reducing the deficit.[37]

Less extreme versions of the block grant were pushed by Republican presidents Nixon, Reagan, Gerald Ford, and George W. Bush. However, the largest and most significant block grant was instituted under Democratic president Bill Clinton in 1996 with the passage of the welfare reform act. This reform changed a categorical grant program called Aid to Families with Dependent Children (AFDC) to a welfare block grant to the states, Temporary Assistance to Needy Families (TANF).

Under TANF, the states have greater leeway in defining many of the rules of their welfare programs, such as qualifications and work requirements. The states do not get a blank check, however; they must continue to spend at certain levels and to adopt some federal provisions, such as the limits on how long a person can stay on welfare. TANF has ended welfare as an entitlement. Under AFDC, all families who qualified were guaranteed benefits—just as people who qualify for Social Security are assured coverage. This guarantee is not part of TANF. If the states run short of money—such as in the current recession—families that might otherwise qualify may not receive welfare benefits. Such decisions, and their repercussions, are left to the individual states.

Congress has generally resisted the block grant approach for both policy and political reasons. In policy terms, many members of Congress fear that the states will do what they want instead of what Congress intends. One member characterized

the idea of putting federal money into block grants as "pouring money down a rat hole,"[38] because it is impossible to control how the states deal with particular problems under block grants.

Congress also has political objections to block grants. When federal funds are not attached to specific programs, they lose their electoral appeal for members of Congress, as they can no longer take credit for the programs. From a representative's standpoint, it does not make political sense to take the heat for taxing people's income, only to turn those funds over in block grants so that governors and mayors get the credit for how the money is spent. In addition, interest groups contribute millions of dollars to congressional campaigns when members of Congress have control over program specifics. If Congress allows the states to assume that control, interest groups have less incentive to make congressional campaign contributions. As a result, the tendency has been to place more conditions on block grants with each annual congressional appropriation.[39]

Categorical grants remain the predominant form of federal aid, amounting to about 80 percent of all aid to state and local governments. The change from AFDC to TANF was an important milestone in welfare policy, but it remains to be seen whether Congress will continue this approach in other policy areas.

- *Option Four: Unfunded Mandates.* The politics of federalism yields one more strategy, shown in the upper right of Table 4.1. When the federal government issues an **unfunded mandate**, it imposes specific policy requirements on the states but does not provide a way to pay for those activities. Here Congress either threatens criminal or civil penalties or promises to cut off other, often unrelated, federal funds if the states do not comply with its directions. A recent example has nearly caused a rebellion in the states. The REAL ID Act was passed by Congress in 2005 following a recommendation of the White House Office of Homeland Security and the 9/11 Commission. This law required regulation of state driver's licenses, typically under control of the states, including verification of an applicant's identity, as well as standardization of watermarks, holograms, and a machine-readable code. These would be required for identification by any citizen doing business with a federal agency, including travelers passing through security at airports. The cost of the program's implementation was estimated to be about $23 billion, with the vast majority of it to be shouldered by the states. Although virtually no one opposes the overall goal of national security, the requirements of the law and its cost led to a potential showdown. As of 2009 fourteen states had passed laws prohibiting implementation of the law, another ten had passed resolutions denouncing REAL ID, and Congress had postponed its enforcement. The result is that Congress has to decide between fulfilling the national security goal of verified identity checks on people and soothing the anger and resistance of the states.[40]

In terms of our math education example, the national government might say to the states that at least 45 percent of the students enrolled in advanced high school math courses must be female and that the states stand to lose 5 percent of their sewage treatment funds if that quota is not met. This requirement could be set with no new federal funding for education at all.

Unfunded mandates are more attractive to members of Congress in periods of ballooning national deficits.[41] Whereas Congress passed unfunded mandates only eleven times from 1931 through the 1960s, it passed fifty-two such mandates in the 1970s and 1980s, a trend that continued into the 1990s.[42] In large part due to complaints from the states Congress passed the Unfunded Mandate Act of 1995, which promised to reimburse the states for expensive unfunded mandates or to pass a separate law acknowledging the cost of an unfunded mandate. This act has limited congressional efforts to pass "good laws" that cost the U.S. Treasury nothing. However, because Congress can define what the states see as an unfunded mandate in several different ways—as a simple "clarification of legislative intent," for example—Congress has continued to push some policy costs on to the states as in the REAL ID legislation discussed above and the No Child Left Behind Act, which required extensive tests and intervention for failing students and schools.[43] In addition, fears of large unfunded mandates played a role in the debates leading up to health care reform. For instance, a version of the reform that expanded Medicaid for low-income people prompted instant criticism from governors because Medicaid is paid for largely by state treasuries. Congress later backed down and provided assistance to the states to meet the new policy.

The current status of federalism is a contradictory mix of rhetoric about returning power to the states and new national initiatives (and program requirements) in the areas of health, education, and the environment. Although many in the states and even the national government say they want the states to have more power, the imperatives of effective policy solutions and congressional and presidential electoral calculations combine to create strong pressures for national solutions to our complex problems.

Advocates for the national government and supporters of the states are engaged in a constant struggle for power, as they have been since the days of the Articles of Confederation. The power of the federal government is enhanced through the mechanisms of cooperative federalism, which give the federal government an increasing role in domestic policy. As the federal government has used the restrictive rules of categorical grants and the economic threats that provide the muscle of unfunded mandates, critics have claimed that cooperative federalism has been transformed into "coercive federalism," in which the states are pressured to adopt national solutions to their local problems with minimal state input.

It is worth remembering, however, that members of Congress who pass the laws are elected in the states and have their primary loyalties to their local constituencies, not to any national audience. Their states have been only too happy to accept federal funds to meet the needs of their residents (and voters) for everything from education to highways to welfare and health care for the poor. However, they also chafe under the rules and regulations that typically come with federal dollars. The conflict is not likely to end any time soon, as the Obama administration takes an activist approach to the massive challenges of the recession and the need to revive the economy, the role of the United States in climate change, and the provision of health care for all Americans.

Where decisions are made—in Washington, D.C., or in the state capitals—makes a big difference in who gets what, and how they get it. The compromise of federalism as it appears in the Constitution, and as it has been interpreted by the Supreme Court, allows the nation, the states, and the citizens to get political benefits that would not be possible under either a unitary or a confederal system, but the balance of power has swung back and forth over the years. Much of the current battle is fought in the halls of Congress, where states pull for a dual federalist interpretation that would give them block grants and devolution, and the national government holds out for a cooperative federalism in which it can award categorical grants and exact unfunded mandates. And under the ideological battle is the political truth that the contestants generally favor the level of government that is most likely to give them what they want.

Who What How

> *amendability* the provision for the Constitution to be changed, so as to adapt to new circumstances

Amending the Constitution
Making it difficult but not impossible

If a constitution is a rule book, then its capacity to be changed over time is critical to its remaining a viable political document. A rigid constitution runs the risk of ceasing to seem legitimate to citizens who have no prospect of changing the rules according to shifting political realities and visions of the public good. A constitution that is revised too easily, however, can be seen as no more than a political tool in the hands of the strongest interests in society. A final feature of the U.S. Constitution that deserves mention here is its *amendability*—that is, the founders' provision for a method of amendment, or change, that allows the Constitution to grow and adapt to new circumstances. In fact, the founders provided for two methods: the formal amendment process outlined in the Constitution, and an informal process that results from the vagueness of the document and the evolution of the role of the courts.

In the more than two hundred years since the U.S. Constitution was written, over 10,000 amendments have been introduced, but it has been formally amended only twenty-seven times. We have passed amendments to expand the protections of civil liberties and rights—to protect freedom of speech and religion, to provide guarantees against abuses of the criminal justice system, to guarantee citizenship rights to African Americans, and to extend the right to vote to blacks, women, and eighteen year olds.

We have also passed amendments on more mechanical matters—to tinker with the rules of the political institutions the Constitution sets up in order to better control the outcomes. To that end, we have made senatorial elections direct, we have limited a president to two terms in office, and we have provided for a succession if the president is unable to serve out his term.

On at least one occasion we have also used the Constitution to make a policy that could more easily have been made through normal legislative channels. With the ratification of the Eighteenth Amendment in 1919 we instituted Prohibition, making the production and sale of alcohol illegal. When our national views on temperance changed, we repealed the amendment in 1933, having to pass a new amendment to do so.

But the Constitution can be changed in more subtle ways by the Supreme Court without an amendment's ever being passed. In the name of interpreting the Constitution, for example, the Supreme Court has extended many of the Bill of Rights protections to state citizens via the Fourteenth Amendment, permitted the national government to regulate business, prohibited child labor, and extended equal protection of the laws to women. In some cases, amendments had earlier been introduced to accomplish these goals but failed to be ratified (like the child labor amendment and the Equal Rights Amendment), and sometimes the Court has simply decided to interpret the Constitution in a new way. Judicial interpretation is at times quite controversial. Many scholars believe that the literal word of the founders should be adhered to, while others claim that the founders could not have anticipated all the opportunities and pitfalls of modern life and that the Constitution should be understood to be a flexible or "living" document.

But these views about whether the Constitution should be changed by amendment or by interpretation are not just matters for academics to solve—they also have political implications and tend to break down along partisan lines. For instance, many recent calls to amend the Constitution have focused on banning abortion, banning gay marriage, banning flag burning, or permitting prayer in school. For the most part, people split into partisan camps in their support of or opposition to those amendments. Democrats tend to oppose such amendments, believing they curtail fundamental individual rights, and Republicans tend to support them, claiming that they promote important traditional values.

But one can go even further in drawing partisan lines around this issue. Democrats, in general, as liberals who believe that change is inevitable and probably a good thing, are more willing to see the Constitution as a flexible, living document that can be altered continually in small, nonpermanent ways by judicial interpretation. Republicans, on the other hand, share, for the most part, the conservative suspicion of change and a belief that the words of the founders ought not to be tampered with by unelected judges. They are willing to change the Constitution, and even to change it in deep and fundamental ways, but they prefer to do it by amendment. We return to this controversy when we look more closely at the courts in Chapter 10.

What Does the Constitution Say?

The Constitution is silent on the subject of judicial interpretation, but in part because it is so silent, especially in Article III, the courts have been able to evolve their own role. On the other hand, Article V spells out in detail the rather confusing procedures for officially amending the Constitution. These procedures are federal; that is, they require the involvement and approval of the states as well as the national government. The procedures boil down to this: Amendments may be proposed either by a two-thirds vote of the House and the Senate or, when two-thirds of the states request it, by a constitutional convention. Amendments must be approved either by the legislatures of three-fourths of the states or by conventions of three-fourths of the states. (See Figure 4.4.) Two interesting qualifications are contained in Article V. No amendment affecting slavery could be made before 1808, and no amendment can deprive a state of its equal vote in the Senate without that state's consent. We can easily imagine the North-South and large state–small state conflicts that produced those compromises.

Possible Alternatives: Making the Constitution Easier or Harder to Amend

The fifty states provide some interesting examples of alternative rules for amending constitutions. Compared to the national government, some states make it harder to amend

their own constitutions. For instance, twelve states require that the amendment pass in more than one session of the legislature—that is, in successive years.

Rules can also make it much easier to amend constitutions. Some states require only simple legislative majorities (50 percent plus one) to propose amendments, and unlike the national Constitution, some states give their citizens a substantial role in the process through mechanisms called referenda and initiatives, which we discuss in the next section. The method by which an amendment is proposed can affect the success of the amendment itself. For instance, amendments limiting the number of terms legislators can serve have been passed in several states with the citizen-controlled initiative, but they have not fared well in states that depend on state legislatures to propose amendments. With opinion polls showing large public majorities favoring term limits, we can safely assume that term limits for Congress would pass much faster if the U.S. Constitution had a provision for a national constitutional initiative. Congress has proven, not surprisingly, reluctant to put restrictions on congressional careers.

One problem with making it too easy to amend a constitution is that public opinion can be fickle, and we

Figure 4.4

Amending the Constitution

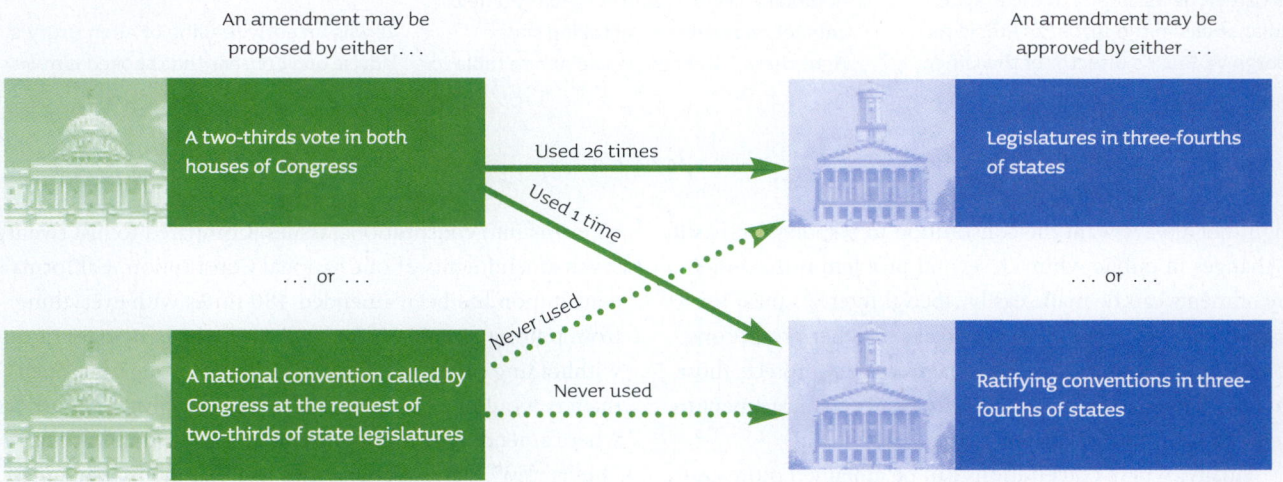

▶ **Profiles in Citizenship: Mitch Daniels**

" . . . if you don't feel grateful for being born into a free society, you better get out and see the world a little bit."

Some politicians are born legislators—they like to argue and deliberate and craft careful compromises. Others are natural executives; they focus on solving problems and clearing hurdles. Count Indiana governor Mitch Daniels among the latter group: despite his folksy manner, he likes to get things done.

And Daniels has been getting things done on all levels of government for most of his career, as assistant to the mayor of Indianapolis in the 1970s, as President George W. Bush's director of the Office

of Management and Budget (OMB) from January 2001 to June 2003, and as governor of the state of Indiana since 2005. He hasn't exactly been squelching rumors that he might run for president in 2012, either—not surprising, given that it is the ultimate office for getting things done in U.S. politics.

When he took on OMB, Daniels expected his new position to be interesting from the start, but the job took on an unanticipated dimension of high-stakes urgency in the days after September 11. He says, "There was one night that won't be replicated maybe ever again . . . this is probably September 13, 14 . . . we're sitting around this long conference table in the Speaker of the House's office. . . . And really, in real time, we're hammering out what will be done about the airlines, which are not flying—they're not going back into the air unless we can get them insurance—the Democrats aren't going to agree to insurance unless you compensate the people in New York City, which had never been done—we didn't do it in Oklahoma City, we're going to do it here . . . and on and on . . . and the first steps toward what became a huge expenditure on homeland security and eventually a new cabinet department. All taking shape right there, all those people at one table.

Right in the middle of the wee hours, it's an amazing thing. But in an atmosphere, again, that won't happen often, of genuine bipartisanship. Just for a little while they all put their sabers away, and it was astonishing."

Astonishing indeed, and in that emotional, keyed-up, history-shaping moment, it was Daniels's job to keep his head—to hold the costs down, to be sure that compensation offered was reasonable and that they didn't set precedents for the future. How on earth do you prepare for such awesome and humbling responsibility?

Sitting in his huge office in the Indiana statehouse, relaxed and thoughtful, Daniels reflects on the extraordinary journey that has taken an Indiana boy to the heights of national politics and business and brought him back home again to run his state's government. His account is peppered with laughter and self-deprecating anecdotes ("Do you have time for a quick story?" he asks more than once), but they can't hide the hard work, the laser intelligence, and the abiding interest in things political that have gotten him where he is.

It was an early reading of Allen Drury's *Advise and Consent* that hooked him on

might not always want the constitution to respond too hastily to changes in public whim. A second problem is that where amendments can be made easily, special interests push for amendments that give them tax breaks or other protections. Constitutional status of their special treatment protects those interests from having to periodically justify that treatment to the public and the legislature.

Finally, where constitutions can be amended more easily, they are amended more frequently. The initiative process in California permits relatively easy translation of citizen

concerns into constitutional issues. Compared to just twenty-seven amendments of our national Constitution, California's constitution has been amended 480 times with everything from putting a cap on taxes, to limiting legislative terms, to withholding public services from illegal immigrants. Such matters would be the subject of ordinary legislation in states where amending is more difficult and thus would not have "higher law" status. Some critics feel that the fundamental importance of a constitution is trivialized by cluttering it with many additions that could be dealt with in other ways.

politics, with its fictionalized account of "the grand theater of the legislative process . . . these large figures and their inner motives and their moments of truth." After his freshman year of college, he was asked by a local precinct committeeman, whose lawn he happened to cut, if he wanted to work on a U.S. Senate campaign. Flattered to be asked, and perhaps with Drury's grand theater in the back of his mind, he said yes.

The campaign put him in touch with Richard Lugar, who went on to become mayor of Indianapolis and U.S. senator. Daniels worked for Lugar (whom he calls "an extraordinary paragon in public service"), mostly as his chief of staff, for thirteen years, before deciding he wanted to move back home. Although he detoured to work as a senior adviser in the Reagan White House, he did get back to Indiana, working in the private sector in Indianapolis before heading back to D.C. and the position at OMB. Today he is very happy to be back in Indiana once again, ensconced in the governor's office. He says, "Governor is the only elected position I can think of that I'd be interested in because it's at a scale big enough to really matter to a lot of people and yet you're in a real position to do things. . . . Things tend to be much more concrete and much more practical, less ideological. Obviously you're closer to the problems here." And solving problems is just what Governor Daniels likes. Other observations:

On citizen wisdom:

In fact, my view has always been that we ought not to have many people spending their entire careers in public life. . . . I think in general people bring the most to public service if they are sort of balanced in their perspective by some other career, or some other professional activity. I think the richness of republican, I'm talking about small "r," republican government comes from the sort of citizen wisdom that you get when people . . . are politicians second and doctors or social workers or small-business people or something else as well.

On keeping the republic:

I subscribe to the view that, as somebody once said, giving some time to public affairs is the rent I owe this country. Number one, if you don't feel grateful for being born into a free society, you better get out and see the world a little bit. . . . And then assuming you do feel as grateful as you should, you owe a little rent, you owe a little something to those who made this possible and so that it remains possible for the folks who follow. Now, the way you pay that rent—you've got a lot of choices. And an elected office or even a government job, government service, is only part of it. . . .

The second thing I'd say is that there are a lot of other ways. . . . The strength of this country to me, maybe the single distinguishing characteristic of American democracy—de Tocqueville sure thought this—is we are joiners in this country and we've got organizations of every kind. . . . And that's every bit as much a way to strengthen a democracy or republic, I think. . . . So I count all of that. Somebody wants to go out and be a leader of the Sierra Club or be a leader of the Heart Association or some civic group, that counts too, to me. . . . And I guess the last thing is, and I said it before, I don't feel the need at all to consider government service a career choice. If you do, that's honorable but you don't need to. And my personal view is the best citizens of all may be those who are grounded elsewhere, who then try to bring what they've learned to the job of building a better society and a more effective government, without being dependent either professionally, financially, or psychologically on that job. ■

Two good reasons, then, why the U.S. Constitution has weathered the passing of time so well are (1) it is not too detailed and explicit, and (2) its amendment procedure, in Madison's words, "guards equally against that extreme facility, which would render the Constitution too mutable; and the extreme difficulty, which might perpetuate its discovered faults."[44]

The founders and the American public had an enormous stake in a Constitution that would survive. The founders had their own reputations as nation-builders at stake, but they and the public also badly wanted their new experiment in self-governance to prove successful, to validate the Enlightenment view of the world. For the Constitution to survive, it had to be able to change, but to change judiciously. The amendment process provided in the Constitution allows for just such change. But occasionally this process is too slow for what the courts consider justice, and they use their broad powers to interpret the existing words of the

**Who
What
How**

Working Toward Equality for All

The Equal Rights Amendment sought to protect equality of rights under the Constitution. Introduced in every Congress from 1923 until its passage in 1972, the amendment fell three states short of the required three-fourths ratification by the states. Times have changes since the late 1970s, when all the protesters were women, and all the media people covering the event were men.

Constitution in light of the changed circumstances of the modern day. That is, they focus not so much on what the founders meant at the time, but on what they would intend if they were alive today. The founders would have been as mixed in support of this practice as are contemporary scholars. Perhaps the focus of so many critical eyes on the Court has served as an informal check on this power.

The Citizens and the Constitution

Limited participation at the national level, enhanced opportunities beyond

Remember Benjamin Franklin's reply to the woman who asked him what he and his colleagues had created? "A Republic, Madam, if you can keep it." In fact, however, the Constitution assigns citizens only the slimmest of roles in keeping

the republic. The founders wrote a constitution that in many respects profoundly limits citizen participation.

The political role available to "the people" moved from "subject" to "citizen" with the writing of the Constitution, and especially with the addition of the Bill of Rights, but the citizen's political options were narrow. It is true that he could vote if he met the tight restrictions that the states might require. His role as voter, however, was and is confined to choosing among competing political elites, in the case of the Senate or the presidential electors, or among competing people like himself who are running for the House, but who will themselves be constrained once in power by a system of checks and balances and the necessity of running for reelection in two years.

The Constitution is not a participatory document. It does not create a democratic society in which individuals take an active part in their own governance. The national political system is remote from most individuals, as the Anti-Federalists claimed it would be, and the opportunities to get

> **initiative** citizen petitions to place a proposal or constitutional amendment on the ballot, to be adopted or rejected by majority vote, bypassing the legislature

> **referendum** an election in which a bill passed by the state legislature is submitted to voters for approval

> **recall elections** votes to remove elected officials from office

involved in it are few and costly in terms of time, energy, and money. In fact, the founders preferred it that way. They did not trust human beings, either to know their own best interests or to handle power without being corrupted. They wanted popular power to serve as a potential check on the elected leaders, but they wanted to impose strict checks on popular power as well, to prevent disturbances like Shays's Rebellion from springing up to threaten the system. The Constitution was the republic's insurance policy against chaos and instability.

But in two crucial ways the Constitution does enhance opportunities for participation. First, because it creates a federal system, participation can flourish at the state and local levels even while it remains limited at the national level. We will see that a variety of less formal options are available to citizens, but three of the formal mechanisms of direct democracy at the state level deserve special mention: the initiative, the referendum, and the recall.

With the **initiative**, citizens can force a constitutional amendment or state law to be placed on the ballot. This is accomplished by getting a sufficient number of signatures on petitions, typically between 3 and 15 percent of those voting in the last election for governor. Once on the ballot, an initiative is adopted with a majority vote and becomes law, *completely bypassing the state legislature.* About half of the states have provisions for the initiative, and in California it has become the principal way to make significant changes to state law.

The **referendum** is an election in which bills passed by the state legislatures are submitted to the voters for their approval. In most states, constitutional amendments have to be submitted for a referendum vote, and in some states questions of taxation do also. A number of the states allow citizens to call for a referendum (by petition) on controversial laws passed by the state legislature, and in many cases the state legislatures themselves can ask for a referendum on matters they believe the voters should decide directly. Referenda are often very complicated and difficult to understand, but they can have large consequences for the citizens who must decipher them and vote on them.

Recall elections are a way for citizens to remove elected officials from office before their terms are up. These, too, require petitions, usually with more signatures than are needed for an initiative (frequently 25 percent of the electorate). Statewide recalls are infrequent, but some are quite notable, like the one that removed Gray Davis as governor of California in 2003, clearing the way for Arnold Schwarzenegger's election.

The record of these three measures of direct democracy is mixed. They do enhance opportunities for individuals to participate, and they give citizens more control over what their government does. However, many citizens do not take advantage of these opportunities, leaving greater power concentrated in the hands of those who do. Furthermore, many of the details of lawmaking can be complicated and hard to understand without careful study—something most citizens don't have time to give them. As a result, the people who do vote can be misled or manipulated by complex or obscure wording, and it is hard for them to know exactly what they are voting on. Finally, direct democracy, by eliminating the checks the founders thought important, makes government more responsive to short-term fluctuations in public opinion, sometimes denying politicians the necessary time to take a long-term approach to problem solving and policymaking.

A second way that the Constitution enhances opportunities for citizen participation, even though it makes such activity difficult at the national level, is by providing political stability. It is precisely because the Constitution has protected the United States from the kind of chaos and instability that existed under the Articles of Confederation that citizens have the luxury of developing a host of citizenship roles that are not prescribed in the Constitution. Citizens participate in local government, on school boards and in parent-teacher organizations, in charitable groups, and in service organizations. They volunteer in congressional and presidential election campaigns, they run for office, and they serve as magistrates. They circulate petitions, take part in fundraising drives, and participate in neighborhood associations. They file lawsuits, they belong to interest groups, and they march in parades and demonstrations. They read papers and watch the news, they call in to radio talk shows, and they write letters to the editor. They surf political sites on the Internet and register their opinions through web site polling.

In twenty-first-century America, the opportunities for community, local, and state participation are only likely to increase, and this at a time when the Internet brings even the national government closer to many homes. All these activities are acts of citizenship, albeit a kind of citizenship on which the Constitution is silent. Our founding document does not endorse a role for citizens, other than that of watchful voter, but it creates a political environment in which a variety of forms of civic participation can flourish.

▶ What's at Stake Revisited

As we have seen in this chapter, the issue of what powers go to the federal government and what powers are reserved to the states has been a hotly contested one since the founding, and one that has no clean, crisp, right answer. As the country and the composition of the Supreme Court have changed, so too have interpretations of states' rights and federal power. All of that means that the issue of medical marijuana, which currently is legal in fourteen states, though illegal nationally, is an excellent example of the messiness that can characterize federal issues in the United States.

For some supporters of the medical marijuana laws, what is at stake is the ability of ill patients to receive the most effective treatment possible. But they are allied with those who want to put limits on national power, some of whom might not approve of medical marijuana on its own merits. In his dissent in *Gonzales v. Raich*, Justice Clarence Thomas said, "No evidence from the founding suggests that 'commerce' included the mere possession of a good or some purely personal activity that did not involve trade or exchange for value. In the early days of the Republic, it would have been unthinkable that Congress could prohibit the local cultivation, possession, and consumption of marijuana." If the national government can regulate this, it can regulate anything.[45]

Opponents of the medical marijuana laws say that as long as the Court has ruled that the state laws violate the commerce clause, the national law should be enforced. Further, some argue that it does touch the issue of interstate commerce because the provision and purchase of medical marijuana "affects the marijuana market generally," and they worry that if the federal government cannot regulate this, then perhaps they will be hampered in other areas, like child pornography, as well.[46]

That there is no clear constitutional resolution of such issues, that it is possible for the Court to produce conflicting rulings on this policy, and that the Bush and Obama administrations would take such differing stances on it explains both how our federal system has found the flexibility to survive so long and so well, and why the debates over where power resides can be so bitterly fought.

To Sum Up

Key terms, chapter summaries, practice quizzes, Internet links, and other study aids are available on the companion web site at http://republic.cqpress.com.

Define | Understand | Practice | Read | Click | Watch

amendability (p. 126)

bicameral legislature (p. 101)

block grant (p. 123)

categorical grant (p. 122)

checks and balances (p. 108)

concurrent powers (p. 111)

confederal systems (p. 112)

cooperative federalism (p. 112)

devolution (p. 121)

dual federalism (p. 112)

Electoral College (p. 103)

enumerated powers of Congress (p. 111)

executive (p. 103)

fusion of powers (p. 110)

Gibbons v. Ogden (p. 119)

initiative (p. 131)

judicial power (p. 105)

judicial review (p. 106)

legislative supremacy (p. 107)

legislature (p. 101)

McCulloch v. Maryland (p. 119)

necessary and proper clause (p. 111)

nullification (p. 119)

parliamentary system (p. 104)

presidential system (p. 104)

recall elections (p. 131)

referendum (p. 131)

republic (p. 101)

separation of powers (p. 108)

supremacy clause (p. 111)

unfunded mandate (p. 124)

unicameral legislature (p. 101)

unitary system (p. 112)

Define | Understand | Practice | Read | Click | Watch

- The Constitution is the rule book of American politics. The great decisions and compromises of the founding were really about the allocation of power among the branches of the government, between the national and state governments, and between government and citizens.

- Congress is given broad lawmaking responsibilities in the Constitution. It is composed of two houses, the House of Representatives and the Senate, each with different qualifications, terms of office, and constituencies. Having two houses of the legislature that are constitutionally separated from the president means that more interests are involved in policymaking and that it takes longer to get things done in the United States than under a parliamentary system.

- The president is elected indirectly by the Electoral College. Compared to the chief executive of parliamentary systems, the U.S. president has less power.

- The Supreme Court today has much greater powers than those named in the Constitution. This expansion derives from the adoption of the principle of judicial review, which gives the Court much more power than its counterparts in most other democracies and also acts as a check on the powers of the president, Congress, and the states.

- The scheme of checks and balances prevents any branch from overextending its own power. It grew out of the founders' fears of placing too much trust in any single source. The system provides a great deal of protection from abuses of power, but it also makes it difficult to get things done.

- The Constitution is ambiguous in defining federalism, giving "reserved powers" to the states but providing a "necessary and proper clause" that has allowed tremendous growth of national powers.

- Our understanding of federalism in the United States has evolved from a belief in dual federalism, with distinct policy responsibilities for the national and state governments, to the more realistic cooperative federalism, in which the different levels share responsibility in most domestic policy areas.

- Alternatives to our federal arrangement are unitary systems, which give all effective power to the central government, and confederal systems, in which the individual states (or other subunits) have primary power. The balance of power adopted between central and subnational governments directly affects the national government's ability to act on large policy problems and the subnational units' flexibility in responding to local preferences.

- The growth of national power can be traced to the early decisions of Chief Justice John Marshall, the constitutional consequences of the Civil War, the establishment of national supremacy in economics with the New Deal, and new national responsibilities in protecting citizens' rights that are associated with the civil rights movement.

- Devolution has required new, and sometimes difficult, agreements between state governments and their citizens. For the most part, state institutions (legislature, courts, governor) have become stronger and more efficient in the process.

- Amending the Constitution—that is, changing the basic rules of politics—is a two-step process of proposal by either Congress or a constitutional convention followed by ratification by the states. Of the thousands of amendments that have been suggested, only twenty-seven have been adopted. The Constitution can also be changed unofficially through the less formal and more controversial process of judicial interpretation.

Define   Understand   **Practice**   Read   Click   Watch

1. **According to this chapter, all governments must have the power to do what three things?**
   a. Legislate, administer laws, and adjudicate laws
   b. Make laws, rewrite laws, and declare laws to be unconstitutional
   c. Check other branches of government, divide powers among the branches equally, and oversee state governments
   d. Engage in war, defend against foreign attack, and make peace
   e. Control the people, control political parties, and control interest groups

2. **The necessary and proper clause is the provision in the Constitution that**
   a. allows each branch of government to exercise some form of control over the others.
   b. empowers the Supreme Court to rule on the constitutionality of laws.
   c. authorizes Congress to make any law required to carry out its powers.
   d. declares that the Constitution is the supreme law of the land.
   e. limits judicial, executive, and legislative powers by assigning them to different persons or groups.

3. **Why did Alexander Hamilton, in *Federalist* No. 78, claim that the judicial branch would be the "least dangerous branch"?**
   a. The Constitution ensures that judicial elections occur only in off-year elections.

   b. The judiciary would hold the power of neither the "sword" nor the "purse."
   c. The judiciary would agree with the president because he appoints its members, which makes it a portion of the executive branch.
   d. The founders made sure that the Constitution would clearly provide the legislative branch with the permanent power of judicial review.
   e. The judiciary holds the power of the "purse" but not the greater power of the "sword."

4. **Which of the following parts of the Constitution is not relevant to understanding federalism?**
   a. The supremacy clause
   b. The elastic clause
   c. The necessary and proper clause
   d. The Tenth Amendment
   e. The Preamble

5. **One reason the federal government's power has increased over state governments is that**
   a. the federal government has increasingly used block grants instead of categorical grants.
   b. more people have begun to support the idea of devolution.
   c. the civil rights movement brought about new federal responsibilities that protect citizens' rights.
   d. states have voluntarily given up power to the federal government.
   e. the supremacy clause doesn't make it clear whether to follow state or federal law when state and federal laws conflict.

Define · Understand · Practice · **Read** · Click · Watch

Beer, Samuel H. 1993. *To Make a Nation: The Rediscovery of American Federalism.* **Cambridge, Mass.: Harvard University Press.** An exceptional historical examination of American federalism with an emphasis on contrasting nation-centered and state-centered federalism.

LaCroix, Alison L. 2010. *The Ideological Origins of American Federalism.* **Cambridge, Mass.: Harvard University Press.** LaCroix traces the origins of American federalism from its colonial beginnings to its emergence in the eighteenth century as the basis for the formation of a multilayered government.

Madison, James. 1969. *Notes of Debates in the Federal Convention of 1787.* **New York: Norton.** A fascinating account of what really happened at the Constitutional Convention from the perspective of James Madison, the father of our Constitution.

Madison, James, Alexander Hamilton, and John Jay. 1961. *The Federalist Papers.* **New York: New American Library** *Madison,* Hamilton, and Jay presented compelling arguments for ratification of the proposed Constitution under the pseudonym Publius. The Federalist Papers may be a bit difficult to understand, but they are some of the most important works ever written in the history of the United States.

Rossiter, Clinton. 1966. *1787: The Grand Convention.* **New York: Macmillan.** In a marvelous account of the Constitutional Convention, Rossiter goes into great detail describing the convention's participants, the debate over ratification, and the early years of the new republic.

Storing, Herbert J. 1981. *What the Anti-Federalists Were For.* **Chicago: University of Chicago Press.** We hear a great deal about those who supported the new Constitution, but what about those who opposed it? This book is a collection of papers written by Anti-Federalists during the constitutional ratification period.

Define · Understand · Practice · Read · **Click** · Watch

The Constitution *www.usconstitution.net. A rewarding site for anyone interested in learning more about the Constitution. This site contains general information about the Constitution, the founders, and other landmark documents in U.S. history. It also contains a section on how current events are influenced by the Constitution, and vice versa.*

National Conference of State Legislatures *www.ncsl.org. This site, dedicated to state-federal issues, includes loads of information on national policies implemented at the state level.*

State Constitutions *www.law.cornell.edu/statutes.html. This site has links to each state's constitution in addition to the U.S. Constitution. These documents provide useful points of comparison to our national "rule book."*

United States Constitution Search *www.law.emory.edu/index .php?id=3080. This site is an excellent source when you need quick answers about the Constitution.*

Define · Understand · Practice · Read · Click · **Watch**

Iron-Jawed Angels *2004. Hilary Swank and Frances O'Connor play two fiery young suffragettes, working for a constitutional amendment guaranteeing women the right to vote. Along the way, they incur the wrath of President Woodrow Wilson and anger other suffragette leaders.*

U.S. Constitution: A Document for Democracy *1988. This documentary looks at the various conflicts that arose during the creation of the U.S. Constitution.*

CONGRESS SHALL MAKE NO LAW

RESPECTING AN ESTABLISHMENT

OF RELIGION, OR PROHIBITING

THE FREE EXERCISE THEREOF;

OR ABRIDGING THE FREEDOM

OF SPEECH, OR OF THE PRESS;

OR THE RIGHT OF THE PEOPLE

PEACEABLY TO ASSEMBLE, AND

TO PETITION THE GOVERNMENT

FOR A REDRESS OF GRIEVANCES

THE FIRST AMENDMENT TO THE CONSTITUTION OF THE UNITED STATES

Chapter 5

Fundamental American Liberties

▶ What's at Stake?

It's usually hard to confuse the ivory towers of academia with the mean streets of the criminal underworld, but when Virginia attorney general Ken Cuccinelli set out to investigate the climate research of Professor Michael Mann, that's just where he was headed.

Mann, currently an environmental science professor at Penn State, had been at the University of Virginia from 1999 to 2005, where he obtained several grants of federal and state money to undertake his research on climate change. In 2009 Mann was one of several researchers working in England whose email was hacked by opponents of the idea that human activities were warming the planet. The hacked emails revealed that some of the researchers were resisting attempts by critics to get a hold of their data under the American and British Freedom of Information Acts, and that they had discussed suppressing some of their data that did not support their global warming thesis. Subsequent investigations by the English university Mann was associated with and by Penn State found that there was no evidence that Mann had suppressed or falsified data.[1]

A Hostile Climate

Virginia attorney general Ken Cuccinelli questioned the legitimacy of climate research carried out by Professor Michael Mann, alleging that Mann falsified data to obtain state funding. Critics of Cuccinelli's investigation called it an assault on academic freedom and an effort by the state to control information it didn't like.

But those investigations were not enough for Cuccinelli, an admitted opponent of climate change science, who wondered if perhaps Mann had deliberately defrauded Virginia taxpayers by using falsified data to obtain state research funds. Cuccinelli sought information from the University of Virginia by issuing "Civil Investigative Demand Letters" that would require school officials to turn over all of Mann's papers, emails, and other documentation from his time at the university. Fraud, if he found it, meant Cuccinelli could prosecute Mann.

Scholars throughout Virginia and the nation immediately protested. The American Association for the Advancement of Science, the American Association of University Professors, the American Civil Liberties Union of Virginia, and the Union of Concerned Scientists all raised their voices against Cuccinelli's efforts, and the *Washington Post*'s editorial board called the action against Mann "Mr. Cuccinelli's Witch Hunt."[2]

In response to the Civil Investigative Demand Letters, the university's lawyers filed suit, arguing that Cuccinelli's efforts were an unwarranted assault on academic freedom. They wrote:

> Academic freedom is essential to the mission of our Nation's institutions of higher learning and a core First Amendment concern. As Thomas Jefferson intended, the University of Virginia has a long and proud tradition of embracing

the "illimitable freedom of the human mind" by fully endorsing and supporting faculty research and scholarly pursuits. Our Nation also has a long and proud tradition of limited government framed by enumerated powers which Jefferson ardently believed was necessary for a civil society to endure. . . .

> Unfettered debate and the expression of conflicting ideas without fear of reprisal are the cornerstones of academic freedom; they consequently are carefully guarded First Amendment concerns. Investigating the merits of a university researcher's methodology, results, and conclusions (on climate change or any topic) goes far beyond the attorney general's limited statutory power.[3]

Cuccinelli, for his part, claimed that his investigation had nothing to do with Mann's research. "We're not investigating his academic work," the Virginia attorney general insisted. "That subpoena is directed at the expenditure of dollars. Whether he does a good job, bad job, or I don't like the outcome—and I think everybody already knows his position on some of this is one that I question. But that's not what that's about."[4]

So what was it about? Were Cuccinelli's actions just an effort to track down some possible misspent state dollars awarded to a researcher long gone to another state university? Or were they, as critics claimed, an effort to use the power of the state to intimidate researchers whose findings were disagreeable to state officials? Why did the university launch such a strong response in rejecting Cuccinelli's claims, and why did one of the nation's top newspapers speak of Cuccinelli's investigation as a "witch hunt"? Just what is at stake in the issue of academic freedom? ∎

civil liberties individual freedoms guaranteed to the people primarily by the Bill of Rights

civil rights citizenship rights guaranteed to the people (primarily in the Thirteenth, Fourteenth, Fifteenth, Nineteenth, and Twenty-sixth Amendments) and protected by the government

The freedoms we consider indispensable to the working of a democracy are part of the everyday language of politics in America.

"Give me liberty," declared patriot Patrick Henry at the start of the Revolutionary War, "or give me death." "Live Free or Die," proudly proclaims the New Hampshire license plate. Americans have always put a lot of stock in their freedom. Certain that they live in the least restrictive country in the world, Americans celebrate their freedoms and are proud of the Constitution, the laws, and the traditions that preserve them.

And yet, living collectively under a government means that we aren't free to do whatever we want. There are limits on our freedoms that allow us to live peacefully with our fellows, minimizing the conflict that would result if we all did exactly what we pleased. John Locke said that liberty does not equal license; that is, the freedom to do some things doesn't mean the freedom to do everything. Deciding what rights we give up to join civilized society, and what rights we retain, is one of the great challenges of democratic government.

What are these things called "rights" or "liberties," so precious that some Americans are willing to lay down their lives to preserve them? On the one hand, the answer is very simple. *Rights* and *liberties* are synonyms; they mean freedoms or privileges to which one has a claim. In that respect, we use the words more or less interchangeably. But when prefaced by the word *civil*, both rights and liberties take on a more specific meaning, and they no longer mean quite the same thing.

Our **civil liberties** are individual freedoms that place limitations on the power of government. In general, civil liberties protect our right to think and act without governmental interference. Some of these rights are spelled out in the Constitution, particularly in the Bill of Rights. These include the rights to express ourselves and to choose our own religious beliefs. Others, like the right to privacy, rest on the shakier ground of judicial decision making. Although government is prevented from limiting these freedoms per se, we will see that sometimes one person's freedom—to speak or act in a certain way—may be limited by another person's rights. Government does play a role in resolving the conflicts between individuals' rights.

Whereas civil liberties refer to restrictions on government action, **civil rights** refer to the extension of government action to secure citizenship rights to all members of society. When we speak of civil rights, we most often mean that the government must treat all citizens equally, apply laws fairly, and not discriminate unjustly against certain groups of people. Most of the rights we consider civil rights are guaranteed by the Thirteenth, Fourteenth, Fifteenth, Nineteenth, and

Twenty-sixth Amendments. These amendments lay out fundamental rights of citizenship, most notably the right to vote but also the right to equal treatment before the law and the right to due process of law. They forbid government from making laws that treat people differently on the basis of race, and they ensure that the right to vote cannot be denied on the basis of race or gender.

Not all people live under governments whose rules guarantee them fundamental liberties. In fact, we argued earlier that one way of distinguishing between authoritarian and nonauthoritarian governments is that nonauthoritarian governments, including democracies, give citizens the power to challenge government if they believe it has denied their basic rights. When we consider our definition of politics as "who gets what, and how," we see that rights are crucial in democratic politics, where a central tension is the power of the individual pitted against the power of the government. What's at stake in democracy is the resolution of that tension. In fact, democracies depend on the existence of rights in at least two ways. First, civil liberties provide rules that keep government limited, so that it cannot become too powerful. Second, civil rights help define who "we, the people" are in a democracy, and they give those people the power necessary to put some controls on their governments.

We will take two chapters to explore the issues of civil liberties and civil rights in depth. In this chapter we begin with a general discussion of the meaning of rights or liberties in a democracy, and then focus on the traditional civil liberties that provide a check on the power of government. In Chapter 6 we focus on civil rights and the continuing struggle of some groups of Americans—like women, African Americans, and other minorities—to be fully counted and empowered in American politics.

As an introduction to the basic civil liberties guaranteed to Americans, in this chapter you will learn about

- **the meaning of rights in a democratic society**
- **the Bill of Rights as part of the federal Constitution, and its relationship to the states**
- **freedom of religion in the United States**
- **freedom of speech and of the press**
- **the right to bear arms**
- **the rights of people accused of crimes in the United States**
- **the right to privacy**

Rights in a Democracy
Limiting government to empower people

The freedoms we consider indispensable to the working of a democracy are part of the everyday language of politics in America. We take many of them for granted: we speak confidently of our freedoms of speech, of the press, of religion, and of our rights to bear arms, to a fair trial, and to privacy. There is nothing inevitable about these freedoms, however.

In fact, there is nothing inevitable about the idea of rights at all. Until the writing of such Enlightenment figures as John Locke, it was rare for individuals to talk about claiming rights against government. Governments were assumed to have all the power, giving their subjects only such privileges as government was willing to bestow. Locke argued that the rights to life, liberty, and the pursuit of property were conferred on individuals by nature, and that one of the primary purposes of government was to preserve the natural rights of its citizens.

This notion of natural rights and limited government was central to the founders of the American system. In the Declaration of Independence, Thomas Jefferson wrote that men are "endowed by their Creator with certain inalienable rights; that among these are life, liberty, and the pursuit of happiness; that, to secure these rights, governments are instituted among men." John Locke could not have said it better himself.

Practically speaking, of course, any government can make its citizens do anything it wishes, regardless of their rights, as long as it is in charge of the military and the police. But in nonauthoritarian governments, public opinion is usually outraged at the invasion of individual rights. Unless the government is willing to dispense with its reputation as a democracy, it must respond in some way to pacify public opinion. Public opinion can be a powerful guardian of citizens' rights in a democracy.

Rights and the Power of the People

Just as rights limit government, they also empower its citizens. To claim a right is to claim a power—power over a government that wants to stop publication of an article detailing its plans for war; power over a school board that wants children to say a Christian prayer in school, regardless of their religious affiliation; power over a state legal system that wants to charge suspects with a crime without guaranteeing that a lawyer can be present; power over a state legislature that says residents can't vote because of the color of their skin or the fact that they were born female.

A person who can successfully claim that he or she has rights that must be respected by government is a citizen of that government; a person who is under the authority of a government but cannot claim rights is merely a subject, bound by the laws but without any power to challenge or change them. This does not mean, as we will see, that a citizen can always have things his or her own way. Nor does it mean that noncitizens have no rights in a democracy. It *does* mean that citizens have special protections and powers that allow them to stand up to government and plead their cases when they believe an injustice is being done.

The power of citizenship is nowhere so clearly illustrated as in the Supreme Court case of *Dred Scott v. Sanford*. Dred Scott was an African American slave who, through a transfer of ownership in 1834, was taken from Missouri, a slave state, into Illinois and the Wisconsin Territory, which Congress had declared to be free areas. Scott argued that living in a free territory made him a free man. The Court's decision, handed down in 1857, denied Scott the legal standing to bring a case before the Supreme Court because, according to the Court, Dred Scott, as an African American and as a slave, could not be considered a citizen of the United States. Although several northern states had extended political rights to African Americans by this time, the ruling declaring Scott a noncitizen denied him access to the courts, one of the primary arenas in which the battle for rights is fought.

When Rights Conflict

Because rights represent power, they are, like all other forms of power, subject to conflict and controversy. Often for one person to get his or her own way, someone else must lose out.

People clash over rights in two ways. The first type of rights conflict occurs between individuals. One person's right to share a prayer with classmates at the start of the school day conflicts with another student's right not to be subjected to a religious practice against his or her will. Our right as citizens to know about the individuals we elect to office might conflict with a given candidate's right to privacy. What is at stake in these disputes might be an inevitable conflict of interest (for instance, candidate versus voter). Or it might be a more fundamental issue—like the role of religion in society, gay rights, or the death penalty—that reflects not just differences in preferences or interests, but deeply held visions of the "right" kind of society. These visions are often so firmly embedded in people's minds that any challenge is intolerable.

The second way rights conflict is when the rights of individuals are pitted against the needs of society and the demands of collective living. The decision to wear a motor-cycle helmet or a seat belt, for instance, might seem like one that should be left up to individuals. But society also has

Are U.S. Rights Universal?

The Constitution gives Americans a number of procedural rights that protect us if we are arrested. Should these protections be extended to those accused of waging war against the United States? Photos of the U.S. military's use of torture against Iraq war prisoners held at Abu Ghraib prison surfaced in 2004 and set off a firestorm of debate. Should the United States extend the same constitutional rights to foreign prisoners as it does to its citizens? What measures will best ensure U.S. national security while maintaining our strong tradition of civil liberties?

an interest in regulating these behaviors because the failure to wear helmets or seat belts is costly to society in more ways than one. The death or serious injury of its citizens deprives society of productive members who might have lived to make important contributions. Through public education and other social programs, society makes a considerable investment in its citizens, which is lost if those citizens die prematurely. In addition, accident victims might require expensive, long-term medical treatment, usually taking place eventually at public expense. The decision about whether to wear a motorcycle helmet might seem to be a private one, but it has many public repercussions. Similarly, individual acts such as carrying a gun or publishing pornography can have consequences for society.

When Rights Conflict—The Case of National Security

One very clear example of how individual rights can conflict with the needs of society is the case of national security. After the terrorist attacks of September 11, 2001, Americans were

deeply afraid. Determined to prevent a repeat of the horrific attacks, the government federalized airport security and began screening passengers, searching luggage, and allowing armed agents on airplanes. Officials scrutinized the backgrounds of tourists and students from the Middle East and kept a close eye on Arab Americans they suspected of having ties to terrorist organizations.

In October 2001 Congress passed and President George W. Bush signed the USA Patriot Act, which, among other things, made it easier for law enforcement to intercept email and conduct roving wiretaps, gave it access to library records and bookstore purchases, and allowed immigrants suspected of terrorist activity to be held for up to seven days (and sometimes indefinitely) without being charged. The Bush administration, fearful that the evidence required in a U.S. court of law might not be forthcoming to convict a suspected terrorist, issued an executive order that non-U.S. citizens arrested on grounds of terrorism could be subject to trial in a military tribunal, where usual rules of due process need not apply.

All these measures may have increased the security of U.S. citizens, but they also reduced their civil liberties. In the immediate aftermath of September 11, such a trade-off struck most Americans as worthwhile. In times of national danger, we are susceptible to calls for locking down our liberties if we believe that doing so can help lock out threats. Somehow a reduction in freedom does not seem like an unreasonable price to pay for a reduction in fear.

But not all Americans were quick to endorse the sacrifice of their rights in favor of a potentially safer society. Immediately after the Patriot Act was passed, organizations including the American Civil Liberties Union (ACLU) criticized the legislation for infringing on Americans' privacy, violating due process, and being discriminatory. Although their efforts failed, some members of Congress tried to repeal sections of the act. Even support among the public began to wane as the events of September 11 became more distant. In January 2002 the country was evenly split when asked whether government should take steps to prevent terrorism even if civil liberties were violated. By November 2003, 64 percent of the public responded that government should take steps to prevent additional terrorist attacks but not violate civil liberties; only 31 percent said that steps should be taken even if civil liberties were violated.[5] Nonetheless, in 2006 Congress voted to reauthorize the 2001 Patriot Act and President Bush signed the bill. In 2010 President Barack Obama signed a one-year extension of some of the act's surveillance measures, despite the objections of civil libertarians who had hoped to find in Obama a stronger supporter of individual rights.

American citizens are not the only ones whose rights may be traded off for greater national security, but Americans are more willing to tolerate the reduction in liberties when they come at the expense of non-U.S. citizens. Those accused of terrorism or of being enemy combatants have been tortured by the U.S. government, imprisoned in ways that violate the Geneva Conventions on the treatment of prisoners of war, and denied the rights of due process that Americans accused of crimes are guaranteed. While large numbers of Americans

object to torture, support for providing terrorists with trials in civilian courts is far less widespread.

The balancing of public safety with individuals' rights is complex. We could ensure our safety from most threats, perhaps, if we were willing to give up all our freedom. With complete control over our movements, with the ability to monitor all our communications, with information on all our spending decisions, government could keep itself informed about which of us was likely to endanger others. The ultimate problem, of course, is that without our civil liberties, we have no protection from government itself.

How Do We Resolve Conflicts About Rights?

Because we are fortunate enough to be political and, we hope, rational beings, we can resolve disputes over rights without necessarily resorting to violence. But that doesn't make their resolution easy or necessarily "fair." Much of the conflict over rights in this country is between competing visions of what is fair. Because so much is at stake, the resulting battles are often politics at its messiest. Adding to the general political untidiness is the fact that so many actors get involved in the process: the courts, Congress, the president, and the people themselves. Although we focus on these actors in depth later in this book, we now look briefly at the role each one plays in resolving conflicts over rights.

The Courts

One of the jobs of the judiciary system is to arbitrate disputes among individuals about such things as rights. In this country, the highest you can go in seeking justice through the courts—that is, the highest court of appeal—is the U.S. Supreme Court. For legal and practical reasons, the Supreme Court can hear only a fraction of the cases that are appealed to it, so the Court agrees to hear cases when it wants to send a message to lower courts about how the Constitution should be interpreted. As we discussed in Chapter 4, the Supreme Court may exercise a power called judicial review, which enables it to decide if laws of Congress or the states are consistent with the Constitution and, if they are not, to invalidate them. Judicial review is generally used sparingly by the Court, but it can offer a remedy when rights conflict.

Thinking Outside the Box

In the delicate balance between security and freedom, on which side should we err?

Even though we typically think of the Supreme Court as the ultimate judge of what is fair in the United States, the truth is that its rulings have varied as the membership of the Court has changed. There is no guarantee that the Court will reach some unarguably "correct" answer to a legal dilemma; the justices are human beings influenced by their own values, ideals, and biases in interpreting and applying the laws. In addition, although the founders had hoped that the Supreme Court justices would be above the political fray, they are in fact subject to all sorts of political pressures, from the ideology of the presidents who appoint them to the steady influence of public opinion and the media. How else can we account for the fact that the same institution that denied Dred Scott his right to use the court system was responsible a century later for breaking down the barriers between blacks and whites in the South? At times in our history the Court has championed what seem like underdog interests that fight the mainstream of American public opinion—for example, ruling in favor of those who refuse to salute the American flag on religious grounds.[6] It has also tempered some of the post–September 11 legislation by ruling, for instance, that U.S. citizens held as enemy combatants do have some due process rights.[7] The Court also rejected the Bush administration's argument that the Supreme Court had no jurisdiction over military tribunals for foreign-born enemy combatants, holding that such tribunals must be authorized by Congress, not executive order.[8] At other times the Supreme Court has been less expansionary in its interpretation of civil liberties, and its rulings have favored the interests of big business over the rights of ordinary Americans, have blocked the rights of racial minorities, and have even put the stamp of constitutional approval on the World War II

Un-American Activity

Preying on American anxieties about communism, Senator Joseph R. McCarthy led an aggressive investigation of suspected communists in the government during the 1950s. Though his investigations, with their sensational and clever tactics, ruined many careers, McCarthy failed to find evidence of even one "card-carrying communist" in the government. He was censured by the Senate in 1954 and died in disgrace in 1957.

incarceration of Japanese Americans in internment camps,[9] an action for which we, as a nation, have since apologized.

Congress

Another actor involved in the resolution of conflicts over rights in this country is Congress. Sometimes Congress has chosen to stay out of disputes about rights. At other times it has taken decisive action either to limit or to expand the rights of many Americans. For example, the Smith Act,

▶ Who, What, How, and WHEN: Civil Liberties Since September 11

We could be totally safe and secure as a nation if we gave up all our civil liberties and let the government lock down society to protect us. While such an extreme loss of freedom is a price Americans refuse to pay, after September 11, national security ramped up and civil liberties were limited as government-issued threat levels moved from yellow to orange to red. Consider the following policies that make trade-offs between freedom and safety:

October 16, 2001

The Patriot Act

The USA Patriot Act (Uniting and Strengthening America by Providing Appropriate Tools Required to Intercept and Obstruct Terrorism) passed soon after the September 11 attacks. It expanded the ability of the U.S. government to search telephone, email, and finance records and made it easier for the government to deport immigrants suspected of terrorism. Despite the complaints of some who believe the act violates civil liberties, most of it was renewed in 2006, and some provisions were again renewed in 2010.

November 19, 2001

Transportation Security Administration (TSA)

The TSA was formed as part of the Department of Homeland Security after September 11 to oversee security in U.S. bus, train, and railroad stations, ports, and airports. TSA employees include airport screeners and U.S. air marshals, among others. The TSA develops rules for air travel, often in response to suspected terrorist threats, such as the "watch list" of names of suspected terrorists and the "3–1–1" rule requiring people to limit liquids in airline carry-on baggage to 3 oz. containers.

2002

Guantánamo Bay

Beginning in 2002 the United States built camps at the U.S. Naval Base at Guantánamo Bay, Cuba, in order to detain suspected terrorists. The Bush administration argued that suspects held at Guantánamo should be tried in military tribunals rather than in courts. Others, including the Supreme Court, have argued instead that the detainees have rights guaranteed by the U.S. Constitution, including habeas corpus. Additionally, some critics protest the treatment of prisoners at the facility.

passed by Congress in 1940, made it illegal to advocate the overthrow of the U.S. government by force or to join any organization that advocated government subversion. A decade later, in the name of national security, the House Un-American Activities Committee investigated and ruined the reputations of many Americans suspected of having sympathy for the Communist Party, sometimes on the flimsiest of evidence.[10] But Congress has also acted on the side of protecting rights. When the courts became more conservative in the 1980s and 1990s, with appointments made by Republican presidents Ronald Reagan and George H. W. Bush, for example, the judiciary narrowed its protections of civil rights issues. The Democratic-led Congress of the time countered with the Civil Rights Act of 1991, which broadened civil rights protection in the workplace. Similarly, in 2010 Congress held hearings on "Don't Ask, Don't Tell," a policy that prevents gay men and lesbians from serving openly in the military, and the legislation was repealed in December 2010.

November 2002

Department of Homeland Security

The new cabinet department of Homeland Security was created from existing government agencies, designed to unite these agencies under one entity responsible for the safety of the United States. Homeland Security absorbed agencies like the Federal Emergency Management Agency and the Immigration and Naturalization Service as well as the newly established Transportation Security Administration. It also established the Homeland Security Advisory System, which uses a color code (red is highest, green is lowest) to indicate the level of terrorist threat the department sees in the United States at any given time.

2005

Foreign Intelligence Surveillance Act (FISA)

FISA was created in 1978 to govern how surveillance was conducted on people in the United States. Following September 11, the Bush administration created a secret program of wiretapping that operated outside of FISA rules; the program was uncovered in 2005. Congress argued that the program had to obtain warrants according to FISA rules, but the administration countered that this would hurt the program's effectiveness. In 2008 Congress passed a bill that allowed expanded surveillance capabilities beyond FISA and gave immunity to phone companies that had cooperated with the secret program.

2007

Michael Mukasey Confirmation Hearings

During the confirmation hearings for Attorney General Michael Mukasey in 2007, a major argument was whether waterboarding was considered a form of torture. The U.S. Justice Department had previously argued in classified memos that it was not torture, and the method was used on terrorist suspects. Others argued the use of waterboarding violated prisoner protections established in the Geneva Convention.

The President

Presidents as well can be involved in resolving disputes over rights. They can get involved by having administration officials lobby the Supreme Court to encourage outcomes they favor. Popular presidents can also try to persuade Congress to go along with their policy initiatives by bringing public pressure to bear. Their influence can be used to expand or contract the protection of individual rights. In the 1950s President Dwight Eisenhower was reluctant to enforce desegregation in the South, believing that it was the job of the states, not the federal government.[11] President John Kennedy chose more active involvement when he sent Congress a civil rights bill in 1963 (it was signed by Lyndon Johnson in 1964). More recently, President Obama moved to close the detention center at Guantánamo Bay that had been the center of so much controversy, but logistical and political difficulties, including action by Congress to block the funds for the transfer of detainees to

habeas corpus the right of an accused person to be brought before a judge and informed of the charges and evidence against him or her

mainland prisons, have left the center open and Obama turned his attention to making some improvements in the prisoners' lives, including the banning of brutal interrogations.

The People

Finally, the American people themselves are actors in the struggle over rights. Individual Americans may use the courts to sue for what they perceive as their rights, but more often individuals act in groups. One of the best known of these groups is the ACLU. The ACLU's goal is to defend the liberties of Americans, whatever their ideological position. Thus the ACLU would be just as likely to fight for the right of the American Nazi Party to stage a march as it would be to support a group of parents and students challenging the removal of books with gay themes from a high school library, and in fact it has been critical of both the Bush administration and the Obama administration for their support of wiretapping and surveillance of individuals.[12] Other interest groups that get involved in the effort to resolve rights conflicts include the National Association for the Advancement of Colored People (NAACP), the National Organization for Women (NOW), the Christian Coalition, Common Cause, environmental groups like the Sierra Club, AARP (formerly the American Association of Retired Persons), and the National Rifle Association (NRA). These groups and many others like them engage in fundraising and public relations activities to publicize their views and work to influence government directly, by meeting with lawmakers and testifying at congressional hearings. Even though individuals may not feel very effective in trying to change what government does, in groups their efforts are magnified, and the effects can be considerable.

Who What How

Citizens of democracies have a vital stake in the issue of fundamental rights. What they stand to gain is more power for themselves and less for government. But citizens also have at stake the resolution of the very real conflicts that arise as all citizens try to exercise their rights simultaneously. And as citizens try to maximize their personal freedoms, they are likely to clash with governmental rules that suppress some individual freedom in exchange for public order. The means for resolving these conflicts are to be found in the Constitution, in the exercise of judicial review by the Supreme Court, in congressional legislation and presidential persuasion, and in the actions of citizens themselves, engaging in interest group activities and litigation.

The Bill of Rights and Incorporation
Keeping Congress and the state governments in check

The Bill of Rights looms large in any discussion of American civil liberties, but the document that today seems so inseparable from American citizenship had a stormy birth. Controversy raged over whether a bill of rights was necessary in the first place, deepening the split between Federalists and Anti-Federalists during the founding. And the controversy did not end once it was firmly established as the first ten amendments to the Constitution. Over a century passed before the Supreme Court agreed that at least some of the restrictions imposed on the national government by the Bill of Rights should be applied to the states as well.

Why Is a Bill of Rights Valuable?

Recall from Chapter 3 that we came very close to not having any Bill of Rights in the Constitution at all. The Federalists had argued that the Constitution itself was a bill of rights, that individual rights were already protected by many of the state constitutions, and that to list the powers that the national government did *not* have was dangerous, as it implied that it *did* have every other power. Alexander Hamilton had spelled out this argument in *Federalist* No. 84, and James Madison agreed, at least initially, calling the effort to pass such "parchment barriers," as he called the first ten amendments, a "nauseous project."[13]

But Madison, in company with some of the other Federalists, came to agree with such Anti-Federalists as Thomas Jefferson, who wrote, "A bill of rights is what the people are entitled to against every government on earth."[14] Even though, as the Federalists argued, the national government was limited in principle by popular sovereignty (the concept that ultimate authority rests with the people), it could not hurt to limit it in practice as well. A specific list of the rights held by the people would give the judiciary a more effective check on the other branches.

To some extent Hamilton was correct in calling the Constitution a bill of rights in itself. Protection of some very specific rights is contained in the text of the document. The national government may not suspend writs of ***habeas corpus***, which means that it cannot fail to bring prisoners, at their request, before a judge and inform the court why they are

bills of attainder laws under which specific persons or groups are detained and sentenced without trial

ex post facto laws laws that criminalize an action after it occurs

incorporation Supreme Court action making the protections of the Bill of Rights applicable to the states

selective incorporation incorporation of rights on a case-by-case basis

being held and what evidence is against them. This provision protects people from being imprisoned solely for political reasons. Both the national and the state governments are forbidden to pass **bills of attainder**, which are laws that single out a person or group as guilty and impose punishment without trial. Neither can they pass **ex post facto laws**, which are laws that make an action a crime after the fact, even though it was legal when carried out. States may not impair or negate the obligation of contracts; here the founders obviously had in mind the failings of the Articles of Confederation. And the citizens of each state are entitled to "the privileges and immunities of the several states," which prevents any state from discriminating against citizens of other states. This provision protects a nonresident's right to travel freely, conduct business, and have access to state courts while visiting another state.[15] Of course, nonresidents are discriminated against when they have to pay a higher nonresident tuition to attend a state college or university, but the Supreme Court has ruled that this type of "discrimination" is not a violation of the privileges and immunities clause.

For the Anti-Federalists, these rights, almost all of them restrictions on the national and state governments with respect to criminal laws, did not provide enough security against potential abuse of government power. The first ten amendments add several more categories of restrictions on government. Although twelve amendments had been proposed, two were not ratified: one concerned the apportionment of members of Congress, and the other barred midterm pay raises for them. (The congressional pay raise amendment, which prevents members of Congress from voting themselves a salary increase effective during that term of office, was passed as the Twenty-seventh Amendment in 1992.) Amendments One through Ten were ratified on December 15, 1791. See Table 5.1 for details on the provisions of the Bill of Rights.

Applying the Bill of Rights to the States

If you look closely at the Bill of Rights, you'll see that most of the limitations on government action are directed toward Congress. "Congress shall make no law . . . ," begins the First Amendment. Nothing in the text of the first ten amendments would prevent the Oregon legislature, for instance, from passing a law restricting the freedoms of Oregon newspaper editors to criticize the government. Until about the turn of the twentieth century, the Supreme Court clearly stipulated that the Bill of Rights applied only to the national government and not to the states.[16]

Not until the passage of the Fourteenth Amendment in 1868 did the Constitution make it possible for the Court to require that states protect their citizens' basic liberties. That post–Civil War amendment was designed specifically to force southern states to extend the rights of citizenship to African Americans, but its wording left it open to other interpretations. The amendment says, in part,

> No state shall make or enforce any law which shall abridge the privileges and immunities of citizens of the United States; nor shall any state deprive any person of life, liberty, or property, without due process of law; nor deny to any person within its jurisdiction the equal protection of the laws.

In 1897 the Supreme Court tentatively began the process of nationalization, or **incorporation**, of most (but not all) of the protections of the Bill of Rights into the states' Fourteenth Amendment obligations to guarantee their citizens due process of law.[17]

Not until the case of *Gitlow v. New York* (1925), however, did the Court begin to articulate a clear theory of incorporation. In *Gitlow*, Justice Edward Sanford wrote, "We may and do assume that freedom of speech and of the press . . . are among the fundamental rights and liberties protected . . . from impairment by the states."[18] Without any great fanfare, the Court reversed almost a century of ruling by assuming that some rights are so fundamental that they deserve protection by the states as well as the federal government. This approach meant that all rights did not necessarily qualify for incorporation; the Court had to consider each right on a case-by-case basis to see how fundamental it was. This was a tactic that Justice Benjamin N. Cardozo called **selective incorporation**. Over the years the Court has switched between a theory of selective incorporation and total incorporation. As a result, almost all the rights in the first ten amendments have been incorporated, with some notable exceptions, such as the Second Amendment (see Table 5.2).

Keep in mind that since incorporation is a matter of interpretation rather than an absolute constitutional principle, it is a judicial creation. What justices create they can also uncreate if they change their minds or if the composition of the Court changes. Like all other judicial creations, the process of incorporation is subject to reversal, and it is possible that such a reversal may currently be under way as today's more

Table 5.1

Protections of the Bill of Rights

The first ten amendments to the Constitution, known as the Bill of Rights, were passed by Congress on September 25, 1789, and ratified two years later, on December 15, 1791. See the Appendix for the actual wording of each amendment.

First Amendment	Prohibits government establishment of religion Protects the free exercise of religion Protects freedom of speech and the press Protects freedom of assembly Protects the right to petition government "for a redress of grievances"
Second Amendment	Protects the right to bear arms in order to maintain a well-regulated militia
Third Amendment	Prohibits the quartering of soldiers in homes during peacetime Requires legal authorization for quartering of soldiers during war
Fourth Amendment	Protects against "unreasonable searches and seizures" Allows judges to issue search warrants only with "probable cause"
Fifth Amendment	Requires a grand jury indictment before a person can be tried for a serious crime Prohibits "double jeopardy" (repeated prosecution for the same offense after being found innocent) Prohibits the government from forcing any person in a criminal case to be a witness against himself or herself Prohibits the government from depriving a person of "life, liberty, or property" without due process Requires that just compensation be paid for property taken for public use
Sixth Amendment	Requires that the accused in a criminal case receive a speedy and public trial, heard by a jury in the district where the crime took place Requires that the accused be informed of the nature and cause of the accusation, be confronted with the witnesses against him or her, have the right to call witnesses who could be favorable to his or her case, and receive the assistance of counsel
Seventh Amendment	Requires a jury trial in civil cases involving more than $20 and requires that juries be the final finders of fact except as provided for by common law
Eighth Amendment	Prohibits excessive bail and excessive fines Prohibits cruel and unusual punishment
Ninth Amendment	States that the rights of the people are not limited to those spelled out in the Constitution
Tenth Amendment	Guarantees that the states or the people retain any powers not expressly given to the national government or prohibited to the states

conservative Court narrows its understanding of the rights that states must protect.

Who What How

Because rights are so central to a democracy, citizens clearly have a stake in seeing that they are guaranteed these rights at every level of government. The Bill of Rights guarantees them at the federal level, but it is through the process of incorporation into the Fourteenth Amendment that they are guaranteed at the state level unless the state constitution also provides guarantees. Incorporation, as a judicial creation, is not on as firm a ground as the Bill of Rights because it can be reversed if the Supreme Court changes its mind.

The Supreme Court also has a stake here. It has considerably expanded its power over the states and within the federal government by virtue of its interpretation of the Fourteenth Amendment and its creation of the process of incorporation.

Freedom of Religion

Limiting Congress to protect both church and state, as well as the individual's right to believe

The First Amendment reads, "Congress shall make no law respecting an establishment of religion, or prohibiting the free exercise thereof; or abridging the freedom of speech, or

Table 5.2

Applying the Bill of Rights to the States

Amendment	Addresses	Case	Year
Fifth	Just compensation	Chicago, Burlington & Quincy v. Chicago	1897
First	Freedom of speech	Gilbert v. Minnesota	1920
		Gitlow v. New York	1925
		Fiske v. Kansas	1927
	Freedom of the press	Near v. Minnesota	1931
Sixth	Counsel in capital cases	Powell v. Alabama	1932
First	Religious freedom (generally)	Hamilton v. Regents of California	1934
	Freedom of assembly	DeJonge v. Oregon	1937
	Free exercise	Cantwell v. Connecticut	1940
	Religious establishment	Everson v. Board of Education	1947
Sixth	Public trial	In re Oliver	1948
Fourth	Unreasonable search and seizure	Wolf v. Colorado	1949
	Exclusionary rule	Mapp v. Ohio	1961
Eighth	Cruel and unusual punishment	Robinson v. California	1962
Sixth	Counsel in felony cases	Gideon v. Wainwright	1963
Fifth	Self-incrimination	Malloy v. Hogan	1964
Sixth	Impartial jury	Parker v. Gladden	1966
	Speedy trial	Klopfer v. North Carolina	1967
	Jury trial in serious crimes	Duncan v. Louisiana	1968
Fifth	Double jeopardy	Benton v. Maryland	1969

of the press; or the right of the people peaceably to assemble, and to petition the government for a redress of grievances." These are the "democratic freedoms," the liberties that the founders believed to be necessary to maintain a representative democracy by ensuring a free and unfettered people. For all that, none of these liberties has escaped controversy, and none has been interpreted by the Supreme Court to be absolute or unlimited. Beginning with freedom of religion, we will look at each clause of the First Amendment, the controversy and power struggles surrounding it, and the way the courts have interpreted and applied it.

The briefest look around the world tells us what happens when politics and religion are allowed to mix. When it comes to conflicts over religion, over our fundamental beliefs about the world and the way life should be lived, the stakes are enormous. Passions run deep, and compromise is difficult.

So far the United States has been spared the sort of violent conflict that arises when one group declares its religion to be the one true faith for the whole polity. One reason for this is that Americans are largely Christian, although they belong to many different sects (see "*Who Are We?* Americans and Religion"), so there hasn't been too much disagreement over basic beliefs. But another reason that violent conflict over religion is limited in the United States is the First Amendment, whose first line guarantees that "Congress shall make no law respecting an establishment of religion or prohibiting the free exercise thereof." Although this amendment has generated a tremendous amount of controversy, it has at the same time established general guidelines with which most people can agree and a venue (the courts) where conflicts can be aired and addressed. The establishment clause and the free exercise clause, as the two parts of that guarantee are known, have become something of a constitutional battleground in American politics, but they have kept the United States from becoming a battleground of a more literal sort by deflecting religious conflict to the courts.

▶ Who Are We?

Americans and religion

America is a religious nation. More of us say we are religious than do citizens in other Western nations (even those with official state churches), and many of us see our religion as a source of our national strength. Yet we are also tolerant of religious views other than our own, and half of us feel that it is possible to live a moral life without believing in God. This combination of faith and tolerance echoes the conflicts inherent in the First Amendment. What is the relationship between religious values and a nation's civic life?

Our Religious Identities: Very religious, but many religions

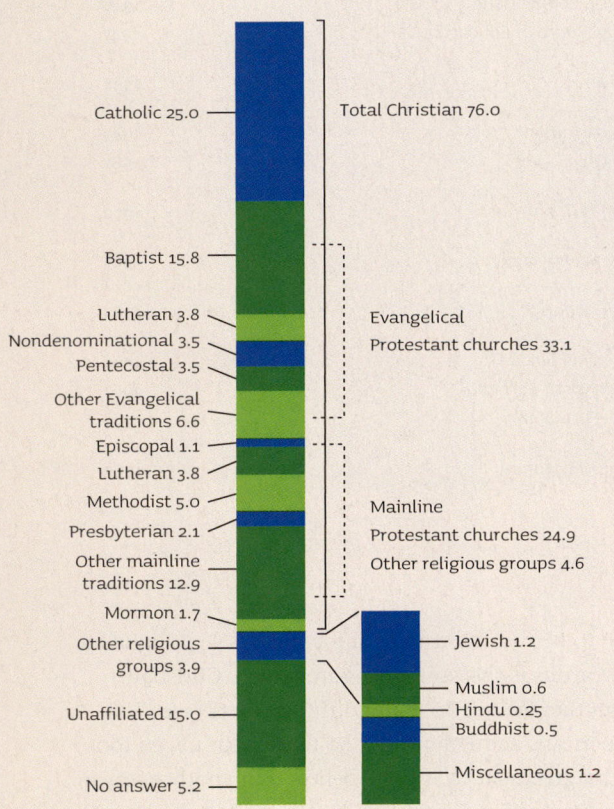

Catholic 25.0 — Total Christian 76.0

Baptist 15.8

Lutheran 3.8
Nondenominational 3.5 — Evangelical
Pentecostal 3.5 — Protestant churches 33.1
Other Evangelical
traditions 6.6
Episcopal 1.1
Lutheran 3.8
Methodist 5.0
Presbyterian 2.1 — Mainline
Other mainline — Protestant churches 24.9
traditions 12.9 — Other religious groups 4.6
Mormon 1.7
Other religious — Jewish 1.2
groups 3.9
— Muslim 0.6
Unaffiliated 15.0 — Hindu 0.25
— Buddhist 0.5
— Miscellaneous 1.2
No answer 5.2

Source: "American Religious Identification Survey 2008," Trinity College, www.americanreligionsurvey-aris.org/reports/ARIS_Report_2008.pdf.

The Strength of Our Belief: Question: How often do you attend religious services?

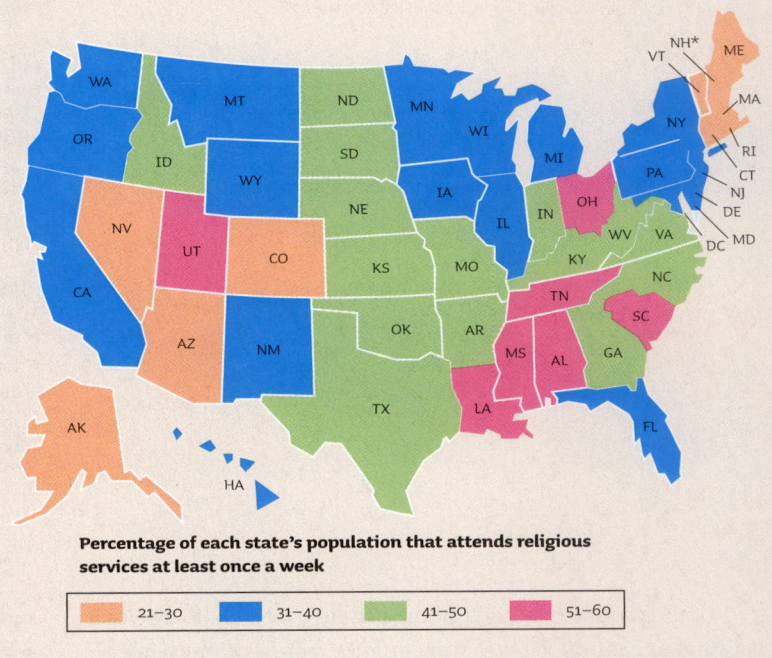

Percentage of each state's population that attends religious services at least once a week

| 21–30 | 31–40 | 41–50 | 51–60 |

Source: The Pew Forum on Religion and Public Life, "U.S. Religious Landscape Survey," http://religions.pewforum.org/maps.

Why Is Religious Freedom Valuable?

While not all the founders endorsed religious freedom for everyone, some of them, notably Jefferson and Madison, cherished the notion of a universal freedom of conscience, the right of all individuals to believe as they pleased. Jefferson wrote that the First Amendment built "a wall of separation between church and state."[19] They based their view of religious freedom on three main arguments. First, history has shown, from the Holy Roman Empire to the Church of England, that when church and state are linked, all individual freedoms are in jeopardy. After all, if government is merely the arm of God, what power of government cannot be justified?

Religious Tolerance and the Role of Religion in American Life: Which is closer to your own views?

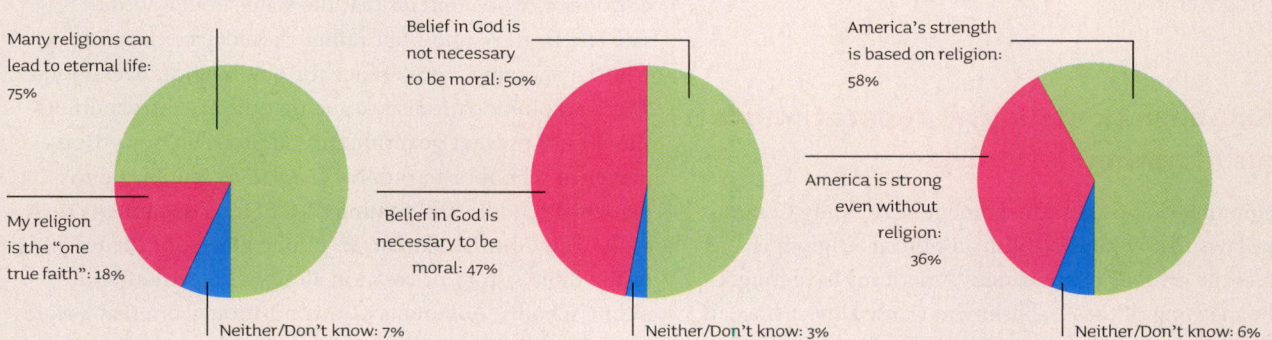

Many religions can lead to eternal life: 75%

My religion is the "one true faith": 18%

Neither/Don't know: 7%

Belief in God is not necessary to be moral: 50%

Belief in God is necessary to be moral: 47%

Neither/Don't know: 3%

America's strength is based on religion: 58%

America is strong even without religion: 36%

Neither/Don't know: 6%

Source: The Pew Forum on Religion and Public Life, "Americans Struggle With Religion at Home and Abroad," press release, March 20, 2002.

Our Religious Beliefs Compared to Other Nations: Americans take religion very seriously.

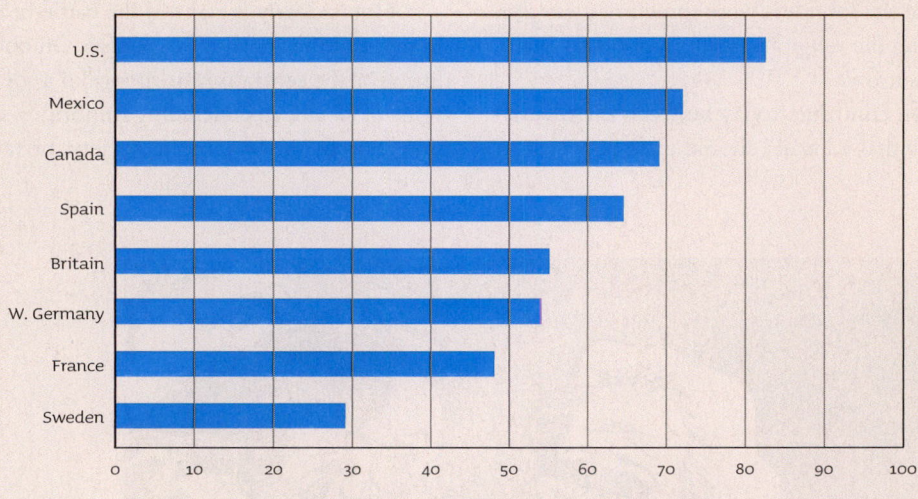

U.S.
Mexico
Canada
Spain
Britain
W. Germany
France
Sweden

0 10 20 30 40 50 60 70 80 90 100

Percentage of people who say they are a "religious person"

Source: *The Public Perspective*, October/November 1997. Survey by the World Values Study Group, 1990–1993.

A second argument for practicing religious freedom is based on the effect that politics can have on religious concerns. Early champions of a separation between politics and religion worried that the spiritual purity and sanctity of religion would be ruined if it mixed with the worldly realm of politics, with its emphasis on power and influence.[20] Further, if religion became dependent on government, in Madison's words, it would result in "pride and indolence in the clergy; ignorance and servility in the laity; in both, superstition, bigotry and persecution."[21]

Finally, as politics can have negative effects on religion, so too can religion have negative effects on politics, dividing society into the factions that Madison saw as the primary threat to republican government. Religion, Madison feared,

establishment clause the First Amendment guarantee that the government will not create and support an official state church

separationists supporters of a "wall of separation" between church and state

accommodationists supporters of government nonpreferential accommodation of religion

could have a divisive effect on the polity only if it became linked to government.

The Establishment Clause: Separationists Versus Accommodationists

The beginning of the First Amendment, forbidding Congress to make laws that would establish an official religion, is known as the **establishment clause**. Americans have fought over the meaning of the establishment clause almost since its inception. While founders like Jefferson and Madison were clear on their position that church and state should be separate realms, other early Americans were not. After independence, for instance, all but two of the former colonies had declared themselves to be "Christian states."[22] Non-Christian minorities were rarely tolerated or allowed to participate in politics. Jews could not hold office in Massachusetts until 1848.[23] It may be that the founders were sometimes less concerned with preserving the religious freedom of others than with guaranteeing their own.

A similar division continues today between the **separationists**, who believe that a "wall" should exist between church and state, and the nonpreferentialists, or **accommodationists**, who contend that the state should not be separate from religion but rather should accommodate it, without showing a preference for one religion over another. These accommodationists argue that the First Amendment should not prevent governmental aid to religious groups, prayer in school or in public ceremonies, public aid to parochial schools, the posting of religious documents such as the Ten Commandments in public places, or the teaching of the Bible's story of creation along with evolution in public schools. Adherents of this position claim that a rigid interpretation of separation of church and state amounts to intolerance of their religious rights or, in the words of Supreme Court Justice Anthony Kennedy, to "unjustified hostility to religion."[24] President Reagan, both Presidents Bush, and many Republicans have shared this view, as have many powerful interest groups such as the Christian Coalition.

A lot is clearly at stake in the battle between the separationists and the accommodationists. On one side of the dispute is the separationists' image of a society in which the rights of all citizens, including minorities, receive equal protection by the law. In this society, private religions

The Devil Is in the Details
Supporters of intelligent design theory seek to replace accounts of evolution in schoolbooks with the idea that the universe was created by a higher power according to a divine plan. Critics of this movement, such as this cartoonist, claim that this asks public schools to take a role in teaching religion, which intelligent design opponents believe is barred by the First Amendment.

Lemon test three-pronged rule used by the courts to determine whether the establishment clause is violated

free exercise clause the First Amendment guarantee that citizens may freely engage in the religious activities of their choice

abound, but they remain private, not matters for public action or support. Very different is the view of the accommodationists, which emphasizes the sharing of community values, determined by the majority and built into the fabric of society and political life.

Recent Rulings on the Establishment Clause

Today U.S. practice stands somewhere between these two images. Sessions of Congress open with prayers, for instance, but a schoolchild's day does not. Religion is not kept completely out of our public lives, but the Court has generally leaned toward a separationist stance. In the 1960s the Court tried to cement this stance, refining a test that made it unconstitutional for the government to pass laws that affect religion unless the laws have a "secular intent" (that is, a nonreligious intent) and "a primary effect that neither advances nor inhibits religion."[25] In two separate cases the Court decided that laws requiring prayer or the reading of biblical verses in public schools violated the Constitution, and that permitting children to be excused did not reduce the unconstitutionality of the original laws.[26] In an earlier case the Court had ruled that even nondenominational prayer could not be required of children in public schools,[27] and in 1968 the Court struck down an Arkansas law prohibiting the teaching of evolution in public schools.[28] With these rulings the Court was aligning itself firmly with the separationist interpretation of the establishment clause.

The Lemon Test

But the Court in the 1960s, under the leadership of Chief Justice Earl Warren, was known for its liberal views, even though Warren, himself a Republican, had been appointed to the Court by President Eisenhower. As the more conservative appointments of Republican presidents Richard Nixon and Reagan began to shape the Court, the Court's rulings moved in a more accommodationist direction. In *Lemon v. Kurtzman* (1971), the Court added to the old test a third provision that a law not foster "an excessive government entanglement with religion."[29] Under the new **Lemon test** the justices had to decide how much entanglement there was between politics and religion, leaving much to their own discretion.

As the current rule in deciding establishment cases, the *Lemon* test is not used consistently, primarily because the justices have not settled among themselves the underlying issue of whether religion and politics should be separate, or

whether state support of religion is permissible.[30] While the justices still lean in a separationist direction, their rulings occasionally nod at accommodationism. In 1984 they allowed a Rhode Island display of a crèche at Christmas (accommodationist);[31] in 1985 they struck down an Alabama law requiring a moment of silence before the public school day began (separationist);[32] in 1987 they rejected a Louisiana law requiring schools to teach creationism (separationist);[33] in 1990 they upheld a federal law (the Equal Access Act of 1984) requiring public high schools to permit religious and political clubs to meet as extracurricular activities (accommodationist);[34] in 1992 they disallowed prayer at graduation ceremonies (separationist);[35] in 2000 they ruled that prayers led by students at high school football games were unconstitutional (separationist);[36] and in 2004 they ruled that a state could keep a state scholarship from a student who wanted to major in pastoral ministries (separationist).[37] Also in 2004, the Supreme Court heard a case on the inclusion of the phrase "one nation under God" in the Pledge of Allegiance. The Court failed to rule on the merits of the case this time, making its decision on other grounds, but the Court will likely have to rule on the constitutionality of the Pledge at some point in the future.

The Free Exercise Clause: When Can States Regulate Religious Behavior?

Religious freedom is controversial in the United States not just because of the debate between the separationists and the accommodationists. Another question that divides the public and justices alike is what to do when religious beliefs and practices conflict with state goals. The second part of the First Amendment grant of religious freedom guarantees that Congress shall make no law prohibiting the free exercise of religion. Seemingly straightforward, the *free exercise clause*, as it is called, has generated as much controversy as the establishment clause. For example, what is the solution when a religious belief against killing clashes with compulsory military service during a war, or when religious holy days are ignored by state legislation about the days individuals should be expected to work? When is the state justified in regulating religions? The Court decided in 1940 that there is a difference between the freedom to believe and the freedom to act on those beliefs.[38] While Americans have an absolute right to believe whatever they want, their freedom to act is subject to government regulation. The state's

> **police power** the ability of the government to protect its citizens and maintain social order

> **compelling state interest** a fundamental state purpose, which must be shown before the law can limit some freedoms or treat some groups of people differently

police power allows it to protect its citizens, providing social order and security. If it needs to regulate behavior, it may. These two valued goods of religious freedom and social order are bound to conflict, and the Court has had an uneasy time trying to draw the line between them.

The Court's ambivalence can be seen in two cases, three years apart, concerning the obligation to salute the flag. In *Minersville School District v. Gobitis* (1940), two children of a Jehovah's Witness family were expelled from school for violating a rule that required them to salute the flag each day.[39] For a Jehovah's Witness, saluting the flag would amount to worshiping a graven image (idol), which their religion forbids. Their father brought suit, claiming that the rule violated his children's freedom of religion. The Court rejected his claim, arguing that children are required to salute the flag to promote national unity, which in turn fosters national security. Within three years, however, the composition of the Court had changed, and several members had changed their minds. In *West Virginia State Board of Education v. Barnette* (1943), children of Jehovah's Witnesses were again expelled for refusing to salute the flag, but this time the Court overturned the school board's rule requiring the salute.[40]

While *Barnette* still holds, the Court has gone back and forth on other religious freedom issues as it has struggled to define what actions the state might legitimately seek to regulate. Under their police power, states have been allowed to require that businesses close on Sundays, or that certain merchandise not be sold then. In *The Blue Law Cases,* the Court argued that the states are within their rights to require Sunday closings as a provision for a day of rest, and that the Sunday closing laws, while religious in origin, no longer contain religious intent.[41] In *Sherbert v. Verner* (1963), however, the Court seemed to contradict itself. A Seventh Day Adventist, for whom Saturday is the Sabbath, was fired from a company for refusing to work on Saturday and was denied unemployment compensation when she refused to take other jobs with compulsory Saturday hours. A lower court ruled in favor of the woman, and the case was appealed to the Supreme Court. The Court upheld *Sherbert,* finding the denial of benefits to be a clear violation of her constitutional rights. The Court wrote that any incidental burden placed on religious freedom must be justified by a **compelling state interest**; that is, the state must show that it is absolutely necessary for some fundamental state purpose that the religious freedom be limited.[42] How the Court determines what is and what is not a compelling state interest is examined in Chapter 6.

The Court rejected this compelling state interest test, however, in *Employment Division, Department of Human Resources v. Smith,* when it upheld a law denying state unemployment benefits to employees of a drug rehabilitation organization who were fired for using peyote, a hallucinogenic drug, for sacramental purposes in religious ceremonies.[43] Here the Court abandoned its ruling in *Sherbert* and held that if the infringement on religion is not intentional but is rather the byproduct of a general law prohibiting socially harmful conduct, applied equally to all religions, then it is not unconstitutional. It found that the compelling state interest test, while necessary for cases dealing with matters of race and free speech, was inappropriate for religious freedom issues. Under the *Smith* ruling, a number of religious practices have been declared illegal by state laws on the grounds that the laws do not unfairly burden any particular religion.

Religious groups consider the *Smith* ruling a major blow to religious freedom because it places the burden of proof on the individual or church to show that its religious practices should not be punished, rather than on the state to show that the interference with religious practice is absolutely necessary. In response to the *Smith* decision, Congress in 1993 passed the Religious Freedom Restoration Act (RFRA). This act, supported by a coalition of ninety religious groups, restored the compelling state interest test for state action limiting religious practice and required that when the state did restrict religious practice, it be carried out in the least burdensome way. However, in the 1997 case of *City of Boerne v. Flores,* the Court held that the RFRA was an unconstitutional exercise of congressional power and that it constituted too great an intrusion on government power.[44] Congress amended the act in 2003 to apply only to the federal government, and many states passed their own RFRAs to protect religious practices at the state level. The Supreme Court in 2006 affirmed the amended federal RFRA when it ruled that the act protected a New Mexico church's use of tea containing an illegal substance for sacramental purposes, reinstating the compelling state interest test.[45]

When Is a Religion a Religion?

Finally, religious freedom is controversial because it raises some thorny questions: What *is* religion? Can any group call itself a religion? If it does so, is it entitled to constitutional protection? Are all its practices protected? Should nonreligion (like atheism or agnosticism) be similarly protected?

In *Reynolds v. U.S.* (1878) and subsequent cases, the Court has upheld a congressional statute prohibiting polygamy against a Mormon who claimed that his religion required him to marry many wives.[46] In *Reynolds*, the Court said that because religion is not defined in the Constitution, the justices must look elsewhere to determine the founders' intentions. A historical analysis led them to the conclusion that, as the Mormon Church did not exist at the time of the founding, and polygamy was not associated with any religion practiced then, it was not a behavior the founders would have meant to protect. The law was constitutional, given government's right to enforce standards of "civilized society."

The Court also confronted the question of what constitutes religion in a number of cases dealing with conscientious objections to serving in war. Here the question was not whether Congress could force someone to go to war against his religious beliefs. Congress had already passed several laws exempting the conscientious objector from military service—first members of well-recognized religious sects like the Quakers and then, in 1940, anyone whose objection was based on "religious training and belief." The Court has had to decide what claims to exemptions under this law were legitimate, and what Congress could and could not exempt without violating anyone's rights. The Court eventually came to argue that "religious training and belief" could be broadly understood, and that even nonreligious objectors could be exempt if they held ethical and moral beliefs parallel to and just as strong as religious convictions.[47] Thus, in some cases, the Court protected the rights of atheists and agnostics as well as members of organized religious groups.

Who What How

All citizens have a stake in a society where they are not coerced to practice a religion in which they do not believe, and where they cannot be prevented from practicing the religion in which they do believe. The rules that help them get what they want here are the establishment clause and the free exercise clause of the First Amendment. There is, however, an inherent conflict between those two clauses. If there truly is a wall of separation between church and state, as the separationists want, then restrictions on religious practice are permissible, which is the opposite of what the accommodationists seek. The only solution is to find a level of separation that the separationists can tolerate that is compatible with a level of protection that accommodationists can agree to.

Freedom of Expression
Checking government by protecting speech and the press

Among the most cherished of American values is the right to free speech. The First Amendment reads that "Congress shall make no law . . . abridging the freedoms of speech, or of the press" and, at least theoretically, most Americans agree.[48] When it comes to actually practicing free speech, however, our national record is less impressive. In fact, time and again, Congress *has* made laws abridging freedom of expression, often with the enthusiastic support of much of the American public. As a nation we have never had a great deal of difficulty restricting speech we don't like, admire, or respect. The challenge of the First Amendment is to protect the speech we despise.

The ongoing controversy surrounding free speech has kept the Supreme Court busy. On the one hand are claims that the right to speak freely should be absolute, that we should permit no exceptions whatsoever. On the other hand are demands that speech should be limited—perhaps because it threatens national security or unity or certain economic interests; because it is offensive, immoral, or hurtful; because it hinders the judicial process; or because it injures reputations. The Supreme Court has had to navigate a maze of conflicting arguments as it has assessed the constitutionality of a variety of congressional and state laws that do, indeed, abridge the freedom of speech and of the press.

Why Is Freedom of Expression Valuable?

It is easier to appreciate what is at stake in the battles over when and what kind of speech should be protected if we think about just why we value free speech so much in the first place. Four arguments for keeping speech free of restrictions deserve our particular attention:

- *An informed citizenry.* In a democracy, citizens are responsible for participating in their government's decisions. Democratic theory holds that, to participate wisely, citizens must have information about what their government is doing. This requires, at the least, a free press, able to report fully on government's activities. Otherwise, citizens are easily manipulated by those people in government who control the flow of information.

The Importance of a Free Press

The reporting of *Washington Post* journalists Bob Woodward (center) and Carl Bernstein (second from left) on the Watergate break-in and cover-up resulted in congressional investigations and, ultimately, President Richard Nixon's 1974 resignation on the brink of his impeachment. Woodward and Bernstein's work drives home the importance of a free press. Here they discuss story developments with publisher Katherine Graham, managing editor Howard Simons, and executive editor Benjamin Bradlee.

- *A watchdog for government.* By being free to voice criticism of government, to investigate its actions, and to debate its decisions, both citizens and journalists are able to exercise an additional check on government that supplements our valued principle of checks and balances. This watchdog function of freedom of expression helps keep government accountable and less likely to step on our other rights. A perfect example of this was the investigation into the Watergate activities by reporters from the *Washington Post* and other newspapers. Had we not had a free press that allowed the investigation of Watergate, the unscrupulous politics or so-called dirty tricks of the Nixon administration would have continued unchecked.

- *A voice for the minority.* Another reason for allowing free speech in society—even (or especially) speech of which we do not approve—is the danger of setting a precedent of censorship. Censorship in a democracy usually allows the voice of the majority to prevail.

One of the reasons to support minority rights as well as majority rule, however, is that we never know when we may fall into the minority on an issue. If we make censorship a legitimate activity of government, we too will be potentially vulnerable to it.

- *Preservation of the truth.* Political theorist John Stuart Mill argued that the free traffic of all ideas, those known to be true as well as those suspected to be false, is essential in a society that values truth. By allowing the expression of all ideas, we discover truths that we had previously believed to be false (the world is not flat, after all), and we develop strong defenses against known falsehoods like racist and sexist ideas.

If free speech is so valuable, why is it so controversial? Like freedom of religion, free speech requires tolerance of ideas and beliefs other than our own, even ideas and beliefs that we find personally repugnant. Those who are convinced that their ideas are eternally true see no real reason to practice toleration, especially if they are in the majority. It is clear to

sedition speech that criticizes the government to promote rebellion

bad tendency test rule used by the courts that allows speech to be punished if it leads to punishable actions

clear and present danger test rule used by the courts that allows language to be regulated only if it presents an immediate and urgent danger

them that language they view as offensive should be silenced, to create the sort of society they believe should exist.

It is the Supreme Court that has had to balance the claims of those who defend the rights of all speakers and those who think they should be limited. The Court has had to make difficult decisions about how to apply the First Amendment to speech that criticizes government, symbolic speech, obscenity, and other offensive speech, as well as about freedom of the press. How the Court arrived at the very complex and rich interpretation that it generally uses today is a political tale.

Speech That Criticizes the Government

Speech that criticizes the government to promote rebellion, called **sedition**, has long been a target of restrictive legislation, and most of the founders were quite content that it should be so. Of course, all the founders had engaged daily in the practice of criticizing their government when *they* were in the process of inciting their countrymen to revolution against England, so they were well aware of the potential consequences of seditious activity. Now that the shoe was on the other foot, and they were the government, many were far less willing to encourage dissent. It was felt that criticism of government undermined authority and destroyed patriotism, especially during wartime.

Early Restrictions on Speech

It didn't take long for American "revolutionaries" to pass the Alien and Sedition Act of 1798, which outlawed "any false, scandalous writing against the government of the United States." In the early 1800s, state governments in the South punished speech advocating the end of slavery and even censored the mail to prevent the distribution of abolitionist literature. Throughout that century and into the next, all levels of government, with the support and encouragement of public opinion, squashed the views of radical political groups, labor activists, religious sects, and other minorities.[49]

By World War I (1914–1918), freedom of speech and of the press were a sham for many Americans, particularly those holding unorthodox views or views that challenged the status quo. War in Europe was seen as partly due to the influence of evil ideas, and leaders in America were determined to keep those ideas out of the United States. Government clamped down hard on people promoting socialism, anarchism, revolution, and even labor unions. By the end of World War I,

thirty-two of forty-eight states had laws against sedition, particularly prohibiting speech that advocated the use of violence or force to bring about industrial or political change. In 1917 the U.S. Congress had passed the Espionage Act, which made it a crime to "willfully obstruct the recruiting or enlistment service of the United States," and a 1918 amendment to the act spelled out what that meant. It became a crime to engage in "any disloyal . . . scurrilous, or abusive language about the form of government of the United States, . . . or any language intended to bring the form of government of the United States . . . into contempt, scorn, contumely, or disrepute."[50] Such sweeping prohibitions made it possible to arrest people on the flimsiest of pretexts.

The Role of the Supreme Court

Those arrested and imprisoned under the new sedition laws looked to the Supreme Court to protect their freedom to criticize their government, but they were doomed to disappointment. The Court did not dispute the idea that speech criticizing the government could be punished. The question it dealt with was just how bad the speech had to be before it could be prohibited. The history of freedom of speech cases is a history of the Court devising tests for itself to determine if certain speech should be protected or could be legitimately outlawed. In four cases upholding the Espionage Act, the Court used a measure it called the **bad tendency test**, which simply required that for the language to be regulated, it must have "a natural tendency to produce the forbidden consequences." That is, if Congress has the right to outlaw certain actions, it also has the right to outlaw speech that is likely to lead to those actions. This test is pretty easy for prosecutors to meet, so most convictions under the act were upheld.[51]

But in two of those cases, *Schenck v. United States* (1919) and *Abrams v. United States* (1919), Justice Oliver Wendell Holmes began to articulate a new test, which he called the **clear and present danger test**. This test, as Holmes conceived it, focused on the circumstances in which language was used.[52] If no immediately threatening circumstances existed, then the language in question would be protected and Congress could not regulate it. But Holmes's views did not represent the majority opinion of the Court, and the clear and present danger test was slow to catch on.

With the tensions that led to World War II, Congress again began to fear the power of foreign ideas, especially communism, which was seen as a threat to the American way of life. The Smith Act of 1940 made it illegal to advocate the

▶ **Profiles in Citizenship: Bill Maher**

"... if you want to teach somebody something, it's got to be like a pill in the dog's food."

Bill Maher is a big fan of the First Amendment. That's because he says what few of us dare to say, what most of us dare not even think. The gasp of laughter that follows the comedian's one-liners is not just shocked amusement, it's shocked recognition that, uncomfortable, unflattering, and unpalatable as his observations are, they're often right on target. Maher has made a career out of mocking the emperor's anatomy, while most of us are still oohing and aahing over the splendor of his new clothes. Usually the First Amendment saves his bacon.

And sometimes it doesn't. On September 17, 2001, he went on his ABC comedy show, *Politically Incorrect*, and said, about the suicide bombing of the World Trade Center: "We have been the cowards, lobbing cruise missiles from miles away. That's cowardly. Staying in the airplane when it hits the building— say what you want about it, it's not cowardly."

Predictably, in those shaky days of national trouble, all hell broke loose.

Asked about Maher's comment at a White House press briefing, then– press secretary Ari Fleischer replied: "All Americans . . . need to watch what they say, watch what they do." Advertisers balked, and Maher's show was canceled.

He's back now, with a cable show called *Real Time With Bill Maher*, where he continues to speak his mind. Still, there are limits. He says: "I can't get up there every week and just rail about the environment and global warming and whatever is going on that I think is most important. But I push it as far as I can. You've got to try to find entertaining ways to get the message through. I always say, in America if you want to teach somebody something, it's got to be like a pill in the dog's food. You've got to wrap it in the bologna . . . stick it right at the back of his throat so he doesn't even know it's there."

violent overthrow of the government or to belong to an organization that did so. Similarly, as the communist scare picked up speed after the war, the McCarran Act of 1950 required members of the Communist Party to register with the U.S. attorney general. At the same time, Senator Joseph McCarthy was conducting investigations of American citizens to search out communists, and the House Un-American Activities Committee was doing the same thing. The suspicion or accusation of being involved in communism was enough to stain a person's reputation irreparably, even if there were no evidence to back up the claim. Many careers and lives were ruined in the process.

Again the Supreme Court did not weigh in on the side of civil liberties. Convictions under both the Smith and McCarran Acts were upheld. The Court had used the clear and present danger test intermittently in the years since 1919, but usually not as originally intended, to limit speech only in the rarest and most dire of occasions. Instead the clear and present danger test came to be seen as a kind of balancing test in which society's interests in prohibiting the speech were weighed against the value of free speech; consequently, the emphasis on an obvious and immediate danger was lost.

The Court's record as a supporter of sedition laws finally ended with the personnel changes that brought Earl Warren to the position of chief justice. In 1969 the Court overturned the conviction of Charles Brandenburg, a Ku Klux Klan leader who had been arrested under Ohio's criminal syndicalism law. In this case the Court ruled that abstract teaching of violence is not the same as incitement to violence. In other words, political speech could be restricted only if it was aimed at producing or was likely to produce "imminent lawless action." Mere advocacy of specific illegal acts was protected unless it led to immediate illegal activity. In a concurring opinion, Justice William O. Douglas pointed out that it was time to get

The trouble, as he sees it, is that Americans want to fit their beliefs into tidy categories of "liberal" and "conservative" as if that sums up the whole debate. Maher wants us to dig our way out of our comfortable platitudes to reach new truths, even if they're unpopular. He recalls getting booed once on the *Tonight Show* after he berated an animal trainer who had appeared with his tiger. "They're like, please, Mr. Comedown. We just enjoyed a delightful animal show, and I pointed out that animals really don't want to be in show business." New rule, as Maher would say today.

Maher is a libertarian, but, true to his own creed, he is also a bit of everything else, believing fiercely in causes like animal rights, the environment, personal responsibility, and civic education. Today, he says, we've lost the thread to the things that matter. Raised by parents who

served in World War II, Maher grew up thinking that there was a common good worth sacrificing for, "that the world had been to the brink and good citizenship was responsible for saving it. And we have nothing like that today. Nothing." Here's more Maher:

On patriotism:

Well, it means being loyal to your country above other countries. And I am. . . . [But] it has to be put in context and also it has to be put side by side with a greater humanity. . . . Americans who say, "This is the greatest country in the world," without having any clue what goes on in any other countries are just pulling it out of nowhere. There are many things that I'm proud of in this country. I'm proud of how my parents and other people stopped fascism and communism. I'm certainly proud of what we started in 1776. It was

a new dawn of freedom and liberty in the world. But I'm not proud of slavery. I'm not proud of the genocide of the Indians. I'm not proud of much of what goes on today. So I still believe in the promise of America, but most of America looks at itself through rose-colored glasses. And that's not healthy.

On keeping the republic:

Take it upon [yourself] to learn the basics. . . . [K]ids need . . . to learn history. Because kids say to me all the time when I say something from history: "How should I know about that, I wasn't born." Oh, really? So nothing happened before you were born? . . . Kids need to learn history so they can put themselves in the proper place, which is of great insignificance. . . . The problem with kids today is not too little self-esteem, it's too much. And history, I think, learning a big picture, is very important in that. ■

rid of the clear and present danger test because it was so subject to misuse and manipulation. Speech, except when linked with action, he said, should be immune from prosecution.[53] The *imminent lawless action test* continues to be the standard for regulating political speech today.

Symbolic Speech

The question of what to do when speech is linked to action, of course, remained. Many forms of expression go beyond mere speech or writing. Should they also be protected? No one disputes that government has the right to regulate actions and behavior if it believes it has sufficient cause, but what happens when that behavior is also expression? When is an action a form of expression? Is burning a draft card, or wearing an armband to protest a war, or torching the American flag an action or an expression? All these questions, and more,

have come before the Court, which generally has been more willing to allow regulation of symbolic speech than of speech alone, especially if the regulation is not a direct attempt to curtail the speech.

We already saw, under freedom of religion, that the Court has decided that some symbolic expression, such as saluting or not saluting the American flag, is a protected form of speech. But drawing the line between what is and is not protected has been extremely difficult for the Court. In *United States v. O'Brien* (1968), the Court held that burning a draft card at a rally protesting the Vietnam War was not protected speech because the law against burning draft cards was legitimate and not aimed at restricting expression. In that case, Chief Justice Earl Warren wrote, "We think it clear that a government regulation is sufficiently justified if it is within the constitutional power of the Government; if it furthers an important or substantial governmental interest; if the governmental interest

imminent lawless action test rule used by the courts that restricts speech only if it is aimed at producing or is likely to produce imminent lawless action

freedom of assembly the right of the people to gather peacefully and to petition government

Miller test rule used by the courts in which the definition of obscenity must be based on local standards

is unrelated to the suppression of free expression; and if the incidental restriction on alleged First Amendment freedoms is no greater than is essential to the furtherance of that interest."[54] Following that reasoning, in 1969 the Court struck down a school rule forbidding students to wear black armbands as an expression of their opposition to the Vietnam War, arguing that the fear of a disturbance was not a sufficient state interest to warrant the suppression.[55]

One of the most divisive issues of symbolic speech that has confronted the Supreme Court, and indeed the American public, concerns that ultimate symbol of our country, the American flag. There is probably no more effective way of showing one's dissatisfaction with the United States or its policies than burning the Stars and Stripes. In 1969 the Court split five to four when it overturned the conviction of a person who had broken a New York law making it illegal to deface or show disrespect for the flag (he had burned it).[56] Twenty years later, with a more conservative Court in place, the issue was raised again by a similar Texas law. Again the Court divided five to four, voting to protect the burning of the flag as symbolic expression.[57] Because the patriotic feelings of so many Americans were fired up by this ruling, Congress passed the federal Flag Protection Act in 1989, making it a crime to desecrate the flag. In *United States v. Eichman*, the Court declared the federal law unconstitutional for the same reasons it had overturned the New York and Texas laws: all were aimed specifically at "suppressing expression."[58] The only way to get around a Supreme Court ruling of unconstitutionality is to amend the Constitution. Efforts to pass an amendment failed by a fairly small margin in the House and the Senate, meaning that despite the strong feeling of many, flag burning is still considered protected speech in the United States.

The Court has recently proved willing to restrict symbolic speech, however, if it finds that the speech goes beyond expression of a view. In a 2003 ruling, the Court held that cross burning, a favored practice of the Ku Klux Klan and other segregationists that it had previously held to be protected speech, was not protected under the First Amendment if it was intended as a threat of violence. "When a cross burning is used to intimidate, few if any messages are more powerful," wrote Justice Sandra Day O'Connor, speaking for a six-to-three majority. "A state may choose to prohibit only those forms of intimidation that are most likely to inspire fear of bodily harm," if the intent to stir up such fear is clear.[59] The Court noted that cross burning would still be protected as symbolic speech in certain cases, such as at a political rally.

Closely related to symbolic speech is an additional First Amendment guarantee, *freedom of assembly*, or "the right of the people peaceably to assemble, and to petition the government for a redress of grievances." The courts have interpreted this provision to mean not only that people can meet and express their views collectively, but also that their very association is protected as a form of political expression. So, for instance, they have ruled that associations like the NAACP cannot be required to make their membership lists public[60] (although groups deemed to have unlawful purposes do not have such protection) and that teachers do not have to reveal the associations to which they belong.[61] In addition, the Court has basically upheld people's rights to associate with whom they please, although it held that public[62] and, in some circumstances, private groups cannot discriminate on the basis of race or sex.[63]

Obscenity and Pornography

Of all the forms of expression, obscenity has probably presented the Court with its biggest headaches. In attempting to define it in 1964, Justice Potter Stewart could only conclude, "I know it when I see it."[64] The Court has used a variety of tests for determining whether material is obscene, but until the early 1970s, only the most hard-core pornography was regulated.

Coming into office in 1969, however, President Nixon made it one of his administration's goals to control pornography in America. Once the Court began to reflect the ideological change that came with Nixon's appointees, rulings became more restrictive. In 1973 the Court developed the **Miller test**, which returned more control over the definition of obscenity to state legislatures and local standards. Under the Miller test, the Court asks "whether the work depicts or describes, in a patently offensive way, sexual conduct specifically defined by state law" and "whether the work, taken as a whole, lacks serious literary, artistic, political or scientific value" (called the SLAPS test).[65] These provisions have also been open to interpretation, and the Court has tried to refine them over time. The emphasis on local standards has meant that pornographers can look for those places with the most lenient definitions of obscenity in which to produce and market their work, and the Court has let this practice go on.

The question of whether obscenity should be protected speech raises some fundamental issues, and has created some unlikely alliances. Justice John Marshall Harlan was quite right

fighting words speech intended to incite violence

political correctness the idea that language shapes behavior and therefore should be regulated to control its social effects

prior restraint censorship of or punishment for the expression of ideas before the ideas are printed or spoken

when he wrote that "one man's vulgarity is another man's lyric."[66] People offended by what they consider to be obscenity believe that their values should be represented in their communities. If that means banning adult bookstores, nude dancing at bars, and naked women on magazine covers at the supermarket, then so be it. But opponents argue that what is obscene to one person may be art or enjoyment to another. The problem of majorities enforcing decisions on minorities is inescapable here. A second issue that has generated debate over these cases is the feminist critique of pornography: that it represents aggression toward women and should be banned primarily because it perpetuates stereotypes and breeds violence. Thus radical feminists, usually on the left end of the political spectrum, have found themselves in alliance with conservatives on the right. There is a real contradiction here for feminists, who are more often likely to argue for the expansion of rights, particularly as they apply to women. Feminists advocating restrictions on pornography reconcile the contradiction by arguing that the proliferation of pornography ultimately limits women's rights by making life more threatening and fundamentally unequal.

Fighting Words and Offensive Speech

Among the categories of speech that the Court has ruled may be regulated is one called **fighting words**, words whose express purpose is to create a disturbance and incite violence in the person who hears the speech.[67] However, the Court rarely upholds legislation designed to limit fighting words unless the law is written very carefully and specifically. Consequently it has held that threatening and provocative language is protected unless it is likely to "produce a clear and present danger of serious substantive evil that rises far above public inconvenience, annoyance, or unrest."[68]

The Court has also ruled that offensive language, while not protected by the First Amendment, may occasionally contain a political message, in which case constitutional protection applies. For instance, the Court overturned the conviction of a young California man named Paul Cohen who was arrested for violating California's law against "maliciously and willfully disturb[ing] the peace or quiet of any neighborhood or person . . . by . . . offensive conduct." Cohen had worn a jacket in a Los Angeles courthouse that had "Fuck the Draft" written across the back, in protest of the Vietnam War. The Court held that this message was not directed to any specific person who was likely to see the jacket and, further,

there was no evidence that Cohen was in fact inciting anyone to a disturbance. Those who were offended by the message on Cohen's jacket did not have to look at it.[69]

These cases have taken on modern-day significance in the wake of the **political correctness** movement that swept the country in the late 1980s and 1990s, especially on college campuses. Political correctness refers to an ideology, held primarily by some liberals, including some civil rights activists and feminists, that language shapes society in critical ways, and therefore racist, sexist, homophobic, or any other language that demeans any group of individuals should be silenced to minimize its social effects. An outgrowth of the political correctness movement was the passing of speech codes on college campuses that ban speech that might be offensive to women and ethnic and other minorities. Critics of speech codes, and of political correctness in general, argue that such practices unfairly repress free speech, which should flourish, of all places, on college campuses. In 1989 and 1991, federal district court judges agreed, finding speech codes on two campuses, the University of Michigan and the University of Wisconsin, in violation of students' First Amendment rights.[70] Neither school appealed. The Supreme Court spoke on a related issue in 1992 when it struck down a Minnesota "hate crime law." The Court held that it is unconstitutional to outlaw broad categories of speech based on its content. The prohibition against activities that "arouse anger, alarm or resentment in others on the basis of race, color, creed, religion or gender" was too sweeping and thus unconstitutional.[71]

Freedom of the Press

The First Amendment covers not only freedom of speech but also freedom of the press. Many of the controversial issues we have already covered apply to both of these areas, but some problems are confronted exclusively, or primarily, by the press: the issue of prior restraint, libel restrictions, and the conflict between a free press and a fair trial.

Prior Restraint

The founders modeled their ideas about freedom of expression on British common law, which held that it is acceptable to censor writing and speech about the government as long as the censorship occurs *after* publication. **Prior restraint**, a restriction on the press before its message is actually published, was seen as a more dangerous form of censorship since the repressed ideas never entered the public domain and their worth could

Solemn Rights

President Barack Obama participates in the transfer home of a fallen U.S. soldier. The Obama administration reversed the policy of former president George W. Bush, which blocked photographs of returning caskets. Supporters of the policy reversal claim that banning photographs allowed the government to suppress evidence of the human costs of the wars in Iraq and Afghanistan and violated freedom of the press, while critics say the ban allowed families to mourn in private and preserved the dignity of the fallen.

not be debated. The Supreme Court has shared the founders' concern that prior restraint is a particularly dangerous form of censorship and almost never permits it. Two classic judgments illustrate their view. In *Near v. Minnesota*, the Court held that a Minnesota law infringed on a newspaper publisher's freedom of the press. Jay Near's newspaper *The Saturday Press* was critical of African Americans, Jews, Catholics, and organized labor. His paper was shut down in 1927 under a state law that prohibited any publication of "malicious, scandalous and defamatory" materials. If he continued to publish the paper, he would have been subject to a $1,000 fine or a year in jail. While extreme emergency, such as war, might justify previous restraint on the press, wrote Justice Charles Evans Hughes, the purpose of the First Amendment was to limit it to those rare circumstances.[72] Similarly, and more recently, in *New York Times Company v. United States*, the Court prevented the Nixon administration from stopping the publication by the *New York Times* and the *Washington Post* of a "top secret" document about U.S. involvement in Vietnam. These so-called Pentagon Papers were claimed by the government to be too sensitive to national security to be published. The Court held that "security" is too vague to be

allowed to excuse the violation of the First Amendment; to grant such power to the president, it ruled, would be to run the risk of destroying the liberty that the government is trying to secure.[73]

Libel

Freedom of the press also collides with the issue of **libel**, the written defamation of character (verbal defamation is called *slander*). Obviously it is crucial to the watchdog and information-providing roles of the press that journalists be able to speak freely about the character and actions of those in public service. But at the same time, because careers and reputations are easily ruined by rumors and innuendo, journalists ought to be required to "speak" responsibly. The Supreme Court addressed this issue in *New York Times v. Sullivan*. In 1960 a Montgomery, Alabama, police commissioner named Sullivan claimed he had been defamed by an advertisement that had run in the *Times*. The ad, paid for by the Committee to Defend Martin Luther King, had alleged that various acts of racism had taken place in the South, one in particular supported by police action on a Montgomery college campus. Sullivan, claiming that as police commissioner he was associated with the police action and was thus defamed, and arguing that there were factual errors in the story (although only minor ones), sued the *Times* for libel and won.

The *Times* was convinced that officials illegally resisting desegregation in the South would use libel cases to deflect attention from the northern press if this judgment were not challenged. The paper brought a unique defense to the case when it appealed to the Supreme Court. It argued that if government officials could claim personal damages when institutions they controlled were portrayed negatively in the press, and if any inaccuracy at all in the story were sufficient to classify the story as false and thus libelous, then libel law would have the same effect that antisedition laws had once had: neither citizens nor the press could criticize the government—dramatically weakening the protection of the First Amendment.[74]

The Supreme Court accepted the *New York Times* argument, and libel law in the United States was revolutionized. No longer simply a state matter, libel became a constitutional issue under the First Amendment. The Court held that public officials, as opposed to private individuals, when suing for libel, must show that a publication acted with "actual malice," which means not that the paper had an evil intent but only that it acted with "knowledge that [what it printed] was false or with reckless disregard for whether it was false or not."[75] Shortly afterward, the Court extended the ruling to include public figures such as celebrities and political candidates—anyone whose actions put them in a public position.

The Court's rulings attempt to give the press some leeway in its actions. Without *Sullivan*, investigative journalism would never have been able to uncover the U.S. role in Vietnam, for instance, or the Watergate cover-up. Freedom of the press, and thus the public's interest in keeping a critical eye on government, is clearly the winner here. The Court's view is that when individuals put themselves into the public domain, the public's interest in the truth outweighs the protection of those individuals' privacy.

The Right to a Fair Trial

Freedom of the press also confronts head-on another Bill of Rights guarantee, the right to a fair trial. Media coverage of a crime can make it very difficult to find an "impartial jury," as required by the Sixth Amendment. On the other side of this conflict, however, is the "public's right to know." The Sixth Amendment promises a "speedy and public trial," and many journalists interpret this provision to mean that the proceedings ought to be open. The courts, on the other hand, have usually held that this amendment protects the rights of the accused, not of the public. But while the Court has overturned a murder verdict because a judge failed to control the media circus in his courtroom,[76] on the whole it has ruled in favor of media access to most stages of legal proceedings. Likewise, courts have been extremely reluctant to uphold gag orders, which would impose prior restraint on the press during those proceedings.[77]

Censorship on the Internet

Lawmakers do not always know how to deal with new outlets for expression as they become available. Modern technology has presented the judiciary with a host of free speech issues the founders never anticipated. The latest to make it to the courts is the question of censorship on the Internet. Some web sites contain explicit sexual material, obscene language, and other content that many people find objectionable. Since children often find their way onto the Internet on their own, parents and groups of other concerned citizens have clamored for regulation of this medium. Congress obliged in 1996 with the Communications Decency Act (CDA), which made it illegal to knowingly send or display indecent material over the Internet. In 1997 the Supreme Court ruled that such provisions constituted a violation of free speech, and that communication over the Internet, which it called a modern "town crier," is subject to the same protections as nonelectronic expression.[78] When Congress tried again with a more narrowly tailored bill, the Child Online Protection Act, the Court struck it down, too.[79]

The Court has not always ruled on the side of a completely unregulated Internet. While not restricting the creation of content, in 2003 the Supreme Court did uphold the Children's Internet Protection Act, which required public libraries that received federal funds to use filtering software to block material that is deemed harmful to minors, such as pornography.[80] However, these filters can create some problems. Many companies and institutions use them to screen offensive incoming email, but such filters often have unwanted consequences. Since the filters cannot evaluate the material passing through, they can end up blocking even legitimate messages and publications. One editor of a newsletter on technology has resorted to intentionally misspelling words (for example, writing "sez" instead of

P. T. Barnum said there's a sucker born every minute—and that was decades before the advent of the Internet. He would have rubbed his hands in glee over the gullibility of people in the electronic age. While freedom of speech is a powerful liberty, as we have seen in this chapter, one consequence is that it makes it very difficult to silence those making fraudulent or misleading claims. We regulate radio and television, of course, but that is because these media were originally (before the days of cable and satellites) held to be scarce resources that belonged to the public. Private publishers can enforce standards of excellence, or accuracy, or style, on what they publish, but when a medium is quasipublic, like the Internet, and access to it is easy and cheap, it is impossible to restrict the views and ideas that are published without also doing some serious damage to freedom of speech. Consequently anything goes, and it is up to us as consumers to sort the grain from the chaff.

Today we have access to more information than we could ever have imagined, but we are not trained to use it critically and competently. Case in point: A father and son traveled six hours from Canada to Mankato, Minnesota, lured by a web site singing the praises of Mankato's sunny beaches and whale watching opportunities.[1] The site turned out to be a spoof perpetrated by winter-weary Mankato residents. Confronted with the reality of more of the frozen north they had just left, the disillusioned dad was angry, but a reasonable target of his anger might have been his own eagerness and willingness to believe unquestioningly what he read on the web.

All of us, of course—professors, students, politicians, journalists, doctors, lawyers, CEOs, and anyone else with access to the web—are potential suckers. The Internet is merely an electronic link between those who have information to give and those who want information—much like the telephone. Anyone who has the small amount of money needed to set up a web page or a blog can get on the Internet and disseminate information.

The fact that some piece of information appears on a computer screen does not confer any special distinction on it, or make it more reliable than any other rumor we may happen to hear. This is not to disparage everything that you find on the Internet. Some of it is terrific, and our ability to surf the web in search of new information expands our intellectual horizons like nothing has since the invention of the printing press. Of the many fascinating sources of information that you can find online, here are three worthy of special note:

- *Blogs.* Blogs are online "weblogs," a forum in which to keep a public journal of sorts on any subject a writer wants to create. Blogs can be about absolutely anything, including cooking, hunting, drinking, personal issues, medical problems, travel, raising kids, and politics. Oh boy, can they be about politics! Bloggers from the left and right battle daily, crossing the line between journalism and activism, with no requirement that they meet the ethical obligations of either. That doesn't make blogs unreliable sources of information (and it doesn't mean you shouldn't set up your own blog if you are so inclined), but it does mean you should be wary of information you find on a blog and you should always try to figure out where the blogger is coming from so that you can see what impact his or her ideological perspective has on the news he or she conveys.

- *Wikipedia.* On first glance Wikipedia looks like a researcher's dream come true—an online encyclopedia that seems to cover every subject under the sun. What could be better for a harried student writing a term paper or just for a curious person seeking to verify the date of an historical event or a person's name? The only catch with Wikipedia is that it is a communal encyclopedia, written by the people who use it. See something that doesn't strike you as right in a Wikipedia entry? Then go ahead and fix it. The check on what you might add or say are the thousands of eyes watching over your shoulder, correcting your mistakes even as you correct theirs. The collaborative power of Wikipedia creates an amazing resource, but one you need to use warily because the information there is only as good as the last person who edited it. Never rely on it without double-checking!

- *Social networking sites and tools.* Increasing numbers of people get their news from social networking sites like Facebook or from tools like Twitter that allow users to tap into a stream of information from sources they choose to follow. Such tools can be great fun for keeping up with friends or family or for tailoring the information you have coming in, but there are a couple of caveats to keep in mind. The information you get is only as good as the sources you follow. Social networking sites are like a giant back fence over which neighbors chitchat endlessly. Treat what you learn like the gossip it is until you have verified it independently. Also remember that what you post to the Internet is there indefinitely. No privacy protections are perfect, and what you post on your own personal domain may find its way to future employers, partners, in-laws, or even your as-yet unborn children. Don't post anything about yourself that you wouldn't want your kids to see some day!

The Internet is clearly the source of good times and scary scenarios. What allows us to rely on what we find on the Internet is our own hard work and careful scrutiny. Here are some tips to help you become a savvy surfer of the World Wide Web:

1. Find out the source of the web site. Examine the web address, or URL, for clues. Web addresses end with .com, .org, .gov, .net, or .edu to indicate, respectively, commercial, nonprofit, government, network, or educational sites. Sites from other countries end with abbreviations of the nation. For example, .kr indicates the site is from Korea and .fr indicates France. Remember, however, that anyone can purchase rights to a web address; an official-looking address does not necessarily confer legitimacy on a site.

2. Check out the author of the site. Sometimes the author is not who it seems to be—many authors try to disguise the source of their sites to gain respectability for their ideas or to lure users further into a site, or they may seem to support groups or individuals who turn out to be their targets. For example, people looking for information on George W. Bush who visited georgewbush.org or bush2004.com might have been surprised to learn that the sites were maintained by critics of the president.[2]

3. If something about a site does not look right (what one author calls the "J.D.L.R.," or the Just Doesn't Look Right, test), investigate more closely.[3] Be suspicious if, for example, you notice lots of misspellings or grammatical errors, or if the site has an odd design. Analyze the site's tone and approach. When a familiar site doesn't look the way you expect it to, consider the possibility that hackers have broken into it and changed its content. Ultimately, remember this: anyone can put up a web site—even you. Are you a reliable enough source to be quoted in a college student's research paper?

4. Find out who is footing the bill. Whoever said there is no such thing as a free lunch might have been speaking of the Internet. Ultimately our access to the glorious world of cyberspace must be paid for, and since we as consumers seem to be singularly unwilling to pay for the information we find, providers of that information are increasingly looking to advertisers to pick up the bill.[4] Commercial interests can shape the content of what we find on the web in any number of ways: links to sponsors' pages may appear prominently on a web page, web sites may promote the products of their advertisers as if they were objectively recommending them without making the financial relationship clear, or the commercial bias may be even more subtle. One author says that "trusting an Internet site to navigate the World Wide Web . . . is like following a helpful stranger in Morocco who offers to take you to the best rug store. You may very well find what you are looking for, but your guide will get a piece of whatever you spend."[5]

5. Use the Internet to evaluate the Internet. You can find out who runs a site by going to www.internic.net and using the "whois" search function. This will give you names and contact information but is not, warns Tina Kelly of the *New York Times*, conclusive. Similarly, she suggests running authors' names through a search engine or http://groups-beta.google.com, which searches newsgroups, to see what you can find out about them. Some browsers will tell you when a site was last updated. And remember that you can always email authors of a site and ask for their credentials.[6] If no contact information for the author is available on the site itself, that alone can tell you something about its reliability. For more information on how to evaluate various types of web sites, check out the Cornell University Library's site at www.library.cornell.edu/olinuris/ref/research/webeval.html.

6. Note the other kinds of information the site directs you to. If you are in doubt about a site's legitimacy, check some of its links to external sites. Are they up-to-date and well maintained? Do they help you identify the ideological, commercial, or other bias the site may contain? If there are no links to other sites, ask yourself what this might mean.

1. Tina Kelly, "Whales in the Minnesota River? Only on the Web, Where Skepticism Is a Required Navigational Aid," *New York Times*, March 4, 1999, D1.
2. Michel Marriot, "Rising Tide: Sites Born of Hate," *New York Times*, March 18, 1999, G1.
3. Kelly, D1.
4. Saul Hansell and Army Harmon, "Caveat Emptor on the Web: Ad and Editorial Lines Blur," *New York Times*, February 26, 1999, A1.
5. Ibid.
6. Kelly, D9.

"sex") to avoid the automatic sensors that screen many of his readers' mail.[81]

The Internet can also have the effect of freeing people from censorship, however. As many people who have worked on their high school newspapers know, the Court has ruled that student publications are subject to censorship by school officials if the restrictions serve an educational purpose. The Internet, however, offers students an alternate medium of publication that the courts say is not subject to censorship. As a result, students have been able to publish such matters as the results of investigations into school elections and campus violence that have been excluded from the hard-copy newspaper.[82] We can probably expect some flux in the laws on Internet censorship as the courts become more familiar with the medium itself and the issues surrounding it. (See "*Consider the Source*: Don't Be Fooled by the World Wide Web" for some tips on how to evaluate what you find on the Internet.)

No less than the success of free democratic government is at stake in the issue of freedom of expression. This First Amendment liberty, we have argued, produces information about government, limits corruption, protects minorities, and helps maintain a vigorous defense of the truth. But something else is at stake as well—preservation of social order; stable government; and protection of civility, decency, and reputation.

Who What How

It has been left to the courts, using the Constitution, to balance these two desired goods: freedom of expression on the one hand, and social and moral order on the other. The courts have devised several rules, or tests, to try to reconcile the competing claims. Thus we have had the bad tendency test, the clear and present danger test, the *Miller* test, and revised libel laws. The tension between freedom and order lends itself not to a permanent solution, since the circumstances of American life are constantly in flux, but rather to a series of uneasy truces and revised tests.

Thinking Outside the Box

How much free speech do we need on our college campuses?

The Right to Bear Arms
Providing for militias to secure the state or securing an individual right?

The Second Amendment to the Constitution reads, "A well regulated militia, being necessary to the security of a free state, the right of the people to keep and bear arms, shall not be infringed." This amendment has been the subject of some of the fiercest debates in American politics. Originally it was a seemingly straightforward effort by opponents of the Constitution to keep the federal government in check by limiting the power of standing, or permanent, armies. Over time it has become a rallying point for those who want to engage in sporting activities involving guns, those who believe that firearms are necessary for self-defense, those who believe an armed citizenry is necessary to check government that might become tyrannical, and those who simply don't believe that it is government's business to make decisions about who can own guns. (See "*Who Are We?*" on the next page.)

Although various kinds of gun control legislation have been passed at the state and local levels, powerful interest groups like the NRA have kept it to a minimum at the federal level. The 1990s, however, saw the passage of three federal bills that affect the right to bear arms: the 1993 Brady Bill, requiring background checks on potential handgun purchasers (see *Who Are We?* feature); the 1994 Crime Bill barring semiautomatic assault weapons; and a 1995 bill making it illegal to carry a gun near a school. The 1995 law and the interim provisions of the Brady Bill, which imposed a five-day waiting period for all gun sales, with local background checks until a national background check system could be established, were struck down by the Supreme Court on the grounds that they were unconstitutional infringements of the national government into the realm of state power.[83] In September 2004, Congress let the ban on semiautomatic weapons expire, largely at the urging of then–House majority leader Tom DeLay. While some Democrats in Congress promised to reintroduce the ban, many members have been reluctant to act, possibly because the NRA continues to target gun control candidates for defeat in reelections.

Why Is the Right to Bear Arms Valuable?

During the earliest days of American independence, the chief source of national stability was the state militia system—armies of able-bodied men who could be counted on

▶ Who Are We?

Gun Ownership in America

When asked, "In general, do you feel that laws covering the sale of firearms should be made more strict, less strict, or kept as they are now?" 44 percent of the public preferred stricter gun control laws, and 43 percent believed laws should remain as they currently are. When asked, "Do you have a gun in your home?" 42 percent of Americans polled said yes. How might these conflicting public beliefs affect the stance that politicians are likely to take on gun control? Have these beliefs altered over time due to legislation like the 1993 Brady Bill?

Gun Ownership in the U.S., 2009

Question: Should laws covering the sales of firearms be made more strict, less strict, or kept as they are now?

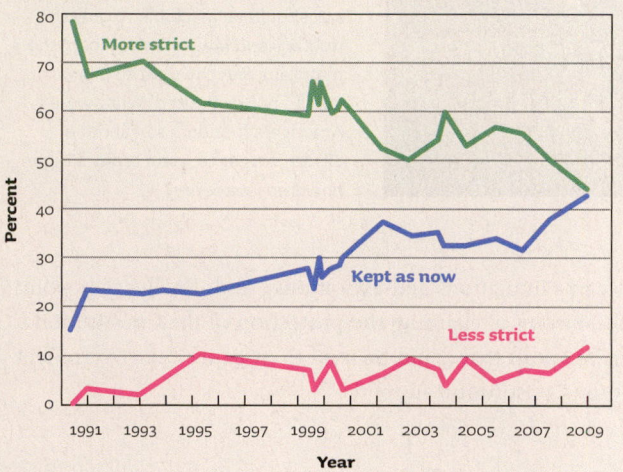

Source: Gallup, "In U.S., Record-Low Support for Stricter Gun Laws," October 9, 2009, www.gallup.com/poll/123596/In-U.S.-Record-Low-Support-Stricter-Gun-Laws.aspx.

Firearms Crimes Before and After Passage of the Brady Bill (1993)

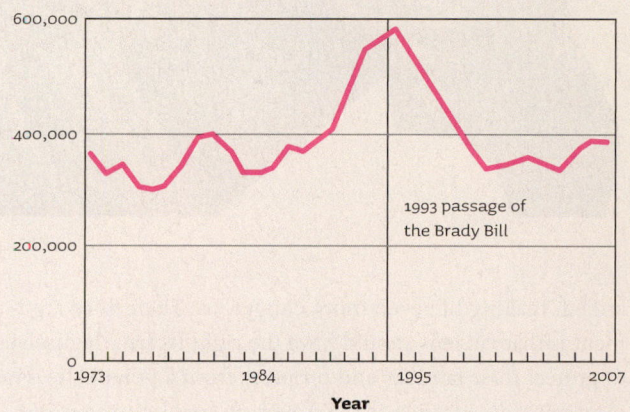

Source: U.S. Department of Justice Bureau of Justice Statistics, "Crimes Committed with Firearms, 1973–2007," http://bjs.ojp.usdoj.gov/content/glance/tables/guncrimetab.cfm.

Note: Crimes included are murder, robbery, and aggravated assault.

---

to assemble, with their own guns, to defend their country from external and internal threats, whether from the British, the Native Americans, or local insurrection. Local militias were seen as far less dangerous to the fledgling republic than a standing army under national leadership. Such an army could seize control and create a military dictatorship, depriving citizens of their hard-won rights. Madison, Hamilton, and Jay devoted five *Federalist Papers* to the defense of standing armies and the unreliability of the militia, but they did not persuade the fearful Anti-Federalists. The Second Amendment was designed to guard against just that tyranny of the federal government.

Arguments in Defense of the Second Amendment Today

The restructuring of the U.S. military, and the growing evidence that under civilian control it did not pose a threat to the liberties of American citizens, caused many people to view the Second Amendment as obsolete. But although the militia system that gave rise to the amendment is now defunct, supporters of rights for gun owners, like the NRA, argue that the amendment is as relevant as ever. They offer at least four reasons the right to bear arms should be unregulated. First, they argue that hunting and other leisure activities involving guns do not hurt anybody (except, of course, the hunted) and are an important part of American culture. They are concerned that even the restriction of weapons not used for hunting, such as assault weapons, will harm their sport by making the idea of regulation more acceptable to Americans and starting society down the slippery slope of gun control. Second, gun rights advocates claim that possession of guns is necessary for self-defense. They believe that gun control means that only criminals, who get their guns on the black market, will be

Serious Shooting
While Americans once used guns for protection, hunting, and sport, changing technology has made high-powered firearms readily accessible to the general public that some say should be available to only the military and law enforcement. Others maintain that the right to bear arms should not be limited. What would America's founders say about a citizen's right to wield today's high-powered weaponry?

armed, making life even more dangerous. Their third argument is that citizens should have the right to arm themselves to protect their families and property from a potentially tyrannical government, just as the American revolutionaries did. Finally, advocates of unregulated gun ownership say that it is not government's business to regulate gun use. The limited government they insist the founders intended does not have the power to get involved in such questions, and any federal action is thus illegitimate.

Arguments Against the Right to Bear Arms

Opponents of these views—such as Handgun Control, Inc., and the Coalition to Stop Gun Violence—counter that none of these claims has anything to do with the Second Amendment, which refers only to the use and ownership of guns by state militia members. They say that gun owners want to make this an issue about rights because that gives their claims a higher status in American discourse, but in fact the issue is merely about their wants and preferences. Americans have long held that wants and preferences can be limited and regulated if they have harmful effects on society. Focusing the debate on rights rather than policy increases the conflict and decreases the chance for resolution.[84] Opponents also assemble facts and comparative data to support their claims that countries with stricter gun control laws have less violence and fewer gun deaths. They remind us that none of the rights of Americans, even such fundamental ones as freedoms of speech and of the press, is absolute, so why should the right to bear arms not

also carry limitations and exceptions? And, finally, they point out the irony of claiming the protection of the Constitution to own weapons that could be used to overturn the government that the Constitution supports.[85]

Judicial Decisions

Until 2008 the Supreme Court had ruled on only a handful of cases that had an impact on gun rights and the Second Amendment, mostly interpreting the Second Amendment as intending to arm state militias, and letting state gun-related legislation stand.[86] The Supreme Court did strike down the legislation concerning possession of guns near schools and reversed one provision of the Brady Bill on federalism, not Second Amendment, grounds. In the close Brady case, four dissenters argued that the burden put on the localities was not disproportionate to the good done by addressing what they called an "epidemic of gun violence."[87] In 2004 the Court let stand a lower court's ruling that supported a California ban on assault rifles on the grounds that the Second Amendment did not protect individual gun owners. The ruling applies only to those states in the Ninth Circuit, however, and does not require a state to ban assault rifles.

In 2008, however, the Supreme Court heard arguments for the first time since 1939 on whether the Constitution guarantees an individual the right to bear arms. In a five-to-four decision, the Court held that it did, striking

Ruling for Gun Rights

Dick Heller, the plaintiff in the Supreme Court case *Heller v. District of Columbia*, holds his gun permit. In 2008 the Court struck down a Washington, D.C. law that banned handgun possession in the home. While the Court relied on a broad interpretation of the Second Amendment, it also noted that the right to bear arms is not unlimited.

down a Washington, D.C., law that banned handgun possession in the home. Although the Court held that the D.C. law violated an individual's right to own a gun for self-protection, the majority was careful to say that the right to own guns is not unlimited. For instance, it does not encompass military-grade weapons, and it does not extend to felons and the mentally ill.[88] In 2010 the Court took the ruling a step further, holding not only that the federal government could not violate an individual's right to bear arms, as it had in the D.C. case, but that neither could a state government.[89]

Some citizens want a protected right to own whatever guns they choose, and others want some regulation on what guns can be owned by private citizens. The rule that should determine who wins and who loses here is the Second Amendment, but though the Supreme Court has been fairly clear that the amendment does not confer an unqualified right to gun ownership on Americans, it also has been reluctant to allow the federal government to impose its will on the states. Consequently the battle is played out in state legislatures and in Congress.

Who What How

> **due process of law** guarantee that laws will be fair and reasonable and that citizens suspected of breaking the law will be treated fairly

The Rights of Criminal Defendants
Protecting the accused from an arbitrary government

A full half of the amendments in the Bill of Rights, and several clauses in the Constitution itself, are devoted to protecting the rights of people who are suspected or accused of committing a crime. These precautions were a particular concern for the founders, who feared an arbitrary government that could accuse and imprison people without evidence or just cause. Governments tend to do such things to shore up their power and to silence their critics. The authors of these amendments believed that, to limit government power, people needed to retain rights against government throughout the process of being accused, tried, and punished for criminal activities. Amendments Four through Eight protect people against unreasonable searches and seizures, self-incrimination, and cruel and unusual punishment, and guarantee them a right to legal advice, a speedy and public trial, and various other procedural protections.

Why Are the Rights of Criminal Defendants Valuable?

As we indicated, a primary reason for protecting the rights of the accused is to limit government power. One way governments can stop criticism of their actions is by eliminating the opposition, imprisoning them or worse. The guarantees in the Bill of Rights provide checks on government's ability to prosecute its enemies.

Another reason for guaranteeing rights to those accused of crimes is the strong tradition in American culture, coming from our English roots, that a person is innocent until proven guilty. An innocent person, naturally, still has the full protection of the Constitution, and even a guilty person is protected to some degree, for instance, against cruel and unusual punishment. All Americans are entitled to what the Fifth and Fourteenth Amendments call due process of law. **Due process of law** means that laws must be reasonable and fair, and that those accused of breaking the law, and who stand to lose life, liberty, or property as a consequence, have the right to appear before their judges to hear the charges and evidence against them, to have legal counsel, and to present

Privacy From Searches?

A police officer is aided by his dog in the search for illegal drugs in lockers at Mound Fort Middle School. Those who advocate these searches, along with other techniques such as random drug testing, argue that the actions are a legitimate means to prevent drug use in schools; opponents say they are a violation of privacy and students' rights. The courts tend to side with the former, allowing searches.

any contradictory evidence in their defense. Due process means essentially that those accused of a crime have a right to a fair trial.

During the 1960s and 1970s the Supreme Court expanded the protection of the rights of the accused and incorporated them so that the states had to protect them as well. And yet the more conservative 1980s and 1990s witnessed a considerable backlash against a legal system perceived as having gone soft on crime—overly concerned with the rights of criminals at the expense of safe streets, neighborhoods, and cities, and deaf to the claims of victims of violent crimes. We want to protect the innocent, but when the seemingly guilty go free because of a "technicality," the public is often incensed. The Supreme Court has had the heavy responsibility of drawing the line between the rights of defendants and the rights of society. We can look at the Court's deliberations on these matters in four main areas: the protection against unreasonable searches and seizures, the protection against self-incrimination, the right to counsel, and the protection against cruel and unusual punishment.

Protection Against Unreasonable Searches and Seizures

The Fourth Amendment says,

> The right of the people to be secure in their persons, houses, papers, and effects, against unreasonable searches and seizures, shall not be violated, and no warrants shall issue but upon probable cause, supported by oath or affirmation, and particularly describing the place to be searched, and the persons or things to be seized.

The founders were particularly sensitive on this question because the king of England had had the right to order the homes of his subjects searched without cause, looking for any evidence of criminal activity. For the most part this amendment has been interpreted by the Court to mean that a person's home is private and cannot be invaded by police without a warrant, obtainable only if they have very good reason to think that criminal evidence lies within.

What's Reasonable?

Under the Fourth Amendment, there are a few exceptions to the rule that searches require warrants. Automobiles present a special case, for example, since by their nature they are likely to be gone by the time an officer appears with a warrant. Cars can be searched without warrants if the officer has probable cause to think a law has been broken, and the Court has gradually widened the scope of the search so that it can include luggage or closed containers in the car.

Modern innovations like wiretapping and electronic surveillance presented more difficult problems for the Court because previous law had not allowed for them. A "search" was understood legally to require some physical trespass, and a "seizure" involved taking some tangible object. Listening in on a conversation—electronically from afar—was simply not covered by the law. In fact, in the first case in which it was addressed, the Court held that bugging did not constitute a search.[90] That ruling held for forty years, until the case of *Katz v. United States* (1967), when it was overturned by a Court that required, for the first time, that a warrant be obtained before phones could be tapped.[91] In the same year, the Court ruled that conversations were included under Fourth Amendment protection.[92] A search warrant is thus needed in order to tap a phone, although, as we noted earlier, the 2001 Patriot Act makes it a good deal easier to get a warrant.

Yet another modern area in which the Court has had to
determine the legality of searches is mandatory random
testing for drug or alcohol use, usually by urine or blood
tests. These are arguably a very unreasonable kind of search,
but the Court has tended to allow them where the violation of
privacy is outweighed by a good purpose, for instance,
discovering the cause of a train accident,[93] preventing drug
use in schools,[94] or preserving the public safety by requiring
drug tests of train conductors and airline pilots.

The Exclusionary Rule

By far the most controversial part of the Fourth Amendment
rulings has been the exclusionary rule. In a 1914 case, *Weeks
v. United States,* the Court confronted the question of what to
do with evidence that had, in fact, been obtained illegally.
It decided that such evidence should be excluded from use
in the defendant's trial.[95] This *exclusionary rule,* as it came
to be known, meant that even though the police might have
concrete evidence of criminal activity, if obtained unlawfully,
it could not be used to gain a conviction of the culprit.

The exclusionary rule has been controversial from the
start. In some countries, including England, illegally obtained
evidence can be used at trial, but the defendant is allowed to
sue the police in a civil suit or bring criminal charges against
them. The object is clearly to deter misbehavior on the part of
the police, while not allowing guilty people to go free. But
the exclusionary rule, while it does serve as a deterrent to
police, helps criminals avoid punishment. The Court itself has
occasionally seemed uneasy about the rule. When the Fourth
Amendment was incorporated, in *Wolf v. Colorado,* the exclusionary rule was not extended to the states. The Court ruled
that it was a judicial creation, not a constitutionally protected
right.[96] Not until the 1961 case of *Mapp v. Ohio* was the
exclusionary rule finally incorporated into state as well as
federal practice.[97]

But extending the reach of the exclusionary rule did not
end the controversy. While the Warren Court (1953–1969)
continued to uphold it, the Burger and Rehnquist Courts
(1969–2005) cut back on the protections it offers. In 1974
they ruled that the exclusionary rule was to be a deterrent to
abuse by the police, not a constitutional right of the accused.[98]
The Court subsequently ruled that illegally seized evidence
could be used in civil trials[99] and came to carve out what it
called a *good faith exception,* whereby evidence is admitted to a
criminal trial, even if obtained illegally, if the police are
relying on a warrant that appears to be valid at the time or on

a law that appears to be constitutional (though either may
turn out to be defective),[100] or on a warrant that is obtained in
error. In 2009 the Roberts Court ruled that to trigger the
exclusionary rule, the police conduct must be deliberate.[101]
The Court's more conservative turn on this issue has not
silenced the debate, however. Some observers are appalled at
the reduction in the protection of individual rights, whereas
others do not believe that the Court has gone far enough in
protecting society against criminals.

Protection Against Self-Incrimination

No less controversial than the rulings on illegally seized evidence are the Court's decisions on unconstitutionally obtained
confessions. The Fifth Amendment provides for a number of
protections for individuals, among them that no person "shall
be compelled in any criminal case to be a witness against
himself." The Supreme Court has expanded the scope of the
protection against self-incrimination from criminal trials, as
the amendment dictates, to grand jury proceedings, legislative
investigations, and even police interrogations. It is this last
extension that has proved most controversial.

Court rulings in the early 1900s ordered that police could
not coerce confessions, but they did not provide any clear rule
for police about what confessions would be admissible. Instead
the Court used a case-by-case scrutiny that depended on "the
totality of the circumstances" to determine whether confessions had been made voluntarily. This approach was not very
helpful to police in the streets trying to make arrests and
conduct investigations that would later hold up in court. In
1966 the Warren Court ruled, in *Miranda v. Arizona,* that police
had to inform suspects of their rights to remain silent and to
have a lawyer present during questioning to prevent them
from incriminating themselves. The *Miranda* rights are familiar
to viewers of police dramas: "You have the right to remain
silent. Anything you say can and will be used against you. . . ."
If a lawyer could show that a defendant had not been "read"
his or her rights, information gained in the police interrogation would not be admissible in court. Like the exclusionary
rule, the *Miranda* ruling could and did result in criminals going
free even though the evidence existed to convict them.

Reacting to public and political accusations that the Warren
Court was soft on crime, Congress passed the Crime Control
and Safe Streets Act of 1968, which allowed confessions to be
used in federal courts not according to the *Miranda* ruling but
according to the old "totality of the circumstances" rule. *Miranda*

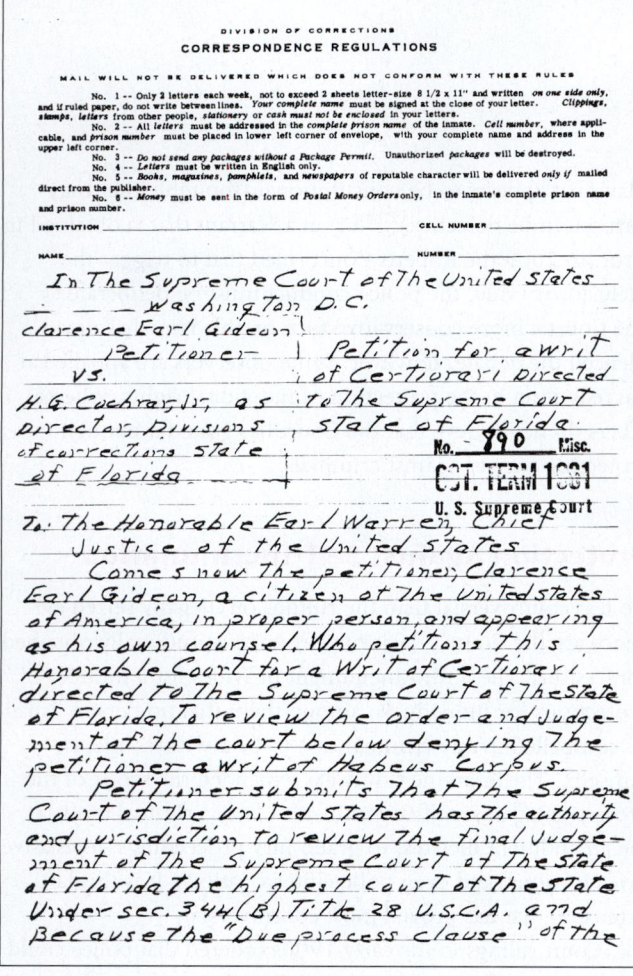

Rights of the Accused
Clarence Earl Gideon spent much of his time in prison studying the law. His handwritten appeal to the Supreme Court resulted in the landmark decision *Gideon v. Wainwright*, which granted those accused of state crimes the right to counsel.

was still effective in the states, however. Vowing to change the liberal tenor of the Warren Court, 1968 presidential candidate Richard Nixon pledged to appoint more conservative justices. True to his campaign promise, once elected he appointed Warren Burger as chief justice. Under the Burger Court, and later the Rehnquist Court, the justices have backed off the *Miranda* decision to some degree. In 2000, despite the fact that some justices had been highly critical of the *Miranda* ruling over the years, the Court upheld the 1966 decision, stating that it had become an established part of the culture, and held the 1968 Crime Control Act to be unconstitutional.[102]

Right to Counsel

Closely related to the *Miranda* decision, which upholds the right to have a lawyer present during police questioning, is

the Sixth Amendment declaration that the accused shall "have the assistance of counsel for his defense." The founders' intentions on this amendment are fairly clear from the 1790 Federal Crimes Act, which required courts to provide counsel for poor defendants only in capital cases—that is, in those punishable by death. Defendants in other trials had a right to counsel, but the government had no obligation to provide it. The Court's decisions were in line with that act until 1938, when in *Johnson v. Zerbst* it extended the government's obligation to provide counsel to impoverished defendants in all criminal proceedings in federal courts.[103] Only federal crimes, however, carried that obligation, until 1963. In one of the most dramatic tales of courtroom appeals, a poor man named Clarence Earl Gideon was convicted of breaking and entering a pool hall and stealing money from the vending machine. Gideon asked the judge for a lawyer, but the judge told him that the state of Florida was not obligated to give him one. He tried to defend the case himself but lost to the far more skilled and knowledgeable prosecutor. Serving five years in prison for a crime he swore he did not commit, he filed a handwritten appeal with the Supreme Court. In a landmark decision, *Gideon v. Wainwright*, the Court incorporated the Sixth Amendment right to counsel.[104]

Not just in Florida, but all over the country, poor people in prison who had not had legal counsel had to be tried again or released. Gideon himself was tried again with a court-appointed lawyer, who proved to the jury not only that Gideon was innocent but that the crime had been committed by the chief witness against him. Conservatives believed that *Gideon* went far beyond the founders' intentions. Again, both the Burger and Rehnquist Courts succeeded in rolling back some of the protections won by *Gideon*, ruling—for instance, that the right to a court-appointed attorney does not extend beyond the filing of one round of appeals, even if the convicted indigent person is on death row.[105]

Though the right to counsel is now seen by most people as an essential right, many argue that this right is in reality often violated because of overworked public defenders or state laws that limit who can receive court-appointed counsel. According to a study by the National Association of Criminal Defense Lawyers, the Bucks County, Pennsylvania, public defender's office handled 4,173 cases in 1980. "Twenty years later, with the same number of attorneys, the office handled an estimated 8,000 cases." In Wisconsin, "more than 11,000 people go unrepresented annually because anyone with an annual income of more than $3,000 is deemed able to pay a lawyer."[106]

Figure 5.1

Capital Punishment by State

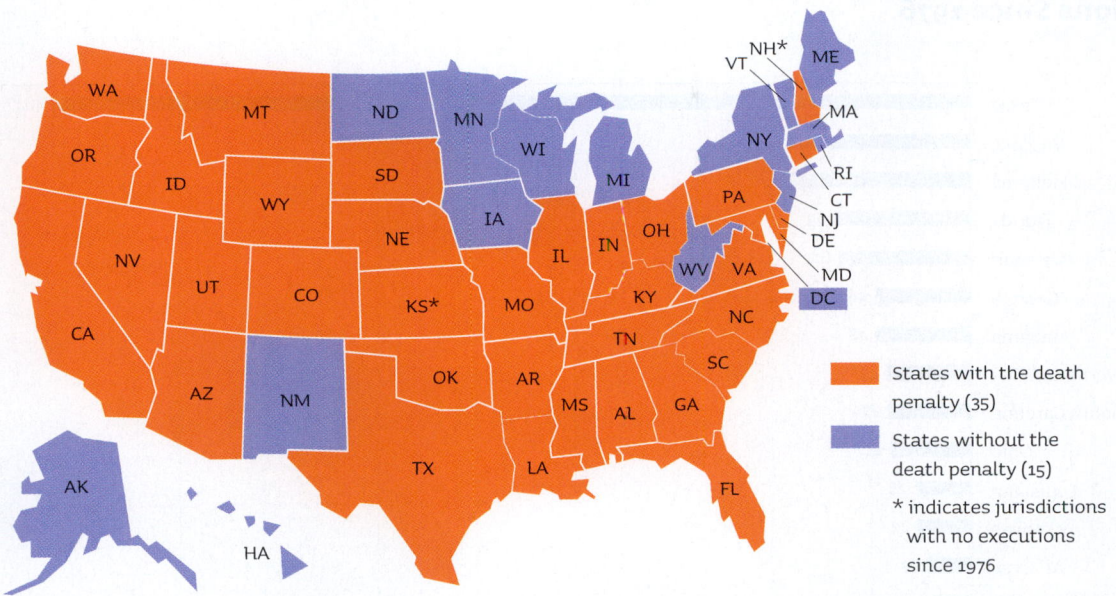

States with the death penalty (35)

States without the death penalty (15)

* indicates jurisdictions with no executions since 1976

Source: Death Penalty Information Center, "Facts About the Death Penalty," May 26, 2010, http://deathpenaltyinfo.org/documents/factsheet.pdf.

Protection Against Cruel and Unusual Punishment

The final guarantee we look at in this section has also generated some major political controversies. The Eighth Amendment says, in part, that "cruel and unusual punishments" shall not be inflicted. Like some of the earlier amendments, this one reflects a concern of English law, which sought to protect British subjects from torture and inhumane treatment by the king. The Americans inherited the concern and wrote it into their Constitution. It is easy to see why it would be controversial, however. What is "cruel"? And what is "unusual"? Can we protect American citizens from cruel and unusual punishment delivered in other countries?

The Court has ruled that not all unusual punishments are unconstitutional, because all new punishments—electrocution or lethal injection, for instance—are unusual when they first appear, but they may be more humane than old punishments like hanging or shooting.[107] Despite intense lobbying on the part of impassioned interest groups, however, the Court has not ruled that the death penalty itself is cruel or unusual (except in the case of mentally retarded individuals,[108] juveniles,[109] and crimes against an individual that do not result in the death of the victim[110]), and the majority of states have death penalty laws (see Figure 5.1).

The strongest attack on the death penalty began in the 1970s, when the NAACP Legal Defense Fund joined with the

ACLU and the American Bar Association to argue that the death penalty was disproportionately given to African Americans, especially those convicted of rape. They argued that this was a violation of the Eighth Amendment, and also the Fourteenth Amendment guarantee of equal protection of the laws. Part of the problem was that state laws differed about what constituted grounds for imposing the death penalty, and juries had no uniform standards on which to rely. Consequently, unequal patterns of application of the penalty developed.

In *Furman v. Georgia* (1972) and two related cases, the Court ruled that Georgia's and Texas's capital punishment laws were unconstitutional, but the justices were so far from agreement that they all filed separate opinions, totaling 231 pages.[111] Thirty-five states passed new laws trying to meet the Court's objections and to clarify the standards for capital punishment. By 1976, six hundred inmates waited on death row for the Court to approve the new laws. That year the Court ruled in several cases that the death penalty was not unconstitutional, although it struck down laws requiring the death penalty for certain crimes.[112] The Court remained divided over the issue. In 1977 Gary Gilmore became the first person executed after a ten-year break. Executions by state since 1976 are listed in Figure 5.2.

In 1987 *McClesky v. Kemp* raised the race issue again, but by then the Court was growing more conservative.[113] It held, five to four, that statistics showing that blacks who murder whites

Figure 5.2

Executions Since 1976

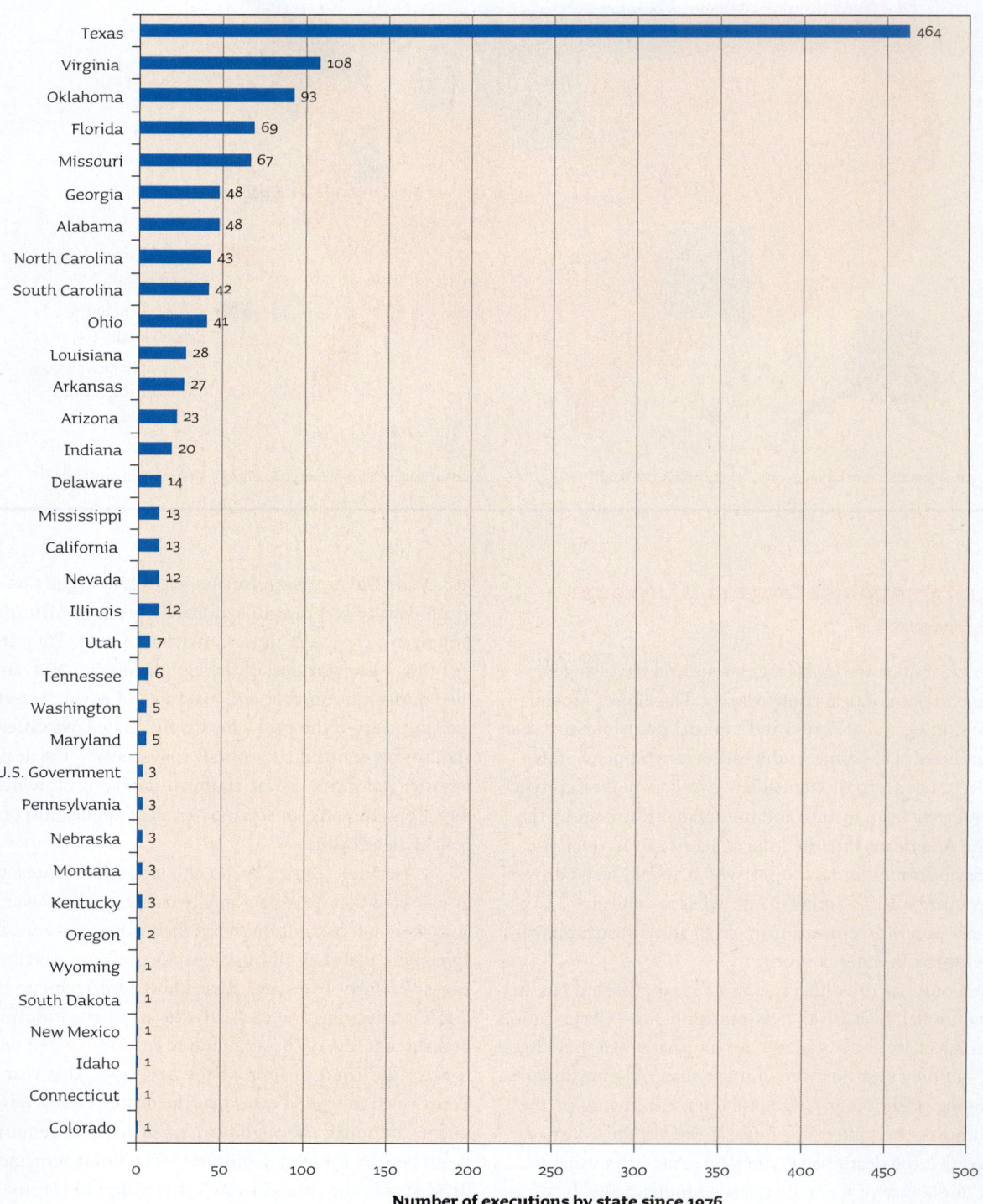

Number of executions by state since 1976

Source: Death Penalty Information Center 2010. "Facts About the Death Penalty," 2010, www.deathpenaltyinfo.org/factsheet.pdf.

Note: Executions through October 2010.

received the death penalty more frequently than whites who murder blacks did not prove a racial bias in the law or in how it was being applied.[114] The Rehnquist Court continued to knock down procedural barriers to imposing the death penalty. In 2006 the Roberts Court held that death row inmates could challenge state lethal injection procedures in lower courts on cruel and unusual punishment grounds. Several of those courts came to different conclusions. In 2008, in *Baze v. Rees*,[115] the Supreme Court upheld Kentucky's lethal injection practice, and other states, waiting for a sign from the Court, went ahead with their own practices.

In recent years public support for capital punishment appears to be softening, not because of opposition in principle but because of fears that the system might be putting innocent people on death row. This feeling grew as DNA testing cleared some death row residents, and careful investigation showed that others, too, were innocent. After thirteen death row convicts in his state were exonerated between 1977 and 2000, Illinois governor George Ryan, a moderate Republican who supported the death penalty in principle, called for a statewide halt to executions. "I cannot support a system, which, in its administration, has proven so fraught with error," Ryan explained, "and has come so close to the ultimate nightmare, the state's taking of an innocent life."[116] Following his lead, then–Maryland governor Parris Glendening issued a moratorium in 2002, but that action was quickly reversed by the new governor, Robert Ehrlich, in January 2003. In 2007 the New Jersey legislature banned the death penalty in the state—the first state to do so since the Supreme Court declared capital punishment constitutional in 1976.[117]

Despite misgivings, the American public continues to favor capital punishment. In 2009 a Gallup poll found 65 percent of the public supporting the death penalty, with 31 percent opposed, even though only 57 percent thought that it was applied fairly.[118]

Who What How

Every citizen has a huge stake in the protection of the rights of criminal defendants. If the government were allowed to arrest, imprison, and punish citizens at will, without legal protections, in secrecy, and without record, then all of us, criminal or not, would be vulnerable to persecution, perhaps for who we are, how we vote, what we say, or what we believe. It is the rules of due process that protect us from an unpredictable and unaccountable legal system.

The Right to Privacy
The personal meets the political

One of the most controversial rights in America is not even mentioned in the Constitution or the Bill of Rights: the right to privacy. This right is at the heart of one of the deepest divisions in American politics, the split over abortion rights, and is fundamental to two other controversial areas of civil liberties: gay rights and the right to die.

Why Is the Right to Privacy Valuable?

Although the right to privacy is not spelled out in the Bill of Rights, it goes hand in hand with the founders' insistence on limited government. Their goal was to keep government from getting too powerful and interfering with the lives and affairs of individual citizens. They certainly implied a right to privacy, and perhaps even assumed such a right, but they did not make it explicit.

The right to privacy, to be left alone to do what we want, is so obviously desirable that it scarcely needs a defense. The problem, of course, is that a right to privacy without any limits is anarchy, the absence of government altogether. Clearly governments have an interest in preventing some kinds of individual behavior—murder, theft, and rape, for example. But what about more subtle behaviors that do not directly affect the public safety but arguably have serious consequences for the public good, like prostitution, drug use, gambling, and even, to take the example we used earlier in this chapter, riding a motorcycle without a helmet? Should these behaviors fall under a right to privacy, or should the state be able to regulate them? The specific issues the Court has dealt with related to this topic are contraception use and abortion, laws restricting the behavior of homosexuals, and laws preventing terminally ill patients from ending their lives.

A right to privacy per se did not enter the American legal system until 1890, when an article called "The Right to Privacy" appeared in the *Harvard Law Review*.[119] In the years after the article appeared, states began to add a privacy right to their own bodies of statutory or constitutional law. The Supreme Court had dealt with privacy in some respects when it ruled on cases under the Fourth and Fifth Amendments, but it did not "discover" a right to privacy until 1965, and whether such a right exists remains controversial. None of the rights guaranteed by the first ten amendments to the Constitution is absolute. All, as we have seen, include limitations and contradictions. The right to privacy, without firm constitutional authority, is the least certain of all.

Reproductive Rights

Throughout the 1940s, people had tried to challenge state laws that made it a crime to use birth control, or even to give out information about how to prevent pregnancies. The Supreme Court routinely refused to hear these challenges until the 1965 case of *Griswold v. Connecticut*. Connecticut had a law on its books making it illegal to use contraceptive devices or to distribute information about them. Under that law, Estelle Griswold, the Connecticut director of Planned Parenthood, was convicted and fined $100 for counseling married couples about birth control.

The Court held that while the right to privacy is not explicit in the Constitution, a number of other rights, notably those in Amendments One, Three, Four, Five, and Nine, create a "zone of privacy" in which lie marriage and the decision to use contraception. It said that the specific guarantees in the Bill of Rights have "penumbras," or outlying shadowy areas, in which can be found a right to privacy. The Fourteenth Amendment applies that right to the states, and so Connecticut's law was unconstitutional.[120] In 1972 the Court extended the ruling to cover the rights of unmarried people to use contraception as well.[121]

Because of the Court's insistence that reproductive matters are not the concern of the government, abortion rights advocates saw an opportunity to use the *Griswold* ruling to strike down state laws prohibiting or limiting abortion. Until the Civil War, such laws were uncommon; most states allowed abortions in the early stages of pregnancy. After the war, however, opinion turned, and by 1910 every state except Kentucky had made abortions illegal. In the 1960s, legislation was again becoming more liberal, but abortions were still unobtainable in many places.

The Court had tried to avoid ruling on the abortion issue, but by 1973 it had become hard to escape. In *Roe v. Wade,* the justices held that the right to privacy did indeed encompass the right to abortion. It tried to balance a woman's right to privacy in reproductive matters with the state's interest in protecting human life, however, by treating the three trimesters of pregnancy differently. In the first three months of pregnancy, it held, there can be no compelling state interest that offsets a woman's privacy rights. In the second three months, the state can regulate access to abortions if it does so reasonably. In the last trimester, the state's interest becomes far more compelling, and a state can limit or even prohibit abortions as long as the mother's life is not in danger.[122]

The *Roe* decision launched the United States into an intense and divisive battle over abortion. States continued to try to limit abortions by requiring the consent of husbands or parents, by outlawing clinic advertising, by imposing waiting periods, and by erecting other roadblocks. The Court struck down most of these efforts, at least until 1977 when it allowed some state limitations. But the battle was not confined to statehouses. Congress, having failed to pass a constitutional amendment banning abortions, passed over thirty laws restricting access to abortions in various ways. For instance, it limited federal funding for abortions through Medicaid, a move the Supreme Court upheld in 1980.[123] Presidents got into the fray as well. President Reagan and the first President Bush were staunch opponents of *Roe* and worked hard to get it overturned. Reagan appointed only antiabortion judges to federal courts, and his administration was active in pushing litigation that would challenge *Roe.*

The balance on the Supreme Court was crucial. *Roe* had been decided by a seven-to-two vote, but many in the majority were facing retirement. When Warren Burger retired, Reagan elevated William Rehnquist, one of the two dissenters, to chief justice, and appointed conservative Antonin Scalia in his place. Reagan's appointees did finally turn the Court in a more conservative direction, but even they did not overturn *Roe.* The 1973 ruling has been limited in some ways, but Rehnquist did not succeed in gathering a majority to strike it down.[124] In 2007 the Roberts Court moved to uphold a ban on partial-birth abortion, but it has not signaled that it would overturn *Roe.*[125]

The debate over abortion in this country is certainly not over. It has long been a rallying point for the Christian Right, which has become a powerful part of the Republican Party. Since 1980 the Republicans have included a commitment to a constitutional amendment banning abortion in their presidential party platform. And while President Obama has expressed support for a woman's right to choose, some Democrats oppose abortion rights as well. In 2010 Michigan representative Bart Stupak refused to support the health care reform bill passed by the Senate because he did not feel it had stringent enough restrictions on the use of federal funds for abortion, though a last-minute compromise satisfied him on this issue. With Americans nearly evenly split on the question of abortion, it is likely to remain a divisive issue in American politics for some time to come.[126]

Gay Rights

The *Griswold* and *Roe* rulings have opened up a variety of difficult issues for the Supreme Court. If there is a right to privacy, what might be included under it? On the whole, the Court has been very restrictive in expanding it beyond the reproductive rights of the original cases. Most controversial was its ruling in *Bowers v. Hardwick* (1986).[127]

Michael Hardwick was arrested under a Georgia law outlawing heterosexual and homosexual sodomy. A police officer, seeking to arrest him for failing to show up in court on a minor matter, was let into Hardwick's house by a friend and directed to his room. When the officer entered, he found Hardwick in bed with another man, and arrested him. Hardwick challenged the law (although he wasn't prosecuted under it), claiming that it violated his right to privacy. The Court disagreed. Looking at the case from the perspective of whether there was a constitutional right to engage in sodomy, rather than from the dissenting view that what took place between consenting adults was a private matter, the Court held five to four that the state of Georgia had a legitimate interest in regulating such behavior.

Justice Lewis Powell, who provided the fifth vote for the majority, said after his retirement that he regretted his vote in the *Bowers* decision, but by then, of course, it was too late. Several states were critical of the Court's ruling. Kentucky's Supreme Court went so far in 1992 as to strike down the state's sodomy law as unconstitutional on the grounds the U.S. Supreme Court refused to use.[128] The Georgia Supreme Court itself struck down Georgia's sodomy law in 1998 on privacy grounds, but in a case involving heterosexual rather than homosexual activity. Not until 2003, in *Lawrence v. Texas*, did the Court, in a six-to-three decision, finally overturn *Bowers* on privacy grounds.[129] Interestingly, despite its long-time reluctance to overturn *Bowers*, the Court in 1996 used the equal protection clause of the Fourteenth Amendment to strike down a Colorado law that would have made it difficult for gays to use the Colorado courts to fight discrimination.[130] Thus the Court can pursue several constitutional avenues to expand the rights of gay Americans, should it want to do so.

The Right to Die

A final right-to-privacy issue that has stirred up controversy for the Court is the so-called right to die. In 1990 the Court ruled on the case of Nancy Cruzan, a woman who had been in a vegetative state and on life-support systems since she was in a car accident in 1983. Her parents asked the doctors to withdraw the life support and allow her to die, but the state of Missouri, claiming an interest in protecting the "sanctity of human life," blocked their request. The Cruzans argued that the right to privacy included the right to die without state interference, but the Court upheld Missouri's position, saying it was unclear that Nancy's wishes in the matter could be known for sure but that when such wishes were made clear, either in person or via a living will, a person's right to terminate medical treatment was protected under the Fourteenth Amendment's due process clause.[131]

The right-to-die issue surged back into national prominence in 2005 by a case involving Terri Schiavo, a young woman who had been in a persistent vegetative state for over fifteen years. Claiming that Schiavo had not wished to be kept alive by artificial measures, her husband asked a state court to have her feeding tube removed. Her parents challenged the decision, but after numerous appeals the court ordered the tube removed in accordance with the precedent set in the Cruzan case. Social conservatives in Congress tried to block the action, but all federal courts, including the Supreme Court, refused to intervene and Schiavo died soon after. Angered by their inability to overturn the state court ruling, conservative groups vowed to fight for federal judicial appointees who would be more likely to intervene in such cases.

The Schiavo case did not change the prevailing legal principles—that this is a matter for individuals to decide and that when their wishes are known they should be respected by the doctors and the courts. In this matter, at least, public opinion seems to be consistent with the law. Polls showed the public strongly opposed to Congress' intervention to prevent Schiavo's death, and large majorities supported the removal of her feeding tube. In the wake of the case, 70 percent of Americans said they were thinking about getting their own living wills.[132]

The question of a person's right to suspend treatment is different from another legal issue—whether individuals have the right to have assistance ending their lives when they are terminally ill and in severe pain. Proponents of this right argue that patients should be able to decide whether to continue living with their conditions, and since such patients are frequently incapacitated or lack the means to end their lives painlessly, they are entitled to help if they want to die. Opponents, on the other hand, say a patient's right to die may require doctors to violate their Hippocratic Oath, and that it is open to abuse. Patients, especially those whose illnesses are chronic and costly, might feel obligated to end their lives out of concern for family or financial matters. In 1997 the

Showing Up and Speaking Out
Quality of life issues play a large role in many assisted-suicide and right-to-die cases, and part of the reason for this is that these issues and values are highly subjective and relative. Those opposed to the practice believe that others can never know the intentions or desires of severely disabled individuals unable to communicate their desires and that everyone has the right to live their lives to the fullest degree possible, even if others see these lives as limited or even not worth living.

Supreme Court ruled that the issue be left to the states and left open the possibility that dying patients might be able to make a claim to a constitutional right to die in the future.[133]

Oregon provided the first test of this policy. In 1997 it passed a referendum allowing doctors under certain circumstances to provide lethal doses of medication to enable terminally ill patients to end their lives. In late 2001 U.S. attorney general John Ashcroft effectively blocked the law by announcing that doctors who participated in assisted suicides would lose their licenses to prescribe federally regulated medications, an essential part of medical practice. In 2004 a federal appellate court ruled that Ashcroft overstepped his authority under federal law, and in early 2006 the Supreme Court upheld the Oregon law.

What's at stake in the right to privacy seems amazingly simple, given the intensity of the debate about it. In short, the issue is whether citizens have the right to control their own bodies in fundamentally intimate matters like birth, sex, and death. The controversy arises when opponents argue that citizens do not have that right, but rather should be subject to religious rules, natural laws, or moral beliefs that dictate certain behaviors with respect to these matters. They promote legislation and constitutional amendments that seek to bring behavior into conformity with their beliefs. The founders did not act to protect this right, possibly because they did not anticipate that they had created a government strong enough to tell people what to do in such personal matters, or possibly because technology has put choices on the table today that did not exist more than two hundred years ago. In the absence of constitutional protection or prohibition of the right to privacy, the rule that provides for it today derives from a series of Court cases that could just as easily be overturned should the Court change its mind.

**Who
What
How**

The Citizens and Civil Liberties

Individual rights yield a collective benefit

In the United States we are accustomed to thinking about citizenship as a status that confers on us certain rights. We have explored many of those rights in detail in this chapter. But as we stand back and ask ourselves why each of these rights is valuable, an interesting irony appears. Even though these are *individual* rights, valued for granting freedoms to individuals and allowing them to make claims on their government, we value them also because they lead to *collective* benefits—we are better off as a society if individuals possess these rights. Democratic government is preserved if criticism is allowed; religion can prosper if it is not entangled in politics; militias may defend the security of a free state if individual citizens are armed; justice will be available to all if it is guaranteed to each.

The collective as well as the individual nature of American civil liberties recalls the argument we made in Chapter 1 that there are two strands of thinking about citizenship in the United States—one focused on individual rights and the self-interest of citizens and the other emphasizing obligations or duties seen as necessary to protect the public interest. We said these traditions have existed side by side throughout our history. They have done so because neither can exist solely by itself in a democracy: obligation without rights is an authoritarian dictatorship, and rights without obligation lead to a state of nature, or anarchy, with no government at all. Citizenship in a democracy plainly carries both rights and duties.

The final section of a chapter on civil liberties is an interesting place to speculate about the duties attached to American citizenship. We have explored the Bill of Rights. What might a Bill of Obligations look like? The Constitution itself suggests the basics. Obligations are very much the flip side of rights; for every right guaranteed, there is a corresponding duty to use it. For instance, the provisions for elected office and the right to vote imply a duty to vote. Congress is authorized to collect taxes, duties, and excises, including an income tax; citizens are obligated to pay those taxes. Congress can raise and support armies, provide and maintain a navy, provide for and govern militias; correspondingly, Americans have a duty to serve in the military. The Constitution defines treason as waging war against the states or aiding or abetting their enemies; citizens have an obligation not to betray their country or state. Amendments Five and Six guarantee grand juries and jury trials to those accused of crimes; it is citizens who must serve on those juries.

As citizenship obligations around the world go, these are not terribly onerous. In Europe such obligations are explicitly extended to include providing for the welfare of those who cannot take care of themselves, for instance. Tax burdens are much higher in most other industrialized nations than they are in the United States. In some countries the obligation to vote is legally enforced, and others have mandatory military service for all citizens, or at least all male citizens.

Still, many people find the obligations associated with American citizenship to be too harsh. For instance, two *Wall Street Journal* reporters wrote, "We [Americans] are a nation of law breakers. We exaggerate tax-deductible expenses, lie to customs officials, bet on card games and sports events, disregard jury notices, drive while intoxicated . . . and hire illegal child care workers. . . . Nearly all people violate some laws, and many run afoul of dozens without ever being considered or considering themselves criminals."[134] While 90 percent of Americans value their right to a trial by jury, only 12 percent are willing to accept the jury duty that makes that right possible.[135] We have already seen that voter turnout in the United States falls far behind that in most other nations.

How much fulfillment of political obligation is enough? Most Americans clearly obey most of the laws, most of the time. When there is a war and a military draft, most draft-aged males have agreed to serve. If we do not pay all the taxes we owe, we pay much of them. If we do not vote, we get involved in our communities in countless other ways. As a nation, we are certainly getting by, at least for now. But perhaps we should consider the long-term political consequences to a democratic republic if the emphasis on preserving civil liberties is not balanced by a corresponding commitment to fulfilling political obligations.

Thinking Outside the Box

Should the founders have provided a Bill of Obligations as well as a Bill of Rights?

▶ What's at Stake Revisited

When Virginia attorney general Ken Cuccinelli attempted to investigate the grants obtained by a former University of Virginia professor whose research findings he disagreed with, he was the darling of conservative opponents of the science of global warming but the object of attacks by academics and liberal critics who warned that his efforts could have a "chilling effect" on academic research. For these critics, the freedom to pursue academic research and studies is a First Amendment issue, and academia requires an atmosphere of open debate in order for it to police itself. The *Washington Post*'s editorial board wrote,

> By equating controversial results with legal fraud, Mr. Cuccinelli demonstrates a dangerous disregard for scientific method and academic freedom. The remedy for unsatisfactory data or analysis is public criticism from peers and more data, not a politically tinged witch hunt or, worse, a civil penalty. Scientists and other academics inevitably will get things wrong, and they will use public funds in the process, because failure is as important to producing good scholarship as success.[136]

Numerous academic investigations into Professor Mann's research and the efforts of fellow researchers to replicate and test his findings found no evidence of fraud, so, the academics believed, that should be the end of it. Political opponents of Mann's findings believed that fellow academics could not be trusted to police Mann's work and sought to discredit his research using the apparatus of the state, something that University of Virginia lawyers pointed out went way beyond the founders' notion of a limited government.

Clearly, the idea of academic freedom is destined to be a controversial one. Academic freedom—traditionally understood as the right of faculty to teach, research, and write about what they think is important without fear of reprisal[137]—is gradually being redefined by both conservatives and liberals on campus as the right not to have to teach or be taught ideas they disagree with or find offensive. Both sides say the issue is about basic civil liberties, and each accuses the other of wanting to indoctrinate students rather than to teach them. The two sets of beliefs are on a collision course, and they may be crashing into each other on a college campus, and maybe even in a state legislature, near you.

As we noted in the *Consider the Source* feature in Chapter 3, liberal critics of campus culture in the late twentieth century argued that academia was dominated by white middle-class males who perpetuated a Eurocentric view of the world. These critics demanded that college curricula, hiring practices, admissions standards, and campus life generally should acknowledge the growing diversity of the United States. Multiculturalism and the political correctness movement (see p. 161 in this chapter) are two of the consequences of that effort to make colleges and universities more representative of American diversity.

But increasingly conservatives argue that the pendulum has swung way too far in that direction. They say that many college professors are too liberal, that students are captive audiences in classes where they are told only one side of the story, and that they are then graded on whether they support the professor's position. They also argue that because students are still developing their opinions about politics and the world, their exposure to liberal professors makes them more likely to leave college with liberal ideas.

Conservative activist David Horowitz feels so strongly about the issue that he created Students for Academic Freedom, an organization that is chartered on more than 130 college campuses and that aims to expose professors who promote their personal beliefs in the classroom. One of the group's goals is to get state legislatures and the U.S. Congress to pass an "Academic Bill of Rights" that urges universities to recognize and promote intellectual diversity on college campuses by promoting ideological diversity in the classroom and encouraging schools to hire more conservative professors.[138] The group has had some success. For instance, the Georgia Senate passed a resolution "encouraging public colleges and universities to refrain from discriminating against students because of their political or religious beliefs."[139]

Not surprisingly, these groups have met with criticism in their own turn. Many students disagree that professors are pushing their views in the classroom. Furthermore, university faculty and administrators claim that the conservative organizations are engaging in a witch hunt to stifle thought and limit speech. The American Association of University Professors opposes the bills pushed by Students for Academic Freedom on the grounds that these bills infringe on what they call academic freedom—that they impose political standards for hiring, for instance, instead of the standards of academic rigor they believe are important, and place external controls over what can be taught in the classroom.

What are liberals and conservatives really battling over? In a sense, each side has grown in response to the other. Each wants to restrict research or speech in the classroom that they find offensive. Liberals want open, honest debate on the failings of the Bush administration's American foreign policy, for instance, but want to limit speech that some minorities might find offensive. Conservatives want open, honest debate on issues such as affirmative action but want to limit speech that suggests that current business practices are environmentally unsustainable. Each side wants to censor the other in the name of academic freedom, but neither of these two sides is really so much about academic freedom as it is about freedom to tell one's story as the dominant story. It's not surprising that college campuses, filled with bright young minds and youthful energy, should have become battlegrounds in this fight, but the stakes there are unusually high. If either side manages to "win" the war, the losers, if John Stuart Mill is to be believed, will be critical thinking, the ability to find and defend the truth, and ultimately, the fate of democracy itself.

To Sum Up

Key terms, chapter summaries, practice quizzes, Internet links, and other study aids are available on the companion web site at http://republic.cqpress.com.

Define **Understand** **Practice** **Read** **Click** **Watch**

accommodationists (p. 152)

bad tendency test (p. 157)

bills of attainder (p. 147)

civil liberties (p. 139)

civil rights (p. 139)

clear and present danger test (p. 157)

compelling state interest (p. 154)

due process of law (p. 169)

establishment clause (p. 152)

ex post facto laws (p. 147)

exclusionary rule (p. 171)

fighting words (p. 161)

free exercise clause (p. 153)

freedom of assembly (p. 160)

habeas corpus (p. 146)

imminent lawless action test (p. 159)

incorporation (p. 147)

Lemon test (p. 153)

libel (p. 162)

Miller test (p. 160)

police power (p. 154)

political correctness (p. 161)

prior restraint (p. 161)

sedition (p. 157)

selective incorporation (p. 147)

separationists (p. 152)

Define | **Understand** | **Practice** | **Read** | **Click** | **Watch**

- Our civil liberties are individual freedoms that place limitations on the power of government. Most of these rights are spelled out in the text of the Constitution or in its first ten amendments, the Bill of Rights, but some have developed over the years through judicial decision making.
- Sometimes rights conflict, and when they do, government, guided by the Constitution and through the institutions of Congress, the executive, and the actions of citizens themselves, is called upon to resolve these conflicts.
- According to the establishment and free exercise clauses of the First Amendment, citizens of the United States have the right not to be coerced to practice a religion in which they do not believe, as well as the right not to be prevented from practicing the religion they espouse. Because these rights can conflict, religious freedom has been a battleground ever since the founding of the country. The courts have played a significant role in navigating the stormy waters of religious expression since the founding.
- Freedom of expression, also provided for in the First Amendment, is often considered the hallmark of our democratic government. Freedom of expression produces information about government, limits corruption, protects minorities, and helps maintain a vigorous defense of the truth. But this right may at times conflict with the preservation of social order and

protection of civility, decency, and reputation. Again, it has been left to the courts to balance freedom of expression with social and moral order.
- The right to bear arms, supported by the Second Amendment, has also been hotly debated—more so in recent years than in the past, as federal gun control legislation has been enacted only recently. Most often the debate over gun laws is carried out in state legislatures.
- The founders believed that to limit government power, people needed to retain rights against government throughout the process of being accused, tried, and punished for criminal activities. Thus they devoted some of the text of the Constitution as well as the Bill of Rights to a variety of procedural protections, including the right to a speedy and public trial, protection from unreasonable search and seizure, and the right to legal advice.
- Though the right to privacy is not mentioned in either the Constitution or the Bill of Rights—and did not even enter the American legal system until the late 1800s—it has become a fiercely debated right on a number of different levels, including reproductive rights, gay rights, and the right to die. In the absence of constitutional protection, the series of court cases on these matters determines how they are to be resolved. Many of these issues are still on shaky ground, as the states create their own legislation and the courts hand down new rulings.

Define | **Understand** | **Practice** | **Read** | **Click** | **Watch**

1. **Because rights represent power in a democratic society,**
   a. rights are subject to the whims of the majority.
   b. a rigid hierarchy of rights exists.
   c. the exercise of rights is inevitably subject to conflict and controversy.
   d. the powerful have a monopoly on rights.
   e. many rights are often limited.

2. **Both freedom of speech and freedom of religion require**
   a. strong acceptance of majority views.
   b. free and periodic elections.
   c. strict regulation by government.
   d. tolerance of ideas that we reject or find repugnant.
   e. limited protection from Congress.

3. **The right to bear arms was initially established**
   a. to keep the federal government in check by limiting the power of permanent armies.
   b. because the right to bear arms has historically been an important element of a free society.

   c. because the right to bear arms was critical to a society that got most of its food from hunting.
   d. to protect the United States from foreign invasion.
   e. because most of the founders were gun owners.

4. **Amendments Four through Eight deal largely with**
   a. rights of expression.
   b. limits on the power of the government to accuse, try, and punish criminal activities.
   c. powers of state government.
   d. limits on the power of government to take or restrict property rights.
   e. voting rights.

5. **This chapter states that citizenship obligations**
   a. are almost never met.
   b. are quite oppressive.
   c. affect the poor and not the wealthy.
   d. are brought to bear more heavily on women and minorities.
   e. are not terribly onerous.

Define **Understand** **Practice** **Read** **Click** **Watch**

Downs, Donald A. 2005. *Restoring Free Speech and Liberty on Campus.* Cambridge, U.K.: Cambridge University Press. *In a book written from his personal experience, Downs argues that academic freedom on college campuses has declined since the 1990s. Downs maintains that constitutional rights and free inquiry will prevail only if individuals or groups stand up to protect them in the face of pressure.*

Epstein, Lee, and Thomas G. Walker. 2007. *Constitutional Law for a Changing America,* 6th ed. Washington, D.C.: CQ Press. *This book presents two detailed yet accessible volumes for beginning constitutional law students.*

Fish, Stanley. 1994. *There's No Such Thing as Free Speech and It's a Good Thing, Too.* New York: Oxford University Press. *Fish, a noted law professor, believes that free speech can be dangerous, making limits necessary for certain kinds of speech.*

Garrow, David. 1994. *Liberty and Sexuality: The Right to Privacy and the Making of Roe v. Wade.* New York: Macmillan. *This book offers a comprehensive historical analysis of the debate surrounding Roe v. Wade, both before and after the decision.*

Hentoff, Nat. 1992. *Free Speech for Me—But Not for Thee: How the American Left and Right Relentlessly Censor Each Other.* New York: HarperCollins. *This book offers an excellent and somewhat frightening account of how both the left and the right attempt to censor speech and publications they oppose.*

Levy, Leonard W. 2001. *Origins of the Bill of Rights.* New Haven: Yale University Press. *Constitutional scholar Levy provides a comprehensive analysis of the history of the Bill of Rights and constitutional provisions that protect it.*

Lewis, Anthony. 2007. *Freedom for the Thought That We Hate: A Biography of the First Amendment.* New York: Basic Books. *Law professor and Pulitzer Prize–winning writer Lewis, formerly of the New York Times, explores the history of the First Amendment and how its legal application and judicial rulings have allowed this liberty to evolve over time.*

Nussbaum, Martha. 2008. *Liberty of Conscience: In Defense of America's Tradition of Religious Equality.* New York: Perseus Publishing. *America has long been heralded as a safe harbor from religious persecution abroad. This historical account of the First Amendment's protection of religious liberty is supported by a wealth of legal precedent.*

Prejean, Helen. 1993. *Dead Man Walking: An Eyewitness Account of the Death Penalty in the United States.* New York: Random House. *Written by a Catholic nun who befriended two inmates on Louisiana's death row, this thought-provoking memoir offers a firsthand glimpse at the harsh realities of the criminal justice system and an impassioned plea to end capital punishment. Adapted for the screen in a 1996 film by Tim Robbins, starring Susan Sarandon and Sean Penn.*

Waldman, Steven. 2008. *Founding Faith: Providence, Politics, and the Birth of Religious Freedom in America.* New York: Random House. *Waldman explores the intentions of the founding fathers and the foundations of religious freedom in early America.*

Define **Understand** **Practice** **Read** **Click** **Watch**

American Civil Liberties Union *www.aclu.org. A fact-filled resource with information on ACLU issues, current events in Congress and the courts, and the history of the organization.*

FindLaw *www.findlaw.com/casecode/supreme.html. This database allows you to search and read the full text of every Supreme Court decision handed down since 1893 and selected earlier cases.*

Note: *The following are just two of the many web sites that address civil liberties issues. For links to other sites, see our web page at http://republic.cqpress.com.*

First Amendment Center *www.firstamendmentcenter.org. This site features comprehensive research and news regarding First Amendment issues and includes commentary and analysis by legal specialists.*

National Rifle Association *www.nra.org. Everything you need to know about the history of the NRA and current gun control legislation; includes links to news commentary on firearms-related stories.*

Define   **Understand**   **Practice**   **Read**   **Click**   **Watch**

Bowling for Columbine   *2002. A controversial and, at times, humorous filmmaker, Michael Moore attempts to uncover why the United States has so many firearms-related deaths.*

Gideon's Trumpet   *1979. An inspiring movie about the 1963 Supreme Court case Gideon v. Wainwright. Based on Anthony Lewis's book published in 1964.*

Michael & Me   *2005. Libertarian talk-radio personality, author, and documentarian Larry Elder attempts to deconstruct Michael Moore's acclaimed Bowling for Columbine, which sought to expose the pitfalls of our gun-toting American society. Borrowing freely from the original documentary, Elder comes to the defense of the Second Amendment in this provocative rebuttal.*

Minority Report   *2002. Adapted from a short story by science fiction writer Philip K. Dick, this film portrays civil liberties gone awry in a grim future where criminals are arrested "precrime."*

The People vs. Larry Flynt   *1996. Director Milos Forman chronicles the notorious publisher's journey from "smut peddler" to champion of free speech, culminating in the Supreme Court's 1988 landmark decision in his favor. Starring Woody Harrelson, Courtney Love, and Edward Norton.*

CONGRESS SHALL MAKE NO LAW

RESPECTING AN ESTABLISHMENT

OF RELIGION , OR PROHIBITING

THE FREE EXERCISE THEREOF;

OR ABRIDGING THE FREEDOM

OF SPEECH, OR OF THE PRESS;

OR THE RIGHT OF THE PEOPLE

PEACEABLY TO ASSEMBLE, AND

TO PETITION THE GOVERNMENT

FOR A REDRESS OF GRIEVANCES

THE FIRST AMENDMENT TO THE CONSTITUTION OF THE UNITED STATES

Chapter 6

The Struggle for Equal Rights

▶ What's at Stake?

The face of presidential politics underwent a sea change in 2008. The lineup on the Democratic primary debate stage said it all. In years past, almost without exception, debate participants, regardless of party, were white men. Sometimes, more recently, black men like Jesse Jackson or Alan Keyes found their way into the mix, but never for long; and everyone watching knew they didn't really have the political backing to be serious contenders for the presidency. Some women had taken a shot at the White House, one as early as 1872 (though women did not win the right to vote until 1920). But while Republican senator Elizabeth Dole made a serious effort in 2000, only Democrat Carol Moseley Braun (2004) made it to the debate stage, and she, an African American, was not seen as having a real chance at the nomination either. And Hispanics for president? Not usually, and never in a debate.

So the participants on the Democratic primary stage as the campaign got under way in 2007 were an

Diverse Choices

As Democrats Bill Richardson, Hillary Clinton, John Edwards, and Barack Obama acknowledged the audience at a debate before the New Hampshire primaries in January 2008, they could just as easily have been taking part in a public service announcement about the opportunities for women and multicultural individuals in twenty-first-century America. Not so very long ago, not all of the individuals on stage would have had the opportunity to vote, much less run for the nation's highest office.

arresting sight. The front-runner was New York senator Hillary Rodham Clinton, a woman with, for the first time, a real opportunity to take her candidacy all the way to the White House. Close behind her in the polls was Illinois senator Barack Obama, whose political backing, particularly among young voters, also gave him a serious chance to win the nomination and the presidency. New Mexico governor Bill Richardson was not running as well in the polls, but he too, with an impressive résumé, seemed like a person who might pull it off, which made him the first serious Hispanic candidate for the presidency.

In the Democrats' apparent eagerness for change, the white men on the stage, John Edwards, Joe Biden, and Chris Dodd, seemed a little unexciting, a little too business-as-usual. Seeming to struggle with a sense that he couldn't compete with the exotic novelty of his opponents as the field narrowed, Edwards began to cite his status as "the white male candidate," almost as if he were the one running at a disadvantage once the field had narrowed to three.[1]

Media commentary focused on whether the country was ready for a female or a black president. A Democratic pollster, writing in

February, wasn't sure. He compared a 1958 poll, in which 53 percent of Americans said they would be unwilling to vote for an African American president and 41 percent said they would not vote for a woman, with recent data in which only 5 percent said they would not support an African American and 11 percent said they would not back a woman. He noted, however, that it was much less socially acceptable to voice one's prejudices today than it used to be, and wondered if the change the polls reflected was a sincere and lasting one.[2]

Certainly there were many complaints about sexism in the media's coverage of the campaign. Clinton supporters (and many Obama supporters as well) noted that Senator Clinton was frequently called "Hillary"; that her wardrobe and makeup were often the subject of discussion and critique; that her laugh was referred to by some as a "cackle," evoking a witch-like image; and that media commentators compared her to everything from a "she-devil," to "everyone's first wife standing outside a probate court."[3] Clinton's campaign drew attention to these slights, hoping to hold the media accountable, but little changed. When John McCain named Sarah Palin as his running mate at the start of the general election, accusations of sexism again flew fast and furiously.

Critical observers claimed that there was racism in the campaign, too. A Republican congressman from Kentucky called the then-forty-six-year-old Obama a "boy."[4] His patriotism and his commitment to Christianity were frequently the subject of Internet rumor and were even questioned in debates, and his opponents occasionally got caught uttering phrases that seemed to feed into racial stereotypes. For example, then-senator Joe Biden praised him as "the first mainstream African-American who is articulate, bright and clean;"[5] former president Bill Clinton seemed to devalue Obama's win in the South Carolina primary by comparing it to Jesse Jackson's;[6] and Senator Clinton made a pitch for support by telling *USA Today* that a poll had found that "Senator Obama's support among working, hard-working Americans, white

Americans, is weakening again, and . . . whites in both states who had not completed college were supporting [her]."[7] The Obama campaign itself sent confusing signals. Cautious about alienating white voters, they played down incidents of racism even as they decried them, leading some observers to claim that they themselves were playing "a race card."[8] Midway through the primary season, media obsession with controversial remarks made by the pastor of his church led Obama to give an entire speech on race, in an effort to put the issue behind him; the attempt was only partly successful.

As the prevalence of sexism and racism in the 2008 Democratic primary and the accompanying media coverage suggest, neither has been eradicated from American culture. Nonetheless, both Clinton and Palin claimed that their candidacies had made major inroads for future women candidates, and Obama's eventual victory over McCain certainly suggests that racism, too, is on the wane. How did that come about? How did the diversity of the electoral field help to change the way Americans saw both gender and race? What was at stake for American civil rights in the 2008 Democratic primary? ■

Despite the deeply held American expectation that the law should treat all people equally, laws by nature must treat some people differently from others.

When you consider where we started, the progress toward racial equality in the United States can look pretty impressive. Just over fifty years ago, it was illegal for most blacks and whites to go to the same schools in the American South or to use the same public facilities, like swimming pools and drinking fountains. Today, for most of us, the segregated South is a distant memory. On August 28, 2008, forty years from the day that civil rights leader Martin Luther King Jr. declared that he had a dream that one day a child would be judged on the content of his character rather than the color of his skin, the nation watched as Barack Obama, born of a white mother from Kansas and an African father from Kenya, accepted the Democratic Party's nomination to the presidency, an office he would go on to win. Such moments, caught in the media spotlight, illuminate a stark contrast between now and then.

But in some ways, the changes highlighted at such moments are only superficial. Though black cabinet members are not uncommon—George W. Bush had two African American secretaries of state, Colin Powell and Condoleezza Rice, and Obama appointed the first black attorney general, Eric Holder—there have been remarkably few blacks in national elected office. *USA Today* pointed out in 2002 that "if the U.S. Senate and the National Governors Association were private clubs, their membership rosters would be a scandal. They're virtually lily white,"[9] and not much has changed since then. Since Reconstruction, only three elected governors and three U.S. senators have been African Americans. Ironically, Obama's election to the presidency in 2008 removed the only black senator serving at the time, although the Illinois governor eventually appointed another African American to replace him.

Even though legal discrimination ended nearly fifty years ago, inequality still pervades the American system and continues to be reflected in economic and social statistics. On average, blacks are less educated and much poorer than whites, they experience higher crime rates, they live disproportionately in poverty-stricken areas, they score lower on standardized tests, and they rank at the bottom of most social measurements. Life expectancy is lower for African American men and women than for their white counterparts, and a greater percentage of African American children live in single-parent homes than do white or Hispanic children. The statistics illustrate what we suggested in Chapter 5—that rights equal power, and long-term deprivation of rights results

civil rights   citizenship rights guaranteed to the people (primarily in the Thirteenth, Fourteenth, Fifteenth, Nineteenth, and Twenty-sixth Amendments) and protected by the government

suspect classification   classification, such as race, for which any discriminatory law must be justified by a compelling state interest

strict scrutiny   a heightened standard of review used by the Supreme Court to assess the constitutionality of laws that limit some freedoms or that make a suspect classification

in powerlessness. Unfortunately, the granting of formal **civil rights**, which we defined in Chapter 5 as the citizenship rights guaranteed by the Thirteenth, Fourteenth, Fifteenth, Nineteenth, and Twenty-sixth Amendments, does not immediately bring about change in social and economic status.

African Americans are not the only group that shows the effects of having been deprived of its civil rights. Native Americans, Hispanics, and Asian Americans have all faced or face unequal treatment in the legal system, the job market, and the schools. Women, making up over half the population of the United States, have long struggled to gain economic parity with men. People in America are also denied rights, and consequently power, on the basis of their sexual orientation, their age, their physical abilities, and their citizenship status. A country once praised by French observer Alexis de Tocqueville as a place of extraordinary equality, the United States today is haunted by traditions of unequal treatment and intolerance that it cannot entirely shake.

In this chapter we look at the struggles of these groups to gain equal rights and the power to enforce those rights. The struggles are different because the groups themselves, and the political avenues open to them, vary in important ways. In order to understand how groups can use different political strategies to change the rules and win power, in this chapter you will learn about

- **the meaning of political inequality**
- **the struggle of African Americans to claim rights denied to them because of race**
- **the struggle of Native Americans, Hispanics, and Asian Americans to claim rights denied to them because of race or ethnicity**
- **women's battle for rights denied to them on the basis of gender**
- **the fight by other groups in society to claim rights denied to them on a variety of bases**
- **the relationship of citizens to civil rights**

The Meaning of Political Inequality
When is different treatment okay?

Despite the deeply held American expectation that the law should treat all people equally, laws by nature must treat some people differently from others. Not only are laws designed in the first place to discriminate *between* those who abide by society's rules and those who don't,[10] but the laws can also legally treat criminals differently once they are convicted. For instance, in all but two states, Maine and Vermont, felons are denied the right to vote for some length of time, and in ten states, felons forfeit voting rights permanently.[11] But when particular groups are treated differently because of some characteristic like race, religion, gender, sexual orientation, age, or wealth, we say that the law discriminates *against* them, that they are denied equal protection of the laws. Throughout our history, legislatures, both state and national, have passed laws treating groups differently based on characteristics such as these. Sometimes those laws have seemed just and reasonable, but often they have not. Deciding which characteristics may fairly be the basis of unequal treatment is the job of all three branches of our government, but especially of our court system.

When Can the Law Treat People Differently?

The Supreme Court has expended considerable energy and ink on this problem, and its answers have changed over time as various groups have waged the battle for equal rights against a backdrop of ever-changing American values, public opinion, and politics. Before we look at the struggles those groups have endured in their pursuit of equal treatment by the law, we should understand the Court's current formula for determining what sorts of discrimination need what sorts of legal remedy.

Legal Classifications

The Court has divided the laws that treat people differently into three tiers (see Table 6.1):

- The top tier refers to those ways of classifying people that are so rarely constitutional that they are immediately "suspect." Suspect classifications require that the government have a *compelling state interest* for treating people differently. Race is a **suspect classification**. To determine whether a law making a suspect classification is constitutional, the Court subjects it to a heightened standard of review called **strict scrutiny**. Strict scrutiny means that the Court looks very carefully at the law and the government interest involved.

> **intermediate standard of review** standard of review used by the Court to evaluate laws that make a quasisuspect classification
>
> **minimum rationality test** standard of review used by the Court to evaluate laws that make a nonsuspect classification

As we saw in Chapter 5, laws that deprived people of some fundamental religious rights were once required to pass the compelling state interest test; at that time, religion was viewed by the Court as a suspect category.

- Classifications that the Court views as less potentially dangerous to fundamental rights fall into the middle tier. These "quasisuspect" classifications may or may not be legitimate grounds for treating people differently. Such classifications are subject not to strict scrutiny but to an *intermediate standard of review*. That is, the Court looks to see if the law requiring different treatment of people bears a substantial relationship to an important state interest. An "important interest test" is not as hard to meet as a "compelling interest test." Laws that treat women differently than men fall into this category.

- Finally, the least-scrutinized tier of classifications is that of "nonsuspect" classifications; these are subject to the *minimum rationality test*. The Court asks whether the government had a *rational basis* for making a law that treats a given class of people differently. Laws that discriminate on the basis of age, such as a curfew for young people, or on the basis of economic level, such as a higher tax rate for those in a certain income bracket, need not stem from compelling or important government interests. The government must merely have had a rational basis for making the law, which is fairly easy for a legislature to show.

The Fight for Suspect Status

The significance of the three tiers of classifications and the three review standards is that all groups that feel discriminated against want the Court to view them as a suspect class so that they will be treated as a protected group. Civil rights laws might cover them anyway, and the Fourteenth Amendment, which guarantees equal protection of the laws, may also formally protect them. However, once a group is designated as a suspect class, the Supreme Court is very unlikely to permit *any* laws to treat them differently. Thus gaining suspect status is crucial in the struggle for equal rights.

After over one hundred years of decisions that effectively allowed people to be treated differently because of their race, the Court finally agreed in the 1950s that race is a suspect class. Women's groups, however, have failed to convince the Court, or to amend the Constitution, to make gender a

suspect classification. The intermediate standard of review was devised by the Court to express its view that it is a little more dangerous to classify people by gender than by age or wealth, but not as dangerous as classifying them by race or religion. Some groups in America—homosexuals, for instance—have not even managed to get the Court to consider them in the quasisuspect category. Although some states and localities have passed legislation to prevent discrimination on the basis of sexual orientation, gays can be treated differently by law as long as the state can demonstrate a rational basis for the law.

These standards of review make a real difference in American politics—they are part of the rules of politics that determine society's winners and losers. Americans who are treated unequally by the laws consequently have less power to use the democratic system to get what they need and want (like legislation to protect and further their interests), to secure the resources available through the system (like education and other government benefits), and to gain new resources (like jobs and material goods). People who cannot claim their political rights have little if any standing in a democratic society.

Why Do We Deny Rights?

People deny rights to others for many reasons, although they are not always candid about what those reasons are. People usually explain their denial of others' rights by focusing on some group characteristic. They may say that the other group is not "civilized" or does not recognize the "true God," or that its members are in some other way unworthy or incapable of exercising their rights. People feel compelled to justify poor treatment by blaming the group they are treating poorly.

But usually there is something other than simple fault-finding behind the denial of rights. People deny the rights of others because rights are power. To deny people rights is to have power over them and to force them to conform to our will. Thus at various times in our history people with power in the United States have compelled slaves to work for their profit, they have denied wives the right to divorce their husbands, and they have driven Native Americans from their homes so that they could develop their land. Denying people their rights is an attempt to keep them dependent and submissive. When they find their voice to demand their rights and the laws change, they soon leave their subservience behind.

Table 6.1

When Can the Law Treat People Differently?

Legal classification	When laws treat people differently because of . . .	The Court applies . . .	The Court asks . . .	Example: Test used to uphold a classification	Example: Test used to strike down a classification
Suspect	Race (or legislation that infringes on some fundamental rights)	Strict scrutiny standard of review	Is there a *compelling state interest* in this classification?	Government had a compelling state interest (national security) in relocating Japanese Americans from the West Coast during World War II. *Korematsu v. United States* (1944)	State government had no compelling reason to segregate schools to achieve state purpose of educating children. *Brown v. Board of Education* (1954)
Quasisuspect	Gender	Intermediate standard of review	Is there an *important state purpose* for this classification, and are the means used by the law substantially related to the ends?	Court upheld federal law requiring males but not females to register for military service (the draft). *Rostker v. Goldberg* (1981)	Court struck down an Alabama law requiring husbands but not wives to pay alimony after divorce. *Orr v. Orr* (1979)
Nonsuspect	Age, wealth, sexual orientation	Minimum rationality standard of review	Is there a *rational basis* for this classification?	Court found a Missouri law requiring public officials to retire at age 70 to have a rational basis. *Gregory v. Ashcroft* (1991)	Court struck down an amendment to the Colorado constitution that banned legislation to protect people's rights on the basis of their sexual orientation because it had no rational relation to a legitimate state goal. *Romer v. Evans* (1996)

People also deny rights to others for another reason. Isolating categories of people—be they recent immigrants who speak English poorly, homosexuals whose lifestyle seems threatening, or people whose religious beliefs are unfamiliar—helps groups to define who they are, who their relevant community is, and who they are *not*. Communities can believe that they, with their culture, values, and beliefs, are superior to people who are different. This belief promotes cohesion and builds loyalty to "people who are like us"; it also intensifies dislike of and hostility to those who are "not our kind." It is only a small step from there to believing that people outside the community do not really deserve the same rights as those "superior" people within.

Different Kinds of Equality

The notion of equality is very controversial in America. The disputes arise in part because we often think that "equal" must mean "identical" or "the same." Thus equality can seem threatening to the American value system, which prizes people's freedom to be different, to be unique individuals. We can better understand the controversies over the attempts to create political equality in this country if we return briefly to a distinction we made in Chapter 2 between substantive and procedural equality.

In American political culture, we prefer to rely on government to guarantee fair treatment and equal opportunity (a *procedural* view), rather than to manipulate fair and equal outcomes (a *substantive* view). We want government to treat everyone the same, and we want people to be free to be different, but we do not want government to treat people differently in order to make them equal at the end. This distinction poses a problem for the civil rights movement in America, the effort to achieve equal treatment by the laws for all Americans. When the laws are changed, which is a procedural solution, substantive action may still be necessary to ensure equal treatment in the future.

> *racism* institutionalized power inequalities in society based on the perception of racial differences

Who What How

In the struggle for political equality, the people with the most at stake are members of groups who, because of some characteristic beyond their control, have been denied their civil rights. What they seek is equal treatment by the laws. The rules the Supreme Court uses to determine if they should have equal treatment are the three standards of strict scrutiny, the intermediate standard of review, and the minimum rationality test.

But minority groups are not the only ones with a stake in the battle for equal rights. Those who support discrimination want to maintain the status quo, which bolsters their own power and the power of those like them. The means open to them are maintaining discriminatory laws and intimidating those they discriminate against.

Thinking Outside the Box

What would a legal system that treated all people exactly the same look like?

Rights Denied on the Basis of Race

The battle to end the legacy of slavery and racism, fought mainly in the courts

We cannot separate the history of our race relations from the history of the United States. Americans have struggled for centuries to come to terms with the fact that citizens of African nations were kidnapped, packed into sailing vessels, exported to America, and sold, often at great profit, into a life that destroyed their families, their spirit, and their human dignity. The stories of white supremacy and black inferiority, told to numb the sensibilities of European Americans to the horror of their own behavior, have been almost as damaging as slavery itself and have lived on in the American psyche— and in political institutions—much longer than the practice they justified. *Racism*, institutionalized power inequalities in society based on the perception of racial differences, is not a "southern problem" or a "black problem"; it is an American problem, and one that we have not yet managed to eradicate from national culture.

Not only has racism had a decisive influence on American culture, it has also been central to American politics. From the start, those with power in America have been torn by the issue of race. The framers of the Constitution were so ambivalent that they would not use the word *slavery*, even while that document legalized its existence. Although some early politicians were morally opposed to the institution of slavery, they were, in the end, more reluctant to offend their southern colleagues by taking an antislavery stand. Even the Northwest Ordinance of 1787, which prohibited slavery in the northwestern territories, contained the concession to the South that fugitive slaves could legally be seized and returned to their owners. Sometimes in politics the need to compromise and bargain can cause people to excuse the inexcusable for political gain.

Blacks in America Before the Civil War

At the time of the Civil War there were almost four million slaves in the American South and nearly half a million free blacks living in the rest of the country. Even where slavery was illegal, blacks as a rule did not enjoy full rights of citizenship. In fact, in *Dred Scott v. Sanford* (1857), the Supreme Court had ruled that blacks could not be citizens because the founders had not intended them to be citizens. "On the contrary," wrote Justice Roger Taney, "they were at that time considered as a subordinate and inferior class of beings, who had been subjugated by the dominant race, and whether emancipated or not, yet remained subject to their authority."[12]

Congress was no more protective of blacks than the Court was. Laws such as the Fugitive Slave Act of 1850 made life precarious even for free northern blacks. When national institutions seemed impervious to their demands for black rights, the abolitionists, a coalition of free blacks and northern whites working to end slavery altogether, tried other strategies. The movement put pressure on the Republican Party to take a stand on political equality and persuaded three state legislatures (Iowa, Wisconsin, and New York) to hold referenda (statewide votes) on black suffrage between 1857 and 1860. The abolitionists lost all three votes by large margins. Even in the North, on the eve of the Civil War, public opinion did not favor rights for blacks.

The Civil War and Its Aftermath: Winners and Losers

We can't begin to speculate here on all the causes of the Civil War. Suffice it to say that the war was not fought simply over

> **black codes** a series of laws in the post–Civil War South designed to restrict the rights of former slaves before the passage of the Fourteenth and Fifteenth Amendments
>
> **Reconstruction** the period following the Civil War during which the federal government took action to rebuild the South
>
> **poll taxes** taxes levied as a qualification for voting

> **literacy tests** tests requiring reading or comprehension skills as a qualification for voting
>
> **grandfather clauses** provisions exempting from voting restrictions the descendants of those able to vote in 1867
>
> **Jim Crow laws** southern laws designed to circumvent the Thirteenth, Fourteenth, and Fifteenth Amendments and to deny blacks rights on bases other than race

the moral evil of slavery. Slavery was an economic and political issue as well as an ethical one. The southern economy depended on slavery, and when, in an effort to hold the Union together in 1863, President Abraham Lincoln issued the Emancipation Proclamation, he was not simply taking a moral stand; he was trying to use economic pressure to keep the country intact. The proclamation, in fact, did not free all slaves, only those in states rebelling against the Union.[13]

It is hard to find any real "winners" in the American Civil War. Indeed the war took such a toll on North and South that neither world war in the twentieth century would claim as many American casualties. The North "won" the war, in that the Union was restored, but the costs would be paid for decades afterward. Politically, the northern Republicans, the party of Lincoln, were in the ascendance, controlling both the House and the Senate, but their will was often thwarted by President Andrew Johnson, a Democrat from Tennessee who was sympathetic toward the South.

The Thirteenth Amendment, banning slavery, was passed and ratified in 1865. In retaliation, and to ensure that their political and social dominance of southern society would continue, the southern white state governments legislated **black codes**. Black codes were laws that essentially sought to keep blacks in a subservient economic and political position by restoring as many of the conditions of slavery as possible. As one scholar describes it, "Twenty years after freedom, a former slave was apt to be a black peasant, apathetically scratching a crop out of exhausted soil not his own, with scrawny mules and rusted plows and hoes that he had neither the incentive nor the means to improve."[14] In all likelihood, he was still working for, or at least on the land of, his former master. "Freedom" did not make a great deal of difference in the lives of most former slaves after the war.

Reconstruction and Its Reversal

Congress, led by northern Republicans, tried to check southern obstruction of its will by instituting a period of federal control of southern politics called **Reconstruction**, which began in 1865. In an attempt to make the black codes unconstitutional, the Fourteenth Amendment was passed, guaranteeing all people born or naturalized in the United States the rights of citizenship. Further, no state could deprive any person of life, liberty, or property without due process of the law, or deny any person equal protection of the law.

As we saw in Chapter 5, the Supreme Court has made varied use of this amendment, but its original intent was to bring some semblance of civil rights to southern blacks. The Fifteenth Amendment followed in 1870, effectively extending the right to vote to all adult males.

At first Reconstruction worked as the North had hoped. Under northern supervision, southern life began to change. Blacks voted, were elected to some local posts, and cemented Republican dominance with their support. But soon southern whites responded with violence. Groups like the Ku Klux Klan terrorized blacks in the South and made them reluctant to claim the rights to which they were legally entitled for fear of reprisals. Lynchings, arson, assaults, and beatings made claiming one's rights or associating with Republicans a risky business. Congress fought back vigorously and suppressed the reign of terror for a while, but its efforts earned accusations of military tyranny, and the Reconstruction project began to run out of steam. Plagued by political problems of their own, the Republicans were losing electoral strength and seats in Congress. Meanwhile, the Democrats were gradually reasserting their power in the southern states. By 1876, Reconstruction was effectively over, and shortly after that, southern whites set about the business of disenfranchising blacks, or taking away their newfound political power.

Segregation and the Era of Jim Crow

Without the protection of the northern Republicans, disenfranchisement turned out to be easy to accomplish. The strategy chosen by the Democrats, who now controlled the southern state governments, was a sly one. Under the Fifteenth Amendment the vote could not be denied on the basis of race, color, or previous condition of servitude, so they set out to deny it on other, legal, bases that would have the primary effect of targeting blacks. **Poll taxes**, which required the payment of a small tax before voters could cast their votes, effectively took the right to vote away from the many blacks who were too poor to pay, and **literacy tests**, which required potential voters to demonstrate some reading skills, excluded most blacks who, denied an education, could not read. Even African Americans who were literate were often kept from voting because a white registrar administered the test unfairly. To permit illiterate whites to vote, literacy tests were combined with **grandfather clauses**, which required passage of such tests only by those prospective voters whose grandfathers

Segregation and the Era of Jim Crow
After Reconstruction, the fever to reestablish and maintain white supremacy in southern and border states led to acts of terror. Between 1882 and 1951, 3,437 African Americans were lynched by mobs. Local authorities usually claimed the killers could not be identified, although the mobs often posed for photographs like this one that were then turned into postcards and saved as macabre souvenirs.

had not been allowed to vote before 1867. Thus, unlike the black codes, these new laws, called **Jim Crow laws**, obeyed the letter of the Fifteenth Amendment, never explicitly saying that they were denying blacks the right to vote because of their race, color, or previous condition of servitude. This strategy proved devastatingly effective, and by 1910, registration of black voters had dropped dramatically, and registration of poor, illiterate whites had fallen as well.[15] Southern Democrats were back in power and had eliminated the possibility of competition.

Jim Crow laws were not just about voting but also concerned many other dimensions of southern life. The 1900s launched a half-century of **segregation** in the South—that is, of separate facilities for blacks and whites for leisure, business, travel, education, and other activities. The Civil Rights Act of 1875 had guaranteed that all people, regardless of race, color, or previous condition of servitude, were to have full and equal accommodation in "inns, public conveyances on land or water, theaters, and other places of public amusement," but the Supreme Court struck down the law, arguing that the Fourteenth Amendment only restricted the behavior of states, not of private individuals.[16] Having survived the legal test of the Constitution, Jim Crow laws continued to divide the southern world in two. But it was not a world of equal halves. The whites-only facilities were

invariably superior to those intended for blacks; they were newer, cleaner, more comfortable. Before long, the laws were challenged by blacks who asked why equal protection of the law shouldn't translate into some real equality in their lives.

One Jim Crow law, a Louisiana statute passed in 1890, required separate accommodations in all trains passing through the state. Homer Plessy, traveling through Louisiana, chose to sit in the white section. Although Plessy often passed as a white person, he was in fact one-eighth black, which made him a black man according to Louisiana law. When he refused to sit in the "Colored Only" section, Plessy was arrested. He appealed his conviction all the way to the Supreme Court, which ruled against him in 1896. In **Plessy v. Ferguson**, the Court held that enforced separation of the races did not mean that one race was inferior to the other. As long as the facilities provided were equal, states were within their rights to require them to be separate. Rejecting the majority view, Justice John Marshall Harlan wrote in a famous dissent, "Our Constitution is color-blind, and neither knows nor tolerates classes among citizens."[17] It would be over fifty years before a majority on the Court shared his view. In the meantime, everyone immediately embraced the "separate," and forgot the "equal," part of the ruling. Segregated facilities for whites and blacks had received the Supreme Court's seal of approval.

segregation the practice and policy of separating races

Plessy v. Ferguson Supreme Court case that established the constitutionality of the principle "separate but equal"

National Association for the Advancement of Colored People (NAACP) an interest group founded in 1910 to promote civil rights for African Americans

The Long Battle to Overturn *Plessy:* The NAACP and Its Legal Strategy

The years following the *Plessy* decision were bleak ones for African American civil rights. The formal rules of politics giving blacks their rights had been enacted at the national level, but no branch of government at any level was willing to enforce them. The Supreme Court had firmly rejected attempts to give the Fourteenth Amendment more teeth. Congress was not inclined to help since the Republican fervor for reform had worn off. Nor were the southern state governments likely to support black rights.

In the early days of the twentieth century, African Americans themselves did not agree on the best political strategy to follow. Booker T. Washington, president of the Tuskegee Institute, a black college, advocated an accommodationist approach. Blacks should give up demanding political and social equality, he said, and settle for economic opportunity. Through hard work and education they would gradually be recognized on their merits and accorded their rights. This philosophy, popular with whites because it asked so little and seemed so unthreatening, angered many other blacks who felt that they had accommodated whites long enough. People like W. E. B. Du Bois took a far more assertive approach. Only by demanding their rights and refusing to settle for second-class treatment, he argued, would blacks ever enjoy full citizenship in the United States.[18]

Du Bois was influential in starting one of a handful of African American groups born in the early 1900s to fight for civil rights. The ***National Association for the Advancement of Colored People (NAACP)***, founded in 1910, aimed to help individual blacks; to raise white society's awareness of the atrocities of contemporary race relations; and most important, to change laws and court rulings that kept blacks from true equality. The NAACP, over time, was able to develop a legal strategy that was finally the undoing of Jim Crow and the segregated South.

By the 1930s, political changes suggested to the legal minds of the NAACP that the time might be right to challenge the Court's "separate but equal" decision. Blacks had made some major political advances in the North, not so much by convincing Republicans to support them again, but by joining the coalition that supported Democratic president Franklin Roosevelt's New Deal. Wanting to woo black voters from the Republican Party, the Democrats gave as much influence to blacks as they dared without alienating powerful southern

Democratic congressmen. The Supreme Court had even taken some tentative steps in the direction of civil rights, such as striking down grandfather clauses in 1915.[19] But after four decades the *Plessy* judgment was still intact.

The Early Education Cases

The NAACP, with the able assistance of a young lawyer named Thurgood Marshall, decided to launch its attack in the area of education. Segregation in education was particularly disastrous for blacks because the poor quality of their schools limited their potential, which in turn reinforced southern beliefs about their inferiority. Knowing that a loss reinforcing *Plessy* would be a major setback, the lawyers at the NAACP chose their cases very carefully. Rather than trying to force the immediate integration of elementary schools, a goal that would have terrified and enraged whites, they began with law schools. Not only would this approach be less threatening, but law schools were clearly discriminatory (most states didn't even have black law schools) and were an educational institution the justices on the Court knew well. The NAACP decision to lead with law school cases was a masterful legal strategy.

The first education case the NAACP took to the Court was *Missouri ex rel Gaines v. Canada*. Lloyd Gaines, a black man, wanted to go to law school in Missouri. Missouri had no law school for blacks but promised to build one. In the meantime, they told him, they would pay his tuition at an out-of-state law school. Gaines sued the state of Missouri, claiming that the facilities open to him under Missouri law were not equal to those available to white students. The Court, in 1938, agreed. It argued that Missouri had failed in its obligation to provide equal facilities and that black students in Missouri had an equal right to go to law school in-state.[20] The *Gaines* case was significant because the Court was looking at something it had ignored in *Plessy:* whether the separate facilities in question were truly equal.

Twelve years later, the *Gaines* decision was expanded in *Sweatt v. Painter*. Again a black law school candidate, Herman Sweatt, applied to a white law school, this time in Texas. The law school denied him admission, but mindful of the Missouri ruling, Texas offered to provide Sweatt with a school of his own in three downtown basement rooms, with a part-time faculty and access to the state law library. Again the NAACP argued before the Court that this alternative would not be an equal facility. But this time it went further and claimed that even if the schools *were* comparable, Sweatt's education would still be unequal because of

Brown v. Board of Education of Topeka Supreme Court case that rejected the idea that separate could be equal in education; catalyst for civil rights movement

the intangible benefits he would lose: the reputation of the school, talking with classmates, and making contacts for the future, for example. The justices agreed. Perhaps they were aware of how different their own legal educations would have been, isolated in three basement rooms by themselves. If the separate education was not equal, they said, it was unconstitutional under the Fourteenth Amendment.[21]

The ruling striking down "separate but equal" laws was aided by an unrelated case that, ironically, had the effect of depriving Japanese American citizens of many of their civil rights during World War II. In *Korematsu v. United States* (1944), Justice Hugo Black articulated the strict scrutiny test described earlier in this chapter: "All legal restrictions which curtail the civil rights of a single racial group are immediately suspect. That is not to say that all such restrictions are unconstitutional. It is to say that courts must subject them to the most rigid scrutiny."[22] After applying strict scrutiny, the Court allowed the laws that limited the civil rights of Japanese Americans to stand because it felt that the racial classification was justified by considerations of national security. The ruling was disastrous for Japanese Americans, but it would give blacks more ammunition in their fight for equal rights. From that point on, a law that treated people differently on the basis of race had to be based on a compelling governmental interest, or it could not stand.

Brown v. Board of Education

By the early 1950s the stage was set for tackling the issue of education more broadly. The NAACP had four cases pending that concerned the segregation of educational facilities in the South and the Midwest. The Court ruled on all of them under the case name **Brown v. Board of Education of Topeka**.

Will Counts Collection: Indiana University Archives

Racial Progress

The scene was chaotic and ugly in 1957 when Elizabeth Eckford and eight other black students integrated Central High School in Little Rock, Arkansas. Forty years later, Eckford and a member of the mob that had taunted her, Hazel Bryan Massery, met again in front of the school, this time on friendly terms (Massery had telephoned Eckford in 1962 to apologize for her part in the disturbance).

In the years since the NAACP's historic fight to overturn *Plessy*, education has indeed been on the rise for all groups. But despite these historic inroads, America's minority groups are still lagging behind whites in education. Higher education is clearly linked to economic success, but even where education levels are similar, minorities and women continue to earn much less than their white male counterparts. Why do these disparities continue to exist?

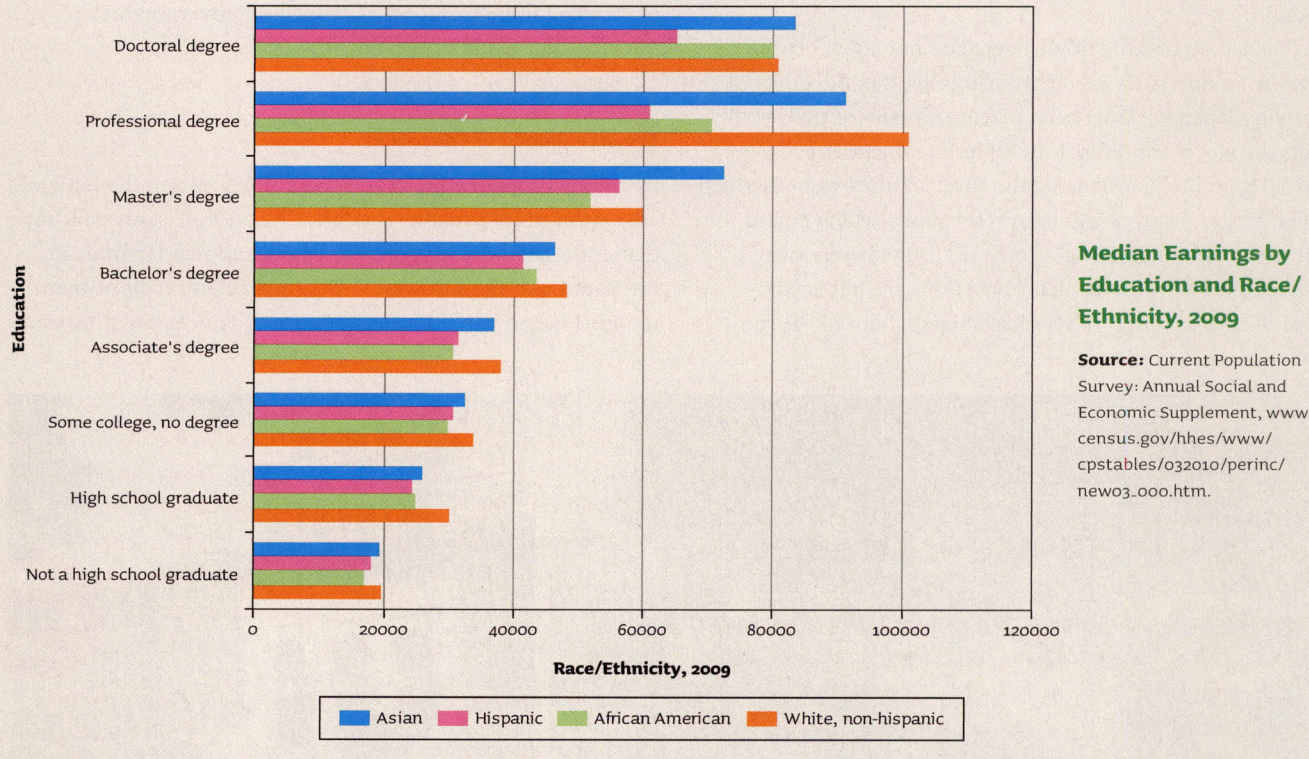

Median Earnings by Education and Race/ Ethnicity, 2009

Source: Current Population Survey: Annual Social and Economic Supplement, www.census.gov/hhes/www/cpstables/032010/perinc/new03_000.htm.

In its now-familiar arguments, the NAACP emphasized the intangible aspects of education, including how black students felt when made to go to a separate school. They cited sociological evidence of the low self-esteem of black schoolchildren and argued that it resulted from a system that made black children feel inferior by treating them differently.

Under the new leadership of Chief Justice Earl Warren, the Court ruled unanimously in favor of Linda Brown and the other black students. Without explicitly denouncing segregation or overturning *Plessy*, lest the South erupt in violent outrage again, the Warren Court held that separate schools, by their very definition, could never be equal because it was the fact of separation itself that made black children feel unequal. Segregation in education was inherently unconstitutional.[23] The principle of "separate but equal" was not yet dead, but it had suffered serious injury.

The *Brown* decision did not bring instant relief to the southern school system. The Court, in a 1955 follow-up to *Brown*, ruled that school desegregation had to take place "with all deliberate speed."[24] Such an ambiguous direction was asking for school districts to drag their feet. The most public and blatant attempt to avoid compliance took place in Little Rock, Arkansas, in September 1957, when Governor

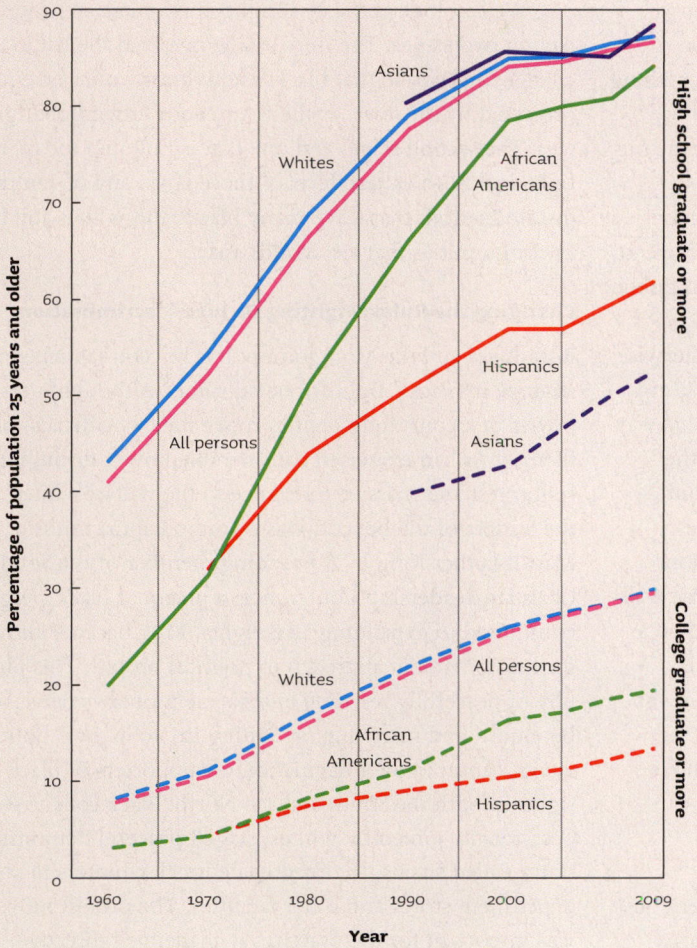

Education Attainment, 1960–2009

Source: U.S. Census Bureau, Historical Tables, "Table A-2: Percent of People 25 Years and Over Who Have Completed High School or College, by Race, Hispanic Origin and Sex: Selected Years 1940 to 2009," www.census.gov/population/www/socdemo/educ-attn.html.

Orval Faubus posted the National Guard at the local high school to prevent the attendance of nine African American children. Rioting white parents, filmed for the nightly news, revealed the faces of southern bigotry. Finally, President Dwight Eisenhower sent one thousand federal troops to guarantee the safe passage of the nine black children through the angry mob of white parents who threatened to lynch them rather than let them enter the school. The *Brown* case, and the attempts to enforce it, proved to be a catalyst for a civil rights movement that would change the whole country. See *"Who Are We? Education in America"* for data on educational disparities that still exist.

The Civil Rights Movement

In the same year that the Court ordered school desegregation to proceed "with all deliberate speed," a woman named Rosa Parks sat down on a bus in Montgomery, Alabama, and started a chain of events that would end with a Court order to stop segregation in all aspects of southern life.

As law required, Parks sat in the black section at the back of the bus. As the bus filled, all the white seats were taken, and the driver ordered Parks and the other blacks in her row to stand. Tired from a fatiguing day as a seamstress, Parks refused. She was arrested and sent to jail.

boycott refusal to buy certain goods or services as a way to protest policy or force political reform

de jure discrimination discrimination arising from or supported by the law

de facto discrimination discrimination that is the result not of law but rather of tradition and habit

Overnight, local groups in the black community organized a **boycott** of the Montgomery bus system. A boycott seeks to put economic pressure on a business to do something by encouraging people to stop purchasing its goods or services. Montgomery blacks, who formed the base of the bus company's clientele, wanted the bus company to lose so much money that it would force the local government to change the bus laws. Against all expectations, the bus boycott continued for over a year. Despite their dependence on public transportation (fewer blacks owned cars than whites), boycotters found the stamina to walk, carpool, and otherwise avoid the buses to make a political statement that was heard around the country. In the meantime, the case wound its way through the legal system, and a little over a year after the boycott began, the Supreme Court affirmed a lower court's judgment that Montgomery's law was unconstitutional.[25] Separate bus accommodations were not equal. (The Montgomery bus boycott was portrayed in the movie *The Long Walk Home*. Watching a historical film—especially one based on a real person or an event—requires critical thinking skills similar to those needed to read a newspaper or surf the web. See "*Consider the Source: Don't Be Fooled by the Movies*" for some suggestions on how to get the most out of the movies you view.)

Two Kinds of Discrimination

The civil rights movement launched by the Montgomery bus boycott confronted two different types of discrimination. **De jure discrimination** (discrimination by law) is created by laws that treat people differently based on some characteristic like race. This is the sort of discrimination most blacks in the South faced. Especially in rural areas, blacks and whites lived and worked side by side, but by law they used separate facilities. Although the process of changing the laws was excruciatingly painful, once the laws were changed and the new laws were enforced, the result was integration.

The second sort of discrimination, called **de facto discrimination** (discrimination in fact), however, produces a kind of segregation that is much more difficult to eliminate. Segregation in the North was of this type because blacks and whites did not live and work in the same places to begin with. It was not laws that kept them apart, but past discrimination, tradition, custom, economic status, and residential patterns. This kind of segregation is so hard to remedy because there are no laws to change; the segregation is woven more complexly into the fabric of society.

We can look at the civil rights movement in America as having two stages. The initial stage involved the battle to change the laws so that blacks and whites would be equally protected by the laws, as the Fourteenth Amendment guarantees. The second stage, and one that is ongoing today, is the fight against the aftereffects of those laws, and of centuries of discrimination, that leave many blacks and whites still living in communities that are worlds apart.

Changing the Rules: Fighting De Jure Discrimination

Rosa Parks and the Montgomery bus boycott launched a new strategy in blacks' fight for equal rights. Although it took the power of a court judgment to move the city officials, blacks themselves had exercised considerable power through peaceful protest and massive resistance to the will of whites. One of the leaders of the boycott was a young Baptist minister named Martin Luther King Jr. A founding member of the Southern Christian Leadership Conference, a group of black clergy committed to expanding civil rights, King became known for his nonviolent approach to political protest. This philosophy of peacefully resisting enforcement of laws perceived to be unjust, and marching or "sitting in" to express political views, captured the imagination of supporters of black civil rights in both the South and the North. Black college students, occasionally joined by whites, staged peaceful demonstrations, called sit-ins, to desegregate lunch counters in southern department stores and other facilities. The protest movement was important for the practices it challenged directly—such as segregation in motels and restaurants, on beaches, and in other recreational facilities—but also for the pressure it brought to bear on elected officials and the effect it had on public opinion, particularly in the North, which had been largely unaware of southern problems.

The nonviolent resistance movement, in conjunction with the growing political power of northern blacks, brought about remarkable social and political change in the 1960s. The administration of Democratic president John F. Kennedy, not wanting to alienate the support of southern Democrats, tried at first to limit its active involvement in civil rights work. But the political pressure of black interest groups forced Kennedy to take a more visible stand. The Reverend King was using his tactics of nonviolent protest to great advantage in the spring of 1963. The demonstrations he led to protest segregation in Birmingham, Alabama, were met with extreme police violence. With an eye to the national media, King included children in the march. When the police turned on

Nonviolent Protests That Worked

In Birmingham, Alabama, a seventeen-year-old demonstrator is attacked by a police dog after defying a city antiparade ordinance on May 3, 1963. This photograph would run on the front page of the *New York Times* the next day and would draw the attention of President John F. Kennedy. As stories and images of such events spread across the country, more and more people demanded that the violence end and blacks be given equal rights and opportunities.

the demonstrators with swinging clubs, vicious dogs, and high-pressure hoses, the horror was brought to all Americans with their morning newspapers. Kennedy responded to the political pressure, so deftly orchestrated by King, by sending to Birmingham federal mediators to negotiate an end to segregation, and then by sending to Congress a massive package of civil rights legislation.

Kennedy did not live to see his proposals become law, but they became the top priority of his successor, Lyndon Johnson. During the Johnson years, the president, majorities in Congress, and the Supreme Court were in agreement on civil rights issues, and their joint legacy is impressive. The Kennedy-initiated Civil Rights Bill of 1964 reinforced the voting laws, allowed the attorney general to file school desegregation lawsuits, permitted the president to deny federal money to state and local programs that practiced discrimination, prohibited discrimination in public accommodations and in employment, and set up the

Equal Employment Opportunity Commission (EEOC) to investigate complaints about job discrimination. Johnson also sent to Congress the Voting Rights Act of 1965, which, when passed, disallowed discriminatory tests like literacy tests and provided for federal examiners to register voters throughout much of the South. The Supreme Court, still the liberal Warren Court that had ruled in *Brown*, backed up this new legislation.[26] In addition, the Twenty-fourth Amendment, outlawing poll taxes in federal elections, was ratified in 1964.

Because of the unusual cooperation among the three branches of government, by the end of the 1960s life in the South, though far from perfect, was radically different for blacks. In 1968, 18 percent of southern black students went to schools with a majority of white students; in 1970 the percentage rose to 39, and in 1972 to 46. The comparable figure for black students in the North was only 28 percent in 1972.[27] Voter registration had also improved dramatically:

Throughout this book, we've made suggestions for films—both dramas and documentaries—that offer some insights into the political events that have shaped our history. Movies like *The Long Walk Home* (1990), which portrays events surrounding the historic Montgomery bus boycott, and *Mississippi Burning* (1988), which dramatizes the murder of three young civil rights workers in the rural South, do indeed stir emotional responses and invite viewers to consider the more human aspects of the civil rights movement in America. But are they good history? Do they enhance the audience's understanding of events? Do they tell the whole truth?

Of course not. Movies are created to make money, to tell stories in a dramatic and compelling manner, and often to promote a particular cause or idea. Stories inspired by real events are retold through the eyes of producers, writers, directors, and actors who bend the truth to create a particular artistic and commercial vision. Even films with no commercial ambitions whatsoever—independent documentaries, for example—are shot (and, perhaps more important, edited) by filmmakers who inevitably have their own agenda. Thus even the most even-handed and objective treatment of an issue is bound to be informed somewhat by the filmmaker's basic feelings. Ken Burns's *Civil War* (1990), for example, is a critically acclaimed, thorough, and fact-based documentation of the war between the states. But it is colored by Burns's own feelings and by the culture in which it was produced. A different filmmaker, living at a different time or in a different place, might have used the same facts and materials to create a very different film.

How then can you distinguish the well-established historical fact from the artist's fancy? Is it possible for a film to enhance our understanding of political events without manipulating us? It is—if you keep a critical eye. The next time you settle in for a movie about politics, history, or social movements, ask yourself the following questions:

1. **What kind of film are you watching?** A Hollywood release such as *The Hurt Locker* (2009) is meant to draw in a huge audience and make lots of money. That often means that factual accuracy is less important than action, romance, or drama. Even films that purport to be inspired by true stories often bend, gloss over, or ignore crucial facts, or even create new ones.

2. **Who made the movie?** Do the producers have a stake in a particular interpretation of events? Does the director have an axe to grind or some personal experience that might inspire or influence his vision? How might a film like *Malcolm X* (1992) have been different had it been made by a white director rather than Spike Lee? Would the story of female baseball players told by Penny Marshall in *A League of Their Own* (1993) have been told differently by a man?

3. **What is the filmmaker's reputation?** Some filmmakers are known for striving to be historically accurate, others for taking artistic license, and still others for using the medium to promote their own beliefs or philosophies. For example, Michael Moore is well known for using his movies, such as *Fahrenheit 9/11* (2004), *Sicko* (2007), and *Capitalism: A Love Story* (2009), to promote his political views; and Mel Gibson used his film *The Passion of the Christ* (2004) to express his interpretation of particular religious events. Oliver Stone's reputation for making movies that dramatize his theories of the nefarious forces behind political and social events (like the 1991 movie *JFK*) no doubt influenced how his 2008 movie *W.*, about President George W. Bush, was received.

4. **Where and when was it made?** Films are informed by the times in which they were produced and must be viewed with that in mind. Movies that were considered progressive at the time they were released might seem racist or sexist now.

5. **What is the primary source for historical material?** Filmmakers often consult historians and other experts to add factual and dramatic accuracy to their movies. For example, Steven Spielberg accomplished his spectacular dramatization of the Allied invasion of Europe during World War II for *Saving Private Ryan* (1998) with the help of noted experts on the subject, including the late Stephen Ambrose, a noted World War II historian.

6. **Who's telling the story?** Consider the movie's perspective. Films about the civil rights movement as seen by the U.S. attorney general, a nonviolent protester, or a southern sheriff would prove very different from beginning to end.

7. **What have the critics said about it?** Thorough reviews of films from reputable critics and historians can offer insights into any hidden agendas. *Mississippi Burning*, for example, is a powerful film, but it has been widely criticized by historians for its grossly misleading account of the investigation into the murder of three civil rights workers in the rural South.

busing achieving racial balance by transporting students to schools across neighborhood boundaries

affirmative action a policy of creating opportunities for members of certain groups as a substantive remedy for past discrimination

from 1964 to 1969, black voter registration in the South nearly doubled, from 36 to 65 percent of adult blacks.[28]

Changing the Outcomes: Fighting De Facto Discrimination

Political and educational advances did not translate into substantial economic gains for blacks. As a group, they remained at the very bottom of the economic hierarchy, and ironically, the problem was most severe not in the rural South but in the industrialized North. Many southern blacks who had migrated to the North in search of jobs and a better quality of life found conditions not much different from those they had left behind. Abject poverty, discrimination in employment, and segregated schools and housing led to frustration and inflamed tempers. In the summers of 1966 and 1967, race riots flashed across the northern urban landscape, leaving death, destruction, and ashes in their wake. Impatient with the passive resistance of the nonviolent protest movement in the South, many blacks became more militant in their insistence on social and economic change. The Black Muslims, led by Malcolm X until his assassination in 1965; the Black Panthers; and the Student Nonviolent Coordinating Committee all demanded "black power" and radical change. These activists rejected the King philosophy of working peacefully through existing political institutions to bring about gradual change.

Northern whites who had applauded the desegregation of the South grew increasingly nervous as angry African Americans began to target segregation in the North. As we explained earlier, the de facto segregation in the North was not the product of laws that treated blacks and whites differently, but instead resulted from different residential patterns, socioeconomic trends, and years of traditions and customs that subtly discriminated against blacks. Black inner-city schools and white suburban schools were often as segregated as if the hand of Jim Crow had been at work.

In the 1970s the courts and some politicians, believing that they had a duty not only to end segregation laws in education but also to integrate the schools, instituted a policy of *busing* in some northern cities. Students from majority-white schools would be bused to mostly black schools, and vice versa. The policy was immediately controversial; riots in South Boston in 1974 resembled those in Little Rock seventeen years earlier.

Not all opponents of busing were reacting from racist motives. Busing students from their homes to a distant school strikes many Americans as fundamentally unjust. Parents seek to move to better neighborhoods so that they can send their children to better schools, only to see those children bused back to the old schools. Parents want their children to be part of a local community and its activities, which is hard when the children must leave the community for the better part of each day. And they fear for the safety of their children when they are bused into poverty-stricken areas with high crime rates. Even many African American families were opposed to busing because of fears for their children's safety and because of the often long bus rides into predominantly white neighborhoods.

The Supreme Court has shared America's ambivalence about busing. Although it endorsed busing as a remedy for segregated schools in 1971,[29] three years later it ruled that busing plans could not merge inner-city and suburban districts unless officials could prove that the district lines had been drawn in a racially discriminatory manner.[30] Since many whites were moving out of the cities, there were fewer white students to bus, and busing did not really succeed in integrating schools in many urban areas. Fifty years after the Brown decision, many schools, especially those in urban areas, remain largely segregated.[31]

Early Efforts at Affirmative Action

The example of busing highlights a problem faced by civil rights workers and policymakers: deciding whether the Fourteenth Amendment guarantee of equal protection simply requires that the states not sanction discrimination or imposes an active obligation on them to integrate blacks and whites. As the northern experience shows, the absence of legal discrimination does not mean equality. In 1965 President Johnson issued Executive Order 11246, which not only prohibited discrimination in firms doing business with the government but also ordered them to take *affirmative action* to compensate for past discrimination. In other words, if a firm had no black employees, it wasn't enough not to have a policy against hiring them; the firm now had to actively recruit and hire blacks. The test would not be federal law or company policy, but the actual racial mix of employees.

Johnson's call for affirmative action was taken seriously not only in employment situations but also in university decisions. Patterns of discrimination in employment and higher education showed the results of decades of decisions by white males to hire or admit other white males. Blacks, as well as other minorities and women, were relegated to low-paying, low-status jobs. After Johnson's executive order, the EEOC decided that the percentage of blacks working in firms should

▶ Who, What, How, and WHEN: Protest and Civil Rights

The battle for civil rights in this country has been a long and sometimes bloody one. One of the strategies that groups have used to gain recognition for their cause is protest. Protests, whether spontaneous or organized in advance, can draw public attention and be a catalyst for change. The following examples are just a few of the protests that have shaped the struggle for equal rights in the United States:

1917 Picketing the White House for Women's Suffrage

Frustrated by President Woodrow Wilson's refusal to back women's suffrage, in 1917 a group of women led by Alice Paul picketed the White House. People were outraged that the women chose to challenge a president during wartime, especially because some of their banners compared Wilson to a dictator. The women were jailed multiple times for their protest, though not charged, and the pickets and subsequent arrests created sympathy for their cause. Eventually Wilson backed what became the Nineteenth Amendment.

1965 Selma-to-Montgomery March

Protesters marching out of Selma, Alabama, to demonstrate for African American voting rights, were stopped by state and local police with clubs and tear gas. Soon after this attempted march, known as Bloody Sunday, the marchers, led by Martin Luther King Jr., tried again after securing court protection for their right to assemble. The march took four days to complete, and by the time they reached Montgomery, people were part of the protest. The protest garnered media attention for civil rights and the Voting Rights Act of 1965.

1966 United Farm Workers Strike

Mexican American activist Cesar Chavez helped organize two events in 1965–1966 to help farm workers, who were paid below the nationally mandated minimum wage. First, he helped organize a strike and boycott against grape growers in Delano, California, until the union he founded, the United Farm Workers, gained a contract with grape producers. Second, he organized a march from Delano to Sacramento to push state legislators to pass laws allowing unionization of farm workers. Later in life, Chavez fasted multiple times to draw more attention to farm workers' rights.

---

reflect the percentage of blacks in the labor force. Many colleges and universities reserved space on their admissions lists for minorities, sometimes accepting minority applicants with grades and test scores lower than those of whites.

Like busing, affirmative action has proved controversial among the American public. We have talked about the tension in American politics between procedural and substantive equality, between equality of treatment and equality of results. That is precisely the tension that arises when Americans are faced with policies of busing and affirmative action, both of which are instances of American policy attempting to bring about substantive equality. The end results seem attractive, but the means to get there—treating people differently—seem inherently unfair in the American value system.

The Court reflected the public's unease with these affirmative action policies when it ruled in *Regents of the University of California v. Bakke* in 1978. A white applicant for admission, Alan Bakke, had been rejected from the medical school at the University of California, Davis, even though minorities with lower grades and scores had been accepted. He challenged Davis's policy, claiming that it denied him admission to medical school on account of his race—effectively resulting in "reverse discrimination." The Court agreed with him, in part. It ruled that a quota system like Davis's, holding sixteen of one hundred spots for minorities, was a violation of the equal protection clause. But it did not reject the idea of affirmative action, holding that schools can have a legitimate interest in having a diversified student body, and that they can take race into account in admissions decisions

Election Day!

1969 **Stonewall Riots**

In June 1969, police raided a gay bar in New York City called the Stonewall Inn. At the time, all states except Illinois had laws against homosexuality and no state guaranteed equal treatment regardless of sexual orientation. Patrons at the bar fought the police raid, and this resistance started protests in Greenwich Village over the treatment of gays and lesbians for the following six days. Many observers believe these protests started the modern gay rights movement in the United States.

1969 **Seizure of Alcatraz**

In 1969 a group of American Indians from several tribes seized the island of Alcatraz in San Francisco Bay. The land once belonged to American Indians but was used by the U.S. government as a prison until 1963. The occupation lasted until 1971 and brought national attention to American Indian causes. After this, the American Indian Movement took over a number of other federal sites, including a replica of the *Mayflower* in Plymouth, Massachusetts. The attention from protest was successful; between 1970 and 1971, Congress passed fifty-two bills restoring Native American self-rule.

---

just as they can take geographical location, for instance.[32] In this and several later cases, the Court signaled its approval of the intent of affirmative action, even though it occasionally took issue with specific implementations.[33]

Few of the presidents who immediately followed Kennedy and Johnson took strong pro–civil rights positions, but none effected a real reversal in policy until Ronald Reagan. The Reagan administration lobbied the Court strenuously to change its rulings on the constitutionality of affirmative action. In 1989 the Court fulfilled civil rights advocates' most pessimistic expectations. In a series of rulings, it struck down a variety of civil rights laws, holding that the Fourteenth Amendment did not protect workers from racial harassment on the job,[34] that the burden of proof in claims of employment discrimination was on the worker,[35] and that

affirmative action was on shaky constitutional ground.[36] The Democratic-led Congress sought to undo some of the Court's late-1980s rulings by passing the Civil Rights Bill of 1991, which made it easier for workers to seek redress against employers who discriminate.

Blacks in Contemporary American Politics

The Supreme Court's use of strict scrutiny on laws that discriminate on the basis of race has put an end to most de jure discrimination. However, de facto discrimination remains, with all the consequences that stem from the fact that tradition and practice in the United States endorse a fundamental inequality of power. In addition, African Americans continue to grapple with issues such as racial profiling, which, like the

▶ Who Are We?

Poverty and prosperity among ethnic and racial groups

A glance at family income and poverty rates shows that, in America, all groups do not fare the same. Asian Americans earn well above the national average, while most other minority groups earn far less. About a quarter of African Americans, Hispanics, and Native Americans live in poverty as defined by the U.S. Census Bureau. This rate is over twice that for whites and Asians. What explanations might account for these differences? Should government play a role in bringing about more equality?

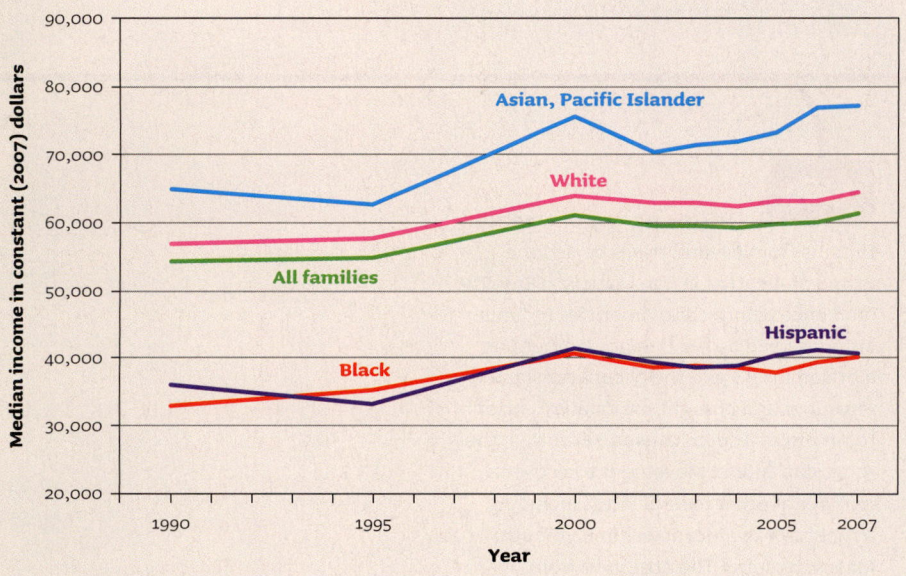

Poverty in America: Median Family Income by Race and Hispanic Origin, 1990–2007

Source: U.S. Census Bureau, "Table 681: Money Income of Families—Median Income by Race and Hispanic Origin in Current and Constant (2007) Dollars: 1990 to 2007," *Statistical Abstract of the United States,* 2010, www.census.gov/compendia/statab/2010/tables/10s0681.pdf.

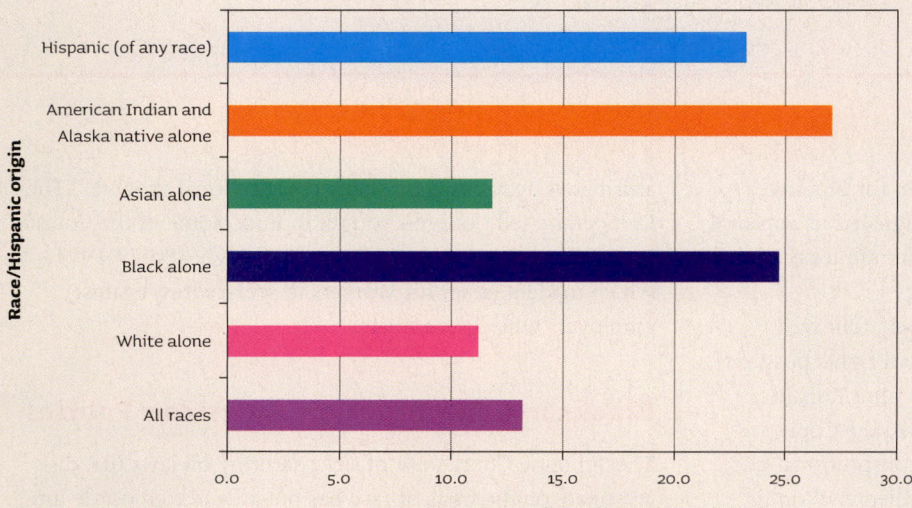

Poverty in America: Poverty Rate by Race and Hispanic Origin, 2008

Source: U.S. Census Bureau, Historical Poverty Tables, Table 24.

inequities in the criminal justice system that we discuss in Chapter 10, mean they often feel that the American political system treats them differently.

Race relations in this country are complicated by the growing diversity within the black community itself. Many blacks in America are in fact not native-born African Americans. They may come from Haiti, or the West Indies, or they may be African immigrants and not Americans at all. In Miami, 48 percent of the black population is West Indian, and a third of New York City blacks are foreign-born immigrants, as are a third of the blacks in Massachusetts and 8 percent of the blacks in Washington, D.C. One researcher points out that "the foreign-born African Americans and native-born African Americans are becoming as different from each other as foreign-born and native-born whites, in terms of culture, social status, aspirations, and how they think of themselves."[37]

This growing diversity signals problems for intraracial relations. Blacks born in other countries, where they were very likely not a minority, often have difficulty identifying with the experience of American blacks and seeing themselves as part of the same group with the same concerns and interests. Their primary identity might be nationality rather than race (they might see themselves as primarily Somali, or Ethiopian, or Jamaican, or Haitian). Native-born black Americans, for their part, often view black immigrants with the same general suspicion and stereotypes that Americans have traditionally directed toward immigrants. As this trend toward diversity grows, it will become even harder than it is now to characterize the "black experience" in America. In this section, we examine some of the other critical issues facing blacks in contemporary American politics.

The Economic Outlook for Blacks

We began this chapter noting that blacks fall behind whites on most socioeconomic indicators, although we should not disregard the existence of a growing black middle class. The median household income for African Americans in 2008 was $34,218; for whites, it was $53,312. Though blacks constituted about 13.5 percent of the U.S. population in 2008, in 2002 they owned only 5 percent of nonfarm U.S. businesses.[38] The racial income gap is blamed, in part, on lack of enforcement of antidiscrimination laws, showing that even when laws change, the results may not.[39] (See *Who Are We? Poverty and Prosperity Among Ethnic and Racial Groups*" for more comparisons.)

But even when overt discrimination is not present, the differences persist. One study by two sociologists uncovered the dispiriting fact that, all other things being equal, African American doctors, lawyers, and real estate managers make less than their white counterparts. Those in securities and financial services fields make seventy-two cents for every dollar earned by a white man in the same job. They speculate that perhaps the gap is due to blacks tending to be assigned by employers to black clients, who are often less financially well off than whites.[40] Such studies show how subtle and yet how pervasive economic inequities can be.

Political Gains and Losses

Because people of lower income and education levels are less likely to vote, African Americans' economic disadvantage has translated into a political limitation as well. And although voting discrimination is clearly illegal now, some racial patterns in disenfranchisement still exist. The most notorious case in point is the 2000 presidential election vote in Florida. Numerous studies show that many people's votes ultimately went uncounted in Florida, most likely costing Vice President Al Gore the election, with African American, Hispanic, and elderly voters especially hard hit.[41]

African Americans have had difficulty overcoming barriers not just on the voting side of the democratic equation. In terms of elected officials, progress has been mixed. By 2001 there were slightly more than nine thousand black elected officials in the United States, in posts ranging from local education and law enforcement jobs to the U.S. Congress. But the number of African Americans is much higher at local levels of government, where the constituents who elect them are more likely to be African American themselves. As the constituencies grow larger and more diverse, the task of black candidates gets tougher. In 2008 there were 642 black mayors,[42] but only two African American governors (Deval Patrick of Massachusetts and David Paterson of New York). In the 111th Congress, elected in 2008, 42 of 435 members of the House of Representatives were black, and there was one black senator, the appointed replacement for Barack Obama, who became only the sixth African American senator in U.S. history.

Indeed, public opinion polls had indicated that more than 140 years after the end of the Civil War, Americans were ready to elect a black president,[43] and in 2008, they did just that. Barack Obama is the nation's first African American president, elected in a campaign that was remarkably free of racial

▶ **Profiles in Citizenship: Ward Connerly**

". . . if I believe in freedom then it's got to be for everybody."

Ward Connerly is a reluctant warrior. He didn't set out to become the go-to guy in the battle against affirmative action; he didn't even want a political life. While he wanted to leave the world a better

place than he found it, he was content to contribute to the political campaigns of others while building his successful California business and enjoying his family. For Connerly, a Republican, the agent of change should be the individual, not government—he was committed to private enterprise and hard work.

That's what he told his friend, Republican governor Pete Wilson, when Wilson asked Connerly to join his administration. Still, Wilson was persuasive, and in 1993 Connerly found himself beginning a twelve-year term as one of the eighteen people on the hugely powerful University of California Board of Regents.

To Connerly, service on the board was "an awesome responsibility." So when the issue of affirmative action came up, he took it seriously. Connerly had had reservations about the policy from the start. Although he grew up poor, his Uncle James and his grandmother had taught him to value the dignity that comes from

self-reliance and the pride that comes from hard work.

Still, he wasn't looking to launch a major controversy when he was approached by the parents of a highly qualified white student who could not gain admission to the UC system. Investigating, he found what he called a system-wide pattern of discrimination against whites and Asians. Affirmative action did not seem to him to be a program of outreach but rather a program of racial preferences, which he found as distasteful when offered to blacks as when offered to whites, and which he believed would weaken black students in the bargain.

The story of how he overturned the UC affirmative action policy is recounted in his book, *Creating Equal*. Although the battle left him feeling bruised, it also strengthened his belief that affirmative action was unfair to whites and debilitating to blacks, and he ended up leading the successful effort to pass

overtones, although Obama did give one speech during the primary campaign that dealt explicitly with race. Obama's administration promised to usher in a much more relaxed attitude to race (he jokingly referred to himself, in his first press conference after his election, as a "mutt"). Although that approach to a subject that has been difficult for Americans to talk about may help to create more ease in the long run, in the short term a disconcerting amount of criticism of the new administration, especially from such right-wing entertainer-commentators as Rush Limbaugh and conservative provoca-teurs such as Andrew Breitbart, comes with a racial tinge.

It's an open question whether this dramatic movement at the top of the ticket will have an overall effect on the numbers of African Americans in American politics. In 2008 black turnout at the polls rose to 16.1 million voters, 2 million more than turned out in 2004.[44] That change, if lasting, might send more black candidates to political office. And in the wake of Obama's election, African Americans appeared to be more optimistic about black progress; a majority (53 percent) said

life will be better for blacks in the future (compared to 44 percent who said so in 2007), and 54 percent of blacks said Obama's election has improved race relations.[45]

But in general, African American candidates continue to face a reality that is daunting. They attribute their difficulties achieving statewide and national office to four factors: the scarcity of blacks in lesser state offices, from which statewide candidates are often recruited; the fact that many good black politicians are mayors, who traditionally have trouble trans-lating urban political success to statewide success; the fact that black politicians have fewer deep pockets from which to raise funds, since they often represent lower-income areas; and "old-fashioned prejudice"—their belief that nonblacks are less likely to vote for them and that party officials are less likely to encourage them to run for higher office because of that.[46]

Affirmative Action Today

Affirmative action continues to be a controversial policy in America. In 1996 voters in California declared affirmative

Proposition 209, an initiative that ended affirmative action statewide in California.

Undaunted, he took on another fight in 1997 over the issue of domestic partner benefits for gays. Originally "close to homophobic," he realized, meeting with long-term gay faculty couples, that "[it was] the real deal, you know. There was no difference except it was two women or two men rather than a man and woman, but it was clear to me that they loved each other, that families can come in different forms and . . . that I needed to rethink my position." Concluding that "if I believe in freedom, then it's got to be for everybody," he led the effort that secured the benefits.

Having infuriated liberals with his stance on affirmative action, Connerly was now annoying his fellow conservatives, including the governor who appointed him. "I was an equal opportunity offender," he says wryly. But the values that informed the one battle underlay the other as well—an abiding commitment to fair play and hard work, to procedural guarantees, not substantive results.

So today, his long term on the board finally ended, Connerly is back to running his own business full-time, but also running the American Civil Rights Institute—a national, not-for-profit organization aimed at educating the public about the need to move beyond racial and gender preferences. Although he tried to leave the issue behind, he could not. "Once you get involved in race you can't extricate yourself from it. It's just something that begins to eat at you, and you can't finish until the job is done. And the job is never done." Here's what else he says:

On having the courage of your convictions:

It requires an awful lot of guts. An awful lot of courage. . . . There will be those who will question whether you're comfortable in your own skin and are you betraying your race and your gender and all of that stuff, which will require that you be very, very secure. . . . [I]t requires you to think hard about who you are, what you want to accomplish. . . . As my grandmother used to often say, "like a tree standing by the water, I shall not be moved." And that was the creed that I adapted and that served me well for those twelve years.

On keeping the republic:

Realize that you live in a great place. And it has been made great by a lot of people over the years who have worked hard to make it great. Every one of your ancestors has made some contribution along the way. . . . [I]t's not the elected official who's made it great, it's the people themselves. . . . That falls on the back of the ordinary citizen. Take it seriously because it's an awesome responsibility. ■

action illegal in their state, and voters in Washington did the same in 1998. In 2006 Michigan voted to ban affirmative action in the state's public colleges and government contracting, and in 2008 affirmative action was on the ballot in Colorado and Nebraska. While the Nebraska ban passed with 58 percent of the vote, it was defeated narrowly in Colorado. The American public remains divided: opinion polls show support for the ideals behind affirmative action, but not if it is perceived to be giving minorities preferential treatment.[47]

The federal courts have taken the notion that race is a suspect classification to mean that any laws treating people differently according to race must be given strict scrutiny. Even though strict scrutiny has traditionally been used to support the rights of racial minorities, when applied consistently across the board, it can also preclude laws that give them special treatment or preferences, even if those preferences are meant to create more equality. That doesn't necessarily mean that the courts throw out the laws, but they do hold them to a higher standard. In a 2001 case rejecting a University of Michigan Law School affirmative action policy, a federal district court judge stated the principle bluntly: "All racial distinctions are inherently suspect and presumptively invalid. . . . Whatever solution the law school elects to pursue, it must be race-neutral."[48] A few months later, a federal appeals court held that the University of Georgia's affirmative action policy was unconstitutional. It said that while a university can strive to achieve a diverse student body, race could not be the only factor used to define diversity.[49]

The University of Michigan Law School case eventually found its way to the Supreme Court, along with another that dealt with Michigan's undergraduate admissions policy. As in *Bakke*, students who had been rejected with higher grade point averages and test scores than some admitted students challenged the constitutionality of Michigan's policies, again on Fourteenth Amendment grounds. The Supreme Court handed down two decisions, the results of which were essentially in line with the *Bakke* decision. The Court threw out the university's undergraduate admissions policy because it was tantamount to racial quotas.[50] In a five-to-four decision, however, the Court held that the law school's holistic approach of taking into account the race of the applicant was constitutional because of the importance of creating a diverse student body.[51]

Despite the controversy, there remains considerable support for affirmative action in the United States. Efforts to end affirmative action have previously failed in state legislatures in New Jersey, Michigan, Arizona, Colorado, and almost a dozen other states. As the 2006 success of the so-called Michigan Civil Rights Initiative and the 2008 defeat of affirmative action in Nebraska show, however, campaigns in the public can succeed where the legislature may balk.

The issues raised by the affirmative action debate in America deserve to be taken seriously by students of American politics. Unlike many earlier debates in American civil rights politics, this one cannot be reduced to questions of racism and bigotry. What is at stake are two competing images of what America ought to be about. On the one side is a vision of an America whose discriminatory past is past and whose job today is to treat all citizens the same. This view, shared by many minorities as well as many white Americans, argues that providing a set of lower standards for some groups is not fair to anybody. Ward Connerly, an African American businessman and a former member of the University of California Board of Regents, whose American Civil Rights Institute is a strong opponent of affirmative action, says that "people tend to perform at the level of competition. When the bar is raised, we rise to the occasion. That is exactly what black students will do in a society that has equal standards for all."[52] (See *Profiles in Citizenship: Ward Connerly.*)

On the other side of the debate are those who argue that affirmative action programs have made a real difference in equalizing chances in society, and although they are meant to be temporary, their work is not yet done. These advocates claim that the old patterns of behavior are so ingrained that they can be changed only by conscious effort. *New York Times* writer David Shipler says, "White males have long benefited from unstated preferences as fraternity brothers, golfing buddies, children of alumni and the like—unconscious biases that go largely unrecognized until affirmative action forces recruiters to think about how they gravitate toward people like themselves."[53]

All Americans have had a great deal at stake in the civil rights movement. Blacks have struggled, first, to be recognized as American citizens and, then, to exercise the rights that go along with citizenship. Lacking fundamental rights, they also lacked economic and social power. Those who fought to withhold their rights knew that recognizing them would inevitably upset the traditional power structure in both the South and the North.

Who What How

The formal citizenship rights granted African Americans by way of the Thirteenth, Fourteenth, and Fifteenth Amendments should have changed the rules of American politics sufficiently to allow blacks to enter the political world on an equal footing with whites. Yet when Congress and the courts failed to enforce the Reconstruction amendments, southern blacks were at the mercy of discriminatory state and local laws for nearly a century. Those laws were finally changed by a combination of tactics that succeeded in eliminating much of the de jure discrimination that had followed the Civil War. However, they were not very effective in remedying the de facto discrimination that persisted, particularly in the North. Efforts to get rid of de facto discrimination generally involve substantive remedies like affirmative action, which remain controversial with procedure-loving Americans. The remnants of past discrimination, in the form of greater poverty and lower education levels for blacks, mean that increased political rights are not easily translated into equal economic and social power.

Rights Denied on the Basis of Race and Ethnicity

Different paths to equality for Native Americans, Hispanics, and Asian Americans

African Americans are by no means the only Americans whose civil rights have been denied on racial or ethnic grounds. Native Americans, Hispanics, and Asian Americans have all faced their own particular kind of discrimination. For historical and cultural reasons, these groups have had different political resources available to them, and thus their struggles have taken shape in different ways.

Native Americans

Native Americans of various tribes shared the so-called New World for centuries before it was discovered by Europeans. The relationship between the original inhabitants of this continent and the European colonists and their governments has been difficult, marked by the new arrivals' clear intent to settle and develop the Native Americans' ancestral lands, and complicated by the Europeans' failure to understand the Indians' cultural, spiritual, and political heritage. The lingering effects of these centuries-old conflicts continue to color the political, social, and economic experience of Native Americans today.

Native Americans and the U.S. Government

The precise status of Native American tribes in American politics and in constitutional law is complicated. The Indians always saw themselves as sovereign independent nations, making treaties, waging war, and otherwise dealing with the early Americans from a position of strength and equality. But that sovereignty has not consistently been recognized by the United States. The commerce clause of the Constitution (Article I, Section 8) gives Congress the power to regulate trade "with foreign nations, among the several states, and with the Indian tribes." The U.S. perception of Indian tribes as neither foreign countries nor states was underscored by Chief Justice John Marshall in 1831. Denying the Cherokees the right to challenge a Georgia law in the Supreme Court, as a foreign nation would be able to do, Marshall declared that the Indian tribes were "domestic dependent nations."[54]

Until 1871, however, Congress continued to treat the tribes outwardly as if they were sovereign nations, making treaties with them to buy their land and relocate them. The truth is that regardless of the treaties, the commerce clause was interpreted as giving Congress guardianship over Indian affairs. The tribes were often forcibly moved from their traditional lands; by the mid-1800s, most were living in western territories on land that had no spiritual meaning for them, where their hunting and farming traditions were ineffective, leaving them dependent on federal aid. The creation of the Bureau of Indian Affairs in 1824 as part of the Department of War (moved, in 1849, to the Department of the Interior) institutionalized that guardian role, and the central issues became what the role of the federal government would be and how much self-government the Indians should have.[55]

Modern congressional policy toward the Native Americans has varied from trying to assimilate them into the broader, European-based culture to encouraging them to develop economic independence and self-government. The combination of these two strategies—stripping them of their native lands and cultural identity, and reducing their federal funding to encourage more independence—has resulted in tremendous social and economic dislocation in the Indian communities. Poverty, joblessness, and alcoholism have built communities of despair and frustration for many Native Americans. Their situation has been aggravated as Congress has denied them many of the rights promised in their treaties in order to exploit the natural resources so abundant in the western lands they have been forced onto, or as they have been forced to sell rights to those resources in order to survive.

Political Strategies

The political environment in which Native Americans found themselves in the mid–twentieth century was very different from the one faced by African Americans. What was at stake were Indians' civil rights and their enforcement, and the fulfillment of old promises and the preservation of a culture that did not easily coexist with modern American economic and political beliefs and practice. For cultures that emphasized the spirituality of living in harmony with lands that cannot really "belong" to anyone, haggling over mining and fishing rights seems the ultimate desecration. But the government they rejected in their quest for self-determination and tribal traditions was the same government they depended on to keep poverty at bay.

Essentially, Native American tribes find themselves in a relationship with the national government that mimics elements of federalism, what some scholars have called "fry-bread federalism."[56] Although that relationship has evolved over time, the gist of it is that American Indians are citizens of tribes as well as citizens of the United States, with rights coming from each. It was not clear what strategy the Native Americans should follow in trying to get their U.S. rights recognized. State politics did not provide any remedies, not merely because of local prejudice but also because the Indian reservations were separate legal entities under the federal government. Because Congress itself has been largely responsible for denying the rights of Native Americans, it was not a likely source of support for their expansion. Too many important economic interests with influence in Congress have had a lot at stake in getting their hands on Indian-held

Gambling on the Future

For Native Americans living on reservations, which often stand on arid and undeveloped land, life can be harsh. Many, such as this woman on the Hopi Indian Reservation in Arizona, live without plumbing and electricity. Since the 1980s, some tribes have established casinos on their reservations to encourage greater economic prosperity. Although gambling and casinos have stirred considerable controversy among Native groups, they also have provided millions of dollars in badly needed funds to improve living and working conditions on reservations.

resources. In 1977 a federal review commission found the Bureau of Indian Affairs guilty of failing to safeguard Indian legal, financial, and safety interests. Nor were the courts anxious to extend rights to Native Americans. Most noticeably in cases concerning religious freedom, the Supreme Court has found compelling state interests to outweigh most Indian claims to religious freedom. In 1988, for instance, the Court ruled that the forest service could allow roads and timber cutting in national forests that had been used by Indian tribes for religious purposes.[57] And in 1990 the Court held that two Native American drug counselors who had been dismissed for using peyote, a hallucinogenic drug traditionally used in Native American religious ceremonies, were not entitled to unemployment benefits from the state of Oregon.[58]

Like many other groups shut out from access to political institutions, Native Americans took their political fate into their own hands. Focusing on working outside the system to change public opinion and to persuade Congress to alter public policy, the Indians formed interest groups like the National Congress of American Indians (NCAI), founded in 1944, and the American Indian Movement (AIM), founded in 1968, to fight for their cause. AIM, for example, staged dramatic demonstrations, such as the 1969 takeover of Alcatraz Island in San Francisco Bay and the 1973 occupation of a reservation at Wounded Knee (the location of an 1890 massacre of Sioux Indians). The American Indian Movement drew public attention to the plight of many Native Americans and, at the same time, to the divisions within the Indian community on such central issues as self-rule, treaty enforcement, and the role of the federal government.

Contemporary Challenges

But for all the militant activism of the sixties and seventies, Native Americans have made no giant strides in redressing the centuries of dominance by white people. They remain at the bottom of the income scale in America, earning less than African Americans on average, and their living conditions are often poor. In 2005, 25.3 percent of American Indians lived in poverty, compared to only 12.6 percent of the total U.S. population.[59] And in 2009 the high school graduation rate of Native Americans was only 51 percent, compared to 70 percent of the overall population.[60] Consider, for example, the Navajos living on and off the reservation in Montezuma Creek, Utah. Sixty percent have no electricity or running water, half don't have jobs, fewer than half have graduated from high school, and 90 percent receive some kind of governmental support.[61]

Since the 1980s, however, an ironic twist of legal interpretation has enabled some Native Americans to parlay their status as semisovereign nations into a foundation for economic prosperity. As a result of two court cases,[62] and Congress' 1988 Indian Gaming Regulatory Act, if a state allows any form of legalized gambling at all, even a state lottery, then Indian reservations in that state may allow all sorts of gambling, subject only to the regulation of the Bureau of Indian Affairs. Many reservations now have casinos that rival Las Vegas in gaudy splendor, and the money is pouring into their coffers. Close to thirty states now allow Indian gambling casinos, and in 2008 they brought in more than $26 billion, more than Native Americans received in federal aid.[63] In 2006 Native American gaming revenue represented 42 percent of all casino gambling revenue nationwide,[64] although many tribes and individuals have no share in it.

Casino gambling is controversial on several counts. Native Americans themselves are of two minds about it—some see gambling as their economic salvation and others as spiritually ruinous. The revenue created by the casinos has allowed Indian tribes to become major donors to political campaigns in states such as California, which has increased their political clout though leaving them open to criticism for making big money donations while many reservations remain poverty stricken. Many other Americans object for economic reasons. Opponents like casino owner Donald Trump claim that Congress is giving special privileges to Native Americans that may threaten their own business interests. Regardless of the moral and economic questions unleashed by the casino boom, for many Native Americans it is a way to recoup at least some of the resources that were lost in the past.

Future Democratic Voters?
Hispanics are a rapidly growing political force in the United States. Both parties have sought their support, but in recent elections, in part due to the parties' stances on immigration, Democrats have been receiving the lion's share of the Latino vote. Hispanics' growing share of the electorate virtually guarantees that politicians of both parties will be increasingly attending to their concerns.

Politically, there is the potential for improvement as well. While recent Supreme Court cases failed to support religious freedom for Native Americans, some lower court orders have supported their rights. In 1996 President Bill Clinton issued an executive order that requires federal agencies to protect and provide access to sacred religious sites of American Indians, which has been a major point of contention in Indian-federal relations. Until the Supreme Court ruled in 1996 that electoral districts could not be drawn to enhance the power of particular racial groups, Native Americans had been gaining strength at the polls, to better defend their local interests. Still, the number of American Indian state representatives has increased slightly in the past few years, although there is currently only one American Indian, Tom Cole of Oklahoma, serving in the House of Representatives. There are no American Indians in the Senate now that Senator Ben Nighthorse Campbell of Colorado retired after his term expired in 2005.

Hispanic Americans

Hispanic Americans, sometimes also called Latinos, are a diverse group with yet another story of discrimination in the United States. They did not have to contend with the tradition of slavery that burdened blacks, and they don't have the unique legal problems of Native Americans, but they face peculiar challenges of their own in trying to fight discrimination and raise their standing in American society. Among the reasons that the Hispanic experience is different are the diversity within the Hispanic population; the language barrier that many face; and the political reaction to immigration, particularly illegal immigration, from Mexico into the United States. Hispanics are the largest minority group in the United States today, making up over 15 percent of the population. Their numbers have more than tripled in the past twenty-plus years, from 14.6 million in 1980 to 46.8 million in 2008.[65] Since 1990 the Hispanic population has grown by 103 percent, compared with an increase of 13.3 percent among non-Hispanics. This population explosion means that the problems facing Hispanics will become much more central to the country as a whole as the twenty-first century unfolds.

Diversity

A striking feature of the Hispanic population is its diversity. While Hispanics have in common their Spanish heritage, they have arrived in the United States traveling different routes, at different times. As illustrated in "*Who Are We? America's Fastest-Growing Minority Groups,*" the current Hispanic population is quite diverse, even though the vast majority

▶ **Who Are We?**

America's fastest-growing minority groups

America is becoming increasingly diverse. Latinos and Asians are the fastest-growing racial and ethnic groups in the United States. By mid-century, Hispanics will make up a quarter of the population, and Asians and Pacific Islanders will have doubled their numbers.

   The different groups that make up the U.S. population are themselves becoming more diverse. Whereas in the past most Hispanics in the United States had origins in Mexico, Puerto Rico, and Cuba, today many can be called the "New Latinos"—immigrants from Central and South America and the Dominican Republic. Meanwhile Asians continue to come from an array of countries, each with quite distinct cultural traditions. Do you think this growing diversity will lead to greater understanding and appreciation for America's rich and diverse heritage, or is it likely to lead to increased intergroup hostility, competition, and racism? Can government do anything to smooth relations among and within groups?

America's Hispanic Population Growth

Hispanic population (in millions) vs *Year*

2050: 24.4%

Percentage of total U.S. population, 2000: 12.1%

Source: U.S. Bureau of the Census.

Note: 2010–2050.

Diversity Among Hispanics

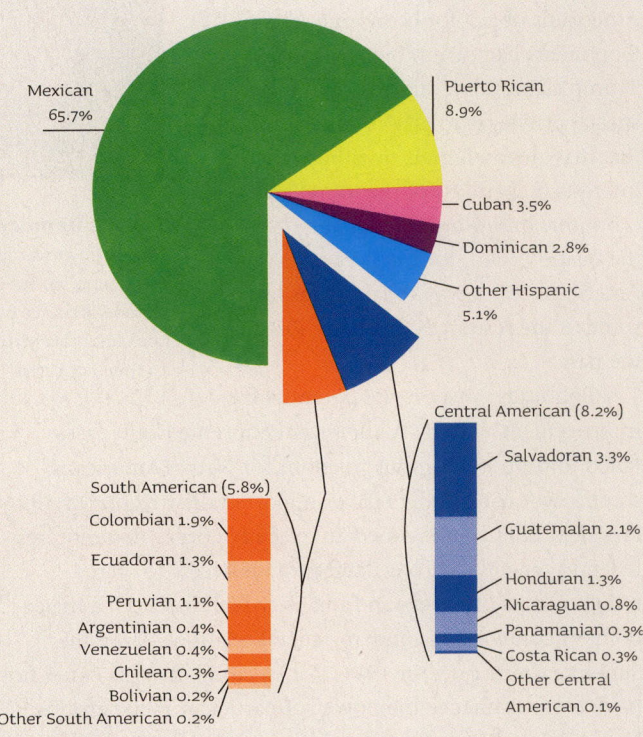

Mexican 65.7%

Puerto Rican 8.9%

Cuban 3.5%

Dominican 2.8%

Other Hispanic 5.1%

Central American (8.2%)
- Salvadoran 3.3%
- Guatemalan 2.1%
- Honduran 1.3%
- Nicaraguan 0.8%
- Panamanian 0.3%
- Costa Rican 0.3%
- Other Central American 0.1%

South American (5.8%)
- Colombian 1.9%
- Ecuadoran 1.3%
- Peruvian 1.1%
- Argentinian 0.4%
- Venezuelan 0.4%
- Chilean 0.3%
- Bolivian 0.2%
- Other South American 0.2%

Source: Pew Hispanic Center, tabulations of 2008 American Community Survey, http://pewhispanic.org/files/factsheets/hispanics2008/Table 6.pdf.

is Mexican. Americans with Mexican backgrounds, called Chicanos or Chicanas, do not necessarily share the concerns and issues of more recent Mexican-born immigrants, so there is diversity even within this group. Immigrants from different countries have settled across the United States. Mexican Americans are concentrated largely in California, Texas, Arizona, and New Mexico; Puerto Ricans are in New York, New Jersey, and other northern states; and Cubans tend to be clustered in South Florida.

These groups differ in more than place of origin and settlement. Cubans are much more likely to have been political refugees, escaping the communist government of Fidel Castro, whereas those from other countries tend to be economic refugees looking for a better life. Because educated, professional Cubans are the ones who fled, they have largely regained their higher socioeconomic status in this country. For instance, almost 25.1 percent of Cuban Americans are college educated, a percentage comparable to

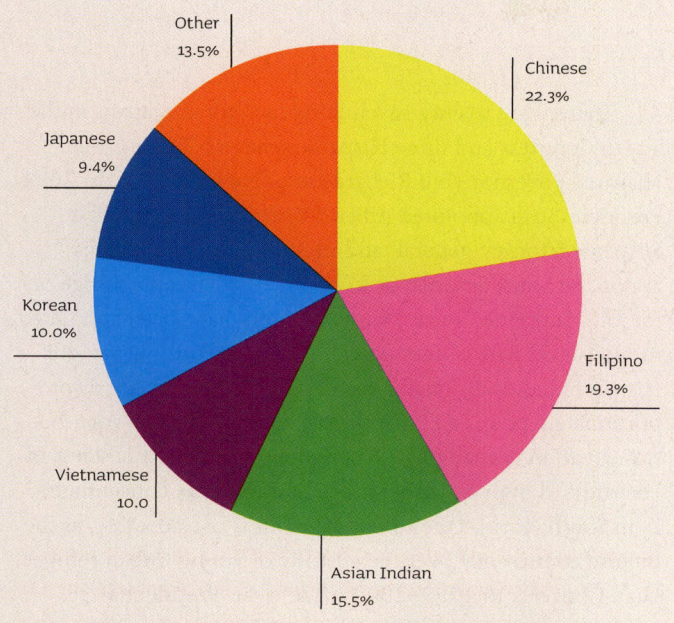

Diversity Among Asians, Native Born

Source: Report by the Lewis Mumford Center for Comparative Urban and Regional Research, University at Albany.

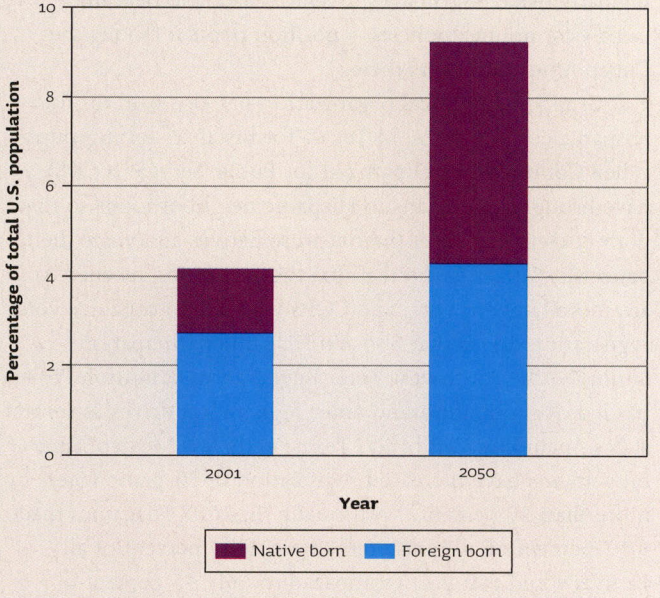

America's Asian Population Growth

Source: U.S. Bureau of the Census, (NP-T5) Projections of the Resident Population by Race, Hispanic Origin, and Nativity, Middle Series, 1999–2100.

that found in the U.S. population as a whole, but only 8.6 percent of Mexican Americans and 15.6 percent of Puerto Ricans are college graduates.[66] Consequently, Cuban Americans also hold more professional and managerial jobs, and their standard of living, on average, is much higher. What this diversity means is that there is little reason for Hispanics to view themselves as a single ethnic group with common interests and thus to act in political concert. While their numbers suggest that if they acted together they would wield considerable clout, their diversity has led to fragmentation and powerlessness.

The English-Only Movement

Language has also presented a special challenge to Hispanics. The United States today ranks sixth in the world in the number of people who consider Spanish a first language, with an active and important Spanish-language media of radio, television, and press. This preponderance of Spanish speakers is

> **English-only movements**   efforts to make English the official language of the United States

probably due less to a refusal on the part of Hispanics to learn English than to the fact that new immigrants are continually streaming into this country.[67] Nonetheless, especially in areas with large Hispanic populations, white Anglos feel threatened by what they see as the encroachment of Spanish, and as we saw in *What's at Stake?* in Chapter 2, many communities have launched **English-only movements** to make English the official language, precluding foreign languages from appearing on ballots and official documents. The English-only controversy is clearly about more than language—it is about national and cultural identity, a struggle to lay claim to the voice of America.

The Controversy Over Immigration

A final concern that makes the Hispanic struggle for civil rights unique in America is the reaction against immigration, particularly illegal immigration from Mexico. As we saw in Chapter 2, illegal immigration is a critical problem in some areas of the country. A backlash against illegal immigration has some serious consequences for Hispanic American citizens, who may be indistinguishable in appearance, name, and language from recent immigrants. They have found themselves suspected, followed, and challenged by the police; forced to show proof of legal residence on demand; and subjected to unpleasant reactions from non-Hispanic citizens who blame an entire ethnic group for the perceived behavior of a few of its members. All this makes acceptance into American society more difficult for Hispanics; encourages segregation; and makes the subtle denial of equal rights in employment, housing, and education, for instance, easier to carry out.

Political Strategies

Though Hispanics face formidable barriers to assimilation, their political position is improving. Like African Americans, they have had some success in organizing and calling public attention to their circumstances. Cesar Chavez, as leader of the United Farm Workers in the 1960s, drew national attention to the conditions under which farm workers labored. Following the principles of the civil rights movement, he highlighted concerns of social justice in his call for a nationwide boycott of grapes and lettuce picked by nonunion labor, and in the process he became a symbol of the Hispanic struggle for equal rights. Groups like the Mexican American Legal Defense and Education Fund (MALDEF) and the League of United Latin American Citizens (LULAC) continue to lobby to end discrimination against Hispanic Americans.

There were twenty-seven Hispanic representatives in the 111th Congress and three Hispanic senators. There is one Hispanic governor (Bill Richardson of New Mexico). In 2004 President Bush appointed Alberto Gonzales to be the first Hispanic attorney general, and in 2009 President Obama appointed Sonia Sotomayor to be the first Hispanic justice on the U.S. Supreme Court. Many Hispanics have been appointed to high-level state offices as well. The voter turnout rate for Hispanics has traditionally been low because they are disproportionately poor and poor people are less likely to vote, but this situation is changing. Where the socioeconomic status of Hispanics is high and where their numbers are concentrated, as in South Florida, their political clout is considerable, as the intense controversy over the custody of young Cuban refugee Elian Gonzalez in 1999–2000 made clear. Presidential candidates, mindful of Florida's twenty-seven electoral votes, regularly make pilgrimages to South Florida to denounce Cuba's communist policies, a position popular among the Cuban American voters there.

Grassroots political organization has also paid off for Hispanic communities. In Texas, for instance, local groups called Communities Organized for Public Service (COPS) have brought politicians to Hispanic neighborhoods so that poor citizens can meet their representatives and voice their concerns. Citizens who feel that they are being listened to are more likely to vote, and COPS was able to organize voter registration drives that boosted Hispanic participation. Similarly, the Southwest Voter Registration Education Project has led over one thousand voter registration drives in several states, including California, Texas, and New Mexico. Such movements have increased registration of Hispanic voters by more than 50 percent.[68] Nationally, in 2008 Hispanics made up 7 percent of all registered voters. Fifty percent of all Latinos voted that year, compared to only 45 percent in 2000.[69]

Because of the increase in the number of potential Hispanic voters, and because of the prominence of the Hispanic population in battleground states such as Florida, New Mexico, Colorado, Nevada, and even in places such as Iowa, where one might not expect a significant Hispanic population, both Barack Obama and John McCain actively courted Hispanic voters in the 2008 presidential election. Each candidate ran several advertisements entirely in Spanish, and Obama considered choosing New Mexico governor Bill Richardson, who is Hispanic, as his running mate.

Asian Americans

Asian Americans share some of the experiences of Hispanics, facing cultural prejudice as well as racism and absorbing some of the public backlash against immigration. Yet the history of Asian American immigration, the explosive events of World War II, and the impressive educational and economic success of many Asian Americans mean that the Asian experience is also in many ways unique.

Diversity

Like Hispanics, the Asian American population is diverse. (See the "Diversity Among Asians" figure in *"Who Are We? America's Fastest-Growing Minority Groups."*) There are Americans with roots in China, Japan, Korea, the Philippines, India, Vietnam, Laos, and Cambodia, to name just a few. Asian Americans vary not only by their country of origin but also by the time of their arrival in the United States. There are Chinese and Japanese Americans whose families have lived here for nearly two centuries, arriving with the waves of immigrants in the early 1800s who came to work in the frontier West. In part because of the resentment of white workers, whose wages were being squeezed by the low pay the immigrants would accept, Congress passed the Chinese Exclusion Act in 1882, halting immigration from China, and the National Origin Act of 1925, barring the entry of the Japanese. It was 1943 before Congress repealed the Chinese Exclusion Act, and 1965 before Asian immigrants were treated the same as those of other nationalities. Asians and Pacific Islanders are currently the fastest-growing immigrant group in America, arriving from all over Asia but in particular from the war-torn countries of Vietnam, Laos, and Cambodia.

Today Asian Americans live in every region of the United States. In 2008 Asians comprised 55.3 percent of the population in Hawaii and 12.1 percent of that in California.[70] New York City has the largest Chinese community outside China. The more recent immigrants are spread throughout the country. The Asian population in the South is especially fast growing; there, from 1980 to 1990, the Asian and Pacific Islander population increased 146 percent, compared to 103 percent in the rest of the country.[71]

Discrimination

Asians have faced discrimination in the United States since their arrival. The fact that they are identifiable by their appearance has made assimilation into the larger European American population difficult. While most immigrants dream of becoming citizens in their new country, and eventually gaining political influence through the right to vote, that option was not open to Asians. The Naturalization Act of 1790 provided only for white immigrants to become naturalized citizens, and with few exceptions—for Filipino soldiers in the U.S. Army during World War II, for example—the act was in force until 1952. Branded "aliens ineligible for citizenship," not only were Asians permanently disenfranchised, but in many states they could not even own or rent property. Female citizens wishing to marry Asian "aliens" lost their own citizenship. The exclusionary immigration laws of 1882 and 1925 reflect this country's hostility to Asians, but at no other time was anti-Asian sentiment so painfully evident than in the white American reaction to Japanese Americans during World War II.

When the United States found itself at war with Japan, there was a strong backlash against Asian Americans. Because most Americans could not tell the difference between people from different Asian heritages, non-Japanese citizens found it necessary to wear buttons proclaiming "I am Korean" or "I am Filipino" to avoid having rocks and racial insults hurled at them.[72] In 1942, however, the U.S. government began to round up Japanese Americans, forcing them to abandon or sell their property, and putting them in detention camps for purposes of "national security." While the government was worried about security threats posed by those with Japanese sympathies, two-thirds of the 120,000 incarcerated were American citizens. Neither German Americans nor Italian Americans, both of whose homelands were also at war with the United States, were stripped of their rights. Remarkably, after they were incarcerated, young Japanese men were asked to sign oaths of loyalty to the American government so that they could be drafted into military service. Those who refused in outrage over their treatment were imprisoned. The crowning insult was the Supreme Court approval of curfews and detention camps for Japanese Americans.[73] Though the government later backed down and, in fact, in 1988 paid $1.25 billion as reparation to survivors of the ordeal, the Japanese internment camps remain a major scar on America's civil rights record.

The Price of Prosperity

One unusual feature of the Asian American experience is their overall academic success and corresponding economic prosperity. Although all Asian groups have not been equally successful (groups that have immigrated primarily as refugees—like the Vietnamese—have higher rates of poverty than do others), median household income in 2008 was $65,637 for Asian and Pacific Islanders, compared with $52,312 for whites, $37,913 for Hispanics, and $34,218 for blacks.[74] A number of factors probably account for this success. Forced out of wage labor in the West in the 1880s by resentful white workers, Asian immigrants developed entrepreneurial skills and many came to own their own businesses and restaurants. A cultural emphasis on hard work and high achievement lent itself particularly well to success in the American education system and culture of equality of opportunity. Furthermore, many Asian immigrants were highly skilled and professional workers in their own countries and passed on the values of their achievements to their children.

High school and college graduation rates are higher among Asian Americans than among other ethnic groups, and are at least as high as, and in some places higher than, those of whites. In 2009, 13 percent of the students at Harvard were Asian, as were 22.5 percent at Stanford, 26 percent at MIT, and 45 percent at the University of California, Berkeley.[75] What their high levels of academic success sometimes mean for Asian Americans is that they become the targets of racist attacks by resentful whites.[76] Asian Americans have accused schools like Stanford, Brown, Harvard, and Berkeley of "capping" the number of Asians they admit, and white alumni who feel that slots at these elite schools should be reserved for their children have complained about the numbers of Asians in attendance. Although the schools deny the capping charges, Asian American students won favorable judgments in sixteen out of forty complaints they filed with the Department of Education between 1988 and 1995, a much higher rate than that achieved by any other racial group.[77] Their success also means that Asian Americans stand in an odd relationship to affirmative action, a set of policies that usually helps minorities blocked from traditional paths to economic prosperity. While affirmative action policies might benefit them in hiring situations, they actually harm Asian Americans seeking to go to universities or professional schools. Because these students are generally so well qualified, more of them would be admitted if race were not taken into account to permit the admission of Hispanic and African American students. Policies that pit minority groups against each other in this way do not promote solidarity and community among them and make racist attitudes even harder to overcome.

Political Strategies

According to all our conventional understanding of what makes people vote in the United States, participation among Asian Americans ought to be quite high. Voter turnout usually rises along with education and income levels, yet Asian American voter registration and turnout rates have been among the lowest in the nation. Particularly in states with a sizable number of Asian Americans such as California, where they constitute 13.4 percent of the population, their political representation and influence do not reflect their numbers.

Political observers account for this lack of participation in several ways. Until after World War II, as we saw, immigration laws restricted the citizenship rights of Asian Americans. In addition, the political systems that many Asian immigrants left behind did not have traditions of democratic political participation. Finally, many Asian Americans came to the United States for economic reasons and have focused their attentions on building economic security rather than learning to navigate an unfamiliar political system.[78]

Some evidence indicates, however, that this trend of nonparticipation is changing. Researchers have found that where Asian Americans do register, they tend to vote at rates higher than those of other groups.[79] In the 1996 election, concerted efforts were made to register and turn out Asian Americans by a national coalition of Asian American interest groups seeking to maximize their impact at the polls. The results included the election of Gary Locke as the first Asian American governor of a mainland state (Washington), and in 1998 there were two thousand elected officials of Asian and Pacific Islander descent—up 10 percent from 1996.[80] About 33 percent of the Asian American voters in California in 1996 were first-time voters.[81] Still, even with the added emphasis on Asian American turnout, they comprised only 4 percent of the electorate in California, New York, and New Jersey in 2004. Only in Hawaii did Asian Americans constitute a larger percentage (26 percent) of the electorate.[82]

One reason for the increasing participation of Asian Americans, in addition to the voter registration drives, is that many Asian Americans are finding themselves more and more affected by public policies. Welfare reform that strips many elderly legal immigrants of their benefits, changes in immigration laws, and affirmative action are among the issues driving Asian Americans to the polls. However, even continued efforts to register this group are unlikely to bring about electoral results as dramatic as those that we are starting to see for Hispanics, because Asian Americans tend to split their votes more or less equally between Democrats and Republicans.[83] Whereas African Americans vote for Democratic candidates over Republicans at a ratio of eight to one, and Hispanics, two to one, Asian Americans favor the Democrats only slightly.[84]

Who What How

Native Americans' rights have been denied through the Supreme Court's interpretation of the commerce clause, giving Congress power over them and their lands. Because neither Congress nor the courts have been receptive to the claims of Native Americans, they have sought to force the American government to fulfill its promises to them and to gain political rights and economic well-being by working outside the system and using the resources generated from running casinos.

Hispanics too have been denied their rights, partly through general discrimination but partly through organized movements such as the English-only movement and anti-immigration efforts. Because of their diversity and low levels of socioeconomic achievement, they have not been very successful in organizing to fight for their rights politically. Tactics that Hispanic leaders use include boycotts and voter education and registration drives.

Finally, Asian Americans, long prevented by law from becoming citizens and under suspicion during World War II, have also had to bear the collective brunt of Americans' discriminatory actions. As diverse as Hispanics, Asian Americans have also failed to organize politically. Their socioeconomic fate, however, has been different from that of many Hispanic groups, and as a group, Asian Americans have managed to thrive economically in their own communities despite political discrimination.

Rights Denied on the Basis of Gender

Fighting the early battles for equality at the state level

Of all the battles fought for equal rights in the American political system, the women's struggle has been perhaps the most peculiar, because women, while certainly denied most imaginable civil and economic rights, were not outside the system in the same way that racial and ethnic groups have been. Most women lived with their husbands or fathers, and many shared their view that men, not women, should have power in the political world. Women's realm, after all, was the home, and the prevailing belief was that women were too good, too pure, too chaste, to deal with the sordid world outside. As a New Jersey senator argued in the late 1800s, women should not be allowed to vote because they have "a higher and holier mission. . . . Their mission is at home."[85] Today there are still some women as well as men who agree with the gist of this sentiment. That means that the struggle for women's rights not only has failed to win the support of all women but also has been actively opposed by some, as well as by many men whose power, standing, and worldview it has threatened.

Women's Place in the Early Nineteenth Century

The legal and economic position of women in the early nineteenth century, though not exactly "slavery," in some ways was not much different. According to English common law, on which our legal system was based, when a woman married, she merged her legal identity with her husband's, which is to say in practical terms she no longer had one. Once married, she could not be a party to a contract, bring a lawsuit, own or inherit property, earn wages for any service, gain custody of her children in case of divorce, or initiate divorce from an abusive husband. If her husband were not a U.S. citizen, she lost her own citizenship. Neither married nor unmarried women could vote. In exchange for the legal identity his wife gave up, a husband was expected to provide security for her, and if he died without a will, she was entitled to one-third of his estate. If he made a will and left her out of it, however, she had no legal recourse to protect herself and her children.[86]

Opportunities were not plentiful for women who preferred to remain unmarried. Poor women worked in domestic service and, later, in the textile industry. But most married women did not work outside the home. For unmarried women, the professions available were those that fit their supposed womanly nature and that paid too little to be attractive to men, primarily nursing and teaching. Women who tried to break the occupational barriers were usually rebuffed, and for those who prevailed, success was often a mixed blessing. When in 1847, after many rejections and a miserable time in medical school, Elizabeth Blackwell graduated at the top of her class to become the first woman doctor in the United States, the only way she could get patients was to open her own hospital for women and children. The legal profession did not welcome women either, because once women were married, they could no longer be recognized in court. In 1860 Belle Mansfield was admitted to the Iowa bar by a judge sympathetic to the cause of women's rights. But when Myra Bradwell became the first woman law school graduate ten years later, the Illinois bar refused to admit her. Rather than support her, the U.S. Supreme Court ruled that admission to the bar was the states' prerogative.[87]

The Birth of the Women's Rights Movement

The women's movement is commonly dated from an 1848 convention on women's rights held in Seneca Falls, New York. There, men and women who supported the extension of rights to women issued a Declaration of Principles that deliberately sought to evoke the sentiments of those calling for freedom from political oppression. Echoing the Declaration of Independence, it stated:

> We hold these truths to be self-evident: that all men and women are created equal; that they are endowed by their Creator with certain inalienable rights; that among these are life, liberty and the pursuit of happiness.

Against the advice of many of those present, a resolution was proposed to demand the vote for women. It was the only resolution not to receive the convention's unanimous support—even among supporters of women's rights, the right to vote was controversial. Other propositions were enthusiastically and unanimously approved, among them calls for the right to own property, to have access to higher education, and to receive custody of children after divorce. Some of these demands were realized in New York by the 1848 Married Women's Property Act, and still others in an 1860 New York law, but these rights were not extended to all American women, and progress was slow.

The women's movement picked up steam after Seneca Falls and the victories in New York, but it had yet to settle on a political strategy. The courts were closed to women, of course, much as they had been for Dred Scott; women simply weren't allowed access to the legal arena. For a long time, women's rights advocates worked closely with the antislavery movement, assuming that when blacks received their rights, as they did with the passage of the Fourteenth Amendment, they and the Republican Party would rally to the women's cause. Not only did that fail to happen, but the passage of the Fourteenth Amendment marked the first time the word *male* appeared in the Constitution. There was a bitter split between the two movements, and afterward it was not unheard of for women's rights advocates to promote their cause, especially in the South, with racist appeals, arguing that giving women the right to vote would dilute the impact of black voters.

In 1869 the women's movement itself split into two groups, divided by philosophy and strategy. The National Woman Suffrage Association took a broad view of the suffrage issue and included among its goals the reform of job discrimination, labor conditions, and divorce law. It favored a federal suffrage amendment, which required work at the national level. Regularly, from 1878 to 1896 and again after 1913, the Susan B. Anthony Amendment, named after an early advocate of women's rights, was introduced into Congress but failed to pass. The American Woman Suffrage Association, on the other hand, took a different tack, focusing its efforts on the less dramatic but more practical task of changing state electoral laws. It was this state strategy that would prove effective and finally create the conditions under which the Susan B. Anthony Nineteenth Amendment would be passed and ratified in 1920.

The Struggle in the States

The state strategy was a smart one for women. Unlike the situation that blacks faced after the war, the national government did not support the women's cause. It was possible for women to have an impact on state governments, however. Different states have different cultures and traditions, and the Constitution allows them to decide who may legally vote. Women were able to target states that were sympathetic to them and gradually gain enough political clout that their demands were listened to on the national level.

Women had been able to vote since 1869 in the Territory of Wyoming. In frontier country, it wasn't possible for women to be as protected as they might be back East, and when they proved capable of taking on a variety of other roles, it was hard to justify denying them the same rights as men. When Wyoming applied for statehood in 1889,

Figure 6.1

Women's Right to Vote Before the Nineteenth Amendment

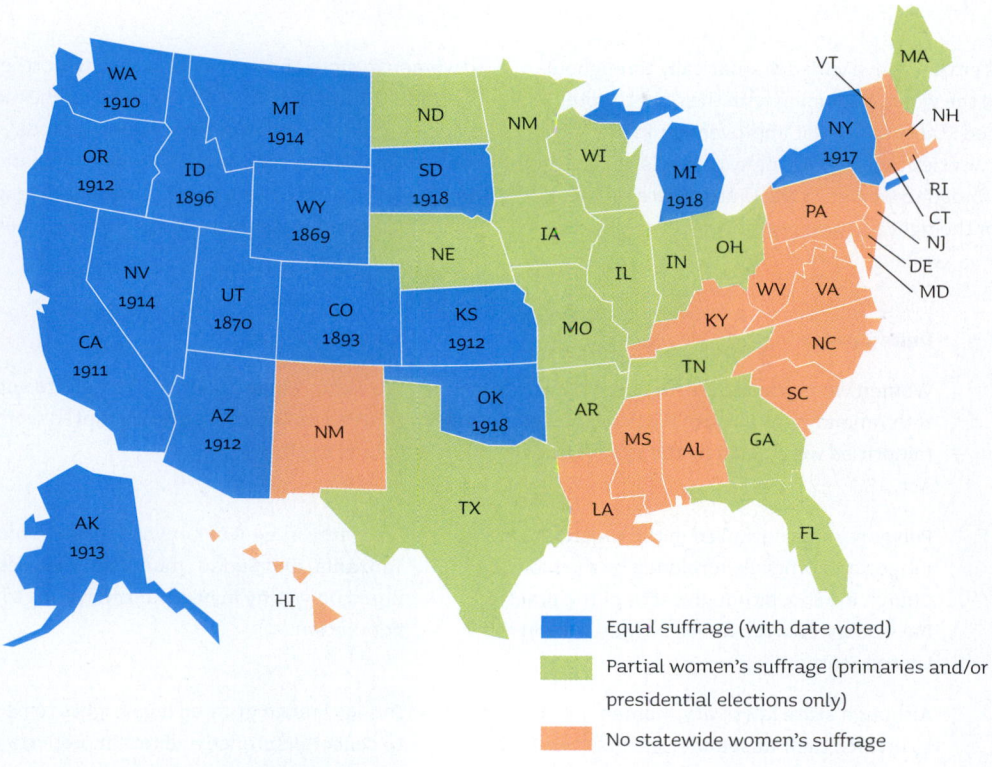

Equal suffrage (with date voted)

Partial women's suffrage (primaries and/or presidential elections only)

No statewide women's suffrage

Congress tried to impose the disenfranchisement of women as the price of admission to the Union. The Wyoming legislature responded, "We will remain out of the Union a hundred years rather than come in without the women."[88] When Wyoming was finally admitted to the United States, it was the first state to allow women to vote.

That success was not to prove contagious, however. From 1870 to 1910, women waged 480 campaigns in thirty-three states, caused seventeen referenda to be held in eleven states, and won in only two of them: Colorado (1893) and Idaho (1896). In 1890 the National and American Woman Suffrage Associations merged, becoming the National American Woman Suffrage Association (NAWSA), and began to refine their state-level strategy. By 1912, women could vote in states, primarily in the West, that controlled 74 of the total 483 Electoral College votes that decided the presidency, but the movement was facing strong external opposition and was being torn apart internally by political differences.

In 1914 an impatient, militant offshoot of NAWSA began to work at the national level again, picketing the White House and targeting the president's party, contributing to the defeat of twenty-three of forty-three Democratic candidates in the western states where women could vote. The appearance of political power lent momentum to the state-level efforts. In 1917 North Dakota gave women presidential suffrage; then Ohio, Indiana, Rhode Island, Nebraska, and Michigan followed suit. Arkansas and New York joined the list later that year. NAWSA issued a statement to members of Congress that if they would not pass the Susan B. Anthony Amendment, it would work to defeat every legislator who opposed it. The amendment passed in the House, but not the Senate, and NAWSA targeted four senators. Two were defeated, and two held on to their seats by only narrow margins. Nine more states gave women the right to vote in presidential elections (see Figure 6.1).

In 1919 the Susan B. Anthony Amendment was reintroduced into Congress with the support of President Woodrow Wilson and passed by the necessary two-thirds majority in both houses. When, in August 1920, Tennessee became the thirty-sixth state to ratify the Nineteenth Amendment, for the required total of three-fourths of the state legislatures, women finally had the vote nationwide. Unlike the situation faced by African Americans, the legal victory ended the battle. Enforcement was not as difficult as enforcement of the Fifteenth

Women's rights as citizens have varied dramatically throughout history and around the world. Beginning with the right to vote, women in the United States saw great improvement in their civil rights during the twentieth century. In many respects, what seem like basic rights afforded to women in the United States—the right to a divorce or the right to own property—are lofty goals to women in more oppressive countries. Nevertheless, women in the United States still do not share some of the more expansive rights granted to women in other countries today—for instance, adequate paid maternity leave. Here, we compare the rights of women in the United States to those around the world to see where the United States fits into the fight for women's rights:

Issue area/right	United States	Around the world
Voting rights	Women were granted the right to vote in the 19th Amendment in 1920; black women and other minorities were aided by the 1965 Voting Rights Act.	Women in Finland gained the right to vote in 1906, in Switzerland in 1971; Kuwait granted women the right to vote in 2005.
Marriage	Polygamy was outlawed in the United States in 1862 and officially forbidden by the Mormon Church in 1890, although cases of the practice have been reported as recently as 2004 in the United States.	Polygamy is legal in Kenya, Senegal, Somalia, Tanzania, and Sudan; moreover, the president of Sudan urged polygamy in his country in 2001 to boost the population.
Divorce	Although state laws vary, women hold the right to divorce their husbands; the first "no-fault" divorce laws in the United States, allowing couples to divorce by mutual consent, were enacted in California in 1969; all states had no-fault laws by 1985.	In 1999 France granted legal rights to people cohabiting to collect insurance and retain property in the event of a separation even without a legal marriage; women in Morocco gained the right to divorce an adulterous husband in 2000; women in Turkey gained the same right in 2002.
Maternity leave	Women in the United States are allowed up to 12 weeks' unpaid medical or maternity leave in a year under the Family and Medical Leave Act of 1993.	Women in France receive 26 weeks' paid maternity leave; women in the Netherlands and Vietnam get 16 weeks' paid leave; women in Germany and Algeria receive 14 weeks' paid leave; women *maquila* (textile) workers in Guatemala are denied health benefits guaranteed by Guatemalan law and can be fired for becoming pregnant.

Amendment, although many women were not inclined to use their newly won right. But until the end, the opposition had been petty and virulent, and the victory was only narrowly won. (See the box, "Comparing Women's Rights in the United States and Around the World.")

Winners and Losers in the Suffrage Movement

The debate over women's suffrage, like the fight over black civil rights, hit bitter depths because so much was at stake. If women were to acquire political rights, opponents feared, an entire way of life would be over. And, of course, in many ways they were right.

The opposition to women's suffrage came from a number of different directions. In the South, white men rejected women's suffrage for fear that women would encourage enforcement of the Civil War amendments, giving political power to blacks. And if women could vote, then of course black women could vote, further weakening the white male position. Believing that women would force temperance on the nation, brewing and liquor interests fought the women's campaign vigorously, stuffing ballot boxes and pouring huge sums of money into antisuffrage efforts. In the

Issue area/right	United States	Around the world
Domestic violence	The Violence Against Women Act, authorized by Congress in 1998, provides funds for training authorities about domestic violence against women, shelters for battered women, and counseling.	In Jordan, men who kill their wives in so-called honor crimes, or because they believe their wives have committed acts that violate social mores (such as adultery), receive reduced penalties from the state; Ecuador outlawed physical and mental assaults against women in 1995.
Workplace rights	Paying women lesser wages than men for the same job was outlawed by the 1963 Equal Pay Act, yet women in the United States earn 76 percent of what men make (and even less for minority women), because women often hold lower-paying jobs.	Women in Turkey were granted the right to get a job without their husband's consent only in 2002; in Sweden, both men and women are eligible for paid leave from their jobs when they have new children.
Violence against women	The first marital rape law, making it illegal for a husband to rape his wife, was put into law in Nebraska in 1976; marital rape is now illegal in all 50 states.	Female genital mutilation, or the practice of removing a women's clitoris and/or stitching the vulva together to discourage sexual contact or promiscuity, is officially forbidden in Somalia, Kenya, Senegal, and Togo, but UNICEF estimates 130 million women worldwide are still subjected to the practice each year, and few measures are taken to prevent the practice effectively.
Dress codes for women	Traditional dress codes for women (prohibiting wearing pants to work, etc.) have effectively fallen out of fashion, but women were not officially given the right to wear pants to work in California until 1995; a 2001 Supreme Court decision upheld a similar 1989 decision making sex-specific dress codes legal in the workplace.	Women under the Taliban regime in Afghanistan were required to wear a *burqa*, or garment that covers them from head to toe with only a mesh opening at the mouth and eyes to see and breathe through, as well as shoes that do not make any noise.

Sources: Human Rights Watch, Women's Human Rights, www.hrw.org/women; National Organization for Women, www.now.org; U.S. Equal Employment Opportunity Commission, www.eeoc.gov; "How We Compare," *The Advertiser* (Australia), December 21, 2001; The Learning Partnership, http://learningpartnership.org; Web Journal of Current Legal Issues, http://webjcli.nclac.uk; Ewan Winning, "Dress Codes: Women Get the Right to Wear Pants," 1997, www.ewin.com/articles/dressed.htm; Find Law's Legal Commentary, http://writ.news.findlaw.com/grossman/20010717.html; UNICEF, www.unicef.org; www.infoplease.com/spot/womenstimeline1.html.

East, industrial and business interests, concerned that voting women would pass enlightened labor legislation, also opposed suffrage. Antisuffrage women's groups, usually composed of upper-class women, claimed that their duties at home were more than enough for women, and that suffrage was unnecessary since men represented and watched out for the interests of women.[89] For some well-to-do women, the status quo was comfortable, and changing expectations about women's roles could only threaten that security.

Everything these opponents feared came to pass eventually, although not necessarily as the result of women voting. In fact, in the immediate aftermath of the Nineteenth Amendment,

the results of women's suffrage were disappointing to supporters. Blacks and immigrants were still being discriminated against in many parts of the country, effectively preventing both males and females from voting. Political parties excluded women, and most women lacked the money, political contacts, and experience to get involved in politics. Perhaps most important, general cultural attitudes worked against women's political participation. Politically active women were ostracized and accused of being unfeminine, making political involvement costly to many women.[90] While the women's rights advocates were clear winners in the suffrage fight, it took a long time for all the benefits of victory

Equal Rights Amendment constitutional amendment passed by Congress but never ratified that would have banned discrimination on the basis of gender

Going to the Dance

In 1919, with the Nineteenth Amendment headed toward final ratification, women began to sense the first signs of real political power.

to materialize. As the battle over the Equal Rights Amendment (ERA) was to show, attitudes toward women were changing at a glacial pace.

The Equal Rights Amendment

The Nineteenth Amendment gave women the right to vote, but it did not ensure the constitutional protection against discrimination that the Fourteenth Amendment had provided for African Americans. Even though the Fourteenth Amendment technically applied to women as well as men, the courts did not interpret it that way. It was not unconstitutional to treat people differently on account of gender. Since the ratification of the Nineteenth Amendment in 1920, some women's groups had been working for the passage of an additional *Equal Rights Amendment* that would ban discrimination on the basis of sex and guarantee women the equal protection of the laws. Objections to the proposed amendment again came

from many different directions. Traditionalists, both men and women, opposed changing the status quo and giving more power to the federal government. But there were also women, and supporters of women's rights, who feared that requiring laws to treat men and women the same would actually make women worse off by nullifying the variety of legislation that sought to protect women. Many social reformers, for instance, had worked for laws that would limit working hours or establish minimum wages for women, which now would be in jeopardy. Opponents also feared that an ERA would strike down laws preventing women from being drafted and sent into combat. Many laws in American society treat men and women differently, and few, if any, would survive under such an amendment. Nonetheless, an ERA was proposed to Congress on a fairly regular basis.

In the 1960s the political omens started to look more hopeful for expanding women's rights. Support for women's rights more generally came from an unlikely quarter, however. Title VII of the Civil Rights Act of 1964, intended to prohibit job discrimination on the basis of race, was amended to include discrimination on the basis of gender, as well, in the hopes that the addition would doom the bill's passage. Unexpectedly, the amended bill passed.

In 1967 the National Organization for Women (NOW) was organized to promote women's rights and lent its support to the ERA. Several pieces of legislation that passed in the early seventies signaled that public opinion was favorable to the idea of expanding women's rights. Title IX of the Education Amendments of 1972 banned sex discrimination in schools receiving federal funds, which meant, among other things, that schools had to provide girls with the equal opportunity and support to play sports in school. The Revenue Act of 1972 provided for tax credits for child care.

In 1970 the ERA was again introduced in the House, and this time it passed. But the Senate spent the next two years refining the language of the amendment, adding and removing provisions that would have kept women from being drafted. Arguing that such changes would not amount to true equality, advocates of equal rights for women managed to defeat them. Finally, on March 22, 1972, the ERA passed in the Senate. The exact language of the proposed amendment read:

1. Equality of rights under the law shall not be denied or abridged by the United States or by any State on account of sex.

2. The Congress shall have the power to enforce, by appropriate legislation, the provisions of this article.

World Class Women

The U.S. women's soccer team celebrates victory against Brazil after the final game of the Athens 2004 Summer Olympics. Many people credit Title IX of the Higher Education Act (aimed at ending discrimination in athletic programs at federally funded institutions) with giving female athletes in the United States the opportunities they needed to make this victory possible.

3. This amendment shall take effect two years after the date of ratification.

When both houses of Congress passed the final version of the amendment, the process of getting approval of three-quarters of the state legislatures began. Thirty states had ratified the amendment by early 1973. But while public opinion polls showed support for the idea of giving constitutional protection to women's rights, the votes at the state level began to go the other way. By 1977 only thirty-five states had voted to ratify, three short of the necessary thirty-eight. Despite the extension of the ratification deadline from 1979 to 1982, the amendment died unratified.

Why did a ratification process that started out with such promise fizzle so abruptly? The ERA failed to pass for several reasons. First, while most people supported the idea of women's rights in the abstract, they weren't sure what the consequences of such an amendment would be, and people feared the possibility of radical social change. Second, the ERA came to be identified in the public's mind with the 1973 Supreme Court ruling in *Roe v. Wade* that women have abortion rights in the first trimester of their pregnancies. Professor Jane Mansbridge argued that conservative opponents of the ERA managed to link the two issues, claiming that the ERA was a rejection of motherhood and traditional values, and turning ERA votes into referenda on abortion.[91]

Finally, the Supreme Court had been striking down some (though not all) laws that treated women differently from men, using the equal protection clause of the Fourteenth Amendment.[92] This caused some people to argue that the ERA was unnecessary, which probably reassured those who approved of the principle of equality but had no desire to turn society upside-down.

Gender Discrimination Today

Despite the failure of the ERA, today most of the legal barriers to women's equality in this country have been eliminated. But because the ERA did not pass, and there is no constitutional amendment specifically guaranteeing equal protection of the laws regardless of gender, the Supreme Court has not been willing to treat gender as a suspect classification, although it has come close at times. Laws that treat men and women differently are subject only to the intermediate standard of review, not the strict scrutiny test. There must be only an important government purpose for laws that discriminate against women, not a compelling interest. Examples of laws that have failed that test, and thus have been struck down by the Court, include portions of the Social Security Act that give benefits to widows but not to widowers, and laws that require husbands but not wives to be liable for alimony payments.[93] Some laws that do treat men and women differently—for instance, statutory rape laws and laws requiring that only males be drafted—have been upheld by the Court.

Thinking Outside the Box

Is it possible to have too much equality?

▶ Who Are We?

Gender and equality

The traditional notion of the male as the sole breadwinner of a household has long been in decline. Today, levels of education among men and women are almost equal. The wage gap between men and women has shrunk, although even for those with similar levels of education, the incomes of men exceed those of women. As women have become more equal in terms of work and income, they have also become a distinctive political group—one that tends to be more Democratic and more liberal than men on many issues. How might the gender gap in wages relate to this ideological gender gap? What social and political changes are likely to follow from the changing economic positions of men and women?

Earning, by Gender and Education: At every level of education, women earn less than men

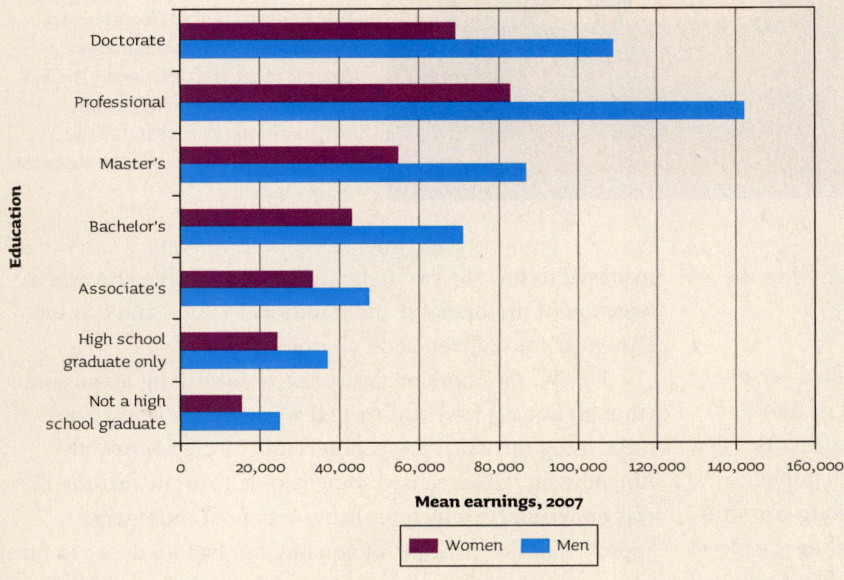

Mean earnings, 2007

■ Women ■ Men

Source: U.S. Census Bureau, "Table 227: Mean Earnings by Highest Degree Earned: 2007," www.census.gov/compendia/statab/cats/education.html.

Percentage of Men and Women in the Work Force: A greater percentage of women are entering the work force

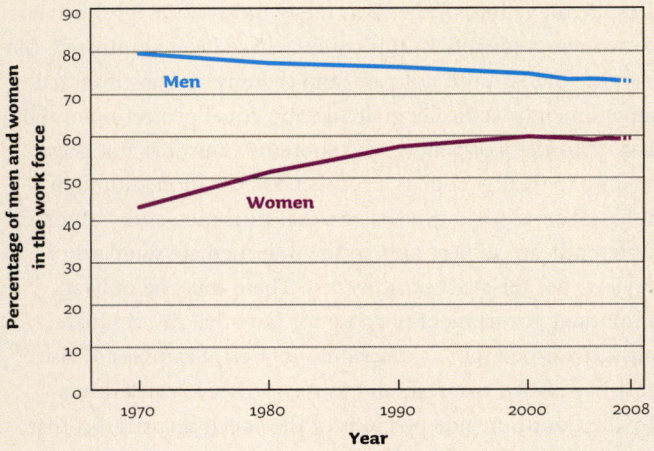

Source: U.S. Census Bureau, "Table 576: Civilian Population—Employment Status by Sex, Race, and Ethnicity," www.census.gov/compendia/statab/cats/labor_force_employment_earnings/labor_force_status.html.

Changes in Median Income, by Sex: The wage gap is shrinking

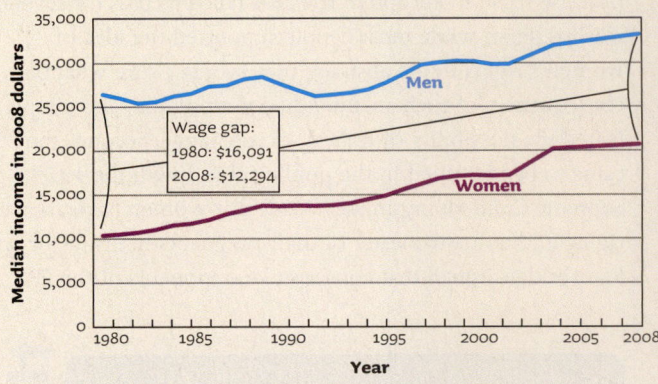

Wage gap:
1980: $16,091
2008: $12,294

Source: U.S. Census Bureau, Historical Income Tables, Table P-8, www.census.gov/hhes/www/income/histinc/incpertoc.html.

sexual harassment unwelcome sexual speech or behavior that creates a hostile work environment

Having achieved formal equality, women still face some striking discrimination in the workplace. (See *"Who Are We? Gender and Equality."*) Women today earn seventy-seven cents for every dollar earned by men, and the National Committee on Pay Equity, a nonprofit group in Washington, calculates that that pay gap may cost women almost a half a million dollars over the course of their work lives.[94] Women's ability to seek remedies for this discrimination has been limited by law. In 2007 the U.S. Supreme Court ruled in a five-to-four decision that a female worker's right to sue for discrimination was constrained by the statutes of limitations in existing civil rights law.[95] On January 29, 2009, the first bill signed into law by President Obama was the Lilly Ledbetter Act, extending the time frame so that workers could still sue even if the wage discrimination against them revealed itself over time. A companion piece to this legislation, the Paycheck Fairness Act, would prohibit discrimination and retaliation against workers who bring discrimination claims. It passed in the House but remained stalled in the Senate as of 2010.

In addition, women are tremendously underrepresented at the upper levels of corporate management, academic administration, and other top echelons of power. Some people argue that women fail to achieve levels of power and salary on a par with men because many women may leave and enter the job market several times or put their careers on hold to have children. Such interruptions prevent them from accruing the kind of seniority that pays dividends for men. The so-called Mommy track has been blamed for much of the disparity between men's and women's positions in the world. Others argue, however, that there is an enduring difference in the hiring and salary patterns of women that has nothing to do with childbearing, or else reflects male inflexibility when it comes to incorporating motherhood and corporate responsibility. These critics claim that there is a "glass ceiling" in the corporate world, invisible to the eye but impenetrable, that prevents women from rising to their full potential. The Civil Rights Act of 1991 created the Glass Ceiling Commission to study this phenomenon, and among the commission's conclusions was the observation that business is depriving itself of a large pool of talent by denying leadership positions to women.

Ever since President Johnson's executive order of 1965 was amended in 1968 to include gender, the federal government has had not only to stop discriminating against women in its hiring practices but also to take affirmative action to make sure that women are hired. Many other levels of government take gender into consideration when they hire, and the Supreme Court has upheld the practice.[96] But it is hard to mandate change in leadership positions when the number of jobs is few to begin with and the patterns of discrimination appear across corporations, universities, and foundations.

Some analysts have argued that the glass ceiling is a phenomenon that affects relatively few women, and that most women today are less preoccupied with moving up the corporate ladder than with making a decent living, or getting off what one observer has called the "sticky floor" of low-paying jobs.[97] While the wage gap between men and women with advanced education is narrowing, women still tend to be excluded from the more lucrative blue collar positions in manufacturing, construction, communication, and transportation.[98]

Getting hired, maintaining equal pay, and earning promotions are not the only challenges women face on the job. They are often subject to unwelcome sexual advances, comments, or jokes that make their jobs unpleasant, offensive, and unusually stressful. Sexual harassment, brought to national attention during the Senate confirmation hearings for Clarence Thomas's appointment to the Supreme Court in 1991, often makes the workplace a hostile environment for women. Now technically illegal, it is often difficult to define and document, and women have traditionally faced retribution from employers and fellow workers for calling attention to such practices. In the late 1990s it became clear that even when the U.S. government is the employer, *sexual harassment* can run rampant. The much-publicized cases of sexual harassment in the military show that progress toward gender equality in the armed forces still has a long way to go, and cases as recent as 2004 against such prominent private employers as Merrill Lynch, Morgan Stanley, and Boeing indicate that the problem continues to plague the private sector too.

Another form of employment discrimination is highlighted in the recent dramatic rise in the number of cases of discrimination reported by pregnant women. Between fiscal years 1992 and 2003, pregnancy discrimination complaints filed with the EEOC jumped 39 percent, outpacing sexual harassment claims.[99] Allegations of pregnant women being unfairly fired or denied promotion have been made against several companies including Wal-Mart and Hooters. In one study, roughly half of the sample of pregnant women stated that their bosses had had negative reactions to the pregnancies.

Nor is employment the only place where women continue to face unequal treatment. A 1995 California law, the Gender Tax Repeal Act, for instance, bans businesses from charging women more than men for the same services, such as haircuts, dry cleaning, and car repairs, and a number of other states are following suit. That such laws are called for is indicated by a

1996 Washington State study: it found that while women generally earn less than men, 36 percent of hair stylists charge women an average of $5.58 more than men for the same basic short cut, and 86 percent of dry cleaners charge women about two dollars more to clean a shirt.[100] Other legal action has tried to correct price differences in catalogs sent to men and women, and the practice of golf courses reserving their best tee times for men.[101] As these examples indicate, the issue of gender equity in America can pop up in unexpected places.

Women in Contemporary Politics

Women have faced discrimination not only in the boardroom and the barbershop but in politics as well. While more women today hold elected office than at any other time in history, women still remain the most underrepresented group in Congress and the state legislatures. In the 111th Congress, only 73 of 435 members of the House of Representatives were female, and there are currently seventeen female senators. As of 2008, there were six female governors. As of 2009, thirty-three cities with populations of more than 100,000 had female mayors.[102]

Women have been underrepresented in government for many reasons. Some observers argue that women may be less likely to have access to the large amounts of money needed to run a successful campaign. A study of U.S. House candidates from the 1970s to the 1990s shows that women candidates raised and spent about three-fourths of what a male candidate did between 1974 and 1980. However, by 1990, women candidates for the House raised and spent *more* money than did male candidates; women candidates raised 111 percent of what male candidates did for the 1992 race.[103] Others argue that women are not as likely as men to want to go into politics. For instance, more women candidates for state legislative office report waiting to wage a campaign until after they were asked to run by a party or legislative official.[104] And, while sexism has abated to some extent, many men (and even some women) are unwilling to vote for a female candidate. In an April 2008 poll, only 63 percent of those surveyed agreed that the United States was ready for a woman president.[105]

However, the representation of women in government is clearly better than it was. Hillary Clinton came very close to winning the Democratic nomination for president in 2008, and polls at the time indicated that she could have beaten Republican John McCain. McCain himself later appointed a woman as his vice presidential running mate. Nancy Pelosi became the first female Speaker of the House in 2006, and three of the last

four secretaries of state have been women. In fact, in 2010 the second and fourth officials in the line of succession to the president of the United States were women (the Speaker of the House follows the vice president, and the secretary of state comes after the president pro tempore of the Senate).

In 1971 women comprised only 2 percent of Congress members and less than 5 percent of state legislators. Today 16.4 percent of Congress members and 23.7 percent of state legislators are female, both all-time highs. In 2005 women held 25 percent of all statewide elective offices, including sixteen lieutenant governorships. While this percentage is below the high of 27.6 in 2001, it is a substantial increase from the 11 percent in 1979.[106] In 2006 women entered ten of the thirty-six gubernatorial races on a major-party ticket (six won, giving the United States a total of eight women governors).[107] Many observers argue that the increase in the number of female candidates running for and winning office expands future electoral opportunities for women. We discuss this issue further in Chapter 8.

Who What How

Supporters and opponents of the women's movement struggled mightily over the extension of rights to women. As in the battles we discussed earlier, at stake were not just civil rights but social and economic power as well.

Because the courts and Congress were at first off-limits to the women's movement, women took their fight to the states, with their more accepting cultures and less restrictive rules. Having finally gained the vote in enough states to allow them to put electoral pressure on national officials, women got the national vote in 1920. The Nineteenth Amendment, however, did not give them the same equal protection of the laws that the Fourteenth Amendment had given blacks. Today the courts give women greater protection of the law, but the failure of the ERA to be ratified means that laws that discriminate against them are still subject to only an intermediate standard of review.

Rights Denied on Other Bases
Challenging other classifications in the courts

Race, gender, and ethnicity, of course, are not the only grounds on which the laws treat people differently in the

United States. Four other classifications that provide interesting insights into the politics of rights in America are sexual orientation, age, disability, and lack of citizenship.

Sexual Orientation

Gays and lesbians have faced two kinds of legal discrimination in this country. On the one hand, overt discrimination simply prohibits some behaviors: gays cannot serve openly in the military, for instance, and in some states they cannot adopt children or teach in public schools. But a more subtle kind of discrimination doesn't forbid their actions or behavior; it simply fails to recognize them legally. Thus in most states gays cannot marry or claim the rights that married people share, such as collecting their partner's Social Security, being covered by a partner's insurance plan, being each other's next of kin, or having a family. Some of these rights can be mimicked with complicated and expensive legal arrangements, some are possible because of the good will of particular companies toward their employees, but others, under the current laws, are out of reach. Being gay, unlike being black or female or Asian, is something that can be hidden from public view, and until the 1970s many gays escaped overt discrimination by denying or concealing who they were, but that too, many people argue, is a serious deprivation of civil rights.[108]

Political Strategies: The Courts

As we discussed in Chapter 5, the case of *Bowers v. Hardwick* (1986) failed to advance the rights of gays and lesbians. The Court ruled that a Georgia statute against sodomy was a legitimate exercise of the state's power and that it met the minimum rationality test described earlier in this chapter.[109] The Court did not require that a law that treated people differently on the basis of sexual orientation had to fulfill either a compelling or an important state purpose; it merely had to be a reasonable use of state power. The four justices who dissented from that opinion did not want to tackle the issue of whether homosexuality was right or wrong. Rather they claimed that, as a privacy issue, what consenting adults do is none of the government's business.

Gay rights again took a hit in 1995, when the Court ruled that the South Boston Allied War Veterans Council did not have to let the Irish-American Gay, Lesbian and Bisexual Group of Boston march in its annual St. Patrick's Day parade under a banner proclaiming its sexual orientation. But the decision did not touch on the rights of homosexuals; it was

An Assault on Marriage?

Newlyweds Sharon Papo (left) and Amber Weiss celebrate after exchanging vows on the first full day of legal same-sex marriages in California, June 17, 2008. Supporters of same-sex marriage did not have long to celebrate. In November 2008, voters passed a referendum banning gay marriage, setting off numerous protests.

based solely on the question of the veterans' group's right to freedom of expression.[110]

More recently, however, gays and lesbians have had some major victories in the courts. In 1996 a bitterly divided Court struck down an amendment to the Colorado constitution that would have prevented gays from suing for discrimination in housing and employment. The amendment had been a reaction on the part of conservative groups to legislation in several cities that would have made it illegal to discriminate against gays in housing, employment, and related matters. The Court ruled that gays could not be singled out and denied the fundamental protection of the laws, that "a state cannot deem a class of persons a stranger to its laws." While the majority on the Court did not rule in this case that sexual orientation was a suspect classification, it did hint at greater protection than the minimum rationality test would warrant.[111] For the first time, it treated gay rights as a civil rights issue.

In 2000 a bare majority on the Court relied on their precedent in the parade case to rule on First Amendment grounds that the Boy Scouts of America had the right to exclude gay leaders because doing so was part of their "expressive message."[112] This ruling did not do anything to limit the more general civil rights issues that the Colorado case advanced.

The two biggest victories for gays and lesbians in a court of law, however, came in 2003. First, in *Lawrence v. Texas*, the Supreme Court overturned the *Bowers* decision, ruling that state sodomy laws were a violation of the right to privacy.[113] Even though many states had already repealed their sodomy laws, or failed to enforce them, the *Lawrence* decision was substantively and symbolically a break with previous judicial opinion that allowed the states to regulate the sexual behavior of gays and lesbians.

The gay and lesbian movement received another unexpected legal victory in 2003, when the Massachusetts Supreme Judicial Court ruled, in an extremely controversial four-to-three decision, that marriage was a civil right and that the state's law banning homosexual marriage violated the equal protection and due process clauses in the Massachusetts constitution.[114] The Massachusetts court ruling sent shockwaves throughout the country as the nation's first legal gay marriages were performed in Massachusetts. (Some local officials in California and New York began to conduct gay marriages as well, though these were later determined to be illegal.)

Critics on the right (and even some on the left) argued that the ruling was an example of judicial activism—of judges trying to legislate from the bench. They claimed that the court had overstepped its bounds and that decisions regarding marriage should be left to the state legislatures. Opponents of the decision also noted that the majority of the public opposed same-sex marriage. Almost immediately after the ruling, President Bush announced his support for an amendment to the Constitution defining marriage as a union between a man and a woman. However, because Congress had already passed a Defense of Marriage Act in 1996 (DOMA) stating that states need not recognize gay marriages performed in other states, the amendment failed to garner much immediate congressional support although conservative groups still strongly support it. That may change, should the Supreme Court strike down DOMA in the future. Also, in reaction to the Massachusetts Supreme Court ruling, eleven states overwhelmingly passed propositions in 2004 that banned same-sex marriage, and a total of twenty-six states currently ban gay marriage by constitutional amendment and forty-three by statute.

Despite the popular backlash in some places, efforts to amend the Massachusetts constitution to ban same-sex marriage were defeated by the state legislature in 2007, and in 2008 the California Supreme Court struck down that state's ban on gay marriage, arguing that the state constitution protected a fundamental right to marry. Unlike the Massachusetts decision, which allowed only residents of that state to marry there, California's decision also allowed nonresidents to marry. In the immediate aftermath of the California decision, New York governor David Paterson instructed all of his state's agencies to recognize same-sex marriages performed elsewhere, clearing the way for New Yorkers marrying in Massachusetts, California, or Canada to have their marriages considered legitimate in New York. Although challenges to Governor Paterson's action are in the works, and California voters amended their constitution to ban gay marriage in 2008, there has clearly been some movement toward an expansion of marriage rights at the state level. Gay marriage is currently legal in Connecticut, Iowa, Massachusetts, New Hampshire, Vermont, and Washington, D.C., and is recognized in New York, Rhode Island, and Maryland.

Political Strategies: Elections

The courts are not the only political avenue open to gays in their struggle for equal rights. Gays have also been effective in parlaying their relatively small numbers into a force to be reckoned with electorally. Although it is difficult to gain an accurate idea of the size of the gay population in the United States,[115] between 4 and 5 percent of the electorate self-identifies as gay, lesbian, or bisexual—a larger portion of the electorate than Hispanics or Jews or other groups that are courted by the political parties.[116] It is not only as individuals that gays wield political power, however. Gays began to organize politically in 1969 after riots following police harassment at a gay bar in New York City, the Stonewall Inn. Today many interest groups are organized around issues of concern to the gay community. The largest, the Human Rights Campaign, made a total contribution to campaigns of nearly $4.5 million in 2008, with $1.3 million going to federal candidates.[117] While in the past gays have primarily supported the Democratic Party, a growing number identify themselves as independent, and a group of conservative gays calling themselves the Log Cabin Republicans have become active on the political right. Openly gay members of Congress have been elected from both sides of the partisan divide.

In 1992, acting on a campaign promise made to gays, President Clinton decided to end the ban on gays in the military with an executive order, much as President Truman had ordered the racial integration of the armed forces in 1948. Clinton, however, badly miscalculated the public reaction to his move. The Christian Right and other conservative and military groups were outraged. In the ensuing storm, Clinton settled instead for a "don't ask, don't tell" (DADT) policy: members of the armed forces need not disclose their sexual orientation, but if they reveal it, or the military otherwise finds out, they can still be disciplined or discharged. For example, shortly after the September 11 attacks, at a time when the military was already facing a shortage of translators who could speak Arabic, six gay army linguists who spoke Arabic were dismissed.[118] In 2008 Barack Obama campaigned on the repeal of DADT, and in 2010 his administration signaled its intention to repeal the policy banning gays in the military.[119] Although down to the wire, a lame duck session of Congress finally broke a Republican filibuster led by Sen. John McCain and repealed the policy in December 2010.

Gays have also tried to use their political power to fend off the earlier-mentioned legislation banning gay marriage. The legislation was prompted in the mid-1990s, by a case in the Hawaiian courts that could have allowed gays to marry in that state. Under the Constitution's "full faith and credit" clause, the other states would have to recognize those marriages as legal. State legislators rushed to create laws rejecting gay marriage, and in 1996 Congress passed DOMA to prevent federal recognition of gay marriage and allow states to pass laws denying its legality. President Clinton, who opposed the idea of gay marriage, signed the bill under protest, claiming that the bill was politically motivated and mean-spirited. In 2000 Vermont passed a law creating civil unions that stop short of achieving the status of marriage but that allow same-sex couples to have all the rights and responsibilities of married couples. Although this law has been deeply divisive in the state, efforts to roll it back have so far proved unavailing and other states, including New Jersey, New Hampshire, and Connecticut, have followed Vermont's lead.

Another issue of active concern to gays is workplace discrimination. The Employment Non-Discrimination Act (ENDA) would make it illegal to discriminate on the basis of sexual orientation in hiring, firing, pay, and promotion decisions. Introduced to Congress for the fifth time in the summer of 2001, it has yet to come up for a vote in the House, and the Senate, while coming within one vote in 1996, has not yet passed it.

The issue of gay rights has come to the forefront of the American political agenda not only because of gays' increasing political power but also because of the fierce opposition of the Christian Right. Their determination to banish what they see as an unnatural and sinful lifestyle—and their conviction that protection of the basic rights of homosexuals means that they will be given "special privileges"— has focused tremendous public attention on issues that most of the public would rather remained private. The spread of AIDS and the political efforts of gay groups to fight for increased resources to battle the disease have also heightened public awareness of gay issues. Public opinion remains mixed on the subject, but tolerance is increasing. In 2010, 69 percent or more of Americans favored lifting the ban on gays in the military, and 46 percent favored permitting gays to adopt (up from 38 percent in 1999).[120] Still, in 2009, 54 percent opposed gay marriage. Interestingly, young people consistently support issues of gay and lesbian rights in far greater numbers than their elders, an indication that change may be on the horizon. For example, whereas 64 percent of those aged 65 years or older opposed gay marriage, only 45 percent of those aged 18–29 years did so.[121]

Age

In 1976 the Supreme Court ruled that age is not a suspect classification.[122] That means that if governments have rational reasons for doing so, they may pass laws that treat younger or older people differently from the rest of the population, and courts do not have to use strict scrutiny when reviewing those laws. Young people are often not granted the full array of rights of adult citizens, being subject to curfews or locker searches at school; nor are they subject to the laws of adult justice if they commit a crime. Some observers have argued that children should have expanded rights to protect them in dealings with their parents.

Older people face discrimination most often in the area of employment. Compulsory retirement at a certain age, regardless of an individual's capabilities or health, may be said to violate basic civil rights. The Court has generally upheld mandatory retirement requirements.[123] Congress, however, has sought to prevent age discrimination with the Age Discrimination Act of 1967, outlawing discrimination against people up to 70 years of age in employment or in the provision of benefits, unless age can be shown to be relevant to the job in question. In 1978 the act was amended to prohibit mandatory retirement before 70, and in 1986 all mandatory retirement policies were banned except in special occupations.

Unlike younger people, who can't vote until they are 18 and don't vote in great numbers after that, older people defend their interests very effectively. Voter participation rates rise with age, and older Americans are also extremely well organized politically. AARP (formerly the American Association of Retired Persons), a powerful interest group with over 30 million members, has been active in pressuring government to preserve policies that benefit older people. In the debates in the mid-1990s about cutting government services, AARP was very much present, and in the face of the organization's advice and voting power, programs like Social Security and Medicare (providing health care for older Americans) remained virtually untouched.

Disability

People with physical and mental disabilities have also organized politically to fight for their civil rights. Advocates for the disabled include people with disabilities themselves, people who work in the social services catering to the disabled, and veterans' groups. Even though laws do not prevent disabled people from voting, staying in hotels, or using public phones, circumstances often do. Inaccessible buildings, public transportation, and other facilities can pose barriers as insurmountable as the law, as can public attitudes toward and discomfort around disabled people.

The 1990 Americans With Disabilities Act (ADA), modeled on the civil rights legislation that empowers racial and gender groups, protects the rights of the more than 44 million mentally and physically disabled people in this country. Disabilities covered under the act need not be as dramatic or obvious as confinement to a wheelchair or blindness. People with AIDS, recovering drug and alcohol addicts, and heart disease and diabetes patients are among those covered. The act provides detailed guidelines for access to buildings, mass transit, public facilities, and communication systems. It also guarantees protection from bias in employment; the EEOC is authorized to handle cases of job discrimination because of disabilities, as well as race and gender. The act was controversial because many of the required changes in physical accommodations, such as ramps and elevators, are extremely expensive to install. Advocates for the disabled respond that these expenses will be offset by increased business from disabled people and by the added productivity and skills that the disabled bring to the workplace. The reach of the act was limited in 2001, when the Supreme Court ruled that state employees could not sue their states for damages under the ADA because of the seldom discussed, but extremely important, Eleventh Amendment,

which limits lawsuits that can be filed against the states.[124] The Court's five-to-four decision was criticized by disability rights advocates as severely limiting the ADA.

Citizenship

The final category of discrimination we discuss is discrimination against people who are not citizens. Should noncitizens have the same rights as U.S. citizens? Should all noncitizens have those rights? Illegal visitors as well as legal? Constitutional law has been fairly clear on these questions, granting citizens and aliens most of the same constitutional rights, except the right to vote. (Even legal aliens who serve in the military are unable to vote.) Politics and the Constitution have not always been in sync on these points, however. Oddly for a nation of immigrants, the United States has periodically witnessed backlashes against the flow of people arriving from other countries, often triggered by fear that the newcomers' needs will mean fewer resources, jobs, and benefits for those who arrived earlier. During these backlashes, politicians have vied for public favor by cutting back on immigrants' rights. The Supreme Court responded in 1971 by declaring that alienage, like race and religion, is a suspect classification, and that laws that discriminate against aliens must be backed by a compelling government purpose.[125] To be sure, the Court has upheld some laws restricting the rights of immigrants, but it has done so only after a strict scrutiny of the facts. In light of the ruling, it has even supported the rights of illegal aliens to a public education.[126]

Among the groups who fight for the rights of immigrants are the Coalition for Humane Immigrant Rights and many politically active Hispanic groups. The people they represent, however, are often among the poorest, and the most politically silent, in society. Illegal immigrants, especially, do not have much money or power, and they are thus an easy target for disgruntled citizens and hard-pressed politicians. However, considerable evidence suggests that while immigrants, particularly the larger groups like Mexicans, tend to be poor, they do become assimilated into American society. The average wages of second- and third-generation Mexican Americans, for instance, rise to about 80 percent of the wages of whites.[127] And their wage levels do not necessarily depress the overall wage levels. In the 1980s wages rose faster in parts of the country with higher immigrant populations.[128] Although many immigrant groups are certainly poor, and a gap remains between their average standards of living and those of longer-term residents, the reaction against immigration in this country may be out of proportion to the problem.

Even groups that already enjoy basic civil rights can face considerable discrimination. Opposition to the extension of more comprehensive rights to these groups comes from a variety of directions.

Who What How

In the case of gays and lesbians, opponents claim that providing a heightened standard of review for laws that discriminate on the basis of sexual orientation would be giving special rights to gays. Gays and lesbians are politically sophisticated and powerful, however, and the techniques they use are often strategies that had originally been closed off to minorities and women. Both they and their opponents use the courts, form interest groups, lobby Congress, and support presidential candidates to further their agendas. In the case of age discrimination, opponents are motivated not by moral concerns but by issues of social order and cost-efficiency. Older people are able to protect their rights more effectively than younger people because of their higher voter turnout.

People resist giving rights to the disabled generally out of concern for the expense of making buildings accessible and the cost-efficiency of hiring disabled workers. Organization into interest groups and effective lobbying of Congress have resulted in considerable protection of the rights of the disabled.

Finally, noncitizens seeking rights face opposition from a variety of sources. Although immigrants themselves are not usually well organized, the biggest protection of their rights comes from the Supreme Court, which has ruled that alienage is a suspect classification and, therefore, laws that discriminate on the basis of citizenship are subject to strict scrutiny.

The Citizens and Civil Rights
The power of group action

The stories of America's civil rights struggles are the stories of citizen action. But clearly, citizens acting individually have not been able to bring about all the changes that civil rights groups have achieved. Although great leaders and effective organizers have played an important role in the battles for rights, the battles themselves have been part of a group movement.

In Chapter 1 we discussed three models of democracy that define options for citizen participation: elite, pluralist, and participatory. Of the three, the pluralist model best describes the actions that citizens have taken to gain the government's protection of their civil rights. Pluralism emphasizes the ways that citizens can increase their individual power by organizing into groups. The civil rights movements in the United States have been group movements, and to the extent that groups have been unable to organize effectively to advance their interests, their civil rights progress has been correspondingly slowed.

As we will see in Chapter 13, what have come to be known as *interest groups* play an increasingly important role in American politics. In fact, from the 1960s through the end of the century, the number of national associations in the United States grew by over 250 percent, to about 23,000, and the number of groups organized specifically to advocate the rights of African Americans, Hispanics, Asian Americans, and women have multiplied by six times during that period.[129] Scholars do not agree on whether this proliferation of groups increases the quality of democracy or skews its results. Groups that are well organized, well financed, and well informed and that have particularly passionate members (who put their votes where their hearts are) are likely to carry greater weight with lawmakers than are groups that are less focused and less well to do. On the one hand, money, information, and intensity of opinion can make interest groups more powerful than their numbers, a fact that seems at odds with notions of political equality and democracy. On the other hand, as we have seen, individuals can accomplish things together in groups that they can only dream of doing alone. In the case of the civil rights movement, democracy would have clearly been impoverished without the power of groups to work on distributing citizenship rights more broadly. We return to the question of how democratic a pluralist society can be in Chapter 13, when we investigate in more depth the role of interest groups in American politics.

Can we end de facto discrimination without imposing substantive solutions?

Thinking Outside the Box

▶ **What's at Stake Revisited**

In this chapter we have learned that the long and difficult battle for civil rights in this country is not yet over. Nonetheless, we began with the observation that the very fact that one of the major parties' slate of candidates included a woman, an African American, and a Hispanic, and that the other party fielded a female vice presidential candidate, was itself a step forward for equality. How could the fact that these individuals ran make a difference, even though only one of them reached the White House? What was at stake in these high-profile candidacies?

America has always been proud to be a nation of equal opportunity, where "any child can grow up to be president." Through more than fifty presidential elections, however, "any child" has turned out to mean any white male child. Girls or kids from other races may have had aspirations, but when they looked at the long lineup of candidates through the years, white male faces were all that they saw. History offered them few or no role models for their hopes for running for president.

In 2008 that changed. As the long primary season drew to an end in the spring of 2008, the candidates and political commentators reflected on what those candidacies had meant.

In closing her concession speech, for instance, Hillary Clinton stopped to consider the impact her campaign had had on race and gender in America:

> Think how much progress we have already made. When we first started, people everywhere asked the same questions:
>
> Could a woman really serve as commander-in-chief? Well, I think we answered that one.

And could an African American really be our president? Senator Obama has answered that one.

Together Senator Obama and I achieved milestones essential to our progress as a nation, part of our perpetual duty to form a more perfect union.

Now, on a personal note—when I was asked what it means to be a woman running for president, I always gave the same answer: that I was proud to be running as a woman but I was running because I thought I'd be the best president. But I am a woman, and like millions of women, I know there are still barriers and biases out there, often unconscious.

I want to build an America that respects and embraces the potential of every last one of us.

I ran as a daughter who benefited from opportunities my mother never dreamed of. I ran as a mother who worries about my daughter's future and a mother who wants to lead all children to brighter tomorrows. To build that future I see, we must make sure that women and men alike understand the struggles of their grandmothers and mothers, and that women enjoy equal opportunities, equal pay, and equal respect. Let us resolve and work toward achieving some very simple propositions: There are no acceptable limits and there are no acceptable prejudices in the twenty-first century.

You can be so proud that, from now on, it will be unremarkable for a woman to win primary state victories, unremarkable to have a woman in a close race to be our nominee, unremarkable to think that a woman can be the president of the United States. And that is truly remarkable.[130]

And while Obama himself did not refer explicitly to race when he claimed the nomination, fellow African Americans did. Writing in the *Washington Post*, Pulitzer Prize–winning columnist Eugene Robinson, like Hillary Clinton, took "a moment to contemplate the mind-bending improbability of what just happened." He wrote:

> A young, black first-term senator—a man whose father was from Kenya, whose mother was from Kansas and whose name sounds as if it might have come from the roster of Guantánamo detainees—has won a marathon of primaries and caucuses to become the presidential nominee of the Democratic Party. To reach this point, he had to do more than outduel the party's most powerful and resourceful political machine. He also had to defy, and ultimately defeat, 389 years of history. . . . Whether he wins or loses, history has been made. Maybe there's more to come, maybe not; but already—after 389 long years—it's safe to say that this nation will never be the same.[131]

The Obama, Clinton, and Richardson candidacies are not important just for what they measure about racism and sexism in America today, but for the impact they will have on generations just coming of age. A diarist on the liberal blog *Daily Kos* pointed out that "my kids will grow up in a world that has always had (in their memories, at least) an African-American as the standard bearer for a major political party,"[132] and the novel experience of seeing people just like themselves at the heights of American politics will be had not only by black kids, but by Hispanic children and girls as well—something that has never before been true in American politics. And that, in Senator Clinton's words, is truly remarkable.

To Sum Up

Key terms, chapter summaries, practice quizzes, Internet links, and other study aids are available on the companion web site at http://republic.cqpress.com.

Define | Understand | Practice | Read | Click | Watch

affirmative action (p. 203)

black codes (p. 194)

boycott (p. 200)

Brown v. Board of Education of Topeka (p. 197)

busing (p. 203)

civil rights (p. 190)

de facto discrimination (p. 200)

de jure discrimination (p. 200)

English-only movements (p. 216)

Equal Rights Amendment (p. 224)

grandfather clauses (p. 194)

intermediate standard of review (p. 191)

Jim Crow laws (p. 195)

literacy tests (p. 194)

minimum rationality test (p. 191)

National Association for the Advancement of Colored People (NAACP) (p. 196)

Plessy v. Ferguson (p. 195)

poll taxes (p. 194)

racism (p. 193)

Reconstruction (p. 194)

segregation (p. 195)

sexual harassment (p. 227)

strict scrutiny (p. 190)

suspect classification (p. 190)

Define | **Understand** | Practice | Read | Click | Watch

- Throughout U.S. history, various groups, because of some characteristic beyond their control, have been denied their civil rights and have fought for equal treatment under the law. All three branches of the government have played an important role in providing remedies for the denial of equal rights.

- Groups that are discriminated against may seek procedural remedies, such as changing the law to guarantee equality of opportunity, or substantive remedies, such as the institution of affirmative action programs, to guarantee equality of outcome.

- African Americans have experienced both de jure discrimination, created by laws that treat people differently, and de facto discrimination, which occurs when societal tradition and habit lead to social segregation.

- African Americans led the first civil rights movement in the United States. By forming interest groups such as the NAACP and developing strategies such as nonviolent resistance, African Americans eventually defeated de jure discrimination.

- De facto discrimination persists in America, signified by the education and wage gap between African Americans and whites. Programs like affirmative action, which could remedy such discrimination, remain controversial. Although African Americans have made great strides in the past fifty years, much inequality remains.

- Native Americans, Hispanics, and Asian Americans have also fought to gain economic and social equality. Congressional control over their lands has led Native Americans to assert economic power through the development of casinos. Using boycotts and voter education drives, Hispanics have worked to stem the success of English-only movements and anti-immigration efforts. Despite their smaller numbers, Asian Americans also aim for equal political clout, but it is through a cultural emphasis on scholarly achievement that they have gained considerable economic power.

- Women's rights movements represented challenges to power, to a traditional way of life, and to economic profit. Early activists found success through state politics because they were restricted from using the courts and Congress; efforts now focus on the courts to give women greater protection of the law.

- Gays, youth, the elderly, and the disabled enjoy the most fundamental civil rights, but they still face de jure and de facto discrimination. While moral concerns motivate laws against gays, social order and cost-efficiency concerns mark the restrictions against youth, the elderly, and disabled Americans.

Define | Understand | Practice | Read | Click | Watch

1. **Suspect classifications are defined as**
   a. ways of ranking criminal behavior as felonies or misdemeanors.
   b. a standard of review in which the Court defines certain laws as most likely unconstitutional and in need of review.
   c. classifications that need review before going into effect.
   d. classifications, such as race or religion, for which a discriminatory law must be justified by a compelling state interest.
   e. classifications for which strict scrutiny is not applied.

2. **In the North, the civil rights movement fought to combat _____ discrimination.**
   a. ex post facto
   b. de facto
   c. de jure
   d. de solis
   e. ad hoc

3. **While significant in numbers, the diversity of Hispanic Americans has**
   a. allowed them to avoid the stereotyping affecting other minority groups.
   b. led to fragmentation and powerlessness.
   c. allowed them to form alliances with other minorities.
   d. limited their ability to assimilate into traditional American society.
   e. made them more likely to compromise.

4. **The Seneca Falls Convention showed that**
   a. support for women's rights existed, but not when it came to voting rights.
   b. African Americans did not support the women's movement.
   c. southerners were supportive of women's rights.
   d. women were not well organized politically.
   e. women actually had more rights than was previously believed.

5. **The model of democracy that best describes the actions American citizens have taken to gain the government's protection of their civil rights is _____ democracy.**
   a. participatory
   b. elite
   c. pluralist
   d. direct
   e. representative

Define | Understand | Practice | Read | Click | Watch

Correspondents of the *New York Times*. 2001. *How Race Is Lived in America: Pulling Together, Pulling Apart*. New York: Times Books. Originally published as a year-long series in the New York Times, this extraordinary compilation offers fifteen provocative and often touching stories that document the way that race is experienced in modern America.

Cushman, Clare, ed. 2002. *Supreme Court Decisions and Women's Rights: Milestones to Equality*. Washington, D.C.: CQ Press/Supreme Court Historical Society. An authoritative, illustrated examination of precedent-setting cases involving women's rights and gender issues.

Deloria, Vine, Jr., and Clifford M. Lytle. 1984. *The Nations Within: The Past and Future of Indian Sovereignty*. New York: Pantheon. A thorough history of federal Indian law, this book effectively lays out the struggles that Native Americans encountered as the United States expanded westward.

Ferriss, Susan, and Ricardo Sandoval. 1997. *The Fight in the Fields: Cesar Chavez and the Farmworkers Movement*. New York: Harcourt Brace. An examination of the life and work of the founder of the United Farm Workers Union. Also a PBS documentary.

Gerstmann, Evan. 2004. *Same-Sex Marriage and the Constitution*. New York: Cambridge University Press. An engaging, clearly written review of the arguments for and against same-sex marriage.

Hacker, Andrew. 1992. *Two Nations: Black and White, Separate, Hostile, Unequal*. New York: Scribner's. A bleak, but unfortunately realistic, account of the differences that exist between black and white Americans. Hacker's book is a must for students interested in race relations.

Ogletree, Charles J., Jr. 2004. *All Deliberate Speed: Reflections on the First Half-Century of Brown v. Board of Education*. New York: Norton. An interesting examination of the Brown decision fifty years later. Ogletree argues that the reforms promised in Brown have been systematically undermined.

Salaita, Steven. 2006. *Anti-Arab Racism in the USA: Where It Comes From and What It Means for Politics Today*. London: Pluto Press. Particularly in the wake of 9/11, to be both Arab and American presents many hardships. The fears that many Americans harbor toward Arabs not only affect Arab Americans socially and economically but also may be reflected in the laws being passed in Congress.

Switzer, Jacqueline Vaughn. 2003. *Disabled Rights: American Disability Power and the Fight for Equality*. Washington, D.C.: Georgetown University Press. A thorough account of the history and politics of the disabilities movement in the United States.

Tatum, Beverly Daniel. 2002. *Why Are All the Black Kids Sitting Together in the Cafeteria? And Other Conversations About Race*. New York: Perseus Publishing. America has made undeniable strides in the area of equal rights for all races, but why are our society and, in particular, our schools still so racially segregated? Tatum suggests that difficulties with discussing racial and ethnic issues honestly must be surmounted first.

Tsesis, Alexander. 2008. *We Shall Overcome: A History of Civil Rights and the Law*. New Haven: Yale University Press. Tsesis traces the legal history of the struggle to achieve civil rights for all Americans.

Wu, Frank H. 2002. *Yellow: Race in America Beyond Black and White*. New York: Basic Books. In this personal account of growing up as an Asian American in the United States, Wu, a law professor at Howard University, adds another dimension to the debate over race.

Define | Understand | Practice | Read | **Click** | Watch

American Indian Movement www.aimovement.org. The AIM web site contains information on the history of the organization, current activities, and commentary on enduring issues in the American Indian community.

Civil Rights in Indian Country www.indiancivilrights.org. Promoting civil rights in Indian Country, this web site also provides information on the group's engagement with civil rights communities in the United States and Canada and the federal mandate for civil rights within Indian Country.

Civilrights.org www.civilrights.org. This web site is a collaboration of the Leadership Conference on Civil Rights and the Leadership Conference on Civil Rights Education Fund with a mission "to serve as the site of record for relevant and up-to-the-minute civil rights news and information."

Human Rights Campaign www.hrc.org. The HRC web site contains information on every major current issue faced by the gay, lesbian, bisexual, and transgender communities. It also includes a scorecard of how well members of Congress rate on these issues.

League of United Latin American Citizens www.lulac.org. The LULAC works toward advancing the civil rights of the U.S. Hispanic population. Its web site contains a wealth of information on the organization's activities and how others can participate in its efforts.

National Association for the Advancement of Colored People www.naacp.org. The NAACP is the country's oldest civil rights organization. Its web site includes information about the organization's history, the various ways in which it is active, and how you can get involved.

National Organization for Women www.now.org. The preeminent women's rights organization, NOW publishes policy briefs on a wealth of issues relevant to bringing about equality for women.

The Rosa Parks Portal http://e-portals.org/Parks/. This web resource directory references Rosa Parks sites online.

U.S. Department of Justice, Civil Rights Division www.usdoj.gov/crt/. This site, representing the Justice Department agency responsible for enforcing the nation's civil rights statutes, includes guides to civil rights laws, cases in which the agency is currently involved, and reports on various topics.

You can connect with many of the other civil rights organizations mentioned in this chapter, as well as additional resources, from the *Keeping the Republic* web site. Just go to http://republic.cqpress.com and select the Chapter 6 Explore section.

Define | Understand | Practice | Read | Click | **Watch**

Glory 1989. Matthew Broderick plays Colonel Robert Gould Shaw, who leads the 54th Massachusetts Volunteer Regiment during the Civil War, the United States' first all-black volunteer company, fighting prejudices of both his own Union army and the Confederates.

I Will Fight No More Forever 1975. This reenactment depicts the flight of Chief Joseph and the Nez Perce after they were forced to abandon their land. After 1,400 miles over the course of three months, the Nez Perce came within 40 miles of Canada, only to find themselves surrounded and left with no choice but to surrender. This true story illustrates the impact of U.S. expansion across North America and how Native American tribes were forcibly relocated to reservations.

Incident at Oglala 1992. Produced and narrated by Robert Redford, this documentary on the 1975 standoff between Indian activists and FBI agents at the Pine Ridge Reservation in South Dakota explores the violent events that took place and questions the conviction of Oglala Sioux political leader Leonard Peltier.

Iron Jawed Angels 2004. Following political activists Alice Paul and Lucy Burns, the film looks at the women's suffrage movement in the early 1900s and the fight to gain women the right to vote.

The Long Walk Home 1990. Set in Montgomery, Alabama, during the 1955 bus boycott lead by Martin Luther King Jr., the film looks at the relationship between a young African American maid and the white woman who employs her.

Malcolm X 1992. A Spike Lee biopic of the controversial and influential African American activist and Black Nationalist leader, with Denzel Washington.

Out of the Past: The Struggle for Gay and Lesbian Rights in America 2005. This documentary explores the gay community with an informative yet entertaining profile of a high school girl who attempted to form a Gay-Straight Alliance in her Salt Lake City community.

Tying the Knot 2003. Following the lives of two homosexual couples, this documentary takes a critical eye to the highly contentious gay marriage debate in the United States.

The Untold Story of Emmett Louis Till 2004. This powerful documentary chronicles the events surrounding a 1950s lynching of a fourteen-year-old black boy. The event resulted in a media frenzy as a shocked nation witnessed not only the brutal crime but also the small Mississippi town's indifference to the brutality.

Chapter 7

Congress

▶ What's at Stake?

In the summer of 2009, with the passage of health care reform in sight, the Democratic Party was on the brink of a historic achievement and Republicans wanted to stop it. Senator Jim DeMint, a Republican from South Carolina, said, "If we are able to stop Obama on this it will be his Waterloo. It will break him."[1]

But the Democrats were equally determined to get the bill through, especially Senator Ted Kennedy, who had been working for years to pass his signature issue of health care reform. With a Democratic president in the White House and Democratic majorities in the House and Senate, reform was nearly a done deal when Kennedy died on August 25, 2009, succumbing to the brain tumor he had been diagnosed with a little more than a year earlier. Massachusetts governor Deval Patrick appointed a Democrat to hold the seat until a special election could be held the following January, and the Senate passed a health care bill on December 24, 2009, by a vote of 60 to 39. All that remained was for the House of Representatives to pass its version of the bill, and then for the two versions to be resolved into a single bill, a final step that would require another vote in each chamber.

In an irony that was not lost on any observers of American politics, Kennedy's death precipitated an event that appeared to give DeMint and his fellow Republicans just the opening they wanted to kill the bill. When the special election took place in January 2010, it was Republican Scott Brown who won the seat that Kennedy had held for almost forty-seven years. The Democrats still had a healthy majority in the Senate—there were still fifty-nine of them after Brown was elected, to only forty-one Republicans—but thanks to a rule called the filibuster, in the Senate fewer than sixty seats might as well be a minority for all the good it does the majority political party.

A filibuster lets a group of senators prevent a vote from taking place on the Senate floor by allowing them to hold an extended debate—essentially

Talk a Bill to Death

In the 1939 movie *Mr. Smith Goes to Washington*, a naïve man appointed to fill a vacant Senate seat soon finds himself amidst the shortcomings of the political process. During a vote on a bill crafted by corrupt politicians, Mr. Smith takes to the Senate floor in a filibuster to defend himself against false charges and stop the bill's passage. The movie's idealistic portrayal of Mr. Smith's filibuster goals is a far cry from today's reality, where partisanship has become entrenched.

"talking a bill to death." And it is death, unless three-fifths of the chamber (that's sixty senators) votes for cloture, that ends the debate and allows the vote to proceed. The end result is that if a minority of the Senate is passionate or ornery enough it can thwart the will of the majority, and of the voters who chose it. With Brown's election depriving the Democrats of their sixtieth vote, Republicans were celebrating Obama's Waterloo.

Democrats, however, were reluctant to see this chance slip away. Unable to muster sixty votes in the Senate in the face of united Republican opposition, the Democratic leadership scrambled and came up with a Plan B. Instead of passing its own bill and then sending it along with the Senate bill to a committee whose job it would be to hammer out a compromise, a step that would require a further vote in the now-unfriendly Senate, the House of Representatives simply passed the Senate's bill on March 21, 2010. The move frustrated many House Democrats who wanted the chamber to pass a more liberal bill, but it enabled President Obama to sign the bill into law, preserving his signature legislation and giving him a major political victory. The House then made the changes it wanted by passing a second bill. Unable to break a filibuster on the second bill, Senate majority leader Harry Reid D-Nev., sent the changes through as part of the budget reconciliation process (all the changes had to be budget related), which required only a simple majority vote. By the skin of its legislative teeth, the U.S. Congress passed reform guaranteeing health care to almost all Americans.

In the aftermath, the filibuster came in for heavy criticism by Democrats even as it was hailed by Republicans. Nancy Pelosi, D-Calif., the Speaker of the U.S. House of Representatives, called it "the 60-vote stranglehold on the future."[2] But Republicans stood by the words of Senate minority leader Mitch McConnell, R-Ky., who said shortly after the Republicans lost their majority in the Senate, "I think we can stipulate once again for the umpteenth time that matters that have any level of controversy about it in the Senate will require 60 votes."[3] Sure enough, Republicans proceeded to block as much of President Obama's agenda as they could, employing the filibuster when they could summon the votes and blocking votes on presidential appointments as well as on policies such as an extension of unemployment benefits, immigration, and the 2010 National Defense Authorization Act, which contained a conditional end to the policy of "Don't Ask, Don't Tell."

Which side is right here? Is the filibuster a good thing, or a bad thing, or does it just depend on where you stand on any particular issue that faces a filibuster? What is at stake in the filibuster, anyway? We'll be able to look at this issue more carefully after we have a better understanding of how Congress works. ∎

If politics is all about who gets what, and how, then Congress is arguably also the center of American national politics.

---

representation the efforts of elected officials to look out for the interests of those who elect them

national lawmaking the creation of policy to address the problems and needs of the entire nation

---

The U.S. Congress is the world's longest-running and most powerful democratic legislature. If politics is all about who gets what, and how, then Congress is arguably also the center of American national politics. Not only does it often decide exactly who gets what, but Congress also has the power to alter many of the rules (or the how) that determine who wins and who loses in American political life.

The Capitol building in Washington, D.C., home to both the House of Representatives and the Senate, has become as much a symbol of America's democracy as are the Stars and Stripes or the White House. We might expect Americans to express considerable pride in their national legislature, with its long tradition of serving democratic government. But if we did, we would be wrong.

Congress is generally distrusted, seen by the American public as incompetent, corrupt, torn by partisanship, and at the beck and call of special interests.[4] Yet despite their contempt for the institution of Congress as a whole, Americans typically revere their representatives and senators and reelect them so often that critics have long been calling for term limits to get new people into office (see the box "Citizens' Love-Hate Relationship With Congress"). How can we understand this bizarre paradox?[5]

There are two main reasons for America's love-hate relationship with Congress. The first is that citizens have conflicting expectations when it comes to the operation of their national legislature. On the one hand, they want their representatives in Washington to take care of their local or state interests and to ensure that their home district gets a fair share of national resources. On the other hand, citizens also want Congress to take care of the nation's business. This can pose a quandary for the legislator because what is good for the home district might not be good for the nation as a whole. Legislators trying to meet both sets of citizens' expectations often end up disappointing someone.

The second reason for citizens' love-hate relationship with Congress is that the rules that determine how Congress works were designed by the founders to produce slow, careful lawmaking that can seem motionless to an impatient public. When citizens are looking to Congress to produce

policies that they favor or to distribute national resources, the built-in slowness can look like intentional foot dragging and partisan bickering. That it is instead a constitutional safeguard is part of a civics lesson most Americans have long forgotten.

Keeping in mind these two dynamics, our legislators' struggle to meet our conflicting expectations and our own frustration with Congress' institutionalized slowness, will take us a long way toward understanding our mixed feelings about our national legislature. In this chapter we explore those dynamics as we look at who—including citizens, other politicians, and members of Congress themselves—gets the results they want from Congress, and how the rules of legislative politics help or hinder them. You will learn about

- **the clash between representation and lawmaking**
- **the powers and responsibilities of Congress**
- **congressional membership and elections**
- **the organization of Congress and the rules of congressional operation**
- **the relationship of citizens to Congress**

Congress
An institutional tension between representation and lawmaking

We count on our elected representatives in both the House and the Senate to perform two major functions: representation and lawmaking. By **representation**, we mean that those we elect should represent, or look out for, our local interests and carry out our will. At the same time, we expect our legislators to address the country's social and economic problems by **national lawmaking**—passing laws that serve the interest of the entire nation.

The functions of representation and lawmaking often conflict. What is good for us and our local community may not serve the national good. One of the chief lessons of this chapter is that the rules under which Congress operates make it likely that when these primary functions do conflict, members of Congress will usually favor their jobs as representatives. That is,

▶ Citizens' Love-Hate Relationship With Congress

Public Feelings Toward Congress

Measured several different ways, the public's attitudes toward Congress are unfavorable: compared to the other branches of government, Congress is more frequently the target of American anger and disgust. Compared to other occupations, members of Congress in general are held in low esteem. However, individual representatives achieve much higher approval ratings by their own constituents than does Congress as a whole. Members' intense efforts at representation result in a situation in which many Americans love their members of Congress but hate their Congress.

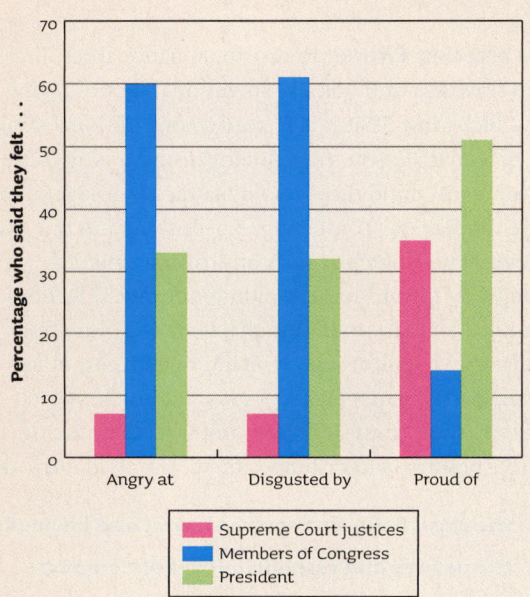

Supreme Court justices
Members of Congress
President

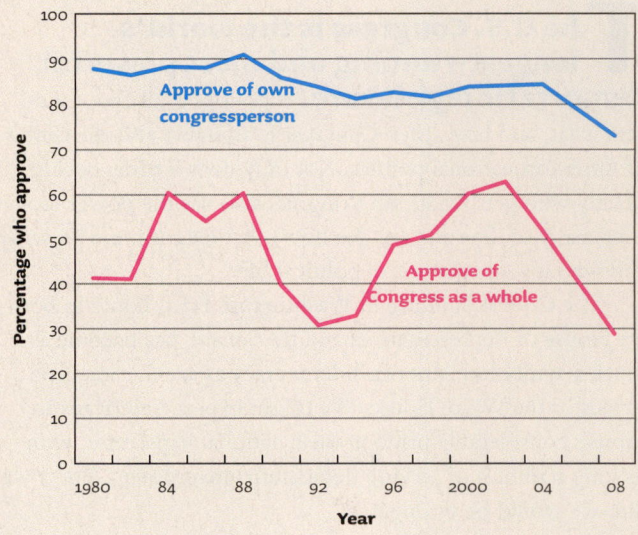

Question: Please tell me how you would rate the honesty and ethical standards of people in these different fields (very high, high, average, low, or very low)? How about . . .

Nurses	83%	College teachers	56%	State governors	15%	HMO managers	9%
Pharmacists	66%	Clergy	51%	Lawyers	14%	Stockbrokers	9%
Medical doctors	65%	Chiropractors	37%	Business executives	12%	Members of Congress	9%
Engineers	65%	Psychiatrists	36%	Advertising practitioners	12%	Car salesmen	6%
Police	63%	Journalists	23%	Senators	12%		
Dentist	57%	Bankers	21%	Insurance salesmen	10%		

Sources: Graph data are from John R. Hibbing and Elizabeth Theiss-Morse, *Congress as Public Enemy* (New York: Cambridge University Press, 1995), 58; American National Election Studies Cumulative File, 1948–2004; National Election Study 2008 Pre-Post Study; ethics ratings data from *USA Today*/Gallup poll, November 20–22, 2009.

Note: Table on ethics ratings shows the percent answering "very high" or "high"; national adult sample of 1,017 respondents; calculated by authors from data obtained from the Roper Center for Public Opinion Research.

a member of Congress will usually do what the local district wants. Thus national problems go unaddressed while local problems get attention, resources, and solutions. No wonder we love our individual representatives but think poorly of the job done by Congress as a national policymaking institution.

Four Kinds of Representation

Representation means working on behalf of one's ***constituency***, the folks back home in the district who voted for the member as well as those who did not. To help us understand this complex job, political scientists often speak about four

constituency the voters in a state or district

policy representation congressional work to advance the issues and ideological preferences of constituents

allocative representation congressional work to secure projects, services, and funds for the represented district

pork barrel public works projects and grants for specific districts paid for by general revenues

casework legislative work on behalf of individual constituents to solve their problems with government agencies and programs

franking the privilege of free mail service provided to members of Congress

symbolic representation efforts of members of Congress to stand for American ideals or identify with common constituency values

types of representation.[6] Most members of Congress try to excel at all four functions so that constituents will rate them highly and reelect them.

Policy Representation

Policy representation refers to congressional work for laws that advance the economic and social interests of the constituency. For example, House members and senators from petroleum-producing states can be safely predicted to vote in ways favorable to the profitability of the oil companies, members from the Plains states try to protect subsidies for wheat farmers, and so on. It is rarer for a member to champion a national interest, since it is in the local constituency that he or she will face reelection, but some members do focus on such issues as foreign policy, campaign finance reform, or the environment.

Allocative Representation

Voters have also come to expect a certain amount of **allocative representation**, in which the congressperson gets projects and grants for the district. Such perks are called **pork barrel** benefits, paid for by all the taxpayers but enjoyed by just a few. Congresspeople who are good at getting pork barrel projects for their districts (for example, highway construction or the establishment of a research institution) are said to "bring home the bacon."

Casework

Senators and representatives also represent their states or districts by taking care of the individual problems of constituents, especially problems that involve the federal bureaucracy. This kind of representation is called **casework**, or constituency service, and it covers things such as finding out why a constituent's Social Security check has not shown up, sending a flag that has flown over the nation's capitol to a high school in the district, or helping with immigration and naturalization problems. To promote their work for constituents, members maintain web pages and send information to the homes of voters through more traditional channels. (See "*Consider the Source: Don't Be Fooled by Your Elected Officials*," for some tips on how to be a savvy consumer of congressional information.) The congressional privilege of **franking** allows members to use the U.S. mail at no charge. This free postal service fulfills the democratic purpose of keeping citizens informed about their lawmakers' activities, but because only positive information about and images of the congressperson are sent out, it is also self-serving.

Symbolic Representation

A fourth kind of representation is called **symbolic representation**. In this elusive but important function, the member of Congress represents many of the positive values Americans associate with public life and government. Thus members are glad to serve as commencement speakers at high school graduations or attend town meetings to explain what is happening in Washington. Equally important are the ways members present themselves to their districts—using colloquialisms such as "y'all" even if they are not from the South and wearing a denim work shirt to county fairs. These appearances are part of a member's "home style" and help to symbolize the message "I am one of you" and "I am a person you can trust; I share your values and interests."[7]

National Lawmaking

As we explained earlier, representation is not the only business of our senators and representatives. A considerable part of their job involves working with one another in Washington to define and solve the nation's problems. We expect Congress to create laws that serve the common good. One scholar calls this view of effective lawmaking "collective responsibility."[8] By this he means that Congress should be responsible for the effectiveness of its laws in solving national problems. A variety of factors go into a representative's calculation of how to vote on matters of national interest. He or she might be guided by conscience or ideology, by the demands of constituents, by interest groups, or by party position. And these considerations may very well be at odds with the four kinds of representation just described, which frequently makes it difficult, if not impossible, for members to fulfill their collective responsibility.

Imagine, for instance, the dilemma of a Democratic congresswoman representing an oil-producing district in Texas who has to vote yes or no on government support for the development of non–fossil fuel technologies. What is good for the nation—to decrease our dependence on fossil fuels so that we are less reliant on foreign sources of oil and to reduce global warming—is not necessarily what is good for the economic interests of her district. The bill would mean higher taxes for her constituents to support a technology that

Being a critical constituent means more than sitting around the dinner table griping about Congress. It means knowing what your representatives are doing so that you can evaluate how well they are representing your interests. How can you learn about your representatives' or senators' performance in Congress? There is an abundance of information, but it is not all equally reliable or equally easy to find. Here is a guide to sources that can help you discover and evaluate what your elected representatives are up to:

1. **Get to know your elected representatives.** Members regularly come home for long weekends in part to maintain contact with constituents. Staff will be happy to reply to your phone call or email to tell you of upcoming town meetings or visits to district offices to meet with constituents. This is harder to arrange for a U.S. senator from a large state, but most citizens can meet with their U.S. representative with just a bit of effort. Members of Congress also maintain their own web sites, and these are great starting points if you want to know what your representative is doing, how he or she voted, or what his or her family looks like. The coverage on these sites, understandably, is glowing, so you need to scrutinize it well.

2. **Don't trust, verify.** Thanks to the Internet there are now several web sites that follow up on what our elected officials say and run fact-checks so that we can know when they are stretching, bending, or outright breaking with the truth. Notable here are politifact.com, run by the esteemed *St. Petersburg Times*, which rates politicians' claims on their "Truth-O-Meter," from "True" to "Half True," to "Pants on Fire." Also good is factcheck.org, operated by the University of Pennsylvania's Annenberg Public Policy Center. One of the best sources for checking up on members of Congress comes from a nonpartisan organization, Project Vote Smart (PVS). PVS collects information on the background, issue positions, campaign finances, and voting records of over 13,000 officeholders and candidates for president, governor, Congress, and the state legislatures. It also tracks performance evaluations for members of Congress from special interest groups that provide them. One big advantage of PVS is that it attempts to provide data on all candidates, not just incumbents, and it makes its information available

during the campaign. All information is free and available online at www.vote-smart.org.

3. **For an overview of the debates going on in Congress, you can find the detailed proceedings of past sessions in the *Congressional Record*, which is available in print at many university libraries and online (www.thomas.loc.gov) for the past few congressional sessions.** The *Congressional Record* is informative, but it can be tedious to read. Moreover, it is not an exact transcript of congressional proceedings. Members are regularly given permission, by unanimous consent, to "extend and revise" their remarks, even to the extent of adding entirely new speeches they never gave. Read this source with some skepticism.

4. **A number of media sources, both local and national, track congressional action.** Your local paper should cover the activities of your state's senators and representatives through articles and editorials and may report on how each representative votes on proposed legislation. The national media may cover your representatives as well, as do *CQ Weekly* and *National Journal* (most college libraries have these publications). You can also go to two highly readable biennial almanacs that provide detailed portraits of members of Congress and their districts and states: the *Almanac of American Politics*, published by National Journal, and *Politics in America*, published by CQ Press.

5. **Follow the money.** A good clue to what your congressperson is up to can be found in the records of who has given money to him or her. Check out www.opensecrets.org, the web site for the Center for Responsive Politics. This center tracks campaign contributions and can even tell you who in your zip code area has given how much money to which political causes or candidates.

Getting the facts is only part of the job of being a critical constituent. Evaluating them is no less important. Any time you engage in evaluation, you need a clear yardstick against which to hold up the thing you are evaluating. Here it may be helpful to remember the twin pressures on a member of Congress to be both a representative and a national lawmaker. Which do you think is more important? What kind of balance should be struck between them? How does your congressperson measure up?

makes their main industry less profitable. In deciding how to vote, our congresswoman would have to consider tough questions that affect the public good, her policy goals, and her reelection.

In this case, what's best for the local district clearly clashes with the national interest. And the scenario holds true again and again for every representative and senator. Thus the potential for conflict is great when one works for one's constituents as well as for the entire nation. We all want a Congress that focuses on the nation's problems, but as voters we tend to reward members for putting constituency concerns first.

Who What How

Both citizens and their representatives have something serious at stake in the tension between representation and lawmaking. Citizens want their local interests protected. But citizens also want sound national policy, and here they are often disappointed. The need to secure reelection by catering to local interests often means that their representatives have fewer incentives to concentrate on national lawmaking.

In fact, members of the House and the Senate face a true dilemma. On the one hand, they want to serve their constituents' local interests and needs, and they want to be reelected to office by those constituents. But they also must face personal, party, and special interest demands to take stands that might not suit the voters back home.

Thinking Outside the Box

Does the local interest have to clash with the national interest?

Congressional Powers and Responsibilities

Expansive powers held in check by the Constitution

The Constitution gives the U.S. Congress enormous powers, although it is safe to say that the founders could not have imagined the scope of contemporary congressional power since they never anticipated the growth of the federal government to today's size. As we will see, they were less concerned with the conflict between local and national interests we have been discussing than they were with the representation of short-term popular opinion versus long-term national interests. The basic powers of Congress are laid out in Article I, Section 8, of the Constitution (see Chapter 4). They include the powers to tax, to pay debts, and to provide

bicameral legislature legislature with two chambers

for the common defense and welfare of the United States, among many other things.

Differences Between the House and the Senate

The term *Congress* refers to the institution that is formally made up of the U.S. House of Representatives and the U.S. Senate. Congresses are numbered so that we can talk about them over time in a coherent way. Each congress covers a two-year election cycle. The 112th Congress was elected in November 2010, and its term runs from January 2011 through the end of 2012. The *bicameral* (two-house) *legislature* is laid out in the Constitution. As we discussed in earlier chapters, the founders wanted two chambers so that they could serve as a restraint on each other, strengthening the principle of checks and balances. The framers' hope was that the smaller, more elite Senate would "cool the passions" of the people represented in the House. Accordingly, while the two houses are equal in their overall power—both can initiate legislation (although tax bills must originate in the House) and both must pass every bill in identical form before it can be signed by the president to become law—there are also some key differences, particularly in the extra responsibilities assigned to the Senate. In addition, the two chambers operate differently, and they have distinct histories and norms of conduct (that is, informal rules and expectations of behavior).[9] Some of the major differences are outlined in Table 7.1.

The single biggest factor determining differences between the House and the Senate is size. With 100 members, the Senate is less formal; the 435-person House needs more rules and hierarchy in order to function efficiently. The Constitution also provides for differences in terms: two years for the House, six for the Senate (on a staggered basis—all senators do not come up for reelection at the same time). In the modern context, this means that House members (also referred to as congresspersons or members of Congress, a term that sometimes applies to senators as well) never stop campaigning. Senators, in contrast, can suspend their preoccupation with the next campaign for the first four or five years of their terms and thus, at least in theory, have more time to spend on the affairs of the nation. The minimum age of the candidates is different as well: members of the House must be at least twenty-five years old, senators thirty. This again reflects the founders' expectation that the Senate would be older, wiser, and better able to deal with national

Table 7.1

Differences Between the House and the Senate

Differences	House	Senate
Constitutional		
Term length	2 years	6 years
Minimum age	25	30
Citizenship required	7 years	9 years
Residency	In state	In state
Apportionment	Changes with population	Fixed; entire state
Impeachment	Impeaches official	Tries the impeached official
Treaty-making power	No authority	2/3 approval
Presidential appointments	No authority	Majority approval
Organizational		
Size	435 members	100 members
Number of standing committees	20	16
Total committee assignments per member	Approx. 6	Approx. 11
Rules Committee	Yes	No
Limits on floor debate	Yes	No (filibuster possible)
Electoral, 2008		
Average winners spent	$1.37 million	$8.5 million
Average losers spent	$493,000	$4.1 million
Most expensive campaign	$7.3 million	$21.8 million
Incumbency advantage	95% reelected	83% reelected
	(93.4% 50-year average)	(80.4% 50-year average)

Sources: Roger H. Davidson, Walter J. Oleszek, and Frances E. Lee, *Congress and Its Members*, 11th ed. (Washington, D.C.: CQ Press, 2008), 63, 209; Federal Election Commission data compiled by the Center for Responsive Politics; Gary C. Jacobson, "Congress: The Second Democratic Wave," in Michael Nelson, ed., *The Elections of 2008* (Washington, D.C.: CQ Press, 2010), Table 5-1.

lawmaking. This distinction was reinforced in the constitutional provision that senators be elected not directly by the people, as were members of the House, but by state legislatures. Although this provision was changed by constitutional amendment in 1913, its presence in the original Constitution reflects the convictions of its authors that the Senate was a special chamber, one step removed from the people.

Budget bills are initiated in the House of Representatives. In practice this is not particularly significant since the Senate has to pass budget bills as well, and most of the time differences are negotiated between the two houses. The budget process has gotten quite complicated, as demonstrated by congressional struggles to deal with the deficit, which called for reductions in spending at the same time that constituencies and interest groups were pleading for expensive new programs. The budget process illustrates once again the constant tension for members of Congress between being responsive to local or particular interests and at the same time trying to make laws in the interest of the nation as a whole.

Other differences between the House and the Senate include the division of power on impeachment of public figures such as presidents and Supreme Court justices. The House impeaches, or charges the official with "treason, bribery, or other high crimes and misdemeanors," and the Senate tries the official. Both Andrew Johnson and Bill Clinton were impeached by the House, but in both cases the Senate failed to find the president guilty of the charges brought by the House. In addition, only the Senate is given the responsibility of confirming appointments to the executive and judicial branches, and of sharing the treaty-making power with the president, responsibilities we explore in more detail later in the text.

Congressional Checks and Balances

The founders were concerned about the abuse of power by the executive and legislative branches, and even by the people. But, as we saw in Chapter 3, they were most anxious to avoid executive tyranny, and so they granted Congress an impressive array of powers. Keeping Congress at the center of national policymaking are the power to regulate commerce; the exclusive power to raise and to spend money for the national government; the power to provide for economic infrastructure (roads, postal service, money, patents); and significant powers in foreign policy, including the powers to declare war, to ratify treaties, and to raise and support the armed forces.

> **congressional oversight** a committee's investigation of the executive and of government agencies to ensure they are acting as Congress intends

As we discussed in Chapter 4, the Supreme Court has generally interpreted the necessary and proper clause of the Constitution quite favorably for the expansion of congressional power. But the Constitution also limits congressional powers through the protection of individual rights and by the watchful eye of the other two branches of government, with which Congress shares power. We look briefly at those relationships here.

Congress and the Executive Branch

Our system of checks and balances means that to exercise its powers, each branch has to have the cooperation of the others. Thus Congress has the responsibility for passing bills, but the bills do not become law unless (1) the president signs them or, more passively, refrains from vetoing them, or (2) both houses of Congress are able to muster a full two-thirds majority to override a presidential veto. While the president cannot vote on legislation or even introduce bills, the Constitution gives the chief executive a powerful policy formulation role in calling for the president's annual State of the Union address and in inviting the president to recommend to Congress "such measures as he shall judge necessary and expedient."

One of the most important functions of Congress is **congressional oversight** of the executive—of the president and the agencies of the bureaucracy that fall under the executive branch. This is usually done through hearings and selective investigations of executive actions whereby Congress attempts to ensure that the president and bureaucracy are carrying out the laws as Congress intended. Executive implementation of congressional legislation is often a point of friction between the two branches. Sometimes the conflict occurs because of differences in presidential and congressional intent. We know, for example, that the number of congressional investigations of executive behavior goes up sharply when the president faces a House of Representatives controlled by the opposition party.[10] For example, as we will see in Chapter 8, when it implemented policy, the administration of George W. Bush frequently ignored or reinterpreted congressional intent when it believed that Congress' actions represented unconstitutional interference in the workings of the executive branch. Despite criticism for its creation of an energy policy with the confidential participation of oil industry executives, a rush to war in Iraq, and numerous alleged misuses of executive power, the Bush administration faced little congressional opposition.[11]

Reluctant to press an administration that had for much of the time following the September 11, 2001, terror attacks enjoyed high public popularity and, moreover, that had returned the Republican Party to the White House after eight years of exile, the Republican-led Congress gave the Bush administration a lot of latitude.

When Congress did in fact question administration officials about their behavior, it tended to accept their explanations, without subpoenaing witnesses, requiring the administration to turn over documents and correspondence, and otherwise pressing them to back up their explanations with facts and evidence. Democrats, however, were chomping at the bit to investigate what they saw as executive excesses and abuse of power. When, in 2006, Republicans lost their majorities in both the House and the Senate, the new Democratic leadership of both houses got busy. "Congress Girds Up for Return to Oversight," read one early 2007 headline in a major paper. "Revival of Oversight Role Sought; Congress Hires More Investigators, Plans Subpoenas," read another.[12] Democrats are not quite as loath to investigate presidents of their own party as are Republicans, but still the GOP was eagerly hoping for a return to power in 2010 to investigate what they saw as signs of corruption in the Obama administration.

Oversight also comes into play when Congress delegates authority to regulatory agencies in the executive branch. Often the agencies do what they are supposed to do, which can make the job of keeping an eye on them boring and unrewarding. If Congress does not keep watch, however, the agencies can develop unhealthy relationships with those they are supposed to be regulating. This was the case with the Securities and Exchange Commission, which failed to protect us from the risky investment practices that resulted in the economic meltdown in late 2008, as well as with the Minerals Management Service, whose failure to adequately police offshore drilling procedures contributed to the ecological disaster in the Gulf of Mexico following the 2010 explosion of BP's *Deepwater Horizon* drilling platform. The Marine Mammal Protection Act and the National Environmental Policy Act were routinely violated by regulators seeking bonuses for encouraging offshore oil drilling.[13] Since these relationships develop far from public scrutiny, we rely on Congress to ensure, through oversight, that agencies do the job they were set up to do, though there is a strong temptation for members to slight congressional responsibility here in favor of splashier and more electorally rewarding activities.

Another congressional check on the executive is the requirement that major presidential appointments—for instance to cabinet posts, ambassadorships, and the federal courts—must be confirmed by the Senate. Historically, most presidential appointments have proceeded without incident, but in recent administrations, appointments have become increasingly political. Senators sometimes use their confirmation powers to do more than "advise and consent" on the appointment at hand. They can, and do, tie up appointments, either because they oppose the nominee on account of his or her ideology or because they wish to extract promises and commitments from the president. Senators may place a "hold" on presidential appointees, which by tradition means that the Senate will not consider the appointment until the hold is lifted. A hold can be suspended, but, like ending the filibuster we read about in *What's at Stake?*, that takes sixty votes. Although senators often agree that the hold process gives undue weight to individual members, they tend to defer to each other, which makes getting the votes needed to break the hold very difficult. In today's highly polarized Congress, senators of the minority party are quick to object to many of a president's appointees. The result is that many appointments languish and high offices in the federal government go unfilled for months or even years. One example among hundreds is the case of Dawn Johnsen, President Obama's choice to head the Office of Legal Counsel at the Justice Department. She was one of the earliest Obama appointees, but her nomination languished for over a year as Republicans objected to work she had done in providing legal counsel to abortion rights groups twenty years earlier and to her criticism of the Bush administration's interrogation and detention policies. She withdrew her name from consideration as it became clear her appointment was not going to get to the floor of the Senate for a vote.[14]

A final built-in source of institutional conflict between Congress and the president is the difference in constituencies. The president looks at each policy in terms of a national constituency and his own policy program, whereas members of Congress necessarily take a narrower view. For example, the president may decide that clean air should be a national priority. For some members of Congress, however, a clean air bill might mean closing factories in their districts because it would not be profitable to bring them up to emissions standards, or shutting down soft coal mines because the bill would kill the market for high-sulfur coal. Often, public policy looks very different from the perspective of congressional offices than it does from the presidential Oval Office at the other end of Pennsylvania Avenue.

Congress and the Judicial Branch

The constitutional relationship between the federal courts and Congress is simple in principle: Congress makes the laws, and the courts interpret them. The Supreme Court also has the lofty job of deciding whether laws and procedures are consistent with the Constitution, although this power of judicial review is not actually mentioned in the Constitution.

We think of the judiciary as independent of the other branches, but this self-sufficiency is only a matter of degree. Congress, for example, is charged with setting up the lower federal courts and determining the salaries for judges, with the interesting constitutional provision that a judge's salary cannot be cut. Congress also has considerable powers in establishing some issues of jurisdiction—that is, deciding which courts hear which cases (Article III, Section 2). And, as we just indicated, in accepting and rejecting presidential Supreme Court and federal court nominees, the Senate influences the long-term operation of the courts.[15]

Congress also exerts power over the courts by passing laws that limit the courts' discretion to rule or impose sentences as judges think best. For example, in the 1980s, Congress passed strict drug laws that required mandatory sentences for offenders; judges could not sentence someone for less than the minimum time that Congress defined in legislation. And finally, though it is hard to do, Congress can remove the ability of federal courts and the Supreme Court to interpret constitutional issues by trying to amend the Constitution itself.

The Constitution gives great power to both the House and the Senate, but it does so in the curiously backhanded way known as checks and balances. The House and the Senate share most lawmaking functions, but the fact that they *both* must approve legislation gives them a check over each other. They in turn are checked by the power of the president and the courts. The legislature is unable to operate without the cooperation of the other two branches unless it can demonstrate unusual internal strength and consensus, allowing it to override presidential vetoes and, in more extreme circumstances, amend the Constitution and impeach presidents.

Who What How

Congressional Elections
Political calculations to define districts and determine who will run

The first set of rules a future congressperson or senator has to contend with are those that govern congressional elections. These, more than any others, are the rules that determine the winners and losers in congressional politics. No matter what a legislator might hope to accomplish, he or she cannot achieve it as a legislator without winning and keeping the support of voters. With House elections every two years and Senate elections every six years, much of the legislator's life is spent running for reelection. In fact, one professor argues that most aspects of Congress are designed to aid the reelection goals of its members.[16] With elections so central, let us take a look at how the rules work, who runs for office, and how the electoral process shapes what members do in Washington.

The Politics of Defining Congressional Districts

As a result of the Great Compromise in 1787, the Constitution provides that each state will have two senators and that seats in the House of Representatives will be allocated on the basis of population. Two important political processes regulate the way House seats are awarded on this basis. One is **reapportionment**, in which the 435 House seats are reallocated among the states after each ten-year census. States whose populations grow gain seats, which are taken from those whose populations decline or remain steady. Figure 7.1 shows

Figure 7.1

House Apportionment for Elections in 2012–2020

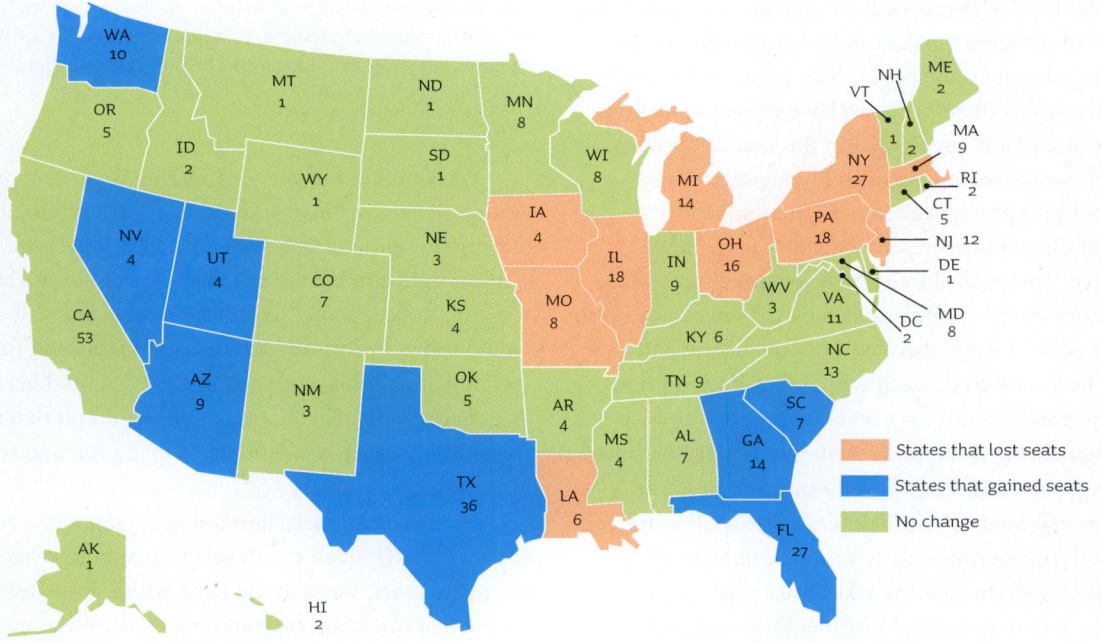

Source: Apportionment Data, U.S. Census, 2010, http://2010.census.gov/2010census/data/apportionment-data-text.php.

> ***redistricting*** process of dividing states into legislative districts
>
> ***gerrymandering*** redistricting to benefit a particular group

> ***racial gerrymandering*** redistricting to enhance or reduce the chances that a racial or an ethnic group will elect members to the legislature

the current apportionment for each state through 2020. The winners are mostly in the rapidly growing Sun Belt states of the South and Southwest; the losers are largely in the Northeast and Midwest.

Since areas that lose population will also lose representatives, just how you count the population becomes critical. Democrats in 2000 proposed using what they claimed was a more precise statistical sampling technique that would allow census workers to get a better estimate of hard-to-count portions of the population such as poor people and immigrants. Fearing that this would add to the population of Democratic districts, and thus increase Democratic representation, Republicans balked. The Supreme Court sided with the Republicans, ruling that the Constitution and the legislation on the books required that, for purposes of reapportionment, the census had to reflect an actual count of the population.

Even more political, however, is the second process that regulates the way districts are drawn. Until the 1960s the states often suffered from malapportionment, the unequal distribution of population among the districts so that some had many fewer residents than others. This, in effect, gave greater representation to those living in lower population districts. This difference is built into the Constitution in the case of the U.S. Senate, but the Supreme Court decided in 1964 that for the U.S. House of Representatives as well as for both houses of the state legislatures, Americans should be represented under the principle of "one person, one vote" and that the districts therefore must have equal populations.[17] The average size of a house district in the year 2000 was 646,952.[18] Districts are equalized following the census through a political process called ***redistricting***, or the redrawing of district lines in states with more than one representative. This procedure, which is carried out by the state legislators (or by commissions they empower), can turn into a bitter political battle because how the district lines are drawn will have a lot to do with who has, gets, and keeps power in the states.

Gerrymandering is the process of drawing district lines to benefit one group or another, and it can result in some extremely strange shapes by the time the state politicians are through. Gerrymandering usually is one of three kinds. Pro-incumbent gerrymandering takes place when a state legislature is so closely divided that members can't agree to give an advantage to one party or the other, so they agree to create districts that reinforce the current power structure by favoring the people who already hold the seats.[19]

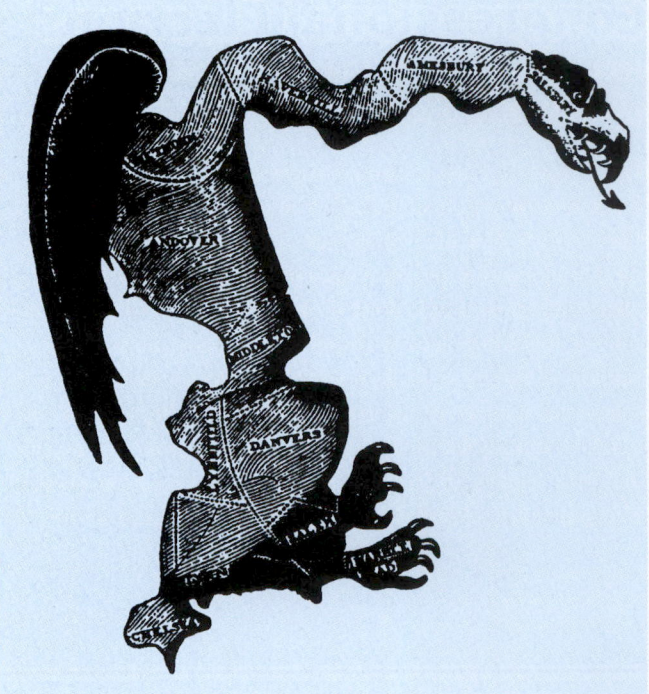

The Politics of Defining Congressional Districts
In 1812, during the administration of Governor Elbridge Gerry, district lines for the Massachusetts senate were drawn to concentrate Federalist Party support in a few districts, thereby helping to elect more Democratic-Republicans. This contemporary cartoon likened one particularly convoluted district to a long-necked monster.

A second kind of gerrymandering is partisan gerrymandering. Generally the goal of the party controlling the redistricting process in a particular state legislature is to draw districts to maximize the number of House seats their party can win. Consequently, Democrats might draw districts that would split a historically Republican district and force an incumbent Republican to run in a new, more liberal district, or even draw districts in a way that would pit two incumbent Republicans in the same district, forcing them to run against each other in a primary.

Finally, ***racial gerrymandering*** occurs when district lines are drawn to favor or disadvantage an ethnic or racial group. For many years, states in the Deep South drew district lines to ensure that black voters would not constitute a majority that could elect an African American to Congress. Since the 1982 Voting Rights Act, the drawing of such lines has been used to maximize the likelihood that African Americans will be

Figure 7.2

Gerrymandering in the 1990s

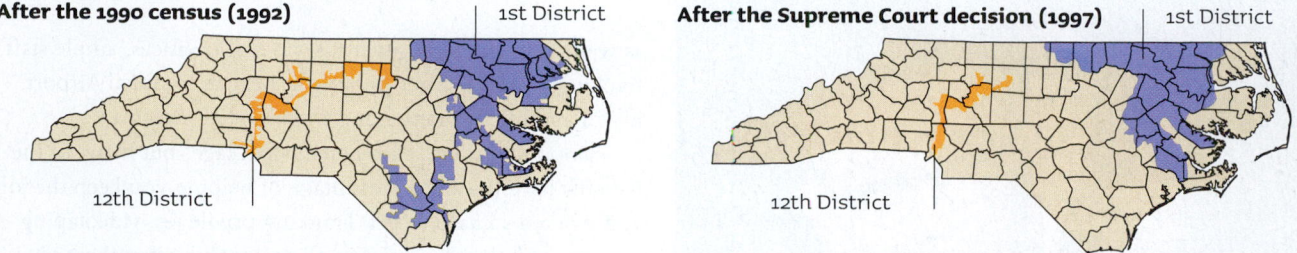

After the 1990 census (1992) · 1st District

12th District

After the Supreme Court decision (1997) · 1st District

12th District

The First and Twelfth Districts of North Carolina were redrawn in 1992 (based on the 1990 census) to consolidate African American communities. The Supreme Court invalidated the gerrymandered districts, and they were redrawn in 1997.

elected to Congress. Both Republicans and African American political activists have backed the formation of *majority-minority districts*, in which African Americans or Hispanics constitute majorities. This has the effect of concentrating enough minority citizens to elect one of their own, and at the same time, it takes these (usually Democratic) voters out of the pool of voters in other districts, thus making it easier for nonminority districts to be won by Republicans.[20] The boundaries for the First and Twelfth Districts of North Carolina, for instance, were redrawn after the 1990 census to consolidate the state's African American population. The Twelfth District was particularly oddly shaped, snaking for over 160 miles along a narrow stretch of Interstate 85 (see Figure 7.2). The gerrymandering accomplished its purpose: two African Americans—the first since 1889—were elected to represent North Carolina in Congress in 1992.[21]

Racial gerrymandering, however, remains highly controversial. While politicians and racial and ethnic group leaders continue to jockey for the best district boundaries for their own interests, the courts struggle to find a "fair" set of rules for drawing district lines. In recent cases the Supreme Court declared that race cannot be the predominant factor in drawing congressional districts. It can be taken into account, but so must other factors, such as neighborhood and community preservation. Since, as we discussed in Chapter 6, race is a suspect classification, it is subject to *strict scrutiny* whenever the law uses it to treat citizens differently, and the law must fulfill a compelling state purpose whether it penalizes them or benefits them.[22] After holding an earlier effort unconstitutional, the Court allowed a later redrawing of the North Carolina district to stand, arguing that where black voters are mostly Democrats, disentangling race from politics can be difficult, and that race can be a legitimate concern in redistricting as long as it is not the "dominant and controlling" consideration.[23]

> *Why is geography a better base for congressional representation than, say, race, religion, gender, occupation, or socioeconomic group?*
>
> **Thinking Outside the Box**

Deciding to Run

Imagine that your interest in politics is piqued as a result of your American politics class. You think the representative from your district is out of touch with the people, too wrapped up in Washington-centered politics, and you start day-dreaming about running for office. What sorts of things should you consider? What would you have to do to win? Even if you never contemplate a life in Washington politics, you will understand much more about how Congress works if you put yourself, temporarily, in the shoes of those who do.

Who Can Run?

The formal qualifications for Congress are not difficult to meet. In addition to the age and citizenship requirements listed in Table 7.1, the Constitution requires that you live in the state you want to represent, although state laws vary on how long or when you have to have lived there. Custom also dictates that if you are running for the House, you live in the district you want to represent. There are no educational requirements for Congress. Although, as we will see, many members of Congress are lawyers, you certainly do not need to be one. In fact, you don't even need to have graduated from college or high school. In many ways, the qualifications for Congress are lighter than for most jobs you might apply for when you

Funny Politics
Comedian and political commentator Al Franken announced his bid to seek Minnesota's Democratic nomination for U.S. Senate in February 2007. After winning the election by barely 250 votes, Franken settled down to serious business in the Senate.

graduate, but you do have to be prepared to expose yourself to the critical scrutiny of your prospective constituents—not a pleasant prospect if you value your privacy!

Why Would Anyone Want This Job?

Like most prospective members of Congress, if you decide to run you are probably motivated by a desire to serve the public. These days, if you are contemplating a run for Congress you are also increasingly likely to be motivated by your ideology—that is, you are probably a conservative Republican or a liberal Democrat who wants to run from a sense of personal conviction and commitment to enact policy that represents your particular, strongly held values.

But your wish to run for Congress may also be enhanced by the fact that it is a very attractive job in its own right. First, there is all the fun of being in Washington, living a life that is undeniably exciting and powerful. The salary, $174,000 in 2010, puts representatives and senators among the top wage earners in the nation, and the "perks" of office are rather nice

as well. These include generous travel allowances, ample staff, franking privileges, free parking at Reagan National Airport, health and life insurance, and a substantial pension.[24]

Not only is this a nice benefits package, but many of the benefits have the added advantage of helping you keep the job you worked so hard to get. Franking privileges, videotaping services, and trips home were all designed by members of Congress to help themselves continue to be members of Congress—all at taxpayer expense.

Along with the benefits and salary comes a certain amount of power and recognition. As a member of Congress you will be among the Very Important People of your community. You will get a title ("The Honorable So-and-So") and will be asked to speak at all sorts of gatherings, from high school graduations to ribbon-cutting ceremonies and Rotary Club meetings. You could build a power base through service to your district or state and try to hold on to your seat as long as possible, or you could use your position and its resources as a jumping-off point for even higher office.

Offsetting these enviable aspects of serving in Congress are the facts that the work is hard and the job security nonexistent. To do the job successfully, you will put in long hours, practice diplomacy, and spend a lot of time away from home and family. And, no matter how hard you work, you are sure to face an opponent in the next election who claims you did not do enough and declares that it's "time for a change." So you have to work all the harder, raise more money, and be even more popular than you were to begin with, just to keep your job.

Also, despite the seemingly high salary, the job of being a member of Congress is expensive. Most members have to maintain two households, one in Washington and one at home. Many find it hard to manage on their congressional salaries.[25] It is also hard on families, who must either divide their time between two homes or live without one parent for part of the year. Finally, more and more members claim that the level of conflict in Congress is so high, and the interest group pressure and fundraising needs so intense, that "the job just isn't any fun any more."[26]

How Can I Win?

To have an outside chance of winning, nonincumbent candidates for Congress need political and financial assets. The key political asset for a potential candidate is experience, including working for other candidates, serving as a precinct chair, or holding an office in the county party organization.

strategic politicians office-seekers who base the decision to run on a rational calculation that they will be successful

incumbency advantage the electoral edge afforded to those already in office

coattail effect the added votes received by congressional candidates of a winning presidential party

midterm loss the tendency for the presidential party to lose congressional seats in off-year elections

Even more helpful is experience in elective office. Those without such experience are called political amateurs and are considered "low-quality" candidates for Congress because they almost never win—unless they happen to be famous sports stars, television personalities, or wealthy businesspeople who have personal resources that can help them beat the odds.[27]

"High-quality" candidates with the requisite political assets need to be careful not to squander them. They do not want to use up favors and political credibility in a losing effort, especially if they have to give up something valuable, like money or an office they currently hold, in order to run. **Strategic politicians** act rationally and carefully in deciding whether a race is worth running. As a strategic candidate yourself, consider these questions:

1. *Is this a district or state I can win?* People want to vote for and be represented by people like themselves, so determine whether you and the district are compatible. Liberals do not do well in conservative parts of the South, African Americans have great difficulty getting elected in predominantly white districts, Republicans have a hard time in areas that are mostly Democratic, and so forth.

2. *Can I beat my opponent?* Whether your opponent is vulnerable is largely governed by the **incumbency advantage**, which refers to the edge in visibility, experience, organization, and fundraising ability possessed by the people who already hold the job. It can make them hard to defeat (see the box "The 112th Congress"). Three possibilities exist:
   a. An incumbent of your party already holds the seat. In this case, winning the nomination is a real long shot. From 1984 through 2008, only fifty-four incumbents lost in primary battles to determine a party's nominee, or about 1 percent of all those seeking reelection.[28]
   b. An incumbent of the opposite party holds the seat. In this case, winning the primary to get your party's nomination may be easier, but the odds are against winning in the general election unless the incumbent has been weakened by scandal, redistricting, or a challenge from within his or her party. Over 96 percent of incumbents running won in their general election contests from 1984 to 2008.[29]
   c. The incumbent is not running. This is an "open seat," your best chance for success. However,

because others know this as well, both the primary and the general elections are likely to be hard fought by high-quality candidates.

3. *Can I get the funds necessary to run a winning campaign?* Modern political campaigns are expensive, and campaigns run on a budget and a prayer are hardly ever successful. Winning nonincumbents over the past decade have spent on average over four times as much as nonincumbents who did not win, and even then the winning nonincumbents could not keep up with the spending of incumbents.[30] Incumbents have access to a lot more political action committee (PAC) money and other contributions than do nonincumbents. (PACs are money-raising organizations devoted to a particular interest group, such as a labor union or trade association; they make donations to candidates that best represent their interests. We'll hear more about PACs in Chapter 13, on interest groups.) As a nonincumbent, you should probably aim at a minimum to raise $1.9 million—the average for challengers who defeated incumbents in 2008.[31] Senate contests, with their much larger constituencies, cost substantially more.

4. *How are the national tides running?* Some years are good for Democrats, some for Republicans. These tides are a result of such things as presidential popularity, the state of the economy, and military engagements abroad. If it is a presidential election year, a popular presidential candidate of your party might sweep you to victory on his or her coattails. The **coattail effect**, less significant in recent elections, refers to the added votes congressional candidates of the winning presidential party receive in a presidential election year as voters generalize their enthusiasm for the national candidate to the whole party.

While the strength of coattails might be declining, there is no arguing with the phenomenon of the **midterm loss**. This is the striking regularity with which the presidential party loses seats in Congress in the midterm elections, also called "off-year" elections—those congressional elections that fall between presidential election years. Before 1998 the presidential party lost seats in the House of Representatives in every midterm election of the twentieth century except in 1934. The 1994 election that brought Republicans to power in Congress for the first time in forty years (see Figure 7.3) was a striking example of the midterm loss: fifty-three seats changed from

▶ **Profiles in Citizenship: Jon Tester**

"The truth is that you can make a difference and it might not take near as much work as you think it's going to take. And second of all, if you get involved, you'll make your community, your county, your state, your country a better place."

Thomas Jefferson, who had a soft spot for farmers, no doubt would have approved of Senator Jon Tester. "Cultivators of the earth," to Jefferson's mind, were the "most virtuous" and "most valuable" of citizens. Senator Tester doesn't talk much about virtue, but he does think it's important

that he leaves Washington every weekend, going home to Montana to get his hands dirty on the farm his family has worked for a century now.

"I think it keeps you real," he says about his determination to keep farming every week. "There's a lot of folks here who treat you, because you got a title in front of your name, they treat you different, they make you think you're special, when we're not. We're not different from anybody. When I go home, when I walk into my shop and I pull my swather out and it's got a flat tire, they don't give a damn if I am a senator or not. It keeps you real and also I think it keeps you grounded with what's going on economically in the country. If the farm quits working, I know that right away; if the market disappears, I know it; fuel prices go up, I know it; cost of equipment goes up or down, I know it."

If politics seems like an unusual occupation for a farmer, consider that Tester is also a former music teacher, holding a degree in music from the College of Great Falls. But he got caught up in

public service early. During a high school trip to the state capital, his imagination had been fired by the state Senate—the grandeur of the building, the enthusiasm of the representatives, and a job that looked "very challenging but very fun." In the back of his mind was the idea that some day he might want to give it a try.

But in a rural community, he says, there is an expectation that citizens will serve on boards and committees. So Tester first did a stint on the school board and his local Soil Conservation Service Committee before following that high school ambition and running for, and winning, a seat in the Montana Senate. It was as much fun as he had thought it might be. "I like public service," says Tester. "It gives you positive vibes all the time. There is a lot of negative, sure there is, but there is a feeling of accomplishment different than working in a field, harvesting a field, picking hay bales or rocks or whatever you are doing on the farm."

In 2006, after eight years in the state Senate, he decided to make the leap to

Democratic to Republican control, making it the largest change of this sort in fifty years.[32] In general, the presidential party losses depend on the president's standing with the public and the state of the economy; an unpopular president and a sour economy spell bad news for congressional candidates of the presidential party in an off-year election.[33]

In 1998 and again in 2002, however, unusual circumstances not only eliminated the midterm loss but also led the president's party to pick up seats. In 1998 the economy was sound and President Clinton's popularity was relatively high. When House Republican leaders pursued impeachment charges against Clinton despite opinion polls demonstrating that most Americans did not want Clinton removed,

Republicans lost five House seats in the midterm election and held even in the Senate. In 2002 President Bush's high popularity ratings following the September 11, 2001, attacks remained strong, and he was able to keep the public focused on national security—an issue that Republicans have historically been seen as better able to handle than Democrats. The combination of beneficial redistricting after the 2000 election, a popular president's rigorous campaigning, and a favorable issue agenda allowed Republicans to pick up seats in both the House and the Senate. However, in 2006 the midterm loss returned true to form; President Bush's approval ratings were lower than any president's ratings save for Richard Nixon's on the eve of his impeachment, and the

national politics. He was a long-shot candidate for the U.S. Senate, and the race was squeaky close—even the day after the election they weren't sure he had actually won—but Tester was philosophical about it, figuring he had done his best and it was in the voters' hands. When the dust settled, he was the new senator from Montana, a job he finds good, but challenging. "This is a great job," he says. "It's a tremendous honor. There's all sorts of good stuff about it."

Down sides? There are those, too, though "there isn't any job out there that doesn't have its ups and downs," he says. The most frustrating part, for him, is the excessive partisanship that the Senate is prone to these days, despite the fact that behind the scenes the senators are collegial and friendly. "I can tell you that there is no doubt in my mind that folks vote in some cases 'yes' or 'no' just to be partisan. That's not what's always best for the country. That's not always best for your constituents, not always what's best for your state." Watching a Senate

vote take place along party lines from the television in his office, he points at the screen. "There is only one hope for what we see on that tube right there, and that's the next generation. They're the ones that can fix this, and if they are willing to allow this to happen, it will never get fixed. It just won't. They can fix it."

Hello, next generation? The ball is in your court. Here is some more of Tester's advice:

On taking risks:

[When I was running for the Senate] I was running in the primary against a guy who had already won statewide who was a millionaire—I'm not. I just thought, if we work hard, like the way I was brought up—if you work hard, and stick to it, to do what you want to do, the good Lord will open the door or he won't. And if you never try it, trust me—there were many times I wanted to get out of the race, many times. But if you never try it, you never know.

On keeping the republic:

[Benjamin] Franklin is right. This place won't work if everybody sits on their hands. And I think it's critically important and I think it's very rewarding for people to get involved. And there is all too many times that I hear people . . . say, 'Oh, I can't make a difference.' You know, 'I can't do this or I can't do that'—well 'can't' shouldn't be a word in somebody's lexicon. The truth is that you can make a difference and it might not take near as much work as you think it's going to take. And second of all, if you get involved, you'll make your community, your county, your state, your country a better place. And I think that's the big issue. It takes some work, but it's very rewarding, and the time I'm talking about is that you don't have to do it eight hours a day. You can do it one evening a month in some cases. And it is very, very important. It's very important to the health of the country, it's very important for you to know what's going on in your community, and it makes life a whole helluva lot more fun. ◼

president's party paid the price as the Democrats won back control of both houses of Congress. Similarly, in 2010, a sputtering economic recovery, high unemployment, and President Obama's correspondingly low approval ratings cost the Democrats the majority in the House. The GOP gain of more than sixty House seats was the largest for that party in six decades, eclipsing the historic 1994 victory and easily wiping out the Democrats' gains in the previous two election cycles. The Democrats were especially vulnerable because they had won in a large number of Republican districts in 2006 and again in 2008. With fewer seats at stake in the Senate, the Democrats lost only six seats, keeping majority control in that chamber, but not by much.

Who Gets Elected?

The founders intended that the House of Representatives, which was elected directly by the people, would be the "people's house," reflecting the opinions and interests of the mass of American citizenry. The Senate was to be a more elite institution, composed of older men of virtue, education, and property like the founders themselves, whom they believed would have the wisdom to balance the impulses of the popularly elected House. In a way, the division of representational duties between the House and the Senate reflects the distinction between the dual tasks of constituent representation on the one hand and national lawmaking on

Figure 7.3

Party Control in the House of Representatives, 1925–2010

After a long period of uninterrupted dominance by the Democratic Party, Republicans controlled the House of Representatives for twelve years following the "Republican Revolution" of 1994. The Democrats won back control of both houses of Congress in 2006 and extended their control in 2008, but lost control of the House in the 2010 midterm elections.

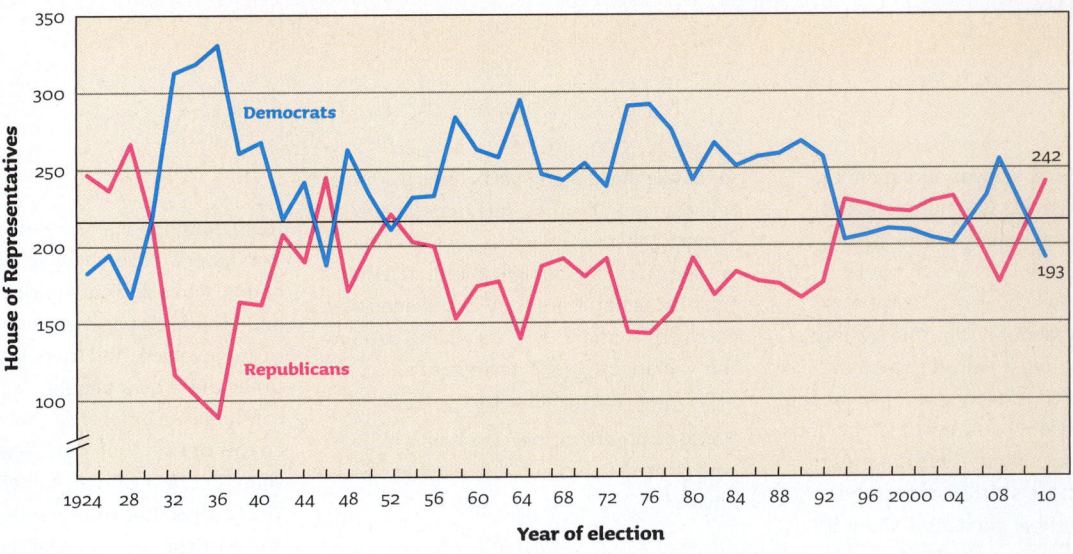

▶ The 112th Congress

Whereas the elections of 2006 and 2008 were big wins for the Democrats, in 2010 the political winds strongly favored Republicans. The combination of the earlier Democratic wins, which had many Democrats defending House seats in Republican or swing districts; unified Democratic control of both houses of Congress and the presidency; and a lingering recession that still produced an unemployment rate of nearly 10 percent made the Democrats an easy target for voters. Disgruntled and angry Republicans and independents turned out in force while disheartened Democrats stayed home. The Republicans took control of the House with a sizable majority, the Democrats retained a bare majority in the Senate, and the prospects were for political gridlock in Washington.

The demographic profile of Congress shifted in ways that are consistent with a large Republican win. The number of women dropped by four, to seventy-three, in the House and by two, to fifteen, in the Senate. The number of Hispanics also decreased to two from three in the Senate and to twenty-three from twenty-seven in the House. No African Americans have been elected to the Senate since President Barack Obama held a seat representing Illinois, but in the House their numbers increased, including the election of two black Republicans from Florida and

South Carolina. The one Native American continued in the House, as did the two Asians in the Senate. The number of Asians in the House increased by two, to a total of nine.

The intense ideological polarization of the parties appears to have increased. Many Republican candidates were backed by the strongly anti-Washington Tea Party movement, drawing them further to the right. Also, because several moderate Republicans lost in the primaries, even those from more competitive districts were discouraged from positioning themselves in the political center. As many of the Democrats who lost were moderates from competitive and Republican districts, the remaining Democrats are a more homogeneously liberal group. Still, as has been usual in the recent past, there is more ideological diversity in the Democratic Party, evidenced by the election of Joe Manchin III, who won the Senate seat in West Virginia by running against much of the Democratic program in Washington. After the election, Manchin became a prime target for Republicans hoping to persuade him to switch parties and join their ranks. The election presents huge challenges for the parties' leaders to govern. Each party has, in both Congress and the electorate, strongly committed bases that will resist much significant compromise.

> **descriptive representation** the idea that an elected body should mirror demographically the population it represents

the other that we have said forms the central dilemma for legislators today.

But today we no longer see the responsibility of making national policy as the sole province of the Senate, nor do we believe that responding to public opinion, interests, and demands is a lower order of representation belonging just to the House. In fact, our expectations about the House and the Senate have changed dramatically since the days of the founding. Most of us have more trust in the people and—as we saw at the outset of this chapter—considerably less regard for politicians, even those with education and property. In this section we look at what kind of legislature the people choose.

The first question we can ask is whether Congress measures up to the definition of what we call **descriptive representation**, in which the legislature is expected to mirror the demographics of those it represents. Founder and president John Adams said a representative assembly "should be in miniature an exact portrait of the people at large. It should think, feel, reason, and act like them."[34] In this regard, Congress fails quite miserably. Congress today, almost as much as the 1787 Constitutional Convention in Philadelphia, is dominated by relatively well-educated, well-to-do white males. The poor, the less educated, women, and minorities are not represented proportionately to their numbers in the population, although there are several trends in the direction of a more demographically representative Congress. (See "*Who Are We?* Our Representatives in Congress.")

Occupations

Americans work in many kinds of jobs. Only a relatively few have professional careers; far more are skilled and semiskilled workers, service economy workers, sales representatives, managers, and clerical workers. Yet this large bulk of the population does not send many of its own to Congress. Rather, Congress is dominated by lawyers and businesspeople and, not surprisingly, politicians. Asked to list their occupations, members of the 111th Congress split about evenly among business and law (38 percent each) and public service and politics (40 percent).[35] While the occupations tend to split more or less evenly between the parties, the Republicans draw much more heavily from business and banking, and the Democrats are more likely to have come from public service careers.

Although being an attorney or a state legislator is frequently listed as a member's prior occupation, many of those serving have more varied and surprising backgrounds. Former occupations of legislators include members of the clergy, sheriffs, a border patrol chief, scientists, radio talk show hosts, an astronaut, several with careers in the military, professional musicians, a comedian, professional athletes, organic farmers, a fruit picker, ski and driving instructors, a casino dealer and prison guard, a coroner, a taxi cab driver, and a former oil field worker. Thus while it is arguable that some *current* professions, especially law, are overrepresented, members also have had experience with many of the jobs of ordinary Americans.[36]

Education and Income

Even though members of Congress have collectively worked at an array of occupations before they got to Capitol Hill, the fact is that they are not representative of their fellow Americans when it comes to education and income. In the adult population

Advocating for African Americans
Founded during the 77th Congress in January 1969, the Democratic Select Committee was renamed the Congressional Black Caucus in 1971. The organization's chair, Rep. Barbara Lee, D-Calif., center, and other members, including Rep. Charles Rangel, D-N.Y., take questions from the media in March 2010 after meeting with President Obama.

▶ **Who Are We?**

Our representatives in Congress

The 111th Congress was the most diverse yet. A record number of women serve in both houses from both parties, and there are more Hispanics than ever before. Despite these advances, both chambers remain predominantly male and almost entirely white. The Senate has seventeen women, no African Americans, and three Hispanics, but this still means that 80 percent of the institution's members remain white males. Is the underrepresentation of women and minorities in Congress something that Americans should be concerned about? Should a legislature look like the people it represents?

Race and Gender in Congress Over Time

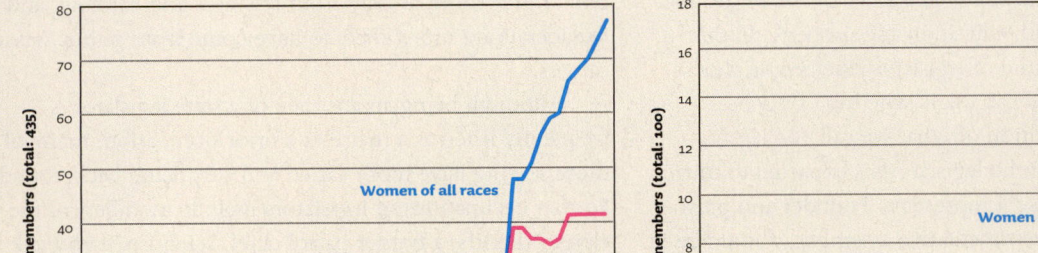

House of Representatives | Senate

Sources: Norman J. Ornstein, Thomas E. Mann, and Michael J. Malbin, *Vital Statistics on Congress, 2001–2002* (Washington, D.C.: AEI Press, 2002), 53–55; various issues of Mildred L. Amer's congressional profiles, Congressional Research Service; and *CQ Today: Guide to the New Congress*, November 6, 2008, 72–73.

---

at large, 26.7 percent graduated from college and only 8.9 percent have advanced degrees. In contrast, 95 percent of Congress' 535 members have a college degree, and three-quarters have graduate degrees. Their income is well above the average American's income as well. Many House members—and an even greater percentage of senators—are millionaires.[37]

By these standards, Congress is an educational, occupational, and income elite. Those lower in the socioeconomic ranks do not have people like themselves in Washington working for them. A hard question to answer is whether it matters. Who can do a better job of representing, say, a working-class man who did not finish high school: people like himself, or those with the education and position to work in the halls of Congress on his behalf? The varied backgrounds of many members do suggest that congressmen and women probably have a good idea of what "ordinary" people's lives

are like and the problems they face. We revisit this question when we look at the representation of women and minorities in Congress.

Race and Gender

Over the long haul, women and minorities have not been well represented in Congress (as indicated in *"Who Are We? Our Representatives in Congress"*). Congress, however, is more representative today than it has been through most of our history. Until the civil rights movement in the 1960s, there were hardly any blacks or Hispanics in the House. Women seemed to have fared somewhat better, partly because of the once-common practice of appointing (and sometimes electing) a congressman's widow to office when the member died. This tactic was thought to minimize intraparty battles for the appointment. Not until the 1970s did female candidates

Senate and House Demographics

Average age:	Members with advanced degrees:	Those with military service:
Senate: 63	Senate: 75 of 100 (78%)	Senate with: 25 Senate without: 69
House: 57	House: 284 of 435 (64%)	House with: 96 House without: 339

Senate and House Occupations

House	111th	House	111th	Senate	111th
Public service/politics	182	Law enforcement	10	Law	54
Business	175	Journalism	7	Public service/politics	32
Law	152	Military	6	Business	26
Education	78	Engineering	6	Education	16
Real estate	35	Science	6	Real estate	6
Agriculture	26	Technical/skilled labor	4	Journalism	5
Medicine/doctor	16	Actor/entertainment	3	Agriculture	5
Labor/blue collar	13	Clergy	1	Medicine/doctor	3
Homemaker	12	Professional sports	1	Labor/blue collar	2
Secretarial/clerical	11	Miscellaneous	1	Artistic/creative	2
Health care	10			Military	1
				Professional sports	1
				Homemaker/domestic	1
				Actor/entertainment	1
				Miscellaneous	1

Sources: CQ.com, www.cq.com/flatfiles/editorialFiles/temporaryItems/2008/cqdailymonitorpdf_20081106.pdf; Mildred Amer and Jennifer E. Manning, "Membership of the 111th Congress: A Profile," Congressional Research Service, December 31, 2008, http://assets.openers.com/rpts/R40086-20081231.pdf.

begin to be elected and reelected on their own in significant numbers.

In the 1990s representation of all three groups, especially blacks and women, began to improve. The reasons, however, are quite different. Women have been coming into their own as candidates, a natural extension of their progress in education and the workplace. Women's political status has also been reinforced by the growing salience of issues that are of particular concern to them, from abortion to family leave policy to sexual harassment. In the 1992 congressional election, following Clarence Thomas's Supreme Court confirmation hearing, where male legislators appeared tone-deaf to the issue of sexual harassment, women were phenomenally successful. In what has been dubbed the "Year of the Woman," women increased their representation in the House by two-thirds (from twenty-eight to forty-seven seats) and tripled their representation in the Senate (from two to six). Experts attribute this success in part to the large number of open seats created by retirements and redistricting following the 1992 census. These open seats created opportunities to run in districts long held by incumbents.[38] Each election since has seen the addition of at least one new female senator, and they have come from both parties (nine Democrats and five Republicans). The House has had a similar increase.

Despite these dramatic changes in women's representation since the 1970s, the number of women in office has still not reached the levels that exist in many other countries. Figure 7.4 shows that the percentage of women in the U.S. Congress still ranks relatively low compared to other countries. These differences exist in part because election rules in some countries, such as Sweden, require parties to run a

Figure 7.4

Percentage of Women in Legislative Bodies in Selected Countries

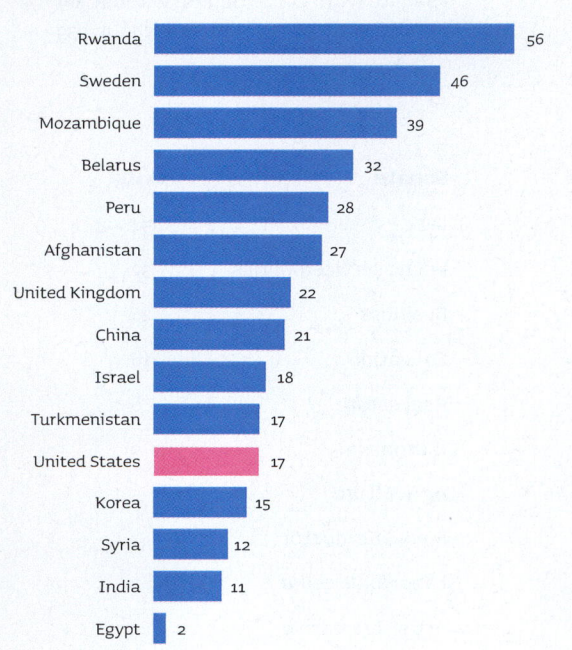

Country	Percentage
Rwanda	56
Sweden	46
Mozambique	39
Belarus	32
Peru	28
Afghanistan	27
United Kingdom	22
China	21
Israel	18
Turkmenistan	17
United States	17
Korea	15
Syria	12
India	11
Egypt	2

Source: Women in National Parliaments, as of June 30, 2010, www.ipu.org/wmn-e/classif.htm.

certain number of women candidates. But new research also highlights the role that the potential pool of candidates for Congress plays. In the United States there are fewer women in the pool of possible candidates than there are men because women tend to be less likely than men to be "self-starters" in running for office; that is, rather than just deciding to run for office and jumping into the campaign, women are more likely to wait to be asked by a party leader or the community. This difference exists even among a pool of potential women officeholders, like attorneys and local officeholders, that is similar to potential male candidates in all other characteristics. Because this is the case at the local and state legislative levels, these lower levels of government produce fewer women to run for office at higher levels like the U.S. Congress.[39]

The pattern of black representation showed steady increases during the 1970s and 1980s, followed by a comparatively large jump in the 1990s with the advent of racial gerrymandering, which we discussed earlier. The constitutionality of racially based districting will depend on future Supreme Court rulings.[40]

Hispanics have been even more underrepresented in Congress than have blacks because Hispanic populations do not tend to be as solidly concentrated as African Americans,

they do not vote as consistently for a single party, and many do not vote at all. Underrepresentation of this group may be poised to change, however. Because the Hispanic population is growing so rapidly in America, both parties have pushed for Hispanics to run for office and have also worked hard to mobilize Hispanics to vote, although Democrats have recently been more successful, with the Obama campaign winning the Hispanic vote in the 2008 elections, especially among the young. What might be a temporary Democratic support could be sealed as one-party loyalty, depending on how the issue of immigration plays out. In 1994 California Republicans backed Proposition 187, which sought to bar illegal immigrants from receiving public services. Although it was later declared unconstitutional, that political move stimulated a rapid rise in Hispanic registration at an eight-to-one Democratic ratio and helped turn California to a solid blue (Democratic) state in national elections. The Republicans' continued support for tough, punitive immigration regulations such as the strict immigration law passed by Arizona in 2010 is likely to continue to push Hispanics toward the Democratic Party.[41]

Does It Matter?

Does descriptive representation of these traditionally under-represented groups matter? For the poor, the answer is not hard to find; there is little or no descriptive representation for the poor, and this does appear to have a substantive effect on how well their interests are represented. Research suggests that the concerns of the poor do not have equal weight with those of the better off. Constituents with higher income and better educations have the resources and skills to communicate their policy preferences to their representatives, and they are more likely to vote and to participate in and contribute to campaigns. The result is that elected officials in general pay less attention to the concerns of the poor in their legislative work. In short, economic inequality carries over to the policy-making process of who gets what.[42]

For race and gender, the answer is that descriptive representation matters, at least at a symbolic level if not in substantive terms. Having "one of our own" as an active participant in the policy process has positive symbolic meaning for women, Hispanics, and African Americans.[43] Results are mixed, however, as to whether the presence of these groups in the legislative process produces better policies for these groups. Members of these demographic groups do tend to put issues of concern to those groups on the political agenda, but when it comes the way they actually vote, the effect is muted.

majority party the party with the most seats in a house of Congress

party polarization greater ideological (liberal versus conservative) differences between the parties and increased ideological consensus within the parties

Women legislators do tend to vote for "women's issues," but they are also Democrats and Republicans, and partisan interest can override gender commitment.[44] The effect of descriptive representation is similarly mixed for minorities. Creating majority-minority districts through racial gerrymandering (typically at least 65 percent African American and Hispanic) has the effect of "bleaching" adjacent districts, particularly in the southern states, which results in whiter, more conservative districts that elect more Republicans and make it harder to pass legislation that is friendly to minority interests.[45] And, as is true for women, although African American and Hispanic legislators add new bills regarding their demographic groups to the agenda and speak about their issues in floor debate, once one takes into account the character of districts, there is little difference in voting on bills between those legislators on the one hand, and their non-Hispanic, white counterparts on the other. The increase in minority legislators elected to Congress has increased the number of bills concerning race, but passage of these bills is contingent on which party is in charge of the legislative process rather than simply the number of minority legislators.[46]

The primary policy effect of descriptive representation seems to be that it brings what might be otherwise neglected perspectives to the legislatures, raising minority-interest issues and anticipating the needs and concerns of fellow minorities when new issues arise.[47] And for groups like the poor, who are not even represented descriptively, even these limited benefits do not exist.

Who What How

Congressional elections are the meeting ground for citizens and their representatives, where each brings his or her own goals and stakes in the process. Citizens want a congressperson who will take care of local affairs, mind the nation's business, and represent them generally on political and social issues. The rules of local representation and electoral politics, however, mean that citizens are more likely to get someone who takes care of local interests and affairs at the expense of national interests and general representation.

Members of Congress want election, and then reelection. Because they make many of the rules that control electoral politics, the rules often favor those already in office. While many members may wish to turn to national affairs, to do what is best for the nation regardless of their local district or state, they have to return continually to the local issues that get them elected.

Congressional Organization

The key role of political parties and congressional committees

Despite the imperatives of reelection and the demands of constituency service, the primary business of Congress is making laws. Lawmaking is influenced a great deal by the organization of Congress—that is, the rules of the institution that determine where the power is and who can exercise it. In this section we describe how Congress organizes itself and how this structure is influenced by members' goals.

The Central Role of Party

Political parties are central to how Congress functions for several reasons. First, Congress is organized along party lines. In each chamber, the party with the most members—the ***majority party***—decides the rules for the chamber and gets the top leadership posts, such as the Speaker of the House, the majority leader in the Senate, and the chairmanships of all the committees and subcommittees.

Party is also important in Congress because it is the mechanism for members' advancement. Because all positions are determined by the parties, members have to advance within their party to achieve positions of power in the House or the Senate, whether as a committee chair or in the party leadership.

Finally, party control of Congress matters because the parties stand for very different things. Across a wide range of issues, Democrats embrace more liberal policies, whereas Republicans advocate more conservative ones. Figure 7.5 shows that on issues from abortion to oil exploration to affirmative action programs, Democratic House candidates are more liberal and Republican House candidates are much more conservative. Upon winning office, these candidates vote very differently from one another. As Figure 7.6 illustrates, Democratic members of the House are increasingly likely to vote with the majority of their party and are opposed by Republican representatives similarly voting as a bloc. Thus, although Americans like to downplay the importance of parties in their own lives, political parties are fundamental to the operation of Congress and, hence, to what the national government does.

Parties have become much more significant in Congress in recent years due to the process of ***party polarization***. This refers to the growing ideological differences between the two

Figure 7.5

Party Differences Among House Candidates on Policy Stances, 2008

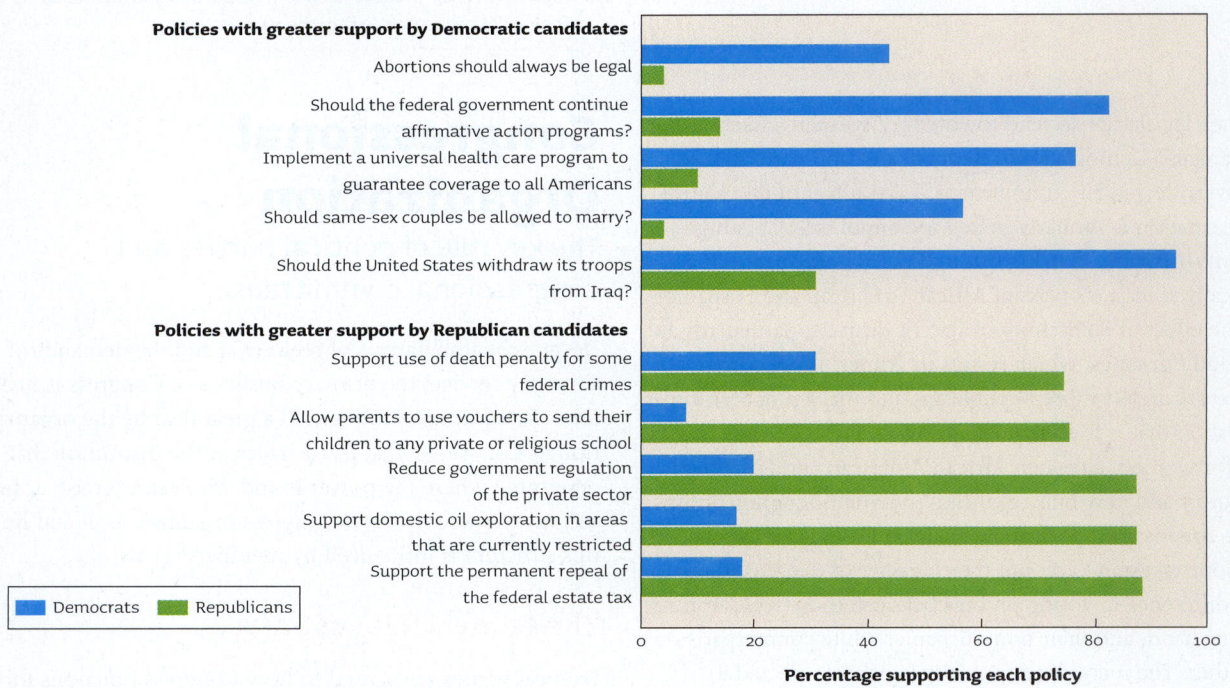

Source: Project Vote Smart, 2008, "Political Courage Test." Calculated by the authors.

Figure 7.6

Party Voting in Congress, 1970–2009

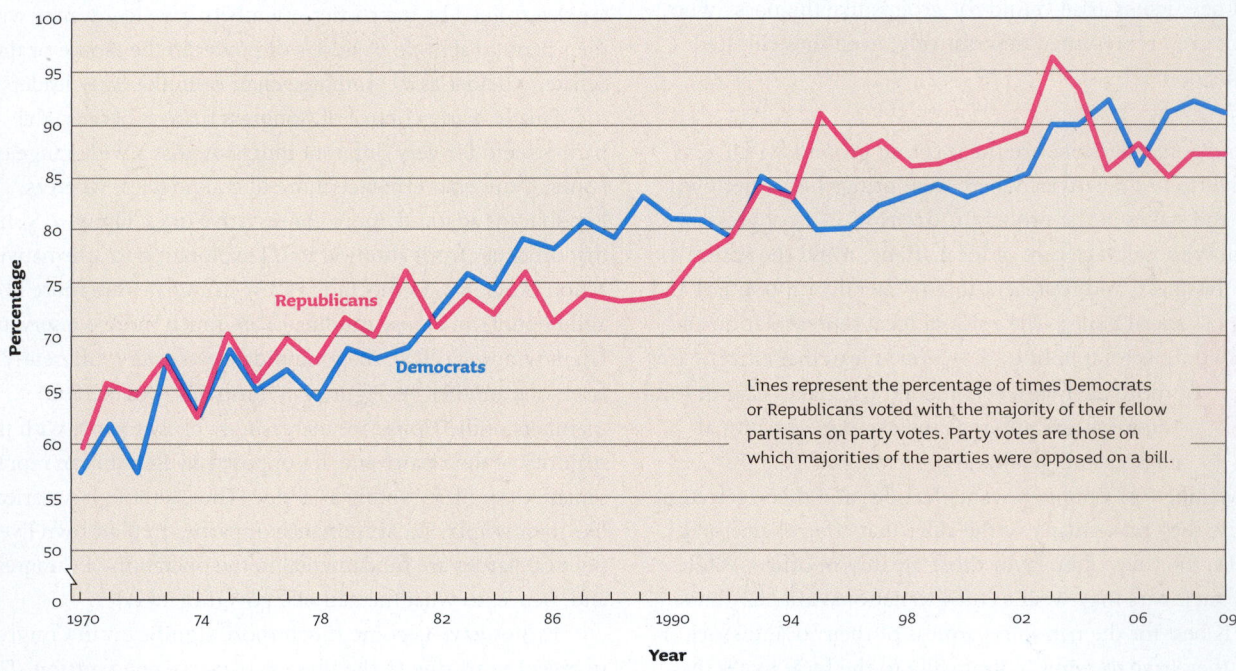

Lines represent the percentage of times Democrats or Republicans voted with the majority of their fellow partisans on party votes. Party votes are those on which majorities of the parties were opposed on a bill.

Sources: Roger H. Davidson, Walter J. Oleszek, and Frances E. Lee, *Congress and Its Members*, 12th ed. (Washington, D.C.: CQ Press, 2010), Figure 9-1; "The U.S. Congress Votes Data Base," *Washington Post*, http://projects.washingtonpost.com/congress/111/ house/party-voters/.

Figure 7.7

Ideological Polarization of the Parties in Congress, 1879–2009

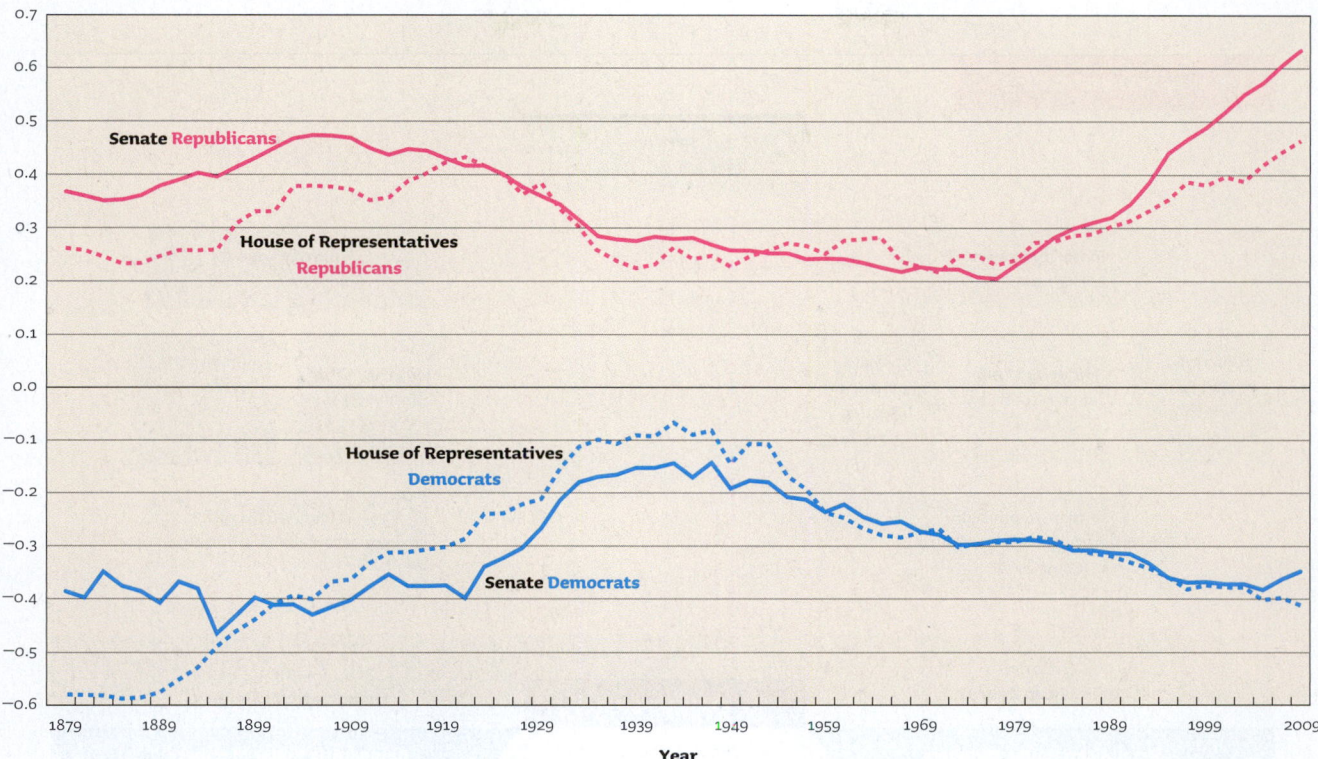

Source: Data on the liberal-conservative measures (DW-NOMINATE scores) developed by Keith Poole and Howard Rosenthal, www.voteview.com. Calculated here by the authors.

parties and the greater ideological agreement within the parties. Today, almost all the Democrats in Congress are pretty liberal, and to an even greater extent the vast majority of congressional Republicans are very conservative. The patterns of party-ideological voting are shown in Figure 7.7. The higher the line, the more conservative the party is in its voting. Notice that the parties in both the Senate and the House of Representatives are further apart ideologically than they have been for over a hundred years. This makes it harder for the parties to work together because their members are committed to such divergent positions across the whole range of issues that Congress must deal with.

Polarization has also been a significant factor in the growing intensity of conflict and rancor that is characteristic of recent congresses. Republican opposition to President Obama's proposals has been quite solid, whereas Obama has been able to count on the support of most congressional Democrats. As we will see later in this chapter, this means the president has been successful in getting his priorities enacted by the House of Representatives only because there are enough Democrats there to get his bills passed even in the face of united Republican opposition. It has been much more difficult for the president to get his policies passed in the Senate, where for most of his term so far the Democrats

have not been able to command sixty votes to break a filibuster without the cooperation of at least one Republican.

The Leadership

The majority and minority parties in each house elect their own leaders, who are, in turn, the leaders of Congress. Strong, centralized leadership allows Congress to be more efficient in enacting party or presidential programs, but it gives less independence to members to take care of their own constituencies or to pursue their own policy preferences.[48] Although the nature of leadership in the House of Representatives has varied over time, the current era is one of considerable centralization of power. Because the Senate is a smaller chamber and thus easier to manage, its power is more decentralized.

Leadership Structure

The Constitution provides for the election of some specific congressional officers, but Congress itself determines how much power the leaders of each chamber will have. The main leadership offices in the House of Representatives are the ***Speaker of the House***, the majority leader, the minority leader, and the whips (see Figure 7.8). The real political choice about who the party leader should be occurs within the party

Figure 7.8

Structure of the House and Senate Leadership in the 112th Congress

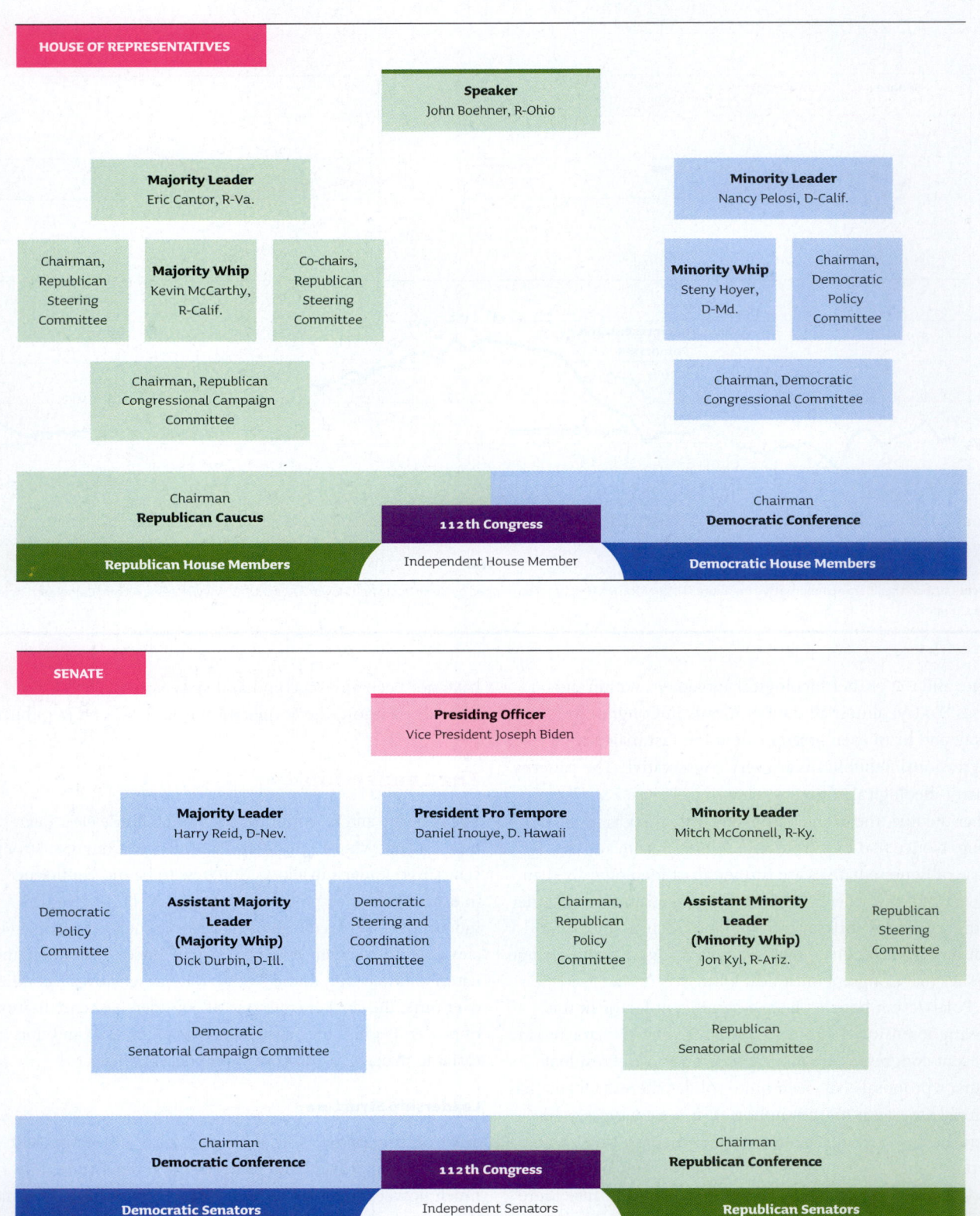

HOUSE OF REPRESENTATIVES

Speaker
John Boehner, R-Ohio

Majority Leader
Eric Cantor, R-Va.

Minority Leader
Nancy Pelosi, D-Calif.

Chairman, Republican Steering Committee

Majority Whip
Kevin McCarthy, R-Calif.

Co-chairs, Republican Steering Committee

Minority Whip
Steny Hoyer, D-Md.

Chairman, Democratic Policy Committee

Chairman, Republican Congressional Campaign Committee

Chairman, Democratic Congressional Committee

Chairman
Republican Caucus

112th Congress

Chairman
Democratic Conference

Republican House Members

Independent House Member

Democratic House Members

SENATE

Presiding Officer
Vice President Joseph Biden

Majority Leader
Harry Reid, D-Nev.

President Pro Tempore
Daniel Inouye, D. Hawaii

Minority Leader
Mitch McConnell, R-Ky.

Democratic Policy Committee

Assistant Majority Leader (Majority Whip)
Dick Durbin, D-Ill.

Democratic Steering and Coordination Committee

Chairman, Republican Policy Committee

Assistant Minority Leader (Minority Whip)
Jon Kyl, R-Ariz.

Republican Steering Committee

Democratic Senatorial Campaign Committee

Republican Senatorial Committee

Chairman
Democratic Conference

112th Congress

Chairman
Republican Conference

Democratic Senators

Independent Senators

Republican Senators

groupings in each chamber. The Speaker of the House is elected by the majority party and, as the person who presides over floor deliberations, is the most powerful House member. The House majority leader, second in command, is given wide-ranging responsibilities to assist the Speaker.

The leadership organization in the Senate is similar but not as elaborate. The presiding officer of the Senate is the vice president of the United States, who can cast a tie-breaking vote when necessary but otherwise does not vote. When the vice president is not present, which is almost always the case, the president pro tempore of the Senate officially presides, although the role is typically performed by a junior senator. Because of the Senate's much freer rules for deliberation on the floor, the presiding officer has less power than in the House, where debate is generally tightly controlled. The locus of real leadership in the Senate is the majority leader and the minority leader. Each is advised by party committees on both policy and personnel matters, such as committee appointments.

In both chambers, Democratic and Republican leaders are assisted by party whips. (The term *whip* comes from an old English hunting expression; the "whipper in" was charged with keeping the dogs together in pursuit of the fox.) Elected by party members, whips find out how people intend to vote so that on important party bills, the leaders can adjust the legislation, negotiate acceptable amendments, or employ favors (or, occasionally, threats) to line up support. Whips work to persuade party members to support the party on key bills, and they are active in making sure favorable members are available to vote when needed.

The Treatment

As Senate majority leader (and later as president), Lyndon B. Johnson was legendary for his ability to cajole, charm, bully, and—by any and all means necessary—persuade others to see things his way. Here, in a light example of "the treatment," Johnson shares a laugh with Supreme Court justice Abe Fortas while invading his personal space.

Leadership Powers

Leaders can exercise only the powers that their party members give them. From the members' standpoint, the advantage of a strong leader is that he or she can move legislation along, get the party program passed, do favors for members, and improve the party's standing. The disadvantage is that a strong party leader can pursue national party (or presidential) goals at the expense of members' pet projects and constituency interests, and he or she can withhold favors.

The power of the Speaker of the House has changed dramatically over time. At the beginning of the twentieth century, the strong "boss rule" of Speaker Joe Cannon (1903–1911) greatly centralized power in the House. Members rebelled at this in 1910 and moved to the **seniority system**, which vested great power in committee chairs instead

of the Speaker. Power followed seniority, or length of service on a committee, so that once a person assumed the chairmanship of a committee, business was run very much at the pleasure of the chair.[49] The seniority system itself was reformed in the 1970s by a movement that weakened the grip of chairs and gave some power back to the Speaker and the party caucuses, as well as to members of the committees, and especially subcommittees.[50]

Speakers' powers were enhanced further with the Republican congressional victories in the 1994 election, when Rep. Newt Gingrich, R-Ga., became Speaker (see the *Profiles in*

Citizenship in Chapter 3). Gingrich quickly became the most powerful Speaker since the era of boss rule. His House Republican colleagues were willing to give him new powers because his leadership enabled them to take control of the House and to enact the well-publicized conservative agenda that they called the *Contract With America*.[51] Gingrich continued as the powerful Republican congressional spokesperson and leader until he resigned in the wake of the almost unprecedented reversal of the 1998 midterm loss, to be replaced by Dennis Hastert, a Republican from Illinois.

When the Democrats won control of the House in 2006, Nancy Pelosi was elected Speaker, the first woman to hold that position. In response to those who wondered if Pelosi could wield power as effectively as her male counterparts, Pelosi herself stated, "Anybody who's ever dealt with me knows not to mess with me."[52] That proved to be an accurate foreshadowing of how she managed the office. Pelosi clearly has her ideological roots in the liberal wing of her party, as one of the "San Francisco–style Democrats" that Republicans like to run against (Pelosi herself is from San Francisco). But as leader, she was, according to one political analyst, "an activist—a decisive and partisan Speaker who often gets involved in the nitty-gritty details of legislation . . . a pragmatist who is unafraid to disappoint her liberal base in the cause of maintaining or even expanding her party's House majority."[53] Pelosi's role in passing Obama's health care reform bill was crucial, and she was effective at maintaining the support and discipline of her Democratic majority in the House, holding on to her leadership position in the party even after the Republicans regained the majority in 2010.[54] One early assessment by a longtime congressional watcher is that she is "entitled to be regarded among the best speakers."[55] John Boehner's lot as Speaker will be more difficult in many ways. His leadership skills will be tested by the challenge of holding his party together as his caucus is divided between traditional Republicans and the newly elected Tea Partiers who come to Congress determined not to compromise in accomplishing their ambitious agenda.

The leaders of the Senate have never had as much formal authority as those in the House, and that remains true today. The traditions of the Senate, with its much smaller size, allow each senator to speak or to offer amendments when he or she wants. The highly individualistic Senate would not accept the kind of control that some Speakers wield in the House. But though the Senate majority leader cannot control senators, he or she can influence the scheduling of legislation, a factor that can be crucial to a bill's success. The majority leader may even pull a bill from consideration, a convenient exercise of authority when defeat would embarrass the leadership.

The current majority leader, Harry Reid of Nevada, is a former middle-weight boxer who brings a boxer's tenacity to his role as leader of the Senate Democrats. Reid proved to be a highly effective manager in the biggest legislative victory of Obama's first years as president, shepherding the health care bill through the Senate and also helping to get major legislation passed in the lame duck session after the 2010 election.[56] One observer claimed that "Obama's presidency has relied on Reid and his orchestration of the Senate more than any other single person."[57] However, the time spent running the Senate rather than attending to his constituents made his bid for reelection in 2010 closer than he would have liked, but he ultimately prevailed.[58]

The Committee System

Meeting as full bodies, it would be impossible for the House and the Senate to consider and deliberate on all of the 10,000 bills and 100,000 nominations they receive every two years.[59] Hence, the work is broken up and handled by smaller groups called committees.

The Constitution says nothing about congressional committees; they are completely creatures of the chambers of Congress they serve. The committee system has developed to meet the needs of a growing nation as well as the evolving goals of members of Congress. Initially, congressional committees formed to consider specific issues and pieces of legislation; after they made their recommendations to the full body, they dispersed. As the nation grew, and with it the number of bills to be considered, this ad hoc system became unwieldy and Congress formed a system of more permanent committees. Longer service on a committee permitted members to develop expertise and specialization in a particular policy area, and thus bills could be considered more efficiently. Committees also provide members with a principal source of institutional power and the primary position from which they can influence national policy.

What Committees Do

It is at the committee and, even more, the subcommittee stage that the nitty-gritty details of legislation are worked out. Committees and subcommittees do the hard work of considering alternatives and drafting legislation. Committees

standing committees permanent committees responsible for legislation in particular policy areas

are the primary information gatherers for Congress. Through hearings, staff reports, and investigations, members gather information on policy alternatives and discover who will support different policy options. Thus committees act as the eyes, ears, and workhorses of Congress in considering, drafting, and redrafting proposed legislation.

Committees do more, however, than write laws. Committees also undertake the congressional oversight we discussed earlier in this chapter; that is, they check to see that the executive and its agencies are carrying out the laws as Congress intended them to. Committee members gather information about agencies from the media, constituents, interest groups, staff, and special investigations (see the discussion of the Government Accountability Office, later in this chapter). A lot of what is learned in oversight is reflected in changes to the laws giving agencies their power and operating funds.

Members and the general public all strongly agree on the importance of congressional oversight; it is part of the "continuous watchfulness" that Congress mandated for itself in the Legislative Reorganization Act of 1946 and reiterated in its Legislative Reorganization Act of 1970. Nevertheless, oversight tends to be slighted in the congressional process. The reasons are not hard to find. Oversight takes a lot of time, and the rewards to individual members are less certain than from other activities like fundraising or grabbing a headline in the district with a new pork project. Consequently, oversight most often takes the form of "fire-alarm" oversight, in which some scandal or upsurge of public interest directs congressional attention to a problem in the bureaucracy rather than careful and systematic reviews of agencies' implementation of congressional policies.[60]

Types of Committees

Congress has four types of committees: standing, select, joint, and conference. The vast majority of work is done by the standing committees. These are permanent committees, created by statute, that carry over from one session of Congress to the next. They review most pieces of legislation that are introduced to Congress. So powerful are the standing committees that they scrutinize, hold hearings on, amend, and, frequently, kill legislation before the full Congress ever gets the chance to discuss it.

The standing committees of the 112th Congress are listed in Table 7.2, and as their names indicate, most deal with issues in specific policy areas, such as agriculture, foreign relations, or justice. Each committee is typically divided into several

Table 7.2

Standing Committees of the 112th Congress

House	Senate
Agriculture	Agriculture, Nutrition, and Forestry
Appropriations	Appropriations
Armed Services	Armed Services
Budget	Banking, Housing, and Urban Affairs
Education and Labor	Budget
Energy and Commerce	Commerce, Science, and Transportation
Financial Services	Energy and Natural Resources
Foreign Affairs	Environment and Public Works
Homeland Security	Finance
House Administration	Foreign Relations
Judiciary	Health, Education, Labor, and Pensions
Natural Resources	Homeland Security and Governmental Affairs
Oversight and Government Reform	Indian Affairs
Permanent Select Committee on Intelligence	Judiciary
Rules	Rules and Administration
Science and Technology	Small Business and Entrepreneurship
Select Committee on Energy Independence and Global Warming	
Small Business	Veterans' Affairs
Standards of Official Conduct	Senate Special or Select Committees
Transportation and Infrastructure	Aging
Veterans' Affairs	Ethics
Ways and Means	Intelligence

subcommittees that focus on detailed areas of policy. There are twenty standing committees and 101 subcommittees in the House. The Senate has seventeen committees and seventy subcommittees. Not surprisingly, committees are larger in the House, with membership rising to more than seventy on some committees, compared to fewer than thirty on the Senate committees. The size of the committees and the ratio of majority to minority party members on each are determined at the start of each Congress by the majority leadership in the House and by negotiations between the majority and minority leaders in the Senate. Standing committee membership is relatively stable as seniority on the committee is a major factor

House Rules Committee the committee that determines how and when debate on a bill will take place

select committee a committee appointed to deal with an issue or a problem not suited to a standing committee

joint committees combined House-Senate committees formed to coordinate activities and expedite legislation in a certain area

conference committees temporary committees formed to reconcile differences in House and Senate versions of a bill

in gaining subcommittee or committee chairs; the chairs wield considerable power and are coveted positions.

The policy areas represented by the standing committees of the two houses roughly parallel each other, but the **House Rules Committee** exists only in the House of Representatives. (There is a Senate Rules and Administration Committee, but it does not have equivalent powers.) The House Rules Committee provides a "rule" for each bill that specifies when it will be debated, how long debate can last, how it can be amended, and so on. Because the House is so large, debate would quickly become chaotic without the organization and structure provided by the Rules Committee. Such structure is not neutral in its effects on legislation, however. Since the committees are controlled by the majority party in the House, and especially by the Speaker, the rule that structures a given debate will reflect the priorities of the majority party.

When a problem before Congress does not fall into the jurisdiction of a standing committee, a **select committee** may be appointed. These committees are usually temporary and do not recommend legislation per se. They are used to gather information on specific issues, like the Select Committee on Homeland Security did after the September 11 terror attacks, or to conduct an investigation, as did the Select Bipartisan Committee to Investigate the Preparation for and Response to Hurricane Katrina.

Joint committees are made up of members of both houses of Congress. While each house generally considers bills independently (making for a lot of duplication of effort and staff), in some areas they have coordinated activities to expedite consideration of legislation. The joint committees in the 111th Congress were on printing, economics, taxation, and the Library of Congress.

Before a bill can become law, it must be passed by both houses of Congress in exactly the same form. But because the legislative process in each house often subjects bills to different pressures, they may be very different by the time they are debated and passed. **Conference committees** are temporary committees made up of members of both houses of Congress commissioned to resolve these differences, after which the bills go back to each house for a final vote. Members of the conference committees are appointed by the presiding officer of each chamber, who usually taps the senior members, especially the chair, of the committees that considered the bill. Most often the conferees are members of those committees.

In the past, conference committees have tended to be small (five to ten members). In recent years, however, as

Congress has tried to work within severe budget restrictions, it has taken to passing huge "megabills" that collect many proposals into one. Conference committees have expanded in turn, sometimes ballooning into gigantic affairs with many "subconferences."[61]

There are times when the conference committee is not used. These instances occur when the differences between the House and Senate versions are negligible and can be worked out informally. However, the major health care reform bill passed in 2010 presented its own challenges. The House and Senate had passed substantially different versions, with the Democrats needing all sixty of their members to end debate and bring it to a vote in the Senate. Leadership decided that Republicans might seize the opportunities offered in conference to sabotage the bill, so they intended to follow a "ping-pong" strategy, whereby the House would amend its bill, bringing it closer to the Senate version, and then the Senate would do the same, and so on until identical bills were passed in each house.[62] Before the process could be undertaken, however, the Democrats lost their sixtieth seat in the Senate in the special election to fill the position held by the late senator Ted Kennedy of Massachusetts. Any bills reaching the Senate could then be filibustered. Instead leaders in both chambers scrambled to come up with a new strategy. Finally, as we saw in the *What's at Stake?* at the beginning of this chapter, the House passed the Senate bill exactly as the Senate had passed it, allowing it to be signed into law, and then minor revisions to it were passed in the Senate under budget reconciliation rules that required only a simple majority, which the Democrats had in both houses, thus allowing them to pass a slightly amended version of the Senate bill.

Getting on the Right Committees

Getting on the right standing committee is vital for all members of Congress because so much of what members want to accomplish is realized through their work on these committees. Political scientist Richard Fenno identified three goals for members—reelection, lawmaking (also called policymaking), and influence in Congress—and argued that committee memberships are the principal means for achieving these goals.[63] Because members are concerned with reelection, they try to get on committees that deal with issues of concern to constituents. Examples of good matches include the Agriculture Committee for farm states' legislators and the Defense Committee for members with military bases or contractors in their districts.

Figure 7.9

Growth in Congressional Staff, 1891–2005

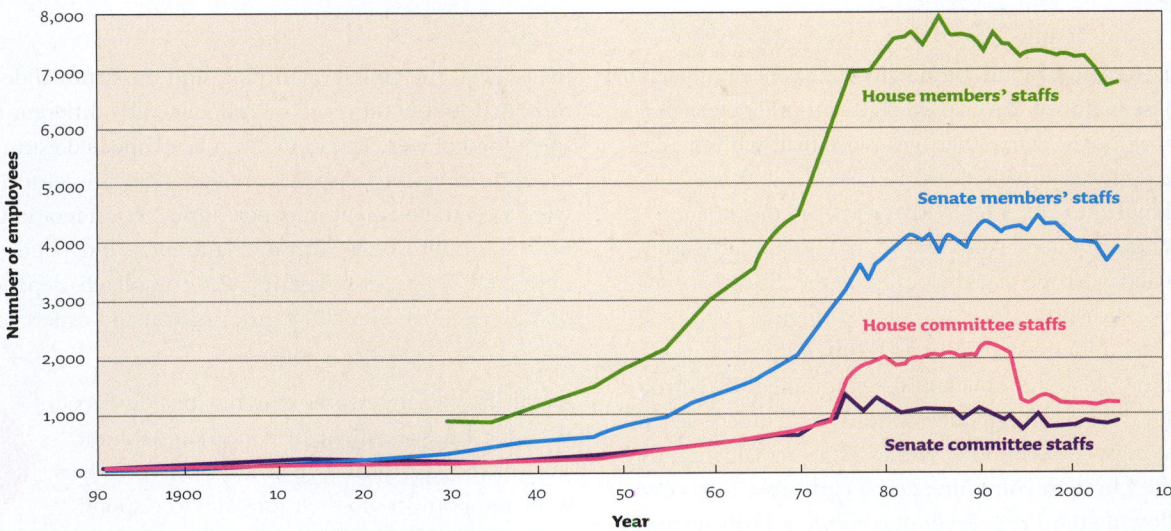

Source: Norman Ornstein, Thomas E. Mann, and Michael J. Malbin, *Vital Statistics on Congress, 2008* (Washington, D.C.: Brookings Institution, 2008), 110.

Members who like to focus on national lawmaking might try to get assigned to committees like Commerce or Foreign Affairs, which have broad jurisdictions and often deal with weighty, high-profile concerns. The House Ways and Means Committee and the Senate Finance Committee, because they deal with taxation—a topic of interest to nearly everyone—are highly prized committee assignments.

When it comes to committee assignments that serve the third goal, achieving power within Congress, an excellent choice is the House Rules Committee. Because it plays the central "traffic cop" role we discussed earlier, its members are in a position to do a lot of favors for members whose bills have to go through Rules. Almost all senators have the opportunity to sit on one of the four most powerful Senate committees: Appropriations, Armed Services, Finance, and Foreign Relations.[64]

Decisions on who gets on what committee vary by party and chamber. Although occasionally the awarding of committee assignments has been used by the parties to reward those who support party positions, in general both the Democrats and the Republicans accommodate their members when they can, since the goal of both parties is to support their ranks and help them be successful.

Committee Chairs

For much of the twentieth century, congressional power rested with the chairmen and chairwomen of the committees of Congress; their power was unquestioned under the seniority system. Today, seniority remains important, but chairs serve at the pleasure of their party caucuses and the party leadership. The committees, under this system, are expected to reflect more faithfully the preferences of the average party member rather than just those of the committee chair or current members.[65]

Congressional Resources

For Congress to knowledgeably guide government lawmaking, it needs expertise and information. Members find, however, that alone they are no match for the enormous amount of information generated by the executive branch, on the one hand, or the sheer informational demands of the policy process—economic, social, military, and foreign affairs—on the other. The need for independent, expert information, along with the ever-present reelection imperative, has led to a big growth in what we call the congressional bureaucracy. Congress has over 22,000 employees, paid for by the federal government. This makes it by far the largest-staffed legislature in the world. Figure 7.9 shows the tremendous growth over time in the number of people working for Congress.

Congressional Staff

The vast majority of congressional staff—secretaries, computer personnel, clericals, and professionals—work for individual members or committees. Notice in Figure 7.9 that a disproportionate amount of the growth has been in personal staff. House members have an average staff of eighteen per member, while the Senate averages twice that, with the sizes of Senate staff varying with state population. Staff members can be assigned to either legislative work or constituency service, at the member's discretion. Those doing primarily constituency work are usually located in the district or state, close to constituents, rather than in Washington.

The committees' staffs (about 2,200 in the House and 1,200 in the Senate) do much of the committee work, from honing ideas, suggesting policy options to members, scheduling hearings, and recruiting witnesses, to actually drafting legislation.[66] In most committees each party also has its own staff. Following the 1994 election, committee staffs were cut by one-third; however, members did not force any cuts in the sizes of their personal staffs.

Congressional Bureaucracy

Reflecting a reluctance dating from Vietnam and Watergate to be dependent on the executive branch for information, Congress has built its own research organizations and agencies to facilitate its work. Unlike personal or committee staffs, these are strictly nonpartisan, providing different kinds of expert advice and technical assistance. The Congressional Research Service (CRS), a unit of the Library of Congress, employs over eight hundred people to do research for members of Congress. For example, if Congress is considering a bill to relax air quality standards in factories, it can have the CRS determine what is known about the effects of air quality on worker health.

The Government Accountability Office (formerly the General Accounting Office but still known as the GAO), with its 3,200 employees, audits the books of executive departments and conducts policy evaluation and analysis. It issues reports such as *Nuclear Safety: NRC's Oversight of Fire Protection at U.S. Commercial Nuclear Reactor Units Could Be Strengthened,* and *Peacekeeping: Thousands Trained but United States Is Unlikely to Complete All Activities by 2010 and Some Improvements Are Needed.*[67] These studies are meant to help Congress determine the nature of policy problems, possible solutions, and what government agencies are actually doing. The GAO studies supplement the already substantial committee staffs working on legislation and oversight.

A third important congressional agency is the Congressional Budget Office (CBO). The CBO is Congress' economic adviser, providing members with economic estimates about the budget, the deficit or surplus, and the national debt, and forecasts of how they will be influenced by different tax and spending policies. The CBO's regularly updated estimates on the costs of various versions of the health care reform plans were a central element in congressional considerations of the bill. Congress has a stronger and more independent role in the policy process when it is not completely dependent on the executive branch for information and expertise.

Who What How

Members of Congress, the congressional leaders, and the parties are all vitally concerned with the rules of congressional organization. The members want autonomy to do their jobs and to respond to their constituents. But they are dependent on their leaders, and thus on their parties, for the committee assignments that enhance their job performance and help them gain expertise in areas that their constituents care about. Without party and leadership cooperation, the individual member of Congress, especially in the House where party control is stronger, is isolated and relatively powerless.

Congressional leaders want tight rules of organization so that they can control what their members do and say. Members of the House and the Senate make their own organizational rules, which give the dominant party in each house power over the internal rules and, consequently, over the policies produced.

How Congress Works
An already complex process, complicated further by internal and external forces

The policies passed by Congress are a result of both external and internal forces. The external environment includes the problems that are important to citizens at any given time—sometimes the economy, sometimes foreign affairs, at other times national security or the federal deficit or the plight of the homeless and so forth. The policy preferences of the president loom large in this external environment as well. It is often said, with some exaggeration but a bit of truth, that "the president proposes, the Congress disposes" of important legislation. Parties, always important, have been increasing their influence in the policymaking arena, and organized interests play a significant role as well.

The Context of Congressional Policymaking

Congress also has a distinct internal institutional environment that shapes the way it carries out its business. Three characteristics of this environment are especially important.

Separate Houses, Identical Bills

First, the Constitution requires that almost all congressional policy has to be passed in identical form by both houses. This requirement, laid out by the founders in the Constitution, makes the policy process difficult because the two houses serve different constituencies and operate under different decision-making procedures. Interests that oppose a bill and lose in one chamber can often be successful at defeating a bill in the other chamber. The opposition has to stop a bill in only one place to win, but the proponents have to win in both. In Congress, it is much easier to play defense than offense.

Fragmentation

The second overriding feature of the institutional environment of Congress as a policymaking institution is its fragmentation. As you read the next section, on how a bill becomes a law, notice how legislation is broken into bits, each considered individually in committees. It is very difficult to coordinate what one bill does with those laws that are already on the books or with what another committee might be doing in a closely related area. Thus we do such seemingly nonsensical things as simultaneously subsidizing tobacco growers and antismoking campaigns. This fragmentation increases opportunities for constituencies, individual members, and well-organized groups to influence policy in those niches about which they really care. The process also makes it very hard for national policymakers—the president or the congressional leaders—who would like to take a large-scale, coordinated approach to our major policy problems.

Norms of Conduct

The third critical feature of the institutional environment of Congress is the importance of *norms*, or informal rules that establish accepted ways of doing things. These are sometimes called "folkways" and are quickly learned by newcomers when they enter Congress. Norms include the idea that members should work hard, develop a specialization, treat other members with the utmost courtesy, reciprocate favors generally, and take pride in their chambers and in Congress. The purpose of congressional norms is to constrain conflict and personal animosity in an arena where disagreements

are inevitable, but they also aid in getting business done. Although congressional norms continue to be important, they are less constraining on members today than they were in the 1950s and 1960s.[68] The extent to which the norms of respect and decorum have been stretched is illustrated by the "You lie!" outburst by Rep. Joe Wilson, R-S.C., during President Obama's nationally televised health care address before a joint session of Congress in 2009. Although Wilson was persuaded by Republican colleagues to apologize, his behavior made him something of a hero on the far right. It is the case that current norms allow for more individualist, media-oriented, and adversarial behavior than in the past.

How a Bill Becomes a Law—Some of the Time

When we see something that seems unfair in business or in the workplace, when disaster strikes and causes much suffering, when workers go on strike and disrupt our lives—whenever a crisis occurs, we demand that government do something to solve the problem that we cannot solve on our own. This means government must have a policy, a set of laws, to deal with the problem. Because so many problems seem beyond the ability of individual citizens to solve, there is an almost infinite demand for new laws and policies, often with different groups demanding quite contradictory responses from the government.

This section considers briefly how demands for solutions become laws. We consider two aspects of congressional policy here: (1) the agenda, or the source of ideas for new policies; and (2) the legislative process, or the steps a bill goes through to become law. Very few proposed policies, as it turns out, actually make it into law, and those that do have a difficult path to follow.

Setting the Agenda

Before a law can be passed, it must be among the things that Congress thinks it ought to do. There is no official list of actions that Congress needs to take, but when a bill is proposed that would result in a significant change in policy, it must seem like a reasonable thing for members to turn their attention to—a problem that is possible, appropriate, and timely for them to try to solve with a new policy. That is, it must be on the *legislative agenda*. Potential new laws can get on Congress' agenda in several ways. First, because public attention is focused so intently on presidential elections and

> **policy entrepreneurship**   practice of legislators becoming experts and taking leadership roles in specific policy areas

campaigns, new presidents are especially effective at setting the congressional agenda. Later in their terms, presidents also use their yearly State of the Union addresses to outline the legislative agenda they would like Congress to pursue. Because the media and the public pay attention to the president, Congress does too. This does not guarantee presidential success, but it means the president can usually get Congress to give serious attention to his major policy proposals. His proposals may be efforts to fulfill campaign promises, to pay political debts, to realize ideological commitments, or to deal with a crisis.

A second way an issue gets on the legislative agenda is when it is triggered by a well-publicized event, even if the problem it highlights is not a new one at all. For example, the 2010 explosion of BP's oil drilling platform *Deepwater Horizon* and the subsequent release of millions of barrels of crude oil into the Gulf of Mexico drew the nation's attention to energy policy, the adequacy of regulatory procedures, and the need to protect the environment. What leaders in Washington will actually do in response to such an event is hard to predict, especially in circumstances in which they are unable to do much of anything (the federal government had neither the technical know-how nor the equipment to plug the oil well, for instance). Nonetheless, such events create a public demand that the government "do something!"

A third way an idea gets on the agenda is for some member or members to find it in their own interests, either political or ideological, to invest time and political resources in pushing the policy. Many members of Congress want to prove their legislative skills to their constituents, key supporters, the media, and fellow lawmakers. The search for the right issue to push at the right time is called *policy entrepreneurship*. Most members of Congress to greater or lesser degrees are policy entrepreneurs. Those with ambition, vision, and luck choose the issues that matter in our lives and

that can bring them significant policy influence and recognition, but most successful policy entrepreneurs are not widely recognized outside of the policy communities in which they operate.[69] Policy entrepreneurship by members is important in setting the congressional policy agenda, and it can reap considerable political benefits for those associated with important initiatives.

Legislative Process: Beginning the Long Journey

Bills, even those widely recognized as representing the president's legislative program, must be introduced by members of Congress. The formal introduction is done by putting a bill in the "hopper" (a wooden box) in the House, where it goes to the clerk of the House, or by giving it to the presiding officer in the Senate. The bill is then given a number (for example, HR932 in the House or S953 in the Senate) and begins the long journey that *might* result in its becoming law. Figure 7.10 shows the general route for a bill once it is introduced in either the House or the Senate, but the details can get messy, and there are exceptions (as Figure 7.11 shows). A bill introduced in the House goes first through the House and then on to the Senate, and vice versa. However, bills may be considered simultaneously in both houses.

Legislative Process: Moving Through Committee

The initial stages of committee consideration are similar for the House and the Senate. The bill first has to be referred to committee. This is largely automatic for most bills; they go to the standing committee with jurisdiction over the content of the bill. A bill to change the way agricultural subsidies on cotton are considered would start, for example, with the House Committee on Agriculture. In some cases, a bill might logically fall into more than one committee's jurisdiction, and here the Speaker exercises a good deal of power. He or she

---

Figure 7.10

How a Bill Becomes Law: Short Version

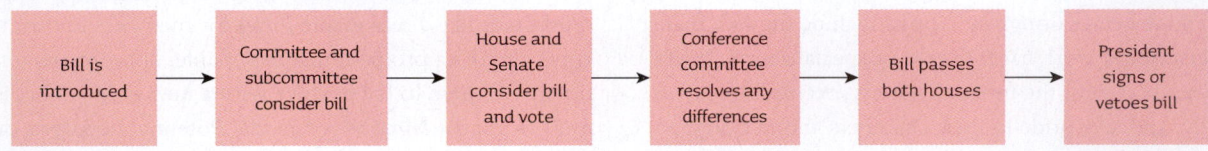

| Bill is introduced | Committee and subcommittee consider bill | House and Senate consider bill and vote | Conference committee resolves any differences | Bill passes both houses | President signs or vetoes bill |

> ***filibuster*** a practice of unlimited debate in the Senate in order to prevent or delay a vote on a bill
>
> ***cloture*** a vote to end a Senate filibuster; requires a three-fifths majority, or sixty votes

can choose the committee that will consider the bill or even refer the same bill to more than one committee. This gives the Speaker important leverage in the House because he or she often knows which committees are likely to be more or less favorable to different bills. Senators do not worry quite as much about where bills are referred because they have much greater opportunity to make changes later in the process than representatives do. We'll see why when we discuss floor consideration.

Bills then move on to subcommittees, where they may, or may not, get serious consideration. Most bills die in committee because the committee members either don't care about the issue (it isn't on their agenda) or actively want to block it. Even if the bill's life is brief, the member who introduced it can still campaign as its champion. In fact, a motivation for the introduction of many bills is not that the member seriously believes the bill has a chance of passing but that the member wants to be seen back home as taking some action on the issue.

Bills that subcommittees decide to consider will have hearings—testimony from experts, interest groups, executive department secretaries and undersecretaries, and even other members of Congress. The subcommittee deliberates and votes the bill back to the full committee. There the committee further considers the bill and makes changes and revisions in a process called *markup*. If the committee votes in favor of the final version of the bill, it goes forward to the floor. Here, however, a crucial difference exists between the House and the Senate.

Getting to the Floor: House Rules

In the House, bills go from the standing committee to the Rules Committee. This committee, highly responsive to the Speaker of the House, gives each bill a "rule," which includes when and how the bill will be considered. Some bills go out under an "open rule," which means that any amendments can be proposed and added as long as they are germane, or relevant, to the legislation under consideration. More typically, especially for important bills, the House leadership gains more control by imposing rules that limit the time for debate and restrict the amendments that can be offered. For example, if the leadership knows that there is a lot of sentiment in favor of action on a tax cut, it can control the form of the tax cut by having a restrictive rule that prohibits any amendments to the committee's bill. In this way, even members who would

like to vote for a different kind of tax cut face pressure to go along with the bill because they can't amend it; it is either this tax cut or none at all, and they don't want to vote against a tax cut. Thus, for some bills, not only can the House Rules Committee make or break the bill, but it can also influence the bill's final content.

Getting to the Floor: Senate Rules

The Senate generally guarantees all bills an "open rule" by default, and unlike in the House, there is no germane rule that says that an amendment must logically relate to the policy being considered. The majority leader, usually in consultation with the minority leader, schedules legislation for consideration. Their control, however, is fairly weak because any senator can introduce any proposal as an amendment to any bill, sometimes called a rider, and get a vote on it. Thus senators have access to the floor for whatever they want in a way that is denied to representatives. Furthermore, whereas in the House the rule for each bill stipulates how long a member can debate, the Senate's tradition of "unlimited debate," as we saw in the *What's at Stake?* that opened this chapter, means that a member can talk indefinitely. Senators opposed to a bill can ***filibuster*** in an effort to tie up the floor of the Senate in nonstop debate to stop the Senate from voting on a bill. A filibuster can be stopped only by ***cloture***. Cloture, a vote to cut off debate and end a filibuster, requires an extraordinary three-fifths majority, or sixty votes. A dramatic example of a filibuster occurred when southern senators attempted to derail Minnesota senator Hubert Humphrey's efforts to pass the Civil Rights Act of 1964. First, they filibustered Humphrey's attempt to bypass the Judiciary Committee, whose chair, a southern Democrat, opposed the bill. This was known as the "minibuster," and it stopped Senate business for sixteen days.[70] It was considered "mini" because from March 30 to June 30, 1964, these same southern Democrats filibustered the Civil Rights Act and created a twenty-week backlog of legislation.[71] Often these senators resorted to reading the telephone book in order to adhere to the rules of constant debate. The consequence of a filibuster, as this example suggests, is that a minority in the Senate is able to thwart the will of the majority. Even one single senator can halt action on a bill by placing a hold on the legislation, notifying the majority party's leadership that he or she plans to filibuster a bill. That threat alone often keeps the leadership from going forward with the legislation.[72]

Figure 7.11

How a Bill Becomes Law: Long Version

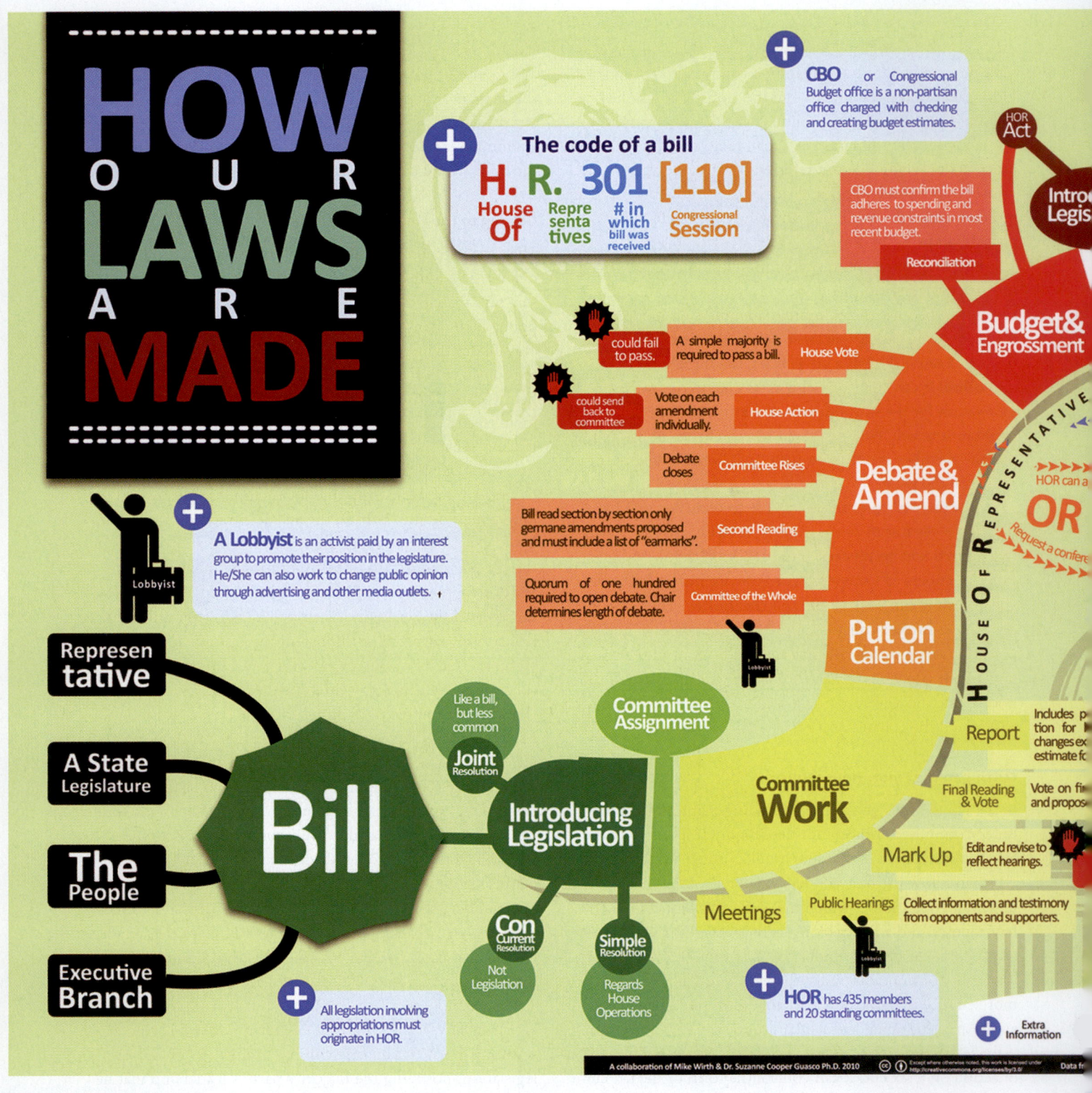

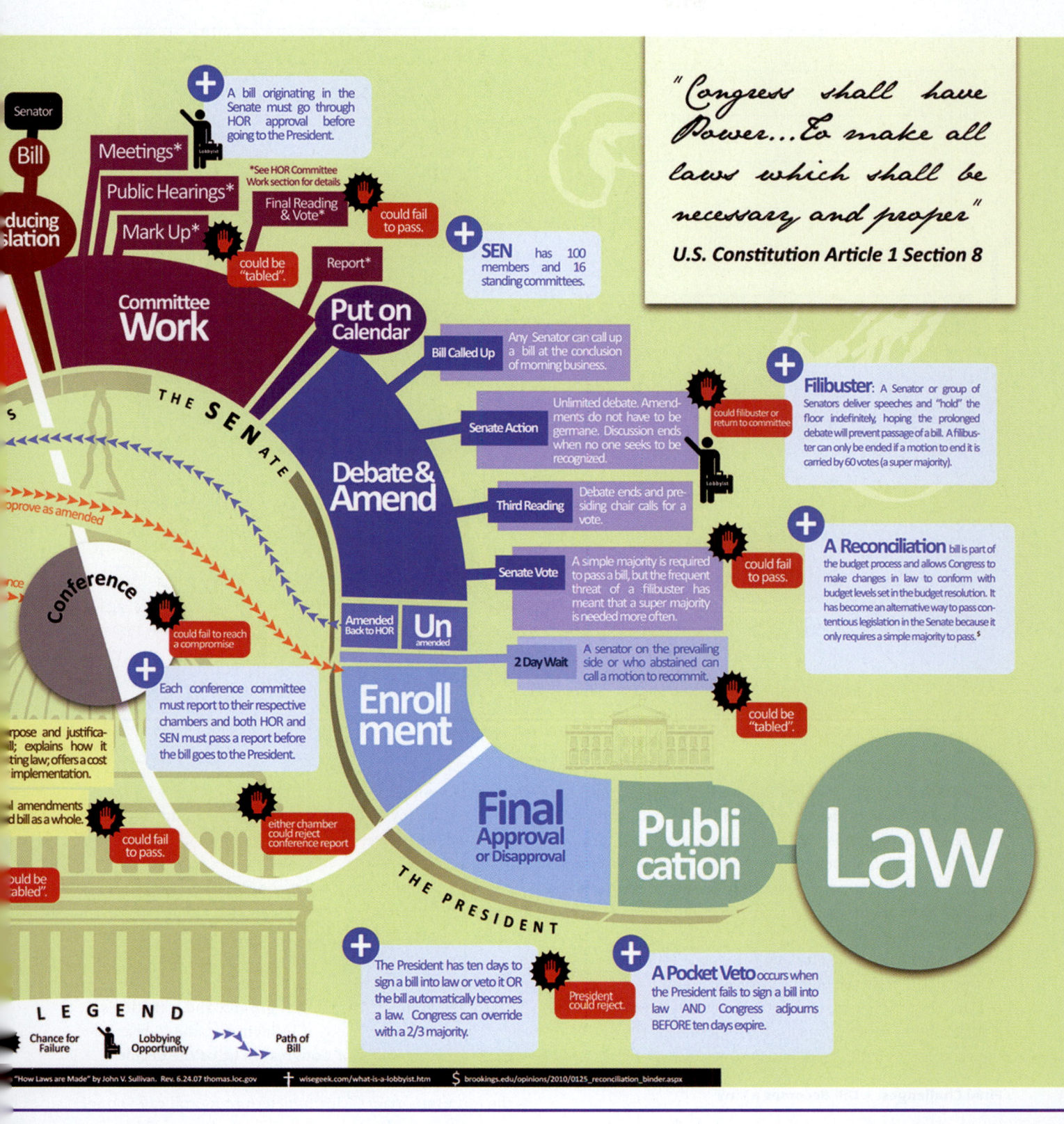

Figure 7.12

Cloture Votes to End Filibusters in the 66th to 111th Congresses (1919–2010)

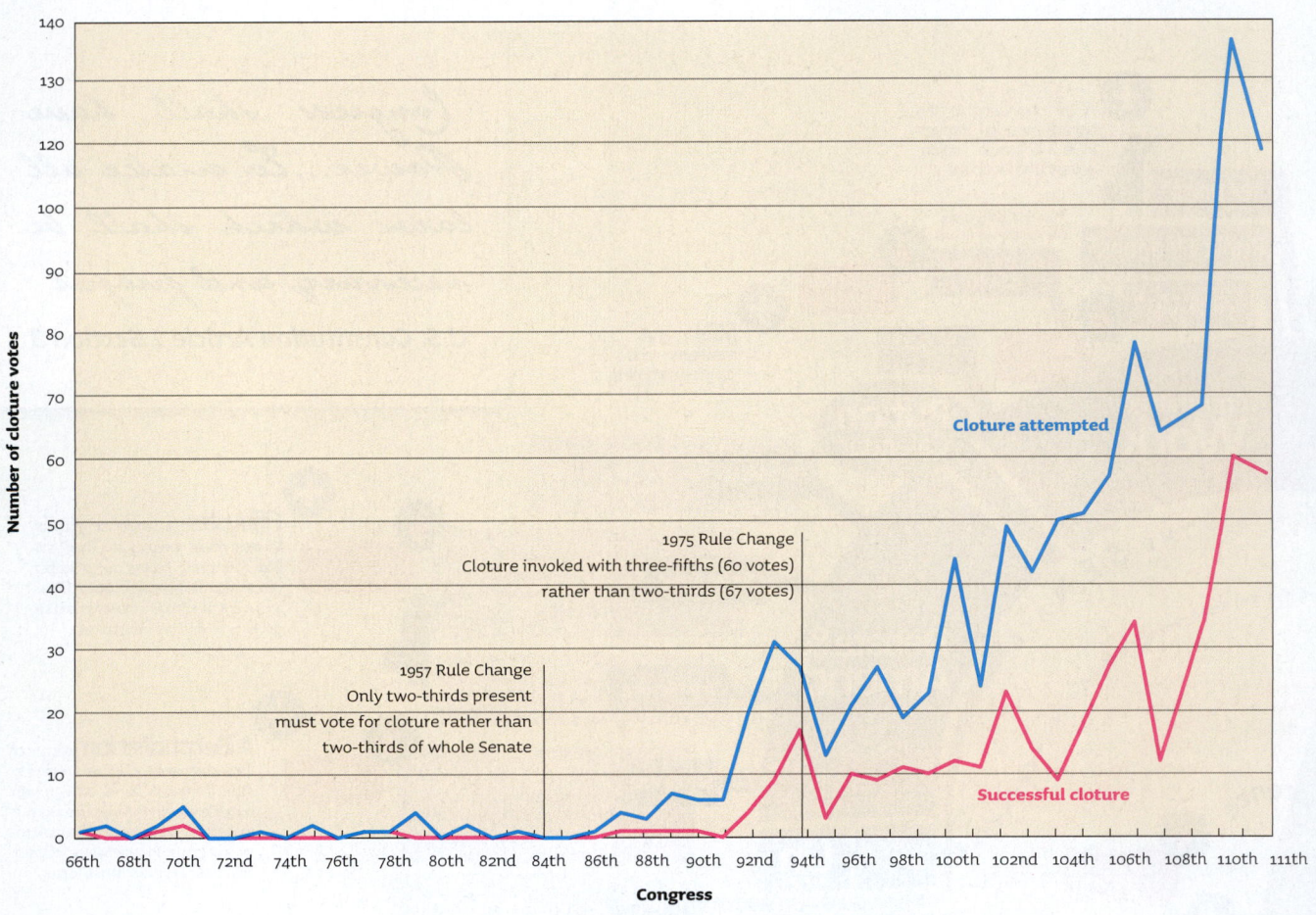

Source: "Senate Action on Cloture Motions," www.senate.gov/pagelayout/reference/cloture_motions/clotureCounts.htm.

Recent congressional sessions have seen a striking increase in the use of the filibuster, as shown in Figure 7.12, with congresses now averaging around forty attempts at cloture. Only about a third of these have been successful in mustering the necessary sixty votes, so a minority has prevailed over the majority most of the time. The use of the filibuster is considered "hardball politics"; its greater use in the past fifteen to twenty years reflects the growing party polarization we discussed earlier. In the highly charged partisan atmosphere of the U.S. Senate today, use of the filibuster and the consequent cloture motions reached an all-time high in the 110th Congress (2006–2008) with little prospect for change.[73]

Final Challenges: A Bill Becomes a Law

Clearly a bill must survive a number of challenges to get out of Congress alive. A bill can be killed, or just left to die, in a subcommittee, the full committee, the House Rules Committee, or any of the corresponding committees in the Senate; and, of course, it has to pass votes on the floors of both houses.

There are multiple ways for the House of Representatives to vote, including a simple voice vote ("all in favor say 'aye'"), but most important legislation requires each member to explicitly vote "yea" or "nay" in what are called **roll call votes**. These are a matter of public record and are monitored by the media, interest groups, and sometimes even constituents. A variety of influences come to bear on the senator or member of Congress as he or she decides how to vote. Studies have long shown that party affiliation is the most important factor in determining roll call voting, but constituency also plays a big role, as does presidential politics. Busy representatives often take cues from other

> **veto override**   reversal of a presidential veto by a two-thirds vote in both houses of Congress
>
> **pocket veto**   presidential authority to kill a bill submitted within ten days of the end of a legislative session by not signing it

> **roll call votes**   publicly recorded votes on bills and amendments on the floor of the House or Senate

members whom they respect and generally agree with.[74] They also consult with their staff, some of whom may be very knowledgeable about certain legislation. Finally, interest groups have an effect on how a member of Congress votes, but studies suggest that their impact is much less than we usually imagine. Lobbying and campaign contributions buy access to members so that the lobbyists can try to make their case, but they do not actually buy votes.[75]

The congressperson or senator who is committed to passing or defeating a particular bill cannot do so alone, however, and he or she looks to find like-minded members for political support. Once a representative or senator knows where he or she stands on a bill, there are a variety of methods for influencing the fate of that bill, many of them effective long before the floor vote takes place. Congressional politics—using the rules to get what one wants—can entail many complex strategies, including controlling the agenda (whether a bill ever reaches the floor), proposing amendments to a bill, influencing its timing, and forming coalitions with other members to pass or block a bill. Knowing how to use the rules makes a huge difference in congressional politics.

If a bill emerges from the roll call process in both houses relatively intact, it goes to the president, unless the chambers passed different versions. If the bills differ, then the two versions go to a conference committee made up of members of both houses, usually the senior members of the standing committees that reported the bills. If the conferees can reach an agreement on a revision, then the revised bill goes back to each house to be voted up or down; no amendments are permitted at this point. If the bill is rejected, that chamber sends it back to the conference committee for a second try.

Finally, any bill still alive at this point moves to the president's desk. He has several choices of action. The simplest choice is that he signs the bill and it becomes law. If he doesn't like it, however, he can veto it. In that case, the president sends it back to the originating house of Congress with a short explanation of what he does not like about the bill. Congress can then attempt a **veto override**, which requires a two-thirds vote of both houses. Because the president can usually count on the support of *at least* one-third of *one* of the houses, the veto is a powerful negative tool; it is hard for Congress to accomplish legislative goals that are opposed by the president. They can,

however, bundle policies together, so that the bill that arrives on the president's desk contains elements that he would typically want to veto along with legislation that is very hard for him to turn down. To get around this practice, Congress introduced and passed in 1996 a controversial line-item veto bill, which would have allowed presidents to strike out spending provisions they didn't like, but the Supreme Court ruled in June 1998 that the line-item veto was unconstitutional.[76]

The president can also kill a bill with the **pocket veto**, which occurs when Congress sends a bill to the president within ten days of the end of a session and the president does not sign it. The bill fails simply because Congress is not in session to consider a veto override. The president might choose this option when he wants to veto a bill without drawing much public attention to it. Similarly, the president can do nothing, and if Congress remains in session, a bill will automatically become law in ten days, excluding Sundays. This seldom-used option signals presidential dislike for a bill but not enough dislike for him to use his veto power.

The striking aspect of our legislative process is how many factors have to fall into place for a bill to become law. At every step there are ways to kill bills, and a well-organized group of members in the relatively decentralized Congress has a good chance, in most cases, of blocking a bill to which these members strongly object. In terms of procedures, Congress is better set up to ensure that bills do not impinge on organized interests than it is to facilitate coherent, well-coordinated attacks on the nation's problems. Once again, we see a balance between representation and effective lawmaking, with the procedures of passage tilted toward the forces for representation.

All American political actors, those in Washington and those outside, have something important at stake in the legislative process. The president has a huge stake in what Congress does in terms of fulfilling his own campaign promises, supporting his party's policy goals, and building his political legacy. He can influence the legislative agenda; try to persuade his fellow party members in Congress to support his policies; take his case to the people; or, once the process is under way, threaten to veto or, in fact, use several different veto techniques.

Who What How

▶ Who, What, How, and WHEN: Congress and Title IX

Hard though it may be to believe today, as recently as forty years ago there were no laws requiring equal education for women. Many law and medical schools admitted only a few women to special spots reserved for them, and women's sports teams were few or nonexistent in high schools and colleges across the country. This began to change in 1972 when Congress passed Title IX, which called for equal treatment of women and men in education. Sometimes passing legislation is only the first step to making significant social or political change. Consider the importance of the events that followed Title IX legislation over time in creating equal educational opportunities for women:

1972   Creation of Title IX

After President Nixon's Task Force on Women's Rights and Responsibilities in 1970 revealed that women lacked employment opportunities because of sex differences in education, members of Congress proposed several bills to end such discrimination. Their compromise bill, Title IX of the Higher Education Amendments, required any school receiving federal funding to end sex discrimination in education. The bill passed in 1972.

1975   Title IX Regulations

After Title IX passed, the Department of Health, Education, and Welfare (HEW) was charged with implementing the law by writing regulations to create equality in education. Writing regulations was controversial; HEW received 9,700 comments about what the regulations should (or should not) be. This was largely because of controversies over how far sex equality in education had to go; textbooks, same-sex education, and especially athletics were all potentially subject to regulation. HEW released the initial regulations in 1974, President Ford signed them in 1975, and Congress reviewed them.

1979   Clarifying Athletic Policy

In response to widespread confusion over the enforcement of Title IX with regard to athletics, in 1979 HEW issued another round of regulations clarifying equality in athletics. Known as the "three-part test," it required schools to demonstrate in one of three ways that they were providing athletic opportunities for women: through having proportions of male and female athletes that were roughly proportional to the student body, through a history of expanding athletic opportunities for women, or through fully accommodating the interests and abilities of women athletes.

But it is Congress that has the most range and flexibility when it comes to passing or stopping legislation. Members want to satisfy constituents, build national reputations or platforms on which to run for future office, and accomplish ideological goals. They have a wealth of legislative tools and strategies at their disposal. But success is not just a matter of knowing the rules. It is personality, luck, timing, and context, as well as political skill in using the rules that make a successful legislator. Repeated filibusters may accomplish a political goal, but if they earn a party a reputation as partisan and uncooperative, they could also cause voter backlash. Legislative politics is a complex balance of rules and processes that favors the skilled politician.

The Citizens and Congress
Public frustration with a slow-moving institution

Academics and journalists spend a great deal of time speculating about what the decline in public support for our political institutions means for American democracy.[77] In this final section we look at the implications for citizens of their increasingly negative views of the U.S. Congress. While public approval of Congress spiked in the wake of September 11,

1984 — Grove City College v. Bell, 1984

Bucking against the changes required under Title IX, Grove City College, in western Pennsylvania, although supporting the equality required by Title IX, argued that the federal assistance received by a few of its students did not subject the entire institution to federal regulation. In *Grove City College v. Bell*, the Supreme Court agreed, saying the regulations could be applied only to programs that directly received federal funding rather than to the entire institution. This ruling severely limited the enforcement of Title IX as of 1984.

1987 — Civil Rights Restoration Act

In response to the decision in *Grove City College*, Congress sought to reinstate the wider interpretation of Title IX as passed in 1972. Several bills were introduced over three years; finally, in 1987 Congress passed the Civil Rights Restoration Act, which specified that any regulations regarding civil rights, such as Title IX, had to apply to the entire institution receiving federal funds and not just the part of the institution that was the recipient. President Reagan vetoed the legislation, but Congress overrode the veto and broad reinforcement of Title IX was reinstated.

2005 — Clarifying Athletic Policy Again

Even after the Civil Rights Restoration Act, controversy over the enforcement of Title IX continued, particularly regarding athletics. In the 1990s new regulations allowed victims of Title IX violations to sue for monetary damages, and a series of lawsuits reinforced the idea that colleges had to provide athletic opportunities for women. However, in 2005 the Department of Education issued a new regulation stating that, if campus surveys showed there was no interest in women's sports among female students, institutions could be considered in compliance with Title IX. This lowered the bar for compliance with the law. As of 2008, it remains to be seen whether Congress will respond.

from 1974 through the 1990s, periodic Gallup polls showed that less than a third of the public "approves of the way Congress is handling its job." In 2010 this proportion dropped to just 16 percent! Part of the blame may be attributed to a general decline in respect for societal institutions ranging from government to organized religion to the media.[78] But the behavior of Congress itself must also be examined.

At least four factors help to explain why citizens are not always very happy with Congress. First, some candidates encourage a negative image of the institution they want to join—running for Congress by running against it, and declaring their intention to fight against special interests, bureaucrats, and the general incompetence of Washington.[79]

Second, in the post-Watergate wave of investigative reporting, media coverage of Congress has become more negative, even though impartial observers say that Congress is probably less corrupt than ever before. Third, since the 1970s, the law requires that information about how much campaigns cost and who contributes to them must be made public, casting a shadow of suspicion on the entire process and raising the concern that congressional influence can be bought. Finally, citizens are turned off by what they see as incessant bickering and partisanship in Congress.

Given the reasons why many Americans are unhappy with Congress, most of the reforms currently on the agenda are not likely to change their minds. One of the most popular

THE BOONDOCKS © 2002 Aaron McGruder. Dist. by UNIVERSAL Uclick. Reprinted with permission. All rights reserved.

reforms being advocated is term limits. The specific proposals vary, but the intent is to limit the number of terms a member of Congress can serve, usually to somewhere between eight and twelve years. Term limits might work if there was evidence that serving in Congress corrupts good people, but there is no such evidence, and thus the reform would not be likely to bring about a "cleaner" institution. Other reforms, however, might make a difference in public support for Congress. Campaign finance reform, for instance, could have a significant impact. Institutional reforms might be able to speed up congressional lawmaking and reduce the need to compromise on details.

Such reforms, however, will probably not fundamentally change how the public feels about Congress. Congress does have the power to act, and when it is unified and sufficiently motivated, it usually does. When Congress reflects a sharply divided society, however, it has a harder time getting things done. It is unable to act *because it is a representative institution*, not because members are inattentive to their districts or in the grip of special interests. Furthermore, Congress has more incentives on a daily basis to be a representative institution than a national lawmaking body. It is important to remember, too, that this slow process is not entirely an accident. It was the founders' intention to create a legislature that would not move hastily or without deliberation. The irony is that the founders' mixed bag of

incentives works so well that Congress today often does not move very much at all.

The truth is that democracy is messy. Bickering arises in Congress because members represent many different Americans with varied interests and goals. It is precisely our bickering, our inefficiency, and our willingness to compromise, to give and take, that preserve the freedoms Americans hold dear. It is the nature of representative government. We conclude where we began. Congress has the dual goals of lawmaking and representation. These goals often and necessarily conflict. The practice of congressional politics is fascinating to many close-up observers but looks rather ugly as we average citizens understand it, based on the nightly news and what we hear during campaigns. It is important to understand, however, that this view of Congress stems from the contradictions in the expectations we place on the body more than the failings of the people we send to Washington.

Thinking Outside the Box

What difference does it make that Americans dislike Congress so much?

▶ What's at Stake Revisited

We've learned enough about politics to know that Congress is a rule-based institution, and as always, the rules determine who wins and who loses. One of the trickier rules is the filibuster, which as we saw in the *What's at Stake?* earlier in this chapter, has its ardent foes as well as its passionate defenders.

But what is true here, of course, is that the opponents and defenders change sides with their electoral fortunes. Republicans love the filibuster when they are in the minority and it enables them to block a Democratic majority, but not so much when it's the other way around. In 2005 Republican Senate majority leader Bill Frist was so frustrated with Democratic filibusters of President Bush's judicial nominees that he threatened to use what Republicans were calling the "nuclear option." Essentially, Frist would have called on the presiding officer of the Senate for a ruling on the constitutionality of the use of the judicial filibuster, and that officer (probably Bush's vice president, Dick Cheney) would have ruled it unconstitutional. Moderate Republicans warned that their party would not always be in the majority and that they would someday regret it if they eliminated the traditional protection for a Senate minority. Along with moderate Democrats, they crafted a compromise that averted the nuclear option. And as that example makes clear, Democrats are not nearly as opposed to the filibuster when they are in the minority as Speaker Pelosi's comments that the filibuster is a

"60-vote stranglehold on the future"[80] would suggest.

The filibuster is a rule that gives the minority power, and both parties are aware that one or the other of them will always be in the minority. As we have seen, however, the use of the filibuster has skyrocketed in the recent past, making it the norm even for routine legislation in the Senate. Rather than debating a bill and registering their disapproval by voting against it, opposing senators prevent the debate from happening in the first place. In summer 2010, Democratic senator Russ Feingold from Wisconsin actually joined a Republican filibuster of financial regulatory reform. Republicans were opposed to the bill because they felt it infringed on the rights of business, and Feingold opposed it because he felt that it didn't infringe enough on the rights of business, but no matter. Politics makes strange bedfellows, and it wasn't until Majority Leader Harry Reid peeled off the support of a couple of Republicans that the vote went through.

Americans are advocates of the idea of supporting a downtrodden minority against a tyrannical majority, but in the case of the filibuster, it is the minority that threatens to become tyrannical, holding a majority of senators and, by implication, the voters who elected them, hostage. One of the reasons that Americans don't like their Congress is because so often legislative business gets mired down in partisan wrangling; the filibuster is one more rule by which this can take place.

In 2007, when the Democrats had only a 51–49 majority in the Senate, former Democratic congressman David Obey said: "They [the public] think we have control of the Senate while we merely have custody. They think that we can control the Senate when in fact we are nine votes short of having the 60 votes that you need to actually run the Senate. So the Senate is a choke point on everything."[81]

Fearing rapid political change, the American founders built a good deal of gridlock into their constitutional design, with checks and balances slowing the policymaking process down to a snail's pace under the best of circumstances. The filibuster can grind the snail's pace to a complete halt. Norm Ornstein of the conservative American Enterprise Institute says, "This is a sharp increase in the use of a filibuster as a routine mechanism. The Senate is set up culturally not to act on anything quickly. That's a good thing. But there can be too much of a good thing."[82]

Politicians, though, are unlikely to agree. Although Democrats have tried to weaken it, changing the number of votes needed for cloture from sixty-seven to an easier-to-achieve sixty in 1975, and although they talk of exercising a nuclear option of their own, the chances of reform are slim. One thing is sure in American politics: although the Democrats didn't lose the majority in the 2010 election, they will lose it someday, and the filibuster will seem like a route to righteous opposition when they do.

To Sum Up

Key terms, chapter summaries, practice quizzes, Internet links, and other study aids are available on the companion web site at http://republic.cqpress.com.

Define | Understand | Practice | Read | Click | Watch

allocative representation (p. 243)

bicameral legislature (p. 245)

casework (p. 243)

cloture (p. 273)

coattail effect (p. 253)

conference committees (p. 268)

congressional oversight (p. 247)

constituency (p. 242)

descriptive representation (p. 257)

filibuster (p. 273)

franking (p. 243)

gerrymandering (p. 250)

House Rules Committee (p. 268)

incumbency advantage (p. 253)

joint committees (p. 268)

legislative agenda (p. 271)

majority party (p. 261)

midterm loss (p. 253)

national lawmaking (p. 241)

norms (p. 271)

party polarization (p. 261)

pocket veto (p. 277)

policy entrepreneurship (p. 272)

policy representation (p. 243)

pork barrel (p. 243)

racial gerrymandering (p. 250)

reapportionment (p. 249)

redistricting (p. 250)

representation (p. 241)

roll call votes (p. 276)

select committee (p. 268)

seniority system (p. 265)

Speaker of the House (p. 263)

standing committees (p. 267)

strategic politicians (p. 253)

symbolic representation (p. 243)

veto override (p. 277)

Define | **Understand** | Practice | Read | Click | Watch

- Members of Congress are responsible for both representation and lawmaking. These two duties are often at odds because what is good for a local district may not be beneficial for the country as a whole.
- Representation style takes four different forms—policy, allocative, casework, and symbolic—and congresspersons attempt to excel at all four. However, since the legislative process designed by the founders is meant to be very slow, representatives have fewer incentives to concentrate on national lawmaking when reelection interests, and therefore local interests, are more pressing.
- The founders created our government with a structure of checks and balances. In addition to checking each other, the House and the Senate may be checked by either the president or the courts. Congress is very powerful but must demonstrate unusual strength and consensus to override presidential vetoes and to amend the Constitution.

- Citizens and representatives interact in congressional elections. The incumbency effect is powerful in American politics because those in office often create legislation that makes it difficult for challengers to succeed.
- Representatives want autonomy and choice committee assignments to satisfy constituent concerns. They achieve these goals by joining together into political parties and obeying their leadership and party rules. House and Senate members make their own organizational rules, which means that the dominant party in each house has great power over the internal rules of Congress and what laws are made.
- Citizens, interest groups, the president, and members of Congress all have a stake in the legislative process. Voters organized into interest groups may have a greater impact on legislative outcomes than may the individual. Yet Congress, with various legislative tools and strategies, holds the most sway over the fate of legislation.

Define   Understand   Practice   Read   Click   Watch

1. **What does it mean that the U.S. Congress is a bicameral legislature?**
    a. It has only one legislative chamber.
    b. It has two legislative chambers, but one (the Senate) has more powers.
    c. It has two legislative chambers, with each having equal power overall.
    d. It has one chamber with legislative power and one chamber with executive power.
    e. It has two legislative chambers with equal power, but they have no checks upon each other.

2. **The reallocation of U.S. House seats among the states every ten years is called**
    a. the census.
    b. reapportionment.
    c. redistricting.
    d. gerrymandering.
    e. partisan gerrymandering.

3. **Which of the following is NOT a factor that explains why citizens today are generally angry at Congress?**
    a. Successful campaigning for Congress often takes the form of running against the institution of Congress.
    b. The media have increased negative coverage of Congress.
    c. The importance of money in campaigns makes the public suspicious of the involvement of special interests in lawmaking.
    d. The public has a poor view of how democracy fares in congressional politics because of such things as long debates, compromise, and deal making.
    e. The public is frustrated with their representatives and senators for putting the national interest in front of their district's or state's interests.

4. **The majority of work done in Congress is done in what type of committee?**
    a. Conference committees
    b. Rules committees
    c. Ethics committees
    d. Standing committees
    e. Select committees

5. **Which of the following statements does NOT describe part of the process of how a bill becomes a law?**
    a. It is difficult for a bill to get on the congressional agenda.
    b. Most bills die in standing committees.
    c. The rules and steps for passage are identical in the House and the Senate.
    d. The process has numerous complex steps with drawbacks at many stages.
    e. A bill might not pass even if a strong majority supports the legislation.

Define   Understand   Practice   Read   Click   Watch

Bell, Lauren Cohen. 2004. *Master the U.S. Congress: A Simulation for Students.* Belmont, Calif.: Wadsworth. *Provides a hands-on simulation of how Congress functions and how representatives and senators behave, given the structure of Congress and the challenges of both representing constituents and making law.*

Caro, Robert A. 2002. *Master of the Senate: The Years of Lyndon Johnson.* New York: Knopf. *The third in a planned series of four books about Johnson. This lengthy book details Johnson's expert use of power to rise to the top leadership position in the Senate.*

CQ's *Politics in America.* 2009. Washington, D.C.: CQ Press. *Make this your first stop when researching individual members of Congress, their districts, or their states. Contains voting records, campaign expenditures, state and district demographics, and more.*

CQ *Weekly.* *The best source for the most recent happenings in Congress. It has especially great election coverage.*

Davidson, Roger H., Walter J. Oleszek, and Frances E. Lee. 2009. *Congress and Its Members,* 12th ed. Washington, D.C.: CQ Press. *Clarifies even the most complex aspects of Congress.*

Dodd, Larry, and Bruce Oppenheimer, eds. 2009. *Congress Reconsidered,* 9th ed. Washington, D.C.: CQ Press. *A rich collection of material related to some of the most pressing issues regarding Congress.*

Fenno, Richard F., Jr. 1978. *Home Style: House Members in Their Districts.* Boston: Little, Brown. *The author hits the campaign trail with several members of Congress to get a better understanding of the congressperson-constituent relationship.*

Herrnson, Paul S. 2008. *Congressional Elections: Campaigning at Home and in Washington,* 5th ed. Washington, D.C.: CQ Press. *An informative book on congressional elections and how their campaigns are waged.*

Jacobson, Gary C. 2009. *The Politics of Congressional Elections, 7th ed. New York: Longman.* An in-depth examination of congressional elections emphasizing challengers' decisions to run for office.

Parker, Glenn R. 1986. *Homeward Bound: Explaining Changes in Congressional Behavior. Pittsburgh: University of Pittsburgh Press.* An insightful and well-documented account of why and when members of Congress visit their home states and districts.

Sinclair, Barbara. 2008. *Unorthodox Lawmaking: New Legislative Processes in the U.S. Congress, 3rd ed. Washington, D.C.: CQ Press.* An inside view of the modern Congress that, as this chapter suggests, illustrates how different lawmaking and politics are in Congress than most "textbook" descriptions suggest.

Define | Understand | Practice | Read | Click | Watch

See "*Consider the Source: Don't Be Fooled by Your Elected Officials*" for useful congressional Internet sources.

The Center on Congress at Indiana University *http:// congress.indiana.edu. This useful web site provides historical and institutional information about the work and role of Congress, especially highlighting the positive role Congress has played in the lives of Americans.*

Thomas *http://thomas.loc.gov. This Library of Congress web site is designed to provide legislative information to the public. It provides voting records, committee reports, and current legislation, and even allows an interested web surfer to search the* Congressional Record *to see what anyone in Congress has said about any particular subject.*

U.S. House of Representatives *www.house.gov. The official web site of the U.S. House of Representatives provides an entry into individual representatives' web sites and those of different House committees, as well as information on the processes, calendar, and votes of Congress.*

U.S. Senate *www.senate.gov. The official Senate web site provides contact information for senators and Senate committees; information on bill traffic and calendars; and quizzes, art history, and facts about this chamber.*

Define | Understand | Practice | Read | Click | Watch

Advise and Consent *1962. Based on the Pulitzer Prize–winning novel of the same name, this political classic starring Henry Fonda examines partisan politics and power as the Senate must determine the suitability of Robert Leffingwell (Fonda) for secretary of state. A fierce debate ensues on the Senate floor, while behind the scenes scandal and bribery flourish.*

The Candidate *1972. Robert Redford plays a charismatic Senate candidate.*

Charlie Wilson's War *2007. Free-wheeling Texas congressman Charlie Wilson (played by Tom Hanks) circumnavigates the* legislative process when he collaborates with a rogue CIA operative (Philip Seymour Hoffman) to assist Afghan rebels in their fight against the Soviet Union.

The Contender *2000. Senator Laine Hanson, played by Joan Allen, vies to be the first female vice president, but a scandal brought on by a political foe threatens to derail her aspirations.*

Mr. Smith Goes to Washington *1939. Frank Capra's classic story about a young politician who is appointed to the Senate and, defying his party's bosses, fights the leaders' corruption.*

Chapter 8
The Presidency

▶ What's at Stake?

When President George W. Bush signed the newly passed reauthorization of the Patriot Act in March 2006, he did so with a public and patriotic flourish. Sitting at a desk behind a banner with the words "Protecting the Homeland" on a red, white, and blue background, he proclaimed that this legislation was "vital to win the war on terror and to protect the American people."[1]

The news cameras that day showed a bunch of men smiling for the cameras. Bush was happy because he had gotten what he wanted from Congress on this bill—among other things, beefed-up police powers for the Federal Bureau of Investigation. Congress was happy because the bill contained carefully crafted oversight provisions to keep those new powers in check: the Justice Department, part of the executive branch, was required to keep Congress informed about how the FBI was using the powers granted to them by the bill. Everyone was happy as they grinned for the cameras while the president wielded his pen.

But out of sight of public view, something was happening that was going to make Congress, or at least the members of it who did not belong to the president's party, extremely unhappy indeed.

Very quietly, without the public display that greeted the bill's signing, the White House issued a document saying that the president didn't really consider himself bound by the requirement that Congress be kept informed, and he reserved the right to withhold information if he deemed that it would "impair foreign relations, national security, the deliberative process of the executive, or the performance of the executive's constitutional duties."[2]

This document, known as a signing statement, was intended to "clarify" the president's understanding of what a bill meant and how he believed it ought to be enforced. Most people in Congress didn't even notice that the signing statement had been added, but those who did were furious. Democratic senator Patrick Leahy from Vermont called the signing statement "nothing short of a radical effort to manipulate the constitutional separation of powers and evade accountability and responsibility for following the law." He added, "The president's constitutional duty is to faithfully execute the

Protecting the Homeland
On March 9, 2006, President George W. Bush shared a laugh with members of Congress as he signed the renewal of the USA Patriot Act at the White House. He was joined for the occasion by (from left to right) Republican senator Pat Roberts of Kansas, Republican representative Peter King of New York, Republican representative F. James Sensenbrenner of Wisconsin, Republican senator Arlen Specter of Pennsylvania, and Republican Speaker of the House of Representatives Dennis Hastert of Illinois.

laws as written by the Congress, not cherry-pick the laws he decides he wants to follow. It is our duty to ensure, by means of congressional oversight, that he does so."[3]

Bush did not invent the signing statement. Since the 1800s, presidents had been issuing statements if they thought a part of a bill they signed was unconstitutional, especially if they thought it unconstitutionally restricted executive power, but these signing statements, recorded in the *Federal Register*, along with the legislation they refer to, had been used only sparingly. Typically presidents used the presidential veto to block legislation they didn't like, whereupon Congress could override the veto if the bill had sufficient support.

But unlike his predecessors, Bush had not vetoed a single bill by the time he issued the Patriot Act signing statement, after more than five years

in office. Instead he had issued a huge number of signing statements, over 750, compared to 232 by his father in his four years in the White House, and only 140 issued by Bill Clinton in his eight years. Bush's successor, President Barack Obama, would veto two bills and issue only about a dozen signing statements in his first two years in office.

Many of Bush's signing statements reflected a strong commitment to the theory of the *unitary executive*, a controversial legal view held by members of the administration that the Constitution requires that all executive power be held only by the president and, therefore, cannot be delegated to or wielded by any other branch. Consequently Bush's signing statements reserved the right to ignore, among other things, an anti-torture law, a law forbidding him to order troops into combat in Colombia, a law requiring him to inform Congress

if he wanted to divert funds from congressionally authorized programs to start up secret operations, a law preventing the military from using intelligence about Americans that was gathered unconstitutionally, a law that required the Justice Department to inform Congress about how the FBI was using domestic wiretapping, laws that created whistleblower protection for federal employees, and laws that required the federal government to follow affirmative action principles.[4]

Critics of the Bush administration howled when they realized what was going on, accusing Bush of doing an end run around Congress and claiming that he was setting up himself, and thus the executive branch, as the ultimate decider of what is constitutional, a function generally thought to belong to the Supreme Court. "There is no question that this administration has been involved in a very carefully thought-out, systematic process of expanding presidential power at the expense of the other branches of government," said one scholar.[5]

Defenders advised calm, saying that Bush didn't actually violate all those laws, but he simply reserved the right to do so as a way of letting Congress and the bureaucracy know how he interprets the legislation he has signed. One law professor who used to work for the Bush administration said of signing statements, "Nobody reads them. They have no significance. Nothing in the world changes by the publication of a signing statement."[6]

Who is right here, critics or champions? Are signing statements terribly damaging wounds to the Constitution, or meaningless pieces of paper? Are all signing statements equal? What exactly was at stake in Bush's expanded use of the tactic, and in his adherence to the unitary theory of the executive? We return to these questions after we look more closely at the powers and limitations of the U.S. president. ■

[O]ne of the most remarkable things about the modern presidency is how much the office has become intertwined with public expectations and perceptions.

Ask just about anyone who the most powerful person in the world is and the answer will probably be "the president of the United States." He, or perhaps someday soon, she, is the elected leader of the nation that has one of the most powerful economies, one of the greatest military forces, and the longest-running representative government that the world has ever seen. Media coverage enforces this belief in the importance of the U.S. president. The networks and news services all have full-time reporters assigned to the White House. The evening news tells us what the president has been doing that day. Even if he only went to church or played a round of golf, his activities are news. This attention is what one scholar calls the presidency's "monopolization of the public space."[7] It means that the president is the first person the citizens and the media think of when anything of significance happens, whether it is a terrorist attack, a natural disaster, or a big drop in the stock market. We look to the president to solve our problems and to represent the nation in our times of struggle, tragedy, and triumph. The irony is that the U.S. Constitution provides for a relatively weak chief executive, and the American public's and, indeed, the world's expectations of the president constitute a major challenge for modern presidents.

The challenge of meeting the public's expectations is made all the more difficult because so many political actors have something at stake in the office of the presidency. Most obviously, the president himself wants to widen his authority to act so that he can deliver on campaign promises and extend the base of support for himself and his party. Although the formal rules of American politics create only limited presidential powers, informal rules help him expand them. Citizens, both individually and in groups, often have high expectations of what the president will do for them and for the country, and they may be willing to allow him more expanded powers to act. An unpopular president, however, will face a public eager to limit his options and ready to complain about any perceived step beyond the restrictive constitutional bounds. Congress, too, stands to gain or lose based on the president's success. Members of the president's party will share some of his popularity, but in general the more power the president has, the less Congress has. This is especially true if the majority party in Congress is different from the president's. So Congress has a stake in limiting what the president may do.

This chapter tells the story of who gets what from the American presidency and how they get it. You will learn about

- *the double expectations gap between what Americans want the president to do and what he can deliver*
- *the evolution of the American presidency from its constitutional origins to the modern presidency*
- *the president's struggle for power*
- *the organization and functioning of the executive office*
- *the role of presidential personality and style*
- *the relationship of citizens to the presidency*

The Double Expectations Gap

Public expectations and the reality of what the president can actually do

Presidential scholars note that one of the most remarkable things about the modern presidency is how much the office has become intertwined with public expectations and perceptions. The implication, of course, is that we expect one thing and get something less—that there is a gap between our expectations and reality. In fact, we can identify two different expectations gaps when it comes to popular perceptions of the presidency. One is between the very great promises that presidents make, and that we want them to keep, on the one hand, and the president's limited constitutional power to fulfill those promises on the other. The second gap is between two conflicting roles that the president is expected to play, between the formal and largely symbolic role of head of state and the far more political role of head of government. These two expectations gaps form a framework for much of our discussion of the American presidency.

The Gap Between Presidential Promises and the Powers of the Office

The first gap between what the public expects the president to do and what he can actually accomplish is of relatively recent vintage. Through the 1930s the presidency in the United

Table 8.1

Length of Time in Office for the Last Nine Presidents

President	Terms served
John F. Kennedy	Assassinated in the third year of his first term.
Lyndon Johnson	Served out Kennedy's term, elected to one term of his own. Chose not to run for reelection, knowing he would lose.
Richard Nixon	Served one full term, reelected, resigned halfway through second term.
Gerald Ford	Served out Nixon's term. Ran for reelection and lost.
Jimmy Carter	Served one full term. Ran for reelection and lost.
Ronald Reagan	Served two full terms.
George H. W. Bush	Served one full term. Ran for reelection and lost.
Bill Clinton	Served two full terms. Impeached but acquitted halfway through second term.
George W. Bush	Served two full terms.

States was pretty much the office the founders had planned, an administrative position dwarfed by the extensive legislative power of Congress. During Franklin Roosevelt's New Deal, however, public expectations of the president changed. Roosevelt did not act like an administrator with limited powers; he acted like a leader whose strength and imagination could be relied on by an entire nation of citizens to rescue them from the crisis of the Great Depression. Over the course of Roosevelt's four terms in office, the public became used to seeing the president in just this light, and future presidential candidates promised similarly grand visions of policy in their efforts to win supporters. Rather than strengthening the office to allow presidents to deliver on such promises, however, the only constitutional change in the presidency weakened it. In reaction to Roosevelt's four elections, the Twenty-second Amendment was passed, limiting the number of terms a president can serve to two.

Today's presidents suffer the consequences of this history. On the one hand, we voters demand that they woo us with promises to change the course of the country, to solve our problems, and to enact visionary policy. On the other hand, we have not increased the powers of the office to meet this greatly expanded job description. Thus, to meet our expectations, the president must wheel, deal, bargain, and otherwise gather the support needed to overcome his constitutional limitations. And if the president doesn't meet our expectations, or if the country doesn't thrive the way we think it should, even if it isn't his fault and there's nothing he could have done to change things, we hold him accountable and vote him out of office. Some evidence of this can be seen in the fates of the past nine presidents; only four have been reelected to a second term, and of those, Richard Nixon resigned after Watergate,

Ronald Reagan faced the Iran-contra scandal and his party lost its majority in the Senate, Bill Clinton was impeached, and George W. Bush won reelection by the smallest margin of any reelected president and left office with the lowest level of public approval of any president finishing two full terms. The inability of some of our most skilled politicians to survive for even two full terms of office (see Table 8.1) suggests that our expectations of what can be done potentially outstrip the resources and powers of the position.

Thinking Outside the Box

How might presidential behavior change if we once again allowed presidents to serve more than two terms?

The Gap Between Conflicting Roles

The second expectations gap that presidents face is in part a product of the first. Since we now expect our presidents to perform as high-level legislators as well as administrators, holders of this office need to be adept politicians. That is, today's presidents need to be able to get their hands dirty in the day-to-day political activities of the nation or, as we just said, to wheel, deal, and bargain. But the image of their president as a politician, an occupational class not held in high esteem by most Americans, often doesn't sit well with citizens who want to hold their president above politics as a symbol of all that is good and noble about America.

> ***head of state*** the apolitical, unifying role of the president as symbolic representative of the whole country

Thus not only must presidents contend with a job in which they are required to do far more than they are given the power to do, but they must also cultivate the talents to perform two very contradictory roles: the essentially political head of government, who makes decisions about who will get scarce resources, and the elevated and apolitical head of state, who should unify rather than divide the public. Few presidents are skilled enough to carry off both roles with aplomb; the very talents that make a president good at one side of this equation often disqualify him from being good at the other.

Head of State

The ***head of state*** serves as the symbol of the hopes and dreams of a people and is responsible for enhancing national unity by representing that which is common and good in the nation. Most other nations separate the head-of-state role from the head-of-government role so that clearly acknowledged symbolic duties can be carried out without contamination by political considerations. One of the clearest examples is Great Britain's monarchy. As head of state, Queen Elizabeth remains a valued symbol of British nationhood. Her Christmas speech is listened to with great interest and pride by the nation, and, despite occasional family troubles, she continues to be an important symbol of what it means to be British. Meanwhile, the prime minister of England can get on with the political business of governing.

That the founders wanted the presidency to carry the dignity, if not the power, of a monarch is evident in George Washington's wish that the president might bear the title "His High Mightiness, the President of the United States and the Protector of Their Liberties."[8] While Americans were not ready for such a pompous title, we nevertheless do put presidents, as the embodiment of the nation, on a higher plane than other politicians. Consequently the American president's job includes a ceremonial role for activities like greeting other heads of state, attending state funerals, tossing out the first baseball of the season, hosting the annual Easter egg hunt on the White House lawn, and consoling survivors

Head of State, Head of Government

The head of government role entails the president getting involved in the details of domestic policy, whereas the head of state role is usually more symbolic. Hosting the annual Easter Egg Roll at the White House (here, President Obama watches a child shoot a basketball at the event) is one such activity. The president got down to serious business as head of government during the February 2010 bipartisan health care summit, where he urged members of both parties, including Vice President Joe Biden (left), Secretary of Health and Human Services Kathleen Sebelius, and Republican senators Mitch McConnell and John Boehner (right), to find ways to reform the system.

Political cartoons are not just for laughs. While they may often use humor as a way of making a political point, that point is likely to be sharp and aimed with uncanny accuracy at political targets. In fact, noted cartoonist Jeff MacNelly, who won a Pulitzer Prize for his work, once said that if cartoonists couldn't draw, most of them would probably have become hired assassins.[1]

Since the first days of our republic, Americans have been using drawings and sketches to say what mere words cannot. Benjamin Franklin and Paul Revere, among others, used pen, ink, and engraving tools to express pointed political views.[2] Moreover, their hapless targets have been acutely aware of the presence of these "annoying little pups, nipping at the heels. . . ."[3] Politicians crave the attention, knowing they have arrived when a cartoonist can draw them without having to indicate their names, but at the same time they dread the sharp sting of the cartoonist's pen.

In the 1870s, Boss Tweed of Tammany Hall (a powerful New York City politician who dominated local party politics) reportedly offered cartoonist Thomas Nast $100,000 to stop drawing cartoons about him (such as the one on page 455 in Chapter 12),[4] saying: "Stop them damn pictures. I don't care so much what the papers write about me. My constituents can't read. . . . But, damn it, they can see pictures."[5] By the early 1900s, legislatures in four states—Pennsylvania, California, Indiana, and Alabama—had introduced anti–cartoon censorship bills to protect the First Amendment freedoms of the political cartoonist.[6]

Political cartoons do more than elicit a laugh or a chuckle. Frequently they avoid humor altogether, going for outrage, indignation, ridicule, or scathing contempt. Their goal is to provoke a reaction from their audience, and they use the tools of irony, sarcasm, symbolism, and shock as well as humor. With this barrage of weapons aimed at you, your critical skills are crucial. The next time you are confronted with a political cartoon, ask yourself these questions:[7]

1. **What is the event or issue that inspired the cartoon?** Political cartoonists do not attempt to inform you about current events; they assume that you already know what has happened. Their job is to comment on the news, and so your first step in savvy cartoon readership is to be up on what's happening in the world. The cartoon shown here assumes that you are familiar with the highly partisan political climate after President Obama won the 2008 election, and his opponents organized in Tea Party demonstrations to protest his administration's efforts to stabilize the economy and reform health care.

2. **Are there any real people in the cartoon? Who are they?** Cartoonists develop caricatures of prominent politicians that exaggerate some gesture or facial feature (often the nose, the ears, or the eyebrows, although cartoonists had a field day with Ronald Reagan's hair) that makes them immediately identifiable.[8] Richard Nixon's ski jump nose and swarthy complexion were frequently lampooned, as was his habit of raising his hands over his head in a victory salute. Clinton often appeared as a bulbous-nosed, chubby-cheeked, childlike figure. Bush was often drawn as a small figure with a monkey-like face, often with huge ears. The ears and nose clued you in that the main figure was meant to be Bush. Obama's ears get skewered often as well—the giant ears on the figure in the Tea Party poster are meant to clue you in that the guy in the Hitler moustache is Obama.

    Many cartoonists do not confine their art to real people. Some will use a generic person sometimes labeled to represent a group (big business, U.S. Senate, environmentalists). Other cartoonists draw stereotypically middle-class citizens, talking television sets, or multipaneled "talking head" cartoons to get their views across.[9]

3. **Are there symbols in the cartoon? What do they represent?** Without a key to the symbols cartoonists use,

---

of national tragedies. The vice president can relieve the president of some of these responsibilities, but there are times when only the president's presence will do.

Head of Government

The president is elected to do more than greet foreign dignitaries, wage war, and give electrifying speeches, however. As *head of government*, he is also supposed to run the government, make law, and function as the head of a political party, all functions that will result in some citizens winning more

than others, some losing, and some becoming angry—all of which work against the unifying image of the head of state. These political roles are the functions that have expanded so greatly since Roosevelt's presidency.

Running the country, as we shall see throughout this chapter, involves a variety of political activities. First, the president is uniquely situated to define the nation's policy agenda—that is, to get issues on the unofficial list of business that Congress and the public think should be taken care of. The media's constant coverage of the president, combined

their art can be incomprehensible. Uncle Sam stands in for the United States, donkeys are Democrats, and elephants are Republicans. Tammany Hall frequently appeared as a tiger in political cartoons of the time. Often these symbols are combined in unique ways. (Here, a dizzy and hung-over looking Uncle Sam is meant to symbolize a nation exhausted by partisan rhetoric and fighting.) However, as politics has focused more on image and personality, symbols, although still important, have taken a back seat to personal caricature.[10]

4. **What is the cartoonist's opinion about the topic of the cartoon?**

Do you agree with it or not? Why? A cartoon is an editorial as surely as are the printed opinion pieces we focused on in Chapter 4. The cartoon has no more claim to objective status than does someone else's opinion, and you need to evaluate it critically before you take what it says to be accurate. In the drawing here, for instance, the cartoonist is likely sharing Uncle Sam's weariness with the endless name-calling and hyperbole that pass for political discourse today. Often evaluation is harder with a cartoon than with text, because the medium can be so effective in provoking a reaction from us, whether it is shock, laughter, or scorn. Furthermore, adding to the difficulty, a single cartoon can be interpreted in multiple ways.

1. Kirkus Reviews, review of *Them Damned Pictures: Explorations in American Political Cartoon Art*, by Roger A. Fischer, January 15, 1996.

2. Richard E. Marschall, "The Century in Political Cartoons," *Columbia Journalism Review*, May–June 1999, 54.

3. Richard Ruelas, "Editorial Cartoonists Nip at the Heels of Society," *Arizona Republic*, June 9, 1996, A1.

4. Marschall, "The Century."

5. Ira F. Grant, "Cartoonists Put the Salt in the Stew," *Southland* (New Zealand) *Times*, February 20, 1999, 7.

6. Marschall, "The Century."

7. Questions are based on the PoliticalCartoons.com teachers' guide, www.cagle.com/teacher.

8. Robert W. Duffy, "Art of Politics: Media With a Message," *St. Louis Post-Dispatch Magazine*, September 2, 1992, 3D.

9. Marschall, "The Century."

10. Ibid.

with the public's belief in the centrality of the office, means that modern presidents have great influence in deciding what policy issues will be addressed.

An effective head of government must do more than simply bring issues to national attention, however. We also expect him to broker the deals, line up the votes, and work to pass actual legislation. This may seem peculiar since Congress makes the laws, but the president is often a critical player in developing political support from the public and Congress to get these laws passed. Thus the president is also seen as the nation's chief lawmaker and coalition builder. An excellent example of the president's role in making law can be seen in President Obama's efforts to pass his major domestic program, "The Patient Protection and Affordable Care Act." Obama brought congressional Democrats and Republicans together in a "health care summit" to try to build a bipartisan coalition in support of the bill. When that effort came to naught, he worked to bring more conservative Democrats aboard, and his White House helped craft the strategy that, as we saw in the *What's at Stake?* in Chapter 7, enabled Democrats

> ***head of government*** the political role of the president as leader of a political party and chief arbiter of who gets what resources

to get the bill passed after Republican Scott Brown took over Ted Kennedy's seat and left the Democrats unable to break a Republican filibuster.

In addition to helping to make the laws, the president is supposed to make government work. When things go okay, no one thinks much about it. But when things go wrong, the president is the one who has to have an explanation—he is accountable. For example, President Obama faced criticism after the BP oil spill in 2010, even though the government didn't cause the spill, and Obama had no real capabilities to fix it. President Harry Truman kept a sign on his desk that read "The Buck Stops Here," which nicely summarizes this view of presidential responsibility.

The president does not just lead the nation; he leads his political party as well. As its head, he appoints the chair of his party's national committee and can use his powers as president—perhaps vetoing a bill, directing discretionary funds, or making appointments—to reward loyalty or punish a lack of cooperation. He also has considerable patronage at his disposal to reward the party faithful, although this practice is fading (see Chapter 9). The president can, if he wants, have a major influence on his party's platform. And, finally, the president is an important fundraiser for his party. By assisting in the election of party members, he helps to ensure support for the party's program in Congress.

We explore the president's powers in greater detail later in this chapter. What is important for our purposes here is that all these roles are *political* aspects of the president's job. Remember that "political" means allocating resources and benefits to some people over others, deciding who wins and who loses. Thus the responsibilities of the office place the president in an inherently and unavoidably contradictory position. On the one hand he is the symbol of the nation, representing all the people (head of state); and on the other he has to take the lead in politics that are inherently divisive (head of government). Thus the political requirements of the president as head of government necessarily undermine his unifying role as head of state.

Presidents want to leave a legacy, a reputation for having led the country in a meaningful way. To do this they make grand promises that they may not necessarily have the power to fulfill. Their job is complicated by the requirement that they serve as head of state, even as they are forced to act as head of government to accomplish their political goals. The people who

Who What How

hold the conflicting expectations of the president are, of course, the American voters. Citizens have a stake in having a successful president, but their expectations make it unlikely that he will succeed. Since voters choose among presidential candidates on the basis of their campaign promises, candidates are only encouraged to make grander promises, in the hopes of getting elected—ultimately increasing the expectations gaps as they are unable to deliver on their extravagant pledges.

Thinking Outside the Box

> **Should the president represent the interests of the people who voted for him, or of all Americans?**

The Evolution of the American Presidency
From restrained administrator to energetic problem-solver

The framers designed a much more limited presidency than the one we have today. The constitutional provisions give most of the policymaking powers to Congress, or at least require power sharing and cooperation. For most of our history, this arrangement was not a problem. As leaders of a rural nation with a relatively restrained governmental apparatus, presidents through the nineteenth century were largely content with a limited authority that rested on the grants of powers provided in the Constitution. But the presidency of Franklin Roosevelt, beginning in 1932, ushered in a new era in presidential politics.

The Framers' Design for a Limited Executive

Since the legislature was presumed by all to be the real engine of the national political system, the presidency was not a preoccupation of the framers when they met in Philadelphia in 1787. The breakdown of the national government under the Articles of Confederation, however, demonstrated the need for some form of a central executive. Nervous about trusting the general public to choose the executive, the founders provided for an Electoral College, a group of people who would be chosen by the states for the sole purpose of electing the president. The assumption was that this body would be made up of leading citizens who would exercise care and good judgment in casting their ballots and who would not make postelection claims on him. Because of their experience with King George III, the founders also wished to avoid the concentration of power that could be abused by a strong executive.

Although the majority's concept of a limited executive is enshrined in the Constitution, Alexander Hamilton's case for a more "energetic" president, found in *Federalist* No. 70, foreshadows many of the arguments for the stronger executive we have today.

Qualifications and Conditions of Office

The framers' conception of a limited presidency can be seen in the brief attention the office receives in the Constitution. Article II is short and not very precise. It provides some basic details on the office of the presidency:

- The president is chosen by the Electoral College to serve four-year terms. The number of terms was unlimited until 1951 when, in reaction to Roosevelt's unprecedented four terms in office, the Constitution was amended to limit the president to two terms.

- The president must be a natural-born citizen of the United States, at least thirty-five years old, and a resident for at least fourteen years.

- The president is succeeded by the vice president if he dies or is removed from office. The Constitution does not specify who becomes president in the event that the vice president, too, is unable to serve, but in 1947 Congress passed the Presidential Succession Act, which establishes the order of succession after the vice president (see Table 8.2). While the rules for succession following vacancies are clear, the rules for replacing a president because of *disability* are not. The Twenty-fifth Amendment states that a vice president can take over when either a president himself or the vice president and a majority of the cabinet report to Congress that the president is unable to serve. If reports are contradictory, two-thirds of Congress must agree

Table 8.2

Who Does the President's Job When the President Cannot?

Presidential order of succession
Vice president
Speaker of the House
President pro tempore of the Senate
Secretary of state
Secretary of the Treasury
Secretary of defense
Attorney general
Secretary of the interior
Secretary of agriculture
Secretary of commerce
Secretary of labor
Secretary of health and human services
Secretary of housing and urban development
Secretary of transportation
Secretary of energy
Secretary of education
Secretary of veterans affairs
Secretary of homeland security

Note: It seems impossible that all in the line of succession could die simultaneously. Nevertheless, during the State of the Union address, when Congress and the cabinet are present with the president and vice president, one cabinet member does not attend in order to ensure that a catastrophe could not render our government leaderless. Some in Congress have pushed legislation that would leapfrog the secretary of homeland security to eighth in line (one behind the attorney general), arguing that because of that secretary's particular familiarity with crises he or she would be best able to lead the country.

that the president is incapacitated.[9] But putting this into practice can be complicated. President Woodrow Wilson, for example, suffered an incapacitating stroke. Because no one wanted to remove a sitting president, his vice president, Thomas Riley Marshall, never came forward, leaving the executive branch essentially unable to function.

> **chief administrator** the president's executive role as the head of federal agencies and the person responsible for the implementation of national policy

> **cabinet** a presidential advisory group selected by the president, made up of the vice president, the heads of the federal executive departments, and other high officials to whom the president elects to give cabinet status

- The president can be removed from office for reasons of "treason, bribery, or other high crimes and misdemeanors." The process of removal involves two steps: First, after an in-depth investigation, the House votes to impeach by a simple majority vote, which charges the president with a crime. Second, the Senate tries the president on the articles of impeachment and can convict by a two-thirds majority vote. Only two American presidents, Andrew Johnson and Bill Clinton, have been impeached (in 1868 and 1998, respectively), but neither was convicted. The Senate failed, by one vote, to convict Johnson and could not assemble a majority against Clinton. The power of impeachment is meant to be a check on the president, but it is often used for partisan purposes. Impeachment resolutions were filed against Reagan (over the invasion of Grenada and the Iran-contra affair), George H. W. Bush (over Iran-contra), and George W. Bush (for a host of offenses ranging from falsifying evidence justifying the war in Iraq to failing to respond adequately to Hurricane Katrina). Republicans have talked about impeaching President Obama for various causes, from allegedly offering a job to a Senate candidate to encourage him not to run, to encouraging manipulation of legislative procedures in order to get health care reform passed.[10] To date, none of the charges against Obama have been filed as impeachment resolutions, however, and few of the resolutions filed about other presidents made it to the floor for a vote in the House, in part because such actions virtually bring governing to a halt and are not popular with the public.[11]

  While impeachment has come to be wielded as a weapon in partisan political battles, the president does sometimes commit actions worthy of impeachment. Nixon would have been impeached had he not resigned in 1974 (the House Judiciary Committee had passed the resolution and there were enough votes to pass the measure on the House floor and to gain conviction in the Senate). In that case there was clear evidence, in the form of conversations taped by the president himself, that Nixon had been involved directly in the cover-up of a burglary at Democratic National Committee headquarters in the Watergate Hotel. During the Reagan administration, a seven-year investigation by an independent counsel revealed that many members of Reagan's national security staff directed or knew about a plan to sell arms to Iran in exchange for American hostages, and to use the proceeds from the sale to assist "contra rebels" fighting against the Marxist Sandinista government in Nicaragua, in direct contradiction to Congress' wishes. While the so-called Iran-contra scandal damaged Reagan's legacy, Reagan himself claimed he knew nothing about it, and no solid evidence surfaced that he did. President George H. W. Bush, calling the investigation a partisan witch-hunt, pardoned six of the fourteen people indicted in the incident.

The Constitutional Power of the President

The Constitution uses vague language to discuss some presidential powers and is silent on the range and limits of others. It is precisely this ambiguity that allowed the Constitution to be ratified by both those who wanted a strong executive power and those who did not. In addition, this vagueness has allowed the powers of the president to expand over time without constitutional amendment. We can think of the president's constitutional powers as falling into three areas: executive authority to administer government, and legislative and judicial powers to check the other two branches.

Executive Powers

Article II, Section 1, of the Constitution begins, "The executive power shall be vested in a president of the United States of America." However, the document does not explain exactly what "executive power" entails, and scholars and presidents through much of our history have debated the extent of these powers.[12] Section 3 states the president "shall take care that the laws be faithfully executed." Herein lies much of the executive authority; the president is the **chief administrator** of the nation's laws. This means that he is the chief executive officer of the country, the person who, more than anyone else, is held responsible for agencies of the national government and the implementation of national policy.

The Constitution also specifies that the president, with the approval of the majority of the Senate, will appoint the heads of departments, who will oversee the work of

> **commander-in-chief**   the president's role as the top officer of the country's military establishment
>
> **chief foreign policy maker**   the president's executive role as the primary shaper of relations with other nations
>
> **treaties**   formal agreements with other countries; negotiated by the president and requiring approval by two-thirds of the Senate

> **executive agreements**   presidential arrangements with other countries that create foreign policy without the need for Senate approval
>
> **State of the Union address**   a speech given annually by the president to a joint session of Congress and to the nation announcing the president's agenda

implementation. These heads, who have come to be known collectively as the **cabinet**, report to the president. Today the president is responsible for the appointments of more than 3,500 federal employees: cabinet and lower administrative officers, federal judges, military officers, and members of the diplomatic corps. His responsibilities place him at the top of a vast federal bureaucracy. But his control of the federal bureaucracy is limited, as we will see in Chapter 9, because although he can make a large number of appointments, he is not able to fire many of the people he hires.

Other constitutional powers place the president, as **commander-in-chief**, at the head of the command structure for the entire military establishment. The Constitution gives Congress the power to declare war, but as the commander-in-chief, the president has the practical ability to wage war. These two powers, meant to check each other, instead provide for a battleground on which Congress and the president struggle for the power to control military operations. After the controversial Vietnam War, which was waged by Presidents Lyndon Johnson and Richard Nixon but never officially declared by Congress, Congress passed the War Powers Act of 1973, which was intended to limit the president's power to send troops abroad without congressional approval. Most presidents have ignored the act, however, when they wished to engage in military action abroad, and since public opinion tends to rally around the president at such times, Congress has declined to challenge popular presidential actions. The War Powers Act remains more powerful on paper than in reality.

Finally, under his executive powers, the president is the **chief foreign policy maker**. This role is not spelled out in the Constitution, but the foundation for it is laid in the provision that the president negotiates **treaties**—formal international agreements with other nations—with the approval of two-thirds of the Senate. The president also appoints ambassadors and receives ambassadors of other nations, a power that essentially amounts to determining what nations the United States will recognize.

While the requirement of Senate approval for treaties is meant to check the president's foreign policy power, much of U.S. foreign policy is made by the president through **executive agreements** with other heads of state, which avoids the slower and more cumbersome route of treaty making.[13] Executive agreements are used much more frequently than treaties; over 10,000 have been executed since 1970,

compared to fewer than 1,000 treaties.[14] This heavy reliance on executive agreements gives the president considerable power and flexibility in foreign policy. Executive agreements are used not only to get around the need for Senate approval. Often they concern routine matters and are issued for the sake of efficiency. If the Senate had to approve each agreement, it would have to act at the rate of one per day, tying up its schedule and keeping it from many more important issues.[15] However, even though the executive agreement is a useful and much-used tool, Congress may still thwart the president's intentions by refusing to approve the funds needed to put an agreement into action.

The framers clearly intended that the Senate would be the principal voice and decision maker in foreign policy, but that objective was not realized even in George Washington's presidency. At subsequent points in our history, Congress has exerted more authority in foreign policy, but for the most part, particularly in the twentieth century, presidents have taken a strong leadership role in dealing with other nations. Part of the reason for this is that Congress has more jealously guarded its prerogatives in domestic policy because those are so much more crucial in its members' reelection efforts. This has changed somewhat in recent years as the worldwide economy has greatly blurred the line between domestic and foreign affairs.

Legislative Powers

Even though the president is the head of the executive branch of government, the Constitution also gives him some legislative power to check Congress. He "shall from time to time give to the Congress information of the state of the union, and recommend to their consideration such measures as he shall judge necessary and expedient." Although the framers' vision of this activity was quite limited, today the president's **State of the Union address**, delivered before the full Congress every January, is a major statement of the president's policy agenda.

The Constitution gives the president the nominal power to convene Congress and, when there is a dispute about when to disband, to adjourn it as well. Before Congress met regularly, this power, though limited, actually meant something. Today we rarely see it invoked. Some executives, such as the British prime minister, who can dissolve Parliament and call new elections, have a much more formidable convening power than that available to the U.S. president.

The Bully Pulpit

The president's State of the Union address is delivered before the full Congress every January and serves as a major statement of the president's policy agenda. President Barack Obama's address in January 2010 evoked strong approval ratings. Later polls, however, showed that his ratings dropped significantly later in his first term.

The principal legislative power given the president by the Constitution is the **presidential veto**. If the president objects to a bill passed by the House and the Senate, he can veto it, sending it back to Congress with a message indicating his reasons. Congress can override a veto with a two-thirds vote in each house, but because mustering the two-thirds support is quite difficult, the presidential veto is a substantial power. Even the threat of a presidential veto can have a major impact in getting congressional legislation to fall in line with the administration's preferences.[16] Table 8.3 shows the number of

> **presidential veto** a president's authority to reject a bill passed by Congress; may be overridden only by a two-thirds majority in each house

bills vetoed since 1933 and the number of successful veto overrides by Congress. The elder President Bush was particularly successful in using the veto—he used it often against the Democratic Congress and was overridden only once. President Clinton never used the veto in 1993 and 1994, when he had Democratic majorities in Congress. However, over the next six years, when he faced a mostly Republican Congress, he attempted to stop thirty-seven bills; Congress was able to override him only twice. With Republican majorities in the House and the Senate for most of his first term; the unusual atmosphere of bipartisanship that appeared in Washington after September 11, 2001; and his practice, noted in *What's at Stake?*, of using signing statements to signal his displeasure with parts of the legislation he signed, George W. Bush joined John Quincy Adams and Thomas Jefferson as the only presidents who did not veto a bill during their first term.[17] With the switch of congressional control to the Democratic Party following the 2006 election, however, things changed, and Bush vetoed a dozen bills, a third of which were overridden by Congress. With a Democratic Congress during his first years in office, President Obama had little cause to veto bills. The first veto he issued in his first two years in office was one that rejected a spending bill similar to one he had already signed;[18] the second a "pocket veto" of a mortgage foreclosure law.

Congress has regularly sought to get around the obstacle of presidential vetoes by packaging a number of items together in a bill. Traditionally, presidents have had to sign a complete bill or reject the whole thing. Thus, for example, Congress regularly adds such things as a building project or a tax break for a state industry onto, say, a military appropriations bill that the president wants. Often presidents calculate that it is best to accept such add-ons, even if they think them unjustified or wasteful, in order to get passed what they judge to be important legislation.

Before it was ruled unconstitutional by the Supreme Court in 1998, the short-lived *line-item veto* promised to provide an important new tool for presidents. Favored by conservatives and by President Clinton, the 1996 line-item veto was supposed to save money by allowing presidents to cut some items, like pork barrel projects, from spending bills without vetoing the entire package. The Supreme Court declared the law unconstitutional because the Constitution says that all legislation is to be passed by both houses and then presented as a whole to the president for his approval.

Another of the president's key legislative powers comes from the vice president's role as presiding officer of the

Table 8.3

Presidential Vetoes, Roosevelt to Obama

Years	President	Total vetoes	Regular vetoes	Pocket vetoes	Vetoes overridden	Veto success rate
1933–1945	Franklin Roosevelt	635	372	263	9	97.6%
1945–1953	Harry Truman	250	180	70	12	93.3
1953–1961	Dwight Eisenhower	181	73	108	2	97.3
1961–1963	John F. Kennedy	21	12	9	0	100.0
1963–1969	Lyndon Johnson	30	16	14	0	100.0
1969–1974	Richard Nixon	43	26	17	7	73.1
1974–1977	Gerald Ford	66	48	18	12	75.0
1977–1981	Jimmy Carter	31	13	18	2	84.6
1981–1989	Ronald Reagan	78	39	39	9	76.9
1989–1993	George H. W. Bush	46	29	17*	1	96.6
1993–2001	Bill Clinton	37	36	1	2	96.4
2001–2009	George W. Bush	12	11	1	4	66.7
2009–	Barack Obama	2	1	1	0	100.0

Sources: Mitchel A. Sollenberger, "The Presidential Veto and Congressional Procedure," in *CRS Report for Congress*, updated February 27, 2004, 4, www.senate.gov/reference/resources/pdf/RS21750.pdf; Joseph J. Schatz, "With a Deft and Light Touch, Bush Finds Ways to Win," *CQ Weekly*, December 11, 2004, 2900–2904; 2005–2008 data from "CRS Report, Regular Vetoes and Pocket Vetoes: An Overview," www.senate.gov/reference/resources/pdf/RS22188.pdf, July 18, 2008. Veto success rate calculated by authors.

*Although they are counted here, Congress did not recognize two of Bush's pocket vetoes and considered the legislation enacted.

Senate. Although the vice president rarely presides over the Senate, Article I, Section 3, says that he may cast a tie-breaking vote when the hundred-member Senate is evenly divided. Some recent examples illustrate just how important this has been to presidential prerogatives. In 1993 Vice President Al Gore voted to break a tie that enabled President Clinton's first budget to pass. The bill included controversial tax increases and spending cuts but ultimately helped create a budget surplus. Eight years later, Vice President Dick Cheney broke a tie vote on Bush's first budget, which ironically undid some of the Clinton tax increases but also included numerous other tax reductions. Both of these pieces of legislation were hallmarks of their respective presidents' agendas. The fact that a president can count on his vice president to break a tie when the Senate is split over controversial legislation is an often underappreciated legislative power.

Although the Constitution does not grant the president the power to make law, his power to do so has grown over time and now is generally accepted. Presidents can issue **executive orders** (not to be confused with the executive agreements he can make with other nations), which are supposed to be clarifications of how laws passed by Congress are to be implemented by specific agencies. Some of the most significant presidential actions have come from executive orders, including President Franklin Roosevelt's order to hold Japanese Americans in internment camps in World War II, President Truman's order that black and white military troops be integrated, President Kennedy's and President Johnson's affirmative action programs, and many of the post–September 11 security measures such as the establishment of military tribunals for cases against terrorists. Perhaps the most contentious arguments in George W. Bush's presidency concerned the administration's executive orders easing environmental

executive orders   clarifications of congressional policy issued by the president and having the full force of law

senatorial courtesy   tradition of granting senior senators of the president's party considerable power over federal judicial appointments in their home states

regulations on businesses, limiting federal funding for stem cell research, or instructing agencies to provide grants for faith-based groups to carry out social services. After the Democrats lost their filibuster-proof majority in the Senate in 2010, President Obama made contingency plans to execute some parts of his agenda—concerning energy, the environment, and fiscal responsibility—via executive order.[19]

Historically, executive orders spike when there are national crises. Patterns also suggest that executive orders are released at a higher rate at the beginning of a president's term as he immediately implements key policies and at the end of his term as he tries to leave his legacy.[20] Indeed, presidents often release particularly symbolic executive orders on their first days in office. Since executive orders are not Congress-made laws, a new president can reverse any of his predecessor's orders that he wants to.[21]

Judicial Powers

Presidents can have tremendous long-term impact on the judiciary, but in the short run their powers over the courts are meager. Their continuing impact comes from nominating judges to the federal courts, including the Supreme Court. The political philosophies of individual judges influence significantly how they interpret the law, and this is especially important for Supreme Court justices, who are the final arbitrators of constitutional meaning. Since judges serve for life, presidential appointments have a long-lasting effect. For instance, today's Supreme Court is considered to be distinctly more conservative than its immediate predecessors due to the appointments made by Presidents Reagan and Bush in the 1980s and early 1990s. Moreover, President Reagan is credited by many with having ushered in a "judicial revolution." He, together with his successor, George H. W. Bush, appointed 550 of the 837 federal judges, most of them conservatives. Clinton appointed moderates to the courts, angering many Democrats, who felt that his appointees should have been more liberal. President George W. Bush revived the conservative trend that was halted under Clinton.[22] Although President Obama's pick of Sonia Sotomayor for the Supreme Court pleased liberals, his nomination of Elena Kagan caused some to worry that his selections would follow Clinton's more moderate record.[23] In general, Obama's choices for the judiciary are fairly liberal, but because he has been slower than Bush to make appointments and the appointments he has made have often been blocked by Republicans in the Senate, he has not yet made as distinctive a mark on the courts.[24]

Presidents cannot always gauge the judicial philosophy of their appointees, however, and they can be sadly disappointed in their choices. Republican president Dwight Eisenhower appointed Chief Justice Earl Warren and Justice William Brennan, both of whom turned out to be more liberal than the president had anticipated. When asked if he had any regrets as president, Eisenhower answered, "Yes, two, and they are both sitting on the Supreme Court."[25]

The presidential power to appoint is limited to an extent by the constitutional requirement for Senate approval of federal judges. Traditionally, most nominees have been approved, with occasional exceptions. Sometimes rejection stems from questions about the candidate's competence, but in other instances rejection is based more on style and judicial philosophy. The Democratic-led Senate's rejection of President Reagan's very conservative Supreme Court nominee Robert Bork in 1987 is one of the more controversial cases.[26] Some observers believe that the battle over the Bork nomination signaled the end of deference to presidents and opened up the approval process to endless challenges and partisan bickering.[27] As we saw in Chapter 7, some of the harshest battles between the president and Congress in recent years came from partisan Senate challenges to judicial nominations. The political polarization we discussed in that chapter has infected the nomination process. The frequent threat of the filibuster and the use of anonymous holds in the Senate allow the party opposing the president to hold up nominations so that many federal judgeships remain open, causing a backlog of cases. Both parties play the game as they try to prevent undesired ideological shifts in the federal courts.[28]

A president's choice of judges for the federal district courts is also limited by the tradition of ***senatorial courtesy***, whereby senior senators of the president's party from the states in which the appointees reside have what amounts to a veto power over the president's choice. If presidents should ignore the custom of senatorial courtesy and push a nomination unpopular with one of the home state senators, fellow senators will generally honor one another's requests and refuse to confirm the appointee.

Although presidents can leave a lasting imprint on the judiciary, in the short run they do little to affect court decisions. They do not contact judges to plead for decisions; they do not offer them inducements as they might a fence-sitting member of Congress. When, as happens rarely, a president criticizes a federal judge for a decision, the criticism is usually poorly received. For example, when spokespeople for President

solicitor general the Justice Department officer who argues the government's cases before the Supreme Court

pardoning power a president's authority to release or excuse a person from the legal penalties of a crime

inherent powers presidential powers implied but not explicitly stated in the Constitution

Clinton went so far as to threaten to ask for the resignation of a federal judge after he made a widely publicized and unpopular decision, a flood of editorials cried foul.[29]

The least controversial way a president can try to influence a court decision is to have the Justice Department invest resources in arguing a case. The third-ranking member of the Justice Department, the **solicitor general**, is a presidential appointee whose job it is to argue cases for the government before the Supreme Court. The solicitor general is thus a bridge between the executive and the judiciary, not only deciding which cases the government will appeal to the Court, but also filing petitions stating the government's (usually the president's) position on cases to which the government is not even a party. These petitions, called *amicus curiae* ("friend of the court") briefs, are taken very seriously by the Court. The government is successful in its litigation more often than any other litigant, winning over two-thirds of its cases in the past half-century, and often having its arguments cited by the justices themselves in their opinions.[30] Elena Kagan, President Obama's second appointment to the Supreme Court, served as his solicitor general before her nomination.

One additional judicial power granted to the president by the Constitution is the **pardoning power**, which allows a president to exempt a person, convicted or not, from punishment for a crime. This power descends from a traditional power of kings as the court of last resort and thus a check on the courts. Pardons can backfire in dramatic ways. After President Gerald Ford pardoned Richard Nixon, in the hopes that the nation would heal from its Watergate wounds more quickly if it didn't have to endure the spectacle of its former president on trial, Ford experienced a tremendous backlash that may have contributed to his 1976 loss to Jimmy Carter. Subsequent presidents have each run into problems with unpopular pardons. When pardons are motivated by political or partisan considerations, rather than as a check on the power of the courts, they tend to be seen by the public and the media as presidential abuses of public trust.[31]

The Traditional Presidency

The presidency that the founders created and outlined in the Constitution is not the presidency of today. In fact, so clearly have the effective rules governing the presidency changed that scholars speak of the era of the *traditional presidency*, from the founding to the 1930s, and the era of the *modern presidency*, from the 1930s to the present. Although the constitutional powers of the president have been identical in both eras, the interpretation of how far the president can go beyond his constitutional powers has changed dramatically.

The founders' limited vision of the office survived more or less intact for a little over one hundred years. There were exceptions, however, to their expectations that echoed Hamilton's call for a stronger executive. Several early presidents exceeded the powers granted in the Constitution. Washington expanded the president's foreign policy powers, Jefferson entered into the Louisiana Purchase, and Andrew Jackson developed the role of president as popular leader. In one of the most dramatic examples, Abraham Lincoln, during the emergency conditions of the Civil War, stepped outside his constitutional role to call up state militias, to enlarge the army and use tax money to pay for it, and to blockade the southern ports. He claimed that his actions, though counter to the Constitution, were necessary to save the nation.[32]

These presidents believed that they had what modern scholars call **inherent powers** to fulfill their constitutional duty to "take care that the laws be faithfully executed." Some presidents, like Lincoln, claimed that national security required a broader presidential role. Others held that the president, as our sole representative in foreign affairs, needed a stronger hand abroad than at home. Inherent powers are not explicitly listed in the Constitution but are implied by the powers that are granted, and they have been supported, to some extent, by the Supreme Court.[33] But most nineteenth- and early-twentieth-century presidents, conforming to the founders' expectations, took a more retiring role, causing one observer to claim that "twenty of the twenty-five presidents of the nineteenth century were lords of passivity."[34] The job of the presidency was seen as a primarily administrative office, in which presidential will was clearly subordinate to the will of Congress.

> **Thinking Outside the Box**
>
> What political impact might it have if, following Washington's wishes, the president were known as "His High Mightiness"?

▶ Who, What, How, and WHEN: Views of the Presidency

The founders may have settled on a president for our chief executive, instead of the more familiar king that reigned in England, but there was by no means a consensus on what the role and powers of the president should be. Even today, though the Constitution puts some limits on the powers associated with it, the office of the presidency continues to evolve and change with the times and the personalities and ambitions of the person holding it. Take a look at just a few presidential incarnations:

1787 — "His High Mightiness, the President of the United States and the Protector of Their Liberties"

During the Constitutional Convention, Alexander Hamilton argued for a president who was appointed by a group of electors and served for life with strong powers. An alternative plan for the presidency was suggested by William Paterson of New Jersey. He proposed a multiperson executive to limit the power of the office. Neither plan took off; the convention instead came up with a limited, elected, single-person executive. Nevertheless, these limits didn't stop George Washington, the first officeholder, from wanting the flowery title of "His High Mightiness."

1906 — The World Player President

Theodore Roosevelt was the first president to travel outside the United States on official presidential business. He went to Panama to check on the construction of the Panama Canal. Later, Woodrow Wilson became the first president to travel to Europe, in part to try to convince the rest of the world to adopt his proposal for a League of Nations. Later, Franklin Roosevelt became the first president to fly in a plane, paving the way for foreign travel to become a regular part of the president's job.

1947 — The Living Room President

Even though Franklin Roosevelt was the first president to appear on TV in the 1930s, not many homes had the new invention. Harry Truman was the first president to appear on TV from the White House when he gave a speech about world hunger. These early appearances opened television as a medium for presidential appearances in election advertisements, debates, and even comedy and late-night shows.

The Modern Presidency

The simple rural nature of life in the United States changed rapidly in the century and a half after the founding. The country grew westward, and the nation became more industrialized. More people worked in factories, fewer on the land. The postal system expanded greatly, and the federal government became involved in American Indian affairs, developed national parks, and enacted policies dealing with transportation, especially the railroads. Government in the nineteenth century sought bit by bit to respond to the new challenges of its changing people and economy, and as it responded, it grew beyond the bounds of the rudimentary administrative structure supervised by George Washington. With the crisis of the Great Depression and Franklin Roosevelt's New Deal solution, the size of government exploded and popular ideas about government changed radically. From being an exception, as it was in our early history, the use of strong presidential power became an expectation of the modern president.

The Great Depression

Nothing in their prior experience had prepared Americans for the calamity of the Great Depression. Following the stock market crash of October 1929, the economy went into a tailspin. Unemployment soared to 25 percent while the gross national product plunged from around $100 billion in 1928 to under $60 billion in 1932.[35] President Herbert Hoover held that government had only limited powers and responsibility

1973 The Imperial President

The "imperial presidency," described by Arthur Schlesinger in a 1973 book, refers to the powerful office held by post–World War II presidents who wielded enormous power in the world and who enjoyed increased prestige and power at home. The term has particularly been applied to Richard Nixon and the activities that led to Watergate and Nixon's resignation, though some observers argue that George W. Bush's presidency was also imperial.

2008 The Glass Ceiling President

Women and minorities have run for president before. Victoria Woodhull ran in 1872 as the Equal Rights Party nominee; Shirley Chisholm competed for the Democratic Party nomination in 1972; and Walter Mondale chose Geraldine Ferraro as his running mate in 1984, although the ticket lost. In 2008, however, the face of presidential politics changed dramatically. Not only were Barack Obama and Hillary Clinton the two main competitors for the Democratic Party nomination, which Obama won, but Republican candidate John McCain chose Sarah Palin, governor of Alaska, as his running mate, virtually ensuring that the winning ticket would be a "first."

to deal with what was, he believed, a private economic crisis. There was no widespread presumption, as there is today, that government was responsible for the state of the economy or for alleviating the suffering of its citizens.

Roosevelt's election in 1932, and his subsequent three reelections, initiated an entirely new level of governmental activism. For the first time, the national government assumed responsibility for the economic well-being of its citizens on a substantial scale. Relying on the theory mentioned earlier, that foreign affairs are thought to justify greater presidential power than do domestic affairs, Roosevelt portrayed himself as waging a war against the Depression and sought from Congress the powers "that would be given to me if we were in fact invaded by a foreign foe."[36] The New Deal programs

he put in place tremendously increased the size of the federal establishment and its budget. The number of civilians (nonmilitary personnel) working for the federal government increased by over 50 percent during Roosevelt's first two terms (1933–1939). The crisis of the Great Depression created the conditions for extraordinary action, and the leadership of Roosevelt created new responsibilities and opportunities for the federal government. Congress delegated a vast amount of discretionary power to Roosevelt so that he could implement his New Deal programs.

Presidential Promises, Popular Expectations

The legacy of the New Deal is that Americans now look to their president and their government to regulate their economy, solve their social problems, and provide political inspiration. No president has had such a profound impact on how Americans live their lives today.[37] Roosevelt's New Deal was followed by Truman's Fair Deal. Eisenhower's presidency was less activist, but it was followed by Kennedy's New Frontier and Johnson's Great Society. All of these comprehensive policy programs did less than they promised, but they reinforced Americans' belief that it is government's and, in particular, the president's job to make ambitious promises. While presidents from Carter to Reagan to Clinton enthusiastically promoted plans for cutting back the size of government, few efforts were successful. Not even President Reagan, more conservative and therefore more hostile to "big government," was able to significantly reduce government size and popular expectations of government action.

"The Imperial Presidency"

The growth of domestic government is not the only source of the increased power of the modern president, however. As early as 1936, the Supreme Court confirmed in *United States v. Curtiss-Wright Corporation* the idea that the president has more inherent power in the realm of foreign affairs than in domestic politics.[38] In the so-called steel seizure case (1952), the Supreme Court struck down a particular exercise of inherent powers on the part of President Truman, but only two of the justices rejected the idea of inherent powers.[39]

These decisions became more significant as the U.S. role in world politics expanded greatly in the post–World War II years. The ascendance of the United States as a world power, its engagement in the Cold War, and its participation in undeclared wars such as Korea and Vietnam made the office very powerful indeed—what historian Arthur Schlesinger called, in a 1973 book, "the imperial presidency."[40] The philosophy behind the imperial presidency was neatly summed up by Richard Nixon, ironically several years after he was forced to resign, when he declared, "When the president does it, that means it's not illegal."[41]

The Presidency Today

Whether or not the power of the modern presidency ever approached "imperial" status at one time, there is no doubt that the political reaction to the Vietnam War and the Watergate scandal in the 1970s made it harder for the modern president to act. Congress, the media, and the courts began to check the president in ways they had not done earlier in the era of the modern presidency.

New Checks on the Presidency

Many in Congress felt that neither the Johnson nor the Nixon administrations had been sufficiently forthcoming over the Vietnam War. Frustration with that, as well as with Nixon's abuse of his powers during Watergate and his unwillingness to spend budgeted money as Congress had appropriated it, led Congress to develop its own mechanisms for getting information about public policy to use as a check on presidential power.[42] Congress also weakened the office of the presidency with the passage of the War Powers Act (1973), which we discussed earlier; the Foreign Intelligence and Surveillance Act (1978), designed to put a check on the government's ability to spy on people within the United States; and the Independent Counsel Act (1978), which was intended to provide an impartial check on a president's activities but which was ultimately left open to abuse by his opponents.

At the same time, fresh from the heady success of the *Washington Post*'s discovery of the Watergate scandal, the Washington press corps abandoned the discretion that had kept them from reporting Franklin Roosevelt's inability to walk or John F. Kennedy's extramarital affairs, and began to subject the president to closer scrutiny. Reporters, eager to make their names as investigative journalists, became far more aggressive in their coverage of the White House.

Even the Supreme Court served to limit the power and stature of the presidency, as when it ruled unanimously in 1997 that a sitting president does not have immunity from civil lawsuits while he is in office, adding that the process of such a case was unlikely to prove a disruption of his duties.[43] Paula Jones's lawsuit against Bill Clinton, of course, proved to be disruptive of his presidency in the extreme, and ended up leading to his impeachment, although on grounds that had nothing to do with the case. Had the Court not made that decision, Clinton's affair with Monica Lewinsky would not have come to light, and he would most likely not have been impeached.

The Bush-Cheney Restoration of the Imperial Presidency

The modern presidency had been weakened by post-Watergate developments and the Clinton impeachment. When the George W. Bush administration came to power,

Bush and his vice president, Dick Cheney, were determined to restore the luster and power of the office. Cheney had been a young staffer in the Nixon White House and chief of staff to Gerald Ford before embarking on a career in Congress. He had seen firsthand the changes in the executive and felt they had gone too far. In January 2002, Cheney remarked that the presidency is "weaker today as an institution because of the unwise compromises that have been made over the last 30 to 35 years," and he highlighted the "erosion of the powers and the ability of the president" of the United States to do his job.[44] Indeed, many of Bush's early executive orders were designed to reinstate those powers, as were claims of executive privilege made by his administration.

The terror attacks of September 11, 2001, provided Bush and Cheney with a strong and persuasive rationale for their desire to create a more muscular presidency. Citing concern about future attacks, the Bush administration increased its efforts to make the office more powerful. Signing statements, as we noted earlier, were used to impose the president's interpretation of legislation over that of Congress; the Foreign Intelligence and Surveillance Act was ignored as the administration undertook an illegal wiretapping program on U.S. soil to detect possible terrorist activity; decisions were taken to torture prisoners of war; the prison camp at Guantánamo Bay, Cuba, was established to hold enemy combatants indefinitely; and military tribunals were set up so that terror suspects could be tried without being given the legal protections of a civil trial. Many of these actions relied on the theory of the unitary executive discussed in *What's at Stake?*

Bush's extraordinarily high approval ratings in the days following September 11 made Congress unwilling to take him on. The Republicans in Congress were supportive of the administration's efforts, and the Democrats feared being seen as soft on terrorism and so went along with Bush's plans. The Patriot Act passed handily in 2001, and only the Supreme Court, in the 2004 case *Hamdi v. Rumsfeld* and the 2006 case *Hamdan v. Rumsfeld*, attempted to put on the brakes. As we argue in this chapter, high approval ratings can give a president more power than the Constitution allows him, and Bush used that power throughout his first administration not only to wage the war on terror in Afghanistan but also to take the war effort to Iraq for reasons that were later shown to have been largely exaggerated and fabricated.

Only after Bush's reelection in 2004, with waning approval ratings, was he seen as vulnerable enough for

Congress to criticize him seriously. By 2006 his approval was so low that Democrats easily won back control of both the House and the Senate and began to undertake the job of congressional oversight that had been largely lacking for the previous six years. (See the *What's at Stake?* feature in Chapter 7 for more on congressional oversight.)

The fate of the Bush administration illustrates the basic themes of this chapter. The Constitution does not give presidents sufficient power to meet their promises and to match expectations of domestic and world leadership, so presidents curry public support to engender a more compliant Congress. Bush chose to stick with his ideological agenda and his slim but cooperative majorities in Congress, and to extend the levers available to extend his ability to act unilaterally: signing statements, executive orders, claims of executive privilege, and politicizing the bureaucracy to achieve policy compliance, especially in regard to the Department of Justice. With the decline in his popularity and his party's losses in Congress, his powers waned and he was a reclusive lame duck during the final months of his presidency.

The Obama Presidency

Overall, it is unlikely that the Bush-Cheney efforts to bulk up the executive will have lasting effect. Obama will no doubt wrestle with the same challenges of office as have all presidents in the modern age, but he is on the record as supporting the traditional checks and balances that limit the president's power. As we saw in *What's at Stake?*, Obama has continued the use of signing statements, though only on a limited basis to protect a president's constitutional prerogatives.[45] Although liberal critics have called out his use of these statements, as well as his failure to close the prison at Guantánamo Bay, his efforts to pursue the war in Afghanistan, and his continuance of some of the Bush administration's national security practices (like secret wiretapping) that they claim infringe on civil liberties,[46] in general Obama has rejected his predecessor's bulked-up presidential aspirations. A former constitutional law professor, Obama seems more aware than many presidents of the necessity of maintaining checks and balances, and he shows no signs of embracing the Bush philosophy of the unitary executive. Scholars and critics on both sides of the ideological divide will watch his administration through the remainder of his term to see whether he feels the need to push the envelope of presidential power or to operate within the limits of the post-Watergate presidency.[47]

> **power to persuade** a president's ability to convince Congress, other political actors, and the public to cooperate with the administration's agenda

The politicians who initially had something important at stake in the rules governing the executive were the founders themselves. Arranged by those, like Alexander Hamilton, who wanted a strong leader and by others who preferred a multiple executive to ensure checks on the power of the office, the constitutional compromise provides for a stronger position than many wanted, but one still limited in significant ways from becoming overly powerful and independent.

Who What How

Until the 1930s, presidents were mostly content to live within the confines of their constitutional restrictions, with only occasional excursions into the realm of inherent powers. But since the 1930s, presidents and citizens have entered into a complex relationship. Seeking effective leadership in an increasingly sophisticated world, citizens have been willing to expand the informal rules of presidential power provided they approve of the ways in which the president uses it. When the powers of the presidency have seemed to have gotten out of hand, however, Congress, the courts, and the media have been quick to limit it, showing how well the founders' system of checks and balances functions.

Presidential Politics

The struggle for power in a constitutionally limited office

Presidential responsibilities and the public's expectations of what the president can accomplish have increased greatly since the start of the twentieth century, but as we have discussed, the Constitution has not been altered to give the president more power. To avoid failure, presidents have to seek power beyond that which is explicitly granted by the Constitution, and even beyond what they can claim as part of their inherent powers, and they do that with varying degrees of success.

The Expectations Gap and the Need for Persuasive Power

Even presidents who have drawn enthusiastically on their inherent powers to protect national security or conduct foreign policy or who support the theory of the unitary executive still cannot summon the official clout to ensure that their legislation gets through Congress, that the Senate approves their appointments, and that other aspects of their campaign promises are fulfilled. Some scholars believe that presidents should be given the power necessary to do the job correctly. Others argue that no one can do the job; it is not a lack of power that is the problem, but rather, no human being is up to the task of solving everyone's problems on all fronts. The solution according to this view is to lower expectations and return the presidency to a position of less prominence.[48]

New presidents quickly face the dilemma of high visibility and status, and limited constitutional authority. Of course, they do not want to fail. It would be political suicide for them to say, "Gee, America, this job is a lot tougher than I thought it would be. The truth is, I don't have the power to do all the stuff I promised." Presidential frustration with the limits of the office is captured nicely by President Truman's remarks about his successor, President Eisenhower, a former general. "He'll sit here," Truman would remark (tapping his desk for emphasis), "and he'll say, 'Do this! Do that!' *And nothing will happen.* Poor Ike—it won't be a bit like the Army. He'll find it very frustrating."[49]

Yet people continue to run for and serve as president, and as we have seen, they deal with the expectations gap by attempting to augment their power with executive orders, executive agreements, claims of executive privilege, signing statements, and the like. All of these give the president some ability to act unilaterally. However, to be successful with larger policy initiatives, presidents seek to develop their primary extraconstitutional power, which is, in one scholar's phrase, the **power to persuade**.[50] To achieve what is expected of them, the argument goes, presidents must persuade others to cooperate with their agendas—most often members of Congress, but also the courts, the media, state and local officials, bureaucrats, foreign leaders, and especially the American public.

Other scholars, however, doubt that it is really persuasion alone that allows a president to get things done. They argue that little evidence indicates that presidents are able to influence important actors, or even the public, to change their policy priorities or preferences, and that presidents' substantial policy successes are due primarily to their ability to see and exploit existing opportunities. These may be political ambitions of members of Congress; latent concerns or yearnings in the public; or changes in public mood or media attention about unexpected events, such as the attacks of September 11, 2001, or the 2010 oil spill in the Gulf of

Mexico. Presidents vary in their ability to capitalize on the political context they face as much as on their ability to single-handedly change minds, either in Washington or in the country at large.[51] Whether they seek to persuade or to take advantage of potential opportunities, presidents have to go beyond their relatively modest constitutional powers if they want to fulfill voter expectations and bring about major policy changes in America.

Going Public

One central strategy that presidents follow in their efforts to influence people "inside the Beltway" (that is, the Washington insiders) to go along with their agenda is to reach out and appeal to the public directly for support. This strategy of **going public** is based on the expectation that public support will put pressure on other politicians to give the president what he wants.[52] Presidents use their powers as both head of government and head of state to appeal to the public.[53] A president's effort to go public can include a trip to an international summit, a town meeting–style debate on a controversial issue, or even the president's annual State of the Union address or other nationally televised speeches.

The Presidency and the Media

At the simplest level of the strategy of going public, the president just takes his case to the people. Consequently, presidential public appearances have increased greatly in the era of the modern presidency. Recent presidents have had some sort of public appearance almost every day of the week, year round. Knowing that the White House press corps will almost always get some airtime on network news, presidents want that coverage to be favorable. Shaping news coverage so that it generates favorable public opinion for the president is now standard operating procedure.[54]

The Ratings Game

Naturally, only a popular president can use the strategy of going public effectively, so popularity ratings become crucial to how successful a president can be. Since the 1930s the Gallup Organization has been asking people, "Do you approve or disapprove of the way [the current president] is handling his job as president?" The public's rating of the president—that is, the percentage saying they approve of how the president is handling his job—varies from one president to the next

Going Public by Going to the People

Presidents' access to the media allows them to present their policy prosposals to the public in the hope that the policies will win popular support that will, in turn, persuade Congress to pass favored legislation. In 2010 President Obama took to the road for a series of talks at automotive plants, including Chrysler's Jefferson North Assembly Plant in Detroit, Michigan, to promote the government bailouts of General Motors and Chrysler as a return on taxpayer investment.

and also typically rises and falls within any single presidential term. The president's ratings are a kind of political barometer: the higher they are, the more effective the president is with other political and economic actors; the lower they are, the harder he finds it to get people to go along. For the modern presidency, the all-important power to persuade is intimately tied to presidential popularity.

Three factors in particular can affect a president's popularity: a cycle effect, the economy, and unifying or divisive current events:[55]

- The **cycle effect** refers to the tendency for most presidents to begin their terms of office with relatively high popularity ratings, which decline as they move through their four-year terms (see Figure 8.1). During the very early months of this cycle, often called the **honeymoon period**, presidents are frequently most effective with Congress. Often, but not always, presidential ratings rise going into reelection, but this seldom approaches the popularity the president had immediately after being elected the first time.

  The post-honeymoon drop in approval demonstrated in Figure 8.1 may occur because, by then, presidents have begun to try to fulfill the handsome

Figure 8.1

Average Quarterly Presidential Approval Ratings, From Eisenhower to Obama

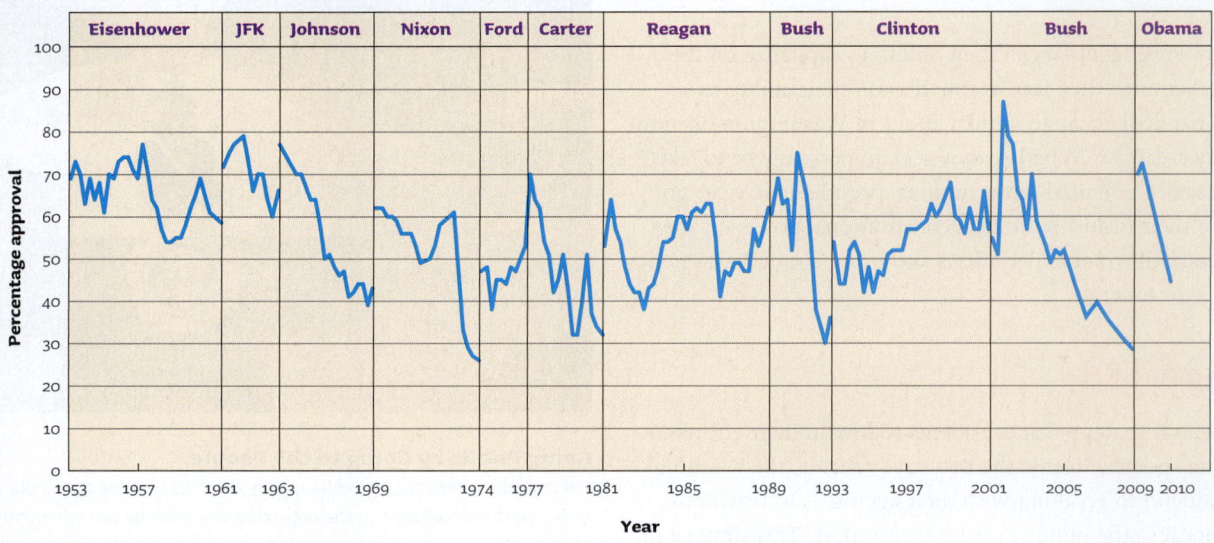

Sources: Quarterly data for 1953–2000 provided by Robert S. Erikson; developed for Robert S. Erikson, James A. Stimson, and Michael B. MacKuen, *The Macro Polity* (Cambridge: Cambridge University Press, 2002); data for 2000–2008 calculated by authors from the Gallup Organization.

Note: Respondents were asked, "Do you approve or disapprove of the way [the current president] is handling his job as president?"

promises on which they campaigned. Fulfilling promises requires political action, and as presidents exercise their head-of-government responsibilities, they lose the head-of-state glow they bring with them from the election. Political change seldom favors everyone equally, and when someone wins, someone else usually loses. Some citizens become disillusioned as the president makes divisive choices, acts as a partisan, or is attacked by Congress and interests that do not favor his policies. For some citizens, the president then becomes "just another politician," not the dignified head of state they thought they were electing. The cycle effect means that presidents need to present their programs early, while they enjoy popular support. Unfortunately, much opportunity available during the honeymoon period can be squandered because of inexperience, as it was at the start of the Clinton administration. In contrast, the Bush team came into office experienced (in part because it benefited from veterans of the previous Bush presidency) and ready to act. Despite the lingering controversy over the contested 2000 election, Republican majorities in both houses of Congress handed Bush several significant legislative victories, including his signature tax cut. Similarly,

President Obama chose as his first chief of staff Rahm Emanuel, a veteran Clinton White House staffer who later served in Congress (see *Profiles in Citizenship*). Emanuel was able to help Obama accomplish an unusually ambitious legislative agenda in the early years of his presidency. Obama continued to be effective with Congress long after his approval ratings left the honeymoon stage, passing in his first two years a major economic stimulus plan, health care reform, and a financial reform bill, along with many less comprehensive pieces of legislation. In fact, his achievements, coming in the context of a highly polarized political environment, probably helped to drive his approval ratings down.

- The second important factor that consistently influences presidential approval is the state of the economy. At least since Franklin Roosevelt, the government has taken an active role in regulating the national economy, and every president promises economic prosperity. In practice, however, presidential power over the economy is quite limited, though we nevertheless hold our presidents accountable for economic performance. President George H. W. Bush lost the presidency in large measure because of the prolonged recession in the latter part of his administration. Clinton won it with a campaign focused on his plan for economic recovery. From 1992, Clinton presided over the nation's longest postwar period of economic growth, and this was a big factor in his relatively easy victory in 1996 and his healthy approval ratings even in the face of the string of embarrassing and headline-grabbing allegations of wrongdoing that led to his impeachment.[56] The economy was troubled for most of President George W. Bush's first term. Growth was slow, especially after the 2001 terror attacks, and because of Bush's tax cuts and the cost of the wars that followed the attacks, the Clinton surplus had turned into the Bush deficit. Bush's approval ratings soared in the wake of the September 11 attacks and in the early days of the Iraq war but dropped throughout the remainder of his presidency as the public became more pessimistic about the war and as the economy cratered toward the end of 2008. As a result of the economic downturn, President Obama came into office during the worst economic recession to hit the nation since the Great Depression of the 1930s. While his ratings reflect a traditional honeymoon effect, they collapsed as unemployment rose and the economic recovery dragged.

- Newsworthy events can influence presidential approval. Sometimes events occur beyond the president's control and he is judged by his response to them. For example, the public and the media looked to President Obama for a response to the BP Gulf oil disaster in 2010. Although the government could do little about the spill because it was dependent on BP for equipment and technological know-how to find a solution, Obama's ratings still took a hit as the oil continued to spill into the Gulf. Events like these are opportunities for establishing presidential leadership, and how presidents perform under such unexpected pressures influences their standing with the public and their long-term effectiveness.

Besides being tests of a president's leadership, newsworthy events can be both divisive and unifying. Political controversy, almost by definition, is divisive and generally hurts presidential ratings. And, of course, controversy in politics is unavoidable even

though the public at large is reluctant to accept this fact of democratic governance.[57] This is part of the reason that presidents' approval ratings seldom maintain their honeymoon highs. Eventually presidents must veto bills, take stands on abortion or stem cell research, raise taxes or oppose a tax break or call for more, or less, regulation. All of these everyday acts of governing give rise to political friction, and this wears down the ratings of a public who prefer not to see their president as a politicking head of government. The drop in ratings for Barack Obama, who was unusually successful at getting his legislative agenda passed, is a textbook example of what happens when a president takes on a political role. Knowing that their cooperation would only bolster Obama, congressional Republicans made a concerted effort to deny him support wherever they could, ensuring that bills that passed on a party-line vote would look controversial and thus unpopular.

On the flip side, unifying events can help presidential ratings. Television footage of the president signing agreements with other heads of state looks "presidential." Similarly, when a president leads the nation in conflict with other countries, at least initially, the public rallies and his approval ratings improve. President George H. W. Bush's rating soared during the 1990–1991 Gulf War, but those were topped by his son's ratings following the terrorist attacks of 2001. George W. Bush's administration framed subsequent legislation in terms of the war on terror, including tax cuts, energy policy, and military spending, all of which were on his agenda before September 11, and his high approval ratings helped him garner support for his agenda even from congressional Democrats.

Thus modern presidents necessarily play the ratings game.[58] Those who choose not to play suffer the consequences: Truman, Johnson, and Ford tended not to heed the polls so closely, and they either had a hard time in office or were not reelected.[59] George W. Bush's plunge in the polls meant that his policy initiatives and preferences were largely ignored by both Congress and the media, especially after his bad poll ratings contributed heavily to the Democrats winning control of Congress in 2006.

> **legislative liaison** executive personnel who work with members of Congress to secure their support in getting a president's legislation passed

> **divided government** political rule split between two parties: one controlling the White House and the other controlling one or both houses of Congress

Working With Congress

Presidents do not always try to influence Congress by going public. Sometimes they deal directly with Congress itself, and sometimes they combine strategies and deal with the public and Congress at the same time. The Constitution gives the primary lawmaking powers to Congress. Thus, to be successful with his policy agenda, the president has to have congressional cooperation. This depends in part on the reputation he has with members of that institution and other Washington elites for being an effective leader.[60] Such success varies with several factors, including the compatibility of the president's and Congress' goals and the party composition of Congress.

Shared Powers and Conflicting Policy Goals

Presidents and members of Congress usually define the nation's problems and possible solutions in different ways. In addition to the philosophical and partisan differences that may exist between the president and members of Congress, each has different constituencies to please. The president, as the one leader elected by the whole nation, needs to take a wider, more encompassing view of the national interest. Members of Congress have relatively narrow constituencies and tend to represent their particular interests. Thus, in many cases, members of Congress do not want the same things the president does.

What can the president do to get his legislation through a Congress made up of members whose primary concern is with their individual constituencies? For one thing, presidents have a staff of assistants to work with Congress. The **legislative liaison** office specializes in determining what members of Congress are most concerned about, what they need, and how legislation can be tailored to get their support. In some cases, members just want their views to be heard; they do not want to be taken for granted. In other cases, the details of the president's program have to be adequately explained. It is electorally useful for members to have this done in person, by the president, complete with photo opportunities for release to the papers back home.

Presidential candidates often claim to be running for office as "outsiders," politicians removed from the politics-as-usual world of Washington and therefore untainted by its self-interest and strife. This can just be a campaign ploy, but when presidents such as Carter and Clinton are elected who truly *do* lack experience in Washington politics, they may fail to understand the sensitivities of members of Congress and

the dynamics of sharing powers. President Carter, even though he had a healthy Democratic majority, had a very difficult time with Congress because he did not realize that, from the perspective of Capitol Hill, what Jimmy Carter believed was good for the nation might not be considered best for each member.[61] Subsequent presidents seem to have learned from Carter's experience. In just the latest example, as we mentioned earlier, President Obama, himself a former senator, picked a legislature-savvy chief of staff to help shepherd his agenda through the lawmaking process.

Partisanship and Divided Government

When the president and the majority of Congress are of the same party, the president is more successful at getting his programs passed. When the president faces **divided government**—that is, when he is of a different party than the majority in one or both houses—he does not do as well.[62] The problem is not just that members of one party act to spite a president of the other party, although that does occur at times. Rather, members of different parties stand for different approaches and solutions to the nation's problems. Democratic presidents and members of Congress tend to be more liberal than the average citizen, and Republican presidents and members of Congress tend to be more conservative.

Figure 8.2 shows a hypothetical example of the position that a Democratic president would take in dealing with a Democratic-led Congress. When the same party controls Congress and the presidency, the two institutions can cooperate relatively easily on ideological issues because the majority party wants to go in the same direction as the president. The president offers his own position, but he is happy to cooperate with the Democratic majority on proposal A because this is much closer to what he wants than is the status quo or the opposition party's proposal. This reflects the situation in 2009 with Democrats gaining the presidency along with continuing control of both houses of Congress. With substantial and sympathetic Democratic majorities in Congress, President Obama set a record for getting his bills through Congress (see Figure 8.3). Consider how drastically the situation changes under divided government—for example, if the Republicans had won control of Congress in 2010. In that case, if Obama were to support a bill similar to proposal A, the Republican Congress would ignore it or amend it to fit more conservative ideological preferences. If a Republican

Figure 8.2

Hypothetical Policy Alternatives Under Unified and Divided Government

It is much easier to pass legislation under unified government, where the president's position and that of Congress start out relatively close together, than under divided government, where there is a large gap between the initial positions of the president and Congress. Presidential success in getting bills passed is much higher under unified government than it is when the opposition party has a majority in Congress.

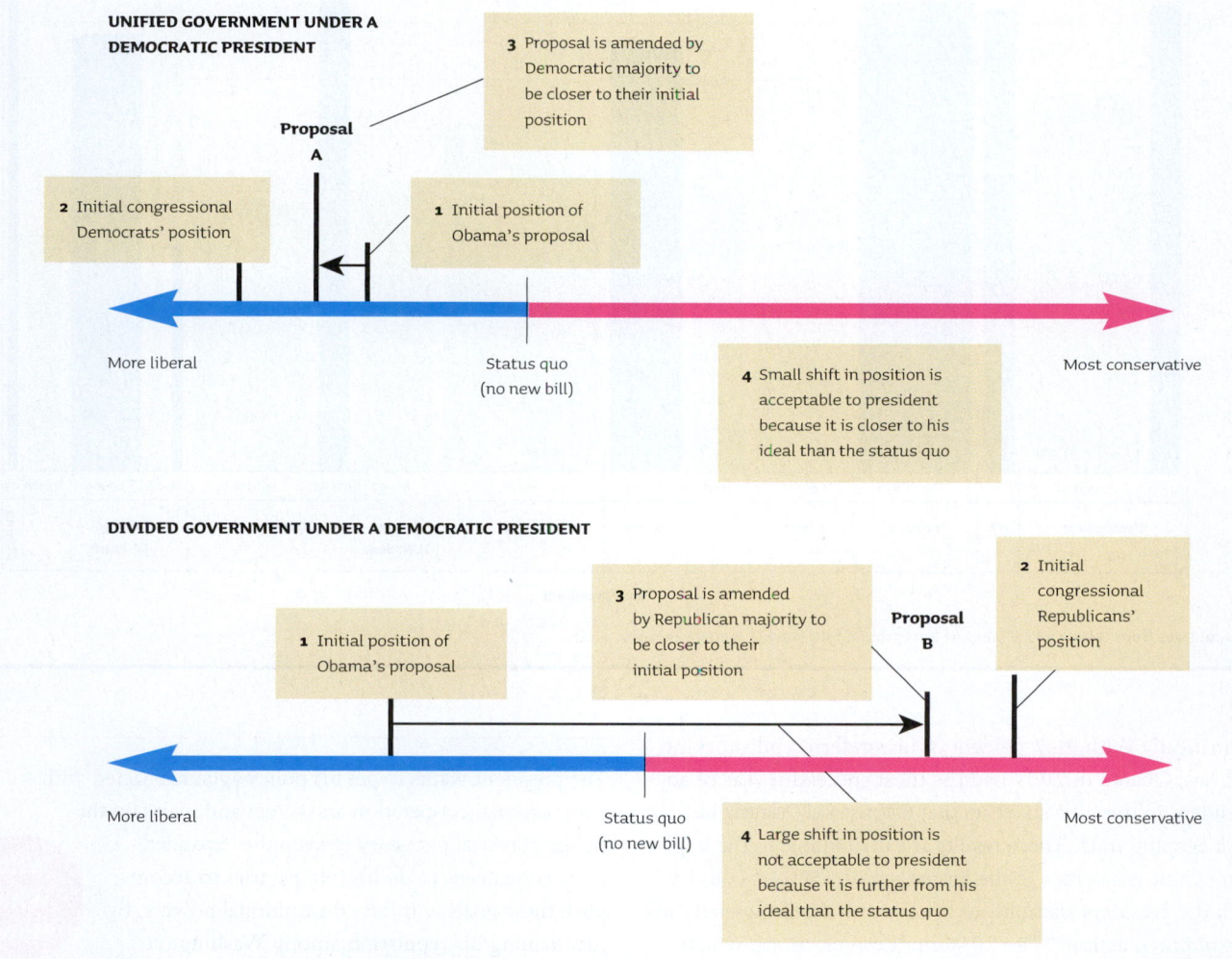

Congress were to send a bill like proposal B to the president, he would veto it because he prefers the alternative of no bill, the status quo, to what Congress passed. Thus, under divided government, Congress tends to ignore what the president wants, and the president tends to veto what the opposition majority party in Congress offers.

Under divided government, presidential success is likely to falter. Figure 8.3 shows the percentage of bills passed that were supported by each president from Eisenhower to Obama. Notice that the success rate is consistently higher under unified government. Dramatic examples of the impact of

divided government can be seen in both the Clinton and George W. Bush administrations. For his first two years in office, Clinton worked with a Democratic majority in both houses, and Congress passed 86 percent of the bills he supported. The next two years (1995–1996) the Republicans had a majority in both houses, and Clinton's success rate dropped to 46 percent.[63] Bush enjoyed impressive success, with his favored bills averaging over three-quarters enacted into law, when he had Republican majorities in Congress. But when he had to deal with a Democratic Congress after the 2006 midterm election, his success rate dropped

Figure 8.3

Presidential Success Under Unified and Divided Government, Eisenhower to Obama

When the president faces a divided government—that is, when the opposing party controls one or both houses of Congress—he usually finds it harder to get his bills passed.

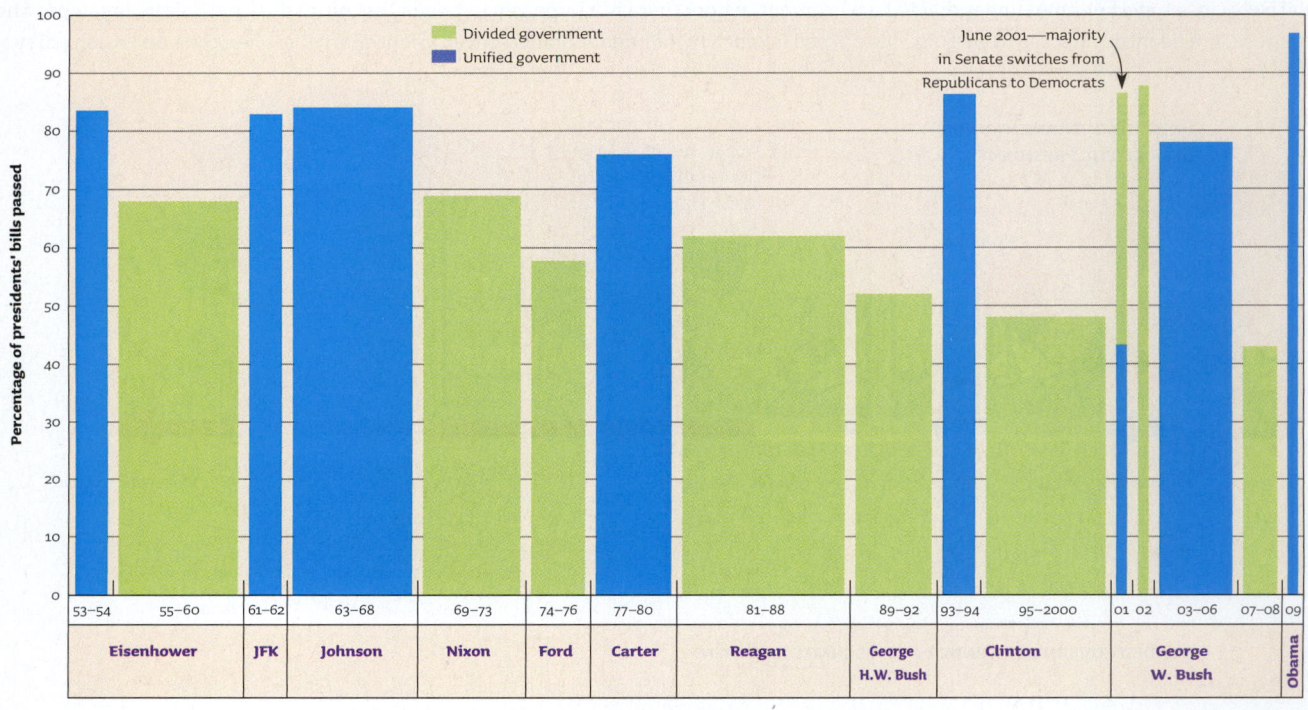

Source: Data from "Presidential Support Background," *CQ Weekly,* January 11, 2010, p. 117.

dramatically. With 96.7 percent of his preferred bills making it into law, Obama in 2009 had the most successful year of any president in the fifty-six years that *Congressional Quarterly* has been keeping track. These results are attributable to the large Democratic majorities in the House and the Senate, coupled with the president's ambitious agenda and a tanking economy that required action.[64] The 2010 midterm elections, which replaced the Democratic majority in the House of Representatives with a conservative Republican majority, inevitably spelled an end to Obama's high rate of success. Whether he can persuade Republicans to work with him, as Clinton did, seems unlikely, given the increased polarization in Congress.

Divided government, however, does not doom Washington to inaction. When national needs are pressing or the public mood seems to demand action, the president and opposition majorities have managed to pass important legislation.[65] For example, the government was divided with a Democrat in the White House and Republicans in control of both houses of Congress when major welfare reform was passed with the Personal Responsibility and Work Opportunity Act of 1996.

The president wants to get his policy agenda enacted with congressional cooperation and to get and maintain the public approval necessary to keep the expanded powers he needs to do his job. He tries to accomplish these goals with his constitutional powers, by maintaining his reputation among Washington elites as an effective leader, by building coalitions among members of Congress, by going public, by skillfully using the media, and by trying to keep the economy healthy.

Citizens have an enormous amount of power in this regard because, distant though Washington may seem to most citizens, presidents are driven by the need for public approval to get most of the things that they want. Congress too has goals: members want to get policy passed so that they may go home to the voters and claim to have supported their interests and to have brought home the bacon. Legislators need to meet the expectations of a different constituency than does the president, but few members of Congress want to be seen by the voters as an obstacle to a popular president. A president who has a strong reputation inside Washington and who has

Who What How

broad popularity outside comes to Congress with a distinct advantage, and members of Congress will go out of their way to cooperate and compromise with him.

Managing the Presidential Establishment

The challenges of supervising an unwieldy bureaucracy

We tend to think of the president as one person—what one presidential scholar calls the "single executive image."[66] However, despite all the formal and informal powers of the presidency, the president is limited in what he can accomplish on his own. In fact, the modern president is one individual at the top of a large and complex organization called the presidency, which itself heads the even larger executive branch of government. George Washington got by with no staff to speak of and consulted with his small cabinet of just three department heads, but citizens' expectations of government, and consequently the sheer size of the government, have grown considerably since then, and so has the machinery designed to manage that government.

Today the executive branch is composed of the cabinet with its fifteen departments, the Executive Office of the President, and the White House staff, amounting altogether to hundreds of agencies and two million civilian employees and almost a million and a half active-duty military employees. The modern president requires a vast bureaucracy to help him make the complex decisions he faces daily, but at the same time the bureaucracy itself presents a major management challenge for the president. The reality of the modern presidency is that the president is limited in his ability to accomplish what he wants by the necessity of dealing with this complex bureaucracy. The executive bureaucracy becomes part of the "how" through which the president tries to get what he wants—for the country, his party, or himself as a politician. But at the same time it becomes another "who," a player in government that goes after its own goals and whose goals can conflict with those of the president.

The Cabinet

Each department in the executive branch is headed by a presidential appointee; collectively, these appointees form the president's cabinet. Today the cabinet comprises fifteen posts heading up fifteen departments. (See Table 9.1 on page 340 for a complete list.) The newest cabinet-level department is the Department of Homeland Security, which was created in 2003. The cabinet is not explicitly set up in the Constitution, though the founders were well aware that the president would need specialty advisers in certain areas. President Washington's cabinet included just secretaries of state, treasury, and war (now called the secretary of defense). The original idea was for the cabinet members to be the president's men overseeing areas for which the president was responsible but that he was unable to supervise personally.

All of that has changed. Today the president considers the demands of organized interests and the political groups and the stature of his administration in putting his cabinet together. The number of departments has grown as various interests (for example, farmers, veterans, workers) have pressed for cabinet-level representation. Appointments to the cabinet have come to serve presidential political goals after the election rather than the goal of helping run the government. Thus the cabinet secretaries typically are chosen to please—or at least not alienate—the organized interests of the constituencies most affected by the departments. Democrats and Republicans will not always choose the same sort of person to fill a cabinet post, however. For example, a Democratic president would be likely to choose a labor leader for secretary of labor, whereas a Republican president would be more likely to fill the post with a representative of the business community.

Presidents may also seek ethnic and gender balance in their cabinet choices. Bill Clinton followed through on his promise to appoint a cabinet of exceptional diversity, and George W. Bush's first- and second-term cabinets followed suit. Bush had two Hispanics, two African Americans, and two Asian Americans serving in his second-term cabinet; four cabinet members were women. In addition, the president chooses cabinet members who have independent stature and reputation before their appointments. President Obama borrowed from Abraham Lincoln's notion building a "team of rivals" when he appointed Hillary Clinton to be his secretary of state and when he retained Bush's secretary of defense, Robert Gates. The president's sense of legitimacy is underscored by having top-quality people working in his administration. Last, but certainly not least, a president wants people who are ideologically similar to him in the policy areas they will be handling.[67] This is not easily achieved (and

> **Executive Office of the President** collection of nine organizations that help the president with policy and political objectives
>
> **Office of Management and Budget** organization within the EOP that oversees the budgets of departments and agencies
>
> **Council of Economic Advisers** organization within the EOP that advises the president on economic matters

> **National Security Council** organization within the EOP that provides foreign policy advice to the president
>
> **White House Office** the approximately four hundred employees within the EOP who work most closely and directly with the president
>
> **chief of staff** the person who oversees the operations of all White House staff and controls access to the president

may not be possible) given the other considerations presidents must weigh.

The combination of these factors in making cabinet choices—political payoffs to organized interests, and the legitimacy provided by top people in the area—often results in a "team" that may not necessarily be focused on carrying out the president's agenda. There are exceptions to the typically guarded relationship between cabinet members and the president, but they prove the rule. President Kennedy appointed his brother Robert as attorney general. George H. W. Bush appointed his very close friend and personal adviser James Baker as treasury secretary. In these cases, however, the close relationship with the president preceded appointment to the cabinet. In general, the political considerations of their appointment, coupled with their independent outlook, mean that cabinet members will provide the president with a variety of views and perspectives. They do not usually, as a group, place loyalty to the president's agenda above other considerations in their advice to the president. Consequently, presidents tend to centralize their decision making by relying more on their advisers in the Executive Office of the President for advice they can trust.[68]

Executive Office of the President

The **Executive Office of the President** (EOP) is a collection of organizations that form the president's own bureaucracy. Instituted by Franklin Roosevelt in 1939, the EOP was designed specifically to serve the president's interests, supply information, and provide expert advice.[69] Among the organizations established in the EOP is the **Office of Management and Budget** (OMB), which helps the president exert control over the departments and agencies of the federal bureaucracy by overseeing all their budgets. The director of OMB works to ensure that the president's budget reflects his own policy agenda. Potential regulations created by the agencies of the national government must be approved by OMB before going into effect. This gives the president an additional measure of control over what the bureaucracy does.

Because modern presidents are held responsible for the performance of the economy, all presidents attempt to bring about healthy economic conditions. The job of the **Council of Economic Advisers** is to predict for presidents where the economy is going and to suggest ways to achieve economic growth without much inflation.

Other departments in the EOP include the **National Security Council** (NSC), which gives the president daily updates about events around the world. The NSC's job is to provide the president with information and advice about foreign affairs; however, the council's role has expanded at times into actually carrying out policy—sometimes illegally, as in the Iran-contra affair.[70] When the existing federal bureaucracy is less than fully cooperative with the president's wishes, some presidents have simply bypassed the agencies by running policy from the White House. One strategy that presidents since Nixon have followed is to appoint so-called policy czars who have responsibility for supervising policy across agencies. Obama has used this strategy extensively to coordinate policy in such areas as health care, energy, and the economy. He made over thirty of these appointments in his first two years to establish firm White House control over the bureaucracy.[71]

White House Staff

Closest to the president, both personally and politically, are the members of the **White House Office**, which is included as a separate unit of the EOP. White House staffers have offices in the White House, and their appointments do not have to be confirmed by the Senate. Just as the public focus on the presidency has grown, so has the size of the president's staff. The White House staff, around 60 members under Roosevelt, grew to the 300–400 range under Eisenhower and in 2010 rested at about 469.[72] The organization of the White House Office has also varied greatly from administration to administration. Presidential scholar James P. Pfiffner has described this organization generally in terms of the following three functional categories: policymaking and coordination, outreach and communications, and internal coordination (see Figure 8.4).

Central to the White House Office is the president's **chief of staff**, who is responsible for the operation of all White House personnel (see "*Profiles in Citizenship: Rahm Emanuel*"). Depending on how much power the president delegates, the chief of staff may decide who gets appointments with the president and whose memoranda he reads. The chief of staff also has a big hand in hiring and firing decisions at the White House. Critics claim that the chief of staff isolates the president by removing him from the day-to-day control of his administration, but demands on the president have grown to

Figure 8.4

Organization of the White House Office

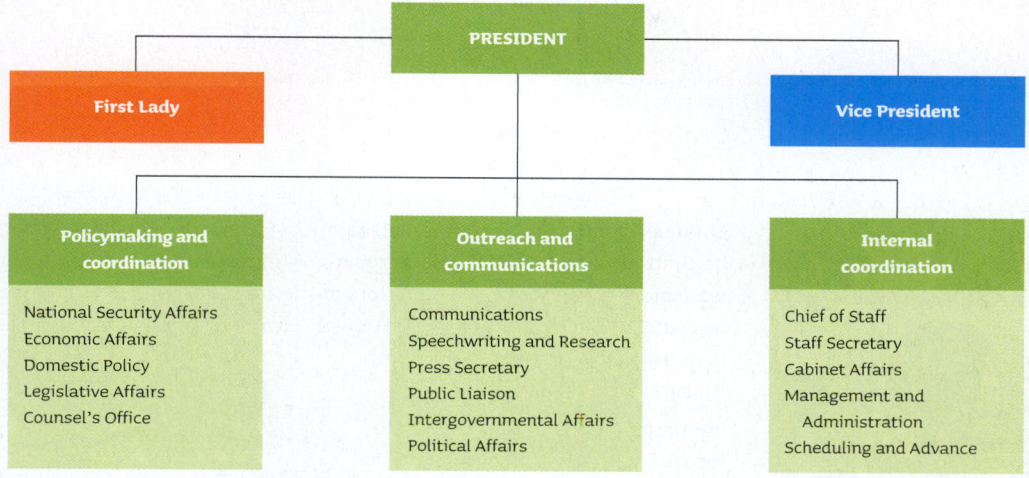

Source: James P. Pfiffner, *The Modern Presidency*, 2nd ed. (New York: St. Martin's, 1998), 87.

the point that a chief of staff is now considered a necessity. Presidents Carter and Ford tried to get by without a chief of staff, but each gave up and appointed one in the middle of his term to make his political life more manageable.[73]

The chief of staff and the other top assistants to the president have to be his eyes and ears, and they act on his behalf every day. The criteria for a good staffer are very different from those for a cabinet selection. First and foremost, the president demands loyalty. That is why presidents typically bring along old friends and close campaign staff as personal assistants. For instance, Barack Obama brought with him several longtime close associates: Rahm Emanuel, a friend and colleague from Chicago politics, who became his first chief of staff, and three senior advisers, David Axelrod, Valerie Jarrett, and Pete Rouse, who replaced Emanuel when he left Washington to run for mayor of Chicago. Rouse was replaced in 2011 by William Daley, son of a former Chicago mayor and himself a former Commerce Secretary in the Clinton administration.

A general principle presidents employ is that their staffs exist only to serve them. When things go well, the president gets the credit; when they do not, the staff take the blame, sometimes even being fired or asked to resign. Such replacements are not unusual at all as presidents change personnel and management strategies to maximize their policy effectiveness and political survival.

The different backgrounds and perspectives of the White House staff and the cabinet mean that the two groups are often at odds. The cabinet secretaries, dedicated to large

departmental missions, want presidential attention for those efforts; the staff want the departments to put the president's immediate political goals ahead of their departmental interests. As a result, the past several decades have seen more and more centralization of important policymaking in the White House, and more decisions being taken away from the traditional turf of the departments.[74]

The Vice President

For most of our history, vice presidents have not been important actors in presidential administrations. Because the original Constitution awarded the vice presidency to the second-place presidential candidate, these officials were seen as potential rivals to the president and were excluded from most decisions and any meaningful policy responsibility. That was corrected with the Twelfth Amendment (1804), which provided for electors to select both the president and the vice president. However, custom for most of the period since then has put a premium on balancing the ticket in terms of regional, ideological, or political interests, which has meant that the person in the second spot is typically not close to the president. In fact, the vice president has sometimes been a rival even in modern times, as when John F. Kennedy appointed Lyndon Johnson, the Senate majority leader from Texas, as his vice president in 1960 in an effort to gain support from the southern states.

Since the Constitution provides only that the vice president act as president of the Senate, which carries no power unless there is a tie vote, most vice presidents have

▶ Profiles in Citizenship: Rahm Emanuel

"...I don't believe every disagreement is partisan...."

As the first appointment President-elect Barack Obama made for his new administration, Illinois representative Rahm Emanuel got lots of media attention, particularly as it took him a couple of days to decide to take the job of White House chief of staff, which he held until October 2010. But Emanuel had worked in the White House before, as a policy adviser for Bill Clinton, and it had been an all-consuming job. And he'd been single at the time. Now with a young family, he had to think twice about returning to the nonstop adrenaline rush that is working in the White House.

Life was simpler, if not less hectic, when we interviewed him in 2005, on a busy day between votes in the House. The clock on the wall buzzed intermittently, signifying an imminent vote in the U.S. House of Representatives. Rep. Rahm

Emanuel didn't want to miss it, and as he chatted with us, one part of his mind was calculating exactly how much longer he could talk before heading to the House floor from his office in the Longworth House Office Building.

But part of his attention was wholly focused on recounting the course his career in public life had taken, this son of an immigrant doctor in Chicago who became a student of child psychology in college, then a player in Chicago politics, a fundraiser for the Clinton campaign in 1992, a senior presidential adviser with an office next to the Oval Office (and, reportedly, the model for Josh Lyman in the television show *The West Wing*), an investment banker, and now (2005, remember) a member of Congress and chair of the DCCC—the Democratic Congressional Campaign Committee.

And all this before he had turned forty-five years old. It should have been astounding, but it wasn't. Emanuel seems to live his life at a faster pace than the rest of us, packing more in and pushing more limits in his impatience and fervor to get things done. He even talks fast, answering questions by telling stories, leaving his listeners to draw their own conclusions as he moves quickly on to his next idea.

Maybe that passion and drive come from his Chicago childhood, where he and his two brothers would read the newspapers to prepare for dinner-table conversation with their parents. The family went to civil rights rallies (his mom ran Chicago CORE—the Congress for Racial Equality), they went to cultural events, and they argued politics at the top of their lungs. (It's an Eastern European–Jewish family thing, Emanuel says. "The decibel level of eight is probably your normal conversation mode.")

In one memorable high-octane family debate in the sixties, Emanuel's mother and maternal grandfather got into a huge argument over a man named Wallace, whom young Rahm took to be Alabama governor George Wallace. Nope, his dad told him, the argument was over Henry Wallace, circa 1948. His family was arguing passionately over a political controversy twenty years old, as if it had just taken place yesterday.

Those are some serious political genes, and they propelled Emanuel into Chicago politics, where he worked closely with Mayor Richard Daley and Senator Paul Simon, and then into Clinton's 1992 campaign for the presidency.

How did he get to the White House while still in his thirties? "I was thirty, thirty-one, single, and I figured you want to do politics and you want to play for the big leagues, the presidential is it. . . . I wanted to be in the White House." So he signed on as a fundraiser for the campaign, and when, against all odds, Clinton won, Emanuel found himself right where he wanted to be.

Okay, so he's clearly driven and goal oriented and ambitious, but it does not appear to be power or, at least, not power for its own sake that drives him. He is dedicated to bringing about a certain community-based vision of society, and the White House was the best platform from which to do it. "In politics and policy [being in the White House] is the Super Bowl. And so there are things that I care about and if you want to make an impact, that's a place you can make a big impact." And a big impact is exactly what he had as he worked on welfare reform, children's health insurance, the Crime Bill, the assault weapons ban, NAFTA, and the balanced budget.

He made the same impact as a representative from Illinois and the guy who took on the job, via the DCCC, of increasing his party's representation in Congress. But though it was his job to strengthen the Democratic Party, Emanuel is cautious about using the word *partisanship*, believing that the media are too quick to chalk up differences to party conflict rather than honest debate and diversity of opinion. It's natural for democracy to be messy and for people to have huge debates about what government should do, but all too often we treat it as pathology rather than a sign of a healthy, functioning democratic system.

Some Republicans criticized his appointment as Obama's first chief of staff, claiming that he was too partisan and that he didn't signal the kind of transformational politics that Obama had talked about. But Emanuel practices what he preaches about party. He can have strong ideological differences with people, but it isn't personal. He has good friends on both sides of the aisle and is respected by many Republicans as well as Democrats.

Without disagreement, politics can't solve problems. Take the issue of Social Security that Congress dealt with shortly after the 2004 election. Emanuel suggests that when the media label a debate as partisan, they trivialize it. But the debate Congress had about Social Security was not mere partisan bickering—it was essential to policymaking. He says, "We're not having a partisan debate about Social Security. We're having an honest-to-God disagreement. They [Republicans] think Social Security should go one way, and we [Democrats] think another, and we're not going to get there with everybody

sitting around singing 'Kum Ba Yah.' An honest fight and debate about that is a good and strong thing. What happens is it gets reported as a partisan fight and just some petty talk. When it's petty and it's partisan, call it. But not every disagreement is partisan."

An Obama White House with Rahm Emanuel as chief of staff may not have been as peaceful as the No Drama Obama presidential campaign, but it was highly effective at accomplishing Obama's political agenda. As Obama said in a statement announcing the pick of his old friend from Illinois, "And no one I know is better at getting things done than Rahm Emanuel." But, he continued, "[t]hough Rahm understands how to get things done in Washington, he still looks at the world from the perspective of his neighbors and constituents on the northwest side of Chicago, who work long and hard, and ask only that their government stand on their side and honor their values." For his part, Emanuel responded, "I'm leaving a job I love to join your White House for one simple reason—like the record amount of voters who cast their ballot over the last month, I want to do everything I can to help deliver the change America needs." Here's what he has to say on partisanship and participation:

On the difference between partisanship and honest political disagreement:

Maybe it comes from growing up in a Jewish home where screaming was the decibel you used, but I don't believe every disagreement is partisan. . . . Now if I say, "Hey, you're a jerk," that's partisan. And that's getting into personal. But what

happens is, and no disrespect, but the elite media make every disagreement a partisan disagreement. It isn't partisan, it's a real policy. And what you can't do, nor should you ever do, is drive politics out of politics. That'd be just bureaucracy. Politics is a good thing. It's how we settle our differences. And through this homogenization of debate, we're saying that every debate is a partisan debate. It isn't. It's a political debate about political differences.

On keeping the republic:

First of all you want to do something with your life. You never know when the Good Lord is going to call your number up. And this is one place in the world, one society where you can leave your thumbprint on this and try to make the world a little better—in your own view better. Second, I see and believe that public service is community service. And when you see the kind of practice my father built and what my mother did, and where I came from and also my grandfather and grandmother on both sides, giving something back to your country and this community is central. . . . Get involved in public service. That could mean a community group, that could be a neighborhood group, that could mean an interest group on some issue, that could mean public office. A campaign. But get involved in your public life. We spend enough time with our iPods, TVs, computers—being individuals. Somewhere else in your life find a way to be part of your community . . . and I think you'll find something that's enriching and also something that allows you to contribute. That's different from anything else you're ever going to do in your life. ■

The Right-Hand Man
Vice presidents traditionally were relegated to ceremonial duties, but that trend has changed significantly in recent administrations. Former vice president Al Gore was a key adviser in the Clinton administration, and Dick Cheney was one of the principal forces in the George W. Bush administration. Joe Biden, shown here with Barack Obama, brings an impressive record of public service, foreign policy experience, and connections to the Obama administration.

tried to make small, generally insignificant jobs seem important, often admitting that theirs was not an enviable post. Thomas Marshall, Woodrow Wilson's vice president, observed in his inaugural address that "I believe I'm entitled to make a few remarks because I'm about to enter a four-year period of silence."[75] Roosevelt's first vice president, John Nance Garner, expressed his disdain for the office even more forcefully, saying that the job "is not worth a pitcher of warm piss."[76]

Ultimately, however, the job of vice president is what the president wants it to be. President Reagan largely ignored George H. W. Bush, for instance, whereas Al Gore, serving under President Clinton, had a central advisory role, in addition to heading up the National Performance Review, which streamlined the bureaucracy and cut government personnel and costs.[77]

Dick Cheney brought a good deal of Washington experience upon which President George W. Bush relied heavily, so much so that many observers have portrayed Cheney as the real power behind the throne.[78]

President Obama's vice president, Joe Biden, brought the heft of a lengthy résumé from six terms in the U.S. Senate and his longtime service on the Senate Foreign Relations Committee. Obama has not relinquished as much authority to

his vice president as Bush did, but Biden has proven to be an effective, independent, and valued policy adviser to the president. He has increasingly been used as an administration spokesperson on a wide range of issues, including his specialty area of foreign relations.[79]

Thus, even though the office of the vice presidency is not a powerful one, vice presidents who establish a relationship of trust with the president can have a significant impact on public policy. The office is important as well, of course, because it is the vice president who assumes the presidency if the president dies, is incapacitated, resigns, or is impeached. Many vice presidents also find the office a good launching pad for a presidential bid. Four of the last ten vice presidents—Lyndon Johnson, Richard Nixon, Gerald Ford, and George H. W. Bush—ended up in the Oval Office, although Al Gore did not enjoy similar success in 2000.

The First Spouse

The office of the "first lady" (even the term seems strangely antiquated in an age when a woman almost won a major party's nomination for the presidency and another was a vice presidential candidate) is undergoing immense changes that reflect the tremendous flux in Americans' perceptions of the appropriate roles for men and women. But the office of first lady has always contained controversial elements, partly the result of conflict over the role of women in politics, but also because the intimate relationship between husband and wife gives the presidential spouse, an unelected position, unique insight into and access to the president's mind and decision-making processes. For all the checks and balances in the American system, there is no way to check the influence of the first spouse. It will be interesting to see whether "first gentlemen" become as controversial as their female counterparts (see the box "Madam President?" for the prospects of a woman president).

First ladies' attempts to play a political role are almost as old as the Republic. In fact, as her husband, John, was preparing to help with the writing of the Constitution, future first lady Abigail Adams admonished him to "remember the ladies," although there is no evidence that he actually did. Much later, in 1919, First Lady Edith Bolling Galt Wilson virtually took over the White House following the illness of her husband, Woodrow, controlling who had access to him and perhaps even issuing presidential decisions in his name. And Eleanor Roosevelt, like her husband, Franklin, took vigorously to political life and kept up an active public role even after his death.

But since the 1960s and the advent of the women's movement, the role of the first lady is seen by the public as less an issue of individual personality and quirks, and more a national commentary on how women in general should behave. As a surrogate for our cultural confusion on what role women should play, the office of the first lady has come under uncommon scrutiny, especially when she takes on a more overtly political role, as did Rosalyn Carter, who even attended cabinet meetings at her husband's request. Public objections to her activities and her position as informal presidential adviser showed that the role of the first lady was controversial even in the late 1970s. Hillary Rodham Clinton shook up public expectations of the first lady's role even more. A successful lawyer who essentially earned the family income while her husband, Bill, served four low-paid terms as governor of Arkansas, Hillary was the target of both public acclaim and public hatred. Her nontraditional tenure as first lady was capped in 2000, at the end of Clinton's second term, by her election as the junior senator from New York. Eight years later she made her own nearly successful run for the Democratic nomination for president and then became Obama's secretary of state.

The politically safest strategy for a first lady appears to be to stick with a noncontroversial moral issue and ask people to do what we all agree they ought to do. Lady Bird Johnson beseeched us to support highway beautification; Nancy Reagan suggested, less successfully, that we "just say no" to drugs; and Laura Bush focused on the issues of education, youth, and literacy.

First Lady Michelle Obama has said flatly that she does not intend to take on an active policymaking role. "I can't do everything," she explains. A committed and active mother to two young children, she wants to keep their lives as normal as possible while living in the White House. Insofar as she takes on a public role, it has thus far been in the noncontroversial styles of Reagan and Bush, as an advocate for working parents, particularly those in the military, who juggle career loads with the demands of raising families, and as a strong supporter of a healthy diet as an antidote to rising childhood obesity rates.[80]

A Package Deal
Barack Obama and his wife, Michelle, share a tender moment on election night, November 4, 2008. First spouses are more than just supportive. They frequently campaign just as hard and serve as advocates for such causes as health care, literacy, and, in Michele Obama's case, childhood nutrition.

The purpose of the executive bureaucracy is to help the president do his job by providing information, expertise, and advice. But while the president's closest advisers are usually focused on his interests, various cabinet officers, staff members, and agency heads may develop agendas of their own that may be at odds with those of the president. He has an easier time controlling members of the EOP, whose job is more clearly to serve him. The vice president and first lady are also more likely to find an agenda that is consistent with the president's.

Who What How

▶ Madam President?

In the United States the idea of Madam President is just that—still an idea—although the 2008 election brought it closer to reality than ever before. In many other countries, however, women chief executives are business as usual. Women have served as elected national leaders or appointed prime ministers in over fifty countries, beginning in 1960 with Sirimavo Bandaranaike of Sri Lanka, the first elected woman prime minister; in 1980 Vigdis Finnbogadottir of Iceland became the first elected woman head of state.[1] The list to the right gives only a sample of the women who have served as national leaders, including several who remain in power today.

Why has the United States lagged behind other nations in electing a woman to its highest political office? American women were among the first women in the world to gain the right to vote, in 1920, well before women living in several of the countries listed in the table. Women leaders have served or are serving in countries such as Pakistan and Senegal, where women currently have fewer civil rights than do women in the United States. Culture does not seem to offer an explanation, because women have been chief executives in Islamic, South American, southern European, Asian, and African countries, where the social and cultural separation between male and female roles has been most pronounced. Furthermore, countries with social and cultural traditions more similar to the United States, such as Britain and Canada, have also had women as national leaders.

So why has the United States not had a female president? In public opinion polls, Americans seem to indicate that they are willing to give it a try. In 2007 a Gallup poll found that 88 percent of Americans would vote for a "well-qualified woman" for president,[2] up from 78 percent in 1984 and only 53 percent in 1969.[3] (See figure.) In addition, 61 percent of Americans think the United States is ready for a woman president.[4] Some people question whether Americans really would support a woman for president, however. One experimental survey found that 26 percent of those polled felt angry about the prospect of a woman president, leading the researchers to believe that some Americans report supporting a woman for president only because they know it is a socially desirable answer.[5]

Another likely explanation for the lack of a woman leader in the United States is that there aren't many women in the pipeline, in jobs like vice president, senator, or state governor, which generate presidential candidates. This is partly because women enter politics on average a decade later than do men, meaning they begin climbing the political ladder later than do most men.[6] The number of female senators from both parties continues to rise, but it remains well below the average percentage of women in American society. Perhaps more important, the number of female governors (four of our past five presidents were governors) has remained limited. Only six women (three Democrats and three Republicans) currently serve as governors. In some ways, 2008 was a groundbreaking year for women candidates. Before then, the only woman candidate for vice president for either party was Geraldine Ferraro, who ran with Walter Mondale in 1984, and only a handful of women (for example, Carol Moseley Braun and Elizabeth Dole) had tried to win the presidential nomination. In 2008 Hillary Clinton nearly won the Democratic nomination, and Sarah Palin, governor of Alaska, was chosen as the vice presidential candidate for the

Leader	Country	Position	Years
Indira Gandhi	India	PM	1966–1977; 1980–1984
Golda Meir	Israel	PM	1969–1974
Margaret Thatcher	UK	PM	1979–1990
Corazon Aquino	Philippines	President	1986–1992
Benazir Bhutto	Pakistan	PM	1988–1990; 1993–1996
Tansu Ciller	Turkey	PM	1993–1996
Chandrika Kumaratunga	Sri Lanka	President	1994–2005
Sheikh Hasina Wajed	Bangladesh	PM	1996–2001; 2009–present
Janet Jagan	Guyana	President	1997–1999
Mary McAleese	Ireland	President	1997–present
Helen Clark	New Zealand	PM	1999–2008
Tarja Halonen	Finland	President	2000–present
Madior Boye	Senegal	PM	2001–2002
Megawati Sukarnoputri	Indonesia	President	2001–2004
Gloria Arroyo	Philippines	President	2001–2010
Yulia Tymoshenko	Ukraine	PM	2005
Angela Merkel	Germany	PM	2005–present
Ellen Johnson-Sirleaf	Liberia	President	2006–present
Pratibha Patil	India	President	2007–present
Cristina Fernandez de Kirchner	Argentina	President	2007–present
Jóhanna Sigurðardóttir	Iceland	PM	2009–present
Jadranka Kosor	Croatia	PM	2009–present
Dalia Grybauskaitė	Lithuania	President	2009–present
Roza Otunbayeva	Kyrgyzstan	President	2010–present
Laura Chinchilla Miranda	Costa Rica	President	2010–present
Kamla Persad-Bissessar	Trinidad and Tobago	PM	2010–present
Mari Kiviniemi	Finland	PM	2010–present
Julia Gillard	Australia	PM	2010–present

Source: Current Women World Leaders, www.guide2womenleaders.com/Current-Women-Leaders.htm.

Note: PM = Prime minister.

Republicans. Though these breakthroughs put, as Clinton stated, cracks in the glass ceiling, they also underscore the paucity of women candidates in the pool; the vast majority of the other contenders for these positions in 2010 were still men.

In general, the overall pool of elected women in the United States remains small. Women legislators hold only 24.4 percent of state legislative seats across the country and even fewer of the national legislative seats in Congress (just over 16 percent of seats in the House of Representatives and 17 percent in the Senate).[7] In this respect, the United States lags far behind other

Question: "If your party nominated a generally well-qualified person for president who happened to be a woman, would you vote for that person?"

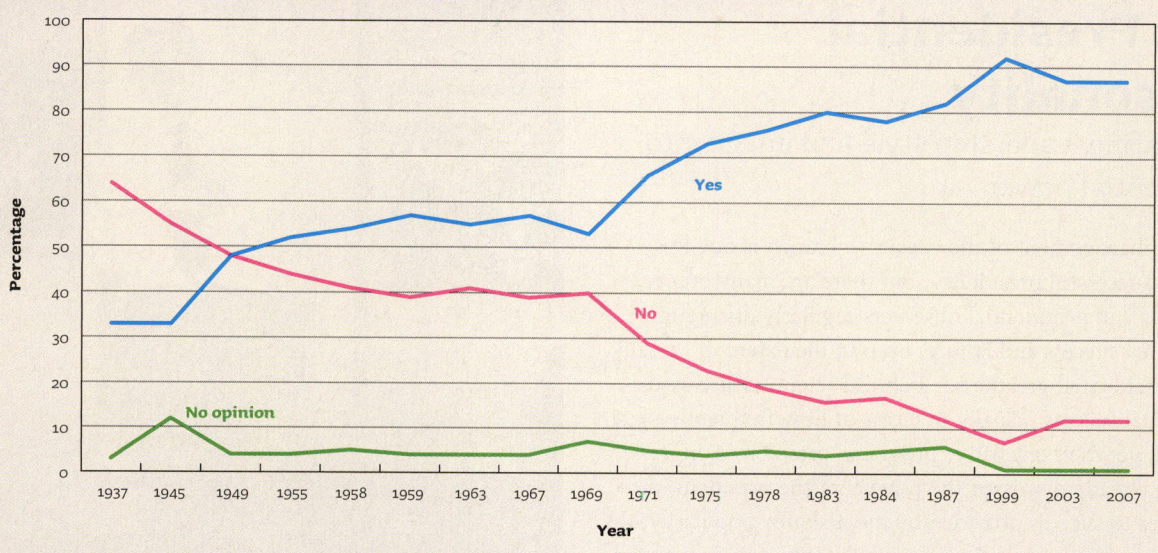

Sources: Authors' update of data from the California State University Social Sciences Research and Instructional Council, www.csubak.edu/ssric/Modules/Others/disk1/gallup.htm; and Gallup/CNN/USA Today poll, June 10, 2003, Roper Center at the University of Connecticut, Public Opinion Online. Data for 2007 from Gallup poll at www.gallup.com/poll/26611/Some-Americans-Reluctant-Vote-Mormon-72YearOld-Presidential-Candidates.aspx.

countries. In 2008, 47 percent of the seats in the lower house of the Swedish legislature were held by women, 49 percent in Rwanda, 40 percent in Argentina, 23 percent in Mexico, 25.5 percent in Iraq, and 27 percent in Australia.[8] In addition, only thirty-five women have ever served in the U.S. Senate, only thirty-one women have served as governors (only twenty-one of whom were elected rather than succeeding another governor),[9] and no woman has ever served as U.S. vice president.[10]

Nevertheless, several researchers point to important advances for women in prominent political positions that may lead to a deeper pool of women candidates for president in the future. Nancy Pelosi, D-Calif., was Speaker of the House of Representatives, the highest leadership position in the House. The continued appointment of women to key executive posts dealing with international affairs, especially including two secretaries of state, also encourages the idea that women can handle crisis-filled political situations. As more women like Clinton and Palin become involved in presidential elections, Americans will grow more accustomed to seeing women in these positions of power.

Several organizations are working toward the goal of electing more women to office, and to the office of president, in the United States. Political action committees like EMILY's List and WISH List work with the primary aim of raising money for women candidates for major political offices. The White House Project (www.thewhitehouseproject.org) is a nonpartisan initiative dedicated to raising the public's awareness of women political leaders in the United States and to putting a woman in the White House.

An important question remains in the issue of a future woman president. Are Americans ready for a "first husband"? Apparently

they are. Ninety-one percent of Americans said that if the president of the United States was a woman, they would find it appropriate for the husband to serve as official host at the White House.[11]

1. The History Net, "Women Prime Ministers and Presidents—20th Century Heads of State," http://womenshistory.about.com/od/rulers20th/a/women_heads.htm.
2. Andrew Kohut, "Are Americans Ready to Elect a Female President," Pew Research Center, http://pewresearch.org/pubs/474/female-president.
3. California State University Social Sciences Research and Instructional Council, "65 Years of Gallup Polling. Mystery Table Three: Willingness to Support a Woman for President," www.csubak.edu/ssric/modules/other/disk1/gallup .htm.
4. Jeffrey M. Jones, "Six in 10 Americans Think U.S. Ready for a Female President," October 3, 2006, www.cawp.rutgers.edu/fast_facts/elections/documents/08-Gallup.6in10.pdf.
5. "Americans' Support for a Female President Is Significantly Exaggerated" (news release), www.niu.edu/pubaffairs/releases/2007/jan/research.shtml.
6. Eleanor Clift and Tom Brazaitis, *Madam President* (New York: Routledge, 2003), 227.
7. Center for American Women and Politics, "Women in Elective Office 2010," www.cawp.rutgers.edu/fast_facts/levels_of_office/documents/elective.pdf.
8. Women in National Parliaments, "World Classification," www.ipu.org/wmn-e/classif.htm.
9. Center for American Women and Politics, "Statewide Elective Executive Women 2009," www.cawp.rutgers.edu/fast_facts/levels_of_office/documents/stwide09.pdf; Center for American Women and Politics, "Women in the U.S. Senate, 1922–2010," www.cawp.rutgers.edu/fast_facts/levels_of_office/documents/senate.pdf.
10. Center for American Women and Politics, "Women in Elective Office 2005," "Women in the U.S. Senate, 1922–2005," and "Statewide Elective Executive Women," www.cawp.rutgers.edu/fast_facts/index.php.
11. *USA Today*/Gallup poll, September 13–15, 2004, iPOLL databank, the Roper Center for Public Opinion Research, University of Connecticut, www.roper center.uconn.edu/data_access/ipoll/ipoll.html.

presidential style image projected by the president that represents how he would like to be perceived at home and abroad

The Presidential Personality

Translating leadership style and image into presidential power

Effective management of the executive branch is one feature of a successful presidency, but there are many others. Historians and presidential observers regularly distinguish presidential success and failure, even to the extent of actually rating presidential greatness.[81] Political scientists also assess presidential success, usually in terms of how frequently presidents can get their legislative programs passed by Congress.[82] We have already discussed the powers of the president, the challenges to success provided by the need for popularity, the difficulties of dealing with Congress, and the enormous management tasks faced by the president. In this section we look at the personal resources of a president that lead to success or contribute to failure. We begin by exploring what kinds of people are driven to become president in the first place.

Classifying Presidential Character

Most presidents share some personality characteristics—giant ambition and large egos, for instance—but this does not mean that they are carbon copies of one another. They clearly differ in fundamental ways. A number of scholars have developed classification schemes of presidential personalities. Each of these schemes is based on the expectation that knowing key dimensions of individual presidential personalities will help explain, or even predict, how presidents will behave in certain circumstances. The most famous of these schemes was developed by James David Barber, who classified presidents on two dimensions: their energy level (passive or active) and their orientation toward life (positive or negative).[83]

Some of our best and most popular presidents have been active-positives. They have had great energy and a very positive orientation toward the job of being president. Franklin Roosevelt, John F. Kennedy, Bill Clinton, and Barack Obama represent this type. Others have had less energy (passives) or have been burdened by the job of being president (negatives). They have acted out their roles, according to Barber, as they thought they should, out of duty or obligation. Ronald Reagan and George W. Bush fit the model of the passive-positive president. They liked being leaders but believed that the job was one of delegating and

The Great Communicator
This was the label many people applied to President Ronald Reagan because of his ability to connect with the American public. His effectiveness as a communicator had little to do with explaining complex policy decisions. Rather, he conveyed a sense of confidence, trustworthiness, and warmth. He made people feel good.

setting the tone rather than of taking an active policymaking role. Richard Nixon is usually offered as one of the clearest examples of an active-negative president; he had lots of energy but could not enjoy the job of being president.

Assessing individual personalities is a fascinating enterprise, but it is fraught with danger. Few politicians fit neatly into Barber's boxes (or the categories of other personality theorists) in an unambiguous way. Although some scholars find that personality analysis adds greatly to their understanding of the differences among presidencies, others discount it altogether, claiming that it leads one to overlook the ways in which rules and external forces have shaped the modern presidency.[84]

Figure 8.5

Presidential Style: A Comparison of the Public's Image of Clinton, Bush, and Obama

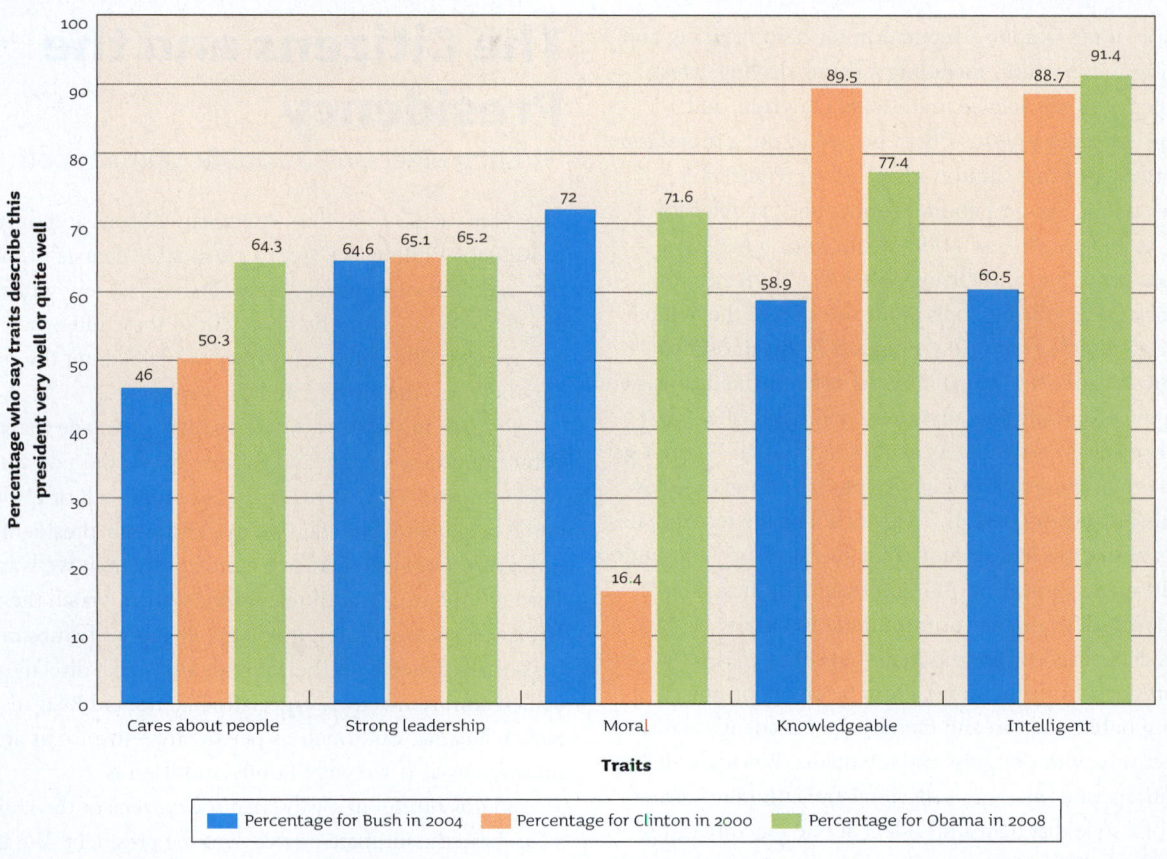

Presidential Style

In addition to their personality differences, each president strives to create a ***presidential style***, or an image that captures symbolically who he is for the American people and for leaders of other nations. These personal differences in how presidents present themselves are real, but they are also carefully cultivated. Each also strives to distinguish himself from his predecessors, to set himself apart, and to give hope for new, and presumably better, presidential leadership.[85]

For example, Harry Truman was known for his straight, sometimes profane, talk and no-nonsense decision making. In contrast, Dwight Eisenhower developed his "Victorious General" image as a statesman above the fray of petty day-to-day politics. John F. Kennedy, whose term followed Eisenhower's, evoked a theme of "getting the country moving again" and embodied this with a personal image of youth and energy.

More recently, in the wake of Watergate and the disgrace of Richard Nixon, Jimmy Carter hit a winning note with a style promising honesty and competent government. Carter was

honest, but his self-doubts and admissions that the United States faced problems that government might not be able to solve disappointed many Americans. In contrast, Ronald Reagan's "it's-morning-in-America" optimism and his calming, grandfatherly presence were soaked up by an eager public.

Bill Clinton's style combined the image of the highly intellectual Rhodes scholar with that of a compassionate leader, famous for "feeling America's pain." That carefully managed image could not disguise the fact that Clinton was also a man of large appetites, however, from his jogging breaks to eat at McDonald's to his extramarital affairs. While people approved of Clinton's leadership through the end of his presidency, a majority of citizens noted concerns about his honesty and moral character.

George W. Bush came into office with an opposite set of characteristics. Widely perceived as a nonintellectual who joked that C students could grow up to be president, he cultivated the image of the chief executive officer he was: a president primarily interested in results, not academic debates, who was willing to set a course and leave others to get the job done. Despite a reputation for hard drinking and high living in his youth, including a drunk driving arrest, Bush's pledge of abstinence, traditional marriage, and frequent references to Jesus Christ helped to put a moral tone on his presidency that Clinton's had lacked. Figure 8.5 compares public opinion about presidential character for Clinton, as he left office in 2000; Bush, during his 2004 reelection campaign; and Obama, after the 2008 election.

Barack Obama brings a placid disposition to the White House. His calm demeanor (symbolized by his unofficial campaign slogan—No Drama Obama) has remained consistent through the economic and environmental crises of the first two years of his presidency. As he says of himself, "I don't get too high when things are going well and I don't get too low when things are going tough."[86] Obama's image incorporates elements of the styles of several of his predecessors, combining Ronald Reagan's optimism, Bill Clinton's braininess, and George W. Bush's faith and commitment to family.

Presidential style is an important but subtle means by which presidents communicate. It can be an opportunity for enhancing public support and thereby the president's ability to deal effectively with Congress and the media. But any style has its limitations, and the same behavioral and attitudinal characteristics of a style that help a president at one juncture can prove a liability later. Furthermore, as Clinton's experience shows, the president does not always have total control over the image of him that the public sees. Political enemies and an investigative press can combine to counter the image the president wants to project. Because public perception is tied so closely to leadership ability, a significant portion of the president's staffers end up concerning themselves with "image management."

Who What How

In the matter of presidential style and personality, the person with the most at stake is undoubtedly the president. His goals are popularity, legislative success, support for his party, and a favorable judgment in the history books. He functions in a number of policy roles as the head of government, but he also serves as our head of state, a role that is merely symbolic at times but that can be of tremendous importance for presidential power in times of national crisis or in conflicts with other nations. Because presidents' formal powers to fulfill these functions are limited, and their informal powers depend on their popularity with citizens and with the Washington elite, the personality and style that allow them to win popularity are crucial.

The Citizens and the Presidency

"Rolling election" by public opinion poll

There are over 300 million American citizens and only one president. While we all have a reasonable chance of meeting our members of Congress, only the luckiest few will actually shake hands with the president of the United States. With connections this remote, how can we talk about the relationship between the citizens and the president?

Perhaps in the days before technology made mass communication so easy and routine, we could not. But today, while we may never dance at an inaugural ball or even wave at the president from afar, we can know our presidents intimately (and often far more intimately than we want to!). Through the medium of television, we can watch them board airplanes, speak to foreign leaders, swing golf clubs or play basketball, dance with their wives, and speak directly to us. Skilled communicators, especially like Ronald Reagan and Barack Obama, can touch us personally—inspire us and infuriate us as if we were family and friends.

So it is fitting, in a way, that the citizens of the United States have the ultimate power over the president. We elect him (and someday her), it is true, but our power goes beyond a once-every-four-years vote of approval or disapproval. Modern polling techniques, as we have seen, allow us to conduct a "rolling election," as the media and the politicians themselves track popular approval of the president throughout his term. The presidential strategy of going public is made possible because all Americans—citizens, president, and members of Congress—know just where the president stands with the public and how much political capital he has to spend.

In 1998 and 1999 we saw perhaps the clearest example of the power that citizens' support can give to a president in the fate of Bill Clinton's imperiled presidency. After a lengthy investigation, independent prosecutor Kenneth Starr sent a report to Congress on September 9, 1998, that he claimed provided grounds for Clinton's impeachment on perjury and obstruction-of-justice charges. As graphic details of Clinton's behavior were made public, Clinton's personal approval ratings sank, yet his job approval ratings stayed high. Questioned on specifics, people said they disapproved of Clinton's moral character and found his behavior (having an affair with a White House intern) repellent, but they thought the impeachment movement was politically motivated and that

Clinton's private behavior had no impact on his ability to do his job. They seemed to find him wanting in the symbolic head-of-state role we discussed earlier in this chapter but continued to approve of him as the head of government. In clear rejection of the investigation of the president, Americans went against tradition on Election Day 1998: instead of handing the president's party its usual midterm loss, they supported the Democrats so strongly that they gained five seats in Congress. The day after Clinton was impeached, on December 11, his approval ratings with the American public hit a high of 73 percent.[87]

Clinton went on to be acquitted in the Senate. Once he was no longer under threat, Clinton's ratings dropped too, to the more normal levels of a popular president near the end of his second term. It is arguable that these polls saved Clinton's political life. Had they fallen it would have been much harder for Democrats and moderates in the House and the Senate to support him and the president may well have lost his job.

In a similar vein, although the details are strikingly different, the presidency of George W. Bush also came to depend on unusually high opinion ratings where one might not have expected to find them. Bush claimed the presidency after a contested election in which he received fewer popular votes than his opponent and that was resolved by the Supreme Court in a five-to-four vote that many believed was politically motivated. Many pundits predicted that his presidency would be a one-term failure. While his early approval ratings showed he was enjoying something on the low end of a traditional honeymoon, by the summer of 2001, his ratings were clearly sinking.

In September, however, the unthinkable happened. When terrorists flew hijacked planes into the World Trade Center and the Pentagon and launched America into the war on terrorism, Bush was given a clean slate on which to write his presidential legacy. Making the war against terrorism the keystone of his presidency, his portrayal of the conflict in simple terms reassured Americans, and his early military successes solidified their support for him. His approval rating hit 90 percent—higher than any other president since records have been kept. With high ratings, Bush was as powerful as, if not more powerful than, if he had won the election in a landslide, and the 2002 election again failed to show the traditional midterm loss as Bush's efforts swept Republicans into Congress—building slightly the majority in the House of Representatives and creating a Republican majority in the Senate.

Bush's approval dropped off steadily afterward, except for a slight turn upward following his initial success with the invasion of Iraq, and then continued to decline into the low 30s, the worst of any president except Richard Nixon. Nevertheless, unlike the situation for Clinton, the American people have tended to approve of Bush more personally than they have approved of how he has performed his job. Moreover, Bush's personal approval and job approval go up and down together, whereas the American public largely separated those judgments for Clinton. Thus the public has linked the head-of-state and head-of-government roles for President Bush much more so than they did for President Clinton. Not surprisingly, when Bush ran for reelection in a tight race, many of the images his campaign focused on were those that tried to remind Americans of the post–September 11 era, when he had high job approval ratings. They also highlighted Bush's personal attributes that the public seemed to prefer over his performance on the job. Even amid a soft economy and a shaky situation in Iraq, the American people returned Bush to office, although with a narrow margin.

How can we understand the very unusual reaction of Americans who showed overwhelming support for a president whom they had only moderately approved of before his involvement in a tawdry sex scandal, and who rejected one president at the election booth only a year before they gave him the highest approval ratings a president has ever received? For one thing, the public judges presidents on different criteria in part because the office has different roles to fill. Which president are they being asked their opinion of? Americans may have disapproved of President Clinton as head of state, but they certainly supported him as head of government. The opposite might be more the case for President Bush. Second, under everyday circumstances, questions concerning presidential job and personal approval seem straightforward, but the strength of the economy, current political conflicts, external events, and the personal foibles of the president can alter the public's assessment of the president in complex ways that either enhance or limit the president's power. Finally, the institution of the American presidency, like most of the rest of the government designed by the framers, was meant to be insulated from the whims of the public. It is an irony that in contemporary politics the president is often more indebted to the citizens for his power than he is to the Electoral College, Congress, the courts, or any of the political elites the founders trusted to stabilize American government.

▶ What's at Stake Revisited

The Constitution may be a study in ambiguity on some issues, but on others it is crystal clear. Congress makes the laws, for instance. Presidents can veto or they can sign, but when they do the latter, it is their job to enforce the law that Congress passed. The principle of checks and balances depends on this back-and-forth power-wielding arrangement. If one branch could impose its will on the others without limit, checks and balances would disappear.

Still, controversy remains about how strong the executive power should be. When George W. Bush started using signing statements to aggressively challenge congressional will, he was putting the brakes on checks and balances. By refusing to veto legislation he didn't like and instead issuing signing statements that enabled him to ignore parts of laws he didn't consider to be constitutional, Bush was bypassing Congress, which then could not exercise its option of overriding a veto, and the courts, which were unable to play their role as the ultimate determinant of what is constitutional. Bush's defenders claimed that the signing statements were just "political chest thumping" that didn't really mean anything,[88] but in fact, the nonpartisan Government Accountability Office found that Bush failed to comply with congressional legislation multiple times.[89]

Many actors have high stakes in such actions. For the Bush administration, what was at stake was a more muscular presidency, one that wasn't, as they thought, emasculated in the wake of the Watergate scandal, and one that was premised on the unitary theory of the executive that said that executive power belongs to the president alone. As we have seen, signing statements were not the only strategy pursued to strengthen the office, but they were a clear attempt to move the presidency beyond its constitutional limits. Other presidents have used signing statements to assert their right to preserve their constitutional powers, but they have not used the statements to expand them.[90]

For Congress, the stakes were painfully high. We have seen what goes into crafting legislation—the compromise, skill, and bargaining involved in creating laws that the people's representatives feel they can sign on to. Bush's signing statements essentially allowed the executive to rewrite the bills, ignoring what he didn't like and keeping what he did, with no way for Congress to guarantee that its actions would count.

And, of course, the stakes could not have been higher for the American public. The point of checks and balances was to limit the power wielded by any one branch, so that the government as a whole would stay limited in power, and to ensure that individual liberties would be safe from government encroachment. The substance of the legislation that Bush felt he could ignore indicates just how much the public stood to lose from his actions; safeguards against wiretapping and torture, and whistleblower protection were jeopardized, among other things.

Citizens also had a stake in the accountability of their elected officials and the smooth running of their democracy. When Congress passes a bill, or overrides a presidential veto, voters have a check. They can hold their representatives accountable and vote them out of office if they don't like what they do. But if the executive alters the laws on the quiet, the lines of accountability are muddied and democracy itself is endangered.

As Bruce Fein, a former official in the Reagan Justice Department, said, "This is an attempt by the president to have the final word on his own constitutional powers, which eliminates the checks and balances that keep the country a democracy. There is no way for an independent judiciary to check his assertions of power, and Congress isn't doing it either. So this is moving us toward an unlimited executive power."[91] Very high stakes, indeed.

To Sum Up

Key terms, chapter summaries, practice quizzes, Internet links, and other study aids are available on the companion web site at http://republic.cqpress.com.

Define | **Understand** | **Practice** | **Read** | **Click** | **Watch**

cabinet (p. 297)

chief administrator (p. 296)

chief foreign policy maker (p. 297)

chief of staff (p. 314)

commander-in-chief (p. 297)

Council of Economic Advisers (p. 314)

cycle effect (p. 307)

divided government (p. 310)

executive agreements (p. 297)

Executive Office of the President (p. 314)

executive orders (p. 299)

going public (p. 307)

head of government (p. 292)

head of state (p. 291)

honeymoon period (p. 307)

inherent powers (p. 301)

legislative liaison (p. 310)

National Security Council (p. 314)

Office of Management and Budget (p. 314)

pardoning power (p. 301)

power to persuade (p. 306)

presidential style (p. 323)

presidential veto (p. 298)

senatorial courtesy (p. 300)

solicitor general (p. 301)

State of the Union address (p. 297)

treaties (p. 297)

White House Office (p. 314)

Define | **Understand** | **Practice** | **Read** | **Click** | **Watch**

- Presidents face a double expectations gap when it comes to their relationship with the American public. The first gap is between what the president must promise in order to gain office and the limitations put on the president by the powers granted by the Constitution. The second gap occurs between conflicting roles. An American president must function as both a political head of government and an apolitical head of state, and often these two roles conflict.

- When it came to defining the functions and powers of the president, the founders devised rules that both empowered and limited the president. While some of the founders argued for a strong leader with far-reaching powers, others argued for several executives who would check each other's power. The constitutional compromise gives us an executive that has certain powers and independence, yet is checked by congressional and judicial power.

- We have seen two periods of presidential leadership so far. The first period, called the traditional presidency, which lasted until the 1930s, describes chief executives who mainly lived within the limits of their constitutional powers. Since then,

in the modern presidency, a more complex relationship has existed between the president and the American citizens, in which presidents branch out to use more informal powers yet remain indebted to public approval for this expansion.

- The president is in a constant struggle with Congress and the public for the furthering of his legislative agenda. The president needs both congressional cooperation and public approval in order to fulfill campaign promises. The chief executive uses several strategies to achieve these goals, including going public and building coalitions in Congress.

- The presidential establishment includes the cabinet, the Executive Office of the President, and the White House Office—a huge bureaucracy that has grown considerably since the days of George Washington's presidency. Although the resources are vast, managing such a large and complex organization presents its own problems for the president. The president's closest advisers are generally focused on his interests, but the variety of other staff and agency heads—often with their own agendas and often difficult to control—can make life difficult for the chief executive.

1. **What best describes the era of the modern presidency?**
   a. Its legacy is that Americans often look to their presidents and government to solve social and economic issues and to inspire the public.
   b. It preceded the Great Depression, which exhausted much of the power of the president to deal with social and economic issues.
   c. It proved that presidents would continue to fulfill the limited role envisioned by the framers.
   d. It occurred during the late eighteenth century and throughout the nineteenth century, when presidents were overshadowed by congressional power.
   e. All of the above.

2. **Which of the following best explains why there has been an increased centralization of important policymaking in the White House in the past several decades?**
   a. The scope of government has decreased, which has lessened the president's need to seek outside advice.
   b. The Twenty-fifth Amendment has given vice presidents much more control than they had prior to its enactment.
   c. The Bipartisan Selection Act of 1960 has centralized the president's policymaking within the Executive Office of the President.
   d. The White House staff have successfully put the president's immediate political goals ahead of the multiple demands placed on him by cabinet secretaries.
   e. The size of government continues to decrease, making it more efficient to concentrate efforts within the White House.

3. **The strategy presidents use to appeal to the public on an issue, in expectation that public pressure will be brought to bear on other political actors, is referred to as**
   a. converting on the expectations gap.
   b. going public.

   c. senatorial courtesy.
   d. the legislative liaison.
   e. presidential approval.

4. **How does the presidential character classification scheme supposedly help presidential scholars and citizens in judging presidents?**
   a. It illustrates how active-positive presidents are always the poorest type of person for the job.
   b. It illustrates how active-negative presidents are always the best type of person for the job.
   c. It proves that the personality of a president has no impact on how a president will perform in office, given the enormous institutional constraints on the presidency.
   d. It alone explains how well a president will perform in office.
   e. It may provide a helpful tool in explaining and predicting how a president may perform in certain circumstances.

5. **Which of the following is NOT true of the double expectations gap?**
   a. The public demands that presidential candidates make numerous promises when running for office.
   b. Presidents do not often have the constitutional powers to fulfill their campaign promises.
   c. Unlike other heads of governments around the world, the president is freed from ceremonial roles carried out by heads of state.
   d. The president must fulfill conflicting roles, which saps his ability to carry out one or more of those roles particularly well.
   e. Presidents struggle to live up to promises and juggle the different roles of the office.

Albright, Madeleine. 2008. *Memo to the President Elect: How We Can Restore America's Reputation and Leadership*. New York: Harper. *Regardless of the outcome of the 2008 presidential election, Albright's timely "memo" offers a Washington insider's look at the many directions that U.S. foreign policy might take under the new administration.*

Drew, Elizabeth. 1996. *Showdown: The Struggle Between the Gingrich Congress and the Clinton White House*. New York: Simon & Schuster. *By drawing on a dramatic conflict between Congress and the president, Drew effectively illustrates how the different agendas of these two branches often collide.*

Gergen, David. 2000. *Eyewitness to Power: The Essence of Leadership: From Nixon to Clinton*. New York: Simon & Schuster. *The journalistic style used in this insider analysis of the four recent presidents for whom Gergen worked makes it very readable.*

Kernell, Samuel. 2007. *Going Public: New Strategies of Presidential Leadership*, 3rd ed. Washington, D.C.: CQ Press. *An interesting book on how recent presidents have bypassed Congress and gone straight to the public for support of presidential initiatives in an attempt to put constituent pressure on Congress.*

Mayer, Kenneth R. 2002. *With the Stroke of a Pen: Executive Orders and Presidential Power*. Princeton: Princeton University Press. *Mayer illustrates how constitutional and institutional powers of the presidency, such as the executive order, allow presidents to follow through on much of their agenda with few checks from Congress.*

McClellan, Scott. 2008. *What Happened: Inside the Bush White House and Washington's Culture of Deception*. New York: PublicAffairs.   The author, who served as White House press secretary during the tenure of George W. Bush, charts the administration's controversial behavior in the run-up to the war in Iraq, and offers an incisive analysis of the well-known "Plame incident."

Milkis, Sidney M., and Michael Nelson. 2007. *The American Presidency: Origins and Development: 1776–2007*, 5th ed. Washington, D.C.: CQ Press.   This engaging book offers a historical look at the American presidency from the Constitutional Convention to George W. Bush and beyond. An enjoyable and informative read for history buffs and casual readers alike.

Neustadt, Richard E. 1990. *Presidential Power and the Modern Presidents: The Politics of Leadership From Roosevelt to Reagan*. New York: Free Press.   In perhaps the most widely cited book on the presidency, Neustadt argues that the persuasive powers of presidents are imperative for accomplishing their goals while in office.

Skowronek, Stephen. 1997. *The Politics Presidents Make: Leadership From John Adams to Bill Clinton*. Cambridge, Mass.: Harvard University Press.   An important book that all students interested in the presidency should read. Skowronek analyzes how political contexts throughout history have contributed to the success or failure of our presidents.

Tulis, Jeffrey K. 1987. *The Rhetorical Presidency*. Princeton: Princeton University Press.   Tulis gives a fascinating account of how the public's demands for a less distant president influenced the behavior of our twentieth-century chief executives.

Woodward, Bob. 2008. *The War Within: A Secret White House History, 2006–2008*. New York: Simon & Schuster.   The fourth installment in the Bush at War series, The War Within offers a well-known and controversial author's take on the Bush administration's handling of the ongoing war in Iraq.

Define   **Understand**   **Practice**   **Read**   **Click**   **Watch**

C-SPAN American Presidents, Life Portraits   *www.americanpresidents.org/classroom. This web site presents educational information about presidents and the presidency from C-SPAN, including curricula and teachers' guides on each president and educational activities.*

Miller Center of Public Affairs   *www.millercenter.org/academic/americanpresident. The Miller Center's American President Online Reference Resource is an information clearinghouse on the U.S. presidency. Profiles of each U.S. president include an at-a-glance section and links to essays, speeches, and additional resources on the president and his administration.*

U.S. National Archives and Records Administration Presidential Libraries   *www.archives.gov/presidential_libraries/addresses/addresses.html. This excellent starting point for research contains links to eleven different presidential libraries and museums, as well as online libraries for twelve presidents.*

White House   *www.whitehouse.gov. The White House home page provides recent presidential addresses, pictures, information on key administration officials and presidential and vice presidential family members, as well as facts about the White House and the executive branch.*

Define   **Understand**   **Practice**   **Read**   **Click**   **Watch**

The American President   *1995. A young, widowed president's relationship with an environmental lobbyist threatens his reelection chances. While this movie is fun, it also has much to say about the relationship between the president, interest groups, and Congress.*

The American President   *1999. This acclaimed PBS documentary explores the lives and careers of the presidents of the United States, offering valuable insights and many little-known facts.*

Frontline   *Not a movie, but this weekly documentary series on PBS often concentrates on issues of the president, the executive branch, and other key aspects of American democracy.*

Man of the Year   *2006. This film, starring Robin Williams, tells the story of a comedian/political talk show host whose television popularity quickly turns into a bid for the presidency. Part political thriller, part comedy, this film offers an interesting (if not entirely factual) take on the U.S. presidency and American electoral politics.*

The West Wing   *(TV series) 1999–2006. An award-winning television series about a fictitious U.S. president and the political issues he and the members of his administration must address.*

Chapter 9

The Bureaucracy

▶ What's at Stake?

What did the chicken that laid your breakfast egg have for *its* breakfast? Was your hamburger once on drugs? And just what is the pedigree of the french fries you ate at lunch? Do you care? Some people do. Those who worry about eating vegetables that have been grown with the aid of pesticides or chemical fertilizers, or meat from animals that were given hormones or antibiotics, or who are concerned about the environmental effects of such practices, form part of a growing number of consumers who look for the label *organic* before they buy food. One estimate says that Americans spent more than $26 billion on organic foods in 2009.[1]

What does it mean to be organic? There is no standardized definition, so states, localities, and private agencies are free to define *organic* as they wish. Usually the standards are stringent. For example, many groups require organic farmers to use land on which no artificial or synthetic fertilizers, pesticides, or herbicides have been used for five years. Such farming techniques favor the small, committed organic farmer and are difficult for large agribusinesses to apply.[2]

In an effort to eliminate the patchwork of local regulations and to assure consumers that organic food purchased anywhere in the country was equally safe, the organic food industry repeatedly asked the U.S. Department of Agriculture (USDA) to nationalize standards. When the USDA revealed its standardized definition of *organic*, however, it was a definition traditional organic farmers and consumers didn't recognize. USDA standards proposed in December 1997 would have allowed the use of genetic engineering, irradiation, antibiotics and hormones, and sewage sludge—techniques that run directly counter to the values of organic farming—in the production of foods to be labeled *organic*. Though strongly supported by the conventional food manufacturers and the developers of biotechnology, these standards were bitterly opposed by the organic food industry and its consumers.

Buying Local
Many of the growing number of consumers who want organic food turn to local farmers markets for produce that is not genetically altered or sprayed with pesticides. Despite the increasing market segment that looks for such products, large agribusiness farms still dominate the landscape and bring their political influence to the table over regulatory processes such as defining what constitutes "organic" food.

Before they issue new regulations, however, all federal agencies must give interested parties and the public the opportunity to be heard. In the battle to win USDA support, the conventional food industry and the food preparers associations had—and used—all the resources of big business; the organic food industry had none. Searching for another strategy for influencing the enormous bureaucracy of the USDA, they began a grassroots campaign, encouraging consumers to write to the USDA objecting to the new standards. Natural food stores posted information and distributed fliers on the proposed regulation, and Horizon Organic Dairy used the back panels of its milk cartons to pass on the information and urge consumer action.[3]

The campaign was successful. Nearly 300,000 letters and emails opposing the proposal were received by the USDA. Even Congress went on record against it.[4] The result was that Secretary of Agriculture Dan Glickman eliminated the provision allowing genetic engineering, crop irradiation, and the use of sewage sludge as fertilizer. Said Glickman, "Democracy will work. We will listen to the comments and will, I am sure, make modifications to the rule."[5]

Depending on where you stand, the moral of this story varies. It might be a David-and-Goliath success, or just a quirky tale about a handful of food fanatics. What is really at stake in the issue of whether the organic food industry should be regulated by the USDA? ■

Bureaucracy . . . is often the only ground on which citizens and politics meet, the only contact many Americans have with government except for their periodic trips to the voting booth.

> **bureaucracy** an organization characterized by hierarchical structure, worker specialization, explicit rules, and advancement by merit

> **neutral competence** the principle that bureaucracy should be depoliticized by making it more professional

Kids have dramatic aspirations for their futures: they want to be adventurers or sports stars, doctors or lawyers, even president of the United States. Almost no one aspires to be what so many of us become: bureaucrats. But bureaucrats are the people who make national, state, and local government work for us. They are the people who give us our driving tests and renew our licenses, who deliver our mail, who maintain our parks, who order books for our libraries. Bureaucrats send us our Social Security checks, find us jobs through the unemployment office, process our student loans, and ensure that we get our military benefits. In fact, bureaucrats defend our country from foreign enemies, chase our crooks at home, and get us aid in times of natural disasters. We know them as individuals. We greet them, make small talk, laugh with them. They may be our neighbors or friends. But as a profession, civil servants are seldom much admired or esteemed in this country. Indeed, they are often the targets of scorn or jokes, and the people who work in the organizations we call bureaucracies are derided as lazy, incompetent, power hungry, and uncaring.

Such a jaded view, like most other negative stereotypes, is based on a few well-publicized bureaucratic snafus and the frustrating experiences we all have at times with the bureaucracy. Waiting in endless lines at the post office or driver's license bureau, expecting in the mail a government check that never arrives, reading about USDA definitions of *organic* that seem preposterous—all these things can drive us crazy. In addition, as demonstrated by the organic food example, the bureaucracy is the source of many of the rules that can help us get what we want from government but that often irritate us with their seeming arbitrariness and rigidity. Though they aren't elected, bureaucrats can have a great deal of power over our lives.

Bureaucracies are essential to running a government. Bureaucracy, in fact, is often the only ground on which citizens and politics meet, the only contact many Americans have with government except for their periodic trips to the voting booth. Bureaucrats are often called "civil servants" because, ultimately, their job is to serve the civil society in which we all live. In this chapter, as we give bureaucracy a closer look, you will learn about

- *the definition of bureaucracy*
- *the evolution, organization, and roles of the federal bureaucracy*
- *politics inside the bureaucracy*
- *the relationship between the federal bureaucracy and the branches of the federal government*
- *the relationship of citizens to the bureaucracy*

What Is Bureaucracy?

A top-down organizational system aiming for competence and fairness

In simplest terms, a **bureaucracy** is any organization that is structured hierarchically—that is, in which orders are given at the top, by those with responsibility for the success of the organization, and followed by those on the bottom. The classic definition comes to us from German sociologist Max Weber. Weber's model of bureaucracy features the following four characteristics:[6]

- *Hierarchy.* A clear chain of command exists in which all employees know who their bosses or supervisors are, as well as whom they in turn are responsible for.

- *Specialization.* The effectiveness of the bureaucracy is accomplished by having tasks divided and handled by expert and experienced full-time professional staffs.

- *Explicit rules.* Bureaucratic jobs are governed by rules rather than by bureaucrats' own feelings or judgments about how the job should be done. Thus bureaucrats are limited in the discretion they have, and one person in a given job is expected to make pretty much the same decisions as another. This leads to standardization and predictability.

- *Merit.* Hiring and promotions are often based on examinations but also on experience or other objective criteria. Politics, in the form of political loyalty, party affiliation, or dating the boss's son or daughter, is not supposed to play a part.

Political scientist Herbert Kaufman says that the closer governments come to making their bureaucracies look more like Weber's model, the closer they are to achieving "neutral competence."[7] **Neutral competence** represents the effort to depoliticize the bureaucracy, or to take politics out of

spoils system the nineteenth-century practice of firing government workers of a defeated party and replacing them with loyalists of the victorious party

patronage system in which a successful candidate rewards friends, contributors, and party loyalists for their support with jobs, contracts, and favors

civil service nonmilitary employees of the government who are appointed through the merit system

Pendleton Act 1883 civil service reform that required the hiring and promoting of civil servants to be based on merit, not patronage

Hatch Act 1939 law limiting the political involvement of civil servants in order to protect them from political pressure and keep politics out of the bureaucracy

administration, by having the work of government done expertly, according to explicit standards rather than personal preferences or party loyalties. The bureaucracy in this view should not be a political arm of the president or of Congress, but rather it should be neutral, administering the laws of the land in a fair, evenhanded, efficient, and professional way.

The Spoils System

Americans have not always been so concerned with the norm of neutral competence in the bureaucracy. Under a form of bureaucratic organization called the **spoils system**, practiced through most of the nineteenth century in the United States, elected executives—the president, governors, and mayors—were given wide latitude to hire their own friends, family, and political supporters to work in their administrations. The spoils system is often said to have begun with the administration of President Andrew Jackson and gets its name from the adage "To the victor belong the spoils of the enemy," but Jackson was neither the first nor the last politician to see the acquisition of public office as a means of feathering his cronies' nests. Such activity, referred to as **patronage**, allowed the elected executive to use jobs to pay off political debts as well as to gain cooperation from the officials who were hired this way, thereby strengthening his base of power.

Filling the bureaucracy with political appointees almost guarantees incompetence because those who get jobs for political reasons are more likely to be politically motivated than genuinely skilled in a specific area. Experts who are devoted to the task of the agency soon become discouraged because advancement is based on political favoritism rather than on how well the job is done. America's disgust with the corruption and inefficiency of the spoils system, as well as our collective distrust of placing too much power in the hands of any one person, led Congress to institute various reforms of the American **civil service**, as it is sometimes called, aimed at achieving a very different sort of organization.

One of the first reforms, and certainly one of the most significant, was the Civil Service Reform Act of 1883. This act, usually referred to as the **Pendleton Act**, created the initial Civil Service Commission, under which federal employees would be hired and promoted on the basis of merit rather

than patronage. It prohibited firing employees for failure to contribute to political parties or candidates. Civil service coverage increased until President Harry Truman in 1948 was successful in getting 93 percent of the federal work force covered under the merit system.

Protection of the civil service from partisan politicians got another boost in 1939 with the passage of the **Hatch Act**. This act was designed to take the pressure off civil servants to work for the election of parties and candidates. It forbids pressuring federal employees for contributions to political campaigns, and it prohibits civil servants from taking leadership roles in campaigns. They cannot run for federal political office, head up an election campaign, or make public speeches on behalf of candidates. However, they are permitted to make contributions, to attend rallies, and to work on registration or get-out-the-vote drives that do not focus on just one candidate or party. The Hatch Act thus seeks to neutralize the political effects of the bureaucracy. However, in doing so, it denies federal employees a number of activities that are open to other citizens.

Why Is Bureaucracy Necessary?

Much of the world is organized bureaucratically. Large tasks require organization and specialization. The Wright brothers may have been able to construct a rudimentary airplane, but no two people or even small group could put together a Boeing 747. Similarly, though we idolize individual American heroes, we know that efforts like the D-Day invasion of Europe, putting a man on the moon, or the war on terrorism take enormous coordination and planning. Smaller in scale, but still necessary, are routine tasks like delivering the mail, evaluating welfare applications, ensuring that Social Security recipients get their checks, and processing student loans.

Obviously many bureaucracies are public, like those that form part of our government. But the private sector has the same demand for efficient expertise to manage large organizations. Corporations and businesses are bureaucracies, as are universities and hospitals. It is not being public or private that distinguishes a bureaucracy; rather, it is the need for a structure of hierarchical, expert decision making. In this chapter we focus on public bureaucracies, in particular, the federal bureaucracy.

> **accountability** the principle that bureaucratic employees should be answerable for their performance to supervisors, all the way up the chain of command

Bureaucracy and Democracy

Decision making by experts may seem odd to Americans, who cherish the idea of democracy, and it may be why so many Americans dislike so much of our public bureaucracy. If we value democracy and the corresponding idea that public officials should be accountable, or responsible, to the people, how can we also value bureaucracy, in which decisions are often made behind closed doors by unelected "experts" who, because of civil service protections, are difficult to hold accountable?

Bureaucratic decision making in a democratic government presents a real puzzle unless we consider that democracy may not be the best way to make every kind of decision. If we want to ensure that many voices are heard from, then democracy is an appropriate way to make decisions. But those decisions will be made slowly (it takes a long time to poll many people on what they want to do), and though the decisions are likely to be popular, they are not necessarily made by people who know what they are doing. When we're deciding whether to have open heart surgery, we don't want to poll the American people, or even the hospital employees. Instead we want an expert, a heart surgeon, who can make the "right" decision, not the popular decision, and make it quickly.

Democracy could not have designed the rocket ships that formed the basis of America's space program, or decided the level of toxic emissions allowable from a factory smokestack, or determined the temperature at which beef must be cooked in restaurants to prevent food poisoning. Bureaucratic decision making, by which decisions are made at upper levels of an organization and carried out at lower levels, is essential when we require expertise and dispatch.

> **Thinking Outside the Box**
>
> ## When does bureaucratic decision making become a threat to democracy?

Accountability and Rules

Bureaucratic decision making does leave open the problem of *accountability*: Who is responsible for seeing that things get done, and to whom does that person answer? Where does the buck stop? Unlike private bureaucracies, where the need to turn a profit usually keeps bureaucrats relatively accountable, the lines of accountability are less clear in public bureaucracies. Because the Constitution does not provide specific rules for the operation of the bureaucracy, Congress has filled in a piecemeal framework for it that, generally speaking, ends up promoting the goals of members of Congress and the interests they represent.[8] The president of the United States, nominally the head of the executive branch of government, also has goals and objectives he would like the bureaucracy to serve. Thus at the very highest level, the public bureaucracy must answer to several bosses who often have conflicting goals.

The problem of accountability exists at a lower level as well. Even if the lines of authority from the bureaucracy to the executive and legislative branches were crystal clear, no president or congressional committee has the interest or time to supervise the day-to-day details of bureaucratic operations. To solve the problem of accountability within the bureaucracy and to prevent the abuse of public power at all levels, we again resort to rules. If the rules of bureaucratic policy are clearly defined and well publicized, it is easier to tell if a given bureaucrat is doing his or her job, and doing it fairly.

What does fairness mean in the context of a bureaucracy? It means, certainly, that the bureaucrat should not play favorites. The personnel officer for a city is not supposed to give special consideration to her neighbors or to her boyfriend's brother. We do not want employees to give preferential treatment to people like themselves, whether that likeness is based on race, ethnicity, religion, partisanship, or even sexual orientation, or to discriminate against people who are different from them. And we do not want people to run their organizations for their own benefit rather than for the public good. In these and many additional ways, we do not want the people carrying out jobs in any bureaucracy to take advantage of the power they have.

Consequences of a Rule-Based System

The centrality of rules in bureaucracies has important trade-offs. According to the goals of neutral competence, we try to achieve fairness and predictability by insisting that the bureaucrats do their work according to certain rules. If everyone follows his or her job description, the supervisor, boss, or policymaker can know what, within some limits, is likely to happen. Similarly, if an important task is left undone, it should be possible to determine who did not do his or her job.

> **red tape** the complex procedures and regulations surrounding bureaucratic activity

On the negative side, the bureaucrats' jobs can quickly become rule-bound; that is, deviations from the rules become unacceptable, and individuality and creativity are stifled. Sometimes the rules that bind bureaucrats do not seem relevant to the immediate task at hand, and the workers are rewarded for following the rules, not for fulfilling the goals of the organization. Rigid adherence to rules designed to protect the bureaucracy often results in outcomes that have the opposite effect. Furthermore, compliance with rules has to be monitored, and the best way we have developed to guarantee compliance is to generate a paper or, these days, an electronic record of what has been done. To be sure that all the necessary information will be available if needed, it has to be standardized—hence the endless forms for which the bureaucracy is so famous.

For the individual citizen applying for a driver's license, a student loan, or food stamps, the process can become a morass of seemingly unnecessary rules, regulations, constraints, forms, and hearings. We call these bureaucratic hurdles **red tape**, after the red tape that seventeenth-century English officials used to bind legal documents.

Rules thus generate one of the great trade-offs of bureaucratic life. If we want strict fairness and accountability, we must tie the bureaucrat to a tight set of rules. If we allow the bureaucrat discretion to try to reach goals with a looser set of rules, or to waive a rule when it seems appropriate, we may gain some efficiency, but we lose accountability. Given the vast number of people who work for the federal government, we have opted for the accountability, even while we howl with frustration at the inconvenience of the rules.[9]

Who What How

The American public is strongly committed to democratic governance, but sometimes decisions need to be made that do not lend themselves to democracy. When what is needed is complex, technical decision making, then some form of specialization and expertise is required. Because we also want accountability and fairness among our decision makers, we want them to stick to a prescribed set of rules. Bureaucratic decision making and administration offer possibilities in governance that democracy cannot, but they also bring their own difficulties and challenges.

The American Federal Bureaucracy

A patchwork of agencies and commissions to meet growing public demands

In 2008 almost two million civilians worked for the federal government, excluding U.S. Postal Service employees, with another million and a half or so in the armed forces. Only a relative handful, 3.3 percent of federal workers, work in the legislative branch or the judiciary. The rest—97 percent of federal workers—are in the executive branch, home of the federal bureaucracy.[10] In this section we look at the evolution of the federal bureaucracy, its present-day organization, and its basic functions.

Evolution of the Federal Bureaucracy

The central characteristic of the federal bureaucracy is that most of its parts developed independently of the others in a piecemeal and political fashion, rather than emerging from a coherent plan. Some government activities are fundamental; from the earliest days of the republic, the government had departments to handle foreign relations, money, and defense. But other government tasks have developed over time as the result of historical forces, as solutions to particular problems, and as a response to different groups who want government to do something for them. The emerging picture is more like a patchwork quilt than the streamlined efficient government structure we would like to have. Thus the nature and duties of the agencies reflect the politics of their creation and the subsequent politics of their survival and growth.[11] We can understand federal agencies as falling into three categories: those designed to serve essential government functions, those crafted to meet the changing needs and problems of the country, and those intended to serve particular clientele groups.[12]

Serving Essential Government Functions

Some departments are created to serve essential government functions, the core operations that any viable government performs. For example, the Departments of State, War, and the Treasury were the first cabinet offices because the activities they handle are fundamental to the smooth functioning of government. The Department of State exists to handle diplomatic relations with other nations. When diplomacy fails, national interests must be protected by force; the

Department of Defense (formerly War) supervises the air force, army, navy, and marines, and, in time of war, the coast guard. All nations have expenses and must extract resources in the form of taxes from their citizens to pay for them. The Department of the Treasury, which oversees the Internal Revenue Service (IRS), performs this key tax collection function. Treasury also prints the money we use and oversees the horrendous job of managing the national debt. Imagine the effort to manage a debt that increases $4.9 billion a day![13]

Responding to Changing National Needs

Other departments and agencies were created to meet the changing needs of the country as we industrialized and evolved into a highly urbanized society. For example, with westward expansion, the growth of manufacturing, and increased commerce came demands for new roles for government. The Department of the Interior was created in 1848 to deal with some of the unforeseen effects of the move westward, including the displacement of Native Americans and the management of western public lands and resources.

Similarly, a number of the negative aspects of industrialization, including child labor abuses, filthy and dangerous working conditions, unsanitary food production, and price gouging by the railroads, led to calls for government intervention to manage the burgeoning marketplace of an industrialized society. Thus began the development of the independent regulatory commissions starting in the late nineteenth century with the Interstate Commerce Commission and continuing into the twentieth century with the Federal Trade Commission, the Federal Reserve System, and others.

Under the New Deal, several new agencies were created and new programs put into place. The federal government's largest single program today, Social Security, was organized under the Social Security Administration as a supplement for inadequate and failed old-age pensions. For the first time, the national government became directly involved in the economic well-being of individual citizens. Related programs like the Works Progress Administration and the Civilian Conservation Corps were sometimes called government "make-work" programs because their primary purpose was to create jobs and get people back to work. The new obligations of the national government did not vanish with postwar prosperity. Americans came to expect that government would play a large role in managing the economy and in ensuring that people could work, eat, and live in decent housing. President Lyndon Johnson's War on Poverty resulted in the creation of the Office

Uncle Sam Lends a Hand

The federal government's response to the Great Depression was Roosevelt's New Deal, which provided assistance to anxious Americans in need of stable work. The Civilian Conservation Corps, featured in this 1941 poster, not only helped preserve the country's forests but also mobilized more than half a million men and women into the labor force.

of Economic Opportunity in 1964 and the Department of Housing and Urban Development (HUD) in 1965.

A changing international environment also created needs that required government to grow. The Cold War between the United States and the Soviet Union launched a multipronged policy effort that included investment in military research, science (the National Science Foundation), education (the National Defense Education Act), and space exploration (the National Aeronautics and Space Administration). Much more recently, the September 11, 2001, terror attacks on the United States led to the establishment of a new cabinet-level Department of Homeland Security to coordinate efforts to protect the country. The new department created a

clientele groups groups of citizens whose interests are affected by an agency or a department and who work to influence its policies

departments one of the major subdivisions of the federal government, represented in the president's cabinet

independent agencies government organizations independent of the departments but with a narrower policy focus

new bureaucratic structure, but also organized under its authority some preexisting agencies and bureaus, including those controlling the U.S. Secret Service, immigration, and emergency management.

Responding to the Demands of Clientele Groups

A number of departments and agencies either were created or have evolved to serve distinct **clientele groups**. These may include interest groups—groups of citizens, businesses, or industry members who are affected by government regulatory actions and who organize to try to influence policy. Or they may include unorganized groups, such as poor people, to which the government has decided to respond. Such departments are sensitive to the concerns of those specific groups rather than focusing on what is good for the nation as a whole. The Department of Agriculture, among the first of these, was set up in 1862 to assist U.S. agricultural interests. It began by providing research information to farmers and later arranged subsidies and developed markets for agricultural products. Politicians in today's budget-cutting climate talk about cutting back on agricultural subsidies, but no one expects the USDA to change its focus of looking out, first and foremost, for the farmer. Similar stories can be told of the Departments of Labor, Commerce, Education, and Veterans Affairs.

Organization of the Federal Bureaucracy

The federal bureaucracy consists of four types of organizations: (1) cabinet-level departments, (2) independent agencies, (3) regulatory boards and commissions, and (4) government corporations. To make the job of understanding the bureaucracy more complicated, some agencies can fit into more than one of those classifications. The difficulty in classifying an agency as one type or another stems partly from Congress' habit of creating hybrids: agencies that act like government corporations, for instance, or cabinet-level departments that regulate. The overall organizational chart of the U.S. government (see Figure 9.1) makes this complex bureaucracy look reasonably orderly. To a large extent the impression of order is an illusion.

Departments

The federal government currently has fifteen **departments**. Table 9.1 lists these departments along with their dates of

creation, budgets, and functions. The heads of departments are known as secretaries—for example, the secretary of state or the secretary of defense—except for the head of the Department of Justice, who is called the attorney general. These department heads collectively make up the president's cabinet, appointed by the president, with the consent of the Senate, to provide advice on critical areas of government affairs such as foreign relations, agriculture, education, and so on. These areas are not fixed, and presidents may propose different cabinet offices. Although the secretaries are political appointees who usually change when the administration changes (or even more frequently), they sit at the heads of the large, more or less permanent, bureaucracies we call departments. Cabinet heads may not have any more actual power than other agency leaders, but their posts do carry more status and prestige.

When a cabinet department is established, it is a sign that the government recognizes its policy area as a legitimate and important political responsibility. Therefore, groups fight hard to get their causes represented at the cabinet level. During the Clinton administration, environmental groups tried to get the Environmental Protection Agency (EPA) raised to the cabinet level. The fact that it was not elevated, despite President Bill Clinton's campaign promises on the matter, was a sign that the business and development interests that opposed environmental regulation were stronger politically. Even though the EPA is not a cabinet-level agency, its director has been asked by some presidents to meet with the cabinet, giving him or her cabinet rank and thus more status, even if the agency is not so elevated. In the Obama administration, the EPA director has cabinet-level rank, as does the White House chief of staff, the director of the Office of Management and Budget, the U.S. trade representative, the ambassador to the United Nations, and the chair of the Council of Economic Advisers.[14]

Independent Agencies

Congress has established a host of agencies outside the cabinet departments (some are listed in Figure 9.1). The **independent agencies** are structured like the cabinet departments, with a single head appointed by the president. Their areas of jurisdiction, however, tend to be narrower than those of the cabinet departments. Congress does not follow a blueprint about how to make an independent agency or a department. Instead, it expands the bureaucracy to fit the case at hand, given the mix of political forces of the moment—that is, given what groups are demanding what action, and with what resources. As a result, the independent agencies vary tremendously in size, ranging from fewer

Figure 9.1

Organizational Chart of the United States Government

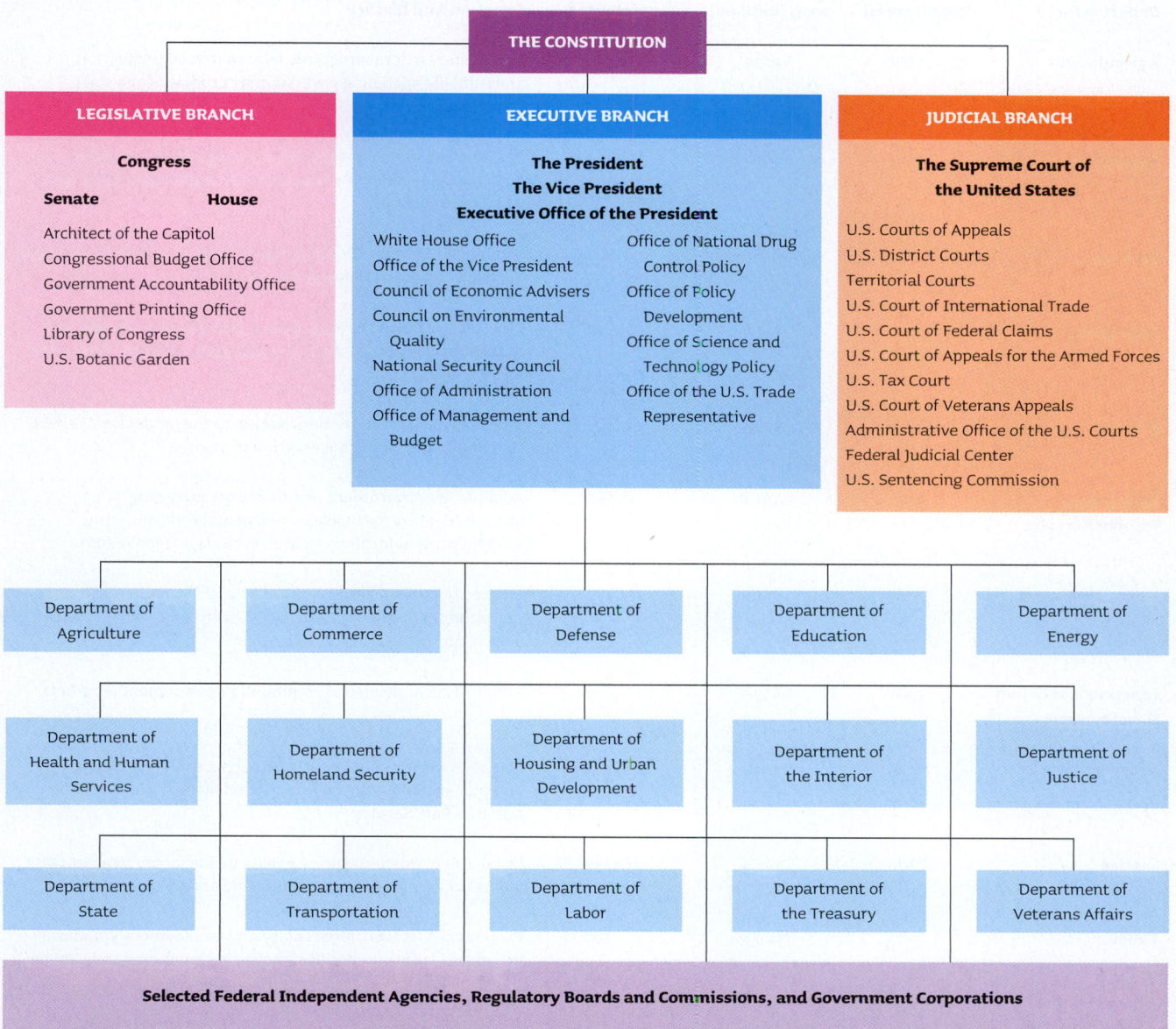

THE CONSTITUTION

LEGISLATIVE BRANCH

Congress

Senate   **House**

Architect of the Capitol
Congressional Budget Office
Government Accountability Office
Government Printing Office
Library of Congress
U.S. Botanic Garden

EXECUTIVE BRANCH

The President
The Vice President
Executive Office of the President

White House Office
Office of the Vice President
Council of Economic Advisers
Council on Environmental
  Quality
National Security Council
Office of Administration
Office of Management and
  Budget

Office of National Drug
  Control Policy
Office of Policy
  Development
Office of Science and
  Technology Policy
Office of the U.S. Trade
  Representative

JUDICIAL BRANCH

**The Supreme Court of
the United States**

U.S. Courts of Appeals
U.S. District Courts
Territorial Courts
U.S. Court of International Trade
U.S. Court of Federal Claims
U.S. Court of Appeals for the Armed Forces
U.S. Tax Court
U.S. Court of Veterans Appeals
Administrative Office of the U.S. Courts
Federal Judicial Center
U.S. Sentencing Commission

Department of Agriculture
Department of Commerce
Department of Defense
Department of Education
Department of Energy

Department of Health and Human Services
Department of Homeland Security
Department of Housing and Urban Development
Department of the Interior
Department of Justice

Department of State
Department of Transportation
Department of Labor
Department of the Treasury
Department of Veterans Affairs

Selected Federal Independent Agencies, Regulatory Boards and Commissions, and Government Corporations

Independent Agencies

Central Intelligence Agency
Equal Employment Opportunity Commission
General Services Administration
National Aeronautics and Space Administration
National Endowment for the Arts
National Endowment for the Humanities
National Science Foundation
Office of Government Ethics
Office of Personnel Management
Peace Corps
Selective Service System
Small Business Administration
Social Security Administration

Regulatory Boards and Commissions

Federal Communications Commission
Federal Labor Relations Authority
Federal Trade Commission (FTC)
Food and Drug Administration
National Labor Relations Board
Nuclear Regulatory Commission
Occupational Safety and Health (OSHA) Review Commission
Securities and Exchange Commission

Government Corporations

Commodity Credit Corporation
Export-Import Bank
Federal Crop Insurance Corporation
Federal Deposit Insurance Corporation (FDIC)
National Railroad Passenger Corporation (Amtrak)
Tennessee Valley Authority
United States Postal Service

Table 9.1

Departments of the United States Government

Department	Year formed	Spending in 2009 (billions)	Number of employees	Function and history
Agriculture	1862	$109.3	100,125	Administers federal programs related to food production and rural life, including price support programs and soil conservation
Commerce	1903	$10.2	118,429	Responsible for economic and technological development; includes Census Bureau; was Commerce and Labor until 1913, when Labor split off
Defense	1789	$636.5	718,802	Manages U.S. Army, Air Force, Navy; created as War Department in 1789; changed to Defense in 1949
Education	1979	$32.4	4,053	Provides federal aid to local school districts and colleges and student college loans; until 1979 was part of Health, Education and Welfare
Energy	1977	$23.9	15,621	Oversees national activities relating to the production, regulation, marketing, and conservation of energy
Health and Human Services	1953	$761.1	65,680	Administers government health and security programs; includes Centers for Disease Control and Food and Drug Administration; formerly Health, Education and Welfare
Homeland Security	2003	$51.6	179,380	Created to prevent terrorist attacks within the United States, make the country less vulnerable to terrorism, and help the nation survive attacks that do occur
Housing and Urban Development	1965	$59.5	630	Administers housing and community development programs
Interior	1849	$11.7	74,362	Manages the nation's natural resources through its eight bureaus, including the Bureau of Land Management and the National Park Service
Justice	1870	$26.6	111,458	Legal arm of executive branch responsible for enforcement of federal laws, including civil rights and antitrust laws
Labor	1903	$109.8	192	Responsible for work force safety and employment standards; originated in Interior in 1884, moved to Commerce and Labor in 1903, split from Commerce in 1913
State	1789	$37.1	36,821	Responsible for foreign policy and diplomatic relations
Transportation	1966	$69.3	56,335	Coordinates and administers overall transportation policy, including highways, urban mass transit, railroads, aviation, and waterways
Treasury	1789	$326.7	116,647	Government's financial agent, responsible for money coming in and going out (including tax collection); advises president on fiscal policy
Veterans Affairs	1989	$94.9	290,079	Administers programs to help veterans and their families, including pensions, medical care, disability, and death benefits

Sources: Office of Management and Budget, *Budget for Fiscal Year 2011*, www.whitehouse.gov/omb/budget/Overview; U.S. Office of Personnel Management, "Table 14: Federal Civilian Employment by Branch, Selected Agency, Pay System and Area, December 2008 and May 2009," www.opm.gov/feddata/html/2009/May/table14.asp.

> **independent regulatory boards and commissions**
> government organizations that regulate various businesses,
> industries, or economic sectors
>
> **regulations** limitations or restrictions on the activities of a
> business or individual

than 400 employees in the Federal Election Commission (FEC) to over 65,000 in the Social Security Administration.

While agencies are called independent because of their independence from cabinet departments, they vary in their independence from the president. This is not accidental, but political. When Congress is not in agreement with the current president, it tends to insulate new agencies from presidential control by making the appointments for fixed terms that do not overlap with the president's, or they remove budgetary oversight from the Office of Management and Budget.[15] Thus some agency heads serve at the president's discretion and can be fired at any time; others serve fixed terms, and the president can appoint a new head or commissioner only when a vacancy occurs. Independent agencies also vary in their freedom from judicial review. Congress has established that some agencies' rulings cannot be challenged in the courts, whereas others' can be.[16]

Independent Regulatory Boards and Commissions

Independent regulatory boards and commissions make regulations for various industries, businesses, and sectors of the economy (see Figure 9.1). **Regulations** are simply limitations or restrictions on the behavior of an individual or a business; they are bureaucratically determined prescriptions for how business is to take place. This chapter opened with the battle over a regulation: the guidelines that must be followed for a product to be labeled "organic." Regulations usually seek to protect the public from some industrial or economic danger or uncertainty. The Securities and Exchange Commission, for example, regulates the trading of stocks and bonds on the nation's stock markets, while the Food and Drug Administration regulates such things as how drugs must be tested before they can be marketed safely and what information must appear on the labels of processed foods and beverages sold throughout the country. Regulation usually pits the individual's freedom to do what he or she wants, or a business's drive to make a profit, against some vision of what is good for the public. As long as there are governments, there will be trade-offs between the two because it is for the purpose of managing citizens' collective lives that governments are formed. How each trade-off is made between individual freedom and public safety is a question of public policy.

There are thirty-eight agencies of the federal government whose principal job is to issue and enforce regulations about what citizens and businesses can do, and how they have to do it. This effort employed nearly 207,000 people and cost

$41 billion in 2005.[17] Given the size of the enterprise, it is not surprising that regulation occasionally gets out of hand. If an agency exists to regulate, regulate it probably will, whether or not a clear case can be made for restricting action. The average cheeseburger in America, for instance, is the subject of over 40,000 federal and state regulations, specifying everything from the vitamin content of the flour in the bun, to the age and fat content of the cheese, to the temperature at which it must be cooked, to the speed at which the ketchup must flow to be certified Grade A Fancy.[18] Some of these rules are undoubtedly crucial; we all want to be able to buy a cheeseburger without risking food poisoning and possible death. Others are informative; those of us on restrictive diets need to know what we are eating, and none of us likes to be ripped off by getting something other than what we think we are paying for. Others seem merely silly. When we consider that adult federal employees are paid to measure the speed of ketchup, we readily sympathize with those who claim that the regulatory function is getting out of hand in American government.

The regulatory agencies are set up to be largely independent of political influence, though some are bureaus within cabinet departments—the federal Food and Drug Administration, for example, is located in the Department of Health and Human Services. Most independent regulatory agencies are run by a commission of three or more people who serve overlapping terms, and the terms of office, usually between three and fourteen years, are set so that they do not coincide with presidential terms. Commission members are nominated by the president and confirmed by Congress, often with a bipartisan vote. Unlike cabinet secretaries and some agency heads, the heads of the regulatory boards and commissions cannot be fired by the president. All of these aspects of their organization are intended to insulate them from political pressures, including presidential influence, in the expectation that they will regulate in the public interest unaffected by current partisan preferences. The number of such agencies is growing, which places the national bureaucracy increasingly beyond the president's control, even as most Americans expect the president to be able to manage the bureaucracy to get things done.[19]

Congress wants to limit presidential influence of regulatory agencies because not all presidential administrations view regulation in the same way, and as they approach the job of appointing regulatory officials accordingly, presidents can have an impact on how the agencies operate during their leaders'

> **government corporations** companies created by Congress to provide to the public a good or service that private enterprise cannot or will not profitably provide

tenures in office. As holders of a conservative ideology that, in general, prefers to see less regulation and to leave control of industry to the market, Republican presidents tend to appoint businesspeople and others sympathetic to the industries being regulated. Democrats, on the other hand, believe that regulation by impartial experts can smooth out many of the externalities of an unregulated market and tend to appoint those with a record of regulatory accomplishment and scientific expertise. This difference in approach could be seen in action when President Barack Obama came into office in 2009. Reversing the trend set by President George W. Bush's administration, he reinvigorated the regulatory mission of agencies such as the EPA, the Occupational Safety and Health Administration, and the Securities and Exchange Commission, in what one progressive author called "the quiet revolution."[20]

Government Corporations

We do not often think of the government as a business, but public enterprises are, in fact, big business. The U.S. Postal Service is one of the larger businesses in the nation in terms of sales and personnel. The Tennessee Valley Authority and the Bonneville Power Administration of the northwestern states are both in the business of generating electricity and selling it to citizens throughout their regions. If you ride the rails as a passenger, you travel by Amtrak, a government-owned corporation (technically called the National Railroad Passenger Corporation). All these businesses are set up to be largely independent of both congressional and presidential influence. This independence is not insignificant. Consider, for example, how angry citizens are when the postal rates go up. Because the Postal Commission is independent, both the president and Congress avoid the political heat for such unpopular decisions. Figure 9.1 lists some examples of the businesses run by the federal government.

Congress created these publicly owned *government corporations* primarily to provide a good or service that is not profitable for a private business to provide. The Federal Deposit Insurance Corporation (FDIC) is a good example. Following the Great Depression, during which financial institutions failed at an alarming rate, citizens were reluctant to put their money back into banks. A "government guarantee," through FDIC, of the safety of savings gave, and continues to give, citizens much more confidence than if the insurance were provided by a private company, which itself could go broke. Similarly, government has acted to bring utilities to rural areas and to ensure that mail is delivered even to the most remote addresses.

The government's ownership of Amtrak came about because a national rail service did not prove profitable for private industry but was seen by Congress as a national resource that should not be lost. The rationale is that providing these services entails not just making a profit but also serving the public interest. However, as in so many other aspects of American government, the public is relatively quiet in speaking up for its interests, and so the politics of government corporations become the politics of interested bureaucrats, clientele groups, and congressional subcommittees.

> **Thinking Outside the Box**
>
> **Are some essential services now provided by the federal bureaucracy better left to the private sector?**

Roles of the Federal Bureaucracy

Federal bureaucrats at the broadest level are responsible for helping the president to administer the laws, policies, and regulations of government. The actual work the bureaucrat does depends on the policy area in which he or she is employed. Take another look at the titles of the cabinet departments and independent agencies listed in Table 9.1 and Figure 9.1. Some part of the bureaucracy is responsible for administering rules and policies on just about every imaginable aspect of social and economic life.

Bureaucrats are not confined to administering the laws, however. Although the principle of separation of powers—by which the functions of making, administering, and interpreting the laws are carried out by the legislative, executive, and judicial branches—applies at the highest level of government, it tends to dissolve at the level of the bureaucracy. In practice, the bureaucracy is an all-in-one policymaker. It administers the laws, but it also effectively makes and judges compliance with laws. It is this wide scope of bureaucratic power that creates the problems of control and accountability that we discuss throughout this chapter.

Bureaucracy as Administrator

We expect the agencies of the federal government to implement the laws passed by Congress and signed by the president.

Operating under the ideal of neutral competence, a public bureaucracy serves the political branches of government in a professional, unbiased, and efficient manner. In many cases this is exactly what happens, and with admirable ability and dedication. The rangers in the national parks help citizens enjoy our natural resources, police officers enforce the statutes of criminal law, social workers check for compliance with welfare regulations, and postal workers deliver letters and packages in a timely way. All these bureaucrats are simply carrying out the law that has been made elsewhere in government.

Bureaucracy as Rule Maker

The picture of the bureaucrat as an impartial administrator removed from political decision making is a partial and unrealistic one. The bureaucracy has a great deal of latitude in administering national policy. Because it often lacks the time, the technical expertise, and the political coherence and leverage to write clear and detailed legislation, Congress frequently passes laws that are vague, contradictory, and overly general. In order to carry out or administer the laws, the bureaucracy must first fill in the gaps. Congress has essentially delegated some of its legislative power to the bureaucracy. Its role here is called ***bureaucratic discretion***. Bureaucrats must use their own judgment, which under the ideal of neutral competence should remain minimal, in order to carry out the laws of Congress. Congress does not say how many park rangers should be assigned to Yosemite versus Yellowstone, for instance; the Park Service has to interpret the broad intent of the law and make decisions on this and thousands of other specifics. Bureaucratic discretion is not limited to allocating personnel and other "minor" administrative details. Congress cannot make decisions on specifications for military aircraft, dictate the advice the agricultural extension agents should give to farmers, or determine whether the latest sugar substitute is safe for our soft drinks. The appropriate bureaucracy must fill in all those details. For example, when Congress passed the Patient Protection and Affordable Care Act in 2010, a key provision barred insurers from implementing "unreasonable premium increases" unless they first submit justifications to federal and state officials. But Congress left it up to the bureaucracy to define "unreasonable," which would have enormous impact on how the law was implemented.

The procedures of administrative rule making are not completely insulated from the outside world, however. Before they become effective, all new regulations must first be publicized in the ***Federal Register***, which is a primary source of information for thousands of interests affected by decisions in Washington. Before adopting the rules, agencies must give outsiders—the public and interest groups—a chance to be heard, as we saw in the examination of organic farming regulation that began this chapter. Similarly, in the case of the rule making concerning the 2010 health care act, the bureaucracy became the focus of intense lobbying efforts by the health insurance industry, which wanted the rule to be defined as favorably for it as possible.[21]

Bureaucracy as Judge

The third major function of governments is adjudication, or the process of interpreting the law in specific cases for potential

OTHER BUREAUCRATS WEIGH IN ON USDA'S NEW FOOD PYRAMID

▶ Who Are We?

The federal bureaucrats

The federal bureaucrats who work for the U.S. government represent a fair cross-section of the American population. But very few women, African Americans, or Hispanics reach the highest grade levels of the civil service ladder. Does this "glass ceiling" make a difference in the way the bureaucracy does its job?

Government Employees by Gender and Race, 2006

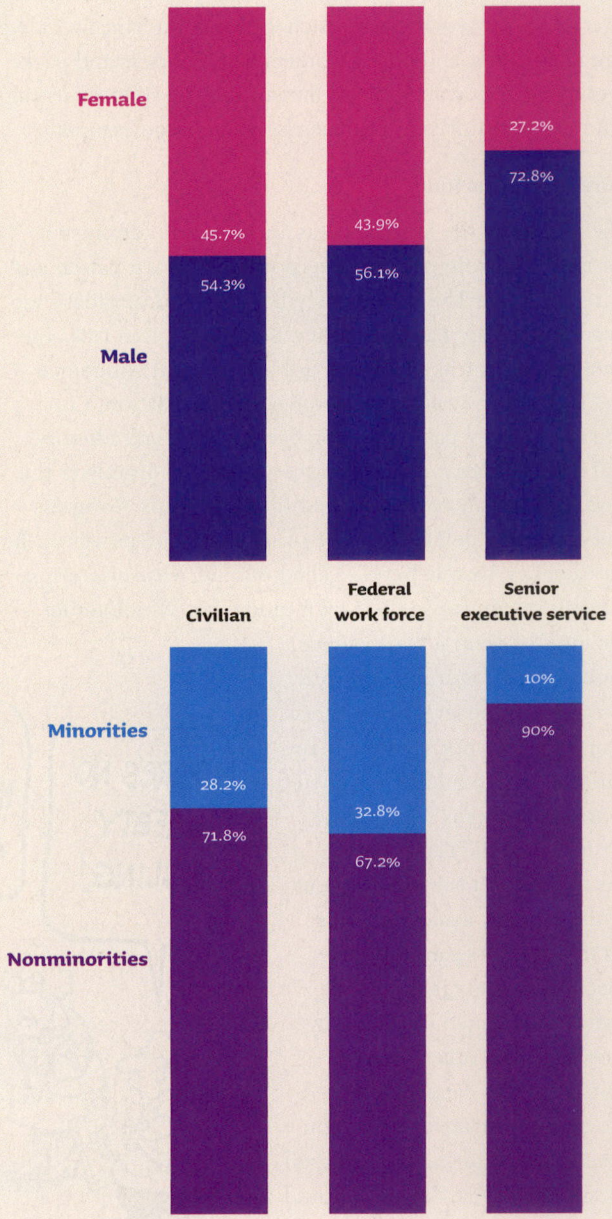

Female

	Civilian	Federal work force	Senior executive service
Female	45.7%	43.9%	27.2%
Male	54.3%	56.1%	72.8%

Male

Civilian — Federal work force — Senior executive service

Minorities

	Civilian	Federal work force	Senior executive service
Minorities	28.2%	32.8%	10%
Nonminorities	71.8%	67.2%	90%

Nonminorities

Minorities in the Civil Service

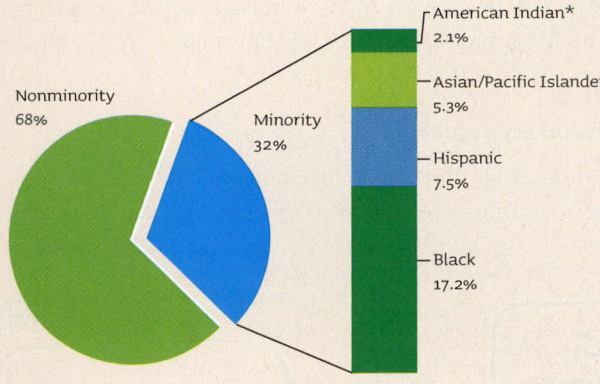

Nonminority
68%

Minority
32%

American Indian*
2.1%

Asian/Pacific Islander
5.3%

Hispanic
7.5%

Black
17.2%

Source: U.S. Office of Personnel Management, "Trends of Employment," in *Federal Civilian Workforce Statistics: The Fact Book*, 2007 Edition, www.opm.gov/feddata/factbook/2007/2007FACTBOOK.pdf, 57.

*American Indian refers to American Indian/Alaska Native.

Source: Author's calculation from *Federal Civilian Workforce Statistics: The Fact Book*, 2007 Edition, www.opm.gov/feddata/factbook/2007/2007 FACTBOOK.pdf.

bureaucratic culture the accepted values and procedures of an organization

violations and deciding the appropriate penalties when violations are found. This is what the courts do. However, a great deal of adjudication in America is carried out by the bureaucracy. For example, regulatory agencies not only make many of the rules that govern the conduct of business but also are responsible for seeing that individuals, but more often businesses, comply with their regulations. Tax courts, under the IRS, for instance, handle violations of the tax codes.

The adjudication functions of the agencies, while generally less formal than the proceedings of the courts, do have formal procedures, and their decisions have the full force of law. In most cases if Congress does not like an agency ruling, it can work to change it, either by passing new legislation or by more subtle pressures. Nevertheless, agencies often issue rulings that could never have overcome the many hurdles of the legislative process in Congress.

Who Are the Federal Bureaucrats?

The full civilian work force of the federal bureaucracy reflects the general work force fairly accurately. For example, 45.7 percent of the U.S. civilian labor force is female and 43.9 percent of the civil service is female. African Americans make up 10 percent of the civilian work force and 17.6 percent of the civil service.[22] The distributions are similar for other demographic characteristics such as ethnic origin or level of education. This representative picture is disturbed, however, by the fact that not all bureaucratic positions are equal. Policymaking is done primarily at the highest levels, and the upper grades are staffed predominantly by well-educated white males. As illustrated in "*Who Are We? The Federal Bureaucrats*," women and minorities are distinctly underrepresented in the policymaking (and higher-paying) levels of the bureaucracy.[23]

Who What How

Government exists, among other reasons, to solve citizens' common problems and to provide goods and services that the market does not or cannot provide. The apparatus for problem solving and service providing is primarily the bureaucracy. Congress and the president define the problems, make the initial decisions, and assign responsibility for solving them to a department, an agency, or a regulatory board.

Citizens or groups of citizens who want something from the government must deal with the bureaucracy as

well. Finally, the bureaucrats themselves have a stake in performing their mandated jobs in a political context where Congress and the president may hedge on the details of what that job actually is. Consequently, bureaucrats need to go beyond administering the laws to making them and judging compliance with them as well. Though we cautiously separate power, and check and balance it among all our elected officials, it is curious that where the officials are unelected and thus not accountable to the people, powers are fused and to a large extent unchecked. The bureaucracy is therefore a very powerful part of the federal government.

Politics Inside the Bureaucracy

Power struggles between political appointees and professional bureaucrats, constrained by cultural norms

Politicians and bureaucrats alike are wary about the effects of politics on decision making. They act as if fairness and efficiency could always be achieved if only the struggle over competing interests could be set aside through an emphasis on strict rules and hierarchical organization. We know, of course, that the struggle can't be set aside. As a fundamental human activity, politics is always with us, and it is always shaped by the particular rules and institutions in which it is played out. Politics within bureaucracies is a subset of politics generally, but it takes on its own cast according to the context in which it takes place.

Bureaucratic Culture

The particular context in which internal bureaucratic politics is shaped is called *bureaucratic culture*—the accepted values and procedures of an organization. Consider any place you may have been employed. When you began your job, the accepted standards of behavior may not have been clear, but over time you figured out who had power, what your role was, which rules could be bent and which had to be followed strictly, and what the goals of the enterprise were. Chances are you came to share some of the values of your colleagues, at least with respect to your work. Those things add up to the

> **bureaucratese** the often unintelligible language used by bureaucrats to avoid controversy and lend weight to their words

culture of the workplace. Bureaucratic culture is just a specific instance of workplace culture.

Knowing the four main elements of bureaucratic culture will take us a long way toward understanding why bureaucrats and bureaucracies behave the way they do. Essentially these elements define what is at stake within a bureaucracy, and what bureaucrats need to do to ensure that they are winners and not losers in the bureaucratic world. To explore bureaucratic culture, let's imagine that you have landed a job working in the U.S. Department of Agriculture. Over time, if you are successful in your job, you will come to share the values and beliefs of others working in your department; that is, you will come to share their bureaucratic culture.

Policy Commitment

As a good bureaucrat in training, the first thing you will do is develop a commitment to the policy issues of agriculture. No matter if you've never thought much about farming before. As an employee of the USDA, you will eventually come to believe that agricultural issues are among the most important facing the country, just as those working at the National Aeronautics and Space Administration place a priority on investigating outer space, and bureaucrats at the National Institutes of Health believe fervently in health research. You share a commitment to your policy area not only because your job depends on it but also because all the people around you believe in it.

Adoption of Bureaucratic Behavior

Not long after you join your department, you will start to see the logic of doing things bureaucratically; you may even start to sound like a bureaucrat. **Bureaucratese**, the formal and often (to outsiders) amusing and sometimes confusing language that many bureaucrats use in their effort to convey information without controversy, may become your second tongue (see "*Consider the Source:* Don't Be Fooled by Bureaucratese"). Part of the reason for the development of bureaucratese is that the use of acronyms and other linguistic shortcuts can make communication more efficient for those in the know, but use of bureaucratese also seems to be an effort to avoid responsibility (for example, use of the passive voice means you don't say who performed the action) or to make the author appear more authoritative by using more and longer words than are really necessary. The elaborate rule structure that defines the bureaucracy will come to seem quite normal to you. You will even depend on it because relying on

the rules relieves you of the responsibility of relying on your own judgment. You will learn that exercising such bureaucratic discretion, as we discussed earlier, can leave you vulnerable if your decisions are not clearly within the rules.

The hierarchical organization of authority will also make a good deal of sense, and you will, in fact, find yourself spending a lot of your time helping to make your superiors look good to their superiors, even as the people working under you will be helping you to look good to your bosses. Remember that in a hierarchy most of your rewards will come from those over you in the power structure; you will be dependent on your superiors for work assignments, promotions, budget allotments, and vacation authorizations. Your superiors will have the same relationships with their bosses.

As you become committed to the bureaucratic structure, you learn that conformity to the rules and norms of the enterprise is the name of the game. Free spirits are not likely to thrive in a bureaucratic environment where deference, cooperation, and obedience are emphasized and rewarded, and the relentless rule orientation and hierarchy can wear down all but the most committed independent souls.

Specialization and Expertise

Early on in your career, you will realize that departments, agencies, and bureaus have specific areas of responsibility. There is not a great deal of interagency hopping; most bureaucrats spend their whole professional lives working in the same area, often in the same department. The lawyers in the Justice Department, scientists at the National Science Foundation, physicians at the National Institutes of Health, and even you as a soybean expert at the USDA all have specialized knowledge as the base of your power. Your power comes from your expertise, and that is tied to the specific policy areas of your agency. To move, you would give that up—and so, not surprisingly, few do.

Because of specialization and expertise, bureaucrats come to know a lot more about their policy areas than do the public or even politicians who must make decisions relevant to those areas. Their possession of critical information gives bureaucrats considerable power in policymaking situations.

Identification With the Agency

All three of the characteristics of bureaucratic culture discussed so far lead to the fourth: identification with and protection of the agency. As you become attached to the interests of agriculture, committed to the rules and structures of the bureaucracy, concerned with the fortunes of your superiors, and appreciative of your own and your colleagues' specialized knowledge, your estimation of the USDA rises also. You begin to think that what is good for Agriculture is good for you, and that threats to the department's well-being become threats to you. You identify with the department, not just because your job depends on it but because you believe in what it does.

Consequences of the Bureaucratic Culture

This pervasive bureaucratic culture breeds a number of political consequences. On the plus side, it holds the bureaucracy together, fostering values of commitment and loyalty to what could otherwise be seen as an impersonal and alienating work environment. It means that the people who work in the federal government, for the most part, really believe in what they do. Members of the Federal Bureau of Investigation (FBI), for example, are strongly attached to the agency's law enforcement mission and are steeped in one of the most distinctive bureaucratic cultures in the nation. This strong commitment to its law enforcement mission has led to major successes, such as the exposure and arrest of major organized crime figures across the country.

But bureaucratic culture can lead to negative consequences as well. As former FBI agent Coleen Rowley pointed out in testimony before the Senate Judiciary Committee in June 2002, this culture very likely had a role in the failure of our law enforcement and intelligence agencies to foresee and prevent the attacks of September 11, 2001. Rowley's office, in Minneapolis, had known that a possible terrorist, Zacarias Moussaoui, was seeking to take flying lessons. Finding his activities suspicious and worrisome, Minneapolis agents tried to get a warrant to search his computer but were unable to do so. In her testimony, Rowley targeted the FBI's hierarchical culture, with its implicit norm that said field agents did not go over the heads of their superiors, who frequently second-guessed their judgment. "There's a certain pecking order, and it's real strong," she told the committee. "Seven to nine levels is really ridiculous."[24]

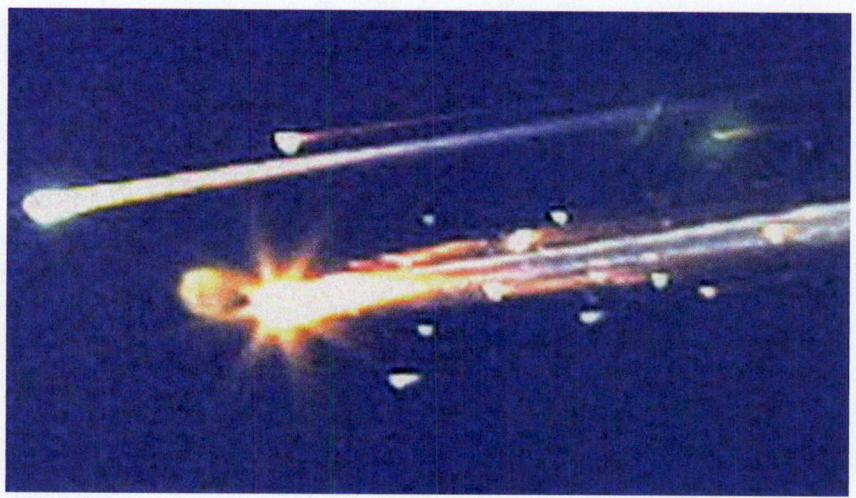

Costly Bureaucratic Mistakes

An entrenched bureaucratic culture and political pressure to meet a deadline were seen as responsible for the 1986 explosion of the space shuttle *Challenger*. The same factors were at play when the damaged space shuttle *Columbia* (seen here as debris streaks across the sky) broke apart upon reentry into the Earth's atmosphere in 2003. Loose foam insulation was the physical cause of damage to the craft, but NASA managers fostered a culture that stifled discussion and led to practices detrimental to safety—the true culprit of the disaster.

Not only did bureaucratic culture keep the FBI from knowing what information it had prior to September 11, but it also kept the FBI and the Central Intelligence Agency (CIA) from communicating with each other about the various pieces of the puzzle they had found. Between them they had much of the information needed to have discovered the plot, but no one "connected the dots." Why? The cultures are different. The FBI is primarily a law enforcement agency; agents are rewarded for making arrests. Its antiterrorist activities prior to September 11 were focused on after-the-fact investigations of terrorist attacks (leading to convictions) but not on preventing such attacks against domestic targets.[25]

The CIA, on the other hand, is focused on clandestine activity to develop information about non-American groups and nations. It is more secretive and less rule-bound, more focused on plans and intentions than on after-the-fact evidence and convictions. Agents focus on relationships, not individual achievement. One reporter covering the two agencies wrote that though the two agencies need to work with each other, "they have such different approaches to life that they remain worlds apart. In fact, they speak such different languages that they can barely even communicate."[26]

The tortured and twisted language our government bureaucrats seem to love can be so awful that it's actually amusing—if you have nothing at stake in figuring out what it means. Try this on for size: "The metropolitan Washington region's transportation system will promote economic sustainability and quality of life through a facilitation of inter- and intra-jurisdictional connectivity of employment and population centers, with a comprehensive multi-modal approach to mobility and utilize available tools to reduce congestion."[1] What a windy way to say that the Washington transportation system will relieve traffic jams by using a variety of methods of transit!

It's no wonder that people have trouble taking what their government says seriously. But what might be merely irritating, or laughable, or just plain stupid when it comes to transportation can assume a lot more importance when it's something we need to know about. Take taxes: failing to accurately calculate and pay one's taxes can lead to a financial penalty, or worse. But what's a taxpayer to do when confronted with something like this? "If the taxpayer's passive activity gross income from significant participation passive activities (within the meaning of section 1.469–2T-(f)(2)(ii) for the taxable year (determined without regard to section 1.469–2T-(f)(2) through (4)) exceeds the taxpayer's passive activity deductions from such activities for the taxable year, such activities shall be treated, solely for purposes of applying this paragraph (f)(2)(i) for the taxable year, as a single activity that does not have a loss for such taxable year." Even a nationwide poll of accountants gave this Internal Revenue Service rule the "Most Incomprehensible Government Regulation" award.[2]

The truth is, translating bureaucratese, the bewildering way that government officials often speak, can be quite a project. It would be nice if we could just avoid dealing with government language altogether, but most of us can't. At some time in our lives we register a car, apply for a student loan, get a marriage license, or file a building permit. We may need to register for Social Security benefits or apply for Medicaid or food stamps.

We may fill out a passport application or a form to bring purchases back through customs after traveling abroad. We may want to read a report from the local school committee or the public transportation board. And one thing is certain: we all have to pay taxes. Here are a few hints for deciphering government jargon:

1. **Translate overly complicated terms that refer to common objects and events.** In bureaucratese, "means of egress" are exits, a "grade separation structure" can turn out to be a bridge, "rail movements" are train trips, "agricultural specialists" are farmers, and an application for an "unenclosed premise permit" is a request to build a patio.[3] Such language may result from an effort to be more specific, from a wish to be less specific, or just from a desire to make something sound more important than it is. Don't be fooled by lofty or euphemistic language.

2. **Watch out for the use of the passive voice.** Bureaucrats often speak passively: "Action is taken," or "Resources are acquisitioned." The passive voice allows the author to avoid saying who is taking the action or acquiring the resources, often key pieces of information you need or want to know.

3. **Don't be intimidated by the insider language bureaucrats may create for themselves.** Be sure you understand what you are reading or being told. When officials at the Department of Housing and Urban Development in Washington talk about having a "pony to ride," they aren't referring to a childhood pet but to a "senior inside official who would walk a controversial project through various obstacles in the department, much like a pony express rider could deliver the mails in the Old West."[4] At the local level, "public assistance benefits insurance" (itself a mouthful of bureaucratese) is called "Benny" or, even more obscurely, "Jack Benny" by county welfare agents in Buffalo, New York. There is no end to the creative shorthand employed by bureaucrats. If you do not understand what you are told, ask.

When an agency is charged with making the rules, enforcing them, and even adjudicating them, it is relatively easy to cover up less catastrophic agency blunders. If Congress, the media, or the public had sufficient information and the expertise to interpret it, this would not be as big a problem. However, specialization necessarily concentrates the expertise and information in the hands of the agencies. Congress and the media are generalists. They can tell something has gone wrong when terrorists attack the United States seemingly without warning, but they cannot evaluate the hundreds of less obvious problems that may have led to the failure to warn that only an expert would even recognize.

Congress has tried to check the temptation for bureaucrats to cover up their mistakes by offering protection to whistleblowers. **Whistleblowers** are employees who expose instances or patterns of error, corruption, or waste in their

4. **Eliminate redundancy—it can make a relatively simple concept sound incredibly complicated.** Bureaucrats are not the only ones guilty of this. An article on writing for lawyers (many of whom go on to work in the government, of course) points out that it is unnecessary to say "green in color," "consensus of opinion," "free gift," or "final outcome."[5] Such wordiness is not only wrong, but it clutters up the language, making it hard to understand what is being said.

5. **Look for nouns that have been turned into verbs.** Bureaucrats are famous for this. Impact, acquisition, and dialogue, for instance, are used as nouns in everyday language but as verbs in bureaucratese. If a word seems out of place, it probably is. Think creatively when translating government documents.

6. **Never speak or write like this yourself!** Bureaucratese is bad enough coming from bureaucrats and lawyers. There is no substitute for good, clear, crisp writing.

Reading and understanding the bloated jargon of government bureaucratese can be quite a challenge. Those of you with a sweet tooth can practice on Official Government Bureaucracy Cookies.[6]

Official Government Bureaucracy Cookies

Output: six dozen cookie units.

Inputs: 1 cup packed brown sugar

1/2 cup butter, softened

2 eggs

2 1/2 cups all purpose flour

1/2 teaspoon salt

1 cup chopped pecans or walnuts

1/2 cup white sugar

1/2 cup shortening

1 1/2 teaspoons vanilla

1 teaspoon baking soda

12 ounces semisweet chocolate chips

Guidance:

After procurement actions, decontainerize inputs. Perform measurement tasks on a case-by-case basis:

1. In a mixing-type bowl, impact heavily on brown sugar, white sugar, butter, and shortening. Coordinate the interface of eggs and vanilla, avoiding an overrun scenario to the best of your skills and abilities.

2. At this point in time, leverage flour, baking soda, and salt into a bowl and aggregate. Equalize with prior mixture and develop intense and continuous liaison among inputs until well coordinated. Associate with chocolate and nut subsystems and execute stirring options.

3. Within this time frame, take action to prepare the heating environment for throughput by manually setting the oven baking unit to a temperature of 375 degrees F.

4. Drop mixture in an ongoing fashion from a teaspoon implement onto an ungreased cookie sheet at intervals sufficiently apart to permit total and permanent throughputs to the maximum extent particular under operating conditions. Position cookie sheet in a bake situation for 8 to 10 minutes or until cooking action terminates.

5. Initiate coordination of outputs with the cooling rack function. Containerize, wrap in red tape and disseminate to authorized staff personnel on a timely and expeditious basis.

1. Walden Siew, "Ready Readers Respond to Our Gibberish Alert," *Washington Times*, December 1, 1997, 1, web version.
2. "Have You Hugged Your 1040 Today?" *Washington Times*, April 15, 1991, D2.
3. Laurel Walker, "Functionaries Should Better Utilize Lexicon: Why Do Bureaucrats Insist on Using So Much Unintelligible Jargon?" *Milwaukee Journal Sentinel*, July 5, 1997, 1–2.
4. Bill McAllister and Maralee Schwartz, " 'A Pony to Ride': Freshly Minted Bureaucratese," *Washington Post*, May 8, 1990, 1.
5. Tom Goldstein and Jethro K. Lieberman, "Double Negative Use Is Not Unavoidable," *Texas Lawyer*, May 28, 1990, 2.
6. Material reprinted with the express permission of: "Ottawa Citizen Group Inc.", a division of Postmedia Network Inc.

agencies. They are just good citizens whose consciences will not permit them to protect their agencies and superiors at the expense of what they believe to be the public good. Coleen Rowley, for instance, was asked to testify before the Senate Judiciary Committee because someone had leaked to the media a memo she had written to FBI director Robert Mueller detailing her concerns about the failure of upper-level agency officials to heed her office's worries and to give permission for the search of Moussaoui's computer. Writing that memo was difficult for her because it required her to break with her loyalty to an agency she loved in order to hold it to standards she believed it should meet (see "*Profiles in Citizenship: Coleen Rowley*").

Whistleblowers are not popular with their bosses, as you can well imagine. The Whistleblower Protection Act of 1989 established an independent agency to protect employees from

▶ **Profiles in Citizenship: Coleen Rowley**

"History has proven over and over that mistakes and problems occur when people fall asleep at the helm. . . ."

Coleen Rowley knew what she wanted to do with her life from the time she was in the fifth grade. Watching TV at home in Iowa, she was enthralled by the exotic adventures of the spies on her favorite show, *Man From U.N.C.L.E.*, and determined to join their ranks as soon as she could.

Even then, Rowley must have been the most goal-oriented, determined person you could ever meet. Having chosen her future career, she set about making it happen—at the age of eleven. She wrote to a local newspaper for more information and was chagrined to find out that U.N.C.L.E. was just a fictional organization. But, the newspaper told her, the United States had a similar agency called the FBI, so young Coleen immediately wrote to it instead.

The FBI responded with a packet of information that she devoured, stoking her interest in joining up. She checked briefly at one question buried in the material: "Why can't women become FBI agents?" The answer was "an elaborate, contrived creative writing exercise," she

says, "about the job being so difficult and demanding . . . requiring agents to be capable of bounding into the room and dominating the situation." But it never said why women couldn't do those things (and, adds Coleen, she's never known a man to bound into a room anyway). "I remember thinking, 'Well, this is dumb. This will have to change.' "

She wasn't deterred for a minute. In preparation for her future career she organized seven or eight girlfriends into the World Organization of Secret Spies Club, where they picked the kind of names they imagined covert agents might have—cool, tough-girl names like Tuesday West and Nicky Slate. Although the WOSS club died out the next year about the time of the first "boy-girl" party in sixth grade, Rowley never gave up her dream of being a government agent.

Right out of college she applied to the FBI (which had reluctantly begun to hire women in 1972) but ended up going on to law school instead. But for her, private law practice held no attractions; it was "government service always." In her last year of law school, she applied to the CIA and the Foreign Service before settling on the FBI.

And so it has been ever since. Coleen Rowley has ended up serving her government in ways she could have never imagined—going from fairly traditional law enforcement officer (she worked for a few years in New York City helping bring organized crime figures to justice) to *Time Magazine* Person of the Year in 2002 (for bringing to light internal FBI failures to connect the dots in its intelligence about potential terrorist activity in the days prior to September 11), to Democratic candidate for Congress in Minnesota's Second District.

Rowley is not heroic or noble about any of this—in fact, she is so phlegmatic and

matter-of-fact that you almost miss how very unusual she is. The fearless, seize-the-initiative stance to the world that she had at eleven years old has only matured and seasoned with time. She no longer has a romantic vision of what government service entails—while there were some exciting moments in her FBI career, she wasn't always living the action-packed dreams inspired by *Man From U.N.C.L.E.* But when push came to shove in the days after September 11, she called on a kind of personal courage and integrity that goes far beyond the ability to bound into a room.

On the courage to make tough decisions:

Keep your head on straight and don't let other people's reactions affect you. It's really ingrained in us that popularity is key. It's key to a lot of success in life [as is] not rubbing people the wrong way. However, if you can figure out constructive ways of addressing wrongs—and there are ways—you will be surprised to see that sometimes it works out. You may pay some price, but I still think it's worth it.

On keeping the republic:

You can serve your country in all kinds of ways. Obviously people think of military service, but there is civilian service and actually citizens serve their country by being informed and being discerning. . . . History has proven over and over that mistakes and problems occur when people fall asleep at the helm and they blindly follow orders. It didn't work in Nuremberg, My Lai Massacre, all these situations. People are afraid to serve their country by rocking the boat and doing the right thing. First you have to discern right from wrong, and many times that's hard. And then when you have discerned it, you've got to have the courage to follow through. I think that's patriotism. ■

whistleblowers individuals who publicize instances of fraud, corruption, or other wrongdoing in the bureaucracy

Thinking Outside
the Box

> **When is rocking the bureaucratic boat (blowing the whistle) a good thing, and when is it not?**

being fired, demoted, or otherwise punished for exposing wrongdoing. The act's intention to protect whistleblowers is certainly a step in the direction of counteracting a negative tendency of organizational behavior, but it does little to offset the pervasive pressure to protect the programs and the agencies from harm, embarrassment, and budget cuts. Moreover, the law has not worked anything like its supporters had hoped. Over the past ten years, complaints of agency punishment by whistleblowers have averaged 835 a year. In almost all these cases, the agency's decisions support the bureaucracy rather than the whistleblower, creating a great career disincentive to speak out when one's agency is guilty of corruption, wrongdoing, or simple incompetence.[27]

Presidential Appointees and the Career Civil Service

Another aspect of internal bureaucratic politics worth noting is the giant gulf between those at the very top of the department or agency who are appointed by the president and those in the lower ranks who are long-term civil service employees. Of the two million civilian employees in the U.S. civil service, about 3,500 are appointed by the president or his immediate subordinates.

Conflicting Agendas

Presidential appointees are sometimes considered "birds of passage" by the career service because of the regularity with which they come and go. Though generally quite experienced in the agency's policy area, appointees have their own careers or the president's agenda as their primary objective rather than the long-established mission of the agency. The rank-and-file civil service employees, in contrast, are wholly committed to their agencies. Minor clashes are frequent, but they can intensify into major rifts when the ideology of a newly elected president varies sharply from the central values of the operating agency. Researchers have found that presidents seek to put their own people, rather than career civil service managers, in

the higher ranks of agencies that do not agree with their policy preferences. Some observers claim this is unjustified "politicalization" of the agencies, whereas others contend that it is one of necessary levers presidents use to achieve some control over the vast federal bureaucracy.[28]

When Ronald Reagan was elected president in 1980, he brought in a distinctly conservative ideology. His appointees to agencies such as the Department of Education and the EPA were charged with reversing the growing federal presence in education and countering the EPA's advocacy of environmental protection over business interests. While President Reagan succeeded in making changes, they were not as extensive as conservatives had hoped, partly because the agencies resisted all the way. President George W. Bush engaged in much the same effort to make bureaucratic appointments loyal to his conservative agenda, and many observers concluded that his efforts were more successful than Reagan's.[29]

Conflicting Time Frames

Political appointees have short-term outlooks; they are viewed by career bureaucrats as "birds of passage."[30] The professionals, in contrast, serve long tenures in their positions; the average upper-level civil servant has worked in his or her agency for over seventeen years, and expects to remain there.[31] Chances are the professionals were there before the current president was elected, and they will be there after he leaves office. Thus, while the political appointees have the advantage of higher positions of authority, the career bureaucrats have time working on their side. Not surprisingly, the bureaucrat's best strategy when the political appointee presses for a new but unpopular policy direction is to stall. This is easily achieved by consulting the experts on feasibility, writing reports, drawing up implementation plans, commissioning further study, doing cost-benefit analyses, consulting advisory panels of citizens, and on and on.

Presidential Strategies

Given the difficulty that presidents and their appointees can have in dealing with the entrenched bureaucracy, presidents who want to institute an innovative program are better off starting a new agency than trying to get an old one to adapt to new tasks. In the 1960s, when President John F. Kennedy wanted to start the Peace Corps, a largely volunteer organization that provided assistance to developing countries by working at the grassroots level with the people themselves, he could have added it to any number of existing departments. He might have argued to have it placed in the State Department (which traditionally works through diplomacy at the highest levels of international politics), or in the CIA (which employs people in other countries in its intelligence-gathering operations), or in the Agency for International Development (which consists of experts at administering foreign aid). The problem was that either these existing agencies were unlikely to accept the idea that nonprofessional volunteers could do anything useful, or they were likely to subvert them to their own purposes, such as spying or managing aid. Thus President Kennedy was easily persuaded to have the Peace Corps set up as an independent agency, a frequent occurrence in the change-resistant world of bureaucratic politics.[32]

Who What How

Life inside the bureaucracy is clearly as political as life outside. Many actors attempt to use the rules to advance themselves and the interests of their agency or clientele group, but the bureaucracy has its own culture in which the rules are played out.

Individual bureaucrats want to succeed in their jobs and promote their agencies. Here time, bureaucratic culture, and the rigid nature of bureaucratic rules are in their favor. Congress has helped bureaucrats who wish to challenge an agency to correct a perceived wrong or injustice by passing the Whistle-blower Protection Act.

The president has an enormous stake in what the bureaucracy does, and so do his political appointees, who have their own agendas for advancement. But the entrenched civil service can often and easily outlast them, and ultimately prevail.

External Bureaucratic Politics

Turf wars among agencies and with the three branches of government

Politics affects relationships not only within bureaucratic agencies but also between those agencies and other institutions. While the bureaucracy is not one of the official branches of government, since it falls technically within the executive branch, it is often called the fourth branch of government because it wields so much power. It can be checked by other agencies, by the executive, by Congress, by the courts, or even by the public, but it is not wholly under the authority of any of those entities. In this section we examine the political relationships that exist between the bureaucracy and the other main actors in American politics.

Interagency Politics

As we have seen, agencies are fiercely committed to their policy areas, their rules and norms, and their own continued existence. The government consists of a host of agencies, all competing intensely for a limited amount of federal resources and political support. They all want to protect themselves and their programs, and they want to grow, or at least to avoid cuts in personnel and budgets.

To appreciate the agencies' political plight, we need to see their situation *as they see* it. Bureaucrats are a favorite target of the media and elected officials. Their budgets are periodically up for review by congressional committees and the president's budget department, the Office of Management and Budget (OMB). Consequently, agencies are compelled to work for their survival and growth. They have to act positively in an uncertain and changing political environment in order to keep their programs and their jobs.

Constituency Building

One way agencies compete to survive is by building groups of supporters. Members of Congress are sensitive to voters' wishes, and because of this, support among the general public as well as interest groups is important for agencies. Congress will not want to cut an agency's budget, for instance, if doing so will anger a substantial number of voters or important interests.

As a result, agencies try to control some services or products that are crucial to important groups. In most cases, the groups are obvious, as with the clientele groups of, say, the USDA. Department of Agriculture employees work hard for farming interests, not just because they believe in the programs but also because they need strong support from agricultural clienteles to survive. Agencies whose work does not earn them a lot of fans—like the IRS, whose mission is tax collection—have few groups to support them. When Congress decided to reform the IRS in 1998, there were no defenders to halt the changes.[33] The survival incentives for bureaucratic agencies do not encourage agencies to work for the broader public interest but rather to cultivate special interests that are likely to be more politically active and powerful.

Even independent regulatory commissions run into this problem. Numerous observers have noted the phenomenon

> **agency capture** process whereby regulatory agencies come to be protective of and influenced by the industries they were established to regulate

of **agency capture**, whereby commissions tend to become creatures of the very interests they are supposed to regulate. In other words, as the regulatory bureaucrats become more and more immersed in a policy area, they come to share the views of the regulated industries. The larger public's preferences tend to be less well formed and certainly less well expressed because the general public does not hire teams of lawyers, consultants, and lobbyists to represent its interests. An excellent case in point is the USDA's proposed definition of *organic*, which seemed designed to benefit big food industries and agribusiness rather than the public and small farmers. The regulated industries have a tremendous amount at stake. Over time, regulatory agencies' actions may become so favorable to regulated industries that in some cases the industries themselves have fought deregulation, as did the airlines when Congress and the Civil Aeronautics Board deregulated air travel in the 1980s.[34]

Guarding the Turf

Agencies want to survive, and one way to stay alive is to offer services that no other agency provides. Departments and agencies are set up to deal with the problems of fairly specific areas. They do not want to overlap with other agencies because duplication of services might indicate that one of them is unnecessary, inviting congressional cuts. Thus, in many instances, agencies reach explicit agreements about dividing up the policy turf to avoid competition and duplication. This does not mean that agencies do not get in one another's way or that their rules and regulations are never contradictory. Rather, to ensure supportive constituencies, they do not want anyone else to do what they do.

This turf jealousy can undermine good public policy. Take, for example, the military: for years, the armed services successfully resisted a unified weapons procurement, command, and control system. Each branch wanted to maintain its traditional independence in weapons development, logistics, and communications technologies, costing the taxpayers millions of dollars. Getting the branches to give up control of their turf was politically difficult, although it was accomplished eventually.

The Bureaucracy and the President

As we discussed in Chapter 8, one of the president's several jobs is that of chief administrator. In fact, organizational charts of departments and agencies suggest a clear chain of command, with the cabinet secretary at the top reporting

A Sticky Situation

Crews suck up oil with vacuum tubes on Grand Terre Island, Louisiana, as part of the clean-up efforts in the wake of BP's *Deepwater Horizon* oil spill in the Gulf of Mexico. In the aftermath of the disaster, fresh scrutiny was directed toward the agencies in charge of regulating the oil industry, as the actions of the agencies seemed to have become more aligned with the industry's interests than those of the public.

directly to the president. But in this case, being "the boss" does not mean that the boss always, or even usually, gets his way. The long history of the relationship between the president and the bureaucracy is largely one of presidential frustration. President Kennedy voiced this exasperation when he said that dealing with the bureaucracy "is like trying to nail jelly to the wall." Presidents have more or less clear policy agendas that they believe they have been elected to accomplish, and with amazing consistency presidents complain that "their own" departments and agencies are uncooperative and unresponsive. The reasons for presidential frustration lie in the fact that, although the president has some authority over the bureaucracy, the bureaucracy's different perspectives and goals often thwart the chief administrator's plans.

Appointment Power

Presidents have some substantial powers at their disposal for controlling the bureaucracy. The first is the power of appointment. For the departments, and for quite a few of the independent agencies, presidents appoint the heads and the next layer or two of undersecretaries and deputy secretaries. These cabinet secretaries and agency administrators are responsible for running the departments and agencies. The president's formal power, though quite significant, is often watered down by the political realities of the appointment and policymaking processes.

▶ Who, What, How, and WHEN: Whistleblowing

Governmental bureaucracy is notoriously slow to change. Whistleblowers can speed up that change, but often at substantial costs to themselves. Though federal legislation protects these employees from being fired or demoted for their actions, it takes a lot of personal courage to expose illegal or unethical activity on the part of one's colleagues. Below are just a few of the people or organizations that have stepped up to blow the whistle in the federal bureaucracy:

1971   Daniel Ellsberg on the Vietnam War

Economist Ellsberg worked for both the Department of Defense and the State Department during the Vietnam War. Because of his war experience and high security clearance, he was able to access documents showing that the U.S. government knew the war in Vietnam was a losing effort that would lead to more casualties, even as it told the American public the opposite. After copying the documents and leaking them to the *New York Times*, Ellsberg hid out for fear of being arrested. President Richard Nixon ordered someone to break into Ellsberg's psychiatrist's office to look for discrediting information. Eventually Ellsberg turned himself in. Though he was accused of conspiracy and espionage, he was not convicted and did not go to jail.

1972   Peter Buxtun on the U.S. Public Health Service

Buxtun was an epidemiologist for the U.S. Public Health Service (PHS). He learned that the PHS had, since 1932, been conducting a study on the consequences of not treating patients who had syphilis. The study, which took place in Tuskegee, Alabama, claimed to offer African American men with syphilis free medical treatment but did not inform them that penicillin had been known to cure the disease since the 1940s. Buxtun appealed to the Centers for Disease Control to stop the study on moral grounds. When they refused, he revealed his story to the *Washington Star*. As a result, the federal government created new standards about how to treat humans involved in clinical trials.

2001   Coleen Rowley on the Federal Bureau of Investigation

After the terrorist attacks on September 11, 2001, FBI agent Rowley wrote a memo to the FBI director detailing how FBI headquarters had mishandled and hindered Minneapolis FBI agents' investigation of Zacarias Moussaoui. Moussaoui had been involved in previous plots involving airplanes and had participated in bizarre flight training behavior. Rowley contended that proper follow-up on this information might have prevented Moussaoui's involvement in September 11. As a result of Rowley's testimony before Congress, the FBI was reorganized and expanded.

Cabinet secretaries are supposed to be "the president's men and women," setting directions for the departments and agencies that serve the president's overall policy goals. The reality is that although the president does select numerous political appointees, many also have to be approved by the Senate. The process begins at the start of the president's administration when he is working to gain support for his overall program, so he doesn't want his choices to be too controversial. This desire for early widespread support means

presidents tend to play it safe and to nominate individuals with extensive experience in the policy areas they will oversee. Their backgrounds mean that the president's men and women are only partially his. They arrive on the job with some sympathy for the special interests and agencies they are to supervise on the president's behalf, as well as loyalty to the president.

As we mentioned, recent presidents have sought to achieve political control over agencies by expanding the numbers of their appointees at the top levels of agencies,

2004 — Joe Darby on Abu Ghraib Prison

Darby was a twenty four-year-old soldier when he decided to report abuses at the Abu Ghraib prison in Iraq. Darby reported the abuses by sending an anonymous note and a CD of pictures to the U.S. Army Criminal Investigation Command. He became known as the whistleblower in the case only after Donald Rumsfeld, then–secretary of defense, identified him in a Senate hearing. Darby has received several awards for his effort but also reported being threatened and shunned for what some see as a betrayal of the military.

2004 — Richard Clarke on September 11

Clarke worked for the executive branch under four presidents, including George W. Bush. When testifying before the 9/11 Commission in 2004, Clarke was the only member of the Bush administration to make a public apology to victims' families for the attacks, which had occurred under his watch. He also testified that the administration had detracted from the war in Afghanistan by focusing too much on Iraq and Saddam Hussein and by trying to build a connection between Iraq and Afghanistan that did not exist. The Bush administration tried to discredit Clarke, but his testimony led to public questioning and doubt about the Iraq–al Qaeda connection.

2010 — WikiLeaks on the Afghan War

WikiLeaks, an international online organization that promises to provide leaked information in a forum that protects the source, published the Afghan War Diary, a collection of over 90,000 classified reports on the Afghan War by U.S. military personnel. The Diary purported to contain news about the conduct of the war from 2004 to 2010, although much of the general outline was already well known. But the leaked documents raised anew questions about the delicate balance between the public's right to know versus national and military security concerns. Critics of the war claimed that the information released proved their point that the war was unwinnable, but Mike Mullen, chair of the Joint Chiefs of Staff, argued that the leaks were made to make a political point by people indifferent to the fact that they were endangering soldiers' and civilian lives as a consequence.

especially those agencies whose missions are not consistent with the administration's policy agenda.[35] President George W. Bush was especially adept at this politicalization of the bureaucracy. For instance, in his second term, he appointed one of his most trusted personal advisers to head the Department of Justice. Officials in the Justice Department fired existing U.S. attorneys and replaced them with conservatives who would be more sympathetic to Republican policy concerns, which blunted the agency's traditionally aggressive enforcement of civil rights laws.[36] This effort was not restricted to Justice. In the wake of criticisms that the CIA had been too lax prior to September 11, Bush appointed Porter Goss as the agency's new director. Goss immediately declared, "We support the administration and its policy in our work." Shortly after, twenty CIA officials resigned, many of whom were replaced with Republican operatives loyal to the administration.[37]

President Obama's appointees have been named with less of an eye to their ideological views than to their scientific expertise. As a Democrat, Obama has attempted to reinvigorate the regulatory purpose and effective competence of the agencies in the bureaucracy, and his appointees have been notable for their experience and credentials. For example, his choice to head the Food and Drug Administration was Margaret Hamburg who, as health commissioner in New York City in the 1990s, developed a program that led to a sharp decline in tuberculosis. For FEMA, Obama selected W. Craig Fugate, who had served as head of emergency management in hurricane-ridden Florida.[38]

The Budget Proposal

The president's second major power in dealing with the bureaucracy is his key role in the budget process. About fifteen months before a budget request goes to Congress, the agencies send their preferred budget requests to OMB, which can lower, or raise, departmental budget requests. Thus the president's budget, which is sent to Congress, is a good statement of the president's overall program for the national government. It reflects his priorities, new initiatives, and intended cutbacks. His political appointees and the civil servants who testify before Congress are expected to defend the president's budget.

And they do defend the president's budget, at least in their prepared statements. However, civil servants have contacts with interest group leaders, congressional staff, the media, and members of Congress themselves. Regardless of what the president wants, the agencies' real preferences are made known to sympathetic members of the key authorizations and appropriations committees. Thus the president's budget is a beginning bargaining point, but Congress can freely add to or cut back presidential requests, and most of the time it does so. The president's budget powers, while not insignificant, are no match for an agency with strong interest group and congressional support. Presidential influence over the bureaucratic budget is generally more effective in terminating an activity that the president opposes than in implementing a program that the agency opposes.[39]

The Presidential Veto

The third major power of the president is the veto. As we argued in Chapter 8, the presidential veto can be an effective weapon for derailing legislation, but it is a rather blunt tool for influencing the bureaucracy. First, many spending bills are bundled together. The president may want a different set of funding priorities for, say, mass transit systems, but such funding is buried in a multibillion-dollar multiagency appropriation. He may not like everything in the bill, but he does not want to risk shutting down the government or starting a public battle. Without a line-item veto, the veto can be used only as a threat in political bargaining. By itself, it does not guarantee the president what he wants.

Government Reorganization

In addition to his other efforts, the president can try to reorganize the bureaucracy, combining some agencies, eliminating others, and generally restructuring the way government responsibilities are handled. Such reorganization efforts have become a passion with some presidents, but they are limited in their efforts by the need for congressional approval.[40]

One recent effort at reorganization was the creation of the Department of Homeland Security in response to the terrorist attacks of September 11, 2001. The goal of the new department was to refocus the activities of multiple agencies whose jurisdictions touched on security issues, bringing them under the leadership of a single organization. More typical of reorganization efforts, in the sense that it was intended to make government leaner and more efficient, was President Clinton's National Performance Review (NPR), which later became the National Partnership for Reinventing Government. The goal of this commission, headed by Vice President Al Gore, was to trim the federal payroll by a quarter of a million jobs and to produce savings of $100 billion by decentralizing, deregulating, and freeing government employees to show more initiative in getting their jobs done.

Powers of Persuasion

The president's final major power over the bureaucracy is an informal one, the prestige of the office itself. The Office of the President impresses just about everyone. If the president is intent on change in an agency, his powers of persuasion and the sheer weight of the office can produce results. Few bureaucrats could stand face to face with the president of the United States and ignore a legal order. But the president's time is limited, his political pressures are many, and he needs to choose his priorities very carefully. The media, for example, will not permit him to spend a good part of every day worrying about a little program that they think is trivial. He will be publicly criticized for wasting time on "minor matters." Thus the president and his top White House staff have to move on to other things. The temptation for a bureaucracy that does not want to cooperate with a presidential initiative is to wait it out, to take the matter under study, to be "able" to

> **iron triangles** the phenomenon of a clientele group, congressional committee, and bureaucratic agency cooperating to make mutually beneficial policy

Figure 9.2

Oil-BOEMRE Iron Triangle

Iron triangles (involving Congress, the bureaucracy, and special interest groups) exist on nearly every subgovernment level. In this example, you can see how the BOEMRE (the Bureau of Ocean Energy Management, Regulation and Enforcement, which depends on the House and Senate for its budget) influences and is influenced by oil company lobbyists, who in turn influence and are influenced by House and Senate committees and subcommittees. This mutual interdependence represents a powerful monopoly of power.

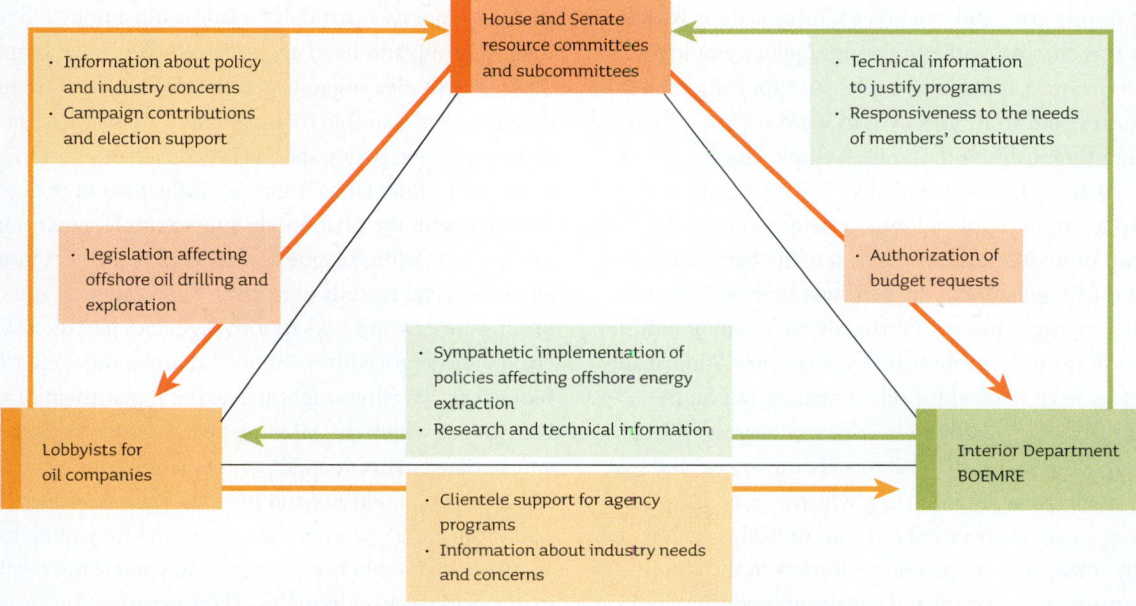

accomplish only a minor part of the president's agenda. The agency or department can then begin the process of regaining whatever ground it lost. It, after all, will be there long after the current president is gone.

The Bureaucracy and Congress

Relationships between the bureaucracy and Congress are not any more clear-cut than those between the agencies and the president, but in the long run individual members of Congress, if not the whole institution itself, have more control over what specific bureaucracies do than does the executive branch. This is not due to any particular grant of power by the Constitution, but rather to informal policymaking relationships that have grown up over time and are now all but institutionalized. That is, much of the influence over the bureaucracy is exercised by Congress, but in highly decentralized agency-by-agency and subcommittee-by-subcommittee sets of relationships.

Iron Triangles

Much of the effective power in making policy in Washington is lodged in what political scientists call **iron triangles**. An iron triangle is a tight alliance among congressional committees, interest groups or representatives of regulated industries, and bureaucratic agencies, in which policy comes to be made for the benefit of the shared interests of all three, not for the benefit of the greater public. Politicians are themselves quite aware of the pervasive triangular monopoly of power. Former secretary of health, education, and welfare John Gardner once declared before the Senate Government Operations Committee, "As everyone in this room knows but few people outside of Washington understand, questions of public policy nominally lodged with the Secretary are often decided far beyond the Secretary's reach by a trinity—not exactly a holy trinity—consisting of (1) representatives of an outside lobby, (2) middle-level bureaucrats, and (3) selected members of Congress."[41]

issue networks complex systems of relationships among groups that influence policy, including elected leaders, interest groups, specialists, consultants, and research institutes

A good example of an iron triangle is the natural resources policy shown in Figure 9.2. In 2010, as oil gushed into the Gulf of Mexico from the ruined oil rig *Deepwater Horizon*, the Minerals Management Service (MMS), an obscure agency that few citizens had heard of, was blasted into the news. The MMS, which was in charge of issuing leases, collecting royalties, and overseeing the dangerous work of offshore drilling for oil and gas on America's continental shelf, was accused of having cozy and even illegal relationships with the industry it was charged with regulating. Agency employees were said to have accepted meals, gifts, and sporting trips from the oil industry, and some agency staff were accused of having had sex and using drugs with industry employees.

At the agency's top sat people like J. Steven Griles, who had worked as an oil industry lobbyist before joining the government. In middle management, the line between the industry and its regulators in the field was blurred.[42] As one MMS district manager put it, "Obviously we're all oil industry . . . . We're all from the same part of the country. Almost all our inspectors have worked for oil companies out on the [Gulf] platforms. They grew up in the same towns."[43] The industry and agency shared a goal of maximizing oil and gas production with hardly more than a whisper of concern for the effects of what was believed to be an unlikely accident. Not surprisingly, many key congressional leaders of the committees with jurisdiction over oil and gas drilling policies are from states with large petroleum interests. The House Committee on Natural Resources and its subcommittee on Energy and Mineral Resources have several members whose districts have major financial interests in oil and gas production, and most of these members receive substantial contributions from the oil and gas industry. The oil- and gas-producing states of Louisiana, Texas, Oklahoma, Colorado, and New Mexico all have members of Congress who receive major contributions from oil and gas industry sources.[44]

Thus the oil industry, the MMS, and members of Congress with responsibility for overseeing the agency all possessed interests in protecting energy production that reinforced one another in a cozy triangle and disregarded the general public's interests in avoiding environmental catastrophe and receiving the appropriate royalties from oil and gas use. The drug and sex scandals, along with the media's relentless coverage of the *Deepwater Horizon* disaster, focused national attention on the problem and spurred the Obama administration to reorganize the agency, now called the Bureau of Ocean Energy Management, Regulation and Enforcement (BOEMRE). However, the forces that created this situation—that is, the intertwined interests among members of Congress who serve on committees that oversee agencies that regulate the industries that affect voters in their districts—are a fundamental part of our political-economic system. As long as citizens and industry are free to "petition Congress for redress of grievances," iron triangles will remain.

The metaphor of the iron triangle has been refined by scholars, who speak instead of *issue networks*.[45] The iron triangle suggests a particular relationship among a fixed interest group and fixed agencies and fixed subcommittees. The network idea suggests that the relationships are more complex than a simple triangle. There are really clusters of interest groups, policy specialists, consultants, and research institutes ("think tanks") that are influential in policy areas. To continue with the offshore drilling example, environmental groups such as the League of Conservation Voters monitor the environmental records of members of Congress, and outside groups use existing laws to force agencies like the MMS to change their procedures. So, for example, the Center for Biological Diversity sought to sue the Department of the Interior (of which the MMS was part) for failing to get appropriate environmental permits required by the Marine Mammal Protection Act and the Endangered Species Act.[46] Thus "outsiders" can use the courts, and they often lobby sympathetic members of Congress to contest the relationships that develop as iron triangles. Their participation shows that the concept of an iron triangle does not always incorporate all the actors in a particular policy area. That is, while the relationships identified by the iron triangle remain important, the full range of politics is frequently better captured by the concept of issue networks.

Congressional Control of the Bureaucracy

Congressional control of the bureaucracy is found more in the impact of congressional committees and subcommittees than in the actions of the institution as a whole. Congress, of course, passes the laws that create the agencies, assigns them their responsibilities, and funds their operations. Furthermore, Congress can, and frequently does, change the laws under which the agencies operate. Thus Congress clearly has the formal power to control the bureaucracy. It also has access to a good deal of information that helps members monitor the bureaucracy. This monitoring process is called *congressional oversight*. Members learn about agency behavior through required reports, oversight hearings and testimony by experts, and reports by congressional agencies such as the Government Accountability Office, and from constituents and organized interests.[47] But

congressional oversight efforts by Congress, especially through committees, to monitor agency rule making, enforcement, and implementation of congressional policies

Congress is itself often divided about what it wants to do and is unable to set clear guidelines for agencies. During the first six years of the Bush administration, the Republican majority was more intent on supporting the president than on protecting congressional prerogatives in the policy process. This aided the president's expansion of control of the bureaucracy.[48] Only when a congressional consensus exists on what an agency should be doing, or at least that Congress should monitor what the agencies do, is congressional control fully effective.

In general, agencies are quite responsive to the congressional committees most directly involved with their authorizations and appropriations. The congressional control that committees and subcommittees exert on the bureaucracy is not the same as the control exercised by Congress as a whole. This is because the subcommittee policy preferences do not always reflect accurately the preferences of the full Congress. Members of Congress gravitate to committees in which they have a special interest—either because of the member's background and expertise or because of the committee's special relevance for the home constituency.[49] Thus, in being responsive to the relevant committees and subcommittees, usually with the support of the organized interests served by the agencies, bureaucrats are clearly less sensitive to the preferences of Congress as a whole, the president, and the general public.

The Bureaucracy and the Courts

Agencies can be sued by individuals and businesses for not following the law. If a citizen disagrees with an agency ruling on welfare eligibility, or the adequacy of inspections of poultry processing plants, or even a ruling by the IRS, he or she can take the case to the courts. In some cases the courts have been important. A highly controversial example involves the timber industry. Environmentalists sued the Department of the Interior and the U.S. Forest Service to prevent logging in some of the old-growth forests of the Pacific Northwest. They sought protection for the spotted owl under the terms of the Endangered Species Act. After a decade-long struggle, logging was greatly restricted in the area in 1992, despite opposition by the economically important timbering interests of the region. However, under the more business-friendly Bush administration, the issue was once again on the agenda and, as the timber industry gained ground, the environmental groups were back in court. In 2009 the Obama administration reversed the Bush administration policy that had doubled the amount of logging allowed.[50]

More often, though, the courts play only a modest role in controlling the bureaucracy. One of the reasons for this limited role is that, since the Administrative Procedure Act of 1946, the courts have tended to defer to the expertise of the bureaucrats when agency decisions are appealed. That is, unless a clear principle of law is violated, the courts usually support administrative rulings.[51] So, for example, while the Supreme Court did restrict some aspects of the Bush administration's policies of unlimited detention of "enemy combatants" held at Guantánamo Bay, it did not go nearly as far as civil liberties advocates wanted.[52]

Another reason is that Congress explicitly puts the decisions of numerous agencies, such as the Department of Veterans Affairs, beyond the reach of the courts. They do this, of course, when members expect they will agree with the decisions of an agency but are uncertain about what the courts might do. Finally, even without these restrictions, the courts' time is extremely limited. The departments and independent agencies make thousands and thousands of important decisions each year; the courts can act on only those decisions about which someone feels sufficiently aggrieved to take the agency to court. Court proceedings can drag on for years, and meanwhile the agencies go about their business making new decisions. In short, the courts can, in specific instances, decide cases that influence how the bureaucracy operates, but such instances are the exception rather than the rule.

All of Washington and beyond have something at stake in bureaucratic politics. The agencies themselves battle over scarce resources, using the tools of constituency building to keep pressure on Congress to maintain their funding levels, and keeping their functions separate from other agencies even if the result is redundancy and inefficiency.

Who What How

The president can employ a variety of techniques to control the bureaucracy, but given time constraints and the weight of bureaucratic norms, he is generally unsuccessful at wresting control from the bureaucrats.

Congress has much at stake in its interactions with the bureaucracy. The bottom line in bureaucratic politics is that the bureaucracy is ultimately responsible to Congress. It is difficult to speak of Congress as a whole institution guided by a common interest, but individual members of Congress certainly have identifiable interests. Because policymaking in Congress so often takes place at the committee and subcommittee levels, and because those committees develop iron triangle relationships with interest groups and the bureaucracies that serve them, members of Congress have quite a lot of input into what the bureaucracy does.

citizen advisory councils citizen groups that consider the policy decisions of an agency; a way to make the bureaucracy responsive to the general public

The Citizens and the Bureaucracy

The tension between transparency and efficiency

The picture that emerges from a look at the politics of the bureaucracy is one of a powerful arm of government, somewhat answerable to the president, more responsible to Congress, but with considerable discretion to do what it wants, often in response to the special interests of clientele groups or regulated industry. If anyone is forgotten in this policymaking arrangement, it is the American public, the average citizens and consumers who are not well organized and who may not even know that they are affected by an issue until the policy is already law. We can look at the relationship between the bureaucracy and the public to determine how the public interest is considered in bureaucratic policymaking.

First, we should figure out what the "public interest" in a democracy really means. Is it the majority preference? If so, then what happens to the minority? Is it some unknown, possibly unpleasant goal that we would favor unanimously if only we could be detached from our particular interests—a sort of national equivalent of eating our spinach because it's good for us? We can imagine some interests that would be disadvantaged by any notion of the public good, no matter how benign. Industries that pollute are disadvantaged by legislation promoting clean air and water; manufacturers of bombs, warplanes, and tanks are disadvantaged by peace. The point here is not to argue that there is no such thing as a "public interest" but to point out that in a democracy it may be difficult to reach consensus on it. To that end, the public interest can probably best be determined by increasing the number of people who have input into deciding what it is. The facts of political life are that the most organized, vocal, and well-financed interests usually get heard by politicians, including bureaucrats. When we speak of the public interest, we usually refer to the interest that would be expressed by the unorganized, less vocal, poorer components of society, if they would only speak. In this final section we look at efforts to bring more people into the bureaucratic policymaking process so as to make policy more responsive to more citizens.

To help increase bureaucratic responsiveness and sensitivity to the public, Congress has made citizen participation a central feature in the policymaking of many agencies.

This frequently takes the form of *citizen advisory councils* that, by statute, subject key policy decisions of agencies to outside consideration by members of the public. There are over 1,200 such committees and councils in the executive branch. The people who participate on these councils are not representative of the citizenry; rather, they are typically chosen by the agency and have special credentials or interests relevant to the agencies' work. Thus citizen advisory councils are hardly a reflection of the general population.

Seven different types of citizen advisory councils have been called over the years (1937 through 1996) to make recommendations on the Social Security system. All have favored the existing programs and recommended expansion. Why? Because members of the councils were carefully selected from among people who already thought highly of Social Security. What political scientist Martha Derthick concluded about the Social Security councils is probably true generally: "The outsiders tended to become insiders as they were drawn into the council's deliberations. . . . Typically, advisory council reports paved the way for program executives' own current recommendations."[53]

Given the chance, such groups can generally be counted on to praise existing efforts—unless they are genuinely flawed or the council is investigating some policy disaster—and then to call for a greater commitment and more resources to deal with whatever problems they are considering. This arrangement serves the interests of the bureaucracy, interest groups, Washington consultants, and elected officials. It probably does not achieve the goal of making public policy more responsive to the broader public interest.

Other reform efforts have attempted to make the bureaucracy more accessible to the public. Citizen access is enhanced by the passage of *sunshine laws* that require that meetings of policymakers be open to the public. Thus the Open Meeting Law was passed in 1976, requiring important agency reviews, hearings, and decision-making sessions to be open to the public, along with most congressional committee and subcommittee meetings. However, most national security and personnel meetings and many criminal investigative meetings are exempted. The right to attend a meeting is of little use unless one can find out that it is being held. The Administrative Procedures Act requires advanced published notices of all hearings, proposed rules, and new regulations so that the public can attend and comment on decisions that might affect them. These announcements appear in the *Federal Register*. In a separate section, the *Federal Register* also contains major presidential documents, including executive orders, proclamations, transcripts of speeches and news conferences, and other White House releases.

With all this information about every meeting, every proposed regulation, and more, the *Federal Register* becomes very large—over 70,000 pages a year. Such size makes it quite forbidding to the average citizen; fortunately, a government booklet, "The *Federal Register*: What It Is and How to Use It," is generally available in libraries and on the Internet, and it greatly eases the task of navigating the *Register*. An online edition of the *Federal Register* is also available (www.gpoaccess.gov/fr/).

A related point of access is the **Freedom of Information Act (FOIA)**, which was passed in 1966 and has been amended several times since. This act provides citizens with the right to copies of most public records held by the agencies. These records include the evidence used in agency decisions, correspondence pertaining to agency business, research data, financial records, and so forth. The agency has to provide the information requested or let the applicant know which provisions of the FOIA allow the agency to withhold the information.

Citizens also receive protection under the **Privacy Act of 1974**, which gives them the right to find out what information government agencies have about them. It also sets up procedures so that erroneous information can be corrected and ensures the confidentiality of Social Security, tax, and related records.

These reforms may provide little practical access for most citizens. Few of us have the time, the knowledge, or the energy to plow through the *Federal Register* and to attend dull meetings. Similarly, while many citizens no doubt feel they are not getting the full story from government agencies, they also do not have much of an idea of what it is they don't know. Hence, few of us ever use the FOIA.

In fact, few Americans try to gain access to the bureaucracy because of negative images that tell us that it is too big, too remote, too complex, and too devoted to special interests. The public does not think well of the bureaucracy or the government, although it does report favorably on its interactions with individual bureaucrats and agencies.[54] One reason for the public disaffection with the bureaucracy may be that it is so constantly under attack by a frustrated president and by members of Congress who highlight the failings of some aspects of government to divert attention from those that are serving their interests only too well.

"Freedom" of Information

The 1966 Freedom of Information Act (FOIA) allows citizens access to declassified documents at the state and federal level. However, provisions contained within the act allow authorities to refuse access to specific information for various reasons. Officials can do this by blacking out content, as in the documents shown here, or by refusing to release them entirely. Critics say that it can be next to impossible to piece together the actual events or facts surrounding an event when access is so frequently denied, and that declassified should mean just that—that it is open to the public for review.

Political scientist Kenneth Meier suggests that although countries usually get bureaucracies no worse than they deserve, the United States has managed to get one that is much better than it deserves, given citizen attitudes and attentiveness toward it. He says that in terms of responsiveness and competency, the U.S. federal bureaucracy is "arguably the best in the world."[55] He places the responsibility for maintaining the quality of the system squarely with the citizens and, to some extent, with the media, suggesting that citizens contact bureaucratic agencies about issues of concern, vote with an elected official's bureaucratic appointments in mind, keep realistic expectations of what government can do, and encourage the media in its watchdog role. Keeping the republic may require public participation in bureaucracy as well as in democracy.

▶ What's at Stake Revisited

Let's go back to the question of what's at stake in the dispute over the USDA's organic food regulation. Remember that regulations are a form of rules, and rules determine who the winners and losers are likely to be. Regulations can serve a variety of interests. They could serve the public interest, simply making it easier for consumers to buy organic food by standardizing what it means to be organic. But regulations can also serve interests besides the public interest. In this case, there were competing business interests as well. Agribusiness and the food preparation industry wanted to use regulations to break into a lucrative market previously closed to them because of the labor-intensive nature of organic farming. For the traditional organic farmers, the proposed regulations spelled disaster.

As far as big business was concerned, this case was like many others. Businesses in the United States are able to lobby the government freely to try to get rules and regulations passed that enhance their positions, and to try to stop those that will hurt them. As we will see in Chapter 11's discussion of interest groups, the larger sums of money that big business can bring to the lobbying effort usually give them an edge in influencing government. If the larger businesses were allowed to compete as organic food producers, the small businesses would lose the only advantage they had, and they would have been forced out of business. In this case, the small businesses were aided by citizen action. This example shows that it is possible to energize a public audience to respond to the bureaucracy. Because those consumers who choose to eat organic foods were a focused, committed, and assertive segment of the population, they were able to follow through with political action.

To Sum Up

Key terms, chapter summaries, practice quizzes, Internet links, and other study aids are available on the companion web site at http://republic.cqpress.com.

Define | Understand | Practice | Read | Click | Watch

accountability (p. 335)

agency capture (p. 353)

bureaucracy (p. 333)

bureaucratese (p. 346)

bureaucratic culture (p. 345)

bureaucratic discretion (p. 343)

citizen advisory councils (p. 360)

civil service (p. 334)

clientele groups (p. 338)

congressional oversight (p. 358)

departments (p. 338)

Federal Register (p. 343)

Freedom of Information Act (FOIA) (p. 361)

government corporations (p. 342)

Hatch Act (p. 334)

independent agencies (p. 338)

independent regulatory boards and commissions (p. 341)

iron triangles (p. 357)

issue networks (p. 358)

neutral competence (p. 333)

patronage (p. 334)

Pendleton Act (p. 334)

Privacy Act of 1974 (p. 361)

red tape (p. 336)

regulations (p. 341)

spoils system (p. 334)

sunshine laws (p. 360)

whistleblowers (p. 348)

Define | **Understand** | **Practice** | **Read** | **Click** | **Watch**

- Bureaucracies are everywhere today, in the private as well as the public spheres. They create a special problem for democratic politics because the desire for democratic accountability often conflicts with the desire to take politics out of the bureaucracy. We have moved from the spoils system of the nineteenth century to a civil service merit system with a more professionalized bureaucracy.

- The U.S. bureaucracy has grown from just three cabinet departments at the founding to a gigantic apparatus of fifteen cabinet-level departments and hundreds of independent agencies, regulatory commissions, and government corporations. This growth has been in response to the expansion of the nation, the politics of special economic and social groups, and the emergence of new problems.

- Many observers believe that the bureaucracy should simply administer the laws the political branches have enacted. In reality, the agencies of the bureaucracy make government policy, and they play the roles of judge and jury in enforcing those policies. These activities are in part an unavoidable consequence of the tremendous technical expertise of the agencies because Congress and the president simply cannot perform many technical tasks.

- The culture of bureaucracy refers to how agencies operate—their assumptions, values, and habits. The bureaucratic culture increases employees' belief in the programs they administer, their commitment to the survival and growth of their agencies, and the tendency to rely on rules and procedures rather than goals.

- Agencies work actively for their political survival. They attempt to establish strong support outside the agency, to avoid direct competition with other agencies, and to jealously guard their own policy jurisdictions. Presidential powers are only modestly effective in controlling the bureaucracy. The affected clientele groups working in close cooperation with the agencies and the congressional committees that oversee them form powerful iron triangles.

- Regardless of what the public may think, the U.S. bureaucracy is actually quite responsive and competent when compared with the bureaucracies of other countries. Citizens can increase this responsiveness by taking advantage of opportunities for gaining access to bureaucratic decision making.

Define | **Understand** | **Practice** | **Read** | **Click** | **Watch**

1. **A bureaucracy is a(n)**
   a. hierarchically structured organization with worker specialization, explicit rules, and advancement by merit.
   b. hierarchically structured organization in which workers have great discretion.
   c. organization of elected officials who work together in a legislative or an executive body of government.
   d. broad organization in which workers have many specialties.
   e. organization in which political supporters are rewarded with public jobs.

2. **Which of the following is NOT a reason why the federal bureaucracy has grown over time?**
   a. To fulfill essential government functions like defense, diplomacy, and currency.
   b. To respond to the changes in society and the economy with westward expansion, industrialization, and the Great Depression.
   c. To respond to the increasing power of the state governments.
   d. To serve particular clientele groups like industries or special interest groups.
   e. To respond to changing international conditions like the Cold War and the September 11, 2001, terrorist attacks.

3. **Which of the following is a characteristic of a bureaucratic culture?**
   a. All departments have a similar culture, but one that differs from that of independent agencies.
   b. Bureaucrats tend to identify with their particular agency and, because of their expertise in the area, they are typically very committed to the particular policies of that agency.
   c. Bureaucrats tend to take on the identity of the judicial branch rather than the executive branch.
   d. Bureaucrats tend to convey information to the public using very clear and accessible language.
   e. Bureaucrats often lack expertise because government workers constantly shift from one agency to another.

4. **In what way do bureaucrats challenge the authority of the president, even though he is their "boss"?**
   a. Bureaucrats tend to have less expertise on most issues than the president.
   b. Bureaucrats often campaign against the president.
   c. Bureaucrats often successfully appoint political heads of their agencies, like cabinet secretaries, who are sympathetic to their own policy interests.
   d. Bureaucrats control the Office of Management and Budget, so they fund the policies they find important and the president is powerless to influence budgetary politics.

e. Bureaucrats often have better established relationships with interest groups and are committed to particular policies, so they often thwart a president's plans to change policies.

5. **What have sunshine laws done for citizens' accessibility to bureaucratic decision making?**
   a. Reduced accessibility, because citizens have access to such information only after the sun has set on a particular administration.
   b. Increased accessibility to bureaucratic decisions regarding defense policy but not environmental policy.
   c. Required public access to most bureaucratic decision-making sessions.
   d. Helped interest groups, but not individual citizens, hold bureaucratic departments accountable.
   e. Added an extra level of bureaucracy, making it more difficult for citizens to access records.

Define | **Understand** | **Practice** | **Read** | **Click** | **Watch**

Downs, Anthony. 1967. *Inside Bureaucracy*. Boston: Little, Brown. *In this groundbreaking work on the bureaucracy, Downs develops a theory of bureaucratic decision making in which bureaucrats are motivated by self-interest.*

Goodsell, Charles T. 2003. *The Case for Bureaucracy: A Public Administration Polemic*, 4th ed. Washington, D.C.: CQ Press. *The majority of the public believes that the bureaucracy is too complex and entangled in red tape. This former bureaucrat takes the opposite view and discusses the positive aspects of bureaucracies.*

Gormley, William T., and Steven J. Balla. *Bureaucracy and Democracy: Accountability and Performance*, 2nd ed. Washington, D.C.: CQ Press. *This accessible textbook provides students with the tools to conduct a systematic assessment of public bureaucracies. Coverage of high-currency issues ranging from Hurricane Katrina to avian flu offer exciting food-for-thought for students interested in learning more about bureaucratic politics and performance.*

Heclo, Hugh. 1977. *A Government of Strangers: Executive Politics in Washington*. Washington, D.C.: Brookings Institution. *The best book written to date on the conflict between appointed officials and career bureaucrats.*

Kettl, Donald F., and James W. Fesler. 2009. *The Politics of the Administrative Process*, 4th ed. Washington, D.C.: CQ Press. *An excellent and easily understandable textbook on public administration that raises several pertinent questions about the bureaucracy.*

Khademian, Anne. 2002. *Working With Culture: The Way the Job Gets Done in Public Programs*. Washington, D.C.: CQ Press. *A short overview of agency culture in federal, state, and local bureaucracies, as well as a demonstration of how management of an agency's culture can lead to successful reform.*

Meier, Kenneth. 2007. *Politics and the Bureaucracy: Policymaking in the Fourth Branch of Government*, 5th ed. Fort Worth, Texas: Harcourt-Brace. *An excellent, readable introduction to politics within the bureaucracy and to the struggles of the bureaucracy with the president and Congress.*

Nelson, William. 2006. *The Roots of the American Bureaucracy, 1830–1900*. Washington, D.C.: Beard Books. *In this interesting commentary on the evolution of the American bureaucracy, Nelson argues that enhancing operational efficiency took second place to restraining executive power among early bureaucrats.*

Pressman, Jeffrey L., and Aaron Wildavsky. 1984. *Implementation*, 3rd ed. Berkeley: University of California Press. *Once a bill is passed in Washington, it still faces a long and difficult journey to be implemented successfully. Pressman and Wildavsky illustrate just how complex and frustrating this process can be.*

Radin, Beryl. 2002. *The Accountable Juggler: The Art of Leadership in a Federal Agency*. Washington, D.C.: CQ Press. *This case study of the Department of Health and Human Services illustrates how bureaucratic bosses must balance the disparate demands of their agencies.*

Reich, Robert. 1997. *Locked in the Cabinet*. New York: Knopf. *Bill Clinton's longtime friend and first secretary of labor gives a firsthand look at the politics behind the Clinton administration.*

Define | **Understand** | **Practice** | **Read** | **Click** | **Watch**

Fed World Information Network *www.fedworld.gov. Sponsored by the Department of Commerce, this site provides a comprehensive central access point for searching, locating, and acquiring government and business information.*

FirstGov *www.firstgov.gov. Billed as the U.S. government's official web portal, this site has links to individual federal agencies, as well as state, local, and tribal governments. There is also a special section "for citizens" to help them navigate services they may need.*

National Archives and Records Administration *www.nara .gov. NARA is an independent federal agency charged with the management of federal records and with ensuring citizen access to the documents that record the rights of American citizens, the actions of federal officials, and the national experience. This site provides electronic access to a huge array of historical documents, including speeches and photos, as well as federal agency records.*

National Whistleblowers Center *www.whistleblowers.org. The National Whistleblowers Center is an advocacy organization that aims to protect the rights of individuals who speak out against wrongdoing and who fear retaliation from their employers. The site contains information on whistleblowers, advocacy efforts, resources, and press releases.*

Define | **Understand** | **Practice** | **Read** | **Click** | **Watch**

The Insider *1999. Based on a true story about a 1994 60 Minutes episode on malpractices in the tobacco industry that was never aired because Westinghouse, the parent company of CBS, objected.*

Silkwood *1983. The true story of a plutonium plant worker who died mysteriously after blowing the whistle on the dangerous conditions in the plant.*

Chapter 10

The American Legal System and the Courts

▶ What's at Stake?

The 2000 presidential election must have set Alexander Hamilton spinning in his grave. In the *Federalist Papers* the American founder confidently wrote that the Supreme Court would be the least dangerous branch of government. Having the power of neither the sword nor the purse, it could do little other than judge, and Hamilton blithely assumed that those judgments would remain legal ones, not matters of raw power politics.

More than two hundred years later, however, without military might or budgetary power, the Supreme Court took into its own hands the very political task of deciding who would be the next president of the United States and, what's more, made that decision right down party lines. On a five-to-four vote (five more conservative justices versus four more liberal ones), the Supreme Court overturned the decision of the Florida Supreme Court to allow a recount of votes in the contested Florida election and awarded electoral victory to Republican George W. Bush.

How did it come to this? The presidential vote in Florida was virtually tied, recounts were required by law in some locations, and voting snafus in several other counties had left untold votes uncounted. Whether those votes should, or even could, be counted or whether voter error and system failure had rendered them invalid was in dispute. Believing that a count of the disputed ballots would give him the few hundred votes he needed for victory, Al Gore wanted the recount. Bush did not. The Florida secretary of

Taking It to the Court
Demonstrators on both sides of the partisan divide rallied as the U.S. Supreme Court decided whether to allow a recount in Florida following the 2000 presidential election.

different standards for counting the vote in different counties, it would amount to a denial of equal protection of the laws. The amount of work required to bring about a fair recount could not be accomplished before the December 12 deadline. A three-person subset of the majority added that the Florida court's order was illegal in the first place.

The dissenters argued instead that the December 12 deadline was not fixed and that the recount could have taken place up to the meeting of the Electoral College on December 18, that there was no equal protection issue, that the Supreme Court should defer to the Florida Supreme Court on issues of state law, and that by involving itself in the political case, the Court risked losing public trust. While the winner of the election was in dispute, wrote Stevens, "the loser is perfectly clear. It is the nation's confidence in the judge as an impartial guardian of the rule of law."

state, a Republican appointed by the governor, Bush's brother, ordered the vote counting finished. The Florida Supreme Court, heavily dominated by Democrats, ruled instead that a recount should go forward.

Bush appealed to the U.S. Supreme Court, asking it to overturn the Florida Supreme Court's decision and to stay, or suspend, the recount pending its decision. A divided Court issued the stay. Justice John Paul Stevens took the unusual route of writing a dissent from the stay, arguing that it was

unwise to "stop the counting of legal votes." Justice Antonin Scalia wrote in response that the recount would pose "irreparable harm" to Bush by "casting a cloud on what he claims to be the legitimacy of his election."

The split between the justices, so apparent in the order for the stay, reappeared in the final decision, where six separate opinions ended up being written. On a five-to-four vote, the majority claimed that if the recount went forward under the Florida Supreme Court's order with

Who was right here? The issue was debated by everyone from angry demonstrators outside the Court to learned commentators in scholarly journals, from families at the dinner table to editorial writers in the nation's press. Was Scalia correct that Bush had really already won and that it was up to the Court to save the legitimacy of his claim to power? Or was Stevens right: that by engaging in politics so blatantly, the Court had done itself irremediable damage in the eyes of the public? What was really at stake for the Court and for America in the five-to-four decision of *Bush v. Gore?* ■

Laws are products of the political process, created by political human beings to help them get valuable resources.

I magine a world without laws. You careen down the road in your car, at any speed that takes your fancy. You park where you please and enter a drugstore that sells drugs of all sorts, from Prozac to LSD to vodka and beer. You purchase what you like—no one asks you for proof of your age or for a prescription—and there are no restrictions on what or how much you buy. There are no rules governing the production or usage of currency either, so you hope that the dealer will accept what you have to offer in trade.

Life is looking pretty good as you head back out to the street, only to find that your car is no longer there. Theft is not illegal, and you curse yourself for forgetting to set the car alarm and for not using your wheel lock. There are no police to call, and even if there were, tracking down your car would be virtually impossible since there are no vehicle registration laws to prove you own it in the first place.

Rather than walk—these streets are quite dangerous, after all—you spot a likely car to get you home. You have to wrestle with the occupant, who manages to clout you over the head before you drive away. It isn't much of a prize, covered with dents and nicks from innumerable clashes with other cars jockeying for position at intersections where there are neither stop signs nor lights and the right of the faster prevails. Arriving home to enjoy your beer in peace and to gain a respite from the war zone you call your local community, you find that another family has moved in while you were shopping. Groaning with frustration, you think that surely there must be a better way!

And there is. As often as we might rail against restrictions on our freedom, such as not being able to buy beer if we are under twenty-one, or having to wear a motorcycle helmet, or not being able to speed down an empty highway, laws actually do us much more good than harm. British philosophers Thomas Hobbes and John Locke, whom we discussed in Chapter 1, both imagined a "prepolitical" world without laws. Inhabitants of Hobbes's state of nature found life without laws to be dismal or, as he put it, "solitary, poor, nasty, brutish and short." And although residents of Locke's state of nature merely found the lawless life to be "inconvenient," they had to mount a constant defense of their possessions and their lives. One of the reasons both Hobbes and Locke thought people would be willing to leave the state of nature for civil society, and to give up their freedom to do whatever they wanted, was to gain security, order, and predictability in life. Because we tend to focus on the laws that stop us from doing the things we want to do, or that require us to do things we don't want to do, we often forget the full array of laws that make it possible for us to live together in relative peace and to leave behind the brutishness of Hobbes's state of nature and the inconveniences of Locke's.

Laws occupy a central position in any political society, but especially in a democracy, where the rule is ultimately by law and not the whim of a tyrant. Laws are the "how" in the formulation of politics as "who gets what, and how"—they dictate how our collective lives are to be organized, what rights we can claim, what principles we should live by, and how we can use the system to get what we want. Laws can also be the "what" in the formulation, as citizens and political actors use the existing rules to create new rules that produce even more favorable outcomes.

In this chapter you will learn about the following aspects of law:

- **the notion of law and the role that it plays in democratic society in general, and in the American legal system in particular**
- **the constitutional basis for the American judicial system**
- **the dual system of state and federal courts in the United States**
- **the Supreme Court and the politics that surround and support it**
- **the relationship of citizens to the courts in America**

Law and the American Legal System

Rules of the game that make collective living possible

Thinking about the law can be confusing. On the one hand, laws are the sorts of rules we have been discussing: limits and restrictions that get in our way, or that make life a little easier. But on the other hand, we would like to think that our legal system is founded on rules that represent basic and enduring principles of justice, that create for us a higher level of civilization. Laws are products of the political process, created by political human beings to help them get valuable resources. Those resources may be civil peace and security, or a particular moral order, or power and influence, or even goods or entitlements. Thus, for security, we have laws that eliminate traffic chaos, enforce contracts, and ban violence. For moral order (and for security as well!), we have laws against murder, incest, and rape. And for political advantage, we have laws like those that give large states greater power in the process of electing a president and those that allow electoral districts to be drawn by the majority party. Laws dealing with more concrete resources are those that, for example, give tax breaks to homeowners or subsidize dairy farmers.

Different political systems produce different systems of laws as well. In small communities where everyone shares values and experiences, formal legal structures may be unnecessary since everyone knows what is expected of him or her, and the community can force compliance with those expectations, perhaps by ostracizing nonconformists. In authoritarian systems, like those of the former Soviet Union, or North Korea or China, laws exist primarily to serve the rulers and the state, and they are subject to sudden change at the whim of the rulers. In systems that merge church and state, such as the Holy Roman Empire, pre-Enlightenment Europe, or some Islamic countries today, laws are assumed to be God-given, and violations of the law are analogous to sin against an all-powerful creator. These sorts of legal systems are not much more convenient for the "ruled" than is Locke's state of nature, though they may be more secure.

In nonauthoritarian countries, where citizens are more than mere subjects and can make claims of rights against the government, laws are understood to exist for the purpose of serving the citizens. That is, laws make life more convenient, even if they have to restrict our actions to do so. But laws, and the courts that interpret and apply them, perform a variety of functions in a democratic society, some of which we commonly recognize, and others of which are less obvious.

The Role of Law in Democratic Societies

For the purpose of understanding the role of law in democratic political systems, we can focus on five important functions of laws:[1]

- The first, and most obvious, function follows directly from Hobbes and Locke: laws *provide security* (for people and their property) so that we may go about our daily lives in relative harmony.

- Laws *provide predictability*, allowing us to plan our activities and go about our business without fearing a random judgment that tells us we have broken a law we didn't know existed.

- The fact that laws are known in advance and identify punishable behaviors leads to the third function of laws in a democracy, that of *conflict resolution*, through neutral third parties known as **courts**.

- A fourth function of laws in a democratic society is *to reflect and enforce conformity to society's values*—for instance, that murder is wrong or that parents should not be allowed to abuse their children.

- A fifth function of laws in a democracy is *to distribute the benefits and rewards society has to offer and to allocate the costs of those good things*, whether they are welfare benefits, civil rights protection, or tax breaks.

The American Legal Tradition

We mentioned earlier that different political systems have different kinds of legal systems—that is, different systems designed to provide order and resolve conflict through the use of laws. Most governments in the industrialized world, including many European countries, South America, Japan, the province of Quebec in Canada, and the state of Louisiana (because of its French heritage), have a legal system founded on a **civil law tradition**, based on a detailed, comprehensive legal code usually generated by the legislature. Some of these codes date back to the days of Napoleon (1804). Such codified systems leave little to the discretion of judges in determining what the law is. Instead, the judge's job is to take an active role in getting at the truth. He or she investigates the facts, asks questions, and determines what has happened. The emphasis is more on getting the appropriate outcome than on maintaining the integrity of the procedures, although fair procedures are still important. While this system is well entrenched in much of the world, and has many defenders, the legal system in the United States is different in three crucial ways.

The Common Law Tradition

To begin, the U.S. legal system, and that of all the states except Louisiana, is based on common law, which developed in Great Britain and the countries that once formed the British Empire. The **common law tradition** relied on royal judges making decisions based on their own judgment and on previous legal decisions, which were applied uniformly, or

> **adversarial system** trial procedures designed to resolve conflict through the clash of opposing sides, moderated by a neutral, passive judge who applies the law
>
> **inquisitorial system** trial procedures designed to determine the truth through the intervention of an active judge who seeks evidence and questions witnesses

commonly, across the land. The emphasis was on preserving the decisions that had been made before, what is called relying on **precedent**, or *stare decisis* (Latin for "let the decision stand"). Judges in such a system have far more power in determining what the law is than do judges in civil law systems, and their job is to determine and apply the law as an impartial referee, not to take an active role in discovering the truth.

The legal system in the United States, however, is not a pure common law system. Legislatures do make laws, and attempts have been made to codify, or organize, them into a coherent body of law. American legislators, however, are less concerned with creating such a coherent body of law than with responding to the various needs and demands of their constituents. As a result, American laws have a somewhat haphazard and hodgepodge character. But the common law nature of the legal system is reinforced by the fact that American judges still use their considerable discretion to decide what the laws mean, and they rely heavily on precedent and the principle of *stare decisis*. Thus, when a judge decides a case, he or she will look at the relevant law but will also consult previous rulings on the issue before making a ruling of his or her own.

The United States as an Adversarial System

Related to its origins in the British common law tradition, a second way in which the American legal system differs from many others in the world is that it is an adversarial system. By **adversarial system**, we mean that our trial procedures are "presumed to reveal the truth through the clash of skilled professionals vigorously advocating competing viewpoints."[2] The winner may easily be the side with the most skilled attorneys, not the side that is "right" or "deserving" or that has "justice" on its side. Judges have a primarily passive role; they apply the law, keep the proceedings fair, and make rulings when appropriate, but their role does not include that of active "truth seeker."

Other legal systems offer an alternative to the adversarial system, and a comparison with these **inquisitorial systems** can help us understand the strengths and weaknesses of our own. The difference can be summed up this way: adversarial systems are designed to determine whether a particular accused person is guilty, whereas inquisitorial systems are intended to discover "who did it."[3] While Britain shares our adversarial tradition, many civil law European countries, like France and Germany, have trial procedures that give a much more active role to the judge as a fact-finder. In these systems, the judge questions witnesses and seeks evidence, and the prosecution (the side bringing the case) and the defense have comparatively minor roles.

In an era when American courtrooms have become theatrical stages and trials are often media extravaganzas, the idea of a system that focuses on finding the truth, that reduces the role of lawyers, that limits the expensive process of evidence gathering, and that makes trials cheaper and faster in general sounds very appealing. There are both cultural and political reasons that we are unlikely to switch to a more inquisitorial system, however. It can be argued, for instance, that the adversarial system makes it easier to maintain that key principle of American law, "innocent until proven guilty." Once a judge in an inquisitorial system has determined that there is enough evidence to try someone, he or she is in fact assuming that the defendant is guilty.[4] In addition, the adversarial system fits with our cultural emphasis on individualism and procedural values, and it gives tremendous power to lawyers, who have a vested interest in maintaining such a system.[5]

The United States as a Litigious System

Not only is the U.S. system adversarial, but it is also *litigious*, which is another way of saying that American citizens sue one another, or litigate, a lot. Legal scholars differ on whether Americans are more litigious than citizens of other nations. Certainly there are more lawyers per capita in the United States than elsewhere (three times as many as in England, for instance, and twenty times as many as in Japan), but other countries have legal professionals other than lawyers who handle legal work, and the number of actual litigators (lawyers who practice in court) is sometimes limited by professional regulations.

Some evidence, however, suggests that Americans do file civil suits—that is, cases seeking compensation from actions that are not defined as crimes, such as medical malpractice or breach of contract—more often than do citizens of many other countries. While the American rate of filing civil suits is roughly the same as the English, Americans file 25 percent more civil cases per capita than do the Germans, and 30 to 40 percent more cases per capita than do the Swedes.[6] Comparisons aside, it remains true that forty-four lawsuits are filed annually for every thousand people in the population.[7]

Why do Americans spend so much time in the courtroom? Scholars argue that the large number of lawsuits in the United States is a measure of our openness and democratic

"So Sue Me . . ."
The label on this coffee cup, "Caution . . . I'm Hot," is not just a benevolent warning to sip carefully, but also the result of a major lawsuit in which a customer sued a chain for serving coffee that was determined to have been dangerously hot. Many criticized the verdict, which favored the plaintiff, saying it represented Americans' propensity to sue, whereas others noted that the plaintiff suffered severe burns that required skin grafts, and the jury award enabled her to pay medical bills. Litigation is one avenue Americans can take to address the risks of everyday life.

concern for the rights of all citizens,[8] and that litigation is unavoidable in democracies committed to individuals' freedoms and to citizens' rights to defend themselves from harm by others.[9] Americans also sue one another a lot because our society has traditionally failed to provide other mechanisms for providing compensation and security from risk. For instance, until health care reform kicks in fully in 2014, many Americans will lack health insurance, a basic security that in many other countries is provided by the government. When disaster strikes, in the form of a car accident or a doctor's error or a faulty product, the only way many individuals can cover expenses has been to sue.

The large number of lawsuits in America, however, has a negative as well as a positive side. Some experts argue that Americans have come to expect "total justice," that everything bad that happens can be blamed on someone, who should compensate them for their harm.[10] In addition, our propensity to litigate means that the courts get tied up with what are often frivolous lawsuits, as when a prisoner filed a million-dollar lawsuit against New York's Mohawk Correctional Facility claiming "'cruel and unusual' punishment for incidents stemming from a guard's refusal to refrigerate the prisoner's ice cream."[11] Such suits are costly not only to the individuals or institutions that must defend themselves, but

> **substantive laws** laws whose content, or substance, define what we can or cannot do
>
> **procedural laws** laws that establish how laws are applied and enforced—how legal proceedings take place
>
> **procedural due process** procedural laws that protect the rights of individuals who must deal with the legal system

also to taxpayers, who support the system as a whole, paying the salaries of judges and legal staff. Politicians make occasional attempts to limit lawsuits (for instance, the recent Republican effort to cap medical malpractice awards), but these efforts often have political motivations and usually come to nothing.

Kinds of Law

Laws are not all of the same type, and distinguishing among them can be very difficult. It's not important that we understand all the shades of legal meaning; in fact, it often seems that lawyers speak a language all their own. Nevertheless, most of us will have several encounters with the law in our lifetime, and it's important that we know what laws regulate what sorts of behavior. To get a better understanding of the various players in the court's legal arena, see *"Consider the Source: Don't Be Fooled When Going to Court."*

Substantive and Procedural Laws

We have used the terms *substantive* and *procedural* elsewhere in this book, and though the meanings we use here are related to the earlier ones, these are precise legal terms that describe specific kinds of laws. **Substantive laws** are those whose actual content or "substance" defines what we can and cannot legally do. **Procedural laws**, on the other hand, establish the procedures used to conduct the law—that is, how the law is used, or applied, and enforced. Thus a substantive law spells out what behaviors are restricted—for instance, driving over a certain speed or killing someone. Procedural laws refer to how legal proceedings are to take place: how evidence will be gathered and used, how defendants will be treated, and what juries can be told during a trial. Because our founders were concerned with limiting the power of government to prevent tyranny, our laws are filled with procedural protections for those who must deal with the legal system—what we call guarantees of **procedural due process**. Given their different purposes, these two types of laws sometimes clash. For instance, someone guilty of breaking a substantive law might be spared punishment if procedural laws meant to protect him or her were violated because the police failed to read the accused his or her rights or searched the accused's home without a warrant. Such situations are complicated by the fact that not all judges interpret procedural guarantees in the same way.

criminal laws laws prohibiting behavior the government has determined to be harmful to society; violation of a criminal law is called a crime

civil laws laws regulating interactions between individuals; violation of a civil law is called a tort

constitutional law law stated in the Constitution or in the body of judicial decisions about the meaning of the Constitution handed down in the courts

statutory laws laws passed by a state or the federal legislature

Criminal and Civil Laws

Criminal laws prohibit specific behaviors that the government (state, federal, or both) has determined are not conducive to the public peace, behaviors as heinous as murder or as relatively innocuous as stealing an apple. Since these laws refer to crimes against the state, it is the government that prosecutes these cases rather than the family of the murder victim or the owner of the apple. The penalty, if the person is found guilty, will be some form of payment to the public—for example, community service, jail time, or even death, depending on the severity of the crime and the provisions of the law. In fact, we speak of criminals having to pay their "debt to society" because in a real sense, their actions are seen as a harm to society.

Civil laws, on the other hand, regulate interactions between individuals. If one person sues another for damaging his or her property, or causing physical harm, or failing to fulfill the terms of a contract, it is not a crime against the state that is alleged but rather an injury to a specific individual. A violation of civil law is called a *tort* instead of a crime. The government's purpose here is not to prosecute a harm to society but to provide individuals with a forum in which they can peacefully resolve their differences. Apart from peaceful conflict resolution, government has no stake in the outcome.

Sometimes a person will face both criminal charges and a civil lawsuit for the same action. An example might be a person who drives while drunk and causes an accident that seriously injures a person in another car. The drunk driver would face criminal charges for breaking laws against driving while intoxicated and might also be sued by the injured party to receive compensation for medical expenses, missed income, and pain and suffering. Such damages are called *compensatory damages*. The injured person might also sue the bar that served the alcohol to the drunk driver in the first place; this is because people suing for compensation often target the involved party with the deepest pockets—that is, the one with the best ability to pay. A civil suit may also include a fine intended to punish the individual for causing the injury. These damages are called *punitive damages*. Reflecting our notion that government poses a bigger threat to our liberties than we do to each other, the burden of proof is easier to meet in civil trials.

Constitutional Law

One kind of law we have discussed often in this book so far is *constitutional law*. This refers, of course, to the laws that are in the Constitution, that establish the basic powers of and limitations on governmental institutions and their

The Road to Nowhere

Drunk driving is one of the leading causes for injury and death on U.S. highways. Here, Brianna Guerrero, left, and Kristin Cash mourn their friend Amanda Laurenson, a junior at Shreveport, Louisiana's Byrd High School who was killed by a man who, police say, was legally drunk. Family members of those injured or killed in such incidents often sue the driver in civil court to receive some sort of compensation for the loss of their loved ones.

interrelationships, and that guarantee the basic rights of citizens. In addition, constitutional law refers to the many decisions that have been made by lower court judges in America, as well as by the justices on the Supreme Court, in their attempts to decide precisely what the Constitution means and how it should be interpreted. Because of our common law tradition, these decisions, once made, become part of the vast foundation of American constitutional law.

All the cases discussed in Chapters 5 and 6 on civil liberties and equal rights are part of the constitutional law of this country. As we have seen, constitutional law evolves over time as circumstances change, justices are replaced, cases are overturned, and precedent is reversed.

Statutory Law, Administrative Law, and Executive Orders

Most laws in the country are made by Congress and the state legislatures, by the bureaucracy under the authority of Congress, and even by the president. *Statutory laws* are those laws that legislatures make at either the state or the national level. Statutes reflect the will of the bodies elected to represent the people, and they can address virtually any behavior. Statutes tell

A cherished principle of our legal system is that everyone is entitled to his or her day in court. If you get into trouble, you are guaranteed access to the courts to redress your wrongs or to defend yourself against false claims. And the way life is in America these days, you are increasingly likely to end up there. If you don't find yourself in court physically, you will certainly watch legal proceedings on television or read about someone's legal travails in a book, newspaper, or magazine. In a society with a heavy emphasis on due process rights, with a litigious disposition to boot, the legal system plays a prominent role in many of our lives at one time or another.

But the legal system is run by lawyers, and legal jargon, like the bureaucratese we studied in Chapter 9, is not easy to understand. In fact, lawyers have a vested interest in our not understanding legalese in the same way that accountants benefit from an incomprehensible tax code. The more we cannot understand the language of the law, the more we need lawyers to tell us what it all means. We cannot condense three years of law school vocabulary here, but we can arm you with some basics to keep in mind if (or when!) you have your day in court.

Entry-Level or Appeals Court?

One critical question, when trying to sort out what is happening in a court of law, is whether we are looking at a proceeding in an entry-level or an appeals court. The personnel and the procedures differ, depending on what kind of court it is.

- **Entry-level court.** This is the court in which a person is initially accused of breaking a criminal or a civil law. The questions to be decided in this court are (1) what is the relevant law and (2) is the person accused guilty of a crime or responsible for violating the civil law? The first question is a question of law, the second a question of fact. The entry-level court produces a verdict based on the application of law to a finding of fact.

- **Appeals court.** This is a court that handles cases when one party to an entry-level proceeding feels that a point of law was not properly applied. Cases are appealed only on points of law, not on interpretations of facts. If new facts are shown to be present, a new trial at the entry level can be ordered.

Who's Who?

It's almost impossible to follow the legal action if you aren't familiar with the players. Here we have grouped them under three headings: the people who are themselves involved in the

dispute, the people who represent them in court, and the people who make the decisions.

People Involved in the Dispute

The parties to the dispute have different names, depending on whether the case is being heard for the first time or on appeal.

- **Plaintiff.** The person bringing the charges or the grievance if the case is in its original, or entry-level, court. If the case is a criminal case, the plaintiff will always be the government, because crimes are considered to be injuries to the citizens of the state, no matter who is really harmed.

- **Defendant.** The person being accused of a crime or of injuring someone.

- **Petitioner.** The person filing an appeal. The petitioner can be either the plaintiff or the defendant from the lower court trial. It is always the loser of that trial, however.

- **Respondent.** The other party in an appeal. As there may be several layers of appeals, the petitioner in one case may later find himself or herself the respondent in a further appeal.

When you see a case name written out it will look like this: Name of Plaintiff v. Name of Defendant, or Name of Petitioner v. Name of Respondent. The names of the cases may switch back and forth as the case moves its way through various appeals. The historic case known as Gideon v. Wainwright, for example, began as a simple criminal case of Wainwright, the prosecutor for Florida, as the plaintiff, against Clarence Gideon, the defendant. When Gideon decided to file his appeal with the Supreme Court, he became the petitioner against Wainwright, now the respondent.

People Who Represent the Parties in Court

- **Lawyers or attorneys.** Professionals who represent the two sides in a dispute. Unlike in other countries, in the United States the same lawyer who works on the case behind the scenes will also represent the client in court.

- **Prosecuting attorney.** The lawyer for the plaintiff. In criminal cases the prosecutor is always a representative of the government—a district or prosecuting attorney at the state level, and a U.S. attorney at the federal level.

- On appeal the government's case is argued by the **state attorney general** (at the state level), the **U.S. attorney** (at the federal level), and the **solicitor general** (if the case goes all the way to the Supreme Court).

- **Defense attorney** (also called a defense counsel). The representative of the defendant. In a criminal case, the Constitution guarantees that a poor defendant be provided with an attorney free of charge, so it can happen that both the prosecutor and the defense counsel are being paid by the same government to represent the two opposing interests in the case.

People Who Make the Decisions

The final group of players are the decision makers. Two kinds of decisions have to be made in a court of law: decisions about facts (what actually happened) and decisions about law. Generally the facts are decided on by citizens, and the law is applied by legal professionals.

- **Juries.** Groups of citizens who decide on the facts in a case. Juries are intended to be a check by citizens on the power of the courts. The Constitution guarantees us a jury of our peers, or equals, although we can waive our right to a jury trial, in which case the judge will make the findings of fact. Lawyers representing the two sides choose from a pool that is representative of the general population, according to a detailed set of rules. In recent years, lawyers have become expert at picking juries that they believe will give maximum advantage to their clients. Questions of fact arise only in entry-level cases, so there are no juries in appeals courts. Citizens can be asked to sit on grand juries (to decide if there is enough factual evidence to warrant bringing a case to trial) or trial juries (to decide whether or not someone is guilty as charged).
- **Jurors.** Participants on a jury, either trial or grand, chosen from a pool of citizens on jury duty at the time.
- **Judges.** Deciders of questions of law. In entry-level courts, judges make rulings on points of law and instruct the jury on the law, so that they know how to use the facts they decide on. If there is no jury, the judge finds facts and applies the law as well. In appeals courts, panels of judges rule on legal questions that are alleged to have arisen from an earlier trial (for example, if a defendant was not given the opportunity to speak to a lawyer, was that a violation of due process?).
- **Justices.** Panels of justices in appeals courts in a state court or the federal Supreme Court. There are no witnesses, and no evidence is presented that would raise any factual questions. If new evidence is thought to be present, the justices order a new trial at the entry level.

Questions to Ask if You Should Find Yourself Having a Day in Court

1. **Does the dispute I am involved in need to be solved in a court of law?** If you have been arrested, you probably have little choice about whether you go to court, but if you are involved in a civil dispute, there are ways to solve conflicts outside the courtroom. Explore options involving mediation and arbitration if you want to avoid a lengthy and possibly acrimonious legal battle.

2. **Do I need a lawyer?** Americans are increasingly getting into the do-it-yourself legal business, but before you take on such a project, carefully evaluate whether hiring a lawyer will serve your interests. Remember that the legal system has been designed by lawyers, and they are trained to know their way around it. Will you be at a disadvantage in resolving your dispute if you don't have a lawyer? It's one thing to draw up your own will, but quite another to undertake your own criminal defense. Disputes such as divorce, child custody, and small claims fall somewhere in between, but as a general rule, if the person whose claims you are contesting has a lawyer, you might want one, too.

3. **Is the case worth the potential cost in money, time, and emotional energy?** Again, if you are in criminal court, you may not have any choice over whether you go to court, but often people enter into civil disputes without a clear idea of the costs involved, seeing them sometimes as a "get-rich-quick" option. Will your lawyer work on a contingency basis (taking a percentage, usually 30 percent, of the settlement he or she wins for you), or will you have to pay an hourly rate? Billable hours can add up quite quickly. Is there a higher principle involved, or is it all about money? Will it be worth it to bring or contest a losing case, only to be left with substantial attorney's fees? You might be willing to sacrifice more for an important cause than for a monetary settlement. Cases can drag on for years, through multiple levels of appeals, and can become a major drain on one's energy and resources.

4. **Should I serve on a jury if called?** Serving on a jury is a good opportunity to see how the system works from the inside, as well as to make a contribution to the nation. Finding a reason to be excused from jury duty sometimes seems like an attractive option when you are besieged by the demands of daily life, but there are real costs to avoiding this civic duty. Since all citizens are entitled to a jury trial, having an active pool of willing jurors is important to the civic health of the nation.

administrative law law established by the bureaucracy, on behalf of Congress

executive orders clarifications of congressional policy issued by the president and having the full force of law

us to wear seatbelts, pay taxes, and stay home from work on Memorial Day. According to the principle of judicial review, judges may declare statutes unconstitutional if they conflict with the basic principles of government or the rights of citizens established in the Constitution.

Because legislatures cannot be experts on all matters, they frequently delegate some of their lawmaking power to bureaucratic agencies and departments. When these bureaucratic actors exercise their lawmaking power on behalf of Congress, they are making **administrative law**. Administrative laws include the thousands of regulations that agencies make concerning how much coloring and other additives can be in the food we buy, how airports will monitor air traffic, what kind of material can be used to make pajamas for children, and what deductions can be taken legally when figuring your income tax. These laws, although made under the authority of elected representatives, are not, in fact, made by people who are directly accountable to the citizens of America. The implications of the undemocratic nature of bureaucratic decision making were discussed in Chapter 9.

Finally, some laws, called **executive orders**, are made by the president himself. These laws, as we explained in Chapter 8, are made without any participation by Congress and need be binding only during the issuing president's administration. Famous executive orders include President Harry Truman's desegregation of the armed forces in 1948 and President Lyndon Johnson's initiation of affirmative action programs for companies doing business with the federal government in 1967.

Thinking Outside the Box

Is justice a matter of enduring principles or the product of a political process?

Who What How

Citizens have a broad stake in a lawful society. They want security, predictability, peaceful conflict resolution, conformity to social norms, and a nondisruptive distribution of social costs and benefits, and they use laws to try to achieve these things. They use the full array of laws and legal traditions available to them in the American legal system to accomplish their goals. The results of the legal process are shaped by the distinctive nature of the American system—its common law roots and its adversarial and litigious nature.

Constitutional Provisions and the Development of Judicial Review

The role of Congress and the courts in establishing the judiciary

Americans may owe a lot of our philosophy of law (called *jurisprudence*) to the British, but the court system we set up to administer that law is uniquely our own. Like every other part of the Constitution, the nature of the judiciary was the subject of hot debate during the nation's founding. Large states were comfortable with a strong court system as part of the strong national government they advocated; small states, cringing at the prospect of national dominance, preferred a weak judiciary. Choosing a typically astute way out of their quandary, the authors of the Constitution postponed it, leaving it to Congress to settle later.

Article III, Section 1, of the Constitution says simply this about the establishment of the court system: "The judicial power of the United States, shall be vested in one supreme court, and in such inferior courts as Congress may from time to time ordain and establish." It goes on to say that judges will hold their jobs as long as they demonstrate "good behavior"—that is, they are appointed for life—and that they will be paid regularly and cannot have their pay reduced while they are in office. The Constitution does not spell out the powers of the Supreme Court. It only specifies which cases must come directly to the Supreme Court (cases affecting ambassadors, public ministers and consuls, and states); all other cases come to it only on appeal. It was left to Congress to say how. By dropping the issue of court structure and power into the lap of a future Congress, the writers of the Constitution neatly sidestepped the brewing controversy. It would require an act of Congress, the Federal Judiciary Act of 1789, to begin to fill in the gaps on how the court system would be organized. We turn to that act and its provisions shortly. First, we look at the controversy surrounding the birth of the one court that Article III does establish, the U.S. Supreme Court.

The Least Dangerous Branch

The idea of an independent judiciary headed by a supreme court was a new one to the founders. No other country had

> **judicial review** the power of the courts to determine the constitutionality of laws
>
> **Marbury v. Madison** the landmark case that established the U.S. Supreme Court's power of judicial review

one, not even England. Britain's highest court was also its Parliament, or legislature. To those who put their faith in the ideas of separation of powers and checks and balances, an independent judiciary was an ideal way to check the power of the president and the Congress. But to others it represented an unknown threat. To put those fears to rest, Alexander Hamilton penned *Federalist* No. 78, arguing that the judiciary was the least dangerous branch of government. It lacked the teeth of the other branches; it had neither the power of the sword (the executive power) nor the power of the purse (the legislative budget power), and consequently it could exercise "neither force nor will, but merely judgment."[12]

For a while, Hamilton was right. The Court was thought to be such a minor player in the new government that several of George Washington's original appointees to that institution turned him down.[13] Many of those who served on the Court for a time resigned prematurely to take other positions thought to be more prestigious. Further indicating the Court's lack of esteem was the fact that when the capital was moved to Washington, D.C., city planners forgot to design a location for it. As a result, the highest court in the land had to meet in the basement office of the clerk of the U.S. Senate.[14]

John Marshall and Judicial Review

The low prestige of the Supreme Court was not to last for long, however, and its elevation was due almost single-handedly to the work of one man. John Marshall was the third chief justice of the United States and an enthusiastic Federalist. During his tenure in office, he found several ways to strengthen the Court's power, the most important of which was having the Court create the power of *judicial review*. This is the power that allows the Court to review acts of the other branches of government and to invalidate them if they are found to run counter to the principles in the Constitution. For a man who attended law school for only six months (as was the custom in his day, he learned the law by serving as an apprentice), his legacy to American law is truly phenomenal.

Federalist No. 78

Marshall was not the first American to raise the prospect of judicial review. While the Constitution was silent on the issue of the Court's power and Hamilton had been quick to reassure the public that he envisioned only a weak judiciary, he dropped a hint in *Federalist* No. 78 that he would approve of a much stronger role for the Court. Answering critics who declared that judicial review would give too much power to

Freedom Fighter
Thurgood Marshall (center) secured his place in legal history when, as special counsel for the National Association for the Advancement of Colored People (NAACP), he convinced the Supreme Court to overturn segregation with the landmark 1954 ruling *Brown v. Board of Education*. In 1967 Marshall himself became a Supreme Court justice, appointed by President Lyndon Johnson.

a group of unelected men to overrule the will of the majority as expressed through the legislature, Hamilton said that in fact the reverse was true. Since the Constitution was the clearest expression of the public will in America, by allowing that document to check the legislature, judicial review would actually place the true will of the people over momentary passions and interests that were reflected in Congress.

Marbury v. Madison

The Constitution does not give the power of judicial review to the Court, but it doesn't forbid the Court to have that power either. Chief Justice John Marshall shrewdly engineered the adoption of the power of judicial review in *Marbury v. Madison* in 1803. This case involved a series of judicial appointments to federal courts made by President John Adams in the final hours of his administration. Most of those appointments were executed by Adams's secretary of state, but the letter appointing William Marbury to be justice of the peace for the District of

Columbia was overlooked and not delivered. (In an interesting twist, John Marshall, who was finishing up his job as Adams's secretary of state, had just been sworn in as chief justice of the United States; he would later hear the case that developed over his own incomplete appointment of Marbury.) These "midnight" (last-minute) appointments irritated the new president, Thomas Jefferson, who wanted to appoint his own candidates, so he had his secretary of state, James Madison, throw out the letter, along with several other appointment letters. According to the Judiciary Act of 1789, it was up to the Court to decide whether Marbury got his appointment, which put Marshall in a fix. If he exercised his power under the act and Jefferson ignored him, the Court's already low prestige would be severely damaged. If he failed to order the appointment, the Court would still look weak.

From a legal point of view, Marshall's solution was breathtaking. Instead of ruling on the question of Marbury's appointment, which was a no-win situation for him, he instead focused on the part of the act that gave the Court authority to make the decision. This he found to go beyond what the Constitution had intended; that is, according to the Constitution, Congress didn't have the power to give the Court that authority. So Marshall ruled that although he thought Marbury should get the appointment (he had originally made it, after all), he could not enforce it because the relevant part of the Judiciary Act of 1789 was unconstitutional and therefore void. He justified the Court's power to decide what the Constitution meant by saying "it is emphatically the province of the judicial department to say what the law is."[15]

The Impact of Judicial Review

With the *Marbury* ruling, Marshall chose to lose a small battle in order to win a very large war. By creating the power of judicial review, he vastly expanded the potential influence of the Court and set it on the road to being the powerful institution it is today. While Congress and the president still have some checks on the judiciary through the powers to appoint, to change the number of members and jurisdiction of the Court, to impeach justices, and to amend the Constitution, the Court now has the ultimate check over the other two branches: the power to declare what they do to be null and void. What is especially striking about the gain of this enormous power is that the Court gave it to itself. What would have been the public reaction if Congress had voted to make itself the final judge of what is constitutional?

Thinking Outside the Box

What would American politics look like today if Chief Justice John Marshall hadn't adopted the power of judicial review?

Aware of just how substantially their power was increased by the addition of judicial review, justices have tended to use it sparingly. The power was not used from its inception in 1803 until 1857, when the Court struck down the Missouri Compromise.[16] Since then it has been used only 158 times to strike down acts of Congress, although it has been used much more frequently (1,261 times) to invalidate acts of the state legislatures.[17]

The Constitution is largely silent about the courts, leaving to Congress the task of designing the details of the judicial system. It was not the Constitution or Congress but John Marshall, the third chief justice, who used the common law tradition of American law to give the Court the extraconstitutional power of judicial review. Once Marshall had claimed the power and used it in a ruling (*Marbury v. Madison*), it became part of the fundamental judge-made constitutional law of this country.

Who What How

Federalism and the American Courts
The structure and organization of the dual court system

In response to the Constitution's open invitation to design a federal court system, Congress immediately got busy putting together the Federal Judiciary Act of 1789. The system created by this act was too simple to handle the complex legal needs and the growing number of cases in the new nation, however, and it was gradually crafted by Congress into the very complex network of federal courts we have today. But understanding just the federal court system is not enough.

Figure 10.1

The Dual Court System

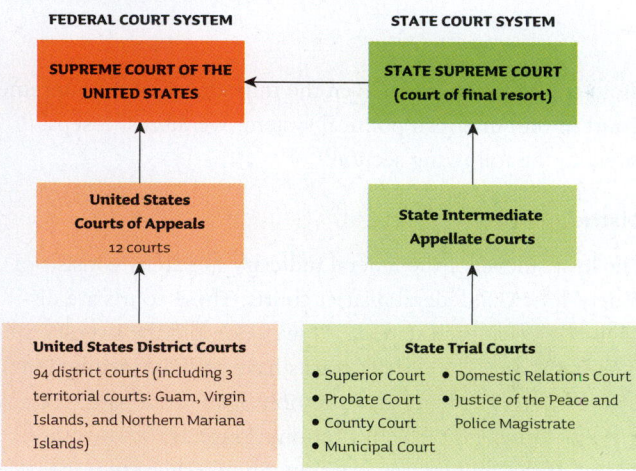

Our federal system of government requires that we have two separate court systems, state and national—and, in fact, most of the legal actions in this country take place at the state level. Because of the diversity that exists among the state courts, some people argue that in truth we have fifty-one court systems. Since we cannot look into each of the fifty state court systems, we will take the "two-system" perspective and consider the state court system as a whole (see Figure 10.1).

Understanding Jurisdiction

A key concept in understanding our dual court system is the issue of *jurisdiction*, the courts' authority to hear particular cases. Not all courts can hear all cases. In fact, the rules regulating which courts have jurisdiction over which cases are very specific. Most cases in the United States fall under the jurisdiction of state courts. As we will see, cases go to federal courts only if they qualify by virtue of the kind of question raised or the parties involved.

The choice of a court, though dictated in large part by constitutional rule and statutory law (both state and federal), still leaves room for political maneuvering. Four basic characteristics of a case help determine which court has jurisdiction over it: the involvement of the federal government (through treaties or federal statutes) or the Constitution, the parties to the case (if, for instance, states are involved), where the case arose, and how serious an offense it involves.[18]

Once a case is in either the state court system or the federal court system, it almost always remains within that system. It is extremely rare for a case to start out in one system and end up in the other. Just about the only time this

occurs is when a case in the highest state court is appealed to the U.S. Supreme Court, and this can happen only for cases involving a question of federal law.

Cases come to state and federal courts under either their original jurisdiction or their appellate jurisdiction. A court's *original jurisdiction* refers to those cases that can come straight to it without being heard by any other court first. The rules and factors just discussed refer to original jurisdiction. *Appellate jurisdiction* refers to those cases that a court can hear on *appeal*—that is, when one of the parties to a case believes that some point of law was not applied properly at a lower court and asks a higher court to review it. Almost all the cases heard by the U.S. Supreme Court come to it on appeal. The Court's original jurisdiction is limited to cases that concern ambassadors and public ministers and to cases in which a state is a party—usually amounting to no more than two or three cases a year.

All parties in U.S. lawsuits are entitled to an appeal, although more than 90 percent of losers in federal cases accept their verdicts without appeal. After the first appeal, further appeals are at the discretion of the higher court; that is, the court can choose to hear them or not. The highest court of appeals in the United States is the U.S. Supreme Court, but its appellate jurisdiction is also discretionary. When the Court refuses to hear a case, it may mean, among other things, that the Court regards the case as frivolous or that it agrees with the lower court's judgment. Just because the Court agrees to hear a case, though, does not mean that it is going to overturn the lower court's ruling, although it does so about 70 percent of the time. Sometimes the Court hears a case in order to rule that it agrees with the lower court and to set a precedent that other courts will have to follow.

State Courts

Although each state has its own constitution, and therefore its own set of rules and procedures for structuring and organizing its court system, the state court systems are remarkably similar in appearance and function (see Figure 10.1). State courts generally fall into three tiers, or layers. The lowest, or first, layer is the trial court, including major trial courts and courts where less serious offenses are heard. The names of these courts vary—for example, they may be called county and municipal courts at the minor level and superior or district courts at the major level. Here cases are heard for the first time, under original jurisdiction, and most of them end here as well.

Occasionally, however, a case is appealed to a higher decision-making body. In about three-fourths of the states, intermediate courts of appeals hear cases appealed from the lower trial courts. In terms of geographic organization, subject matter jurisdiction, and number of judges, courts of appeals vary greatly from state to state. The one constant is that these courts all hear appeals directly from the major trial courts and, on very rare occasions, directly from the minor courts as well.

Each of the fifty states has a state supreme court, although again the names vary. Since they are appeals courts, no questions of fact can arise, and there are no juries. Rather, a panel of five to nine *justices*, as supreme court judges are called, meet to discuss the case, make a decision, and issue an opinion. As the name suggests, a state's supreme court is the court of last resort, or the final court of appeals, in the state. All decisions rendered by these courts are final unless a case involves a federal question and can be heard on further appeal in the federal court system.

Judges in state courts are chosen through a variety of procedures specified in the individual state constitutions. The procedures range from appointment by the governor or election by the state legislature to the more democratic method of election by the state population as a whole. Thirty-nine states hold elections for at least some of their judges. Judicial elections are controversial, however. Supporters argue that they give people a voice, while holding judges accountable and keeping them in line with public opinion. Critics, however, say judicial elections can create a conflict of interest. For example, in 2002 the U.S. Chamber of Commerce and the Business Roundtable, two organizations that regularly appear in court, spent $25 million to influence judicial elections across the country.[19] Others argue that few people are able to cast educated votes in judicial elections and that the threat of defeat may influence judges' rulings.

Federal Courts

The federal system is also three-tiered. There is an entry-level tier called the district courts, an appellate level, and the Supreme Court at the very top (see Figure 10.1). In this section we discuss the lower two tiers and how the judges for those courts are chosen. Given the importance of the Supreme Court in the American political system, we discuss it separately in the following section.

District Courts

The lowest level of the federal judiciary hierarchy consists of ninety-four U.S. federal district courts. These courts are distributed so that each state has at least one and the largest states each have four. The district courts have original jurisdiction over all cases involving any question of a federal nature or any issue that involves the Constitution, Congress, or any other aspect of the federal government. Such issues are wide-ranging but might include, for example, criminal charges resulting from a violation of the federal anticarjacking statute or a lawsuit against the Environmental Protection Agency.

The district courts hear both criminal and civil law cases. In trials at the district level, evidence is presented, and witnesses are called to testify and are questioned and cross-examined by the attorneys representing both sides. In criminal cases the government is always represented by a U.S. attorney. U.S. attorneys, one per district, are appointed by the president, with the consent of the Senate. In district courts, juries are responsible for returning the final verdict.

U.S. Courts of Appeals

Any case appealed beyond the district court level is slated to appear in one of the U.S. courts of appeals. These courts are arranged in twelve circuits, essentially large superdistricts that encompass several of the district court territories, except for the twelfth, which covers just Washington, D.C. (see Figure 10.2). This Twelfth Circuit Court hears all appeals involving government agencies, and so its caseload is quite large even though its territory is small. (A thirteenth Federal Circuit Court hears cases on such specialized issues as patents and copyrights.) Cases are heard in the circuit that includes the district court where the case was originally heard. Therefore, a case that was initially tried in Miami, in the southern district in Florida, would be appealed to the Court of Appeals for the Eleventh Circuit, located in Atlanta, Georgia.

The jurisdiction of the courts of appeals, as their name suggests, is entirely appellate in nature. The sole function of these courts is to hear appeals from the lower federal district courts and to review the legal reasoning behind the decisions reached there. As a result, the proceedings involved in the appeals process differ markedly from those at the district court level. No evidence is presented, no new witnesses called, and

Figure 10.2

The Federal Judicial Circuits

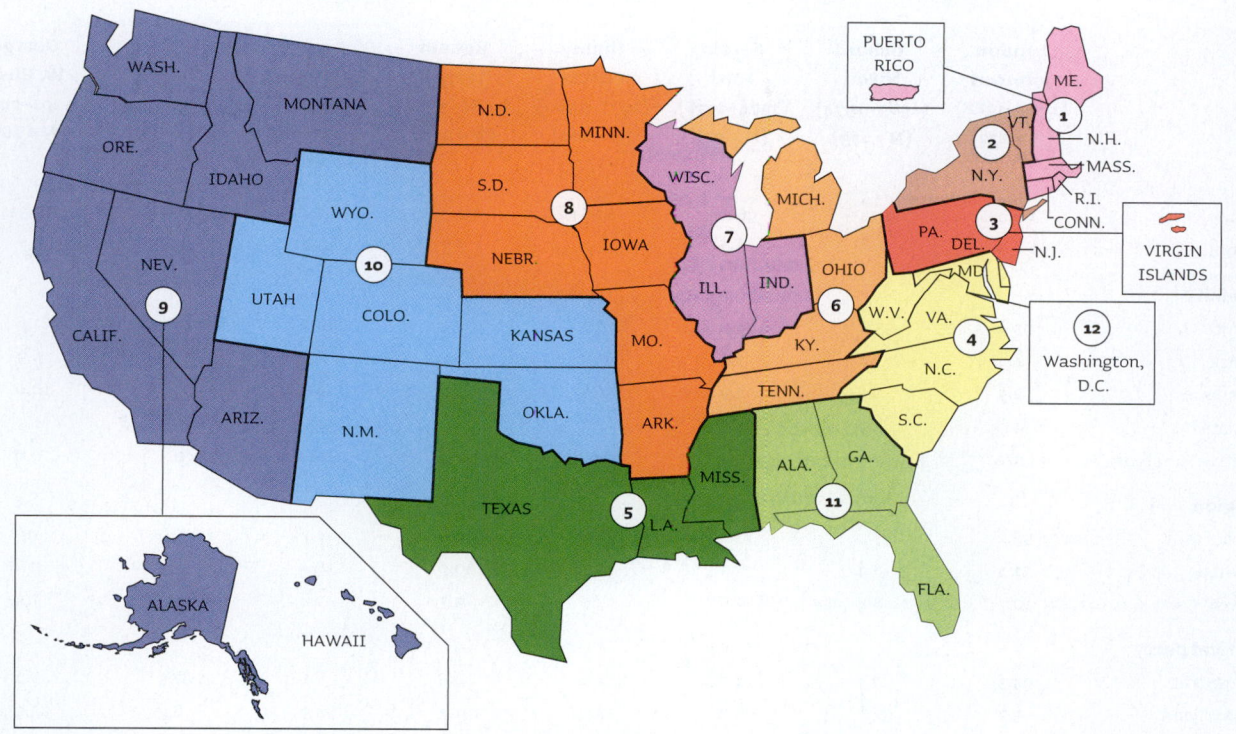

Source: Administrative Office of the United States Courts.

no jury impaneled. Instead, the lawyers for both sides present written briefs summarizing their arguments and make oral arguments as well. The legal reasoning used to reach the decision in the district court is scrutinized, but the facts of the case are assumed to be the truth and are not debated.

The decisions in the courts of appeals are made by a rotating panel of three judges who sit to hear the case. Although many more than three judges are assigned to each federal appeals circuit (the Court of Appeals for the Ninth Circuit, based in San Francisco, has forty-seven), the judges rotate in order to provide a decision-making body that is as unbiased as possible. In rare cases where a decision is of crucial social importance, all the judges in a circuit will meet together, or *en banc*, to render a decision. Having all the judges present, not just three, gives a decision more legitimacy and sends a message that the decision was made carefully.

Selection of Federal Judges

The Constitution is silent about the qualifications of federal judges. It specifies only that they shall be appointed by the president, with the advice and consent of the Senate, and that they shall serve lifetime terms under good behavior. They can

be removed from office only if impeached and convicted by the House of Representatives and the Senate, a process that has resulted in only thirteen impeachments and seven convictions in more than two hundred years.

Traditionally, federal judgeships have been awarded on the basis of several criteria, including rewarding political friendship, supporting and cultivating future support, especially of a gender or ethnic or racial group, and ideology. You can see the demographic, cultural, and political characteristics of the last eight presidents' appointments to the U.S. District Courts in Table 10.1.

Throughout most of the country's history, the courts have been demographically uniform—white, male, and predominantly Christian. President Jimmy Carter broke that trend, vowing to use his nominations to increase the diversity in the federal courts. President Bill Clinton renewed that commitment: nearly half of his appointees were women and minorities, compared to 35 percent under Carter, 14 percent under Ronald Reagan, and 27 percent under George H. W. Bush.[20] President George W. Bush, while not quite emulating Clinton's record, still made a point of nominating a diverse slate of candidates, especially increasing the number of Hispanics on

Table 10.1

Characteristics of Presidential Appointees to U.S. District Court Judgeships (by presidential administration, 1963–2008)

	Lyndon Johnson (1963–1968) (N = 122)	Richard Nixon (1969–1974) (N = 179)	Gerald Ford (1974–1976) (N = 52)	Jimmy Carter (1977–1980) (N = 202)	Ronald Reagan (1981–1988) (N = 290)	George H. W. Bush (1989–1992) (N = 148)	Bill Clinton (1993–2000) (N = 305)	George W. Bush (2001–2008) (N = 261)
Sex								
Male	98.4%	99.4%	98.1%	85.6%	91.7%	80.4%	71.5%	79.3%
Female	1.6	0.6	1.9	14.4	8.3	19.6	28.5	20.7
Ethnicity								
White	93.4	95.5	88.5	78.7	92.4	89.2	75.1	81.6
Black	4.1	3.4	5.8	13.9	2.1	6.8	17.4	6.9
Hispanic	2.5	1.1	1.9	6.9	4.8	4.0	5.9	10.0
Asian	0.0	0.0	3.9	0.5	0.7	0.0	1.3	1.5
Native American	n/a	n/a	n/a	n/a	n/a	n/a	0.3	0.0
Religion								
Protestant	58.2	73.2	73.1	60.4	60.3	64.2	n/a	n/a
Catholic	31.1	18.4	17.3	27.7	30.0	28.4	n/a	n/a
Jewish	10.7	8.4	9.6	11.9	9.3	7.4	n/a	n/a
Political party								
Democrat	94.3	7.3	21.2	91.1	4.8	6.1	87.5	8.0
Republican	5.7	92.7	78.8	4.5	91.7	88.5	6.2	83.0
Independent/other	0.0	0.0	0.0	4.5	3.4	5.4	6.2	3.4
ABA rating								
Exceptionally well/ well qualified	48.4	45.3	46.1	50.9	53.5	57.4	59.0	70.1
Qualified	49.2	54.8	53.8	47.5	46.6	42.6	34.4	28.4
Not qualified	2.5	0.0	0.0	1.5	0.0	0.0	1.0	1.5

Sources: Sheldon Goldman, "Reagan's Judicial Legacy: Completing the Puzzle and Summing Up," *Judicature* 72 (April–May 1989): 320, 321, Table 1; Sheldon Goldman and Elliot Slotnick, "Clinton's First Term Judiciary: Many Bridges to Cross," *Judicature* 80 (May–June 1997): 261. Table adapted by *Sourcebook* staff, Bureau of Justice Statistics, *Sourcebook of Criminal Justice Statistics, 1996* (Washington, D.C.: U.S. Department of Justice, 1996), Table 1.77, 62; Harold W. Stanley and Richard G. Niemi, *Vital Statistics on American Politics, 2007–2008* (Washington, D.C.: CQ Press, 2008), 281–282; Sheldon Goldman, Sara Schiavoni, and Elliot Slotnick, "George W. Bush's Judicial Legacy: Mission Accomplished," *Judicature* 92 (May/June 2009): 279.

Note: Percentages may not add to 100 because of rounding. ABA = American Bar Association; n/a = not available.

the bench.[21] As of September 2010, only forty-three of President Barack Obama's nominees to the federal bench had been confirmed. Of those, twenty-two (just over 50 percent) were women and nearly 40 percent were minorities (eleven African American, four Asian American, and two Hispanic American, a number that included Supreme Court Justice Sonia Sotomayor).[22]

These days an increasingly important qualification for the job of federal judge is the ideological or policy positions of the appointee. Beginning with Richard Nixon in the 1970s, presidents have become more conscious of the political influence of these courts and have tried to use the nomination process to further their own political legacies.

As presidents have taken advantage of the opportunity to shape the courts ideologically, the Senate confirmation process has become more rancorous (see Figure 10.3). While Republican presidents Richard Nixon, Ronald Reagan, and George H. W. Bush made a conscious effort to redirect what they saw as the liberal tenor of court appointments in the years since the New Deal, and Democrat Jimmy Carter countered with liberal appointees, the moderate ideology of most of Democratic president Bill Clinton's appointees meant that the courts did not swing back in a radically liberal direction.[23] Clinton's appointees were what one observer called "militantly moderate"—more liberal than Reagan's and Bush's, but less liberal than Carter's, and

Figure 10.3

Number and Percentage of Judges Confirmed, Truman–Obama

Judicial confirmation rates

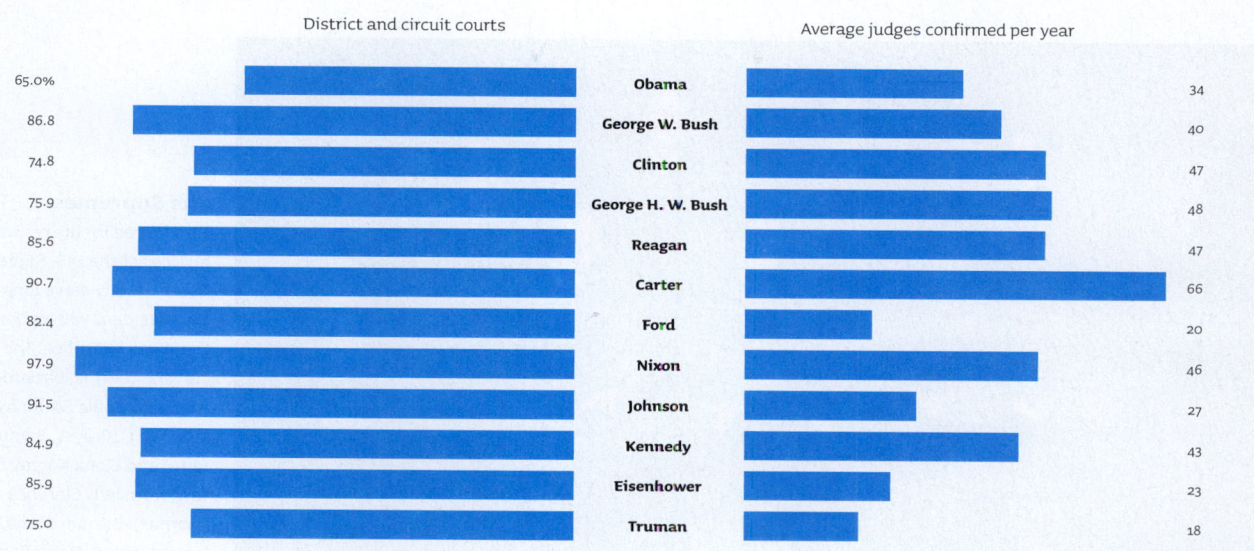

Sources: Mitchell Sollenberger, "Judicial Nomination Statistics: U.S. District and Circuit Courts, 1945–1976," Congressional Research Service, October 22, 2003; Denis Rutkus and Mitchell Sollenberger, "Judicial Nomination Statistics: U.S. District and Circuit Courts, 1977–2003," Congressional Research Service, February 23, 2004; Denis Steven Rutkus, Kevin M. Scott, and Maureen Bearden, "U.S. Circuit and District Court Nominations by President George W. Bush during 107th–109th Congresses," Congressional Research Service, January 23, 2007; "Judicial Nominations: 110th Congress," U.S. Department of Justice Archive, www.justice.gov/archive/olp/judicialnominations.htm.

Note: Data from *CRS Reports* include nominations to territorial district courts in the U.S. Virgin Islands, Guam, and Northern Mariana Islands, as well as resubmitted nominations.

similar ideologically to the appointments of Republican president Gerald Ford.[24] In conjunction with the fact that, by the end of George W. Bush's second term, 56.2 percent of the authorized judicial positions had been filled by Republicans,[25] this means that today's federal bench tilts in a solidly conservative direction.

The increasing politicization of the confirmation process means that many of a president's nominees face a grueling battle in the Senate, and even if they get through the Senate Judiciary Committee hearings, they are lucky if they can get as far as a vote on the floor. Senators of the opposing party can put a hold on a nomination, requiring a vote of sixty senators to bring the nomination to a vote. While both parties use this tactic to stall those nominations of the other party's president to which they object, the Republicans have recently been more effective. Observers chalk this up to the greater discipline among Republican senators. Says one liberal advocate, "Republican senators have voted in lock step to confirm every judge that Bush has nominated. The Democrats have often broken ranks."[26] That Republican unity has continued into the Obama years. While the politicization of the process means that each party has objected to the more

ideological appointments of the other side, in 2009 and 2010 Republicans were blocking votes on all Obama nominations, even moderate ones that would typically have enjoyed bipartisan support, in order to stall the Obama administration's efforts and to gain leverage for other things they wanted.[27] Ironically, when those nominations do eventually come to a vote, they pass with the support of many of the Republicans who supported a filibuster to delay the vote in the first place. While these delay tactics may help the party score a short-term political victory, many federal judgeships are going unfilled as a consequence, contributing to a backlog of cases in the courts.

Another, related influence on the appointment of federal judges is the principle of **senatorial courtesy**, which we discussed in Chapter 8. In reality, senators do most of the nominating of district court judges, often aided by applications made by lawyers and state judges. Traditionally, a president who nominated a candidate who failed to meet with the approval of the state's senior senator was highly unlikely to gain Senate confirmation of that candidate, even if he was lucky enough to get the Senate Judiciary Committee to hold a hearing on the nomination. The

senatorial courtesy tradition of granting senior senators of the president's party considerable power over federal judicial appointments in their home states

The Supremes
Nominated for life terms, the justices of the U.S. Supreme Court usually serve long after the president who appointed them has left office. The current Court is, back row, from left: Sonia Sotomayor, Stephen G. Breyer, Samuel Alito, and Elena Kagan; front row, from left: Clarence Thomas, Antonin Scalia, Chief Justice John G. Roberts Jr., Anthony M. Kennedy, and Ruth Bader Ginsberg.

practice of senatorial courtesy was weakened somewhat by the Bush administration and Senate Republicans, who forced confirmation hearings despite the objections of Democratic home state senators.[28] Once President Barack Obama was elected, however, Senate Republicans sought to restore the policy, sending a letter to the White House promising to block any appointments that didn't meet with the home state senator's approval.[29]

The growing influence of politics in the selection of federal judges does not mean that merit is unimportant. As the nation's largest legal professional association, the American Bar Association (ABA) has had the informal role since 1946 of evaluating the legal qualifications of potential nominees. While poorly rated candidates are occasionally nominated and confirmed, perhaps because of the pressure of a senator or a president, most federal judges receive the ABA's professional blessing. The ABA's role has become more controversial in recent years, as Republicans are convinced that it has a liberal bias, and in 2001 the Bush administration announced that it would no longer seek the ABA's ratings of its nominees, breaking a tradition that goes back to Dwight Eisenhower. The ABA continued to rate the nominees (and the Bush White House boasted that the vast majority of its nominees were rated qualified or well qualified), but it did so independently.[30] In March 2009, the Obama administration restored the ABA's traditional role in the nomination process.

The dual court system in America is shaped by rules that ultimately determine who will win and lose in legal disputes. Because our common law tradition gives the judge a great deal of power to interpret what the law means, the selection of judges is critical to how the rules are applied. Both the president and the Senate are involved in the selection of federal judges, and both have a stake in creating a federal judiciary that reflects the views they think are important—and rewards the people they feel should be rewarded. The rules that determine whether the president or the Senate is successful come partly from the Constitution (the nomination and confirmation processes) and partly from tradition (senatorial courtesy).

Who What How

Thinking Outside the Box

How would the federal judiciary be different if judges were elected rather than appointed?

The Supreme Court
A political institution

At the very top of the nation's judicial system reigns the Supreme Court. While the nine justices do not wear the elaborate wigs of their British colleagues in the House of Lords, the highest court of appeals in Britain, they do don long black robes to hear their cases and sit against a majestic background of red silk, perhaps the closest thing to the pomp and circumstance of royalty that we have in American government. Polls show that even after its role in the contested presidential election of 2000, the Court gets higher ratings from the public than does Congress or the president, and that it doesn't suffer as much from the popular cynicism about government that afflicts the other branches.[31]

The American public seems to believe that the Supreme Court is indeed above politics, as the founders wished it to be. Such a view, while gratifying to those who want to believe in the purity and wisdom of at least one aspect of their government, is not strictly accurate. The members of the Court themselves are preserved by the rule of lifetime tenure from continually having to seek reelection or reappointment, but they are not removed from the political world around them. It is more useful, and closer to reality, to regard the Supreme Court as an intensely political institution. In at least four critical areas—how its members are chosen, how those members choose which cases to hear, how they make decisions, and the effects of the decisions they make—the Court is a decisive allocator of who gets what, when, and how. Reflecting on popular idealizing of the Court, scholar Richard Pacelle says that "not to know the Court is to love it."[32] In the remainder of this chapter, we get to know the Court, not to stop loving it but to gain a healthy respect for the enormously powerful political institution it is.

How Members of the Court Are Selected

In a perfect world, the wisest and most intelligent jurists in the country would be appointed to make the all-important constitutional decisions faced by members of the Supreme Court. In a political world, however, the need for wise and intelligent justices needs to be balanced against the demands of a system that makes those justices the choice of an elected president, and confirmed by elected senators. The need of these elected officials to be responsive to their constituencies means that the nomination process for Supreme Court justices is often a battleground of competing views of the public good. Merit is certainly important, but it is tempered by other considerations resulting from a democratic selection process.

On paper, the process of choosing justices for the Supreme Court is not a great deal different from the selection of other federal judges, though no tradition of senatorial courtesy exists at the high court level. Far too much is at stake in Supreme Court appointments to even consider giving any individual senator veto power. Because the job is so important, the president himself gets much more involved than he does in other federal judge appointments. As the box "Packing the Courts" highlights, the composition of the Court has serious political consequences.

The Constitution, silent on so much concerning the Supreme Court, does not give the president any handy list of criteria for making these critical appointments. But the demands of his job suggest that merit, shared ideology, political reward, and demographic representation all play a role in this choice.[33] We can understand something about the challenges that face a president making a Supreme Court appointment by examining each of these criteria briefly.

Merit

The president will certainly want to appoint the most qualified person and the person with the highest ethical standards who also meets the other prerequisites. Scholars agree that most of the people who have served the Court over the years have been among the best legal minds available, but they also know that sometimes presidents have nominated people whose reputations have proved questionable.[34] The ABA passes judgment on candidates for the Supreme Court, as it does for the lower courts, issuing verdicts of "well qualified," "qualified," "not opposed," and "not qualified." The Federal Bureau of Investigation (FBI) also checks out the background of nominees, although occasionally critical information is missed. In 1987 the Reagan administration, which had widely publicized its Just Say No campaign against drug use, was deeply embarrassed when National Public Radio reporter Nina Totenberg broke the story that its Supreme Court nominee, appeals court judge Douglas Ginsburg, had used marijuana in college and while on the Harvard Law School faculty. Ginsburg withdrew his name from consideration. More controversial was the 1991 case of Clarence Thomas, already under attack for his lack of judicial experience and low ABA rating, who was accused of sexual harassment by a former employee, law professor Anita Hill. Although Thomas was confirmed,

▶ Packing the Courts

The Supreme Court was a thorn in President Franklin Roosevelt's side. Faced with the massive unemployment and economic stagnation that characterized the Great Depression of the 1930s, Roosevelt knew he would have to use the powers of government creatively, but he was hampered by a Court that was ideologically opposed to his efforts to regulate business and industry and skeptical of his constitutional power to do so. In Roosevelt's view, he and Congress had been elected by the people, and public opinion favored his New Deal policies, but a majority of the "nine old men," as they were called, on the Supreme Court consistently stood in his way. Six of the justices were over age seventy, and Roosevelt had appointed none of them.

Roosevelt proposed to change the Court that continually thwarted him. The Constitution allows Congress to set the number of justices on the Supreme Court, and indeed the number has ranged from six to ten at various times in our history. Roosevelt's answer to the recalcitrant Court was to ask Congress to allow him to appoint a new justice for every justice over age seventy who refused to retire, up to a possible total of fifteen. Thus he would create a Court whose majority he had chosen and that he confidently believed would support his New Deal programs.

Most presidents try to pack the Court, building their own legacies with appointees who they hope will perpetuate their vision of government and politics. But Roosevelt's plan was dangerous because it threatened to alter the two constitutional principles of separation of powers and checks and balances. Roosevelt would have made into a truism Hamilton's claim that the judiciary was the least dangerous branch of government, while raising the power of the presidency to a height even Hamilton had not dreamed of. The American people reacted with dismay. Public opinion may have backed his policies, but it turned on him when he tried to pack the Court.

No other president has attempted to pack the Court as blatantly as Roosevelt did, and none has failed so ignominiously. The public backlash may have contributed to the slowing of the New Deal and the Republican victories in 1938 that left Roosevelt with a weakened Democratic majority in Congress. His audacious

Precedent for the President
Historical Figures—a 1937 *Herblock cartoon.*

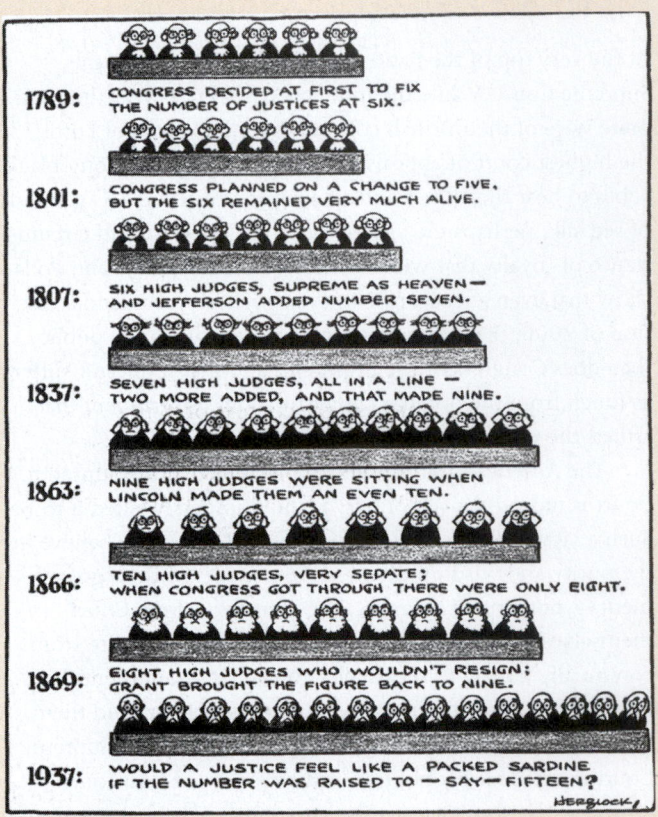

plan had risked the very policy success he was trying so hard to achieve.

In the end, Roosevelt was reelected two more times. The Court, ironically, did an about-face. One justice started voting with the Roosevelt supporters; another retired. Eventually he made eight appointments to the Supreme Court, putting his stamp on it more effectively than any other president since Washington. The Court was, in essence, packed by Roosevelt after all.

the hearings brought to center stage ethical questions about Court nominees.

Political Ideology

Although a president wants to appoint a well-qualified candidate to the Court, he is constrained by the desire to find a candidate who shares his views on politics and the law. Political ideology here involves a couple of dimensions. One is the traditional liberal–conservative dimension. Supreme Court justices, like all other human beings, have views on the role of government, the rights of individuals, and the relationship between the two. Presidents want to appoint justices who look at the world the same way they do, although they are occasionally surprised when their nominee's ideological stripes turn out to be different than they had anticipated. Republican president Dwight Eisenhower called the appointment of Chief Justice Earl Warren, who turned out to be quite liberal in his legal judgments, "the biggest damn fool mistake I ever made."[35] Although there have been notable exceptions, most presidents appoint members of their own party in an attempt to get ideologically compatible justices. Overall, roughly 90 percent of Supreme Court nominees belong to the president's party.

But ideology has another dimension when it refers to the law. Justices can take the view that the Constitution means exactly what it says it means and that all interpretations of it must be informed by the founders' intentions. This approach, called **strict constructionism**, holds that if the meaning of the Constitution is to be changed, it must be done by amendment, not by judicial interpretation. Judge Robert Bork, a Reagan nominee who failed to be confirmed by the Senate, is a strict constructionist. During his confirmation hearings, when he was asked about the famous reapportionment ruling in *Baker v. Carr* that the Constitution effectively guarantees every citizen one vote, Bork replied that if the people of the United States wanted their Constitution to guarantee "one man one vote," they were free to amend the document to say so. In Bork's judgment, without that amendment, the principle was simply the result of justices' rewriting the Constitution. When the senators asked him about the right to privacy, another right enforced by the Court but not specified in the Constitution, Bork simply laughed.[36] The opposite position to strict constructionism, what might be called **judicial interpretivism**, holds that the Constitution is a living document, that the founders could not possibly have anticipated all possible future circumstances, and that justices should interpret the Constitution in light of social changes. When the Court, in *Griswold v. Connecticut*, ruled that while there is no right to privacy in the Constitution, the Bill of Rights can be understood to imply such a right, it was engaging in judicial interpretation. Strict constructionists would deny that there is a constitutional right to privacy.

While interpretivism tends to be a liberal position because of its emphasis on change, and strict constructionism tends to be a conservative position because of its adherence to the status quo, the two ideological scales do not necessarily go hand in hand. For instance, even though the Second Amendment refers to the right to bear arms in the context of militia

membership, many conservatives would argue that this needs to be understood to protect the right to bear arms in a modern context, when militias are no longer necessary or practical—not a strict constructionist reading of the Constitution. Liberals, on the other hand, tend to rely on a strict reading of the Second Amendment to support their calls for tighter gun controls.

Even though it is often hard for a president to know where a nominee stands on the strict constructionist–interpretivist scale, especially if that nominee does not have a large record of previous decisions in lower courts, this ideological placement can be very important in the decision-making process. This was the case, for instance, with President Richard Nixon, who was convinced that interpretivist justices were rewriting the Constitution to give too many protections to criminal defendants, and with President Reagan, who faulted interpretivist justices for the *Roe v. Wade* decision legalizing abortion on the grounds of the right to privacy. But in neither case have all of these presidents' appointees adhered to the desired manner of interpreting the Constitution.

In the George W. Bush administration, another ideological element rose in importance along with the strict constructionist–interpretivist divide. Bush was concerned with finding nominees who not only would interpret the Constitution strictly but also would support a strengthening of executive power. As we saw in Chapter 8, many members of the Bush administration supported the unitary theory of the executive, which claims that the Constitution permits only the president to wield executive power. Under this theory, efforts by Congress to create independent agencies outside of the president's purview are unconstitutional. The administration also objected to efforts by Congress and the courts to limit or interpret executive power in matters of national security.

When Sandra Day O'Connor announced her retirement from the Supreme Court in July 2005, Bush appointed John G. Roberts Jr. to replace her. When then–chief justice William Rehnquist died that September, Bush renominated Roberts as chief justice and was again looking for a replacement for O'Connor, settling in the end on Samuel Alito. In both Roberts and Alito, Bush nominated candidates who were supporters of a strong executive office.

President Obama's Supreme Court nominees will likely reflect his own center-left, interpretivist ideology. His first nomination, Sonia Sotomayor, who joined the Court in September 2009, was more controversial for remarks she had

made about her ethnicity and gender than for her judicial views. When former solicitor general Elena Kagan was nominated by Obama for the Court in 2010, however, her lack of a history of clear judicial rulings left her ideology something of a mystery, and many liberals feared that she would end up being a moderate voice on the Court.[37]

Reward

More than half of the people who have been nominated to the Supreme Court have been personally acquainted with the president.[38] Often nominees are either friends of the president, or his political allies, or other people he wishes to reward in an impressive fashion. Harry Truman knew and had worked with all four of the men he appointed to the Court, Franklin Roosevelt appointed people he knew (and who were loyal to his New Deal), John F. Kennedy appointed his longtime friend and associate Byron White, and Lyndon Johnson appointed his good friend Abe Fortas.[39] While several FOBs (Friends of Bill) appeared on Clinton's short lists for his appointments, none was actually appointed. Though George W. Bush tried to appoint his friend and White House counsel Harriet Meiers to the Court, she was forced to withdraw her name amid criticism that she wasn't sufficiently qualified. Barack Obama had a longtime working relationship with one of his nominees, Elena Kagan, who had been his first solicitor general.

Representation

Finally, the president wants to appoint people who represent groups he feels should be included in the political process, or whose support he wants to gain. Lyndon Johnson appointed Thurgood Marshall at least in part because he wanted to appoint an African American to the Court. After Marshall retired, President George H. W. Bush appointed

Clarence Thomas to fill his seat. While Bush declared that he was making the appointment because Thomas was the person best qualified for the job, and not because he was black, few believed him. In earlier years, presidents also felt compelled to ensure that there was at least one Catholic and one Jew on the Court. This necessity has lost much of its force today as interest groups seem more concerned with the political than the denominational views of appointees, but Hispanic groups rejoiced when President Obama made Sonia Sotomayor the first Hispanic member of the Court in 2009. The issue of ethnic representation on the Court was put front and center during Sotomayor's confirmation hearings when she drew fire from Republicans who noted a line in a speech she had given in 2001, where she had argued that "I would hope that a wise Latina woman with the richness of her experiences would more often than not reach a better conclusion than a white male who hasn't lived that life."[40]

Table 10.2 shows the composition of the Supreme Court. There are six men on the Court and three women. Six justices are Catholic, and three Jewish; only Judeo-Christian religions have been represented on the Court so far. Five of the justices were appointed by Republicans, four by Democrats. They have attended an elite array of undergraduate institutions and law schools. In 2010 their ages ranged from fifty to seventy seven, with the average being sixty four. There have never been any Native Americans or Asian Americans on the Court, and only a total of two African Americans, whose terms did not overlap, and one Hispanic. The overwhelmingly elite, white male Christian character of the Court raises interesting questions. We naturally want our highest judges to have excellent legal educations (although John Marshall barely had any); but should the nation's highest court represent demographically the people whose Constitution it guards? Some observers (including Justice Sotomayor) have suggested that

Table 10.2

Composition of the Supreme Court, 2010

Justice	Year born	Year appointed	Political party	Appointing president	Home state	College/ law school	Religion	Position when appointed
John G. Roberts Jr.	1955	2005	Rep.	W. Bush	Maryland	Harvard/ Harvard	Catholic	U.S. Appeals Court Judge
Antonin Scalia	1936	1986	Rep.	Reagan	D.C.	Georgetown/ Harvard	Catholic	U.S. Appeals Court Judge
Anthony M. Kennedy	1936	1988	Rep.	Reagan	California	Stanford/ Harvard	Catholic	U.S. Appeals Court Judge
Clarence Thomas	1948	1991	Rep.	Bush	Georgia	Holy Cross/Yale	Catholic	U.S. Appeals Court Judge
Ruth Bader Ginsburg	1933	1993	Dem.	Clinton	New York	Cornell/Columbia	Jewish	U.S. Appeals Court Judge
Stephen G. Breyer	1938	1994	Dem.	Clinton	California	Stanford, Oxford/ Harvard	Jewish	U.S. Appeals Court Judge
Samuel A. Alito Jr.	1950	2006	Rep.	W. Bush	New Jersey	Princeton/Yale	Catholic	U.S. Appeals Court Judge
Sonia Sotomayor	1954	2009	Ind.	Obama	New York	Princeton/Yale	Catholic	U.S. Appeals Court Judge
Elena Kagan	1960	2010	Dem.	Obama	New York	Oxford/Harvard	Jewish	Solicitor General

Source: Supreme Court of the United States, "The Justices of the Supreme Court," www.supremecourtus.gov/about/biographies.aspx.

women judges may be sensitive to issues that have not been salient to men and may alter behavior in the courtroom; the same may be true of minority judges as well. In a different vein, what message is sent to citizens when the custodians of national justice are composed primarily of a group that is itself fast becoming a minority in America?

Confirmation by the Senate

As with the lower courts, the Senate must approve presidential appointments to the Supreme Court. Here again, the Senate Judiciary Committee plays the largest role, holding hearings and inviting the nominee, colleagues, and concerned interest groups to testify. Sometimes the hearings, and the subsequent vote in the Senate, are mere formalities, but increasingly, as the appointments have become more ideological and when the Senate majority party is not the party of the president, the hearings have had the potential to become

political battlefields. Even when the president's party controls the Senate, the minority party can still influence the choice through the filibuster unless the Senate Republicans renew their 2005 effort to halt this tradition. The Bork and Thomas hearings are excellent examples of what can happen when interest groups and public opinion get heavily involved in a controversial confirmation battle. These political clashes are so grueling because so much is at stake.

Choosing Which Cases to Hear

The introduction of political concerns into the selection process makes it almost inevitable that political considerations will also arise as the justices make their decisions. Politics makes an appearance at three points in the decision-making process, the first of which is in the selection of the cases to be heard.

writs of certiorari formal requests by the U.S. Supreme Court to call up the lower court case it decides to hear on appeal

Figure 10.4

Pathway to and Through the Supreme Court

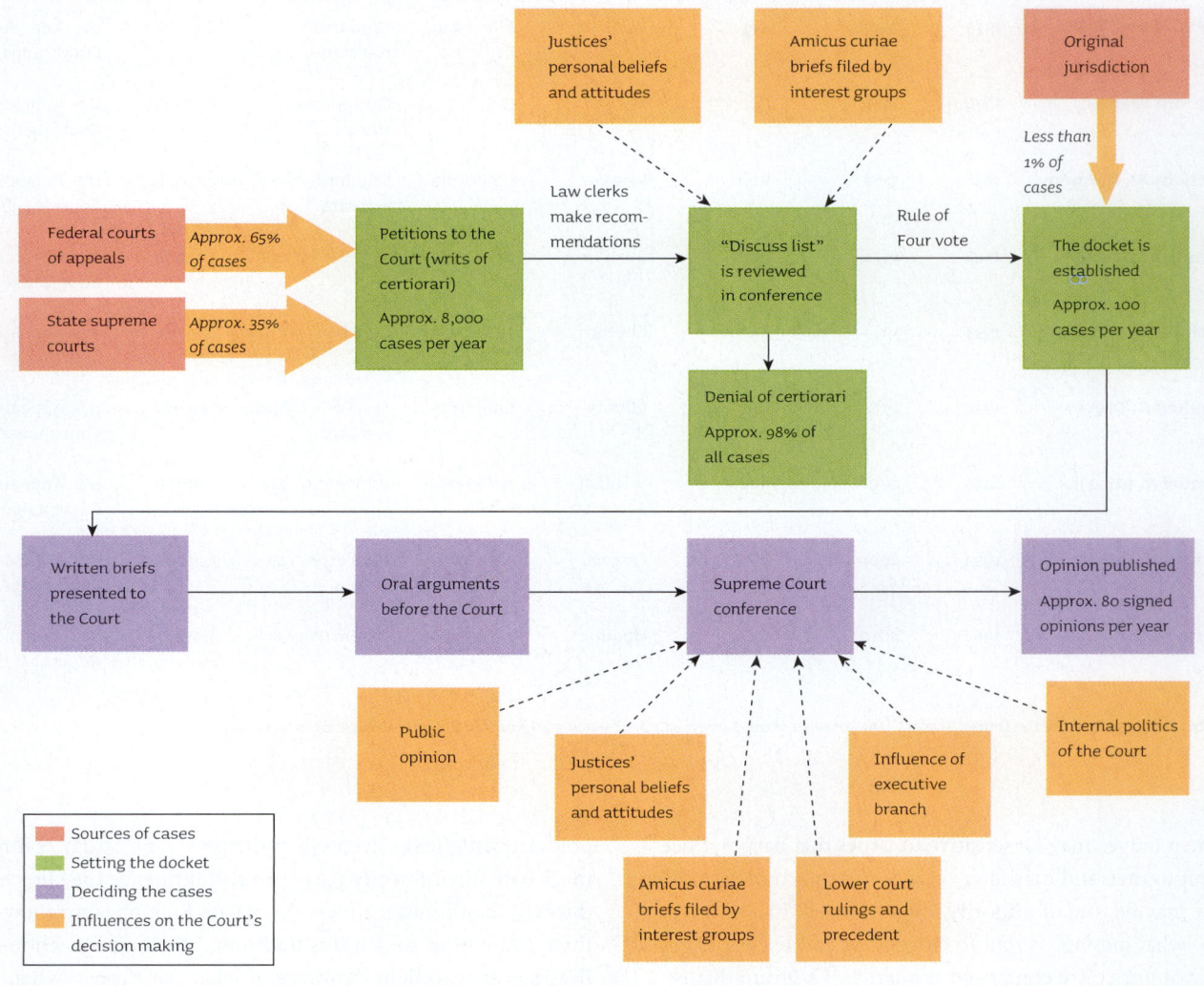

Sources of cases
Setting the docket
Deciding the cases
Influences on the Court's decision making

Source: Administrative Office of the United States Courts.

The Supreme Court could not possibly hear the roughly eight thousand petitions it receives each year.[41] Intensive screening is necessary to reduce the number to the more manageable eighty to ninety that the Court finally hears (see Figure 10.4). This screening process is a political one; having one's case heard by the Supreme Court is a scarce resource. What rules and which people determine who gets this resource and who doesn't?

Petitioning the Supreme Court

Almost all the cases heard by the Court come from its appellate, not its original, jurisdiction, and of these virtually all arrive at the Court in the form of petitions for *writs of certiorari*, in which the losing party in a lower court case explains in writing why the Supreme Court should hear its case. Petitions to the Court are subject to strict length, form, and style

Rule of Four the unwritten requirement that four Supreme Court justices must agree to grant a case certiorari in order for the case to be heard

solicitor general Justice Department officer who argues the government's cases before the Supreme Court

amicus curiae briefs "friend of the court" documents filed by interested parties to encourage the Court to grant or deny certiorari or to urge it to decide a case in a particular way

requirements, and must be accompanied by a $300 filing fee. Those too poor to pay the filing fee are allowed to petition the Court *in forma pauperis*, which exempts them not only from the filing fee but also from the stringent style and form rules. In the 2008 term, 6,142 of the 7,738 case filings were *in forma pauperis*.[42] The Court's jurisdiction here is discretionary; it can either grant or deny a writ of certiorari. If it decides to grant certiorari and review the case, then the records of the case will be called up from the lower court where it was last heard.

For a case to be heard by the Court, it must be within the Court's jurisdiction, and it must present a real controversy that has injured the petitioner in some way, not just request the Court's advice on an abstract principle. In addition, it must be an appropriate question for the Court—that is, it must not be the sort of "political question" usually dealt with by the other two branches of government. This last rule is open to interpretation by the justices, however, and they may not all agree on what constitutes a political question. But these rules alone do not narrow the Court's caseload to a sufficiently small number of cases, and an enormous amount of work remains for the justices and their staffs, particularly their law clerks.

The Role of Law Clerks

Law clerks, usually recent graduates from law school who have served a year as clerk to a judge on a lower court, have tremendous responsibility over certiorari petitions, or "cert pets," as they call them. They must read all the petitions (thirty pages in length plus appendixes) and summarize each in a two- to five-page memo that includes a recommendation to the justices on whether to hear the case, all with minimal guidance or counsel from their justices.[43] Some justices join a "cert pool"—each clerk reads only a portion of the whole number of submitted petitions and shares his or her summaries and evaluations with the other justices. Currently eight of the nine justices of the Court are in a pool; one justice, Justice Samuel Alito, requires his clerks to read and evaluate all the petitions.

The memos are circulated to the justices' offices, where clerks read them again and make comments on the advisability of hearing the cases. The memos, with the clerks' comments, go on to the justices, who decide which cases they think should be granted cert and which denied. The chief justice circulates a weekly list of the cases he thinks should be discussed, which is known unimaginatively as the "discuss list." Other justices can add to that list the cases they think should be discussed in their Friday afternoon meetings.

The Rule of Four

Once a case is on the discuss list, it takes a vote of four justices to agree to grant it certiorari. This **Rule of Four** means that it takes fewer people to decide to hear a case than it will eventually take to decide the case itself, and thus it gives some power to a minority on the Court. The denial of certiorari does not necessarily signal that the Court endorses a lower court's ruling. Rather, it simply means that the case was not seen as important or special enough to be heard by the highest court. Justices who believe strongly that a case should not be denied have, increasingly in recent years, engaged in the practice of "dissenting from the denial" in an effort to persuade other justices to go along with them (since dissension at this stage makes the Court look less consensual) and to put their views on record. Fewer than 5 percent of cases appealed to the Supreme Court survive the screening process to be heard by the Court.

Other Influences

The decisions to grant cert, then, are made by novice lawyers without much direction, who operate under enormous time and performance pressures, and by the justices, who rely on the evaluations of these young lawyers while bringing to the process the full array of values and ideologies for which they were, in part, chosen. Naturally the product of this process will reflect these characteristics, but there are other influences on the justices and the decision-making process at this point as well.

One factor is whether the United States, under the representation of its lawyer, the **solicitor general**, is party to any of the cases before it. Between 70 and 80 percent of the appeals filed by the federal government are granted cert by the justices, a far greater proportion than for any other group.[44] Researchers speculate that this is because of the stature of the federal government's interests, the justices' trust in the solicitor general's ability to weed out frivolous lawsuits, and the experience the solicitor general brings to the job.[45] Justices are also influenced by **amicus curiae briefs**, or "friend of the court" documents, that are filed in support of about 8 percent of petitions for certiorari by interest groups that want to encourage the Court to grant or deny cert. The amicus briefs do seem to affect the likelihood that the Court will agree to hear a case, and since economic interest groups are more likely to be active here than are other kinds of groups, it is their interests that most often influence the justices to grant cert.[46] As we will see, amicus curiae briefs are also used further on in the process.

▶ **Profiles in Citizenship: Sandra Day O'Connor**

"... every new generation has to learn all over again the foundations of our government ... and every individual's role in it."

Even though she's told the story many times, Sandra Day O'Connor's voice still echoed with the frustration of that first job hunt. But there was irony in her voice, too—after all, the story had a happy ending, though it's one she never imagined when she graduated from law school back in 1952.

Really, all she wanted then was to work as a lawyer. She was getting married that summer, and her husband-to-be still had a year left in law school. Since, she said dryly, they both liked to eat, she thought getting a job would be a good idea.

But she reckoned without the prejudice against hiring women that pervaded the country in those days. There were positions galore posted on the jobs board at Stanford Law School, where she'd graduated third in her class of 102, but none of the firms was willing to hire a woman. She'd even parlayed an undergraduate friendship into an interview at a friend's father's firm, but all that resulted were questions about her office skills.

The former Supreme Court justice's story sounded both ludicrous and poignant when we interviewed her the year before her retirement in her impressive law chambers, with their rich polished woods and warm leather furniture, the walls lined with thick volumes of legal wisdom. As this most distinguished of American women recounted that long-ago interview in her precise, forceful voice, her snowy white hair and soft blue suit not blunting at all the effect of the power she radiated, it was hard not to find the incongruity a

little amusing, even as one imagined the bitter disappointment of the young lawyer she once was.

"Well, Miss Day, how do you type?" asked the partner who interviewed her. Just so-so, she replied. "If you can type well enough, maybe I can get you a job here as a legal secretary," he suggested. "But, Miss Day, our firm has never hired a woman as a lawyer. I don't see the day when we will—our clients wouldn't accept it."

Having run into a brick wall in the private sector, Sandra Day, soon to be Sandra Day O'Connor, set to work convincing the San Mateo County attorney to hire her; because he was engaged in public law, "he wasn't afraid to have a woman in his office." With that first job—initially undertaken without pay and in a shared office—she launched herself on a public career that coursed through years in the state attorney general's office in Arizona, the Arizona state senate, and the state bench, and would finally hit its dramatic peak twenty-nine years later, when President Ronald Reagan appointed her as the first female justice on the U.S. Supreme Court.

Don't you just wish you could have seen her girlfriend's father's partner's face when that announcement was made?

Deciding Cases

Once a case is on the docket, the parties are notified and they prepare their written briefs and oral arguments for their Supreme Court appearance. Lawyers for each side get only a half-hour to make their cases verbally in front of the Court, and they are often interrupted by justices who seek clarification, criticize points, or offer supportive arguments. The half-hour rule is generally followed strictly. In one case, two justices got up and walked out as the oral argument cut into their lunch hour, even though the lawyer

who was speaking had been granted an extension by the chief justice.[47]

The actual decision-making process occurs before and during the Supreme Court conference meeting. Conference debates and discussions take place in private, although justices have often made revealing comments in their letters and memoirs that give insight into the dynamics of conference decision making. A variety of factors affect the justices as they make decisions on the cases they hear. Some of those factors come from within the justices—their attitudes, values, and beliefs—and some are external.

But maybe it's too easy to blame Sandra Day O'Connor's extraordinary career in public law on the stubborn sexism of the private legal profession in 1950s America. She might have taken that path anyway—her decision to go to law school in the first place was in part idealistic, inspired by a professor she'd taken a law class from as an undergraduate. "He was the first one who persuaded me that the individual could make a difference in this big world of ours," she remembered. By "the individual" he meant not just a president or governor or other person with power, but even someone "at the bottom of the totem pole." "The person at the bottom will sometimes have the best understanding of how to make something work. If you are sincere about it and determined enough, you can hang in there and see to it that it happens."

And those are the recurring themes in the life of Sandra Day O'Connor: sincerity in her efforts, determination to make a difference, persistence in the face of opposition, and independence in charting her path.

Perhaps all these qualities were honed from an early age, as she grew up on her family's Lazy B Ranch on the border of New Mexico and Arizona. There the fact that their herd grazed on federal land taught her early about the interrelationship between citizens and government. The harsh, isolated beauty of the land taught her other things as well. As she has written, the ranch was "a place where the wind always blows, the sky forms a dome overhead, and the clouds make changing patterns against the blue, and where the stars at night are brilliant and constant, a place to see the sunrise and sunset, and always to be reminded how small we are in the universe but, even so, how one small voice can make a difference."[1]

And there is that idealism again, an optimism about the potential of human beings that is tempered, when she talks, with a strong no-nonsense manner and a brisk practicality, a moderation and pragmatism that was reflected in her judgments on the Court. She's clearly never suffered fools gladly but at the same time is not without hope that we can save ourselves from foolishness. Here is some of her advice:

On what she'd tell today's students about how one person can make a difference:

Of course [you] have to have courage, you have to learn to believe in yourself, and to do that you have to develop some skills. So learn to read fast, and to write well, that's what you need to learn to do as a student. I have to read something like 1,500 pages a day. Now I couldn't do that if I hadn't taken speed reading. And that's important. I'm serious. You don't realize how important it is to be able to read fast. Because if you can read fast, think of all you can learn. . . . And then have courage to believe that, yes, you are equipped to do something, and go do it.

On keeping the republic:

You know, I've always said that we don't inherit our knowledge and understanding through the gene pool. And every new generation has to learn all over again the foundations of our government, how it was set up and why, and what is every individual's role in it. And we have to convey that to every generation . . . [i]f every young generation of citizens [doesn't] have an understanding of this, we can't keep our nation in decent order for the future.

1. Sandra Day O'Connor and H. Alan Day, *Lazy B: Growing Up on a Cattle Ranch in the American Southwest* (New York: Random House 2002), 302. ■

Judicial Attitudes

Justices' attitudes toward the Constitution and how literally it is to be taken are clearly important, as we saw earlier in our discussion of strict constructionism and interpretivism. Judges are also influenced by the view they hold of the role of the Court: whether it should be an active law- and policymaker, or should keep its rulings narrow and leave lawmaking to the elected branches of government. Those who adhere to *judicial activism* are quite comfortable with the idea of overturning precedents, exercising judicial review, and otherwise making decisions that shape government policy. Practitioners of *judicial restraint*, on the other hand, believe more strongly in the principle of *stare decisis* and reject any active lawmaking by the Court as unconstitutional.

These positions seem at first to line up with the positions of interpretivism and strict constructionism, and often they do. But exceptions exist, as when liberal justice Thurgood Marshall, who had once used the Constitution in activist and interpretivist ways to change civil rights laws, pleaded for restraint among his newer and more conservative colleagues who were eager to roll back some of the earlier decisions by overturning precedent and creating more conservative law.[48]

In recent years, especially in the wake of a Massachusetts Supreme Court decision that said forbidding gays the right to marry violates the Massachusetts constitution, conservatives have lambasted what they call the activism or "legislating from the bench" of courts who they say take decision making out of the hands of the people. But activism is not necessarily a liberal stance, and restraint is not necessarily conservative. Activism or restraint often seems to be more a function of whether a justice likes the status quo than it does of any steady point of principle.[49] A justice seeking to overturn the *Roe v. Wade* ruling allowing women to have abortions during the first trimester of pregnancy would be an activist conservative justice; Justice Thurgood Marshall ended his term on the Court as a liberal restraintist.

In addition to being influenced by their own attitudes, justices are influenced in their decision making by their backgrounds (region of residence, profession, place of education, and the like), their party affiliations, and their political attitudes, all of which the president and the Senate consider in selecting future justices.[50]

External Factors

Justices are also influenced by external factors.[51] Despite the founders' efforts to make justices immune to politics and the pressures of public opinion by giving them lifetime tenure, political scientists have found that they usually tend to make decisions that are consistent with majority opinion in the United States. Of course, this doesn't mean that justices are reading public opinion polls over breakfast and incorporating their findings into judicial decisions after lunch. Rather, the same forces that shape public opinion also shape the justices' opinions, and people who are elected by the public choose the justices they hope will help them carry out their agenda, usually one that is responsive to what the public wants.

Political forces other than public opinion exert an influence on the Court, however. The influence of the executive branch, discussed earlier, contributes to the high success rate of the solicitor general. Interest groups also put enormous pressure on the Supreme Court, although with varying success. Interest groups are influential in the process of nomination and confirmation of the justices, they file amicus curiae briefs to try to shape the decisions on the certiorari petitions, and they file an increasingly large number of briefs in support of one or the other side when the case is actually reviewed by the Court.

According to one scholar, the number of amicus briefs filed by interest groups is increasing. In the 2004 term the average number of such briefs in cases with oral arguments was 7.99, compared to 4.23 during the 1986–1995 terms.[52] Some 149 briefs were filed in connection with the University of Michigan affirmative action cases discussed in Chapter 6.[53] Interest groups also have a role in sponsoring cases when individual petitioners do not have the resources to bring a case before the Supreme Court. The National Association for the Advancement of Colored People (NAACP), the American Civil Liberties Union (ACLU), and the Washington Legal Foundation are examples of groups that have provided funds and lawyers for people seeking to reach the Court. While interest group activity has increased tremendously since the 1980s, researchers are uncertain whether it has paid off in Court victories. Their support does seem to help cases get to the Court, however, and they may reap other gains, such as publicity.

A final influence on the justices worth discussing here is the justices' relationships with one another. While they usually (at least in recent years) arrive at their conference meeting with their minds already made up, they cannot afford to ignore one another. It takes five votes to decide a case, and the justices need each other as allies. One scholar who has looked at the disputes among justices over decisions, and who has evaluated the characterization of the Court as "nine scorpions in a bottle," says that the number of disagreements is not noteworthy.[54] On the contrary, what is truly remarkable is how well the justices tend to cooperate, given their close working relationship, the seriousness of their undertaking, and the varied and strong personalities and ideologies that go into the mix.

Writing Opinions

Once a decision is reached, or sometimes as it is being reached, the writing of the opinion is assigned. The *opinion* is the written part of the decision that states the judgment of the majority of the Court; it is the lasting part of the process, read by law students, lawyers, judges, and future justices. As the living legacy of the case, the written opinions are vitally important for how the nation will understand what the decision means. If, for instance, the opinion is written by the least enthusiastic member of the majority, it will be weaker and less authoritative than if it is written by the most passionate member. The same decision can be portrayed in different ways, can be stated broadly or narrowly, with implications for many future cases or for fewer. If the chief justice is in

concurring opinions documents written by justices expressing agreement with the majority ruling but describing different or additional reasons for the ruling

dissenting opinions documents written by justices expressing disagreement with the majority ruling

the majority, it is his or her job to assign the opinion-writing task. Otherwise, the senior member in the majority assigns the opinion. So important is the task that chief justices are known to manipulate their votes, voting with a majority they do not agree with in order to keep the privilege of assigning the opinion to the justice who would write the weakest version of the majority's conclusion.[55] Those justices who agree with the general decision, but who do so for reasons other than or in addition to those stated in the majority opinion, may write *concurring opinions*, and those who disagree may write *dissenting opinions*. These other opinions often have lasting impact as well, especially if the Court changes its mind, as it often does over time and as its composition changes. When such a reversal occurs, the reasons for the about-face are sometimes to be found in the dissent or the concurrence for the original decision.

The Political Effects of Judicial Decisions

The last area in which we can see the Supreme Court as a political actor is in the effects of the decisions it makes. These decisions, despite the best intentions of those who adhere to the philosophy of judicial restraint, often amount to the creation of public policies as surely as do acts of Congress. Chapters 5 and 6, on civil liberties and the struggle for equal rights, make clear that the Supreme Court, at certain points in its history, has taken an active lawmaking role. The history of the Supreme Court's policymaking role is the history of the United States, and we cannot possibly recount it here, but a few examples should show that rulings of the Court have had the effect of distributing scarce and valued resources among people, affecting decisively who gets what, when, and how.[56]

It was the Court, for instance, under the early leadership of John Marshall, that greatly enhanced the power of the federal government over the states by declaring that the Court itself has the power to invalidate state laws (and acts of Congress as well) if they conflict with the Constitution;[57] that state law is invalid if it conflicts with national law;[58] that Congress' powers go beyond those listed in Article I, Section 8, of the Constitution;[59] and that the federal government can regulate interstate commerce.[60] In the early years of the twentieth century, the Supreme Court was an ardent defender of the right of business not to be regulated by the federal government, striking down laws providing for maximum working hours,[61] regulation of child labor,[62] and minimum

wages.[63] The role of the Court in making civil rights policy is well known. In 1857 it decided that slaves, even freed slaves, could never be citizens;[64] in 1896 it decided that separate accommodations for whites and blacks were constitutional;[65] and then it reversed itself, declaring separate but equal to be unconstitutional in 1954.[66] It is the Supreme Court that has been responsible for the expansion of due process protection for criminal defendants,[67] for instituting the principle of one person–one vote in drawing legislative districts,[68] and for establishing the right of a woman to have an abortion in the first trimester of pregnancy.[69] In 2010 the Court ruled that campaign finance legislation could not limit the money spent by corporations on electioneering broadcasts because corporations have First Amendment protections.[70] And, of course, there was the case of *Bush v. Gore*, with which we began this chapter. Each of these actions has altered the distribution of power in American society in ways that some would argue should be done only by an elected body.

Who What How

The Supreme Court is a powerful institution, and all Americans have a great stake in what it does. Citizens want to respect the Court and to believe that it is the guardian of American justice and the Constitution.

The president wants to create a legacy and to build political support with respect to his Supreme Court appointments, and he wants to place justices on the Court who reflect his political views and judicial philosophy. Occasionally he also wants to influence the decisions made by the Court.

Members of the Senate also have an interest in getting justices on the Court who reflect their views and the views of their parties. They are also responsive to the wishes of their constituents and to the interest groups that support them. Confirmation hearings can consequently be quite divisive and acrimonious. Interest groups, which want members on the Court to reflect their views, can lobby the Senate before and during the confirmation hearings, and can prepare amicus curiae briefs in support of the parties they endorse in cases before the Court.

Finally, the justices themselves have a good deal at stake in the politics of the Supreme Court. They want a manageable caseload and are heavily reliant on their law clerks and the rules of court procedure. They want to make significant and respected decisions, which means that they have to weigh their own decision-making criteria carefully.

▶ Who, What, How, and WHEN: Branch Clash

The founders may have wanted us to think of the Supreme Court as above politics, but as we have seen, that is far from the truth. The Supreme Court is as political as the other two branches and clashes with them frequently, making decidedly political decisions that have substantial effects on the powers of the executive and Congress. Here are just a few examples of this "branch clash":

1803 — *Marbury v. Madison (The Court Versus the President)*

William Marbury was appointed justice of the peace in Washington, D.C., by President John Adams shortly before he left office, but the appointment was never delivered. When the new president, Thomas Jefferson, and his secretary of state, James Madison, refused to deliver the appointment, Marbury brought his case to the Supreme Court. Chief Justice John Marshall concluded the Supreme Court did not have the power to decide whether Marbury got the appointment, since judicial appointment power rested with the executive and the Senate according to the Constitution. In giving up the small power to decide Marbury's fate, Marshall gave the Court the big power of deciding what the Constitution means by establishing *judicial review*.

1935 — *Schechter Poultry Corp. v. United States (The Court Versus the President)*

The Schechter Poultry Corporation challenged several provisions of the National Industrial Recovery Act (NIRA), part of Franklin Roosevelt's New Deal. The Supreme Court struck down part of the act, saying Congress overstepped its authority to regulate commerce and the president cannot make decisions that are Congress' responsibility. This was only one of several cases in which the Court struck down provisions of the New Deal because of extraordinary presidential power, leading FDR to try to "pack the court," or increase the number of justices, so that he could appoint justices more sympathetic to New Deal provisions.

The Citizens and the Courts

Equal treatment and equal access?

In this chapter we have been arguing that the legal system and the American courts are central to the maintenance of social order and conflict resolution, and are also a fundamental component of American politics—who gets what, and how they get it. This means that a crucial question for American democracy is, Who takes advantage of this powerful system for allocating resources and values in society? An important component of American political culture is the principle of equality before the law, which we commonly take to mean that all citizens should be treated equally by the law, but which also implies that all citizens should have equal access to the law. In this concluding section we look at the questions of equal treatment *and* equal access.

1974 — ***United States v. Nixon (The Court Versus the President)***

Prosecutors appointed to investigate the Watergate break-in repeatedly subpoenaed audiotapes Richard Nixon had secretly made in the Oval Office. At first Nixon refused to hand over any of the tapes; later, he handed over some of them with large gaps of silence, claiming it was his *executive privilege* as president to keep Oval Office communication a secret from other branches. The Supreme Court rejected his argument, and Nixon was forced to hand over the tapes. He resigned from office shortly thereafter.

2000 — ***Bush v. Gore (The Court Versus the State Courts)***

The decision in this case stopped the statewide recount ordered by the Florida Supreme Court in the 2000 presidential race, declaring it unconstitutional. With this decision, George W. Bush—determined by the Florida secretary of state to be the winner of Florida and thus of the highly controversial 2000 election—became president. While some observers praised the Court's decision, others argued that it was highly political and would damage the legitimacy of the election's results, and of the Court itself.

Equal Treatment by the Criminal Justice System

In Chapter 6, on civil rights, we examined in depth the issue of equality before the law in a constitutional sense. But what about the day-to-day treatment of citizens by the law enforcement and legal systems? Citizens *are* treated differently by these systems according to their race, their income level, and the kinds of crimes they commit. That African Americans and whites have very different views of their treatment by law enforcement and the courts was brought home to Americans by their very different reactions to the verdict in the first, criminal trial of O. J. Simpson. When the "not guilty" verdict was read, a camera caught the faces of black and white students watching television together on a college campus (see photo). The black faces were elated, the white faces stunned. On reflection, the difference seemed to be this: blacks have become so used to a law enforcement system that treats them with suspicion and hostility, and some of the Los Angeles police who arrested Simpson were, in fact, so obviously

The Verdict
Reactions of black and white college students in Rock Island, Illinois, to the O. J. Simpson criminal trial verdict announced on October 3, 1995, contrasted sharply, indicating still-potent tensions around the issue of race relations.

racist, that blacks had no difficulty believing that the evidence against Simpson was trumped up and that the system was out to bring him down simply for being a successful African American man. Whites, on the other hand, who have had far less reason to distrust the police and the courts, saw in the Simpson case a straightforward instance of violent spousal abuse that ended in murder. The "disconnect" on the issue between the races was huge and highlights a compelling truth about our criminal justice system.

African Americans and white Americans do not experience our criminal justice system in the same ways, beginning with what is often the initial contact with the system, the police. In a poll taken during the O. J. Simpson criminal trial, months before the verdict was reached, only 33 percent of blacks said they believed the police testify truthfully, and only 18 percent said they would believe the police over

other witnesses at a trial. Sixty-six percent of blacks said they think the criminal justice system is racist, as opposed to only 37 percent of whites.[71] Blacks are often harassed by police or treated with suspicion simply because they are black, and they tend to perceive the police as persecutors rather than protectors.

In fact, blacks are more likely to be arrested than whites, and they are more likely to go to jail, where they serve harsher sentences. In part, this is because blacks are more likely to be poor and urban, and to belong to a socioeconomic class where crime not only doesn't carry the popular sanctions that it does for the middle class, but where it may provide some of the only opportunities for economic advancement. But studies show that racial bias and stereotyping also play a role in the racial disparities in the criminal justice system.[72]

Race is not the only factor that divides American citizens in their experience of the criminal justice system. Income also creates a barrier to equal treatment by the law. Over half of those accused of felonies in the United States have court-appointed lawyers. These lawyers are likely to be less than enthusiastic about these assignments: the pay is modest and sometimes irregular. Many lawyers do not like to provide free services *pro bono publico* ("for the public good") because they are afraid it will offend their regular corporate clients. Consequently the quality of the legal representation available to the poor is not of the same standard available to those who can afford to pay well. Yale law professor John H. Langbein is scathing on the role of money in determining the legal fate of Americans. He says, "Money is the defining element of our modern American criminal-justice system." The wealthy can afford crackerjack lawyers who can use the "defense lawyer's bag of tricks for sowing doubts, casting aspersions, and coaching witnesses," but "if you are not a person of means, if you cannot afford to engage the elite defense-lawyer industry—and that means most of us—you will be cast into a different system, in which the financial advantages of the state will overpower you and leave you effectively at the mercy of prosecutorial whim."[73]

Equal Access to the Civil Justice System

While the issue with respect to the criminal justice system is equal treatment, the issue for the civil justice system is equal access. Most of us in our lifetimes will have some legal problems. While the Supreme Court has ruled that low-income defendants must be provided with legal assistance in state and federal criminal cases, there is no such guarantee for civil cases. That doesn't mean, however, that less affluent citizens have no recourse for their legal problems. Both public and private legal aid programs exist. Among others, the Legal Services Corporation (LSC), created by Congress in 1974, is a nonprofit organization that provides resources to over 138 legal aid programs around the country with more than 900 local offices. The LSC helps citizens and some immigrants with legal problems such as those concerning housing, employment, family issues, finances, and immigration. This program has been controversial, as conservatives have feared that it has a left-wing agenda and Republicans have tried to limit it when they have been in the congressional majority.

Does the fact that these services exist mean that more citizens get legal advice? Undoubtedly it does. Every year LSC programs handle nearly a million cases.[74] Still, there is no question that many of the legal needs of the less affluent are not being addressed through the legal system.[75]

Clearly a bias in the justice system favors those who can afford to take advantage of lawyers and other means of legal assistance. And since people of color and women are much more likely to be poor than are white males (although white men are certainly represented among the poor), the civil justice system ends up discriminating as well.

These arguments do not mean that the U.S. justice system has made no progress toward a more equal dispensation of justice. Without doubt, we have made enormous strides since the days of *Dred Scott*, when the Supreme Court ruled that blacks did not have the standing to bring cases to court, and since the days when lynch mobs dispensed their brand of vigilante justice in the South. The goal of equal treatment by and equal access to the legal system in America, however, is still some way off.

▶ What's at Stake Revisited

Since the divisive outcome of *Bush v. Gore*, the nation has calmed down. The pickets and the angry voices are quiet. The stunning national crisis that began with the terrorist attacks on September 11, 2001, has put things into a broader perspective, and a Court-decided election no longer seems as great a danger as the possibility of being caught without any elected leader at all at a critical time. Public opinion polls show that trust in all institutions of government, including the Supreme Court, ran high after September 11, and Bush's legitimacy no longer rested with the Court's narrow majority but rather with the approval ratings that hit unprecedented heights in the aftermath of the terrorist attacks and with his successful reelection in 2004.

But changed national circumstances and subsequent elections do not mean that the Court's unusual and controversial move in resolving the 2000 election should go unanalyzed. What was at stake in this extraordinary case?

First, as Justice Stevens pointed out, the long-term consequences of people's attitudes toward the Court are unknown. The Court, as we have seen, has often engaged in policymaking, and to believe that it is not a political institution would be a serious mistake. But part of its own legitimacy has come from the fact that most people do not perceive it as political, and it is far more difficult now to maintain that illusion. In the immediate aftermath of the decision,

the justices, speaking around the country, tried to contain the damage and reassure Americans; some of the dissenting justices emphasized that the decision was not made on political or ideological grounds. Only in the longer term will we see if that case was persuasive to the American public. It would be ironic indeed if the Court moved to ensure Bush's legitimacy at the expense of its own.

Also at stake in such a deeply divided decision was the Court's own internal stability and ability to work together. While the confidentiality of the justices' discussions in arriving at the decision has been well guarded, the decision itself shows that they were acrimonious. Again, in the aftermath, the justices have tried to put a unified front on what was clearly a bitter split. Members of the majority have continued to socialize with dissenters, and as Justice Scalia himself told one audience, "If you can't disagree without hating each other, you better find another profession other than the law."[76] While the stakes in this case may have been more directly political than in most other cases, the members of the Supreme Court are used to disagreeing over important issues and probably handle the level of conflict more easily than do the Americans who look up to them as diviners of truth and right.

Another stake in the pivotal decision was the fundamental issue of federalism itself. The federal courts, as Justice Ruth Bader Ginsburg wrote in her dissent, have a long tradition

of deferring to state courts on issues of state law. Indeed, many observers were astounded that the Court agreed to hear the case in the first place, assuming that the justices would have sent it back to be settled in Florida. Normally it would have been the ardent conservatives on the Court—Rehnquist, Scalia, and Thomas—whom one would have expected to leap to the defense of states' rights. It has been made clear, however, that the *Bush v. Gore* decision did not signal a reversal on their part. If the opinions of the Court about federalism have changed at all since 2000, it will probably be due more to the imperatives of the war on terrorism, as we suggested in Chapter 2, than to the dictates of the election case.

Some observers argue that the majority of the Court saw something else at stake that led them to set aside their strong beliefs in states' rights and to run the risk that they might be seen as more Machiavelli than King Solomon, more interested in power than wisdom. The majority saw the very security and stability of the nation at stake. Anticipating a long recount of the votes that might even then be inconclusive, they thought it was better to act decisively at the start rather than to wait until a circus-like atmosphere had rendered impossible the most important decision a voting public can make. Whether they were right in doing so, and whether the stakes justified the risks they took, politicians, partisans, and historians will be debating for years to come.

To Sum Up

Key terms, chapter summaries, practice quizzes, Internet links, and other study aids are available on the companion web site at http://republic.cqpress.com.

Define | Understand | Practice | Read | Click | Watch

administrative law (p. 376)
adversarial system (p. 371)
amicus curiae briefs (p. 391)
appeal (p. 379)
appellate jurisdiction (p. 379)
civil law tradition (p. 370)
civil laws (p. 373)
common law tradition (p. 370)
concurring opinions (p. 395)
constitutional law (p. 373)
courts (p. 370)
criminal laws (p. 373)
dissenting opinions (p. 395)
executive orders (p. 376)
inquisitorial systems (p. 371)
judicial activism (p. 393)
judicial interpretivism (p. 387)

judicial restraint (p. 394)
judicial review (p. 377)
jurisdiction (p. 379)
Marbury v. Madison (p. 377)
opinion (p. 394)
original jurisdiction (p. 379)
precedent (p. 371)
procedural due process (p. 372)
procedural laws (p. 372)
Rule of Four (p. 391)
senatorial courtesy (p. 383)
solicitor general (p. 391)
statutory laws (p. 373)
strict constructionism (p. 387)
substantive laws (p. 372)
writs of certiorari (p. 390)

Define | Understand | Practice | Read | Click | Watch

- Laws serve five main functions in a democratic society. They offer security, supply predictability, provide for conflict resolution, reinforce society's values, and provide for the distribution of social costs and benefits.
- American law is based on legislation, but its practice has evolved from a tradition of common law and the use of precedent by judges.
- The American legal system is considered to be both adversarial and litigious in nature. The adversarial nature of our system implies that two opposing sides advocate their position with lawyers in the most prominent roles, while the judge has a relatively minor role in comparison.
- Laws serve many purposes and are classified in different ways. Substantive laws cover what we can or cannot do, while procedural laws establish the procedures used to enforce law generally. Criminal laws concern specific behaviors considered undesirable by the government, while civil laws cover interactions between individuals. Constitutional law refers to laws included in the Constitution as well as the precedents established over time by judicial decisions relating to these laws. Statutory laws, administrative laws, and executive orders are established by Congress and state legislatures, the bureaucracy, and the president, respectively.

- The founders were deliberately vague in setting up a court system so as to avoid controversy during the ratification process. The details of design were left to Congress, which established a layering of district, state, and federal courts with differing rules of procedure.
- The Constitution never stated that courts could decide the constitutionality of legislation. The courts gained the extra-constitutional power of judicial review when Chief Justice John Marshall created it in *Marbury v. Madison*.
- The political views of the judge and the jurisdiction of the case can have great impact on the verdict. The rules of the courtroom may vary from one district to another, and the American dual court system often leads to more than one court having authority to deliberate.
- The U.S. Supreme Court reigns at the top of the American court system. It is a powerful institution, revered by the American public but as political an institution as the other two branches of government. Politics is involved in how the Court is chosen and how it decides a case, and in the effects of its decisions.
- While the U.S. criminal justice system has made progress toward a more equal dispensation of justice, minorities and poor Americans have not always experienced equal treatment by the courts or had equal access to them.

Define   **Understand**   **Practice**   **Read**   **Click**   **Watch**

1. **According to this chapter, one purpose of courts in a democracy is to**
   a. make laws that are fair to all.
   b. ensure that no innocent person goes to jail.
   c. protect the values of democracy.
   d. resolve conflicts.
   e. protect citizens from the government.

2. **In *Federalist No. 78*, Alexander Hamilton argued for establishing an independent judiciary by referring to the judiciary as**
   a. potentially dangerous to the liberties of citizens.
   b. the most important branch of government.
   c. the smallest branch of government.
   d. the least dangerous branch of government.
   e. the most powerful branch of government.

3. **The importance of judicial review is that it**
   a. significantly expanded the power of the courts.
   b. established the dual court system.
   c. keeps unelected officials from making laws.
   d. limits the ability of judges to let their personal opinions guide their rulings.

   e. increases the courts' dockets because they now must review all laws.

4. **The American dual court system is an application of**
   a. the English legal system.
   b. federalism.
   c. checks and balances.
   d. separation of powers.
   e. judicial review.

5. **Concerning equal treatment of citizens by the U.S. criminal justice system,**
   a. enormous strides have been made since the days of *Dred Scott*, but the goal of equality is still some way off.
   b. despite the court reform efforts since the days of *Dred Scott*, little progress has been made toward the goal of equality in our courts.
   c. as long as white men are the majority of judges in the American courts, women and minorities can expect little help from the courts in their quest for equality.
   d. the efforts.to reform our justice system ensure equal justice for all today.
   e. the courts have made great strides toward ensuring equality for African Americans but not for women.

Define   **Understand**   **Practice**   **Read**   **Click**   **Watch**

Baum, Lawrence. 2008. *American Courts: Process and Policy*, 6th ed. Boston: Houghton Mifflin. *An extremely informative text on the American court system and how it influences policy.*

Baum, Lawrence. 2007. *The Supreme Court*, 9th ed. Washington, D.C.: CQ Press. *The definitive book for understanding the Supreme Court as a political institution.*

Bork, Robert H. 1990. *The Tempting of America: The Political Seduction of the Law*. New York: Free Press. *One of the country's most controversial Supreme Court nominees discusses his interpretations of the Constitution as well as the events that led to his unsuccessful attempt to sit on the Supreme Court.*

Carp, Robert A., Ronald Stidham, and Kenneth L. Manning. 2007. *Judicial Processes in America*, 7th ed. Washington, D.C.: CQ Press. *The Constitution was written so that judges would be impartial observers and not be influenced by politics. The authors, however, argue that justices are actually quite involved in the policymaking process.*

Daley, James, ed. 2006. *Landmark Decisions of the U.S. Supreme Court*. New York: Dover. *This edited volume contains unabridged accounts of thirteen key cases decided before the U.S. Supreme Court.*

O'Brien, David M. 1999. *Storm Center: The Supreme Court in American Politics*, 5th ed. New York: Norton. *A wonderful narrative on the workings of the Supreme Court in the past as well as the present.*

O'Brien, David M., ed. 2008. *Judges on Judging: Views From the Bench*, 3rd ed. Washington, D.C.: CQ Press. *Judges at all levels of the judicial process, from Supreme Court justices to state court judges, offer their viewpoints on the functioning of the American legal system and U.S. courts.*

Pacelle, Richard L. 2001. *The Supreme Court in American Politics: The Least Dangerous Branch*. Boulder: Westview Press. *Focusing on the role of the Court as a nonelected institution within a representative democracy, Pacelle examines the ways in which appointed judges shape national law.*

Rosenberg, Gerald N. 1991. *The Hollow Hope: Can Courts Bring About Social Change?* Chicago: University of Chicago Press. *A powerful and somewhat controversial book about the* inability of many court rulings to bring significant change to people's lives.

Shesol, Jeff. 2010. *Supreme Power: Franklin Roosevelt Versus the Supreme Court*. New York: Norton.   A detailing of Roosevelt's efforts to reorganize the federal judiciary, set into the political context of the day, and the battle that ensued.

Tushnet, Mark V., ed. 2001. *Thurgood Marshall: His Speeches, Writings, Arguments, Opinions, and Reminiscences*. Chicago: Lawrence Hill Books.   A collection of writings and speeches from the trailblazing NAACP lawyer and the first African American Supreme Court justice.

Walker, Thomas G. 2008. *Eligible for Execution: The Story of the Daryl Atkins Case*. Washington, D.C.: CQ Press.   The workings of the U.S. judicial system come to life in this engaging narrative, which charts Daryl Atkins's journey through the U.S. legal system, with the Supreme Court ruling on whether executing the mentally handicapped is cruel and unusual punishment.

Define   Understand   Practice   Read   Click   Watch

CQ Supreme Court Collection   *http://library.cqpress.com/scc. Have a question about the Supreme Court? You will find your answer here. This is a wonderful collection of information regarding the history of the Court, justices, and cases. The site is password-protected, but many schools' libraries have a subscription.*

FindLaw   *www.findlaw.com. This site is an exceptional source for information on federal court decisions.*

U.S. Courts   *www.uscourts.gov. This web site offers a plethora of information on the federal courts.*

U.S. Government Web Site on the U.S. Court System   *http:// uspolitics.america.gov/uspolitics/government/constitution.html. This web site offers a succinct overview of the U.S. judiciary and its constitutionally derived powers. The site also contains an archive of articles on the U.S. judicial system (accessible via the web site or RSS).*

Define   Understand   Practice   Read   Click   Watch

ABC News Nightline Public Defenders: Counsel for the Poor   *2007. This made-for-TV documentary explores the interplay between socioeconomic factors and the U.S. judicial system, arguing that guilty verdicts and poverty often go hand in hand.*

A Civil Action   *1999. A captivating account of a court case detailing lawyer Jan Schlichtmann's maddening legal battle against two corporations accused of industrial pollution in New England.*

Erin Brockovich   *2000. This film, starring Julia Roberts and based on a true story, tells the tale of one woman's struggle against a* large corporation responsible for polluting the water supply of a small town and, in the process, exposes the difficulties of navigating the American legal system.

First Monday in October   *1981. A romantic comedy about the first woman appointed to the Supreme Court. This movie was released the same year that Sandra Day O'Connor became the first woman to sit on the Court.*

Twelve Angry Men   *1957. A classic movie about the tough decisions that a jury has to make as it deliberates the verdict in a murder trial.*

Chapter 11

Public Opinion

▶ What's at Stake?

How much responsibility do you want to take for the way you are governed? Most of us are pretty comfortable with the idea that we should vote for our rulers (although we don't all jump at the chance to do it), but how about voting on the rules? Citizens of some states—California, for instance—have become used to being asked for their votes on new state laws through referenda and voter initiatives. But what about national politics—do you know enough or care enough to vote on laws for the country as a whole, just as if you were a member of Congress or a senator? Should we be governed more by public opinion than by the opinions of our elected leaders? This is the question that drives the debate about whether U.S. citizens should be able to participate in such forms of direct democracy as the national referendum or initiative.

Not only do many states (twenty-seven out of fifty) employ some form of direct democracy, but many other countries do as well. In the past several years alone, voters in Slovenia were asked to decide about the establishment of a tribunal to resolve a border dispute with Croatia, in Bolivia about whether there should be limits to individual landholdings, in Azerbaijan about amending the constitution, in Sierra Leone about choosing a president (in the first democratic elections since 1967), and in Iceland about terms of payment on the national debt.

In 1995 former senator Mike Gravel, D-Alaska, proposed that the United States join many of the world's nations in adopting a national *plebiscite*, or popular vote on policy. He argued that Americans should support a national initiative he called "Philadelphia II" (to evoke "Philadelphia I," which was, of course, the Constitutional Convention), which would set up procedures for direct popular participation in national lawmaking.[1] Such participation could take place through the ballot box (the Swiss go to the polls four

Take It to the People

On November 4, 2010, Californians cast their votes against Proposition 19, which sought to legalize marijuana in the state. California is one of the states that permit a fair amount of direct democracy in making laws and amending the constitution.

times a year to vote on national policy) or even electronically, as some have suggested, with people voting on issues by computer at home. Experts agree that the technology exists for at-home participation in government. And public opinion is overwhelmingly in favor of proposals to let Americans vote for or against major national issues before they become law.[2]

Do you agree with Gravel and the roughly three-quarters of Americans who support more direct democracy at the national level? Should we have rule by public opinion in the United States? How would the founders have responded to this proposal? And what would be the consequences for American government if a national plebiscite were passed? Just what is at stake in the issue of direct democracy at the national level? ■

[T]he very legitimacy of the U.S. government, like that of all other democracies, rests on the idea that government exists to serve the interests of its citizens.

> **public opinion** the collective attitudes and beliefs of individuals on one or more issues

> **public opinion polls** scientific efforts to estimate what an entire group thinks about an issue by asking a smaller sample of the group for its opinion

It is fashionable these days to denounce the public opinion polls that claim to tell us what the American public thinks about this or that political issue. The American people themselves are skeptical—65 percent of them think that the polls are "right only some of the time" or "hardly ever right."[3] (You might believe that finding, or you might not.) Politicians can be leery of polls, too—or even downright scornful of them. Disdainful of the Clinton years, when the president's team of pollsters openly tested the public on various issues, including his approval ratings, the Bush administration was cagey about the fact that they watched polls at all. Bush himself frequently said things like "I really don't worry about polls or focus groups; I do what I think is right."[4] Matthew Dowd, the Bush administration's chief of polling at the Republican National Committee, echoed that stance with an emphatic "We don't poll policy positions. Ever."[5] Of course, the Bush administration did look at polls, and conducted them, too, just like every other administration has since the advent of modern polling, and just as the Obama administration continues to do today.[6]

These reactions to public opinion raise an interesting question. What is so bad about being ruled by the polls in a democracy, which, after all, is supposed to be ruled by the people? If politics is about who gets what, and how they get it, shouldn't we care about what the "who" thinks? **Public opinion** is just what the public thinks. It is the aggregation, or collection, of individual attitudes and beliefs on one or more issues at any given time. **Public opinion polls** are nothing more than scientific efforts to measure that opinion—to estimate what an entire group of people thinks about an issue by asking a smaller sample of the group for its opinions. If the sample is large enough and chosen properly, we have every reason to believe that it will provide a reliable estimate of the whole. With today's technology, we can keep a constant finger on the pulse of America and know what its citizens are thinking at almost any given time. And yet, at least some Americans seem torn about the role of public opinion in government today. On the one hand, we want to believe that what we think matters, but on the other hand, we'd like to think that our elected officials are guided by unwavering principles.

In this chapter we argue that public opinion *is* important for the proper functioning of democracy, that the expression of what citizens think and what they want is a prerequisite for their ability to use the system and its rules to get what they want from it. But the quality of the public's opinion on politics, and the ways that it actually influences policy, may surprise us greatly. Specifically, in this chapter you will learn about

- *the role of public opinion in a democracy*
- *what our opinions are—do we think like the "ideal democratic citizen"?*
- *where our opinions come from*
- *how public opinion can be measured*
- *the relationship of citizenship to public opinion*

The Role of Public Opinion in a Democracy

Keeping the government of the people informed by the people

Public opinion is important in a democracy for at least two reasons. The first reason is normative: we believe public opinion *should* influence what government does. The second is empirical: a lot of people behave as if public opinion does matter, and to the degree that they measure, record, and react to it, it does become a factor in American politics.

Why Public Opinion Ought to Matter

The presence of "the people" is pervasive in the documents that create and support the American government. In the Declaration of Independence, Thomas Jefferson wrote that a just government must get its powers from "the consent of the governed." Our Constitution begins, "We, the People. . . ." And Abraham Lincoln's Gettysburg Address hails our nation as "government of the people, by the people, and for the people." What all of this tells us is that the very legitimacy of the U.S. government, like that of all other democracies, rests on the idea that government exists to serve the interests of its citizens.

Keeping in Touch
Members of Congress often face the problem that voters feel they have "lost touch" with their districts. They try to counter this perception with speeches, town hall meetings, and other appearances in their districts. Here, San Francisco mayor Gavin Newsom and Rep. Loretta Sanchez (second right) greet union members at a Labor Day luncheon.

Since the beginning of the republic, there has been a shift in our institutions toward a greater role for the citizenry in politics. We can see this in the Seventeenth Amendment to the Constitution (1913), which took the election of the U.S. Senate from the state legislatures and gave it to the citizens of the states. We can see it in the altered practice of the Electoral College. Once supposed to be a group of enlightened citizens who would exercise independent judgment, in recent decades it almost always follows the vote of the people (with the dramatic exception of the 2000 election). We can see it in state politics, where the instruments of direct democracy—the initiative, referendum, and recall—allow citizens to vote on policies and even remove officials from office before their terms are up. These changes reflect views like those of political scientist V. O. Key, who observed, "Unless mass views have some place in the shaping of policy, all talk about democracy is nonsense."[7]

But how to determine whose views should be heard? As we saw in Chapter 1, different theories of democracy prescribe different roles for "the people," in part because these theories disagree about how competent the citizens of a country are to govern themselves. Elitists suspect that citizens are too ignorant or ill informed to be trusted with major political decisions; pluralists trust groups of citizens to be competent on those issues in which they have a stake, but they think that individuals may be too busy to gather all the information they need to make informed

decisions, and proponents of participatory democracy have faith that the people are both smart enough and able to gather enough information to be effective decision makers.

As Americans, we are also somewhat confused about what we think the role of the democratic citizen should be. We introduced these conflicting notions of citizenship in Chapter 1. One view, which describes what we might call the *ideal democratic citizen*, is founded on the vision of a virtuous citizen activated by concern for the common good, who recognizes that democracy carries obligations as well as rights. In this familiar model a citizen should be attentive to and informed about politics, exhibit political tolerance and a willingness to compromise, and practice high levels of participation in civic activities.

A competing view of American citizenship holds that Americans are *apolitical, self-interested actors.* According to this view, Americans are almost the opposite of the ideal citizen: inattentive and ill informed, politically intolerant and rigid, and unlikely to get involved in political life.

We argue in this chapter, as we have earlier, that the American public displays both of these visions of citizenship. But we also argue that there are mechanisms in American politics that buffer the impact of apolitical, self-interested behavior, so that Americans as a *group* often behave as ideal citizens, even though as *individuals* they do not.

Why Public Opinion Does Matter

Politicians and media leaders act as though they agree with Key's conclusion, which is the practical reason public opinion matters in American politics. Elected politicians, for example, overwhelmingly believe that the public is keeping tabs on them. When voting on major bills, members of Congress worry quite a lot about public opinion in their districts.[8] Presidents, too, pay close attention to public opinion. In fact, recent presidents have had in-house public opinion experts whose regular polls are used as an important part of presidential political strategies. And, indeed, the belief that the public is paying attention is not totally unfounded. Although the public does not often act as if it pays attention or cares very much about politics, it can act decisively if the provocation is sufficient. For instance, in the 2006 midterm election, voters showed their frustration with Republicans' support for the war in Iraq (despite polls that said a majority of Americans had come to oppose the war) by handing the Democrats enough seats in the House and the Senate to give them control in both chambers.[9] And in 2008 and 2010, elections were primarily about voter angst over a depressed economy, a worry that first enhanced and then diminished the Democrats' control of Congress.

Politicians are not alone in their tendency to monitor public opinion as they do their jobs. Leaders of the media also focus on public opinion, making huge investments in polls and devoting considerable coverage to reporting what the public is thinking. Polls are used to measure public attitudes toward all sorts of things. Of course, we are familiar with "horse race" polls that ask about people's voting intentions and lend drama to media coverage of electoral races. Sometimes these polls themselves become the story the media covers. With the availability of a twenty-four-hour news cycle and the need to find something to report on all the time, it is not surprising that the media have fastened on their own polling as a newsworthy subject. Public opinion, or talk about it, seems to pervade the modern political arena.

Public opinion is important in theory—in our views about how citizens and politicians *should* behave—and in practice— how they actually *do* behave. American political culture contains two views of citizenship, an idealized view and a self-interested view. These two views seem to be at odds, and Americans are ambivalent about the role public opinion should play in politics. The founders of the American polity developed constitutional rules to hold the power of citizens in check. Many of those rules, however, have changed over the intervening two hundred years as consensus has grown that citizens should play a stronger role in government.

Who What How

Politicians and the media act as if they think the public is very powerful indeed. Politicians usually try to play it safe by responding to what the public wants, or what they think it will want in the future, while the media often cover public opinion as if it were a story in itself, and not just the public's reaction to a story.

Citizen Values
How do we measure up?

At the beginning of this chapter we reminded you of the two competing visions of citizenship in America: one, the ideal democratic citizen who is attentive and informed, holds reasoned and stable opinions, is tolerant and participates in politics, and two, the apolitical, self-interested actor who does not meet this ideal. As we might expect from the fact that Americans hold two such different views of what citizenship is all about, our behavior falls somewhere in the middle. For instance, some citizens tune out political news but are tolerant of others and vote regularly. Many activist citizens are informed, opinionated, and participatory but are intolerant of others' views, which can make the give and take of democratic politics difficult. We are not ideal democratic citizens, but we know our founders did not expect us to be. As we will see by the end of this chapter, our democracy survives fairly well despite our lapses.

Political Knowledge and Interest

The ideal democratic citizen understands how government works, who the main actors are, and what major principles underlie the operation of the political system. Public opinion pollsters periodically take readings on what the public knows about politics, and the conclusion is always the same: Americans are not very well informed about their political system.[10]

Knowledge of key figures in politics is important for knowing whom to thank—or blame—for government policy, key information if we are to hold our officials accountable. Virtually everyone (99 percent of Americans) can name the president, but knowledge falls sharply for less central offices.[11] In 2004 most Americans (86 percent) knew that Dick Cheney was the vice president of the United States. This compares with the less than one-third who could identify William Rehnquist as the then–chief justice of the United States and the 11 percent who correctly identified Dennis Hastert as the then–Speaker of the House of Representatives.[12] Americans have a reasonable understanding of the most prominent aspects of the governmental system and the most visible leaders but are ignorant about other central actors and key principles of political life.

Interest in politics is also highly variable in the United States. For example, just under 44 percent of the electorate

Learning About Politics the Easy Way
Quite a few people now get their political news with a side of humor. One example is Comedy Central's popular *The Daily Show*, with comedian Jon Stewart. Stewart "reports" current political news with biting satire, hilarious correspondents, and interviews with major players in business, the arts, and politics, including an appearance by President Barack Obama in the runup to the 2010 midterm elections.

in 2008 said they were "very much interested" in the election campaign, whereas 41 percent were only "somewhat interested."[13] Taken together the moderate levels of political knowledge and interest indicate that the American public does not approach the high levels of civic engagement recommended by civics texts, but neither is it totally ignorant and unconcerned. In fact, as we will see, the public separates itself into different strata of political engagement, with only a minority who are seriously involved in following and trying to influence politics and government.

Tolerance

A key democratic value is tolerance. In a democracy, with many people jockeying for position and competing visions of the common good, tolerance for ideas different from one's own and respect for the rights of others provide oil to keep the democratic machinery running smoothly. It is a prerequisite for compromise, an essential component of politics generally, and democratic politics particularly.

How do Americans measure up on the important democratic requirement of respect for others' rights? The record is mixed. As we saw in Chapters 5 and 6, America has a history of denying basic civil rights to some groups, but clearly tolerance is on the increase since the civil rights movement of the 1960s. Small pockets of intolerance persist, primarily among such extremist groups as those who advocate violence against doctors who perform abortions, the burning of black churches in the South, or anti-Arab and anti-Muslim incidents following

the terrorist attacks on the World Trade Center and the Pentagon on September 11, 2001.[14] Such extremism, however, is the exception rather than the rule in contemporary American politics.

In terms of general principles, Most Americans support the values of freedom of speech, religion, and political equality. For instance, 90 percent of respondents told researchers they believed in "free speech for all, no matter what their views might be." Subsequent studies, such as those by the First Amendment Center, show similar data. However, when citizens are asked to apply these principles to particular situations in which specific groups have to be tolerated (especially unpopular groups like the American Nazi Party preaching race hatred or atheists preaching against God and religion), the levels of political tolerance drop dramatically.[15]

In studies of political tolerance, the least politically tolerant are consistently the less educated and less politically sophisticated. For example, one study found that on a civil liberties scale designed to measure overall support for First Amendment rights, only 24 percent of high school graduates earned high scores, compared with 52 percent of college graduates.[16]

Such findings have led some observers to argue that elites are the protectors of our democratic values. According to this view, the highly educated and politically active are the ones who guard the democratic process from the mass of citizens who would easily follow undemocratic demagogues (like Adolf Hitler). Critics of this theory say that educated people simply know what the politically correct responses to polls are and therefore can hide their intolerance better. In practice, the mass public's record has not been bad, and some of the worst offenses of intolerance in our history, from slavery to the incarceration of the Japanese in America during World War II, were led by elites, not the mass public. Nevertheless, the weight of the evidence does indicate that democratic political tolerance increases with education.

Participation

One of the most consistent criticisms of Americans by those concerned with the democratic health of the nation is that we do not participate enough. And indeed, as participation is usually measured, the critics are right. Figure 11.1 shows that

Figure 11.1

Comparison of Voter Turnout Among Select Nations

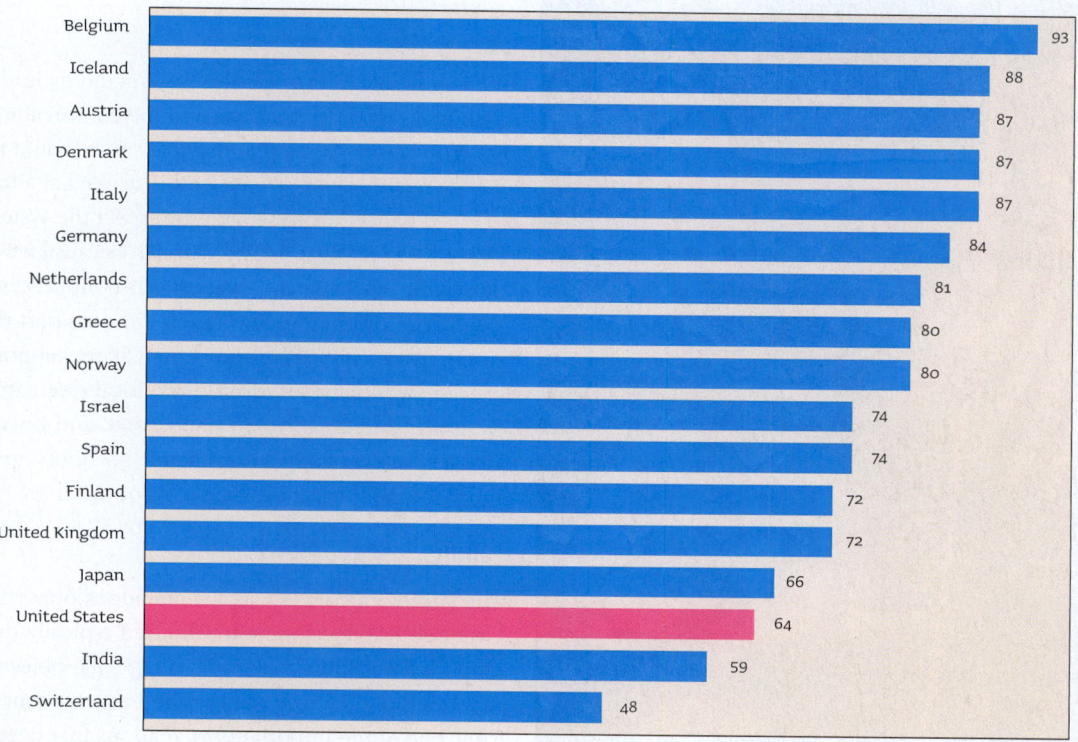

Nation	Turnout
Belgium	93
Iceland	88
Austria	87
Denmark	87
Italy	87
Germany	84
Netherlands	81
Greece	80
Norway	80
Israel	74
Spain	74
Finland	72
United Kingdom	72
Japan	66
United States	64
India	59
Switzerland	48

Source: Data calculated by authors with data from the Institute for Democracy and Electoral Assistance, www.idea.int/vt/.

for voter turnout in national elections, the United States ranks almost last among industrialized nations. Various explanations have been offered for the low U.S. turnout, including the failure of parties to work to mobilize turnout and obstacles to participation such as restrictive registration laws, limited voting hours, and the frequency of elections. We examine who votes and why in Chapter 14, but for now the fact remains that, among industrialized nations, the United States has one of the lowest levels of voter turnout in national elections.

Who What How

In a nation that claims to be ruled by the people, all American citizens have a stake in ensuring that "the people" are as close to being public-spirited ideal democratic citizens as they can be. It is also the case, however, that the primary incentive that drives each citizen is concern for his or her own interests, and that although many citizens do exhibit some of the characteristics of the ideal democratic citizen, they rarely exhibit all of them. Consequently, most citizens do not fit the model of the theoretical ideal. Those who do fit the model achieve that status through political education, the practice of toleration, and political participation.

Thinking Outside the Box

Of the four traits of the ideal citizen we discuss here—knowledge, ideology, tolerance, and participation—which is most important for the health of democracy?

What Influences Our Opinions About Politics?

Sources of continuity and division in the American public

So far, we have learned that many, but by no means all, Americans exhibit the characteristics of our so-called ideal democratic citizen, and we have discovered that the traits of ideal

Little Patriots
Early political socialization can be happy unintentionally. Parents take youngsters to parades to enjoy the music and the colorful pageantry. Once there, though, children begin to develop an emotional response to political celebrations (like the Fourth of July) and national symbols (like the American flag).

democratic citizenship are not distributed equally across the population. The implication of our analysis, that education and socioeconomic status have something to do with our political opinions and behaviors, still does not tell us where our opinions come from. In this section we look at several sources of public opinion: political socialization, economic self-interest, partisanship and ideology, education, demographics, and geographic region of residence. All these things affect the way we come to see politics, what we believe we have at stake in the political process, and the kind of citizenship we practice.

Political Socialization: How We Learn the Rules of the Game

Democracies and, indeed, all other political systems depend for their survival on each new generation picking up the values and allegiances of previous generations—beliefs in

political socialization the process by which we learn our political orientations and allegiances

the legitimacy of the political system and its leaders, and a willingness to obey the laws and the commands of those leaders. You can well imagine the chaos that would result if each new generation of citizens, freshly arrived at adulthood, had to be convinced from scratch to respect the system and obey its laws. In fact, that doesn't happen because we all learn from our cradles to value and support our political systems, which is why the children in France or China support their leaders as surely as the children of the United States support theirs. The process by which we learn our political orientations and allegiances is called *political socialization*, and it works through a variety of agents, including family, schools, group memberships, and the major public events of our lives.

Family

The family, of course, has a tremendous opportunity to influence political development. Children typically develop an emotional response to some fundamental objects of government before they really understand much about those objects. Thus one of the important orientations that develops in the preschool years is nationalism, a strong emotional attachment to the political community. Children saluting the flag or watching fireworks at Independence Day celebrations easily absorb the idea that being American is something special. The greatest impact of the family—though one that has weakened somewhat in recent years—is on party identification.[17] Children tend to choose the same political party as their parents.[18] Interestingly, when parents disagree in their partisanship, the child identifies more often with the party affiliation of the mother. The family has a weaker effect on attitudes such as racial relations or welfare.

Schools and Education

Schools, where many children begin their day with the Pledge of Allegiance, and where schoolbooks emphasize stories of patriotism and national heroes, are an important agent of political learning and the development of citizen orientations. Most school districts include as part of their explicit mission that the schools should foster good citizenship.[19] In many districts, U.S. history or civics is a required course, and some state legislatures require a course or two in U.S. and state politics for all college students in the state system.

Early on in school, children develop basic citizenship skills, such as learning fundamental civic precepts—like "Always obey the laws" and "Be helpful to others."[20] Political training also continues in the schools with the establishment

spiral of silence the process by which a majority opinion becomes exaggerated because minorities do not feel comfortable speaking out in opposition

of class officers, mock presidential elections, and, at the upper grades, a widening array of clubs and extracurricular activities whose byproducts include training in leadership and group skills, group decision making, cooperation, and problem solving. All these experiences help foster essential citizenship skills in a society that depends largely on grassroots organization and voluntary compliance with political decisions.

Groups

Shared values and experiences help define families, friends, and social groups, and research backs up the common notion that peer groups have a lot of influence on individuals' social and political attitudes. People who attend the same church tend to have similar political attitudes, as do individuals who live in the same neighborhoods. These tendencies can be traced in part to the ways people select themselves into groups, but they are reinforced by social contacts. The processes of talking, working, and worshiping together lead people to see the world similarly.[21]

Groups can also influence members by simple peer pressure. Researchers have documented the effects of peer pressure as a phenomenon they call the *spiral of silence*, a process by which a majority opinion becomes exaggerated.[22] In many contexts, when there is a clearly perceived majority position, those holding minority positions generally do not speak up or defend their views. This relative silence tends to embolden the advocates of the majority opinion to speak even more confidently. Thus what may begin as a bare majority for a group's position can become the overwhelming voice of the group through this spiral of silence.

Political and Social Events

Major political and social events can have a profound socializing influence on the political orientations of the public and, because most of us experience these events largely, if not exclusively, through the filter of the media, those in the news and entertainment business have a potentially strong influence over how our views are shaped.

Divisive political events can cause levels of trust in government to decline; unifying events can cause them to rise. For example, coming out of World War II and into the prosperity of the 1950s, many Americans had a rosy picture of the United States; their good feelings were manifested as strong approval of government. However, the divisive events of the 1960s, including the civil rights movement and the unpopular Vietnam War, followed by the scandal of

Watergate and the resignation of President Richard Nixon in the 1970s, had visible consequences in declining levels of trust in government, as Figure 11.2 shows.[23]

The partisan politics of the 1990s, including the impeachment of President Bill Clinton and the contested presidential election of 2000, should have caused levels of trust to fall even further. That they did not probably reflects citizens' generally positive assessment of government's role in the economic prosperity of the era. The events of September 11, 2001, and the ensuing war on terror caused Americans to see their government in an even more positive light. As is evident from Figure 11.2, however, as Americans' attention focused on domestic issues and partisan politics returned to business as usual, expressions of trust fell to their pre–September 11 levels.

Sources of Divisions in Public Opinion

Political socialization produces a citizenry that largely agrees with the rules of the game and accepts the outcomes of the national political process as legitimate. That does not mean, however, that we are a nation in agreement on most or even very many things. There is a considerable range of disagreement in the policy preferences of Americans, and those disagreements stem in part from citizens' self-interests, ideology, education, age, gender, race, and religion—even the area of the country in which they live.

Economic Self-Interest

People's political preferences often come from an assessment of what is best for them economically, from asking, "What's in it for me?" So, for instance, as Figure 11.3 shows, those in the lowest income brackets are the least likely to agree that too much is being spent on welfare, while those with more income are more likely to agree. Similarly, as incomes increase so does the feeling that one is paying too much in taxes. These patterns are only tendencies, however. Some wealthy people favor the redistribution of wealth and more spending on welfare; some people living in poverty oppose these policies. Even on these straightforward economic questions, other factors are at work. Similarly, those with lower incomes are generally more favorable than the wealthy to government attempts to narrow the income gap between rich and poor.

Partisanship and Ideology

Much of the division in contemporary American public opinion can be described in ideological (liberal or conservative) or

Figure 11.2

Trust in Government, 1958–2010

Public levels of trust in government response to major political events

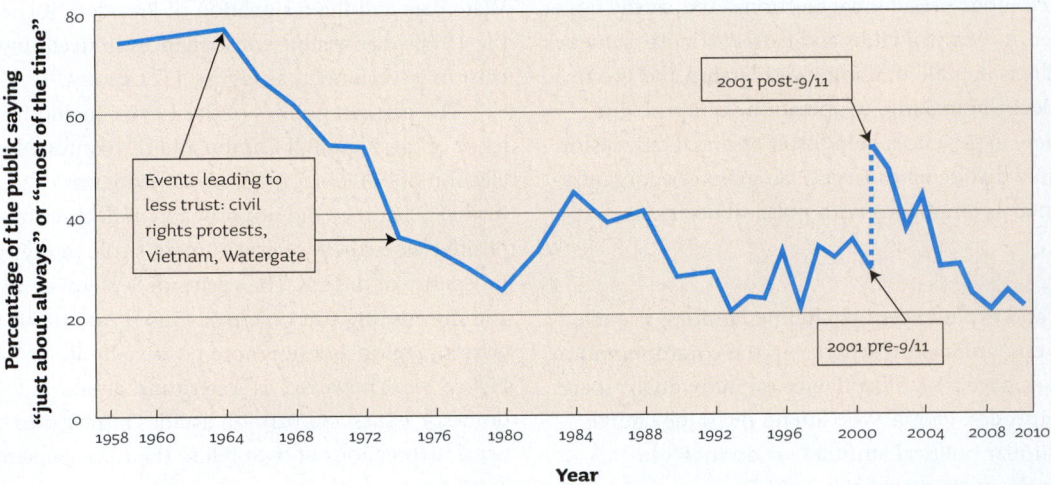

Question: How much of the time do you trust the government in Washington to do what is right?—Just about always, most of the time, or only some of the time?

Sources: National Election Studies, 1958–2000; various polls from the Roper Center, 1994–2004. Yearly averages calculated by the authors with separate averages for 2001 (before and after September 11). Data from 2005 are gathered from thirty-five national polls by CBS News/*New York Times*, CNN/Opinion Research Corp, Gallup/CNN/*USA Today*, NBC News/*Wall Street Journal*, Pew Research Center for the People and the Press, and Quinnipiac University Polls.

Figure 11.3

Attitudes Toward Welfare Spending and Taxes by Income

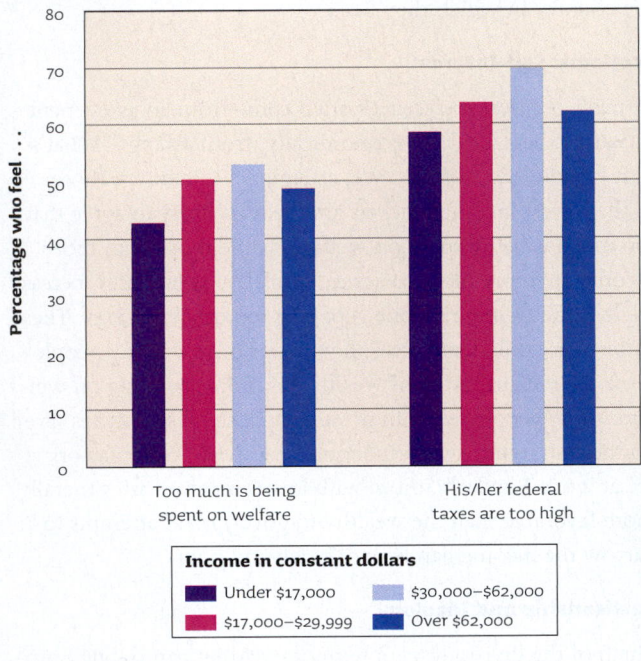

Source: General Social Survey, 2006.

partisan (Democrat or Republican) terms. How we adopt the labels of current political conflict has a good deal of influence on the policy positions we take, and even on how we perceive political personalities and events.

As we saw in Chapter 2, ideologies are sets of ideas about politics, the economy, and society that help us deal with the political world. For many Americans today, liberalism stands for faith in government action to bring about equitable outcomes and social tolerance, while conservatism for many represents a preference for limited government and traditional social values. A whole host of policy controversies in contemporary American politics are widely discussed in liberal-conservative terms.

Party identification, as we will see in Chapter 12, refers to our relatively enduring allegiances to one of the major political parties; for many of us it is part of what defines us.[24] Party labels provide mental cues that we use in interpreting and responding to personalities and news.

Identification as a Democrat or Republican strongly influences how we see the political world. Research shows that uncertainty about new policies or personalities is usually resolved to be consistent with our partisanship. Even our view of objective events is affected by partisanship. Toward the end of Republican president Ronald Reagan's second term in office, a poll asked Americans whether inflation and unemployment had gotten better or worse over the eight years of his administration. In fact, both had improved, but Democrats and Republicans were miles apart in their perceptions of the objective facts: a majority of the Democrats said inflation was worse and only 8 percent acknowledged it was better. Among Republicans only 13 percent thought it had gotten worse, and fully 47 percent thought it had improved.[25] In a more recent example, just fourteen days into the Obama administration, a poll asked if Americans approved or disapproved of the way Obama was handling his job as president. Objectively, it would be hard for anyone to tell much after only two weeks, but partisans had formed their opinions: fully half of the Republicans polled already disapproved, compared to only 2 percent of Democrats.[26] Clearly we see the world through a partisan lens.

Because party elites and candidates have become ideologically polarized in recent decades—that is, Republicans are increasingly associated with a very conservative ideology and Democrats with a very liberal one, with less common ground left in the middle—citizens find it increasingly easy to sort themselves into one party or the other.[27] As a result, average Democrats and Republicans are much further apart ideologically than was the case in previous decades (see Figure 11.4). The result for politics is that fewer people are likely to swing between candidates because fewer come to contemporary elections with a fully open mind. Most voters are predisposed one way or the other by the combination of ideological and partisan identifications.

An important ideological group in the electorate includes those who are "philosophical conservatives" but "operational liberals." When asked, they identify themselves as conservatives, attached to the concept of limited government and an unregulated market, but they also support many of the programs that accompany contemporary liberalism, such as Social Security, Medicare, and environmental protection. Of course, politicians try to play on this, with Republicans appealing to such citizens' loyalty to "conservative principles" while Democrats avoid ideological labels and try to focus attention on specific favored programs.

Education

As we suggested earlier in our discussion of the ideal democratic citizen, a number of political orientations change as a person attains more education. One important study looked in depth at how education influences aspects of citizenship, separating citizen values into "democratic enlightenment" and "democratic engagement."[28] *Democratic enlightenment* refers to a citizen's ability to hold democratic beliefs, including

Figure 11.4

The Effects of Education on Democratic Enlightenment and Engagement

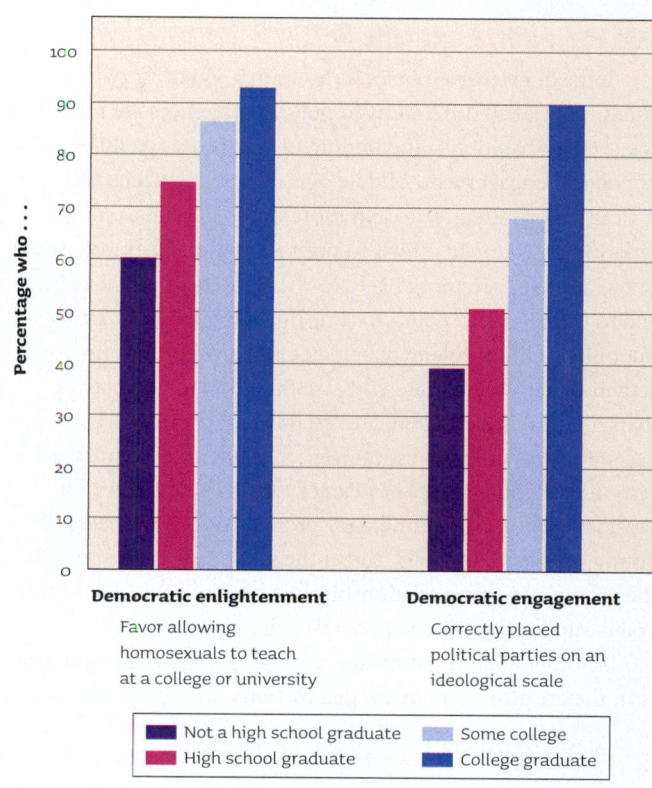

Source: Calculated by the authors from the General Society Survey, 2008, and the American National Election Study, 2008.

the acceptance that politics is about compromise and that sometimes the needs of the whole community will conflict with and override one's individual preferences. *Democratic engagement* refers to a citizen's ability to understand his or her own interests and how to pursue those interests in politics. Both democratic dimensions are tied to education: better-educated citizens are more likely to be tolerant and committed to democratic principles and are more likely to vote, to be informed about politics, and to participate at all levels of the political system (see Figure 11.4).[29] In short, those who graduate from college have many more of the attributes of the idealized active democratic citizen than do those who do not graduate from high school.

Age

We might expect that people change their opinions as they age, that our experiences over time affect how we see the political world. There is, however, precious little evidence for the common view that masses of people progress from youthful idealism to mature conservatism.

> ***political generations***   groups of citizens whose political views have been shaped by the common events of their youth

Indeed, extensive research shows that, on most political issues, only small differences in policy preferences are related to age.[30] One exception is the finding of consistent age differences in political engagement. Middle-age and older citizens are typically more attentive to and more active in politics: they report more frequent efforts to persuade others, they vote more often, and they are more likely to write letters to public officials and to contribute to political campaigns. It seems that acting out one's political role may be part and parcel of the array of activities that we associate with "settling down," such as marrying, having children, and establishing a career. This exception was mitigated somewhat in 2008 with the unusual response of young people to Barack Obama's candidacy for president. The Obama candidacy brought record numbers of young people to the polls, and at the same time created one of the sharpest age-vote relationships we have seen, with younger voters supporting Obama in overwhelming numbers.[31]

Another area in which age plays a role in public opinion is in the creation of ***political generations***, groups of citizens who have been shaped by particular events, usually in their youth, and whose shared experience continues to identify them throughout their lives. One of the most distinctive of such groups is the New Deal generation—those who came of age during the Great Depression. They are distinctly more Democratic in their party orientations than preceding generations.[32] Young people are likely to be more influenced by current political trends since they carry less political baggage to offset new issues that arise. Thus, for example, environmental issues and gay rights are currently prominent on the political agenda. On both of these issues, as we can see in Figure 11.5, younger citizens are markedly more liberal than their elders, for whom accepted attitudes on these issues were rather different when they came of age politically. Thus political events and age intersect, forming lasting imprints on younger groups, who tend to continue with the attitudes formed as they entered the electorate. As older groups die, overall opinion among the citizenry changes. This is the process of generational replacement.

Figure 11.5

The Effect of Income on Political Orientation

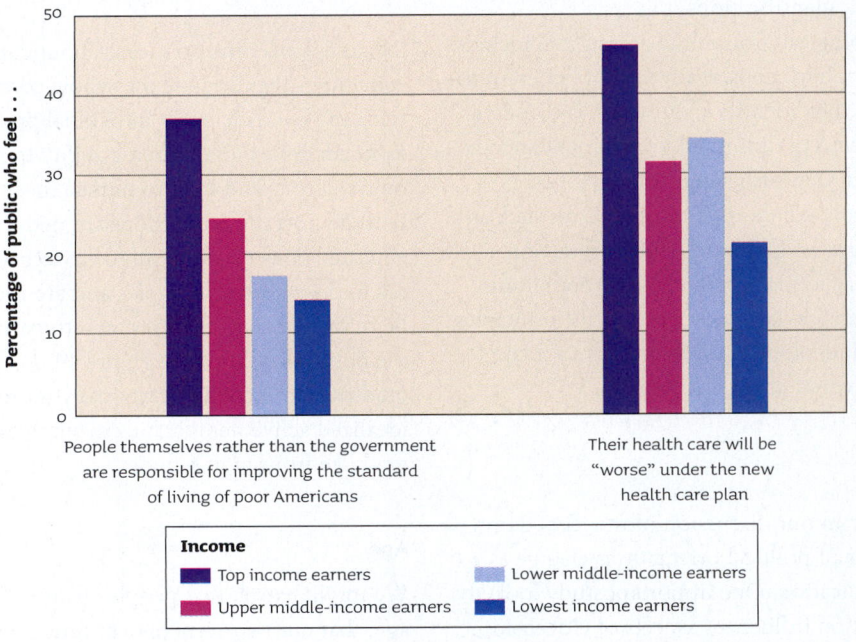

Source: General Social Survey, 2008, calculated by the authors.

> **gender gap** the tendency of men and women to differ in their political views on some issues

Gender

For many years, one's gender had almost no predictive power in explaining opinions and behavior—except that women were less active in politics and usually less warlike in their political attitudes. Just after World War II, in the United States there was a strong presumption that the man was the bread-winner and the woman's place was in the home (see Table 11.1). Since the 1960s, however, there has been something of a revolution in our expectations about the role of women in society and in politics. As women gained more education and entered the work force, they also increased their levels of participation in politics. Whereas in the 1950s women trailed men in voter turnout by over 12 percent,[33] by 2006 women voted at a slightly higher rate than did men.

Interestingly, in the last quarter of the twentieth century, as men and women approached equality in their levels of electoral participation, their attitudes on issues diverged. This tendency for men and women to take different issue positions or to evaluate political figures differently is called the **gender gap**. In almost all cases, it means that women are more liberal than men. The ideological stances of women overall have not changed significantly since the 1970s, but those of men

Table 11.1

Postwar Attitudes, 1945

Question asked of the general public:	
Do you think married women whose husbands earn enough to support them should or should not be allowed to hold jobs if they want to?	
Should be allowed	24%
Should not be allowed	60
Depends (volunteered)	13

Source: *Public Perspective*, The Roper Center for Public Opinion Research.

have shifted steadily, as more call themselves conservatives (see Figure 11.6). The gap is substantial (10 percent or larger) on the death penalty and spending on space exploration (see Table 11.2). In general, the gender gap has been found to be especially large on issues that deal with violence.[34] The gender gap also has electoral consequences. Women are more likely than men to vote for Democratic candidates. In fact, in every presidential election from 1980 to 2008, women have been more supportive of the Democratic candidate than men. Clearly there is something of a gender divide in U.S. national elections.[35]

The differences between men and women might be explained by their different socialization experiences and by

Figure 11.6

The Effect of Gender on Political Ideology

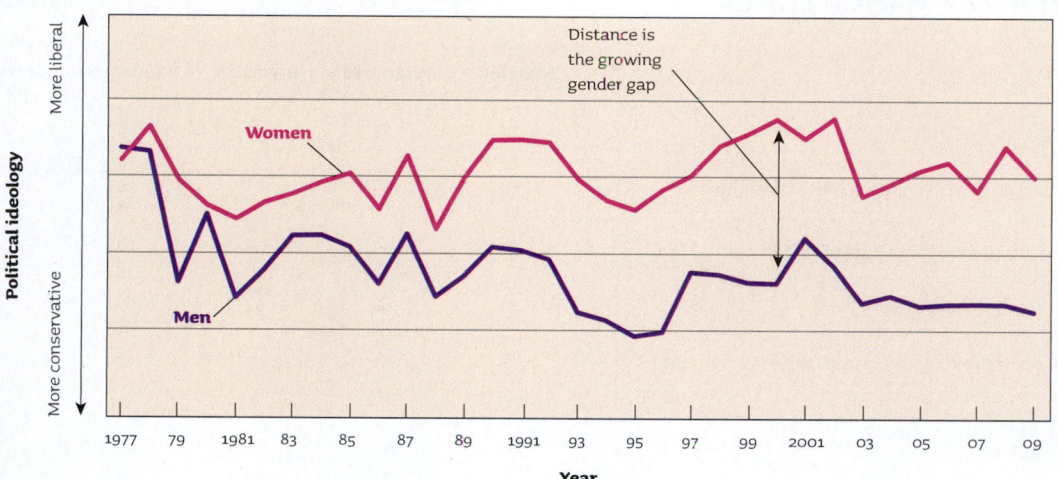

Source: Calculated by the authors from CBS News/*New York Times* national polls, 1976–2009.

marriage gap the tendency for married people to hold political opinions that differ from those of people who have never married

Table 11.2

Gender Differences on Selected Political Issues

Issue	Men	Women	Gap
Favor allowing abortion for any reason	41	34	−2
Oppose death penalty for murder	29	36	−7
Agree government spends "too much" on space exploration	34	46	12
Agree that employers should hire and promote women because of past discrimination	57	71	14
Democratic presidential vote			
Vote for Gore 2000	39	49	10
Vote for Kerry 2004	45	52	7
Vote for Obama 2008	49	56	7

Sources: General Social Survey Cumulative File, National Election Studies Cumulative File, National Election Pool 2008 General Election Exit Polls.

the different life situations they face. The impact of one's life situation has emerged recently in what observers are calling the *marriage gap*. This refers to the tendency for different opinions to be expressed by those who are married or widowed versus those who have never been married. "Marrieds" tend toward more traditional and conservative values; "never marrieds" tend to have a more liberal perspective. The "never marrieds" are now sufficiently numerous that in many localities they constitute an important group to which politicians must heed in deciding which issues to support. The effect of the marriage gap in terms of specific issues is shown in Table 11.3.

Race and Ethnicity

Race has been a perennial cleavage in American politics. Only in recent decades have blacks achieved the same political rights as the white majority, and yet disparity in income between whites and blacks continues. When we compare by race the answers to a question about spending to improve the condition of blacks, the responses are quite different. African Americans are more favorable to such spending than are whites. We see a similar pattern in whether respondents would support a community bill to bar discrimination in housing. African Americans tend to favor such a law; whites

Table 11.3

Policy Positions by Marital Status

	Married	Widowed	Divorced	Separated	Never married
Favor death penalty	70	65	65	51	64
Allow homosexuals to teach in colleges and universities	80	65	83	70	84
Allow women to have an abortion for any reason	37	30	47	27	48
Approve of Bible prayer in public schools	59	65	57	69	46
"Too little" spent on improving and protecting environment	65	51	65	67	70
Ideology					
Liberal (all categories)	21	21	26	29	41
Moderate	27	44	40	47	35
Conservative (all categories)	40	35	33	24	24

Source: General Social Survey, 2008.

Figure 11.7

Differences in Policy Views, by Race and Ethnicity

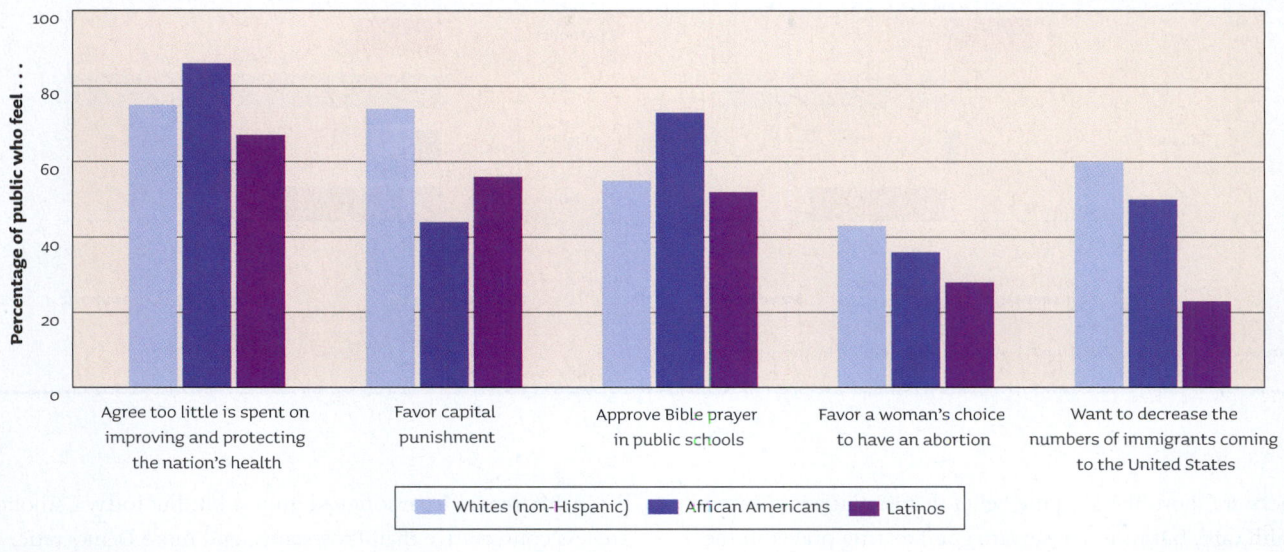

Source: General Social Survey, 2008.

are more likely to side with the owner's right to sell a house to whomever he or she chooses. These differences, some of which are shown in Figure 11.7, are typical of a general pattern. On issues of economic policy and race, African Americans are substantially more liberal than whites. However, on social issues like abortion and prayer in schools, the racial differences are more muted.

The root of the differences between political attitudes of blacks and whites most certainly lies in the racial discrimination historically experienced by African Americans. Blacks tend to see much higher levels of discrimination and racial bias in the criminal justice system, in education, and in the job market. Undeniably a very large gulf exists between the races in their perceptions about the continuing frequency and severity of racial discrimination.[36]

Finally, reflecting the very different stands on racial and economic issues the parties have taken, African Americans are the most solidly Democratic group in terms of both party identification and voting. Interestingly, as income and other status indicators rise for whites, they become more conservative and Republican. The same does not happen among African Americans. Better-educated and higher-income blacks actually have stronger racial identifications, which results in distinctly liberal positions on economic and racial issues and solid support for Democratic candidates.[37]

Some signs indicate that this may be changing, however. The increasing number of black conservatives, exemplified perhaps by former secretary of state Condoleezza Rice, Supreme Court Justice Clarence Thomas, former California Board of Regents member Ward Connerly (see *Profiles in Citizenship* in Chapter 6), and Michael Steele, the head of the Republican National Committee, show that the assumptions once made about African Americans and the Democratic Party are not universally true. Nevertheless, the rise of Democrat Barack Obama to become the first black president of the United States has undoubtedly reinforced the bond between African Americans and the Democratic Party.

Or course Americans differ by ethnicity as well as by race, and these factors interact in interesting ways to influence the opinions we hold on different policies. Figure 11.7 compares the views of non-Hispanic whites, blacks, and Hispanics or Latinos on five policies. Unfortunately, the numbers of Asians in typical national surveys are too small to achieve reliable estimates, but studies have shown that there is little consensus among Asians as a group across a wide range of issues. It is interesting that whites, blacks, and Latinos are not consistent in terms of contemporary liberalism-conservatism. For example, whites are most conservative on the death penalty, with almost three-quarters favoring capital punishment, compared to about half of African Americans and Latinos.

Figure 11.8

Ideological and Party Identification by Major Religious Denominations

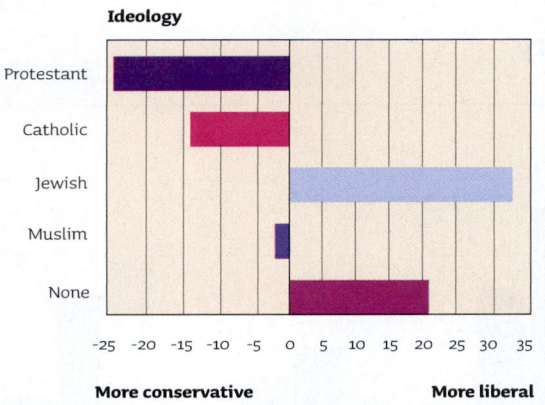

Ideology

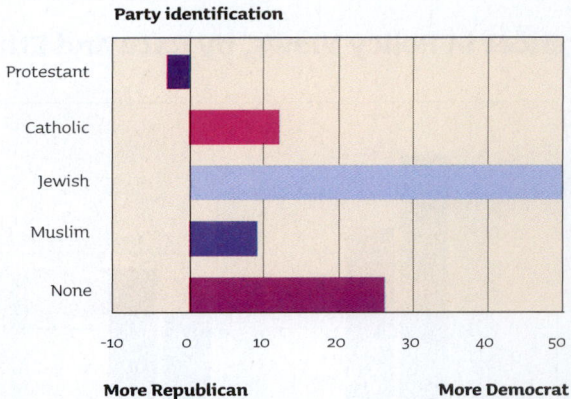

Party identification

Source: CBS News/*New York Times*, 2007–2009. Calculated by the authors.

Blacks are most liberal in the belief that too little is spent on health care, but most conservative in favoring prayer in the schools. Latinos stand out in their opposition to abortion and in not favoring a reduction in the numbers of immigrants allowed into the country. While the pattern is not one of ideological consistency, these differences make sense in terms of the particular histories and contexts of America's racial and ethnic mix.

Religion

Many political issues touch on matters of deep moral conviction or values. In these cases the motivation for action or opinion formation is not self-interest but one's view of what is morally right. The question of morals and government, however, is tricky. Many people argue that it is not the government's business to set moral standards, although it is increasingly becoming the position of conservatives that government policy ought to reflect traditional moral values. In addition, government gets into the morals business by virtue of establishing policies on issues of moral controversy, like abortion, assisted suicide, and organ transplants. These questions are often referred to as social issues, as opposed to economic issues, which center more on how to divide the economic pie.

Our views of morality and social issues are often rooted in our differing religious convictions and the values with which we were raised. We often think of religion in terms of the three major faiths in America: Protestantism, Catholicism, and Judaism. Following the New Deal realignment, there were major political differences in the preferences of these groups, with non-southern Protestants being predominantly Republican, and Catholics and Jews being much more likely to be Democrats and to call themselves liberals. Over the years

those differences have softened quite a bit, but today Catholics are less conservative than Protestants, and more Democratic, while Jews and the not religious are clearly more liberal and Democratic than the other groups (see Figure 11.8). Interestingly, Muslims are more liberal than Protestants and Catholics but are more conservative than Jews.[38]

Specific religious affiliations may no longer be the most important religious cleavage for understanding citizen opinions on social issues. Since the 1970s a new distinction has emerged in U.S. politics, between those in whose lives traditional religion plays a central role and those for whom it is less important. In this alignment, those who adhere to traditional religious beliefs and practices (frequent church-goers, regular Bible readers, "born-again Christians") tend to take conservative positions on an array of social issues (like homosexuality and abortion), compared with more liberal positions taken on those issues by what may be called "seculars." This tendency is suggested in Figure 11.8. Among those who say they are not religious, Democrats outnumber Republicans and liberals outnumber conservatives.

Geographic Region

Where we live matters in terms of our political beliefs. People in the Farm Belt talk about different things than do city dwellers on the streets of Manhattan. Texans appreciate subtle assumptions that are not shared by Minnesotans. Politicians who come from these areas represent people with different preferences, and much of the politics in Congress is about being responsive to differing geography-based opinions.[39] For instance, scholars have long argued that "the South is different." The central role of race and its plantation past for a long time gave rise to different patterns of public opinion compared to the non-southern

Table 11.4

Where We Live Makes a Difference

	Big city	Suburbs	Small town	Rural
Party identification				
Democrat	39	32	29	31
Republican	20	30	31	29
Ideology				
Liberal	32	26	22	19
Conservative	30	36	35	38
Policy				
Too little spending to help blacks	41	31	25	25
Too little spending on education	77	70	69	69
Too little spending on environment	65	63	61	57
Allow abortion for any reason	44	42	33	25
Disagree with homosexuals having the right to marry	48	51	59	68

Source: General Social Survey Cumulative File, 1972–2008. Results cover years 2000–2008.

Note: The middle categories of "independent" and "moderate" have been omitted for party identification and ideology.

states. The South today is not the Old South, but the region does retain some distinctive values. Opinions in the South—by which we mean the eleven states of the Confederacy—remain more conservative on civil rights but also on other social issues. (See the *Who Are We?* feature in Chapter 4, which shows how the states vary in terms of political ideology.)

Whether we live in the city, the suburbs, or the country also has an effect on our opinions. City dwellers are more Democratic in their political preferences and more liberal on issues like spending to help minorities and to improve education. On other issues, such as the environment, abortion, and a proposed constitutional amendment to ban same-sex marriages, rural residents stand out as distinctly conservative compared to other residential groups (see Table 11.4).

Political socialization helps to fuel and maintain the political system by transferring fundamental democratic values from one generation to the next. More specific values come from demographic characteristics—our age, race, and gender—and from our life experiences—education, religious affiliation, and where we live.

Who What How

As citizens find themselves in different circumstances, with differing political ideas, these differences are mined by interest groups, political parties, and candidates for office who are looking for support, either to further their causes or to get elected. Thus the differences in policy preferences that a complex society inevitably produces become the stuff of political conflict.

Measuring and Tracking Public Opinion

Using science to discover what people are thinking about political issues

Given the central role that public opinion plays in democracy, finding out what the public thinks is an important business, and one at which social scientists have gotten very adept over the years. While public opinion polls are sometimes discounted by politicians who don't like their results, the truth is that today most social scientists and political pollsters conduct public opinion surveys according to the highest standards of scientific accuracy, and their results are for the most part reliable. In this section we look at the ways that we are able to gauge what the public thinks on issues important to our civic and political lives.

Learning About Public Opinion Without Polls

You undoubtedly know what your friends and family think about many issues, even though you have never conducted an actual poll on their beliefs. We all reside in social communities that bring us into contact with various types of people. Simply by talking with them, we get a sense of their ideas and preferences. Politicians, whose careers depend on voters, are necessarily good talkers and good listeners. They learn

▶ Who, What, How, and WHEN: Presidential Polling

In an election year, opinion polling gives the public a way to track the candidates' ups and downs. Famous polling organizations such as Gallup, Rasmussen, and Zogby, and news organizations such as CBS/*New York Times* and ABC/*Washington Post*, all keep tabs on how the candidates are doing, helping to perpetuate a "horse race" view of what elections are all about. When it comes to predicting the winners, pollsters get it right most of the time. But, as you can see below, sometimes they don't:

1916 — Hughes and Wilson Presidential Election

The magazine *Literary Digest* conducted its first presidential straw poll by sending out ballots to their subscribers asking who would win the election: Charles Evans Hughes or President Woodrow Wilson. They correctly predicted Wilson from the 2,500 ballots that were returned.

1936 — Landon and Roosevelt Presidential Election

In 1936 the *Literary Digest* tried again to predict who would win the presidential election between then-president Franklin Roosevelt and challenger Alf Landon. They sent ballots to a list of people from the telephone book, car registration records, and their own subscription records, and a phenomenal 2.4 million people returned the ballots. They predicted Alf Landon by 14 percent, but Roosevelt won by a landslide. Their mistake was sampling only people who could afford cars, telephones, or magazine subscriptions in the middle of the Great Depression and, therefore, oversampling Republicans, who were likely to vote for Landon. On the other hand, George Gallup, who used a more random sample to forecast FDR's win, went on to head up a famous polling organization.

1948 — Dewey and Truman Presidential Election

Gallup wasn't always perfect, however. In 1948 the organization tried a technique called "quota sampling," which attempted to predict the presidential vote based on interviews with a certain number of people from different groups: men, women, African Americans, and various income groups. They, as well as other pollsters, also stopped polling a week before the presidential election, leading them to miss last-minute decisions by voters and causing them to predict, incorrectly, that Dewey would defeat Truman in the presidential election. The *Chicago Tribune* even preprinted the election results they expected from the polls. To Truman's delight, they were wrong: he won by 3.5 percent.

constituent opinion from the letters, phone calls, and emails they receive. They visit constituents, make speeches, attend meetings, and talk with community leaders and interest group representatives. Elected politicians also pick up signals from the size of the crowds that turn out to hear them speak and from the way those crowds respond to different themes. All these interactions give them a sense of what matters to people and how citizens are reacting to news events, economic trends, and social changes. Direct contact with people puts politicians in touch with concerns that could be missed entirely by the most scientifically designed public opinion poll. That poll might focus on issues of national news that are on the minds of national politicians or pollsters, while citizens may be far more concerned about the building of a dam upriver from their city or about teacher layoffs in their school district.

Thus politicians are fond of saying that they do not believe in polls or that they do not trust them. Perhaps what they are actually saying is that polls are no substitute for their own sampling of what is on their constituents' minds. It is

2000 **Bush and Gore Presidential Election**

Though exit polls had been used since 1980 to enable the media to predict presidential election outcomes by state before all the votes were counted, this practice hit a big snag in the 2000 election. Based on faulty exit poll data, networks "called" the state of Florida incorrectly for Gore, only to retract and then call it incorrectly for Bush (recall that the Florida results were so close that the election was ultimately decided by the Supreme Court). The resulting mayhem led to the dismantling of the Voter News Service, the organization that had supplied the exit polls to the networks, after the 2002 congressional election.

2008 **Obama and McCain Presidential Election**

Pollsters in 2008 worried about the Bradley effect. This effect, named for former Los Angeles mayor Tom Bradley, suggests that some election polls may overstate the vote for an African American candidate, perhaps because respondents are unwilling to tell an interviewer they will not vote for the African American, or perhaps because those who refuse to answer polls are more likely to vote along racial lines. If such an effect ever did exist, however, there was no sign of it in 2008. In the primaries, in fact, Obama outperformed the polls in the states where he won, suggesting that a "reverse" Bradley effect might have occurred, and in the general election, the polls were remarkably accurate on the whole. Several pollsters came close to nailing the final vote tally of 53 to 46 for Obama.

natural to want to rely on our personal experiences with people (see Figure 11.9).

While informal soundings of public opinion may be useful to a politician for some purposes, they are not very reliable for gauging how everyone in a given population thinks because they are subject to sampling problems. A **sample** is the portion of the population a politician or pollster surveys on an issue. Based on what that sample says, the surveyor then makes an estimation of what everyone else thinks. This may sound like hocus-pocus, but if the sample is

scientifically chosen to be representative of the whole population, it actually works very well. Pollsters are trained to select a truly representative sample—that is, one that does not overrepresent any portion of the population and whose responses can therefore be safely generalized to the whole. When a sample is not chosen scientifically and has too many people in it from one portion of the population, we say it has a problem of **sample bias**. When trying to judge public opinion from what they hear among their supporters and friendly interest groups, politicians must allow for the bias of

sample the portion of the population that is selected to participate in a poll

sample bias the effect of having a sample that does not represent all segments of the population

straw polls polls that attempt to determine who is ahead in a political race

Figure 11.9

Congressional Sources of Public Opinion Information

A survey of members of Congress found that they use a mix of sources to learn about public opinion, with opinion polls being fairly far down the list.

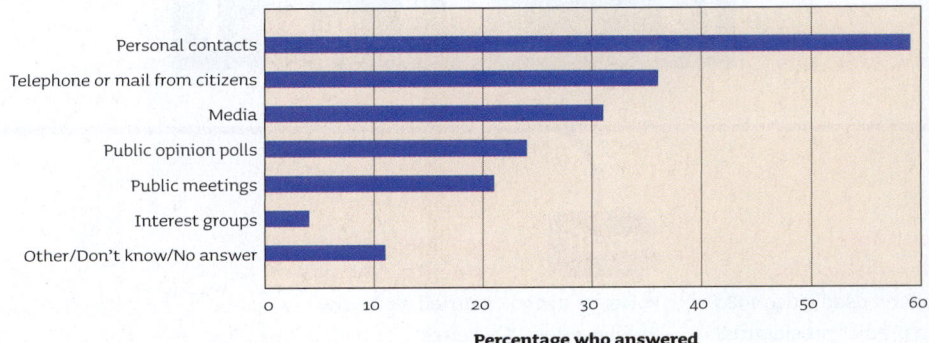

Source: Data from the Pew Research Center for the People and the Press, Trust in Government Study, October 1997 and February 1998.

Note: Eighty-one members of Congress were asked, "What is your principal source of information about the way the public feels about issues?"

their own sampling. If they are not effective at knowing how those they meet differ from the full public, they will get a misleading idea of public opinion.

The Development of Modern Public Opinion Polls

The scientific poll as we know it today was developed in the 1930s. However, newspapers and politicians have been trying to read public opinion as long as we have had democracies. The first efforts at actually counting opinions were the **straw polls**, dating from the first half of the nineteenth century and continuing in a more scientific form today.[40] The curious name for these polls comes from the fact that a straw, thrown up into the air, will indicate which way the wind is blowing.[41] These polls were designed to help politicians predict which way the political winds were blowing and, more specifically, who would win an upcoming election. Before the modern science of sampling was well understood, straw polls were conducted by a variety of hit-or-miss methods, and though their results were often correct, they were sometimes spectacularly wrong.

The experience of the *Literary Digest* illustrates this point dramatically. The *Literary Digest* was a highly popular magazine that conducted straw polls in the 1920s and 1930s. It mailed millions of questionnaires during presidential

election campaigns asking recipients who they planned to vote for and then tabulated the mailed-in results. The *Digest* polls were quite successful in predicting the election winners in 1920 through 1932 and received wide recognition and publicity. However, in 1936 the magazine predicted that President Franklin Roosevelt would be defeated by Alf Landon by a wide margin. Instead, Roosevelt won handily. The poll was wrong for several reasons. First, people change their minds often during an election campaign, with some remaining undecided until the final days, and the *Digest* poll was unable to record last-minute voting decisions. Second, there was a clear (in retrospect) sample bias: the *Digest* poll had included too many Republican voters in its sample because it drew names from lists of automobile registrations, telephone directories, and different clubs and organizations. The sample thus overrepresented the middle-class, financially well-off population, since at that time most families could not afford cars or telephones. Although this bias had not been a problem in the past, by 1936 these voters were becoming more identified with the Republican Party.[42] The sample bias was compounded because respondents had to mail in their questionnaires. Not only were they not representative to begin with, but the more political, intense, and involved voters who self-selected themselves by mailing back the questionnaire further skewed the results.

sampling error a number that indicates within what range the results of a poll are accurate

random samples samples chosen in such a way that any member of the population being polled has an equal chance of being selected

Polling errors led to an even more well-known polling fiasco in 1948, one whose results were captured in a photograph of a smiling and victorious President Harry Truman holding up a copy of the *Chicago Daily Tribune,* whose headline declared "Dewey Defeats Truman." By this time, pollsters had learned more about sampling requirements but not enough about changing voter minds. Having polled the public early on and established that Dewey held a substantial lead, few polling organizations bothered to follow up. The *Tribune* used old data, and polls again failed to capture last-minute changes in voters' decisions.

The Quality of Opinion Polling Today

Today, polling is big business and a relatively precise science. Political polls are actually a small portion of the marketing business, which tries to gauge what people want and are willing to buy. Many local governments also conduct surveys to find out what their citizens want and how satisfied they are with various municipal services. All polls face the same two challenges, however: (1) getting a good sample, which entails both sampling the right number of people and eliminating sample bias, and (2) asking questions that yield valid results.

How Big Does a Sample Need to Be?

No sample is perfect in matching the population from which it is drawn, but it should be close. Confronted with a critic who did not trust the notion of sampling, George Gallup is said to have responded, "Okay, if you do not like the idea of a sample, then the next time you go for a blood test, tell them to take it all!" While it might seem counterintuitive, statisticians have determined that a sample of only one thousand to two thousand people can be very representative of the entire 300 million residents of the United States.

Sampling error is a number that indicates how reliable the poll is; based on the size of the sample, it tells within what range the actual opinion of the whole population would fall. Typically a report of a poll will say that its "margin of error" is plus or minus 3 percent. That means that, based on sampling theory, there is a 95 percent chance that the real figure for the whole population is within 3 percent of that reported. For instance, when a poll reports a presidential approval rating of 60 percent and a 3 percent margin of error, this means that there is a 95 percent chance that between 57 and 63 percent of the population approve of the president's job performance. A poll that shows one candidate leading another by 2 percent of the projected vote is really too close

Pollsters Get a Black Eye

Harry Truman laughed last and loudest after one of the biggest mistakes in American journalism. The *Chicago Daily Tribune* relied on a two-week-old Gallup poll to predict the outcome of the 1948 presidential race, damaging polling's image for decades. With polls today conducted all the way up to Election Day—and exit polls tracking how ballots are actually cast—similar goofs are much less likely.

to call since the 2 percent might be due to sampling error. The larger the sample, the smaller the sampling error, but samples larger than two thousand add very little in the way of reliability. Surveying more people, say five thousand, is much more expensive and time-consuming but does not substantially reduce the sampling error.

Dealing With the Problem of Sample Bias

Because of fiascos like the *Literary Digest* poll, modern polls now employ systematic **random samples** of the populations whose opinions they want to describe. In a systematic random sample, everyone should have the same chance to be interviewed. Since almost all households now have telephones, it is possible to get a representative sample in telephone polls. Some pollsters argue that respondents are more candid and cooperative when they are interviewed in person. But achieving a representative sample for in-person interviewing is much more difficult since it requires interviewers to make personal contact with specific individuals chosen in advance.

Because reputable survey firms use scientific sampling strategies, sampling bias is not generally a problem that plagues modern pollsters, but there is one way it can sneak in through the back door. The chief form of sample bias in current surveys is nonresponse. Response rates to telephone surveys have dropped considerably over the years; in current surveys sometimes as few as one-quarter of those intended to be included in surveys actually participate. The reasons for this drop include hostility to telemarketers; the increasing use of caller ID; the growing use of cell phones (which are more difficult for pollsters to call since they are not allowed to autodial them); and the simple fact that people are busier, are working more, and have less time and inclination to talk to strangers on the phone.[43] As a result, most telephone polls, unless corrected, will have too many elderly women and too few younger men because the former are typically at home to answer the phone when the interview calls, and the latter are more frequently out. One consequence of the nonresponse problem is that the most reluctant respondents—those likely to be missed in a typical survey—seem to be less racially tolerant than the average population, meaning that a standard survey might yield responses that are slightly more liberal on racial matters than might be the population as a whole.[44]

Pollsters deal with the problem of differential response rates, which yield a sample that does not look demographically like the population that is being sampled—perhaps there are too many whites or old people, or not enough college graduates or young adults—by *weighting* the sample to match what the census says the population looks like. This is done during the analysis of the results; under- or overrepresented groups are multiplied by values that bring them up to their actual numbers in the population. Surprisingly, though, studies of differential response rates, which one might think would cause serious sample biases, find that well-constructed telephone polls continue to provide accurate information on citizens' responses to most questions about politics and issues.

The Importance of Asking the Right Questions

Asking the right questions in surveys is a surprisingly tricky business. Researchers have emphasized three main points with respect to constructing survey questions:

- *Respondents should be asked about things they know and have thought about.* Otherwise, they will often try to be helpful but will give responses based on whatever cues they can pick up from the context of the interview or the particular question. For example, some researchers from the University of Cincinnati did a local survey in which they asked respondents whether they favored a nonexistent "Public Affairs Act of 1974." Almost a quarter of the respondents were willing to give an opinion![45] However, researchers also have found that if questions provide a "don't know" option, only about 10 percent of respondents will choose it.[46]

- *Questions should not be ambiguous.* One highly controversial example comes from a 1992 survey that reported that over a third of the American public either did not believe or doubted that the Holocaust had even happened.[47] One newspaper called the American public "willfully stupid"; Holocaust survivor, author, and Nobel laureate Elie Wiesel was "shocked" by the results.[48] The uproar, however, was largely the product of a bad question. Respondents were asked, "Does it seem possible or does it seem impossible to you that the Nazi extermination of the Jews never happened?" To say that one believed the Holocaust happened, the respondent had to agree to a double negative—that it was "impossible" that it "never" happened. There was

Doonesbury

Figure 11.10

Asking the Right Question

Comparison of results from two versions of school choice questions

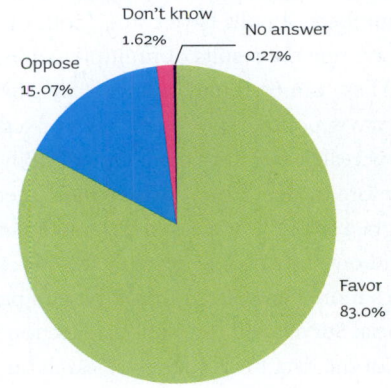

Version A

Question: Do you favor or oppose allowing students and parents to choose a private school to attend at public expense?

Don't know 1.53%

No answer 0.18%

Oppose 54.24%

Favor 44.04%

Version B

Question: A proposal has been made that would allow parents to send their school-age children to any public, private, or church-related school they choose. For those parents choosing non-public schools, the government would pay all or part of the tuition. Would you favor or oppose this proposal in your state?

Don't know 1.62%

No answer 0.27%

Oppose 15.07%

Favor 83.0%

Source: PDK/Gallup 33rd Annual Survey of the Public's Attitude Towards Public Schools, 2001.

plenty of room for confusion. Other respondents were asked a more straightforward version of the question: "The term *Holocaust* usually refers to the killing of millions of Jews in Nazi death camps during World War II. Do you doubt that the Holocaust actually happened, or not?" With this wording, only 9 percent doubted the Holocaust and 4 percent were unsure.[49]

- *Similar questions can yield surprisingly different answers.* For instance, do a majority of Americans support school choice, in which the government will pay the costs of children attending the schools the parents select? Notice in Figure 11.10 how two rather similar questions on this topic yield very different conclusions. In the shorter version, a majority are opposed to school choice, whereas in the longer version, which asks almost the same thing but with greater detail, an overwhelming majority are in favor of it. Words like *proposal* may connote some legitimacy in respondents' minds, or perhaps the injection of religion or the mention of "school-age children" brings to mind different "considerations" that affect how the questions are interpreted.[50] Why do you think people would be more likely to answer more positively to the second wording?

There are still other considerations that pollsters should take into account. Studies have shown, for instance, that the order in which questions are asked can change the results, as

can such a simple factor as the number of choices offered for responses. Clearly, good surveys can tell us a lot about public opinion, but they will hardly ever produce the final word. And, of course, just as soon as they might, public opinion would probably shift again in any case.

Types of Polls

Many people and organizations report the results of what they claim are measures of public opinion. To make sense of this welter of claims, it is useful to know some basic polling terminology and the characteristics of different types of polls.

National Polls

National polls are efforts to measure public opinion within a limited period of time using a national representative sample. The time period of interviewing may be as short as a few hours, with the results reported the next day, or extended over a period of weeks, as in academic polls. The underlying goal, however, is the same: to achieve scientifically valid measures of the knowledge, beliefs, or attitudes of the adult population.

Many national polls are conducted by the media in conjunction with a professional polling organization. These polls regularly measure attitudes on some central item, such as how the public feels about the job that the president or Congress is doing. Several of these organizations make their *benchmark poll* initial poll on a candidate and issues on which campaign strategy is based and against which later polls are compared

tracking polls ongoing series of surveys that follow changes in public opinion over time

exit polls election-related questions asked of voters right after they vote

polls available through the Internet.[51] Some of the polls that regularly collect data in large national samples include the following: the ABC News/*Washington Post* poll, the CBS News/*New York Times* poll, the NBC News/*Wall Street Journal* poll, the CNN/*USA Today*/Gallup poll, and the *Los Angeles Times* poll. With the growing numbers of polls have come "polls of polls," which seek to average the results of multiple polling organizations' efforts. These can be found online, at sites like www.pollster.com, www.pollingreport.com, www.fivethirtyeight.com, and www.realclearpolitics.com. Other polling organizations provide more in-depth surveys than these media polls. Some are designed to see how people feel about particular topics or to find out how people develop attitudes and evaluate politics more generally. Two of these in particular, the General Social Survey and the National Election Studies, provide much of the data for academic research on public opinion in America (and much of what we say in this chapter about public opinion).[52]

Campaign Polls

A lot of polling is done for candidates in their efforts to win election or reelection. Most well-funded campaigns begin with a *benchmark poll*, taken of a sample of the population, or perhaps just of the potential voters, in a state or district to gather baseline information on how well the candidate is known, what issues people associate with the candidate, and what issues people are concerned about, as well as assessments of the opposition, especially if the opponent is an incumbent. Benchmark polls are instrumental in designing campaign strategy.

Presidential campaigns and a few of the better-funded statewide races (for example, those for governor or U.S. senator) conduct *tracking polls*. These follow changes in attitudes toward the candidates by having ongoing sets of interviews. Such daily samples are too small to allow reliable generalization, but groups of these interviews averaged over time are extremely helpful. The oldest interviews are dropped as newer ones are added, providing a dynamic view of changes in voters' preferences and perceptions.

A sudden change in a tracking poll might signal that the opponent's new ads are doing damage or that interest group endorsements are having an effect. Campaign strategies can be revised accordingly. More recently, the news media have undertaken tracking polls as part of their election coverage. In the 2004 presidential election, tracking polls were conducted by several polling organizations and were reported widely in

the media. Several tracking polls showed a very close race with none quite anticipating the size of Bush's three-percentage-point victory on election night. By 2008 there were even more tracking polls—up to nine pollsters were reporting daily results by the time of the election, and several web sites were aggregating the results. The averaging process of the aggregators helps to smooth out individual pollsters' house effects (biases or patterns that might be built into an individual pollster's methodology) and differences in their assumptions about turnout. Their "track record" was a good one—the folks at pollster.com and fivethirtyeight.com missed the individual state results by less than 2.5 points, and fivethirtyeight.com's formula of weighting and averaging poll data in conjunction with other data patterns missed the actual vote tally of 52.5 to 46.2 by a hair: their final prediction was 52.3 to 46.2.

On election night the media commentators often "call" a race, declaring one candidate a winner, sometimes as soon as the voting booths in a state are closed but well before the official vote count has been reported. These predictions are made, in part, on the basis of *exit polls*, which are short questionnaires administered to samples of voters in selected precincts after they vote. Exit polls focus on vote choice, a few demographic questions, some issue preferences, and evaluations of candidates. In addition to helping the networks predict the winners early, exit polls are used by network broadcasters and journalists to add explanatory and descriptive material to their election coverage. Because exit polls are expensive to conduct, media organizations have banded together in recent years to share the costs of conducting national exit polls.

Exit polls, however, have a mixed record in recent elections, leading news agencies to become cautious about how the results are used.[53] For example, in 2000 flawed data led the networks to mistakenly "call" Florida for Vice President Al Gore (which would have meant that he'd won the presidency); then to switch the call to George W. Bush; and finally, late in the evening, to conclude that the state was too close to call at all. Exit poll defenders argue that these polls are being misused by the public and the media; they are not intended to predict the elections in progress but to explain the vote after the election by providing information on what groups voted for which candidates. The challenges faced by those conducting exit polls are the same as those the preelection pollsters must contend with: it is very difficult to obtain a fully representative sample of voters. As a result of

Profiles in Citizenship: Nate Silver

"Don't underestimate your ability to come up with an idea that nobody else has. It happens all the time. Quit being a consumer and be a producer."

© Melissa Ann Pinney

A lot of public opinion polls were published in the days leading up to the 2008 presidential election, and a lot of political predictions were based on those polls. While many pollsters got the big call right, forecasting an Obama win, it's ironic that Nate Silver, who came closest to nailing the Electoral College count—calling the correct results in forty-nine out of fifty states—wasn't a pollster at all.

But then, Nate Silver is a very smart guy, a guy who deals in numbers and mathematical models and predictions all the time. He wasn't long out of college before he had developed the PECOTA (Player Empirical Comparison and Optimization Test Algorithm) system—a model for predicting the performance of baseball players that became associated with a web site called *Baseball Prospectus* that Silver managed. Baseball is a long way from politics, however, and by 2008 Silver had given up *Baseball Prospectus* and was concentrating his mathematical prowess on primaries and electoral votes, writing on the new blog that he called fivethirtyeight.com (after the total number of votes in the Electoral College).

If you ask him how he got to here from there, the answer is about what you'd expect from this young, brilliant, and quirky man. He got into politics because of Internet poker, of course. Doesn't everyone?

Some context here is that Silver is the son of a political scientist, so the world was one he was well familiar with and he liked it. "I was more into politics as compared to a normal person," he says, "because it was interesting, kind of like a big game show." But still, Internet poker?

"In 2006 I was playing poker mostly online. The outgoing Republican Congress passed a law where they basically made online poker illegal, but it was not very effective. What they technically did, more or less, is say you can play poker, but you can't deposit money in and out, so that had a chilling effect on the game . . . that got me following congressional procedure." Besides, he had gone to the University of Chicago, and a member of the Chicago law faculty, Senator Barack Obama, was running for president. "That was kind of cool," he says. "I actually had like a hometown candidate now."

Goodbye baseball, hello politics.

Silver started blogging on the liberal *Daily Kos* site under the pseudonym Poblano, and then he started fivethirtyeight.com. What Silver added that other analysts didn't was a model that aggregated the existing polling and, based on those numbers as well as demographic and other data, ran computerized simulations of the various primary and general election races. If Obama and Hillary Clinton were facing off in a primary in North Carolina, for instance, Silver could simulate the election 100 times and tell you what percentage of the time Obama would win and what percentage Clinton would. His predictions were uncannily accurate, and soon Silver's readership soared and he was on cable TV, analyzing polls and races. Two years after the election, Silver signed a three-year contract with the *New York Times*, on whose web site you can currently find fivethirtyeight.com.

Today Silver is writing a book on predictions (in all realms, from sports, to weather, to politics), waiting for the next election, and maintaining his site. What does he want people to get from his blog? "I want to inform people, I want people to think more critically about things. Basically, I want people to not be intimidated by numbers and statistics, to not just assume that something that they hear, whether it's from a politician or from Fox News or from another writer in the *New York Times*, is necessarily true. I just want to encourage people to use their brains."

Here's some other advice from Nate Silver:

On patriotism:

You probably have some family members who have their flaws and idiosyncrasies and probably a few distant relatives who are even fairly screwed-up people, but you still love them, anyway. I think that's what patriotism is really, saying, "Look, this is where I was born, or I migrated to the United States, this is where my loyalty is. . . ." You don't have a choice, it doesn't matter how unhappy you are, you know? It's your family, and you are stuck with it.

On keeping the republic:

People just have to be willing to put in the work. It's a big, complicated world now, and as many people that there are, there are more things to be done. Don't underestimate your ability to come up with an idea that nobody else has. It happens all the time. Quit being a consumer and be a producer. Start your own blog, start your own political organization. Have fun with it—there is nothing wrong with that at all. ■

push polls   polls that ask for reactions to hypothetical, often false, information in order to manipulate public opinion

these problems, networks are now relatively cautious in declaring winners without corroborating evidence from the actual vote returns; there were no mistakes in "calling" the states in the 2004 presidential election.[54]

Pseudo-Polls

A number of opinion studies are wrongly presented as polls. More deceptive than helpful, these pseudo-polls range from potentially misleading entertainment to outright fraud. Self-selection polls are those, like the *Literary Digest*'s, in which respondents, by one mechanism or another, select themselves into a survey rather than being chosen randomly. Examples of self-selection polls include viewer or listener call-in polls and Internet polls. These polls tell you only how a portion of the media outlet's audience (self-selected in the first place by their choice of a particular outlet) who care enough to call in or click a mouse (self-selected in the second place by their willingness to expend effort) feel about an issue.

When the CNN web site asks users to record their views on whether the United States should engage in military action with Iraq, for instance, the audience is limited, first, to those who own or have access to computers; second, to those who care enough about the news to be on the CNN site; and third, to those who want to pause in their news reading for the short time it takes for their vote to be counted and the results to appear on the screen. Further, nothing stops individuals from recording multiple votes to make the count seem greater than it is. Results of such polls are likely to be highly unrepresentative of the population as a whole. They should be presented with caution and interpreted with a great deal of skepticism.

Another, increasingly common kind of pseudo-poll is the push poll, which poses as a legitimate information-seeking effort but is really a shady campaign trick to change people's attitudes. **Push polls** present false or highly negative information, often in a hypothetical form, and ask respondents to react to it. The information, presented as if true or at least possible, can raise doubts about a candidate and even change a voter's opinion about him or her. Insofar as they have a legitimate function, "push questions" are used on a limited basis by pollsters and campaign strategists to find out how voters might respond to negative information about the candidate or the opposition. This is the kind of information that might be gathered in a benchmark poll, for example. Less scrupulous consultants, working for both political parties, however, sometimes use the format as a means of propaganda. As an example, a pollster put this question to Florida voters:

Please tell me if you would be more likely or less likely to vote for Lt. Governor Buddy MacKay if you knew that Lt. Gov. Buddy MacKay plans to implement a new early-release program for violent offenders who have served a mere 60 percent of their sentences if he is elected governor?[55]

MacKay had no such plans, and to imply that he did was false. Moreover, the goal of this "poll" was not to learn anything but rather to plant negative information in the minds of thousands of people. By posing as a legitimate poll, the push poll seeks to trick respondents into accepting the information as truthful and thereby to influence the vote. Such polls are often conducted without any acknowledgment of who is sponsoring them (usually the opponents of the person being asked about). The target candidate often never knows that such a poll is being conducted, and because push polls frequently pop up the weekend before an election, he or she cannot rebut the lies or half-truths. A key characteristic of push polls is that they seek to call as many voters as they can with little regard to the usual care and quality of a legitimate representative sample. "Push polling for me is marketing," said Floyd Ciruli, a Denver-based pollster. "You call everybody you can call and tell them something that may or may not be true."[56]

Legislation against push polling has been introduced in several state legislatures, and the practice has been condemned by the American Association of Political Consultants.[57] There is a real question, however, about whether efforts to regulate push polls can survive a First Amendment test before the Supreme Court.

Survey Experiments

A final category of polls are those conducted by social scientists not so much to gauge and measure public opinion about elections or current events as to deepen our understanding of public attitudes, especially on controversial issues such as race, gender, and civil liberties, where respondents know what the socially acceptable answer to the survey questions is and so are less likely to disclose their true opinions. In survey experiments, the survey questions are manipulated in an effort to get respondents to disclose more information than they think they are disclosing.

A pioneering example of such work is an experiment in the study of racial attitudes in which researchers sought to find out if the way a question is framed affects how respondents feel about a particular group. In this case, researchers wondered if the mention of affirmative action, which many people do not like, would influence respondents' attitudes toward African Americans. A sample of white respondents were randomly put into two groups, a control group that was only asked a question about their feelings toward blacks, and a group that first was asked about their view of affirmative action and then their attitude toward blacks. They found that the mere mention of affirmative action excited more negative responses toward blacks in the second group,[58] which helped researchers to understand the complex sets of issues that lie behind racial attitudes in American public opinion and told them something about the impact of framing on racial attitudes. The advent of Internet polling has made the use of survey experiments even more widespread because administration over the Internet allows the use of images, sounds, and other multimedia in addition to the words used in a typical survey.[59]

New Technologies and Challenges in Polling

Technology is a pollster's friend, but it can also create unexpected challenges. In the early days of polls, surveys were done in-person, on the door stoop or in the living room. That method was superseded by telephone interviewing as almost all households got telephones and in light of the obvious efficiency of calling people on the phone versus sending interviewers to far-flung places for face-to-face interviews. With the advent of computer technology has come the substitution of computers for humans to do the interviewing. The computers dial the numbers (autodialing) and deliver recorded messages, even "interacting" by asking questions that are answered by pushing buttons on a touch-tone phone. This technology, called "robo calling," is much cheaper than using human interviewers, but it is also controversial. It is easily abused, especially when combined with push poll methods.[60] Legitimate polling firms also use robo calls and have collected more information on more political subjects than has been available in the past, such as the state-by-state results provided by SurveyUSA.[61]

Computers provide another challenge (and opportunity) for pollsters in the form of online surveys. Here we do not mean the polls that CNN or others put up asking for volunteers to click in their opinions on some issue. Pollsters create panels of Internet users who regularly log in to deliver their opinions on matters the pollsters select. Although some critics argue that the online polls have no scientific basis because they do not rely on strict probability samples, proponents argue that with

appropriate adjustments, the Internet polls nicely match results from traditional telephone interviewing. They have the advantage of garnering fewer refusals, and for some kinds of questions, respondents to online surveys appear to be more candid in admitting to things that might be embarrassing to confess to a human interviewer.[62]

Pollsters also face a growing challenge as increasing numbers of citizens, especially younger people, rely on cell phones. The U.S. Telephone Consumer Protection Act limits the technologies that can be used in contacting cell phone users—forbidding autodialing, for instance. Those contacted by cell phones are also more likely to refuse to answer polls. As pollsters adapt to these newer technologies, research and regulations are likely to lead to changes in contacting cell phone users.[63]

How Accurate Are Polls?

For many issues, such as attitudes toward the environment or presidential approval, we have no objective measure against which to judge the accuracy of public opinion polls. With elections, however, polls do make predictions, and we can tell by the vote count whether the polls are correct. The record of most polls is, in general, quite good. For example, all the major polls have predicted the winner of presidential elections correctly since 1980, except in the incredibly close 2000 election. They are not correct to the percentage point, nor would we expect them to be, given the known levels of sampling error, preelection momentum shifts, and the usual 15 percent of voters who claim to remain undecided up to the last minute. Polls taken closer to Election Day typically become more accurate as they catch more of the late deciders.[64] Even in the 2000 presidential election, most of the polls by election eve had done a fairly good job of predicting the tightness of the race. Read "*Consider the Source: Don't Be Fooled by the Polls*" for some tips on how you can gauge the reliability of poll results you come across.

Citizens, politicians and their staffs, the media, and professional polling organizations are all interested in the business of measuring and tracking public opinion. Citizens rely on polls to monitor elections and get a sense of where other Americans stand on particular issues. Their interest is in fair polling techniques that produce reliable results.

Who What How

▶ Consider the Source: Don't Be Fooled by the Polls

In the heat of the Clinton impeachment hearings, angry conservative Republicans could not believe the polls: over 65 percent of Americans still approved of the job the president was doing and did not want to see him removed from office. Their conclusion? The polls were simply wrong. "The polls are targeted to get a certain answer," said one Floridian. "There are even T-shirts in South Florida that say 'I haven't been polled.'"[1]

Do we need to know people personally who have been polled in order to trust poll results? Of course not. But there are lots of polls out there, not only those done carefully and responsibly by reputable polling organizations but also polls done for marketing and overtly political purposes—polls with an agenda, we might say. How are we, as good scholars and citizens, to know which results are reliable indications of what the public thinks, and which are not? One thing we can do is bring our critical thinking skills to bear by asking some questions about the polls reported in the media. Try these:[2]

1. **Who is the poll's sponsor?** Even if the poll was conducted by a professional polling company, it may still have been commissioned on behalf of a candidate or company. Does the sponsor have an agenda? How might that agenda influence the poll, the question wording, or the sponsor's interpretation of events?

2. **Is the sample representative?** That is, were proper sampling techniques followed? What is the margin of error?

3. **From what population was the sample taken?** There is a big difference, for instance, between the preference of the general public for a presidential candidate and the preference of likely voters, especially if one is interested in predicting the election's outcome! Read the fine print. Sometimes a polling organization will weight responses according to the likelihood that the respondent will actually vote in order to come up with a better prediction of the election result. Some polls survey only the members of one party, or the readers of a particular magazine, or people of a certain age, depending on the information they are seeking to discover. Be sure the

sample is not self-selected. Always check the population being sampled, and do not assume it is the general public.

4. **How are the questions worded?** Are loaded, problematic, or vague terms used? Could the questions be confusing to the average citizen? Are the questions available with the poll results? If not, why not? Do the questions seem to lead you to respond one way or the other? Do they oversimplify issues or complicate them? If the survey claims to have detected change over time, be sure the same questions were used consistently. All these things could change the way people respond.

5. **Are the survey topics ones that people are likely to have information and opinions about?** Respondents rarely admit that they don't know how to answer a question, so responses on obscure or technical topics are likely to be more suspect than others.

6. **What is the poll's response rate?** A lot of "don't knows," "no opinions," or refusals to answer can have a decided effect on the results.

7. **Do the poll results differ from those of other polls, and if so, why?** Check out www.pollster.com, www.fivethirtyeight.com, or www.realclearpolitics.com for some context. Don't necessarily assume that a change in individual poll numbers means that public opinion has changed. What is it about this poll that might have caused the discrepancy?

8. **What do the results mean?** Who is doing the interpreting? What are that person's motives? For instance, pollsters who work for the Democratic Party will have an interpretation of the results that is favorable to Democrats, and Republican interpretation will favor Republicans. Try interpreting the results yourself.

1. Melinda Henneberger, "Where G.O.P. Gathers, Frustration Does Too," *New York Times*, February 1, 1999, 3.
2. Some of these questions are based in part on similar advice given to poll watchers in Herbert Asher, *Polling and the Public: What Every Citizen Should Know*, 7th ed. (Washington, D.C.: CQ Press, 2007), 206–209.

To win elections, politicians must know what citizens think and what they want from their officials. They need to know how various campaign strategies are playing publicly and how they are faring in their races against other candidates. Politicians and their campaign consultants evaluate face-to-face contact with voters and their correspondence and calls, but they also pay attention to national media and party or campaign polls.

The media want current and accurate information on which to base their reporting. They also have an interest in keeping and increasing the size of their audiences. To build their markets, they create and publish polls that encourage their audiences to see elections as exciting contests.

Finally, professional pollsters have an interest in producing accurate information for their clients. The quality of their surveys rests with good scientific polling techniques.

rational ignorance the state of being uninformed about politics because of the cost in time and energy

on-line processing the ability to receive and evaluate information as events happen, allowing us to remember our evaluation even if we have forgotten the specific events that caused it

two-step flow of information the process by which citizens take their political cues from more well-informed opinion leaders

opinion leaders people who know more about certain topics than we do and whose advice we trust, seek out, and follow

Thinking Outside **the Box**

Do frequent opinion polls enhance or diminish democracy?

The Citizens and Public Opinion

Informational shortcuts that save democracy from our lack of care and attention

We have seen ample evidence that although politicians may act as if citizens are informed and attentive, only some Americans live up to our model of good citizenship, and those who do often belong disproportionately to the ranks of the well educated, the well-off, and the older portions of the population. This disparity between our ideal citizen and reality raises some provocative questions about the relationships among citizens, public opinion, and democracy. Were the founders right to limit the influence of the masses on government? Do we want less informed and coherent opinions represented in politics? Can democracy survive if it is run only by an educated elite?

Earlier in this chapter we suggested that all would not be lost for American democracy if only some of us turned out to be ideal citizens, and that it was possible to argue that although Americans as individuals might not fit the ideal, Americans as a group might behave as that ideal would predict. How is such a trick possible? The argument goes like this.

It may not be rational for all people to be deeply immersed in the minutiae of day-to-day politics. Our jobs, families, hobbies, and other interests leave us little time for in-depth study of political issues, and unless we get tremendous satisfaction from keeping up with politics (and some of us certainly do), it might be rational for us to leave the political information gathering to others. Social scientists call this idea **rational ignorance**.

This does not mean that we are condemned to make only ignorant or mistaken political decisions. Citizens are generally pretty smart. In fact, studies show that voters can behave much more intelligently than we could ever guess from their answers to surveys about politics. A great many of us use shortcuts to getting political information that serve us quite well, in the sense that they help us make the same decisions we might have made had we invested considerable time and energy in collecting that political information ourselves.[65]

Shortcuts to Political Knowledge

One shortcut is the **on-line processing** of information.[66] (On-line here does not refer to time spent on the Internet, as you will see.) Many of the evaluations we make of people, places, and things in our lives (including political figures and ideas) are made on the fly. We assemble impressions and reactions while we are busy leading our lives. When queried, we might not be able to explain why we like or dislike a thing or a person, and we might sound quite ignorant in the sense of not seeming to have reasons for our beliefs. But we do have reasons, and they may make a good deal of sense, even if we can't identify what they are.

A second important mental shortcut that most of us use is the **two-step flow of information**. Politicians and the media send out massive amounts of information. We can absorb only a fraction of it, and even then it is sometimes hard to know how to interpret it. In these circumstances, we tend to rely on **opinion leaders**, who are more or less like ourselves but who know more about the subject than we do.[67] Opinion leaders and followers can be identified in all sorts of realms besides politics. When we make an important purchase, say, a computer or a car, most of us do not research all the scientific data and technical specifications. We ask people who are like us, who we think should know, and whom we can trust. We compile their advice, consult our own intuition, and buy. The result is that we get pretty close to making an optimal purchase without having to become experts ourselves. The two-step flow allows us to behave as though we were very well informed without requiring us to expend all the resources that being informed entails.

Thinking Outside **the Box**

Is a democracy that depends on citizen "shortcuts" weaker than one that does not?

The Rational Electorate

Politicians deal with citizens mostly in groups and only rarely as individuals. Elected officials think about constituents as whole electorates ("the people of the great state of Texas") or as members of groups (women, environmentalists, developers, workers, and so forth). Groups, it turns out, appear to be better behaved, more rational, and better informed than the individuals who make up the groups, precisely because of the sorts of shortcuts we discussed in the previous section. This doesn't seem to make sense, so perhaps a nonpolitical example will clarify what we mean.

Consider the behavior of fans at a football game. People seem to cheer at the appropriate times; they know pretty much when to boo the referees; they oooh and aaaah more or less in unison. We would say that the crowd understands the game and participates effectively in it. However, what do the individual spectators know? If we were to do a football survey, we might ask about the players' names, the teams' win-loss records, the different offensive and defensive positions, the meaning of the referees' signals, and so forth. Some fans would do well, but many would probably get only a few questions right. From the survey, we might conclude that many people in this crowd do not know football at all. But because they take their cues from others, following the behavior of those who cheer for the same team, they can act as if they know what they are doing. Despite its share of football-ignorant individuals, in the aggregate—that is, as a group—the crowd acts remarkably football-intelligent.

Similarly, if we were to ask people when national elections are held, for instance, only a handful would be able to say it is the Tuesday after the first Monday in November of evenly numbered years. Some people would guess that they occur in November, others might say in the fall sometime, and others would admit they don't know. Based on the level of individual ignorance in this matter, it would be surprising if many people ever voted at all, since you can't vote if you don't know when Election Day is. But somehow, as a group, the electorate sorts it out, and almost everyone who is registered and wants to vote finds his or her way to the polling place on the right day. By using shortcuts and taking cues from others, the electorate behaves just as if it knew all along when the election was. More substantively, even though many voters may be confused about which candidates stand where on specific issues, groups of voters do a great job of sorting out which party or candidate best represents their interests. Members of the religious right vote for Republicans, and members of labor unions vote for Democrats, for instance. Even though there are undoubtedly quite a few confused voters in the electorate in any particular election, they tend to cancel each other out in the larger scheme of things, although understandably, some biases remain.[68] As a

whole, from the politician's point of view, the electorate appears to be responsive to issues and quite rational in evaluating an incumbent's performance in office.[69]

So even though citizens do not spend a lot of time learning about politics, politicians are smart to assume that the electorate is attentive and informed. In fact, this is precisely what most of them do. For example, studies have shown that state legislators vote in accordance with the ideological preferences of their citizens, just as if the citizens were instructing them on their wishes.[70] The states with the most liberal citizens—for example, New York, Massachusetts, and California—have the most liberal policies. And the most conservative states, those in the South and the Rocky Mountains, have the most conservative policies. Other studies confirm a similar pattern in national elections.[71]

We began this chapter by asking why polling is routinely disparaged by politicians. Why don't we have more confidence in being ruled by public opinion? After all, in a democracy where the people's will is supposed to weigh heavily with our elected officials, we have uncovered some conflicting evidence. Many Americans do not model the characteristics of the ideal democratic citizen, but remember that the United States has two traditions of citizenship—one much more apolitical and self-interested than the public-spirited ideal. The reality in America is that the ideal citizen marches side by side with the more self-interested citizen, who, faced with many demands, does not put politics ahead of other daily responsibilities. But we have also argued that there are mechanisms and shortcuts that allow even some of the more apolitical and self-interested citizens to cast intelligent votes and to have their views represented in public policy. This tells us that at least one element of democracy—responsiveness of policies to public preferences—is in good working order.

We should not forget that political influence goes hand in hand with opinion formation. Those who are opinion leaders have much more relative clout than do their more passive followers. And opinion leaders are not distributed equally throughout the population. They are drawn predominantly from the ranks of the well educated and the well-off. Similarly, even though the shortcuts we have discussed allow many people to vote intelligently without taking the time to make a personally informed decision, many people never vote at all. Voters are also drawn from the more privileged ranks of American society. The poor, the young, and minorities—all the groups who are underrepresented at the voting booth—are also underrepresented in policymaking. There cannot help but be biases in such a system.[72]

▶ What's at Stake Revisited

We have argued in this chapter that public opinion is important in policymaking and that politicians respond to it in a variety of ways. But what would happen if we more or less bypassed elected officials altogether and allowed people to participate directly in national lawmaking through the use of a national referendum or initiative? What is at stake in rule by public opinion?

On the one hand, voters would seem to have something real to gain in such lawmaking reform. It would give new meaning to government "by the people," and decisions would have more legitimacy with the public. Certainly it would be harder to point the finger at those in Washington as being responsible for bad laws. In addition, as has been the experience in states with initiatives, citizens might succeed in getting legislation passed that legislators themselves refuse to vote for. Prime examples are term limits and balanced budget amendments. Term limits would cut short many congressional careers and balanced budget amendments force politicians into hard choices about taxation and spending cuts that they prefer to avoid.

On the other side of the calculation, however, voters might be worse off. While policies like the two mentioned above clearly threaten the jobs of politicians, they also carry unintended consequences that might not be very good for the nation as a whole. Who should decide— politicians who make a career out of understanding government, or people who pay little attention to politics and current events and who vote from instinct and outrage? Politicians who have a vested interest in keeping their jobs, or the public who can provide a check on political greed and self-interest? The answer changes with the way you phrase the question, but the public might well suffer if left to its own mercy on questions of policy it does not thoroughly understand.

There is no doubt that the founders of the Constitution, with their limited faith in the people, would have rejected such a referendum wholeheartedly. Not only does it bring government closer to the people, but it wreaks havoc with their system of separation of powers and checks and balances. Popular opinion was supposed to be checked by the House and the Senate, which were in turn to be checked by the other two branches of government. Bringing public opinion to the fore upsets this delicate balance.

In addition, many scholars warn that the hallmark of democracy is not just hearing what the people want, but allowing the people to discuss and deliberate over their political choices. Home computer voting or trips to the ballot box do not necessarily permit such key interaction.[73] Majority rule without the tempering influence of debate and discussion can quickly deteriorate into majority tyranny, with a sacrifice of minority rights.

The flip side may also be true, however. Since voters tend to be those who care more intensely about political issues, supporters of a national referendum also leave themselves open to the opposite consequence of majority tyranny: the tyranny of an intense minority who care enough to campaign and vote against an issue that a majority prefer, but only tepidly.

Finally, there are political stakes for politicians in such a reform. As we have already seen, the passage of laws they would not have themselves supported would make it harder for politicians to get things done. But on the positive side, a national referendum would allow politicians to avoid taking the heat for decisions that are bound to be intensely unpopular with some segment of the population. One of the reasons that national referenda are often used in other countries is to diffuse the political consequences for leaders of unpopular or controversial decisions.

Direct democracy at the national level would certainly have a major impact on American politics, but it is not entirely clear who the winners and losers would be, or even if there would be any consistent winners. The new rules would benefit different groups at different times. The American people believe they would enjoy the power, and various groups are confident they would profit, but in the long run the public interest might be damaged in terms of the quality of American democracy and the protections available to minorities. Politicians have very little to gain. If such a reform ever does come about, it will be generated not by the elite but by public interest groups, special interest groups, and reformers from outside Washington.

To Sum Up

Key terms, chapter summaries, practice quizzes, Internet links, and other study aids are available on the companion web site at http://republic.cqpress.com.

Define | Understand | Practice | Read | Click | Watch

benchmark poll (p. 428)

exit polls (p. 428)

gender gap (p. 417)

marriage gap (p. 418)

on-line processing (p. 433)

opinion leaders (p. 433)

political generations (p. 416)

political socialization (p. 412)

public opinion (p. 407)

public opinion polls (p. 407)

push polls (p. 430)

random samples (p. 425)

rational ignorance (p. 433)

sample (p. 423)

sample bias (p. 423)

sampling error (p. 425)

spiral of silence (p. 413)

straw polls (p. 424)

tracking polls (p. 428)

two-step flow of information (p. 433)

weighting (p. 426)

Define | **Understand** | Practice | Read | Click | Watch

- The role of public opinion in politics has been hotly debated throughout American history. The founders devised a Constitution that would limit the influence of the masses. Today, some changes in the rules have given the public a greater role in government.

- Politicians and the media watch public opinion very closely. Elected officials look for job security by responding to immediate public desires or by skillfully predicting future requests. The media make large investments in polls, sometimes covering public attitudes on a candidate or issue as a story in itself.

- There are two competing visions of citizenship in America. The ideal democratic citizen demonstrates political knowledge, possesses an ideology (usually liberal or conservative), tolerates different ideas, and votes consistently. At the other extreme lies the apolitical, self-interested citizen. Most Americans fall somewhere between these extremes, but factors such as age, higher education, and improved socioeconomic status seem to contribute to behavior that is closer to the ideal.

- Political socialization—the transfer of fundamental democratic values from one generation to the next—is affected by demographic characteristics such as race and gender, and by life experiences such as education and religion. Interest groups, political parties, and candidates all attempt to determine the political ideas shared by various groups in order to gain their support.

- While most politicians pay attention to their own informal samplings of opinion, they have also come to rely on professional polling. Such polls are based on scientific polling methods that focus on getting a good sample and asking questions that yield valid results.

- Even though Americans do not measure up to the ideal of the democratic citizen, there is much evidence to support the idea that public opinion does play a large role in government policy. While some citizens may seem apolitical and disinterested, many use rational information shortcuts to make their voting decisions. Policymakers have responded by staying generally responsive to public preferences.

Define **Understand** **Practice** **Read** **Click** **Watch**

1. **According to supporters of pluralist democracy, citizens' opinions**
   a. should be ignored by politicians because the people are too uninformed to make important political decisions.
   b. should be reflected through groups that fight for their members' interests.
   c. should influence politicians on local issues, but not national issues.
   d. should be followed closely by politicians because individuals are informed enough to be effective decision makers.
   e. should influence politicians only on domestic policy, but not on foreign policy.

2. **Which of the following is NOT true regarding political participation?**
   a. Minorities have lower participation rates than do whites.
   b. The older someone is, the more likely he or she is to participate.
   c. Compared to other industrialized countries, the United States ranks toward the bottom regarding voter turnout.
   d. Women are less likely to vote than men.
   e. The more education one has, the more likely he or she is to vote.

3. **Which of the following is NOT true about political socialization?**
   a. The spiral of silence can occur because of peer pressure.
   b. Children develop nationalism before they enter school.
   c. Children generally learn their basic citizenship skills from the family.
   d. Political events, such as the Clinton impeachment, can significantly influence people's political orientations.
   e. Race relations is an area in which the family has a weaker effect on attitudes.

4. **———— polls are an ongoing series of surveys that follow public opinion over time.**
   a. Exit
   b. Straw
   c. Following
   d. Benchmark
   e. Tracking

5. **People who know more about certain topics than we do and whose advice we trust, seek out, and follow are known as**
   a. opinion formers.
   b. opinion leaders.
   c. rational cue providers.
   d. on-line processors.
   e. opinion elites.

Define **Understand** **Practice** **Read** **Click** **Watch**

Asher, Herbert. 2007. Polling and the Public: What Every Citizen Should Know, 7th ed. Washington, D.C.: CQ Press. *An easy-to-understand and extremely informative source on the problems with public opinion polling undertaken by both candidates and the news media.*

Clawson, Rosalee A., and Zoe M. Oxley. 2008. Public Opinion: Democratic Ideals, Democratic Practice. Washington, D.C.: CQ Press. *Answering the question "What role does public opinion play in governmental decision making?" this text offers an in-depth analysis of democratic theory and the disjuncture between democratic ideals and practice.*

Delli Carpini, Michael X., and Scott Keeter. 1996. What Americans Know About Politics and Why It Matters. New Haven: Yale University Press. *In this detailed examination of the American public's political knowledge, the authors discuss the problems that can exist in a democracy when the vast majority of the public are uninformed and disinterested in the political process.*

Erikson, Robert S., and Kent L. Tedin. 2007. American Public Opinion: Its Origins, Content, and Impact, 7th ed. New York: Pearson Longman. *The authors examine how the public thinks, why they think this way, what kinds of differences exist among Americans with different demographic backgrounds, and what influence public opinion has on public policy.*

Gallup, George, and Saul Forbes Rae. 1940. The Pulse of Democracy. New York: Simon & Schuster. *This is a hopeful account of the processes and promise of polling by perhaps the most important figure behind the development of the polling industry as we know it today. Gallup provides an insightful and candid view of polling in its infancy and with it wonderful insights into the politics of the early days of the New Deal era.*

Key, V. O., Jr. 1961. *Public Opinion and American Democracy.* **New York: Knopf.**   A classic work by one of America's most influential political scientists. Key challenges the conventional wisdom and argues that the public is capable of making tough political decisions.

Lippmann, Walter. 2004 [1922]. *Public Opinion.* **Mineola, N.Y.: Dover Publications.**   A classic work on the theoretical and philosophical issues surrounding public opinion, the public's limited knowledge of government, and how government synthesizes public views into a distilled pro or anti stance for policy purposes.

McClosky, Herbert, and Alida Brill. 1983. *Dimensions of Tolerance: What Americans Believe About Civil Liberties.* **New York: Russell Sage.**   A heavily empirical but engaging analysis of both the mass public's and the elites' support for unpopular minorities.

Page, Benjamin I., and Robert Y. Shapiro. 1992. *The Rational Public: Fifty Years of Trends in Americans' Policy Preferences.* **Chicago: University of Chicago Press.**
A comprehensive examination of American public opinion over time and across various demographic groups. Page and Shapiro argue that—contrary to popular belief—public opinion is quite stable, and when changes do occur, they do so for rational reasons.

Stimson, James A. 1999. *Public Opinion in America: Moods, Cycles, and Swings,* **2nd ed. Boulder: Westview Press.**   This pathbreaking work takes a new approach in public opinion research by constructing an overall measure of the public "mood" for more or less government activism and tracing these changes over the last half of the twentieth century.

Define **Understand** **Practice** **Read** **Click** **Watch**

ABC News/*Washington Post* Polls *abcnews.go.com/US/ PollVault/ and www.washingtonpost.com/wp-dyn/content/politics/ polls/. Analysis of the most recent ABC News/Washington Post polls.*

The Gallup Organization *www.gallup.com. The home page for the world's most famous polling company.*

Los Angeles Times Polls *www.latimes.com/news/custom/time spoll. Descriptions and analyses of polls about current issues and elections.*

New York Times Polls *www.nytimes.com/ref/us/polls_index.html. Analysis of the most recent New York Times polls and surveys.*

Two great sites, **The Pew Research Center for the People and the Press** *(www.people-press.org)* and **Public Agenda** *(www.publicagenda.org),* provide information about polls dealing with a variety of issues.

PollingReport.com *An independent, nonpartisan resource on public opinion trends. Summarizes results from major public opinion surveys, including national and congressional elections.*

The Roper Center for Public Opinion Research *www.roper center.uconn.edu. Provides access to hundreds of public opinion data sets about many current topics.*

World Public Opinion's "Americans and the World Digest" *www.americans-world.org/default.cfm. A repository of U.S. public opinion on issues of international concern ranging from globalization and trade to biotechnology and human rights.*

Chapter 12

Political Parties

▶ What's at Stake?

In spring 2010, pundits said Senate majority leader Harry Reid was a dead man walking. Seen as one of the Democrats' most vulnerable incumbents as the 2010 midterm elections approached, his poll numbers were sinking fast. Reid had done much of the heavy work of getting President Barack Obama's agenda passed through the Senate, and some of those policies, notably the stimulus bill and health care reform, were not popular in his home state of Nevada, where the economic recovery was dragging its feet and unemployment was higher than the national average. Sue Lowden, a Nevada state senator and businesswoman with a moderately conservative record, looked likely to win the Republican primary and the Reid camp was seriously worried that they would lose the election to her in the fall.

But a funny thing happened on the way to November 2. Lowden made some campaign gaffes that spring that caught national attention (suggesting that cash-strapped patients pay their medical bills with chickens through the barter system, for instance). When the dust cleared the day after the Republican primary in June, Tea Party favorite Sharron Angle was the winner by fourteen points, a woman the *New York Times* called "a largely unknown former state lawmaker with 10 grandchildren, whose fondness for weightlifting and for her .44 Magnum won the ardor of the Republican Party base."[1]

Reid's camp took a deep, relieved breath at the reprieve. They knew that if Reid was running as President Obama's surrogate against the economy in hard-hit Nevada he was in serious electoral danger, but running against an ideologically extreme candidate whose positions fell far outside the Nevadan mainstream, he had a fighting chance. They quickly moved to frame Angle's views in a way that voters would find unacceptable.

Down to the Wire
The 2010 race between Nevada senator Harry Reid and Tea Party challenger Sharron Angle, shown here during an October 14, 2010, debate, had Reid fighting for his political life as voters took an anti-incumbent attitude to the polls.

In the primary, Angle's web site had highlighted some of her more controversial positions—support for the privatization of Social Security and Medicare, for a Scientology-based program that would have provided massages to prisoners, for the elimination of the Departments of Education and Energy, for U.S. withdrawal from the United Nations, for unregulated oil drilling within the United States and off its shores, and for the shipping of nuclear waste to Nevada for reprocessing.[2] Those positions appealed strongly to her Tea Party base but were not as popular throughout the state, even among Republicans.

Shortly after her primary win, mention of these positions was scrubbed from her web site.

Reid's campaign, however, had captured the missing pages and published them on a site they called TheRealSharronAngle.com. Angle sent them a cease-and-desist letter claiming Reid was seeking to deceive voters, but after briefly taking down the archived information, Reid's people resurrected it and continued to run an aggressive advertising campaign, painting Angle as a fringe candidate, too conservative for Nevada.[3] Reid began to pull even in the polls, and by July 16 one of them showed him with a seven-point lead.[4]

Reid was not out of danger, but, through no actions of his own, the race had gone from a near-certain loss to one in which he had a fighting chance. Nevada was not an isolated instance. In Kentucky the mainstream candidate for the Republican Senate nomination, who had been backed by Senate minority leader Mitch McConnell, lost to libertarian and Tea Party–backed Rand Paul. In Florida, the Tea Party–favored Marco Rubio defeated moderate governor Charlie Crist in the Republican Senate primary. Both primary results turned what were seen as certain Republican wins to races in which the outcome was up for grabs.

Still, these were heady days for the Tea Partiers. Minnesota representative Michele Bachmann formed a Tea Party Caucus in the House and invited fellow conservatives to join. Some did with enthusiasm, but some mainstream Republicans cringed and analysts pointed out that what were seen as victories for the Tea Party in the Republican primaries of 2010 might not turn into victories for the Republican Party in the longer term, even if they won seats in the anti-incumbent election in November. One article said of the Tea Party fervor that "the tea party movement is a loaded political weapon for Republicans heading into the midterm elections."[5]

Just whom did they think the loaded weapon was pointed at? What is really at stake for a political party in tying its fortunes to its more ideologically extreme members? We will return to these questions after we learn more about just how political parties work. ■

Who wins and who loses in American politics is determined not just by the Constitution but also by more informal rules, and chief among these are the rules produced by the political parties.

---

political gridlock the stalemate that occurs when political rivals, especially parties, refuse to budge from their positions to achieve a compromise in the public interest

political party a group of citizens united by ideology and seeking control of government in order to promote their ideas and policies

---

Americans have always been of two minds about political parties. While partisan passions can burn long and brightly, fueling public service and civic action, we are also cynical about partisan bickering and the *political gridlock*, or stalemate, that can result when rival parties stubbornly refuse to budge from their positions to achieve a compromise in the public interest. Skepticism about political parties, in fact, has been a major feature of American politics since the drafting of the Constitution. When James Madison wrote in *Federalist* No. 10 that "liberty is to faction what air is to fire," he conceded that factions, whether in the form of interest groups or political parties, are a permanent fixture within our representative system, but he hoped to have limited their effects by creating a large republic with many and varied interests. President George Washington echoed Madison's concerns when he warned "against the baneful effects of the spirit of party generally" in his farewell address as president in 1796.

But it was already too late. In the presidential election of 1796, Washington's vice president, John Adams, was backed by the Federalist Party, and his opponent, Thomas Jefferson, was supported by the Democratic-Republicans. The degree to which Madison, as primary author of the Constitution, overestimated the new republic's ability to contain the effects of faction is shown by the fact that the Constitution originally awarded the presidency to the top Electoral College vote-getter, and the vice presidency to the runner-up. In 1796 this meant that Federalist John Adams found himself with Democratic-Republican Jefferson as his vice president. (The Constitution was amended in 1804 to prevent this unhappy partisan consequence from becoming a regular occurrence.) Parties have been entrenched in American politics ever since.

Despite popular disenchantment with political parties and politicians' occasional frustration with them, most political observers and scholars believe that parties are essential to the functioning of democracy in general, and American democracy in particular. Despite Madison's opinion of factions, parties have not damaged the Constitution. They provide an extraconstitutional framework of rules and institutions that enhance the way the Constitution works. Who wins and who loses in American politics is determined not just by the Constitution but also by more informal rules, and chief among these are the rules produced by the political parties.

We can define a *political party* as a group of citizens united under a label who recruit, nominate, and elect candidates for office in order to control the government in accordance with their ideas and policies. In this chapter you will learn more about parties themselves, their role in American politics, their history, and the peculiar nature of American parties. Specifically, you will learn about

- **what political parties are, and whether they live up to our expectations of their role in a democracy**
- **what parties stand for in America, and whether they offer us a choice**
- **the history of political parties in America**
- **how the functions of parties developed in the American context and what they do today—how they conduct two central functions of democratic politics: electioneering and governing**
- **characteristics of the American party system, and how it compares to party systems in other countries**
- **the relationship of citizens to parties, in particular the popular unhappiness with partisanship and parties in the United States**

What Are Political Parties?

Organizations seeking to influence government policy by controlling the apparatus of government

Probably because Madison hoped that they would not thrive, political parties—unlike Congress, the presidency, the Supreme Court, and even the free press—are not mentioned in the Constitution. As we will see, in fact, many of the rules

partisanship loyalty to a political cause or party

party organization the official structure that conducts the political business of parties

party-in-government members of the party who have been elected to serve in government

party-in-the-electorate ordinary citizens who identify with the party

party identification voter affiliation with a political party

that determine the establishment and role of the parties have been created by party members themselves. Although the founding documents of American politics are silent on the place of political parties, keen political observers have long appreciated the fundamental role that political parties play in our system of government.[6] According to one scholar, "Political parties created democracy, and . . . democracy is unthinkable save in terms of parties."[7]

The Role of Parties in a Democracy

Our definition of parties—that they are organizations that seek, under a common banner, to promote their ideas and policies by gaining control of government through the nomination and election of candidates for office—underscores a key difference between parties and interest groups. While both interest groups and parties seek to influence governmental policies, only parties gain this influence by sponsoring candidates in competitive elections. For political parties, winning elections represents a means to the end of controlling democratic government. Parties are crucial to the maintenance of democracy for three reasons:

- *Political linkage.* Parties provide a linkage between voters and elected officials, helping to tell voters what candidates stand for and providing a way for voters to hold their officials accountable for what they do in office, both individually and collectively.

- *Unification of a fragmented government.* Parties help overcome some of the fragmentation in government that comes from separation of powers and federalism. The founders' concern, of course, was to prevent government from becoming too powerful. But so successful were they in dividing up power that without the balancing effect of party to provide some connection between state and national government, for instance, or between the president and Congress, American government might find it very hard to achieve anything at all. Parties can lend this coherence, however, only when they control several branches or several levels of government.

- *A voice for the opposition.* Parties provide an articulate opposition to the ideas and policies of those elected to serve in government. Some citizens and critics may decry the **partisanship**, or taking of political sides, that sometimes seems to be motivated by possibilities for

party gain as much as by principle or public interest. Others, however, see partisanship as providing the necessary antagonistic relationship that, like our adversarial court system, keeps politicians honest and allows the best political ideas and policies to emerge.

To highlight the multiple tasks that parties perform to make democracy work and to make life easier for politicians, political scientists find it useful to divide political parties into three separate components: the party organization, the party-in-government, and the party-in-the-electorate.[8]

Party Organization

The **party organization** is what most people think of as a political party. The party organization represents the system of central committees at the national, state, and local levels. At the top of the Democratic Party organization is the Democratic National Committee, and the Republican National Committee heads the Republican Party. Underneath these national committees are state-level party committees, and below them are county-level party committees, or county equivalents (see Figure 12.1). These party organizations raise money for campaigns, recruit and nominate candidates, organize and facilitate campaigns, register voters, mobilize voters to the polls, conduct party conventions and caucuses, and draft party platforms. This may seem like a lot; however, this is only a fraction of what party organizations do, as we will see at the end of this chapter.

Party-in-Government

The **party-in-government** comprises all the candidates for national, state, and local office who have been elected. The president, as the effective head of his party, the Speaker of the House of Representatives, the majority and minority leaders in the House and the Senate, the party whips in Congress, and state governors are all central actors in the party-in-government, which plays an important role in organizing government and in translating the wishes of the electorate into public policies.

Party-in-the-Electorate

The **party-in-the-electorate** represents ordinary citizens who identify with or have some feeling of attachment to one of the political parties. Public opinion surveys determine **party identification**, or party ID, by asking respondents if they think of themselves as Democrats, Republicans, or independents.

Figure 12.1

Organizational Structure of the Party System

You can see two clear trends in party identification over time in Figure 12.2. Overall, voter attachments to the parties have declined; the percentages identifying as independents increased in the 1960s and the 1970s so that today more people consider themselves independents than identify with either of the political parties. The second trend to note in Figure 12.2 is the loss of the large numerical advantage the Democratic Party had among identifiers in the 1950s so that now the parties are about even.

Most voters who identify with one of the political parties "inherit" their party IDs from their parents, as we suggested in our discussion of political socialization in Chapter 11.[9] Party identifiers generally support the party's basic ideology and policy principles. These policy principles usually relate to each party's stance on the use of government to solve various economic and social problems.

Voters in most states can choose to register their party preferences for the purpose of voting in party primaries (elections to choose candidates for office). These voters are not required to perform any special activities, to contribute money to the political party, or for that matter, even to vote in the primaries. However, while voters do not have a strong formal role to play in the party organization, parties use identifiers as a necessary base of support during elections. In virtually every presidential election, both of the major-party candidates win the votes of an overwhelming percentage of those who identify with their respective parties. But just capturing one's ***party base*** is not sufficient to win a national election since neither party has a majority of the national voters. As we will see later in this chapter, candidates are often pulled between the ideological preferences of their base and the more moderate preferences of independents.

> ***responsible party model*** party government when four
> conditions are met: clear choice of ideologies, candidates pledged
> to implement ideas, party held accountable by voters, and party
> control over members

Figure 12.2

Party Identification, 1952–2008

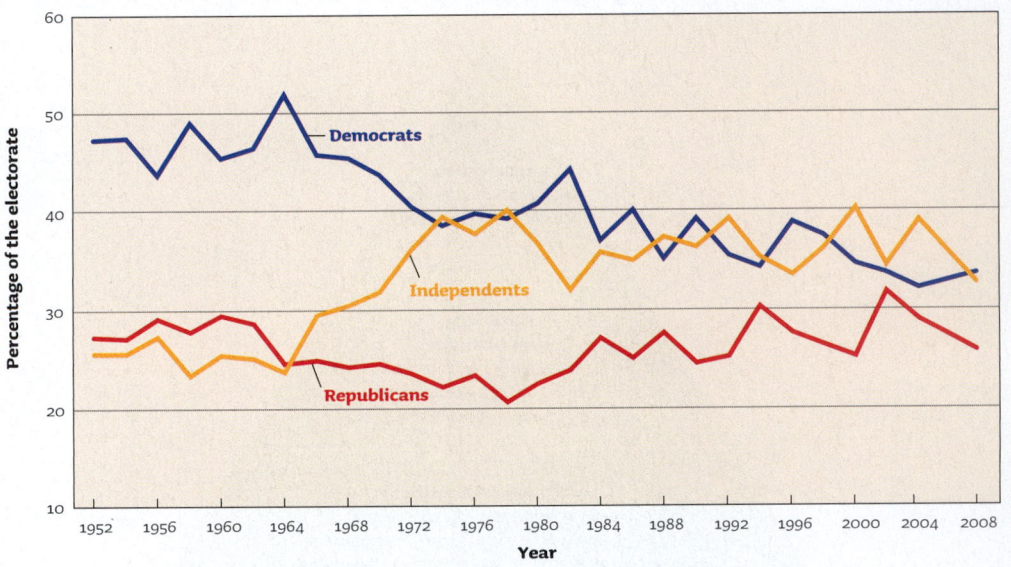

Sources: American National Election Studies, University of Michigan; data made available by the Inter-University Consortium for Political and Social Research.

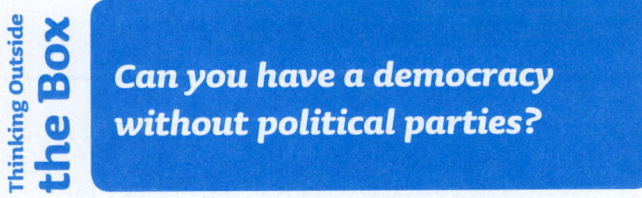

Can you have a democracy without political parties?

The Responsible Party Model

Earlier we said that one of the democratic roles of parties is to provide a link between the voters and elected officials, or, to use the terms we just introduced, between the party-in-the-electorate and the party-in-government. There are many ways in which parties can link voters and officials, but for the link to truly enhance democracy—that is, the control of leaders by citizens—certain conditions have to be met. Political scientists call the fulfillment of these conditions the responsible party model.[10] Under the ***responsible party model:***

- Each party should present a coherent set of programs to the voters, consistent with its ideology and clearly different from those of the other party.

- The candidates for each party should pledge to support their party's platform and to implement their party's program if elected.

- Voters should make their choices based on which party's program most closely reflects their own ideas and hold the parties responsible for unkept promises by voting their members out of office.

- While governing, each party should exercise control over its elected officials to ensure that party officials are promoting and voting for its programs, thereby providing accountability to the voters.

The responsible party model proposes that democracy is strengthened when voters are given clear alternatives and hold the parties responsible for keeping their promises. Voters can, of course, hold officials accountable without the assistance of parties, but it takes a good deal more of their time and attention. Furthermore, several political scientists have noted that while individuals can be held accountable for their own actions, many, if not most, government actions are the product of many officials. Political parties give us a way of holding officials accountable for what they do collectively as well as individually.[11]

Holding Parties Accountable

Continued U.S. military involvement overseas and the growing unpopularity of President George W. Bush were among the reasons Democrats swept back into the majority in the 2006 midterm elections after twelve years out of power, making Nancy Pelosi the first woman Speaker of the House. What goes around in politics comes around, however, and in 2010, anger over a stubborn recession returned Republicans to the majority in the House.

The responsible party model—which fits some systems, such as Great Britain, quite well—has been used by political scientists in the past to critique the American parties, which during the middle decades of the twentieth century were seen as too unfocused and undisciplined.[12] Changes in our system over the past twenty years or so have brought the American parties closer to a responsible parties system—especially in the distinctive policy programs the parties have come to represent. Almost inevitably, however, in practice the American system falls short of the idealized model. Voters do not fit the responsible party model well; they do not vote solely on party or issues, relying on other considerations like candidate experience and personality. In addition, the legislative link breaks down because legislators have to respond to their constituents' interests or risk getting voted out of office; congressional party loyalty will not be perfect on every issue. So, for example, Senators Olympia Snowe and Susan Collins of Maine and Senator Scott Brown of Massachusetts, whose constituents are more liberal than are those of most other Republican senators, must occasionally break ranks to vote

with the Democrats to keep their northeastern constituents happy. Even though it doesn't fit the American case perfectly, the responsible party model is valuable because it underscores the importance of voters holding the parties accountable for governing, and it provides a useful yardstick for understanding fundamental changes in the U.S. two-party system.

Political parties seek to control government and to promote their ideologies and policies. They do this by creating rules that allow them to control the nomination, campaign, and election processes and by trying to control the actions of their members elected to office. Politicians obviously have something at stake here, too. Parties provide a mechanism that helps them get nominated for office, win elections, and run government—but winning requires the support of nonparty members as well.

Who What How

American citizens also have a big stake in what political parties do. Parties provide a link between citizens and government, cohesion among levels and branches of government, and an articulate opposition to government policy.

Do American Parties Offer Voters a Choice?

The party base and the general electorate as countervailing forces on a party's issue positions

A key feature of the responsible party model is that the parties should offer voters a choice between different visions of how government should operate. Barry Goldwater, the 1964 Republican presidential nominee, stated this more bluntly: political parties, he said, should offer "a choice, not an echo." Offering voters a choice is the primary means through which parties make representative democracy work. In America the policy differences between the two major parties, the Democrats and the Republicans (often also called the GOP for "Grand Old Party"), are narrower than in some democracies around the world, particularly those with many parties spread across the ideological spectrum. Increasingly, however, voters do see clear policy choices between the Democratic and Republican Parties.[13] In this section we investigate what the two major parties stand for, including competing forces that draw the parties apart to ideologically distinct positions, and push them together to take more moderate stances.

What Do the Parties Stand For?

Although it may seem to voters that members of the two parties are not very different once they are elected to office, the parties can be considered quite distinct in three areas: their ideologies, their memberships, and the policies they stand for.

Party Ideology

Each major party represents a different ideological perspective about the way that government should be used to solve problems. Ideologies, as we have said before, are broad sets of ideas about politics that help to organize our views of the political world, the information that regularly bombards us, and the positions we take on various issues. As we saw in Chapter 2, liberalism and conservatism today are ideologies that divide the country sharply over issues such as the role of government in the economy, in society, and in citizens' private lives. In general, conservatives look to government to provide social and moral order, but they want the economy to remain as unfettered as possible in the distribution of material resources. Liberals encourage government action to solve economic and social problems but want government to stay out of their personal, religious, and moral lives, except as a protector of their basic rights.

At least since the New Deal of the 1930s, the Democratic Party, especially outside the South, has been aligned with a liberal ideology and the Republican Party with a conservative perspective.[14] Since the 1960s the parties have become more consistent internally with respect to their ideologies. The most conservative region in the country is the South, but because of lingering resentment of the Republican Party for its role in the Civil War, the South was for decades tied tightly to the Democratic Party. In the 1960s, however, conservative southern Democratic voters began to vote for the Republican Party, and formerly Democratic politicians were switching their allegiances as well. By the 1990s the South had become predominantly Republican. This swing made the Democratic Party more consistently liberal and the Republicans more consistently conservative. To illustrate, so-called "consistents," liberal Democrats and conservative Republicans, made up only 33 percent of party identifiers in 1977, while "inconsistents," conservative Democrats and liberal Republicans, made up 21 percent. Consistency between party ideology and beliefs of party members has increased over the years so that, by 2009, consistents made up 49 percent of party identifiers while inconsistents made up only 10 percent.[15]

This greater alignment of party and ideology gives the party activist bases more power within each party because they do not have to do battle with people of different ideological persuasions. The stronger activist core is able to exert more internal pressure within the parties, nominating candidates through primaries but also calling for ideological conformity in the parties in Congress. The Tea Party example with which we opened the chapter is a case in point. That is not to say, however, that all Democrats think the same or that all Republicans think the same. Each party has its ideological and moderate factions, but the divisions within the parties are much smaller today.[16] Table 12.1 shows how party ID matches up with a number of issue positions.

Party Membership

Party ideologies attract and are reinforced by different coalitions of voters. This means that the Democrats' post–New Deal liberal ideology reflects the preferences of its coalition of working- and lower-class voters, including union members, minorities, women, the elderly, and urban dwellers. The Republicans' conservative ideology, on the other hand, reflects the preferences of upper- to middle-class whites, those who are in evangelical and Protestant religions, and suburban voters. Table 12.2 shows how each party's coalition differs based on group characteristics. There is nothing inevitable about these coalitions, however, and they are subject to change as the parties' stances on issues change and as the opposing party offers new alternatives. Differences between men and women used to be insignificant, but the gender gap has grown and endured as the parties have taken contrasting positions on a series of issues on which men and women tend to feel differently (see discussion of the gender gap in Chapter 11).

Policy Differences Between the Parties

When the parties run slates of candidates for office, those candidates run on a **party platform**—a list of policy positions the party endorses and pledges its elected officials to enact as policy. A platform is the national party's campaign promises, usually made only in a presidential election year. If the parties are to make a difference politically, then the platforms have to reflect substantial differences that are consistent with their ideologies. The responsible party model requires that the parties offer distinct platforms, that voters know about them and vote on the basis of them, and that the parties ensure that their elected officials follow through in implementing them.

The two major parties' stated positions on some key issues from their 2008 platforms appear in "*Consider the Source:*

Table 12.1

Party Identification and Issue Positions, 2008

Issue position	Democrats	Independents	Republicans
Ideological self-identification			
Liberal	54%	25%	4%
Moderate	28	42	13
Conservative	17	32	82
Gay marriage			
Agree gays and lesbians should be allowed to marry	47	45	18
Health care policy			
Government should provide health insurance for all	62	54	22
Defense spending			
Defense spending should be increased	34	41	60
Abortion			
By law, a woman should always be able to obtain an abortion as a matter of personal choice	51	42	26
Social spending			
Prefer more services in health and education even if it means an increase in spending	68	51	24
Torture			
Favor use of torture for suspected terrorists to try to get information	16	26	34

Source: Calculated by the authors from the 2008 National Election Studies data set; data made available by the Inter-University Consortium for Political and Social Research at the University of Michigan.

Note: Compare across columns. For example, 54 percent of Democrats compared to only 4 percent of Republicans considered themselves liberal.

Table 12.2

Party Identification by Groups

Social groups	Democrats	Independents	Republicans	Party Difference
Religious group				
Protestants	30%	28%	42%	−12%
Catholics	38	35	27	+11
Jews	70	10	20	+50
Other	44	36	20	+24
Sex				
Men	31	41	28	+3
Women	42	31	27	+15
Race/ethnicity				
Whites	29	37	34	−5
Blacks	72	25	3	+69
Hispanics	51	35	14	+37
Asians	31	49	20	+11
Household income				
Less than $35,000	43	39	18	+25
$35,000–89,999	35	38	27	+8
$90,000+	27	25	48	−21

Sources: Calculated by the authors from the 2008 National Election Studies data set. The figures for Asians are based on the 2004–2008 surveys for enough cases for a reliable estimate.

Note: In each row, the cell entries for the three party identifications sum to 100 percent. For example, 30 percent of the Protestants are Democrats, 28 percent are independents, and 42 percent are Republicans. The figures in the last column show the relative partisan balance for each group, with positive values indicating more Democrats among that group.

Think of it as an invitation to a party—so to speak. In their platforms, political parties make a broad statement about who they are and what they stand for in the hope that you will decide to join them. The excerpts below from the Democratic and Republican platforms of 2008 show differing positions on several key issues. The full text of these platforms can be found on the web sites of the parties' national committees. When you read a party's platform, keep these questions in mind:

1. **Whose platform is it, and what do you know about that party's basic political positions?** Understanding the basics will help you to interpret key phrases. For instance, how might the terms *family values* and *religious freedom* be defined differently in the Democratic and Republican platforms?

2. **Who is the audience?** Parties direct their platforms to two different groups—the party faithful and potential new supporters. For example, Democrats want to keep their traditional supporters, like union members, but they also want to broaden their appeal to the middle class and to small-business owners. Republicans want to keep their base (including pro-life activists) happy but also want to attract more women in an effort to close the gender gap. How does this dual audience affect how parties portray themselves?

3. **Which statements reflect values, and which are statements of fact?** First, get clear about the values you are being asked to support. Parties tend to sprinkle their platforms liberally with terms like *fundamental rights*. Everybody is in favor of fundamental rights. Which ones do they actually mean, and do you consider them fundamental rights? What are the costs and benefits of agreeing to their value claims? Then evaluate the facts. Are they accurate? Check out statistics. Do they seem reasonable? If not, look them up.

4. **Do you think the party can deliver on its policy proposals?** What resources (money, power, and so on) would it need? Can it get them? Would enacting the promised policies achieve what the party claims it would? Who would win, and who would lose?

5. **What is your reaction to the platform?** Could you support it? How does it fit with your personal values and political beliefs? Is the appeal of this platform emotional? Intellectual? Ideological? Moral? Remember that party platforms are not just statements of party principles and policy proposals; they are also advertisements. Read them with all the caution and suspicion you would bring to bear on any other ad that attempts to convince you to buy, or buy into, something. *Caveat emptor!* (Let the buyer beware!)

Democratic Platform

Adopted by the Democratic National Committee

August 25, 2008

Affirmative Action: Democrats will fight to end discrimination based on race, sex, ethnicity, national origin, language, religion, sexual orientation, gender identity, age, and disability in every corner of our country, because that's the America we believe in. . . . We support affirmative action, including in federal contracting and higher education, to make sure that those locked out of the doors of opportunity will be able to walk through those doors in the future.

Gay Rights: We support the full inclusion of all families, including same-sex couples, in the life of our nation, and support equal responsibility, benefits, and protections. We will enact a comprehensive bipartisan employment non-discrimination act. We oppose the Defense of Marriage Act and all attempts to use this issue to divide us.

Republican Platform

Adopted by the Republican National Committee

September 1, 2008

Affirmative Action & Civil Rights: We consider discrimination based on sex, race, age, religion, creed, disability, or national origin to be immoral, and we will strongly enforce anti-discrimination statutes. As a matter of principle, Republicans oppose any attempts to create race-based governments within the United States. Precisely because we oppose discrimination, we reject preferences, quotas, and set-asides, whether in education or in corporate boardrooms.

Gay Rights: We call for a constitutional amendment that fully protects marriage as a union of a man and a woman, so that judges cannot make other arrangements equivalent to it. In the absence of a national amendment, we support the right of the people of the various states to affirm traditional marriage through state initiatives.

Abortion: The Democratic Party strongly and unequivocally supports *Roe v. Wade* and a woman's right to choose a safe and legal abortion, regardless of ability to pay, and we oppose any and all efforts to weaken or undermine that right. The Democratic Party also strongly supports access to comprehensive affordable family planning services and age-appropriate sex education which empower people to make informed choices and live healthy lives.

Gun Control: We recognize that the right to bear arms is an important part of the American tradition, and we will preserve Americans' Second Amendment right to own and use firearms. We believe that the right to own firearms is subject to reasonable regulation . . . like closing the gun show loophole, improving our background check system, and reinstating the assault weapons ban. . . .

Iraq/War on Terror: The central front in the war on terror is not Iraq, and it never was. We will defeat al Qaeda in Afghanistan and Pakistan, where those who actually attacked us on 9-11 reside and are resurgent. . . . We must first bring the Iraq war to a responsible end.

Taxes: We will eliminate all federal income taxes for seniors making less than $50,000 per year. . . . We will exempt all start-up companies from capital gains taxes and provide them a tax credit for health insurance. . . . We will not increase taxes on any family earning under $250,000 and we will offer additional tax cuts for middle class families. For families making more than $250,000, we'll ask them to give back a portion of the Bush tax cuts to invest in health care and other key priorities.

Energy Policy/Climate Change: The energy threat we face today may be less immediate than threats from dictators, but it is as real and as dangerous. We know we can't drill our way to energy independence . . . we will invest in advanced energy technologies, to build the clean energy economy and create millions of new, good "Green Collar" American jobs . . . we will call on businesses, government, and the American people to make America 50 percent more energy efficient by 2030. . . . We will implement a market-based cap and trade system to reduce carbon emissions . . . to lower the price of gasoline, we will crack down on speculators who are driving up prices beyond the natural market rate.

Abortion: We assert the inherent dignity and sanctity of all human life and affirm that the unborn child has a fundamental individual right to life which cannot be infringed. We support a human life amendment to the Constitution, and we endorse legislation to make clear that the Fourteenth Amendment's protections apply to unborn children.

Gun Control: We uphold the right of individual Americans to own firearms, a right which antedated the Constitution and was solemnly confirmed by the Second Amendment. We call for education in constitutional rights in schools, and we support the option of firearms training in federal programs serving senior citizens and women. Gun ownership is responsible citizenship, enabling Americans to defend themselves, their property, and communities.

Iraq/War on Terror: A stable, unified, and democratic Iraqi nation is within reach. Our success in Iraq will deny al Qaeda a safe haven, limit Iranian influence in the Middle East, strengthen moderate forces there, and give us a strategic ally in the struggle against extremism. That outcome is too critical to our own national security to be jeopardized by artificial or politically inspired timetables that neither reflect conditions on the ground nor respect the essential advice of our military commanders. . . .

Taxes: Sound tax policy alone may not ensure economic success, but terrible tax policy does guarantee economic failure. . . . Along with making the 2001 and 2003 tax cuts permanent. . . . Republicans will lower [the American family's tax burden by] doubling the exemption for dependents . . . we support a major reduction in the corporate tax rate . . . we support a plan to encourage employers to offer automatic enrollment in tax deferred savings programs.

Energy Policy: Our current dependence on foreign fossil fuels threatens both our national security and our economy and could also force drastic changes in the way we live. We must aggressively increase our nation's energy supply, in an environmentally responsible way, and do so through a comprehensive strategy that meets both short and long term needs. . . . We support accelerated exploration, drilling and development in America. . . . Alternate power sources must enter the mainstream. . . . While we grow our supplies, we must also reduce our demand—not by changing our lifestyles but by putting the free market to work and taking advantage of technological breakthroughs.

Source: John T. Woolley and Gerhard Peters, *The American Presidency Project* (online), Santa Barbara: University of California (hosted), Gerhard Peters (database). Available from www.presidency.ucsb.edu/ws/?pid=78283.

party activists the "party faithful"; the rank-and-file members who actually carry out the party's electioneering efforts

Don't Be Fooled by Political Party Platforms." These differences between the Democratic and Republican platforms in 2008 are typical, and they are what make it possible for the electorate to bring about meaningful policy changes. When the parties' programs are clearly different, electing a new majority party to Congress can result in substantial changes in the policy directions pursued by the national government. That is, party differences are necessary for popular control of the overall directions of government policy.

Forces Drawing the Parties Apart and Pushing Them Together

Political parties in our system have a dilemma—how to keep the core ideological base satisfied while appealing to enough more moderate voters that they can win elections in diverse constituencies. In a small, homogenous district this is not likely to be a problem. Conservative Republicans and liberal Democrats can be nominated and elected and party members are happy. As constituencies get larger and more diverse, parties have a choice. They can be moderate and win elections, or stay ideologically pure and lose. In other words, there are internal forces that draw the parties away from each other, to the opposite ends of the ideological spectrum, but external, electoral forces can push them together. These forces are central to understanding electoral politics in America today. In this section we look more closely at these complex relationships.

The Pull Toward Extremism

As we have seen so far in this chapter, there are major forces within the parties that keep them distinct: the need to placate party activists, to raise money, and to keep the candidates true to their own beliefs as well as to those of their base. On key issues, although presidents seek to portray their proposals as serving the interests of the general public, in fact the specific policy solutions are almost always consistent with their party's ideological perspective and policy agenda.

The main players in political parties are often called the "party faithful," or ***party activists***, people who are especially committed to the values and policies of the party, and who devote more of their resources, in both time and money, to the party's cause. The activists are part of the party base, but their support for the party goes beyond simply voting. They also volunteer their time, donate their money, and stay actively involved in party politics. Although these party activists are not an official organ of the party, they represent a party's lifeblood. Compared to the average voter, party activists tend to be more

ideologically extreme (more conservative or more liberal even than the average party identifier) and to care more intensely about the party's issues. Their influence can have significant effects on the ideological character of both parties.[17]

Party activists play a key role in keeping the parties ideologically distinct because one of the primary goals of their participation and support is to ensure that the party advocates their issue positions. Because they tend to be concerned with keeping the party pure, they can be reluctant to compromise on their issues,[18] although they also care a great deal about winning.[19] Liberal activists kept the Democratic Party to the left of most Americans during the 1970s and 1980s; the only Democratic candidate who won a presidential election during that time was Jimmy Carter, in the immediate aftermath of the Watergate scandal that drove Republican Richard Nixon from office. Republicans sought to keep alive the impression that the Democrats were a party of crazed left-wing activists in 1988 by making *liberal*, or "the L-word" as they referred to it, such a derogatory term that Democrats would not use it to describe themselves for fear of turning off voters. The Democratic Party dealt with this problem by restructuring its internal politics and giving more weight to moderates like Bill Clinton and Al Gore. The Republicans got caught in the same trap of appearing to be as conservative as their most activist members in the religious right and, later, in the Tea Party.

The need to please party activists gives candidates a powerful incentive to remain true to the party's causes. Activists are poised to work hard for candidates who promote their political, social, economic, or religious agendas and, conversely, to work just as hard against any candidate who does not pass their litmus test.[20] This means that candidates who moderate too much or too often risk alienating the activists who are a key component of their success. For instance, John McCain, in his primary race to become the 2008 Republican presidential nominee, was seen as an outsider by many of the Republican base and was not able to generate the enthusiasm and contributions he probably would have received if he had been consistently appealing to the party base over the years. His pick of Sarah Palin as his running mate went some way to healing that breach, but at the cost of alienating many voters in the middle of the ideological spectrum.

Active support and contributions by those with strong ideological policy preferences help to keep candidates from converging to the ideological position of the moderate voter (see Figure 12.3, bottom). Thus the likely winner of most Democratic primaries is going to be more liberal than the

Figure 12.3

External and Internal Forces on the Parties

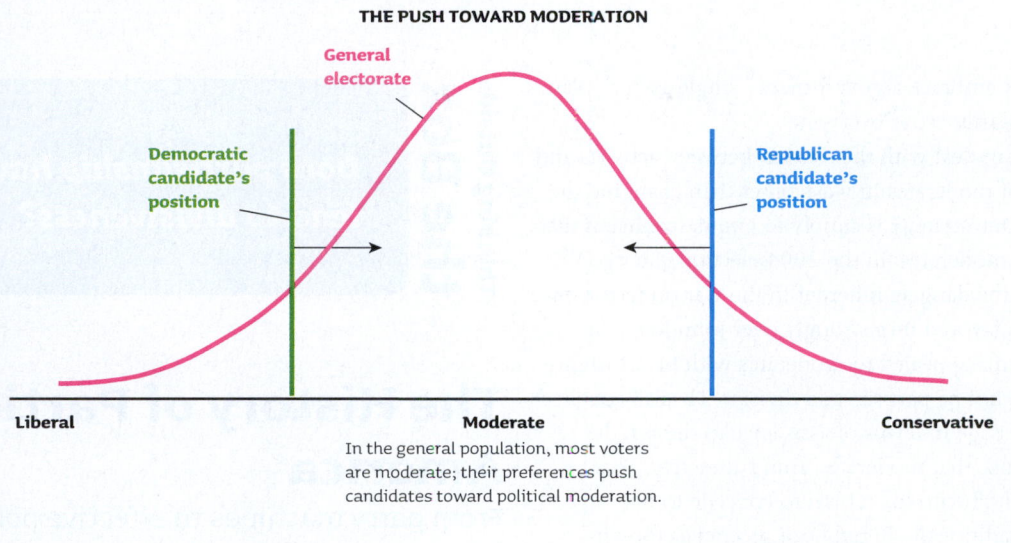

THE PUSH TOWARD MODERATION

General electorate

Democratic candidate's position

Republican candidate's position

Liberal　　　　　　　　Moderate　　　　　　　　Conservative

In the general population, most voters are moderate; their preferences push candidates toward political moderation.

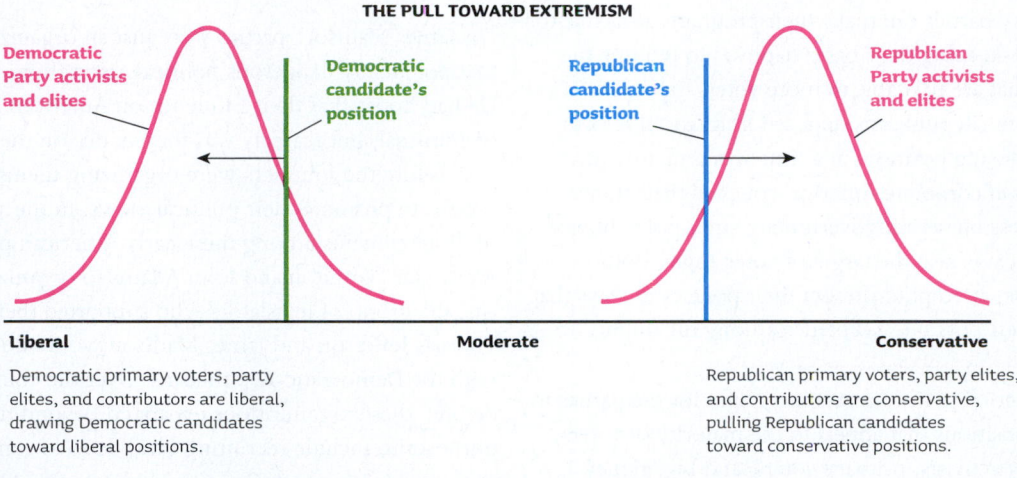

THE PULL TOWARD EXTREMISM

Democratic Party activists and elites

Democratic candidate's position

Republican candidate's position

Republican Party activists and elites

Liberal　　　　　　　　Moderate　　　　　　　　Conservative

Democratic primary voters, party elites, and contributors are liberal, drawing Democratic candidates toward liberal positions.

Republican primary voters, party elites, and contributors are conservative, pulling Republican candidates toward conservative positions.

average voter in the general election, and the likely winner of most Republican primaries will be more conservative. Even though candidates do win some votes by taking more moderate stands, they are nevertheless mindful of their bases and tend not to stray very far from their roots once in office.[21] This means that few politicians are willing to be truly moderate and work with the other side. Since the 1980s, an increased ideological polarization between the parties has yielded more intense partisan conflict and sometimes policy gridlock.

The Push Toward Moderation

Ideological purists do not always win the day, however. Obviously, if a candidate is going to win an election, he or she must appeal to more voters than does the opposing candidate.

On any policy or set of policies, voters' opinions range from very liberal to very conservative; however, in the American two-party system, most voters tend to be in the middle, holding a moderate position between the two ideological extremes (see Figure 12.3, top, on this page). In diverse districts, the party that appeals best to the moderate and independent voters usually wins most of the votes. Thus, even though the ideologies of the parties are distinct, the pressures related to winning a majority of votes can lead both parties to campaign on the same issue positions, thus making them look similar to voters.[22] As a result, at various times the Republicans moved from their initial opposition to join the majority of voters in supporting Social Security, Medicare, and Medicaid. Similarly, the Democrats, while wanting to expand health care coverage, did not embrace a government "single-payer" plan that would necessarily cover everyone.

The parties can deal with the tension between activists and the larger body of moderates in ways other than changing the party positions. One strategy is simply to emphasize issues that are popular with moderates. In the 2004 election, George W. Bush focused on the dangers inherent in the war on terror, on which moderates favored him strongly over John Kerry. In 2008 Barack Obama appealed to moderates with his insistence that politics need not be partisan and divisive. He also couched his economic message in terms of assistance to the middle class, another stance that moderates found attractive. That approach, combined with his refusal to concede to his opponent such traditionally Republican ground as foreign policy and national security, helped him win the election.

Another way parties can make their programs attractive to moderates while keeping their bases happy is to reframe the issues in ways that are palatable to more voters. In the 2010 midterm elections, Republicans opposed to financial reform and regulation, losing positions at a time when many Americans were angry at corporate America, couched their stance not as probusiness but as antigovernment, since polls showed that government was also the target of voter anger. Both parties, of course, attempt to present their policies in ways that will get the widest possible acceptance among the public.

Who What How

The rules of electoral politics create incentives for the parties to take moderate positions that appeal to the majority of voters, but party activists, primary voters, and big-money donors, who tend to be more ideological and issue oriented, push party policy agendas back toward their extremes. As a consequence, parties and their candidates tend to remain true to their respective party's ideological perspective, promoting policy solutions that are consistent with the party's ideology. Thus Democratic candidates espouse a policy agenda that reflects the liberal interests of the coalition of groups that represent their most ardent supporters. Likewise, Republican candidates advocate a policy agenda that reflects the conservative interests of the coalition of groups that are their most ardent supporters. In this way, both parties, in most elections, offer voters "a choice, not an echo," but they also contribute to the growing partisanship of American politics. The real losers in this situation may be the party moderates and independents who, less intense and active than the party base, find themselves poorly represented at the end of the day.[23]

party machines   mass-based party systems in which parties provided services and resources to voters in exchange for votes

Thinking Outside the Box

Does partisanship have to lead to divisiveness?

The History of Parties in America
From party machines to effective political organizations

For James Madison, parties were just an organized version of that potentially dangerous political association, the faction. He had hopes that their influence on American politics would be minimal, but scarcely was the ink dry on the Constitution before the founders were organizing themselves into groups to promote their political views. In the 1790s a host of disagreements among these early American politicians led Alexander Hamilton and John Adams to organize the Federalists, the group of legislators who supported their views. Later, Thomas Jefferson and James Madison would do the same with the Democratic-Republicans. Over the course of the next decade, these organizations expanded beyond their legislative purposes to include recruiting candidates to run as members of their party for both Congress and the presidency. The primary focus, however, was on the party-in-government and not on the voters.[24]

The Evolution of American Parties

The history of political parties in the United States is dominated by ambitious politicians who have shaped their parties in order to achieve their goals.[25] Chief among those goals, as we have seen, are getting elected to office and running government once there. In 1828 Martin Van Buren and Andrew Jackson turned the Democratic Party away from a focus on the party-in-government, creating the country's first mass-based party and setting the stage for the development of the voter-oriented party machine. *Party machines* were tightly organized party systems at the state, city, and county levels that kept control of voters by getting them jobs, helping them out financially when necessary, and in fact becoming part of their

party bosses party leaders, usually in an urban district, who exercised tight control over electioneering and patronage

patronage system in which successful party candidates reward supporters with jobs or favors

party primary nomination of party candidates by registered party members rather than party bosses

party eras extended periods of relative political stability in which one party tends to control both the presidency and Congress

critical election an election signaling a significant change in popular allegiance from one party to another

realignment substantial and long-term shift in party allegiance by individuals and groups, usually resulting in a change in policy direction

lives and their communities. This mass organization was built around one principal goal: taking advantage of the expansion of voting rights to all white men (even those without property) to elect more Democratic candidates.[26]

The Jacksonian Democrats enacted a number of party and governmental reforms designed to enhance the control of party leaders, known as **party bosses**, over the candidates, the officeholders, and the campaigns. During the nomination process the party bosses would choose the party's candidates for the general election. The most common means for selecting candidates was the party caucus, a special meeting of hand-picked party leaders who appointed the party's nominees. Any candidate seeking elective office (and most offices were elective) would have to win the boss's approval by pledging his loyalty to the party boss and supporting policies that the party boss favored.

Winning candidates were expected to hire only other party supporters for government positions and reward only party supporters with government contracts. This largesse expanded the range of people with a stake in the party's electoral success. The combination of candidates and people who had been given government jobs and contracts meant that the party had an army of supporters to help recruit and mobilize voters to support the party. Moreover, because party bosses controlled the nomination process, any candidate who won elective office but did not fulfill his pledges to the party boss would be replaced by someone who would. This system of **patronage**, which we discussed in Chapter 9, on bureaucracy, rewarded faithful party supporters with public office, jobs, and government contracts and ensured that a party's candidates were loyal to the party or at least to the party bosses.

Because the Democratic Party machine was so effective at getting votes and controlling government, the Whig Party (1830s through 1850s), and later the Republican Party (starting in the mid-1850s), used these same techniques to organize. Party bosses and their party machines were exceptionally strong in urban areas in the East and Midwest. The urban machines, while designed to further the interests of the parties themselves, had the important democratic consequence of integrating into the political process the masses of new immigrants

coming into the urban centers at the turn of the twentieth century. Because parties were so effective at mobilizing voters, the average participation rate exceeded 80 percent in most U.S. elections prior to the 1900s.

However, the strength of these party machines was also their weakness. In many cases, parties would do almost anything to win, including directly buying the votes of people, mobilizing new immigrants who could not speak English, and resurrecting dead people from their graves to vote in the elections. In addition, the whole system of patronage, based on doling out government jobs, contracts, and favors, came under attack by reformers in the early 1900s as representing favoritism and corruption. Political reforms such as the **party primary**, in which the party-in-the-electorate rather than the party bosses chose between competing party candidates for a party's nomination, and civil service reform, under which government jobs were filled on the basis of merit instead of party loyalty, did much to ensure that party machines went the way of the dinosaur.

"THAT'S WHAT'S THE MATTER."

BOSS TWEED. "As long as I count the Votes, what are you going to do about it? say?"

Figure 12.4

A Brief History of Party Eras

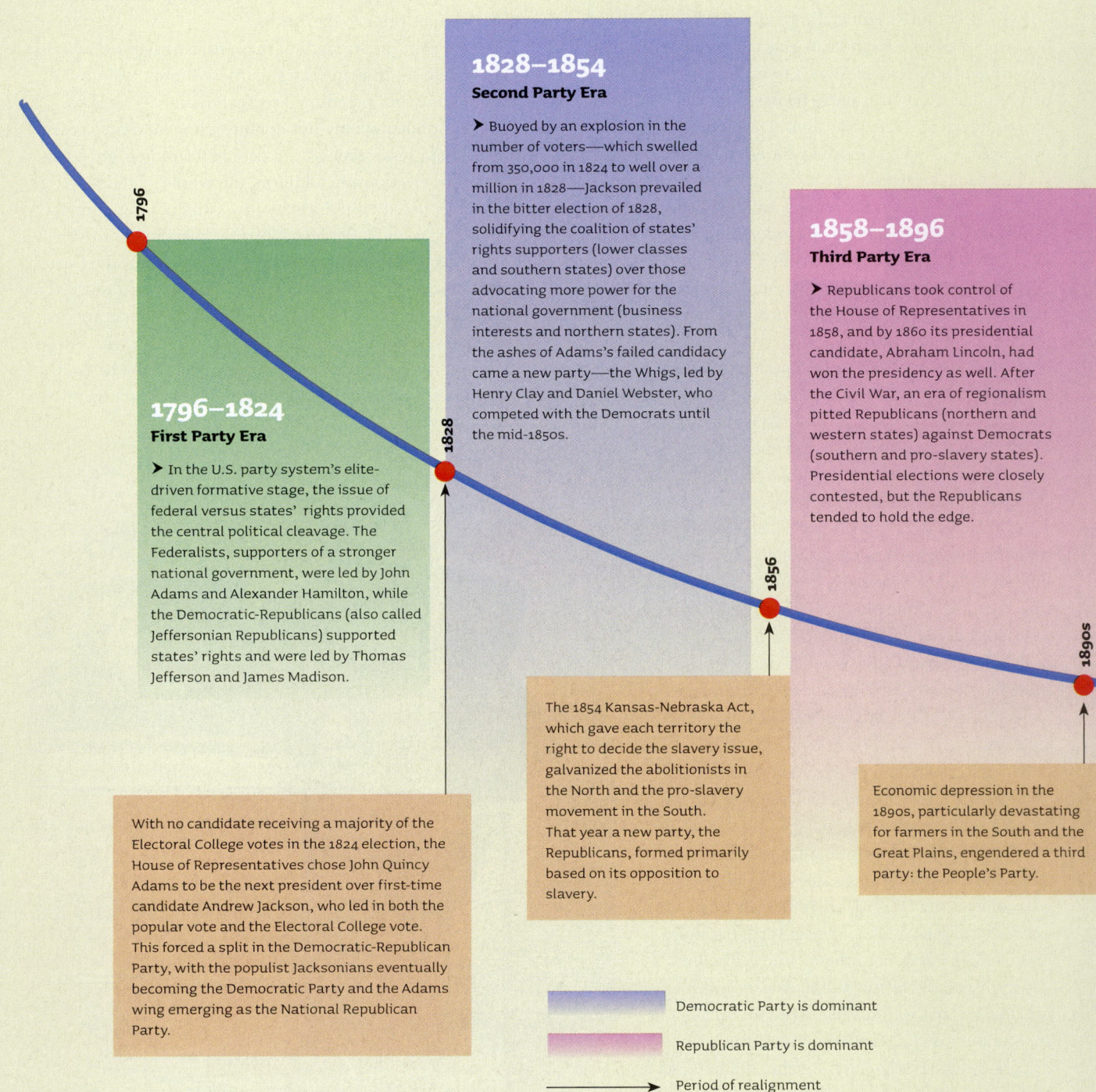

1828–1854
Second Party Era

➤ Buoyed by an explosion in the number of voters—which swelled from 350,000 in 1824 to well over a million in 1828—Jackson prevailed in the bitter election of 1828, solidifying the coalition of states' rights supporters (lower classes and southern states) over those advocating more power for the national government (business interests and northern states). From the ashes of Adams's failed candidacy came a new party—the Whigs, led by Henry Clay and Daniel Webster, who competed with the Democrats until the mid-1850s.

1858–1896
Third Party Era

➤ Republicans took control of the House of Representatives in 1858, and by 1860 its presidential candidate, Abraham Lincoln, had won the presidency as well. After the Civil War, an era of regionalism pitted Republicans (northern and western states) against Democrats (southern and pro-slavery states). Presidential elections were closely contested, but the Republicans tended to hold the edge.

1796–1824
First Party Era

➤ In the U.S. party system's elite-driven formative stage, the issue of federal versus states' rights provided the central political cleavage. The Federalists, supporters of a stronger national government, were led by John Adams and Alexander Hamilton, while the Democratic-Republicans (also called Jeffersonian Republicans) supported states' rights and were led by Thomas Jefferson and James Madison.

1796

1828

1856

1890s

With no candidate receiving a majority of the Electoral College votes in the 1824 election, the House of Representatives chose John Quincy Adams to be the next president over first-time candidate Andrew Jackson, who led in both the popular vote and the Electoral College vote. This forced a split in the Democratic-Republican Party, with the populist Jacksonians eventually becoming the Democratic Party and the Adams wing emerging as the National Republican Party.

The 1854 Kansas-Nebraska Act, which gave each territory the right to decide the slavery issue, galvanized the abolitionists in the North and the pro-slavery movement in the South. That year a new party, the Republicans, formed primarily based on its opposition to slavery.

Economic depression in the 1890s, particularly devastating for farmers in the South and the Great Plains, engendered a third party: the People's Party.

Democratic Party is dominant

Republican Party is dominant

⟶ Period of realignment

1896–1928
Fourth Party Era

➤ Although William Jennings Bryan, a Nebraska Democrat, attempted to merge the Democratic Party with the People's Party in the presidential elections of 1896, he failed to amass enough farmers and industrial labor voters to win. The splitting of votes between the People's Party and the Democrats strengthened the Republican Party. As economic issues subsided in the late 1890s, the regional bases of Republicans and Democrats intensified.

1896

1932–1964
Fifth Party Era

➤ The coalition of voters supporting the New Deal included southern Democrats, Catholic immigrants, blue collar workers, and farmers. Republicans maintained support among business owners and industrialists, and strengthened their regional support in the Northeast and Plains states.

1932

1968–2010
Sixth Party Era?

➤ While there is much controversy about whether we have entered a new partisan era at all, and no single critical election has marked the realignment, incremental changes have occurred that are large and so far long-lasting. A realigning process has mobilized African Americans and other minorities into the Democratic Party and southern whites into the Republican Party, creating a greater consistency between partisanship and ideological and issue preferences. The current era is characterized by a narrowly divided nation, intense party competition, and increased gridlock in government.

2010

1968

The stock market crash of 1929 led to the Great Depression, which produced massive unemployment, property foreclosures, and bank failings. Desperate people looked to the federal government for relief, and in 1932 Franklin Roosevelt and the Democrats' New Deal campaign swept the Republicans out of office.

Republicans became identified with a conservative position during the civil rights era of the 1950s and 1960s. Democrats championed minority, women's, and gay rights and other liberal issues from the 1970s through the 1990s.

Continued realignment

Analysts debate whether this period of highly competitive parties is one of transition to a new party era, or whether it is its own era, breaking with the patterns of clear party dominance that have defined such periods in the past.

> **dealignment**   a trend among voters to identify themselves as independents rather than as members of a major party

A Brief History of Party Eras

A striking feature of American history is that, while we have not had a revolutionary war in America since 1776, we have several times changed our political course in rather dramatic ways. One of the many advantages of a democratic form of government is that dramatic changes in policy direction can be effected through the ballot box rather than through bloody revolution. Over the course of two centuries, the two-party system in the United States has been marked by twenty-five- to forty-year periods of relative stability, with one party tending to maintain a majority of congressional seats and controlling the presidency. These periods of stability are called **party eras**. Short periods of large-scale change—peaceful revolutions, as it were, signaled by one major **critical election** in which the majority of people shift their political allegiance from one party to another—mark the end of one party era and the beginning of another. Scholars call such a shift in party dominance a **realignment**. In these realignments the coalitions of groups supporting each of the parties change to a new alignment of groups. Though it is not always the case, realignments generally result in parallel changes in governmental policies, reflecting the policy agenda of each party's new coalition. Realignments have been precipitated by major critical events like the Civil War and the Great Depression. Sometimes decisive realignments are not apparent, but rather the old period of stability gradually breaks down without a critical precipitating event in a period of **dealignment**, slowly re-forming into a new and different party era. The United States has gone through six party eras in its two-hundred-years-plus history. The timeline in Figure 12.4 summarizes the six party eras and the realigning elections associated with the transitions between them.

The Parties Today

As Figure 12.4 indicates, the New Deal coalition supporting the Fifth Party Era has changed, but no single critical election has marked a clear realignment. Rather, a dealigning process has occurred that includes the massive migration of white southerners to the Republican Party and the less massive but still notable trend for Catholics to be less solidly Democratic than they were at the formation of the New Deal. Similarly, African Americans have shifted from somewhat favoring the Democratic Party to overwhelming Democratic identification, a trend solidified with Barack Obama's nomination as the Democratic candidate for the presidency in 2008. The geographic bases of the parties have also changed: the South used to be referred to as the "Solid South," meaning solidly Democratic; it is now the most dependable region for the Republican Party in presidential elections (see Figure 12.5). In recent elections, Democrats have been more likely to win in New England and the mid-Atlantic states—areas where the Republicans were stronger in the 1940s. However, since the 1980s, party identification has strengthened, but along more consistent ideological and less regional lines.[27] In recent years these changes have been labeled as differences between "Red" and "Blue" America, which refers to the southern, midwestern, and mountain support for the Republican Party set against a pattern of coastal and industrial Northeast support for Democrats (see *"Who Are We? Red Versus Blue States"* in Chapter 14).

The current party era is thus characterized by major changes that have mobilized African Americans and other minorities into the Democratic Party and southern whites into the Republican Party, and a system in which neither party has a clear, enduring majority. These phenomena have led to a much higher incidence of divided government at the national and state levels, with the executive and legislative branches in the hands of different parties. One of the hallmarks of divided government is the gridlock we mentioned earlier, as each party moves to prevent the other from enacting its policy goals. Gridlock and even the unified government with tiny governing majorities, such as President George W. Bush had for most of his administration, make it much harder for the presidential party to achieve its agenda because it is easily blocked by the other party. Citizens, as a consequence, do not know which party to hold accountable if they are dissatisfied with government policy or inaction.

Early political leaders designed parties as elite-driven institutions that served their own interests in governing. Laws that gave the vote to all white males, however, meant that politics was less of an elite activity and inspired leaders to create the mass-based political machine. These machines continued to allow leaders total control over the party, but with the perhaps unexpected consequence of politicizing new generations of American immigrants and strengthening American democracy.

Reformers wanted more political accountability—more power for the voters and less for the party bosses. They broke the machines with civil service reform and primary elections. The American party system, although it is not perfect, has

Who What How

electioneering the process of getting a person elected to public office

---

Figure 12.5

Changing Party Identification of White Voters in and Outside the South, 1952–2008

The data provide a picture of the transformation of the New Deal alignment. Party identification among white southerners shows clear evidence of a fundamentally changed system over the past fifty years, from clear dominance by Democrats to near equality for the major parties. Outside the South, the parties are now highly competitive as well, but this came about with much less change than occurred in the southern states.

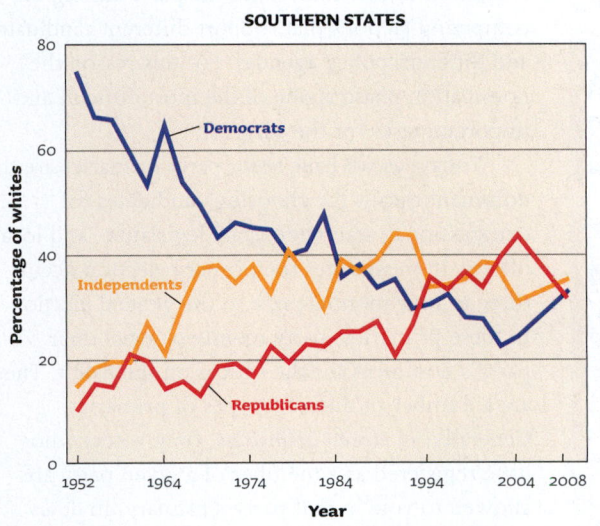

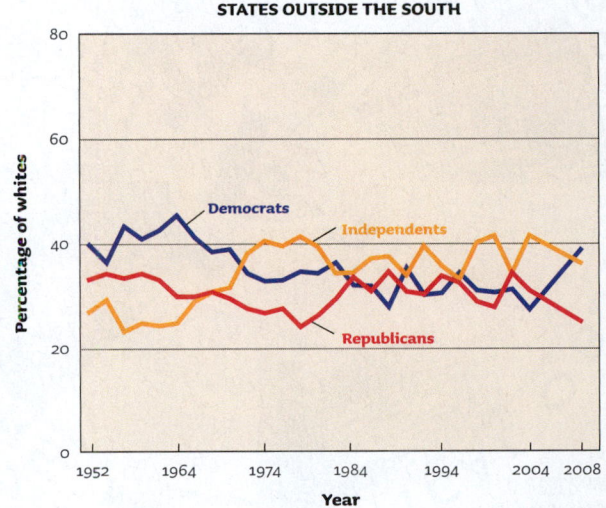

Source: Calculated by the authors from National Election Studies data.

---

allowed citizens to repeatedly change their government, at times radically, without resort to violence or bloodshed.

What Do Parties Do?

Enhancing democracy by linking citizens and government

We have said that, in general, parties play an important role in American democracy by providing a link between citizens and government, coherence in government, and a vocal opposition. These roles are closely tied to the two main activities of parties: electioneering and governing. Generally, party organizations handle tasks related to electioneering, and the party-in-government handles tasks related to governing. In this section we look at each of these two party functions.

Electioneering

Electioneering involves recruiting and nominating candidates, defining policy agendas, and getting candidates elected.

According to an old saying in politics, "before you can save the world, you must save your seat." One of the primary reasons for the existence of party organizations is to help candidates get and save their seats.

Who Should Run? Recruiting Candidates

Each party's electioneering activities begin months before the general election with the first step of finding candidates to run. There is usually no shortage of ambitious politicians eager to run for high-profile offices like state governor and U.S. senator, but the local parties have to work hard to fill less visible and desirable elective offices like those in the state legislature and county government. It is especially difficult to recruit candidates to run against a current officeholder because incumbents enjoying the advantages of having previously assembled a winning coalition and having a name voters recognize are hard to beat. Incumbents also tend to have a financial advantage; donors and interest groups are more likely to give money to candidates who have proven themselves by winning than to challengers who are largely untested. Unless

Mudslinging Back in the Fourth Party Era

Tough campaigns aren't new to American politics. During the 1896 presidential race, one very partisan novelty item attempted to show what a vote for either candidate would mean: a vote for William McKinley, "Protection to American Industries"; a vote for William Jennings Bryan, "Repudiation, Bankruptcy, and Dishonor."

there is a strong indication that an incumbent is vulnerable, it is hard to recruit opposing candidates.[28]

In response to this reality, parties have begun to target races they think they can win and to devote their resources to those elections. Although they generally try to run candidates in most races, they will target as especially winnable those contests where the seat is open (no incumbent is running), or where the incumbent has done something to embarrass himself or herself (perhaps a scandal), or where strong electoral indicators suggest that the party has a good chance of winning the seat (perhaps the party's previous gubernatorial candidate won a strong majority of votes in the district). In these targeted races the party attempts to recruit quality candidates—perhaps known community leaders—and to direct campaign contributions and aid to the targeted contests.[29]

Nominating Candidates

The nomination phase is a formal process through which the party chooses a candidate for each elective office to be contested that year. The nomination phase can unite the party behind its candidates, or it can lead to division within the party among the competing factions that support different candidates and different policy agendas. For this reason the nomination phase is one of the most difficult and important tasks for the party.

Today, as we have seen, party primaries are the dominant means for choosing candidates for congressional, statewide, state legislative, and local offices. In most states the primary election occurs three to four months prior to the general election. In these primaries, party members select their party's nominees for the offices on the ballot. There are a number of different types of primaries. Generally, in ***closed primaries***, only voters who have registered as a member of a given party are allowed to vote in that party's primary. In ***open primaries***, voters simply request one party's ballot on the day of the primary or choose which party's primary they wish to participate in after they enter the polling booth.[30]

Many party officials complain about the open primary system because it permits members of the other party to get involved in the nomination process. This occurred on an organized basis in the 2008 presidential primaries, when conservative radio talk show host Rush Limbaugh launched his "Operation Chaos," encouraging Republican voters to cross over and vote in the Democratic primary for Senator Hillary Clinton since McCain was already clearly the Republican nominee. People disagree whether the goal was simply to prolong the battle for the Democratic nomination or to promote the election of the candidate many conservatives thought would be easier to defeat. Regardless, there is some evidence that Limbaugh's electoral mischief may have cost Barack Obama primary wins in Texas and Indiana.[31] Because voters who are not necessarily loyal to a party are allowed to vote, open primaries can weaken political parties.[32]

In presidential primaries, voters do not choose the actual candidates they want to run for president; rather, they elect delegates. Delegates are usually party activists who support a candidate and run for the opportunity to go to the party's

> **nominating convention** formal party gathering to choose candidates

national **nominating convention** the summer before the election and cast a vote for him or her. We discuss the mechanics of presidential election nominating conventions in more detail in Chapter 14.

In addition to nominating candidates, party conventions have the important function of bringing the party faithful together to set the policy priorities of the party, to elect party officers, and, not least, to provide a sense of solidarity and community for the activists. After working long and hard all year in their communities, party activists find it restoring and rejuvenating to come together with like-minded people to affirm the principles and policies they hold in common.

The primary process and the practice of televising convention proceedings have dramatically changed the nature of these national conventions. Before reforms in the late 1960s that ensured that candidates would be chosen by elected delegates rather than party bosses, national conventions were filled with political bargaining and intrigue and conflict over platform issues. Delegates going into the convention did not always know who would be the party's nominee.[33] By 1972, when many states had adopted the primary system, delegates were committed to presidential candidates before the convention began, meaning that there was little question about who would get the nomination. Floor battles at the convention can still happen, however, as they did in 1980 during the late Massachusetts senator Ted Kennedy's challenge to President Jimmy Carter for the Democratic nomination. The prospect of such a divisive move can throw party members into a panic, as it did toward the end of the primaries in 2008, when Democrats feared Senator Clinton would take her battle for the nomination all the way to the August convention. But generally speaking, today's presidential nominating conventions merely rubber-stamp the primary victor.

The influence of television on the national conventions has been considerable as well. In the 1950s the new medium of television began covering the national conventions. With a national audience watching, the parties began to use these conventions as a public springboard for the presidential campaign. It was important that the party appear to be strong and unified, to maximize its electoral chances. The riot-torn 1968 Democratic convention in Chicago highlights the importance of party unity: young people, most of them Democrats, protested the Vietnam War and the selection process that led to the nomination of Vice President Hubert H. Humphrey, a supporter of U.S. involvement in the war. The protests, conflict, and disarray of the Democratic convention,

By Invitation Only

As part of his 2004 reelection campaign, President George W. Bush frequently held town meetings during which he took questions from members of the public. Meetings using this format are typically staged for television to present the candidate as dealing with real people and their concerns. The twist developed by the Bush campaign was to carefully screen the "public" allowed into the events, which effectively prevented the president from having to deal with embarrassing questions on contentious issues.

which television brought into America's living rooms, may have played a role in Humphrey's loss to Richard Nixon in the general election.

Even though skirmishes between the ideological wings within both parties flare up occasionally, for the most part, conventions have turned into choreographed events, designed to show, in prime time, that the party is unified behind its presidential candidate. In fact, conventions have generally become so routine and predictable that since 2000 the networks have devoted very little prime-time coverage to

soft money unregulated campaign contributions by individuals, groups, or parties that promote general election activities but do not directly support individual candidates

General Elections

In the election phase the role of the party changes from choosing among competing candidates within the party and developing policy agendas to getting its nominated candidates elected. Traditionally the party's role here was to "organize and mobilize" voters, but increasingly they are becoming the providers of extensive services to candidates.

The advent of mass communication—radio, television, and most recently the Internet—has changed the way a party and its candidates relate to voters. When party organizations were the major source of information about a candidate, elections were party centered. Now, with mass communication, elections are more candidate centered. Candidates can effectively run their own campaigns with their own staffs—buying television and radio ad time and presenting themselves on their own terms—and party affiliation is just one of the many characteristics of a candidate, not the sole identifying feature. This shift toward candidate-centered politics is part of a larger transformation in campaigning from the labor-intensive campaigns of the past, which depended on party workers getting out the vote for the party's candidates, to today's capital-intensive campaigns, which depend on the tools of mass communication and money to buy airtime.[35] It does depend, however, on the candidate. In 2008 Barack Obama's unprecedented fundraising ability meant that he had the wherewithal to conduct his own campaign, whereas John McCain, until his choice of Sarah Palin as his running mate energized his base, was more dependent on his party's efforts on his behalf.[36]

Consistent with this change toward capital-intensive campaigns, today's political parties primarily offer candidate services, including fundraising and training in campaign tactics, instruction on compliance with election laws, and public opinion polling and professional campaign assistance.[37]

Money, of course, is central in a capital-intensive campaign, and the parties are major fundraising organizations. Because of a loophole in the campaign finance laws that allowed parties to collect contributions of unlimited size from donors, parties became major banks for candidates in the 1990s (see Chapter 14). These unlimited funds, called ***soft money***, were used by the parties for party-building efforts such as voter registration and issue development activities.[38] Both parties distributed money to candidates either by giving cash directly to the candidates or by supplementing the campaign efforts of candidates with television and radio issue advertising. Although this issue advertising was supposed to represent an "independent" expenditure of money—candidates were not allowed

The National Party Nominating Conventions

The national presidential nominating conventions have evolved into full-blown spectacles exploding with fireworks, confetti, streamers, and 24-7 information, action, and events. In 2008 the Democratic Party's choice for president, Barack Obama, and his running mate, Joe Biden, took the stage with their families at Invesco Field in Denver, Colorado, as more than 70,000 supporters looked on.

them, although the cable stations have picked up the slack. In 2008, however, things were a little more exciting and networks and cable stations alike showed the major convention speeches, with Obama's and McCain's acceptance speeches garnering more than 38 million viewers each.[34]

Defining Policy Agendas

After a political party nominates its candidates, one of the party's main roles is to develop a policy agenda, which represents policies that a party's candidates agree to promote when campaigning and to pursue when governing. The development of such an agenda involves much politicking and gamesmanship as each faction of the party tries to get its views written into the party platform, which we discussed earlier. Whoever wins control over the party platform has decisive input on how the campaign proceeds.

> *governing* activities directed toward controlling the distribution of political resources by providing executive and legislative leadership, enacting agendas, mobilizing support, and building coalitions

to participate in the decisions about how the money was spent or direct the content of the issue ads—in practice, there was generally much correspondence between the issue ads of the party and the campaign ads of the candidates, because parties simply mimicked the ads of their candidates.

Soft money raising was seriously limited by campaign finance reform legislation passed in 2002 called the Bipartisan Campaign Reform Act, or BCRA. Especially important to the parties was the provision that did away with their ability to collect unlimited soft money contributions. Nevertheless, collecting many individual contributions (called "bundling") by political action committees (PACs) to make larger donations and other apparent loopholes allow the parties to continue their role as major providers of campaign services to candidates.[39]

In congressional elections, both parties spend a great deal of money on the targeted contests we discussed earlier.[40] For targeted seats the parties supplement their issue ads by sending party leaders into the district to raise money for the candidate. This move has the added benefit of giving the candidate greater media visibility. When the president's popularity is high, he is a positive campaign presence for his party's congressional candidates. If his approval ratings have fallen by the midterm, his congressional campaign appearances are more limited to fundraising events for his party's congressional candidates in closed gatherings of the party faithful with whom he typically remains a big draw. For the party that does not control the presidency, congressional leaders and presidential hopefuls (sometimes one and the same) usually fill this void.

Governing

Once a party's candidates have been elected to office, attention turns to the matter of governance. **Governing** involves the two major jobs of controlling government by organizing and providing leadership for the legislative and/or executive branches and enacting the party's policy agendas. Party governance gives voters a means to make officeholders accountable for failed and successful governing policies,[41] and it can provide an extraconstitutional framework that can lend some coherence to the fragmentation produced by separation of powers and federalism.

Controlling Government

When parties "control" government at the national level and in the states, it means that the party determines who occupies the leadership positions in the branch of government in which

the party has a majority. Thus, when Barack Obama won the presidency in 2008, he—and, by extension, the Democrats—controlled the top leadership positions in the executive branch of the government (cabinet secretaries and undersecretaries of agencies and the White House staff). For the first two years of Obama's administration, his party also controlled the legislative branch. This means the Democrats selected the majority leader in the Senate and the Speaker of the House, controlled committee assignments, selected chairs of legislative committees, and had a majority of seats on each committee. Controlling government also means that the legislative leadership controls the legislative calendar and the rules governing legislative debate and amendments (especially in the House). When then–Pennsylvania senator Arlen Specter left the Republican Party in April 2009, Democrats even gained a filibuster-proof majority in the Senate for a brief period of time, until Senator Ted Kennedy's seat was filled by Republican Scott Brown in January 2010. After the 2010 midterm elections, Democrats still maintained a small majority in the Senate, but control of the House of Representatives passed to the Republicans. With a divided government, the job of governing became a challenge for both parties.

Execution of Policy Agendas and Accountability

Of course the ultimate goal of a political party is not only to choose who occupies the leadership positions in government

Getting the Job Done
Soon-to-be Speaker of the House John Boehner, R-Ohio, gives a teary thumbs up after the 2010 midterm elections, in which Republicans took back a majority of the House. Once in power, parties must deliver on their campaign promises to prove to the public that their votes were well spent.

▶ **Profiles in Citizenship: David Frum**

"It's not that partisanship is intrinsically evil; in Britain it's fine. . . . But in America, partisanship is a problem because the government can't govern."

David Frum is a waiter. And no, that doesn't mean the former Bush speechwriter, author of six books and editor of the *Frum Forum*, a website "dedicated to the modernization and renewal of the Republican party and the conservative movement"[1] has opted for a second career in restaurant service.

According to Frum the political world is divided into two types of people: waiters and chasers. "A waiter is somebody who has a vision of where his country is going and parks himself at that position to wait for the country. Churchill was a waiter, Reagan was a waiter, but also Lyndon LaRouche was a waiter—it's not necessarily a good thing to be a waiter. Every crackpot, crank, and lunatic is also a waiter. The chasers are those always trying to catch up to where they think the people are at that moment." Chasers—Frum mentions Newt Gingrich, Bill Clinton, and Rush Limbaugh—adopt the values of the constituency they want to lead; waiters believe the world will eventually come around to adopting their view.

It is being a waiter that enables Frum to be at once an ardent member of the Republican Party and also one of its toughest critics. At least one criticism recently cost him a job. In the wake of the passage of the Obama health care bill, he argued publicly that by refusing to work with Democrats on the bill in hopes of denying Obama a victory, Republicans ended up having to swallow a more liberal policy than they would have if they had negotiated with Democrats. In response, he was fired from his position as a fellow at the American Enterprise Institute, which caused him to be even more critical of the party, arguing that the Republican practice of not tolerating dissent among its members was leading to a closed system that would ultimately weaken the party.

It wasn't a comfortable position for Frum, but discomfort is part of the job of being a waiter.

Born into a liberal Canadian family (he became a U.S. citizen in 2007), Frum moved right in college "under the impact of events." He says, "The late 1970s felt like the end of the world, the end of western civilization. . . . Then came the Reagan years and the battle to turn that situation around and all of us young Reaganites felt that the Reagan people did a very good job of keeping us mobilized and motivated. . . ." He went on to law school at Harvard, and by the late 1980s he had become an editorial writer at the *Wall Street Journal*. It was there that he got his first taste of running counter to party orthodoxy, exploring the criticism of U.S. economic trends that it had benefited the wealthiest Americans but had left the least wealthy falling farther behind. "It was a very important debate, and as I plunged into the study of this thing, it became very clear to me that it was true. . . . And then I was also struck by the inability of my conservative colleagues to process this information. That is, if something is true, you can either say, 'it's a bad thing,' in which case you need to figure what we do about it, or 'it doesn't matter, we don't

but also to execute its policy agenda—the party's solutions to the nation's problems. Whether the problem is defined as a lack of affordable health care, insufficient national security, high taxes, distressed communities, unemployment, illegal immigration, or a failing economy, each party represents an alternative vision for how to approach and solve problems.

We have already noted that significant differences exist between the platforms and policy agendas of the two major parties. The question here is whether the parties actually implement their policy agendas. On this score, parties do fairly well. About two-thirds of the platform promises of the party that controls the presidency are implemented.[42]

The classic example of a party fulfilling its campaign promises was the first hundred days of the New Deal under the Democratic Party. Running on a platform that called for an activist national government, Franklin Roosevelt and the congressional Democrats were elected in a landslide in 1932. Under Roosevelt's leadership, Congress proceeded to pass New Deal legislation designed to regulate the economy and banking industry, and to provide government programs to help farmers and the unemployed. After maintaining control of Congress in 1934, the Democrats went on to pass one of the most important pieces of legislation in American history, the Social Security Act (1935). Similarly, recent presidents

care whether it is true,' but you don't have the option of just saying, 'I don't see it, it's not there.'" His work on the successes and limits of the Reagan Revolution resulted in his first book, *Dead Right*.

His writing brought him to the attention of the incoming George W. Bush administration in 2000, and he was offered a job as a White House speechwriter, where he was credited with the famous "axis of evil" phrase that justified Bush's foreign policy. His service put him in an uncomfortable position again when, in 2005, Bush nominated Harriet Miers to fill a vacancy on the Supreme Court. Frum's work with Miers in the White House, where she served as staff secretary, convinced him that she was not Supreme Court caliber. "It reflected a deep problem," he says. "[Bush] nominates her in October 2005 so this is after that bloody summer in Iraq, and after Hurricane Katrina, and it begins to raise the question—are these things all accidents? Or is something going wrong with the way this administration makes decisions?"

His willingness to criticize the administration of which he had once been a part made him a target in Republican circles, chiefly on Fox News, where the attacks got personal. And it cemented Frum's role

as a waiter, a role he maintains today. Unlike some disaffected Republicans, like Andrew Sullivan (see Profiles in Citizenship, p. 588), who continue to call themselves conservative but who have left the Republican Party behind, Frum says, "I have not given up on the movement. I am not going to." Though he adds ruefully, "They may give up on me." Even if that happens, however, Frum knows what to do.

While he waits, here are some of his observations on American politics:

On partisanship:

It's a question about in whose interest do you govern, how do you govern, how do you solve problems, how do you work with people that disagree with you? How important is consensus? This is not a parliamentary political system and if you try to run it like a parliamentary system you wreck it. In a parliamentary system the government has enormous power. . . . The job of the other side is to shoot you down, embarrass you, and trip you up— but the other side of the political aisle cannot interfere with the working of the government. There's no filibuster, there's no veto, and the government governs. The other side tries to bring them down and they usually succeed and at that point

you have these very rapid alternations of power. . . .

In the congressional system, the ability to sabotage, to stop the government from governing is very great, and the American system appears to work best with a high degree of consensus. It's not that partisanship is intrinsically evil; in Britain it's fine. In Britain it's indispensible; if you didn't have intense partisanship in Britain, the government would be too strong. But in America, partisanship is a problem because the government can't govern.

On keeping the republic:

Do not entrap yourself in a closed information system. Closed information systems require the complicity of the audience because information now is so abundant that it takes great effort to avoid coming into contact with it. Political science suggests that people are working harder and harder to avoid coming into contact with unwelcome information. And as I look at the Republican Party, many of these problems are not problems of leadership but of followership and the citizens also need to work harder at their job.

1. "About," *FrumForum*, www.frumforum.com/about. ■

have been successful in passing the signature issues of their campaigns. Important examples include President George W. Bush's tax cuts and the No Child Left Behind Act, and President Obama's Patient Protection and Affordable Care Act and the financial reform bill. These were major changes in the direction of national policy.

The greater competitiveness of the parties in the current era, however, means that divided government happens much more frequently than in earlier party systems, and as we saw in Chapter 8, presidential success typically plummets when the president's party loses control of Congress. This was certainly the case for Presidents Bush and Clinton following

the midterm elections that brought them divided government for parts of their administrations and is likely to be the case for President Obama as well.

Within the context of the responsible party model, the ability of a party to accomplish its stated agenda is extremely important for voter accountability. As the party in power promotes its policy agenda and its ideas for how government should solve problems, it provides voters with an opportunity to hold the party responsible for its successes or failures. Voters then determine if a party's candidates should be rewarded through reelection or punished by "throwing the rascals out." In 1932 the persistence of the Depression convinced voters that the GOP policies had failed and led them to replace the Republicans with the Democrats and their solutions. After seeing Democrats implement the New Deal in 1933 and 1934, the voters cast their ballots to keep Roosevelt and his party in power, thus rewarding the party for its efforts to deal with the Great Depression. As we have pointed out, such clear accountability is more difficult under divided government, when voters do not know which party to hold accountable.

Who What How

It is hard to imagine any actors in American politics *not* having a stake in the activities of electioneering and governing. For political parties, the stakes are high. They want electoral victory for their candidates and control of government. They try to achieve these goals by using the rules they themselves have created, as well as the electoral rules imposed by the state and federal governments.

Candidates seeking to get elected to office, and to build a reputation once there, engage in candidate-centered campaigns with the assistance of the party organization and the party-in-the-electorate. They also encourage the election of other members of their party.

Party activists want to gain and keep control of the party's agenda, to ensure that it continues to serve the causes they believe in. They participate in primaries and hold the elected officials accountable.

Citizens value their limited government, but paradoxically they also get impatient when government seems to grind to a halt in a morass of partisan bickering. The policy efficiency and coherence that parties can create can dissolve the gridlock, but this comes at the potential cost of a more powerful government. When voters elect a divided government, gridlock is almost inevitable.

Characteristics of the American Party System
Ideologically moderate and decentralized

Party systems vary tremendously around the world. In some countries, only one major party exists in the governmental structure. This single party usually maintains its power through institutional controls that forbid the development of opposition parties (totalitarian states like China and the old Soviet Union), or through corruption and informal means of physical coercion (Mexico, until recently), or through military control (Burma, Libya, and Sudan). These systems essentially prevent any meaningful party competition. Without choices at the ballot box, democracy is impossible. Some countries, on the other hand, have so many parties that often no single party can amass enough votes to control government. When that happens, the parties may try to cooperate with other parties, governing together as a coalition. Parties can represent ideological positions, social classes, or even more informal group interests. Parties can put tight constraints on what elected leaders can do, making them toe the "party line," or they can give only loose instructions that leaders can obey as they please. The truth is, there is no single model of party government.

Among all the possibilities, the American party system is distinctive, but it too fails to fit a single model. It is predominantly a two-party system, although third-party movements have come and gone throughout our history. The American system also tends toward ideological moderation, at least compared with other multiple-party countries. And finally, our two-party system has decentralized party organizations and fluctuating levels of party discipline. We explore each of these characteristics in this section.

Two Parties

As we have seen, the United States has a two-party system. Throughout most of the United States' history, in fact, two specific parties, the Democrats and the Republicans, have been the only parties with a viable chance of winning the vast majority of elective offices. As a consequence, officeholders representing these two parties dominate the governing process.

Why a Two-Party System?

The United States—along with countries like Great Britain and New Zealand—stands in sharp contrast to other democratic party systems around the world, such as those found in Sweden, France, Israel, and Italy, which have three, four, five, or more major political parties, respectively. The United States has experienced few of the serious political splits—stemming from such divisive issues as language, religion, or social conflict—that are usually responsible for multiple parties. The lack of deep and enduring cleavages among the American people is reinforced by the longevity of the Democratic and Republican Parties themselves. Both parties predate the Industrial Revolution, the urbanization and suburbanization of the population, and the rise of the information age, and they have weathered several wars, including the Civil War and two world wars, as well as numerous economic recessions and depressions. One scholar compared each party to a "massive geological formation composed of different strata, with each representing a constituency or group added to the party in one political era and then subordinated to new strata produced in subsequent political eras." Proponents from one era may continue to support a political party even if it undergoes changes in issue positions. These political parties persist not just because of the support they can attract today but because of the accumulation of support over time.[43]

But the most important reason that the United States maintains a two-party system is that the rules of the system, in most cases designed by members of the two parties themselves, make it very difficult for third parties to do well on a permanent basis.[44] As we saw in Chapter 4, for instance, democracies that have some form of proportional representation are more likely to have multiple parties. These governments distribute seats in the legislature to parties by virtue of the proportion of votes that each party receives in the election. For example, if a party receives 20 percent of the vote, it will receive roughly 20 percent of the seats in the legislature. Countries with proportional representative systems have more parties than those with single-member plurality-vote systems, because small parties can still participate in government even though they do not get a majority of the votes. The U.S. Constitution, on the other hand, prescribes a single-member district electoral system. This means that the candidate who receives the most votes in a defined district (generally with only one seat) wins that seat, and the loser gets nothing, except perhaps some campaign debt. This type of winner-take-all system creates strong incentives for voters to cast their ballots for one of the two established parties because voters know they are effectively throwing away their votes when they vote for a third-party candidate.

The United States has other legal barriers that reinforce the two-party system. In most states, legislators from both parties have created election laws that regulate each major party's activities, but these laws also protect the parties from competition from other parties. For example, state election laws ensure the place of both major parties on the ballot and make it difficult for third parties to gain ballot access. Many states require that potential independent or third-party candidates gather a large number of signature petitions before their names can be placed on the ballot. Another common

state law is that before a third party can conduct a primary to select its candidate, it must have earned some minimum percentage of the votes in the previous election.

Third parties are also hampered by existing federal election laws. These laws regulate the amount of campaign contributions that presidential candidates can receive from individuals and PACs and provide dollar-for-dollar federal matching money for both major parties' presidential campaigns, if the candidates agree to limit their spending to a predetermined amount. However, third-party candidates cannot claim federal campaign funds until after the election is over, and even then their funds are limited by the percentage of past and current votes they received. As an additional hurdle, they need to have gained about 5 percent or more of the national vote in order to be eligible for federal funds.[45]

Access to the national media can also be a problem for third parties. Even though regulations are in place to ensure that the broadcast media give candidates equal access to the airwaves, Congress has insisted on a special exception that limits participation in televised debates to candidates from the two major parties, which kept Ross Perot out of the debates in 1996,[46] Ralph Nader and Patrick Buchanan out in 2000, Nader out again in 2004 and 2008, and Bob Barr out in 2008.

Third-Party Movements

Just because the Democrats and the Republicans have dominated our party system does not mean that they have gone unchallenged. Over the years, numerous third-party movements have tried to alter the partisan make-up of American politics. These parties have usually arisen either to represent specific issues that the parties failed to address, like Prohibition in 1869, or to promote ideas that were not part of the ideological spectrum covered by the existing parties, like socialist parties, never very popular here, or the Libertarian Party. In general, third parties have sprung up from the grassroots or have broken off from an existing party (the latter are referred to as splinter parties). In the case of the current Tea Party movement, the new party is not actually distinct from the Republican Party (most Tea Party members identify themselves as conservative Republicans), and as long as the Republican Party adopts most of the issues the Tea Partiers care about, they are not likely to separate and form an organized party of their own. In many cases third parties have been headed up by a strong leader who carries much of the momentum for the party's success on his or her own shoulders (for example, Teddy Roosevelt, George Wallace, and Ross Perot). Table 12.3

Table 12.3

Third-Party Movements in America

Third party	Year est.	Most successful presidential candidate	History and platform
National Republican Party	1824	John Quincy Adams	Split off from Democratic-Republicans to oppose Andrew Jackson's campaign for the presidency.
Anti-Masonic Party	1826	William Wirt	Held the first American party convention in 1831. Opposed elite organizations (the Masons in particular), charging they were antidemocratic.
Free Soil Party	1848	Former president Martin Van Buren	Fought for cheap land and an end to slavery. The antislavery members eventually became supporters of Lincoln's Republican Party.
Know-Nothing Party	1849	Millard Fillmore	Promoted native-born Protestants' interests, claiming that Catholics were more loyal to the pope than to the United States.
Prohibition Party	1869	James Black	Advocated the prohibition of alcohol manufacture and use. The party continues to run candidates.
Populist Party	1891	James Weaver	Appealed to farmers during the depressed agricultural economy period by blaming railroads and eastern industrialists for unfair prices.
Socialist Party of America	1901	Eugene V. Debs	Fought for an end to the capitalist economic system in the United States. When jailed for sedition in 1920, Debs ran for president from prison and received 3.4% of the popular vote.
Bull Moose Party (Progressive Party)	1912	Former president Teddy Roosevelt	As the most successful third-party candidate in American presidential election history, Roosevelt campaigned as a progressive crusader and received 27.4% of the vote.
States' Rights Party (Dixiecrats)	1948	Strom Thurmond (later 8-term senator from S.C.)	Split from the Democratic Party in 1948 over civil rights; advocated segregation and used the Democratic Party infrastructure in southern states to gain 2.4% of the vote.
American Independent Party	1968	George Wallace	Former Democrat Wallace began his own party, which attacked civil rights legislation and Great Society programs. He received 13.5% of the vote.
Libertarian Party	1971	Ed Clark	Fights for personal liberties and opposes all welfare state policies. Clark won 1.1% of the vote in 1980.
Reform Party	1995	Ross Perot	Perot received 19% of the presidential vote as an independent in 1992, and he began this party to formalize a third-party challenge. Perot won 8% of the vote in 1996. Reform candidate Jesse Ventura was elected governor of Minnesota in 1998.
Green Party	1984/ 1996	Ralph Nader	Really two parties. Green Party USA was founded on a platform of eliminating the Senate and breaking up the nation's 500 largest corporations. The Association of State Green Parties (ASGP) broke off in the mid-1990s to promote more mainstream social justice and environmental issues. Nader, a member of neither, ran as the ASGP candidate in 2000, winning less than 3% of the vote. The ASGP backed another candidate in 2004.

shows some key third-party movements that have made their mark on U.S. history.

Third parties can have a dramatic impact on presidential election outcomes. When the winning margins are large, third parties may be merely a blip on the screen, but when the electorate is narrowly divided, the presence of third-party candidates is fraught with peril for Democrats and Republicans. After he voted for Nader in 2000, Green Party member Matt Duss got telephone calls from Democrats. "Are you !#%!b GREENS out of your !# minds?" they screamed into his ear.[47] Some joked that GREEN stood for "Get Republicans Elected Every November." Did Ralph Nader cost Al Gore the election? Perhaps he did, but that oversimplifies a complex event. As one analyst put it, Nader undoubtedly cost Gore many votes, but Pat Buchanan's Reform Party candidacy cost Bush as well. Although Buchanan won only 450,000 votes overall, had he not been in the race, Bush arguably could have won narrow victories in Iowa, New Mexico, Oregon, and Wisconsin, and won the Electoral College without the help of Florida.[48] Many Republicans believe that Bush's father was also hurt in his 1992 reelection bid against Bill Clinton by the candidacy of Ross Perot. Third-party challenges are not just a lose-lose proposition for the major parties, however. In an effort to prevent third parties from taking crucial support away from them, many major-party candidates, as we saw earlier, try to appropriate their issues, thereby broadening their base of support. Thus, although third parties are, in most cases, short-lived, they nonetheless fill a significant role in the American party system.

Gentlemanly Combat

Debates are one way for voters to learn where presidential hopefuls stand on the issues and how they conduct themselves under pressure. Following one such debate in October 2007 in Dearborn, Michigan, Senator John McCain, R-Ariz., second from right, shakes hand with Senator Sam Brownback, R-Kan. Other participants shown in this image are, from left, Mike Huckabee, Mitt Romney, Rudy Giuliani, and Duncan Hunter, behind McCain.

from the communist-based Democratic Left Party to the ultra-conservative neo-Fascist National Alliance Party—the United States has a fairly limited menu of viable parties: the moderately conservative Republican Party and the moderately liberal Democratic Party. Neither the Democrats nor the Republicans promote vast changes to the U.S. political and economic systems. Both parties support the Bill of Rights, the Constitution and its institutions (presidency, Congress, the courts, and so on), the capitalist free-enterprise system, and even basic governmental policies like Social Security and the Federal Reserve system. This broad agreement between the two parties in major areas is a reflection of public opinion. Surveys show broad public support for the basic structure and foundations of the U.S. political and economic systems. It is within this agreement on the broad contours of the political system that we see clear polarization of the parties on specific issues and on the solutions to the nation's problems. On these the parties are clearly more ideologically distinct than in past decades, but still they accept the basic parameters of American politics.

Thinking Outside the Box

Are the American people well represented by a two-party system?

Ideological Moderation

Compared with many other party systems—for instance, the Italian system, which offers voters a variety of choices ranging

Decentralized Party Organizations

In American political parties, local and state party organizations make their own decisions. They have affiliations with

▶ Who, What, How, and WHEN: Third-Party Influence

The United States may have a firmly entrenched two-party system, but that doesn't mean third parties never get out of the gate. The rules are stacked against any of **them crossing the finish line, but there have been some notable attempts:**

1912 — Progressive (Bull Moose) Party

Teddy Roosevelt formed the Progressive Party in 1912 after losing the Republican presidential nomination. He won 27 percent of the popular vote and eighty-eight Electoral College votes, beating Taft, the Republican nominee, but was defeated by Woodrow Wilson, the Democrat. The party faded after the 1912 election but resurfaced in the 1920s with support for reforms such as recall elections.

1912 — Socialist Party of America

Even though the Socialist Party of America was formed in 1901 and managed to elect several mayors and congressional candidates across the country, its biggest impact on the presidential race was in 1912. Candidate Eugene V. Debs got 6 percent of the popular vote. In 1920 Debs ran again—from jail, where he had been sentenced for violating the Sedition Act—and got 3.4 percent of the vote.

1968 — American Independent Party

In the 1968 presidential election, the American Independent Party nominated George Wallace, a former Alabama governor. He ran on a platform that opposed civil rights. The party gained 13.5 percent of the popular vote, won five southern states, and got forty-six Electoral College votes, making the American Independent Party the last third party to win any Electoral College votes.

---

the national party organization but no obligations to obey its dictates other than selecting delegates to the national convention. Decision making is dispersed across the organization rather than centralized at the national level; power tends to move from the bottom up instead of from the top down. This means that local concerns and politics dominate the lower levels of the party, molding its structure, politics, and policy agendas. Local parties and candidates can have a highly distinctive character and may look very different from the state or national parties. Political scientists refer to this as a *fragmented party organization.*

American parties are organized (or disorganized) into several major divisions spread across the national, state, and local levels. Most visible are the national committees, the Republican National Committee (RNC) and the Democratic National Committee (DNC). They are responsible for taking care of the national parties' business between their national

presidential nominating conventions. They provide a good deal of campaign support and fundraising assistance, especially to presidential candidates. After these are the congressional campaign committees, one for each party in the House and in the Senate, which are responsible for trying to elect party members with the goal of keeping or gaining party control.

At the subnational level, there are state and local party organizations. Since the 1970s the state organizations have become more professionally organized and staffed, providing increased levels of support, often with funds from the national committees. Increasingly, the state legislative leaders have what are called "leadership PACs," which they use to gather funds from activists and interest groups and funnel those into competitive contests in their efforts to gain partisan majorities in the state legislatures. Finally, there are local party organizations, which are generally much weaker, often

1971 **Libertarian Party**
Founded in 1971, the Libertarian Party promoted a platform that emphasized limited government intervention in both economic policy and personal freedoms, such as the right to carry a weapon or to smoke in a public building. Though they have not had much success at the presidential level (their candidates have never gained more than 1 percent of the popular vote), they have elected candidates to local office and even the Alaska state legislature, and are the third largest political party in the United States today.

1996 **Reform Party**
The Reform Party was founded by Ross Perot following his strong showing as an independent candidate in the 1992 presidential election (Perot garnered almost 19 percent of the popular vote in 1992). The Reform Party was able to secure federal funding in 1996, but Perot was not allowed to participate in debates with the major-party candidates. He received 8 percent of the vote in 1996. The party's biggest success came when Jesse Ventura won the governorship of Minnesota in 1998.

2000 **Green Party**
The Green Party was organized in the United States in the 1990s with a platform centered around environmentalism and social justice issues. Its biggest presidential election impact came in 2000, however, when Ralph Nader, the Green Party nominee, was on the ballot in forty-four states and received 2.7 percent of the popular vote. Splits occurred within the party over whether Nader would be the nominee in 2004; he was not. Some also worried that the Green Party was a spoiler in the 2000 election and tried to keep the party off the ballot in the states in 2004.

existing only on a part-time basis staffed by volunteers. The local organizations have such a structure because the vast majority of local elections, like those for city councils and school boards, are nonpartisan.[49]

The decentralized character of American parties means that the national organization does not have financial or, especially, ideological control of the state and local organizations. This makes it possible for new factions within the parties to capture local and then state organizations as a base for influencing the directions of the parties more generally. Consider, for example, the successful efforts of the Christian Right in the Republican Party in the late 1980s. Building upon dedicated local volunteers and church networks, the movement established itself as a powerful force in the Republican Party nationally. The Tea Party movement today is attempting to follow a similar strategy, although national media attention helps it focus its efforts at nonlocal levels as well.

The consequences of decentralization can also be seen in the occasional frustration of national officials when an embarrassing candidate is able to pull off a primary victory. Among many examples is David Duke, a former Ku Klux Klan member who ran for governor of Louisiana in 1991, and Alvin Greene, an unemployed army veteran without a campaign or even a web site, who captured the Democratic nomination for the U.S. Senate in South Carolina in 2010. In these cases, the national organizations are powerless to do anything other than withhold support. Usually, as in these cases, the embarrassing candidate just loses and is forgotten.

The biggest reason for the fragmentation of control of American parties is federalism and political reforms like the direct primary. All of our candidates, even the president and vice president, are elected in state (or local) elections that are to some extent governed by state laws. Thus members of the

> *party discipline* ability of party leaders to bring party members in the legislature into line with the party program

state legislatures and Congress are attached primarily to the state parties that constitute much of the electoral base. Of course, even their ability to run depends on surviving the local context of contested district or state primary elections, and the national parties have only indirect influence at best on these.

Decentralization, however, does not mean that local parties are necessarily different from their national counterparts. Consider the possible effect of party activists. While their influence means that the base may control the leadership (decentralization) rather than the other way around, power may be less fragmented as the base strengthens its hold on the entire party. The more conservative base of the Republican Party has long had greater control at the local level, but national Republican policy was tempered by the need to get along with Democrats in Congress and to appeal to the moderate voter in national elections. When the party took control of Congress in 1994, however, members of Congress were better able to impose their more ideological perspective at the upper levels of the party.

Changes in Party Discipline Over Time

Historically, American party organizations have been notable for their lack of a hierarchical (top-down) power structure, and the officials elected to government from the two parties have not felt compelled to take their orders from the top. This looseness within the parties was a continuing source of frustration for the advocates of the responsible party model of government. They wished for greater *party discipline*—the ability of party leaders to keep members voting together in a cohesive way—which was more typical of European parliamentary parties. This lack of party unity among legislators in the United States reflected the diversity of opinions within the parties, both among activists and among rank-and-file identifiers. We have seen, however, that significant changes have occurred in the parties' base coalitions, especially in the movement of southern conservatives from the Democratic to the Republican Party. This shift, with similar but less dramatic ideological alignment in the non-southern states, has resulted in a party system in which we have greater ideological agreement within the parties and greater ideological distance between them.

These changes in the electoral environment of Congress have helped create the conditions for greatly heightened partisanship in Congress. One factor is simply the greater ideological agreement within the parties coupled with an increased (and seemingly increasing) ideological gulf between the parties. This is reinforced by stronger party leadership made possible by rules changes in the House of Representatives in the 1970s.[50] For example, in 2006, Democrat Nancy Pelosi became the first woman Speaker of the House and led the Democrats with a firm and expert hand. She gained a reputation among some as "one of the most powerful Speakers in modern history."[51] Pelosi's ability to lead the House Democrats and to pass President Obama's program was made possible by the increased ideological homogeneity within the Democratic Party that is an important aspect of the polarized political parties of the contemporary era.[52] The Republican victories in 2010 made John Boehner, R-Ohio, the new Speaker of the House. Boehner has a substantial Republican majority, which should be an asset, but the heightened energy and greater conservatism of the new Republicans elected to Congress pose a challenge for him if he tries to negotiate differences with House Democrats and the Obama Administration to reach policy agreements.

The United States' two-party system is a direct result of first, the kind of electoral system that the founders designed, and second, the rules that lawmakers in the two parties have put into place to make it difficult for third parties to thrive. This does not stop the drive for third parties, however, when dissatisfied voters seek representation of ideas and issues that the two major parties do not address.

The American parties are, in general, ideologically moderate. Activists want parties to take more extreme stances and to act on their principles. Voting in primaries has enabled

Who What How

them to pull the parties in a more extreme, but also more disciplined, direction. The losers here are the general voting public, who cannot always find a moderate alternative to vote for. Some scholars argue that these voters may register their wishes for moderation by splitting their tickets, resulting in a divided government that is less able to act decisively.[53]

The Citizens and Political Parties

Learning to tolerate the messiness of democracy

We began this chapter by noting that, for all their importance to the success of democracy, political parties have been perennially unpopular with the public. Scholars tell us that one reason for this unpopularity is that voters are turned off by partisan bickering and each party's absorption with its own ideological agenda instead of a concern for the public interest.[54] In this section we suggest the possibility that politics is *about* bickering, and that bickering may itself be a major safeguard of American democracy.

We defined politics at the start of this book as the struggle over who gets what and how they get it in society, a process that involves cooperation, bargaining, compromise, and trade-offs. We remarked at the outset that politics is often seen as a dirty business by Americans, but that it is really our saving grace since it allows us to resolve conflict without violence. The difficulty is that Americans do not see politics as our saving grace. Perhaps we have enjoyed relative domestic tranquility for so long that we do not know what it is like to have to take our disagreements to the streets and the battlefields to resolve them. Some researchers have found that when Americans look at government, they do not focus primarily on the policy *outcomes* but on the political *process* itself. Although policies themselves are increasingly complex and difficult to grasp, most of us are able to understand the way in which the policies are created, the give and take, the influence of organized interests, and the rules of the game. In other words, finding the *what* of politics to be complicated, most citizens focus their attention and evaluation on the *how*. We are not helped out here by the media, which, rather than explaining the substance of policy debate to American citizens, instead treat politics like one long, bitterly contested sporting event.

Given citizen dissatisfaction with partisan politics in America, where do we go from here? What is the citizen's role in all this, if it is not to stand on the sidelines and be cynical about partisan politics? Political scientists John Hibbing and Elizabeth Theiss-Morse argue that the problem lies with a lack of citizen education—education not about the facts of American government but about the process. "Citizens' big failure," they claim, "is that they lack an appreciation for the ugliness of democracy."[55] Democratic politics is messy by definition; it is authoritarian government that is neat, tidy, and efficient. Perhaps the first thing we as citizens should do is to recognize that partisanship is not a failure of politics; it is the heart of politics.

At the beginning of this chapter, we said there were three ways in which parties enhanced democracy in America. We have given considerable attention to the first two: the linkage between citizen and government and the coherence among the branches of government that parties can provide. The third way parties serve democracy is in providing for a vocal opposition, an adversarial voice that scrutinizes and critiques the opposite side, helping to keep the process and the people involved honest. This is akin to the watchdog function the media are said to serve, but it is more institutionalized, a self-monitoring process that keeps both parties on their toes. To be sure, this self-monitoring certainly can, and does, deteriorate into some of the uglier aspects of American democracy, but it also serves as the guardian of political freedom. Where such partisan squabbling is not allowed, political choice and democratic accountability cannot survive either.

There are three things citizens can do to offset their frustration with the partisan course of American politics:

1. *Get real.* Having realistic expectations of the process of democratic government can certainly help head off disillusionment when those expectations are not met.

2. *Get involved.* Parties, because of their decentralized nature, are one of the places in American politics to which citizens have easy access. The only reason the more extreme ideologues hold sway in American politics is that the rest of us allow them to, by leaving the reins in their hands.

3. *Don't split your ticket.* If you are truly disturbed at what you see as government paralysis, try voting for a straight party ticket. Even if you vary the party from election to election, you will be able to hold the party accountable for government's performance.

▶ What's at Stake Revisited

We began this chapter by looking at the Nevada Senate race between Harry Reid and Sharron Angle, and asking what is at stake when a party chooses to be represented by its more extreme members. As it happens, Reid eked out a victory in the race that even his own staffers thought he might lose when his likely opponent was a moderate Republican. The "dead man walking" lived to fight another day as Senate majority leader for the Democrats, and in fact he helped lead his party to a several dramatic victories in the lame duck session just weeks after the election.

In the wake of the 2010 midterm elections the verdict on the Tea Party faction of the Republican Party is mixed. While many Tea Party candidates such as Sharron Angle, Joe Miller in Alaska, and Christine O'Donnell in Delaware lost, many others were successful, including Marco Rubio in Florida and Rand Paul in Kentucky. With a new Republican majority in the House and a larger number of Republicans in the Senate, Tea Partiers are celebrating a victory and flexing their muscles in the party.

But while many in the Tea Party are doing a victory dance there is reason to believe that the election wins may not have furthered the Republican Party's interests in the long term. Although the Tea Party is made up almost entirely of Republican voters, they are the most conservative of Republicans. Extreme ideological candidates can win in small homogeneous constituencies, such as congressional districts, but as the constituency gets larger, as in Senate and presidential elections, candidates usually have to moderate their most extreme positions in order to win. In fact, although the election likely would have produced Republican wins for the Kentucky and Florida senate seats even without the Tea Party movement, the Nevada and Delaware elections likely would have been Republican pickups if more mainstream Republican candidates had run. Instead, candidates perceived as out of the mainstream won the primaries and the Democrats held on to seats many thought they should have lost.

To Sum Up

Key terms, chapter summaries, practice quizzes, Internet links, and other study aids are available on the companion web site at http://republic.cqpress.com.

Define | Understand | Practice | Read | Click | Watch

closed primaries (p. 460)
critical election (p. 455)
dealignment (p. 455)
electioneering (p. 459)
governing (p. 463)
nominating convention (p. 461)
open primaries (p. 460)
partisanship (p. 444)
party activists (p. 452)
party base (p. 445)
party bosses (p. 455)
party discipline (p. 472)
party eras (p. 455)

party identification (p. 444)
party-in-government (p. 444)
party-in-the-electorate (p. 444)
party machines (p. 454)
party organization (p. 444)
party platform (p. 448)
party primary (p. 455)
patronage (p. 455)
political gridlock (p. 443)
political party (p. 443)
realignment (p. 455)
responsible party model (p. 446)
soft money (p. 462)

Define | **Understand** | **Practice** | **Read** | **Click** | **Watch**

- Political parties make a major contribution to American government by linking citizens and government, overcoming some of the fragmentation of government that separation of powers and federalism can produce, and creating an articulate opposition.
- American political parties offer the average voter a choice in terms of ideology, membership, and policy positions (platform). The differences may not always be evident, however, because electoral forces create incentives for parties to take moderate positions, drawing the parties together. At the same time, party activists who are committed to the values and policies of a particular party play a key role in pushing the parties apart and keeping them ideologically distinct.
- The two primary activities of parties are electioneering (getting candidates elected) and governing (all the activities related to enacting party policy agendas in government).
- American history reveals at least five distinct party eras. These are periods of political stability when one party has a majority of congressional seats and controls the presidency. A realignment, or new era, occurs when a different party assumes control of government. Party politics today may be undergoing both a realignment and a dealignment, resulting in greater numbers of voters identifying themselves as independents.
- America's two-party system is relatively moderate, decentralized, and increasingly disciplined. Although the rules are designed to make it hard for third parties to break in, numerous third-party movements have arisen at different times to challenge the two dominant parties.
- While public disenchantment with political parties may be on the increase, parties remain one of the most accessible avenues for citizen participation in government.

Define | **Understand** | **Practice** | **Read** | **Click** | **Watch**

1. **Which of the following is NOT a condition of the responsible party model?**
   a. The parties offer a clear choice of ideologies.
   b. The candidates pledge to implement their parties' programs.
   c. The party is held accountable by voters.
   d. The party has control over its elected officials.
   e. The party gives campaign contributions to all of its candidates.

2. **_____ are least likely to be members of the Democratic Party.**
   a. Women
   b. African Americans
   c. Jews
   d. Protestants
   e. Union members

3. **A _____ is a trend among voters to identify themselves as independent rather than as members of a major party.**
   a. dealignment
   b. critical election
   c. party era
   d. realignment
   e. partisan reshuffling

4. **The Bipartisan Campaign Reform Act limited the power of parties because it**
   a. eliminated bundling.
   b. eliminated a party's ability to collect unlimited soft money donations.
   c. made it harder for parties to hand-pick their nominees.
   d. increased the power of interest groups by subjecting issue advocacy ads to fewer regulations.
   e. prohibited parties from running television commercials in support of their candidates.

5. **According to researchers, most American citizens focus on the _____ of politics rather than on the _____.**
   a. how, what
   b. who, how
   c. how, who
   d. who, what
   e. what, how

Define   **Understand**   **Practice**   **Read**   **Click**   **Watch**

Adkins, Randall E., ed. 2008. *The Evolution of Political Parties, Campaigns, and Elections: Landmark Documents, 1787–2007*. Washington, D.C.: CQ Press. A handy primer, this edited volume explores the evolution of political parties through fifty primary source documents that offer readers a firsthand introduction to this exciting topic.

Aldrich, John H. 1995. *Why Parties? The Origin and Transformation of Political Parties in America*. Chicago: University of Chicago Press. In one of the most insightful books written in recent years on political parties in America, Aldrich argues that parties are still quite strong and remain so because of their ability to overcome collective action problems.

Bibby, John F., and Brian F. Schaffner. 2007. *Politics, Parties, and Elections in America*. New York: Wadsworth. A what's-what of political parties, covering all the basics.

Hershey, Marjorie Randon. 2008. *Party Politics in America*, 13th ed. New York: Pearson Longman. A comprehensive text on parties in America. Earlier editions elucidated the distinction among party-in-government, party-in-the-electorate, and party organization.

Hetherington, Marc J., and William J. Keefe. 2006. *Parties, Politics, and Public Policy in America*. Washington, D.C.: CQ Press. This text examines the continued vitality of American political parties.

Jewel, Malcolm, and Sarah Morehouse. 2001. *Political Parties and Elections in American States*, 4th ed. Washington, D.C.: CQ Press. Two distinguished scholars of state politics present a unique view of the party system, focusing on differences across the fifty states in the roles of the political parties in the electoral process for the state legislatures and governorships. The authors consider campaign finance, rules governing the parties and elections, and state political cultures to conclude that the parties are alive and well in states, and that competition between the parties is increasing in several of the states.

Key, V. O., Jr. 1949. *Southern Politics in State and Nation*. New York: Random House. A seminal work on the one-party South. Key is a must-read for anyone interested in understanding the current state of southern politics.

Nader, Ralph. 2002. *Crashing the Party: How to Tell the Truth and Still Run for President*. New York: St. Martin's Press. The vigilant muckraker and Green Party candidate gives a blow-by-blow account of his 2000 run for the White House and offers theories on what he sees as the failure of the two-party system.

Schattschneider, E. E. 1942. *Party Government*. New York: Holt, Rinehart, and Winston. A classic book on the need for strong, centralized parties in order for democracy to prosper.

Wattenberg, Martin P. 1996. *The Decline of American Political Parties, 1952–1994*. Cambridge: Harvard University Press. Wattenberg presents an interesting argument about how the rise of candidate-centered elections has severely limited the influence and power of political parties.

Define   **Understand**   **Practice**   **Read**   **Click**   **Watch**

National Republican Senatorial Committee, National Republican Congressional Committee, Democratic Senatorial Campaign Committee, and Democratic Congressional Campaign Committee www.nrsc.org, www.nrcc.org, www.dscc.org, and www.dccc.org. Want to know how policy issues are being framed in congressional campaign and fundraising efforts? These four sites give you the partisan line.

Politics 1's Directory of U.S. Political Parties www.politics1.com/parties.htm. Interested in learning more about some of the lesser-known parties in the United States? This site offers brief descriptions of numerous lesser-known political parties as well as links to their web sites.

Republican and Democratic National Committees www.rnc.org and www.democrats.org. These two sites will answer all your questions about the two major parties.

VoteSmart.org's Political Resources www.votesmart.org/resource_political_resources.php?category=1. Another comprehensive directory of U.S. political parties. Party contact information is clearly displayed below each entry.

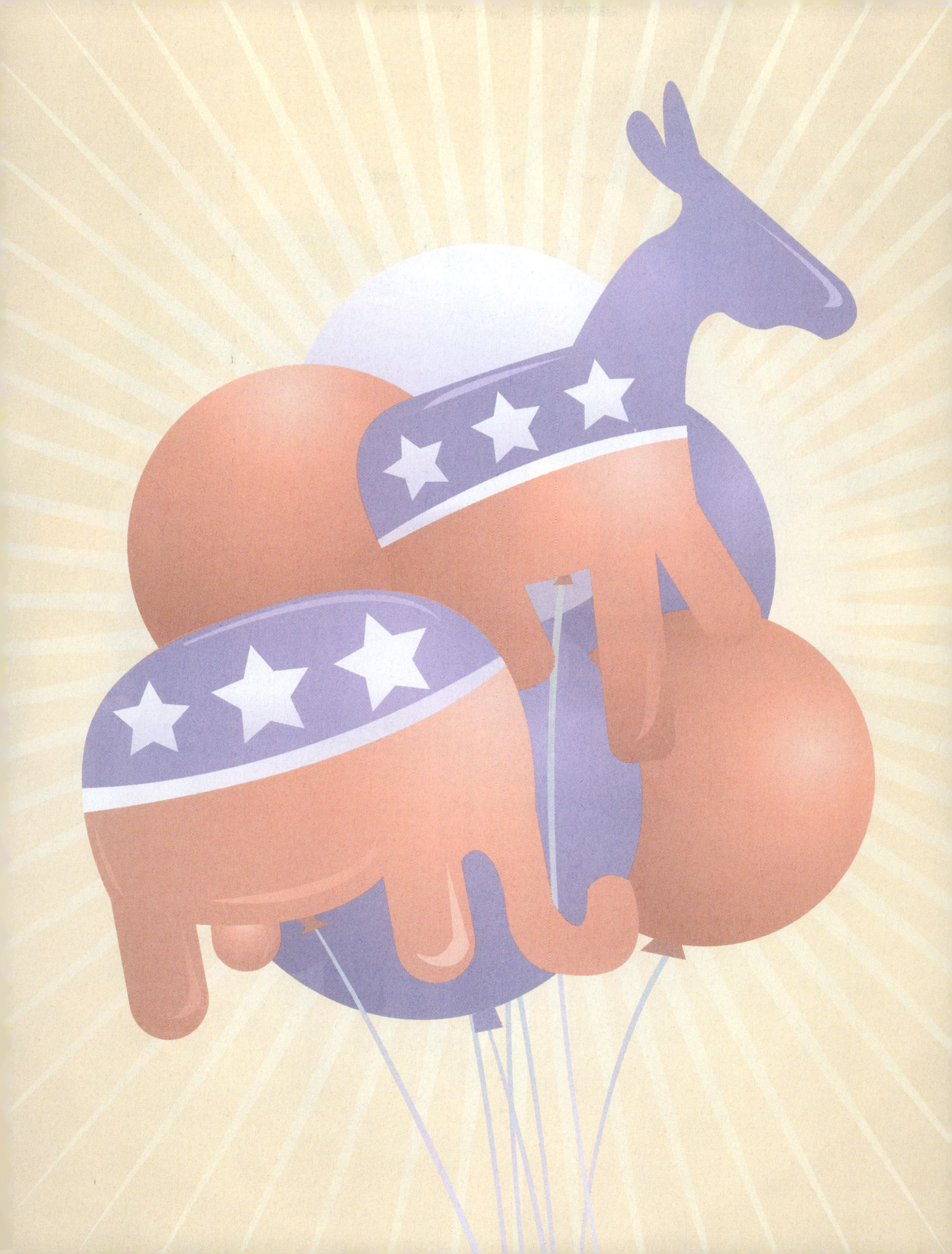

Chapter 13

Interest Groups

▶ What's at Stake?

Harry and Louise killed health care reform in 1994, and in 2009 President Barack Obama's chief of staff at the time, Rahm Emanuel, was determined that they wouldn't do it again.

Emanuel had been working in the Clinton White House when the insurance industry set out to stop health care reform in 1994, spending millions on TV advertising, including the infamous "Harry and Louise" commercials that featured a worried couple sitting at their kitchen table, discussing their fears over government-run health care plans. An apprehensive public was easily persuaded to share Harry and Louise's concerns, and the health care industry scored a major victory. Health care reform was dead for at least the next sixteen years.

Emanuel had watched the Clintons in 1994, and he thought he knew where they had gone wrong. President Bill Clinton had assigned his wife, Hillary, the task of coming up with a comprehensive health care plan. Hillary Clinton consulted experts and worked for a year before delivering a hefty plan to her husband, who in turn gave it to Congress with instructions to pass the bill. Congress, however, doesn't take that kind of instruction well. Allegedly the late senator Daniel Patrick Moynihan (whose New York seat Hillary Clinton would later win) took one look and said, "I'm not even going to read it."[1]

Members of Congress weren't the only powerful opponents of the Clinton bill. The insurance, medical, and pharmaceutical industries were all opposed and immediately spent millions on an advertising campaign to defeat it, as well as on intensive lobbying efforts to convince an already skeptical Congress to ignore the bill. It never even came up for a vote.

Getting Everyone on Board
President Barack Obama speaks about health care in May 2009 while leaders from the insurance, hospital, and other medical industries stand with him. Earlier efforts at health care reform floundered, in part because Congress and relevant interest groups were excluded from the process.

As far as Emanuel was concerned, the lessons learned were first, get Congress involved from the start, and second, do something to bring the relevant interest groups to the table.

The Obama team took these lessons to heart. From the beginning, Congress invested heavily in the reform bill's design. And in March 2009, the White House invited members of all the affected industries to meet with President Obama and members of Congress. Out of the public eye the president's negotiators met with representatives of the health care industry and deals were made. For example, America's Health Insurance Plans (AHIP), an industry interest group that represents the insurance companies, agreed to sign on to a plan of universal insurance coverage for all Americans, regardless of preexisting health conditions, in exchange for the White House's agreement that any plan it endorsed would require every American who could afford it to buy insurance and would not include a public competitor to the private health insurance plans. Similarly, the representatives of the pharmaceutical industry agreed to make $80 billion in cuts on drug prices in exchange for the White House's agreement not to push for further cuts. Though this situation would change before the health care reform bill became law, the Obama administration had, at least initially, co-opted two of the loudest and richest voices that had brought down the Clinton health care plan.

But at what cost? Republicans had already determined that their strategy would be to deny Obama any legislative victories they could, so they were all opposed to health care reform for political, if not policy, reasons. In addition, by making deals with the health care industry, Obama, who had promised a change in the way Washington did business, alienated many in his own party. Some of the strongest criticism of his plan came from disillusioned liberals who were resentful that the bill would require them to buy insurance from private companies, and who believed that Obama had sold out the so-called "public option" and the opportunity to accrue cost savings by reducing drug costs further. The clamor of criticism nearly drowned out the victory celebration when the president finally signed the law on March 23, 2010.

Was it worth it? Was Emanuel's calculation correct that the bill would not pass at all if special interest groups torpedoed it? Was the political cost of seeming to be "consorting with the enemy" too great to bear? Just what was at stake in the Obama administration's decision to bring health groups into the reform process at an early stage? ■

Although they have long existed, interest groups, unlike political parties, were not a major force in American politics until the beginning of the twentieth century.

faction a group of citizens united by some common passion or interest and opposed to the rights of other citizens or to the interests of the whole community

interest group an organization of individuals who share a common political goal and unite for the purpose of influencing government decisions

political action committees (PACs) the fundraising arms of interest groups

French observer Alexis de Tocqueville, traveling in America in the early 1830s, noted a peculiar (he thought) tendency of Americans to join forces with their friends, neighbors, and colleagues. He said, "Americans of all ages, all conditions, and all dispositions, constantly form associations. They have not only commercial and manufacturing companies, in which all take part, but associations of a thousand other kinds—religious, moral, serious, futile, general or restricted, enormous or diminutive."[2] Figure 13.1 shows that Americans are indeed among the top "joiners" in the world.

While Tocqueville's remarks did not refer specifically to political groups, James Madison was concerned about the American propensity to form political associations, or what he called factions. As we saw in Chapter 3, Madison defined a **faction** as a group of citizens united by some common passion or interest, and opposed to the rights of other citizens or to the interests of the whole community.[3] He feared that factions would weaken and destabilize a republic, but he also believed, as he argued in *Federalist* No. 10, that a large republic could contain the effects of factions by making it hard for potential members to find one another and by providing for so many potential political groups that, if they did find each other and organize, their very numbers would cancel each other out.

Modern political scientists have a different take on factions, which they call by the more neutral term *interest groups*. An **interest group** is an organization of individuals who share a common political goal and unite for the purpose of influencing public policy decisions.[4] (Parties, as you may recall from the previous chapter, also seek to influence policy, but they do so by sponsoring candidates in elections.) The one major difference between this definition and Madison's is that many political scientists do not believe that all interest groups are opposed to the broad public interest. Rather, they hold that interest groups play an important role in our democracy, ensuring that the views of organized interests are heard in the governing process.[5] That is, interest groups are an essential part of the "who" in our formulation of politics as who gets what and how. We saw in Chapter 1 that interest groups play a central role in the pluralist theory of democracy, which argues that democracy is enhanced when citizens' interests are represented through group membership. The group interaction ensures that members' interests are represented but also that no group can become too powerful.

Although they have long existed, interest groups, unlike political parties, were not a major force in American politics until the beginning of the twentieth century. When the Progressive reformers at the turn of the century opened up the political process to the people, political parties were weakened and interest groups were correspondingly strengthened. By the 1960s, Washington, D.C., was awash in interest group activity as the federal government continued to expand its New Deal and Great Society programs,[6] and the growth has continued to the present day. While precise data on the number of interest groups do not exist, according to one author, from 1970 to 1990, an average of ten interest groups were formed every week.[7]

The increase in the number of interest groups accelerated after 1974, when the Federal Election Campaign Act was passed in an effort to curb campaign spending abuses. Seeking to regulate the amount of money an interest group could give to candidates for federal office, the law provided for **political action committees (PACs)** to serve as fundraisers for interest groups. As we will see later in this chapter, PACs are limited in how much money they can donate to a candidate, but a number of loopholes allow them to get around some of the restriction, and recent court cases have lifted limitations on how much money these groups can spend on a candidate's behalf.[8] Although many PACs are creatures of interest groups, others are independent and act as interest groups in their own right. Though their activities are limited to collecting and distributing money, PACs have become extremely powerful players in American politics. Today there are about 4,210 PACs,[9] and they typically contribute a substantial portion of candidates' campaign funds, although Obama broke the pattern of campaign reliance on PACs in 2008.

The explosion of interest group activity has probably caused Madison and the other founders to roll over in their

Figure 13.1

Americans Like to Belong

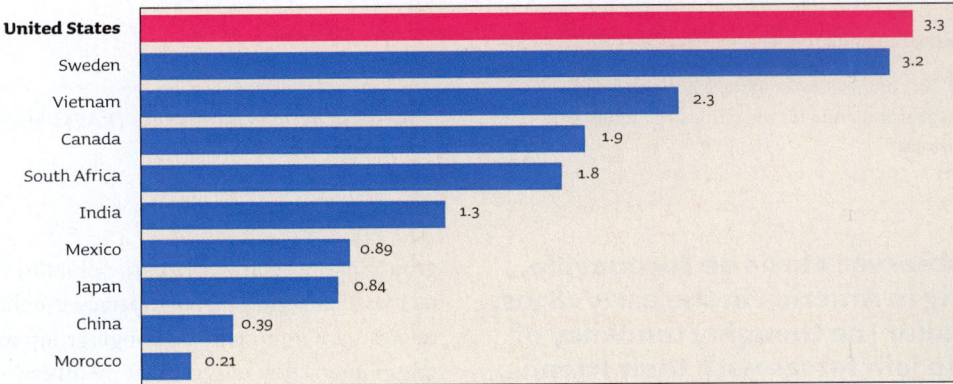

United States	3.3
Sweden	3.2
Vietnam	2.3
Canada	1.9
South Africa	1.8
India	1.3
Mexico	0.89
Japan	0.84
China	0.39
Morocco	0.21

Source: World Values Survey. Respondents interviewed in 1999–2001 were asked about the organizations, clubs, and groups they belonged to. Calculated by the authors.

graves. After all, Madison believed that he had secured the republic against what he called the "mischiefs of faction." He could not have envisioned a day when mass transportation and communication systems would virtually shrink the large size of the republic that he had believed would isolate interest groups. In today's world, dairy farmers in Wisconsin can easily form associations with dairy farmers in Pennsylvania; coal producers in the East can organize with coal producers in the Midwest; citrus growers in Florida can plan political strategy with citrus growers in California. Nor would Madison have foreseen the development of the Internet, which allows hundreds of thousands of people to organize and to voice their concerns to their representatives almost instantaneously.

Critics argue that interest groups have too much power, that they don't effectively represent the interests of groups that don't organize (the poor, the homeless, or the young, for instance), and that they clog up the vital arteries of American democracy, leading to gridlock and stagnation.[10] Supporters echo Madison's pluralist hopes—that group politics can preserve political stability by containing and regulating conflict and by providing checks on any one group's power. In this chapter we examine these two perspectives on interest group politics. Specifically, you will learn about

- *the various roles interest groups play in the U.S. political system and the ways they organize*
- *the many types of interest groups and the kinds of interests they represent*

- *how interest groups attempt to exert their influence through lobbying and campaign activities*
- *the resources that different interest groups bring to bear on influencing governmental decisions*
- *the relationship of citizens to interest groups in American politics—and the question of whether interest group politics is biased in favor of certain groups in society*

The Roles and Formation of Interest Groups

Organizing around common political goals to influence policy from outside the apparatus of government

Whether we approve or disapprove of the heavy presence of interest groups in the United States, it is undeniable that they play a significant role in determining who gets what in American politics. In this section we consider the various political roles that interest groups play, and the conditions and challenges they have met in order to organize in the first place.

lobbying interest group activities aimed at persuading policymakers to support the group's positions

Roles of Interest Groups

Negative images of interest groups abound in American politics and the media. Republicans speak of the Democrats as "pandering" to special interest groups like labor unions and trial lawyers; in their turn, Democrats claim that the Republican Party has been captured by big business and the religious right. In both cases, the parties charge each other with giving special treatment to some groups at the expense of the public good. The truth is that, as Madison guessed, interest groups have become an integral part of American politics, and neither party can afford to ignore them. In this section we go beyond the negative stereotypes of interest groups to discuss the important roles they play in political representation, participation, education, agenda building, provision of program alternatives, and program monitoring.[11]

- *Representation.* Interest groups play an important role in representing their members' views to Congress, the executive branch, and administrative agencies. Whether they represent teachers, manufacturers of baby food, people concerned with the environment, or the elderly, interest groups ensure that their members' concerns are adequately heard in the policymaking process. The activity of persuading policymakers to support their members' positions is called *lobbying*. Lobbying is the central activity of interest groups.

- *Participation.* Interest groups provide an avenue for citizen participation in politics that goes beyond voting in periodic elections. They are a mechanism for people sharing the same interests or pursuing the same policy goals to come together, pool resources, and channel their efforts for collective action. Whereas individual political action might seem futile, participation in the group can be much more effective.

- *Education.* One of the more important functions of interest groups is to educate policymakers regarding issues that are important to the interest group. Members of Congress must deal with many issues and generally cannot hope to become experts on more than a few. Consequently they are often forced to make laws in areas where they have scant knowledge. Interest groups can fill this void by providing details on issues about which they are often the experts.

In addition, sometimes interest groups must educate their members about important issues that may affect them.

- *Agenda building.* We can think of those issues that Congress, the executive branch, or administrative agencies will address as an informal political agenda. It is the role of an interest group to alert the proper government authorities about its issue; get the issue on the political agenda; and, finally, make the issue a high priority for action.

- *Provision of program alternatives.* Interest groups can be effective at supplying alternative suggestions for how issues should be dealt with once they have been put on the agenda. From this mix of proposals, political actors choose a solution.[12]

- *Program monitoring.* Once laws are enacted, interest groups keep tabs on their consequences, informing Congress and the regulatory agencies about the effects, both expected and unexpected, of federal policy. For example, the Children's Defense Fund has been active in drawing the attention of the national government to the effect of federal policies on the well-being of children.[13] Program monitoring helps the government decide whether to continue or change a policy, and it also helps to keep politicians accountable by ensuring that someone is paying attention to what they do.

> **Thinking Outside the Box**
>
> **Does it distort democracy for interest groups to bring different resources to the political process?**

Why Do Interest Groups Form?

Many of us can imagine public problems that we think need to be addressed. But despite our country's reputation as a nation of joiners, most of us never act, never organize a group, and never even join one. Social scientists call this the *problem of collective action*: the difficulty of getting people to work

Slow Food Nation

Slow Food USA is an interest group that represents people who want to preserve local, authentic ways of growing and preparing food. An offshoot of the international Slow Food movement, and the brainchild of interest group entrepreneur Carlo Petrini, Slow Food advocates eating regionally, seasonally, and convivially.

together to achieve a common goal. The problem of collective action can be overcome, in part, by the shared perception of a serious common problem or threat, an abundance of time and money to support a cause, and effective leadership.

Common Problem or Threat

Most interest groups seem to be organized around shared interests, but many people who share interests never come together at all. What causes some groups to organize? For one noted scholar, the key triggering mechanism for interest group formation is a disturbance in the political, social, or economic environment that threatens the members of a group—for instance, governmental action to regulate businesses and professions.[14] This threat alerts the group's

> **interest group entrepreneurs** effective group leaders who are likely to have organized the group and can effectively promote its interests among members and the public

members that they need to organize to protect their interests through political action.

Resource Advantage

While this explanation helps us understand interest group formation, it focuses on the external threats to a group rather than the internal resources that the potential group has. Researchers have long observed that some interest groups organize more easily than others and that some interest groups have formed without an external threat.[15] The resources available to prospective interest group members seem to be the key. Those with more money can pay for the direct-mail campaigns, publicity, legal assistance, and professional lobbying help that get the message to Washington and the public that the group means business. Perhaps just as important, those with greater resources are more likely to understand the political process, to have the confidence to express their views, and to appreciate the value of organizing into an interest group to push their policy positions.[16] This suggests that individuals with more wealth and more knowledge of the political system have a natural advantage in using the interest group process to pursue their policy goals. This also can explain why business and professional groups are more prevalent than those that represent the homeless, welfare recipients, and the unemployed.

Effective Leadership

Even though wealthy groups have an advantage over groups whose pockets are not as well lined, an effective and charismatic leader can help redress the balance. The strong, effective leadership of what one scholar has called **interest group entrepreneurs** can be crucial to a group's ability to organize, no matter what its resources are.[17] These entrepreneurs have a number of important characteristics, among them that they shoulder much of the initial burden and costs of organizing the group, and that they can convince people that the interest group will be able to promote the group's interests and influence the policies that affect it.[18] Such inspirational leaders have included César Chavez, who organized the United Farm Workers; Ralph Nader, who began a number of consumer interest groups; and Candy Lightner, who established Mothers Against Drunk Driving (MADD).

The Free Rider Problem

External threats, financial resources, and effective leadership can spur interest group formation, but they are usually not

> ***free rider problem*** the difficulty groups face in recruiting when potential members can gain the benefits of the group's actions whether they join or not
>
> ***collective good*** a good or service that, by its very nature, cannot be denied to anyone who wants to consume it
>
> ***selective incentives*** benefits that are available only to group members as an inducement to get them to join

> ***material benefits*** selective incentives in the form of tangible rewards
>
> ***solidary benefits*** selective incentives related to the interaction and bonding among group members
>
> ***expressive benefits*** selective incentives that derive from the opportunity to express values and beliefs and to be committed to a greater cause

enough to overcome what we called earlier the problem of collective action. Another name for this is the ***free rider problem***: why should people join you to solve the problem when they can free ride—that is, reap the benefits of your action whether they join or not?[19] The free rider problem affects interest groups because most of the policies that interest groups advocate involve the distribution of a collective good. A ***collective good*** is a good or benefit that, once provided, cannot be denied to others. Public safety, clean air, peace, and lower consumer prices are all examples of collective goods that can be enjoyed by anyone. When collective goods are involved, it is difficult to persuade people to join groups because they are going to reap the benefits anyway. The larger the number of potential members involved, the more this holds true, because each will have trouble seeing that his or her efforts will make a difference.

Many groups overcome the free rider problem by supplying ***selective incentives***—benefits available to their members that are not available to the general population. There are three types of these incentives:[20]

- ***Material benefits*** are tangible rewards that members can use. One of the most common material benefits is information. For example, many groups publish a magazine or a newsletter packed with information about issues important to the group and pending legislation relevant to the group's activities. The American Bankers Association provides two publications (*Banking Journal* and *Banking News*) as well as email and fax service to select members who desire immediate information about banking issues that develop in Washington (*ABA Insider*). In addition to information, interest groups often offer material benefits in the form of group activities or group benefit policies. The National Rifle Association (NRA) sponsors hunting and shooting competitions and offers discounted insurance policies. The Sierra Club offers a package of benefits that includes over 250 nature treks throughout the United States.

- ***Solidary benefits*** come from interaction and bonding among group members. For many individuals, politics is an enjoyable activity, and the social interactions occurring through group activities provide high levels of satisfaction and, thus, are a strong motivating force. Solidary incentives can come from local chapter meetings,

Breaking the Fast

Inspirational leaders attract attention to their causes, making their appeals difficult to ignore. César Chavez, founder of the United Farm Workers, went on a twenty-five-day fast in 1968 to reaffirm the importance of nonviolence in union organizing. The bread-breaking ceremony that ended his fast drew a crowd of four thousand farm workers, supporters like Senator Robert F. Kennedy, and widespread media coverage.

lobbying missions to Washington or the state capital, or group-sponsored activities. The significant point is that the interest group provides the venue through which friendships are made and social interactions occur.

- ***Expressive benefits*** are those rewards that come from doing something that you strongly believe in, from affiliating yourself with a purpose to which you are deeply committed—essentially from the *expression* of your values and interests. Many people, for example, are attracted to the American Civil Liberties Union (ACLU) because they passionately believe in protecting individual civil liberties. People who join the National Right to Life Committee believe strongly in making all abortions illegal in the United States. Their membership in the group is a way of expressing their views and ideals.

> **economic interest groups** groups that organize to influence government policy for the economic benefit of their members

Group leaders often use a mixture of incentives to recruit and sustain members. Thus the NRA recruits many of its members because they are committed to the cause of protecting an individual's right to bear arms. The NRA reinforces this expressive incentive with material incentives like its magazine and with solidary incentives resulting from group fellowship. The combination of these incentives helps make the NRA one of the strongest interest groups in Washington.

Who What How

While they may have any number of goals, interest groups primarily want to influence policy. To accomplish this goal, they employ representation, participation, education, agenda building, alternative policy proposals, and program monitoring. To get anything done at all, however, they must organize and convince members to join. If all of the benefits of membership are collective goods, then potential members may free ride on the efforts of others while still enjoying the product of the group's success. Thus interest groups offer selective benefits to entice members: material benefits, solidary benefits, and expressive benefits.

Types of Interest Groups
Organizing around shared interests, passions, and identities

There are potentially as many interest groups in America as there are interests, which is to say the possibilities are unlimited. Therefore, it is helpful to divide them into different types, based on the kind of benefit they seek for their members. Here we distinguish between economic, equal opportunity, public, and government (both foreign and domestic) interest groups. Depending on the definitions that they use, scholars have come up with different schemes for classifying interest groups, so do not be too surprised if you come across these groups with different labels at various times.

Economic Interest Groups

Economic interest groups seek to influence government for the economic benefit of their members. Generally these are players in the productive and professional activities of the nation—businesses, unions, other occupational associations,

agriculturalists, and so on. The economic benefits they seek may be higher wages for a group or an industry, lower tax rates, bigger government subsidies, or more favorable regulations. What all economic interest groups have in common is that they are focused primarily on pocketbook issues.

Corporations and Business Associations

Given that government plays a key role in regulating the economy and defining the ground rules for economic competition, it should not surprise us that corporations and business groups are the most numerous and the most powerful of all interest groups. About 70 percent of all the interest groups that have their own lobbies in Washington, D.C., or hire professionals there, are business related.[21] The primary issues that they pursue involve taxes, labor, and regulatory issues. However, business interests have also been active in the areas of education, welfare reform, and health insurance.

Economic interest groups may be corporations like British Petroleum (BP) or Monsanto, which lobby government directly. More than six hundred corporations keep full-time Washington offices to deal with government relations, and that doesn't count the companies that hire out this function to independent lobbyists, or whose attempts to influence policy are made in cooperation with other businesses.[22] Such cooperation may take the form of industry associations, like the Tobacco Institute, the American Sportfishing Association, or the National Frozen Pizza Institute.

At a more general level, businesses may join together in associations like the National Association of Manufacturers or the Business Roundtable, representing major corporations.[23] The most diverse of these major business lobbies is the Chamber of Commerce, which represents a whole host of businesses (three million) ranging from small mom-and-pop stores to large employers.[24] In the 2010 midterm elections, the Chamber of Commerce was especially active, promising to spend $75 million, primarily to elect Republicans who support its opposition to the Democrats' health care and tax policies.[25]

Unions and Professional Associations

Interest groups often organize in response to one another. The business groups we just discussed organized not only as a way to deal with the increased regulatory powers of the federal government but also because labor was organized. Although labor organizations do not represent the force in society that they once did (membership has declined dramatically since the early 1950s, when over 35 million workers were unionized),[26] they can still be a formidable power when they decide to influence government, especially at the state level. The American Federation of Labor–Congress of Industrial Organizations (AFL-CIO) is by far the largest American union organization, with 11.5 million members from fifty-six trade and industrial unions.[27] In 2005, the year of the AFL-CIO's fiftieth anniversary, two of its most influential member unions, the Brotherhood of Teamsters and Service Employees International Union, left the AFL-CIO with two other unions, depriving the organization of one-third of its members.[28] The United Auto Workers and the United Mine Workers of America also represent major segments of the labor force.[29]

Another large segment of America's work force represented by unions are public employees. The American Federation of Government Employees represents federal workers, while the American Federation of State, County and Municipal Employees represents workers at lower levels of government. Teachers, firefighters, police, and postal workers, among others, also have large unions that wield significant influence on matters of policy in their particular areas of interest.

Unions are not the only organizations to represent economic interests along occupational lines. Many occupations that require much training or education have formed professional associations. Their basic purposes are to protect the profession's interests and to promote policies that enhance its position. For example, the American Medical Association has lobbied vigorously to lower the amount of medical malpractice awards.[30] The American Bar Association not only represents attorneys' interests (as do groups like the Association of Trial Lawyers of America) but, over the years, also has actively promoted structural and procedural reforms of the courts.

Agricultural Interest Groups

Farming occupies an unusual place in American labor politics. It is the one occupation on which everyone in the nation depends for food, but it is also the one most subject to the vagaries of climate and other forces beyond human control. To keep farmers in business and the nation's food supply at affordable levels, the U.S. government has long regulated and subsidized agriculture. Consequently, although less than 2 percent of the U.S. work force is involved in farming, a large network of interest groups has grown up over the years to pursue policies favorable to agriculture. These include the

Thinking Outside **the Box**

Are there ways to get people to pay for collective goods?

American Farm Bureau, the largest national organization representing farmers, and other groups like the American Agriculture Movement and the National Farmers Union, which represents small farmers.[31]

The agricultural community has evolved over the years to include agribusiness interests ranging from growers' associations (wheat, corn, fruit) to large multinational corporations like Archer Daniels Midland (ADM is a major grain processor), Altria (made up of the Philip Morris tobacco company and Kraft Foods), and ConAgra Foods, Inc. These agribusiness interests are not very different from the corporate interests we discussed earlier, even though their business is agriculture.

Equal Opportunity Interest Groups

Equal opportunity interest groups organize to promote the civil rights of groups that do not believe that their members' interests are being adequately represented and protected in national politics through traditional means. Because in many cases these groups are economically disadvantaged, or are afraid that they might become disadvantaged, these groups also advocate economic rights for their members. Equal opportunity groups believe that they are underrepresented not because of *what they do* but because of *who they are*. They may be the victims of discrimination, or see themselves as threatened. These groups have organized on the basis of age, race, ethnic group, gender, and sexual orientation. Membership is not limited to people who are part of the demographic group because many people believe that promoting the interests and rights of various groups in society is in the broader interest of all. For this reason, some scholars classify these groups as public interest groups, a type we explore in the next section.

Age

One of the fastest-growing segments of the U.S. population is composed of people aged sixty-five and older, as we saw in Chapter 2. Established in 1961, the American Association of

Retired Persons (now known simply as AARP) has a membership of more than 40 million Americans, more than one-half of all Americans over fifty years old. Despite its name, ironically, almost half of AARP's members still work.[32] Why does a group that claims to represent retired Americans have so many workers? Because a mere $16 a year is all it takes to become a member of AARP and to enjoy its numerous material benefits, like reduced health insurance rates and travel discounts.

With the motto of "Leave No Child Behind," the Children's Defense Fund (CDF) is strikingly different from AARP, and not just in the ages of those it represents. The CDF is funded from foundation grants and private donations. Indeed, because its constituents are not adults, it does not have any formal members. To combat this, the CDF regularly holds media events in which it issues reports and displays the results of its sponsored research. Through these media events, the CDF hopes to draw the public's attention to the plight of children in poverty and enhance the public's support for programs that address their needs.[33] The CDF does not have the support of a legion of dues-paying members to get its proposed legislation passed. Supporters of children's rights and well-being suggest that this lack of effective advocates is precisely the reason that children are the largest group in the United States living in poverty.

Race and Ethnicity

Many equal opportunity groups promote the interests of racial or ethnic minorities. Among such groups, none can match the longevity and success of the National Association for the Advancement of Colored People (NAACP). Founded in 1909 in response to race riots in Springfield, Illinois (the home of Abraham Lincoln), the NAACP has had a long history of fighting segregation and promoting the cause of equal opportunity and civil rights for African Americans. Its Legal Defense and Educational Fund is responsible for litigating most of the precedent-setting civil rights cases, including the famous *Brown v. Board of Education*. (See Chapter 6 for details on the struggle for equal rights.) Today the NAACP is by far the largest race-based equal opportunity group, with a membership of over 500,000.[34]

Many other equal opportunity interest groups are similar to the NAACP but focus on the civil rights of other races or ethnic minorities. The League of United Latin American Citizens (LULAC) has worked for over seventy-five years to advocate the rights of Hispanics in the United States with respect to such issues as education, employment, voter registration, and housing.[35] The Mexican American Legal Defense and Educational Fund (MALDEF) is dedicated to the protection of Latinos in the United States, working through the courts and the legislatures on issues of language, immigration, employment, and education.[36] In a similar vein the American Indian Movement (AIM) has for over forty years promoted and protected the interests of Native Americans. Founded on a philosophy of self-determination, AIM has worked to support legal rights, educational opportunities, youth services, job training, and other programs designed to eliminate the exploitation and oppression of Native Americans.[37] Likewise, numerous groups represent the concerns of Asian Americans. For example, the Southeast Asia Resource Action Center (SEARAC) is an umbrella organization coordinating the efforts of several networks supporting Asian Americans. SEARAC is a national and regional advocate for Cambodian, Laotian, and Vietnamese Americans on public policies concerning health care, economic growth, civil rights, and increased political participation.[38]

Gender

Issues dealing with the equal treatment of women are a major feature of the American political landscape. Among women's groups, the National Organization for Women (NOW) is the largest, with over 500,000 members nationwide.[39] Funded by membership dues, NOW maintains an active lobbying effort in Washington and in many state capitals, builds coalitions with other women's rights groups, and conducts leadership training for its members. However, NOW has been a lightning rod for controversy among women because of its strong support for women's reproductive rights. Other groups that have drawn fire for having a feminist ideological agenda include EMILY's List, which stands for Early Money Is Like Yeast (it makes the dough rise). EMILY's List is a PAC that contributes money to Democratic women candidates.

Whereas NOW and groups like EMILY's List have ties to liberal interests, other groups like the National Women's Political Caucus have sprung up to support the efforts of all women to be elected to public office, no matter what their partisan affiliation. Still others are conservative. For every group like NOW or EMILY's List, there is a conservative counterpart that actively opposes most, if not all, of what is seen as a liberal feminist agenda. For instance, Republican women have formed WISH (Women in the Senate and House). Another prominent conservative women's group is the Eagle Forum, led by Phyllis Schlafly. Since 1972 the Eagle

public interest groups groups that organize to influence government to produce collective goods or services that benefit the general public

Forum has campaigned against reproductive rights, the Equal Rights Amendment, and the societal trend of women working outside the home.[40]

In addition to these women's groups, there are groups that promote equal opportunity for men. The American Coalition for Fathers and Children and the National Congress for Fathers and Children have formed around the issue of promoting divorced men's custodial rights.[41] These men's groups pale in comparison, however, to the women's groups when it comes to funding, membership, and national exposure.

Sexual Orientation

With the sexual revolution of the late 1960s and early 1970s, a number of gay and lesbian groups formed to fight discriminatory laws and practices based on sexual orientation. Their activities represent a two-tier approach to advocating equal opportunities for gays and lesbians. First, there is a focus on local and state governments to pass local ordinances or state laws protecting the civil rights of gays and lesbians. Groups that have made efforts at the local and state levels include the Gay and Lesbian Activists Alliance, which has been active in the mid-Atlantic states around Washington, D.C., since 1971, and the Gay and Lesbian Advocates and Defenders, a group composed of individuals from New England. On the national level, groups like the National Gay and Lesbian Task Force tend to focus their efforts on opposing federal policies that are intolerant of gays and lesbians (for example, exclusion of gays and lesbians from the military or a constitutional amendment to ban gay marriage) and on promoting funding for AIDS research.

While most gay and lesbian groups are officially nonpartisan, many have close ties to the Democratic Party. To promote gay and lesbian issues within the Republican Party, activists within the GOP have formed groups like the Log Cabin Republicans to provide campaign contributions to GOP candidates who support equal opportunity for gays and lesbians, and to lobby Republican representatives and senators on gay and lesbian issues.[42]

Public Interest Groups

Public interest groups try to influence government to produce noneconomic benefits that cannot be restricted to the interest groups' members or denied to any member of the general public. The benefits of clean air, for instance, are available to all, not just the members of the environmental group that

Not Keeping It Buried

Lt. Dan Choi, an Iraq war army veteran discharged under the U.S. military's Don't Ask, Don't Tell policy, cleans the gravestone of Sgt. Leonard Matlovich, a Vietnam veteran also discharged for being gay, in November 2010. Matlovich's headstone reads, "They gave me a medal for killing two men and discharge for loving one." Don't Ask Don't Tell was repealed by Congress in December 2010, in part because of the activism of Choi and gay rights groups, who kept the issue on Congress' and the president's agenda.

fought for them. In a way, all interest group benefits are collective goods that all members of the group can enjoy, but public interest groups seek collective goods that are open to all members of society or, in some cases, the entire world.

Public interest group members are usually motivated by a view of the world that they think everyone would be better off to adopt. They believe that the benefit they seek is good for everyone, even if individuals outside their group may disagree or even reject the benefit. While few people would dispute the value of clean air, peace, and the protection of human rights internationally, there is no such consensus about protecting the right to an abortion, or the right to carry concealed weapons, or the right to smoke marijuana. Yet each of these issues has public interest groups dedicated to procuring and enforcing these rights for all Americans. Because they are involved in the production of collective goods for very large populations and the individual incentive to contribute may be particularly difficult to perceive, public interest groups are especially vulnerable to the free rider problem. That has not stopped them from organizing, however. The number of these groups grew dramatically in the 1960s and again in the 1980s.[43]

People are drawn to public interest groups because they support the groups' values and goals; that is, expressive benefits are the primary draw for membership. Often when events occur that threaten the goals of a public interest group, membership increases. For example, fearing that the Republicans would dismantle environmental laws after Ronald Reagan was elected president, new members flocked to environmental interest groups like the Sierra Club and the National Wildlife Federation; these organizations gained about 150,000 members from 1980 to 1985.[44] Likewise, after President Clinton signed the Brady Bill in 1993—which required a waiting period before gun purchases, among other regulations—the NRA saw its membership increase by half a million, and it shot up again in 2008 when, in anticipation of Barack Obama's election to the presidency, the NRA claimed that Obama would ban guns if elected (even though Obama's record on gun rights is hardly one designed to please gun control advocates).[45]

While many members are initially attracted by expressive benefits, public interest groups seek to keep them active by offering material benefits and services ranging from free subscriptions to the group's magazine to discount insurance packages.

Environmental Groups

Starting with Earth Day in 1970, environmentally based interest groups have been actively engaged in promoting environmental policies. The Clean Air and Water Acts, the Endangered Species Act, and the creation of the Environmental Protection Agency all represent examples of their successes during the 1970s. Today the Sierra Club, National Audubon Society, and Natural Resources Defense Council maintain active and professional lobbying efforts in Washington, as do environmental groups such as Greenpeace. On the extreme fringes of the environmental movement are more confrontational groups like Earth First! Their members take a dim view of attempts to lobby members of Congress for "green" laws. Instead, their calls for direct action have included building and living in aerial platforms in old-growth redwood forests in California so as to dissuade the timber industry from felling the trees. Activists have also protested by taking over the offices of local members of Congress.[46]

Consumer Groups

The efforts of Ralph Nader and his public interest group Public Citizen have become synonymous with the cause of

consumer protectionism. Since his path-breaking book *Unsafe at Any Speed* (1965) documented the safety problems with Chevrolet's Corvair, Nader has been exposing the hazards of a variety of other consumer products and addressing unsafe practices in the nuclear power, airline, and health care industries.[47] Another consumer advocacy group is Consumers Union, the nonprofit publisher of *Consumer Reports* magazine. Consumers Union testifies before state and federal government agencies, petitions government, and files lawsuits to protect consumer interests.[48]

Religious Groups

Religious groups in America have had a long history of interest group activity, dating back to the abolitionist movement. In more recent times, religious groups have developed and grown in response to what they describe as the moral decay and decadence of American society. The Christian Coalition, for example, with two million members the most powerful religious fundamentalist group in American politics,[49] lobbies on political issues and provides members with voters' guides. Pat Robertson, who had chaired the Christian Coalition's board, also developed the Christian Broadcasting Network in 1976, which, along with other large Christian media sources like James Dobson's *Focus on the Family* radio broadcast, helps to educate and mobilize evangelical Christians on political issues nationwide. These groups have become a major force in national politics and an important part of the coalition supporting the Republican Party.[50]

Fundamentalist Christian groups are not the only religiously affiliated interest groups. The United States Conference of Catholic Bishops also lobbies on particular issues, and the Anti-Defamation League promotes a broad set of foreign, domestic, and legal issues that combat worldwide anti-Semitism and discrimination against Jewish Americans.

Second Amendment Groups

Based on its interpretation of the Second Amendment to the Constitution, the NRA is opposed to almost any effort to control and regulate the sale and distribution of firearms. Overall, the NRA has had considerable policy success. Despite public opinion polls that show a clear majority of Americans favoring gun control, the level of regulation of gun purchases remains minimal. The NRA's success can be credited to its highly dedicated members who are willing to contribute their time, resources, and votes to those candidates who support the NRA's positions—and, conversely, to a credible threat of retribution to officeholders who cross the NRA. In the 1994 elections, one year after passage of the Brady Bill, NRA voters contributed to the coalition of voters who ousted moderate Democratic representatives, and Brady supporters, across the South.[51]

One group that has challenged the power of the NRA is Handgun Control, Inc., an interest group founded by Brady Bill namesake James Brady, who was severely wounded in the 1981 attempted assassination of President Reagan, and his wife, Sarah. Handgun Control, Inc., now known as the Brady Campaign to Prevent Gun Violence, was instrumental in getting the waiting-period legislation passed in 1993. In 1994 Congress followed the Brady Bill with the Violent Crime Control and Law Enforcement Act, which banned nineteen types of automatic or semiautomatic assault rifles.[52] With the election of a Republican majority in 1994, gun control efforts had less success in Congress and when the assault weapons ban lapsed in 2004, they were able to keep it from being renewed.[53]

Reproductive Rights Groups

The Supreme Court's decision in *Roe v. Wade* (1973), granting women the right to an abortion, generated a number of interest groups. On the pro-choice side of this debate are the National Abortion Rights Action League (NARAL) and Planned Parenthood. These groups have mounted a public relations campaign aimed at convincing policymakers that a majority of Americans want women to have the right to choose safe and legal abortions.[54]

On the pro-life side of the debate are the National Right to Life Committee and its more confrontational partner, Operation Rescue. The National Right to Life Committee lobbies Congress and state legislatures to limit abortions, hoping ultimately to secure the passage of a constitutional amendment banning them altogether. Operation Rescue attempts to prevent abortions by blocking access to abortion clinics, picketing clinics, and intercepting women who are considering abortions. In recent years, pro-life groups have shifted from a single focus on abortion to other issues they see as similar, such as opposing stem cell research and, in 2005, protesting the removal of a feeding tube from a brain-damaged woman.

Other Public Interest Groups

Other public interest groups target the issue of human rights. The ACLU is a nonprofit, nonpartisan defender of individual

Research for Cures Makes Waves

Many scientists and medical experts believe that stem cells have the potential to treat and cure serious diseases, including Parkinson's, Alzheimer's, and other neural disorders. Actor Michael J. Fox (shown here with Senator John Kerry) was diagnosed with Parkinson's in 1991 and for years has lobbied state and federal officials for legislation opening the avenues for further stem cell research. Critics, however, argue that the use of stem cells, especially those from embryos, is unethical and immoral.

rights against the encroachment of a powerful government. The ACLU supports the rights of disadvantaged minorities and claims to be the "nation's guardian of liberty."[55] Another human rights group, Amnesty International, promotes human rights worldwide, with over 1.5 million members in 150 countries. In the United States, Amnesty International lobbies on issues such as the death penalty, arms control, and globalization.[56]

Interest groups have also taken up the cause of animal rights. The most well-known of these groups is the Humane Society. Beyond providing local animal shelters, the Humane Society researches animal cruelty and lobbies governments at all levels on issues ranging from domestic pet overpopulation and adoption to farm animal treatment and wildlife habitat protection (see "*Profiles in Citizenship*: Wayne Pacelle"). In recent years a number of actors and actresses have used their celebrity status to protect animals. People for the Ethical

▶ **Who, What, How, and WHEN: Interest Groups and Women's Rights**

Alexis de Tocqueville said Americans were a nation of joiners, and there do seem to be interest groups in the United States for almost every issue imaginable. For some groups, interest group formation has been especially important for helping the public see as political the issues that they take for granted in their daily lives. Consider the impact of these interest groups on women's rights over time:

1873 — **Women's Christian Temperance Union**

The WCTU began as an organization dedicated to the prohibition of and abstinence from alcohol and drugs. But the organization saw this cause as closely related to women's rights since alcohol abuse was linked to domestic battery and rape, and laws at the time did little to protect women from these problems. Women lacked the political power to change the laws to protect themselves; they could not vote, and in many states women could not hold property or maintain custody of their children in a divorce. The WCTU endorsed women's suffrage and was one of the first interest groups to maintain a professional lobbyist in Washington, D.C.

1890 — **National American Woman Suffrage Association**

The National Woman Suffrage Association (NWSA) and the American Woman Suffrage Association (AWSA) both formed in the mid-1800s to campaign for women's suffrage. Although they took different approaches (for instance, the NWSA allowed only women members while the AWSA allowed men) and sometimes worked in opposition to each other, in 1890 they merged to form a united front toward their goal. They lobbied Congress and various presidents and organized at the state and local levels to help women gain the right to vote in 1920.

1966 — **National Organization for Women**

Title VII of the 1964 Civil Rights Act called for equality between women and men in employment; however, the Equal Employment Opportunity Commission, the organization established to enforce this standard, continued to allow newspapers to publish advertisements for jobs with sex as a qualification (for example, a job opening for a woman secretary). NOW lobbied successfully to end sex-segregated job advertising. It continues to lobby for issues such as the Equal Rights Amendment, equal pay for women, improvements in rape laws, and pro-choice efforts.

Treatment of Animals (PETA) is a leading national interest group promoting the rights of animals. Its grassroots campaigns include attacking major health and beauty corporations like Procter & Gamble for using animals for product testing, assailing circuses and rodeos for using animals as entertainment, and condemning fur coat manufacturers for the cruel ways they kill animals.[57] Other groups like the Animal Rights Law Project at Rutgers University and the Animal Liberation Front also advocate animal rights. Animal rights activists often use civil disobedience in their attempts to stop hunting and end the use of animals for biomedical and product safety tests.[58]

Government Interest Groups

Foreign governments also lobby Congress and the president. Typically some lobbyists' most lucrative contracts come from foreign governments seeking to influence foreign trade policies. The Japanese government maintains one of the more active lobbying efforts in Washington, hiring former members of Congress and bureaucrats to aid in their efforts to keep U.S. markets open to Japanese imports.[59] In recent years, ethics rules have been initiated to prevent former government officials from working as foreign government lobbyists as soon as they leave office, but lobbying firms

1967 **Eagle Forum**
Lawyer Phyllis Schlafly founded the conservative Eagle Forum, which a few years later became Stop ERA, a coalition opposed to the ratification of the Equal Rights Amendment. Schlafly believed it would have negative repercussions for women such as a loss of the traditional family relationship. Together with states' rights organizations, Stop ERA was successful in defeating the ratification of the amendment. The Eagle Forum continues to lobby today for pro-life causes and against same-sex marriage, feminist proposals, the possible ratification of the ERA, and other conservative causes.

1988 **Coalition Against Trafficking in Women**
Developed as a nongovernmental organization to combat trafficking in women, CATW works to prevent movement of women across state or international borders for the purposes of forced prostitution. It has lobbied the United Nations and various national governments, including the United States, for policies that punish those who participate in trafficking. In 2000 it lobbied Congress to pass the Trafficking Victims Protection Act—a policy that garnered support from such wide-ranging interests as feminists against prostitution and conservative Christian groups.

continue to hire them when they can because of their contacts and expertise.[60]

Domestic governments have also become increasingly involved in the business of influencing federal policy. With the growing complexities of American federalism, state and local governments have an enormous stake in what the federal government does, and often try to gain resources, limit the impact of policy, and otherwise alter the effects of federal law. All fifty states have government relations offices in Washington to attempt to influence federal policy directly. In addition, the "Big Seven" major intergovernmental interest groups—the National Governors Association, the Council of State Governments, the National Conference of State Legislatures, the National League of Cities, the National Association of Counties, the United States Conference of Mayors, and the International City/County Management Association—all either lobby for benefits for subnational governments or otherwise represent the interests of intergovernmental actors.[61]

All citizens stand to win or lose a great deal from government action. If it goes their way, producing policy that benefits them, they win. But if it produces policy that helps other

Who What How

▶ **Profiles in Citizenship: Wayne Pacelle**

"... making the world a better place—that's the bottom line."

In the midst of one of his finest moments, Wayne Pacelle got himself thrown out of the gallery of the House of Representatives.

He was watching the vote on a budget amendment he had lobbied hard for, an amendment to cut millions of dollars of taxpayer money spent to promote the sale of U.S.-made mink coats in Italy, China,

and France. He needed 218 votes to win, and everyone thought they were going to be trounced. He watched the scoreboard light up with vote after vote. When they got to 232, he couldn't help it. He let out a yell and pumped his fist. But the House frowns on emotional displays in the gallery, and out he went. Was he abashed? Hardly. "It didn't take the smile off my face," he says, grinning even now at the memory.

It was a great win, but every single triumph matters to Pacelle—it's how he feeds his spirit and keeps himself going in the face of the often daunting odds and unimaginable stories of animal abuse he confronts daily in his job as CEO of the Humane Society of the United States. Each law enacted by Congress to protect animals (fifteen in the past few years), each state bill passed (more than 150), each statewide ballot measure approved (fifteen so far), each animal life saved, each creature relieved of pain and suffering—he tallies them all. "I celebrate the positive action because it's easy to get burned out," he says. "It's easy to get demoralized. . . . And for me, I just tell people you've got to celebrate every little victory, it makes a big difference."

"For us, it's not an all-or-nothing game," he explains. "We can't solve all of the issues in the world, we never will. . . . But if we solve it for a million, or 10 million, or a billion creatures, that's a 100-percent victory for each of those animals. And just that one act of merciful behavior or the shielding of an animal from abuse or cruelty can mean all the difference between a good quality of life and a miserable, tormented existence for that creature."

Pacelle has felt that kind of enormous, compassionate connection to animals ever since he was two or three years old. "It was a purely emotional, altruistic response that I had toward other creatures. I just saw them as powerless and I saw them as peers at that age, and they looked to me like they were composed of the same spark of life that people were."

He carried that empathy and awareness with him as he got older and, as he read philosophy and learned more about the world, he began to fit it into a broader context of what it meant to him to be a responsible citizen. He started an animal rights group in college in the 1980s, at

citizens at their expense, or passes the cost of expensive policy onto them, or reduces their ability to use the system to get what they want, then they lose. Economic actors want to protect their financial interests; members of disadvantaged or threatened groups want to protect their legal and economic interests; ideologically motivated people want to promote their vision of the good society; and governments want a good relationship with the U.S. federal government. All these actors promote their goals through the formation of different types of interest groups.

Interest Group Politics
Strategies for influencing different branches of government

The term *lobbying* comes from seventeenth-century England, where representatives of special interests would meet members of the English House of Commons in the large anteroom, or lobby, outside the Commons floor to plead their cases.[62] Contemporary lobbying, however, reaches far beyond the lobby of the House or Senate. Interest groups do indeed

the same time that he was active in the antiapartheid movement to limit U.S. investment in South Africa and in protests of U.S. involvement in Central America. Ask him what the common thread is and he is clear: "I'm broadly interested in making the world a better place," he says. "That's the bottom line. Public policy is just the means to achieve the end of a more fair, a more just society."

A huge and saintly ambition, but Pacelle doesn't look like a zealot or a crusader when he says it. Actually, he looks like, well, a movie star, or a relative of a famous American political family (possessing what the *Washington Post* once called "John Kennedy, Jr. good looks"). He is polished, articulate, and funny (it must run in the family—his brother, Richard, is the funniest political scientist we know), and the animals couldn't ask for a more dedicated or committed advocate.

How has he kept that idealism and commitment in the face of the giant sums of money that Washington lobbyists traffic in these days? He may be an optimist, but he's a realist, too.

"You'd be naive to think money doesn't have an impact," he says. "It does. It gains access, and it builds loyalty. But, ultimately, money is a means to an end. Money is there to have resources to deliver a message to influence voting behavior. So if you've got people who can organize around a principle and you can deliver votes based on that set of ideas, then you don't need money." Well, maybe not as much, anyway. Here are some of his thoughts:

On the positive side of lobbying:

There's a reason in Washington, D.C., that there are thousands of lobbyists and thousands of interest groups. They're not here for fun; it's not just a big party. They're here because it does make a difference and participation can have a measurable impact on public policy. I think for me, just being determined and dogged about it, just not relenting, just basically treating this as if it's a full court press all the time. . . . I mean when we're not on defense, we're on the offense. It's almost a very crusading sort of attitude. I don't like to infuse it with religious sorts of notions, but it's a powerful, ethical

construct. And having enough imagination to see that things can be different. That we're not just locked into our present set of social relationships and circumstances, that we can aspire to do things better.

On keeping the republic:

No one's going to hand you a key to change everything, but if you're smart and if you're determined you can make a real difference in the world. I've seen it happen thousands and thousands of times. And anybody who tells me differently just isn't paying attention to what's going on. And don't count on somebody else to do it, you know, don't count on a group like the Humane Society of the United States to do it. When I go around and I talk to people I say, "Listen, we can help." And our staff of four hundred, we've got great experts and we do a lot of amazing stuff, but you make the difference. It's the collective action of people of conscience that really can have a meaningful impact on society. And again, the history is of people stepping up and calling themselves to action. And leadership and citizenship are such important values in this culture. And if not them, who? ◼

contact lawmakers directly, but they no longer confine their efforts to chance meetings in the legislative lobby or to members of the legislature.

Today, lobbyists target all branches of government and the American people as well. The ranks of those who work with lobbyists have also swelled. Beginning in the 1980s, interest groups, especially those representing corporate interests, have been turning to a diverse group of political consultants, including professional Washington lobbyists, campaign specialists, advertising and media experts, pollsters, and academics. Lobbying today is a big business in its own right.

There are two main types of lobbying. **Direct lobbying** (sometimes called inside lobbying) is interaction with actual decision makers within government institutions. While we tend to think of Congress as the typical recipient of lobbying efforts, the president, the bureaucracy, and even the courts are also the focus of heavy efforts to influence policy. **Indirect lobbying** (or outside lobbying) attempts to influence policymakers by mobilizing interest group members or the general public to contact elected representatives on an issue. Some groups have resorted to more confrontational indirect methods, using political protests, often developing into

direct lobbying direct interaction with public officials for the purpose of influencing policy decisions

indirect lobbying attempts to influence government policymakers by encouraging the general public to put pressure on them

revolving door the tendency of public officials, journalists, and lobbyists to move between public and private sector (media, lobbying) jobs

full-blown social movements, to make their demands heard by policymakers. Recently, corporations and other, more traditional interest groups have been combining tactics—joining conventional lobbying methods with the use of email, computerized databases, talk radio, and twenty-four-hour cable television—to bring unprecedented pressure to bear on the voting public to influence members of government.

Direct Lobbying: Congress

When interest groups lobby Congress, they rarely concentrate on all 435 members of the House or all 100 members of the Senate. Rather, lobbyists focus their efforts on congressional committees, where most bills are written and revised. Because the committee leadership is relatively stable from one Congress to the next (unless a different party wins a majority), lobbyists can develop long-term relationships with committee members and their staffs.

Strategies for Congressional Lobbying

Interest groups use many strategies to influence members of Congress:

- *Personal contacts.* Personal contacts, including appointments, banquets, parties, lunches, or simply casual meetings in the hallways of Congress, are the most common and the most effective form of lobbying.

- *Professional lobbyists.* Interest groups frequently need professional help to navigate the increasingly complex world of government regulations and benefits. As a result, much of modern lobbying involves the use of professional lobbyists, either in-house employees dedicated to advancing the interests of a particular group, or contract lobbyists who work for lobbying firms that address a variety of groups' needs.

  Because access to power and knowledge about how government works is key to successful lobbying, some of the most effective lobbyists are former government officials. Rotating into lobbying jobs from elected or other government positions is known as passing through the ***revolving door***, a concept we meet again in Chapter 15. It refers to public officials who leave their posts to become interest group representatives (or media figures), parlaying the special knowledge and contacts they gathered in government into lucrative salaries in the private sector. Such assistance

can be so invaluable to their clients that even legislative aides can make their fortune lobbying, commanding starting salaries of upwards of $300,000 a year.[63] The liberal advocacy group Public Citizen reported that 37 percent of lawmakers who have gone into the private sector since 1998 have taken up lobbying.[64] Current law passed in 2007 requires that senators wait two years before lobbying Congress; members of the House must wait just one year. Former Senate staffers cannot lobby the Senate for a year after they leave their positions, and House staffers cannot lobby the actual offices or committees where they worked.

Still, more than a third of congressional staffers who left government service in 2008 became professional lobbyists.[65] Other government officials also face new restrictions on when they can lobby the agencies for which they once worked.[66] President Obama felt so strongly that the revolving door was a breach of the public trust that early in his administration he signed an executive order prohibiting presidential appointees from working as lobbyists for two years after leaving their posts and from returning to lobby the executive branch during his time in office.[67]

Examples of the revolving door abound. One Washington lobbying firm employs two one-time Senate majority leaders, former Republican senator Bob Dole and former Democratic senator Tom Daschle. Although neither of the retired senators actually goes to the Hill to lobby directly for clients, they are available to dispense political wisdom; to share their experience, knowledge, and contacts; and to provide access to their one-time colleagues. It makes sense for lobbying firms to hire former officials from both parties so that they can maximize their access to the halls of power.

Revolving-door activity is subject to occasional attempts at regulation and frequent ethical debate, as it was in 2007, because it raises questions about whether people should be able to convert public service into private profit, and whether such an incentive draws people into public office for motives other than serving the public interest.

- *Expert testimony.* Interest groups lobby decision makers by providing testimony and expertise and sometimes even draft legislation on the many issue areas in which policymakers cannot take the time to become expert.[68] Information is one of the most important resources lobbyists can bring to their effort to influence Congress. Providing valid information to representatives and staffers becomes a tool that lobbyists use to build long-term credibility with members of Congress.

For example, in 2003, with support from a president and a vice president who were former energy company executives, Republicans in Congress worked closely with energy companies to develop legislation that would increase oil exploration, coal mining, and nuclear plant development. One industry lobbyist said of the energy bill: "This is the mother lode."[69] Democrats, locked out of the conference committee that was considering the bill, were so frustrated by the influence of the energy lobbyists that then-senator Bob Graham, D-Fla., fumed, "at this point, industry lobbyists are effectively writing this bill."[70] Of course, in their turn energy companies had been frustrated with the Clinton administration's pro-environmental positions on energy exploration, claiming that they listened only to conservationists and environmental groups.[71]

- *Campaign contributions.* Giving money to candidates is another lobbying technique that helps interest groups gain access and a friendly ear. The 1974 Federal Election Campaign Act that was passed in an effort to curb campaign spending abuses was aimed at regulating the amount of money an interest group could give to candidates for federal office, by providing for PACs to serve as fundraisers for interest groups. Subsequent campaign finance legislation has limited how much money PACs can donate to candidates, but as the *What's at Stake?* in this chapter illustrates, there are always loopholes that let them circumvent the restrictions in order to support the candidates of their choice. Figures 13.2 and 13.3 show how the major types of interest groups divide their money between the Democratic and Republican Parties.

- *Coalition formation.* Interest groups attempt to bolster their lobbying efforts by forming coalitions with other interest groups. While these coalitions tend to be based on single issues, building coalitions in favor of or against specific issues has become an important strategy in lobbying Congress. In 2009, for example, the Coalition to Advance Health Care Reform brought together over sixty business groups to advocate for market-based solutions to rising health care costs.[72]

Attempts at Lobbying Reform

Many attempts have been made to regulate the tight relationship between lobbyist and lawmaker. The difficulty, of course, is that lawmakers benefit from the relationship with lobbyists in many ways and are not enthusiastic about curtailing their opportunities to get money and support. In 1995 Congress completed its first attempt in half a century to regulate lobbying when it passed the Lobbying Disclosure Act. The act required lobbyists to report how much they are paid, by whom, and what issues they are promoting.[73] Also in 1995, the Senate and the House passed separate resolutions addressing gifts and travel given by interest groups to senators and representatives.[74] Partly in reaction, in September 2007, after the Democrats took back the majority in the House and the Senate in 2006, Congress passed and President Bush signed the Honest Leadership and Open Government Act, which tightened travel and gift restrictions and included, among other things, the following provisions:[75]

- Prohibits senators, members of the House, and their aides from receiving any gifts, meals, or travel in violation of their chamber's rules. While these rules are complex, basically any gifts from registered lobbyists are forbidden and gifts from other sources must have a monetary value of under $50.

- Increases the frequency with which lobbyist disclosures must be filed.

- Requires lawmakers to disclose when lobbyists "bundle" or collect from clients more than $15,000 in campaign contributions in a six-month period.

- Requires disclosure of "earmarks"—that is, special projects of individual legislators often hidden in legislation, and their sponsors.

- Forbids members of Congress to influence lobbying firms to hire members of a particular party.

Ethics reforms can cast a definite chill on lobbyist activity, but members of Congress and lobbyists quickly learn where they can bend the rules.[76] As soon as the 2007 reform was passed, lobbying groups scrambled to find new ways to provide travel for lawmakers they wanted to influence, and ways to make free meals acceptable (perhaps calling them receptions, which are legal if widely attended, or fundraisers).[77]

Figure 13.2

Spending by Type of PAC, 1989–2008 (in millions)

300
250
200
150
100
50
0
Dollars spent, in millions
1989–1990
1991–1992
1993–1994
1995–1996
1997–1998
1999–2000
2001–2002
2003–2004
2005–2006
2007–2008
Year
Type of PAC
Cooperative and corp. w/o stock
Trade/membership/health
Labor
Corporate

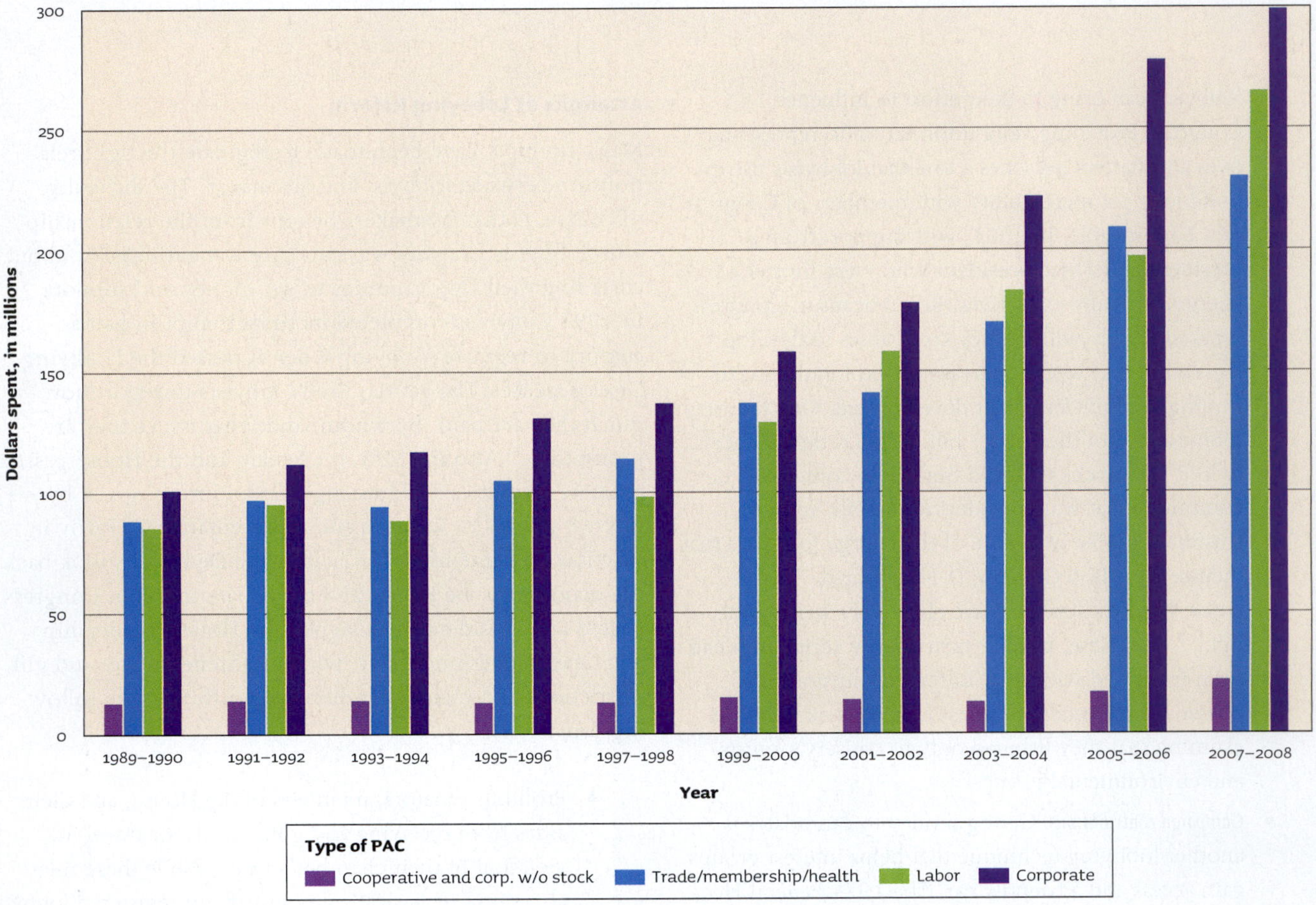

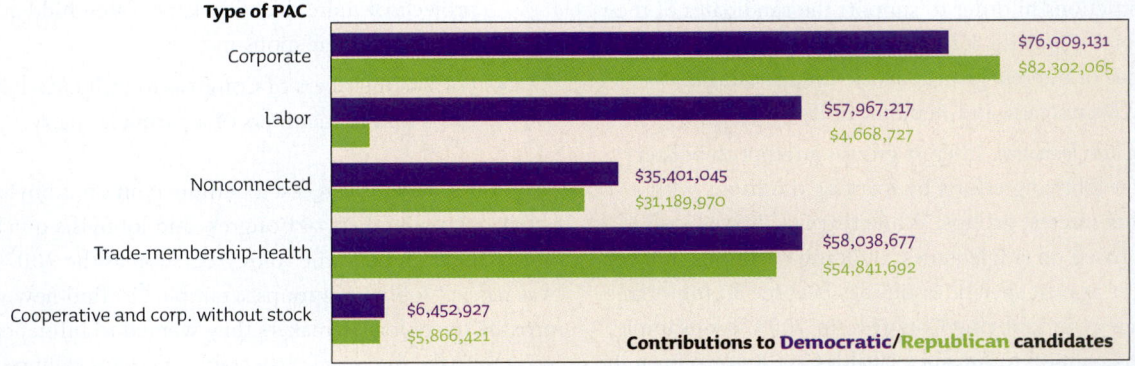

Source: Harold W. Stanley and Richard G. Niemi, "Table 2-12: Contributions and Independent Expenditures, by Type of PAC, 1999–2008," *Vital Statistics on American Politics 2009–2010* (Washington, D.C.: CQ Press, 2010), 94–95.

Figure 13.3

PAC Contributions to All Congressional Candidates by Type of PAC and Candidate Party, 2008

Type of PAC
Corporate
$76,009,131
$82,302,065
Labor
$57,967,217
$4,668,727
Nonconnected
$35,401,045
$31,189,970
Trade-membership-health
$58,038,677
$54,841,692
Cooperative and corp. without stock
$6,452,927
$5,866,421
Contributions to Democratic/Republican candidates

Source: Federal Election Commission press release, "Growth in PAC Financial Activity Slows; Table 2: PAC Contributions 2007–2008 Through December 31, 2008," www.fec.gov/press/press2009/20090415PAC/20090424PAC.shtml.

Direct Lobbying: The President

As we saw in the *What's at Stake?* that opened this chapter, lobbyists also target the president and the White House staff to try to influence policy. As with Congress, personal contacts within the White House are extremely important, and the higher up in the White House, the better. Nor has the White House been exempt from the revolving-door phenomenon. At least two Clinton cabinet members, the late secretary of commerce Ron Brown and trade representative Mickey Kantor, had been professional lobbyists, and this despite Clinton's unusually tough stance against lobbying.[78] Similarly, former senator Tom Daschle was in line to take a high-profile role in health care reform in the Obama administration until it became known that he had failed to disclose compensation (in the form of a car and driver) he received from a lobbying firm. Despite Obama's seemingly uncompromising stance against the revolving door, he had to relax his rules somewhat to fill some executive branch positions.[79] Part of the difficulty is that the practice of the revolving door is so pervasive, with one party's appointees joining lobbying forms while their party is out of power, that a president is hard pressed to find stellar appointees who *haven't* been lobbyists at some point.

The official contact point between the White House and interest groups is the Office of Public Liaison. Its basic purpose is to foster good relations between the White House and interest groups in order to mobilize these groups to support the administration's policies. Given the highly partisan and ideologically charged nature of most presidencies, it should not be surprising that the groups each White House administration cultivates are those with which it feels most ideologically comfortable.

Direct Lobbying: The Bureaucracy

While opportunities for lobbying the president may be somewhat limited, opportunities for lobbying the rest of the executive branch abound. Interest groups know that winning the legislative battle is only the first step. The second, and sometimes most important, battle takes place in the bureaucracy, where Congress has delegated rule-making authority to federal agencies that implement the law.[80] When, for instance, the Occupational Safety and Health Administration (OSHA) decreed that workplace design must take into account the physical abilities of workers in order to avoid repetitive motion injuries, groups like organized labor supported the effort, although they believed the new standards did not go

Apologizing for the Apology

While the Gulf Coast was slick with spilled oil in June 2010, Rep. Joe Barton, R-Texas, apologized to the CEO of BP over the way the company had been treated by the U.S. government, saying it had been subject to a "$20 million shakedown" to compensate those affected by the spill, an apology he later retracted. The oil spill was in part the result of the tight relationship between regulators and the regulated industry that characterizes an iron triangle.

far enough, while business groups lobbied heavily against it, claiming that the standards were unnecessary, unsupported by medical evidence, and expensive to implement.[81]

Interest groups often try to gain an advantage by developing strong relations with regulating agencies. Because many of the experts on a topic are employed by the interests being regulated, it is not unusual to find lobbyists being hired by government agencies, or vice versa, in an extension of the revolving-door situation we discussed earlier. The close relationships that exist between the regulated and the regulators, along with the close relationships between lobbyists and congressional staffers, lead to the creation of the iron triangles we talked about in Chapter 9 (see especially Figure 9.2 on page 357). In addition to iron triangles working against an open policy-making environment by limiting the participation of actors not in the triangle, they also have the potential for presenting conflicts of interest. Although recent laws prevent former government employees from lobbying their former agencies for five years after they leave their federal jobs, government agencies are sometimes forced to recruit personnel from within the businesses they are regulating because that is often where the experts are to be found.

Direct Lobbying: The Courts

Interest groups also try to influence government policy by challenging the legality of laws or administrative regulations

WHEN ALL THE BODIES HAVE BEEN BURIED IN DARFUR, HOW WILL HISTORY JUDGE US?

GENOCIDE IS HAPPENING RIGHT NOW IN DARFUR. YOU CAN HELP END IT.
400,000 people dead. 2.5 million displaced. Untold thousands raped, tortured and terrorized. Men. Women. Children. Ending the horror will take a strong UN peacekeeping force and a no-fly zone. And that will take leadership from world leaders, including President Bush.

LOG ON TO DEMAND ACTION. | www.SaveDarfur.org

SAVEDARFUR

Mourning Those Lost

Darfur, a region in Sudan, has been in the middle of an ethnic and tribal conflict since early 2003. The United Nations estimates that more than a half million individuals have been killed and 2.5 million more displaced. Images such as the one in this issue advocacy ad are a powerful way for humanitarian groups to convey the seriousness of a particular situation they want to draw public attention to.

in the courts. These legal tactics have been used by groups like the NAACP (challenging segregation laws), the ACLU (freedom of speech, religion, and civil liberties cases), the Sierra Club (environmental enforcement), and Common Cause (ethics in government). As soon as campaign finance reform was passed in 2002, the NRA, the ACLU, the AFL-CIO, and other groups immediately went into action to challenge the new law in court. Sometimes groups bring cases directly, and sometimes they file amicus curiae ("friend of the court") briefs asking the courts to rule in ways favorable to their positions.

Indirect Lobbying: The Public

One of the most powerful and fastest-growing kinds of lobbying is indirect lobbying, in which the lobbyists use

public opinion to put pressure on politicians to do what they want.[82] In this section we examine the various ways in which interest groups use the public to lobby and influence government decision makers. These efforts include educating the public by disseminating information and research, mobilizing direct citizen lobbying efforts, and organizing demonstrations or protests.

Educating the Public

Interest groups must get their issues onto the public's agenda before they can influence how the public feels about them. Many interest group leaders are sure that the public will rally to their side once they know "the truth" about their causes.[83] Interest groups often begin their campaigns by using research to show that the problem they are trying to solve is a legitimate one. For example, the Tax Foundation is a conservative group promoting tax cuts. To dramatize its point that American taxes are too high, every year the foundation announces "Tax Freedom Day"—the day on which the average wage earner finishes paying the amount of taxes he or she will owe and starts working for his or her own profit. In 2010, that day was April 9.[84] The foundation believes that this information is so compelling that the public will jump to the conclusion that their taxes are too high.

Of course, all the research in the world by the Tax Foundation, or any other interest group, does no good if the public is unaware of it. For this reason, interest groups cultivate press coverage. They know that people are more likely to take their research seriously if it is reported by the media as legitimate news, but getting news coverage can be difficult for interest groups because they are in competition with every other group, not to mention with actual news stories. Many of them turn to expensive public relations firms to help them get their message out, using tactics ranging from TV commercials to direct-mail campaigns. (See "*Consider the Source: Don't Be Fooled by Direct Mail*.")

A popular way for interest groups to get out their message is through the use of *issue advocacy ads*. These commercials encourage constituents to support or oppose a certain policy or candidate without directly telling citizens how to vote. In the past, as long as these ads did not specifically promote the election or defeat of a particular candidate, issue advocacy ads were not subject to any limitations, meaning a PAC could spend all the money it wanted on ads promoting an issue and, by implication, the candidates of its

The NRA knows where you live—but it's not gunning for you; it's after your money. So are the Brady Campaign to Prevent Gun Violence, the Humane Society, the Sierra Club, and Save the Children. You can only be glad that you are probably too young for AARP to take an interest in you yet. Our mailboxes, once a repository for letters from mom and a handful of bills, have become a battleground for interest groups after our hard-earned cash, and now our email inboxes are filling fast, too. Welcome to the age of direct-mail solicitations.

If it hasn't happened to you yet, no doubt as you become gainfully employed, give money to a cause or two you admire, and become integrated into your community, you too will become the target of "personalized" written requests from interest groups for the donations that they need to keep financially afloat. Direct mail is big business, run by professionals whose job it is to design the impassioned pleas that encourage you to open your wallet or write that check. Because interest groups have so much at stake in their direct-mail solicitations (in many cases, their very survival depends on it), they pull out all the stops in their letters to you. How can you evaluate these dramatic requests so that you can in fact support the legitimate groups whose causes you believe in, but not fall (as they hope you will) for over-the-top exaggeration and provocatively embellished prose? When presented with a plea for funds, ask yourself the following questions:

1. **What is this group?** What does it stand for? Sometimes direct-mail writers spend the majority of their time telling you what they are against, or whom they oppose, in the hopes that you will share their animosities and therefore support them. Many groups give a web address. Check them out, but remember that the web site is also written by supporters and may not give you a full or unbiased view. Look the group up in a newspaper archive and get some objective information (that is, information not written by the group itself!).

2. **How did it get your address?** Does it treat you as a long-lost friend? Often a group will buy a mailing list from some other group. You can occasionally trace your name by the particular spelling (or misspelling), use of a maiden name or nickname, or some other characteristic that does not appear on your standard mailing address. Knowing how a group got your name can sometimes tell you what its connections are and what it is about. A simple mail order purchase of hiking boots can get you on the mailing lists of sports outfitters, and a short step later onto the lists of the NRA, which hopes that outdoorsy people will hunt and thus support its cause. In addition, as mailing techniques get more sophisticated, interest groups are able to personalize their requests for support. If you belong to the local humane society and other groups that would indicate your love for animals, and if the interest group got your name from their lists, it can target you with a fundraising letter that plays on your concern for animal life. If the letter seems to be directed to your deepest values, harden your heart until you have checked out the group independently.

3. **What claims does it make?** Direct mail is designed to make you sit down and write a check now. From some letters, you get the sense that Armageddon is at hand and the world will soon self-destruct without your donation. Do not believe everything you read in a fundraising letter. Verify the facts before you send any money. The more persuasive and amazing the claim appears to be, the more it requires verification!

4. **What is it asking for?** It is almost always money, but a group may also ask you to write your congressperson, make a phone call, wear a ribbon, or otherwise show support for a cause. Be clear about what you are being asked to do and what you are committing to do. If possible, check out the interest group's record for effective action. If most of the money it gets goes to administrative costs, you won't be furthering your cause much by contributing your dollars.

5. **What do you get for your money?** What material benefits does the group offer? Do you receive a newsletter? Discounts on products or services? Special offers for the group? We are not advising free ridership here, but it is wise to know exactly what you are getting before you part with your cash.

choice. The passage of the 2002 Bipartisan Campaign Reform Act (also called the McCain-Feingold Act) put a temporary chill on these ads, but several recent Supreme Court rulings, culminating with the 2010 decision in *Citizens United v. Federal Election Commission*, have lifted the restrictions, and in fact, issue advocacy ads can now directly advocate for or against candidates as well as for their issue positions.[85]

Even under the restraining hand of the McCain-Feingold Act, so-called **527 groups** like the Swift Boat Veterans for Truth, which effectively attacked John Kerry during his 2004

527 groups   groups that mobilize voters with issue advocacy advertisements on television and radio but may not directly advocate the election or defeat of a particular candidate

social protest   public activities designed to bring attention to political causes, usually generated by those without access to conventional means of expressing their views

campaign for the presidency, are able to raise unlimited amounts of money from labor unions, corporations, and interest groups to mobilize voters with issue advocacy ads on television and radio, so long as they do not directly advocate the election or defeat of a candidate.[86] Organized under section 527 of the Internal Revenue Code, they are not subject to laws that the Federal Election Commission regulates.[87] In the wake of the *Citizens United* ruling, these groups are less important than they were because the 527 loophole is no longer needed for groups to spend unlimited money, but they still exist.

Groups can also get information to the public through the skillful use of the Internet, whether through carefully designed advocacy web sites and blogs, through social networks, or through web-based videos, creating messages that go "viral," spreading quickly by email and hitting targeted audiences. Internet-savvy interest groups are increasingly turning to YouTube, the video-sharing web site in place only since 2005, for a cheap and efficient way to get their message out.

Mobilizing the Public

The point of disseminating information, hiring public relations firms, creating web sites, and running issue ads is to motivate the public to lobby politicians themselves. On most issues, general public interest is low, and groups must rely on their own members for support. As you might suspect, groups like AARP, the Christian Coalition, and the NRA, which have large memberships, have an advantage because they can mobilize a large contingent of citizens from all over the country to lobby representatives and senators. Generally this mobilization involves encouraging members to write letters, send emails or faxes, or make phone calls to legislators about a pending issue.

Professional lobbyists freely admit that their efforts are most effective when the people "back home" are contacting representatives about an issue.[88] Although considerable evidence indicates that members of Congress do monitor their mail and respond to the wishes of their constituents, there is also some evidence that as these tactics have become more prevalent, they are being met with increasing skepticism and resistance on Capitol Hill.[89] To combat congressional skepticism, many interest groups have begun to deliver on their threats to politicians by mobilizing their members to vote. The religious right has long been able to do this, mobilizing

conservative voters from the pulpit, but more recently liberals—for example, the "netroots," liberal activist groups like MoveOn.org and ActBlue that challenge establishment politicians and interest groups—have gotten into the game via the Internet.

Unconventional Methods, Social Protest, and Mass Movements

A discussion of interest group politics would not be complete without mention of the unconventional technique of social protest. Throughout our history, groups have turned to *social protest*—activities ranging from planned, orderly demonstrations to strikes and boycotts, to acts of civil disobedience—when other techniques have failed to bring attention to their causes. The nonviolent civil rights protests beginning with the Montgomery, Alabama, bus boycott discussed in Chapter 6 illustrate the types of actions such groups have used to bring their concerns to national attention.

Like other grassroots lobbying techniques, the techniques of social protest provide a way for people to publicly express their disagreement with a government policy or action. At the same time, their use often signals the strength of participants' feelings on an issue—and, often, outrage over being closed out from more traditional avenues of political action. Thus demonstrations and protests have frequently served an important function for those who have been excluded from the political process because of their minority, social, or economic status. While social protest may have the same objective as other types of indirect lobbying—that is, educating the public and mobilizing the group's members—demonstrations and spontaneous protests also aim to draw in citizens who have not yet formed an opinion or to change the minds of those who have. Such actions may turn a political action into a mass movement, attracting formerly passive or uninterested observers to the cause.

Social protest in the United States did not begin with the civil rights movement, although many activists since then have followed the strategies used by civil rights leaders. The labor movement of the late nineteenth century used demonstrations and strikes to attract more members to unions, with the goal of improving working conditions and wages. The women's suffrage movement of the late nineteenth and early twentieth centuries, discussed in Chapter 6, used social protest to fight for voting rights for women. Social movements have been used to change both private and government

Napping for Trees
Citizens engage in political actions both conventional and unconventional. Here, an Earth First! activist passes the time in a northern California forest, suspended from a tree he is trying to protect from being harvested.

behavior. The prohibition (or temperance) movement of the late nineteenth and early twentieth centuries, for example, was aimed at stopping one particular behavior: the drinking of alcohol.

Modern mass movements employ many of the same tactics as those used in earlier days, but they have also benefited greatly from the opportunities offered by the modern media. The increasingly widespread medium of television was important to the success of the civil rights movement in the 1950s and early 1960s, as the protests and demonstrations brought home the plight of southern blacks to other regions of the country. Especially significant to the TV audience was the coverage of police brutality. Viewers were shocked by the beatings with nightsticks and the use of high-pressure hoses on demonstrators. In the 1970s mass demonstration was used effectively by peace groups protesting American involvement in the Vietnam War. Americans at home could not help but be impressed by the huge numbers of students gathered at such protests—burning draft cards, marching on the Pentagon, or staging college sit-ins or teach-ins to protest the government's policy. Month

after month, a complete recap of the day's major protest activities on the evening news forced most people to at least confront their own views on the situation.

The possibilities for using the media to support mass movements have exploded with the advent of the Internet. High-tech flash campaigns have helped groups like Censure and Move On (now MoveOn.org, a citizen action group originally formed in 1998 to pressure Congress not to impeach President Clinton) mobilize hundreds of thousands of citizens to lobby Congress by setting up relatively inexpensive and efficient "cyberpetitions" on their web sites.[90] Less conventional outlets of the traditional media can also get involved in social protest. Since the beginning of the Obama administration, Fox News has helped to foment protest on the right with publicity for and encouragement of the Tea Party movement.[91] In response, in 2010 Jon Stewart and Stephen Colbert staged a dual Rally for Sanity/Keep Fear Alive event, drawing an estimated 215,000 people to Washington's National Mall.

Today a number of groups continue in the tradition of unconventional social protest. Operation Rescue, which

> ***grassroots lobbying*** indirect lobbying efforts that spring from widespread public concern
>
> ***astroturf lobbying*** indirect lobbying efforts that manipulate or create public sentiment, "astroturf" being artificial grassroots

opposes abortion rights, tends to be the most active in using unconventional techniques to influence public opinion and, through harassment and intimidation, to discourage both providers and those seeking abortions. More recently, as we indicated earlier, the group extended its tactics to protest the termination of medical treatment to a brain-damaged woman.[92] Although Operation Rescue's tactics tend to be the most extreme, even more traditional mainstream abortion groups like the National Right to Life Committee (on the pro-life side) and NOW (a pro-choice group) take an active role in organizing annual marches in Washington to promote their respective causes.

"Astroturf" Political Campaigns: Democratic or Elite Driven?

The indirect lobbying we have discussed is often called ***grassroots lobbying***, meaning that it addresses people in their roles as ordinary citizens. It is the wielding of power from the bottom (roots) up, rather than from the top down. Most of what we refer to as grassroots lobbying, however, does not spring spontaneously from the people but is orchestrated by elites, leading some people to call it ***astroturf lobbying***— indicating that it is not really genuine. Often the line between real grassroots and astroturf lobbying is blurred, however. A movement may be partly spontaneous but partly orchestrated. After MoveOn.org's success as a spontaneous expression of popular will spread by "word of mouse" over the Internet, its organizers began other flash campaigns, notably one called "Gun Safety First," urging people to support gun control measures. This was less clearly a spontaneous popular movement, but it still involved mobilizing citizens to support a cause they believed in. Similarly, the current Tea Party movement has been, in part, the project of Dick Armey, a former Republican House majority leader whose organization, FreedomWorks, promotes low taxes and small government. FreedomWorks and several other conservative groups, as well as prominent individuals including some commentators at Fox News, have lent their organizational expertise to the Tea Partiers but deny that they are orchestrating an astroturf movement.[93] Regardless of how it started out, the Tea Party movement has certainly acquired a life and mind, perhaps several minds, of its own.

At the astroturf extreme, there was nothing spontaneous at all about the pharmaceutical industry's 2003 efforts to oppose the importation of cheaper drugs from Canada. The Pharmaceutical Research and Manufacturers Association (PhRMA), the industry's lobbying group, spent over $4 million on such tactics as persuading seniors that their access to medicine would be limited if reimportation of these American-made drugs were allowed and convincing members of a Christian advocacy group that prescription drug importation might lead to easier access to the controversial morning-after pill.[94] Concerned citizens were then coached by a PhRMA-hired public relations firm on how to contact legislators to weigh in against the proposed law. Such a strategy is obviously an attempt to create an opinion that might not otherwise even exist, playing on popular fears about drug availability and sentiments about abortion to achieve corporate ends.

While pure grassroots efforts are becoming increasingly rare, a good deal of indirect lobbying is done to promote what a group claims is the public interest, or at least the interest of the members of some mass-based group like AARP. One observer who works for a public interest group says, "Grassroots politics has become a top-down corporate enterprise," and speculates that there is very little genuine grassroots-type lobbying left.[95] More often than not, astroturf lobbying uses the support of the public to promote the interest of a corporation or business. In many cases the clients of astroturf lobbying efforts are large corporations seeking tax breaks, special regulations, or simply the end of legislation that may hurt the corporation's interest. To generate public support, clients employ armies of lobbyists, media experts, and political strategists to conduct polls, craft multimedia advertising campaigns, and get the message out to "the people" through cable and radio news talk shows, the Internet, outbound call centers, fax machines, or some combination of these. Astroturf campaigns are very expensive.

One prominent campaign media consultant predicts that direct lobbying will become less important as indirect lobbying gains in effectiveness and popularity.[96] While indirect lobbying seems on its face to be more democratic, to the extent that it manipulates public opinion, it may in fact have the opposite effect. And as multimedia campaigns get more and more expensive, the number of groups that can afford to participate will undoubtedly decline. Ironically, as lobbying moves away from the closed committee rooms of Congress and into the realm of what appears to be popular politics, it may not get any more democratic than it has traditionally been.

Interest groups exist to influence policy. Because of the complexity of the American system, these groups can accomplish their goals in a number of ways. They can engage in direct lobbying, by working from inside the government to influence what the government does, or by working on the public rather than on government officials to influence policy. Sometimes interest group organizers will inspire their members to use unconventional methods to try to influence government, including social protests, mass resistance or demonstrations, and Internet communication. Increasingly, lobbyists are combining strategies and taking advantage of the new communication technologies to create innovative, expensive, and often successful campaigns to influence public policy.

Who What How

Thinking Outside the Box

Are there any lobbying techniques that should be off limits in a democracy?

Interest Group Resources
Using money, leadership skills, size, and intensity to make their voices heard

Interest group success depends in large part on the resources a group can bring to the project of influencing government. The pluralist defense of interest groups is that all citizens have the opportunity to organize, and thus all can exercise equal power. But all interest groups are not created equal. Some have more money, more effective leadership, more members, or better information than others, and these resources can translate into real power differences that give groups a better chance of influencing government policy than, say, the Children's Defense Fund. In this section we examine the resources that interest groups can draw on to exert influence over policy-making: money, leadership, membership, and information.

Money

Interest groups need money to conduct the business of trying to influence governmental policymakers. Money can buy an

Table 13.1

The Lobbying Groups With the Most Clout in Washington

Lobbying group	Rank
National Rifle Association	1
AARP	2
National Federation of Independent Business	3
American Israel Public Affairs Committee	4
Association of Trial Lawyers	5
AFL-CIO	6
Chamber of Commerce	7
National Beer Wholesalers Association	8
National Association of Realtors	9
National Association of Manufacturers	10
National Association of Home Builders	11
American Medical Association	12
American Hospital Association	13
National Education Association	14
American Farm Bureau Federation	15
Motion Picture Association of America	16
National Association of Broadcasters	17
National Right to Life Committee	18
Health Insurance Association of America	19
National Restaurant Association	20
National Governors Association	21
Recording Industry Association	22
American Bankers Association	23
Pharmaceutical Research and Manufacturers Association	24
International Brotherhood of Teamsters	25

Source: Jeffrey Birnbaum and Russell Newell, "Fat & Happy in D.C.," *Fortune*, May 28, 2001, 94.

interest group the ability to put together a well-trained staff, to hire outside professional assistance, and to make campaign contributions in the hopes of gaining access to government officials. Having money does not guarantee favorable policies, but not having money just about guarantees failure.

Staff

One of the reasons money is important is that it enables an interest group to hire a professional staff, usually an executive director, assistants, and other office support staff. The main job of this professional staff is to take care of the day-to-day operations of the interest group, including pursuing policy initiatives; recruiting and maintaining membership; providing membership services; and, of course, getting more money through direct mailings, telemarketing, web site donations, and organizational functions. Money is important for creating an organizational infrastructure that can in turn be used to raise additional support and resources.

Professional Assistance

Money also enables the interest group to hire the services of professionals, such as a high-powered lobbying firm. These firms have invested heavily to ensure that they have connections to members of Congress.[97] A well-endowed group can also hire a public relations firm to help shape public opinion on a policy, as was done with the Harry and Louise campaign discussed earlier, and a skilled person to handle Internet operations.

Campaign Contributions

Interest groups live by the axiom that to receive, one must give—and give a lot to important people. The maximum that any PAC can give to a candidate is $5,000 for each separate election, or $15,000 to a political party per year. In the 2008 cycle, PACs gave a total of $385.9 million to congressional candidates up for election, an all-time high for PAC contributions.[98] While some PACs give millions to campaigns, most PACs give less than $50,000 to candidates for each election cycle, focusing their contributions on members of the committees responsible for drafting legislation important to their groups.[99] In the wake of the *Citizens United* decision, however, considerable money can be spent by groups on a candidate's behalf, and the groups don't have to disclose the donors who have contributed the money. In the days before the 2010 midterm elections, it was apparent that though the actual

changes to campaign finance law made by the *Citizens United* decision were small, it had the psychological effect of giving a "green light" to those who wanted to spend lavishly on an election.[100]

PAC spending is usually directed toward incumbents of both parties, with incumbents in the majority party, especially committee chairs, getting the greatest share. This dramatic difference is shown in Figure 13.4, which illustrates not only that most of the PAC money goes to incumbents, but that this huge imbalance has increased over the past decade. About 80 percent of PAC contributions go to incumbent members of Congress.[101] While most PACs want to curry favor with incumbents of either party, some tend to channel their money to one party. For instance, business interests, the American Medical Association, pro-life groups, Christian groups, and the NRA tend to support Republican candidates; and labor groups, the Association of Trial Lawyers of America, the National Education Association, and environmental and pro-choice groups give primarily to Democrats.

The ability to make sizable and strategically placed campaign contributions buys an interest group access to government officials.[102] Access gives the interest group the ability to talk to a representative and members of his or her staff and to present information relevant to the policies they seek to initiate, change, or protect. Access is important because representatives have any number of competing interests vying for their time. Money is meant to oil the door hinge of a representative's office so that it swings open for the interest group. For instance, the Clinton administration was well known in its early years for allowing major donors to stay in the Lincoln bedroom of the White House. The access bought by campaign contributions is usually less blatant, but officials know who has supported their campaigns, and they are unlikely to forget it when the interest group comes knocking at their doors.

The relationship between money and political influence is extremely controversial. Many critics argue that this money buys more than just access; rather, they charge, it buys votes. The circumstantial evidence is strong. For instance, in the Senate deliberations on a public option in health care, which would have provided individuals with an alternative to private health care insurance, the thirty senators who supported the public option had received an average of $15,937 in contributions from the health care industry in the previous six years, compared to the $37,322 that was received, on average, by the seventy senators who opposed it.[103]

Figure 13.4

PAC Contributions to Congressional Campaigns by Type of Contest, 1998–2008

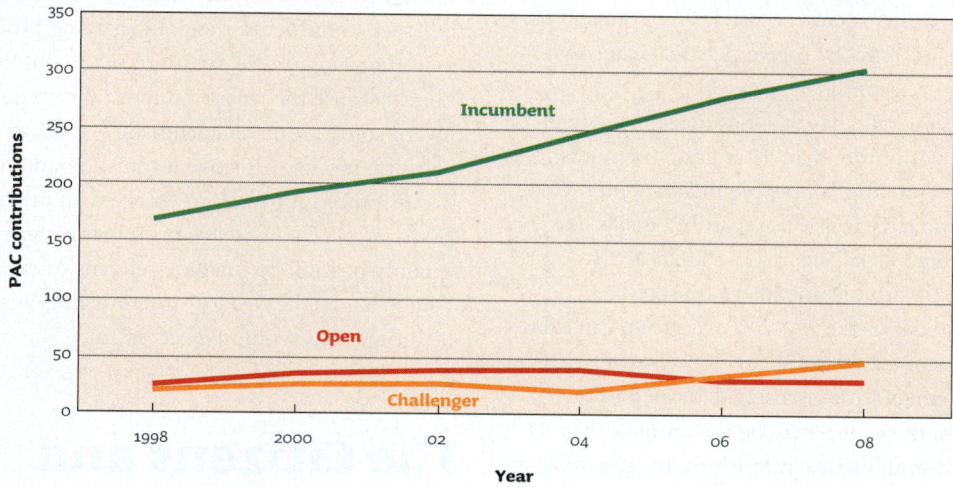

Source: Federal Election Commission, "Growth in PAC Financial Activity Slows," April 24, 2009, http://fec.gov/press/press2009/20090415PAC/20090424PAC.shtml.

However, in the matter of vote buying, systematic studies of congressional voting patterns are mixed. These studies show that the influence of campaign contributions is strongest in committees, where most bills are drafted. However, once the bill reaches the floor of the House or the Senate, there is no consistent link between campaign contributions and roll-call voting.[104] This suggests that campaign contributions influence the process of creating and shaping the legislation, and thus defining the policy alternatives. Nonetheless, the final outcome of a bill is determined by political circumstances that go beyond the campaign contributions of interest groups.

Leadership

Leadership is an intangible element in the success or failure of an interest group. We mentioned earlier that an effective and charismatic leader or interest group entrepreneur can help a group organize even if it lacks other resources. In the same way, such a leader can keep a group going when it seems to lack the support from other sources. Candy Lightner's role in MADD and César Chavez's leadership of the United Farm Workers are excellent cases in point. But professional interest group leadership can come at a cost. As the mass membership interest groups that characterized this country in the past century give way to highly professional groups whose power comes more from their organizational skills than from their active members, some observers have argued that the groups no longer serve as training grounds for citizenship and are more elite driven than democratic. Says one, "The result is a new civic America largely run by advocates and managers without members and marked by yawning gaps between immediate involvements and larger undertakings."[105] Ultimately, professional group leadership can leave the mass citizenry with fewer paths to civic engagement, eliminating one of the characteristics of interest group politics that leads pluralists, for instance, to claim that interest groups can enhance democracy.

Membership: Size and Intensity

The membership of any interest group is an important resource in terms of its size, but the level of intensity that members exhibit in support of the group's causes is also critical. Members represent the lifeblood of the interest group because they generally fund its activities. When an interest group is trying to influence policy, it can use its members to write letters, send emails, and engage in other forms of personal contact with legislators or administrative officials. Often interest groups try to reinforce their PAC contributions by encouraging their members to give personal campaign contributions to favored candidates.

Larger groups generally have an advantage over smaller ones. For instance, with more than 40 million members, AARP can mobilize thousands of people in an attempt to influence elected officials' decisions regarding issues like mandatory retirement, Social Security, or Medicare. In addition, if an interest group's members are spread throughout the country, as are AARP's, that group can exert its influence on almost every member of Congress.

If a group's members are intensely dedicated to the group's causes, then the group may be far stronger than its numbers would indicate. Intense minorities, because of their willingness to devote time, energy, and money to a cause they care passionately about, can outweigh more apathetic majorities in the political process. For instance, although a majority of Americans favor some form of gun control, they are outweighed in the political process by the intense feeling of the just over four million members of the NRA, who strongly oppose gun control.[106]

Information

Information is one of the most powerful resources in an interest group's arsenal. Often the members of the interest group are the only sources of information on the potential or actual impact of a law or regulation. The long struggle to regulate tobacco is a case in point. While individuals witnessed their loved ones and friends suffering from lung diseases, cancer, and heart problems, it took public health interest groups like the American Cancer Society, the Public Health Cancer Association, and the American Heart Association to conduct the studies, collect the data, and show the connection between these life-threatening illnesses and smoking habits. Of course the tobacco industry and its interest group, the Tobacco Institute, presented their own research to counter these claims. Not surprisingly, the tobacco industry's investigations showed "no causal relationship" between tobacco use and these illnesses.[107] Eventually, the volume of information showing a strong relationship overwhelmed industry research suggesting otherwise. In 1998 the tobacco industry reached a settlement

with states to pay millions of dollars for the treatment of tobacco-related illnesses.

Again, there is no mystery about what interest groups want: they seek to influence the policymaking process. Some interest groups are clearly more successful than others because the rules of interest group politics reward some group characteristics—such as size, intensity, money, effective leadership, and the possession of information—more than others (perhaps social conscience or humanitarianism). It is certainly possible to imagine reforms or rule changes that would change the reward structure and, in so doing, change the groups that would be successful.

Who What How

The Citizens and Interest Groups
The people versus the powerful

Defenders of pluralism believe that interest group formation helps give more power to more citizens, and we have seen that it certainly can enhance democratic life. Interest groups offer channels for representation, participation, education, defining policy solutions, and public agenda building, and they help to keep politicians accountable. Pluralists also believe that the system as a whole benefits from interest group politics. They argue that if no single interest group commands a majority, interest groups will compete with one another and ultimately must form coalitions to create a majority. In the process of forming coalitions, interest groups compromise on policy issues, leading to final policy outcomes that reflect the general will of the people as opposed to the narrow interests of specific interest groups.[108] In this final section we examine the claims of critics of interest group politics who argue that it skews democracy—giving more power to some people than to others—and particularly discriminates against segments of society that tend to be underrepresented in the first place (the poor and the young, for instance).

We have seen in this chapter that a variety of factors—money, leadership, membership, information—can make an interest group successful. But this raises red danger flags for American democracy. In American political culture, we value political equality, which is to say the principle of one person, one vote. And as far as voting goes, this is how we practice democracy. Anyone who attempts to visit the polls twice on Election Day is turned away, no matter how rich that person is, how intensely he or she feels about the election, or how eloquently he or she begs for another vote. But policy is made not only at the ballot box. It is also made in the halls and hearing rooms of Congress; in the conference rooms of the bureaucracy; and in corporate boardrooms, private offices, restaurants, and bars. In these places interest groups speak loudly, and since some groups are vastly more successful than others, they have the equivalent of extra votes in the policy-making process.

We are not terribly uncomfortable with the idea that interest groups with large memberships should have more power. After all, democracy is usually about getting the most votes in order to win. But when it comes to the idea that the wealthy have an advantage, or those who feel intensely, or those who have more information, we start to balk. What about the rest of us? Should we have relatively less power over who gets what because we lack these resources?

It is true that groups with money, and business groups in particular, have distinct advantages of organizational access. Many critics suggest that business interests represent a small, wealthy, and united set of elites who dominate the political process,[109] and much evidence supports the view that business interests maintain a special relationship with government and tend to unite behind basic conservative issues (less government spending and lower taxes). Other evidence, however, suggests that business interests are often divided regarding governmental policies and that other factors can counterbalance their superior monetary resources.

Because business interests are not uniform and tightly organized, groups with large memberships can prevail against them. While corporate money may buy access, politicians ultimately depend on votes. Groups with large memberships have more voters. A good example of this principle occurred in 1997 when President Clinton proposed trimming $100 billion in Medicare spending over five years. Instead of raising premiums on the elderly, the Clinton administration proposed cuts in Medicare reimbursements

to hospitals and doctors. This proposal sparked an intensive lobbying campaign pitting the American Medical Association and the American Hospital Association, two of the most powerful and well-financed lobbies in Washington, against AARP, representing more than 40 million older Americans. Fearing the voting wrath of AARP, the Republican-led Congress struck a deal with the administration to cut Medicare reimbursements for hospitals and doctors.[110] As this example suggests, when a group's membership is highly motivated and numerous, it can win despite the opposition's lavish resources.[111]

While interest group politics today in America clearly contains some biases, it is not the case that any one group or kind of group always gets its way. After years of collecting government subsidies and benefiting from favorable policies, the tobacco industry has at last been stripped of its privilege, illustrating that even corporate giants can be brought low.[112] Similarly the less wealthy but very intense NRA, which kept gun control off the American law books for decades, has finally been confronted by angry citizens' groups that have put the issue of gun control firmly on the public's agenda, though with mixed success.[113]

What has helped to equalize the position of these groups in American politics is the willingness on the part of citizens to fight fire with fire, politics with politics, organization with organization—an effort made more accessible with the widespread use of the Internet. It is, finally, the power of participation and democracy that can make pluralism fit the pluralists' hopes. For some groups, such as the poor, such advice may be nearly impossible to follow. Lacking the knowledge of the system and the resources to organize in the first place, poor people are often the last to be included in interest group politics. Neighborhood-level organizing, however, such as that done by the Southwest Voter Registration Education Project and Hermandad Mexicana Latinoamericana, can counteract this tendency. Other groups left out of the system, such as the merely indifferent, or young people who often regard current issues as irrelevant, will pay the price of inattention and disorganization when the score cards of interest group politics are finally tallied.

▶ What's at Stake Revisited

In this chapter we have seen that Madison's fear of factions was not unfounded. Interest groups may not be able to buy votes, per se, but they certainly can buy access and influence, and the politician who ignores them does so at his or her peril.

Having seen what happened when President Clinton failed to get the health industry groups on board, the Obama team was determined to avoid Clinton's mistakes. What was at stake for the Obama administration, for interest groups, for the political parties, and for the nation as a whole in the White House's decision to bring these groups in at the ground level in the effort to reform the country's health care system?

The stakes for the White House were huge. President Obama had made health care a signature issue of his campaign and had promised as well a new way of governing—lean, effective, bipartisan. Republicans could deny him the "bipartisan label," but he didn't want to cede ground on whether government could be an effective actor as well. Most observers agreed that if health care reform failed to pass this time around, it could be years before it had another shot. White House communications director Dan Pfeiffer said that what was on the line was whether government could still solve big problems, whereas former Senate majority leader Tom Daschle said that a failure to get the bill passed

would amount to a failure to govern. The way to succeed was to get all the concerned actors on board. "The President said that having people at the table is better than having them throw stuff at the table," said Pfeiffer.[114]

For industry interest groups, the stakes were substantial as well. If they stayed outside of the process but were unable to stop health care reform, they risked being stuck with a policy they hated. And many groups agreed with one of the basic tenets of the reformers—that the status quo in health care, with its rising costs, was unsustainable. If they joined the reform effort, they could have a say in shaping the solution to the problem. America's Health Insurance Plan (AHIP), recognizing that its members would be required to cover preexisting conditions, made the "universal mandate"—the condition that all who could afford it be required to buy insurance—the price of their cooperation. The drug companies were able to head off more severe cuts in drug coverage and competition from cheaper drug companies abroad by voluntarily offering to reduce costs. As *New Republic* writer Jonathan Cohn put it, for interest groups the choice was simple: you can be at the table or you can be on the menu.[115]

The value of the strategy the interest groups followed is suggested by the fate of the Republican Party, which did stay outside the process and refused to compromise. After

reform passed, conservative author and former George W. Bush speechwriter David Frum criticized the Republican strategy, saying that Republican participation could have pulled the plan in a direction more consistent with conservative principles. By refusing to play at all, the Republicans ceded influence over the final product—they went for all the marbles and ended with none.[116] By getting involved early, interest groups got a good share of the marbles.

Which, of course, is what so annoyed President Obama's liberal critics. Obama gave away the store, they argued, making concessions before he had to and giving up the public option, a key element of reform near and dear to their hearts.[117] For them, what was at stake in Obama's deal-making with the health care industry was the very integrity of reform. No less than the Republicans, Democratic critics believed that to compromise was to water down their principles. Had they insisted on purity, however, there likely would have been no health care bill at all. Though the House of Representatives managed to pass a bill with a weak version of the public option, without Republican support, Senate majority leader Harry Reid needed every Democrat on board, as well as independent senator Joe Lieberman of Connecticut. Lieberman tends to vote with the Democrats, but he made it clear that he would not support a public option, and the legislative effort to provide it died.[118]

The *political* stakes were high for the actors, like the president, who stood to face a crippled agenda if he could not bring off the reform he had promised, and for the Republicans, who had sworn to bring Obama to his Waterloo over the issue. For the health care industry, the stakes were more substantive—how much would they have to give away to keep reform within tolerable limits? The stakes for the American people were more substantive as well. For the uninsured and the uninsurable, the stakes were the difference between regular access to quality care and a patchwork of critical care cobbled together in emergency rooms and free clinics. For all Americans, the insured as well as the uninsured, the stakes were runaway health care costs that limit our ability to spend money on other necessities, or costs brought under control, with savings ultimately reducing the federal deficit. Those on the left and the right seem to believe that, by holding out, their side could have achieved all their goals, but the truth is that American politics is about compromise, and a health care reform proposal that didn't try to incorporate multiple views and goals was probably not going to be passed at all, especially given the tenuous nature of the Democratic majority in the Senate. What was at stake in bringing the industry groups to the table in the health care reform effort was the very fate of health care in America. Whether or not the reform was strong enough to improve it remains to be seen.

To Sum Up

Key terms, chapter summaries, practice quizzes, Internet links, and other study aids are available on the companion web site at http://republic.cqpress.com.

Define | **Understand** | **Practice** | **Read** | **Click** | **Watch**

astroturf lobbying (p. 504)
collective good (p. 485)
direct lobbying (p. 495)
economic interest groups (p. 486)
equal opportunity interest groups (p. 487)
expressive benefits (p. 485)
faction (p. 481)
527 groups (p. 501)
free rider problem (p. 485)
grassroots lobbying (p. 504)
indirect lobbying (p. 495)

interest group (p. 481)
interest group entrepreneurs (p. 484)
issue advocacy ads (p. 500)
lobbying (p. 483)
material benefits (p. 485)
political action committees (PACs) (p. 481)
public interest groups (p. 489)
revolving door (p. 496)
selective incentives (p. 485)
social protest (p. 502)
solidary benefits (p. 485)

Define | **Understand** | **Practice** | **Read** | **Click** | **Watch**

- Government will always distribute resources in ways that benefit some at the expense of others. People who want influence on the way that government policy decisions are made form interest groups. To accomplish their goals, interest groups lobby elected officials, rally public opinion, offer policy suggestions, and keep tabs on policy once enacted. Interest groups also must organize and convince others to join, often offering selective benefits to members.

- Interest groups come in all different types. Economic groups like business associations or trade unions want to protect and improve their status. Public interest groups advocate their vision of society, and equal opportunity groups organize to gain, or at least improve, economic status and civil rights. Governments form associations to improve relations among their ranks.

- Lobbyists are the key players of interest groups. They influence public policy either by approaching the three branches of government (direct lobbying) or by convincing the people to pressure the government (indirect lobbying).

- The success of individual interest groups is often affected by factors like funding, quality of leadership, membership size and intensity, and access to information.

- Critics of interest groups fear that the most powerful groups are simply those with the most money, and that this poses a danger to American democracy. However, interest group formation may also be seen as a way to give more power to more citizens, offering a mechanism to keep politicians accountable by offering additional channels for representation, participation, education, creation of policy solutions, and public agenda building.

Define | **Understand** | **Practice** | **Read** | **Click** | **Watch**

1. **Which of the following is NOT a role played by interest groups?**
   a. Education
   b. Contesting elections
   c. Providing program alternatives
   d. Agenda building
   e. Program monitoring

2. **The free rider problem is**
   a. a good or service that, by its very nature, cannot be denied to anyone who wants to consume it.
   b. a problem arising when an interest group rides on the coattails of its patron political party when passing legislation.
   c. a benefit that is available only to group members as an inducement to get them to join.
   d. the difficulty groups face in recruiting when potential members can gain the benefits of the group's actions whether or not they join.
   e. the difficulty groups face when an interest group entrepreneur uses a group to benefit financially.

3. **Which of the following is a type of interest group that organizes to influence government to produce collective goods or services that benefit the general public?**
   a. Public interest groups
   b. Equal opportunity interest groups
   c. Economic interest groups
   d. Economic interest groups, except for unions and professional organizations
   e. Government interest groups

4. **What is the key difference between direct lobbying and indirect lobbying?**
   a. Direct lobbying involves interest groups interacting with the legislative branch, whereas indirect lobbying involves interest groups interacting with the executive branch.
   b. Direct lobbying involves interest groups interacting with public officials, whereas indirect lobbying involves interest groups giving campaign contributions to public officials.
   c. Direct lobbying involves interest groups interacting with public officials, whereas indirect lobbying involves interest groups trying to influence government policymakers by encouraging the general public to put pressure on them.
   d. Direct lobbying involves interest groups funding a lawmaker's travel on fact-finding trips, whereas indirect lobbying involves interest groups funding a lawmaker's reelection with campaign contributions.
   e. Direct lobbying involves interest groups lobbying a congressperson in his or her office, while indirect lobbying involves interest groups providing testimony at a hearing.

5. **Which of the following is NOT an important resource for interest groups?**
   a. Money
   b. Leadership
   c. Intensity of membership
   d. Information
   e. Contacts with political parties

Define Understand Practice **Read** Click Watch

Berry, Jeffrey M., and Clyde Wilcox. 2009. *The Interest Group Society*, 5th ed. New York: Longman. In one of the most comprehensive books on interest groups available, Berry and Wilcox cover all the bases, including PACs, lobbying, and the problems that interest groups bring to the policymaking process.

Birnbaum, Jeffrey. 1992. *The Lobbyists: How Influence Peddlers Work Their Way in Washington*. New York: Random House. A journalist takes the reader into the halls of the Capitol and examines the role that lobbyists play in the political arena.

Cigler, Allan J., and Burdett A. Loomis, eds. 2011. *Interest Group Politics*, 8th ed. Washington, D.C.: CQ Press. A noteworthy collection dealing with the many facets of interest group politics.

Feldman, Richard. 2007. *Ricochet: Confessions of a Gun Lobbyist*. Hoboken, N.J.: Wiley. An unprecedented insider's view of the National Rifle Association, written by a former NRA regional political director and gun lobbyist.

Olson, Mancur, Jr. 1971. *The Logic of Collective Action: Public Goods and the Theory of Groups*. Cambridge: Harvard University Press. The classic work on collective action problems. Olson argues that groups must offer selective incentives in order to attract members, but they remain vulnerable to free rider problems.

Rauch, Jonathan. 1994. *Demosclerosis: The Silent Killer of American Government*. New York: Crown. This fascinating book argues that the growth in interest groups has had negative effects on the development of public policy.

Truman, David B. 1971. *The Governmental Process: Political Interests and Public Opinion*, 2nd ed. New York: Knopf. A classic work on the formation of pluralist theory.

Define Understand Practice Read **Click** Watch

Center for Responsive Politics www.opensecrets.org. This excellent source of up-to-the-minute data on money and politics contains a wealth of information on lobbyists and PACs, politician and congressional committee profiles, campaign donation lists, and much more.

Federal Election Commission www.fec.gov. This web site lists the official reports regarding campaign finance. With a little research, the user can gain access to how much PAC money was spent in recent as well as past elections.

Political Advocacy Groups: A Directory of U.S. Lobbyists http://van-ezproxy.vancouver.wsu.edu/pag/index.html. A frequently updated directory of U.S. interest groups and lobby organizations. Each interest group's entry includes contact information and a copy of its mission statement.

Senate Office of Public Records www.senate.gov/pagelayout/legislative/g_three_sections_with_teasers/lobbyingdisc.htm. This web site for the Senate's lobby filing disclosure program provides a searchable function that allows the researcher to read the midyear and year-end Lobbying Disclosure Reports for all the interests that have lobbied Congress. Specifically, one can see how much each interest group spent lobbying Congress.

U.S. Public Interest Research Group (PIRG) www.uspirg.org. U.S. PIRG is a self-styled "advocate for the public interest" that seeks to combat the actions of special interest lobbyists. The web site offers overviews of various issues, ranging from product safety to media reform and Internet freedom.

Define Understand Practice Read Click **Watch**

The Best Congress Money Can Buy 2007. Dan Rather Reports (New York: CBS). This film analyzes the extent of interest groups' control over congressional decision making. A unique look at how much government legislation money can really buy.

Buried in the Fine Print 2006. 60 Minutes (New York: CBS). This brief documentary explores the shadowy relationship between interest groups and legislative earmarks.

Dangerous Prescription 2003. Frontline (Boston: WGBH). This is an interesting documentary on the Food and Drug Administration's difficulty regulating medicines. The lobbying strengths and influence of the pharmaceutical industry are highlighted.

Thank You for Smoking 2006. This Golden Globe–nominated film follows the efforts of Nick Naylor—chief spokes person for a major tobacco lobby—to paint cigarette use in a more positive light, and the heated public debate that ensues.

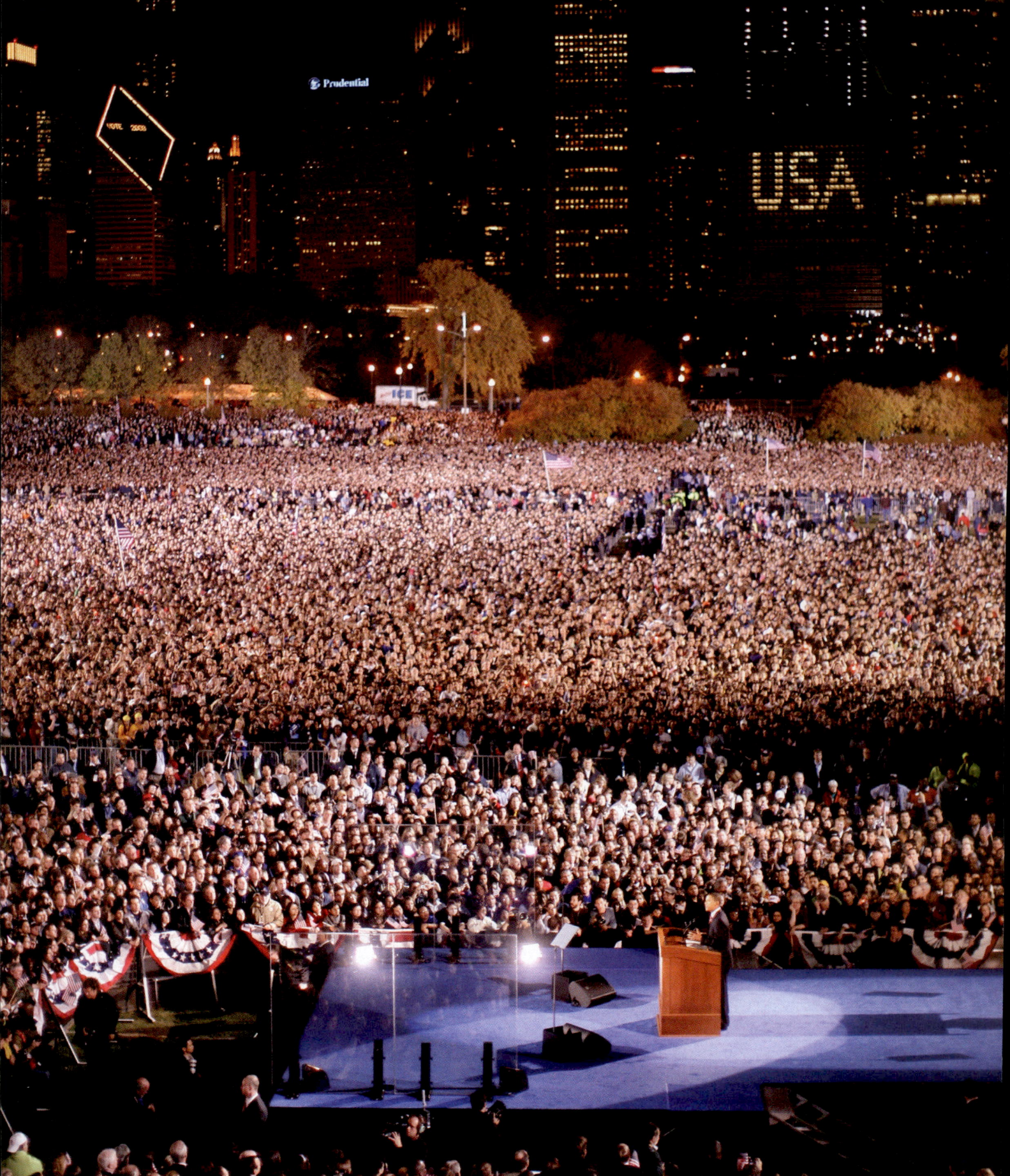

Chapter 14

Voting, Campaigns, and Elections

▶ What's at Stake?

State of the Union addresses are well-attended affairs. In 2010, as Barack Obama stood at the podium with the Speaker of the House and the vice president sitting behind him, he looked out on an august assembly that included six black-robed members of the nation's highest court sitting in the very front rows.

Imagine the justices' surprise when the president took the highly unusual step of calling them out in front of the entire nation for a decision he said was "wrong." Targeting a ruling the Court had just handed down in a case called *Citizens United v. Federal Election Commission*, Obama said:

> Last week, the Supreme Court reversed a century of law to open the floodgates for special interests—including foreign companies—to spend without limit in our elections. Well, I don't think American elections should be bankrolled by America's most powerful interests, and worse, by foreign entities. They should be decided by the American people, and that's why I'm urging Democrats and Republicans to pass a bill that helps to right this wrong.

The *Citizens United* case reversed a significant part of the Bipartisan Campaign Reform Act of 2002 (BCRA), also known as the McCain-Feingold Act, that had been passed after much debate in 2002. The act had prevented corporations and unions from spending money from their treasuries (as opposed to specially created political action committees) on television

Alito Shakes Head When Obama Criticizes Campaign Finance Decision

tpmtv 3,277 videos Subscribe

THE PLACE FOR POLITICS 'LIVE msnbc

STATE OF THE UNION

TPM

A Public Rebuke

In his 2010 State of the Union address, President Obama stated that the Supreme Court's ruling in the *Citizens United* case "open[ed] the floodgates for special interests—including foreign corporations—to spend without limit in our elections," causing Justice Samuel Alito (circled above) to shake his head and mouth the words "Not true." This ruling and others by the Supreme Court have thwarted Congress' efforts to limit campaign donations, allowing money to play a dominant role in American elections.

advertising for or against political candidates immediately before an election. While the ruling left earlier restrictions on corporate election spending in place, the majority penned a broadly worded decision that endorsed the free speech rights of corporations. The *New York Times* called it "a sharp doctrinal shift" that "will have major political and practical consequences," that would "reshape the way elections were conducted."[1]

The president's remarks were immediately controversial, starting with the words "not true" apparently mouthed by a head-shaking Justice Samuel Alito.[2] Commentators debated the propriety of the president of the United States publicly criticizing the actions of another branch of government. Some thought he had overstepped his bounds, and others argued that the words were a well-deserved rebuke of the Court.

No doubt knowing that his remarks would cause a firestorm, Obama nonetheless chose to make them in an unmistakably severe tone. Were they deserved? Was the *Citizens United* decision really that big a deal? What was at stake after all in the decision to allow corporate interests to spend without restraint in U.S. elections? We return to this question after we examine the way that elections are held, and funded, in the United States. ■

The mechanism that connects citizens with their governments, by which they signify their consent and through which they accomplish peaceful change, is elections.

Although we pride ourselves on our democratic government, Americans seem to have a love-hate relationship with the idea of campaigns and voting. On the one hand, many citizens believe that elections do not accomplish anything, that elected officials ignore the wishes of the people, and that government is run for the interests of the elite rather than the many. Voters in 2008 were unusually motivated, with a turnout rate of higher than 60 percent, but typically only about half of the eligible electorate votes.

On the other hand, when it is necessary to choose a leader, whether the captain of a football team, the president of a dorm, or a local precinct chairperson, the first instinct of most Americans is to call an election. Even though there are other ways to choose leaders—picking the oldest, the wisest, or the strongest; holding a lottery; or asking for volunteers—Americans almost always prefer an election. We elect over half a million public officials in America.[3] This means we have a lot of elections—more elections more often for more officials than in any other democracy.

In this chapter we examine the complicated place of elections in American politics and American culture. You will learn about

- *what the founders were thinking when they established a role for elections, and the potential roles that elections can play in a democracy*

- *Americans' ambivalence about the vote and the reasons that only about half of the citizenry even bother to exercise what is supposed to be a precious right*

- *how voters go about making decisions, and how this in turn influences the character of presidential elections*

- *the organizational and strategic aspects of running for the presidency*

- *what elections mean for citizens*

Voting in a Democratic Society

A nonviolent means for political change

Up until the last couple hundred years, it was virtually unthinkable that the average citizen could or should have any say in who would govern. Rather, leaders were chosen by birth, by the church, by military might, by the current leaders, but not by the mass public. Real political change, when it occurred, was usually ushered in with violence and bloodshed.

Today, global commitment to democracy is on the rise. Americans and, increasingly, other citizens around the world believe that government with the consent of the governed is superior to government imposed on unwilling subjects and that political change is best accomplished through the ballot box rather than on the battlefield or in the streets. The mechanism that connects citizens with their governments, by which they signify their consent and through which they accomplish peaceful change, is elections. Looked at from this perspective, elections are an amazing innovation—they provide a method for the peaceful transfer of power. Quite radical political changes can take place without blood being shed, an accomplishment that would confound most of our political ancestors.

As we saw in Chapter 1, however, proponents of democracy can have very different ideas about how much power citizens should exercise over government. Elite theorists believe that citizens should confine their role to choosing among competing elites; pluralists think citizens should join groups that fight for their interests in government on their behalf; and participatory democrats call for more active and direct citizen involvement in politics. Each of these views has consequences for how elections should be held. How many officials should be chosen by the people? How often should elections be held? Should people choose officials directly, or through representatives whom they elect? How accountable should officials be to the people who elect them?

We have already seen, in Chapter 11, that though Americans hardly resemble the informed, active citizens prescribed by democratic theory, that does not mean they are unqualified to exercise political power. At the end of this chapter, when we have a clearer understanding of the way that elections work in America, we will return to the question of how much power citizens should have and what different answers to this question mean for our thinking about elections. We begin our study of elections, however, by examining the functions that they can perform in democratic government. First we look at the very limited role that the founders had in mind for popular elections when they designed the American Constitution, and then we evaluate the claims of democratic theorists more generally.

A Hard-Won Right
Democracy is nothing if it is not about citizens choosing their leaders. In 1966 black voters in Peachtree, Alabama, lined up to vote for the first time since passage of the Voting Rights Act of 1965.

The Founders' Intentions

The Constitution reflects the founding fathers' fears that people could not reliably exercise wise and considered judgment about politics. Consequently the founders built a remarkable layer of insulation between the national government and the will of the people. The president was to be elected not directly by the people but by an electoral college, which was expected to be a group of wiser-than-average men who would use prudent judgment. In fact, only the House of Representatives, one-half of one-third of the government, was to be popularly elected. The Senate and the executive and judicial branches were to be selected by different types of political elites who could easily check any moves that might arise from the whims of the masses. In the founders' view, the government needed the support of the masses, but it could not afford to be led by what they saw as the public's shortsighted and easily misguided judgment.

The Functions of Elections

Despite the founders' reluctance to entrust much political power to American citizens, we have since altered our method of electing senators to make these elections direct, and the Electoral College, as we shall see, almost always endorses the popular vote for president. As we said in the introduction to this chapter, elections have become a central part of American life, even if our participation in them is somewhat uneven. Theorists claim that elections fulfill a variety of functions in modern democratic life: selecting leaders, giving direction to policy, developing citizenship, informing the public, containing conflict, and legitimizing and stabilizing the system. Here we examine and evaluate how well elections fill some of those functions.

Selection of Leaders

Like our founders, many philosophers and astute political observers have had doubts about whether elections are the best way to choose wise and capable leaders. Philosophers from Plato to John Stuart Mill have expressed doubts about citizen capability, arguing that you cannot trust the average citizen to make wise choices in the voting booth.[4] More recent critics also focus on the other side of the equation, claiming that democratic elections often fail to produce the best leaders because the electoral process scares off some of the most capable candidates. Running for office is a hard, expensive, and bruising enterprise. Many qualified people are put off by the process, though they might be able to do an

Thinking Outside the Box

Are elections the best way to choose our leaders?

excellent job and have much to offer through public service. The simple truth is that elections ensure only that the leader chosen is the most popular on the ballot. There is no guarantee that the best candidate will run, or that the people will choose the wisest, most honest, or most capable leader from the possible candidates.

Policy Direction

Democracy and elections are only partially about choosing able leadership. The fears of the founders notwithstanding, today we also expect that the citizenry will have a large voice in what the government actually does. Competitive elections are intended in part to keep leaders responsive to the concerns of the governed, since they can be voted out of office if voters are displeased.

The policy impact of elections, however, is indirect. For instance, at the national level, we elect individuals, but we do not vote on policies. Although citizens in about half the states can make policy directly through initiatives and referenda, the founders left no such option at the national level. Rather, they provided us with a complicated system in which power is divided and checked. Those who stand for election have different constituencies and different terms of office. Thus the different parts of the national government respond to different publics at different times. The voice of the people is muted and modulated. At times, however, especially when there is a change in the party that controls the government, elections do produce rather marked shifts in public policy.[5] The New Deal of the 1930s is an excellent case in point. The election of a Democratic president and Congress allowed a sweeping political response to the Depression, in sharp contrast to the previous Republican administration's hands-off approach to the crisis.

The electoral process actually does a surprisingly good job of directing policy in less dramatic ways as well. A good deal of research demonstrates, for example, that in the states, elections achieve a remarkable consistency between the general preferences of citizens and the kinds of policies that the states enact.[6] At the congressional level, members of the House and the Senate are quite responsive to the overall policy wishes of their constituents, and those who are not tend to suffer at the polls.[7] At the presidential level, through all of the hoopla and confusion of presidential campaigns, scholars have found that presidents do, for the most part, deliver on the promises that they make and that the national parties do accomplish much of what they set out in their platforms.[8] Finally, elections speed up the process by which changes in public preferences for a more activist or less activist (more liberal or more conservative) government are systematically translated into patterns of public policy.[9]

Citizen Development

Some theorists argue that participation in government in and of itself—regardless of which leaders or policy directions are chosen—is valuable for citizens and that elections help citizens feel fulfilled and effective.[10] When individuals are unable to participate in political affairs, or fail to do so, their sense of **political efficacy**, of being effective in political affairs, suffers. In studies of the American electorate, people who participate more, whether in elections or through other means, have higher senses of political efficacy.[11] From this perspective, then, elections provide a mechanism by which individuals can move from passive subjects who see themselves pushed and pulled by forces larger than themselves to active citizens fulfilling their potential to have a positive effect on their own lives.

Informing the Public

When we watch the circus of the modern presidential campaign, it may seem a bit of a stretch to say that an important function of elections, and the campaigns that precede them, is to educate the public. But ideally the campaign is a time of deliberation when alternative points of view are aired openly so that the citizenry can judge the truth and desirability of competing claims and the competence of competing candidates and parties. The evidence is that campaigns do in fact have this impact. People learn a good deal of useful political information from campaign advertisements and for the most part choose the candidates who match their value and policy preferences.[12] As citizens, we probably know and understand a lot more about our government because of our electoral process than we would without free and competitive elections.

Vote Smart

Volunteer members of Project Vote Smart, liberals and conservatives alike, reach out to citizens to inform them about the voting records and backgrounds of thousands of candidates and elected officials so that voters can make informed decisions. The group accepts no funding from any organization, special interest group, or industry as part of its effort to maintain its neutral, nonbiased platform.

Containing Conflict

Elections help us influence policy, but in other ways they also limit our options for political influence.[13] When groups of citizens are unhappy about their taxes, or the quality of their children's schools, or congressional appropriations for AIDS research, or any other matter, the election booth is their primary avenue of influence. Of course, they can write letters and sign petitions, but those have an impact only because the officials they try to influence must stand for reelection. Even if their candidate wins, there is no guarantee that their policy concerns will be satisfied. And those who complain are likely to hear the systemwide response: If you don't like what's going on, vote for change.

If elections help reduce our political conflicts to electoral contests, they also operate as a kind of safety valve for citizen discontent. There is always a relatively peaceful mechanism through which unhappy citizens can vent their energy. Elections can change officials, replacing Democrats with Republicans or vice versa, but they do not fundamentally alter the underlying character of the system. Without the electoral vent, citizens might eventually turn to more threatening behaviors like boycotts, protests, civil disobedience, and rebellion.

Legitimation and System Stability

A final important function of elections is to make political outcomes acceptable to participants. By participating in the process of elections, we implicitly accept, and thereby legitimize, the results. The genius here is that participation tends to make political results acceptable even to those who lose in an immediate sense. They do not take to the streets, set up terrorist cells, or stop paying their taxes. Rather, in the overwhelming majority of instances, citizens who lose in the electoral process shrug their shoulders, obey the rules made by the winning representatives, and wait for their next chance to elect candidates whose policies are more to their liking. Even many supporters of Al Gore in 2000 came to accept Bush's Electoral College victory as conferring legitimacy on him, despite his loss of the popular vote. The beauty of elections is that they can bring about change, but without grave threats to the stability of the system.

Who What How

Those with the greatest stake in the continued existence of elections in America are the citizens who live under their rule. At stake for citizens is, first, the important question of which candidates and parties will govern. However, by viewing elections in a broader perspective, we can see that elections also contribute to the quality of democratic life: they help to define a crucial relationship between the governed and those they choose as leaders, to influence public policy, to educate the citizenry, to contain conflict, and to legitimize political outcomes and decisions.

Exercising the Right to Vote in America

The costs of not voting

We argued in Chapter 11 that even without being well informed and following campaigns closely, Americans can still cast intelligent votes reflecting their best interests. But what does it say about the American citizenry when, in a typical presidential election, barely half of the adult population votes? In off-year congressional elections, in primaries, and in many state and local elections held at different times from the presidential contest, the rates of participation drop even lower.

How do we explain this low voter turnout? Is America just a nation of political slackers? This is a serious and legitimate question in light of the important functions of democracy we have just discussed, and in light of the tremendous struggle many groups have had to achieve the right to vote. Indeed, as we saw in Chapter 6, the history of American suffrage—the right to vote—is one struggle after another for access to the ballot box.

Voting varies dramatically in its importance to different citizens. For some, it is a significant aspect of their identities as citizens. Eighty-seven percent of American adults believe that voting in elections is a "very important obligation" for Americans.[14] Thus many people vote because they believe they should and because they believe the vote gives them a real influence on government. However, only about half the electorate has felt this way strongly enough to vote in recent presidential elections.

Who Votes and Who Doesn't?

Many political observers, activists, politicians, and political scientists worry about the extent of nonvoting in the United States.[15] When people do not vote, they have no voice in choosing their leaders, their policy preferences are not registered, and they do not develop as active citizens. Some observers fear that their abstention signals an alienation from the political process.

From survey data, we know quite a lot about who votes and who doesn't in America in terms of their age, gender, income, education, and racial and ethnic make up:

- *Age.* Older citizens consistently vote at higher rates. For example, 69 percent of those aged forty-five to sixty years reported voting in the 2008 election, compared to 51 percent of those aged eighteen to twenty-nine years. This gap of 18 percent, however, is a bit smaller than it had been in previous elections (for example, 21 percent in 2004).[16]

- *Gender.* Since 1984 women have been voting at a higher rate than men, although the differences are typically only 3 or 4 percent. For example, in the 2008 presidential election the turnout rates for women and men were 65.7 and 61.5 percent, respectively.[17]

- *Income.* The likelihood of voting goes up steadily with income. For example, in 2008 only 49 percent of those making $10,000 or less reported voting, compared to 82 percent of those earning $150,000 or more.[18]

- *Education.* Education is consistently one of the strongest predictors of turnout. For instance, in the 2008 election, only 39 percent of those with less than a high school education voted, compared to almost 72 percent of those who attended some college or got a bachelor's degree; 82.7 percent of those with advanced degrees voted.

- *Race and ethnicity.* Turnout among members of racial and ethnic minority groups has traditionally been lower than that of whites. But that changed in 2008, with an African American as the Democratic nominee. Turnout for blacks was 65 percent, virtually tied with non-Hispanic whites. Hispanic turnout increased in 2008 to 49 percent, the same level as Asians for that year.[19]

When we add these characteristics together, the differences are quite substantial. Compare, for example, the turnout among eighteen- to twenty-four-year-old males with less than a high school education (only 25.5 percent) with the turnout rate for females aged sixty-five to seventy-four years with advanced degrees (87.6 percent).[20] By virtue of their different turnout rates, some groups in American society are receiving much better representation than others. The same patterns hold true and are even more pronounced for types of political engagement other than voting, such as actively working for a party or candidate in distributing literature, staffing the phone banks during a get-out-the-vote drive, or making financial contributions.[21] The upshot is that our elected officials are indebted to and hear much more from the higher socioeconomic ranks in society. They do not hear from and are not elected by the low-participation "have nots."[22]

Figure 14.1

Voter Turnout in Presidential and Midterm House Elections, 1932–2008

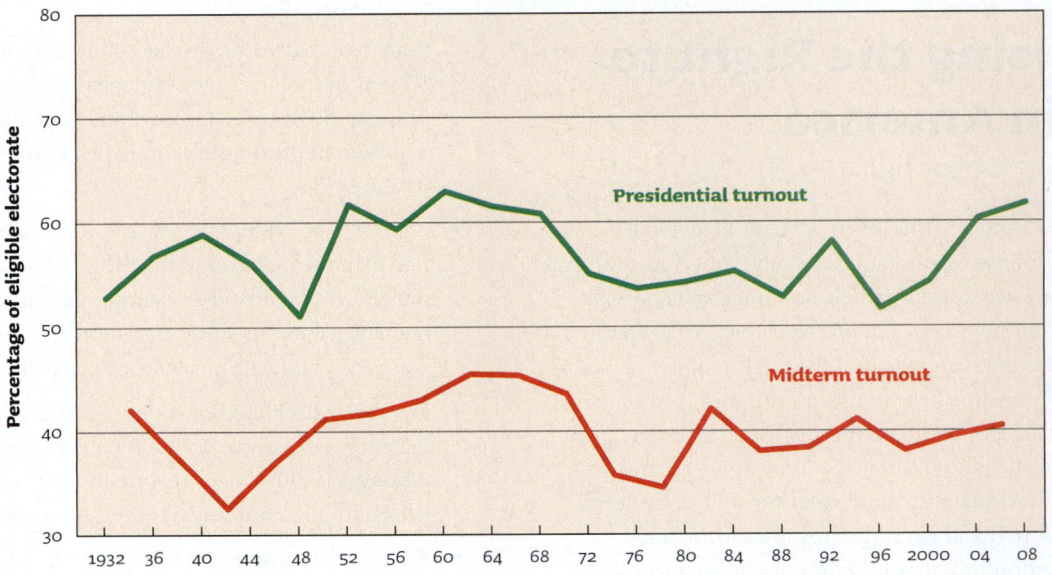

Sources: Presidential data through 2000 from 2005, *The New York Times Almanac*, 114; midterm data through 1998 from U.S. Census Bureau, *2000 Statistical Abstract*, 291; 2004 and 2008 presidential data from United States Election Project, "Voter Turnout," http://elections.gmu.edu/voter_turnout.htm; 2002 and 2006 midterm data from United States Election Project, "2002 Voting-Age and Voting-Eligible Population Estimates and Voter Turnout," http://elections.gmu.edu/voter_turnout_2002.htm, and "2006 Voting-Age and Voting-Eligible Population Estimates and Voter Turnout," http://elections.gmu.edu/voter_turnout_2006.htm.

Why Americans Don't Vote

As we have noted elsewhere, compared with other democratic nations, the United States has low voter turnout levels (see Figure 11.1, on page 411). Despite overall increases in education, age, and income, which generally increase the number of voters, presidential election turnout rates have barely gotten over the 60 percent mark for more than thirty years (and midterm congressional turnout rates have been much lower)[23] (see Figure 14.1). What accounts for such low turnout rates in a country where 82 percent of adults say voting is important to democracy[24]—indeed, in a country that often prides itself on being one of the best and oldest examples of democracy in the world? The question of low voter turnout in the United States poses a tremendous puzzle for political scientists, who have focused on six factors to try to explain this mystery.

Thinking Outside the Box

Should there be penalties for those who don't vote?

Legal Obstacles

Voter turnout provides a dramatic illustration of our theme that rules make a difference in who wins and who loses in politics. The rules that govern elections vary in democracies around the world, yielding very different rates of turnout. So, for example, in many other democracies it is the government, not the individual voter, that bears the responsibility for registering citizens to vote, and in some countries—Australia, Belgium, and Italy, for example—voting is required by law. Turnout rates in these countries are high.[25] But in the United States, several election rules actually make it more difficult for voters to exercise their right to vote, not only by requiring advance registration but also by limiting voting to a single weekday when most people have to work. U.S. laws also allow for many elections, and evidence suggests that frequency of elections results in "voter fatigue." The low turnout that results may be an accidental consequence of laws intended for other purposes, but in some cases politicians support those laws in the belief that high turnout will benefit the other party or be harmful to stable government.

A number of reform efforts have attempted to ease the burden of casting a ballot. Congress passed the National Voter

Motor Voter Bill legislation allowing citizens to register to vote at the same time they apply for a driver's license or other state benefit

voter mobilization a party's efforts to inform potential voters about issues and candidates and to persuade them to vote

Registration Act of 1993, or the **Motor Voter Bill** as it is more commonly called, which requires the states to take a more active role in registering people to vote, including providing registration opportunities when applying for a driver's license or at the welfare office. In addition, some states have instituted the option to register on an election day, and Oregon has even gone as far as having its elections by mail. Each reform has marginally increased the numbers of people voting, but on the whole the results have been a disappointment to reformers. An exhaustive review of the research concluded that, even with obstacles to voting removed, "for many people, voting remains an activity from which there is virtually no gratification— instrumental, expressive, or otherwise." [26]

Politicians have been reluctant to pass major electoral reforms because of fears about whom the beneficiaries of such changes might be. The conventional wisdom is that Democrats would benefit from efforts to increase turnout because Republicans are already motivated enough to turn out under current laws, but this expectation (or fear) does not seem to have been borne out by our experience with the Motor Voter Bill. Still, such worries continue and some efforts are being made to make it harder for some people to vote. For example, a recently passed voter identification law in Indiana states that in order to vote one must provide a government-issued picture ID card such as a driver's license or passport. True to form, Republicans argued that this was to prevent (as yet not documented) voter fraud and Democrats claimed the law was a ploy to reduce turnout among the poor and less educated (who generally tend to vote Democratic). The Supreme Court ruled that the law does not violate the U.S. Constitution, and neither party is likely to be vindicated in its claims; studies of its effects have not revealed any impact on either voter fraud or turnout.[27]

Attitude Changes

Political scientists have found that some of the low voter turnout we can see in Figure 14.1 is accounted for by changes over time in psychological orientations or attitudes toward politics.[28] For one thing, if people feel that they do not or cannot make a difference and that government is not responsive to their wishes, they often don't bother to vote. Lower feelings of political efficacy lead to less participation.

A second orientation that has proved important in explaining low turnout is partisanship. There was a distinct decline in Americans' attachments to the two major political parties in the 1960s and 1970s. With a drop in party identification came a drop in voting levels. This decline, however, has leveled off, and in recent years there has even been an increase in the percentage of citizens saying they identify as Democrats or Republicans. This slight increase in partisanship may have stemmed the decline in turnout that was apparent from the late 1960s through the 1980s.

Attitudes, of course, do not change without some cause; they reflect citizens' reactions to what they see in the political world. It is easy to understand why attitudes have changed since the relatively tranquil 1950s. Amid repeated scandal and increasing partisanship, our public airwaves have been dominated by negative information about and images of the leadership in Washington, D.C. The Bush administration did enjoy a period of good feeling in the aftermath of the September 11 attacks as the nation rallied against the threat of terrorism, but that dissipated as politics got back to usual. President Obama ran successfully by raising expectations for a more inclusive, cleaner, and less partisan politics. Many in the electorate bought the message of hope, and the United States saw the highest turnout levels in decades. However, while Obama was able to pass quite a bit of legislation, the deep partisan differences that divide the parties and the complexities of our economic and environmental problems dashed the (perhaps unrealistic) hopes of many voters. In 2010 Democratic voter turnout, especially among young voters, was down, possibly reflecting in part frustration with Obama's inability to change the tone as he had promised and with the continued partisanship in politics, but the election of a Republican majority to the House did not seem designed to reduce the divisiveness.

Voter Mobilization

Another factor that political scientists argue has led to lower turnout from the 1960s into the 1990s is a change in the efforts of politicians, interest groups, and especially political parties to make direct contact with people during election campaigns.[29] **Voter mobilization** includes contacting people— especially supporters—to inform them about the election and to persuade them to vote. It can take the form of making phone calls, knocking on doors, or even supplying rides to the polls. As the technology of campaigns, especially the use of television, developed and expanded in the 1980s and 1990s, fewer resources were used for the traditional shoe-leather efforts of direct contact with voters, but solid evidence now indicates that personal contacts do a better job of getting out the vote than do mass mailing and telephone calls.[30]

> **social connectedness**   citizens' involvement in groups and their relationships to their communities and families

Lining Up to Be Heard

Americans are asked to cast their ballots more often than people in most other democracies, and in the face of such demand, a lot of people choose to just stay home. Mobilization efforts like early voting and mail-in ballots aim to eliminate would-be voters' excuses and boost electoral participation by making the process easier.

Television is certainly useful for reaching large numbers of citizens with a campaign message, but it is less effective at motivating people to vote. As television grew so did the use of negative attack ads, which turn people off and hurt turnout.[31] In recent campaigns, both Democrats and Republicans have increased their efforts at voter mobilization. They and a growing number of interest groups are combining computer technology with personal contacts as an integral part of their overall campaigns.[32] The increases in turnout that we have seen in the last couple presidential elections (see Figure 14.1) are attributable, at least in part, to these efforts.[33]

Decrease in Social Connectedness

Some of the overall decline in voter turnout toward the end of the last century is due to larger societal changes rather than to citizen reactions to parties and political leaders. *Social connectedness* refers to the number of organizations people participate in and how tightly knit their communities and families are—that is, how well integrated they are into the society in which they live. The evidence indicates that people are increasingly likely to live alone and to be single, new to their communities, and isolated from organizations. As individuals loosen or altogether lose their ties to the larger community, they have less of a stake in participating in communal decisions—and

less support for participatory activities. Lower levels of social connectedness have been an important factor in accounting for the low turnout in national elections.[34]

Generational Changes

Events occurring in the formative years of a generation continue to shape its members' orientation toward politics throughout their lives, and can account for varying turnout levels. This is different from the observation that people are more likely to vote as they get older. For instance, those age groups (cohorts) that came of age after the 1960s show much lower levels of attachment to politics, and they vote at lower rates than do their parents or grandparents. Some research suggests that generational differences account for much or most of the turnout decline at the end of the 1990s. That is, people who once voted have not stopped voting; rather, they are dying and are being replaced by younger, less politically engaged voters. The result is lower turnout overall.[35] Of course it is possible for this trend to be reversed as events and personalities politicize and mobilize new generations of citizens.

The Rational Nonvoter

A final explanation for the puzzle of low voter turnout in America considers that, for some people, not voting may be the rational choice. This explanation suggests that the question to ask is not "Why don't people vote?" but rather "Why does anyone vote?" The definition of *rational* means that the benefits of an action outweigh the costs. It is rational for us to do those things from which we get back more than we put in. Voting demands our resources, time, and effort. Given those costs, if someone views voting primarily as a way to influence government and sees no other benefits from it, it becomes a largely irrational act.[36] That is, no one individual's vote can change the course of an election unless the election would otherwise be a tie, and the probability of that happening in a presidential election is small (though, as the 2000 election showed, it is not impossible).

For many people, however, the benefits of voting go beyond the likelihood that they will affect the outcome of the election. In fact, studies have demonstrated that turnout decisions are not really based on our thinking that our votes will determine the outcome. Rather, we achieve other kinds of benefits from voting. It feels good to do what we think we are supposed to do or to help, however little, the side or the causes we believe in. Plus, we get social rewards from our politically involved friends for voting (and avoid sarcastic remarks for not voting). These benefits accrue no matter which side wins.

Does Nonvoting Matter?

What difference does it make that some people vote and others do not? There are two ways to tackle this question. One approach is to ask whether election outcomes would be different if nonvoters were to participate. The other approach is to ask whether higher levels of nonvoting indicate that democracy is not healthy. Both questions, of course, concern important potential consequences of low participation in our elections.

Consequences for Election Outcomes

Studies of the likely effects of nonvoting come up with contradictory answers. A traditional, and seemingly logical, approach is to note that nonvoters, being disproportionately poor and less educated, have social and economic characteristics that are more common among Democrats than among Republicans. Therefore, were these people to vote, we could expect that Democratic candidates would do better. Some polling results support this thinking. Pollsters asked registered voters a number of questions to judge how likely it was that they would actually vote in elections for House members. When the voting intentions of all registered voters and the subset of likely voters were compared, the likely voters were

distinctly more Republican. If this were to hold true generally, we could conclude that nonvoting works to the disadvantage of Democratic candidates. One political scholar found some evidence of this for the 1980 presidential election and concluded that a much higher turnout among nonvoters would have made the election closer and that Jimmy Carter might even have won reelection.[37] Similarly, when political scientists have run simulations to test whether full turnout would alter the results in elections for the U.S. Senate, the share of the vote for Democratic candidates is increased, but given that these elections are not particularly close, the extra votes would seldom change the winner of the elections.[38]

Undermining this interpretation are findings from most other presidential elections that nonvoters' preferences are quite responsive to short-term factors, so they go disproportionately for the winning candidate. Because these voters are less partisan and have less intensely held issue positions, they are moved more easily by the short-term campaign factors favoring one party or the other. In most presidential elections, nonvoters' participation would have increased the winner's margin only slightly or not changed things at all.[39] Interviews taken shortly after the two most recent presidential elections suggest that those who did not vote would have broken for the winner, Bush in 2004 and Obama in 2008.[40] The potential effects of nonvoters being mobilized, therefore, are probably not as consistently pro-Democratic as popular commentary suggests.

Consequences for Democracy

Although low turnout might not affect who wins an election, we have made it clear that elections do more than simply select leaders. How might nonvoting affect the quality of democratic life in America? Nonvoting can influence the stability and legitimacy of democratic government. The victor in close presidential elections, for example, must govern the country, but as critics often point out, as little as 25 percent of the eligible electorate may have voted for the winner. When a majority of the electorate sits out of an election, the entire governmental process may begin to lose legitimacy in society at large. Nonvoting can also have consequences for the nonvoter. As we have noted, failure to participate politically can aggravate already low feelings of efficacy and produce higher levels of political estrangement. To the extent that being a citizen is an active pursuit, unhappy, unfulfilled, and unconnected citizens seriously damage the quality of democratic life for themselves and for the country as a whole.

Is our democracy stronger if more Americans vote?

All political actors are not equal on Election Day. Some reduce their power considerably by failing to turn out to vote. Two things are at stake in these turnout patterns. The first is a question of representation and political power: while many politicians would like to attend to the needs of all constituents equally, when push comes to shove and they have to make hard choices, voters are going to be heeded more than silent nonvoters. A second issue at stake in low and declining turnout rates is the quality of democratic life we spoke of earlier—and the stability and legitimacy of the system. Nonvoting is tied to citizen estrangement from the political process, and, in this view, the quality of democratic life itself depends on active citizen participation.

**Who
What
How**

How the Voter Decides
Many factors determine the final choice

Putting an X next to a name on a ballot or pulling a lever on a voting machine or even putting your finger on a party icon on a touch-screen monitor to register a preference would seem like a pretty simple act. But although the action itself may be simple, the decision process behind the choice is anything but. A number of considerations go into our decision about how to vote, including our partisan identification and social group membership; our gender, race, and ethnicity; our stance on the issues and our evaluation of the job government has been doing generally; and our opinions of the candidates. In this section we examine how these factors play out in the simple act of voting.

Partisanship and Social Group Membership

The single biggest factor accounting for how people decide to vote is *party identification*, a concept we discussed in Chapter 12. For most citizens, party ID is stable and long-term, carrying over from one election to the next in what one scholar has called "a standing decision."[41] In 2008, for example, 89 percent of those identifying with the Democratic Party voted for Barack Obama, and 90 percent of those identifying with the Republican Party voted for John McCain.[42]

Clearly, party ID has a strong and direct influence on identifiers' voting decisions. Scholars have demonstrated that party ID also has an important indirect influence on voting decisions, because voters' party ID also colors their views on policy issues and their evaluation of candidates, leading them to judge their party's candidate and issue positions as superior.[43] Under unusual circumstances, social group characteristics can exaggerate or override traditional partisan loyalties. The 1960 election, for instance, was cast in terms of whether the nation would elect its first Catholic president. In that context, religion was especially salient, and fully 82 percent of Roman Catholics supported John F. Kennedy, compared to just 37 percent of Protestants—a difference of 45 percentage points. Compare that to 1976, when the Democrats ran a devout Baptist, Jimmy Carter, for president. The percentage of Catholics voting Democratic dropped to 58 percent, while Protestants voting Democratic increased to 46 percent. The difference shrank to just 12 percent.

Gender, Race, and Ethnicity

It is not clear what impact gender plays in voting decisions. In Chapter 11 we discussed the gender gap in the positions men and women take on the issues, which has generally led women to be more likely to support the Democratic candidate. Since 1964, women have been more supportive of the Democratic candidate in every presidential election but one (they were not more likely to support Carter in 1976).[44] But women do not vote monolithically; for instance, married women are more conservative than single women.

It's an open question whether the gender of a candidate affects the women's vote. In statewide races, there is some evidence that Republican and independent women will cross party lines to vote for Democratic women candidates, though the opposite is not true for Republican women candidates.[45] In the Super Tuesday 2008 Democratic primaries, a larger percentage of women than men voted for Hillary Clinton in fourteen out of sixteen states.[46] However, despite the speculation that the nomination of Sarah Palin as the Republican vice presidential candidate might have swayed some women to support the McCain-Palin ticket, there was little evidence in the 2008 exit polls to support that idea.

prospective voting basing voting decisions on well-informed opinions and consideration of the future consequences of a given vote

retrospective voting basing voting decisions on reactions to past performance; approving the status quo or signaling a desire for change

African Americans have tended to vote Democratic since the civil rights movement of the 1960s. In fact, African Americans have averaged just under 90 percent of the two-party vote for the Democratic candidate in recent presidential elections (1988 to 2004).[47] The nomination of Barack Obama, the first black to receive a major party's presidential nomination, increased the solidarity of the African American vote even further in 2008. This was evident in the Democratic primaries, where the African American vote was a major factor, with 82 percent of it going for Obama, compared to 16 percent for Hillary Clinton. Having a black presidential candidate heightened the role of race in the general election as well. African American support for the Democratic ticket reached a record 95 percent, and the gap between black and white support for the Democratic ticket was substantially larger in 2008 (52 percent) than in 2004 (37 percent).[48]

Ethnicity is less predictive of the vote than race, partly because ethnic groups in the United States become politically diverse as they are assimilated into the system. Although immigrant groups have traditionally found a home in the Democratic Party, dating back to the days when the party machine would provide a one-stop shop for new immigrants seeking jobs, homes, and social connections, recent immigrant groups today include Asians and Hispanics, both of which comprise diverse ethnic communities with distinct identities and varying partisan tendencies.[49] These diverse groups tend to support the Democratic Party, but each has subgroups that are distinctly more Republican: Vietnamese, in the case of Asians, and Cubans, among Latino groups.[50] That said, in 2008 Obama received the overwhelming portion of Hispanic votes. Nationally 67 percent of Latino voters supported Obama, but this support varied by state, from 74 percent in California to 57 percent in Florida. However, this was a substantial shift in the Florida Latino vote—which is largely Cuban—from a mere 44 percent for John Kerry in 2004.

Issues and Policy

An idealized view of elections would have highly attentive citizens paying careful attention to the different policy positions offered by the candidates and then, perhaps aided by informed policy analyses from the media, casting their ballots for the candidates who best represent their preferred policy solutions. In truth, as we know by now, American citizens are not "ideal," and the role played by issues is less obvious and more complicated than the ideal model would predict.

The role of issues in electoral decision making is limited by the following factors:

- People are busy and, in many cases, rely on party labels to tell them what they need to know about the candidates.[51]

- People know where they stand on "easy" issues like capital punishment or prayer in schools, but some issues, like economic policy or health care, Social Security reform, or foreign policy in the Middle East, are complicated, and many citizens tend to tune them out.[52]

- The media do not generally cover issues in depth. Instead, they much prefer to focus on the horse-race aspect of elections, looking at who is ahead in the polls rather than what substantive policy issues mean for the nation.[53]

- As we discussed in Chapter 11, people process a lot of policy-relevant information in terms of their impressions of candidates (on-line processing) rather than as policy information. They are certainly influenced by policy information, but they cannot necessarily articulate their opinions and preferences on policy.

Although calculated policy decisions by voters are rare, policy considerations do have a real impact on voters' decisions. To see that, it is useful to distinguish between prospective and retrospective voting. The idealized model of policy voting with which we opened this section is *prospective voting*, in which voters base their decisions on what will happen in the future if they vote for a candidate—what policies will be enacted, what values will be emphasized in policy. Prospective voting requires a good deal of information that average voters, as we have seen, do not always have or even want. While all voters do some prospective voting and, by election time, are usually aware of the candidates' major issue positions, it is primarily party activists and political elites who engage in the full-scale policy analysis that prospective voting entails.

Instead, most voters supplement their spotty policy information and interest with their evaluation of how they think the country is doing, how the economy is performing, and how well the incumbents are carrying out their jobs. They engage in *retrospective voting*, casting their votes as signs of approval or to signal their desire for change.[54]

Oh, it's time for some campaignin'

Taking a Jab
The campaign between Barack Obama and John McCain was targeted in this JibJab video, which lampooned the candidate's images—McCain's as a gravel-voiced, crazed former POW and Obama's as a unicorn-riding, change-loving peacenik. Political satire can have a potent effect on defining a candidate's image, as Sarah Palin found out in 2008, when she became the focus of Tina Fey's impressions on Saturday Night Live.

In presidential elections this means that voters look back at the state of the economy, at perceived successes or failures in foreign policy, and at domestic issues like education, gun control, or welfare reform. In 1980 Ronald Reagan skillfully focused on voter frustration in the presidential debate by asking voters this question: "[A]re you better off than you were four years ago?"[55] Politicians have been reprising that question ever since. In 2008 the situation was more complicated, as no incumbent was running, but nonetheless Democrat Barack Obama tried to make the election a retrospective referendum on the Bush years, tying Republican John McCain to Bush's record whenever he could. The effort was partially successful; fully 67 percent of the almost three-quarters of the electorate who disapproved of how Bush was handling his job voted for Obama. But in the 2010 midterm elections Republicans managed to turn the strategy back on Obama, pegging the stubbornly bad economy to his policies and tapping into voter angst about the economy to turn Democrats out of office.

Retrospective voting is considered to be "easy" decision making as opposed to the more complex decision making involved in prospective voting because one only has to ask, "How have things been going?" as a guide to whether to support the current party in power. Retrospective voting is also seen as a useful way of holding politicians accountable, not for

what they said or are saying in a campaign, but for what they or members of their party in power *did*. Some scholars believe that this type of voting is all that is needed for democracy to function well.[56] In practice, voters combine elements of both these voting strategies.

The Candidates

In addition to considerations of party, personal demographics, and issues, voters also base their decisions on judgments about candidates as individuals. What goes into voters' images of candidates?

Some observers have claimed that voters view candidate characteristics much as they would a beauty or personality contest. There is little support, however, for the notion that voters are won over merely by good looks or movie-star qualities. Consider, for example, that Richard Nixon almost won against John F. Kennedy, who had good looks, youth, and a quick wit in his favor. Then, in 1964, the awkward, gangly Lyndon Johnson defeated the more handsome and articulate Barry Goldwater in a landslide. In fact, ample evidence indicates that voters form clear opinions about candidate qualities that are relevant to governing, such as trustworthiness, competence, experience, and sincerity. Citizens also make judgments about the ability of the candidates to lead the nation and withstand the pressures of the presidency. Ronald Reagan, for example, was admired widely for his ability to stay above the fray of Washington politics and to see the humor in many situations. By contrast, his predecessor, Jimmy Carter, seemed overwhelmed by the job.

The 2008 campaign allowed voters to develop quite distinct images of Barack Obama and John McCain. Many more agreed that McCain "has the right experience to be president" (54 percent versus 36 percent for Obama). However, this potential advantage was trumped by Obama's success with his "change" theme. Fifty-four percent agreed that Obama "can bring the kind of change the county needs," compared to just 39 percent who felt that statement applied to McCain. Voters also perceived differences in temperament. Obama achieved a substantial advantage on having "a better personality and temperament to be president" (55 percent to McCain's 37 percent). One of the many things that made Ronald Reagan popular was the slogan "It's morning again in America," which symbolized for many his optimistic outlook for the country. On this dimension, when voters were asked which candidate "is more optimistic," Obama fared very well, with

invisible primary early attempts to raise money, line up campaign consultants, generate media attention, and get commitments for support even before candidates announce they are running

62 percent of respondents (versus 30 percent for McCain).[57] It is no surprise that Obama stuck with the theme of "change you can believe in," while McCain tried to convince voters to put more weight on experience and service to the country.

Who What How

Citizens have a strong interest in seeing that good and effective leaders are elected and that power transfers peacefully from losers to winners. By the standard of highly informed voters carefully weighing the alternative policy proposals of competing candidates, the electorate may seem to fall short. However, by a realistic standard that considers the varying abilities of people and the frequent reluctance of candidates and the media to be fully forthcoming about policy proposals, the electorate does not do too badly. Voters come to their decisions through a mix of partisan considerations, membership in social groups, policy information, and candidate image.

Presidential Campaigns
The long, expensive road to the White House

Being president of the United States is undoubtedly a difficult challenge, but so is getting the job in the first place. In this section we examine the long, expensive, and grueling "road to the White House," as the media like to call it.

Getting Nominated

Each of the major parties (and the minor parties, too) needs to come up with a single viable candidate from the long list of party members with ambitions to serve in the White House. How the candidate is chosen will determine the sort of candidate chosen. Remember, in politics the rules are always central to shaping the outcome. Prior to 1972, primary election results were mostly considered "beauty contests" because their results were not binding. But since 1972, party nominees for the presidency have been chosen in primaries, taking the power away from the party elite and giving it to the activist members of the party who care enough to turn out and vote in the party primaries.

The Pre-primary Season

It is hard to say when a candidate's presidential campaign actually begins. Potential candidates may begin planning and

The Shake That Launched a Dream?
What inspires a person to want to become president? Having the opportunity to shake the hand of a sitting president—especially one he particularly admired—clearly meant a lot to the teenaged Bill Clinton.

thinking about running for the presidency in childhood. Bill Clinton is said to have wanted to be president since high school, when he shook President Kennedy's hand. At one time or another, many people in politics consider going for the big prize, but there are several crucial steps between wishful thinking and running for the nomination. Candidates vary somewhat in their approach to the process, but most of those considering a run for the White House go through the following steps:

1. Potential candidates usually test the waters unofficially. They talk to friends and fellow politicians to see just how much support they can count on, and they often leak news of their possible candidacy to the press to see how it is received in the media. This period of jockeying for money, lining up top campaign consultants, generating media buzz, and getting commitments of potential support from party and interest group notables even before candidates announce they are running is called the *invisible primary*. Some

party caucus local gathering of party members to choose convention delegates

presidential primary an election by which voters choose convention delegates committed to voting for a certain candidate

open primary primary election in which eligible voters need not be registered party members

closed primary primary election in which only registered party members may vote

candidates may have an interest but find during the invisible primary that there is not enough early support among the powerful or the public to support a presidential run.[58]

2. If the first step has positive results, candidates file with the Federal Election Commission (FEC) to set up a committee to receive funds so that they can officially explore their prospects. The formation of an *exploratory committee* can be exploited as a media event by the candidate, using the occasion to get free publicity for the launching of the still-unannounced campaign.

3. It costs a lot of money for a candidate to be taken seriously. Some well-positioned candidates, like Hillary Clinton in 2008, are able to raise large amounts of money before they officially enter the race, whereas others are forced to scramble to catch up. In previous years analysts argued that serious candidates needed to raise at least $20 million by the first caucus or primary,[59] but 2008 set new records for the financial challenges of the invisible primary. Clinton and Obama each had raised over $100 million by the time the primary season began in January, and among Republicans, Mitt Romney raised $88.5 million (though $35 million was self-funded), Rudy Giuliani raised $60.9 million, and eventual nominee John McCain had $42 million.[60]

4. The potential candidate must use the pre-primary season to position himself or herself as a credible prospect with the media. It is no coincidence that in the last eight elections, the parties' nominees have all held prominent government offices and have entered the field with some media credibility. Incumbents especially have a huge advantage here.

5. The final step of the pre-primary season is the official announcement of candidacy. Like the formation of the exploratory committee, this statement is part of the campaign itself. Promises are made to supporters, agendas are set, media attention is captured, and the process is under way.

Primaries and Caucuses

The actual fight for the nomination takes place in the state party caucuses and primaries in which delegates to the parties' national conventions are chosen. In a **party caucus**, grassroots members of the party in each community gather in selected locations to discuss the current candidates. They then vote for delegates from that locality who will be sent to the national convention, or who will go on to larger caucuses at the state level to choose the national delegates. Attending a caucus is time consuming, and participation rates are frequently in the single digits.[61] However, 2008 marked a big change, with most states setting records for primary and caucus turnout, especially on the Democratic side, where the heated nomination battle between Barack Obama and Hillary Clinton sparked unusual levels of interest. Most states still hold primary elections, but in recent years there has been a trend toward caucuses, the method used in fifteen states.[62]

The most common device for choosing delegates to the national conventions is the **presidential primary**. Primary voters cast ballots that send delegates committed to voting for a particular candidate to the conventions. Presidential primaries can be either open or closed, depending on the rules the state party organizations adopt, and these can change from year to year. Any registered voter may vote in an **open primary**, regardless of party affiliation. At the polling place, the voter chooses the ballot of the party whose primary he or she wants to vote in. Only registered party members may vote in a **closed primary**. A subset of this is the semi-open primary, open only to registered party members and those not registered as members of another party.

The Democrats also send elected state officials, including Democratic members of Congress and governors, to their national conventions. Some of these officials are "superdelegates," able to vote as free agents, but the rest must reflect the state's primary vote.[63]

In addition to varying in terms of whom they allow to vote, the parties' primary rules also differ in how they distribute delegates among the candidates. The Democrats generally use a method of proportional representation, in which the candidates get the percentage of delegates equal to the percentage of the primary vote they win (provided they get at least 15 percent). Republican rules run from proportional representation, to winner-take-all (the candidate with the most votes gets all the delegates, even if he or she does not win an absolute majority), to direct voting for delegates (the delegates are not bound to vote for a particular candidate at the convention), to the absence of a formal system (caucus participants may decide how to distribute the delegates).

> ***front-loading*** the process of scheduling presidential primaries early in the primary season

State primaries also vary in the times at which they are held, with various states engaged in ***front-loading***, vying to hold their primaries first in order to gain maximum exposure in the media and power over the nomination. By tradition and state law, the Iowa caucus and the New Hampshire primary are the first contests for delegates. As a result, they get tremendous attention, from both candidates and the media—much more than their contribution to the delegate count would justify. This is why in 1998 other states began moving their primaries earlier in the season.[64] The process of moving primary dates up continued in 2008 so that on February 5, twenty-four states plus American Samoa had their primaries and caucuses in an event that some termed "tsunami Tuesday."

The consequence of such front-loading is that candidates must have a full war chest and be prepared to campaign nationally from the beginning. Traditionally, winners of early primaries could use that success to raise more campaign funds to continue the battle. With the primaries stacked at the beginning, however, this becomes much harder. When the winner can be determined within weeks of the first primary, it is less likely that a dark horse, or unknown candidate, can emerge. The process favors well-known, well-connected, and, especially, well-funded candidates. Again, incumbents have an enormous advantage here.

The heavily front-loaded primary has almost no defenders, but it presents a classic example of the problems of collective action that politics cannot always solve.[65] No single state has an incentive to hold back and reduce its power for the good of the whole; each state is driven to maximize its influence by strategically placing its primary early in the pack. Since states make their own laws, subject to only a few regulations laid down by the parties, they are able to schedule the primary season pretty much as they want, regardless of what system would produce the best nominees for national office.

In the fierce battle that the primaries have become, incumbents, of course, have a tremendous advantage. No incumbent has been seriously challenged since Ronald Reagan gave Gerald Ford a good scare in 1976. While the incumbent's advantage is most powerful here, most serious presidential contenders have at least held some major elected office. As Table 14.1 shows, of the two major parties' nominees over the past ten presidential elections, seven were incumbent presidents, three were former or incumbent vice presidents, five were senators, and five were governors. Governors, with executive experience and the ability to claim that they are untainted by the gridlock politics of Washington, have recently had the edge, with four of those five former governors going on to win the presidency.

Table 14.1

Highest Previously Held Offices of Presidential Nominees

Year	Democratic nominee	Previous office	Republican nominee	Previous office
1972	George McGovern	U.S. senator	Richard Nixon	Incumbent president
1976	Jimmy Carter	Governor (Georgia)	Gerald Ford	Incumbent president
1980	Jimmy Carter	Incumbent president	Ronald Reagan	Governor (California)
1984	Walter Mondale	Former vice president	Ronald Reagan	Incumbent president
1988	Michael Dukakis	Governor (Massachusetts)	George H. W. Bush	Incumbent vice president
1992	Bill Clinton	Governor (Arkansas)	George H. W. Bush	Incumbent president
1996	Bill Clinton	Incumbent president	Bob Dole	U.S. senator
2000	Al Gore	Incumbent vice president	George W. Bush	Governor (Texas)
2004	John Kerry	U.S. senator	George W. Bush	Incumbent president
2008	Barack Obama	U.S. senator	John McCain	U.S. senator

> **front-runner**   the leading candidate and expected winner of a nomination or an election
>
> **momentum**   the widely held public perception that a candidate is gaining electoral strength

In most of the crowded primaries in recent years there has been a clear **front-runner**, a person who many assume will win the nomination before the primaries even begin. Early front-runner status is positive because it means the candidate has raised significant money, has a solid organization, and receives more media coverage than his or her opponents. But success in primaries comes not just from getting a majority of the votes but also from being perceived as a winner, and front-runners are punished if they fail to live up to lofty expectations—the fate shared by Republican Rudy Giuliani and Democrat Hillary Clinton in 2008. The goal for all the other candidates is to attack the front-runner so as to drive down his or her support, while maneuvering into position as the chief alternative. Then if the front-runner stumbles, as often happens, each of the attacking candidates hopes to emerge from the pack.

Generally a candidate's campaign strategy becomes focused on developing **momentum**, the perception by the press, the public, and the other candidates in the field that one is on a roll, and that polls, primary victories, endorsements, and funding are all coming one's way. Since all candidates in a primary are from the same party, voters cannot rely on partisanship as a cue in making up their minds. Considerations of electability—which candidate has the best chance to triumph in November—are important as voters decide whom to support, and here candidates who seem to have momentum can have an advantage. Developing momentum helps to distinguish one's candidacy in a crowded field and is typically established in the early primaries.

Consequently, who actually "wins" in the primaries is not always the candidate who comes in first in the balloting. An equally critical factor is whether the candidate is seen to be improving or fading—the matter of momentum and expectations. Much of the political credit that a candidate gets for an apparent "win" depends on who else is running in that primary and what the media expectations of that candidate's performance were.

Figure 14.2 shows the changes in Democrats' preference between leading Democratic contenders for the party's

Figure 14.2

Preferences for 2008 Democratic Presidential Candidates

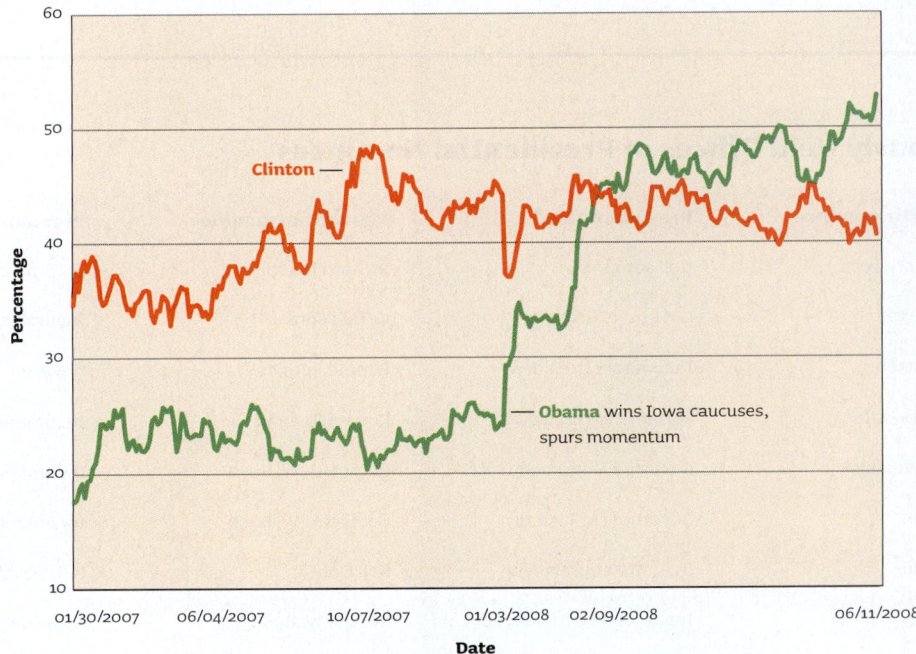

Source: Real Clear Politics, "RCP Poll Average: Democratic Presidential Nomination," www.realclearpolitics.com/epolls/2008/president/us/democratic_presidential_nomination-191.html.

nomination in 2008. Clinton entered the primary season with a clear lead among Democrats nationally, but Obama's strong showing in Iowa initiated a momentum that quickly allowed him to gain an advantage that eventually resulted in his winning the nomination.

The Convention

Since 1972, delegates attending the national conventions have not had to decide who the parties' nominees would be. However, two official actions continue to take place at the conventions. First, as we discussed in Chapter 12, the parties hammer out and approve their platforms, the documents in which parties set out their distinct issue positions. Second, the vice presidential candidate is named officially. The choice of the vice president is up to the presidential nominee. Traditionally the choice was made to balance the ticket (ideologically, regionally, or even, when Democrat Walter Mondale chose Geraldine Ferraro in 1984, by gender). Bill Clinton's choice of Al Gore was a departure from this practice, as he tapped a candidate much like himself—a Democratic moderate from a southern state. In 2000 George W. Bush picked Dick Cheney, a man whose considerable experience in the federal government could be expected to offset Bush's relative lack of it. In 2004 liberal Bostonian John Kerry returned to the regional and ideological balancing principle, choosing moderate North Carolina senator John Edwards as his running mate, though he broke with tradition by announcing his choice three weeks before his party's convention.

In 2008 Barack Obama chose Delaware senator Joe Biden as his running mate, going for an experienced hand with a foreign policy background to shore up his own record. Democrats applauded his pick of Biden as one that balanced the ticket and showcased Obama's own judgment and decision-making skills. They had barely finished cheering their new nominee, however, when John McCain upstaged Obama with his own pick, Alaska governor Sarah Palin, who he felt would bolster his maverick credentials, help him energize his base, and bolster his standing with women. The choice was immediately controversial; wildly popular with religious conservatives, it was viewed with surprise and skepticism by Democrats and media commentators. There is no clear evidence that the vice presidential choice has significant electoral consequences, but the presidential nominees weigh it carefully nonetheless. If nothing else, the caliber of the nominee's choice for vice president is held to be an indication of the kind of appointments the nominee would

Enjoying the Party

Republican presidential candidate John McCain and his running mate, Alaska governor Sarah Palin, greet the crowd at the Republican National Convention in St. Paul, Minnesota, on September 4, 2008. While Palin's speech at the convention electrified the party faithful, ultimately her seeming unpreparedness for office hurt McCain's candidacy.

make if elected. Although McCain's pick of Palin as his running mate was popular initially, with 20 percent more of the public having positive than negative feelings toward her, a cascade of bad news stories about her soon engulfed the McCain campaign. By the time of the election, Palin's negatives were 7 percent higher than her positives. This all rebounded on the campaign amid charges that McCain could hardly have been following his slogan of "putting country first" with such a selection.

Although their party business is limited, the conventions still provide the nominee with a "convention bump" in the polls. The harmonious coverage, the enthusiasm of party supporters, and even the staged theatrics seem to have a positive impact on viewers. The result is that candidates have usually, though not always, experienced a noticeable rise in

swing voters the approximately one-third of the electorate who are undecided at the start of a campaign

the polls immediately following the conventions. Both Obama and McCain received bounces from their conventions in 2008, though McCain's was slightly larger. McCain briefly achieved a lead in the polls after his convention, but the negative publicity surrounding Palin and then the economic crisis that began in mid-September put Obama back on top, where he stayed until the election.

The General Election Campaign

After the candidates are nominated in late summer, there is a short break, at least for the public, before the traditional fall campaign. When the campaign begins, the goal of each side is to convince supporters to turn out and to get undecided voters to choose its candidate. Most voters, the party identifiers, will usually support their party's candidate, although they need to be motivated by the campaign to turn out and cast their ballots. Most of the battle in a presidential campaign is for the ***swing voters***, the one-third or so of the electorate who have not made up their minds at the start of the campaign and who are open to persuasion by either side. As one would expect given the forces described in Chapter 12 (see Figure 12.3, page 453), this means that for both parties, the general election strategy differs considerably from the strategy used to win a primary election. To win the general election, the campaigns move away from the sharp ideological tone used to motivate the party faithful in the primaries and "run to the middle" by making less ideological appeals.

In the general campaign, each side seeks to get its message across, to define the choice in terms that give its candidate the advantage. This massive effort to influence the information to which citizens are exposed requires a clear strategy, which begins with a plan for winning the states where the candidate will be competitive.

The Electoral College

The presidential election is not a national race; it is a race between the candidates in each of the fifty states and the District of Columbia (see "*Who Are We?* Red versus blue states"). The reasons for the Electoral College's existence may seem outdated sometimes, but it nevertheless drives campaign strategy. Because our founders feared giving too much power to the volatile electorate, we do not actually vote for the president and vice president in presidential elections. Rather, we cast our votes in November for electors (members of the Electoral College), who in turn vote for the president in

December. The Constitution provides for each state to have as many electoral votes as it does senators and representatives in Congress. Thus Alaska has three electoral votes (one for each of the state's U.S. senators and one for its sole member of the House of Representatives). By contrast, California has fifty-five electoral votes (two senators and fifty-three representatives). In addition, the Twenty-third Amendment gave the District of Columbia three electoral votes. There are 538 electoral votes in all; 270 are needed to win the presidency. Figure 14.3 shows the distribution of electoral votes among the states today.

Electors are generally activist members of the party whose presidential candidate carried the state. In December, following the election, the electors meet and vote in their state capitals. In the vast majority of cases, they vote as expected, but there are occasional "faithless electors" who vote for their own preferences. The results of the electors' choices in the states are then sent to the Senate, where the ballots are counted when the new session opens. If no candidate achieves a majority in the Electoral College, the Constitution calls for the House of Representatives to choose from the top three electoral vote winners. In this process, each state has one vote. Whenever the vote goes to the House, the Senate decides on the vice president, with each senator having a vote. This has happened only twice (the last time was in 1824), although some observers of the 2000 election speculated that that election, too, could have been decided in the House of Representatives if Florida's election had not been decided in the courts.

The importance of the Electoral College is that all the states but Maine and Nebraska operate on a winner-take-all basis. Thus the winner in California, even if he or she has less than a majority of the popular vote, wins all of the state's fifty-five electoral votes. The loser in California may have won 49 percent of the popular vote but gets nothing in the Electoral College. It is possible, then, for the popular vote winner to lose in the Electoral College. This has happened only three times in our history, most recently in 2000, when Bush received an Electoral College majority even though Gore won the popular vote by more than half a million votes. Usually, however, the opposite happens: the Electoral College exaggerates the candidate's apparent majority. The 2008 election is typical of this exaggeration of the victory margin in the Electoral College. Obama got 52.9 percent of the popular vote, but his majority in the Electoral College was 67.8 percent. This exaggeration of the winning margin has the effect of legitimizing the winner's

Figure 14.3

Electoral College in 2012

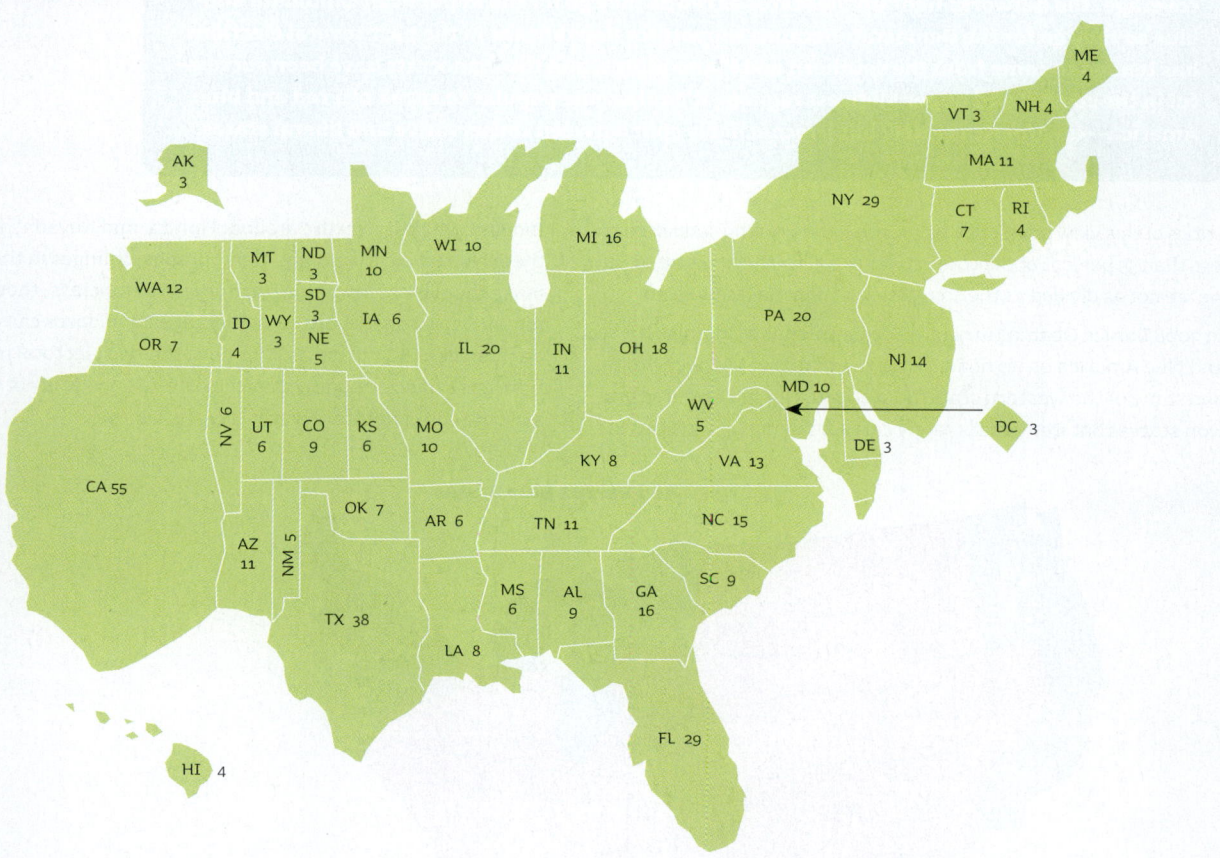

Note: This distorted map, in which the states are sized according to their number of electoral votes, demonstrates the electoral power of the more populous states. Total electoral votes = 538.

victory and allowing him or her to claim that he or she has a *mandate*—a broad popular endorsement—even if he or she won by a small margin of the popular vote.

The rules of the Electoral College give greater power to some states over others. The provision that all states get at least three electoral votes in the Electoral College means that citizens in the smaller states get proportionately greater representation in the Electoral College. Alaska, for example, sent one elector to the Electoral College for every 223,000 people, while California had one elector for every 645,000 residents.

However, this "advantage" is probably offset by the practice of winner-take-all, which focuses the candidates' attention on the largest states with the biggest payoffs in electoral votes, especially the competitive, or "battleground," states. Small states with few electoral votes or those that are safely in the corner of one party or the other are ignored

(although California, a reliably Democratic state, still received sixty visits from McCain, forty-one of them for fundraising purposes).[66] Perennial battlegrounds get the most candidate attention. Ohio, for instance, saw forty-two campaign visits by McCain and forty-five by Obama. Indiana, until 2008 a safely Republican state, had rarely seen a presidential candidate in person or even in a commercial. But following his strong primary campaign in Indiana, Obama showed some strength in the Hoosier State (which neighbors his home state of Illinois) and targeted it with visits and heavy media advertising. The McCain campaign assumed that Indiana was safe and largely ignored it until it was too late. Indiana saw little of McCain, but a lot of Barack Obama, and he won the state by less than 1 percent and received all eleven of its electoral votes, turning it blue for the first time since 1964.

Over the years, hundreds of bills have been introduced in Congress to reform or abolish the Electoral College, an

▶ Who Are We?

Red versus blue states

In our Electoral College system, presidential elections are won state by state. In election night coverage, the networks light up the states as red as they go for the Republican candidate and blue as they go for the Democrat. Because support for Republicans in the past several elections has tended to come from the southern and Plains states, and the Democrats have been successful in the coastal and upper Midwest regions, it has become popular to speak of a red and blue America—an America closely but irreconcilably split between conservative and liberal states.

Critics of this view point out that, in 2004, the winning candidate got less than 55 percent of the vote in twenty-four of the fifty states, so we are not as divided as the conventional map makes us seem.

In 2008 Barack Obama turned the conventional wisdom about red and blue America on its head. While the states of the deep South and some of the western states stayed red, Obama targeted and won states that Democrats rarely carry, chalking up victories in

Indiana, Virginia, North Carolina, Florida, and Nevada, and turning them blue on election night. Demographic changes in those states make them more favorable territory for Democrats, though it remains to be seen if future Democratic candidates can capitalize on them like Obama did. But for now, the two electoral maps here from 2004 and 2008 show that the blue-red divide is not as fixed as some commentators would have us believe.

Red Versus Blue States

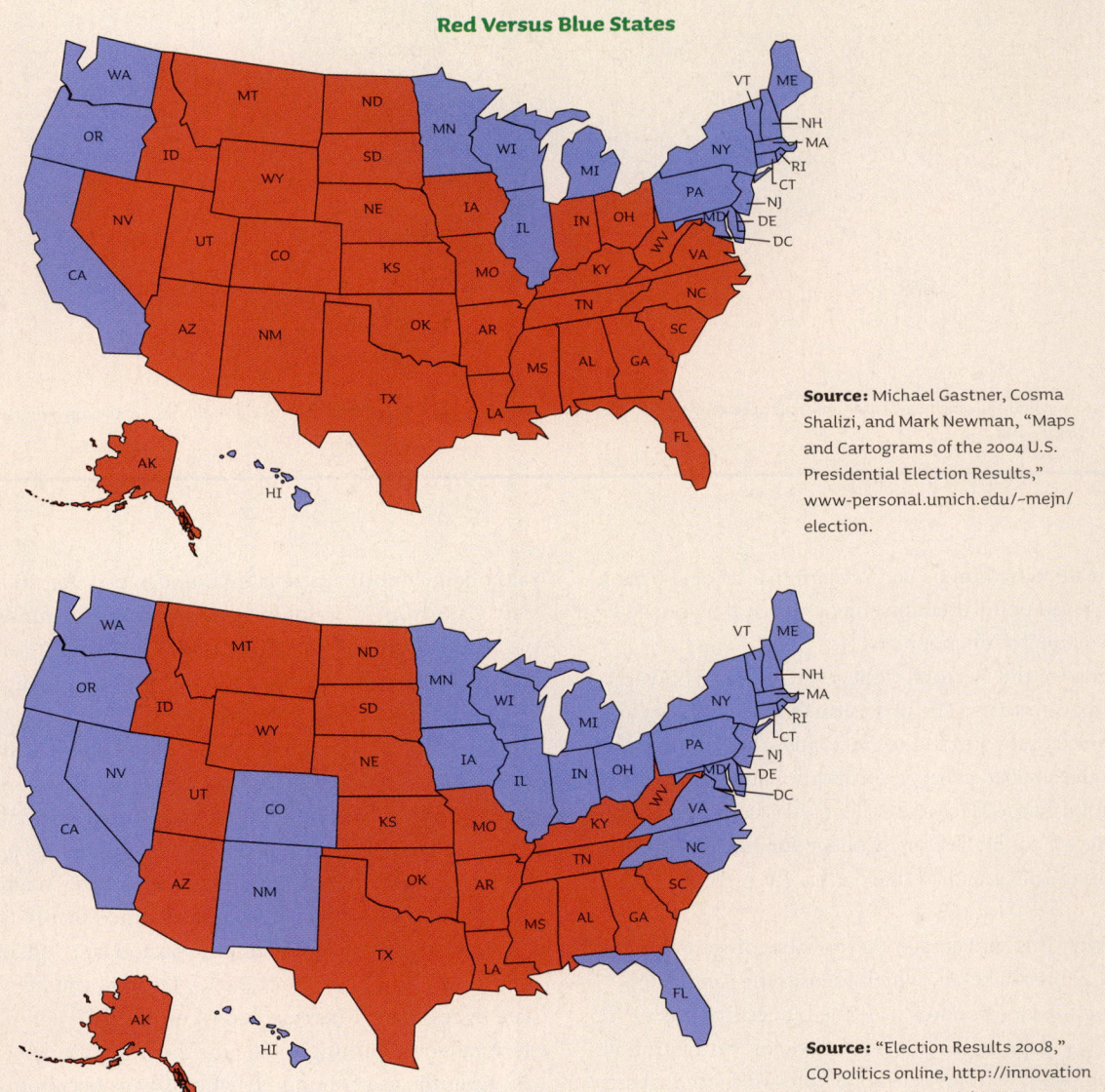

Source: Michael Gastner, Cosma Shalizi, and Mark Newman, "Maps and Cartograms of the 2004 U.S. Presidential Election Results," www-personal.umich.edu/~mejn/election.

Source: "Election Results 2008," CQ Politics online, http://innovation .cq.com/election_night08.

especially urgent project for many Democrats after the 2000 election.[67] Major criticisms of the current system include the following:

- The Electoral College is undemocratic because it is possible for the popular winner not to get a majority of the electoral votes.

- In a very close contest, the popular outcome could be dictated by a few "faithless electors" who vote their consciences rather than the will of the people of their states.

- The Electoral College distorts candidates' campaign strategies. The winner-take-all provision in all but two states puts a premium on a few large, competitive states, which get a disproportionate share of the candidates' attention.

Few people deny the truth of these charges, and hardly anyone believes that if we were to start all over, the current Electoral College would be chosen as the best way to elect a president. Nevertheless, all the proposed alternatives also have problems, or at least serious criticisms.

Who Runs the Campaign?

Running a modern presidential campaign has become a highly specialized profession. Most presidential campaigns are led by an "amateur," a nationally prestigious chairperson who may serve as an adviser and assist in fundraising. However, the real work of the campaign is done by the professional staff the candidate hires, and who themselves become important figures not only in the campaigns but often in the administrations as advisers and, later, as political commentators. For example, James Carville, Bill Clinton's campaign strategist (see the *Profiles in Citizenship* feature on pages 538–539), continues to appear frequently on television as a campaign commentator, as has Karl Rove, who ran both of George W. Bush's successful campaigns and worked as a policy adviser in the Bush White House. Obama's campaign trust included David Axelrod, who continued as a political adviser in the White House; Robert Gibbs, who took the job as Obama's press secretary; and David Plouffe, who continued to consult on the 2010 midterm elections and wrote a book about the presidential campaign. Campaign work at the beginning of the twenty-first century is big business.

Some of the jobs include not only the well-known ones of campaign manager and strategist but also more specialized components tailored to the modern campaign's emphasis on

information and money. For instance, candidates need to hire research teams to prepare position papers on issues so that the candidate can answer any question posed by potential supporters and the media. But researchers also engage in the controversial but necessary task of *oppo research*—delving into the background and vulnerabilities of the opposing candidate with an eye to exploiting his or her weaknesses. Central to the modern campaign's efforts to get and control the flow of information are pollsters and focus group administrators, who are critical for testing the public's reactions to issues and strategies. Media consultants try to get free coverage of the campaign whenever possible, and to make the best use of the campaign's advertising dollars by designing commercials and print advertisements.

Candidates also need advance teams to plan and prepare their travel agendas, to arrange for crowds (and the signs they wave) to greet the candidates at airports, and even to reserve accommodations for the press. Especially in the primaries, staff devoted to fundraising are essential to ensure the constant flow of money necessary to grease the wheels of any presidential campaign. They work with big donors and engage in direct-mail and Internet campaigns to solicit money from targeted groups. Much of the success of the Obama campaign rested on its effectiveness at communicating with and mobilizing its supporters electronically. Assisted by the inventor of Facebook, among others, the Obama campaign raised more money and had many more volunteers than its competitor campaigns, which did not benefit from such skilled use of the Internet.[68]

Finally, of course, candidates need to hire a legal team to keep their campaigns in compliance with the regulations of the FEC and to file the required reports. In general, campaign consultants are able to provide specialized technical services that the parties' political committees cannot.[69]

Presenting the Candidate

An effective campaign begins with a clear understanding of how the candidate's strengths fit with the context of the times and the mood of the voters. To sell a candidate effectively, the claims to special knowledge, competence, or commitment must be credible.[70] In 1992 the Clinton campaign contrasted its candidate's fresh, young, energetic image with the public's perceptions of the incumbent, President George H. W. Bush, as lacking a clear policy direction or vision. The Clinton campaign headquarters (which staffers called "The War Room") prominently displayed a sign—"It's the Economy, Stupid"—to

▶ Profiles in Citizenship: James Carville

". . . don't confuse the right to do something with the right thing to do."

James Carville found his calling and his salvation in his love affair with politics. "You know, I was never that great at anything," he says in that manic Louisiana drawl familiar to anyone who has watched the movie *The War Room* or seen him on CNN. "The only thing I was great at was being kind of, you know, a horrible student—a worse than bad lawyer. I sat in my office one day and said if I had to hire a lawyer I wouldn't hire me."

But the man loved politics—had done so since he was a kid, when larger-than-life figures walked the Louisiana landscape of his youth, people like Gov. Earl Long ("There's a great man! He's my guy!") and characters called "Pinhead Willie," "Coozan Dud," and "Wild Bill, Big Bad Bill Dodd." Ask him if politics was a big deal in his family when he was growing up in Carville, Louisiana (a town named for his postmaster grandfather), and he gives a single-word answer: "Huge."

So politics was the path he chose to get himself away from lawyering. He set up as a political consultant, finding the pace of electoral politics perfectly suited to his personal occupational challenges ("I have pretty serious attention problems and dyslexia and the whole dictionary of fashionable childhood diseases"). It was a life made to measure for him: "You're really determining something that profoundly matters to people all across the spectrum and it's something that, if you're like me and you've got a lot of energy left over—if you're a sprinter, not a distance runner—it's perfect. And you know at the end of the day if you've won or lost. How can you beat it? There's nothing that could be more fun."

With his brilliant mind and intuitive understanding of politics, Carville ran a couple of winning Pennsylvania campaigns and caught the attention of Bill Clinton in his 1992 run for the presidency. Carville headed up the Little Rock "War Room" and kept attention focused on the campaign's famous mantra—"It's the Economy, Stupid." Of course, Clinton won—and now Carville was at the top of his game. "And there was a time—it certainly passed—there was a time in my life where if I had to hire a political consultant I would have hired me. Now that's a great feeling. . . . And it was particularly great on the heels of knowing that I was a bad lawyer. It's not a very satisfying way to go through life, being bad and not liking what you do."

Carville's life must be superbly satisfying now. No longer running campaigns (he says he has become a victim of his own success, drawing more attention than the candidates he would work for), he is still active in the Democratic Party, appearing frequently as a commentator on television and with his wife, Republican Mary Matalin, on the lecture circuit.

Matalin was working for the first president Bush when she and Carville met (they ran

help keep the campaign on track. In 2000 and 2004, George W. Bush's campaign staff were able to portray him as an effective "decider" as opposed to the more ineffective and flip-flopping images they created of Al Gore and John Kerry.

The 2008 Obama presidential campaign is considered by many observers to be one of the best-run campaigns in modern American politics. It paired near complete message control with an unprecedented use of technology and a massive and very well-organized volunteer component. The campaign capitalized on a national weariness with the Bush years and crafted a campaign theme emphasizing change that was well suited to Obama's apparent competence, his skills as a speaker, and his relative outsider status (he had served only

two years in the U.S. Senate when he decided to run for president). He highlighted his change theme by continually linking McCain to the unpopular Bush administration and its policies, arguing that McCain was running for Bush's third term. The Obama campaign could have been distracted by the nomination of Sarah Palin for vice president, but it exercised the message discipline to ignore most of the Palin hoopla and keep with the main theme of the campaign.

As the campaigns struggle to control the flow of information about their candidates and influence how voters see their opponent, oppo research comes into play, sometimes complete with focus groups and poll testing. In fact, oppo research has become a central component in all elections, leading to the

opposing campaigns in 1992), and she has worked for Vice President Dick Cheney since that time. If you think "politics makes strange bedfellows," read their book, *All's Fair: Love, War, and Running for President*, to see just how strange. With the high-octane life their parents lead, it would seem that politics could hardly help being as "huge" for their two kids as it was for Carville (although he says since it's "the family business," they are not too impressed).

But it's hard to imagine that they will remain wholly unmoved by their father's powerful feelings about politics. Nobody could be. Leafing though a book of photographs of his beloved Louisiana, Carville talks about politics with the passion and reverence of a man recalling a first love. His voice gets hushed with the intensity of his memories, reading passages out loud and getting so eager to share the stories that he impulsively gives us the book to keep.

Impulsive and emotional Carville may be, but when it comes to assessing the day-to-day stake of politics, he is a sharp-eyed realist. He knows powerful people would prefer us to check out and let them have their way. "All these decisions are going to

get made—doesn't matter whether you're involved in them," he says. "The school's going to go on, somebody's going to have the hiring policy, somebody's going to decide the curriculum, the hospitals are going to get built, somebody's going to have to decide where they are, who gets served, etc., etc. . . . the taxes are going to get collected. Whatever. Okay. Now what a lot of powerful people would like to tell you is, you don't worry your pretty little head with that. We'll take care of all these things and you don't need to, you know, you just have a couple of beers and eat some Doritos and watch the game."

He is amazed that people fall for the idea that they can't figure out complex issues. "None of this stuff is impenetrable. The only way that the political golden rule operates—that those who have got the gold make the rules—is if it's by default," that is, if people fail to pay attention. More Carville wisdom:

On why politics matters:

There's a lot of things you can say about politics and politicians . . . some are corrupt and some are liars . . . but the one thing you can't say is that what they

do doesn't matter. Because it matters profoundly. From where you put the intersection, to the park, to the taxes, to the bonds, you name it. Abortion, euthanasia, it doesn't matter. On a sliding scale of does the bridge get built or not, all of this is decided by politicians. So every criticism that a young person has of politics is valid until they get to the point that it doesn't matter. Then that's where the whole argument completely falls apart. Right on its face.

On keeping the republic:

The first thing we need to do is remove this thing that participating in public affairs in whatever form you want to is some kind of chore. I don't think it really is. I think it's kind of a privilege and it's fun. . . . I tell young people you have the right not to participate, but don't confuse the right to do something with the right thing to do. They are two distinct things. I think the biggest thing that young people can do is, when it comes to this, be guided by your passion. . . . It's a hell of a lot of fun. And it's a really fascinating thing. And you learn a lot. But the biggest thing you do is you actually get to make a difference. ■

negative campaigning so prevalent in recent years.[71] Astute candidates also have oppo research done on themselves; knowing that their opponent will be studying them, they hope to forestall any unpleasant surprises. With his checkered youth in mind, Texas governor George W. Bush hired people to do oppo research on him twice during his runs for governor. The benign results then convinced him later that he had nothing to fear from the close scrutiny of a national campaign.

The Issues

Earlier we indicated that issues matter to voters as they decide how to vote. This means that issues must be central to the candidate's strategy for getting elected. From the candidate's

point of view, there are two kinds of issues to consider when planning a strategy: valence issues and position issues.

Valence issues are policy matters on which the voters and the candidates share the same preference. These are what we might call "motherhood and apple pie" issues, because no one opposes them. Everyone is for a strong, prosperous economy; for America having a respected leadership role in the world; for fighting terrorism; for thrift in government; and for a clean environment. Similarly, everyone opposes crime and drug abuse, government waste, political corruption, and immorality.

Position issues have two sides. On abortion, there are those who are anti-abortion and those who are pro-choice.

valence issues issues on which most voters and candidates share the same position

position issues issues on which the parties differ in their perspectives and proposed solutions

wedge issue a controversial issue that one party uses to split the voters in the other party

issue ownership the tendency of one party to be seen as more competent in a specific policy area

Politics Makes Strange Bedfellows

Each of the political parties hires professional campaign consultants whose fortunes rise and fall with the victories and losses of the candidates whose campaigns they run. Among the most famous of these in recent years is the defiantly liberal James Carville, who ran Bill Clinton's successful 1992 presidential campaign. Carville is married to Mary Matalin, who was deputy campaign manager in George H. W. Bush's failed 1992 reelection bid, a conservative commentator on CNN, and, from January 2001 through the end of 2002, Vice President Dick Cheney's top public relations strategist. Carville and Matalin are regular guests on NBC's *Meet the Press*.

On military engagements such as Vietnam, Iraq, or Afghanistan, there are those who favor pursuing a military victory and those who favor just getting out. Many of the hardest decisions for candidates are on position issues—although a clear stand means that they will gain some friends, it also guarantees that they will make some enemies. Realistic candidates who want to win as many votes as possible try to avoid being clearly identified with the losing side of important position issues. For instance, although activists in the Republican Party fought to keep their strong anti-abortion plank in the party platform in 2008, and while his nomination of Sarah Palin for his vice presidential running mate reignited the anti-abortion advocates in the Republican base, John McCain seldom mentioned the issue during the campaign because a majority of the national electorate is opposed to such a strong position.

When a candidate or party does take a stand on a difficult position issue, the other side often uses it against them as a

wedge issue. A **wedge issue** is a position issue on which the parties differ and that proves controversial within the ranks of a particular party. For a Republican, an anti–affirmative action position is not dangerous, since few Republicans actively support affirmative action. For a Democrat, though, it is a very dicey issue, because liberal party members endorse it but more moderate members do not. An astute strategy for a Republican candidate is to raise the issue in a campaign, hoping to drive a wedge between the Democrats and to recruit to his or her side the Democratic opponents of affirmative action.

The idea of **issue ownership** helps to clarify the role of policy issues in presidential campaigns. Because of their past stands and performance, each of the parties is widely perceived as better able to handle certain kinds of problems. For instance, the Democrats may be seen as better able to deal with education matters, and the Republicans as more effective at solving crime-related problems. The voter's job then is not so much to evaluate positions on education and crime, but rather to decide which problem is more important. If education is pressing, a voter might go with the Democratic candidate; if crime is more important, the voter might choose the Republican.[72] From the candidate's point of view, the trick is to convince voters that the election is about the issues that his or her party "owns."

An example of how issue ownership operated in the 2008 presidential election can be seen in exit poll data. Voters were asked which of five issues was the most important facing the country. Table 14.2 shows that three of those issues worked to the advantage of Barack Obama. Two of them—the economy and health care—are Democratic-owned issues, and Obama received clear majorities on both. John McCain owned just one issue, terrorism. Unfortunately for McCain, only 9 percent of the electorate felt that was the most important issue. We might have suspected that McCain would also command an advantage on the war in Iraq issue, but by 2008 the war was relatively unpopular and Obama had initially claimed attention in the Democratic field by being an early critic of the war, and thus got the support of most of these voters. What is clear is that Obama benefited electorally from the economic crisis that directed voters' attention to that issue.

Because valence issues are relatively safe, candidates stress them at every opportunity. They also focus on the position issues that their parties "own" or on which they have majority support. What this suggests is that the real campaign is not about debating positions on issues—how to reduce the deficit or whether to restrict abortion—but about which

Table 14.2

Issue Ownership in the 2008 Election

"Which Issue Mattered the Most in How You Voted for President?"

Naming issue	Most important	Voted for Obama	Voted for McCain
Obama's issues			
The economy	63%	53%	44%
Health care	9	73	25
McCain's issues			
Terrorism	9	13	86
Claimed by both candidates			
The war in Iraq	10	59	39
Energy policy	7	5	46

Source: ABC News exit polls, http://abcnews.go.com/pollingunit/exitpolls2008#pres_all.

issues should be considered. Issue campaigning is to a large extent about setting the agenda.

The Media

It is impossible to understand the modern political campaign without appreciating the pervasive role of the media. Even though many voters tend to ignore campaign ads—or at least they tell survey interviewers that they do—we know that campaign advertising matters. It has increased dramatically with the rise of television as people's information source of choice. Studies show that advertising provides usable information for voters. Political ads can heighten the loyalty of existing supporters, and they can educate the public about what candidates stand for and what issues candidates believe are most important. Ads also can be effective in establishing the criteria on which voters choose between candidates.

One of the best examples of this effective advertising came from the 1988 presidential campaign. Because George H. W. Bush was behind in the polls and perceived as not very sympathetic to average citizens, his campaign sought to change the way people were thinking about him and his opponent, Michael Dukakis. The campaign came up with an effective ad showing criminals walking in and out of a prison through a turnstile. A voice-over claimed that Dukakis's "revolving door prison policy" had permitted first-degree murderers to leave on weekend furloughs. At the same time, a pro-Bush group called the National Security PAC ran the more controversial Willie Horton ad, which focused on the mug shot of Horton, showing (without saying so) that he was African American. Implying that Dukakis bore some responsibility for the events described, the commercial coolly told

negative advertising campaign advertising that emphasizes the negative characteristics of opponents rather than one's own strengths

how Horton, who was serving a life sentence for murder, had stabbed a man and raped his girlfriend while on a weekend pass.[73] The Dukakis campaign failed to respond to this one-two punch, and subsequent surveys showed that those who saw the commercials came to think of crime as an important issue in the campaign. Bush's standings began to climb, and, of course, he went on to win the election.[74] (See *"Consider the Source:* Don't Be Fooled by Campaign Advertising" for some advice on how to critically evaluate the political ads that come your way.) Although **negative advertising** may turn off some voters and give the perception that politics is an unpleasant business, the public accepts accurate attacks on the issues. As long as it does not go too far, an attack ad that highlights negative aspects of an opponent's record actually registers more quickly and is remembered more frequently and longer by voters than are positive ads.[75] Experts have suggested that requiring candidates to appear in their own ads would discourage negativity. Negative ads, however, continue to be the rule, rather than the exception, though not all candidates resort to them equally. During the heat of the 2008 campaign, in one week, nearly 100 percent of the McCain campaign's ads were negative, compared to 34 percent of Obama's ads during the same time period.[76]

Because paid media coverage is so expensive, a campaign's goal is to maximize opportunities for free coverage while controlling, as much as possible, the kind of coverage it gets. The major parties' presidential candidates are accompanied by a substantial entourage of reporters who need to file stories on a regular basis, not only for the nation's major newspapers and television networks but also to keep reporters and commentators on the cable news stations like CNN, MSNBC, and Fox busy. These media have substantial influence in setting the agenda—determining what issues are important and, hence, which candidates' appeals will resonate with voters.[77] As a result, daily campaign events are planned more for the press and the demands of the evening news than for the actual in-person audiences, who often seem to function primarily as a backdrop for the candidates' efforts to get favorable airtime each day. The campaigns also field daily conference calls with reporters to attack their opponents and defend their candidates and to try to control, or "spin," the way they are covered. In 2008 a strategy for getting on the news without spending a lot of money was to produce negative "web ads" designed for Internet circulation, which, if catchy enough, could get endless coverage by the networks, the cable stations, and the blogs.

► Consider the Source: Don't Be Fooled by Campaign Advertising

"Sticks and stones may break my bones," goes the old childhood rhyme, "but words can never hurt me." Try telling that to the innumerable targets of negative advertising, sloganeering that emphasizes the negative characteristics of one's opponents rather than one's own strengths. Negative advertising has characterized American election campaigns since the days of George Washington. George Washington? His opponents called him a "dictator" who would "debauch the nation."[1] Thomas Jefferson was accused of having an affair with a slave, a controversy that has outlived any of the people involved; Abraham Lincoln was claimed to have had an illegitimate child; and Grover Cleveland, who admitted to fathering a child out of wedlock, was taunted with the words, "Ma, Ma, where's my Pa?"[2] (His supporters had the last laugh, however: "Gone to the White House, ha, ha, ha.")

Like it or not (and most Americans say they do not), the truth is that negative campaign advertising works, and in the television age it is far more prevalent than anything that plagued Washington, Jefferson, or Lincoln. People remember it better than they do positive advertising; tracking polls show that after a voter has seen a negative ad eight times, he or she begins to move away from the attacked candidate.[3] Some candidates claim that their advertising is not really negative but rather "comparative," and indeed a candidate often needs to compare his or her record with another's in order to make the case that he or she is the superior choice. Negative advertising is nonetheless unpopular with voters, who often see it as nasty, unfair, and false. In fact, advertising that is proved to be false can frequently backfire on the person doing the advertising. But how is a savvy media consumer to know what to believe? Be careful, be critical, and be fair in how you interpret campaign ads. Here are some tips. Ask yourself these questions:

1. **Who is running the ad?** What do they have to gain by it? Look to see who has paid for the ad. Is it the opponent's campaign? An interest group? A political action committee (PAC) or a 527 group? What do they have at stake, and how might that affect their charges? If the ad's sponsors do not identify themselves, what might that tell you about the source of the information? About the information itself?

2. **Are the accusations relevant to the campaign or the office in question?** If character is a legitimate issue, questions of adultery or drug use might have bearing on the election. If not, they might just be personal details used to smear this candidate's reputation. Ask yourself, What kind of person should hold the job? What kinds of qualities are important?

3. **Is the accusation or attack timely?** If a person is accused of youthful experimentation with drugs or indiscreet behavior

Celebrity
John McCain's campaign used Britney Spears (shown) and Paris Hilton in a campaign ad to compare Barack Obama's well-known status worldwide with that of celebrities.

in his or her twenties but has been an upstanding lawyer and public servant for twenty-five years, do the accusations have bearing on how the candidate will do the job?

4. **Does the ad convey a fair charge that can be answered, or does it evoke unarticulated fears and emotions?** A 1964 ad for Lyndon Johnson's presidential campaign showed a little girl counting as she plucked petals from a daisy. An adult male voice gradually replaced hers, counting down to an explosion of a mushroom cloud that obliterated the picture. The daisy commercial never even mentioned Johnson's opponent, Barry Goldwater, though the clear implication was that the conservative, promilitary Goldwater was likely to lead the nation to a nuclear war. Amid cries of "Foul!" from Goldwater's Republican supporters, the ad was aired only once, but it became a classic example of the sort of ad that seeks to play on the fears of its viewers.

5. **Is the ad true?** FactCheck.org, a project of the Annenberg Public Policy Center, is an excellent resource for monitoring factual accuracy in campaign ads. Other media outlets like the *New York Times* will often run "ad watches" to help viewers determine if the information in an advertisement is true. If it is not (and sometimes even if it is), you can usually count on hearing a response from the attacked candidate rebutting the charges. Occasionally candidates have chosen not to respond, claiming to take the high road, but as Michael Dukakis's dismal performance in the 1988 election showed, false attacks left unanswered can be devastating. Try to conduct your own "ad watch." Study the campaign ads and evaluate their truthfulness.

1. Alexandra Marks, "Backlash Grows Against Negative Political Ads," *Christian Science Monitor*, September 28, 1995, 1.
2. Roger Stone, "Positively Negative," *New York Times*, February 26, 1996, 13.
3. Ibid.

Although the candidates want the regular exposure, they do not like the norms of broadcast news, which they see as perpetuating horse-race journalism, focusing on who is ahead rather than on substantive issues.[78] In addition, the exhausting nature of campaigns, and the mistakes and gaffes that follow, are a source of constant concern because of the media's tendency to zero in on them and replay them endlessly. The relationship between the campaigns and the media is testy. Each side needs the other, but the candidates want to control the message, and the media want stories that are "news"— controversies, changes in the candidates' standings, or stories of goofs and scandals. We discuss the complex relationship between the media and the candidates at greater length in Chapter 15.

Candidates in recent elections have turned increasingly to "soft news" and entertainment programming to get their messages across. Candidates have been especially effective in appealing across party lines to reach the less engaged voters in the soft news formats. Many 2008 candidates, including John McCain, Barack Obama, Ron Paul, and Hillary Clinton appeared on NBC's *Saturday Night Live* and Comedy Central's *The Daily Show With Jon Stewart* and *The Colbert Report* (even Michelle Obama made a stop at the latter two). Such appearances give the candidates more unedited airtime and allow them to evade the hard news tendency to interpret all events in horse-race terms.

In 2008 the Internet came into its own as a source of news. Mainstream media outlets like the *New York Times*, the *Washington Post*, *Time* magazine, and the major networks maintained blogs that joined independent bloggers like Josh Marshall of Talkingpointsmemo.com and National Review Online in updating campaign news and poll results throughout the day. And with everyone having a cell phone camera or a video camera in his or her pocket, YouTube helped to transform the electoral landscape as well. A recorded gaffe or misstatement by a candidate or a campaign surrogate could go viral—reaching millions of viewers with the quick clicks of many mouses. Politicians accustomed to a more conventional way of campaigning were often caught in the YouTube trap. Bill Clinton, for instance, campaigning for his wife in the Democratic primary, was several times captured on tape saying something ill-advised that spread quickly before he could attempt damage control. Even the more media-savvy Obama found a tape of his words about frustrated voters becoming bitter, spoken at what he thought was a closed fundraiser, making the Internet and then the mainstream media rounds at lightning speed.

Presidential Politics Enters the Media Age

The first televised debates were held in 1960 between then–Vice President Richard Nixon and the younger and less experienced Senator John F. Kennedy. Many believe that television made the difference in Kennedy's razor-thin victory. Kennedy appeared relaxed and charismatic compared with the brooding Nixon— reinforced by the latter's unfortunate five o'clock shadow. Today, the presidential debates are an expected and anticipated feature of presidential campaigns.

Presidential Debates

Since 1976 the presidential debates have become one of the major focal points of the campaign. The first televised debate was held in 1960 between Senator John F. Kennedy and Vice President Richard Nixon. The younger and more photogenic Kennedy came out on top in those televised debates, but interestingly, those who heard the debates on the radio thought that Nixon did a better job.[79] In general, leading candidates find it less in their interest to participate in debates because they have more to lose and less to win, and so for years debates took place on a sporadic basis.

More recently, however, media and public pressure have all but guaranteed that at least the major-party candidates will participate in debates, although the number, timing, and format of the debates are renegotiated for each presidential election season. Recent elections have generated two or three debates, with a debate among the vice presidential contenders worked in as well. Third-party candidates, who have the most to gain from the free media exposure and the legitimacy that debate participation confers on a campaign, lobby to be included but rarely are. Ross Perot was invited in 1992 because both George H. W. Bush and Bill Clinton hoped to woo his supporters. Ralph Nader and Pat Buchanan were shut out of all three debates in 2000.

Do the debates matter? Detailed statistical studies show, not surprisingly, that many of the debates have been standoffs. However, some of the debates, especially those identified with

▶ Who, What, How, and WHEN: Money in Elections

Since the U.S. founding, people have complained that those with money have too much influence in politics. The federal government has passed laws to limit the influence of money, but each time new loopholes have opened to keep the money flowing into politicians' pockets. Below is a brief look at some efforts to limit the influence of money in politics:

1883   **Pendleton Civil Service Act**

The spoils system thrived in the nineteenth century, when campaigns were often financed through an "assessment" to the party in exchange for government jobs if the party won. The Pendleton Act made civil service jobs merit-based rather than patronage-based, depriving parties of a big funding source.

1925   **Federal Corrupt Practices Act**

When contributions from government employees were limited, businesses stepped in, leading to increasing concern about too much business influence on government. After the Teapot Dome Scandal, in which government officials were bribed in exchange for leasing rights on naval oil reserves, the Corrupt Practices Act created campaign spending limits and disclosure requirements. No one enforced them, however, and the rules were widely ignored.

1974   **Federal Election Campaign Act**

With existing financing rules neglected and campaign costs soaring, the Federal Election Campaign Act (FECA), begun in 1971, was strengthened in 1974, after the Watergate scandal. The act created donation limits, disclosure rules, an agency to monitor them (the Federal Election Commission), and public financing for presidential elections. In 1976 FECA was refined in the Supreme Court case *Buckley v. Valeo*. The Court ruled parties could raise and spend money on behalf of candidates, outside of the money candidates themselves raised and reported to the FEC. This case cleared the way for *soft money* spending in elections.

---

significant candidate errors or positive performances, have moved vote intentions 2 to 4 percent, which in a close race could be significant.[80] In addition, a good deal of evidence indicates that citizens learn about the candidates and their issue positions from the debates.[81] The presidential debates in 2008 were unusually important. Many Americans were relatively unfamiliar with the candidates, especially with Obama, who was new on the national scene and the target of rumors that made him seem unusual and foreign. But in the debates he displayed a calm demeanor and deliberative tone that reassured viewers and undercut John McCain's arguments that Obama was "too risky" or "too liberal." Indeed, during the debates there were negative trends in McCain's ratings as viewers concluded that he was mostly attacking his opponent rather than addressing the issues people were concerned about.

When voters are less familiar with the candidates, as in 2008, the debates can have a significant impact on how the candidates are seen.

Money

Winning—or even losing—a presidential campaign involves serious money. The presidential candidates in 2008 spent a total of $1.3 billion, more than double what was spent by the presidential candidates in 2004, which had doubled what was spent in 2000. The data in Figure 14.4 show this striking upward trend, which came about despite significant fundraising limits put into place by BCRA.

This torrent of cash is used to cover the costs of all the activities just discussed: campaign professionals, polling and travel for the candidates and often their spouses (along with

www.swiftvets.com

2002 **Bipartisan Campaign Reform Act (BCRA)**

Soft money became more and more influential in politics after the *Buckley* decision, particularly in 1996 as issue ads paid for by soft money became common. BCRA limited the raising and spending of soft money by political parties and put stricter rules on "electioneering communications," or advertisements during the campaign. This legislation is still controversial, particularly as groups like 527s have emerged to test their limits.

2003 **McConnell v. Federal Election Commission**

In the first big Supreme Court case to test BCRA, the Court upheld most of the provisions of the law. One it overturned, however, was the BCRA prohibition on campaign donations by people under the age of seventeen. The Court determined this was a violation of free speech. This decision allowed those under age seventeen to donate to campaigns but also inadvertently allowed parents to make additional donations in their children's names to bypass BCRA limits. Though the FEC discourages these types of donations, it is hard for the FEC to monitor how often they occur.

2010 **Citizens United v. Federal Election Commission**

This landmark case, decided on a 5–4 vote, struck down another provision of BCRA—one that limited corporate spending on elections. The Court held that the First Amendment protects the rights of corporations to run political advertisements. Amidst a flurry of political controversy, the decision immediately unleashed a wave of corporate spending in the 2010 midterm elections.

the accompanying staff and media), with the biggest share going to the production and purchase of media advertising. The campaign costs for all federal offices in 2008 came in at about $5.3 billion, or just over $18 for every man, woman, and child in the country.[82] Of course, the 2008 expenditures easily top all previous records.

Where does all this money come from? To make sense of the changing world of election campaign finance, we need to start by defining the different kinds of campaign contributions, each with different sources and regulations:

- *Government matching funds* are given, in the primary and general election campaigns, to qualified presidential candidates who choose to accept them and to spend only that money. The funds come from citizens who have

checked the box on their tax returns that sends $3 ($6 on joint returns) to fund presidential election campaigns. The idea behind the law is to more easily regulate big money influence on campaign finances, ensure a fair contest, and free up candidates to communicate with the public. For primary elections, if a candidate raises at least $5,000 in each of twenty states and agrees to abide by overall spending limits (about $50 million in 2008), as well as state-by-state limits, the federal government matches every contribution up to $250.

This same fund fully finances both major-party candidates' general election campaigns and subsidizes the two national party nominating conventions. John McCain opted to participate in the 2008 federal campaign financing and faced a spending limit of

Figure 14.4

Increase in Total Spending in Presidential Campaigns, 1976–2008

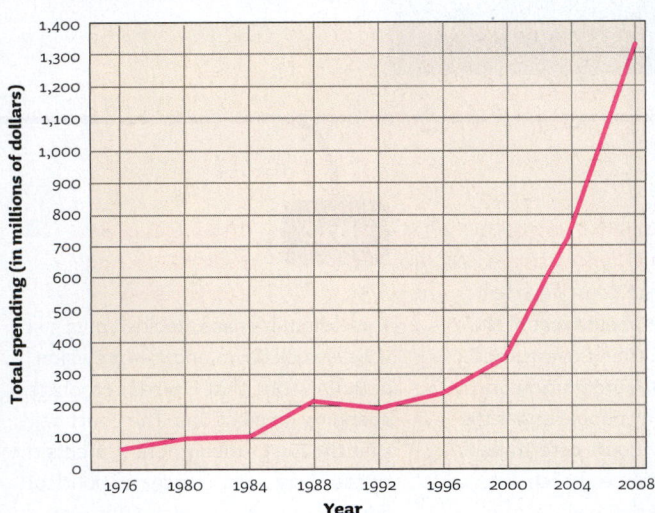

Sources: Center for Responsive Politics, "Presidential Fund-raising and Spending, 1976–2008, www.opensecrets.org/pres08/totals.php?cycle=2008, and "Banking on Becoming President," http://opensecrets.org/pres08/index.php.

$84.1 million. Barack Obama chose not to participate in the general election federal financing, arguing that by relying on small donors, his campaign was essentially publicly funded anyway. This meant that his campaign had to raise all the funds it would spend rather than receiving the federal subsidy, but it also meant that the Obama campaign was not limited in the amount it could spend. If presidential candidates accept this public funding, and Obama is the first major-party candidate not to have done so for the general election campaign, they may not raise any other funds or use any leftover funds raised during the primary campaign. Third parties that received at least 5 percent of the vote in the previous presidential campaign may also collect public financing. Unlike the two major parties, however, the money a third party receives depends on the number of votes the party received in the previous election. Ross Perot was eligible to receive $29 million for his 1996 presidential campaign after his party won 19 percent of the vote in 1992, while the two major parties received $61.8 million each.[83]

- **Hard money** refers to the funds given directly to candidates by individuals, political action committees (PACs), the political parties, and the government. The spending of hard money is under the control of the candidates, but its collection is governed by the rules of the Federal Election Campaign Act (FECA) of 1971, 1974, and its various amendments. This act established the FEC and was intended to stop the flow of money from large contributors (and thus limit their influence) by outlawing contributions by corporations and unions, and by restricting contributions from individuals. The campaign finance reform bill passed in 2002 actually raised the hard money limits. Under that law, individuals can give a federal candidate up to $2,300 per election and can give a total of $108,200 to all federal candidates and parties in a two-year election cycle.[84] The limit on the parties' hard money contributions to candidates was held to be unconstitutional in a 1999 Colorado district federal court decision but was later upheld in a five-to-four Supreme Court decision.[85]

  However, in the 2010 decision in *Citizens United v. Federal Election Commission*,[86] which we discussed in the *What's at Stake?* feature that opened this chapter, the Supreme Court struck down a provision of the McCain-Feingold Act that prohibited corporations (and by implication unions and interest groups) from sponsoring broadcast ads for or against specific candidates. Corporations and unions are thus free to engage in broadcast campaigns, although provisions requiring disclosure and limitations on direct contributions to candidates were retained. Experts disagreed about the likely consequences of the far-reaching decision, but mirroring the Court's five-to-four breakdown on the ruling, it was generally decried by liberals and supported by conservatives.[87]

- **Soft money** is unregulated money collected by parties and interest groups in unlimited amounts to spend on party-building activities, get-out-the-vote drives, voter education, or issue position advocacy. Prior to the passage of campaign finance reform in 2002, as long as the money was not spent to tell people how to vote or coordinated with a specific candidate's campaign, the FEC could not regulate soft money. This allowed corporate groups, unions, and political parties to raise unlimited funds often used for television and radio advertising, especially in the form of issue advocacy

issue advocacy ads advertisements paid for by soft money, and thus not regulated, that promote certain issue positions but do not endorse specific candidates

get-out-the-vote (GOTV) drives efforts by political parties, interest groups, and the candidate's staff to maximize voter turnout among supporters

ads. As we discussed in Chapter 13, *issue advocacy ads* are television or radio commercials run during an election campaign that promote a particular issue, usually by attacking the character, views, or position of the candidate the group running the ad wishes to defeat. The courts have considered these ads protected free speech and have held that individuals and organizations could not be stopped from spending money to express their opinions about issues, or even candidates, so long as they did not explicitly tell viewers how to vote.

Most observers thought that BCRA would remove unregulated money from campaigns and curb negative advertising. While it limited the spending of PACs and parties, new groups, called 527 groups after the loophole (section 527) in the Internal Revenue Code that allows them to avoid the regulations imposed by BCRA, sprang up in their stead (see Chapter 13). Like groups that raised and spent soft money prior to BCRA, 527s can raise unlimited funds for issue advocacy or voter mobilization so long as they do not openly promote any candidate or openly try to defeat any particular candidate. BCRA does forbid all groups, even 527s, from running such ads funded by soft money within sixty days of a general election, or within thirty days of a primary election. The 2010 *Citizens United* case loosened the regulations further, lifting the sixty-day limit. For upcoming elections it appears that interest groups, corporations, and unions will have greater leeway in how and when they campaign for candidates. Even so, they are still limited in making direct (hard money) contributions; most of their efforts will be as independent expenditures (efforts that cannot be coordinated with the candidates' campaigns). Moreover, it can be argued that the new decision will not affect our elections in a major way as these entities found plenty of ways to attempt to influence campaigns under the old laws. In any case, given that such contributors do not share a single common ideology or set of issue preferences, some observers argue that any effects will largely cancel each other out. Only with the unfolding of future elections will we know for sure.[88]

Getting Out the Vote

Get-out-the-vote (GOTV) drives refer to the voter mobilization efforts we discussed earlier in this chapter, an increasingly important part of any presidential campaign. As we noted, in the 1980s and 1990s, such efforts concentrated mostly on television advertising. The expense of these "air wars" meant that parties and campaigns worried less about knocking on

doors and the shoe-leather efforts associated with a campaign's "ground war." Parties mistakenly associated GOTV with "get on television" rather than its traditional meaning of "get out the vote."[89] Beginning in 1998 the campaigns renewed efforts to contact potential voters face-to-face. This is consistent with research that shows that decreased party mobilization efforts were a substantial part of the reason that voter turnout had been decreasing.[90]

In 2008, however, the Obama campaign rewrote the strategy book for modern campaigns. Not only did it reawaken efforts at direct contacting, but it tied such contact to advances in Internet technology, from regular ads on YouTube, to recurring emails and text messages to contributors, to highly sophisticated and coordinated volunteer efforts at voter mobilization.[91] Rather than sending in staff and volunteers in the last couple of weeks of the campaign, the Obama campaign had paid staff and dozens, even hundreds, of offices and thousands of volunteers across all the battleground states. One high-level Republican campaign official said of it: "This is the greatest ground game they've ever put together. It's scary."[92] It created a new model for effective campaigns: engaging everyday citizens as integral parts of the campaigns rather than just as spectators and voters. The Obama campaign's successful mobilization efforts were even able to turn typically Republican states like Indiana to the Democratic column, at least for 2008.[93]

What is particularly interesting about these grassroots efforts is that they are not just a return to a bygone era. Rather, mobilization efforts combine old-school door-to-door campaigning with modern technology.[94] Vast computer databases tell volunteers whose doors to knock on, and these volunteers often have hand-held personal electronic devices that have detailed information on each voter.[95] This allows parties and groups to target swing voters and their base voters. Campaigns and interest groups also flood supporters' email in-boxes and tie up the phone lines. Seventy-six percent of voters in battleground states reported that they had been contacted and urged to vote a particular way.[96] In their zeal to seek out all possible voters, campaigns have reached out to poorer voters in both urban and rural areas who have not received either party's attention in recent decades.[97]

Interpreting Elections

After the election is over, when the votes are counted, and we know who won, it would seem that the whole election season is finally finished. In reality, the outcomes of our

> *electoral mandate* the perception that an election victory signals broad support for the winner's proposed policies

collective decisions cry for interpretation. Probably the most important interpretation is the one articulated by the victor. The winning candidate in presidential elections inevitably claims an *electoral mandate*, maintaining that the people want the president to do the things he campaigned on and that the election is all about the voters' preference for his leadership and policy programs. Presidents who can sell the interpretation that their election to office is a ringing endorsement of their policies can work with Congress from a favored position. To the extent that the president is able to sell his interpretation, he will be more successful in governing. In contrast, the losing party will try to argue that its loss was due to the characteristics of its candidate or specific campaign mistakes. Party members will, predictably, resist the interpretation that the voters rejected their message and their vision for the nation. In general, Congress responds less to presidential declarations of a mandate and more to indications of changes in public preferences signaled by a change in which party wins the presidency or a large legislative seat turnover, especially one that produces a change in party control of Congress.[98]

The media also offer their interpretations of elections. In fact, research shows that of the many possible explanations that are available, the mainstream media quickly—in just a matter of weeks—hone in on an agreed-upon standard explanation of the election.[99] In 2000 the media, in explaining the closeness of the race, focused on how much more likable voters found George W. Bush, despite the majority's agreement with Al Gore on the issues, and on what they claimed to be Gore's badly run campaign. In 2004 the media decided quickly that, although the nation was closely divided, moral-values voters in red states put Bush over the top. In 2008 the media story was that President Bush's rock-bottom approval ratings were dragging down McCain and that, with the economy in collapse, the Republican was facing insurmountable odds while the voters were hungry for change. The media, assisted by the left-leaning blogosphere, also maintained that Obama had run a reasonably positive campaign, but that Republicans were stirring up anger and mob-like sentiments with their insinuations that Obama was "un-American" and "risky." These explanations offer parts of the truth, but they oversimplify reality and do not give us a complete understanding of the complex decisions made by the American electorate.

In the matter of presidential elections, the parties, their elites, party activists, and the candidates all have something vital at

stake. The traditional party leaders fared best under the old rules and closed-door decision making that yielded seasoned and electable politicians as the parties' nominees. Activists, with a broader agenda than simply winning power, seek control of the platform and the nomination, and may well have goals other than electability in mind. The primary system allows them to reap the fruits of the considerable time and resources they are willing to invest in politics.

Candidates seeking the nomination must answer to both the traditional party leaders and the activist members. This often puts them in a difficult position. Once nominated and pursuing a national bipartisan victory, the candidate needs to hold on to party supporters while drawing in those not already committed to the other side. Here the candidate makes use of the rules of the Electoral College, professional staff, strategic issue positions, the media, fundraising, and voter mobilization.

Who What How

The Citizens and Elections

Do too many informed voters lead to too much conflict?

At the beginning of this chapter we acknowledged that the American citizen does not look like the ideal citizen of classical democratic theory. Nothing we have learned in this chapter has convinced us otherwise, but that does not mean that Americans are doomed to an undemocratic future. In the first chapter of this book we considered three models of citizen activity in democracies, which we revisit here.

The first model we discussed is the elite model, which argues that as citizens we can do no more (or are fitted to do no more) than choose the elites who govern us, making a rather passive choice from among remote leaders. The second model of democratic politics, the pluralist model, sees us as participating in political life primarily through our affiliation with different types of groups. Finally, the participatory model of democracy is perhaps more prescriptive than the other two models, which it rejects because it believes that it is unsatisfactory for the majority of the citizenry to play a largely passive role in the political system. This model holds that we grow and develop as citizens through being politically active. In fact, rather than fitting any of these models exclusively, the American citizen's role in elections seems to borrow elements from all three models in a way that might be called a fourth model. As we shall see, American citizens, though they do not meet the ideals of democratic theory, do make a difference in American politics through the mechanism of elections.

A Fourth Model?

The early studies of voting that used survey research found that most citizens had surprisingly low levels of interest in presidential election campaigns. These studies of the 1944 and 1948 presidential elections found that most citizens had their minds made up before the campaigns began and that opinions changed only slightly in response to the efforts of the parties and candidates. Instead of people relying on new information coming from the campaigns, people voted according to the groups to which they belonged. That is, income, occupation, religion, and similar factors structured who people talked to, what they learned, and how they voted.

The authors of these studies concluded that democracy is probably safer without a single type of citizen who matches the civics ideal of high levels of participation, knowledge, and commitment.[100] In this view, such high levels of involvement would indicate a citizenry fraught with conflict. Intense participation comes with intense commitment and strongly held positions, which make for an unwillingness to compromise. This revision of the call for classic "good citizens" holds that our democratic polity is actually better off when it has lots of different types of citizens: some who care deeply, are highly informed, and participate intensely; many more who care moderately, are a bit informed, and participate as much out of duty to the process as commitment to one party or candidate; and some who are less aware of politics until some great issue or controversy awakens their political slumber.

The virtue of modern democracy in this *political specialization view* is that citizens play different roles and that together these roles combine to form an electoral system that has the attributes we prefer: it is reasonably stable; it responds to changes of issues and candidates, but not too much; and the electorate as a whole cares, but not so intensely that any significant portion of the citizenry will challenge the results of an election. Its most obvious flaw is that it is biased against the interests of those who are least likely to be the activist or pluralist citizens—the young, the poor, the uneducated, and minorities.[101]

Do Elections Make a Difference?

If we can argue that most Americans do take more than a passive role in elections and that, despite being less-than-ideal democratic citizens, most Americans are involved "enough,"

then we need to ask whether the elections they participate in make any difference. We would like to think that elections represent the voice of the people in charting the directions for government policy. Let us briefly discuss how well this goal is attained. At a minimal but nevertheless important level, elections in the United States do achieve electoral accountability. By this we mean only that by having to stand for reelection, our leaders are more or less constantly concerned with the consequences of what they do for their next election. The fact that citizens tend to vote retrospectively provides incumbent administrations with a lot of incentive to keep things running properly, and certainly to avoid policies that citizens may hold against them. Thus we begin by noting that elections keep officeholders attentive to what they are doing.

We can also ask if elections make a difference in the sense that it matters who wins. The answer is yes. Today the parties stand on opposite sides of many issues, and given the chance, they will move national policy in the direction they believe in. Thus in 1980 the election of Ronald Reagan ushered in conservative policies—especially his tax cuts and domestic spending reductions—that Jimmy Carter, whom Reagan defeated, would never have even put on the agenda. Looking at elections over time, scholars Robert S. Erikson, Michael MacKuen, and James A. Stimson observe a direct relationship between national elections and the policies that government subsequently enacts. Electing Democrats results in more liberal policies; electing Republicans results in more conservative policies.[102] This same generalization can be seen in the politics of the American states, where we find that more liberal states enact more liberal policies and more conservative states enact more conservative policies. Policy liberalism, which is a composite measure of things like the tax structure, welfare benefits, educational spending, voting for the Equal Rights Amendment, and so forth, is higher as the states become more liberal.[103] There is much solid evidence that elections are indeed crucial in bringing about a degree of policy congruence between the electorate and what policymakers do.

Just because elections seem to work to bring policy into rough agreement with citizen preferences does not mean that all citizens know what they want and that candidates know this and respond. Some citizens do know what they want; others do not. Some candidates heed the wishes of constituents; others pay more attention to their own consciences or to the demands of ideological party activists and contributors. Averaged over all these variables, however, we do find that policy follows elections. Citizens, even with the blunt instrument of the ballot, can and do change what government does.[104]

▶ **What's at Stake Revisited**

When, during his 2010 State of the Union address, President Obama criticized the Supreme Court's *Citizens United* ruling, he was expressing a sentiment held widely by Democrats. By contrast, Republicans generally hailed the Court's decision that corporations' campaign spending was protected speech as a good thing. Congressional Democrats later attempted to make the spending of corporate money on elections more transparent through legislation they called the Disclose Act. The act would have required corporations to make public who they are and how they spend their money, but it was defeated by a Republican filibuster in the Senate.

We have seen that reforming campaign finance law has been a tough job for Congress, one that it has tried to accomplish more than once without great success. The McCain-Feingold Act was a bipartisan effort to rein in campaign spending, but the issue continues to divide Americans along partisan lines. Why is the spending of corporate money on campaigns such a hot-button issue in American politics? Who stands to win and who to lose?

Democrats say that everyday Americans have a stake in the matter, that corporations have too much influence in American electoral politics, and that corporate dollars swamp the preferences of ordinary citizens. In their view, regular Americans lose when they cannot summon equal resources to fight political battles.[105] Of course, Democratic politicians themselves have a stake as well. Since they tend not to be the party that supports big business, those unlimited corporate dollars are more likely to go toward promoting their Republican opponents. Naturally they'd like the playing field evened out.

By the same token, Republicans will be winners here because that corporate money most often serves their electoral interests. They claim broader stakes, however, arguing that something fundamental is at risk here. In their view, the *Citizens United* decision is a victory for free speech and corporate freedom from government regulation. As Senate minority leader Mitch McConnell, R-Ky., put it, "For too long, some in this country have been deprived of full participation in the political process. With this monumental decision, the Supreme Court took an important step in the direction of restoring the First Amendment rights of these groups by ruling that the Constitution protects their right to express themselves about political candidates and issues up until Election Day."[106]

In truth, this is not just a partisan issue, because Republicans and Democrats are both right—the issue is about unequal power and it is about fundamental freedoms. As long as the Supreme Court equates the right to spend money to promote a political cause to be equivalent to the right to free speech, Americans will have to grapple with the real consequence that some people will be able to speak very much more loudly than others. Whether this violates the rights of ordinary Americans or whether limiting such spending violates the rights of corporations (and whether corporations are indeed entitled to the same rights as individuals) are issues that are not cut and dried even for the Court, as the five-to-four vote in *Citizens United* makes clear.

To Sum Up

Key terms, chapter summaries, practice quizzes, Internet links, and other study aids are available on the companion web site at http://republic.cqpress.com.

Define | Understand | Practice | Read | Click | Watch

closed primary (p. 530)
electoral mandate (p. 548)
front-loading (p. 531)
front-runner (p. 532)
get-out-the-vote (GOTV) drives (p. 547)
government matching funds (p. 545)
hard money (p. 546)
invisible primary (p. 529)
issue advocacy ads (p. 547)
issue ownership (p. 540)
momentum (p. 532)
Motor Voter Bill (p. 523)
negative advertising (p. 541)
open primary (p. 530)

oppo research (p. 537)
party caucus (p. 530)
political efficacy (p. 519)
position issues (p. 539)
presidential primary (p. 530)
prospective voting (p. 527)
retrospective voting (p. 527)
social connectedness (p. 524)
soft money (p. 546)
swing voters (p. 534)
valence issues (p. 539)
voter mobilization (p. 523)
wedge issue (p. 540)

Define | **Understand** | Practice | Read | Click | Watch

- Elections represent the core of American democracy, serving several functions: selecting leaders, giving direction to policy, developing citizenship, informing the public, containing conflict, and stabilizing the political system.
- Voting enhances the quality of democratic life by legitimizing the outcomes of elections. However, American voter turnout levels are typically among the lowest in the world and may endanger American democracy. Factors such as age, income, education, and race affect whether a person is likely to vote.
- Candidates and the media often blur issue positions, and voters realistically cannot investigate policy proposals on their own. Therefore, voters make a decision by considering party identification and peer viewpoints, prominent issues, and campaign images.
- The "road to the White House" is long, expensive, and grueling. It begins with planning and early fundraising in the pre-primary phase and develops into more active campaigning

during the primary phase, which ends with each party's choice of a candidate, announced at the party conventions. During the general election the major-party candidates are pitted against each other in a process that relies increasingly on the media and getting out the vote. Much of the battle at this stage is focused on attracting voters who have not yet made up their minds.
- The Electoral College demonstrates well the founders' desire to insulate government from public whims. Citizens do not vote directly for the president or vice president but rather for an elector who has already pledged to vote for that candidate. Except in Maine and Nebraska, the candidate with the majority of votes in a state wins all the electoral votes in that state.
- Although American citizens do not fit the mythical ideal of the democratic citizen, elections still seem to work in representing the voice of the people in terms of citizen policy preferences.

Define   **Understand**   **Practice**   **Read**   **Click**   **Watch**

1. **Which of the following groups of people are generally LEAST likely to vote?**
   a. eighteen to twenty-four year olds
   b. Women
   c. The wealthy
   d. Those with advanced degrees
   e. Whites

2. **Which of the following is the single biggest factor accounting for how people decide to vote?**
   a. The issue positions of the candidates
   b. A candidate's personal characteristics
   c. Whether the candidate is an incumbent
   d. The candidate's party affiliation
   e. The candidate's experience

3. **Scholars usually refer to a candidate gaining "momentum" during the**
   a. pre-primary season.
   b. primary season.
   c. national convention.
   d. presidential debates.
   e. general election.

4. **A position issue is**
   a. an issue on which most voters and candidates share the same position.
   b. a controversial issue that one party uses to split the voters in the other party.
   c. the tendency of one party to be seen as more competent in a specific policy area.
   d. an issue that is perceived to be unimportant by the electorate.
   e. an issue on which the parties differ in their perspectives and proposed solutions.

5. **Which of the following is NOT a key function of elections?**
   a. They provide legitimacy to the government.
   b. They allow government to change policy direction or to keep with the current policy direction.
   c. They allow disaffected citizens to remove all their representatives at one time.
   d. They educate the public.
   e. They increase political efficacy.

Define   **Understand**   **Practice**   **Read**   **Click**   **Watch**

Adkins, Randall E. 2008. *The Evolution of Parties, Campaigns, and Elections: Landmark Documents from 1787–2007.* Washington, D.C.: CQ Press. *Examines parties and elections over history through primary documents such as speeches, letters, court cases, legislation, and documentary photographs.*

Anonymous (Joe Klein). 1996. *Primary Colors: A Novel of Politics.* New York: Random House. *A "fictional" account of a southern governor running for president whose campaign is constantly plagued by scandal. Fun to read!*

Campbell, Angus, Philip E. Converse, Warren E. Miller, and Donald E. Stokes. 1960. *The American Voter.* New York: Wiley. *This classic in voting studies shows the importance of party identification in electoral behavior. These surveys developed into the National Election Studies, which continue to serve as the chief source of data for academic electoral research in the United States.*

Conway, M. Margaret, Gertrude A. Steuernagel, and David W. Ahern. 2005. *Women and Political Participation: Cultural Change in the Political Arena,* 2nd ed. Washington, D.C.: CQ Press. *A succinct overview of the various ways in which women participate in politics.*

Fiorina, Morris P. 1981. *Retrospective Voting in American National Elections.* New Haven: Yale University Press. *In an intriguing analysis of voting behavior, Fiorina argues that citizens vote based on retrospective evaluations of the incumbent and, if the issues are clear, prospective evaluations of the candidates' positions.*

Herrnson, Paul S. 2008. *Congressional Elections: Campaigning at Home and in Washington,* 5th ed. Washington, D.C.: CQ Press. *A systematic analysis of congressional campaign dynamics and the fight for votes and financial resources among electoral candidates.*

Polsby, Nelson W., and Aaron Wildavsky. 2004. *Presidential Elections: Strategies and Structures of American Politics,* 11th ed. Lanham, Md.: Rowman & Littlefield. *A great text on presidential elections.*

Raymond, Allen (author), and Ian Spiegelman (contributor). 2008. *How to Rig an Election: Confessions of a Republican Operative.* New York: Simon & Schuster. *Written by Republican campaign adviser Allen Raymond, this highly acclaimed book offers an insider's perspective on the "dark" side of electoral campaigns.*

Semiatin, Richard J., ed. 2008. *Campaigns on the Cutting Edge.* Washington, D.C.: CQ Press. *A detailed look at the changing face of modern political campaigns, with an emphasis on the increasingly prominent role played by digital media.*

Suarez, Ray. 2007. *The Holy Vote: The Politics of Faith in America.* **New York: Harper.** *A National Public Radio commentator's analysis of separation of church and state in America and its implications for voting behavior in American elections.*

Toobin, Jeffrey. 2001. *Too Close to Call: The Thirty-Six-Day Battle to Decide the 2000 Election.* **New York: Random House.** *This in-depth, dramatic account of the 2000 election mess follows the activities of the Bush and Gore camps from election night through the U.S. Supreme Court's decision to stop the recount in Florida thirty-six days later.*

Wattenberg, Martin P. 1991. *The Rise of Candidate-Centered Politics: Presidential Elections of the 1980s.* **Cambridge: Harvard University Press.** *Wattenberg examines the weakened role of parties in presidential elections and argues that candidates now play a more central role in the campaigns.*

Define **Understand** **Practice** **Read** **Click** **Watch**

AllPolitics *www.cnn.com/politics. A great source for up-to-the-minute analysis of current elections.*

Center for Responsive Politics *www.opensecrets.org. This web site keeps tabs on campaign finance, offering multiple ways to research contributions to candidates and the spending patterns in presidential elections.*

Declare Yourself *www.declareyourself.com. This interactive, media-filled web site includes a comprehensive FAQ on various aspects of U.S. elections and the voting process, a press room, and a blog with frequent (and often entertaining) updates.*

Electoral College Home Page *www.archives.gov/federal-register/electoral-college/. A fascinating compendium of information on the Electoral College, including history, procedures, and presidential and vice presidential "box scores" for 1789 through 2004.*

FactCheck.org: A Project of the Annenberg Public Policy Center *www.factcheck.org. This web site separates fact from fiction in campaigns and everyday politics. Both articles and podcasts are available.*

The Living Room Candidate: Presidential Campaign Commercials *www.livingroomcandidate.org. This is an excellent site from which to view old and new presidential campaign commercials. The historical value of comparing past commercials to current commercials is especially useful.*

Project Vote Smart *www.vote-smart.org. This useful site will answer just about any question you might have about current elections and candidates.*

U.S. Government Voting and Elections *www.usa.gov/Citizen/Topics/Voting.shtml. This web site contains a variety of information to help you get involved in the voting process. Get started by learning about elections and voting, registering to vote, and contacting elected officials.*

Vote411.org: Election Information You Need *www.vote411.org. Find out the basic information you need as a voter, including how to register, whom to contact in your state with questions, when and where debates will be held, and exactly what will be appearing on your ballot in upcoming elections.*

Define **Understand** **Practice** **Read** **Click** **Watch**

American Blackout *2005. Winner of the Special Jury Prize at the 2006 Sundance Film Festival, this controversial documentary situates itself at the intersection of race and voting, exploring African Americans' systematic exclusion from the voting process.*

The Candidate *1972. The son of a former California politician is persuaded by his party to challenge a popular incumbent senator. The candidate speaks his mind and surprises everyone in the polls.*

Hacking Democracy *2006. This well-received HBO documentary explores the dangers inherent in America's increasing reliance on computerized voting machines, with a specific focus on those created by the Diebold Corporation.*

Journeys With George *2003. Comical Emmy-winning documentary of a reporter (and filmmaker) and the presidential candidate—George W. Bush—with whom she travels during the 2000 campaign.*

The Perfect Candidate *1996. A superb documentary on the 1994 Virginia Senate race between Oliver North and Charles Robb. The cameras take you on the campaign trail for a behind-the-scenes look at how campaigns are run.*

Uncounted: The New Math of American Elections *2007. An eye-opening documentary that exposes the extent of fraud during the 2004 U.S. presidential election.*

The War Room *1992. This excellent documentary puts you at the heart of Clinton's 1992 presidential campaign.*

Chapter 15

The Media

▶ What's at Stake?

Portions of this *What's at Stake?* were written on the author's iPhone, when inspiration struck at a moment when she was away from her computer. She emailed them to herself, and later pasted them into the document she was writing. When, still away from her desk, she needed to check a source, she looked up the book on Amazon.com, downloaded it to the Kindle on her phone, and did a little research, highlighting the material she needed to come back to. All news sources and most of the research for this chapter were accessed over the Internet. The one thing you can guarantee about this technology, some of which would have seemed downright astounding a year or two before, is that by the time this book comes out it will seem like no big deal at all. We are in the midst of a media revolution, and the only thing we know for sure is that things will change, quickly and inevitably. Hang on for the ride.

For anyone born after the 1960s, it might sound laughable, but news used to enter the average American's life at only a couple of neatly defined and very predictable points during the day. The local morning paper arrived before dawn, there to be read over coffee and breakfast. The afternoon paper (yes, most cities had two papers back then) was waiting for you when you came home from work. Big city papers like the *New York Times* and the *Washington Post* were available only to those who lived in New York or Washington, D.C., unless you ordered a copy of the paper to be mailed to you at great expense, arriving several days late (no FedEx, no overnight delivery). In 1960 the evening news came on all three TV stations at 7:30 P.M., and TV-owning America (87 percent of households in 1960) got their last news of the day from Chet Huntley and David Brinkley on NBC, John Daly on ABC, or Douglas Edwards on CBS (Edwards was to be followed two years later by Walter Cronkite, also known as "Uncle Walter," the most trusted face in news). That was pretty much it for news in 1960s America, unless a special event (a space shot, for instance) or a tragedy (like JFK's assassination) occurred that required a special bulletin.

That was then. Fifty years later, readership of newspapers is way, way down. Whereas a third of Americans bought a daily paper in 1941, only 13 percent did so in 2009.[1] Figures released in October 2009 showed circulation down

I DON'T KNOW IF NEWSPAPERS ARE REALLY DYING, BUT I DON'T LIKE THE LOOKS OF THE NEW PAPERBOY.

By permission of Dave Coverly and Creators Syndicate, Inc.

nearly 11 percent in the previous six months alone.[2] Most towns have only one paper, if they have any at all. Meanwhile, in addition to the three original networks, which continue to broadcast news as well as a variety of programming, there are now more than a dozen television stations around the world that are devoted to nothing but news, 24–7, many of which can be accessed from the United States. In addition, there are hundreds of talk radio stations around the country, and of course there is the glorious, chaotic marketplace of ideas and information called the Internet.

Today we take for granted that we can access most information sources not only from newspapers, magazines, books, radios, and the television, but also from our computers. More portably, we can be linked to the world of information from our phones, our electronic

books, and our wireless notebooks, which we can use to read the news, follow a blog, download a book, or watch a movie.

Carry around a newspaper? Why on earth would we want to do that?

A web site called newspaperdeathwatch.com, dedicated to "chronicling the decline of newspapers and the rebirth of journalism," keeps tabs on the papers that have ceased publication or moved to a print-online hybrid or simply an online existence, among them, the *Tucson Citizen*, the *Rocky Mountain News*, the *Baltimore Examiner*, the *Seattle Post-Intelligencer*, the *Detroit News/Free Press*, and the *Christian Science Monitor*. You can check it out yourself to see the latest list of the dead and dying.[3]

As we begin the second decade of the century, it is not unusual to hear people say that the day of the print media is over. If you are feeling

inclined to irony, you can Google "the newspaper is dead" and you will get tens of thousands of hits, with all people insisting (1) that it is true, (2) that it isn't, (3) that it matters, and (4) that it doesn't. In further irony, many of the most thriving news web sites—online journals like the *Drudge Report* and the *Huffington Post* that traffic in "breaking news"—are often merely linking to the reporting of others—often to reporting done by those same dinosaur newspapers whose deaths they are quick to proclaim.

What's the truth here? Is the newspaper an anachronism, a dinosaur left over from another era, or an essential institution whose demise is unimaginable? A writer at *LA Observed*, an online site that touts its independent reporting and commentary, jumped in with both feet: "Not that I'm happy about this, but I'll say it. Newspapers don't matter. Otherwise people would be reading them."[4] Less cavalierly, a journalist writing in *USA Today* (one of the endangered papers), speculated recently that "[s]ometime soon, millions of people may find themselves unwittingly involved in a test that could profoundly change their daily routines, local economies and civic lives. They'll have to figure out how to keep up with City Hall, their neighborhoods and their kids' schools—as well as store openings, new products and sales—without a 170-year-old staple of daily life: a local newspaper."[5]

Does it matter? No less a grand thinker than Thomas Jefferson said, "The basis of our governments being the opinion of the people, the very first object should be to keep that right; and were it left to me to decide whether we should have a government without newspapers or newspapers without a government, I should not hesitate a moment to prefer the latter."[6] Are newspapers that fundamental? Can a democratic world survive without newsprint? Just what is at stake in the declining importance of the American newspaper? ■

Democracy demands that citizens be informed about their government, that they be able to criticize it, deliberate about it, change it if it doesn't do their will. Information, in a very real sense, is power.

It's hard to imagine anyone today voting for a presidential candidate without checking out the candidate's web site or Facebook page, seeing him or her give a speech on streaming video, or watching a fundraising pitch on YouTube. But most of those who voted for George Washington for president, or for Abraham Lincoln, had never even heard the voice of the candidate they chose, and they might have had only a vague idea of what the candidate looked like. While photographs of Lincoln were available, only portraits, sketches, or cartoons of Washington could reach voters. And while Franklin Roosevelt's voice reached millions in his radio "fireside chats," and his face was widely familiar to Americans from newspaper and magazine photographs, his video image was restricted to newsreels that had to be viewed in the movie theater. Not until the advent of television in the mid–twentieth century were presidents, senators, and representatives beamed into the living rooms of Americans, and their smiling, moving images made a part of the modern culture of American politics.

Fast forward fifty years. The electronic age in which we live today has made politics immediate and personal in a way that would leave even these later politicians stunned and bemused. Our information-oriented culture means we are bombarded 24–7 with news flashes, sound bites, web ads, blog posts, commercials, comedy routines, text messages, podcasts, and requests to join networks of those who want our friendship and support. Politicians scramble to stay on top of electronic innovations that continually shape and alter the political world. President George W. Bush's use of the words *internets* and *the Google* signaled his discomfort with the changing electronic world, much as his father's unfamiliarity with a grocery scanner revealed his eight years before. President-elect Barack Obama's confident use of networking strategies and text messaging in his campaign for the presidency put him at an advantage over his older and less tech-savvy opponent, John McCain.

Democracy demands that citizens be informed about their government, that they be able to criticize it, deliberate about it, change it if it doesn't do their will. Information, in a very real sense, is power. Information must be available, and it must be disseminated widely. This was fairly easy to accomplish in the direct democracy of ancient Athens, where

the small number of citizens were able to meet together and debate the political issues of the day. Because their democracy was direct and they were, in effect, the government, there was no need for anything to mediate *between* them and government, to keep them informed, to publicize candidates for office, to identify issues, and to act as a watchdog for their democracy.

In some ways our democratic political community is harder to achieve today. We don't know most of our fellow citizens personally, we cannot directly discover the issues ourselves, and we have no idea what actions our government takes to deal with issues unless the media tell us. We are dependent on the mass media to connect us to our government, and to create the only real space we have for public deliberation of issues. But increasing technological developments make possible ever-newer forms of political community and more immediate access to information. Networking sites like Facebook, LinkedIn, and Twitter allow people to reach out and interact socially, and politicians have not been shy about using such strategies to create networks of supporters. Chat rooms and blogs allow people with common interests to find each other from the far reaches of the world, and allow debate and discussion on a scale never before imagined.

Some visionaries talk of the day when we will all vote electronically on individual issues from our home computers (or maybe even our phones). If we have not yet arrived at that day of direct democratic decision making, changes in the media are nonetheless revolutionizing the possibilities of democracy, much as the printing press and television did earlier, bringing us closer to the Athenian ideal of political community in cyberspace, if not in real space.

In this chapter you will learn about this powerful entity called the media as we focus on

- *the sources of our information*
- *the historical development of the ownership of the American media and its implications for the political information we get*
- *the role of journalists themselves—who they are and what they believe*
- *the link between the media and politics*
- *the relationship of citizens to the media*

> **mass media** means of conveying information to large public audiences cheaply and efficiently

Where Do We Get Our Information?

Increasingly from a combination of sources

Media is the plural of *medium*, meaning in this case an agency through which communication between two different entities can take place. Just as a medium can be a person who claims to transmit messages from the spiritual world to earthbound souls, today's **mass media**, whether through printed word or electronic signal, convey information cheaply and efficiently from the upper reaches of the political world to everyday citizens. And what is just as important in a democratic society, the media help carry information back from citizens to the politicians who lead, or seek to lead, them.

The news media in the twenty-first century increasingly rely on new technology. The printing press may have been invented in China over a thousand years ago, but almost all of the truly amazing innovations in information technology—telegraphs, telephones, photography, radio, television, computers, faxes, cell phones, and the Internet—have been developed in the past two hundred years, and most of them have come into common use only in the past fifty. What that means is that our technological capabilities sometimes outrun our sophistication about how that technology ought to be used or how it may affect the news it transfers.

Understanding who gets information, where it comes from, and how that information is affected by the technology that brings it to us is crucial to being a knowledgeable student of politics, not to mention an effective democratic citizen. In this section we examine the sources that we in America turn to for the news and the consequences that follow from our choices.

Who Gets What News From Where?

In a recent study, most Americans (84 percent) reported that they enjoyed keeping up with the news, and a bare majority (52 percent) even enjoyed it a lot. Young people were less likely to feel this way—only a third of those aged eighteen to twenty-four fell into the "a lot" category, compared to nearly two-thirds of those aged fifty and older—but even a majority of them enjoyed the news at least somewhat.[7] Even though about 80 percent of Americans will get some news on a given day, only 34 percent say they get it from reading a newspaper (down from 48 percent ten years earlier). Television news

Welcome to the Information Age: 24-7 News and Views
In 1968 President Lyndon Johnson was able to watch all of the national news with three television sets tuned to the three networks: ABC, CBS, and NBC. Today, cable stations, blogs, and other 24-7 outlets provide a wealth of news and views to inform, satisfy, challenge, and frustrate almost every opinion or stance on the political spectrum.

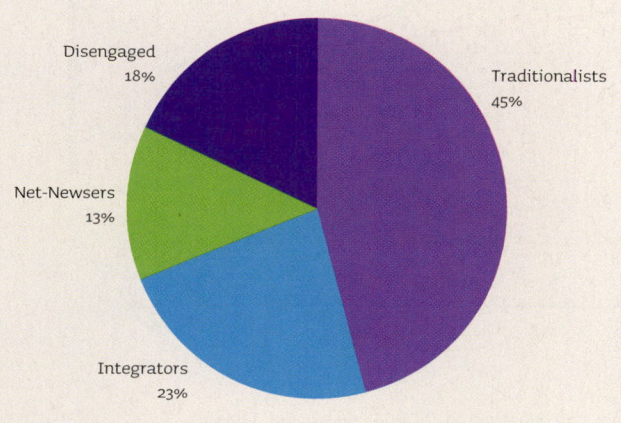

Who Are We?

Consumers of the news

All news-getters are not the same. Many of us are old-fashioned when it comes to technology, some are on the cutting edge, and still others are caught in between. Which profile fits you? How does that affect what you know about the world?

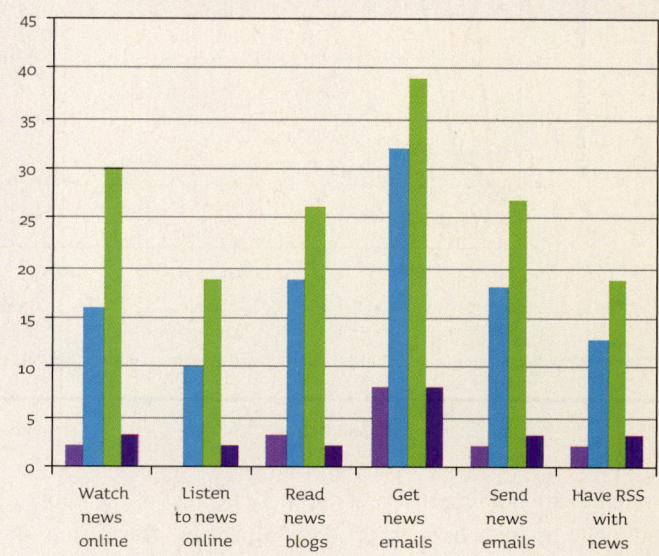

Online News Use by Audience Segments

Traditionalists

- Older, less educated, and less affluent
- Heavy reliance on television news
- Most have computer, but few get news online
- Understand news better by seeing pictures
- Strong interest in weather; little interest in science or technology

Integrators

- Middle aged, well educated, and affluent
- Television is their main source of news, but they also get news online on a typical day
- Spend the most time with the news on a typical day
- Greater interest in political news and sports

Net-Newsers

- Relatively young, well educated, and affluent
- Regularly read political blogs and watch television news
- Web news use soars during the day
- Frequent online news viewers
- Strong interest in technology news

Disengaged

- Less educated and less affluent
- Do not follow the news closely on a daily basis
- More likely to follow weather and local news

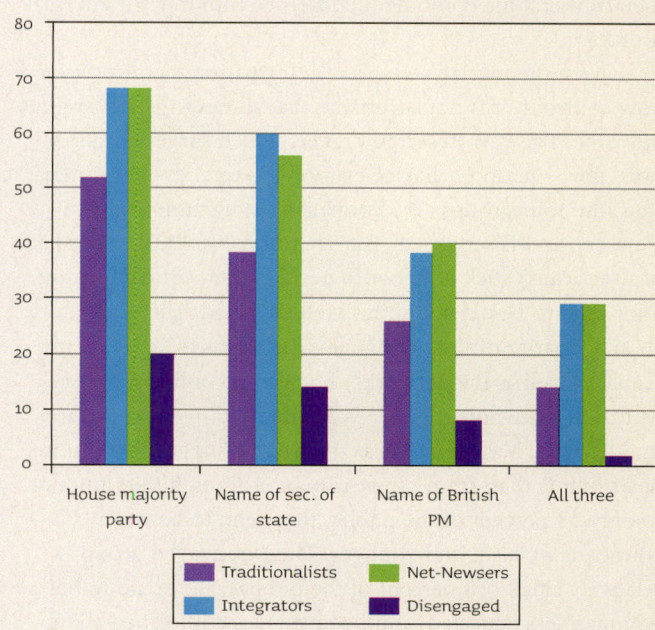

Knowledge of Current Events by Audience Segment

Source: Pew Research Center, "Key News Audiences Now Blend Online and Traditional Sources," August 17, 2008, http://pewresearch.org/pubs/928/key-news-audiences-now-blend-online-and-traditional-source.

Figure 15.1

Newspaper Circulation as a Percentage and Number of Newspapers, 1850-2007

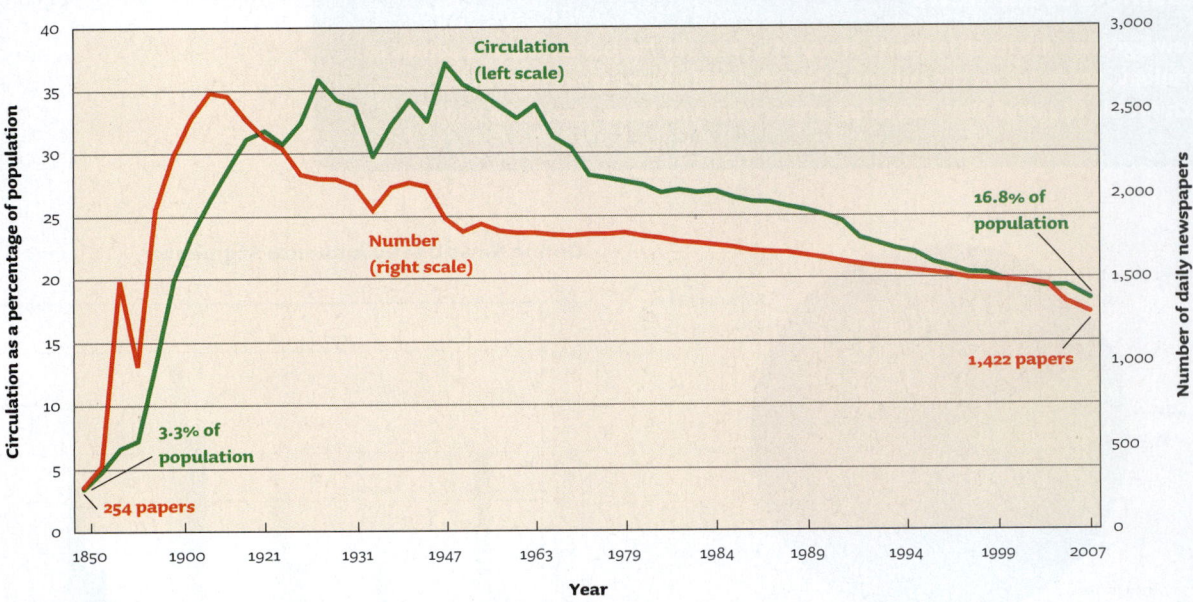

Source: Harold W. Stanley and Richard G. Niemi, *Vital Statistics on American Politics, 2009–2010* (Washington, D.C.: CQ Press, 2009), Table 4.2.

watchers are holding steady at about 57 percent of the public, but radio listeners have dropped to 35 percent, down from 49 percent ten years ago. The news source that shows growth is the Internet—37 percent of the public get some news online, up from only 13 percent in 1998. Many of those who do get their news online combine the Internet with more traditional sources.[8]

Given the myriad sources of information that Americans now confront, it is not surprising that all news-getters are not the same. The Pew Research Center, which surveys Americans' news-getting behavior every two years, divides Americans into four groups: Traditionalists, Integrators, Net-Newsers, and Disengaged. The Traditionalists (just under half of Americans) stick to network news as their primary source. They tend to be older and less well educated. The Integrators, about a quarter of the public, get their news from television (cable as well as the networks) but also go online for news daily. On the whole they are well educated, well-to-do, and middle aged. Net-Newsers, as their name suggests, get more news online than from other sources. Although they amount to only 13 percent of the public, they tend to be well educated, well off, and younger. The Disengaged group is relatively small (18 percent of the public); they tend to be younger, less educated, and by far the least informed about American politics.[9] The *"Who Are We? Consumers of the News"* feature shows the demographic characteristics and news habits of each group.

Despite the fact that most of the American public is exposed to some news, and some people are exposed to quite a lot of it, levels of political information in this country are not high. In one study, only about half of the public could correctly answer questions about domestic politics and public figures.[10] These politically informed people are not evenly distributed throughout the population, either. Older Americans, those with more education, and men were more likely to answer the questions correctly.[11]

Newspapers and Magazines

As we indicated in *What's at Stake?*, American newspaper readership is currently at a historical low (see Figure 15.1), and as Figure 15.2 shows, it is also lower than in most other industrialized nations.[12] Today only about a dozen cities have more than one daily paper. But several major newspapers—the *Wall Street Journal*, *USA Today*, the *New York Times*, the *Washington Post*, and the *Los Angeles Times*—have achieved what amounts to national circulation, providing even residents of single-daily cities with an alternative. Those major papers gather their own news, and some smaller papers that cannot afford to station correspondents around the world can subscribe to their news services. Practically speaking, this means that most of the news that Americans read on a daily basis comes from very few sources: these outlets or wire services like the Associated Press (AP) or Reuters.

Figure 15.2

U.S. Newspaper Circulation Compared to Other Countries

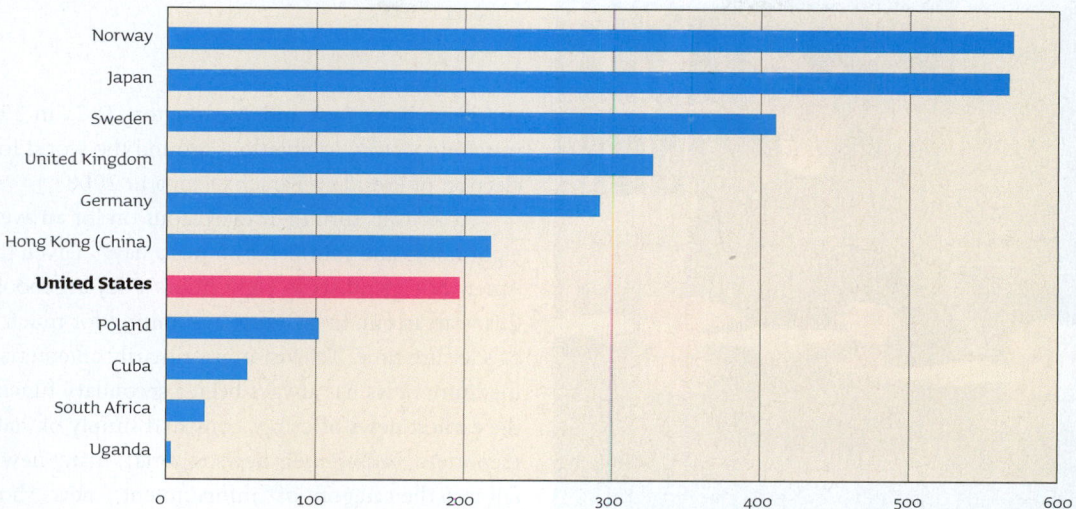

Total average circulation per 1,000 inhabitants in 2000

Source: Harold W. Stanley and Richard G. Niemi, *Vital Statistics on American Politics, 2005–2006* (Washington, D.C.: CQ Press, 2005), 174–175.

Newspapers cover political news, of course, but many other subjects also compete with advertising for space in a newspaper's pages. Business, sports, entertainment (movies and television), religion, weather, book reviews, comics, crossword puzzles, advice columns, classified ads, and travel information are just some of the kinds of content that most newspapers provide in an effort to woo readers, although increasingly many of these are available online. Craigslist, for instance, has done much to make the classified sections of newspapers redundant, and some observers argue that the site is at least partly responsible for making newspapers an endangered species.[13] Generally the front section and especially the front page are reserved for major current events, but these need not be political in nature. Business deals, sporting events, and even sensational and unusual weather conditions can push politics farther back in the paper.

Magazines can often be more specialized than newspapers. While the standard weekly news magazines (*Time, U.S. News and World Report*, and the new, weekly *Christian Science Monitor*, for example) carry the same eclectic mix of subjects as major newspapers, they can also offer more comprehensive news coverage because they do not need to meet daily deadlines, giving them more time to develop a story. These popular news magazines tend to be middle of the road in their ideological outlook. Other magazines appeal specifically to liberal readers—for instance, the *New Republic* and the *Nation*—and to conservatives—for instance, the *National Review* and the *American Spectator*.

Radio

The decline in the number of newspapers that began in the early 1900s was probably due in part to the emergence of radio. Although radios were expensive at first, one in six American families owned one by 1926,[14] and the radio had become a central part of American life. Not only was radio news more up-to-the-minute, it was also more personal. Listeners were able to hear a session of Congress for the first time in 1923 and a presidential inauguration in 1925.[15] Disasters such as the 1937 crash of the airship *Hindenburg* were brought into Americans' homes with an immediacy that newspapers could not achieve. Franklin Roosevelt used his "fireside chats" to sell his New Deal policies directly to the public, without having to go through the reporters he viewed as hostile to his ideas.[16]

Today, 99 percent of American households own at least one radio,[17] and more than 11,000 radio stations offer entertainment and news shows through commercial networks and their local affiliates. There are also two noncommercial networks, National Public Radio and Public Radio International, funded in small part by the U.S. government but also by private donations from corporations and individuals. Since the 1980s the radio call-in talk show has grown in popularity, allowing the radio hosts and their guests, as well as the audience, to air their opinions on politics and creating a sense of political community among their primarily conservative listeners.

Political Commentary With a Bite

Many go to the radio for music or news, but political talk shows are also popular and effective. Progressive political commentator and syndicated radio host Rachel Maddow (shown here with *Newsweek*'s Howard Fineman) proved so popular in guest appearances on such televised news shows as *Countdown With Keith Olbermann* that she was approached to do her own show for MSNBC in September 2008.

Television

The impact of radio on the American public, however dramatic initially, cannot compare with the effects of television, which grew into a national medium almost immediately thanks to the previously established radio networks. American ownership of television sets skyrocketed from 9 percent of households in 1950 to 98 percent in 1975, a statistic that continues to hold firm. In fact, 82 percent of American homes have more than one TV set and 40 percent own three or more; over 80 percent receive cable or satellite transmission.[18]

Politicians were quick to realize that, like radio, television allowed them to reach a broad audience without having to deal with print reporters and their adversarial questions. The Kennedy administration was the first to make real use of television, a medium that might have been made for the young, telegenic president. And it was television that brought the nation together in a community of grief when Kennedy was assassinated.

Television carried the Vietnam War (along with its protesters) and the civil rights movement into Americans' homes, and the images that it created helped build popular support to end the war abroad and segregation at home. Television can create global as well as national communities, an experience many Americans shared as they sat captive before their television sets in the days following the terrorist

> **narrowcasting** the targeting of specialized audiences by the media

attacks on New York and Washington, D.C., in 2001, or watching victory celebrations around the world following the election of President Barack Obama in 2008.

Americans turn their televisions on for an average of eight hours and fourteen minutes a day.[19] Given that most Americans spend six to eight hours a day at school or at work, this is an astounding figure, accounting for much of America's leisure time. Television is primarily an entertainment medium; news has always been a secondary function. While the earliest news offerings consisted simply of "talking heads" (reporters reading their news reports), many newscasts now fall into the category of "infotainment," news shows dressed up with drama and emotion to entice viewers to tune in. Once given a choice of only three networks, in 2008 the typical American home received nearly 120 television channels.[20] Rather than pursuing broad markets, stations are now often focusing on specific audiences such as people interested in health and fitness, sports, or travel. This practice of targeting a small, specialized broadcast market is called **narrowcasting**.[21] The competition for viewers is fierce, and as we will see, the quality of the news available can suffer as a consequence.

There are many television shows whose primary subject is politics. Many cable stations and C-SPAN, sometimes called "America's Town Hall," offer news around the clock, although not all the news concerns politics. Weekend shows like *Meet the Press* highlight the week's coverage of politics, and the cable news stations frequently showcase debates between liberals and conservatives on current issues. Some stations, such as the music channel MTV, direct their political shows to a specific age group (here, young people), and others, like *America's Voice*, to those holding particular ideologies (conservatism, in this case).

Like radio, television has its call-in talk shows. And politics is often the subject of the jokes on such shows as *Saturday Night Live, The Daily Show With Jon Stewart, The Colbert Report, Late Show With David Letterman,* and *The Tonight Show*. Sometimes the line between fun and fact gets blurred, as when in 2003 Democratic senator John Edwards announced his candidacy for the presidency on Stewart's show, prompting Stewart to say, "I guess I should probably tell you now that we're a fake show. So, I want you to know that this may not count." Since at least 2000 the major presidential candidates and their wives have regularly sat down to chat with Larry King, Jay Leno, Letterman, and Oprah Winfrey (who took the unprecedented step of endorsing Barack Obama in 2008). Sometimes the performance is forced, but candidates who can convey an image of themselves as a regular, likable person can win in a big way. John McCain has been a mainstay of late-night TV, where by joking about his own age ("I am so old," he told Leno, "my Social Security number is eight"), he managed to take some of the sting out of criticisms that he was too old to be president, and during the 2008 primary season, Hillary Clinton used an appearance on *Saturday Night Live* to soften her image. Although Sarah Palin, too, appeared on *Saturday Night Live* later in 2008, it was after Tina Fey had already become a national sensation by creating a punishing caricature of her as a beauty queen candidate, and it's questionable whether her own performance helped change her image at all.

It is not just candidates who make appearances on late-night comedy shows. In late October 2010, just days before the midterm elections, President Barack Obama sat down with Jon Stewart for an interview on *The Daily Show*. Sometimes the comedians take more overt political roles. Days after Obama's appearance, Stewart and Stephen Colbert held a rally in Washington, D.C.—a merger of Stewart's "The Rally to Restore Sanity" and Colbert's "The March to Keep Fear Alive." Clearly meant to be spoofs on the angry conservative Tea Party rallies and Glenn Beck's "Restoring Honor" rally, they were taken seriously enough by real news organizations that most forbade their reporters from attending unless they were there in a political capacity on the grounds that these were political events.[22]

The Internet

The most recent new medium to revolutionize the way we get political news is the Internet, or the web (for World Wide Web), which connects home or business computers to a global network of sites that provide printed, audio, and visual information on any topic you can imagine. In 2010 some 80 percent of American adults used the Internet, over 66 percent had a broadband connection at home, and 60 percent went online wirelessly from their laptops or phones.[23] Sixty-one percent of Americans in 2010 said they got some news from the Internet on a typical day—more than five times the number from a decade ago—and 25 percent did so from their phones. Fifty-nine percent of adult Americans say they get their news from a combination of on- and offline sources. Twenty-eight percent of Americans have a customizable web page that feeds them news, and 37 percent of Internet users have socially interacted with others concerning the

Friending the President?
Around 80 percent of Americans use the Internet, and they are increasingly doing so to obtain their news. Media and politicians alike are making use of technology to reach out to readers in new ways. President Barack Obama has his own Facebook page. Newspapers run feeds on Twitter. Readers now can interact with their news sources via comments, "likes," and links in ways they never could before.

news—creating it, commenting on it, or disseminating it through social networking sites like Facebook or Twitter.[24] It is not too much to say that the Internet is revolutionizing the way we get information.

The mainstream media take advantage of the web, but mostly to replicate or supplement the information that they publish through traditional means. All the major newspapers and the AP have web sites, usually free, where all or most of the news in their print versions can be found. (Visit http://republic.cqpress.com and choose Chapter 15 for links to major news sites.) Many magazines and journals are also available

▶ Who, What, How, and WHEN: Media and Politics

Today we have multiple ways of following politics—we can read a paper, listen to the radio, watch television, or surf the web. Hard to believe there was a time when a dog-eared pamphlet and a church sermon were the only ways of accessing information about the political world. As the media through which we get political information have become more sophisticated, they have changed the way politics itself is practiced. Here are some of the major transitions in the media-politics connection:

1803 — The Penny Press

While political pamphlets of the eighteenth century represented the advent of the printed word (think Thomas Paine's *Common Sense*, an effort to convince colonists to declare independence from the British), it was the tabloid newspapers of the early 1800s that epitomized the heyday of the printed word. They were significantly less partisan than previous newspapers, since they were independent rather than party funded. Because they were cheap and readily available, they reached a much larger audience. While still years away from "objective" media sold to the masses, the penny press changed politics by opening up both readership and the information available to the public.

1933–1944 — Fireside Chats

The early twentieth century witnessed the advent of the radio, with nearly 90 percent of U.S. households owning one by the 1930s. President Franklin Roosevelt used this medium effectively to address the American people with his fireside chats during his four terms as president. Designed to be intimate, conversational talks with the president, these chats brought politics right into the living room. Listeners sent millions of letters to the White House, and Americans began to see politicians as people with whom they might have a personal connection.

1960 — Kennedy-Nixon Debates

The television set eclipsed the radio in the 1960s as the medium that most affected Americans' political behavior. Richard Nixon and John F. Kennedy participated in the first televised presidential debate before the November 1960 election. While a majority of the 70 million people who watched the debate on television thought Kennedy won, people who listened to the debate on the radio thought Nixon won. Kennedy, tan and well rested, seemed more presidential than the nervous Nixon, whose visible five o'clock shadow gave him a sinister appearance. More than half of voters surveyed said the debates influenced their vote, and the influence of television in creating a political image was born.

online. By searching for the topics we want and connecting to links with related sites, we can customize our web news. Politics buffs can bypass nonpolitical news, and vice versa. True politics junkies can go straight to the source: the federal government makes enormous amounts of information available at its www.whitehouse.gov and www.senate.gov sites.

In addition to traditional media outlets that provide online versions, myriad other sources of information are available on the web. Online sources like *Slate*, *Salon*, the *Huffington Post*, and the *Drudge Report* exist solely on the Internet and may or may not adopt the conventions, practices, and standards of the more traditional media. Web logs, or **blogs**,

1982–2005 · *Crossfire* Airs

The idea of pitting one conservative speaker with a liberal speaker to challenge each other's opinions on a television show actually began on the radio, with Tom Braden and Pat Buchanan in 1978. CNN offered the pair a show in 1982 and *Crossfire* the TV series was born, featuring partisan battles on the air. The show foundered in 2005 due to increased competition from *Hannity & Colmes* on Fox and *Hardball* on MSNBC, and most famously with Jon Stewart's appearance in 2004, when he said, "It's not so much that it's bad, as it's hurting America. . . . Stop, stop, stop hurting America." Opinion-driven shows like *The O'Reilly Factor* also were driving stations like CNN, which strived for neutrality, to give airtime to less objective journalists like Lou Dobbs and Jack Cafferty. With a twenty-four-hour news cycle and multiple outlets for defending partisan views and actions, the "permanent campaign" became part of the American political landscape.

2005 · The Introduction of YouTube

The Internet was already revolutionizing the way we get our news—with continuously updated versions of print newspapers like the *New York Times* and the *Washington Post*, with elaborate sites for network and cable stations, and with political blogs of every ideological stripe—when YouTube burst on the scene in 2005. A web site that enables anyone to upload and share a video, YouTube made it easy to capture and expose politicians in moments that might have previously sunk into oblivion. When Republican senator George Allen, of Virginia, used a racial slur to refer to an audience member at a campaign event, the video was not only replayed endlessly on cable news but also went viral on YouTube. The on-demand replay helped to usher Allen to a narrow defeat to Democrat Jim Webb and ended speculation that he would run for president in 2008. It also reminded all politicians that, in the age of YouTube, words once spoken are in the public domain instantly and forever.

have become increasingly popular as well. Blogs—online journals, like the one discussed by Andrew Sullivan in this chapter's *Profile in Citizenship*—can be set up by anyone with a computer and an Internet connection. They can be personal, political, cultural, or anything in between; they run the gamut from individual diaries to investigative journalism. In fact, anyone can put up a blog or a web page and distribute information on any topic. This makes the task of using the information on the web challenging. It gives us access to more information than ever before, but the task of sorting and evaluating that information is solely our own responsibility (see *Consider the Source* in Chapter 5).

> *blogs* web logs, or online journals, that can cover any topic, including political analysis

Not only does the web provide information, but it is also interactive to a degree that far surpasses talk radio or television. The social networking sites Facebook, MySpace, and Twitter, as well as many other web sites and blogs, have chat rooms or discussion opportunities where all sorts of information can be shared, topics debated, and people met. Although this can allow the formation of communities based on specialized interests or similar views, it can also make it very easy for people with fringe or extreme views to find each other and organize.[25] In 2008 political campaigns took advantage of this, using online technology and social networking principles to organize, raise funds, and get out the vote. It was Democratic senator Barack Obama's early use of the Internet for his campaign, borrowing from the innovative 2004 campaign of Howard Dean, that gave him an edge over Senator Hillary Clinton in the presidential primaries. The Internet has the potential to increase the direct participation of citizens in political communities and political decisions, though the fact that not all Americans have access to the web means that multiple classes of citizenship could form.

Who What How

From newspapers to radio, television, and, most recently, the Internet, Americans have moved eagerly to embrace the new forms of technology that entertain them and bring new ways of communicating information. But the deluge of political information requires consumers to sort through and critically analyze the news they get—often a costly exercise in terms of time, effort, and financial resources. Consequently, although the amount of political information available to Americans has increased dramatically, Americans do not seem to be particularly well informed about their political world.

Who Owns the Media, and How Does That Affect Our News?

From government control to corporate control

The ownership structure of the American media has changed dramatically since the days of the nation's founding. The media have gone from dependence on government for their very existence to massive corporate ownership that seems to rival government for its sheer power and influence on the citizenry. In this section we look at the ways in which the ownership of those media has changed the kind of news we get.

The Early American Press

In its earliest days, the press in America was dependent on government officials for its financial, and sometimes political, survival. Under those circumstances, the press could hardly perform either the watchdog function of checking up on government or the democratic function of empowering citizens. It served primarily to empower government or, during the Revolution, the patriots who had seized control of many of the colonial presses.

During colonial times, printers were required to obtain government approval and thus tended to avoid controversial political reporting so that they could stay in business. But the radical patriot movement was aggressive and violent in its methods of securing a supportive press. As public opinion swung toward independence, printers who favored British rule or aimed to treat both sides objectively were targeted with letters and criticism, and their print shops were raided, vandalized, and burned. Angry mobs burned the loyalist printers in effigy and frequently forced them to change their viewpoints or shut down their presses.

After the American Revolution, with independence firmly in hand, Americans celebrated their "freedom of the press," which they enshrined in the First Amendment to the Constitution. The debates over the Constitution itself took place in newspapers and pamphlets, producing works such as the *Federalist Papers*. Most revolutionaries concluded that, without the press, independence could not have been won and liberty could not survive. It is ironic that the victory they celebrated was founded on the vigorous suppression of their opponents' freedom of the press.

The press that grew up in the early American republic continued to be anything but free and independent. Because the newspaper business was still a risky financial proposition, it was an accepted practice for a politician or a party to set up a newspaper and support it financially—and expect it to support the appropriate political causes in return. Andrew Jackson, elected in 1828, carried the patronage of the press to new lengths. Like his predecessors, he offered friendly papers the opportunity to print government documents and denied it to his critics. But Jackson's administration heralded an age of mass democracy. Voter turnout doubled between 1824 and 1828.[26] People were reading newspapers in unheard of numbers, and those papers were catering to their new mass audiences with a blunter and less elite style than they had used in the past.

Growing Media Independence

The newspapers after Jackson's day were characterized by larger circulations, which drew more advertising and increased their financial independence. As newspapers sought to increase their readership, they began to offer more politically impartial news coverage in the hope that they would not alienate potential readers. This effort to be objective, which we see as a journalistic virtue today, came about at least partly as the result of the economic imperatives of selling newspapers to large numbers of people who do not share the same political views.

Prior to 1833, newspapers had been expensive; a year's subscription cost more than the average weekly wages of a skilled worker.[27] But in that year, the *New York Sun* began selling papers at only a penny a copy. Its subject matter was not an intellectual treatment of complex political and economic topics but rather more superficial political reporting of crime, human interest stories, humor, and advertising. As papers began to appeal to mass audiences rather than partisan supporters, they left behind their opinionated reporting and strove for more objective, "fairer" treatment of their subjects that would be less likely to alienate the readers and the advertisers on whom they depended for their livelihood. This isn't to say that newspaper editors stayed out of politics, but they were not seen as being in the pocket of one of the political parties, and the news they printed was considered to be evenhanded. In 1848 the AP was organized as a wire service to collect foreign news and distribute it to member papers in the United States. This underscored the need for objectivity in political reporting so that the news would be acceptable to a variety of papers.[28]

After the Civil War, the need for newspapers to appeal to a mass audience resulted in the practice of *yellow journalism*, the effort to lure readers with sensational reporting on topics like sex, crime, gossip, and human interest. With the success of such techniques, newspapers became big business in the United States. Newspaper giant Joseph Pulitzer's *World* was challenged by William Randolph Hearst's *New York Journal*, and the resulting battle for circulation drew the criticism that there were no depths to which journalists wouldn't sink in their quest for readers. The irony, of course, is that sensationalism did win new readers and allowed papers to achieve independence from parties and politicians, even as they were criticized for lowering the standards of journalism.

The Media Today

Today the media continue to be big business, but on a scale undreamed of by such early entrepreneurs as Pulitzer and Hearst. No longer does a single figure dominate a paper's editorial policy; rather, all the major circulation newspapers in this country, as well as the national radio and television stations, are owned by major conglomerates. Often editorial decisions are matters of corporate policy, not individual judgment. And if profit was an overriding concern for the editor-entrepreneurs, it is gospel for the conglomerates. Interestingly, journalists freed themselves from the political masters who ruled them in the early years of this country, only to find themselves just as thoroughly dominated by the corporate bottom line.

Media Monopoly

The modern media get five times as much of their revenue from advertising as from circulation. Logic dictates that advertisers will want to spend their money where they can get the biggest bang for their buck: the papers with the most readers and the stations with the largest audiences. Because advertisers go after the most popular media outlets, competition is fierce, and outlets that cannot promise advertisers wide enough exposure fail to get the advertising dollars and go out of business. Competition drives out the weaker outlets, corporations seeking to maximize market share gobble up smaller outlets, and to retain viewers, they all stick to the formulas that are known to produce success. What this means for the media world today is that there are fewer and fewer outlets, they are owned by fewer and fewer corporations, and the content they offer is more and more the same.[29]

In fact, today, ten corporations, among them Time-Warner, Disney, National Amusements (owner of both Viacom and CBS Corporation), News Corporation Limited, and General Electric, own the major national newspapers, the leading news magazines, the national television networks including CNN and other cable stations, as well as publishing houses, movie studios, telephone companies, entertainment firms, and other multimedia operations. Most of these corporations are also involved in other businesses, as their familiar names attest. Figure 15.3 shows in detail the media empires that own the five major television networks. These

Figure 15.3

Who Owns the News?

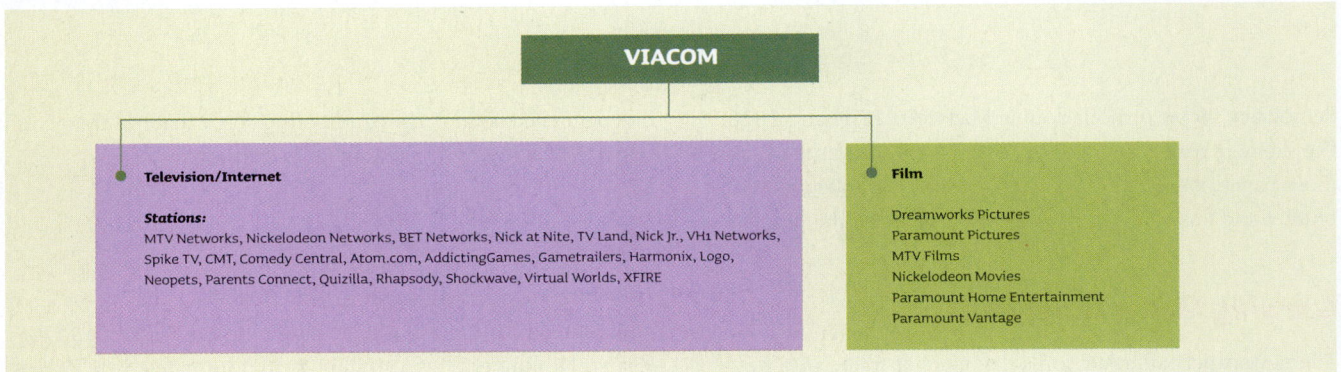

VIACOM

Television/Internet

Stations:
MTV Networks, Nickelodeon Networks, BET Networks, Nick at Nite, TV Land, Nick Jr., VH1 Networks, Spike TV, CMT, Comedy Central, Atom.com, AddictingGames, Gametrailers, Harmonix, Logo, Neopets, Parents Connect, Quizilla, Rhapsody, Shockwave, Virtual Worlds, XFIRE

Film

Dreamworks Pictures
Paramount Pictures
MTV Films
Nickelodeon Movies
Paramount Home Entertainment
Paramount Vantage

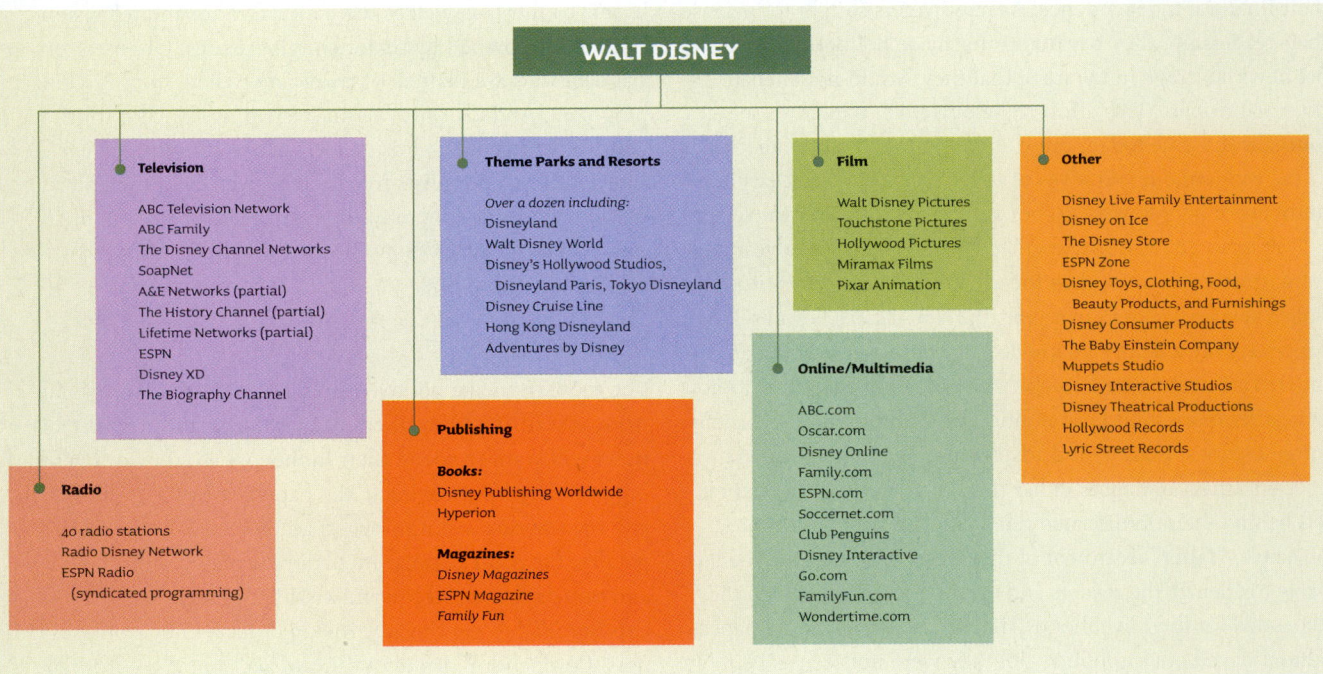

WALT DISNEY

Television

ABC Television Network
ABC Family
The Disney Channel Networks
SoapNet
A&E Networks (partial)
The History Channel (partial)
Lifetime Networks (partial)
ESPN
Disney XD
The Biography Channel

Theme Parks and Resorts

Over a dozen including:
Disneyland
Walt Disney World
Disney's Hollywood Studios,
    Disneyland Paris, Tokyo Disneyland
Disney Cruise Line
Hong Kong Disneyland
Adventures by Disney

Film

Walt Disney Pictures
Touchstone Pictures
Hollywood Pictures
Miramax Films
Pixar Animation

Other

Disney Live Family Entertainment
Disney on Ice
The Disney Store
ESPN Zone
Disney Toys, Clothing, Food,
    Beauty Products, and Furnishings
Disney Consumer Products
The Baby Einstein Company
Muppets Studio
Disney Interactive Studios
Disney Theatrical Productions
Hollywood Records
Lyric Street Records

Radio

40 radio stations
Radio Disney Network
ESPN Radio
    (syndicated programming)

Publishing

Books:
Disney Publishing Worldwide
Hyperion

Magazines:
Disney Magazines
ESPN Magazine
Family Fun

Online/Multimedia

ABC.com
Oscar.com
Disney Online
Family.com
ESPN.com
Soccernet.com
Club Penguins
Disney Interactive
Go.com
FamilyFun.com
Wondertime.com

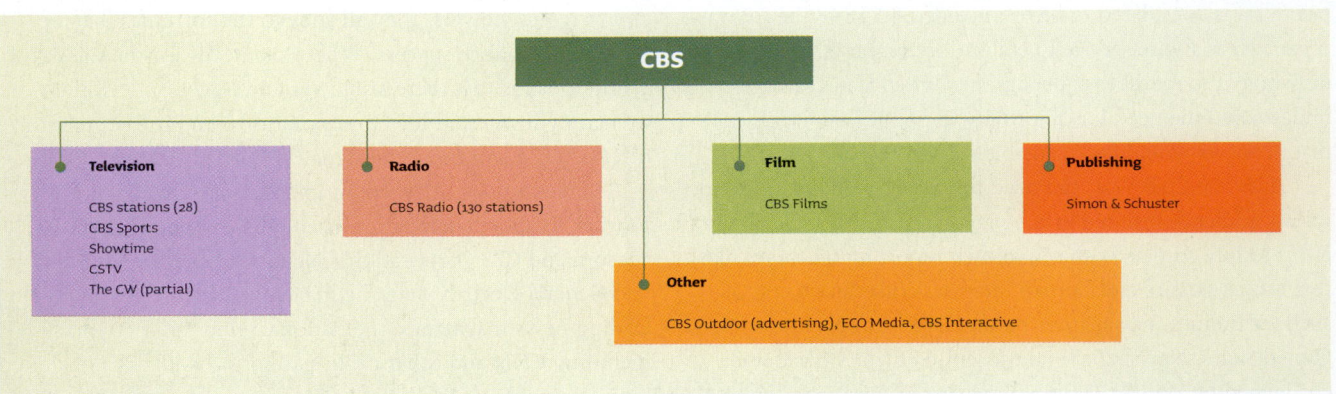

CBS

Television

CBS stations (28)
CBS Sports
Showtime
CSTV
The CW (partial)

Radio

CBS Radio (130 stations)

Film

CBS Films

Publishing

Simon & Schuster

Other

CBS Outdoor (advertising), ECO Media, CBS Interactive

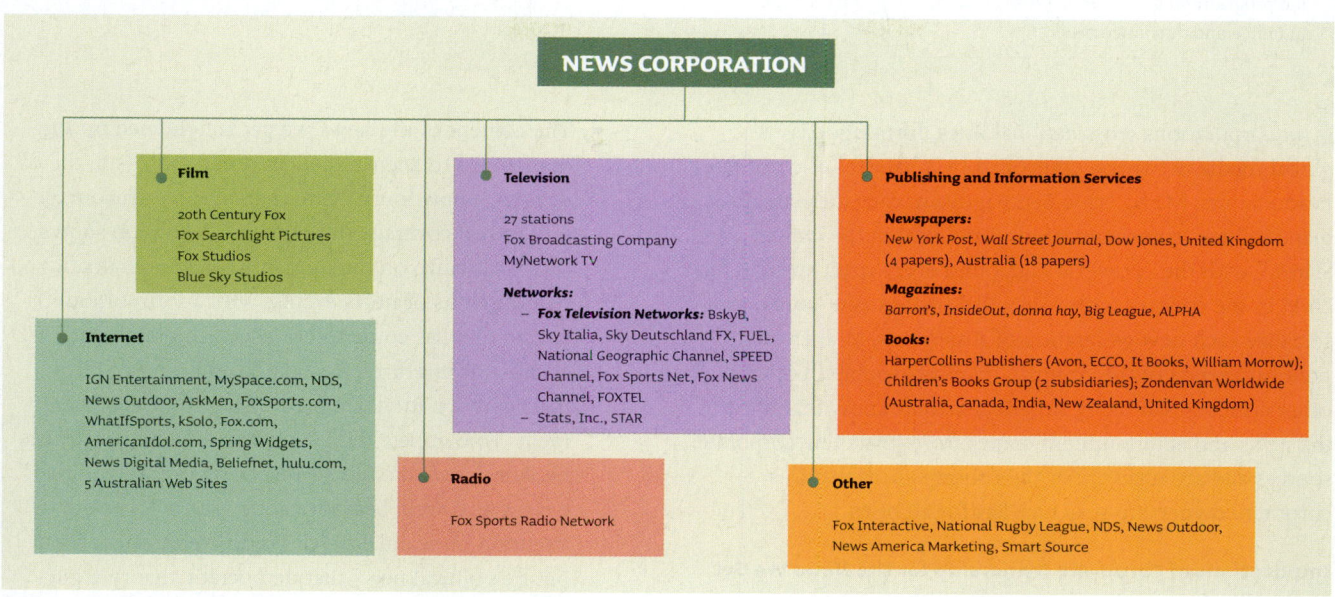

NEWS CORPORATION

Film
- 20th Century Fox
- Fox Searchlight Pictures
- Fox Studios
- Blue Sky Studios

Internet

IGN Entertainment, MySpace.com, NDS, News Outdoor, AskMen, FoxSports.com, WhatIfSports, kSolo, Fox.com, AmericanIdol.com, Spring Widgets, News Digital Media, Beliefnet, hulu.com, 5 Australian Web Sites

Television

27 stations
Fox Broadcasting Company
MyNetwork TV

Networks:
- **Fox Television Networks:** BskyB, Sky Italia, Sky Deutschland FX, FUEL, National Geographic Channel, SPEED Channel, Fox Sports Net, Fox News Channel, FOXTEL
- Stats, Inc., STAR

Radio

Fox Sports Radio Network

Publishing and Information Services

Newspapers:
New York Post, Wall Street Journal, Dow Jones, United Kingdom (4 papers), Australia (18 papers)

Magazines:
Barron's, InsideOut, donna hay, Big League, ALPHA

Books:
HarperCollins Publishers (Avon, ECCO, It Books, William Morrow); Children's Books Group (2 subsidiaries); Zondenvan Worldwide (Australia, Canada, India, New Zealand, United Kingdom)

Other

Fox Interactive, National Rugby League, NDS, News Outdoor, News America Marketing, Smart Source

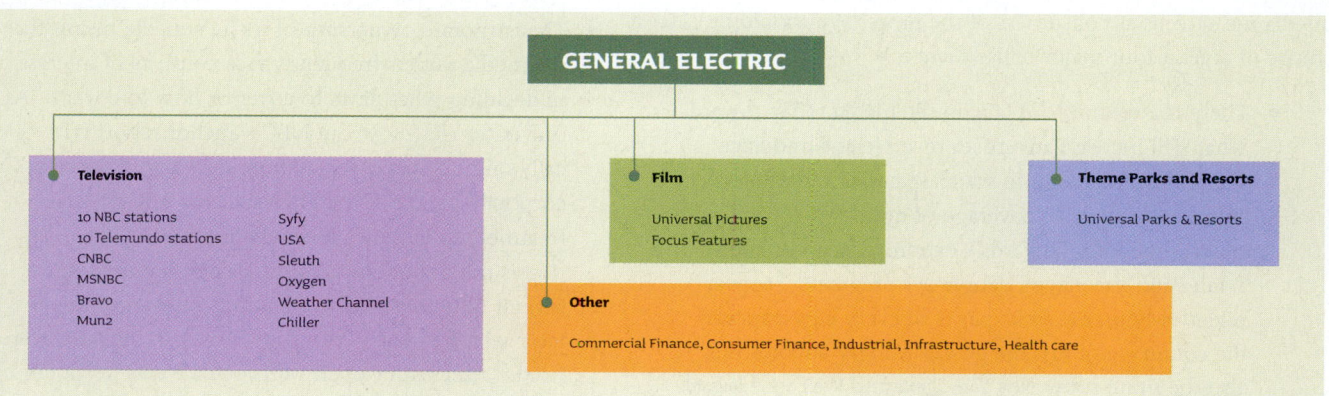

GENERAL ELECTRIC

Television

10 NBC stations	Syfy
10 Telemundo stations	USA
CNBC	Sleuth
MSNBC	Oxygen
Bravo	Weather Channel
Mun2	Chiller

Film

Universal Pictures
Focus Features

Theme Parks and Resorts

Universal Parks & Resorts

Other

Commercial Finance, Consumer Finance, Industrial, Infrastructure, Health care

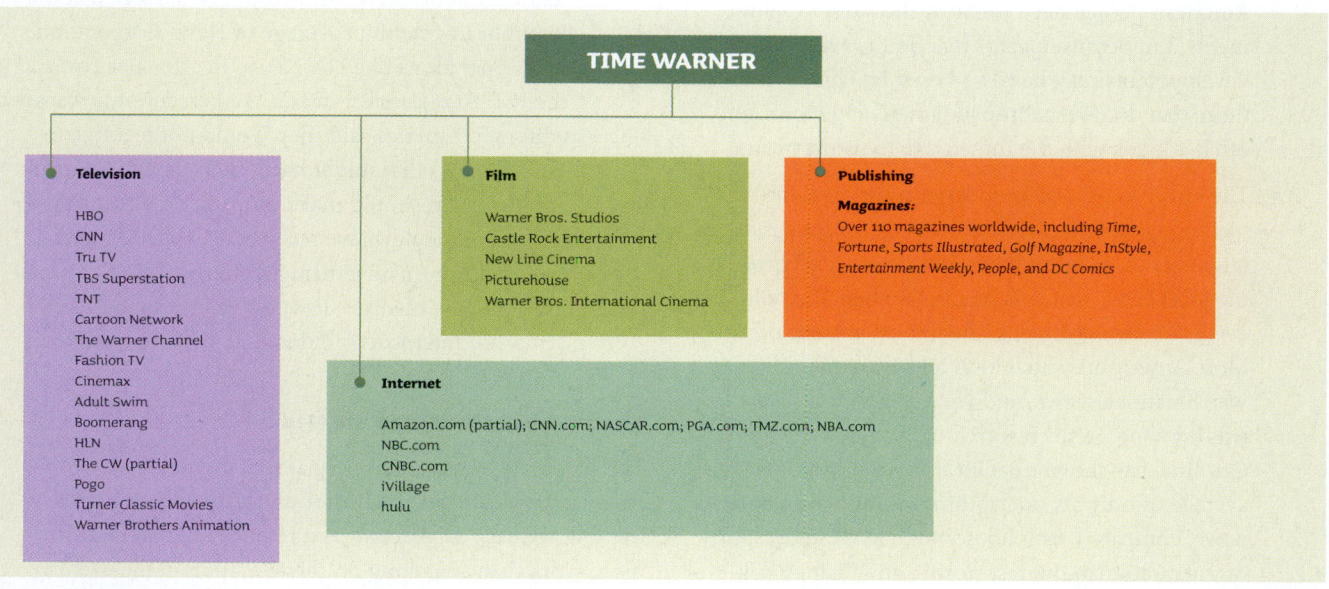

TIME WARNER

Television

HBO
CNN
Tru TV
TBS Superstation
TNT
Cartoon Network
The Warner Channel
Fashion TV
Cinemax
Adult Swim
Boomerang
HLN
The CW (partial)
Pogo
Turner Classic Movies
Warner Brothers Animation

Film

Warner Bros. Studios
Castle Rock Entertainment
New Line Cinema
Picturehouse
Warner Bros. International Cinema

Internet

Amazon.com (partial); CNN.com; NASCAR.com; PGA.com; TMZ.com; NBA.com
NBC.com
CNBC.com
iVillage
hulu

Publishing

Magazines:
Over 110 magazines worldwide, including *Time, Fortune, Sports Illustrated, Golf Magazine, InStyle, Entertainment Weekly, People,* and DC Comics

> **commercial bias** the tendency of the media to make coverage and programming decisions based on what will attract a large audience and maximize profits

giant corporations cross national lines, forming massive global media networks, controlled by a handful of corporate headquarters. Media critic Ben Bagdikian calls these media giants a "new communications cartel within the United States," with the "power to surround every man, woman, and child in the country with controlled images and words, to socialize each new generation of Americans, to alter the political agenda of the country."[30] What troubles him and other critics is that many Americans don't know that most of the news and entertainment comes from just a few corporate sources and are unaware of the consequences that this corporate ownership structure has for all of us.

Implications of Corporate Ownership for the News We Get

What does the concentrated corporate ownership of the media mean to us as consumers of the news? We should be aware of at least four major consequences:

- There is a **commercial bias** in the media today toward what will increase advertiser revenue and audience share. People tune in to watch scandals and crime stories, so extensive coverage of nonnewsworthy events, like John Edwards's extramarital affair and Sarah Palin's teenaged daughter's pregnancy, appear relentlessly on the front pages of every newspaper in the country, not just the gossip-hungry tabloids but also the more sober *New York Times* and *Wall Street Journal*. It may not be because an editor has decided that the American people need to know the latest developments, but because papers that don't reveal those developments may be passed over by consumers for those that do. Journalistic judgment and ethics are often at odds with the imperative to turn a profit.

- The effort to get and keep large audiences, and to make way for increased advertising, means a reduced emphasis on political news. This is especially true at the local level, which is precisely where the political events that most directly affect most citizens occur. More Americans watch local television news than watch national news, and yet one political scientist, drawing on his research of local news in North Carolina, has shown that local news shows spend an average of only six out of thirty minutes on political news, compared with hot topics like weather, sports, disasters, human interest stories, and "happy talk" among the newscasters.[31]

- The content of the news we get is lightened up and dramatized to keep audiences tuned in.[32] As in the days of yellow journalism, market forces encourage sensational coverage of the news. Television shows often capitalize on the human interest in dramatic reenactments of news events, with a form of journalism that has come to be called "infotainment" because of its efforts to make the delivery of information more attractive by dressing it up as entertainment. To compete with such shows, the mainstream network news broadcasts increase the drama of their coverage as well. Sensational newscasts focus our attention on scandalous or tragic events rather than on the political news that democratic theory argues citizens need.

- The corporate ownership of today's media means that the media outlets frequently face conflicts of interest in deciding what news to cover or how to cover it. As one critic asks, how can NBC's anchor report critically on nuclear power without crossing the network's corporate parent, General Electric, or ABC give fair treatment to Disney's business practices?[33] The question is not hypothetical: after Disney acquired ABC, several ABC employees, including a news commentator who had been critical of Disney in the past, were fired.[34] And with Rupert Murdoch's News Corporation giving a million dollars to the Republican Governors Association in 2010, who would be surprised at the Republican-friendly coverage of News Corporation's news operations like Fox News, the *New York Post*, and the *Wall Street Journal*?[35] In fact, 33 percent of newspaper editors in America said they would not feel free to publish news that might harm their parent company,[36] a statistic that should make us question what is being left out of the news we receive. A further conflict of interest arises in advertising matters. Note, as just one example, the media's slowness to pick up on stories critical of the tobacco industry, a major advertiser.[37]

Alternatives to the Corporate Media

The corporate media monopoly affects the news we get in serious ways. Citizens have some alternative news options, but few are truly satisfactory as a remedy, and all require more work than switching on the television in the evening. One alternative is public radio and television. Americans tend to assume that media wholly owned or controlled by the government serve the interests of government rather than the citizens. This was certainly true in our early history and is true in totalitarian countries such as the former Soviet Union or today's China. But as we have seen, privately owned media are not necessarily free either.

And, in fact, government-controlled media are not necessarily repressive. Great Britain and other European countries have long supported a media system combining privately owned (and largely partisan) newspapers with publicly owned radio and television stations. Although such stations now find themselves competing with cable rivals, some, including the British Broadcasting Company (BBC), are renowned for their programming excellence. Sometimes, then, publicly owned media may be even "freer" than privately owned media if they allow producers to escape the commercial culture in which most media shows exist. The United States has public radio and television networks, but they are not subsidized by the government at sufficient levels to allow them complete commercial freedom. Rather, they are funded by a combination of government assistance and private or corporate donations. These donations sound very much like commercials when announced at the start and finish of programming and could arguably affect the content of the shows.

Another choice for citizens is the *alternative press*. Born of the counterculture and antiwar movement in the 1960s, these local weekly papers, like the (New York) *Village Voice* and the SF (San Francisco) *Weekly*, were intended to offer a radical alternative to the mainstream media. Usually free and dependent on advertising, these papers have lost their radical edge and become so profitable that, in an ironic turn of events, they themselves are now getting bought up by chains like New Times, Inc.[38] Rejecting the alternative press as too conventional, there is now even an "alternative to the alternative press" aimed at a younger audience and coveted by advertisers.[39]

Nevertheless, an independent press does continue to thrive without the support of corporate owners. A few investigative magazines, like *Mother Jones* (published by the Foundation for National Progress) and *Consumer Reports* (published by Consumers Union), rely on funding from subscribers and members of their nonprofit parent organizations. However, unless they are completely free from advertising (as is *Consumer Reports*), even these independent publications are not entirely free from corporate influence. Other alternative newsletters and magazines, such as the liberal *Nation* or the conservative *National*

Review, cover issues and policies often ignored by the mainstream press, but they do so from a perspective that supports their own political agendas.

A final, but rapidly growing, alternative to the mainstream corporate media is, of course, the Internet. The Internet offers myriad sources for political news. Although, as we saw in *Consider the Source* in Chapter 5, it takes time and effort to figure out which of these sources are accurate and trustworthy, and in many cases the news options on the web are dominated by the same corporate interests as are the rest of the media, the Internet provides a way for the motivated individual to get around the biases of the mainstream media and to customize the news in a way that was previously impossible. Not only are there news feeds and web portals that allow users to get the news they want, when they want it, but the growing number of blogs presents news readers with a new and independent option for finding news online—one that allows them to go around the corporate barriers in their quest for news. Although in 2008 only 10 percent of the public reported regularly reading blogs for information about current events and politics, that remains a huge number of Americans who are logging on to get their political news from this alternative source.[40] In addition, the growing number of cell phone users offers another way for people to access customized news, with owners of smart phones notable for their heavy news consumption.[41] The fact that these tech-savvy news readers are disproportionately well educated and young suggests that America's news-reading habits may be changing dramatically, and that the web may come closer to realizing its potential for offering a truly democratic, practical, and "free" alternative to the corporate-produced news we now receive.

> ## *Can a corporately owned press be a free press?*
>
> **Thinking Outside the Box**

Regulation of the Media

The media in America are almost entirely privately owned, but they do not operate without some public control. Although the principle of freedom of the press keeps the print media almost free of restriction (see Chapter 5), the

Net Neutrality

Many people feel that the World Wide Web, or Internet, should be a free service everyone can access, as this poster illustrates.

broadcast media have been treated differently. In the early days of radio, great public enthusiasm for the new medium resulted in so many radio stations that signal interference threatened to damage the whole industry. Broadcasters asked the government to impose some order, which it did with the passage of the Federal Communications Act, creating the Federal Communications Commission (FCC), an independent regulatory agency, in 1934.

Because access to the airwaves was considered a scarce resource, the government acted to ensure that radio and television serve the public interest by representing a variety of viewpoints. Accordingly, the 1934 bill contained three provisions designed to ensure fairness in broadcasting:

- *The equal time rule.* The *equal time rule* means that if a station allows a candidate for office to buy or use airtime outside of regular news broadcasts, it must allow all candidates that opportunity. On its face, this provision seems to give the public a chance to hear from candidates of all ideologies and political parties, but in actuality, it often has the reverse effect. Confronted with the prospect of allowing every

candidate to speak, no matter how slight the chance of his or her victory and how small an audience is likely to tune in, many stations instead opt to allow none to speak at all. This rule has been suspended for purposes of televising political debates. Minor-party candidates may be excluded and may appeal to the FCC if they think they have been unfairly left out.

- *The fairness doctrine.* The *fairness doctrine* extended beyond election broadcasts; it required that stations give free airtime to issues that concerned the public and to opposing sides when controversial issues were covered. Like the equal time rule, this had the effect of encouraging stations to avoid controversial topics. The FCC ended the rule in the 1980s, and when Congress tried to revive it in 1987, President Ronald Reagan vetoed the bill, claiming it led to "bland" programming.[42]

- *The right of rebuttal.* The *right of rebuttal* says that individuals whose reputations are damaged on the air have a right to respond. This rule is not strictly enforced by the FCC and the courts, however, for fear that it would quell controversial broadcasts, as the other two rules have done.

All of these rules remain somewhat controversial. Politicians would like to have the rules enforced because they help them to air their views publicly. Theoretically, the rules should benefit the public, though as we have seen, they often do not. Media owners see these rules as forcing them to air unpopular speakers who damage their ratings and as limiting their abilities to decide station policy. They argue that given all the cable and satellite outlets, access to broadcast time is no longer such a scarce resource and that the broadcast media should be subject to the same legal protections as the print media.

Many of the limitations on station ownership that the original act established were abolished with the 1996 Telecommunications Act in order to open up competition and promote diversity in media markets. The act failed to rein in the media giants, however, and, in fact, ended up facilitating mergers that concentrated media ownership even more. The law permits ownership of multiple stations as long as they do not reach more than 35 percent of the market, and nothing prevents the networks themselves from reaching a far larger market through their collective affiliates. The 1996 legislation also opened up the way for ownership of cable stations by network owners, and it allows cable companies to offer many services previously supplied only by telephone

> **gatekeepers** journalists and media elite who determine which news stories are covered and which are not
>
> **muckrakers** investigative reporters who search for and expose misconduct in corporate activity or public officials

companies. The overall effect of this deregulation has been to increase dramatically the possibilities for media monopoly.

Some users favor a policy of *net neutrality* that would ensure that telecommunication companies cannot use their control over Internet access to restrict or limit content with price discrimination, and would keep the Internet unfettered and open to innovation. Opponents argue such a policy would reduce incentives for companies to innovate. In 2007 the Federal Trade Commission declined to recommend regulation, issuing a report disparaging the subject of regulation generally and arguing that the industry is a young one and the effects of regulation on consumers and providers are unknown.[43] In 2008, however, several net neutrality bills were introduced in Congress (of which the "netroots," such as the posters at *Daily Kos*, were in favor, and the telecom and cable companies in opposition), and in December 2010, the FCC approved rules of net neutrality along party lines, Democrats on the Commission voting in favor, Republicans opposed.[44]

Who What How

The ownership of the media has historically influenced whether the news is objective, and thus serves the public interest, or is slanted to serve a particular political or economic interest. Democratic theory and American political tradition tell us that democracy requires a free press to which all citizens have access. We have a free press in this country, and we also have a free market, and these two worlds produce clashing rules in which the press has largely been the loser to economic imperative.

Who Are the Journalists?

Gatekeepers who decide what news gets covered and how

Corporate ownership does not tell the whole story of modern journalism. Although the mass media are no longer owned primarily by individuals, individuals continue to be the eyes, ears, nose, and, in fact, legs of the business. Journalists are the people who discover, report, edit, and publish the news in newspapers and magazines and on the radio, television, and the Internet. To understand the powerful influence the media exert in American politics, we need to move beyond the ownership structure to the question of who American journalists are and how they do their job.

What Roles Do Journalists Play?

Journalism professors David Weaver and Cleveland Wilhoit have asked journalists about their perceptions of the roles they play in American society. Based partly on their work, we can distinguish four journalistic roles: the gatekeeper, the disseminator, the interpretive/investigator, and the public mobilizer.[45] Often these roles coexist in a single journalist.

- *Gatekeepers* decide, in large part, the details about what news gets covered (or not) and how. Not all journalists share this enormous power of gatekeeping equally. Managers of the wire services, which determine what news gets sent on to member papers; editors who decide what stories should be covered or what parts of a story should be cut; and even reporters who decide how to pitch a story are all gatekeepers, though to varying degrees.

- *Disseminators* confine their role to getting the facts of the story straight and moving the news out to the public quickly, avoiding stories with unverified content, and reaching as wide an audience as possible. The disseminator role is open to the criticism that, in a complex society, simple dissemination does nothing to help citizens understand the news. In the words of veteran journalist Eric Sevareid, in merely reporting the facts, journalists "have given the lie the same prominence and impact the truth is given."[46]

- *Interpretive/investigators* developed their role in reaction to this criticism and to the growing sophistication of the issues confronting the American public. This role combines the functions of investigating government's claims, analyzing and interpreting complex problems, and discussing public policies in a timely way. Such interpretation is related to investigation, or the actual digging for information that is not readily apparent or available. Such a role is not new to journalism. The *muckrakers* of the early twentieth century exposed abuses of public and private power ranging from corporate monopolies, to municipal corruption, to atrocious conditions in meatpacking plants, to political dishonesty, and their work inspired a wide array of political reforms. Bob Woodward and Carl Bernstein, the two young reporters for the *Washington Post* who uncovered the Watergate scandal in the 1970s, brought the spirit of investigative journalism to the

civic journalism a movement among journalists to be responsive to citizen input in determining what news stories to cover

Should the media be driven by what consumers want to know or what they need to know?

present day. The public legacy of muckraking is alive in journalism today as reporters uncover shameful migrant worker conditions, toxic waste dumps near residential areas, and corruption in local officials. Many online journalists, like blogger Josh Marshall of *Talking Points Memo*, carry on the muckraking tradition.

- *Public mobilizers* develop the cultural and intellectual interests of the public, set the political agenda, and let the people express their views. This role is closely aligned with a contemporary movement in the American media called public or civic journalism. *Civic journalism* is a movement among journalists to be responsive to citizen input in determining what news stories to cover. It is a reaction to the criticism that the media elite report on their own interests and holds that, instead, the media

ought to be driven by the people and their interests. The movement is controversial in American journalism because, while on its face it is responsive to the citizens, it is also seen as condescending to them, with the potential for manipulation. With the growing presence of the Internet as a space where people can communicate and organize, public mobilization is becoming a much more grassroots affair.

Who Chooses Journalism?

The vast majority of journalists in this country (just over two-thirds) work in the print media, and about one-third are in broadcast journalism. Journalists live throughout the country, although those with more high-powered jobs tend to be concentrated in the Northeast. The gender, education, ethnic backgrounds, and religious affiliations of American journalists are examined in "*Who Are We? U.S. Journalists.*"

Does this demographic profile of journalism make any difference? Does a population need to get its news from a group of reporters that mirrors its own gender, ethnic, and religious characteristics in order to get an accurate picture of what is going on? Not surprisingly, this question generates controversy among journalists. Some insist that the personal profile of a journalist is irrelevant to the quality of his or her news coverage, but some evidence suggests that the life experiences of journalists do influence their reporting. For instance, most mainstream media focus on issues of concern to white middle-class America and reflect the values of that population, at the expense of minority issues and the concerns of poor people. General reporting also emphasizes urban rather than rural issues and concentrates on male-dominated sports. Women journalists, on the other hand, tend to report more on social issues that are of more concern to women.[47]

What Do Journalists Believe?

It is not the demographic profile of journalists, but their ideological profile—that is, the political views that they hold—that concerns many observers. Political scientists know that the more educated people are, the more liberal their views tend to be. Because professional journalists are a well-educated lot on the whole, their views tend to be to the left of the average American's, particularly on social issues.[48] Women and minority journalists are more likely to be Democrats than the average American, though of course there are Republicans and independents in the profession as well (see Table 15.1).[49]

Chalk Show Host
Conservative media talk show host Glenn Beck uses a chalkboard to illustrate a theory as he speaks at the National Rifle Association annual meeting in May 2010. The growing partisan tone in many news outlets attracts primarily like-minded audiences, and, having demonized the other side, makes political compromise difficult.

► Who Are We?

U.S. journalists

Do American journalists mirror the American population? In terms of race and ethnic background, journalists do not reflect the general labor force, although they do come closer to reflecting the demographics of the labor force who hold college degrees. How might this lack of representation in journalism affect the news we receive?

Age (years)	Percentage of journalists in age group	Percentage of civilian labor force in age group
20–24	4.4%	10.2%
25–34	29.3	22.1
35–44	27.9	25.0
45–54	28.3	22.7
55–64	7.8	11.8
65+	2.3	3.3
Gender	**Gender of journalists**	**Gender of U.S. civilian labor force**
Male	67.0%	53.4%
Female	33.0	46.6
Ethnic origin	**Ethnic origins of U.S. journalists**	**Ethnic origins of U.S. population**
African American	3.7%	12.7%
Hispanic	3.3	13.4
Asian American	1.0	4.2
American Indian	0.4	0.9
White (non-Hispanic)	85.4	67.0
Religion	**Journalists' religions**	**Religions of U.S. adult population**
Protestant	46.2%	53.0
Catholic	32.7	25.0
Jewish	6.2	2.0
Other/none	14.8	20.0

Sources: For data on U.S. journalists: David H. Weaver, Randal A. Beam, Bonnie J. Brownlee, Paul S. Voakes, and G. Cleveland Wilhoit, *The American Journalist in the 21st Century* (Mahwah, N.J.: Lawrence Erlbaum Associates, 2006); for data on the U.S. adult population: U.S. Census Bureau, *Statistical Abstract of the U.S. 2004–2005*, Tables No. 15, 67, 570, 572.

Note: Column totals may not add to 100 percent due to rounding. Persons of Hispanic or Latino origin may be of any race.

Still, even though they have ideological inclinations of their own, most members of the so-called "mainstream media" in the United States strive to leave their values outside the newsroom and to do objective work. Indeed, studies show that there is no discernible overall ideological bias in the media. To the extent that some outlets are slightly tilted to the left, they are offset by others that lean slightly to the right.[50] Most journalists, aware that their values are more liberal than the average American's, try hard to keep their coverage of issues balanced. Some Democratic candidates for president have even accused the press of being harder on them to compensate for their personal preferences. Ben Bradlee, then–executive editor of the *Washington Post*, said that when Ronald Reagan became president, the journalists at the *Post* thought, "Here comes a true conservative. . . . And we are known—though I don't think justifiably—as the great liberals. So [we thought] we've got to really behave ourselves here. We've got to not be arrogant, make every effort to be informed, be mannerly, be fair. And we

Table 15.1

Political Party Identification of U.S. Journalists Compared With U.S. Adult Population (percentage in each group)

Political leanings	Journalists				U.S. adult population			
	1971	1982–1983	1992	2002	1971	1982–1983	1992	2002
Democrat	35.5%	38.5%	44.1%	37.0%	43.0%	45.0%	34.0%	32.0%
Republican	25.7	18.8	16.4	18.6	28.0	25.0	33.0	31.0
Independent	32.5	39.1	34.4	33.5	29.0	30.0	31.0	32.0
Other/don't know/refused	6.3	3.7	5.1	10.5	–	–	3.0	5.0

Sources: David H. Weaver et al., *The American Journalist in the 21st Century* (Mahwah, N.J.: Lawrence Erlbaum Associates, 2006); Gallup/CNN/*USA Today* survey, July 29–31, 2002.

did this. I suspect in the process that this paper and probably a good deal of the press gave Reagan not a free ride, but they didn't use the same standards on him that they used on Carter and Nixon."[51] In addition to this sort of self-restraint, the liberal tendencies of many journalists are tempered by the undoubtedly conservative nature of news ownership and management we have already discussed. The editorial tone of many papers is conservative; for instance, generally more papers endorse Republican candidates for president than they do Democrats (see Figure 15.4). However, in the run-up to the 2008 presidential election, Barack Obama beat John McCain in endorsements 287 to 159, including over fifty papers that had backed Bush four years earlier.[52]

Interestingly, despite the studies showing no discernible partisan bias in the media, people today, both liberals and conservatives, tend to perceive a bias against their own views, especially to the extent that they talk with others with similar views about that bias.[53] Until the mid-1980s, citizens were not convinced that there was an ideological bias in the media—55 percent believed that the media were basically accurate and only 45 percent thought the press was biased in its reporting. Today large percentages are skeptical about the media sources they follow—both print and broadcast.[54]

Not surprisingly, the rise in the perception that the media are biased coincides with the growth of a more partisan tone in the media. A concerted conservative effort to bring what they believe is a much-needed balance to the news has resulted in a host of talk radio shows, including those of Rush Limbaugh and Glenn Beck, the Fox News Channel on TV, and the online *Drudge Report,* to join already existing conservative media outlets like the *Wall Street Journal* editorial page. The rise of the conservative media has led to what two scholars call a conservative "echo chamber," "a self-protective enclave

Figure 15.4

Newspaper Endorsements of Presidential Candidates, 1932–2008

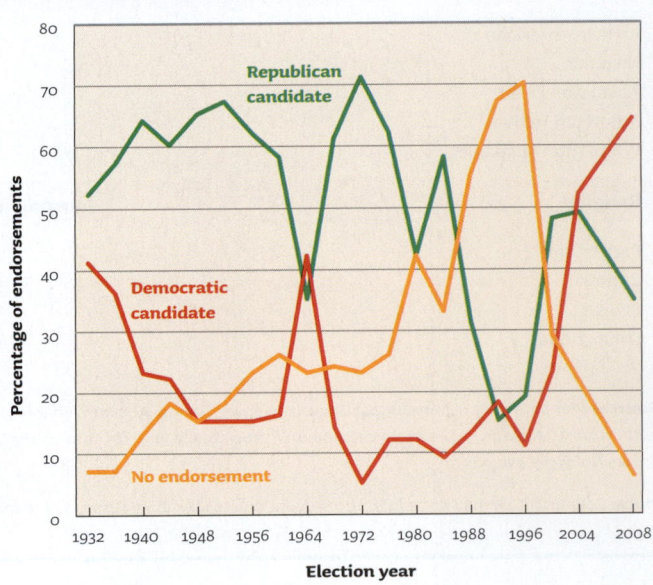

Source: Harold W. Stanley and Richard G. Niemi, *Vital Statistics on American Politics, 2009–2010* (Washington, D.C.: CQ Press, 2009), Table 14.7.

hospitable to conservative beliefs" that "reinforces the views of these outlets' like-minded audience members, helps them maintain ideological coherence, protects them from counter-persuasion, reinforces conservative values and dispositions . . . and distances listeners, readers, and viewers from 'liberals' in general and Democrats in particular."[55]

revolving door the tendency of public officials, journalists, and lobbyists to move between public and private sector (media, lobbying) jobs

pundit a professional observer and commentator on politics

The increasing effectiveness of this Republican media machine has led liberals, especially after media coverage of the Clinton impeachment, the 2000 election recount, the swift-boating of John Kerry, and the rise of the Tea Party movement, to argue that the media are biased against them.[56] Their response, in the form of shows—like *Countdown With Keith Olbermann* and the *Rachel Maddow Show* on MSNBC, and the online *Huffington Post* (among other blogs and liberal web sites)—now contributes a powerful liberal voice, but one nowhere nearly as effective politically as the conservative voice already in place. This is due partly to the different values that conservatives and liberals bring to the table. Liberals can't settle on a single truth to promote and often argue as much among themselves as with their ideological opponents. Conservatives, on the other hand, are more willing to silence their own party members who don't conform to the conservative ideal they believe Ronald Reagan embodied.[57]

When Americans, most of whom hold moderate views somewhere in the political center, listen to these overtly partisan media sources, it is no wonder that they perceive the media as biased in one direction or another. In 2010, at his "Rally to Restore Sanity and/or Fear," held on the Washington Mall, comedian Jon Stewart blasted what he called the "24-hour political pundit perpetual panic conflictinator," accusing cable news outlets on both sides of demonizing each other so severely that they were creating a political environment in which compromise and cooperation are well nigh impossible.

The Growth of the Washington Press Corps

From a news-gathering perspective, America is organized into beats, identifiable areas covered by reporters who become familiar with their territories, get to know the sources of their stories, and otherwise institutionalize their official bit of journalistic "turf." Typical beats include the police, politics, business, education, and sports, and these can be broken down into even more specialized areas, such as the White House, Congress, and the Supreme Court. News that doesn't fit neatly into a preexisting beat may not get well covered or may turn up in unexpected places. For instance, in the 1960s, political news about women was rare. When the National Organization for Women was formed in 1966, the *Washington Post* did not mention it and the *New York Times* ran its story on the "Food, Fashion, Family, and Furnishings" page under a recipe for roasting turkey.[58]

The beat system, however, is well entrenched in American journalism, and at the top echelon of American journalists are those who cover the national political beat in Washington. National politics takes place in Washington—not just the interactions of Congress, the president, and the courts but also the internal workings of political parties and the rival lobbying of interest groups, including states, major corporations, and other national organizations. For a political reporter, Washington is the coveted place to be.

The Revolving Door

As the *Washington Post*'s David Broder points out, the concentration of politics, politicians, and reporters in Washington leads to "a complex but cozy relationship between journalists and public officials."[59] Washington journalists share an interest in politics with politicians, they have similar educations, they often make about the same amount of money, and they are in many ways natural colleagues and friends. So much do journalists and politicians have in common that they often exchange jobs with ease, in a trend that Broder calls the "revolving door."

The ***revolving door***, like the practice we discussed in Chapter 13, refers to the practice of journalists taking positions in government and then returning to journalism again, or vice versa, perhaps several times over. The number of prominent journalists who have gone through this revolving door is legion, including such notables as George Stephanopoulos, a Clinton adviser who now hosts *Good Morning America* on ABC; Karl Rove, President George W. Bush's political adviser who is now a commentator on Fox; and the late Tony Snow, who went from a career in television to being Bush's press secretary, to name only a few.[60]

The Rise of the Pundit

Many of those who return to the media through the revolving door find themselves joining the ranks of the journalists and academics who have earned the unofficial and slightly tongue-in-cheek title of ***pundit***. A pundit is traditionally a learned person, someone professing great wisdom. In contemporary media parlance, it has come to mean a professional observer and commentator on politics—a person skilled in the ways of the media and of politics who can make trenchant observations and predictions about the political world and help us untangle the complicated implications of political events. The twenty-four-hour news cycle and the growth in cable news shows means there is a nearly insatiable demand for bodies to fill the

© Edward Koren/The New Yorker Collection/www.cartoonbank.com.

political "panels," and sometimes the ones who appear have pretty tenuous claims to expertise. Because of the media attention they get, many pundits join the unofficial ranks of the celebrity journalists who cross over from reporting on public figures to being public figures themselves, thus raising a host of questions about whether they themselves should be subject to the same standards of criticism and scrutiny that they apply to politicians. Because they receive wide media coverage from their fellow journalists, the pronouncements of the punditry carry considerable power. The pundits, as journalists, are meant to be a check on the power of politicians, but who provides a check on the pundits?

American journalists do not mirror American society; they are more male, more white, and more liberal than the average population, although some elements of that picture are changing. It is not clear, however, how much difference this profile makes in the public's perception of the news it gets. In the high-stakes world of Washington journalism, the tight relationship between journalists and politicians provides citizens with more information and a more complete context in which to understand it. But the link also requires citizens to be skeptical about what they hear and who they hear it from.

Who What How

The Media and Politics
Manipulating information to influence who gets what and how

As we have seen, the American media make up an amazingly complex institution. Once primarily a nation of print journalism, the United States is now in the grip of the electronic media. Television has changed the American political landscape, and now the Internet promises, or threatens, to do the same. Privately owned, the media have a tendency to represent the corporate interest, but that influence is countered to some extent by the professional concerns of journalists. Still, some of those at the upper levels of the profession, those who tend to report to us on national politics, have very close links with the political world they cover, and this too influences the news we get. What is the effect of all this on American politics? In this section we look at four major areas of media influence on politics: the shaping of public opinion, the portrayal of politics as conflict and image, the use of public relations strategies by politicians, and the reduction in political accountability.

The Shaping of Public Opinion

As we saw in Chapter 11, the media are among the main agents of political socialization: they help to transfer political values from one generation to the next and to shape political views in general. We have already looked at the question of bias in the media and noted that not only is there a corporate or commercial bias, but that Americans are also increasingly convinced that the news media are ideologically biased. Political scientists acknowledge that ideological bias may exist, but they conclude that it isn't so much that the media tell us what to think as that they tell us what to think *about*. These scholars have documented four kinds of media effects on our thinking: agenda setting, priming, framing, and persuasion by professional communicators.[61]

Agenda Setting

Most of us get most of our news from television, but television is limited in the number of the many daily political events it can cover. As political scientists Shanto Iyengar and Donald Kinder say, television news is "news that matters,"[62] which means that television reporters perform the function of agenda setting. When television reporters choose to cover an event, they are telling us that out of all the events happening,

priming the way in which the media's emphasis on particular characteristics of people, events, or issues influences the public's perception of those people, events, or issues

framing process through which the media emphasize particular aspects of a news story, thereby influencing the public's perception of the story

this one is important and we should pay attention. A classic example of agenda setting in television news concerns the famine in Ethiopia that hit the American airwaves in 1984 in the form of a freelance film that NBC's Tom Brokaw insisted on showing on *The Nightly News*. Although the Ethiopian famine had been going on for over a decade, it became news only after NBC chose to make it news, and the famine was a major concern for the American public for almost a year. U.S. government food aid rose from $23 million in 1984 to $98 million after the NBC broadcast.[63]

The agenda-setting role of the media is not the last word, however. When Americans lost interest in the famine, the network coverage ceased, although the famine itself did not. Often the media will be fascinated with an event that simply fails to resonate with the public. Despite extensive media coverage of President Bill Clinton's affair with White House intern Monica Lewinsky in 1998, public opinion polls continued to show that the public did not think it was an issue worthy of the time the media spent on it.

Priming

Closely related to agenda setting, *priming* refers to the ways that the media influence how people and events should be evaluated by things that they emphasize as important. The theory of priming says that if the media are constantly emphasizing crime, then politicians, and particularly the president, will be evaluated on how well they deal with crime. If the media emphasize the environment, then that will become the relevant yardstick for evaluation. During George W. Bush's presidential campaign, the media emphasized the intelligence of the candidates, causing many of Bush's verbal gaffes to be seen as indications of his intelligence. He continued to misspeak in the same ways after he became president, but once the war on terrorism began, those in the media chose to emphasize different yardsticks—such as leadership and calmness—for evaluating Bush's performance, and his intelligence was no longer seen as an issue. In effect, according to this concept, the media tell us not only what to think about but also how to think about those things. Priming has been supported with empirical evidence,[64] although it is clearly not in effect all the time on all the issues.

Framing

A third media effect on our thinking is called *framing*. Just as a painting's appearance can be altered by changing its frame, a political event can look different to us depending on how the media frame it—that is, what they choose to

emphasize in their coverage. For example, people view a war differently depending on whether the coverage highlights American casualties or military victories. Similarly, the story of a mother on welfare can emphasize the circumstances of her personal life, leading to the conclusion that she is responsible for her plight, or it can emphasize national data on education, poverty levels, and unemployment, implying that social forces are to blame. The important point about framing is that how the media present a political issue or event may affect how the public perceives that issue, whether they see it as a problem, and who they view as responsible for solving it.

Persuasion by Professional Communicators

Finally, some political scientists argue that the media affect public opinion because viewers, who often don't have the time or background to research the issues themselves, sometimes change their minds to agree with trusted newscasters and expert sources.[65] Familiar with this phenomenon, when President Lyndon Johnson heard popular CBS news anchor Walter Cronkite take a stand against American involvement in Vietnam, he told an aide it was "all over." Predicting that the public would follow the lead of one of the most trusted figures in America, he knew there would be little support for a continued war effort. Often, however, especially in the age of cable news and multiple broadcast choices, the communicators on whom the media rely are not revered figures like "Uncle Walter," but people who regularly pass through the revolving door and whose objectivity cannot be taken for granted.

Do Media Effects Matter?

The effects of agenda setting, priming, framing, and expert persuasion should not be taken to mean that we are all unwitting dupes of the media. In the first place, these are not iron-clad rules; they are tendencies that scholars have discovered and confirmed with experimentation and public opinion surveys. That means that they hold true for many but not all people. Members of the two major political parties, for instance, are less affected by agenda setting than are independents, perhaps because the latter do not have a party to rely on to tell them what is important.[66]

Second, we bring our own armor to the barrage of media effects we face regularly. We all filter our news watching through our own ideas, values, and distinct perspectives. Scholars who emphasize that audiences are active, not passive, consumers of the media say that people counter the effects of the media by setting their own agendas and processing the

Where you get your news matters. One of the more interesting media studies done in recent years showed a clear relationship between where people get their news and the accuracy of their beliefs about the war in Iraq. A series of three polls taken from June through September 2003 found that a surprising number of U.S. adults had the following misperceptions on aspects of the situation in Iraq:

- Evidence of links between Iraq and al Qaeda has been found. [No evidence has been found.]

- Weapons of mass destruction have been found in Iraq. [No such weapons have been found.]

- World public opinion favored the United States going to war with Iraq. [World opinion was strongly opposed to the U.S. invasion of Iraq.]

The figure shows the relationship between having misperceptions on these issues and respondents' primary media sources. The highest rates of misperceptions occurred among Fox News viewers, among whom 80 percent had at least one of the above items wrong. The most accurate perceptions were among the Public Broadcasting System (PBS) and National Public Radio (NPR) audience, in which just 23 percent had any misperceptions on the above items. Interestingly, these media source effects held up

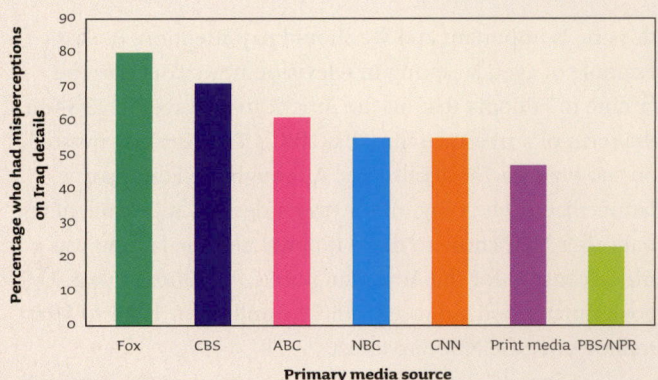

Source: Steve Kull, "Misperceptions, the Media and the Iraq War," the PIPA/Knowledge Networks Poll, October 2, 2003, www.pipa.org.

even when levels of education and partisanship were taken into account. Researchers have not been able to determine causality here. That is, they do not know whether Fox's support of the Bush administration's war effort led to the misperceptions being held, or whether supporters of the president who already held the misperceptions decided to watch Fox.

news in light of those agendas. That is, viewers exercise *selective perception*; they filter information through their own values and interests, thereby determining the news items they will pay attention to, the items they will remember, and the items they will forget.[67] If people do not seem to be well informed on the issues emphasized by the media, it may be that they do not see them as having an effect on their lives. The point is that as consumers, we do more than passively absorb the messages and values provided by the media.

This same point can be made with respect to ideological bias in the news. While researchers have tried to look at whether the ideological slant of a news source makes a difference to one's perception of the news, it is a difficult question to answer since people seem to gravitate to the sources that they agree with. Are their views shaped by bias in the news, or do they choose the bias they prefer to be exposed to? A 2003 study looking at misperceptions about the Iraq war (specifically, beliefs that there was evidence of links between al Qaeda and Saddam Hussein, that weapons of mass destruction had been found in Iraq, and that world opinion favored U.S. action in Iraq) concluded that the frequency with which those beliefs were held varied dramatically with the

primary source of a person's news. Watchers of the Fox News Channel (which tended to be more supportive of the Bush administration) held those misperceptions much more frequently than did those who got their news from other sources.[68] (See the box, "Media and Misperception.")

The Portrayal of Politics as Conflict and Image

In addition to shaping public opinion, the media also affect politics by their tendency to portray complex and substantive political issues as questions of personal image and contests between individuals. Rather than examining the details and nuances of policy differences, the media tend to focus on image and to play up personalities and conflicts even when their readers and viewers say they want something quite different. The effect of this, according to some researchers, is to make politics seem negative and to increase popular cynicism.

Horse-Race Journalism

Horse-race journalism refers to the media's tendency to see politics as competition between individuals. Rather than

selective perception the phenomenon of filtering incoming information through personal values and interests

horse-race journalism the media's focus on the competitive aspects of politics rather than on actual policy proposals and political decisions

sound bite a brief, snappy excerpt from a public figure's speech that is easy to repeat on the news

feeding frenzy excessive press coverage of an embarrassing or scandalous subject

reporting on the policy differences between politicians or the effects their proposals will have on ordinary Americans, today's media tend to report on politics as if it were a battle between individual gladiators or a game of strategy and wit but not substance. This sort of journalism not only shows politics in the most negative light, as if politicians cared only to score victories off one another in a never-ending fight to promote their own self-interests, but it also ignores the concerns that citizens have about politics.

As journalist James Fallows points out, when citizens are given a chance to ask questions of politicians, they focus on all the elements of politics that touch their lives: taxes, wars, Social Security, student loans, education, and welfare.[69] But journalists focus on questions of strategy, popularity, and relative positioning in relation to real or imagined rivals. Fallows gives the following example of coverage of the 1996 presidential campaign. When interviewed by former CBS anchor Dan Rather about Bill Clinton's reelection campaign, Senator Ted Kennedy, D-Mass., started to speak about the balanced budget amendment, which was supported by many Americans but not by the president. Rather responded, "Senator, you know I'd talk about these things the rest of the afternoon, but let's move quickly to politics. Do you expect Bill Clinton to be the Democratic nominee for reelection in 1996?"[70] The obsession with who is winning makes the coverage of campaigns, or of partisan battles in Congress, or of disputes between the president and Congress far more trivial than it needs to be, and far less educational to the American public. ("*Consider the Source: Don't Be Fooled by the Media*" will help you get beyond the horse-race coverage in much of today's media.)

The Emphasis on Image

Television is primarily an entertainment medium and, by its nature, one that is focused on image: what people look like, what they sound like, and how an event is staged and presented. Television, and to some extent its competitors in the print media, concentrates on doing what it does well: giving us pictures of politics instead of delving beneath the surface. This has the effect of leading us to value the more superficial aspects of politics, even if only subconsciously. An early and telling example was the 1960 presidential debate between Richard Nixon and John F. Kennedy, when the young and telegenic Kennedy presented a more presidential image than the swarthy and sweating Nixon and won both the debate and the election. Combine this emphasis on image with horse-race journalism, and the result is a preoccupation with appearance

and strategy at the cost of substance. In their coverage of the 2000 presidential debates, the media focused on candidate Al Gore's impatient behavior as he rolled his eyes and heaved sighs of exasperation while Bush was speaking, rather than on the substance of what either candidate had to say. History repeated itself in the coverage of the 2008 debates, when commentators fixed on the contempt that John McCain showed for Barack Obama, manifested in grimaces, rolling eyes, and a refusal to look at his opponent. Viewers named the calmer, more comfortable-looking Obama the winner of the debates by a large margin.

The words of politicians are being similarly reduced to the audio equivalent of a snapshot, the **sound bite**. A sound bite is a short block of speech by a politician that makes it on the news. Like the film clips of Gore's debate behavior, these are often played repetitively and can drown out the substance of the message a politician wishes to convey. Occasionally they can come back to haunt a politician, as did George H. W. Bush's famous 1988 promise, "Read my lips, no new taxes," broken in 1992 when, as president, he did, in fact, support a tax hike. The amount of time that the electronic media devote to the actual words a politician utters is shrinking. In 2000 the average length for a sound bite from a presidential candidate on the nightly network news was 7.3 seconds, down from 10 seconds in 1992 and 42 seconds in 1968.[71] Journalists use the extra time to interpret what we have heard and often to put it into the horse-race metaphor we just discussed.[72]

The emphasis on superficial image is exacerbated by the competition among media outlets. Ratings wars have led television news shows to further reduce the substance of their coverage under the assumption that audiences want more "light" news. To make way for the human interest features—such as medical advances, pet stories, and scandals—that they believe will attract viewers, networks must reduce the time available for the major news events of the day—what one critic calls an effort to "dumb down the content" of news.[73]

Scandal Watching

Reporters also tend to concentrate on developing scandals to the exclusion of other, possibly more relevant, news events. At the end of the summer of 2008, when former Democratic candidate John Edwards revealed that he had had an affair with a campaign staffer, media attention focused immediately and obsessively on Edwards, who had been out of the race for months, rather than on the two candidates, Obama and McCain, who were still contending for the presidency. Political scientist Larry Sabato refers to this behavior as a **feeding frenzy**:

As we have seen in this chapter, many forces are working to make the citizen's job difficult when it comes to getting, following, and interpreting the news. But forewarned is forearmed, and the knowledge you have gained can turn you into the savviest of media consumers. Journalist Carlin Romano says, "What the press covers matters less in the end than how the public reads. Effective reading of the news requires not just a key—a Rosetta stone by which to decipher current clichés—but an activity, a regimen." [1] When you read the paper, watch the news, listen to the radio, or surf the Internet, try to remember to ask yourself the following questions. This will be a lot more work than just letting the words wash over you or pass before your eyes, but as a payoff you will know more and be less cynical about politics; you will be less likely to be manipulated, either by the media or by more knowledgeable friends and family; and, as a bonus, you will be a more effective, sophisticated, and satisfied citizen. Here are the questions. Keep a copy in your wallet.

1. **Who owns this media source?** Look at the page in newspapers and magazines that lists the publisher and editors. Take note of radio and television call letters. Check out Figure 15.3 and see if the source is owned by one of the media conglomerates shown there. Look to see who takes credit for a web site. What could be this owner's agenda? Is it corporate, political, ideological? How might that agenda affect the news?

2. **Who is this journalist (reporter, anchor, webmaster, etc.)?** Does he or she share the characteristics of the average American or of the media elite? How might that affect his or her perspective on the news? Has he or she been in politics? In what role? How might that affect how he or she sees current political events? Some of this information might be hard to find at first, but if a particular journalist appears to have a special agenda, it might be worth the extra research to find out.

3. **What is the news of the day?** How do the news stories covered by your source (radio, TV, newspaper, magazine, or web) compare to the stories covered elsewhere? Why are these stories covered and not others? Who makes the decisions? How are the stories framed? Are positive or negative aspects emphasized? What standards do the journalists suggest you use to evaluate the story—that is, what standards do they seem to focus on?

4. **What issues are involved?** Can you get beyond the "horse race"? For instance, if reporters are focusing on the delivery of a politician's speech and his or her opponent's reactions to it, try to get a copy of the speech to read for yourself. Check the web or a source like the *New York Times*. Similarly, when the media emphasize conflict, ask yourself what underlying issues are involved. Look for primary (original) sources whenever possible, ones that have not been processed by the media for you. If conflicts

---

"the press coverage attending any political event or circumstance where a critical mass of journalists leap to cover the same embarrassing or scandalous subject and pursue it intensely, often excessively, and sometimes uncontrollably."[74] Many such feeding frenzies have been over scandals that have proved not to be true or seemed insignificant with the passing of time, and yet the media have treated them with the seriousness of a world crisis. Reputations have been shredded, justly or unjustly, but once the frenzy has begun, it is difficult to bring rational judgment to bear on the case. After such attacks, the media frequently indulge in introspection and remorse, until the next scandal starts to brew.

Growing Negativism, Increased Cynicism

Political scientist Thomas Patterson attributes the phenomenon of the feeding frenzy to an increased cynicism among members of the media. He argues that it is not a liberal or a conservative bias among reporters that we ought to worry about. Rather, it is their antigovernment views—focusing on the adversarial and negative aspects of politics to the exclusion of its positive achievements—that foster a cynical view of politics among the general public. Most presidents and presidential candidates are treated by the press as fundamentally untrustworthy, when in fact most do precisely what they say they are going to do. Clinton, in his first year, was plagued by press criticism despite the fact that he kept a majority of his campaign promises and was more successful in getting his legislative packages through Congress that year than Kennedy, Nixon, Ford, Carter, Reagan, or Bush had been in their best years. Yet in the first six months of his presidency, 66 percent of his news evaluations were negative.[75] Since it takes time and energy to investigate all the claims that a president or a candidate makes, the media evaluate political claims not with their own careful scrutiny but with statements from political

are presented as a choice between two sides, ask yourself if there are other sides that might be relevant.

5. **Who are the story's sources?** Are they "official" sources? Whose point of view do they represent? Are their remarks attributed to them, or are they speaking "on background" (anonymously)? Such sources frequently show up as "highly placed administration officials" or "sources close to the senator." Why would people not want their names disclosed? How should that affect how we interpret what they say? Do you see the same sources appearing in many stories in different types of media? Have these sources been through the "revolving door"? Are they pundits? What audience are they addressing?

6. **Is someone putting spin on this story?** Is there visible news management? Is the main source the politician's press office? Is the story based on a leak? If so, can you make a guess at the motivation of the leaker? What evidence supports your guess? What is the spin? That is, what do the politician's handlers want you to think about the issue or event?

7. **Who are the advertisers?** How might that affect the coverage of the news? What sorts of stories might be affected by the advertisers' presence? Are there potential stories that might hurt the advertiser?

8. **What are the media doing to get your attention?** Is the coverage of a news event detailed and thorough, or is it "lightened up" to make it faster and easier for you to process? If so, what are you missing? What is on the cover of the newspaper or magazine? What is the lead story on the network? How do the media's efforts to get your attention affect the news you get? Would you have read or listened to the story if the media had not worked at getting your attention?

9. **What values and beliefs do you bring to the news?** What are your biases? Are you liberal? Conservative? Do you think government is too big, or captured by special interests, always ineffective, or totally irrelevant to your life? Do you have any pet peeves that direct your attention? How do your current life experiences affect your political views or priorities? How do these values, beliefs, and ideas affect how you see the news, what you pay attention to, and what you skip? List all the articles or stories you tuned out, and ask yourself why you did so.

10. **Can you find a news source that you usually disagree with, that you think is biased or always wrong?** Read it now and again. It will help you keep your perspective and ensure that you get a mix of views that will keep you thinking critically. We are challenged not by ideas we agree with but by those that we find flawed. Stay an active media consumer.

1. Carlin Romano, "What? The Grisley Truth About Bare Facts," in Robert Karl Manoff and Michael Schudson, eds., *Reading the News* (New York: Pantheon Books, 1986), 78.

opponents. This makes politics appear endlessly adversarial and, as Patterson says, replaces investigative journalism with attack journalism.[76]

Consequences of the Emphasis on Conflict and Image

A consequence of the negative content of political coverage is that voters' opinions of candidates have sunk, and citizen dissatisfaction with the electoral process has risen.[77] Not only is the public becoming more cynical about the political world, but it is also becoming more cynical about the media. A recent public opinion poll shows that half or more of the American public now thinks that the news is too biased, sensationalized, and manipulated by special interests, and that reporters offer too many of their own opinions, quote unnamed sources, and are negative.[78] Two scholars argue that the "conflict-driven sound-bite-oriented discourse of politicians," in conjunction with the "conflict-saturated strategy-oriented structure of press coverage," creates a mutually reinforcing lack of confidence in the system that they call the "spiral of cynicism."[79] But as we argued at the beginning of this chapter, the media have a real and legitimate role to play in a democracy: disseminating information, checking government, and creating political community. If people cease to trust the media, the media become less effective in playing their legitimate roles as well as their more controversial ones, and democracy becomes more difficult to sustain.

Another consequence, and one that may alleviate the first somewhat, is that new forms of the media are opening up to supplement or even replace the older ones. Television talk shows, radio call-in shows, and other outlets that involve public input and bypass the adversarial questions and negative comments of the traditional media allow the public, in some ways, to set the agenda. In fact, a study of the 1992 election showed that television talk shows focused more on substantive

permanent campaign the idea that governing requires a continual effort to convince the public to sign on to the program, requiring a reliance on consultants and an emphasis on politics over policy

policy issues and presented more balanced and positive images of the candidates than did the mainstream media.[80]

Politics as Public Relations

There is no doubt that the media portray politics in a negative light, that news reporting emphasizes personality, superficial image, and conflict over substantive policy issues. Some media figures argue, however, that this is not the media's fault, but rather the responsibility of politicians and their press officers who are so obsessed with their own images on television that they limit access to the media, speak only in prearranged sound bites, and present themselves to the public in carefully orchestrated "media events."[81] Media events are designed to limit the ability of reporters to put their own interpretation on the occasion. The rules of American politics, which require a politician to have high public approval to maximize his or her clout, mean that politicians have to try to get maximum exposure for their ideas and accomplishments while limiting the damage the media can do with their intense scrutiny, investigations, and critical perspectives. This effort to control the media can lead to an emphasis on short-term gain over long-term priorities and the making of policy decisions with an eye to their political impact—a tendency that has come to be known as the ***permanent campaign***.[82] A first-rate example of how the permanent campaign drove events in the George W. Bush administration can be found in *What Happened: Inside the Bush White House and Washington's Culture of Deception*, the memoirs of Bush's former press secretary, Scott McClellan.[83]

THE CHRISTIAN SCIENCE MONITOR *Bennett*

'...Political campaigns have become so simplistic and superficial...
In the 20 seconds we have left, could you explain why?..

News Management

News management describes the chief mechanism of the permanent campaign, the efforts of a politician's staff—media consultants, press secretaries, pollsters, campaign strategists, and general advisers—to control the news about the politician. The staff want to put their own issues on the agenda, determine for themselves the standards by which the politician will be evaluated, frame the issues, and supply the sources for reporters, so that they will put their client, the politician, in the best possible light. In contemporary political jargon, they want to put a **spin**, or an interpretation, on the news that will be most flattering to the politician whose image is in their care. To some extent, modern American politics has become a battle between the press and the politicians and among the politicians themselves to control the agenda and the images that reach the public. It has become a battle of the "spin doctors." The classic example of news management is the rehabilitation of the image of Richard Nixon after he lost the 1960 election to the more media-savvy Kennedy campaign. Inspired by the way the Kennedy administration had managed the image of Kennedy as war hero, patriot, devoted father, and faithful husband, when at least one of those characterizations wasn't true, Nixon speechwriter Ray Price saw his mission clearly. Noting that Nixon was personally unpopular with the public, he wrote in a 1967 memo, "We have to be very clear on this point: that the response is to the image, not to the man, since 99 percent of the voters have no contact with the man. It's not what's there that counts, it's what's projected— and it's not what he projects but rather what the voter receives. It's not the man we have to change, but rather the received impression."[84] With the help of an advertising executive and a television producer, among others, Nixon was repackaged and sold to voters as the "New Nixon." He won election as president in 1968 and 1972, and that he had to resign in 1974 is perhaps less a failure of his image makers than the inevitable revelation of the "real" Nixon underneath.

News Management Techniques

The techniques that Nixon's handlers developed for managing his image have become part of the basic repertoire of political staffs, particularly in the White House but even to some extent for holders of lesser offices. They can include any or all of the following:[85]

- *Tight control of information.* Staffers pick a "line of the day"—for instance, a focus on education or child care—and orchestrate all messages from the administration around that theme. This strategy frustrates journalists who are trying to follow independent stories. But it recognizes that the staff must "feed the beast" by giving the press something to cover, or they may find the press rebelling and covering stories they don't want covered at all.[86]

- *Tight control of access to the politician.* If the politician is available to the press for only a short period of time and makes only a brief statement, the press corps is forced to report the appearance as the only available news.

- *Elaborate communications bureaucracy.* The Nixon White House had four offices handling communications. In addition to the White House press secretary, who was frequently kept uninformed so that he could more credibly deny that he knew the answers to reporters' questions, there was an Office of Communications, an Office of Public Liaison, and a speech-writing office.

- *A concerted effort to bypass the White House press corps.* During Nixon's years this meant going to regional papers that were more easily manipulated. Today it can also include the so-called new media of television talk shows and late-night television, and other forums that go directly to the public, such as town hall meetings. Part and parcel of this approach is the strategy of rewarding media outlets that provide friendly coverage and punishing those that do not.

- *Prepackaging the news in sound bites.* If the media are going to allow the public only a brief snippet of political language, the reasoning goes, let the politician's staff decide what it will be. In line with this, the press office will repeat a message often, to be sure the press and the public pick up on it, and it will work on phrasing that is catchy and memorable.

Thinking Outside the Box

Should journalists rely on anonymous sources?

> **leaks** confidential information secretly revealed to the press
>
> **trial balloon** an official leak of a proposal to determine public reaction to it without risk

- *Leaks.* A final and effective way that politicians attempt to control the news is with the use of leaks, secretly revealing confidential information to the press. **Leaks** can serve a variety of purposes. For instance, a leak can be a **trial balloon**, in which an official leaks a policy or plan in order to gauge public reaction to it. If the reaction is negative, the official denies he or she ever mentioned it, and if it is positive, the policy can go ahead without risk. Bureaucrats who want to anonymously stop a practice they believe is wrong may use a "whistleblower leak." Information can be leaked to settle grudges, or to curry favor, or just to show off.[87] The Bush administration, for instance, annoyed at former ambassador Joe Wilson's views on the Iraq war, leaked the identity of his wife, Valerie Plame, as a CIA agent to discredit Wilson's opinions on the Iraq war, a classic example of leaking information in an effort to control the news.

Not all presidential administrations are equally accomplished at using these techniques of news management, of course. Nixon's was successful, at least in his first administration, and Reagan's has been referred to as a model of public relations.[88] President Clinton did not manage the media effectively in the early years of his first administration; consequently, he was at the mercy of a frustrated and annoyed press corps. Within a couple of years, however, the Clinton staff had become much more skilled, and by his second administration were adeptly handling scandals that would have daunted more seasoned public relations experts.

News Management in the Bush Administration and Beyond

The George W. Bush administration did a superb job of news management, especially in Bush's first term. For instance, most of Bush's public events were open only to Bush supporters; where there was audience interaction, he received questions only from those who endorsed his programs and goals. In addition, in 2005 it was revealed that the Bush administration had paid several journalists to report favorably on the president's policies, and the administration expanded a Clinton-era program of government-produced videos touting administration achievements that were distributed to local television stations, which showed them as actual news.[89] The Government Accountability Office has said that such videos may be "covert propaganda" and cannot be made if they do not disclose who made them, but the Department of Justice

Behind the Scenes of the Permanent Campaign
Karl Rove (shown behind President George W. Bush) was the president's chief political adviser and deputy chief of staff until his resignation in August 2007 in response to allegations of his involvement in several illegal and unethical events. Scott McClellan, White House press secretary from 2003 until his resignation in 2006, would write about some of those activities, and much more, in his book *What Happened.*

and the Office of Management and Budget has said that the agencies may ignore that finding.[90] Finally, reporters who could be trusted to ask supportive questions were favored in White House news briefings and press conferences.[91] Supporters defended the Bush White House's news management strategy as efficient and praiseworthy. Critics, on the other hand, claimed that the White House had become a "propaganda machine" to serve the president's political goals.[92] "George W. Bush doesn't really want people to get the news unfiltered. He wants people to get the news filtered by George W. Bush," said one.[93]

All indications in the first two years of his administration are that Barack Obama's White House will be as disciplined as Bush's was. During the presidential campaign, the Obama camp was famous for avoiding leaks and controlling its

> **political accountability** the democratic principle that political leaders must answer to the public for their actions

message and, although that perfect discipline has not been maintained in the White House, it is still remarkably free of public infighting and leaks. Obama's press secretary, Robert Gibbs, is a senior adviser to the president and has uncommon access and a dedication to protecting Obama's interests.[94] One difference between the Obama administration and its predecessors is the elaborate electronic communication network it has set up, which allows administration officials to talk directly to supporters and to bypass the traditional media if they want to.

There is a real cost to the transformation of politics into public relations, no matter whose administration is engaging in the practice (and with varying degrees of expertise, they all do). Not only does the public suffer from not getting the straight story to evaluate government policies that affect their lives, but politicians must spend time and energy on image considerations that do not really help them serve the public. And the people who are skilled enough at managing the press to get elected to office have not necessarily demonstrated any leadership skills. The skills required by an actor and a statesperson are not the same, and the current system may encourage us to choose the wrong leaders for the wrong reasons and discourage the right people from running at all.

Reduction in Political Accountability

A final political effect of the media, according to some scholars, is a reduction in political accountability. *Political accountability* is the very hallmark of democracy: political leaders must answer to the public for their actions. If our leaders do something we do not like, we can make them bear the consequences of their actions by voting them out of office. The threat of being voted out of office is supposed to encourage them to do what we want in the first place.

Some political scientists, however, argue that Americans' reliance on television for their news has weakened political accountability, and thus democracy as well.[95] Their arguments are complex but compelling.

First, they say that television has come to reduce the influence of political parties, since it allows politicians to take their message directly to the people. Parties are no longer absolutely necessary to mediate politics—that is, to provide a link between leaders and the people—but parties have traditionally been a way to keep politicians accountable.

Second, television covers politicians as individuals, and as individuals, they have incentives to take credit for what the public likes and to blame others for what the public doesn't

like. And because they are covered as individuals, they have little reason to form coalitions to work together.

Third, television, by emphasizing image and style, allows politicians to avoid taking stances on substantive policy issues; the public often does not know where they stand and cannot hold them accountable.

Finally, the episodic way in which the media frame political events makes it difficult for people to discern what has really happened politically and whose responsibility it is.

The result is that the modern media, and especially television, have changed the rules of politics. Today it is harder for citizens to know who is responsible for laws, policies, and political actions, and harder to make politicians behave responsibly.

Who What How

Where the worlds of politics and the media intersect, there are many actors with something serious at stake. Journalists, of course, want bylines or airtime, the respect of their peers, and professional acclaim, at the same time that they want to help keep their news organizations competitive and profitable. Their goals and rules clash with those of politicians, who need to communicate with the public; to present themselves as attractive, effective leaders; and to make their ideas and proposed policies clear to voters. The clash of journalists' and politicians' goals means that each side often feels exploited or treated unfairly by the other, making for an uneasy relationship between the two.

What is at stake for citizens is not only their ability to get information on which to base their political decisions, but also their ability to see good as well as bad in government, to know their leaders as they really are and not just their public relations images, and to hold them accountable. The rules put the burden of responsibility on citizens to be critical consumers of the media.

The Citizens and the Media

Growing citizen access increases engagement but blurs lines of journalism

We have been unable to talk about the media in this chapter without talking about citizenship. Citizens have been a constant "who" in our analysis because the media exist, by

"[W]hat bloggers do is completely new—and cannot be replicated on any other medium. . . . It's genuinely new. And it harnesses the web's real genius—its ability to empower anyone to do what only a few in the past could genuinely pull off."

It's hard not to feel like a stalker when you are meeting a blogger whose work you have followed for a decade. You have seen his wedding pictures, laughed at his dogs' antics, know all about his health status, and keep up with his political views. He, on the other hand, may have read and even answered some of your emails over the years but, really, he has no clue who you are. So, getting the chance to sit down for coffee with Andrew Sullivan, the founder and editor of the *Daily Dish* (www .andrewsullivan.com), which marked its ten-year anniversary in 2010, is just a little creepy, in a nice and reassuring way—like meeting a total stranger who has the face of an old friend.

But Sullivan, the man who describes his job as "having a conversation with 1.2 million people a month," totally gets that. He knows that his job is breaking down traditional boundaries between journalism and political activism, between reporting and analysis, between the personal and the public, and yes, between stranger and friend.

But blogging seems to be a perfect medium for Sullivan, who has in his time aspired to be both politician and writer. He is Oxford educated, with a Ph.D. in government from Harvard, and before turning thirty, he was the editor of the *New Republic*. But his academic heft and considerable brilliance is balanced with a passionate zeal for the issues he cares about. Blogging lets him combine advocacy and fact-sifting in a form of journalism that, when done well, breaks with the old models of news-gathering and dissemination in startling ways.

So, Sullivan is not at all shy about airing his opinions—he is a prolife Catholic, a conservative, British-born, America-loving, married gay man who is a civil libertarian and a fiscal conservative with a deep thread of compassion and humanitarianism running through it all. But while opinionated, he is not a partisan (though he claims an affinity for British Toryism). He refuses to appear on partisan cable television shows (though he is a frequent guest on *Real Time With Bill Maher*), and he shows a remarkable ability to change his mind about deeply held views if new evidence appears or he meets a persuasive counterargument. He was a strong supporter of George W. Bush and the Iraq war in its early years, for instance, and then an even stronger opponent of both when he began to doubt the evidence that had brought us to invade Iraq. Likewise, he is pro-life, but when his readers' stories convinced him that his position against late-term abortion was wrong, he changed his position on that, too.

What Sullivan calls his "readership of extraordinarily smart and humane and interesting people" is the lifeblood of his blog. When he seeks information, they provide it; when he is wrong, they correct him; when something is happening in the world that he cares about, they gather round in a virtual community to share the incoming news. After the 2009 Iranian election resulted in streets full of green-garbed protesters demonstrating against the regime, his site became the go-to place for updates on what was happening. Facing local news blackouts,

definition, to give information to citizens and to mediate their relationship to government. But if we evaluate the traditional role of the media with respect to the public, the relationship that emerges is not a particularly responsive one. Almost from the beginning, control of the American media has been in the hands of an elite group, whether party leaders, politicians, wealthy entrepreneurs, or corporate owners. Financial concerns have meant that the media in the United States have been driven more by profit motive than by public interest. Not only are ownership and control of the media far removed from the hands of everyday Americans, but the reporting of national news is done mostly by reporters who do not fit the profile of those "average" citizens and whose concerns often do not reflect the concerns of their audience.

Citizens' access to the media has been correspondingly remote. The primary role available to them has been passive:

demonstrators blogged, tweeted, and texted information that found its way to Sullivan and, in solidarity with a revolution he supported passionately, he turned his site green for the duration.

He says: "We were also, amazingly, the prime source of information for people in Iran itself because their networks were being stymied. People who were in Lebanon and Syria who couldn't get to their news sites went to me. My colleagues Patrick and Chris, we took eight-hour shifts around twenty-four hours. . . . And in one of the more iconic moments when Neda [Agha-Soltan, a bystander at the protests] was shot by a government sniper and fell to the ground, I got this staggering picture on the blog. We were among the first to broadcast it within minutes of it occurring. Now that's to bring a moment in a revolution instantly to a global audience of millions . . . it was totally an organic process in which we were essentially a filter and I think it was a breakthrough moment for the media."

For Sullivan, blogging is a democratic as well as a journalistic phenomenon. In 2002 he wrote in the *London Times* that "what bloggers do is completely new—and cannot be replicated on any other medium. It's somewhere in between writing a column and talk radio.

It's genuinely new. And it harnesses the web's real genius—its ability to empower anyone to do what only a few in the past could genuinely pull off. In that sense, blogging is the first journalistic model that actually harnesses rather than merely exploits the true democratic nature of the web. It's a new medium finally finding a unique voice.

Stay tuned as that voice gets louder and louder."[1]

Here are some other thoughts from Andrew Sullivan:

On patriotism:

It's not the same thing as nationalism. It is not that your country is always right. . . . I think at some level it is simply loving—and I mean that in a deep sense—the culture, tradition, constitution, and people of the place you call home. In a way I must say I have two patriotisms—of the country I came from and the country I'm still trying to become a citizen of. And patriotism, yes, does mean sometimes dissenting from one's country's leadership, but I think it's too facile to say it's the highest form. I think another equally valid form is supporting your country when the chips are down, even when it isn't perfect, even when it does make mistakes, because it's yours.

On keeping the republic:

America is actually in I think a quite extraordinary crisis right now—spiritually, politically, and economically. I don't think it's been this acute since maybe the late 70s or 60s. . . . I do think people have to understand if they are not there the discourse will be captured by someone else. And you have a responsibility—I've lived long enough to understand that. And it's easy to insulate oneself and delude oneself into thinking it doesn't really matter or I don't have to do something—but in fact you do.

One of the ways this really struck home for me was, personally, in the late 80s, early 90s, the AIDS crisis. I realized if I didn't help these people who were dying no one would. . . . And then when I contracted it, and thought I was given a few years, I sat down and wrote [his book] *Virtually Normal*, because I wanted to leave behind a contribution to an argument [about gay rights]. . . . I had nothing to lose because I thought I was going to die. But why should I have had to get to that point? So imagine that you have a couple of years left on this earth, what are you waiting for?

1. Andrew Sullivan, "A Blogger's Manifesto," *Sunday Times of London*, February 24, 2002. ■

that of reader, listener, or watcher. The power they wield is the power of switching newspapers or changing channels, essentially choosing among competing elites; but this is not an active, participatory role. While freedom of the press is a right technically held by all citizens, there is no right of access to the press. Citizens have difficulty making their voices heard, and, of course, most do not even try. Members of the media holler long and loud about their right to publish what they want, but

only sporadically and briefly do they consider their obligations to the public to provide the sort of information that can sustain a democracy. If active democracy requires a political community in which the public can deliberate about important issues, it would seem that the American media are failing miserably at creating that community.

The rapid changes in information technology that we have discussed throughout this chapter offer some hope that the media can be made to serve the public interest more effectively. As we saw in this chapter's *What's at Stake?* feature, the media are in flux and, while the future of the print media is in question, some of the new media that are replacing it are remarkably more open and responsive. The term *new media* refers to the high-tech outlets that have sprung up to compete with traditional newspapers, magazines, and network news. Some of these, such as cable news, specialized television programs, and Internet news, allow citizens to get fast-breaking reports of events as they occur and even to customize the news that they get. Talk radio and call-in television shows—new uses of the "old" media—allow citizen interaction, as do Internet chat rooms and other online forums. Many web sites allow users to give their opinions of issues in unscientific straw polls. Some analysts speculate that it is only a matter of time until we can all vote on issues from our home computers. The one thing that these new forms of media have in common is that they bypass the old, making the corporate journalistic establishment less powerful than it was but perhaps giving rise to new elites and raising new questions about participation and how much access we really want citizens to have.

One of the most significant developments in the new media is the proliferation of web logs, or blogs (see *Profiles in Citizenship:* Andrew Sullivan), which we mentioned earlier. It is truly citizen journalism—the cyber-equivalent of giving everyday people their own printing presses and the means to publish their views. While blogs can be on any subject, the ones that interest us here are the ones that focus on politics and media criticism. As is true of any unregulated media source, there is a good deal of inaccurate and unsubstantiated information in the so-called blogosphere. There is no credentialing process for bloggers, they are not usually admitted to the White House or other official news conferences unless they also report for a more traditional media outlet, and they generally lack the resources required to do a great deal of investigative reporting.

But blogs can also do many things that their more mainstream brethren cannot, and there is some truly first-rate journalism to be found on blogs. Since bloggers are not (usually) indebted to deep corporate pockets, they can hold the mainstream media accountable. For example, when CBS's Dan Rather reported in the fall of 2004 on documents that seemed to support the claim that President Bush had used influence to escape the draft, it was bloggers who discovered that the evidence was fraudulent. It is the job of the consumer to scrutinize the reporting of bloggers as scrupulously as they do the rest of the media, however. There is no substitute for critical evaluation of the news, but blogs are a media form that is truly independent, open, and democratic in a way that no other media source can be.

▶ What's at Stake Revisited

In this chapter we have seen that the world of information has undergone enormous, one might almost say revolutionary, change in the last half century, and the roller coaster ride hasn't come to an end. There are so many new ways to get information that the real challenge seems to be processing it and evaluating it. Worrying about the fate of something as old-fashioned as a newspaper seems almost beside the point.

But what is at stake in the impending demise of newspapers as a business model is more than it might seem on its face. The issue is not about newspapers, per se—but about the news they report. As Clay Shirky, an Internet expert and writer, says, "Society doesn't need newspapers. What we need is journalism."[96] By this he means information, well researched and objective, about the world we live in, about the things our elected officials are doing in our name, about the consequences of the public choices we make.

Journalism has traditionally been paid for by newspapers that have either had their own news bureaus around the world or subscribed to and supported a news service like the AP. The money they paid for news-gathering came from advertisers who paid their rates because they had no other way to reach their markets. Now that those advertisers have multiple, cheap outlets in which to market their wares, newspapers, and thus journalism, are in danger. But journalism today is also in danger from forces within. As we have seen, the mainstream media, the conventional media of which print is the backbone, are concentrated in corporate ownership and driven by their quest for advertising dollars to simplify and "dummy down" the news, often becoming uncomfortably close to their sources in the process. The quality of journalism has been threatened by more than the decline of the print media.

Shirky argues that we are in the midst of a revolution, "where the old stuff gets broken faster than the new stuff is put in its place,"[97] so we don't know what journalism will look like in a new, post-newspaper age. But Shirky thinks it's a mistake to assume that we aren't transitioning to such an age, that those who proclaim loudly that the old newspaper model can be saved are whistling past the graveyard, refusing to acknowledge that printing presses are costly to run and that the model of newspaper-centered news is

obsolete in a world where the Internet makes it impossible for them to charge for or to retain control over the work they do.

And as we saw, some observers believe that the revolution is bringing positive changes. Media critic Dan Gillmor argues that a powerful, citizen-driven journalism is taking the place of a complacent, ratings-driven corporate journalism, that information is gathered and disseminated in real time with multiple researchers on the job to correct and assist each other, a sort of Wikipedia journalism, perhaps.[98] This is the model, for instance, of Andrew Sullivan, who "live blogged" the Iranian uprising in 2009, passing on to his readers information tweeted to him from the front lines, information that could not have been easily gathered even with a news bureau in Tehran. Sullivan would agree with Gillmor, arguing that blogging is "the first journalistic model that actually harnesses rather than exploits the true democratic nature of the web."[99]

For Sullivan, the demise of the old media and the rise of the new is a positive development, making him more hopeful for democracy, not less. He says,

> But what distinguishes the best of the new media is what could still be recaptured by the old: the mischievous *spirit* of journalism and free, unfettered inquiry. Journalism has gotten too pompous, too affluent, too self-loving, and too entwined with the establish-ment of both wings of American politics to be what we need it to be.

We need it to be fearless and obnoxious, out of a conviction that more speech, however much vulgarity and nonsense it creates, is always better than less speech. In America, this is a liberal spirit in the grandest sense of that word—but also a conservative one, since retaining that rebelliousness is tending to an ancient American tradition, from the Founders onward.[100]

Shirky is optimistic as well:

> For the next few decades, journalism will be made up of overlapping special cases. Many of these models will rely on amateurs as researchers and writers. Many of these models will rely on sponsorship or grants or endowments instead of revenues. Many of these models will rely on excitable 14 year olds distributing the results. Many of these models will fail. No one experiment is going to replace what we are now losing with the demise of news on paper, but over time, the collection of new experiments that do might give us the journalism we need.[101]

And then again, they may not—Shirky's optimism does not seem misplaced in light of the work of writers such as Gillmor and Sullivan, but the truth is that what's at stake in the end of the newspaper model may be the very information we need to make the intelligent decisions that allow democracy to thrive. The jury is out on this one, but the open, innovative nature of the medium allows each of us to engage in the experimentation and work that might bring the answers. The late media critic Marshall McLuhan wrote in the 1960s that "the medium is the message." In the Internet age, that has the potential to be true as never before.

To Sum Up

Key terms, chapter summaries, practice quizzes, Internet links, and other study aids are available on the companion web site at http://republic.cqpress.com.

Define | Understand | Practice | Read | Click | Watch

blogs (p. 564)

civic journalism (p. 574)

commercial bias (p. 570)

feeding frenzy (p. 581)

framing (p. 579)

gatekeepers (p. 573)

horse-race journalism (p. 580)

leaks (p. 586)

mass media (p. 558)

muckrakers (p. 573)

narrowcasting (p. 562)

new media (p. 590)

news management (p. 585)

permanent campaign (p. 584)

political accountability (p. 587)

priming (p. 579)

pundit (p. 577)

revolving door (p. 577)

selective perception (p. 580)

sound bite (p. 581)

spin (p. 585)

trial balloon (p. 586)

Define | Understand | Practice | Read | Click | Watch

- Mass media are forms of communication—such as television, radio, the Internet, newspapers, and magazines—that reach large public audiences. More media outlets and more information mean that Americans must devote ever-increasing time, effort, and money to sort out what is relevant to them.

- Media ownership can influence the kind of news we get. Early political parties and candidates created newspapers to advocate their issues. When newspapers suddenly became cheap and thus accessible to the general public in the 1830s, papers aimed for objectivity as a way to attract more readers. Later, newspaper owners used sensationalist reporting to sell more newspapers and gain independence from political interests. Today's media, still profit driven, are now owned by a few large corporate interests.

- The 1934 Federal Communications Act, which created the Federal Communications Commission, imposed order on multiple media outlets and attempted to serve the public interest through three provisions: the equal time rule, the fairness doctrine, and the right of rebuttal.

- Journalists, playing four roles, have great influence over news content and presentation. Gatekeepers decide what is news and what is not. Disseminators determine relevant news and get it out to the public quickly. The investigator role involves verifying the truth of various claims or analyzing particular policies. Finally, as public mobilizers, journalists try to report the people's interests rather than their own.

- Public skepticism of the media has increased in recent decades. Some critics believe the homogeneous background of journalists—mostly male, white, well educated, with northeastern roots—biases the press, as does their predominantly liberal ideology. Others claim that the revolving door, the practice of journalists taking government positions but later returning to reporting, severely damages news objectivity.

- Citizen access to the media has been primarily passive, but the rise of new, interactive media and the growth of the civic journalism movement may help to transform citizens into more active media participants.

Define **Understand** **Practice** **Read** **Click** **Watch**

1. **Compared to most industrialized countries,**
   a. American newspapers are more ideological.
   b. newspaper circulation is much lower in the United States.
   c. newspaper circulation is much higher in the United States.
   d. U.S. cities are more likely to have two major newspapers.
   e. Americans rely more on newspapers to receive their news.

2. **The increase in the use of blogs is significant because**
   a. the news communicated through blogs is much more accurate than other news sources.
   b. the web may realize its potential for offering a truly democratic and "free" alternative to the corporate-produced news we now receive.
   c. it is easier for the poor to obtain political news.
   d. it will lessen the effects of feeding frenzy.
   e. it is a strictly regulated news source.

3. **The journalistic reporting of Bob Woodward and Carl Bernstein in uncovering the Watergate scandal is an example of**
   a. muckraking.

   b. yellow journalism.
   c. civic journalism.
   d. exploitation.
   e. investigative journalism.

4. **Civic journalism is the**
   a. belief that it is a journalist's job to teach the public basic facts about government.
   b. movement among journalists to be responsive to citizen input in determining what news stories to cover.
   c. movement toward making news coverage more positive.
   d. movement toward making news coverage more objective.
   e. movement toward increasing the number of blogs.

5. **The process through which the media emphasize particular aspects of a news story, thereby influencing the public's perception of the story, is known as**
   a. priming.
   b. agenda setting.
   c. news management.
   d. selective perception.
   e. framing.

Define **Understand** **Practice** **Read** **Click** **Watch**

Alterman, Eric. 2004. *What Liberal Media? The Truth About Bias and the News.* New York: Basic Books. *Alterman takes Goldberg (see below) to task and argues that the real problems with the media are corporate ownership and a conservative "punditocracy."*

Bagdikian, Ben H. 2004. *The New Media Monopoly.* Boston: Beacon Press. *Bagdikian provides an engaging analysis of the evils of large media corporations and their domination of American news, entertainment, and popular culture.*

Chester, Jeff. 2008. *Digital Destiny: New Media and the Future of Democracy.* New York: New Press. *In this eye-opening book, Chester explores the FCC's connections to media lobbyists and interest groups, arguing for a new wave of media regulation.*

Crouse, Timothy. 1973. *The Boys on the Bus: Riding With the Campaign Press Corps.* New York: Ballantine. *One of the most exciting books you'll find on media coverage of political campaigns. The author takes you behind the scenes during the 1972 presidential election.*

Downie, Leonard, Jr., and Robert G. Kaiser. 2002. *The News About the News: American Journalism in Peril.* New York: Knopf. *Two Washington Post veterans share their take on what is wrong with the American news media. Among their targets: television news, civic journalism, and corporately owned media outlets.*

Freedman, Des. 2008. *The Politics of Media Policy.* Cambridge, U.K.: Polity. *A handy and comprehensive introduction to the world of media policymaking.*

Goldberg, Bernard. 2003. *Bias: A CBS Insider Exposes How the Media Distort the News.* New York: Perennial. *CBS news veteran Goldberg claims that the media are overwhelmingly liberally biased, shares stories from his days at CBS, and goes after Dan Rather.*

Graber, Doris A. 2006. *Mass Media and American Politics,* 7th ed. Washington, D.C.: CQ Press. *Graber argues that the mass media have become increasingly important and powerful players in the American political process.*

Hertsgaard, Mark. 1988. *On Bended Knee: The Press and the Reagan Presidency*. New York: Farrar, Straus & Giroux. *In crafting this wonderful account of Reagan's relationship with the press, Hertsgaard interviewed 175 senior Reagan officials, journalists, and news executives to get an in-depth look at the Great Communicator's dealings with the media.*

Iyengar, Shanto, and Donald R. Kinder. 1987. *News That Matters: Television and American Opinion*. Chicago: University of Chicago Press. *A relatively short book with a compelling message: that television news educates the American public and shapes our perception of political life.*

Sabato, Larry J. 1991. *Feeding Frenzy: How Attack Journalism Has Transformed American Politics*. New York: Free Press. *A thought-provoking analysis of how the press's preference for sensationalized news has changed the way politics is played.*

Schaefer, Todd, and Thomas Birkland. 2007. *Encyclopedia of Media and Politics*. Washington, D.C.: CQ Press. *An authoritative guide to the relationship between media and politics, this reference covers diverse topics ranging from media-related legislation to profiles of influential media outlets.*

Walsh, Kenneth T. 1996. *Feeding the Beast: The White House Versus the Press*. New York: Random House. *A well-known White House reporter's engaging account of how the White House and the press use each other to achieve their goals.*

West, Darrell M. 2009. *Air Wars: Television Advertising in Election Campaigns, 1952–2008*, 5th ed. Washington, D.C.: CQ Press. *A comprehensive and informative source on the use of television advertising in campaigns and how political ads have changed over time.*

Define Understand Practice Read **Click** Watch

Columbia Journalism Review *www.cjr.org/about_us/mission_statement.php. Billing itself as "a watchdog and a friend of the press in all its forms," the* Columbia Journalism Review *frequently publishes articles on issues that lie right at the intersection of media and politics.*

Drudge Report and Buzzflash *www.drudgereport.com and www.buzzflash.com. Conservative Drudge and liberal Buzzflash provide up-to-the-minute summaries of a variety of political stories, events, and rumors.*

ETalkingHeads' Political Blog Directory *http://directory.etalkinghead.com. Are you interested in exploring how pundits and novices alike use new forms of digital media to talk politics? This comprehensive political blog directory offers links to political blogs sorted by political orientation (for example, left-leaning, right-leaning, moderate).*

Poynter Online *www.poynter.org. The web site for the Poynter Institute, a nonprofit school for journalists and teachers of journalists, offers useful information on issues of diversity, ethics, and interpreting the media.*

Define Understand Practice Read Click **Watch**

All the President's Men *1976. The story of how two young Washington Post journalists' investigative reporting led to the downfall of Richard Nixon. After the movie (as well as the book) was released, the number of people entering the field of journalism increased dramatically.*

The Colbert Report *(Comedy Central). A hip, irreverent, and smart comedic take on the media and politics, with Stephen Colbert as the "conservative" host.*

The Daily Show With Jon Stewart *(Comedy Central). A hip, irreverent, and smart comedic take on the media and politics.*

Good Night and Good Luck *2006. George Clooney's well-known portrayal of CBS newscaster Edward R. Murrow's fight against*

McCarthyism and the wave of anticommunist sentiment that pervaded American society in the early 1950s.

A Mighty Heart *2007. This well-received film artfully explores the relationship between media and politics through the real-life story of Daniel Pearl, a* Wall Street Journal *reporter who was brutally murdered at the hands of Pakistani militants in 2002.*

Wag the Dog *1998. The president "creates" a war on television to distract the public from a recent scandal, raising interesting questions about the strength of our democracy, given the enormous influence of the media and other elites.*

Chapter 16

State and Local Politics in a Federal System

▶ What's at Stake?

As original protests go, smearing swastikas on the Arizona state capitol building with refried beans is right up there.[1] The Nazi emblem, symbol of a fascist government and a political ideology that celebrated one race as superior to others, was intended to show contempt for the new immigration law that Republican governor Jan Brewer had just signed; the refried beans signaled Hispanic American fears that the new law would reduce *them* to second-class citizens.

The law that stirred their concern and anger was SB 1070, an Arizona statute that required police to detain those they had reason to suspect might be in the country illegally, and to verify their citizenship status. It also made it a state crime to fail to carry documentation of that status, a portion of the law that could target not only those in the country illegally but also those who had followed legal channels to enter the country and even those who were born in the United States. Opponents of the law argued that it would lead to racial profiling, that the very fact of having brown skin or a Hispanic appearance would be enough to get them detained.

The law immediately caused an uproar. Not only was it controversial on civil rights grounds, but federal officials, including President Barack Obama, made clear that they believed the Constitution authorized the national government alone to handle immigration. Arizona's law, they claimed, like a previous state law that required employers to verify their employees' citizenship status electronically and punished

those who hired illegal aliens, was unconstitutional because it usurped federal power.[2]

Arizona officials, on the other hand, responded that if it was the federal government's job to deal with immigration, then it needed to act. Thanks to a border that makes Arizona the most popular point of entry for those trying to get from Mexico to the United States without the proper documentation, the state is home to an estimated 460,000 illegal immigrants.[3] Most Arizonans support the law, claiming that the influx of undocumented workers leads to higher crime rates and a drain on social services.

There was fury on both sides. Opponents challenged the law in court, on both civil rights and federalism grounds, and organized boycotts of the state. Supporters defended the law and blamed President Obama. His one-time opponent in the battle for the presidency, Arizona senator John McCain, said, "The law is a response to the president's and the administration's failure to secure our borders. The federal government has a responsibility to secure the borders and they have not."[4]

Who was right in this contentious debate? Had the state overstepped its bounds in tackling immigration and authorizing state officials to enforce federal law? Had the federal government failed to enforce that law? If so, why? What exactly was at stake in this debate over stopping undocumented workers from crossing the Arizona border? We return to this question after we learn more about how state and local governments work in the U.S. federal system. ■

As the state-federal relationship changes, so too do the arenas in which citizens and their leaders make the decisions that become government policy.

devolution the transfer of powers and responsibilities from the federal government to the states

dual federalism the federal system under which the national and state governments were responsible for separate policy areas

Usually when we refer to "the government," we mean the one in Washington, D.C. If ever we fret about government getting out of control, it is generally the one on the banks of the Potomac that we have in mind. After all, the founders went to great lengths to limit the power of the national government, and they warned us about the dangers of letting it get too big, too powerful. By contrast, our state governments seem manageable, friendly, close to home.

How ironic is it, then, that the government with by far the greatest day-to-day effect on our lives is the one right in our own state capital? The state issues birth certificates and death certificates and most of the other legal documents in between: from driver's licenses, to marriage licenses, to licenses to practice medicine or law or even to sell insurance. State laws control most of our behavior even though the federal government also has significant influence on how we live our lives. The struggle between national and state government defines many of the important conflicts in American politics.

It's been that way from the start. The Federalists and the Anti-Federalists fought intensely over the balance between national and state powers in our federal system. Debates over the Articles of Confederation and the Constitution show that the founders were well aware that the rules dividing the power between the states and the national government were crucial in determining who would be the winners and the losers in the new country. Where decisions are made—in Washington, D.C., or in the state capitals—would make a big difference in "who gets what, and how."

In this chapter we focus on the challenges that states and localities face in the context of American federalism, both today and historically. Specifically, in this chapter you will learn about

- **the structure of federalism today, and the ways the national government tries to secure state cooperation (recap from Chapter 4)**

- **the political cultures that exist in different states and the policy differences these cultures generate**

- **the variety of rules established by state constitutions, and how those rules affect the progress of devolution**

- **state political institutions and the changes in those institutions as they evolve to manage the new tasks that states take on**

- **local government and its relationship to state politics**

- **the relationship of citizens to their state and local governments**

The Federal Context of State and Local Politics

Political motivations for preferring action at the state or national level

As we explained in Chapter 4, federalism is a continually renegotiated compromise between the advocates of strong national government on the one hand, and advocates of state power on the other. Since the New Deal of the 1930s, the powers of all levels of government have increased in this country, but the power of the national government has increased much more quickly than that of the states.

Ronald Reagan was elected president in 1980 in part as a reaction to the expansion of the national government and a wave of strong anti-Washington sentiment that continued to grow throughout the 1990s. Reacting to the demands for change, many Republicans advocated a process called **devolution**, the shifting of more power and responsibility back to state governments.

More recently, however, as Republicans became more accustomed to holding the reins of power in Washington, with their various congressional majorities and their hold on the presidency from 2000 to 2008, their zeal for returning responsibilities to the states became less urgent, slowing the devolutionary trend. Devolution becomes a popular issue these days primarily for strategic reasons when the other party holds control at the national level.

As the state-federal relationship changes, so too do the arenas in which citizens and their leaders make the decisions that become government policy. Fundamental shifts usually mean changes in the probable winners and losers of American politics. We gained some insight into the problems and challenges of contemporary federalism in Chapter 4. In this section we review some of the basics of federalism.

The Structure of Federalism

As we saw, the practice and understanding of federalism for the first 150 years of U.S. history can best be described as a system of **dual federalism**, in which the national and state governments were responsible for different policy areas. Under dual federalism, the national, or federal, government had responsibility for foreign affairs, and the states, for domestic policy. That is, most of the laws that directly affect citizens on a day-to-day basis were the responsibility of the states. Federalism was a relatively simple matter, at least in

Getting a Second Chance

Chastened by the anger and criticism generated by the lack of action and inept handling of resources following Hurricane Katrina in 2005, federal and state governments took no chances when Hurricane Gustav approached landfall in mid-2008. National Guard units such as this one in Louisiana helped evacuate residents and assisted in preparing the region for the storm.

theory, because the two levels of government were seen as dealing with distinct and separate matters.

Beginning with the New Deal in the 1930s, however, all levels of government, but especially the national government, got much more involved in domestic policy, including regulation of the economy and efforts to improve the lives of citizens in ways that had previously not been considered legitimate business for the federal government. In response to growing citizen expectations of government in the 1960s and 1970s, the implementation of new policies dealing with civil rights, poverty, transportation systems, the problems of the cities, and the environment, to name just a few, led to a federalism that is today very different from anything the founders envisioned. The current arrangement is called *cooperative federalism*, which means that rather than each level being responsible for its own special set of policies, as in dual federalism, the levels of government share responsibilities in most domestic policy areas.

> ***cooperative federalism*** the federal system under which the national and state governments share responsibilities for most domestic policy areas

Thinking Outside **the Box**

Who should have primary responsibility in case of emergencies or natural disasters: the local, state, or national government?

Cooperative federalism in today's government is apparent in data that describe the relative size of all levels of government over time. Figure 16.1 shows the growth of state and local governments (in terms of employees) compared with the federal government, reflecting the process of today's federalism: the national government tends to provide the money and directions for policies, which are then carried out, to a large extent, by employees of the states and cities. Thus the two levels of government are jointly carrying out functions that, most likely, would not have even been assigned to government before the 1930s. The Medicaid program is an excellent example. Medicaid is a federally funded program to provide health care to the poor. Before the New Deal, the idea that government would provide health care to any of its citizens would have seemed like an illegitimate use of its power. Now the federal government supplies the money and establishes the basic requirements and the base amounts that states will provide for health care. States can build on that amount, or apply for a waiver to provide innovative health services, as states like Oregon have done. Although the money comes from the federal government and the federal government continually audits the states, Medicaid is administered completely by state and local employees.

Federal Incentives to State Action

Even though cooperative federalism implies a degree of collaboration and teamwork between national and state government, the relationship is not always as easy as the concept makes it sound. From the perspective of the fifty states, the national government can appear to be an intrusive presence—the 800-pound gorilla in the room. States have to attend to their constitutional responsibilities for public safety, education, economic development, and many other policies that affect our daily lives, but they cannot ignore the demands that Washington makes on them. From the perspective of the national government, the task is to coordinate and regularize

Figure 16.1

The Growth of Local, State, and Federal Government, 1982–2009

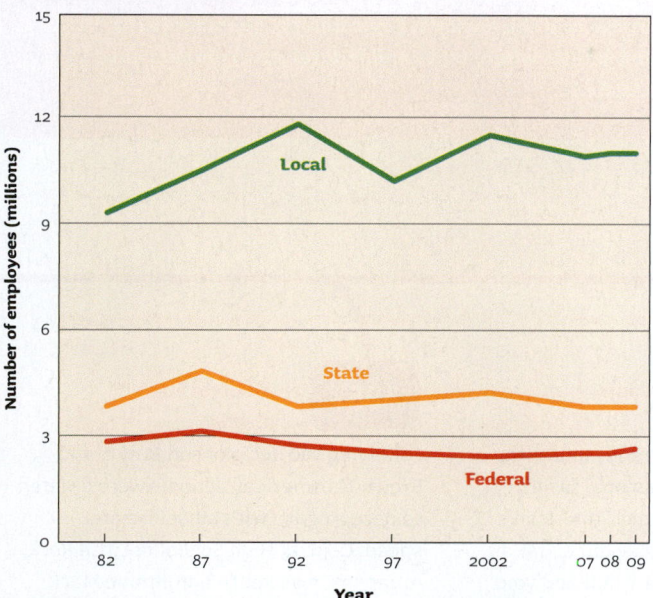

Sources: Harold W. Stanley and Richard G. Niemi, *Vital Statistics on American Politics, 2009–2010* (Washington, D.C.: CQ Press, 2009), 312; and U.S. Census Bureau, Government Employment & Payroll, www.census.gov/govs/apes/historical_data.html. Used by permission.

categorical grants federal funds provided for a specific purpose, restricted by detailed instructions, regulations, and compliance standards

block grants federal funds provided for a broad purpose, unrestricted by detailed requirements and regulations

unfunded mandates federal orders under which states operate and pay for programs created at the national level

the activities of fifty separate entities. There are several different ways it can make this happen.

It will be helpful as we learn about state and local government in this chapter if we keep the federal context in mind (see Table 16.1, which is a reprint of Table 4.1). The national government can of course leave states to their own devices with little federal guidance. But if it wants to encourage (or coerce) state behavior, it has essentially three choices: to provide strict instructions and the money to carry out those instructions in the form of **categorical grants**, to provide broad goals and guidelines and the money for the states to meet those goals (**block grants**), or to provide specific rules and obligations with no money to help the states meet them (**unfunded mandates**).

The preferred option of states is to be left alone, or to be given money with a broad mandate to spend it. Congress, of course, would prefer to give orders with no funding. More often than not, the federal-state relationship ends up being a combination of these different policy options. We said in

Table 16.1

How the National Government Influences the States

		Provide Federal Funds?	
		Yes, Federal grants as incentives	No Federal funding
How strict are the rules?	Strict and specific requirements	**Categorical Grants:** • Good for congressional credit taking. • Ensures state compliance and policy uniformity. • Heavy federal regulatory burden ("red tape"). • National policy requirements may not be appropriate for local conditions.	**Unfunded Mandates:** • Very cheap for the federal government. • Easy way for members of Congress to garner favor. • States complain about unfairness and burdensome regulations. • Undermines state cooperation.
	No rules, or broad grants of power within program areas	**Block Grants:** • Greater state flexibility, program economy. • State politicians love money without "strings." • Greater program innovation. Undermines congressional credit taking. • Grants become highly vulnerable to federal budget cuts. • Leads to policy diversity and inequality, meeting state rather than national goals.	**No Federal Influence:** • States have autonomy and pay for their own programs. • Results in high diversity of policies, including inequality. Promotes state competition and its outcomes. • Calls for congressional and presidential restraint in exercising their powers

▶ Who, What, How, and WHEN: Tension Between State and Local Power

Federalism is a clever power-sharing arrangement, but as laid out in the U.S. Constitution there are plenty of opportunities for conflict and rivalry between the states and the national government. Consider just a few points where state and federal governments have clashed:

1819 — *McCulloch v. Maryland*

The state of Maryland challenged Congress' power to create a bank because it was not a power explicitly given to Congress in the Constitution. The Supreme Court declared that Congress did have the power to open the bank because of the necessary and proper clause in the Constitution. Moreover, Maryland could not tax the bank because federal law was supreme over state law. The case was a giant step in the direction of stronger national power.

1832 — Nullification Crisis

Dependent on foreign trade, southern states opposed congressional tariffs in 1828 designed to protect American products. South Carolina went so far as to declare the federal law null and void within the state. Congress authorized the use of force to bring about South Carolina's compliance, but before force was used, a lower tariff was negotiated and the crisis was over. The conflict between the federal government and the southern states was not, however. Thirty years later, South Carolina and ten other southern states seceded from the federal government and formed their own confederacy, starting the Civil War.

1957 — Central High Crisis

Following the decisions in *Brown* and *Brown II*, American schools were ordered to desegregate with all deliberate speed. Central High School in Little Rock, Arkansas, was set to admit nine black students, when the governor used the Arkansas National Guard to keep them out of the school. In response, President Eisenhower took over the Arkansas National Guard and used the U.S. Army to patrol the school and allow the nine black students to attend class. The confrontation highlighted the power of the federal courts to force a state to follow national policy.

Chapter 4 that federalism today has been moving in a devolutionary direction but with mixed results. States would like to gain more power, and they are frequently backed by a majority on the Supreme Court, but members of Congress have mixed feelings on the subject. For many years, Democrats had the upper hand in Washington and Republicans called for more state control. This began to change when the Republicans won control of Congress in 1994, with Democrats arguing that decisions should be left to the states, where they had comparatively more influence. In recent years, as control of Congress has shifted back and forth, the future of devolution as a matter of principle as opposed to a political strategy for getting what you want is uncertain.

How the states deal with their challenges and provide for their citizens—indeed what their citizens even want—varies a good deal from state to state. We look at these differences in the next section by examining the context of state politics as a prelude to a discussion of the institutions of state government and some of their important political actors.

Many actors have a stake in the shifting balance of federal power, and in where political decisions get made. Those who control the national government naturally want the rules to favor national power. No matter who controls Washington, a fundamental tension exists between national and state government, with the national government preferring to control what the states do and the states struggling for more power to do things their own way. Various policies—categorical grants, block grants, and unfunded mandates—define the relationship, but the constitutional deck is ultimately stacked in favor of the national government.

Who What How

1987 **Yucca Mountain Nuclear Waste Depository**

The U.S. government suggested federal land in Nevada's Yucca Mountains as a place to store nuclear waste. Currently, nuclear waste is kept at plants around the country, many of which are near cities. However, the people of Nevada have sued the U.S. government numerous times to stop the project. They worry about leakage from the waste, especially in Las Vegas. The waste has yet to be moved because, as of 2010, the problem remains unresolved.

2004 **Definitions of Marriage**

A 2004 ruling by the Massachusetts Supreme Judicial Court made gay marriage legal in Massachusetts. In 2008, California and Connecticut followed suit, although in 2008 California voters passed Proposition 8, making such marriages unconstitutional, a measure still being challenged in court. As of 2010, same-sex marriages were legal in Connecticut, Iowa, Massachusetts, New Hampshire, Vermont, and the District of Columbia. Additionally, New York, New Jersey, Maryland, and Rhode Island, while not permitting gay marriages themselves, recognize those unions performed elsewhere. But in 1996, Congress had passed the Defense of Marriage Act, which declared that no state had to recognize a same-sex marriage performed in another state and that the federal government did not recognize same-sex marriage. So is a couple married in Iowa still married in the state of Indiana? The two laws remain in conflict, even as other states decide to outlaw or allow gay marriages under their constitutions.

The Context of State Politics

Culture and policy producing measurable differences among states

When the federal government passes a law, it tends to follow the philosophy that "one size fits all," that one policy solution will be appropriate for all the states. But the states often do not like the fit; they are fifty very different places, after all. The states are different in their climates, their physical geography, ethnic and religious make-up, and their economies and wealth. For example, annual per-capita income in Mississippi was less than $45,000 in 2007, compared with Connecticut's $81,421. Imagine the different challenges those income levels present to policymakers. Or compare the economic interests of tobacco-producing states, which make a lot of money from tobacco sales, with the concerns of states that have to pay higher medical costs, especially for their poorer residents, due to the harmful effects of smoking. Similarly, the older population of the Sun Belt states leads politicians in those states to take strong stands in support of Social Security and Medicare. States with great reserves of natural resources favor public lands policies that permit timber cutting out west or oil drilling in Alaska, policies that, to many Americans, seem to exploit the environment. The presence of large numbers of immigrants in states like Texas, California, and Florida means that those states deal with problems in education, welfare, and employment that other states might not share. All these differences make national policymaking difficult and have implications for the policy choices made by the states.

individualistic political culture a political culture that distrusts government, expects corruption, downplays citizen participation, and stresses individual economic prosperity; found in the mid-Atlantic region, the lower Midwest, and the West Coast

traditionalistic political culture a political culture that expects government to maintain existing power structures and sees citizenship as stratified, with politicians coming from the social elite; found in the South and Southwest

moralistic political culture a political culture that expects government to promote the public interest and the common good, sees government growth as positive, and encourages citizen participation; found in New England, the upper Midwest, and the Pacific Northwest

State Political Cultures

States differ not only in measurable ways, like population age, ethnicity, and economic interests, but also in their political cultures. These distinctions in turn lead to a host of other political differences, including differences in rules, institutions, and policies.

As we saw in Chapter 1, people in all nations have shared political cultures: beliefs and expectations about the political world that include opinions about the proper role of government, the duties of the citizen, what is acceptable and not acceptable in public life, and what one can legitimately demand of government. Although we talked in Chapter 2 about a national political culture, Professor Daniel Elazar has provided a framework for identifying three political subcultures within the broader American culture.[5] The values of these subcultures are rooted in the ethnic and religious traditions of the immigrants to the United States who carried these basic values with them as they settled in different parts of the nation.

The *moralistic political culture*, rooted in the values of the Puritans, began in New England. From there it fanned out across the upper Midwest, reinforced by subsequent immigration waves from Scandinavia, where the political culture emphasizes government action to achieve equality and a high quality of life for all citizens. Its distinctive feature is an expectation that the role of government is to promote a common good and that growth in government is thus a positive thing. There are expectations that citizens will participate in government, that politics will revolve around issues, and that both elected officials and bureaucrats will be free of corruption and economic self-interest. The conception of citizenship is very inclusive in the moralistic political culture; it encourages equality and widespread participation in a vigorous public life.

The *individualistic political culture* stems from the English and German groups who initially settled the mid-Atlantic states. With a strong emphasis on the Protestant work ethic, the fundamental values in this political culture are a belief that the marketplace, and not government, is the best mechanism for distributing resources, and that the role of government is to serve the interests of individuals as they (not government) define it. Their westward migration spread the values of limited government and the priority on individual economic prosperity through the lower Midwest and border states to the West Coast. Citizens in this political culture are more like consumers who shop for what they want than committed members of an inclusive community. Participation is entirely voluntary—government is something one can take or leave. Elazar reports that in the individualistic culture, both bureaucracy and public service are expected to be tainted and corrupt, as is politics generally, so they are best minimized.

The *traditionalistic political culture* grows from the values and beliefs of those who settled the southern colonies. It is strongest in the southern states but was carried westward into areas of the Southwest by subsequent migrations. The plantation traditions of the Old South encouraged a highly stratified view of society in which the role of government was to maintain the existing (traditional) power structures. Change is suspect rather than embraced, and government should not interfere, even to improve society, as this would upset existing social and economic arrangements. Politicians were expected to come from the social elite, and participation by the common man, and especially African Americans and women, was discouraged. Citizenship is highly stratified with people having very different, and unequal, roles in the traditionalistic political culture.

Figure 16.2 shows the parts of the country in which each of the three political cultures is strongest; in many of the states a hybrid of two of the cultures has developed. Quite a number of differences characterize the state political cultures. Here are just some of the differences that researchers have found:

- Political participation is highest in the states with moralistic cultures and lowest in states with traditionalistic cultures.[6]

- Politics is "cleaner," or more honest, in the moralistic states, as indicated by the values of elected officials and fewer convictions for political corruption.[7]

- The Democratic and Republican Parties are more ideologically polarized in moralistic states than in the other two cultures, where party differences are smaller.[8]

- The traditionalistic and individualistic cultures place less emphasis on merit systems in staffing their bureaucracies than do the moralistic states.[9]

- Spending on welfare is more generous in moralistic states, and the traditionalistic states have the lowest per-capita welfare expenditures.[10]

Figure 16.2

The Regional Distribution of Political Cultures Within the States

Although we tend to think of the United States as one large political community, scholars have traced distinct political traditions, or "subcultures," within the country that reflect the east-to-westward migrations of different religious and ethnic communities. The most frequently used classification is that of Daniel Elazar, with three dominant subcultures: the moralistic, the individualistic, and the traditionalistic.

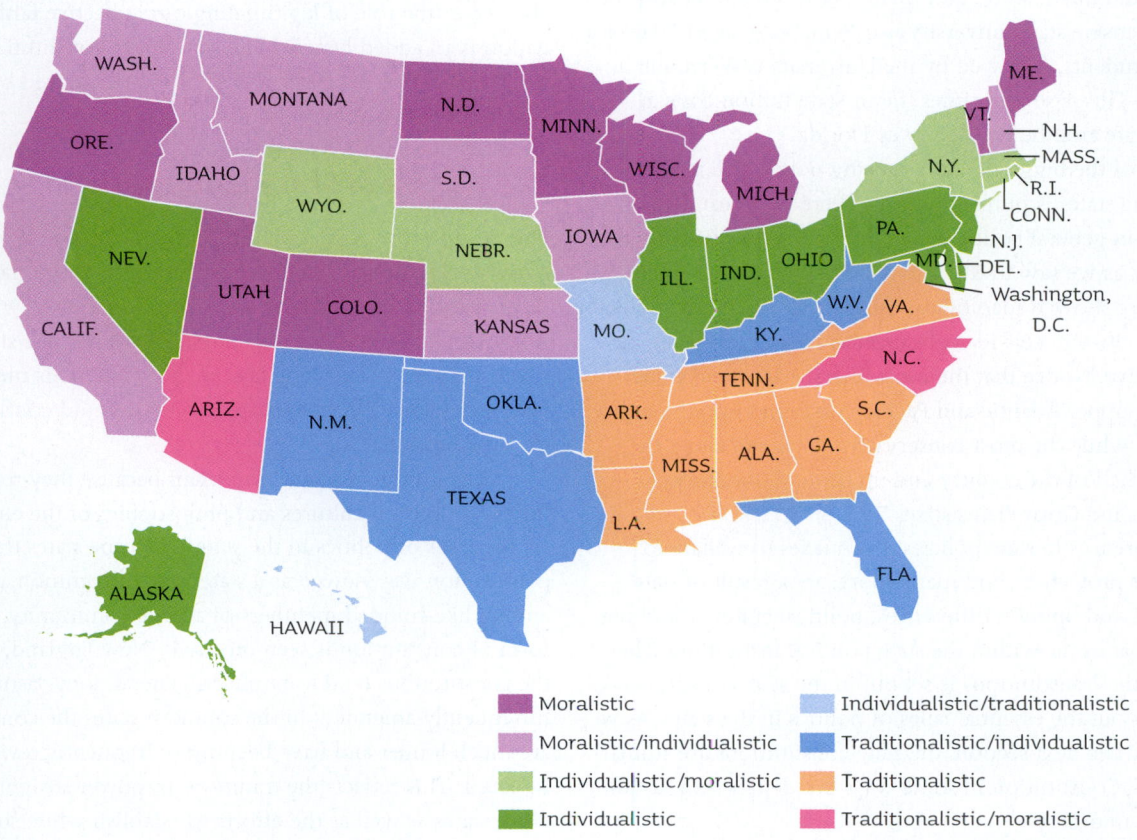

Legend:
- Moralistic
- Moralistic/individualistic
- Individualistic/moralistic
- Individualistic
- Individualistic/traditionalistic
- Traditionalistic/individualistic
- Traditionalistic
- Traditionalistic/moralistic

Source: Figure 5.4, p. 135 from *American Federalism: A View from the States*, 3rd ed. by Daniel J. Elazar. © 1984 by Harper & Row, Publishers, Inc. Reprinted by permission of Pearson Education, Inc.

More generally, the values that people bring to politics in the states do not reflect just their income, race, age, or other social characteristics. Research shows that these characteristics do not adequately explain differences in policy preferences; real differences in political attitudes persist that can be explained only by political culture. Where one lives, and was raised, has a genuine impact on what one believes.[11] State cultures matter in the things citizens want and demand from government.

Culture and Policy in the States

The states are certainly influenced by the federal government under cooperative federalism. As a result, their policies today are more similar to one another than they were fifty years ago. Nevertheless, policies in the states are hardly the same. State values are reflected in crime policy, for example, in the maximum penalty given for committing crimes. Some states, such as Hawaii, Iowa, and Wisconsin, do not execute anyone for any reason, whereas others, including Florida, Georgia, New Jersey, and Texas, have laws that permit executions for several categories of crime including committing murder during a rape or robbery, hijacking and kidnapping, committing multiple murders, and so on.

Perhaps closer to home, the states vary a good deal in how much it costs residents to attend a public college or university. For example, in the 2006–2007 school year, tuition and fees for freshmen varied a great deal across state colleges and universities. Not including room and board, the most expensive state university was Penn State, at $12,164 for in-state students, followed by the University of Vermont, at $11,324. This is several times the in-state tuition costs at Florida State and the University of Florida.[12]

One of the biggest factors causing policy differences among the states is public opinion. There is a great deal of variation in general political liberalism or conservatism across the states, as we saw in the *Who Are We?* figure in Chapter 4. That figure showed ideological differences among the states based on citizens' self-identification as liberal, moderate, or conservative. Notice that the most liberal states tend to be along the upper Atlantic and Pacific coasts and into the upper Midwest, while the most conservative states run along the southern half of the country and up through the Rocky Mountain and Great Plains states.

Differences in state policies, from taxes to welfare to consumer protection, and many more, are a result of state economic and opinion differences, political cultures, and the politics that occur within the state political institutions. The shape of these institutions is set out in the state constitutions, which lay out the essential rules of politics in the states. As we will see in the next section, the state constitutions are similar to the U.S. Constitution in some ways but depart from it quite markedly in others.

The policies made at the state level are not just products of demographic, geographic, or economic characteristics. Citizens and politicians want to make laws that reflect the deep values they hold about the proper role of government in their lives. As citizens of the United States, we want our national policies to reflect our national cultural values, but we have cultural identities we want represented as state citizens as well. State political cultures help to shape rules, institutions, and behaviors that result in policies noticeably different from those of other states. Only by understanding these cultural differences can we thoroughly understand state policy differences.

Who What How

Rules of the Game
The legitimizing role of constitutions

The U.S. Constitution is treated in popular culture as an icon; it is considered by the citizenry to be an almost holy document produced by the "miracle of Philadelphia." Of course, as we have seen, the Constitution is a highly political blueprint for the rules of American national politics. That it also serves the role of legitimating our collective faith in the nation is an added benefit. The states have constitutions, too, but none inspire awe. More often they are ignored by the public and scorned by politicians and scholars.

The Nature of State Constitutions

One study shows that a majority of citizens do not even know that their states have constitutions.[13] But in fact, each of the fifty states does have a constitution and they are important in several respects. First, of course, the state constitutions are the supreme law of the states. This means they take precedence over any state law that would conflict with the constitution.

Constitutions also are important because they reflect the different political cultures and philosophies of the elites who set the rules of politics in the states. In some states the constitution was viewed as a statement of common agreement among like-minded members of a large community. This form of constitution is seen mostly in New England, where the constitutions tend to be short, general, long-lasting, and infrequently amended. In the southern states the constitutions are much longer and have been more frequently revised and replaced. This reflects the traditions of power struggles in those states as well as the efforts to establish white supremacy after the Civil War. In other states, such as those of the mid-Atlantic states, for example, the constitutions are seen as contracts guaranteeing rights and protections for different groups. Thus, as new groups have achieved power, the constitutions have grown lengthier and more complex, reflecting the shifting balance of political forces.[14]

Further, state constitutions are of practical importance because they lay out the basic guidelines for state government, elections, and lawmaking, the rules that determine who gets what, where, and how in state politics. Included, among other things, are the terms of office, candidate qualifications, the structure of the court system, guidelines for local governments, and procedures for amending the constitution.

super legislation the process of amending state constitutions to include interest groups' policy preferences

In broad outline, the state constitutions provide for rather similar institutional frameworks in the states, even though writing these constitutions is one thing that is wholly up to each individual state. For instance, they all call for the separation of powers with independently elected executives and legislative branches. All have an independent judiciary that has the power of judicial review. All the states have bicameral legislatures that are dominated in various balances by one of the two major parties—except for Nebraska, which has a unicameral, nonpartisan legislature. None of the states has opted for a parliamentary system, in which the legislature and executive would be joined. In addition, all the states have their own bills of rights, and many of these include rights that go further than the U.S. Constitution's Bill of Rights. For example, nineteen state constitutions contain explicit guarantees against gender discrimination, and others include less obvious rights such as the right to an education or the right to fish in public waters.

In many cases, state constitutions guarantee procedures favored by particular groups, which can lead to frivolous entries. For example, certain provisions in Maryland's constitution specify the details of off-street parking in Baltimore, Alabama's constitution deals with the issue of compensation for peanut farmers whose crops suffer damage due to a particular type of fungus or freezing temperatures, and South Dakota's constitution establishes a twine and cordage plant at the state prison. More frequent are the constitutional limitations on taxation for different groups of citizens or classes of property.

The process of putting a group's policy preferences into state constitutions is called **super legislation**. The idea here is that if an interest group can gain constitutional status for a preferred government policy, that policy is safer than if it is simply legislation that can be changed by a majority in the next legislature. As a result of the politics of super legislation, most of the state constitutions have many very specific provisions, which means the constitutions are constantly being amended, either to add a protection or grant a favor, or to deal with the unmanageable consequences of previous amendments.[15] In fact, about 250 state constitutional amendments are considered each year.[16] When a constitution becomes too unwieldy, it may be cast aside in favor of a newly written document; the fifty states have had a total of 146 different constitutions while the national government has had only one (or two if you count the Articles of Confederation).

One remarkable feature of the state constitutions as a consequence of this super legislation is their length. Whereas the U.S. Constitution has just 8,700 words, the average state constitution runs on for 26,000 words. Topping the list is Alabama's at a monstrous 220,000—about the length of your average college textbook (see the cartoon above).[17] These long constitutions and their hundreds of provisions restrict action by the states so much that many states cannot respond efficiently to new circumstances. Some commentators refer to them as "straightjackets" that hamper as much as help the states in serving their citizens.

Waves of Reform

Since the time of the nation's founding, state politics has experienced several waves of reform. Interestingly, each wave has been prompted by unintended consequences from the previous reform. The lesson here, as we will see, is that rules do matter in determining who the winners and losers will be, but changing the rules can be a gamble: who gets what, and how, over time is not always predictable.

State governments in this country were based initially on the general distrust of government felt by the Anti-Federalists, who were strongest at the state level of politics, and on a reaction to the strong powers of the recently ousted British governors. The state constitutions therefore largely limited political power and provided for weak governors. However, there was much work to be done at the state level: roads needed to be built, schools to be maintained, and the public peace to be protected. To coordinate and exercise what little power there was in state government, political parties grew in prominence and influence. They could mobilize the electorate and provide leadership and coordination among the disparate parts of the governments. By controlling nominations and resources, they could strike the deals, do the favors, and deliver

The Constitution—the official Constitution of the United States of America—may not be the only constitution in your life. The state you live in surely has its own constitution, and if you belong to any social, professional, or charitable organizations, chances are good that they are founded on principles set out in a constitution or a set of bylaws.

These constitutions serve the same purpose as our national document—they establish who can make decisions, how business will proceed, and how power is transferred. They may or may not also set out what rights the members of the organization possess. Because, as we have seen in this book, constitutions are the product of what is usually an intensely political process, we cannot always rely on them to state clearly what they mean and to mean what they say.

Here are some tips you can use when scrutinizing the constitutions of groups to which you belong so that you can see who the rules are going to benefit, and how they will shape the outcomes:

1. **What is the body being constituted?** Who is bound by the document? In the case of the Articles of Confederation, the states were bound into a confederation of state governments, while the Constitution of 1787 bound individuals into a nation. The consequences of each were very different; as we have seen, it was much easier to enforce the provisions of a constitution against individuals than against states. Who is bound by the constitutions in your personal life? If you are in a sorority, fraternity, or residence hall, are only residents bound by the bylaws, or do visitors or nonresident members also come under the group's jurisdiction? If you belong to a sport's club, do the rules apply only to paying members, or to guests and visitors as well?

2. **Are parts of the constitution ambiguous?** If so, is the vagueness intentional, as in Article III of the Constitution on the judiciary, perhaps signaling the authors' inability to agree on the provisions? Does it indicate that the authors were ashamed or embarrassed, as the U.S. founders were over the constitutional references to slavery? Or is the ambiguity a result of the fact that when the group's operating laws were put together the authors simply weren't concerned about the issue, or thought it would never come up? It can be argued that the U.S. founders' failure to provide an amendment in the Bill of Rights protecting privacy was a result of the fact that they never intended the government to get so powerful that it could make serious inroads on citizens' private lives.

3. **Does the constitution provide lists of powers, or rights, or responsibilities?** If so, is the list comprehensive—does it include every power or right or responsibility that can be possessed or is it merely suggestive? Does the list limit power, or expand it? The list of congressional powers in Article I, Section 8, would be far more limiting on Congress if it were not for the Elastic Clause, which provides Congress with any powers not listed if they are necessary and proper to performing its job.

4. **Can the constitution be changed?** If so, how and by whom? Is change easy or difficult? How does that affect how the constitution can be used as a political document?

5. **Who is in charge of deciding what the constitution means?** When the U.S. Constitution failed to address that, it left the door open for the Supreme Court to grab the power of judicial review in *Marbury v. Madison*. Whoever decides what the rules mean has an enormous amount of power. Watch that person or group carefully.

---

the services needed to make government work. However, as we saw in Chapter 12, the growth of political parties also led to a good deal of electoral fraud and corruption.

The Populist and Progressive movements, active in the early 1900s, grew up in reaction to this corruption, to the dominance of political parties by big business, and to the sense that politics was not serving the interests of the common people and the common good. Reformers successfully advocated for a number of measures to clean up government, break the stranglehold of the political parties on politics, and establish a direct link between the policy process and the people. To achieve these goals, reformers attacked on several fronts:

- *Nonpartisanship* was a goal of a number of reforms, all based on the belief that the political parties stood in the way of fair-minded officials relying on expert advice and serving the public interest. Activists fought for merit-based hiring systems (the civil service) in the belief that administration should be separated from politics. At the state level, many executive functions were turned over to independent, nonpartisan boards and commissions, thus taking away from the political parties their ability to make decisions regarding contracts (spending) and patronage (jobs).

> **initiative** a citizen petition to place a proposal or constitutional amendment on the ballot, to be adopted or rejected by majority vote, bypassing the legislature
>
> **referendum** an election in which a bill passed by the state legislature is submitted to voters for approval
>
> **recall election** a vote to remove an elected official from office

Taking the Law Into Their Own Hands
Here, supporters of gay marriage rally against California Proposition 8. After the California Supreme Court legalized same-sex marriage in 2008, opponents of gay marriage fought to get Proposition 8 on the ballot. The measure, which passed in November of that year, amended the California constitution to recognize only the union between a man and a woman as a valid marriage within the state. The measure is currently being challenged in the courts.

- *Electoral reforms* included reforms of the actual voting process, such as the use of the secret ballot and changes in the layout of ballots. These reforms made it harder to vote a straight party line and thus weakened the control of the parties. Local reformers were successful in gaining nonpartisan appointed executives and nonpartisan elections for local legislative bodies. One of the most important Progressive-era reforms was to take the nomination process away from the party elites with the use of the direct primary. In the direct primary, party nominees for the general election are chosen in a preliminary election by the voters rather than at party conventions run by party officials.

- *Direct democracy reforms* allowed citizens to take charge of lawmaking themselves, rather than having to accept the decisions of the state legislatures, which may resist some of the policies the public wants. These reforms include initiatives, referenda, and recall elections.

Direct Democracy Today

The direct democracy reforms of the Progressives changed the political landscape in a number of states. We discussed these reforms earlier, in the section in Chapter 4 on "The Citizens and the Constitution." The **initiative** allows citizens in about half the states to place a constitutional amendment or state law on the ballot, completely bypassing the state legislature. The **referendum** is an election in which bills passed by the state legislatures are submitted to the voters for their approval. Both initiatives and referenda are frequently complicated and difficult to understand, but they can have large consequences for the citizens who must decipher them and vote on them.

In Maine, for example, voters were asked in 2003 to deal with a question of whether the state government should pay 55 percent of the costs of public education, which would shift much of the burden for financing schools from a primary reliance on property taxes. What would seem to be a straightforward question became pretty confusing. Voters were presented with a citizen initiative (called Question 1A), and an alternative proposal in the form of a referendum formulated by the state legislature (called Question 1B). The ballot also had a Question 1C, which was a vote against the previous two proposals as follows:

1A Citizen Initiative
Do you want the State to pay 55% of the cost of public education, which includes all special education costs, for the purpose of shifting costs from the property tax to state resources?

1B Competing Measure
Do you want to lower property taxes and avoid the need for a significant increase in state taxes by phasing in a 55% state contribution to the cost of public education and by providing expanded property tax relief?

1C Against A and B
Against both the Citizen Initiative and the Competing Measure.

None of the three choices received a majority of votes.[18] However, because it received more than 33 percent of the vote (38 percent), under Maine's election rules, Question 1A appeared on the ballot again in the 2004 election. It passed.

Recall elections allow citizens to remove elected officials from office before their terms are up. Recalls don't happen very often. Although a variety of less-prominent officials such as judges, mayors, and city council members have been recalled, only three governors have met that fate. The most recent and nationally visible was the recall of California's

Democratic governor Gray Davis, who was replaced by actor Arnold Schwarzenegger. That campaign started off slowly, inspired by the poor California economy and general unpopularity of Governor Davis. It got a huge boost when multimillionaire representative Darrell Issa decided to back the movement and former muscleman and actor Arnold Schwarzenegger announced on the *Tonight Show* that he would run. Interpretations of the law by the secretary of state made it relatively easy to get names on the ballot, which ended up with 135 candidates. Nevertheless, Schwarzenegger was elected easily with more than 48 percent of the vote.

The initiative, referendum, and recall are tools of direct democracy; they allow the people to influence state government directly. Their use has varied a good deal over time. Notice in Figure 16.3 the pattern of the use of initiatives that were put on the ballot by citizens. They were popular when they were first adopted, fell into a long period of relative disuse, and have enjoyed a rebirth since the 1970s. The big turning point was the passage of Proposition 13 in California in 1978, which called for massive cuts in property taxes, which had been escalating wildly due to the boom in property values. Since then, citizens and interest groups in some states, especially California and Oregon, have been quick to turn to the initiative to get what they want. The initiative is more important today than it has ever been. In California it has become the principal way to make significant changes in the law as, in the words of one journalist, "the voters do their thing by passing initiatives that determine taxes, set budget priorities and chart social policy—all the big questions."[19] In recent years Californians have used the initiative to decide the following:[20]

1996   Proposition 209 prohibited affirmative action by state agencies, including colleges and universities.

Proposition 215 permitted the medical use of marijuana.

1998   Proposition 5 allowed tribal-state compacts for tribal casinos.

2000   Proposition 38 denied school vouchers and state funds for private and religious schools.

2002   Proposition 49 mandated state grants for before- and after-school programs.

2004   Proposition 71 funded stem cell research.

2006   Proposition 83 placed residential restrictions and required lifetime GPS monitoring on convicted sex offenders.

2008   Proposition 8 eliminated the right of same-sex couples to marry.

2010   Proposition 19 defeated; would have legalized marijuana and allowed government to regulate it.

The instruments of direct democracy have the obvious advantage of bringing government closer to the people. It would seem antidemocratic to argue that the people should not be allowed to vote on the important matters of public policy. In practice, the record is mixed. In some instances, the initiative does exactly what the reformers had wanted by bringing about changes in the law that politicians might not support. The term limits movement is a good example. Term limits specify a number of years elected officials can serve in office before they are forced to retire or run for another office. They are almost always opposed by state legislators but have been passed in states with the initiative. In states without the initiative, legislators have blocked the policy, which most opinion polls show is overwhelmingly popular with voters.[21]

Critics of direct democracy argue, however, that the initiative leads to bad laws and is primarily a tool for special interests. Many legislative proposals are extremely complicated, and they can be seriously distorted when presented to the public (as we saw in the Maine example, above). The public may be easily swayed, for instance, by the language in which a proposition is presented. As mentioned in Chapter 11, initiatives expressed as anti–affirmative action measures do not do well with voters, but the same measures presented as efforts to eliminate discrimination have a reasonable chance of passing. Similarly, antitax initiatives can be open to manipulation. They are almost always led by a charismatic spokesperson posing as the defender of the little guy against the avarice of government. Typically, research shows, he or she is working with special interests that remain well hidden in the background. An example is Florida's Amendment 1, passed by 70 percent of the voters in 1996. It required a statewide election and approval of two-thirds of those voting before any new tax could be added to the state constitution. The public champion was David Biddulph, who campaigned throughout the state from his Winnebago, claiming to be working for the citizens against government greed. But the campaign was not Biddulph's; it was the sugar industry's.

> **citizen legislators** part-time state legislators, who also hold other jobs in their community while serving in the statehouse

Figure 16.3

Initiatives in the United States, 1904–2009

The initiative and referendum enjoyed great popularity immediately after they were first enacted in many states, early in the twentieth century. After a period of decline, they are once again being used frequently by citizens and interest groups to achieve policy changes that might not otherwise be passed in state legislatures.

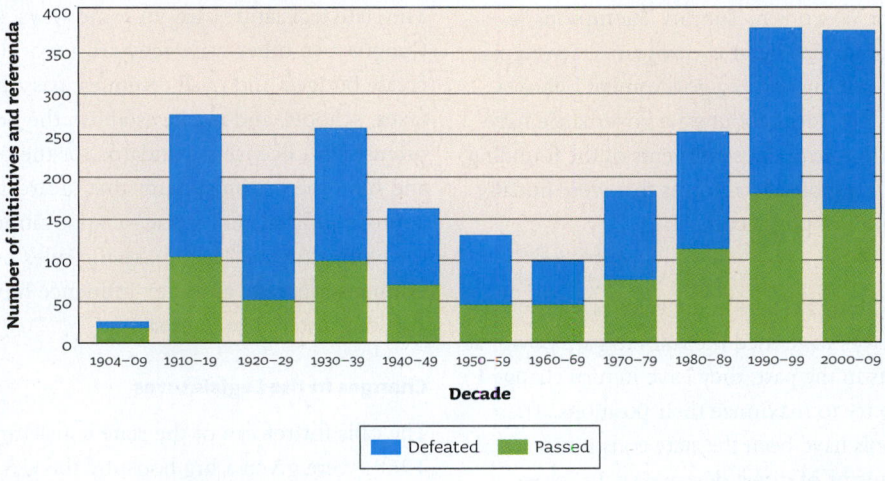

Source: Initiative and Referendum Institute at University of Southern California.

According to an early treasurer of the committee behind the initiative, the effort "was paid for by sugar, written by sugar, and taken to court by sugar."[22] And of the apparent antitax crusader: "Biddulph is paid by Big Sugar. . . . He's paid to give the speeches he gives. He's a hired puppet."[23] Although the specifics vary from state to state, this seems to be a general pattern among the antitax initiatives that citizens have been approving.[24]

Well-funded special interests have the resources to hire the firms that now specialize in direct democracy, argue critics. These firms use paid employees to get the required signatures and then hire professional ad agencies to develop effective media campaigns to sell the initiatives. The critics argue that this one-sided information barrage dupes the public into supporting bad policies that the better-informed state legislators would not approve.[25]

Another concern voiced by critics is that the initiative is overly responsive to majority whims and thus is frequently used against weak, unpopular, or minority groups, ignoring the protection of rights and interests that are more easily accommodated in the traditional legislative process.[26] Certainly the passage of an initiative prohibiting affirmative action in universities and government hiring in California in 1996, as well as the passage of anti–gay marriage initiatives in all thirty-one states where the issue has been put to a public vote are consistent with this concern. But some evidence indicates that this criticism is misplaced: a study of California initiatives demonstrated that minority voters are no more likely than whites to be on the losing side of initiative votes.[27]

Direction of Current Reforms

Many of the earliest direct democracy reforms are still in place in most state governments, now flanked by a newer generation of such reforms. At the same time, however, a set of reforms has developed that counters the reliance of state governance on citizens and **citizen legislators**, the part-time lawmakers who have served their states while also working at regular jobs in their communities. The effort to "get things done" at the state level has demanded more effective state government.

The sentiment behind this latest wave of reform represents a belief, new at the state level, that government has an important role and that the states need strong, competent governors and well-informed, capable state legislators.[28] Calls for renewed power at the state level have signaled, not a revival of populist, participatory ideology, but support for state government as energetic as the national government was after the New Deal. In fact, one author calls the administration of the former Republican governor of Wisconsin, Tommy Thompson, "a kind of mini–New Deal for proliferating programs, acronyms, and slogans," central planning and big government but on a state-sized scale.[29] In effect, ideas about state governance have finally reversed the antigovernment sentiments of the founding, in part and ironically in response to reforms that were initially intended to keep that philosophy secure.

Who What How

Many actors have something at stake in the rules of state politics. As different actors have used the rules to gain power at various points in the past, they have in turn changed the rules to try to maximize their positions. Their primary tools have been the state constitutions and the mechanisms of direct democracy. In some regions, the state elites used the state constitutions to establish their ideas about the fundamental purposes and values of government. In others, constitutions became the route by which disadvantaged groups could assert their claims to rights and power in the government. In a perversion of this practice, special interest groups essentially used state constitutions as a way to give their policy preferences special constitutional status, in a form of super legislation.

When state governments seemed to be falling victim to corrupt parties and officials, some states' citizens decided to take power back into their own hands by creating and using the tools of direct democracy: referenda, initiatives, and recall. These new rules gave greater power to the people but also left them open to manipulation by organized interests and to accusations of amateurish and inefficient governing.

State Institutions
Able to handle more power and responsibility?

From the perspective of effective governability, state government has improved dramatically since the 1960s. Many legislatures are more professional, the governors are better able to lead their states, and the courts are more coordinated in their operations. These changes are not spread evenly across the states, however, and one of the big questions of devolution is whether the states are prepared to deal with the challenges of governing more of their own affairs.

The Legislators and the Legislatures

The state legislatures are, in some ways, small versions of Congress. In other ways they are a world apart. They have to create budgets and raise revenues; pass the laws that govern taxes, schools, and roads; establish the penalties for different offenses; set licensing standards for the professions and trades; and fund the prison systems that incarcerate offenders. They approve judicial and executive appointments and represent their constituents. They make the rules by which local governments operate, and they influence how federal programs are administered in their states.

Changes in the Legislatures

The calls for reform of the state legislatures of the 1950s and 1960s were given a big boost by the U.S. Supreme Court in its 1962 *Baker v. Carr* decision, in which the Court ruled that state legislative districts had to be roughly equal in populations—"one man, one vote." Before this, many of the state legislatures were grotesquely malapportioned so that the rural counties were overrepresented at the expense of the cities and suburbs. The reapportioned legislatures of the 1960s were more sympathetic to the calls for changes to meet the growing policy needs of the states—particularly the changes in the cities and the massive growth of the suburbs.[30]

A primary concern of the reformers of the 1950s and 1960s was a widespread belief that state legislatures could not do their jobs effectively. This is where the state legislatures have differed so markedly from the modern Congress. They were plagued by high turnover and filled with part-timers who had little or no staff. They met infrequently, usually once every two years, and for limited sessions. As a result they were dependent on lobbyists and the executive branch for ideas and information. They lacked the time and capability to exercise effective oversight of the state agencies, to deal effectively as representatives when their constituents had problems with state government, and to gain enough expertise to make effective choices about what was best for their states. In short, they were seen as weak and ineffective.

The reforms brought higher salaries, and more and better professional staff; extended the length of legislative sessions; and in most states led to yearly meetings of the legislatures. The largest states, like California, Michigan, New York, and Pennsylvania, have full-time legislatures, and some of the others are approaching this. Most of the smaller, rural states retain citizen legislatures, which are part-time with low pay, small staffs, and high turnover. Examples of the latter include Montana, New Hampshire, North Dakota, South Dakota, Utah, and Wyoming.[31]

All these improvements have resulted in significant changes in the make-up of state legislatures. State legislators today are better educated, younger, more motivated, and more independent politicians. Fewer are lawyers and small businessmen, and more are women and minorities: 24 percent are female, 9 percent are black, and 3 percent are Hispanic.[32] Now that the reforms of the fifties and sixties are paying off in the sense that the states have increasingly capable legislatures, it is noteworthy that public opinion is swinging in the opposite direction. We seem to be reverting to our original and recurring distrust of government. Popular opinion clearly reflects the view that a lot of what is wrong with government is due to "professional politicians" who have lost touch with their constituents. The term limits movement, whereby citizens in states with initiatives have been limiting the number of terms that their state legislators may serve, works against the new professionalization of state legislatures by ousting their members just as they gain experience and "learn the ropes." Thus, in a highly professionalized state like California, term limits means that the state legislature, which is well funded and staffed, is becoming composed of largely inexperienced elected representatives, undermining some of the positive gains in legislative competence achieved via the professionalization movement.[33] The growing verdict of research on the impact of term limits is that they have not achieved the goals of their advocates.[34] Elections are not more competitive, and rather than empowering citizens it appears that term limits have enhanced the power of governors, the bureaucracy, legislative staff, and perhaps interest groups.[35] Many legislators lament the loss of institutional memory as freshmen or one-term legislators assume leadership positions and committee chairmanships because the veterans who understand the policies and history have been forced out.[36]

The term limits movement does seem to be waning. Only fifteen states currently have term limits in place. Laws have

been repealed in six states, four by their state supreme courts and two by their legislatures. Citizens, however, are not yet convinced, as they voted down legislative referenda in Arkansas, California, and Montana that would have increased the number of terms before legislators would be forced to leave.[37] South Dakotans voted in 2008 not to repeal the state's term limits on state legislators.

A final legislative reform to consider is size. The nation's 7,382 state legislators work in chambers of remarkably different sizes. They range from tiny New Hampshire's lower house with four hundred members, to Alaska's Senate of just twenty members. There is no relationship between the size of a state and the size of its legislature. We saw in Chapter 7 that the difference in the size of the House of Representatives and the Senate is one factor in determining the need for a tighter organization of the House. The same holds true for the state legislatures. More members means greater complexity, and institutions develop rules and hierarchy in order to get things done. In addition, some observers argue that the complexity of larger legislatures provides more openings for special interests.[38]

Legislative reformers generally prefer more modest-sized legislatures, large enough to have an effective committee system but small enough that members can work together informally, negotiate, and know what each other is up to. This reform does not come easily. Legislators are happy to have outsiders suggest that they get larger salaries and more staff, but they tend to ignore suggested reforms like reduced size (and term limits) that would put some of them out of work. Nevertheless, Rhode Island in 2000 followed through on a 1994 bill and reduced the size of its legislature from a total of 150 members to 113.

Representation

We have already seen that the states have very different political cultures. Among other things, these cultures shape what

A State's Interest

California governor Arnold Schwarzenegger meets with British prime minister David Cameron in October 2010 to share ideas about conservatism. As heads of their states, governors may interact with foreign leaders when state interest is involved, and state laws and regulations can impact federal foreign policy.

citizens want from government. Some want a vigorous state government that actively protects groups like the poor and consumers, and that enforces equality; others advocate a small government sector that leaves individuals free to make their own way. Some have populations that promote cultural pluralism and embrace alternative lifestyles; others want the state to favor traditional values of family and church.

Candidates who run for legislative seats in the different states, therefore, have to make their pitches in quite different opinion contexts, knowing, of course, that they will be assessed on what they produce. It turns out that, across a broad range of issues, state legislators do a very good job of translating state opinion into public policy. There is a very strong tendency for the most liberal states to also have the most liberal public policies and for the most conservative states to have the most conservative policies.[39] And even on specific issues like abortion, welfare spending, the death penalty, and environmental protection, the states tend to follow their citizens' preferences.[40] Overall the state legislatures appear quite responsive to citizens' preferences on issues, at least on those issues the general public cares about.

The people who run for and serve in the state legislatures are less representative demographically than they are ideologically. The candidates for the state legislatures are overwhelmingly white, middle- to upper-middle-class males. Most have not held prior elective or appointive office, though many

(about half) have held positions in their local or state party organizations.[41]

The Governors

A central theme in our discussion of the presidency was that the public has high expectations of the president but that he has relatively limited constitutional powers. The governors have the same problem, only more so. Despite their constitutional handicaps, however, today's governors seem poised to provide the kind of leadership that, in fact, may enable the states to meet the policy challenges ahead. Indeed, the governors are providing much of the policy leadership in the nation today.

Changes in the Governorship

The governorship is by far the most visible office in the states. Governors are known and recognized by their constituents; only the president of the United States is more visible among the citizenry.[42] The governor is seen by citizens as the head of their state and is held responsible for how things are going there.

The problem for governors is that they do not have a great deal of control over state policymaking. They are limited by a tradition in the states that is deeply suspicious of executive power. Early governors were not elected but rather were selected by the state legislatures (and before that, colonial governors were chosen by the king). Then as popular elections became the rule, many governors were still held on the short leash of one-year terms and were limited to running for reelection only once. In addition, the power of the executive was, and continues to be, split among a number of elected offices. We may think of the governor as the chief executive and expect him or her to "run" the administrative branch, but in most states the governor has no constitutional power over the attorney general, the secretary of state, the education commissioner, and other elective statewide offices. State attorneys general and secretaries of state frequently use their positions to advance their own political careers, often for a run for the governor's office. Thus they may have very different agendas than does the current governor. In some cases they are even members of different political parties.

As late as the 1960s, the limitations and fragmentation of executive powers produced many state chief executives who ranged from mediocre to awful. Without the resources to lead, the office attracted what political scientist Larry Sabato calls "good-time Charlies," affable men who could get elected but who did not contribute measurably to making effective policy in their states.[43] In 1949 one observer summarized a widespread sentiment: "There are some enlightened, honest, and well-intentioned governors . . . but they are pathetically few in number."[44]

Fortunately for the states, the movement of the 1960s for stronger state governments included an effort to develop the leadership capabilities of the governors. These reforms included centralizing power in the governorship, increasing the governors' powers of appointment and veto, increasing their salaries and the lengths of their terms of office, and giving them greater control over formulating the state budget. One outcome of these reforms is that more capable people, what Sabato refers to as the "new breed" of governors, have been attracted to the office.[45] They are competent and innovative, and they believe that the states can and should provide new solutions to the problems of their citizens.

The reformers have been less successful in unifying the executive branch under the control of the governor. Most states have several independently elected heads of departments, and many require that various department heads report to independent commissions and boards rather than to the governor. The states also tend to place strong limits on the governors' appointment powers for the top nonelected jobs in the state bureaucracies. Often the governor does not even make the nominations; he or she only gets to approve those forwarded by the legislatures or by an independent commission. Of course, the governor's ability to pick an administrative team is central to his or her ability to gain some control over the state bureaucracy.[46] The trend is toward greater gubernatorial control, and constitutional changes in such states as New York and Illinois have greatly increased the governor's appointive powers.[47] Ohio and Pennsylvania come close to approximating the federal executive, in which the president appoints his cabinet. In most states, however, the governor's official powers are far from equivalent to the president's at the national level. One place where the governors do have an advantage is in the line-item veto. With this power, which varies in detail across the states, forty-three of the states' governors can eliminate parts of the state budget with which they disagree. Where the governor has more control over the budgetary process, he or she is more successful at overriding local legislative interests to deal with statewide problems.[48]

The powers of the governor are important because highly fragmented power gives small, well-organized interests multiple avenues to stop, change, or otherwise influence policy. Without adequate constitutional authority, governors stand little chance of meeting the high expectations that voters have of them as the states' top leaders.

Electing the Governor

Despite the difficulty governors have in effecting change, the governorship is still considered one of the plum jobs of American electoral politics. It has been called the "greatest job in the world," by former Massachusetts governor Michael Dukakis.[49] Besides being at the center of important activities in the states, the governorship is also a prime launching pad for higher office. Many governors are successful in bids for the U.S. Senate, and the experience also provides a good base for a presidential run. Four of our last six presidents—Carter, Reagan, Clinton, and George W. Bush—had been governors. They could campaign on their successes as capable chief executives, while claiming to be "outsiders" at a time when the public was disenchanted with Washington politics. The office is so desirable that candidates are willing to spend a fortune, literally, to obtain it. The average campaign expenditures by the fourteen governors elected in 2007–2008 was over $15 million, and some states greatly exceeded the average. For example, expenditures in the races in North Carolina, Louisiana, and Kentucky all surpassed $30 million, and later the 2009 and 2010 races continued the trend, with California gubernatorial candidate Meg Whitman spending a whopping $170 million in her losing effort against Jerry Brown (who spent a "mere" $40 million).[50]

The outcomes of gubernatorial elections are influenced by at least three factors. One factor is what an incumbent governor does in office. Voters have reasonably clear policy images of gubernatorial candidates, and the media provide good coverage of their activities, at least compared with that given to U.S. senators.[51] Governors who raise taxes, for example, suffer at the polls, and incumbents who have been judged poorly by experts are less likely to be returned to office.[52] Incumbents are even held responsible for things— good and bad—not directly within their control. For instance, when voters judge the state economy to be doing well, the incumbent governor gets a clear boost in votes.[53] Incumbency itself gives candidates an edge; their reelection rates are currently a bit over 70 percent.[54]

> *Why are governors so much more successful than legislators in their quest for the presidency?*

Another factor that counts is the context of the election. National tides influence voting for governor. The strong partisan tides generated by public dissatisfaction with the Bush administration in the 2006 elections had a big effect on the down-the-ticket gubernatorial races. The Republicans lost control of six seats, giving Democrats a majority of the governorships for the first time since 1994. Similarly, the recession in President Obama's first year in office contributed to gubernatorial losses for the Democrats in both New Jersey and Virginia. These elections support studies that find that the public's assessment of presidential performance and the health of the economy are important factors in how many people vote for governor. If the president is doing well in the polls and the economy is thriving, so too will those in his party who are running for governor.[55]

Finally, campaigns matter, too. How much candidates spend—and how they spend—influences voters' decisions. In a close contest the campaign issues that candidates choose to stress can spell the difference between victory and defeat.[56]

The State Courts

As we saw in Chapter 10, the United States has a dual court system. There is a system of federal courts and, independent of this, fifty systems of state courts. The state courts handle far more cases than do the federal courts. When we deal with the law, chances are most of us deal with some part of our state court system. This is because the states retain jurisdiction over most things that touch our lives in a direct way. Laws governing property, marriage and divorce, most contracts and business dealings, murder, land use, traffic, and even pollution are generally state laws. Of course, anyone who violates a federal law can be tried in federal courts. But when a crime violates both federal and state laws, such as dealing in illegal drugs or kidnapping, the case can go to either. Most cases with overlapping jurisdiction end up in state court.

The Significance of the State Courts

The primary purpose of the state courts is to settle disputes, whether between the community and an individual accused of breaking some law (criminal cases) or between private individuals or businesses that have a disagreement they can't resolve (civil cases). In the process of dispute settlement, however, the state courts also make public policy. They do this because they inevitably need to interpret existing statutes in a particular circumstance, and when they do, they set precedents that govern subsequent court decisions. The state courts also have the power of judicial review, which gives them the authority to overrule state legislative and executive decisions.

In some cases this leads to major changes in state politics. One recurring and controversial example is the courts' decisions on the redistricting plans that follow each decennial census. As we saw in Chapter 7, in order to conform to the U.S. Supreme Court's dictates for "one man, one vote," state and congressional district lines must be redrawn following each census. New district boundaries are drawn up by the state legislatures or, in some cases, by special redistricting commissions in the redistricting process we discussed earlier. If a party feels it has been treated unfairly, or that some procedural rules have been violated—or simply that it is going to lose seats—it often sues in either federal or state court. The courts have played a role in almost half the redistricting plans for the 1990s and in sixteen states following the 2000 and 2002 elections. This topic is so controversial because the redistricting plan that is accepted often determines which party will control one or both houses of the state legislatures as well as the partisan balance of the state's congressional delegation.

Another important example of how the state courts influence policy is through interpreting the state constitutions. In a 1973 decision the New Jersey Supreme Court ruled that the inequality of spending on local schools violated the state constitution. When the legislature refused to adopt state taxes to equalize school funding, the court closed the state school system. This forced the state to adopt a state income tax, which it would not otherwise have done.[57] It also resulted in more equal funding for the schools of New Jersey but not to the complete satisfaction of the New Jersey Supreme Court. The case continued for thirty years as New Jersey's courts and its politicians wrangled about the meaning of the state's constitutional guarantee to a "thorough and efficient" education. In early 2008 the New Jersey state legislature

> **unified state court systems** court systems organized and managed by a state supreme court
>
> **merit system of judicial selection** the attempt to remove politics—either through elections or appointments—from the process of selecting judges

passed Governor Jon Corzine's "Formula for Success: All Children, All Communities," which increases the state's share of school funding. The plan may put an end to the standoff between the Supreme Court and the legislature if the Court agrees that the formula complies with the state constitution's requirement.

The most recent example of policymaking by the state courts to receive significant national attention was the Massachusetts Supreme Court's 2004 finding that the state constitution provided no basis for denying gays and lesbians the right to marry. Beyond the obvious extension of the right to marry to gays and lesbians in Massachusetts, the decision raised the profile of this divisive issue in the 2004 presidential campaign, motivated President Bush's supporters,[58] and added fuel to the movement for a national constitutional ban on same-sex marriages. The state courts can clearly be a catalyst for important changes in policy, just as the U.S. Supreme Court has been with respect to such fundamental issues as race, representation, and federal-state power relationships, which influence the outcome of many battles for who gets what and how.

Reforms of the State Court System

The different courts in the states developed as part of the individual communities they serve rather than being set up as components of unified and coordinated state court systems. As a result, they are highly decentralized. These fragmented systems vary in their details from state to state, but most have a trilevel system of local, appellate, and supreme courts. Two problems have contributed to calls for reforms in the state court systems. First, the decentralized character of the courts has meant that decisions are handled differently from one jurisdiction to the next. And second, with urbanization and population growth, the courts have become increasingly backlogged in their handling of cases. Much like the critics of the legislatures and the executive, court reformers have strong ideas about how to centralize and professionalize decision making and how to make it more efficient and evenhanded, and less political.

The reformers have had two goals. One is the creation of **unified state court systems**, in which the state supreme court manages the full state court system. With the help of professional administrators, this centralization of authority is supposed to reduce the number of different kinds of courts and the overlapping jurisdictions. The goal is to achieve coherent and uniform policies for the practice of law and

Politicking for the Court

Mississippi is one of fourteen states that select their supreme court judges through nonpartisan elections. When would-be judges have to campaign for a seat on the court, the doors are open for organized interests to try to influence voters. The U.S. Chamber Institute for Legal Reform, for instance, spends millions of dollars during an election season on television advertisements supporting judicial candidates it considers pro-business in different states, including Mississippi.

court procedure across the state rather than leaving these matters up to the local courts to set as they please. Only a handful of states have fully unified systems, but quite a few have made incremental moves in that direction.

The second of the reformers' goals is to change the selection, retention, and evaluation of state court judges. Traditionally, judges have been selected either by election (different states have both partisan and nonpartisan elections) or by elected officials (the governor or the state legislature). This, of course, means that political considerations—partisan, electoral, or both—have played an influential role in the selection of judges. In an attempt to place judges "above politics," reformers pushed successfully for **merit systems of judicial selection**. The merit system (which is frequently called the Missouri Plan for the first state to adopt it) usually works something like this: The governor chooses a panel of legal experts who create a list with the names of three prospective judicial candidates. The governor then chooses one from this slate. After a period of time, the voters may have a chance to vote on whether or not they think a particular judge should be retired. It is not entirely clear that these reforms have succeeded in eliminating the politics from judicial selection.[59]

The expansion of the merit system stalled in the 1990s at the same time that more judicial races were becoming electorally competitive. Some observers see as troubling the trend toward high-cost judicial elections in which the chief contributors are the interests groups, litigants, and lawyers who will be appearing before the victorious judge. The campaigns have become more competitive and more expensive, with ever greater interest group involvement. From 2000 to 2006, the percentage of state supreme court elections featuring television advertising increased from 22 percent to 91 percent. Expenditures in contested judicial contests have soared to more than $206 million, which has more than doubled the $83 million judges raised in the 1990s. Contests for the state supreme courts have become expensive and highly competitive.[60] This reflects the increased levels of politicization of the judiciary that we see at the national level in the form of contentious confirmation battles in the U.S. Senate.

Does it matter how a judge is selected? Critics of judicial elections, such as Supreme Court Justice Ruth Bader Ginsburg and former Justice Sandra Day O'Connor, worry that elections can undermine judicial independence.[61] One concern is whether public opinion should play a role in how judges decide a case. Critics believe that determinations of justice should be independent of public opinion and they point with concern to findings like the fact that, when rulings in capital punishment cases are compared, elected judges are more likely to uphold the death sentence, a likelihood that increases as the judges' reelections draw near.[62] Supporters of judicial elections, on the other hand, say that judges should be accountable to the public for the decisions they make.

Critics also worry about the corrupting influence of the rapidly increasing flow of campaign contributions in judicial elections. For instance, in an infamous 2004 West Virginia Supreme Court election, the CEO of one of the state's large coal mining companies spent $3 million to support the campaign of a relatively unknown candidate, Brent Benjamin,

who challenged the state supreme court justice who had presided over a $50 million verdict against the coal company. Benjamin won and subsequently joined the majority in a three-to-two decision to overturn that judgment. Although the U.S. Supreme Court eventually ruled (five to four) that Benjamin should have recused himself, many observers remain concerned that with the huge increases in campaign expenditures for these judicial seats, cases are being settled at election time instead of by impartial judges applying the rule of law.[63]

The New Judicial Federalism

Although judicial reforms may not be restructuring state politics, one significant change in state judicial practice is the increasing tendency for state supreme court justices to rely on the state constitutions rather than just the federal Constitution in important rulings. In doing so, these justices are influencing state policymaking beyond the guarantees and limitations provided by the U.S. Constitution.

There are two reasons for this change. First, the national Supreme Court has become more conservative as a result of the Reagan and Bush appointments, narrowing its interpretation of citizens' rights. This is the area where the state supreme court justices have been most active in expanding interpretations of their state constitutions to provide greater protections than individuals might receive following recent U.S. Supreme Court rulings.[64] Second, the state supreme courts have generally chosen to be participants in the revitalization of state governments by following an activist judicial philosophy. In doing so, they have been willing policymakers, generally cooperating with the legislative and executive branches, in achieving new policy goals for the states.[65]

This new judicial federalism has had a noticeable impact in the area of school financing, one of the central functions of state government. Schools are most often financed by local property taxes and because housing values vary a great deal from one community to another, unless the state steps in to equalize the imbalance, some districts have a lot more to spend on their schools than others. Many cases have been brought to the U.S. Supreme Court claiming that this inequality violates the Constitution. However, the Court has consistently ruled that there is no constitutional right to education, and, therefore, grossly unequal expenditures in different schools within a state or jurisdiction are not unconstitutional. Some state supreme court justices, however, have found a basis in state constitutions to push the executive and legislative branches into widespread equalization programs. The New Jersey case mentioned earlier is an example. That action follows from the pivotal *Serrano v. Priest* case in California, in which the California Supreme Court openly broke with the U.S. Supreme Court's reluctance to find that the state has a duty to provide equal educations for all its citizens.[66] Since then at least ten state supreme courts have held that existing school financing systems are unconstitutional.

The state courts have also expanded rights in the areas of privacy, criminal rights, obscenity, and even free speech that go beyond protections afforded by the U.S. Constitution.[67] For example, in 1998 the Georgia Supreme Court struck down the state's sodomy law on privacy grounds, an action the U.S. Supreme Court had refused to take in *Bowers v. Hardwick*.[68] In 1999 the Vermont Supreme Court ruled that the state is constitutionally required to extend to same-sex couples the same benefits and protections granted to married opposite-sex couples under Vermont law,[69] and as we just discussed, the Massachusetts Supreme Court took that stance one step further in 2004, ruling that the state constitution provided no basis for the legislature to ban same-sex marriages.[70] These rulings were followed up in May 2008 by a four-to-three California Supreme Court ruling that struck down the state's ban on same-sex marriages. However, in November 2008, California voters chose narrowly to make the ban part of the state constitution. Gay marriage advocates immediately challenged the California amendment in federal court, and in August 2010 a Federal District Court judge overturned it but put a stay on further gay marriages in California until appeals in the case are resolved.

Who What How

State institutions provide the primary state-level arenas for political actors to struggle over the scarce resources of subnational politics. Citizens, along with elected and appointed state officials, are among those with the most at stake in those struggles, and the rules that are embedded in those institutions are critical to the outcomes. Some of the most significant political struggles have been over the rules that shape the institutions themselves.

Citizens have an interest in effective and efficient government that is not corrupt. Unfortunately, these may be conflicting goals. As citizens of some states have relied increasingly on reforms like term limits, referenda, and initiatives to provide checks on their elected officials, they

have made it more difficult for those officials to govern. The more recent reforms involve giving back some of the power to state officials that was taken away in an effort to reduce corruption.

Governors also have more powers today than they did before the 1960s but not the full array of powers that reformers (and many governors) believe is needed. Governors want the power to lead their states effectively and the latitude to be politically innovative in the policy solutions they design. To achieve their goals they take advantage of the rules that have increased their power with respect to the other state institutions, and they use the means of increasingly expensive elections to publicize their ideas and their records.

Finally, the courts at the state level want to settle disputes and protect the rights of state citizens, but they also want to take a more active role in shaping state policy. As devolution continues, the executive and legislative branches will be caught between the need to provide services that the federal government no longer funds on the one hand, and strong state sentiments against raising taxes on the other. In many instances, the losers in these battles will take their cases to the courts, primarily the state courts.

Local Governments
Creations of the states in a variety of legal forms

Cities, towns, and counties form the bottom tier of American government, but they do not have any constitutional status. Unlike the states, which have a guaranteed constitutional position, the localities are not even mentioned in the Constitution; they exist completely at the mercy of the state governments. Since 1900, most of the states have allowed their larger cities (typically those with populations of at least 2,500) to opt to govern themselves. Many state-local government arrangements are laid out in the state constitutions, so the localities also have some protection there. For the most part, however, the powers of the localities are given to them by the states, and the states can take them away.

A Multiplicity of Forms

The outstanding feature of American local government is the variety of its sizes and structures. In terms of the cities and towns, two types of governing structures are most common.

> **mayoral government** form of local government in which a mayor is elected in a partisan election
>
> **council-manager government** form of local government in which a professional city or town manager is appointed by elected councilors

> **commission** the basic component of the county form of government; combines executive and legislative functions over a narrow area of responsibility

In big cities nationally, as in the older, and especially eastern cities, the dominant form is the **mayoral government**. Partisan elections determine the mayor, who serves as the chief executive, and city council members, who are usually elected from districts within the cities. This form provided the basis for the now largely extinct urban political party machines. These "machines" were political organizations effective at mobilizing the immigrants and other people drawn to the industrializing cities. The political machines provided favors, jobs, and services in exchange for political support, with not a little graft and corruption tossed in to grease the wheels.

The Progressives had a substantial influence on the form of local government in those areas where they were popular, and also on the cities that have been incorporated since the early part of the twentieth century. They advocated a form of city governance called **council-manager government**. The chief executive in this system is an *appointed* professional manager who brings administrative expertise and nonpartisanship to the position rather than wheeling and dealing in government contracts in exchange for political support. In its pure form, the council-manager form of government also uses nonpartisan at-large districts for city council elections; all members run citywide rather than from separate districts.

While the political machines are largely extinct, controversy continues about the forms of city government. The issue today is whether at-large elections create a bias against the election of minorities. Since minorities tend to be residentially segregated, they have a stronger chance of electing one of their own from districts that encompass just one part of a city or town where they may constitute a majority than from citywide districts where they may always be minorities.[71] Advocates of at-large elections argue that these are better for selecting council members with a concern for the overall good of the cities rather than just narrow constituencies.

In addition to the towns and cities, there are literally thousands of other local governments that provide services and extract taxes. There are 3,033 county governments—called "parishes" in Louisiana and "boroughs" in Alaska—in the United States whose primary responsibility is to govern and provide basic services for the areas not covered by cities and towns. The counties are a wonderful study in how not to design a government. The most common structure is the **commission**, in which the executive and legislative functions are shared by three to fifty elected commissioners, generally with each being responsible for different parts of county government. In addition, the counties typically have a host of additional elected executive department heads, such as the coroner, treasurer, county assessor, and district attorney, often creating confusion in terms of accountability and coordination.

Finally, there are the other types of jurisdictions, including 13,051 school districts, 19,492 municipal governments, 16,519 townships, and 37,381 special districts, which include narrow authorities that deal with water, sewage, solid waste, flood control, public housing, electrical power, and other issues.[72] These mini-governments tend to work in secret because the general public is largely unaware of their existence. The officers are usually elected, but since they are seldom in the limelight, they make decisions and extract taxes (usually as an invisible part of the property taxes) without much public attention. The difficulty with all the special districts is that they fragment power and make coordinated solutions to problems exceedingly difficult to find.

We see in local government today the legacy of earlier efforts to keep government close to the people. Having lots of jurisdictions and elective offices does, in theory, give the people a great deal of direct control. Unless citizens make a real effort to get involved, however, the local governments are sufficiently distant from their lives—and there are so many of them—that they tend to function largely on their own. Their very number means that special interests can find opportunities to exert influence, and because their jurisdictions are often so narrow, few elected officials are in a position to plan and make policy in the overall public interest.

The Special Problems of the Cities

The existence of the automobile combined with America's new federally funded interstate highway system permitted the growing cities of the mid–twentieth century to expand well past their pre–World War II boundaries. The new suburbanites tended to be the more economically successful, and the towns that grew to accommodate them developed as politically independent jurisdictions. Over time this has resulted in central cities that are poorer, older, and disproportionately nonwhite.[73] In the 1980s, for instance, the flight of better-off, primarily white residents from the city of East St. Louis, Illinois, to the suburbs, and the departure of manufacturing and other blue collar jobs, meant that property values fell, and thus property taxes brought in less money for city services. The city was unable to pick up garbage, replace police cars, and repair broken sewer lines. This fate was not reserved

metropolitan-wide government a single government that controls and administers public policy in a central city and its surrounding suburbs

for East St. Louis. Inner cities everywhere have faced similar challenges.

Flight to the suburbs has created significant problems as the central cities, which tend to be Democratic and liberal, must rely on a shrinking tax base to deal with problems of urban decay, education, crime prevention, and aging transportation systems. The surrounding, predominantly Republican, and more conservative suburbs are usually not anxious to share their affluence with the inner cities,[74] even though the inner-city problems of poverty and crime can spill over into their borders and many suburbanites commute to work in the cities and confront their problems daily.

Urban reformers find a solution in **metropolitan-wide government**. A single government that includes the cities and surrounding suburbs can represent all interests and, in particular, draw on the healthy tax bases of the suburbs to deal with the inner-city problems. If successful, all are better off.[75] This consolidation is working in about a dozen of our major cities, including Jacksonville and Dade County, Florida; Indianapolis, Indiana; and Minneapolis–St. Paul, Minnesota. More frequently, however, suburbanites have successfully resisted joining politically with their central cities. They perceive such consolidation as a threat to their identities, independence, lifestyles, and tax bases.[76]

The state governments certainly could, in theory, step in to exercise leadership in finding solutions to the problems of urban decay, crime, and poverty; sometimes they do. The "Unigov" consolidation of Indianapolis and its surrounding Marion County was imposed by the state legislature in 1969. However, the general difficulty is that many more people now live in the suburbs than in the central cities, so most state legislators do not represent urban citizens. To use the distinction between legislative roles that we developed in Chapter 7, as lawmakers, they would need to impose some sacrifices on their constituents to achieve healthy cities, which are in the interest of the whole state. However, as representatives, they find such calls to be incompatible with their goals of reelection. It is tough to sell the suburbanites on the idea that they should be taxed to pay for fixing inner-city problems. Even reformers acknowledge that the movement toward metropolitan consolidation is largely dead.[77]

In practice, the federal government has provided the bulk of the aid to the cities. Such aid has come in several packages, including the urban renewal efforts of the 1960s, subsidies for urban mass transportation, and many of the programs of the Department of Housing and Urban Development (HUD),

Combating Urban Blight
Construction gets underway on the Gateway Project in Detroit, Michigan. The major economic development project will connect area freeways to the Ambassador Bridge, which is the busiest international border crossing in North America, and Detroit's Mexicantown neighborhood. Such development efforts are integral to promoting city vitality, limiting flight to the suburbs, and combating the problems of urban decay.

such as the current community development block grants. Federal aid to the cities also takes the form of the largest federal grant-in-aid programs of welfare and medical care (the recipients of which are disproportionately found in the cities). While there is a great deal of competition for federal dollars and the political clout of the cities has declined, they do better under Democratic administrations in large part because the cities provide strong support for the party's candidates for president and Congress.

State and Local Relations

We mentioned earlier that virtually all the power in state-local relations lies with the state governments. The states generally tell the localities what kinds of laws they can pass; how high their property taxes can be; what kinds of building ordinances they can pass; how much time their children must spend in school; what kinds of training their firefighters, police officers, and teachers must have; and so on.

The degree of local power does, however, vary. It is stronger in the New England states, which historically have had very vigorous, and relatively powerful, local

► **Profiles in Citizenship: Bill Richardson**

"To have power is a good thing. But you have to use it for the right purposes."

Bill Richardson's fraternity, in the late sixties, was all about fun, beer, and parties. Richardson wasn't against any of that, mind you (on the contrary, his eyes twinkle when he remembers those days), but it seemed to him that his fraternity could be more sensitive to the community, more relevant and philanthropic. And so this apolitical student, with dreams of playing baseball after college, ran for president of his fraternity on a platform of relevance. And, to his surprise, he won.

Sitting today, some forty years later, relaxed on the couch in his office in the beautiful New Mexico state house in Santa Fe, still wearing the beard he grew after he withdrew from the primary race for the Democratic presidential nomination, Governor Richardson reminisces about that first, early election. "I was the shadow candidate. I was unknown, and I found that if you worked hard and had a good message, you could win. . . . And then I was able to achieve, in that year I was president, a few things. And that was the first time I realized that maybe this was something I was good at. Because I was a mediocre student." ("Though I was a good baseball player," he hastens to add with a grin.)

"To have power is a good thing. But you have to use it for the right purposes."

If his tenure as president of his fraternity turned him on to the idea that he could make a difference, it was a speech by Minnesota senator Hubert Humphrey that he heard on a class trip to Washington, D.C., that encouraged him to make his career in public service. "I remember some of the things he said," recalls Richardson. "He said care about Africa. Care about those regions of the world that are on nobody's radar screen. Give of yourself. You can make a difference. You can help people. And there's no more noble cause. . . . And I think there was something special about it being in the U.S. Senate, you know, elected representatives, people elected by their constituents. And I thought—I may want to do that."

And so Richardson launched what has proven to be an amazingly eclectic and diverse public career—beginning as an assistant to a member of Congress, then as a staff member in the Department of State, on to seven terms as a U.S. representative from New Mexico (serving for a time as chairman of the Congressional Hispanic Caucus), then to U.S. ambassador to the United Nations, then secretary of energy, and now governor of New Mexico with a run for the Democratic nomination for the presidency tucked in there in 2007–2008. And the man is only in his early sixties, so don't look for him to retire from public life anytime soon.

governments based on the "town meeting," in which all citizens are eligible to participate. In contrast, local power is weaker in southern states, where we find highly central-ized policymaking, funding for education, and other important functions. Moreover, the cities complain about unfunded mandates from the states, just as the states complain when these mandates come from the federal government.[78]

The political relationships are similar as well. Many people fear that as the federal government cuts back on services, it will continue to put more pressure on the state governments to provide them. Similarly, fiscal pressure on state governments has caused them to pass on additional requirements and regulations to the localities. The local governments, unfortunately, do not have any lower level of government to which they can pass their problems.

Citizens want effective local government, especially delivery of essential services, but they want to guard against corrup-tion. They are more likely to get efficiency with a council-manager form of government than with a mayoral system, in which energy can be deflected from governance to partisan squabbling. Citizens have far greater opportunities for participation at the local level of government than at the federal or even state level, which would allow them to check corruption

Who What How

He began by going to graduate school and getting a master's degree in international affairs. When he got out, he looked for work in Congress. He had no inside track, no friends in high places to ease his way. In fact, he says, "I didn't know anybody, so I wrote letters to 435 members of Congress." Only one responded, offering him a position as an unpaid intern. Richardson took it and, by virtue of his hard work, turned it into a paying job. With that he began to build an impressive résumé that has spanned the levels of the federal government. He has held positions at both state and national levels and, if you count his stint at the United Nations, at international levels, as well.

His work at the UN, representing the country before 185 other nations, may have been, he thinks, the most fun job he has held. Richardson thrives on the international stage, and indeed, he has a reputation as a diplomat extraordinaire. Even as a governor he has taken time out to negotiate with foreign leaders, resolving conflicts and bargaining for the release of hostages. He credits his childhood for equipping him for this role: "The fact that I was raised in a bilingual household in Mexico by a mother [who] would only speak Spanish to me and a father who would only speak English, . . . the fact that I lived in two worlds, you know, a Mexican world and an American world, spoke two languages almost simultaneously." His upbringing in those two worlds created a man who, seeing both sides, can find common ground and create a bridge to understanding and agreement, the very essence of political skill.

Here's what else he has to say about his multifaceted career in public service:

On being a state governor and the role of power:

The job I think I've made more of a difference in has been governor of New Mexico because as a governor, you set the agenda. It's probably the most powerful position in American government. Because you set the agenda, for a smaller group of people. You know, when I was in the Cabinet, UN ambassador, secretary of energy, you know they're very powerful positions, but you're basically answering to either the White House or the Congress or constituencies. Your flexibility is limited to convey your ideas. As the governor, you set the agenda. . . . And it's a powerful position to do something good.

And I think it's important that your students realize that power is a good thing. To have power is a good thing. But you have to use it for the right purposes.

On keeping the republic:

Know the values of the country, of individualism, of patriotism, and civil liberties. . . . And you know one of our big problems right now internationally is that we've lost our moral compass, and what we've done in terms of these efforts to eavesdrop on ourselves, and torture and illegal detentions has undermined our position morally, more than any other war might. And so it's important that students be good citizens, be informed, participate, vote, stay in school. Learn. . . . Getting involved in political races, getting involved in referendums, trying to make a difference locally, trying to clean up the environment locally. . . . You can do it in your own town or county as a citizen. ■

and keep an eye on what officials do, but many people do not take advantage of those opportunities, leaving local government to proceed largely out of the public eye.

Citizens also want an improved quality of life, which means, for those who can afford it, that they leave the inner urban areas and move to the suburbs, causing a host of problems for those who are left behind. One solution that has had some success is the creation of metropolitan-wide governments that allow urban areas to share the wealthier tax base of their suburbs. Local governments, which want to solve local problems effectively, are often limited in their efforts by their dependence on the states for power and resources.

The Citizens and State and Local Government
Democracy, up close and personal

State and local governments are closer to their citizens than is the federal government. Whereas federal governance may often seem like it takes the form of elite democracy, run by people far removed from everyday citizens, state and local governments allow far more opportunities for participatory governance, if citizens only choose to get involved. Citizens may vote for initiatives and referenda, run for local office, sit on school boards and other advisory boards, even take part in citizen-volunteer judicial boards and community-run probation programs.[79]

But there is another way that citizens can shape state and local policies as surely as when they vote in the polling place, and that is by voting with their feet. In a kind of political pressure that the federal government almost never has to confront, citizens can move from a state or locality they don't like to one that suits them better. Consider this: few Americans ever think seriously about changing countries. Other nations may be nice to visit, but most of us, for better or worse, will continue to live under the government of the United States. But at the same time, far fewer of us will live in the same state or city throughout our lives. We move for jobs, for climate, for a better quality of life. When we move, we can often choose where we want to relocate. Businesses also move—for better facilities, to be closer to suppliers or transportation routes, for more favorable tax rates, to have access to better labor forces, and so on—and they are also in a position to choose where they want to go. This mobility of people and business enterprises creates incentives for competition and cooperation among the states and among the localities that influence how they operate in important ways. Although we do not conventionally consider the decision to move to be a political act, it affects policy just as much as more traditional forms of citizen participation.

Competition and Policy in the States and Localities

States and localities thus face a problem the federal government doesn't have to deal with; they must compete with one another. Indeed, states and communities now compete openly for middle-class residents by advertising themselves as wonderful places to raise a family (good schools, clean environment, and low taxes) and for businesses by plugging the economic development programs and subsidies they will provide to companies that move in. This competition can be seen in the scramble among larger cities to woo professional sports teams with tax breaks and new stadiums, and in states' and communities' efforts to recruit auto plants and other manufacturing enterprises. In addition, cities compete for people. For example, Hattiesburg, Mississippi, is part of

the Hometown Retirement Program, which is conducted by the Mississippi Development Authority. The city has spent over a quarter of a million dollars on guides and advertisements to entice retirees to relocate to Hattiesburg, including offering tax exemptions for retirees on their annuities and other retirement benefits. Many people have accepted the tempting promise of the town's web site: "Your retirement dollar goes a long way in the Greater Hattiesburg Area. . . . You'll never be bored in Hattiesburg."[80] Retirees can bring substantial resources into a community; their incomes may not be high, but they often have considerable savings and investments.[81]

This race for new businesses and middle-class, tax-conscious citizens makes state legislators and local councils especially wary of new taxes that would support higher levels of welfare, job training for the unemployed, drug treatment programs, prenatal care for the poor, or the like. One effect of competition, liberal critics of devolution argue, is that it creates an incentive for a "race to the bottom" in terms of providing for the poor. Even highly sympathetic localities cannot afford to do much more for their poor than can surrounding jurisdictions because if they did, they would lose middle-class taxpayers and businesses while perhaps gaining more poor people attracted by the city's relatively generous benefits.[82] Critics of the 1996 welfare reform bill, with its greater state responsibility for the poor, are especially concerned that future economic hard times may cause states to accelerate the race to the bottom.

Competition can also be good for geographic regions, however. Voting with our feet can have positive consequences for states and localities. If parents "shop" for neighborhoods based on the quality of schools, parks, and amenities, then cities and towns have to work harder to keep their populations. They have to be inventive in delivering services or risk losing people and businesses to more efficient jurisdictions. If they let their roads go, allow building without green spaces, or permit too much pollution, they will lose people and businesses to other places. Thus the competition among cities and states stands as a continuing incentive for policy innovation. It means that city managers, mayors, state legislators, and governors are constantly on the lookout for better ways to serve their citizens. Then when more effective programs are developed and tested, they generally spread quickly to other locations.[83]

interstate compacts agreements between two or more states, frequently formed to manage a common resource

Intergovernmental Cooperation

Citizens' abilities to choose and move among states and localities increases competition between those regions, but the increased competition also highlights areas of cooperation in solving common problems. Cooperation and communication are often facilitated by the intergovernmental associations that bring together individuals in similar circumstances to share information and to develop cooperative solutions to common problems. The number of formal associations of different officers, regions, levels of government, and policy interests among the states and cities is quite amazing. Along with the improved capacities of the state legislatures and the governors, the organizations of intergovernmental cooperation are an important element in equipping the states and localities to deal with the increasing challenges of devolution.

Almost every component, activity, and office of state government has its own national association. Heading this list is the National Governors Association (NGA), of which former president Bill Clinton was chair while he was governor of Arkansas. It provides a forum for the exchange of ideas among the nation's governors, but it also has become an important influence in its own right. For example, in June 2005, the NGA presented to Congress a proposal to improve Medicaid, one of the fastest growing and most costly of state programs. The governors' proposal bore a great deal of legitimacy, given that it was the product of a bipartisan effort and came from those who have to deal directly with the problem of health care for the poor.[84] The effectiveness of the NGA over the years has led some observers to view it as Congress' "third house."[85]

The Council of State Governments provides a wide array of services and information for the states, as does the National Conference of State Legislatures. At the local level the National Municipal League has long been an effective forum for the cities. In addition, cooperation is fostered by policy area–specific associations like the Educational Commission of the States, which provides analyses and information to the state governments on all sorts of questions about educational finance and policy trends. Similar associations exist in most of the major policy areas. Governments cooperate on a regional basis as well.

There are also dozens of *interstate compacts*, which are agreements between two or more states, requiring congressional approval to form an organization to manage a common resource such as a seaport or public transportation infrastructure. The Port Authority of New York and New Jersey, and the Washington Metropolitan Area Transportation Authority (Maryland, Virginia, and Washington, D.C.) are just two examples.

Intergovernmental cooperation even extends beyond our national boundaries. States and cities along both the Mexican and Canadian borders have entered into associations and agreements with their sister governments across the border to address common problems. Following the terrorist attacks of September 11, 2001, the Border Legislative Conference was organized. It provides state legislators in Mexico and the United States a mechanism to promote collaboration and communication on common problems facing the U.S.-Mexico border region. It was fostered by existing state legislative organizations and is funded with grants from the U.S. Agency for International Development.[86]

Although states and localities may cooperate on many dimensions, the bottom line of their relationships is competition for citizens, businesses, and resources. This gives citizens a unique method of influencing state and local policy—the power of the consumer to purchase a competing product—that is not available to them as national citizens.

▶ **What's at Stake Revisited**

Officials in Arizona were stymied by the problem of undocumented workers crossing illegally into their state from Mexico. In an effort to deal with it, former governor (now secretary of homeland security) Janet Napolitano signed a bill in 2007 that would crack down on employers who hire undocumented workers and require them to verify electronically that the people they hired were in the country legally. Three years later, Gov. Jan Brewer signed a bill that would empower local police to enforce federal immigration standards, requiring those it thought might be here illegally to produce documentation and imposing state sanctions on those who could not produce such documentation. Both pieces of legislation were challenged in the courts. Setting aside the civil rights issues involved, which have their own political stakes, what was at stake for federalism in the passage of these two laws?

For the state of Arizona, what was at stake was the management of a problem with implications that are economic (where cheap immigrant labor is available, legal workers have to work for a similarly cheap rate or go unemployed), social (a heightened crime rate), and political (anger over both of the former problems threatens to unseat officials who are unresponsive to those issues). Secretary Napolitano, arguing from inside the federal government now, claimed that the law she signed was necessary to manage illegal

immigration and should not be challenged.[87] Governor Brewer said that the law she had signed "represents another tool for our state to use as we work to resolve a crisis we did not create and the federal government has refused to fix."[88] Other states share Arizona's stakes and echo its concerns; almost all have passed or attempted to pass legislation dealing with some aspect of immigration.

For the federal government, however, the stakes were equally critical. Federal law imposes sanctions on employers who hire undocumented workers and on immigrants who do not carry their documentation, but it forbids states to impose their own sanctions. "While we understand the frustration of Arizonans with the broken immigration system, a patchwork of state and local policies would seriously disrupt federal immigration enforcement and would ultimately be counterproductive," federal Justice Department officials said. "States can and do play a role in cooperating with the federal government in its enforcement of immigration laws, but they must do so within our constitutional framework."[89] If states were to create their own legal systems for dealing with this problem, there would be fifty separate sets of rules and sanctions for federal officials to navigate.

But Arizonans were right that the federal government had not effectively dealt with the issue of illegal immigration, which is a

constant problem for states along that extensive and porous border. In general, as we saw in Chapter 2, the federal government has had difficulty passing a comprehensive immigration bill in recent years. Although people like Senator McCain blame President Obama, it was President Bush who first tried to update our immigration laws. He was ultimately defeated by the more conservative members of his party, who want a tougher stance on undocumented workers, preferring to ship them back to Mexico rather than create a formal guest worker program that would give workers a legal way to come to the United States and help fill our labor needs. Bush's plan, like the Development, Relief and Education for Alien Minors (DREAM) Act debated off and on in Congress since 2001, provides a path by which some illegal immigrants already here (students, in the case of the DREAM Act) can eventually earn citizenship. The DREAM Act passed the House of Representatives in 2010 but failed to pass in the Senate. With Senator John McCain, once a friend to immigration reform, now taking a hard line that borders must be secured before reform can be addressed, and with a Republican majority in the House of Representatives in 2011, the impasse in Washington seems irresolvable.

In August 2010, President Obama signed the Southwest Border Security Bill, which allocates $600 million to help secure the border between the United States and Mexico, but absent more comprehensive reform, it is unlikely to stop the flow of workers here in search of opportunities.[90] Frank Sharry, executive director of America's Voice, a national interest group that lobbies for comprehensive immigration reform, summarizes the state of immigration reform this way: "Years ago, you had President George W. Bush and Mexican President Vicente Fox talking about how to modernize immigration policy between the two countries so that, as they put it in their own words, immigration became safe, legal and orderly. And now, you have Arizona politicians saying, 'Kick them out and keep them out.' The vision of a 21st-century immigration policy that delivered control and promised humanity has been replaced by hard-edged rhetoric and mean-spirited policies that have strained relations between the two countries."[91]

Clearly, the current state of immigration reform at the national level has also strained relations between states and the federal government, illustrating that although federalism can enhance flexibility it can also blur the lines of responsibility. Particularly when problems seem to be intractable, lack of clear lines of accountability can increase acrimony and finger-pointing, as the parties try to avoid taking the blame for problems that are difficult to fix.

What's at stake here is the ability of states to step in and attempt to manage a problem that approaches crisis proportions for some of them, and the federal government's ability to apply uniform standards and rules to immigrants in all fifty states. The issue remains unresolved, awaiting an answer from the courts. The law concerning employer sanctions already reached the Supreme Court, which had not dealt with a case concerning federalism and immigration since 1976. It heard arguments in December 2010. In that case, the newest justice, Elena Kagan, who was solicitor general when the case came up, recused herself, leaving only eight justices to decide the case. If it should be a tie, then the lower court judgment, which favored Arizona, will stand. In July 2010, a federal judge blocked part of the law that Brewer signed, and the judgment is being appealed. Eventually it may also reach the Supreme Court, though the first ruling may solve that issue, as well.

To Sum Up

Key terms, chapter summaries, practice quizzes, Internet links, and other study aids are available on the companion web site at http://republic.cqpress.com.

Define Understand Practice Read Click Watch

block grants (p. 601)

categorical grants (p. 601)

citizen legislators (p. 611)

commission (p. 620)

cooperative federalism (p. 600)

council-manager government (p. 620)

devolution (p. 599)

dual federalism (p. 599)

individualistic political culture (p. 604)

initiative (p. 609)

interstate compacts (p. 625)

mayoral government (p. 620)

merit system of judicial selection (p. 617)

metropolitan-wide government (p. 621)

moralistic political culture (p. 604)

recall election (p. 609)

referendum (p. 609)

super legislation (p. 607)

traditionalistic political culture (p. 604)

unfunded mandates (p. 601)

unified state court systems (p. 617)

| Define | **Understand** | Practice | Read | Click | Watch |

- Federalism reflects a continually changing compromise between advocates of a strong national government and those who advocate strong state government.
- Under dual federalism, national and state governments were thought to be responsible for separate policy areas. With cooperative federalism (our current arrangement), the state and national governments share responsibility for most domestic policy areas.
- State cultural identities (individualistic, moralistic, and traditionalistic) contribute to the policy differences among the states.
- The primary tools used to influence the rules of state politics have been the state constitution and mechanisms of direct democracy, including referenda, initiatives, and recall elections.
- Contemporary federalism has required new, and sometimes difficult, agreements between state governments and their citizens. For the most part, state institutions (legislatures, governors, courts) have become stronger and more efficient in the process.
- American local government—towns, cities, and counties—may take many forms. Like the state-federal power struggles, localities frequently ask states for more independence to address local problems such as urban blight.
- State and local governments provide citizens with many opportunities for participation should they choose to get involved. Even if they don't participate in the usual ways, citizens exert a unique kind of power over their states and localities: they can move away, or vote with their feet.

| Define | Understand | **Practice** | Read | Click | Watch |

1. **What is the key difference between dual federalism and cooperative federalism?**
   a. The federal government has more power under dual federalism than under cooperative federalism.
   b. Most laws that affect citizens under dual federalism are the responsibility of the federal government, whereas most laws that affect citizens under cooperative federalism are the responsibility of the state government.
   c. In cooperative federalism, the federal government is much more involved in domestic policy, regulation of the economy, and social welfare than it is under dual federalism.
   d. Compared to dual federalism, cooperative federalism has significantly less sharing of any responsibility in domestic policy areas between state and federal governments.
   e. Cooperative federalism is much more in line with what the founders envisioned than is dual federalism.

2. **Of the types of political cultures among states, which of the following best reflects the moralistic political culture?**
   a. The marketplace, and not government, is the best mechanism for distributing resources.
   b. The role of government is to maintain the existing power structures.
   c. It is built on the plantation traditions of the Old South that eventually spread across the South and Southwest.
   d. It emphasizes that the common good can be achieved through government action to bring equality and a high quality of life to all citizens.
   e. It strongly emphasizes the Protestant work ethic.

3. **The process of putting a group's policy preferences into state constitutions rather than just passing laws to favor the group's preferences is called**
   a. super legislation.
   b. block grants.
   c. constitutionalizing legislation.
   d. preference constitutions.
   e. specialized legislation.

4. **What was one major problem facing state legislatures in the 1950s and 1960s that led to major reforms?**
   a. Alaska's and Hawaii's statehoods had lowered all the states' powers vis-à-vis the federal government.
   b. State legislatures often couldn't get the federal government to fund their initiatives.
   c. Legislatures lacked the time and capability to exercise effective oversight of state agencies.
   d. Legislatures had members who were younger, more educated, and more diverse than the different states' general populations.
   e. Legislatures disregarded the ideas and information that were provided to them from interest groups.

5. **According to the text, what is the most outstanding feature of American local government?**
   a. The forms of government consistently follow the urban political party machine model.
   b. Local governments generally follow a single structural model.
   c. Unlike the federal government, local governments do not tax citizens.
   d. Most decisions regarding citizens' rights are made at the local level.
   e. Local governments come in a large variety of sizes and structures.

Define Understand Practice Read Click Watch

Council of State Governments. 2008. *The Book of the States,* **Vol. 40. Lexington, Ky.: Council of State Governments.** This annual volume contains comparative data on the states.

Donahue, John D. 1997. *Disunited States.* **New York: Basic Books.** A former bureaucrat argues that the trend toward devolution may undermine national interests.

Elazar, Daniel J. 1984. *American Federalism: A View From the States,* **3rd ed. New York: Harper & Row.** The classic work on state political culture. Elazar's innovative distinctions among traditionalistic, moralistic, and individualistic cultures have generated much controversy among scholars.

Erikson, Robert S., Gerald C. Wright, and John P. McIver. 1993. *Statehouse Democracy: Public Opinion and Policy in the American States.* **New York: Cambridge University Press.** The authors report strong evidence for the health of democracy in the states. Their analysis shows how public opinion influences state policy.

Gray, Virginia, and Russell Hanson, eds. 2008. *Politics in the American States: A Comparative Analysis,* **9th ed. Washington, D.C.: CQ Press.** An excellent set of readings by experts on the full array of topics in state government and policy. Each provides a broad overview and incorporates the latest research on the topics.

Jewell, Malcolm, and Marcia Lynn Whicker. 1994. *Legislative Leadership in the American States.* **Ann Arbor: University of Michigan Press.** A pioneering examination of the changing nature of legislative leadership in the states, full of examples and descriptions about what makes legislative leadership effective.

Rosenthal, Alan. 2009. *Engines of Democracy: Politics and Policymaking in State Legislatures.* **Washington, D.C.: CQ Press.** A sympathetic and insightful comprehensive overview of the state legislatures by a highly respected longtime observer. Rosenthal explains the policymaking process, how legislators represent and leaders lead, and the challenges legislators face.

Sabato, Larry. 1983. *Goodbye to Good-time Charlie: The American Governor Transformed,* **2nd ed. Washington, D.C.: CQ Press.** This book traces the transformation of the governorship.

Define Understand Practice Read Click Watch

Council of State Governments *www.csg.org.* This organization is designed to provide all three branches of state governments with analysis of policy trends and forecasting.

Governing.com *www.governing.com.* The online version of Governing magazine, which covers issues related to state and local politics.

GovSpot.com's State Government Directory *www.govspot .com/state/.* This in-depth directory offers links for each state sorted by branches of government, departments and agencies, elections, laws, licenses, permits, records, taxes, and travel and recreation.

National Conference of State Legislatures *www.ncsl.org.* This site contains a wealth of information about state legislatures, federal-state relations, and policy issues before the legislatures.

National Governors Association *www.nga.org.* This organization provides information on governors and lobbies the federal government on their behalf.

USA.gov's State Government Directory *www.usa.gov/ Agencies/State_and_Territories.shtml.* This web site offers a link to each state's and territorial government's home page so that you can more easily access information on state and local government.

Define Understand Practice Read Click Watch

Bury My Heart at Wounded Knee *2007.* This HBO film tells the story of the tension-fraught relationship between the U.S. government and Native American tribesmen seeking to preserve their right to indigenous territory in the face of a federal push toward deeper integration.

Chapter 17

Social and Environmental Policy

▶ What's at Stake?

In the spring and summer of 2010, Americans watched, horrified, as oil gushed into the Gulf of Mexico from a ruined oil rig, the *Deepwater Horizon*, leased by British Petroleum off the coast of Louisiana. It was the worst offshore oil spill in U.S. history. For weeks, and then months, the oil company and the U.S. government were stymied in their efforts to stop the leak by a lack of technology, equipment, and know-how. As TV commentators covered the wreckage in the Gulf, they turned time and again to a question of just how horrified we really were. Would the vision of oil-soaked birds and dead fish do anything to quench America's seemingly insatiable thirst for oil? Would it encourage us to be more frugal in our consumption of fossil fuels and spur us to invest more in alternative sources of energy?

Not really. In a country like the United States, where so much development took place after the invention of the automobile, we can't get along without our cars, and as an auto-dependent nation, we're at the mercy of gas prices, which have climbed in recent years to well over $2.00 or even $3.00 a gallon. Many factors can cause gas prices to rise, but a central one is the availability of oil: oil prices account for roughly half the cost of gasoline.[1] Most of the oil we use in the United States comes from outside this country. In early 2008, 66 percent came from abroad and that figure is expected to rise by an additional two-thirds by 2025.[2]

How do we insulate ourselves from the vagaries of the oil market? Should we develop alternative sources of energy, build hybrid cars, brew up

Deepwater Inferno

Clouds of smoke billow into the sky following an explosion at the BP *Deepwater Horizon* oil well in the Gulf of Mexico. The well spewed oil into the Gulf for three months and released the equivalent of nearly 5 million barrels of crude oil, affecting the environment and wildlife along the Gulf Coast. While a massive clean-up effort was mounted and fingers were pointed at Washington and within the oil industry, concern grew over the effects of offshore drilling and the need for alternative sources of energy.

fuel from corn or other common resources, or just encourage Americans to use less gas, perhaps by carpooling or biking to work? Conservationists insist that we are devoting far too little time and money to promoting such environmentally friendly solutions.[3] Others argue, however, that the answer is much more straightforward and obvious—we should simply look for more oil on our own shores.

The question of whether we should offset our oil dependence by pursuing more domestic sources of oil—via offshore drilling or drilling in the Arctic National Wildlife Refuge (ANWR)—has long been a hot-button issue in American politics. Although the *Deepwater Horizon* oil spill changed public opinion about offshore drilling, the public remained closely divided on the issue.[4] And while a majority had opposed drilling

in ANWR, as gas prices rose, so did approval of tapping our Alaskan reserves.[5] Highlighting the divisive nature of the issue, support for drilling broke down along party lines: during the 2008 presidential campaign the Republican position was summed up by the chant "Drill, Baby, Drill"; the Democrats' view, by a less catchy determination to do no such thing. President Barack Obama, seeking to bridge the gap, made the development of alternate forms of energy a priority for his administration, but he also supported the growth of offshore drilling as an interim measure until those alternate sources could be tapped.

The case of ANWR, a massive amount of land in Alaska that is the nation's largest wildlife preserve, provides a good example of the political challenges involved in trying to augment our oil supply at home. Environmentalists have battled with

advocates of drilling in ANWR for more than thirty years, beginning in the Carter administration. In 1995 Congress approved drilling, only to have President Bill Clinton veto the measure. The election of George W. Bush in 2000 provided drilling advocates with their best chance to date to remove restrictions in ANWR. Although President Bush made opening up ANWR a key legislative priority through both his terms in office, these attempts were consistently controversial and ultimately thwarted.

Concerned interest groups have lined up on both sides of the issue, spending millions to convince lawmakers to see things their way. Arctic Power, an organization whose members include Exxon Mobil and which has been endorsed by the Alaska state legislature, has been at the forefront of the pro-drilling fight, as have been the Alaska Chamber of Commerce and the International Brotherhood of Teamsters. On the other side, the U.S. Public Interest Research Group opposes drilling, as does the Sierra Club and smaller groups like the Alaska Wilderness League.[6] Those supporting drilling in ANWR were energized in 2008 with Senator John McCain's choice of then–Alaska governor Sarah Palin as his running mate. Though McCain disagreed with the policy, Palin has been a vocal advocate of drilling in her state.

Why has the effort to open drilling in Alaska been so hard fought, and why do its foes remain so bitterly opposed? What exactly is at stake in the battle over drilling for oil here at home? We return to these questions after we look more closely at the policymaking process and at environmental policymaking, in particular. ■

Public policy can encourage or discourage behaviors in order to solve a problem that already exists or to avoid creating a future problem.

public policy a government plan of action to solve a problem

" **T**he quality of this air is horrible," we say as we gasp for breath while jogging in a local park. "Someone ought to do something about this."

"It's intolerable that homeless people are allowed to sleep in the public library. Why doesn't somebody do something?"

"How tragic that so many young children don't have health care. Can't anyone do anything about it?"

When we utter such cries of disgust, frustration, or compassion, we are not calling on the heavens to visit us with divine intervention. Usually the general somebody/anybody we call on for action is our government, and what government *does* or *doesn't do*, at the end of the day, is called public policy. In fact, public policy has been a focus of discussion throughout this book. When we ask what's at stake, as we do at the beginning of each chapter, or pause within a chapter to reflect on who, what, and how, the *what* is almost always a government action or policy. The study of public policy is inseparable from the study of American politics.

In this chapter we focus specifically on what public policy is and how the parts of government we have studied come together to create it. But government is not something "out there," something external to us. We have seen in this book that in many ways American government is very responsive to us as citizens, either individually as voters or collectively as interest groups. Although we do not dictate the details, the broad outlines of American public policy are largely what we say they should be. In some policy areas, such as social welfare reform and crime policy, politicians have responded to public opinion by limiting welfare and getting tougher on criminals. In other areas, notably Social Security and health care, they have responded to the powerful demands of organized interest groups. In still other policy areas, primarily economic policy, some of the political decisions have been taken out of the hands of elected officials precisely because they tend to respond to what voters and interest groups want, or what they imagine voters want.

In the next three chapters we look at the who, what, and how of American policymaking—who makes it, who benefits, and who pays, and how different sets of rules or incentive structures shape the policy that is produced and help to determine the winners and losers. In this chapter we examine domestic public policy. Specifically, you will learn about

- **what policy is, who makes it, and how it is made**
- **social policy, focusing primarily on the issues of Social Security, welfare, and health care**
- **environmental policy, examining the history of environmental programs in the United States and their effect on the environment today**
- **the responsiveness of public policy to citizens' wishes**

Making Public Policy
How government attempts to solve collective problems

Our lives are regulated by policies that influence nearly everything we do. For example, many stores have a no-return policy on sales merchandise. Restaurant owners alert customers to their policy toward underdressed diners with the sign "No shirt, no shoes, no service." Your college or university may have a policy requiring a minimum grade point average for continued enrollment.

These are private, nongovernmental policies, adopted by individuals, businesses, or organizations to solve problems and to advance individual or group interests. Stores want to sell their new merchandise, not last season's leftovers; restaurant owners want a certain clientele to dine in their establishments; and institutions of higher education want to maintain standards and give students an incentive to excel. The problems of the clothing store, the restaurant, and the university are straightforward. Addressing these problems with a policy is pretty easy. Creating public policies, however, is more difficult than creating policies on merchandise returns, dining attire, and acceptable grades.

Public policy is a government plan of action to solve a problem that people share collectively or that they cannot solve on their own. That is not to say that the intended problem is always solved, or that the plan might not create more and even worse problems. Sometimes government's plan of action is to do nothing; that is, it may be a plan of inaction, with the expectation (or hope) that the problem will go away on its own, or in the belief that it is not or should not be government's business to solve it. Some issues may be so controversial that policymakers would rather leave them alone, confining the

Cuz It's Cool
There are many ways for government officials to achieve the goals of public policies, including regulations, fines, fees, changes in the tax code, jail time, or just influencing public opinion. Here is one of four hundred billboards the Pennsylvania Department of Public Health placed around the state to convince young people that smoking—which costs individuals and government millions each year in increased health costs—is not cool at all.

scope of a policy debate to relatively "safe" issues.[7] But, by and large, we can understand public policy as a purposeful course of action intended by public officials to solve a public problem.[8] When that problem occurs here in the United States, we say that the government response is domestic policy; when it concerns our relations with other nations, we call it foreign policy, a topic we discuss in Chapter 19. (You can find the wealth of rules and regulations that make up American public policy in the *Federal Register*. See *Consider the Source* on page 636 for some suggestions on how to navigate that massive repository of the nation's laws.)

Solving Public Problems

Public policies differ from the restaurant's "No shirt, no shoes, no service" policy because they are designed to solve common problems, not to address the concerns of a single business or institution. We think of problems as public when they cannot be handled by individuals, groups, businesses, or other actors privately, or when they directly or indirectly affect many citizens. Public problems might include the need for collective goods that individuals alone cannot or will not produce, such as highways, schools, and welfare. Public problems can include harm caused to citizens by the environment, foreign countries, dangerous products, or each other. Sometimes the very question of whether or not a problem is public becomes the subject of political debate. When people suggest that government ought to do something about violent crime, or about drug use, or about poor school quality, they are suggesting that government should create a policy to address a public problem.

Government can address public problems directly, by building schools, prisons, or highways, for example, but a great deal of public problem solving entails offering incentives to individuals or groups to get them to behave the way government wants them to behave. In other words, public policy can encourage or discourage behaviors in order to solve a problem that already exists or to avoid creating a future problem. For instance, government has an interest in having well-educated, property-owning citizens, since the conventional wisdom is that such people are more stable and more likely to obey the laws—in short, to be good citizens. Consequently, government policy encourages students to go to college by offering low-interest college loans and generous tax credits. It encourages homeownership in the same way. These various forms of federal assistance provide incentives for us to behave in a certain way to avoid creating the problem of an uneducated, rootless society.

On the other hand, government may discourage behavior that it considers socially undesirable. For example, most people serving time in a federal penitentiary have been convicted of drug-related crimes. Public officials hope that arresting people who sell or use drugs will discourage other citizens from using drugs. Public service announcements on television and educational campaigns in public schools are other ways that government seeks to curb the use of drugs among its citizens.

Public policies are part and parcel of our modern lives. Consider the last time you traveled by car or bus to another state. You probably used at least one interstate highway en route. Before Congress passed the Federal-Aid Highway Act in 1956, interstate highways didn't exist. President Eisenhower saw the need for citizens to have easy access by car to other states and for the country's defense resources to be mobile. The problem, as President Eisenhower and others viewed it, was slow and uncertain travel on state highways. The solution: a new national policy for interstate travel. Later formally named the Dwight D. Eisenhower System of Interstate and Defense Highways, these 42,000 miles of high-quality highways tie the nation together and represent the largest public works project in U.S. history. Despite its high price tag, many Americans would agree that this part of the nation's transportation policy has accomplished its goal.

Difficulties in Solving Public Problems

Despite the good intentions of policymakers, however, public problems can be difficult to solve. First, as we have already suggested, people have different ideas about what constitutes a problem. The definition of a public problem is not something that can be looked up in a dictionary. It is the product of the values and beliefs of political actors and, consequently, is frequently the subject of passionate debate. The very fact that we are talking about public problems means that a variety of voices and opinions are involved, as opposed to a private problem, on which no broad consensus is required.

The need for facilitating interstate travel was relatively easy to see and agree upon, although the policy was not without its critics.

Other issues are not viewed so commonly as public problems. For instance, people debate endlessly about whether the health care system in this country represents a problem that needs to be solved. Some observers argue that the fact that so many people remain uninsured is a travesty in a rich country like ours; others believe that America's health care system is the best in the world and shouldn't be fundamentally restructured. Even something that seems as obviously problematic as poverty can be controversial. To people who believe that poverty is an inevitable though unfortunate part of life, or to those who feel that poor people should take responsibility for themselves, poverty may not be a problem requiring a public solution.

A second reason that solving public problems can be hard is that solutions cost money—often a lot of money. Finding the money to address a new problem usually requires shifting it out of existing programs or raising taxes. With an eye toward the next election, politicians are reluctant to spend tax dollars to support new initiatives. This is especially true when these new initiatives are not widely supported by citizens, which is often the case with policies that take money from some citizens in order to benefit others, such as the welfare policy discussed later in this chapter.

Public problems can also be difficult to solve because often their solutions generate new problems. Policies tough on crime can jam up the courts and slow the criminal justice system. Policies to help the poor can create dependence on government among the disadvantaged. And environmental policies can impair a business's ability to compete. Often the problems caused by policy require new policies to solve them in turn.

A final reason that problems can be hard to solve has to do with their complexity. Seldom are there easy answers to any public dilemma. Even when policymakers can agree on a goal, they often lack the knowledge they need to reach it. Competing solutions may be proposed, with no one knowing definitively which will best solve the problem. And some public problems may in reality be multiple problems with multiple causes—further muddying the effort to find adequate solutions. Policymaking in the American context is made even more complex by the federal system. Whose responsibility is it to solve a given problem—the federal, state, or local government's?

Imagine you own a manufacturing business and the Environmental Protection Agency (EPA) has just implemented new regulations regarding how many pollutants factories can emit. Or maybe you are concerned about health issues and the Food and Drug Administration (FDA) has new guidelines for what counts as organically grown produce. Or maybe you work for Planned Parenthood and the U.S. president has just signed an executive order designed to limit the number of abortions. The media may cover a few of these policies, but in many cases the actions of government are so numerous, specific, and dull that they never receive any press coverage. Where do you go to find out how the government's actions affect your business or your life?

Fortunately, the *Federal Register* publishes all the information you will ever need about government policies, including all executive agency rules and notices (for example, from the Department of Agriculture or the Environmental Protection Agency) as well as presidential documents, such as executive orders.

The *Federal Register* covers an enormously complex system of rules and regulations, organized into four sections:

- Presidential documents include all executive orders (see Chapter 8 for more on executive orders) or proclamations signed that day by the president. For example, a president may issue a proclamation honoring a historical person, such as Martin Luther King Jr., or observing a special event, such as the sixtieth anniversary of the end of World War II.

- Proposed rules are published to allow for public comment before a new rule is implemented. If citizens or interest groups are upset with, say, the FDA's proposed pesticides rule, they have the chance to make their voices heard.

- Rules and regulations are published after the time for comments expires. Once the rule is published, it amends the Code of Federal Regulation (CFR). The CFR is simply a listing of all federal regulations and is updated four times a year.

- Notices describe official actions and functions that provide important information but do not amend the CFR. For example, meetings of certain government groups are posted or federal grant opportunities are announced.

Be forewarned, the *Federal Register* is not the easiest or most compelling reading you will ever do. The language can often be difficult to comprehend largely because the subject matter is usually quite complex. But when government decisions touch your life and affect your ability to make a living, it is essential that you know what you are up against. Here are the steps you can follow to help you navigate the maze and find information in the *Federal Register*:

1. **Access the Internet.** The wonderful thing about the Internet is that citizens have access to enormous amounts of information quickly. Instead of having to wait about a week for a university library to receive the *Federal Register*, as was once the case, you can simply go to the Government Printing Office web site (www.gpoaccess.gov/index.html), click on "Federal Register," and immediately get a copy from any date between 1994 and the present. (To obtain older versions, you must go to a federal depository or academic library, whose records might be incomplete.)

2. **Perform a keyword search or browse.** Once online, you may then perform a search by keyword, agency, date, or section (for example, "Notices" or "Proposed rules"). If you want to browse a particular day of the *Federal Register*, the table of contents lists all documents by agency name in alphabetical order and is then arranged by section. The table of contents also presents a brief description of each document's subject matter. At the back of each issue of the *Federal Register*, you will find a reader aid that, among other things, reminds you about rules going into effect that day, lists recently enacted public laws, and gives customer service information.

3. **Examine the heading.** Each section of the *Federal Register* has a standard format to make it easier for readers to follow and obtain the information they need. The heading lists the agency name (and subagency if one exists), the parts of the CFR that will or would be affected (this is not included for notices or presidential documents), and the subject matter.

4. **Read the entry.** If after reading the heading you decide that you want more information on the proposed rule, enacted regulation, or notice, you can read the different sections of the entry. Next to "AGENCY" you will find the name of the agency proposing or implementing the rule, announcing a meeting, or the like. Next to "ACTION" you will see the section under which the entry falls (for example, "Final rule; Treasury decision"). The "SUMMARY" provides a brief explanation of the issues involved and the rulemaking objectives; in other words, what the agency did and why. The "DATES" section lists the date of a meeting, hearing, comment deadline, or when a regulation will go into effect. You will also see contact information, including the name, address, phone number, and email address of a knowledgeable person involved in the rule or notice. Finally, under "SUPPLEMENTARY INFORMATION" you will find background on the issue, the rulemaking objectives (if it is a proposed rule), the purpose of the meeting (if it is a notice), a response to comments made about the proposed rule (if it is a final rule), and the part of the CFR that is affected.

Here you will find a sample entry to put a "face" on the *Federal Register* regarding new regulations on production, taxation, and advertising of flavored malt beverages (that's beer, to you). To give you an idea of how detailed the entries in the *Federal Register* can be, this final rule is forty-five pages long.

DEPARTMENT OF THE TREASURY

Alcohol and Tobacco Tax and Trade Bureau

27 CFR Parts 7 and 25

[TTB T.D.–21; Re: TTB Notice No. 4]

RIN 1513–AA12

Flavored Malt Beverage and Related Regulatory Amendments (2002R–044P)

AGENCY: Alcohol and Tobacco Tax and Trade Bureau, Treasury.

ACTION: Final rule; Treasury decision.

SUMMARY: The Department of the Treasury and its Alcohol and Tobacco Tax and Trade Bureau adopt as a final rule certain proposed changes to the regulations concerning the production, taxation, composition, labeling, and advertising of beer and malt beverages.

This final rule permits the addition of flavors and other nonbeverage materials containing alcohol to beers and malt beverages, but, in general, limits the alcohol contribution from such flavors and other nonbeverage materials to not more than 49% of the alcohol content of the product. However, if a malt beverage contains more than 6% alcohol by volume, not more than 1.5% of the volume of the finished product may consist of alcohol derived from flavors and other nonbeverage ingredients that contain alcohol. This final rule also amends the regulations relating to the labeling and advertising of malt beverages, and adopts a formula requirement for beers.

We issue this final rule to clarify the status of flavored malt beverages under the provisions of the Internal Revenue Code of 1986 and the Federal Alcohol Administration Act related to the production, composition, taxation, labeling, and advertising of alcohol beverages. This final rule also will ensure that consumers are adequately informed about the identity of flavored malt beverages.

DATES: This rule is effective January 3, 2006.

FOR FURTHER INFORMATION CONTACT: Charles N. Bacon, Alcohol and Tobacco Tax and Trade Bureau, Regulations and Procedures Division, P.O. Box 5056, Beverly Farms, MA 01915; telephone (978) 921–1840.

SUPPLEMENTARY INFORMATION:

Table of Contents

Notes to Readers

A. ATF–TTB Transition

Effective January 24, 2003, section 1111 of the Homeland Security Act of 2002 (Public Law 107–296, 116 Stat. 2135), divided the Bureau of Alcohol, Tobacco and Firearms (ATF) into two new agencies, the Alcohol and Tobacco Tax and Trade Bureau (TTB) in the Department of the Treasury, and the Bureau of Alcohol, Tobacco, Firearms and Explosives in the Department of Justice. The regulation and taxation of alcohol beverages remains a function of the Department of the Treasury and is the responsibility of TTB. References to the former ATF and the new TTB in this document reflect the time frame, before or after January 24, 2003.

B. Use of Plain Language

In this document, "we," "our," and "us" refer to the Department of the Treasury and/or the Alcohol and Tobacco Tax and Trade Bureau (TTB). "You," "your," and similar words refer to members of the alcohol beverage industry and others to whom TTB regulations apply.

I. Background Information

Flavored malt beverages are brewery products that differ from traditional malt beverages such as beer, ale, lager, porter, stout, or malt liquor in several respects. Flavored malt beverages

---

Color key	
🟩 Department or agency	
🟦 Parts of the Code of Federal Regulations affected	
🟪 Subject matter	
🟥 Agency	
🟪 Action	
🟧 Summary	
🟧 Dates	
⬜ Contact information	
🟩 Supplementary information	

> ***redistributive policies*** policies that shift resources from the "haves" to the "have-nots"

the Box

What problems require public solutions, and what problems should be left to individuals to solve?

Consider, for example, the public problem of homelessness. If you live in an urban area, chances are good that you've seen people living on the street, under bridges, in parks, or in subway tunnels. Most people would agree that this is not desirable, but because the problem has many causes, there are many possible solutions. Should government create more jobs or provide job training assistance? Build more homeless shelters? Provide public money so that homeless families can live in low-income apartments? What if some of the homeless people suffer from mental disorders or drug and alcohol addiction? Should government provide counseling and therapy? Most likely, some combination of these and other strategies will be needed to address the needs of homeless Americans. Determining the appropriate combination of strategies is not easy.

Types of Public Policy

In an effort to make sense of all the policies in contemporary politics, some political scientists divide them into types—redistributive, distributive, or regulatory—depending on who benefits and who pays, what the policy tries to accomplish, and how it is made.[9] Although this classification, summarized in Table 17.1, is not perfect (it turns out, for instance, that sometimes a policy can fit into more than one category), it does help us to think about policy in a coherent way.

Redistributive policies attempt to shift wealth, income, and other resources from the "haves" to the "have-nots." Like Robin Hood, government acting through redistributive policies seeks to help its poorer citizens. The U.S. government's income tax policy is redistributive because it is based on a progressive tax rate. People who earn more pay a higher percentage of their incomes to the federal government in taxes. (The progressivity of the income tax, however, is tempered by other elements of the U.S. tax code.) Programs such as Medicaid or food assistance are redistributive policies because they shift dollars away from people with relatively larger incomes to people with smaller or no incomes. As we see later in this chapter, U.S. social welfare policy is largely redistributive. Health care policy in the United States is also redistributive, since the government, through taxation, provides for the cost of health care for some of those who cannot afford it.

Redistributive policies are generally politically difficult to put in place because they take resources away from the affluent segments of society who are most likely to be politically active, to vote regularly, and to contribute to political campaigns or interest groups. These attentive constituents individually or

Table 17.1

Types of Policy

Type of policy	Policy goal	Who promotes this policy?	Who benefits? (wins)	Who pays? (loses)	Examples
Redistributive	To help the have-nots in society	Public interest groups, officials motivated by values	Disadvantaged citizens	Middle- and upper-class taxpayers	Medicaid; food stamps
Distributive	To meet the needs of various groups	Legislators and interest groups	Members of interest groups and the legislators they support	All taxpayers	Homeowners' tax deductions; veterans' benefits; anticrime policies; education reform
Regulatory	To limit or control actions of individuals or groups	Public interest groups	Public	Targeted groups	Environmental policy

> *distributive policies* policies funded by the whole taxpayer base that address the needs of particular groups

> *regulatory policies* policies designed to restrict or change the behavior of certain groups or individuals

collectively contact their congressional representatives to express their views. In contrast, the recipients of redistributive policies, far lower on the socioeconomic scale, tend to vote less often and lack the resources to donate to political campaigns or form interest groups. Their causes may be taken up by public interest groups, professional organizations representing social workers, or legislators who believe that it is government's job to help the needy. In the battle of who gets what in politics, policies that redistribute wealth are relatively rare because the people who must pay for the policies are better equipped than the poor to fight political battles.

Distributive policies, on the other hand, are much easier to make, because the costs are not perceived to be borne by any particular segment of the population. Tax deductions for interest on home mortgage payments, agriculture price supports, interstate highway policies, federal grants for higher education, even programs that provide for parks and recreation are examples of distributive policies. The common feature of distributive policies is that while they provide benefits to a recognizable group (such as homeowners or the families of college students), the costs are widely distributed. In other words, all taxpayers foot the bill.

Distributive policies are often associated with pork barrel politics in which legislators try to secure federal dollars to support programs in their home districts (see Chapter 7). Since the costs are distributed among all taxpayers, and no one group bears the brunt of the expense, it's hard to block the adoption of the policy. This is especially true when a program has good media appeal. Consider, for example, the country's disaster relief policy. Through the Federal Emergency Management Agency (FEMA), people can receive grants to help restore private property lost due to earthquakes, floods, hurricanes, or other catastrophic events. However, the money that goes to crisis victims comes from the public treasury. Some critics of federal disaster relief policy question the high costs associated with rebuilding whole communities after natural disasters—especially the rebuilding of homes in high-risk areas (such as beachfront property)—and argue that individual homeowners should take more responsibility for their losses. However, as we saw in 2005 when Hurricane Katrina hit the Gulf Coast, it's hard for any politician to argue to reduce funding for any disaster relief program when the nightly news shows devastated communities. Also, because no one segment of the population bears the brunt of the cost, no clear voices are raised in opposition.

Regulatory policies differ from redistributive and distributive policies in that they are designed to restrict or change the behavior of certain groups or individuals. Whereas redistributive and distributive policies work to increase assistance to particular groups, regulatory policies tend to do just the opposite. They limit the actions of the regulatory target group—the group whose behavior government seeks to control. Most environmental policies, for example, are regulatory in nature. Business owners face myriad air emissions limitations and permit requirements that must be met in order to avoid government sanctions, including the possibility of civil fines or a criminal trial. Since the groups being regulated frequently have greater resources at their disposal than the groups seeking the regulation (often public interest groups), the battle to regulate business can be a lopsided one, as we indicated in Chapter 13.

The politics surrounding the creation of regulatory policies are highly confrontational. The "losers" in regulatory policy are often the target groups. Business doesn't want to pay for environmental controls, nor do manufacturers want to be monitored for compliance by government. By contrast, interest groups representing the beneficiaries of the policy argue just as strongly for the need for regulatory control. To continue our environmental policy example, the Environmental Defense Fund and the American Lung Association are repeat players in policy developments under the Clean Air Act. These groups have frequently sued the U.S. Environmental Protection Agency to compel it to lower the acceptable levels of airborne pollutants.[10] We return to environmental policy later in this chapter.

Who Makes Policy?

All the political actors we have studied in this book have a hand in the policymaking process. Government actors inside the system—members of Congress, the president, the courts, and bureaucrats—are involved, as are actors outside the system—interest groups, the media, and members of the public.

Policies are usually created by members of Congress in the form of one or more new laws. Sometimes what we think of as a single policy is really a bundle of several laws or amendments to laws. Environmental policy and social welfare policy are prime examples of bundles of programs and laws. National environmental policy is included in more than a dozen laws, among them the Clean Air Act, the Clean Water

Act, and the Safe Drinking Water Act. Social welfare policy consists of more than direct financial assistance to poor families. Also included are programs that subsidize food purchases, provide day-care for children, and offer job training and education for the parents.

The role of Congress in creating and legitimating policy through its laws is critically important to understanding national public policy. Recall from Chapter 7 that members of Congress are often most attentive to what their constituencies and the interest groups that support their campaigns want. Nonetheless, many members of Congress also follow their own values and consciences when making difficult political decisions. Rep. Jay Inslee, D-Wash., who lost his seat in 1994 over his vote in favor of gun control (before winning it back in 1998), puts it this way: "It was bitter and it was painful . . . but I have not regretted that vote for one minute. No Congressman's seat is worth a child's life." [11]

The president may also create policy, perhaps by putting an issue on the public agenda, by including it (or not) in his budget proposal, by vetoing a law made by Congress, or by issuing an executive order that establishes a new policy or augments an existing one. Executive orders sometimes make profound changes in policy. One such executive order created affirmative action. When Congress passed the Civil Rights Act in 1964, banning employment discrimination against women and minorities, the law did not require that employers actively seek to employ persons within these protected classes. Arguing that America must seek "equality as a fact and equality as a result," President Lyndon Johnson issued Executive Orders 11246 and 11375, requiring federal contractors to develop affirmative action programs to promote the hiring and advancement of minorities and women.

Government bureaucracies at the federal, state, or local level may also create or enhance policy through their power to regulate. Administrative agencies are crucial to the policymaking process, helping to propose laws, lobbying for their passage, making laws of their own under authority delegated from Congress, and implementing laws. We saw in Chapter 9 that when a broadly worded bill is passed by Congress, it is the bureaucracy that creates the regulations necessary to put the law into action. Moreover, agencies have enormous control over policy simply by how they enforce it.

Finally, the courts are policymakers as well. We saw clearly in Chapter 10 that the Supreme Court has been responsible for some of the major changes in policy direction in this country with respect to business regulation, civil rights, and civil liberties, to name just a few. When the courts rule on what the government can or should do (or not do), they are clearly taking an active policymaking role. In addition, they are often asked to rule on the implementation of policy decisions made elsewhere in the government, on affirmative action, for example, or welfare policy, or education.

National policies are best thought of as packages made by several actors. Congress passes a law that establishes a policy. In turn, federal and/or state agencies respond by writing regulations and working with individuals who are affected by the policy. The president may want to emphasize (or deemphasize) a policy in several ways. He or she may publicize the new policy through public statements—most notably the State of the Union address. The president may issue formal (executive orders) or informal instructions to agencies that highlight policy goals. So, although a law may initially establish a plan of action for a public problem, policies tend to evolve over time and contain many elements from all branches of government. These various components (laws, regulations, executive orders, agency actions, and so on) taken as a whole form the government's policy.

Steps of the Policymaking Process

Political scientists have isolated five steps that most policymakers follow in the process of trying to solve a public problem. Figure 17.1 illustrates the policymaking process.

Agenda Setting

The first step in creating policy is agenda setting. Agenda setting occurs when problems come to the attention of people who can address them (usually members of Congress). These problems can be brought to Congress' attention by individual members, the president, interest groups, the media, or public opinion polls.

Why is it that some issues capture the attention of Congress and other policymakers, while other issues don't? Sometimes an issue explodes onto the agenda because of a *triggering event*. For instance, the terrorist attacks of September 11, 2001, stunned the nation and made national security an immediate priority, propelling Congress to pass the USA Patriot Act, discussed in Chapter 5, almost immediately. It

Figure 17.1

The Policymaking Process

Policymaking begins with agenda setting and ends with policy evaluation, which often cycles back to the creation of new policy initiatives.

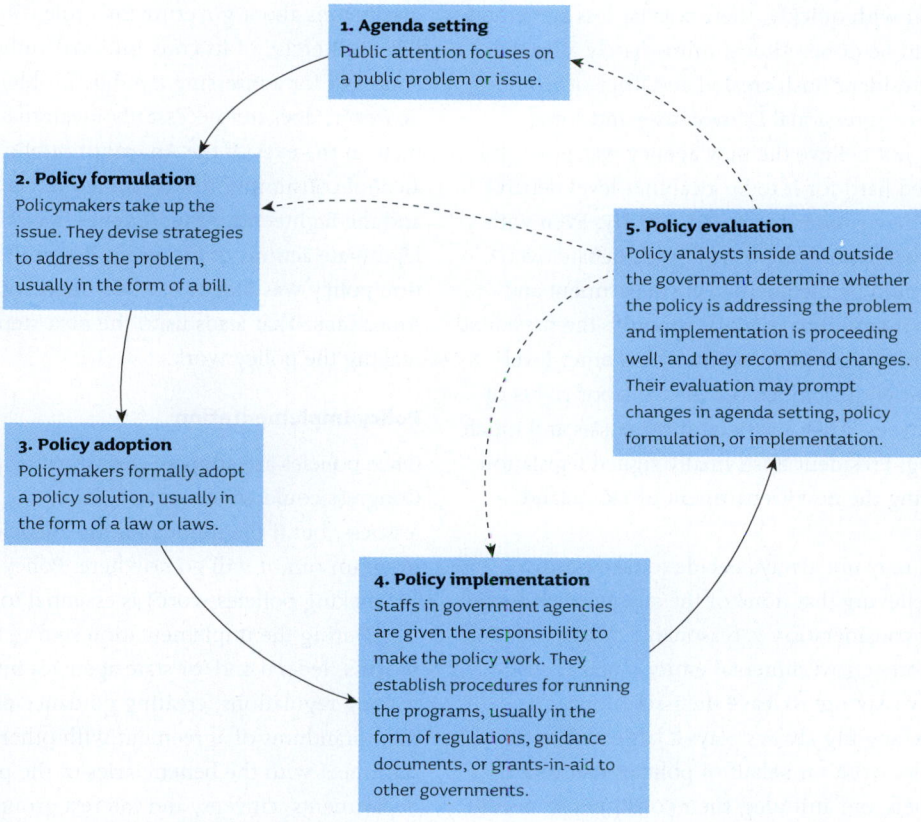

1. Agenda setting
Public attention focuses on a public problem or issue.

2. Policy formulation
Policymakers take up the issue. They devise strategies to address the problem, usually in the form of a bill.

3. Policy adoption
Policymakers formally adopt a policy solution, usually in the form of a law or laws.

4. Policy implementation
Staffs in government agencies are given the responsibility to make the policy work. They establish procedures for running the programs, usually in the form of regulations, guidance documents, or grants-in-aid to other governments.

5. Policy evaluation
Policy analysts inside and outside the government determine whether the policy is addressing the problem and implementation is proceeding well, and they recommend changes. Their evaluation may prompt changes in agenda setting, policy formulation, or implementation.

is rare for legislation to pass this quickly without a dramatic or compelling triggering event.

Sometimes issues reach the public agenda not because of one particular event but because they have prominent political supporters within Congress or the administration. These individuals, known as policy or interest group entrepreneurs (see Chapter 13), fight to get members of Congress to pay attention to their pet issues and concerns.[12] Consider the fact that despite George W. Bush's promise to veto increased federal funding for stem cell research and the Republican congressional majority's disinclination to cross a president who had helped many of them get into office, Congress passed legislation to do just that in 2005. The issue had stayed on the public agenda in the face of considerable effort by social conservatives to remove it, in part because of the sponsorship of former first lady Nancy Reagan and actors Michael J. Fox and the late Christopher Reeve.[13]

Policy Formulation

The second step in the policymaking process is called policy formulation. At this step, several competing solutions to the policy problem or objective are developed and debated in Congress. These alternative strategies often take the form of bills—perhaps proposed by the president or an administrative agency—that are introduced into Congress and sent to committees for deliberation. Dozens of bills may be introduced in each congressional session on any particular policy area, each offering a different approach to addressing the public problem. Congressional committees decide which of the alternatives offers the most promise for solving the problem and which will be acceptable to the whole Congress. As you'll recall from Chapter 7, most bills die in committee, and the ones that survive are almost always "marked up," or changed, before going to the floor.

Following September 11 and the clear consensus that homeland security was a problem that Congress needed to deal with, and deal with quickly, there was far less agreement on how that should be done. Almost immediately after the terrorist attacks, President Bush created an Office of Homeland Security, but congressional Democrats—and some Republicans—did not believe the new agency was powerful enough and pushed hard for it to be a cabinet-level department, something the president opposed initially. Even with the president's new support, there was much debate over which agencies would be included in the department and how much power it would have. And, although the president changed his tune regarding the creation of a cabinet-level position, he fought with Democrats over the labor rights of department employees. After a variety of proposals and much political wrangling, President Bush finally signed legislation in late 2002 creating the new Department of Homeland Security.[14]

Policymakers may not always decide to take positive action. Instead, believing that none of the strategies presented by the bills under consideration is reasonable or that the issue is better left to another governmental entity (such as state government), they may opt to leave the issue alone. Of course, political wrangling always plays a large part in this process as members work on behalf of policies that reflect their personal beliefs and attitudes, their constituents' needs, and their party's overall goals and agenda.

Policy Adoption

If a preferred policy alternative emerges from the policy formulation stage, it must be legitimized through formal governmental action. Policies—some trivial, some enormously important—are continually being adopted by all three branches of government. In just a few short months in the spring of 2005, policy was adopted by congressional legislation (for instance, the passage of the bankruptcy reform bill that made it more difficult for people to avoid debts by filing for federal bankruptcy protection),[15] by executive order (as when President Bush directed that the government could impose quarantines on people arriving in the United States to prevent outbreaks of bird flu),[16] by federal bureaucratic decision (the creation of the new food pyramid by the Food and Drug Administration, instructing Americans about how to achieve a healthy diet),[17] and by court ruling (the U.S. Supreme Court's decision that minors cannot be subject to the death penalty).[18]

The key point about policy adoption is that the policy has now moved beyond debates over possible options and discussions about government's role. Government has, by formal exercise of its constitutional authority, legitimized its approach for addressing a public problem. Policy adoption, however, does not necessarily mean that the policy is legitimate in the eyes of the American public. During the 1920s, alcohol consumption was banned through the Volstead Act and the Eighteenth Amendment—legal and constitutionally legitimate actions of Congress. Politically, however, Prohibition policy was illegitimate, or unacceptable, to many Americans. That leads us to the next step, which involves making the policy work.

Policy Implementation

Once policies are adopted they must be put into practice. Congress could create a good policy for addressing homelessness, but if the implementing agencies don't make the program run, it will go nowhere. Policy implementation (or making policies work) is essential to policy success.

During the implementation step of the policymaking process, federal and/or state agencies interpret the policy by writing regulations, creating guidance documents, or drafting memorandums of agreement with other agencies. Agency staff meet with the beneficiaries of the policy, staff in other departments, citizens, and interest groups in an attempt to devise a workable plan for putting the policy into action.

Implementation of public policy is neither easy nor guaranteed. Early studies of policy implementation suggested that policymakers and citizens could not assume that, just because a policy was adopted, it would be put into place.[19] Several scholars argue that policy implementation will go more smoothly if: (1) a law has clear, unambiguous goals, (2) Congress has provided sufficient funding and staffing resources, and (3) the policy enjoys the support of policymakers, agency officials, and the public.[20] Also important, according to these scholars, is the degree of behavioral change demanded by the policy and the nature of the target group—the people, organizations, governments, or businesses that will have to change their behavior. When the behavioral change is great and the size of the target group is large, they argue, policy implementation will stall because members of the group will resist complying with the policy.

It is also essential for the bureaucrats who are implementing the policy to agree with it. If people who are responsible for implementation don't believe the policy is

> **cost-benefit analysis** an evaluation method in which the costs of the program are compared to the benefits of the policy

sound, they will resist or ignore it. Scholars argue that real implementation power rests with street-level bureaucrats—people who run the program "on the ground"—not with the makers of public policy.[21] For instance, despite President Clinton's executive order creating the "don't ask, don't tell" policy with regard to gays in the military, officials who disagreed with the policy continued to seek out and use information about the sexual orientation of members of the armed forces, leading to efforts to repeal the policy.[22] (DADT was repealed in December 2010.)

Finally, implementing policy often becomes complicated when it involves federal, state, and local governments. Policy goals may not be shared by all levels of government, and states may have different capacities to respond to the demands of putting a new program into place.[23]

Policy Evaluation

The last step in the policymaking process is to evaluate the policy. Since creating a perfect policy and choosing the best strategy for addressing a public problem are virtually impossible, government should analyze what is working and what needs to be changed. If policy evaluation is done correctly, it is likely that policy change will occur—new laws will be created to "fix" or improve the existing policy, agencies will issue new regulations or change procedures, and implementation obstacles will be identified and, if possible, corrected. At the heart of policy evaluation is saving the good parts of a current policy while identifying the gaps between policy goals and on-the-ground outcomes.

Policy evaluation requires the policy analyst to ask several fundamental questions. Does the policy as currently constructed address the initial public problem? Does it represent a reasonable use of public resources? Would other strategies be more effective? Has it produced any undesirable effects?

One way to evaluate policy is to conduct a **cost-benefit analysis**. On the surface, this looks simple. The analyst adds up the costs of the program and then compares these costs to the benefits of the policy. If cost-benefit analysis is conducted as a way of choosing among alternative directions in policy, then the alternative with the greatest net benefit should be chosen. However, cost-benefit analysis has a number of pitfalls.[24] First, the analyst must be able to quantify, or put a monetary value on, all costs and benefits of the policy. How does one determine the value of clean air? Of feeling safe on the streets? These intangible values defy easy dollars-and-cents translation.

What Is a Life Worth to Us?

Policy evaluation involves assessing the tradeoff of a program's costs to taxpayers versus the benefits of its outcomes. The dilemma is figuring out how much value to place on the life of someone like Carolyn Bieber. Homeless with her boyfriend on the streets of Santa Monica, California, her body was weakened by epilepsy, pregnancy, and alcoholism. Two days after this photo was taken she had a seizure and died. Can a policy planner put a cost on that?

A second problem with cost-benefit analysis, and with other policy evaluation techniques, is that public problems are fraught with uncertainties. We just don't have enough information to predict all the possible results of policy. In addition, outcomes may be years away. Take, for example, the national government's policy that lands disturbed by coal mining be reclaimed to their approximate original contour and that habitats be restored for the plants and animals that used to live there. Experts now know that it may take two decades to discover whether our national coal-mining reclamation policy is working, and we may never know if groundwater disturbances caused by coal mining can be reversed.[25]

A final limitation of cost-benefit analysis is that it only allows the analyst to ask of a policy whether it is *efficient*: is the policy delivering the most bang for the buck? However, efficiency is just one factor by which a policy can be evaluated. Enacted policies could also be evaluated in terms of social acceptability—that is, the degree to which the public accepts and supports the policy. For example, an efficient policy may call for increased surveillance in private areas, but the public may oppose this policy on privacy grounds. Others evaluate policies based on their feasibility since even the best policy will have little effect if it is too controversial to enact or too complicated to implement. Yet another concern rests with how *equitable*, or fair, a policy may be. An environmental policy that regulates hazardous waste may be very efficient (waste is removed at low cost) and effective (waste is prevented from entering the environment), but it may fail when equity is used as an evaluative yardstick (the hazardous waste incinerator is located in a low-income community where primarily persons of color reside).

Policy evaluation is conducted inside government by agencies such as the U.S. Government Accountability Office, the Congressional Budget Office, the Office of Management and Budget, and the Congressional Research Service. Congress also conducts oversight hearings in which agencies that implement programs report their progress toward policy goals. For example, each year the Office of Family Assistance presents an annual report to Congress on the status of the Temporary Assistance for Needy Families (TANF) welfare program that we discuss later in this chapter. The report is quite detailed, including data and information on caseloads, expenditures, child poverty, and worker participation rates.[26]

Even if an agency does not make a formal presentation before a congressional committee, it will often document the successes and failures of a program in a report. One thing to keep in mind about government reports, however, is that the agency creating the report may have a stake in how the policy is evaluated. The people working for a government agency on a specific program likely have a great deal invested in the program (perhaps their jobs or their funding), or a new presidential administration may not have a commitment to a program and wants to see it fail. It is important to remember, as we discussed in Chapter 9, that, in theory, bureaucrats are supposed to be apolitical and neutral. However, that is not always the case.

Because of the potential lack of neutrality of government officials, groups outside government also evaluate policy. Although some, such as the Bill and Melinda Gates Foundation, are nonpartisan and funded by philanthropic organizations, others, like the think tanks we discussed in Chapter 13, often have more political agendas. Groups like the Brookings Institution, Common Cause, the Heritage Foundation, and the Cato Institute examine policies that are in place to determine whether the desired outcomes are being achieved. Organizations that opposed a particular law or new program also monitor their effects and are especially vocal if the law or program has had negative consequences for them. For example, on the tenth anniversary of the enactment of the North American Free Trade Agreement (NAFTA), an agreement

social policies distributive and redistributive policies that seek to improve the quality of citizens' lives

> ## Thinking Outside the Box
>
> ### To what extent should future generations be considered when government sets out to solve public problems for current citizens?

among the United States, Mexico, and Canada to make the trading of goods among the countries easier, Public Citizen, a nonprofit consumer advocacy group, released a scathing report accusing the program of, among other things, eliminating American jobs and reducing wages.[27]

Public policies are government's strategies for addressing public problems or changing behaviors. The governmental actors involved in devising policy solutions to public problems seek to solve those problems through agenda setting, formulation, adoption, implementation, and evaluation. Nongovernmental actors engage in all the forms of political participation and lobbying that we have discussed throughout this book. Citizens, in their role as voters, also seek to influence the solutions to public problems by voting for candidates who they believe will be responsive to their wishes. In the remainder of this chapter, we will see how these various actors seek to solve public problems by creating, implementing, and evaluating policy in two critical areas: social and environmental policy.

Who What How

The Case of Social Policy
Government efforts to improve citizens' lives

As we have seen, in the United States we have public policies to address every imaginable public problem, from transportation, to crime, to education. We can't discuss every public policy in this short chapter, but we can zero in on a few to give you a clearer idea of how the policy process works—who the actors are, what they want, and how they go about getting it. In this section we look at *social policies*—primarily distributive and redistributive policies that seek to improve the quality of citizens' lives.

poverty threshold the income level below which a family is considered to be "poor"

social welfare policies public policies that seek to meet the basic needs of people who are unable to provide for themselves

means-tested programs social programs whose beneficiaries qualify by demonstrating need

social insurance programs programs that offer benefits in exchange for contributions

Social policies focus on a variety of quality-of-life problems—most of them centered on the problem of how we can improve people's standards of living. As we will see, social policies can benefit people at all levels of income and wealth, but most frequently they deal with the issue of poverty.

Poverty is a particularly difficult issue for societies to deal with because there is no universally accepted definition of who is poor. If you look up *poverty* in the dictionary, you will find no absolute income level below which people are poor and above which they are not. Deciding what is poverty— who is poor and who isn't—is itself a policy decision made by the government through the agency of the Census Bureau. The Census Bureau calculates the minimum cost for a family of four to live, assuming that a third of its income is spent on food. In 2010 the **poverty threshold**, or poverty line, for a family of four was a pretax income of $22,050.[28] This calculation focuses only on income and does not include noncash benefits like food assistance or family assets like a home or a car. Keep in mind that there is no guarantee that a family of four can live on this amount—numerous individual circumstances can raise a family's expenses. In 2008 the U.S. poverty rate was 13.2 percent, and the number of people with family incomes below the official poverty level was 40 million.[29] (See "*Who Are We?* Poverty and the American People.") More than 19 percent of American children live in poverty—a rate much higher than in most other Western industrialized nations.[30] Nearly 30 percent of female-headed, single-parent households are poor, compared to only 4.6 percent of married-couple households. The percentages are even higher for Hispanic and black female-headed, single-parent households (37.1 percent and 34.3 percent, respectively).[31]

Whether they address poverty by ignoring it and leaving the issue to private charities (remember that not taking action is a policy as surely as is taking specific steps to make a problem go away) or by building an extensive welfare state, all societies have a policy on how to take care of the economically vulnerable. One way to address the problem is with **social welfare policies**, government programs that provide for the needs of those who cannot, or sometimes will not, provide for themselves—needs for shelter, food and clothing, jobs, education, old-age care, and medical assistance. Most social welfare policies are redistributive; they transfer resources, in the form of financial assistance or essential services, from those with resources to those without. Policies

such as these are usually **means-tested programs**, that is, beneficiaries must prove that they lack the necessary means to provide for themselves, according to the government's definitions of eligibility. As we said earlier, redistributive programs can be politically divisive and can open the way to partisan battle.

A second way societies deal with the problem of caring for the economically vulnerable is through **social insurance programs** that offer benefits in exchange for contributions made by citizens to offset future economic need. Social Security is an example of a social insurance program. While welfare policies are usually designed to be temporary solutions for helping the poor, social insurance programs cover longer-range needs. Social insurance programs are distributive because broad segments of the population pay into and benefit from the system at some point in their lives.

Although welfare and Social Security were originally designed to aid the needy—poor children in the first case and the elderly poor in the second—they have evolved in different directions because of who is involved and how they go about trying to get what they want from the system. Today the differences are substantial.

Social Security is a hugely popular program whose benefit levels are guarded zealously, whereas welfare has been reformed to end its thirty-year guarantee that no American child would go hungry. Social Security promises a lifetime of benefits to recipients, even though most draw far more money out of the system than they ever put in, whereas welfare laws now limit recipients to two years at a time on the program, with a lifetime total of five years. Why the differences? The answer lies in the identity of the beneficiaries of the two programs and those who pay for them (the *who*), what the two programs try to accomplish (the *what*), and the politics under which each policy is produced (the *how*). In this section we look at each of these elements more closely.

Social Security

When extended families lived together and grown children took care of their aging parents, care for the elderly wasn't considered to be a public problem. But in modern society, with its mobile populations and splintered families, people often do not live in the same state as their parents, let alone in the same town or house. Although people are living longer and longer, American culture no longer emphasizes the responsibility of each generation to care for the previous one

▶ Who Are We?

Poverty and the American people

Americans have long viewed the United States as the land of opportunity, but millions of U.S. residents live in poverty. As we discussed in Chapter 6, a greater percentage of African Americans, Hispanic Americans, and American Indians live in poverty than do whites. One can also see the effects of poverty when looking at families. Families with a single householder, especially if that person is female, are far more likely to live in poverty than are families with two parents. Children, foreign-born citizens, noncitizens, and those who live in the South are more apt to live in poverty as well. Do differences in poverty rates among these groups present a problem that elected officials should deal with, or should we just accept that some people will always be better off than others?

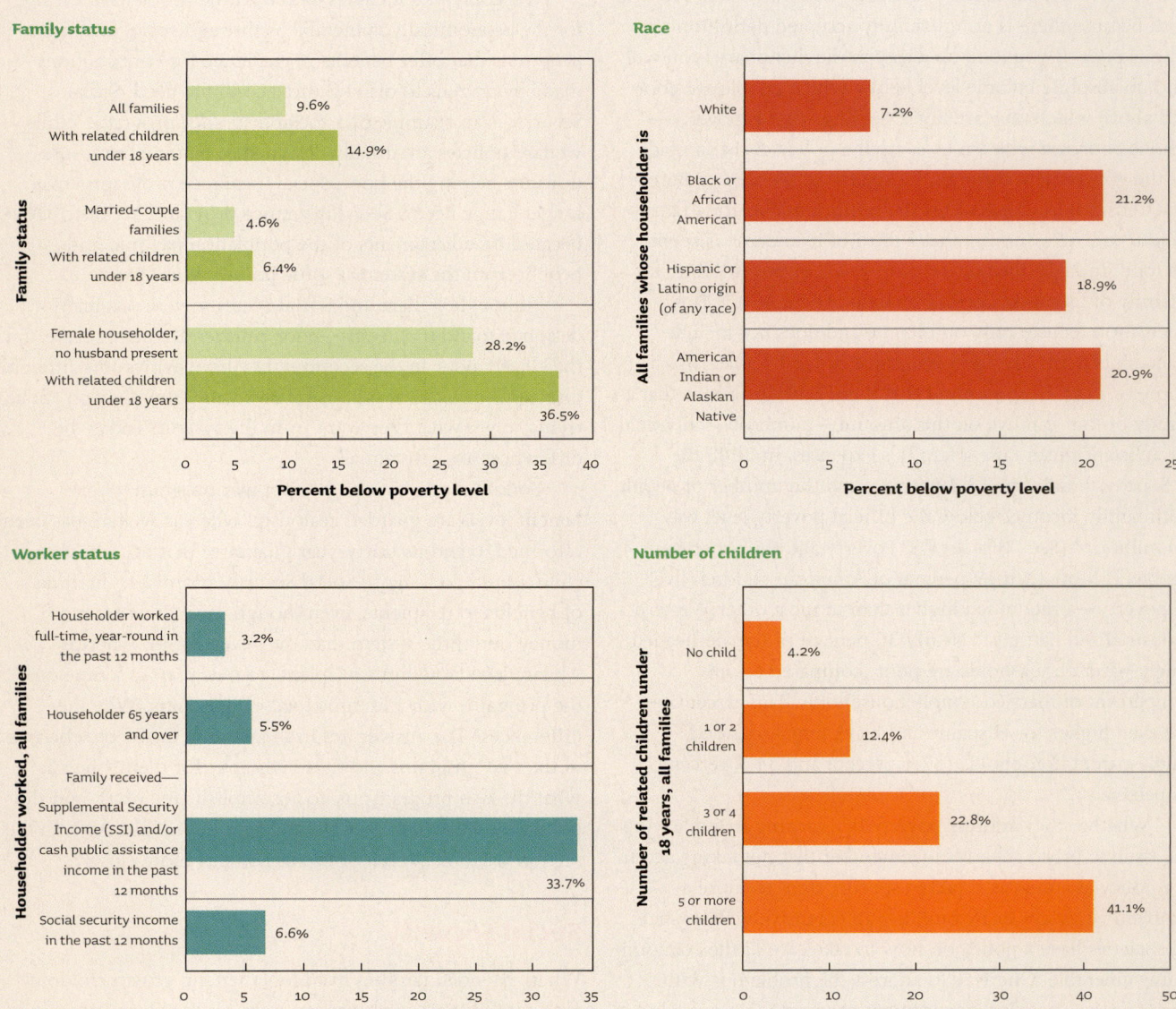

Family status

Family status

- All families — 9.6%
- With related children under 18 years — 14.9%
- Married-couple families — 4.6%
- With related children under 18 years — 6.4%
- Female householder, no husband present — 28.2%
- With related children under 18 years — 36.5%

Percent below poverty level

Race

All families whose householder is

- White — 7.2%
- Black or African American — 21.2%
- Hispanic or Latino origin (of any race) — 18.9%
- American Indian or Alaskan Native — 20.9%

Percent below poverty level

Worker status

Householder worked, all families

- Householder worked full-time, year-round in the past 12 months — 3.2%
- Householder 65 years and over — 5.5%
- Family received—Supplemental Security Income (SSI) and/or cash public assistance income in the past 12 months — 33.7%
- Social security income in the past 12 months — 6.6%

Percent below poverty level

Number of children

Number of related children under 18 years, all families

- No child — 4.2%
- 1 or 2 children — 12.4%
- 3 or 4 children — 22.8%
- 5 or more children — 41.1%

Percent below poverty level

Source: U.S. Census Bureau, "Poverty Status in Past 12 Months of Families, 2006–2008," American Community Survey 3-Year Estimates, Table S1702, http://factfinder.census.gov/.

or of individuals to save money for their own old age. Social Security—essentially a forced savings program for workers, whose own contribution is matched by an equal contribution from their employers—has become the national policy solution to the problem of providing a secure retirement for those who, because of bad financial planning, low incomes, or unforeseen economic crises, cannot secure it for themselves.

Social Security was born in the midst of the Great Depression, when so many older Americans found themselves facing an impoverished retirement that Franklin Roosevelt's New Deal administration passed the Social Security Act in 1935. The act had three components: Aid to Families With Dependent Children (which we discuss later, in the section on welfare policy), Old Age Survivors and Disability Insurance (Social Security), and unemployment insurance. Social Security provided what is essentially a guaranteed pension for workers. Lyndon Johnson's amendment to the act added health care benefits for the elderly in the form of Medicare. These programs have brought financial security to many retired people, but they are costly programs, especially as the baby boomer generation approaches retirement age.

How It Works

As we indicated, ***Social Security*** is a social insurance program: people contribute to Social Security during their working lives in order to receive benefits when they retire. Consequently most people see Social Security in a positive light—as if they are receiving something they have earned and to which they are entitled, not as a government handout. As we will see, that is only part of the story.

On its face, Social Security looks very different from the social welfare programs we mentioned earlier, where income or resources are transferred from one group to another. Recipients contribute a portion of their income, matched by their employers, directly into a fund for Social Security. If you receive a paycheck, your Social Security contribution appears as a withholding called FICA (Federal Insurance Contributions Act). Workers contribute 7.7 percent of the first $106,800 (in 2010) of their salaries in FICA taxes and their employers match that amount, to a total of 15.3 percent.

That money you contribute does not sit in an account with your name on it but rather goes to pay the benefits of those who are currently retired. Because there are more people working right now than are needed to pay current retirement benefits, the excess funds are paid into a Social Security Trust Fund. That money is not sitting around either.

The government borrows it for various other expenses and has to pay it back with interest.

Retirees receive monthly checks from the Social Security Administration, based on how much money they paid into the system. Retirement age is based on when you were born: those who were born before 1937 can retire at sixty-five and receive full benefits, or retire early (at sixty-two) and get 80 percent of their benefits. Since people are living longer than they did when the Social Security Act was passed, and since they continue to receive benefits as long as they are alive (and their surviving spouses after that), Congress has altered these ages to make the plan more financially viable. For example, those born after 1960 retire with full benefits at age sixty-seven, and if they choose early retirement, they receive only 70 percent of their benefits.

In early 2010 the average monthly payment for all retired workers was $1,164.[32] What you receive can vary by as much as a thousand dollars, depending on what your salary was during your working life.[33] In 2007, 88 percent of married couples and 86 percent of nonmarried persons aged sixty-five or older received Social Security benefits. Social Security was the major source of income (providing at least 50 percent of total income) for 53 percent of retired couples and 73 percent of nonmarried beneficiaries.[34]

Is Social Security Going Broke?

Social Security today is in hot water. That is due partly, as we will see, to ideological reasons but partly also to its finances. The short explanation is that the program is running out of money, but why that is so requires a deeper understanding of how it is funded.

We call Social Security an insurance program, but it is different from real insurance in critical ways. Because life is uncertain, many of us choose to buy insurance against future risk, to pay money now while we are able to offset future catastrophe—that we might have a car accident, get sick, or die. We pool that money with others, and if we are unlucky enough to be struck by disaster, that money comes to our aid or that of our survivors. If we are living a charmed life and stay whole and healthy, we probably never see that money again—we are subsidizing someone else's misfortune.

Although we contribute to Social Security, there is really no uncertainty about the future. We will all get old (at least we hope we will), and we will all receive benefits. There will be no lucky retirees subsidizing the lives of unlucky retirees—Social Security has to pay for all of us, meaning that the risk-sharing advantages of insurance don't come into play here. In that sense, Social Security is more like a forced savings plan than an insurance plan. The government requires that we save our money each month so that we can draw on it in our retirement.

But if Social Security is a forced savings account, it is a magical one indeed because it never runs out as long as we or our spouses are alive. We continue to receive payments long after we've gotten back the money we put in, even including the interest we might have earned had it been in a real savings account. The average Social Security recipient gets back what he or she put into the program within the first seven years of receiving benefits.[35] And since there is no means-test for Social Security, not only poor recipients but also billionaires can continue to collect this direct subsidy from taxpayers. And since billionaires and other wealthy people paid Social Security taxes only on the first $90,000 of their income, they did not even contribute proportionately.

How is this bottomless Social Security savings account possible? Why doesn't it run out like a regular savings account does, when all the money is spent? So far it has worked because the number of people in the work force has been able to cover the retirement expenses of those leaving it. The Social Security Trust Fund has gotten fat because the pool of workers has grown faster than the pool of retirees. That is about to change, however, as the baby boomers get older and begin to retire. Between 2010 and 2030, the number of Americans over age sixty-five will increase by 72 percent, while the number of working-age Americans (those aged twenty to sixty-four) will increase by only 4 percent.[36]

The Social Security Trust Fund now receives more in FICA taxes than is paid out in benefits, but by 2017 that will change as the number of retirees grows and the fund is tapped to pay their benefits. That means that the federal government, which has been borrowing that money, will need to pay it back, with interest. If nothing is done to change the way Social Security works (for example, by cutting benefits, increasing Social Security taxes, or raising the retirement age), the Social Security Board of Trustees estimates that the trust fund will run out of money by the year 2041 and that the only funds available to pay retirees' benefits will be the money simultaneously paid in by current workers. Social Security recipients would receive only about 74 percent of the benefits they are owed, according to the current promise of the program.[37]

Unless the law changes that promise, the government will have to pay benefits whether or not the money is there. This is because Social Security is an **entitlement program**, which means that benefits must be paid to people who are entitled to receive them. Funding entitlement programs is nondiscretionary for government: once the entitlement is created, recipients who qualify must receive their benefits.

Entitlements comprise an increasing share of the federal budget. In 1963, spending for entitlement programs (of which Social Security is the largest) was about 25 percent of the federal budget. By 2007 entitlement spending was almost 55 percent of the budget, and it continues to grow. Social Security itself is the government's largest program, paying approximately $587 billion in benefits, or about 21 percent of the federal budget, in 2007.[38] Combining entitlement spending with a net interest expense of almost 7 percent leaves less than 40 percent for discretionary spending.[39] As interest rates continue to rise, the percentage of discretionary spending will continue to decline. Think about that for a moment. If things don't change, every other program of the national government—national defense, education, environmental protection, veterans' programs, disaster assistance, even national parks—will have to be funded with the remaining 30 or 35 percent of tax revenues.

The Politics of Social Security Today

Many older Americans continue to need the economic protection that Social Security provides, but the system is clearly not sustainable into the indefinite future in its present form. It could be made sustainable if benefit levels were cut, or if taxes were increased, or if the $90,000 cap on income for Social Security taxes were lifted, or if the program were means-tested, or if the retirement age were raised. Each of these solutions would work, but they are politically unpalatable. If they were enacted, people would have to pay more or get less or both, and no one wants to do those things.

Social Security has been shielded from hard decisions by AARP, a powerful organization of older Americans that protects the interests of retirees. Not only does AARP bring the skills and resources of a high-powered interest group to bear to protect its members' interests, but older people are also far more likely to vote than are younger citizens, making elected politicians extremely reluctant to cross their will. Through the end of the twentieth century, that reluctance held. Politicians went to unusual lengths to profess their loyalty to keeping Social Security intact; in the 2000 presidential campaign,

Social Security Act the New Deal Act that created AFDC, Social Security, and unemployment insurance

candidate Al Gore became a joke on late-night television for the number of times he promised to protect Social Security funds by putting them in a "lock box."

After winning reelection in 2004, President Bush claimed that he had won a mandate for change and was going to spend some of his political capital on reforming Social Security. Conservative Republicans had never been thrilled with the New Deal's assumption of government responsibility for America's retirement, and they viewed Bush's second term as a chance to begin to unravel some of that governmental role by returning responsibility to individuals.[40] Bush proposed that people be allowed to invest some portion of the Social Security taxes they pay in private stock market accounts. He focused much of his appeal on young people for whom retirement seemed a long way off, and for whom the chance to buy into stock market investments seemed more attractive than risky. By emphasizing Social Security's economic woes and reiterating the possibility that the program would be broke before young people retired, he tried to change the perception of the program from one of a distributive program where everyone would benefit, to a redistributive one where money was transferred from the young to subsidize the old.

However, critics responded that such private accounts would do nothing to save the financial fortunes of Social Security and would in fact worsen it by requiring the government to borrow an estimated $1 trillion or more to give young people something to invest while their actual taxes were going to make the payments to current retirees.[41] They claimed further that such accounts would be subject to all the volatility of the stock market when Social Security is supposed to protect people from risk and that Bush's reform was meant to fill the coffers of stock brokers and would eventually end Social Security as a guarantor of a secure retirement.[42]

When polls showed that the American people were not enchanted with the idea of privatizing Social Security and didn't believe that Bush's reforms would save the system money, Bush relabeled his proposal as "personal accounts." These would still be private accounts invested in the stock market with the same price tag, however. This plan remained unpopular with AARP and Bush's Democratic critics.[43] And despite the high priority placed on this issue by the Bush administration, Social Security reform went down as Bush's first major legislative defeat. Although the issue of Social Security is likely to stay on the public agenda until its financial problems are addressed, the question of how to finance the program remains a controversial area of debate.[44]

Welfare Policy in the United States

Social Security is a program designed to protect people's long-term financial futures, but it is not designed to alleviate poverty in the short term. In fact, through the greater part of our history, poverty was not considered a public problem requiring government action. Rather, it was thought to be the result of individual failings. Whatever collective responsibility might exist was private, belonging to churches and charities but not to the government. It was not until the Great Depression of 1929 forced large numbers of previously successful working and middle-class people into poverty that the public view shifted and citizens demanded that government step in. In this section we look at some of the key ways American government today tries to improve the quality of life for its poorest citizens through social welfare policies, focusing particularly on economic security for children.

New Deal Welfare Programs

Proposed policy solutions varied tremendously in the early years of the Depression. In 1930 Senator Huey Long, D-La., advanced a strongly redistributive policy. Long's solution, which he called "Share Our Wealth," proposed limiting annual incomes to $1 million while guaranteeing all families at least $5,000 per year. By confiscating the wealth of the nation's richest people, Long argued that "every man could be king."[45] On the other side of the spectrum, President Herbert Hoover and Secretary of the Treasury Andrew Mellon did not believe that the Depression was a symptom of a public problem that needed solving by the national government. Rather, Hoover called for charity and volunteerism to alleviate economic suffering. His ideas were largely out of tune with public perceptions of the gravity of the problem, and he lost his bid for reelection to Franklin Roosevelt in 1932.

President Roosevelt ushered in the New Deal, a period of the most extensive economic security policy this country had ever seen. Chief among the New Deal programs was the same **Social Security Act** we discussed earlier, which, in addition to guaranteed pensions for older Americans, included Aid to Families With Dependent Children (AFDC), based on the commitment that no child would ever go hungry in America. AFDC was a means-tested program that provided benefits for families with children who could demonstrate need, to keep the children fed and to tide over the adults until they could find work and provide for their children themselves. The federal government contributed more than half the AFDC

▶ **Who, What, How, and WHEN: Meeting Public "Needs"**

People look to their government to provide the things they need but cannot get on their own. Sometimes government tries to meet those needs, sometimes it doesn't; how the government defines what "needs" it should meet changes over time. Here are a few examples of how the definition of "needs" and public efforts to meet those needs has altered over time:

1852 **Free Public Education**

Public schools existed in the United States well before the Revolution; however, they were primarily for the wealthy and funded haphazardly. In 1852 Massachusetts became the first state to provide free public education statewide and to require that students attend elementary school. By about the end of the nineteenth century, all states had free public schools, though legislation in the twentieth century finally opened these schools to all races and required public schools to treat girls and boys equally.

1935 **Social Security Act**

Before 1935 the United States had programs to offer certain groups of people economic security. For example, the government provided pensions for widows, orphans, and disabled veterans of the Civil War. However, these programs were not universal and left many groups, particularly the elderly, susceptible to economic fluctuations. At the height of the Depression in 1934, by some estimates, over half the elderly people in the United States couldn't support themselves and the federal government decided that this was a need that should be met. The Social Security Act created an insurance system by which workers paid a tax on their paycheck and then received payments after they retired at age sixty-five—"insurance" that they would always have some income.

1958 **National Defense Education Act**

Though elementary education became a government-provided good in the nineteenth century, college was considered a benefit only for those who could afford it, not a need that government should subsidize. When competition between the United States and the Soviet Union began to heat up in the Cold War, the U.S. government looked for a way to find talented Americans to work in the space program. The National Defense Education Act provided student loans for college for this purpose; it was followed by the creation of work-study, the Federal Stafford Loan program, and student loan consolidation.

---

payments, and the states supplied the balance, managed the program, and determined who was eligible and how much they received. Even though states retained a role, with AFDC, for the first time, the federal government assumed responsibility for the economic well-being of its citizens.

It is important to note, however, what AFDC did not promise. Assistance here was primarily to dependent children—their parents were aided only secondarily, and the intention was to get them back to work. We had not become a society that easily accepted the notion that the haves are responsible for the have-nots. Redistributive policies that transfer money from the working people to children might seem acceptable; policies that subsidize able-bodied adults are much less palatable. The United States has never kept pace with the Western European welfare states that have promised their citizens security from cradle to grave (or from womb to tomb, as some have more graphically put it). American welfare policy has had far more limited aspirations, and even those have been controversial. By the 1990s, even liberals were clamoring for reform of a welfare system that seemed to have lost sight of its ideals and that, rather than propping up people until they could return to work, produced a culture of dependency that became increasingly difficult for recipients to escape.

At the center of the controversy was AFDC. By 1996, over four million families were receiving aid, with an average

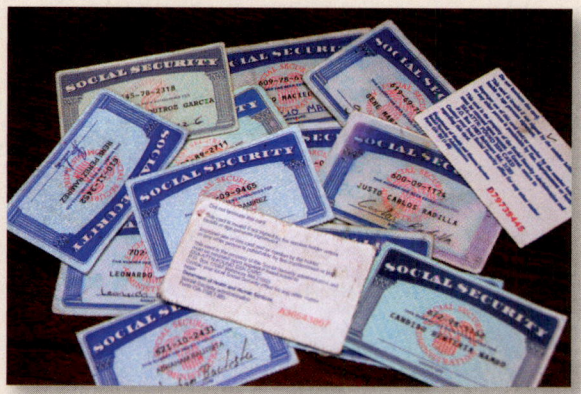

1964 **Food Stamp Act**

Like Social Security, temporary food stamp programs had been around to feed the hungry since 1939. Food stamps supplement the food budget of low-income people who can prove their need. The Food Stamp Act of 1964 made the stamps permanent, although qualifications for receiving them have changed over the years and the program's name was changed to the Supplemental Nutrition Assistance Program on October 1, 2008. In 2009 about 15.2 million households participated in the program in an average month.

1965 **Medicare**

Though repeated efforts to create a national health care program failed until 2010, the government has long provided health care benefits to the elderly, the disabled, and children. Medicare began in 1965 and offers hospitalization, health insurance, and prescription drugs (as of 2006) for people over age sixty-five. Medicaid offers some of the same benefits for low-income people and the disabled. The State Children's Health Insurance Program, started in 1997, provides money to states to offer health care to some uninsured children. Politicians are still debating whether health care for working-age adults is a need that government should address.

2010 **Patient Protection and Affordable Care Act**

In March 2010 President Obama signed a bill into law that would accomplish what presidents had been trying to do since FDR—make health care insurance accessible to most Americans. The bill required all Americans to purchase health insurance, providing assistance for those unable to afford it. Among other provisions, the bill created incentives for small businesses to insure employees and made it easier for people to buy insurance on the open market, making it illegal for insurers to deny coverage for preexisting conditions or to drop coverage for people once they had become ill.

monthly payment of $377. According to government statistics, the majority of AFDC recipients in the 1990s were primarily young unmarried mothers (aged nineteen to thirty), unemployed, residing in central cities.[46] AFDC was designed to raise above the poverty line those families hurt by economic downturns. President Roosevelt and the New Deal architects believed that the government should provide some temporary support when the economy slumped. Yet the explosive growth of the program, particularly in the last quarter of the twentieth century, prompted many policy-makers to question its success. From 1970 to 1995, enrollment increased by over 50 percent from 1.9 million to 4.9 million families. In fiscal year 1994, enrollment and benefits rose to an all-time high with a monthly average of 14.2 million persons receiving benefits totaling $22.8 billion. Studies also indicated that many families were moving on and off AFDC rolls over longer periods of time.[47] Opponents of AFDC posed the question: how long is "temporary"?

Welfare Today

AFDC was criticized because it contained no work require-ments and set no time limits for remaining on welfare. As a redistributive program, it seemed to transfer money from a hard-working segment of the population to one that did nothing to earn it. Also, many states provided additional cash assistance for each additional child, leading some critics to

> **Temporary Assistance to Needy Families (TANF)** a welfare program of block grants to states that encourages recipients to work in exchange for time-limited benefits

Help the Hungry

Most welfare programs were dismantled or limited under the Welfare Reform Act of 1996, making food kitchens like this one in San Francisco a vital resource for the homeless and others in dire straits during hard times like the recent recession, which has seen higher unemployment than at any time since the Great Depression.

Figure 17.2

Population Receiving Welfare (AFDC and TANF), 1960–2010

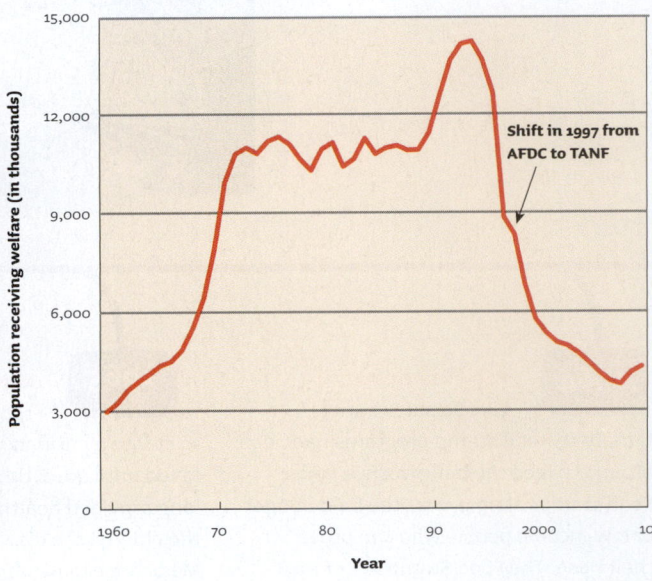

Source: Data obtained from the U.S. Department of Health and Human Services, Administration for Children and Families, Office of Family Assistance, www.acf.hhs.gov/programs/ofa/data-reports/index.htm#tanfdata/.

claim the program encouraged irresponsible child-bearing, especially among unwed mothers, and fostered a culture of dependence in which people came to believe that they had a right to welfare as a way of life. Public opinion polls showed that many Americans believed that welfare recipients were unwilling to work, living off the generosity of hard-working taxpayers. Reports of fraud gave rise to stereotypes of the "welfare queen" driving a Cadillac to the post office to pick up her welfare check. Since lower-income people are less likely to organize for political purposes, welfare recipients put up no coordinated defense of their benefits. While Republicans had traditionally been more critical of welfare policy, even some Democrats began to heed the calls of their constituents for welfare reform, arguing that the welfare system created disincentives for recipients to become productive members of society. On August 22, 1996, President Clinton signed the Personal Responsibility and Work Opportunity Reconciliation Act, fulfilling his promise to "end welfare as we know it."

With Clinton's signature, AFDC was replaced by the **Temporary Assistance to Needy Families (TANF)** block grant to state governments. This reform gives states greater control

over how they spend their money but caps the amount that the federal government will pay for welfare. The law requires work in exchange for time-limited benefits. Most recipients must find a job within two years of going on welfare and cannot stay on the welfare rolls for more than a total of five years altogether (or less, depending on the state). Moreover, many states cap family benefits when an additional child is born to a family on welfare.

More than a decade after the heated debates surrounding its adoption, the controversy over welfare reform has waned. Few observers dispute that the program has successfully reduced the welfare rolls—the Department of Health and Human Services reports that, from August 1996 to October 2009, the number of welfare recipients fell from 12.2 million to around 4.3 million (see Figure 17.2). Most states met their 2004 goals in putting 50 percent of single parents to work for thirty hours per week and 90 percent of two-parent families to work for thirty-five hours per week.[48]

But although studies of families who have left welfare have found that nearly two-thirds are employed in any given month and that more than three-fourths have worked since leaving welfare,[49] some critics argue that even where jobs are found, wages are so low that many people are unable to lift

Table 17.2

Other Programs to Help the Poor or Unemployed in the United States

Program name	Description
Earned income tax credit	Supplements the incomes of working people with low or moderate incomes. Those eligible for the credit receive a payment from the government or a rebate on their taxes that effectively raises their take-home pay.
Housing assistance	Subsidizes rents for families whose income falls below a certain level. Program is federally funded, with monies allocated directly to the cities and towns that administer the funds.
School lunch/ breakfast programs	Provide nutritionally balanced, low-cost or free meals to schoolchildren whose families are income eligible.
State child care subsidies	Subsidize working families receiving TANF and other low-income working families. Funded by the federal government but distributed by states. Programs vary by state, but generally states will reimburse the family for the cost of child care up to a maximum amount.
Supplemental Security Income (SSI)	Makes cash payments to poor people who are old, disabled, or blind. Originally part of the Social Security Act of 1933, SSI benefits today are given to people with low income or capital who are 65 or older, disabled people with an impairment that would keep them from working, or disabled children who are also poor. The program is paid for by the general revenues of the United States and, in states that supplement SSI, from state funds.
Unemployment insurance	Provides economic security to workers who become unemployed through no fault of their own (e.g., when they are laid off). Monthly benefits depend on length of employment, base pay, and average weekly wage. The program is funded by a tax on employers and is run by states, which can set the amount of benefits, the length of time that workers can receive benefits, and eligibility requirements.

their families out of poverty.[50] They also point to the large number of single mothers living in poverty (28 percent in 2008). The inadequacy of work as a means of raising low-wage workers out of poverty is even more pronounced in the current economic climate characterized by high unemployment. These challenges were the focus of a recent national poverty conference in which one expert reported, "We have a work-based safety net without work. We're really in a pickle."[51]

Extended families, especially grandmothers, pick up some of the burden when mothers with small children have lost their benefits but remain unable to hold down a job or care for their children. Nationwide, about 1.4 million children are living in "skip generation" households, which represents a 52 percent increase since 1990.[52] (See "*Who Are We? What Our Families Look Like*" for a survey of family structures today.) One study shows that although the number of children living in single-parent families has fallen since the late 1990s, there was a disturbing rise in the number of inner-city children living in homes without either parent.[53] Another study found that, despite lawmakers' intention to encourage more traditional two-parent families, as more women were forced to find work, the chances that they would get married actually declined.[54]

The 1996 legislation expired in October 2002 and had to be renewed by Congress. After a lengthy and contentious reauthorization process, Congress finally enacted changes to TANF three years later in the Deficit Reduction Act of 2005. The difficulty in agreeing on the shape of welfare reform highlights the difference between the parties and nearly guarantees that the issue will remain controversial and on the political agenda for years to come. The reforms enacted in the Deficit Reduction Act further emphasized the work focus of the TANF program, by increasing the proportion of recipients who must be working and defining more narrowly what counts as "work." These debates continued as Congress worked on the 2010 reauthorization of the program.[55] TANF is not the only policy intended to solve the problem of poverty in the United States. In addition to the food assistance and educational programs discussed in the following sections, a variety of other government plans are designed to reduce poverty (see Table 17.2).

Food Assistance Programs

Another set of social welfare programs is administered within the U.S. Department of Agriculture (USDA). USDA's domestic food assistance programs affect the daily lives of millions of

Changes in Births, Marriage, and Divorce, 1960–2007

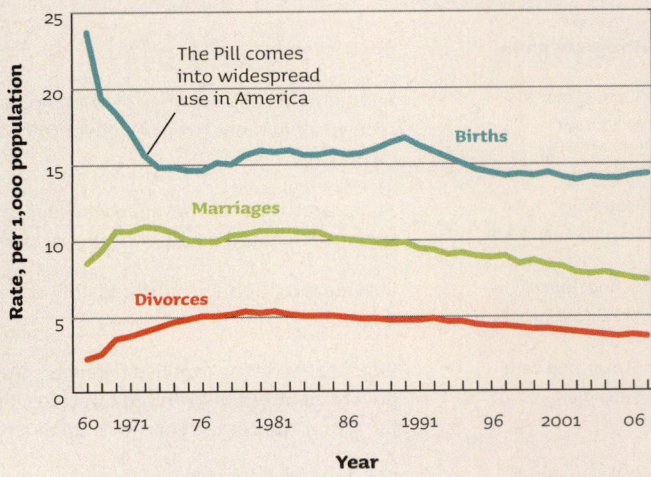

Source: U.S. Census Bureau, 2010 Statistical Abstract of the United States, Table 78: Live Births, Deaths, Marriages, and Divorces, www.census.gov/compendia/statab/cats/births_deaths_marriages_divorces/births.html.

Types of Households, 2008: Just barely half the households in America fit our traditional notion of a husband and wife and a couple of children.

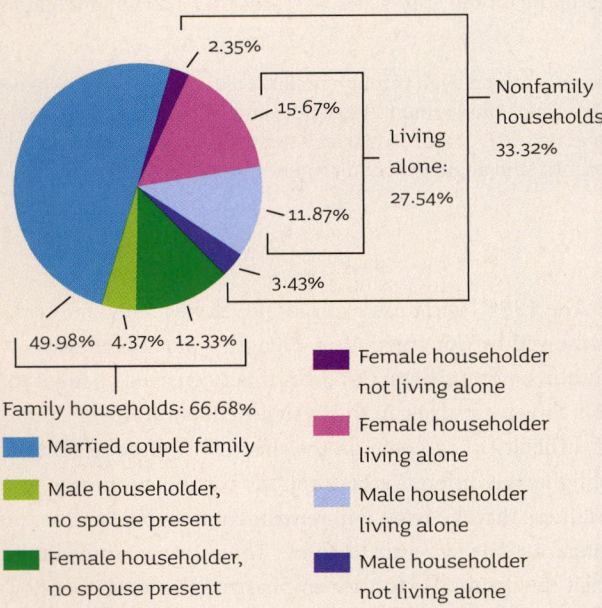

Female householder not living alone
Female householder living alone
Male householder living alone
Male householder not living alone

Family households: 66.68%

Married couple family
Male householder, no spouse present
Female householder, no spouse present

Sources: U.S. Census Bureau, 2008 Statistical Abstract of the United States, Table 61, www.census.gov/compendia/statab/tables/08s0061.pdf; U.S. Census Bureau, Current Population Reports, P20–561, and earlier reports; and "America's Families and Living Arrangements, 2007," September 2009, http://www.census.gov/prod/2009pubs/p20–561.pdf.

Size of Households, 1960–2007: A lower birthrate means smaller families and smaller households.

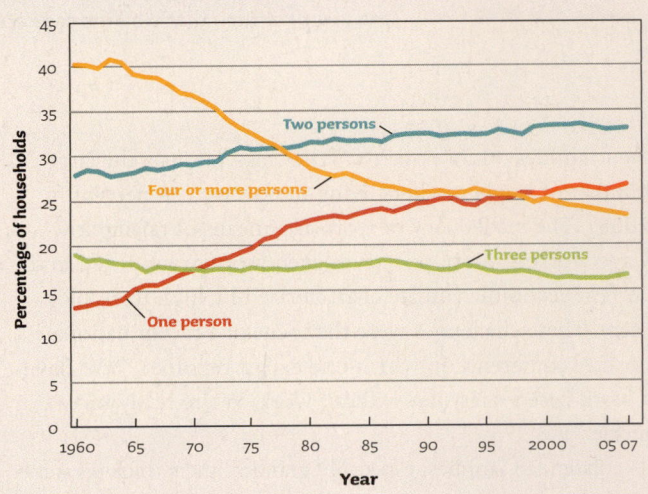

Source: U.S. Census Bureau, 2010 Statistical Abstract of the United States, Table 61: Households and Persons per Household by Type of Household, www.census.gov/compendia/statab/cats/population.html.

people. About one in four Americans participates in at least one food assistance program at some point during a given year.[56] Expenditures for food assistance account for more than half of the USDA's budget. In 2009 these expenditures totaled almost $79 billion—a nearly 30 percent increase from the previous year. In fact, 2009 saw the largest increase in demand for food assistance in thirty-four years.[57] These efforts include a set of more targeted programs focused on particular populations with special nutrition needs (such as the National School Lunch and Breakfast Programs and the Special Supplemental Nutrition Program for Women, Infants, and Children). But the largest food assistance program is the

> **Supplemental Nutrition Assistance Program (SNAP)**
> a federal program that provides vouchers to the poor to help them buy food

Figure 17.3

Payments for Individuals by Category and Major Program, 1990–2009

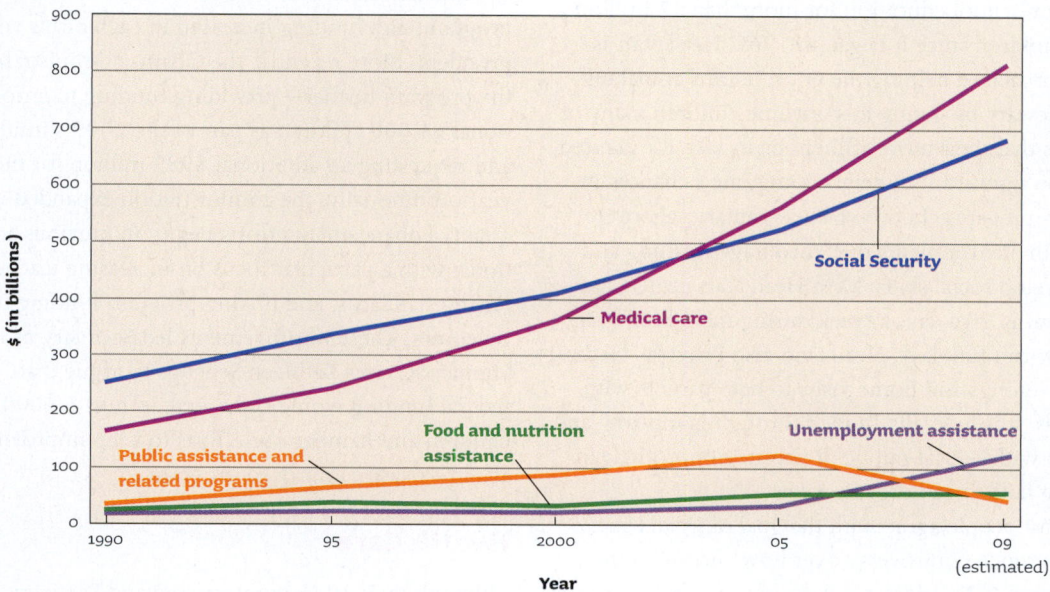

Source: U.S. Office of Management and Budget, Budget of the United States Government, Historical Tables, Table 11.3, www.whitehouse.gov/sites/default/files/omb/budget/fy2011/assets/hist.pdf.

Note: In billions of dollars (585.7 represents 585,700,000,000). Medical care includes Medicare, the State Children's Health Insurance Program, Medicaid, Veterans Administration hospitals, and Indian Health among other programs. Food and nutrition assistance includes SNAP and the Child Nutrition and Special Milk and Special Supplemental Feeding programs (WIC and CSFP).

Supplemental Nutrition Assistance Program (SNAP), previously called the Food Stamp program. In 2009, 33.7 million Americans participated in SNAP each month—with more than one in ten Americans participating at any given time during the year.[58]

SNAP provides low-income families with vouchers to purchase food (typically dispersed via an electronic system using a plastic card similar to a bank debit card). For most poor families, the vouchers cover only part of the food budget. Families also spend some of their own cash to buy enough food for the month. The amount of food assistance that households receive is indexed to family income. In 2009 these benefits averaged $124 per person, which is 23 percent higher than in the previous year (see Figure 17.3). This

increase was due in part to additional funding provided by the American Recovery and Reinvestment Act of 2009 (the stimulus package), which used SNAP as one way to increase short-term spending in local communities in which food assistance recipients live.

If everyone in a household receives TANF or Supplemental Security Income (see Table 17.2), the household qualifies for SNAP benefits. Otherwise, qualifications are based on the number of people in a household and the household's gross (total) and net (the amount remaining after deductions) monthly income. Through September 30, 2010, a four-person household would qualify for SNAP benefits if the household's gross monthly income was less than $2,389 and the net monthly income was less than $1,838.[59]

Head Start

Head Start—along with programs such as Medicare and Medicaid, which we turn to in a moment—was a major component of Lyndon Johnson's War on Poverty. The program has provided preschool education for more than 27 million low-income children since it began in 1965. Head Start is a different approach to helping the poor; it aims at making welfare unnecessary by giving low-income children many of the advantages that their more affluent peers take for granted, and that can be significant in determining one's chances in life. Head Start prepares children for elementary school by putting them in environments that encourage learning and help them develop social skills. Most Head Start centers are half-day programs, five days a week during the school year, although a few run full days. Head Start also provides medical and dental screenings and home visits to help parents with parenting skills. It is federally funded through grants to—and in partnership with—local public or private nonprofit agencies, including faith-based organizations.

While most people agree with the goal of Head Start, there has been much controversy over how successful the program has been.[60] To address this debate, in 1998 Congress determined, as part of Head Start's reauthorization, that the Department of Health and Human Services should conduct a random-assignment national study to determine the impact of Head Start on the children it serves. This study is currently following children randomly assigned to receive (or not receive) Head Start services into their elementary school years. Findings suggest that children who attended Head Start receive more enriching preschool experiences than they would otherwise, and score better on several measures of language skills (pre-reading, pre-writing, vocabulary, and parent reports of children's literacy skills) at the end of Head Start. However, only a few of the advantages Head Start children gained before entering school were still significant at the end of first grade.[61] These findings of limited return on investment, paired with the increasing costs (in 2009 the average cost per child was $7,864),[62] made many critics call for scaling back Head Start.

Supporters of Head Start, however, continue to believe that the program is essential to furthering the development of low-income students, many of whom belong to racial or ethnic minorities. The central claim made by those who support Head Start is no longer that it increases student intelligence, but that it changes students' "social methods of relating to peers and teachers, which helps them become

more effective at dealing with life."[63] Supporters also argue, although with limited empirical evidence, that the programs have positive long-term effects including increasing children's health and reducing teen pregnancy, crime, and welfare dependence. President George W. Bush was committed to the program, and funding increased in each of his years as president. More recently, the Obama administration expanded the program further—providing funding to enroll an additional 64,000 children as part of the 2009 stimulus package and requesting an additional $989 million for the next fiscal year. Additionally, the administration expanded many of the quality enhancement efforts begun in previous administrations, with a particular focus on increasing teacher training, raising standards, and linking program funding to program outcomes. These improvements led Secretary of Health and Human Services Kathleen Sebelius to argue that "denying federal funding would only serve to hurt 60,000 poor children and hamper our efforts to keep improving what is already a vastly improved program."[64]

Health Care

Although in 2010 Congress passed and President Obama signed the Patient Protection and Affordable Care Act, which will make access to health insurance more available and affordable for most Americans by 2014, the United States stands out among industrialized nations as the only one that doesn't have a universal health care system guaranteeing minimum basic care to all. Ironically, of those nations, it also spends the most on health care: 16 percent of the U.S. gross domestic product (GDP) went to health care in 2008, compared to an average of 9.0 percent in countries such as Canada and Germany, which have comprehensive health care for their citizens.[65] And this spending is expected to increase to approximately $3.6 trillion (18.7 percent of the GDP) by 2014.[66]

Before health care reform was passed in 2010, the federal government's role in health care was confined to the provision of Medicare and Medicaid. Like Social Security, Medicare is a social insurance program designed to help the elderly pay their medical costs. Like TANF, Medicaid is a means-tested welfare program to assist the poor—especially children—with their medical costs. Many Americans do not qualify for either of these two programs and are left uninsured, either unable to provide insurance for themselves, or willing to gamble that they will not need it. Indeed, an estimated 46.3 million Americans, or 15.4 percent of the population, were without coverage in 2008.[67]

Medicare

Signed into law by President Johnson in 1965 as an amendment to the Social Security Act, **Medicare** extended health care coverage to virtually all Americans who are over sixty-five, disabled, or suffering from permanent kidney failure. The idea was that workers would pay a small Medicare tax (collected as a payroll tax like FICA) while they were healthy in order to receive medical health insurance when they retired.

Medicare has two parts. Part A provides hospital insurance, limited stays at skilled nursing facilities, home health services, and hospice care. Medicare Part B, for which beneficiaries pay a monthly premium ($96.40 in 2008) helps pay for doctors' services, outpatient hospital services (including emergency room visits), ambulance transportation, diagnostic tests, laboratory services, and a variety of other health services.[68]

In 2008, about 45 million aged and disabled people, or more than 15 percent of the U.S. population, were on Medicare.[69] As the population ages and lives longer, and as medical costs skyrocket, Medicare has become an extraordinarily expensive program. The program's current budget of $504 billion (in 2010) represents 15 percent of the federal budget, with costs projected to double over the next decade to $916 billion.[70] For this reason, the trustees for the Medicare Trust Fund estimate that full benefit payments can be made only until 2020, twenty-one years sooner than the Social Security Trust Fund is expected to experience a shortfall.[71] Because of this, many people argue that the really urgent crisis for policymakers is not Social Security but Medicare.[72]

In 2003 Congress passed and President Bush signed the Medicare Modernization Act, which provided the elderly with prescription drug coverage under Medicare for the first time and gave private insurance companies a much greater role in the program. Democrats criticized the cost of the program (estimated to be $724 billion over the next ten years), argued that the plan gave too much power to health maintenance organizations (HMOs), and attacked Bush for not allowing the importation of less expensive drugs from Canada, claiming that the plan is a windfall for the pharmaceutical industry.

Medicaid

Medicaid was also enacted as an amendment to the Social Security Act in 1965, as part of President Johnson's Great Society program. A federally sponsored program that provides medical care to the poor, Medicaid is funded jointly by the national and state governments and covers hospitalization, prescription drugs, doctors' visits, and long-term nursing care.

Before the 1996 passage of welfare reform, needy people who were poor enough to qualify for Medicaid were already receiving some kind of cash assistance—either as welfare or Supplemental Social Security payments. Since the reforms, however, Medicaid and welfare have been delinked—families that are not eligible under TANF may still qualify for Medicaid if they meet previous AFDC requirements. Moreover, since part of TANF requires that recipients get a job, families who move from welfare to work are eligible for transitional Medicaid assistance for six to twelve months. Also recently established is the State Children's Health Insurance Program. This program allows states to expand family eligibility for Medicaid to up to 200 percent of the poverty line. States can also establish more generous eligibility requirements for Medicaid than those under TANF. For example, states can choose to increase income and personal asset limits, thereby insuring more families. In most states, families with young children that have incomes equal to or less than 133 percent of the poverty line are eligible. States can choose to disregard personal assets, such as the family car, in calculating eligibility. This delinking of welfare and Medicaid means that it is now possible for poor families to receive medical care without receiving welfare. This is a tremendous advantage over the former system, under which medical benefits depended on qualification for AFDC, and welfare recipients would lose their children's health coverage if they took a job, giving them a disincentive to get off the welfare rolls.

Rising medical costs are a concern to state and national policymakers who worry about the states' ability to continue to fund Medicaid, a program that costs states around one-fourth of their budgets. Because of these rising costs, President Bush in 2005 recommended scaling back the number of people eligible for Medicaid as well as the expenses that would be covered under the program. According to Bush, these changes would have saved the government $60 billion over ten years.[73] But governors from both parties were concerned that the reductions would add to the budget deficits of the states, which would have to pick up the costs of the cuts. Others believed Bush's proposal would reduce the number of poor people covered under Medicaid. Because of these concerns, the Senate refused to back the proposed cuts.

The Patient Protection and Affordable Care Act

U.S. policymakers have consistently hesitated to create a national health care system to serve all Americans. Fears of excessive government control, large costs, and inefficient

Stamp of Approval—For Now

President Obama signs the Patient Protection and Affordable Care Act into law on March 23, 2010. The legislation provides national health care reform, one of the Obama administration's main domestic policy priorities and one subject to great partisanship. Republicans, having gained control of the House in the 2010 midterm elections, have vowed to repeal the act.

services have doomed reform efforts. This may have something to do with the two sides of our uniquely American political culture, something we discussed in Chapter 2. Recall that we described Americans as both procedural and individualistic. In other words, Americans value rules over results and individual choice over the collective good.

The failure of President Clinton's 1993–1994 health care reform effort, a precursor to the act that did pass in 2010, is a good example of how our political culture can make social policy very difficult to formulate. In September 1993 President Clinton presented his "Health Security" plan to give every citizen at least some basic health care services. He wanted all Americans to have the ability to purchase health care at a reasonable price without fear of losing their coverage if they changed jobs or developed a serious medical condition. Also, in keeping with his deficit-reduction goals, he aimed to slow the rate of growth in health care expenditures, specifically Medicare and Medicaid. Concerned interest groups objected strenuously to Clinton's plan, running television ads to convince the public that the plan would damage the quality of their medical care and frantically lobbying Congress, whose Democratic leaders never even brought the doomed legislation up for a vote.

The reaction to the Clinton reform effort demonstrates the uneasy feelings concerning health care reform shared by both Americans and special interest groups, such as physicians, hospitals, HMOs, and pharmaceutical companies. The principal beliefs supporting the American system are that the free market and the ability to choose our physicians and hospitals will provide the best health care. Proponents of universal health care found it difficult to eliminate the perception that government control will harm the quality and raise the cost of health care services.

Nonetheless, rising health care costs for everyone and concern over the high number of Americans who had no health care insurance at all made federal health care reform a key issue in the 2008 election, both in the Democratic primary campaign, and later in the general election. But though Obama, an advocate of making health insurance available to all, won the presidency, there was no guarantee that health care reform would proceed as he had hoped. The economic crash of 2008 and the expensive financial bailout and stimulus plans made spending money on social programs much less attractive to politicians. Despite this context, the Obama administration continued to push health care reform as its primary domestic policy priority. Adopting lessons from failed efforts to reform our nation's complex health care insurance and delivery system, Obama did not propose the creation of a single-payer or unified national health care plan like those in Europe. Instead, he endorsed a range of separate policy changes that he argued would combine together to expand access to health insurance, slow the growth of health care costs, and provide more patient protections—particularly for the hard-to-insure such as those with preexisting conditions.[74]

One of the most controversial reform elements in the run up to the passage of reform was whether the bill should include the so-called public option. The public option refers to a proposed government-sponsored health insurance plan that would compete with the plans offered by private health insurance companies. Proponents of the public option viewed it as central to increasing competition in the market and bringing down the high cost of health insurance. On the other hand, more conservative opponents viewed the public option as a threat to the viability of the private insurance market—one that would bankrupt private companies that could not compete with the government-financed public plan.[75]

After a contentious year-long debate, this massive reform bill—the Patient Protection and Affordable Care Act—was

2010

- Young adult coverage is expanded to allow them to stay on their parents' plans until age twenty-six.

- Tax credits that help small businesses provide insurance benefits to workers are implemented.

- Those uninsured because of a preexisting condition can buy coverage through a Pre-Existing Condition Insurance Plan.

2011

- Health care premium costs decrease because 85 percent of premiums must be spent on health care, not administrative costs.

- The Center for Medicare and Medicaid Innovation and the Children's Health Insurance Program (CHIP) target improvements in health care quality and efficiency.

- The Independent Payment Advisory Board will explore new measures to reduce health care costs and expand quality care.

2012

- Integrated health systems will be fostered to improve communication and collaboration with doctors engaged in patient care.

- Paperwork and administrative costs will be reduced by shifting to secure, electronic records.

2013

- Preventive health coverage will be expanded through new funding of state Medicare programs.

2014

- Individuals and small businesses will be able to buy health insurance directly in a Health Insurance Exchange, a competitive insurance marketplace for qualified plans. Members of Congress also begin to receive their health insurance through exchanges.

- Individuals who can afford it will be required to obtain basic health insurance coverage (if not already covered) or to pay a fee to offset the costs of caring for uninsured Americans. Exemptions will be available to those who cannot afford to pay.

- Annual cap on the amount of coverage that an individual may receive will be eliminated.

- Reforms will prohibit the denial of the sale of health insurance due to preexisting conditions.

- The small business insurance tax credit will increase.

2015

- Physician payments will be tied to the quality of care physicians provide.

Source: HealthCare.gov, "Understanding the Affordable Care Act, Timeline: What's Changing and When," www.healthcare.gov/law/timeline/index .html#event1-pane.

signed into law in March 2010. It did not include a public option, because the Speaker of the House and majority leader in the Senate were unable to put together a winning coalition to vote for its inclusion. The bill, however, includes many provisions aimed at expanding insurance coverage through a requirement that employers with fifty or more employees provide health insurance and that most Americans outside that system purchase health insurance for themselves. To make these mandates affordable, the bill expands Medicaid to more low-income individuals and provides subsidies and tax credits to individuals and small businesses to reduce the burden of insurance premiums.

The reform bill also creates state-based American Health Benefit Exchanges and Small Business Health Options Exchanges, which will serve as vehicles for individuals and small businesses to purchase qualified health insurance in a competitive market. These exchanges will be administered by a government agency or nonprofit organization—under the governance of the states. Additionally, Consumer Operated and Oriented Plans (CO-OPs) will allow for the creation of nonprofit, member-run health insurance companies in all fifty states.[76] The various elements of the health care reform bill will be phased in gradually over the next five to ten years.

The hard-won victory for the Democrats was made more difficult by the refusal of any Republican to support the bill and by the death of longtime health care reform advocate Senator Ted Kennedy of Massachusetts. After a grueling battle in the House and the subsequent legislative maneuvers required to align the House bill with the Senate version, the public was frustrated with the partisan debate. Approval of health care reform had fallen, though it began to creep back

subsidy financial incentive given by the government to corporations, individuals, or other government jurisdictions or institutions

up in some polls in the months following the bill's passage and leveled off at a near tie, with a narrow plurality still disapproving.[77] While Republicans decried the bill and insisted they would work to repeal it, Democrats scrambled to get some key provisions into effect before the 2010 midterm elections so that voters could see what the reforms might mean in their lives. Though experts said the bill would mean long-term savings for the health care system, a recession-weary nation, tired of government spending and leery of giving too much power to federal officials, remained skeptical in the months before the election.[78] After the Republicans won control of the House they vowed to roll back the program by denying it funding if they couldn't repeal it outright, though it was going to be a challenge for them with the Democrats retaining control of the Senate and the White House.

Middle Class and Corporate Welfare

Social policies include not only what we typically think of as welfare—programs to assist the poor—but also programs that increase the quality of life for the middle class. Clearly this is true of the social insurance programs of Social Security and Medicare, which go to all contributors, rich and poor, in amounts that generally exceed their contributions. But a number of other distributive policies benefit workers, middle-class homeowners, students, and members of the military. These policies help a particular group in society at the expense of all taxpayers by giving that group a subsidy. A *subsidy* is a financial incentive such as a cash grant, a tax deduction, or a price support given by the government to corporations, individuals, or other government jurisdictions or institutions usually to encourage certain activities or behaviors (such as homeownership and going to college). Even though these subsidies are designed to achieve government's ends, they have long since fallen into the category of benefits to which groups feel entitled. It would be a brave congressperson, for instance, who decided to incur the wrath of middle-class homebuyers by removing the income tax deduction for mortgage interest!

In this section we look briefly at three different kinds of subsidies, all of which benefit groups that we wouldn't typically associate with social welfare policies.

Education Subsidies

A well-educated citizenry is a valuable asset for a nation, and government encourages education through the use of various subsidies. For instance, education subsidies provide funds to local school systems for certain types of educational programs but allow the school districts themselves to manage the programs. The federal government also provides direct student loans and guarantees loans made to students by private lenders such as banks and credit unions. To further encourage low-income students to attend college, Congress in 2001 eliminated the five-year limit on the period that former students can deduct interest on college loans from their taxable income. Interest can now be deducted over the life of the loan.[79] And additional reforms in 2010 eliminated fees paid to private banks that provide loans, using the cost savings to expand the federal Pell grant program—raising the maximum grant to $5,975 and expanding the number of grants awarded by 820,000 in 2010. The same reform package also makes it easier for students to repay loans after graduating. If students keep making payments, any outstanding balance will be forgiven after twenty years, or after just ten years for those working in public service (that is, teaching, military service).[80]

More recently government has provided tax credits as incentives to help citizens with the cost of higher education. These include the American Opportunity Tax Credit (previously called the HOPE Scholarship) and Lifetime Learning Credit. For tax year 2010, these credits could total up to $2,000 per return (for the Lifetime Learning Credit) or $2,500 per eligible student, as long as the family's adjusted gross income was below a certain amount (the limit to receive the full credit was $80,000 for single taxpayers and $160,000 for married taxpayers filing jointly). The size of the credit is phased-out for taxpayers with incomes over these limits.[81]

Homeownership Subsidies

Homeownership is encouraged through a set of tax credits. The mortgage interest tax deduction allows homeowners to deduct the cost of their mortgage interest payments from their taxable income, which resulted in an $80 billion revenue loss in 2009. Together with direct spending programs that helped Americans purchase homes or avoid foreclosure in the depths of the recession, the federal government spent roughly $230 billion in 2009 on the goal of promoting (and stabilizing) homeownership. This investment is more than four times what is spent to support rental affordability.[82] Because homeowners must meet a certain income level to receive most of these tax breaks, this federal housing policy helps taxpayers primarily in the middle- and upper-class income brackets.

Corporate "Welfare" Subsidies

U.S. corporations are also beneficiaries of social subsidies. According to some analysts, an estimated $170 billion is funneled to American corporations through direct federal subsidies and tax breaks each year.[83] Many subsidies are linked to efforts to create jobs. However, many of these programs have little oversight, and there are many instances of subsidies going to companies that are downsizing or—in the case of many high-tech companies—moving jobs overseas. Business leaders also claim that subsidies for research and development are needed to keep American companies afloat in the global marketplace. Business is heavily subsidized in some countries, and business lobbyists claim that U.S. subsidies are essential to the development of new technology. But others say that corporate America has become too dependent on federal handouts. The biggest winners are agribusiness, the oil industry, and energy plants. For instance, the Environmental Working Group, a nonpartisan group that studies farm subsidies, reports that between 1995 and 2009 the federal government spent $245.2 billion in direct payment subsidies to farmers, with three-quarters of the total subsidy going to only 10 percent of America's farms: the largest and richest 10 percent. In contrast, 62 percent of American farmers received no subsidy. During this time, Riceland Foods, Inc., alone received more than $554 million in subsidies.[84] States have also gotten into the corporate welfare business, handing out millions of dollars to fund corporations that stay within their borders in the defense, high-tech, and science and medical industries.

Who What How

Economic security policy, such as Social Security, welfare, and health care, is a high-stakes policy area. As citizens, we all have a stake in creating a society in which no one goes hungry or lives in need. As Americans, we are also imbued with the culture of individualism we discussed in Chapter 2, and we believe that people should take responsibility for themselves and their own economic well-being. These conflicting ideas meet in the area of welfare policy, where we want programs that will help people but not help them so much that they become dependent on the assistance. When it comes to care for the elderly, our beliefs about personal responsibility are tempered by our conviction that Social Security is an insurance program (not just "something for nothing"), and our belief that we too will benefit from it when our time comes.

Poor people have a stake in their own economic security, but they are less likely to have the political skills that would enable them to put pressure on elected officials to enact policy in their favor, and few organizations lobby for the needs of the poor. Programs like TANF, SNAP, and Medicaid are redistributive policies, which means that they are generally unpopular among voters as a whole, many of whom ascribe blame to the poor individual for his or her own lack of resources.

In contrast, the elderly, many of whom receive a great deal more from Social Security than they ever contribute, are well organized and are more likely to vote. Elected officials respond to their strength and numbers by treating Social Security as the "sacred cow" of American politics. They are afraid to touch it lest it costs them money and votes. They are also reluctant to limit corporate welfare or subsidies that help wealthy or middle-class Americans because these groups may provide large donations to candidates' campaigns or substantial numbers of votes on Election Day.

The Case of Environmental Policy
Regulating the world we live in

The policies discussed so far in this chapter have been primarily redistributive or distributive policies. As we mentioned earlier, however, public policies may also be regulatory. In the next chapter we examine regulatory policies more closely as they relate to the economy, but here we look at regulatory policies as part of our efforts to improve the quality of the physical world in which we live. Here, as with other policies we have looked at, the debates focus on the appropriate role of government—should it take positive steps to reach substantive goals or merely confine itself to creating and maintaining a fair playing field on which political actors can do battle?

Bad Seafood

A sign posted at the Wyckoff/Eagle Harbor Superfund site in Bainbridge Island, Washington, warns that fish and seafood taken from Eagle Bay may not be safe for consumption. The primary reason for the warning, in place since 1985, is the high levels of the chemical creosote present in the water and soil from the decades when the site was used for treating wood.

The problem of pollution and the push to protect the environment have been on the public agenda (that is, defined as public problems) for a relatively short period of time. When the rapid economic growth and industrialization of the post–World War II era led to increasing pollution and consumption of natural resources, it took some time—and several triggering events—for Americans to recognize the environmental costs of expansion. The publication of Rachel Carson's 1962 bestseller *Silent Spring* provided the first major warning of the dangers of pesticides (in particular, DDT, which was used universally by American farmers at that time). Around the same time, thousands of acres mined for coal lay unreclaimed in many coal-producing states. In 1969, Americans were alarmed by the news accounts of a raging fire in the Cuyahoga River in Cleveland, Ohio, fueled by the

enormous amounts of ignitable pollutants discharged into it. Reports that America's national emblem, the bald eagle, teetered on the brink of extinction increased the public outcry.

On the heels of these events, and others like them, environmental groups and citizens began to call upon the government to develop a comprehensive **environmental policy**. Believing that state governments would be unwilling to control industrial activity for fear of losing business to more accommodating states, these groups appealed to the national government instead. When Congress acted to protect the environment, it did so by passing a flurry of environmental laws beginning with the National Environmental Policy Act in 1969. This act required government agencies to issue an environmental impact statement listing the effects any new regulation would have on the environment. This was followed by the Clean Air Act (1970), the Federal Water Pollution Control (Clean Water) Act (1972), the Endangered Species Act (1973), and the Safe Drinking Water Act (1974), among others. President Richard Nixon established the U.S. Environmental Protection Agency (EPA) in 1970 by executive order to implement most of the major pollution control laws. The level of legislative, regulatory, and administrative activity necessary to create national environmental policy was enormous—larger in scope than any previous activity, except the programs created under Roosevelt's New Deal. It's no wonder that environmental policy scholars call the 1970s America's first environmental decade.

Major Programs in Place

Nearly all the new laws enacted in the 1970s were regulatory in nature. They controlled the polluting actions of businesses by requiring businesses to get a permit to pollute. For example, the **Clean Air Act** required the EPA to set national ambient air quality standards for common air pollutants and required states to set emissions limitations on companies that were polluting the air. The law also required automobile manufacturers to reduce tailpipe emissions from cars, a requirement that manufacturers resisted bitterly through most of the 1970s.

Many business owners criticized the costs of complying with the myriad environmental laws and regulations. In the early 1980s they were pleased to find in President Reagan a more sympathetic ear. The Reagan administration chose to slash funding and staffing levels in federal agencies responsible for running environmental programs and to appoint agency heads who were sensitive to the concerns of business. But attempts by the Reagan administration to diminish regulations were short lived. Membership in environmental groups increased dramatically during the 1980s, as public sentiment still favored environmental protection over regulatory relief. Congress responded to its constituents by passing amendments to existing environmental laws that, in general, strengthened rather than relaxed compliance provisions.[85]

One of the most significant pieces of environmental legislation passed during this period was the Comprehensive Environmental Response, Compensation, and Liability Act (CERCLA) in 1980, amended in 1986 by the Superfund

amendments of the Reauthorization Act. The purpose of this legislation, commonly referred to as **Superfund**, was to oversee the cleanup of toxic waste disposal sites—and to make liable for the cost of cleanup the persons responsible for the waste (those who generated or transported the wastes to that site, or the owners of the land at the time the waste was disposed there, or the current owner of the site). Superfund cleanups require an enormous amount of cooperation among federal, state, and local officials and politicians, as well as legal, engineering, and environmental experts. As a result, these projects can take years to complete.

Environmental Policy Issues on the Horizon

In the 1990s environmental policy began to take new directions as our understanding about the nature of environmental problems grew, giving more control to states and focusing on changing individual behavior as well as on regulating business.

Environmental Justice

Environmental justice has emerged as a concern for environmental policy, requiring that all Americans be afforded the same protection from environmental hazards regardless of race, ethnicity, or national origin. Studies suggest that hazardous waste and solid waste treatment facilities are more likely to be located in low-income minority neighborhoods and that minorities and people with low incomes face greater environmental risks than do white, affluent citizens.[86] In response, President Clinton issued an executive order in 1994 requiring state environmental agencies and the EPA to ensure that their practices are not discriminatory. That order remains in place and, although critics claimed that it was not implemented fully during the Bush administration, most environmental justice advocates are pleased at the progress President Obama has made in that area.[87]

Regulatory Takings

Another hot-button issue is regulatory takings, the ability of the government to prevent property owners from using their land. The U.S. Supreme Court has ruled that when a property owner is denied all of the economic value of the land, he or

The Winds of Change?
Many, including President Obama, believe that part of the answer to America's energy problems lies in harnessing alternative energy sources, such as this wind farm in San Gorgonio, California. The Renewable Energy and Energy Efficiency Export Initiative is part of the effort to meet the challenge of decreasing our reliance on fossil fuels and make the United States a leading exporter of clean energy technologies.

she must be compensated or it is a violation of Fifth Amendment rights. However, a regulatory taking that deprives a property owner of *some* of the value of the land is not unconstitutional. Two environmental laws, the Endangered Species Act and the wetlands provision of the Clean Water Act, potentially restrict the ability of property owners to build on their land. Some citizens argue that they should be compensated for any restriction on their land; environmentalists argue that compensating landowners who are affected by regulatory takings would be too costly, and would work against environmental protection. This topic will likely be debated for many years to come.

U.S. Dependence on Fossil Fuels

Recent environmental concerns have focused on problems stemming from our high demands for fossil fuels. Many lawmakers continue to worry that the United States, as the country that uses the most oil in the world, is too dependent on oil and the foreign countries that produce it. This concern was voiced by President Bush, a former oilman, in his 2006 State of the Union address when he declared that "Americans are addicted to oil,"[88] and President Obama has made the reduction of our reliance on oil a key component of his energy plans. Our excessive use of fossil fuels is a problem not only because there is no sustainable supply, but because of the consequences. Our foreign policy goals are often overshadowed by our need to keep access to oil supplies, the air in our cities is filled with toxic chemicals despite the constraints placed on air pollution in the 1970s, and scientists argue that global warming is putting the future of the entire planet in jeopardy.

One way to address the problem of American dependence on fossil fuels is with a gas tax and stricter standards on cars that use a lot of it. Though the United States has the lowest gas prices in the world, increasing taxes on gasoline is immensely unpopular.[89] Because everyone pays the same tax rate, some observers claim that gas taxes are regressive—in other words, they hurt the poor more than the wealthy. In addition, although Americans tend not to support tax increases in general, raising the gas tax is especially disliked because Americans are more dependent on their cars than are people in other countries and their wallets feel the impact daily. As a result, politicians are hesitant to raise the gas tax. In fact, during the 2008 presidential campaign,

Senators Clinton and McCain called for a gas tax holiday, even though experts declared universally that it would not save Americans much money and might in fact cause gas prices to rise even more.

Because of the unpopularity of gas tax increases, it is not surprising that politicians prefer to focus instead on the issue of fuel efficiency standards for automobiles. The Bush administration pushed for the passage of an Energy Bill in December 2007 that included tougher corporate average fuel efficiency (CAFE) requirements for cars, SUVs, and light trucks.[90] In 2010 President Obama announced even tougher standards, moving up the compliance deadlines of the 2007 bill by four years and establishing the first nationwide regulation for greenhouse gases.[91]

Another possible solution to our energy problem involves developing technology that doesn't require using oil for energy, such as electric cars.[92] Even with their slightly higher costs, gasoline-electric hybrid cars have become increasingly common, and more car companies are offering fuel-efficient alternatives. However, recent sales figures (approximately 290,000 hybrid cars sold in 2009) suggest that sales are leveling off at about 3 percent of the market share,[93] despite government-created incentives to buy the cars. In 2005, new hybrid owners could claim a one-time tax deduction of $2,000. The tax deduction was set to fall to $500 for new hybrid owners in 2006 and then expire after that. However, additional clean-car credits were incorporated into the 2005 Energy Bill, which allows for a credit of $250–$3,400, depending on the fuel economy and the weight of the hybrid vehicle. However, this remains a short-term benefit, since the tax credit will be phased out for each manufacturer once that company has sold 60,000 eligible vehicles.[94] Further, hybrid vehicles purchased after December 31, 2010, are not eligible. States have tried to encourage consumers to buy hybrid vehicles, as well. For example, Connecticut eliminated the sales tax on cars that average more than forty miles per gallon.[95] States including Colorado, Maine, and New Mexico have also passed laws giving tax credits for the purchase of some hybrid cars.[96]

Yet another solution to our energy demands focuses on developing alternatives to America's dependence on foreign oil. As we discussed in the *What's at Stake?* feature at the beginning of this chapter, some people believe that the answer to our energy independence lies in the search for oil

within our own borders, in places such as the Gulf of Mexico and the Arctic National Wildlife Refuge in Alaska. ANWR has been protected by environmental conservation legislation because it houses a number of endangered species. Throughout his two terms, President Bush advocated opening a small area of this refuge for drilling but faced strong objections from Democrats—and some Republicans— in Congress.[97]

The Obama Record on the Environment

When Barack Obama came into office, environmentalists were full of hope that with a Democrat in the White House, some of their long-standing concerns would be addressed, and to some extent their hopes have been met. Initially, they were pleased. Among other promising signs, President Obama nominated people to environmental posts who were seen as strong advocates for the cause, he called for tougher standards on automobile emissions and generally ordered his administration to be more stringent in its enforcement of environmental regulation, he put a moratorium on drilling for oil on public land, and he encouraged the House of Representatives to pass a cap and trade bill that would cap factory and power plant emissions but preserve some flexibility by allowing companies to buy and sell emissions credits.[98] The initial enthusiasm some environmentalists felt for Obama began to wane, however, in 2010. The president, long an advocate of nuclear power, proposed a budget that tripled federal loan guarantees for new nuclear reactors; he announced support for "clean coal technology" in his State of the Union address; and, just weeks before the *Deepwater Horizon* oil rig blew up, he announced a plan to lift the moratorium on offshore drilling. The president also was criticized for his failure to urge the Senate to push through a cap and trade bill like the one the House had passed in the summer of 2009. The fact that political realities would have made passage of the bill difficult if not impossible in the face of the refusal of Republican senators to support it did not soften environmentalists' disillusioned belief that Obama had not led forcefully enough.[99] Nor did the fact that, following the *Deepwater Horizon* disaster, his administration put a ban on expansion of offshore drilling. On environmental issues, Obama has taken a stand more notable for a liberal pragmatist, looking for solutions that can garner bipartisan support, than for the aggressively progressive stance some supporters had hoped to see him take.

► **Profiles in Citizenship: Christine Todd Whitman**

"Democracy is not a spectator sport . . . if we don't participate you lose the ability to make decisions."

Christine Todd Whitman has had a lot of opportunities in her life, but the luxury of being politically indifferent wasn't one of them. Not for her was the option of saying, "Politics doesn't matter. It has nothing to do with me." Since the day her parents met (at the Republican National Convention, of all places, in 1932), her fate was sealed. How do you disdain politics when it's the mainstay of every dinner-table conversation, when you go to political meetings as a little girl with your mom, and when you attend your first political convention at the age of nine (and have been to every single one of them since)?

Nope, political apathy wasn't in the cards for Whitman. Growing up listening to the debates between her ultra-conservative dad who believed that government should stay out of people's lives, and her more socially conscious Republican mom who saw a role for government to help people improve themselves, she forged the moderate philosophy that has taken her from New Jersey freeholder, to two-term governor of the state, to President Bush's first director of the Environmental Protection Agency, and back to private life.

Whitman articulated that philosophy in her 2005 book, *It's My Party, Too*, a passionate effort by a pro-environment, pro-choice, fiscally conservative Republican to reclaim the party she loves from the extremist forces she thinks have hijacked its traditional principles. "It's amazing that those who seem to be the most conservative can't seem to find enough ways to get the federal government involved in your life," she says wryly.

Sitting in the huge paneled barn of an office she uses today, with its heart-stopping views of the fields that extend beyond the New Jersey home she grew up in, she talks about the necessity of moderation and compromise in governance. Even her voice is measured—matter-of-fact and judicious—as she recounts the barriers that extreme partisanship threw in her way at the EPA. "It's when you want to take people by the hair and shake them and say, 'Look, if you say you care so much about this issue, then quit yelling and start solving problems.'"

Problem solving is what she is all about—it's why being governor suited her to a tee. "Just being in the executive branch to start with is more satisfying to me than the legislative. . . . [A]s governor you really can, in this state particularly, see a problem, say, 'That's the problem I want to solve, here's how we're thinking about doing it. . . .' And then you can get it done."

Her stint at the EPA was maddening to her precisely because her efforts to get things done were hampered, partly by politics (in her book she recounts how some of her efforts were undermined by the Bush administration) and partly by the fact that the environmental legislation passed by Congress left her little room to maneuver. Before taking the job, she hadn't realized "how constrained the agency is by the enabling legislation. How specific Congress was in the Clean Air Act and the Clean Water Act as to what the agency could and couldn't do. And so your ability to be innovative is amazingly

After nearly forty years of environmental protection, most Americans are breathing cleaner air and swimming in cleaner lakes and rivers. However, as the controversies over current environmental policies make clear, tough sustainability problems remain. Issues of land-use patterns, non-point-source pollution, private property rights, environmental justice, oil consumption, and reducing pollutants in a cost-effective way will likely top the agenda for environmental policy for the foreseeable future. Determining America's proper role in protecting the global environment from overpopulation; greenhouse gases; and a loss of rain forests, pristine habitats, and natural resources will also be critical if we are to ensure that future generations are able to enjoy the environment.

narrowed. And when you try to do it at all, you get hauled into court by one side or the other. That gets really frustrating."

Because states have little control over the pollution that crosses their borders from neighboring states, often they can't meet stringent clean air standards, especially on the timetable set by the legislation. When Whitman tried to buy them some time so that the states could find ways to improve their air quality, even if they couldn't meet the standards, she was accused of watering down those standards and "undoing the Clean Air Act." With some disappointment, she decided to leave the EPA in May 2003.

Since leaving the administration, she has written her book and focused her efforts on bolstering the moderate element of her party, which she thinks has a fundamental role to play in bringing American politics back to the center, and in mentoring Republican women who want to be involved in politics: she believes that women can make a distinctive contribution in American politics, and that there needs to be more of them at every level. Every level? She hasn't said what her future political ambitions are, but she does allow as how she is frequently approached by people who tell her they'd vote for her if she ever runs for president. So we ask, "Do you think there will be a woman president in your lifetime?" She smiles. "I think there will be. It may take a while, but . . . ," she shrugs. No promises. Here's what else she has to say:

On changing the tone of American politics:

Well, I think we need to change the rhetoric. I think part of what's turning off young people today is the rhetoric of the parties, is the fact that nobody's doing anything because they're too busy yelling at one another. And you may like the "Crossfires" but they're starting to lose some of their popularity and I think it's because, particularly young people are saying, "I'm not getting anywhere." That's why they go to the *Daily Show*, you know, Jon Stewart. He doesn't yell. He has his opinion and he will push it, but you can hear back and forth and you can get to hear the other side and he happens to be very bright and makes his political points with a smile. Which is what people like.

On keeping the republic:

Democracy is not a spectator sport, as I have said over and over again. And if we don't participate you lose the ability to make decisions. . . . [Y]ou look at the environmental movement. And the modern-day environmental movement was started by one woman and a book.

Rachel Carson wrote *Silent Spring* and that changed the entire country's approach to the environment and awareness of the importance of environmental action and governance. And so when people say to me, "I can't make a difference, I'm only one person and what can I do?" my pushback is . . . throughout history it has been a few people who have, in fact, because of their willingness to put themselves out there, made an enormous difference. That doesn't mean everybody has to be a Rachel Carson, because she paid a terrible price. . . . But you can make a difference if you get involved and it is about your life. Whether you're talking about education for children or the air you breathe, decisions are being made every day that affect you. . . . [Y]ou don't have to care about everything, but if the environment is what turns you on or if the arts are what turns you on, then take a look at what's happening in those areas around you. . . . If there's something in there that's happening that bothers you or something that you think is good, let people know that. Every officeholder at every level has someone that looks at the mail if they don't look at it themselves. And they tally up what's coming in, and they'll tell them, "Hey, Senator, this is what your constituents are writing about, this is what they care about," and it does affect behavior. ■

Who What How

We all have something at stake regarding the environment. After all, everyone wants to breathe clean air and drink clean water.

But not everyone is in agreement over how best to balance a clean environment with business interests. Environmental groups, like the Sierra Club and the World Wildlife Fund, want stricter regulations on pollutants and more protection of wildlife. Business interests push for less restrictive regulations. They also support incentives—such as tax breaks—for buying, say, environmentally friendly equipment. Both sides donate substantial amounts of money and do a great deal of lobbying to try to convince elected officials or bureaucrats to support their positions. Because of the lobbying ability of both sides, environmental policy is destined to remain a central debate in American politics.

The Citizens and Social Policy

The influence of the public's opinions on policymaking

In this book we have discussed elite, pluralist, and participatory theories of how democracy works. As we have seen, each theory explains some aspect of policymaking in the United States, but pluralism is especially prominent when it comes to domestic social policy. Social Security is a good example of the role pluralism plays in the policy process. Even though society as a whole might be better off with more stringent rules on who gets what from Social Security, older Americans, in the guise of AARP, have lobbied successfully to maintain the generous and universal benefits that make Social Security so expensive. It is also true, however, that individual Americans, in their roles as voters and responders to public opinion polls, have a decisive influence on policymaking. Though they may not participate in the sense of getting deeply involved in the process themselves, there is no doubt that politicians respond to their preferences in creating public policy.

As we saw in Chapters 11 and 16, public opinion matters in politics. State legislators, for instance, vote in accordance with the ideological preferences of their citizens.[100] States with more liberal citizens, for example, New York, Massachusetts, and California, have more liberal policies, and more conservative states, those in the South and the Rocky Mountain region, have more conservative policies. We noted that other studies have found a similar pattern in national elections.[101] What these findings, and others like them, tell us is that for all the cynicism in politics today, when it comes to who gets what, and how they get it, American democracy works to a remarkable degree.

▶ What's at Stake Revisited

The public debate over offshore drilling that followed the disaster on the *Deepwater Horizon* in 2010 only underscored the controversial nature of drilling at home that was already deeply familiar to the advocates of drilling in the Arctic National Wildlife Refuge. With soaring gas prices and growing public concern, the issue of drilling in ANWR had returned to the federal agenda two years before the *Deepwater Horizon* spill, in May 2008, when President Bush again asked Congress to allow oil and natural gas drilling in the refuge. But the Democratic-controlled Senate voted 56 to 42 against the proposal, with opponents refusing to consider tapping new domestic sources of oil as part of a broad energy approach.[102] Under the plan pushed by President Bush, drilling would occur in roughly 1.5 million acres of the 19-million-acre refuge. Why so much fuss over a small slice of land inhabited by 256 people?[103] What was at stake in drilling in ANWR?

Plenty, argue opponents, who claim that drilling in the Arctic is dangerous because it is more environmentally fragile than the Gulf, where results of an oil spill were bad enough. Drilling offshore in the Arctic would be even worse.[104] Although the drilling would only occur in roughly 8 percent of the refuge, opponents argued that it will degrade air and water quality and destroy the pristine land that is home to many animals, including migratory birds, caribou, polar bears, and oxen. Furthermore, they argue that it contains a six-month supply of oil at the most and will never supply more than 2 percent of the national demand.[105] Critics are also concerned about setting dangerous precedents, that drilling in ANWR would potentially lead to greater support for offshore drilling, especially in places such as the waters off California's coast. Finally, they claim that drilling offers short-term gain at the cost of developing the alternative resources that could solve our energy problems for the long haul. According to drilling opponents, instead of searching for more oil, the United States should focus on lowering oil consumption by continuing to produce more fuel-efficient vehicles and developing alternative sources of energy.[106] These same arguments arose again in the aftermath of the *Deepwater Horizon* oil spill.

For the oil industry, arctic drilling is a win-win proposition. According to one estimate by the American Petroleum Institute, drilling in ANWR could produce 1.5 million barrels of oil a day for twenty years (roughly the amount of oil the U.S. imports from Saudi Arabia), reduce the trade deficit by $19 billion annually, and create thousands of new jobs.[107] Drilling advocates claimed that the environmental impact of drilling would be minimal. They argued that the land where the drilling would take place is limited: "Production would come from a portion of ANWR consisting of only 2,000 acres, an area about the size of a regional airport in a refuge the size of South Carolina."[108] They were not convinced that wildlife would be adversely affected, especially with the new techniques of directional drilling that would be used, which makes it possible to drill in virtually any direction for miles.[109] From the perspective of supporters of the drilling, what's not to like about a policy that produces so much oil and is good for the economy?

The deeper philosophical issues here go beyond the issues we see on the surface. What is interesting about the fundamental stakes in the ANWR and domestic offshore drilling issue, and in environmental policy generally, is how it turns our conventional definitions of liberal and conservative on their heads. Here it is conservatives who argue for progress and change and put their faith in technology to solve the problems of the future and liberals who argue that we should preserve our traditional ways, slow down, consider consequences, and not act rashly.

For proponents of drilling, it is about a philosophy of economic development, progress, and profit-making. From their perspective, it is silly not to use the resources we have at hand, and they claim that those objecting are not the people who live in Alaska, who stand to gain financially, but do-gooder environmentalists who use the "protect the land" argument at the expense of developing land that will be beneficial to the country. For opponents, on the other hand, the core issues are long-term planning versus short-term indulgence. They fear that drilling will distract us from what we ought to be focusing on, conservation and technology to make us independent of foreign oil in the future. Drilling today (and possibly tomorrow, if precedent is set) allows us to remain SUV-driving gasaholics, addicted to a resource we will eventually run out of, damaging not only our own lives but those of our children as well. For now, anyway, the balance of power in Washington sides with the former, and the disasters like the *Deepwater Horizon* spill put environmentalists in the unenviable position of being able to test empirically whether their gloomy prognostications of environmental catastrophe come true.

To Sum Up

Key terms, chapter summaries, practice quizzes, Internet links, and other study aids are available on the companion web site at http://republic.cqpress.com.

Define | Understand | Practice | Read | Click | Watch

Clean Air Act (p. 663)

cost-benefit analysis (p. 643)

distributive policies (p. 639)

entitlement program (p. 648)

environmental policy (p. 662)

means-tested programs (p. 645)

Medicaid (p. 657)

Medicare (p. 657)

poverty threshold (p. 645)

public policy (p. 633)

redistributive policies (p. 638)

regulatory policies (p. 639)

social insurance programs (p. 645)

social policies (p. 644)

Social Security (p. 647)

Social Security Act (p. 649)

social welfare policies (p. 645)

subsidy (p. 660)

Superfund (p. 663)

Supplemental Nutrition Assistance Program (SNAP) (p. 655)

Temporary Assistance to Needy Families (TANF) (p. 652)

triggering event (p. 640)

Define | **Understand** | Practice | Read | Click | Watch

- Public policy is a government plan of action to solve a common social problem. Social problems may affect many citizens and require government action because individuals, groups, businesses, or other private actors either cannot handle these problems or have no incentive to address them.

- Public policy can be difficult to create for several reasons. There are often competing views about what constitutes a problem, most problems are complex and difficult to solve, and solutions can be costly and often create new problems.

- Public policy is generally one of three types: redistributive, distributive, or regulatory. Redistributive policies attempt to shift wealth, income, and other resources from the haves to the have-nots. Distributive policies address particular needs of an identifiable group, and the costs are shared among all taxpayers. Regulatory policies limit the actions of a specific, targeted group.

- Creating public policy involves many steps (agenda setting, formulation, adoption, implementation, and evaluation) and a multitude of groups (including Congress, the president, the courts, the bureaucracy, special interests, and the public).

- Social policies include government programs that seek to provide economic security for people who cannot help themselves, as well as other government assistance that improves the quality of life for individuals. Social policies, including Social Security and welfare, may be redistributive or distributive, taking from the whole pool of resources to help particular groups of citizens. While social policies generally are thought of as programs that help the poor, they can help the wealthy and middle class as well, as education subsidies, corporate welfare, and Medicare illustrate.

- Environmental policy is a regulatory policy that often leads to debates on balancing the protection of the environment with the protection of business. Although environmental policy is commonly discussed today, it did not become a major national issue until the 1970s. Today's major environmental debates revolve around issues of environmental justice, regulatory takings, and the use of fossil fuels.

- Pluralism is the most prominent theory of democracy in social policy. Citizens' interests are often represented when groups lobby elected officials. Participatory democracy also explains some aspects of the policymaking process, as citizens in their roles as voters and respondents to surveys can influence elected officials. Perhaps somewhat surprisingly, public policy usually reflects public opinion, an indication that American democracy works quite well.

Define Understand **Practice** Read Click Watch

1. A _____ policy is funded by the whole taxpayer base and addresses the needs of particular groups.
   a. redistributive
   b. regulatory
   c. means-tested
   d. distributive
   e. social welfare

2. Which of the following is NOT a step of the policymaking process?
   a. agenda setting
   b. policy formulation
   c. policy implementation
   d. policy evaluation
   e. policy revision

3. _____ is NOT an example of a means-tested program.
   a. TANF
   b. Social Security
   c. Head Start
   d. Medicaid
   e. SNAP

4. Due to significant strides in legislative and regulatory activity during this time, environmental scholars call the _____ America's first environmental decade.
   a. 1950s
   b. 1960s
   c. 1970s
   d. 1980s
   e. 1990s

5. The _____ theory of democracy best reflects how domestic policymaking works in the United States.
   a. pluralist
   b. participatory
   c. direct
   d. elite
   e. indirect

Define Understand Practice **Read** Click Watch

Carson, Rachel. 1962. *Silent Spring*. Boston: Houghton Mifflin. This book is credited by many as sparking the environmental movement in the United States. Carson was the first to warn of the dangers of harmful pesticides used by farmers at the time of the book's publication.

DeWitt, Larry W., Daniel Béland, and Edward D. Berkowitz, eds. 2008. *Social Security: A Documentary History*. Washington, D.C.: CQ Press. This incisive volume is your go-to source for all there is to know about the U.S. Social Security system since its founding in 1935.

Gingrich, Newt. 2005. *Winning the Future: A 21st Century Contract with America*. Washington, D.C.: Regnery Press. This former Speaker of the House offers innovative conservative strategies for dealing with such social problems as Social Security and health care.

Howard, Christopher. 2007. *The Welfare State Nobody Knows: Debunking Myths About U.S. Social Policy*. Princeton: Princeton University Press. Readers are sure to discover something useful (and perhaps unexpected) in this fact-versus-fiction analysis of the U.S. welfare state.

Katz, Michael B. 1995. *Improving Poor People: The Welfare State, the "Underclass," and Urban Schools as History*. Princeton: Princeton University Press. An examination of the problems of welfare and education policy and why neither has done much to help the poor.

Kingdon, John. 1984. *Agendas, Alternatives, and Public Policies*. Boston: Little, Brown. An easy-to-read, provocative account of the players in the policymaking process, with an emphasis on how, why, and when issues get put on the political agenda.

Kraft, Michael E., and Scott R. Furlong. 2009. *Public Policy: Politics, Analysis, and Alternatives*, 3rd ed. Washington, D.C.: CQ Press. This book offers a striking approach to the most urgent American public policy challenges by focusing on the policy process and policy analysis in substantive policy areas.

Patel, Kant, and Mark E. Rushefsky. 2000. *Health Care Politics and Policy in America*, 2nd ed. Armonk, N.Y.: M. E. Sharpe. A well-written text on health care policy that covers all the major issues on the topic.

Peters, B. Guy. 2007. *American Public Policy: Promise and Performance*, 7th ed. Washington, D.C.: CQ Press. Peters argues that the primary reason citizens should be concerned about government—in any country—is because of public policy, "the outcome of the political process." In addition to describing in detail the structure and process of public policy making, he looks closely at the policy areas we discuss in this chapter, along with many others.

Rosenbaum, Walter A. 2008. *Environmental Politics and Policy,* **7th ed. Washington, D.C.: CQ Press.** Rosenbaum's widely respected text on environmental policy is a great first place to turn when investigating politics and the environment.

Scheberle, Denise. 1997. *Federalism and Environmental Policy: Trust and the Politics of Implementation.* **Washington, D.C.: Georgetown University Press.** An in-depth examination of the relationship between the federal and state governments and their roles in the implementation of environmental policy. Using extensive survey and interview data, Scheberle stresses the importance of trust between the different levels of government.

Whitman, Christine Todd. *It's My Party Too: The Battle for the Heart of the GOP and the Future of America.* **New York: Penguin.** A highly thought-provoking book, by the former Republican governor of New Jersey and head of the EPA, who argues that her party has moved too far to the right, which, in her mind, threatens the viability of the Republican Party in the future. She calls for the party to return to its core values of less government, lower taxes, and creating more jobs in the private sector, instead of running on issues such as opposition to abortion and stem-cell research.

Define	Understand	Practice	Read	Click	Watch

Centers for Medicare and Medicaid Services *www.cms.hhs.gov.* The CMS answers questions that people have about the health care programs in the United States and provides links to recent media articles discussing these programs.

Department of the Interior's Office of Environmental Policy and Compliance *www.doi.gov/oepc.* A handy resource for those interested in learning more about U.S. compliance with various environmental standards and regulations.

Environmental Protection Agency *www.epa.gov.* This site will provide you with up-to-date information about environmental policy and allows you to check the air quality in your area.

HealthCare.gov *www.healthcare.gov/law/introduction/index.html.* Learn about the Affordable Care Act, the timeline under which its provisions will be rolled out, and what it means for you.

Public Agenda Online *www.publicagenda.org.* Public Agenda is a nonpartisan, public opinion research and citizen education organization. Its Briefing Guides provide excellent background on the major policy issues affecting Americans today.

Sierra Club *www.sierraclub.org.* One of the country's oldest environmental groups, Sierra Club makes it easy for visitors to its web site to contact their members of Congress about a variety of environmental issues. Individuals also can check out candidates and judicial nominees whom the group supports, as well as track how their representatives voted on environmental issues.

Social Security Administration *www.ssa.gov.* Have a question about Social Security? Worried that you won't receive benefits when you retire? Want to view your Social Security statement? This site will answer all your questions and is particularly helpful at examining the future of Social Security.

Supplemental Nutrition Assistance Program *www.fns.usda.gov/snap/.* Located in the Food and Nutrition Service of the U.S. Department of Agriculture, this program's site contains information on qualifying for the program, research and statistics, and other materials.

White House in Focus Feature *www.whitehouse.gov/infocus.* This section of the White House web site contains a wealth of information on U.S. social policy in such diverse issue areas as health care, environmental preservation, and education.

Define **Understand** **Practice** **Read** **Click** **Watch**

A Civil Action 1998. This film is based on the true story of a lawyer who represented the families of children who died from leukemia after two large corporations leaked toxic chemicals into the water supply of a New England town.

An Inconvenient Truth 2006. This well-known and highly regarded documentary on global warming by former vice president Al Gore is a must-see for those interested in environmental politics in the United States and abroad.

Food Inc. 2008. This documentary examines our nation's food supply, with a focus on the large corporations making up most of the food industry; government's regulatory agencies (USDA and FDA); and the role for farmers, workers, and consumers in the production of the food we eat.

Flintown Kids 2005. A documentary portraying Flint, Michigan, as one of the worst poverty-stricken urban areas in the United States, revealing in particular the severely neglected public school system.

The Grapes of Wrath 1940. The poverty, desperation, and hopelessness of the Great Depression are brought to life in this film, adapted from the classic John Steinbeck novel of the same name.

In America 2003. An intimate portrayal of an Irish immigrant family in New York, struggling with poverty and cultural isolation.

red equities.
Energy prices continued their long mo

Tough times

650
240

global supply and

Chapter 18

Economic Policy

▶ What's at Stake?

As the new century kicked in, many Americans thought they were on to a sure thing. The housing market was booming, and nearly 70 percent of Americans owned a home in 2006. As the demand for houses went up, American home values increased, rising 124 percent between 1997 and 2006.[1] With houses increasing in value and credit cheap, everyone wanted to own one (or more), certain that even if they couldn't afford the initial outlay, the houses would appreciate and make them money.

Mortgage companies helped things along with an orgy of subprime lending, that is, giving mortgages to people who couldn't qualify for traditional mortgages and who were at high risk of defaulting, or giving borrowers terms that they could afford initially but that would rise later. By 2006, a fifth of all new mortgages in the United States were subprime.[2] Fueled by the housing boom, Americans went on a buying jag, spending borrowed money as if it were their own. The economy, flush with cash, prospered.

The trouble with bubbles, of course, is that they always burst. When this one popped in 2005–2006, those who had borrowed on their homes frequently owed far more than the houses were worth. Stuck making large mortgage payments, they were unable to sell the homes to get out from under the load of debt. Many of those with subprime loans defaulted or found they could refinance their variable mortgages only at higher rates that they could not afford. Many people lost their homes; foreclosures were filed on nearly 1,300,000 properties in 2007 alone.[3]

But that was just the tip of a much scarier iceberg. In the fall of 2008 the investment banking industry collapsed, creating panic in the financial sector, sending stocks crashing around the globe, driving politicians into emergency mode, impacting the course of a presidential election, and necessitating a giant bailout by the federal government, to the tune of at least $700 billion. Economists spoke of a crisis as bad as the Great Depression.

What the heck had happened? How did some bad loans turn into total financial chaos? What is really at stake in living on borrowed funds? We'll revisit this question after we take a closer look at how economic policy works. ■

When Wall Street Came Tumbling Down
As a perfect storm of circumstances sent the stock market spiraling down in late 2008, the federal government scrambled to stabilize sinking financial institutions. Yet even the multibillion-dollar bail-out effort ultimately put into place was unable to prevent world markets and economies from reeling, sparking fears of a global recession, if not depression.

Economic policy addresses the problem of economic security, not for some particular group or segment of society, but for society as a whole.

economic policy   all the different strategies that government officials employ to solve economic problems

Do you have big financial plans for your future? Fantasies of becoming a successful entrepreneur? Running your own business? Making a killing in the stock market someday? Perhaps your goals are more humble: you may just want to make some money and then backpack around the world, or buy a home, get your kids through college, and save money for a comfortable retirement. Maybe you just want to get a good job and pay off those student loans! Whatever your financial ambitions, your fate will be at least partly in the hands of economic policy makers. Therefore, it is essential that you understand the economic policy process.

Economic policy addresses the problem of economic security, not for some particular group or segment of society, but for society as a whole. Economic prosperity is undoubtedly a lot better than economic misery. Not only does economic hardship make life difficult for those who suffer business losses or reduced standards of living, but it also makes trouble for incumbent politicians who, as we have seen, are held accountable by the public for solving economic problems. In Chapter 1, we said that the United States has an economic system of regulated capitalism. That is, the U.S. economy is a market system in which the government intervenes to protect rights and make procedural guarantees. All of the different strategies that government officials, both elected and appointed, employ today to solve economic problems, to protect economic rights, and to provide procedural guarantees to help the market run smoothly, are called **economic policy**.

For much of our history, policymakers have felt that government should pursue a hands-off policy of doing very little to regulate the economy, in effect letting the market take care of itself, guided only by the laws of supply and demand. This was in keeping with a basic tenet of capitalism, which holds that the economy is already regulated by millions of individual decisions made each day by consumers and producers in the market. The principle of laissez-faire, discussed in Chapter 1, was supposed to allow what eighteenth-century economist Adam Smith called "the invisible hand" of the marketplace to create positive social and economic outcomes.[4]

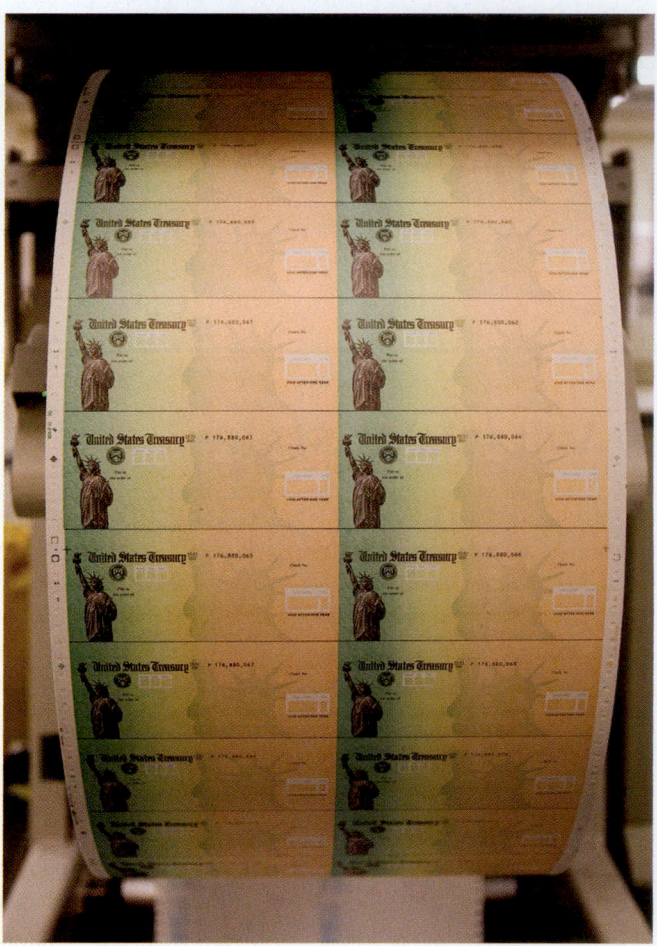

Making Money
In an effort to jumpstart a flagging economy, the federal government approved an economic stimulus plan that put $168 billion back in the hands of Americans in the form of rebate checks beginning in spring 2008. About 130 million households were eligible to receive up to $1,200 per couple.

The Great Depression of the 1930s, however, changed the way government policymakers viewed the economy. Since that economic disaster, the goal of economic policy makers has been to even out the dramatic cycles of inflation and recession without undermining the vitality and productivity of a market-driven economy. In Figure 18.1, we can see the difference in smoothness of the economic cycles before and after government began to intervene actively in the 1930s. The challenge for government is to achieve a balance of steady growth—growth that is not so rapid that it causes prices to rise (inflation), nor so sluggish that the economy slides into the doldrums (a recession or depression).

In this chapter you will learn more about how government has tried to meet the challenge of steady growth through economic policy. Specifically, you will learn more about

- *basic economic principles*
- *monetary policy and fiscal policy*
- *economic regulatory policy, with a focus on antitrusts, unions, and trade*
- *the relationship of economic policy to the citizens*

A Beginner's Guide to Understanding the Economy
Learning the fundamentals

Anyone who has read the financial pages of a newspaper or filled out a tax return knows that understanding the economy and economic policy can drive you around the bend. Learning a few basic principles and terms relating to the economy can take you a long way to better understanding how it works. The goal of this section is to give you some background on

Figure 18.1

Government: A Steadying Influence on Gross Domestic Product

The zero line in this figure represents no economic growth (and no decline). The ideal for economic prosperity is steady, positive economic growth, or a change in the gross domestic product just a few percentage points above the zero line. Notice here that with strong government intervention in the economy beginning in the late 1930s, the radical swings between growth and decline were substantially diminished. The depth of the recent recession is indicated by the actual drop in GDP in 2009.

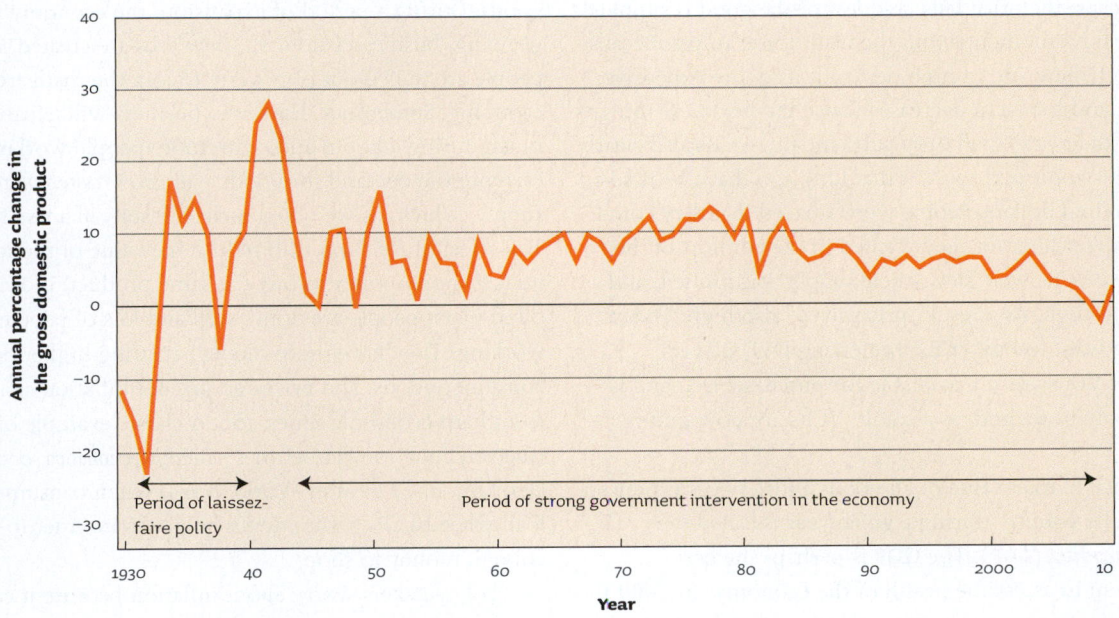

Source: U.S. Department of Commerce, Bureau of Economic Analysis, www.bea.gov/national/txt/dpga.txt.

laws of supply and demand   basic principles that regulate the economic market and influence the price of a good

gross domestic product (GDP)   total market value of all goods and services produced by everyone in a particular country during a given year

economic boom   a period of fast economic growth in GDP, signaling prosperity

economic bust   a period of steep decline in GDP, signaling recession

business cycle   the peaks and valleys of the economy between boom and bust

inflation   an increase in the price of goods

recession   a decline in GDP for two consecutive quarters

certain fundamental economic terms, which will make it much easier to grasp the economic policies we discuss in this chapter. The *Consider the Source* feature on page 680 is devoted to understanding key economic indicators as well.

We begin with the *laws of supply and demand*, the basic principles that regulate the economic market. They are called laws not because they have been passed by lawmakers but because they represent relationships in the economic world that hold true so consistently that we can count on them to occur unless something happens to change the conditions under which they operate. They are more like the law of gravity than the law that says you must wear a seat belt. The law of demand tells us that people will buy more of something the cheaper it is, and less of it the more expensive it is. The law of supply says that producers of goods and services are willing to produce more of a particular good or service as its price increases and less of it as its price goes down. Together these two economic principles should regulate the free capitalist market, ensuring that as consumer demand for a good goes up, more of that good will be supplied and the price will rise until it hits a point at which consumers are unable or unwilling to purchase the good, at which time the demand drops, the price falls, and less of the good is supplied.

Think for a moment about the iPad, for example. Because it is relatively new and in high demand, iPads are expensive. As the demand for them decreases (once the next new thing is invented), their price will drop substantially. VCRs also clearly illustrate this concept. It wasn't that long ago that a VCR cost several hundred dollars. People were amazed that they could watch movies whenever they wanted in the comfort of their own homes. VCRs were new, their supply was limited, and demand was high. As a result, prices were also high. Today, few people want to buy VCRs, preferring DVD players instead, yet VCRs are still available for purchase. Demand is down, supply is up, and, as a result, VCRs are now quite cheap.

The total market value of all goods and services produced in a particular country during a given year is called the *gross domestic product (GDP)*. The GDP is perhaps the best measurement to assess the health of the economy. In 2009 the GDP of the United States was $14.1 trillion dollars, the largest GDP in the world by far. China had the second largest GDP ($8.7 trillion), followed by Japan ($4.2 trillion), India ($3.6 trillion), Germany ($2.8 trillion), and the United Kingdom

($2.1 trillion). Niue, a tiny independent island in the South Pacific, had a GDP of only $10 million.[5] As we discussed earlier, one widely shared goal for the economy is to have a smooth, positive rate of growth in economic activity, and this translates into a steady growth in the GDP. Figure 18.1 shows annual percentage changes in the U.S. GDP since 1930.

But economies rarely follow a smooth or steady path. They go through peaks and valleys or, in economic terms, booms and busts. An *economic boom* is a period of fast economic growth in GDP, signaling a prosperous economy. An *economic bust* is a period of steep decline in GDP, signaling a recession. The alternation of periods between boom and bust is known as a *business cycle*. Fluctuations in the economy vary in length and intensity, and are often—although not always—linked to economic conditions in other countries.

Because cyclical economic effects can wreak havoc on businesses, not to mention on individual lives, the modern government tries to create policies that will minimize the impact of the business cycle and maximize economic prosperity. One of the biggest problems that government faces is controlling inflation. *Inflation* is an increase in the price of goods. During a period of expansion, the economy is growing, businesses flourish, new jobs are created, and people are pulled out of poverty to join the mainstream economy. Sometimes, however, business will expand so much during a boom and, with more people working and earning, the demand for goods will grow faster than the supply, which, as we stated earlier, results in a rise in prices. The effect of inflation is to reduce the value of money, so that it takes more money to buy the same product. It occurs most often when people are doing well and lots of people are working. They have more money, creating higher demand for consumer goods, and prices go up. But inflation can result from hard economic times, too. A classic example of high runaway inflation, sometimes called *hyperinflation*, occurred in Germany in 1923 after World War I, when consumers had to load wheelbarrows with deutsche marks in order to have enough money to shop.

Policymakers worry about inflation because it can slow the economy. A *recession* is a slowdown in economic growth, specifically a decline in GDP for two consecutive quarters (there are four quarters in a year). When prices get too high because of inflation, people can no longer afford to keep

▶ Who Are We?

Personal debt and consumption

The American government isn't alone in racking up large debts. As we noted earlier, more than 75 percent of all American families are in debt. Most of that debt comes from investment in the future, such as homeownership and education loans, and from the purchase of basic necessities like health care. However, a significant proportion of American families go into debt because of consumption that is not likely to bring future benefits. In 2007, only 56.5 percent of families actually saved money.[1] How does being in debt constrain the future choices a family makes?

A Public in Debt:

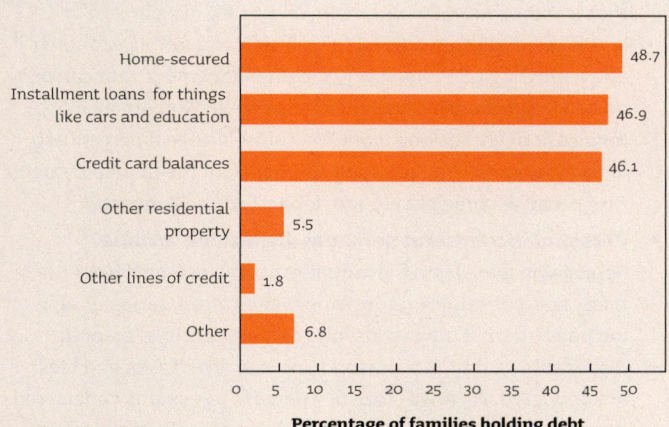

Percentage of families holding debt

Home-secured — 48.7
Installment loans for things like cars and education — 46.9
Credit card balances — 46.1
Other residential property — 5.5
Other lines of credit — 1.8
Other — 6.8

Median value of family debt (thousands of 2007 dollars)

Home-secured — 107
Installment loans for things like cars and education — 13
Credit card balances — 3
Other residential property — 100
Other lines of credit — 2
Other — 6.8

A Consuming Public:

Average annual household expenditures, 2009 (in dollars)

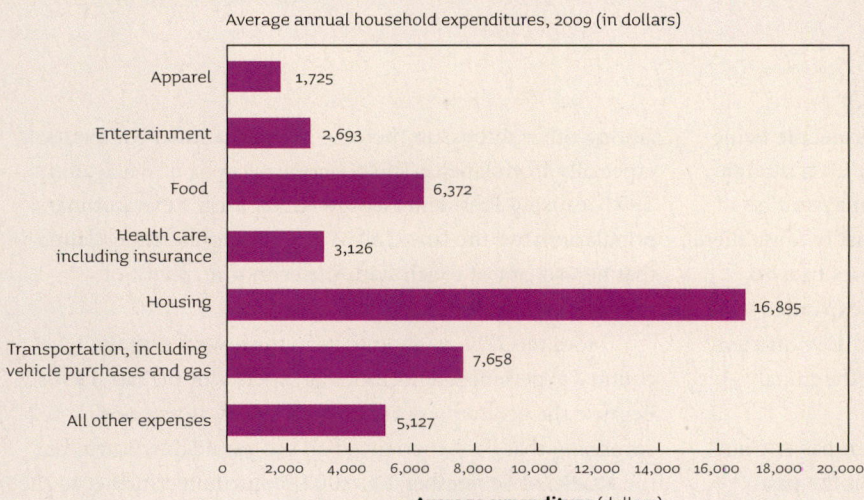

Apparel — 1,725
Entertainment — 2,693
Food — 6,372
Health care, including insurance — 3,126
Housing — 16,895
Transportation, including vehicle purchases and gas — 7,658
All other expenses — 5,127

Average expenditure (dollars)

Source (above): U.S. Federal Reserve, "Changes in U.S. Family Finances: Evidence From the 2004 and 2007 Survey of Consumer Finances," www.federalreserve.gov/PUBS/bulletin/209.pdf.scf09.pdf.

Source (left): U.S. Department of Labor, "Table A. Composition of Consumer Unit: Average Annual Expenditures and Characteristics of All Consumer Units and Percent Changes, Consumer Expenditure Survey, 2007–2009," www.bls.gov/news.release/pdf/cesan.pdf.

1. U.S. Federal Reserve, "Changes in U.S. Family Finances: Evidence From the 2004 and 2007 Survey of Consumer Finances," www.federalreserve.gov/PUBS/bulletin/209.pdf.scf09.pdf.

Keeping up with the economy, in good times or bad, can be a challenge, especially when politicians are trying to persuade you to see things their way. As one guide to understanding the economy put it, "Economic figures can be manipulated to demonstrate almost anything."[1] Politicians are wont to spin those figures to support their arguments and to attract voters to their side.

Critical consumers of politics have some tools available to help them sort through the political spin and figure out how the economy is doing. Objective measures of the economy are of two kinds: *coincident economic indicators* help us understand how the economy is currently functioning, and *leading economic indicators* predict how it will look in the future. Coincident economic indicators include such variables as employment, personal income, and industrial production. Leading economic indicators focus on variables that indicate a reemergence from a recession and growth in the economy, like consumer confidence, stock market prices, and "big-ticket purchases" such as automobiles and homes. Understanding these two kinds of economic indicators can help us figure out how the economy is really doing and can arm us against the persuasive words of politicians.

Here we examine just a few of literally dozens of these variables. You can find the most recent data from these leading economic indicators and others at www.economicindicators.gov. For a more complete guide to understanding a wide range of economic indicators, you might want to consult a reference book, such as *The Economist's Guide to Economic Indicators*.[2]

- **Real GDP.** The real gross domestic product (GDP) is the total economic activity in constant prices. Because of inflation, it is important to put all prices on the same scale. In other words, to see how much the economy has grown from 2000 to 2010, you would want to convert 2010 dollars into 2000 dollars. Because real GDP uses constant prices, it is a useful measure to track economic growth over time. A real GDP growth of around 3 percent per year is a good sign for the American economy.[3] A rise in real GDP shows that production and consumption are increasing.

- **Unemployment.** The unemployment rate is the percentage of the labor force (defined as those aged sixteen and older) that is out of work. An unemployment rate of 5 percent or less is generally considered to be a sign of a strong economy and a growing GDP. However, the unemployment rate can be misleading because it includes only people who are available for and actively seeking work. Therefore, the real percentage of those unemployed is usually higher than the unemployment rate because some people are not actively seeking jobs.

- **Personal income and personal disposable income.** Personal income is an individual's income received from many sources but primarily from wages and salaries. It also includes interest, dividends, and Social Security. Personal disposable income is a person's income after taxes and fees are deducted. A growth rate of 3 percent per year is considered to be a healthy increase in personal income, although growth should be steady. Too rapid an increase in personal income can lead to inflation.[4] These two measures predict the ability of citizens to consume and save.

- **Consumer spending.** The amount of goods that people are buying is another way to measure the health of the economy buying. Demand slows, which results in fewer people being employed, and the economy stops expanding. Even though the economy slows during a recession, there may still be a pattern of overall economic growth; that is, just because there is a slowdown does not mean the economy goes back to square one. In other words, an economy that expanded substantially in a single year and then has two slow quarters may still be in better shape than it was before the initial expansion.

The United States has been fortunate that it has encountered for the most part few severe recessions in the past half-century. The economy struggled during the 1970s, when inflation and unemployment rose at the same time, something that was highly unusual. Later, President Ronald Reagan was forced to combat recession early in his term because of, among other things, an increase in international competition, especially from Japan.[6] The economy slowed down again in 1991, causing President George H. W. Bush's extraordinary popularity after the first Gulf War to evaporate amid claims that he was out of touch with the economic plight of everyday Americans.

More recently, economic growth slowed after the country experienced enormous prosperity in the late 1990s. Because the economy goes through cycles, it was not surprising that we experienced an economic downturn, but the attacks of September 11, 2001, contributed further to the faltering economy. Signs of economic recovery emerged in 2004 as the GDP once again began to rise, but by the end of 2007, triggered by the collapse of the housing market and the subprime mortgage crisis, and exacerbated by rising fuel

because it is the key factor in the increase or decrease of the GDP. One way to measure consumer spending is by the Department of Labor's Consumer Expenditure Survey, which asks American consumers questions about their buying habits on items such as food, apparel, housing, and entertainment. Consumer spending accounts for approximately 70 percent of the GDP and has a big impact on job growth.[5]

- **Stock market price indexes.** A stock market price index measures the overall change in stock prices of corporations traded on U.S. stock markets. There are many different stock market price indexes, including the New York Stock Exchange (NYSE) Composite Index, the NASDAQ Composite Index, and the Dow Jones Industrial Average Index. The Dow Jones Industrial Average Index, for instance, provides the average price per share of thirty large companies' stocks on the NYSE. The NYSE Composite Index covers the prices of approximately 2,900 companies listed on the NYSE. A strongly performing stock market affects consumer and investment spending. If the stock market is performing well, people are more optimistic about the economy and are more likely to buy or invest.

- **Home and motor vehicle sales.** The purchases of these major items are good indicators of consumer demand, as well as of construction and manufacturing activity. The number of homes and motor vehicles sold can change depending on the time of year (for example, car sales are likely to increase when companies decrease prices to sell older models to make way for the new models), which makes it a smart idea to take two or three months together and compare that with similar periods of previous years.

To avoid being duped, ask yourself the following questions when you hear these indicators bandied about by a politician with an agenda. They may help you become a critical consumer of economic information.

- **Whose numbers are they?** Who is reporting the numbers? Is it a government agency? A political party? A business or consumer group? A newspaper? How might the source influence the interpretation of the numbers?

- **What were the expectations?** As important as the actual numbers is whether the numbers met the expectations of economic forecasters. An increase of 50,000 new jobs might seem like positive growth, but not if forecasters projected an increase of 250,000. (Also ask yourself who the forecasters are, and what agenda they might have.)

- **Are the numbers affected by seasonality?** Consumer spending and sales rise and fall at certain times of the year. For example, few people are building houses in the winter, which means that a decline in the number of home sales from August to December does not necessarily mean a drop-off in the economy. For seasonal variables it is best to compare numbers to previous years.

1. *The Economist's Guide to Economic Indicators: Making Sense of Economics*, 5th ed. (Princeton, N.J.: Bloomberg Press, 2003), 1.
2. Ibid.
3. Ibid, 47.
4. Ibid, 85.
5. Norman Frumkin, *Guide to Economic Indicators*, 3rd ed. (Armonk, N.Y.: M. E. Sharpe, 2000).

prices, the economy headed back into recession.[7] The National Bureau of Economic Research dates this most recent recession from December 2007 to June 2009, though its after-effects continued to be felt because the recovery was less than robust.[8]

A particularly serious and prolonged recession is called a *depression*. A depression is a sharp reduction in a nation's GDP for more than a year and is accompanied by high unemployment. The last depression in the United States occurred when the stock market crashed in 1929. The United States spent much of the 1930s in a period of high unemployment and low production. By 1932, industrial production had declined 51 percent from its peak in 1929, and 25 percent of the work force was out of a job.[9] Because the human and corporate costs of this crisis were so high, the U.S. government

had to play a more active economic role to cushion the effects and provide some relief, a role it has played ever since.

In theory, at least, the market is self-regulating. A *self-regulating market* should correct itself when it moves in an inflationary or a recessionary direction. If it moves into a period of inflation, then prices for goods will get too high, people will not be able to afford them, and they will buy less. Or if a recession hits and people are out of work, they should be willing to work for lower wages and there should be lower demand and lower prices for the components a business uses to make a product. Left alone, the economy does in fact go through "natural" cycles of inflation and recession.

Although recessions and depressions are normal, citizens don't like the discomfort and hardship that can come with them. Since the Great Depression, people have come to look

depression a sharp reduction in a nation's GDP for more than a year, accompanied by high unemployment

self-regulating market an ideal market that corrects itself when it moves in an inflationary or recessionary direction

fiscal policy economic policy in which government regulates the economy through its powers to tax and spend

Keynesianism an economic theory that government could stimulate a lagging economy by putting more money into it or cool off an inflationary economy by taking money out

balanced budget a budget in which expenditures equal revenues

deficits shortfalls in the budget due to the government's spending more in a year than it takes in

surpluses the extra funds available because government revenues are greater than its expenditures

to the government to help smooth out the cycles of boom and bust, inflation and recession. (Once again, Figure 18.1 shows the difference in economic stability once government became involved.) Policymakers try to do this through the use of fiscal policy and monetary policy, which allow them to regulate the economy by manipulating taxes and interest rates. You will learn more about these two economic tools in the next section.

Who What How

It is not difficult to imagine who has something at stake in the economy. Consumers, workers (and the unemployed), businesses, investors, and elected officials all want a strong economy. Consumers would like to limit inflation to keep prices low, so that their dollar has more buying power. Workers and those looking for work want the economy to do well so that they can stay employed or new jobs can be created. Businesses want a prosperous economy so that consumption will rise, increasing production and profits as well. Investors, of course, stand to make a great deal of money when the economy is booming and lose a great deal when it is not. Elected officials benefit from a booming economy because they are more likely to be reelected if their constituents are happy; they often pay the electoral cost even when economic hardship is not their fault.

Since the 1930s these groups have come to expect government actors to use the tools of fiscal policy and monetary policy to regulate the economy and keep it prosperous.

Fiscal Policy and Monetary Policy

Using government strategies to regulate the economy

Even before the stock market crash of 1929 that precipitated the Great Depression, economic reformers had begun to question the ability of the unregulated market to guard the public interest. They argued that some government intervention in the economy might be necessary—not only to improve the public welfare and protect people from the

worst effects of the business cycle but also to increase the efficiency of the market itself. Such intervention could take one of two forms: fiscal policy, which enables government to regulate the economy through its powers to tax and spend, or monetary policy, which allows government to manage the economy by controlling the money supply through the regulation of interest rates. Each of these strategies, as we will see, has political advantages and costs, and both play an important role in contemporary economic policy.

One of the strongest advocates of government action in the 1930s was British economist John Maynard Keynes (pronounced "canes"), who argued that government can and should step in to regulate the economy by using *fiscal policy*—the government's power to tax and spend. According to *Keynesianism*, government could stimulate a lagging economy by putting more money into it (increasing government spending and cutting taxes) or cool off an inflationary economy by taking money out (cutting spending and raising taxes).

Keynes argued, contrary to most other economists at the time, that it is not essential to achieve a *balanced budget* in the national economy—that is, a budget in which government spends no more money than it brings in through taxes and revenues. Rather, for Keynes, *deficits* (shortfalls due to the government spending more in a year than it takes in) and *surpluses* (extra funds because government revenues are greater than its expenditures) were tools to be utilized freely to fine-tune the economy.

To illustrate, let us assume that the economy is prosperous—people are employed and have plenty of money to spend. Aggregate demand is rising and is about to set off a wave of inflation as prices rise and workers need more wages to keep pace. Rather than let the cycle run its course, government can raise taxes, which takes money out of the hands of consumers and causes aggregate demand to drop because people have less money to spend. Government can also spend less. If government buys fewer uniforms for the military, or delays placing orders for fleets of cars, or just freezes its own hiring, it can avoid stimulating the economy and thus raising aggregate demand. By taxing more and spending less, government is likely to run a surplus. Similarly, if a recession sets in, the Keynesian response is for government to cut taxes (to promote consumer and business

> **monetary policy** economic policy in which government regulates the economy by manipulating interest rates to control the money supply
>
> **interest rates** the cost of borrowing money, calculated as a percentage of the money borrowed

spending) and to increase its own spending. This would create a deficit, but in the process it would stimulate the economy. Cutting taxes leaves more money for citizens and businesses to spend, thereby increasing the demand for products. Increasing government spending directly influences demand, at least for the products and services that government buys. As these sectors get moving, they create demand in other sectors.

The Keynesian strategy of increasing government spending during recessionary periods and cutting back during expansionary periods gradually became the primary tool of economic policy in the period between 1930 and the 1970s. Franklin Roosevelt used it to lead the country out of the Depression in the 1930s. His New Deal created federal agencies to help businesses recover, jobs programs to put people back to work, and social programs to restore the buying power of consumers. Subsequent presidents made fiscal policy the foundation of their economic programs until the late 1970s, when the economy took a turn that fiscal policy seemed unable to manage. During this period the U.S. economy was characterized by inflation and, *at the same time*, unemployment. Keynesian theory was unable to explain this odd combination of economic events, and economists and policymakers searched for new theories to help guide them through this difficult economic period. Taxing and spending are limited in their usefulness to politicians because they are usually redistributive policies (see Chapter 17), necessarily requiring that they reward or punish members of the population by lowering or raising their tax burden, or spending more or less money on them. This can be politically tricky for elected officials who want to maximize their chances at reelection. Their temptation is to lower taxes and increase spending, which can result in a sizable national debt, and which loses sight of the goal of leveling out the cycles of a market economy.

Many people looking at the high inflation and growing unemployment of the 1970s began to turn to monetary policy as a way to manage the economy. **Monetary policy** regulates the economy by controlling the money supply (the sum of all currency on hand in the country plus the amount held in checking accounts) by manipulating interest rates. The monetarists believed that the high inflation of the 1970s was caused by too much money in the economy, and they advocated cutting back on the supply of money. How is this

The Health of the Nation
When we focus on the big picture numbers of GDP, inflation rates, and unemployment figures, it's easy to overlook the human impact of these data. The wife and children of a sharecropper in Washington County, Arkansas, in 1935, during the height of the Great Depression, certainly felt the hardship and dislocation of the era's record unemployment, bank closings, and the dramatic drops in GDP, industrial production, and other indicators of economic health.

accomplished? We often think that there is a fixed amount of money out there and that at different times the lucky among us simply have more of it. But money is a commodity with a price of its own—what we call **interest rates**—and by changing interest rates, the government can put more money into circulation, or take some out. When there is a lot of money, people can borrow it cheaply—that is, at low interest rates—and they are more likely to spend it, raising aggregate demand. When money is scarce (and interest rates are high), people borrow less because it costs more; thus they spend less and drive down aggregate demand. By raising and lowering interest rates, government can regulate the cycles of the market economy just as it does by taxing and spending. As a tool of economic policy, however, monetary policy can be somewhat hard to control. Small changes can have big effects. Reducing the money supply might lower inflation, but too great a reduction can also cause a recession, which is what

Economic Bust
The subprime mortgage crisis was a primary factor in the drastic increase in foreclosures and the steep decline in new home sales beginning in late 2007. Foreclosures have continued as the U.S. economy suffers in a recession that has seen more than 9 percent of Americans out of work.

happened in the early 1980s. Changes need to be made in narrow increments rather than in broad sweeps.

Today policymakers use a combination of fiscal and monetary policy to achieve economic goals. As Figure 18.1 on page 677 shows, from the 1940s, when the federal government made a full commitment to regulate the gyrations of the business cycle, the highs and lows of boom and bust have been greatly tempered. There are still fluctuations in inflation, unemployment, and GDP, but they lack the punishing ferocity of the earlier unregulated period.

As we have indicated, however, the two kinds of policy are not equally easy for government to employ. Most significantly, the instruments of monetary policy are removed from the political arena and are wielded by actors who are not subject to electoral pressures. By contrast, fiscal policy is very much at the center of enduring political struggles. Many voters would prefer to pay less in taxes but also to have government spend more on their needs. We explore the politics of these two types of policy in the sections that follow.

The Politics of Monetary Policy

We can thank the politicians of the early twentieth century for divorcing monetary policy from politics. Controlling interest rates is a regulatory policy (Chapter 17) that would generate heavy lobbying from businesses and corporations, which have

Federal Reserve System independent commission that controls the money supply through a system of twelve federal banks

a huge stake in the cost of money. Realizing that Congress and the president could probably not agree on interest rates any more effectively than on taxes, spending, or anything else, Congress established the **Federal Reserve System** in 1913, as an independent commission, to control the money supply. The Fed, as it is known, is actually a system of twelve federal banks. It is run by a Board of Governors, seven members appointed by the president and confirmed by the Senate who serve fourteen-year staggered terms. The Fed chair is appointed by the president and serves a four-year term that overlaps the president's term of office. The current chair, serving since 2006, is Ben Bernanke. Bernanke followed on the heels of Alan Greenspan, who served nearly twenty years, from 1987 to 2006.

How does the Fed influence the economy? By controlling the amount of money that banks and other institutions have available to loan. When they have a lot of money to loan, interest rates tend to drop and people borrow more, thus increasing levels of economic activity, which includes everything from buying a new car to investing in an automobile manufacturing plant. When lending institutions have less to loan (smaller reserves), they charge more for their money (higher interest rates) and, at every level of demand for money, economic activity slows down. The Fed controls the supply of money by controlling the interest rates at which banks borrow money, by limiting the amount the banks have to hold in reserve, and by buying government securities.

When the Fed is trying to hold back inflationary pressures, it is most likely to adopt a *tight monetary policy*, keeping money in short supply. When the economy is headed for a recession, the Fed is more likely to adopt a *loose monetary policy*, getting more money into the economy. The Fed must confront a number of challenges that make economic policy making a difficult task. Unexpected events such as labor stoppages, agricultural shortfalls or surpluses, or international crises, as well as normal change, can make it very difficult to control the economy or even to determine the impact of different policy decisions. Beliefs about how the economy works also change. Before the 1990s, most experts argued that we would not be able to have a sustained period of economic growth without strong inflationary pressures. But by the century's end, these pressures had not appeared—in part because of globalization of the economy and in part because of unanticipated increases in productivity.

Economic policy making must also try to take into account unpredictable psychological factors; economic behavior depends not just on the real condition of the economy but also on what people expect to happen. Watch the newspaper and you'll see economic pundits regularly trying to read between the lines of every Bernanke speech for hints of what the Fed is going to do. A collective misreading can set off a chain of economic decisions that can actually cause the Fed to act, perhaps even to do the opposite of what was expected in the first place.

Because elected officials try to respond to constituent pressures, and because economic policy remedies can be painful to citizens in the short run, monetary policy has been insulated from the turmoil of partisan politics. Thus, as an independent agency, the Fed can make its decisions with an eye only on general economic policy goals, and is influenced much less by partisan or electoral constituency considerations. Also, because the Fed only has to worry about monetary policy, it can react more quickly than Congress and the president. This is especially important because if economic policy decisions are forecast far in advance, markets, investors, and consumers may adjust their behavior in ways that undermine the intended results. Further, the ability to act quickly can enable the Fed to take action based on early indicators of economic instability, before the forces of inflation or recession do much damage.

The Politics of Fiscal Policy

Monetary policy, while subject to its own challenges, can avoid the political pitfalls for which those making fiscal policy must regularly watch out. This is primarily because fiscal policy makers, as elected officials, try to respond to their constituents' demands, or what they anticipate their constituents' demands will be. Imagine, for example, how difficult it would be for lawmakers to try to quell inflationary pressures by telling older citizens that their Social Security checks would need to be cut in order to fix the economy. Similarly, most of us do not want our taxes increased even if it means that the national economy will be better off.

Fiscal policy is made by Congress and the president, through the budget process. Budgets may seem tedious and boring, reminding us of our own efforts at financial responsibility. But government budgets are where we find the clearest indications, in black and white, of politics—who gets what,

and who pays for it. The government budget process also exemplifies the conflict we discussed in Chapter 7 between the needs for lawmaking and the electoral imperatives of representation. Members of Congress and the president, as lawmakers, have an interest in maintaining a healthy economy and should be able to agree on appropriate levels of taxes and spending to see that the economy stays in good shape. But as elected leaders they are also accountable to constituencies and committed to ideological or partisan goals. From a representative's perspective the budget is a pie to be divided and fought over.

For the budget to serve its national fiscal policy goals, as a lawmaking perspective dictates, the process must be coordinated and disciplined. Of course, coordination and discipline imply a need for control, perhaps even centralized control, of the budget process. But representatives deplore such control and much prefer a decentralized budget process. They stand a far better chance of getting a tax favor for a local industry or a spending program that benefits constituents when the budget is hammered out in the relative secrecy of the congressional subcommittees.

History of the Budget Process

Before 1921 there was no formal budget process. As American society became more complex and the role of the government expanded, Congress decided that someone needed to be in charge, or at least to take an overall view of the budget process. Congress gave the president the responsibility for preparing and delivering to Congress a national budget with the Budget and Accounting Act of 1921. The act created the Bureau of the Budget, today the Office of Management and Budget (OMB), to assist the president (see *Profiles in Citizenship* for former OMB directors Peter Orzsag, in this chapter, and Mitch Daniels, in Chapter 4). The president's budget sets the agenda for congressional action. It is a plan of spending, reflecting existing programs and new presidential initiatives as well as economic estimates of revenues and projections for deficits and surpluses in future years.

The preparation of the president's budget begins over a year before it is submitted to Congress. OMB asks all the federal agencies to submit their requests for funding, along with justifications for the requests. OMB acts as the president's representative and negotiates for months with the agencies and departments in fashioning a budget that reflects the president's priorities but at the

"I think the single most important thing at this point is to resist the strong trend towards polarization that is hollowing out the middle of the political spectrum and making evidence-based debate difficult."

Though Americans don't much like to admit it, governments cost money. The collective projects they undertake are expensive, largely paid for by tax revenue. We think of public servants as glad-handing politicians, friendly police officers and brave firefighters. But sometimes they are the brainiacs at the computers, running the numbers and trying to balance the books. In the case of Peter Orszag, former director of the Congressional Budget Office (CBO) and the Office of Management and Budget (OMB), the job was even more complex. Trying to get the right *policy* answer while balancing the pressure from politicians

to get the right *political* answer was a challenge. Orszag is back in the private sector, at least for now, but he reflected for us on his years of government service and how he got there.

Orszag's family wasn't very political, but he grew up in Lexington, Massachusetts, with an acute sense of history fed by his fascination with the local reenactments of the famous Revolutionary War battles. His private-school education emphasized the value of service, culminating in his high school internship in the office of a then-new Senator Tom Daschle, D-S.D. (who would go on in time to serve as the Senate majority leader.) Since the office was just finding its feet, Orszag's experience was not a run-of-the-mill internship; while his friends in other Senate offices were opening mail and running errands, he was writing speeches and working with Daschle's newly minted chief of staff, Pete Rouse.

From there Orszag went to Princeton where he got hooked on economics. Orszag says, "At its most fundamental, I have always been interested in combining rigor and relevance, so it's what attracted me to economics in the first place. There was a book that Alan Blinder, a professor at Princeton, wrote in 1987, called *Hard Heads, Soft Hearts: Tough-Minded Economics for a Just Society*. I had been sensing that I liked this combination, but that captured it, and I love that book and

it's what drew me to economics, because you are applying this ostensibly rigorous tool to real-world situations." Orszag took an introductory class from Professor Blinder at Princeton, graduated as an econ major and headed to England with a Marshall Scholarship to earn a master's and a Ph.D. in economics from the London School of Economics.

Before long, Orszag was able to put some of his economic theory to the test when he returned to the United States to work as an economic advisor in the second Clinton administration. He did a brief stint in the private sector after that, setting up a consultancy business with his younger brother. When they sold the business he went to work at the Brookings Institution, a liberal think tank, and then to CBO as its director.

CBO is an arm of the legislature that is charged with providing economic analysis to Congress to help it make policy and budgetary decisions. Orszag really enjoyed his work there; he found it "remarkably independent to a degree that was refreshing and astonishing." Because it was nonpartisan it was mostly free of political pressure. He was able to restructure staff and process in the office to make it more responsive to Congress.

Orszag would have liked to have stayed at CBO, but after the 2008 election, with the economy in freefall, President Obama

same time does not inflame entrenched constituencies (see Figure 18.2).

Congress' job is to approve the budget, but it does not accept everything that the president requests. Congressional consideration of the budget has become increasingly complex, particularly since the 1970s. Before that, all bills

involving expenditures were considered in a dual committee process: first expenditures were authorized by a substantive standing committee of the House (for example, the House Committee on Education and the Workforce), and then the relevant House Appropriations Subcommittee would go over the same requests, often hearing from the same agency

asked him to take on the directorship of OMB. As he says, "When the president of the United States asks you to do something, unless you have a very strong counter argument, it's typically what you do." So to OMB he went, adding a dose of politics into the economics mix, something unlike what he had been used to at CBO, even though he had been working for politicians in Congress. Of the difference he says, "CBO is correctly seen by the press as being a pretty impartial neutral arbiter and playing it straight, so that was not hard. The OMB job is a more challenging combination because it's got part where you are supposed to be analytical and rigorous and bringing evidence to bear, but you are also part of the president's economics team, and you're a west wing staffer. But you're also in the Cabinet, Senate-confirmed, and have external responsibilities. So that can get a little awkward." He dealt with the awkward dance between politics and policy by adopting a rule: "I would only say true things but everything that was true I didn't need to say."

At OMB, Orszag was instrumental in shaping the health care reform bill that Obama signed in 2010, shortly after which he announced his resignation and moved on. Currently he is a Vice Chairman of Global Banking at Citigroup, a position he sees not as his final career move, but as an important one. He told us: "I'm going

to go five to ten years into the private sector. Have a different set of experiences and then—I believe very firmly that people who have different experiences whether it's within government—not staying in the same agency but going legislative versus executive or changing topics and areas—or just government versus the private sector—as long as you are actually doing something new, it leads to more insight. One of the things that I've enjoyed so much at CBO and OMB is being able to do different things and bring insights from one field to another, and I have always found that people who have a breadth of experience are the most interesting and can bring a lot to whatever task that they are currently doing. So it's time for me to do something different and I'm going to do it."

On public versus private service:

"The thing I would say about government versus business and applying what you have learned, is that especially in places like the Council of Economic Advisors or the National Economic Council, etc., the breadth and depth is unmatched compared to most other settings. In terms of getting exposure to lots of different areas, it's difficult to beat. On top of that, is of course whatever benefit one derives psychologically from a sense of public service. What I say is as long as you feel like you are contributing to forward

progress, the return in terms of your sense of self is extraordinarily high."

On keeping the republic:

"I think the single most important thing at this point is to resist the strong trend towards polarization that is hollowing out the middle of the political spectrum and making evidence-based debate difficult. So that means toning down the volume on either left or right medium streams on cable news and on the blogosphere. And there is a broader point to that too, which is that most of us have grown up, and I think it's still the case for college freshmen, where the mental attitude that one takes towards something that's written on a piece of paper or something that is said on the airwaves, the default is that it is true. We've been trained that if we read something in the newspaper or see it on the Internet it must be true. The probability that it is correct is not anywhere as near as high as it was at some point. We need to move to an attitude where when we see something or hear something or read something we don't automatically assume and give it the benefit of the doubt, unless it's coming from a certain trusted source . . . [T]his is a huge problem I think because it is difficult to have the kind of democracy that we want and need, when the debate often occurs at this level where it's just kind of bombs being thrown back and forth. ∎

officials, and recommend that the funds be appropriated by the Appropriations Committee. The process was the same in the Senate.

Then in 1974 Congress passed the Congressional Budget and Impoundment Act, which, among other things, created a new committee layer: the House and Senate Budget

Committees. These committees were meant to achieve some coherence in the congressional budget process because they were required to approve an overall general plan, and then provide the standing committees with target levels for expenditures, given the expected revenues. As part of this process, the House and the Senate have to pass a joint budget

> *supply side economics* President Ronald Reagan's economic plan, by which tax cuts would ultimately generate more, not less, government revenues by allowing for increased investments and productivity

Figure 18.2

The Budget Process

Fiscal policy making is a complex process involving both the executive and legislative branches of government. It begins with the president, who solicits budget requests from federal agencies (see step 1) and ends with the passage of a budget resolution in Congress, and the appropriation of funds (see steps 6, 7, and 8). In between, there is a great deal of analysis, discussion, and negotiation.

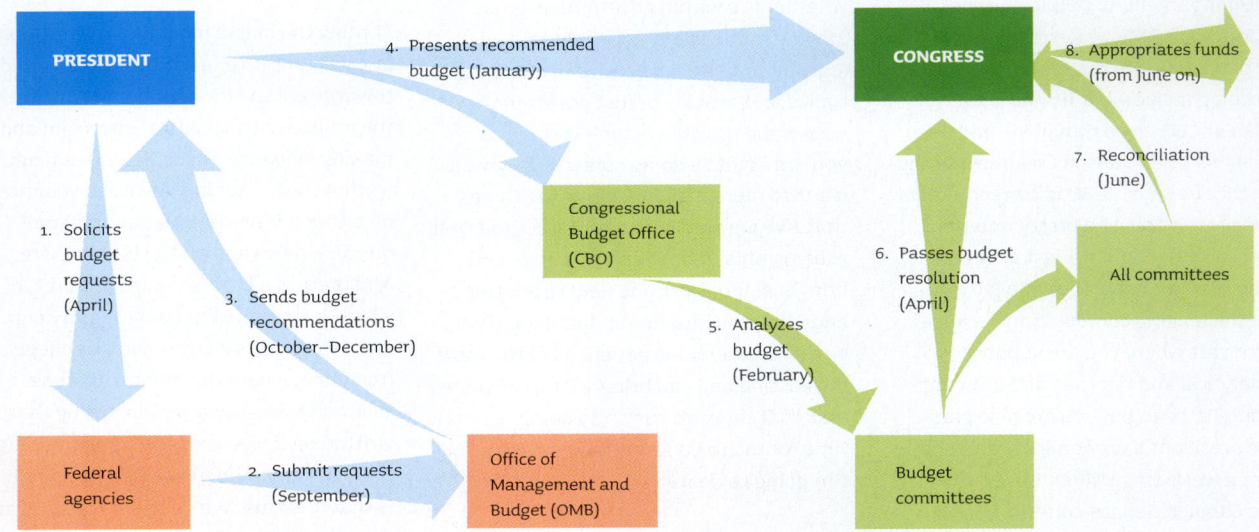

Source: William Boyes and Michael Melvin, *Fundamentals of Economics*, 4th ed. (Boston: Houghton Mifflin, 1999). © 2009 South-Western, a part of Cengage Learning, Inc. Reproduced by permission. www.cengage.com/permissions.

resolution, supposedly early in the budget process, so that both chambers are working within the same budgetary framework. This process worked until the 1980s and the election of President Reagan.

Early in his tenure as president, Reagan got Congress to agree to a large tax cut, arguing that the added funds in the economy would ultimately generate more government revenue to replace what was lost by lower taxation. The idea behind Reagan's plan, called *supply side economics*, was that tax cuts, especially if targeted at the wealthy, would result in greater investment, which would mean more production without inflation. This turned upside down the principles of fiscal policy, which held that decreased taxation would lead to growth and inflation. Supply side economics may have been an incentive for investment, but it did not produce more revenue; instead, the government faced increasing budget deficits. If less revenue is coming in as taxes, the only way to balance the budget is to spend less money. The Democrats in

Congress refused to accept Reagan's cuts in social programs, although they went along with most of his suggested increases in defense spending. The outcome was a budget badly out of whack and a government deeply in debt (see Figure 18.3).

Congress struggled in vain to bring spending into alignment with revenues. The 1985 Gramm-Rudman Act (amended in 1987) set up a mechanism calling for automatic 10-percent cuts on existing programs should Congress not be able to move toward a balanced budget in a given year. It did not work. Congress was too divided to be able to raise taxes or cut programs enough to bring expenditures down. Rather they used accounting tricks to avoid the automatic cuts—or just changed the targets. As one expert put it, "When the game is too hard . . . members of Congress change the rules."[10] The forces for representation were too strong for members to inflict such pain on their core constituents and to risk the electoral consequences for themselves.

> ***national debt*** the total of the nation's unpaid deficits, or simply the sum total of what the national government owes

Figure 18.3

U.S. Federal Budget Deficit/Surplus and Debt

The annual budget deficit (left) is the amount by which government spending exceeds tax revenues. If tax revenue is greater than the government spending, a budget surplus results. In the 1970s and 1980s the United States ran larger budget deficits (in the billions), but the trend was reversed briefly in the 1990s. What stands out, however, is the result of the government's efforts to stimulate the economy to fight the 2007/2008 recession with recent very large deficits. The federal debt (right) represents the total amount of outstanding loans owed by the U.S. government, here presented as a percentage of our Gross Domestic Product. The current debt is approaching 100 percent of the GDP, which has not occurred since the massive national spending that financed our participation in World War II.

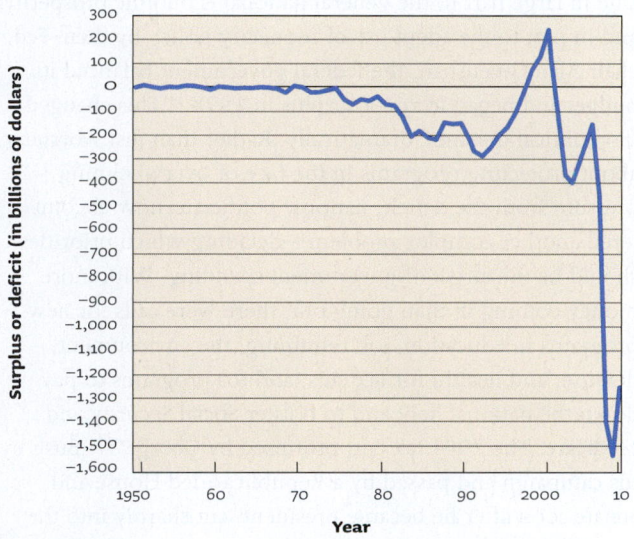
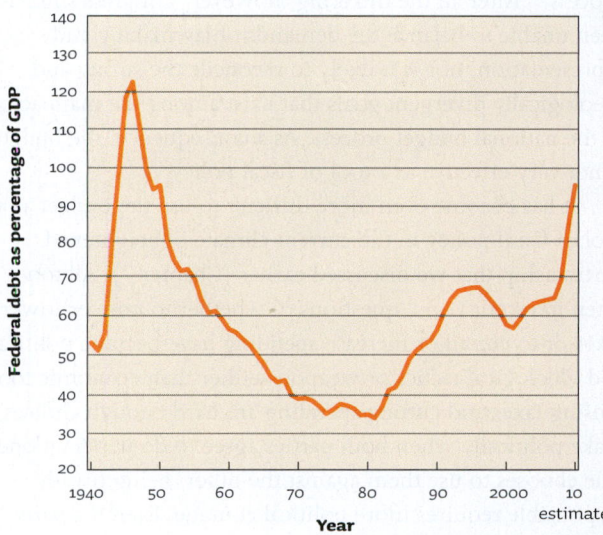

Source: Office of Management and Budget, Historical Tables, "Table 1.1: Summary of Receipts, Outlays, and Surpluses or Deficits" and "Table 7.1: Federal Debt at the End of Year: 1940–2015," www.whitehouse.gov/omb/budget/Historicals/.

Politics in an Era of Expanding Debt

The deficit began to loom large again in the 1980s and the 1990s. When the government uses fiscal policy to stimulate a slow economy, it generally runs a deficit for a few years (as it does any time it spends more than it brings in). As the shortfalls accumulate, the government amasses the ***national debt*** (see right side, Figure 18.3), which is the total of the nation's unpaid deficits, or simply the sum total of what the national government owes. The national debt grew during the New Deal period as the federal government attempted to use fiscal policy, especially massive spending on domestic programs such as the Works Project Administration and the Civilian Conservation Corps, to stimulate the economy out of the Great Depression. It continued to rise as the government borrowed heavily to finance our participation in World War II. But by the time the war was over, the economy was moving again and the growing economy generated additional revenues, permitting the government to pay down a portion of the national debt. Deficits started rising again in the 1980s, and by 2010 the national debt had climbed to almost $14 trillion, more than $43,000 per citizen. Just like citizens who carry a credit card balance or borrow money to buy a car, the government pays interest on the national debt. In 2010, roughly 5 percent of our taxes went simply to pay interest on the national debt, the lowest percentage since 1968.[11]

However, because interest rates are likely to rise from their historic lows, it is expected that the percentage of taxes paid on this interest will rise again.

The 1980s and 1990s became known as the era of *deficit politics*.[12] All federal program decisions were made in the light of their impact on the deficit. This changed the character of the politics involved and helped to increase the power of the leadership, particularly in the House of Representatives; dealing with the deficit called for more coordination and discipline. Congress then developed a dizzying array of informal mechanisms in an effort to streamline the budgetary process.[13] After all the tinkering, however, Congress still has been unable to balance the demands of lawmaking and representation, nor is it likely to reconcile the strong and ideologically divergent goals that exist among the main actors in the national budget process. As a consequence, the budget is not very effective as a tool of fiscal policy.

It has become even more difficult to use the budget as a tool of fiscal policy in the current climate of heightened partisanship that we discussed earlier (Chapter 7). All too often in recent years, questions of whether to raise or lower taxes or to curtail or increase spending have become political and ideological tactics or weapons rather than economic tools. Raising taxes and cutting spending are hard enough choices to make politically when both parties agree to do it. When one side chooses to use them against the other, being fiscally responsible requires more political courage. Even if a party has the determination to act, it can be difficult to get things done. When the president and majorities of both houses of Congress are of the same party, they are likely to agree on the general direction national policy should take to achieve a coherent budget. With the increased use of the filibuster, however, a party usually needs a super-majority in the Senate to be able to make budget decisions. Under conditions of divided government, even that much coherence is difficult to achieve.

The election of Republican Ronald Reagan to the presidency while the Democrats retained control of the House of Representatives brought about the gridlock that led to the era of deficit politics, as Reagan pushed tax cuts and the Democrats refused to cut spending. Similarly, the results of the 1994 election pitted a highly ideological and conservative Republican majority in Congress against Democratic president Bill Clinton. The Republicans were certain they had been elected to curtail what they called the "tax and spend" habits of the Democrats, sending a budget in 1995 that President Clinton vetoed because of cuts to popular Democratic programs. In the ensuing standoff, the government went into a partial shutdown. Clinton, who argued that popular programs needed to be protected, won the battle for public opinion over the congressional Republicans, who argued they would not budge over principle. Mindful of that public relations disaster, Republican leaders gave Clinton much of what he wanted in his 1996 budget and were criticized by their own party members for being too compliant in an election year.

Budget politics took a new turn at the end of the 1990s. Due in large part to the general national economic prosperity, and in part to the adept use of monetary policy by then–Fed chair Alan Greenspan, the federal government balanced its budget and began to run a surplus in 1998.[14] This changed the political dynamic dramatically. Rather than just worrying about protecting programs in the face of overwhelming pressure from the deficit, national politicians now encountered another complex problem—deciding which priorities should be the target of government spending. With more money coming in than going out, there were calls for new programs in education, job retraining, the environment, defense, and health; for tax cuts; and for programs to pay down the national debt and to bolster Social Security and Medicare. The 2001 tax cut, promised by George W. Bush in his campaign and passed by a Republican-led House and Senate soon after he became president, cut sharply into the surplus. It also signaled a different philosophy of tax policy. Rather than just trying to restrain spending and balance the budget, as was the traditional Republican goal, the new Republican strategy was to provide incentives for saving and investment (through tax cuts for the wealthy) and to favor "starving the beast" (that is, shrinking government by cutting off its money supply) rather than focusing on the deficit.[15] As economic growth slowed and the prosperity of the 1990s began to wind down, government revenues dropped from earlier estimates. By mid-2002 the deficit had returned.[16] To help stimulate the economy, the president endorsed additional tax cuts in 2003, which contributed further to the rising deficit. Finally, the wars in Afghanistan and Iraq had cost the government over $500 billion during the Bush administration (headed toward $1 trillion by 2010).

The deficit grew quickly, and the economy did not improve. In October 2008, with economic disaster on the immediate horizon, the Bush administration oversaw the passage of the Troubled Assets Relief Program (TARP) to bail

excise taxes consumer taxes levied on specific merchandise, such as cigarettes or alcohol

progressive taxes taxes whose rates increase with income

out financial institutions deemed "too big to fail." Although much of the funds had been repaid by 2010, the cost of the program was still about $30 billion, although it was possible that it might ultimately end up making a profit for the government.[17] The American Recovery and Reinvestment Act of 2009 (commonly known as the stimulus bill) added nearly $900 billion of spending on tax relief for individuals and businesses, extensions of unemployment insurance, infrastructure development, and various other projects designed in the Keynesian economic tradition to kick the economy into gear. Supporters of these efforts to soften the blow of economic recession and jumpstart the economy claimed that TARP and the stimulus package headed off a much worse decline in the economy, while detractors argued, from the right, that they simply bailed out big corporations while leaving the taxpayers to pay a mounting load of debt, and from the left, that the stimulus needed to be even bigger than it was.[18] The nonpartisan Congressional Budget Office, however, estimated that the program was on track to meeting the goal of saving 3.5 million jobs by the end of 2010.[19]

With the 2010 deficit projected to be $1.3 trillion (just below the record $1.42 trillion of 2009), the issues of spending and taxing were back at the heart of partisan battles as the 2010 midterm elections approached.[20] Republicans declared that the stimulus bill was a failure because it hadn't created enough jobs to pump up the economy, and said that a recession was no time for government to spend money. They deplored the recklessness of running up the deficit by spending, while insisting that the Bush tax cuts, scheduled to lapse in 2010, be made permanent.[21] The Democrats, on the other hand, argued that a recession was the very time that government should spend money and demanded an end to the Bush tax cuts for the top 2 percent of the population.[22]

The American public is quite concerned about the large budget deficit and the increasing national debt, but it is not necessarily willing to make sacrifices in spending to combat these problems. According to one poll, 89 percent of the public said that reducing the budget deficit was a "top priority" or an "important" problem for the country, but 47 percent also wanted to see more spending to help the economy recover.[23] Without popular pressure to curtail spending and balance the budget, politicians are unlikely to make the hard choices such action would entail.

Tax Policy

Taxation is part of the federal budgetary process. Much is at stake in making tax policy; a decimal point here, a deleted line in the tax code there, can mean millions for industries. Politicians at all levels are loath to raise taxes, but sooner or later most do so to pay for the services their constituents demand.

The U.S. government takes in a lot of money in taxes every year, estimated to be $2.3 trillion in 2010.[24] Figure 18.4 shows the major sources of revenue for the federal government. The largest single source is individual federal income taxes. The next largest is contributions to social insurance, and by far the largest component of this is Social Security, with funds coming equally from our paychecks and employers. One of the smallest categories is **excise taxes**—taxes levied on specific items like cigarettes and alcohol—but it still represents roughly $66.3 billion.[25]

One of the features of the U.S. tax code is that some money is earmarked for particular purposes whereas other taxes go into the general fund. Thus Social Security taxes cannot be used to purchase new jets for the air force and highway trust funds cannot be used to supplement Medicare costs. An apparent exception is when the government borrows money from itself with a promise to pay it back. This has been the practice in recent years when the Social Security Trust Fund was running large surpluses. The national government borrowed money from the trust fund to pay for other things, vowing to reimburse Social Security in the future out of general fund revenues.

Personal income taxes in the United States are **progressive taxes**, which means that those with higher incomes not only pay more taxes but they also pay at a higher rate. Taxes are paid on all the income an individual or household receives, including wage and salary income, interest and dividends, rents on property owned, and royalties. The amount owed depends on your tax rate and the amount of your taxable income, which is your total income minus certain exemptions and deductions. Deductions can include interest payments on

What kinds of individual behavior should government encourage with economic policy?

Thinking Outside
the Box

regressive taxes taxes that require poor people to pay a higher proportion of their income than do the well off

Figure 18.4

Major Sources of Income (Revenues) and Expenditures (Outlays) in the 2011 Estimated U.S. Budget (in billions)

For the year 2011 the U.S. government will collect roughly $2.6 trillion and spend almost $3.4 trillion. Revenues come from taxes (primarily individual income and social insurance payroll taxes[1]). Outlays fall into two major spending categories: mandatory spending (budget items like Social Security, which the government has already committed to pay for) and nonmandatory, or discretionary, spending (budget items that are determined by government policy).

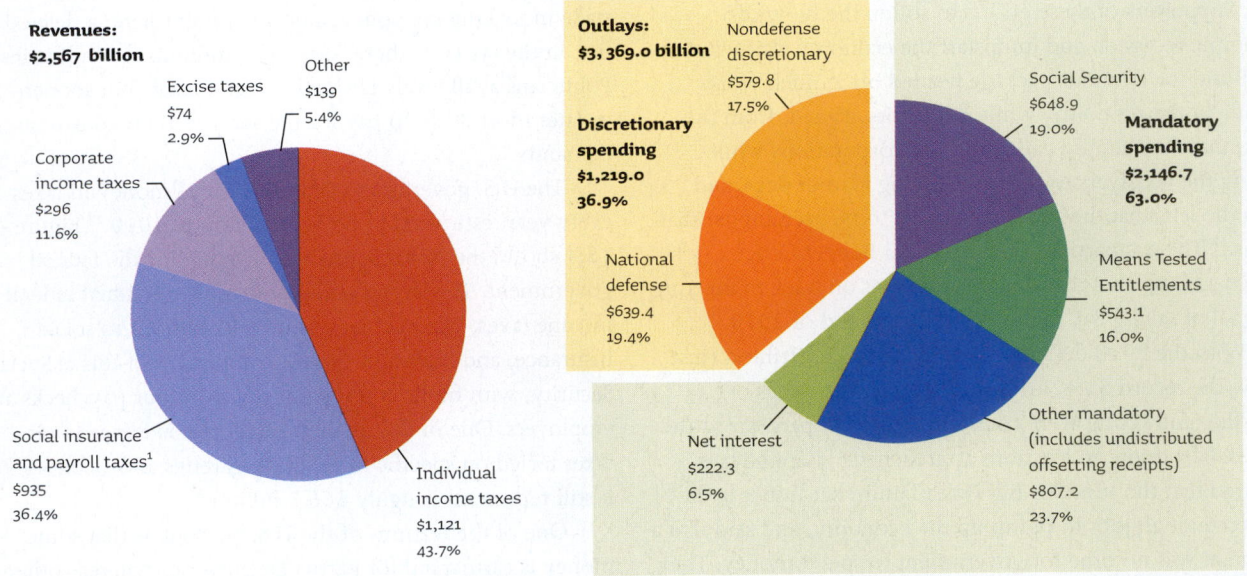

Source: Office of Management and Budget, "Historical Tables: Budget of the United States Government," Fiscal Year 2011," Table 2.1—Receipts by Source: 1934–2015, Table 2.2—Percentage Composition of Receipts by Source: 1934–2015, Table 8.2—Outlays by Budget Enforcement Act Category in Constant (FY 2005) Dollars: 1962–2015, Table 8.3—Percentage Distribution of Outlays by Budget Enforcement Act Category: 1962–2015, http://www.whitehouse.gov/sites/default/files/omb/budget/fy2011/assets/hist.pdf.

1. Social insurance taxes include Social Security taxes, Medicare taxes, unemployment insurance taxes, and federal employee retirement payments.

a home mortgage or charitable contributions. In 2010, single taxpayers were allowed a standard deduction of $5,700 ($11,400 for married couples). Everyone is subject to the same rate of taxation for some base amount, and incomes over that amount are subject to progressively higher percentages of tax. The range of taxable income at each tax bracket determines your marginal tax rate. For example, if you are in a 35-percent tax bracket, it does not mean that you pay 35 percent of all your income in taxes, but that you pay 35 percent on everything you make above the tax bracket

beneath you—and a lower percentage on the income made under that base amount (see Table 18.1).

Other taxes are called **regressive taxes**, even if they are fixed percentages, because they take a higher proportion of income from a poor person's income than from those who are well off. Sales taxes are often argued to be regressive, particularly when they are levied on necessities like food and electricity. If a poor person and a rich person each buy an air conditioner for $200, with a sales tax of 5 percent, the resulting $10 tax is a bigger chunk of the poor person's

Table 18.1

How Progressive Income Taxing Works

Progressive income taxing means the more you make, the higher a percentage of your income you pay in taxes. Here's how you would calculate the amount due for a married couple filing jointly (based on 2009 projections) at various income levels. The highest tax bracket, for those with taxable incomes over $372,950, is 35 percent. That doesn't mean that 35 percent is paid on the entire income, however. Notice how the percentage paid goes up for each increment of income, so that the 35 percent is paid only on the amount over $372,950.

TAXABLE INCOME: if your income, after all deductions, is more than	but not more than	you will pay this amount	plus this percentage	on the amount over
$0–	$16,700	$0	10%	$0
16,700	67,900	1,670	15	16,700
67,900	137,050	9,350	25	67,900
137,050	208,850	26,638	28	137,050
208,850	372,950	46,742	33	208,850
372,950		100,895	35	372,950

Let's look at the calculations based on three families' incomes.

TAXABLE INCOME (income after deductions for children, charitable contributions, mortgage interest, and the like)	A Tax on first $16,700	B Tax on next $51,200	C Tax on next $69,150	D Tax on next $71,800	E Tax on next $164,100	F Tax on income over $372,950	Total tax owed
$30,000	$1,670	($30,000−16,700) X 0.15 = $1,995	—	—	—	—	$3,665 (A + B)
$75,000	$1,670	$51,200 x 0.15 = $7,680	($75,000−67,900) X 0.25 = $1,775	—	—	—	$11,125 (A + B + C)
$1,000,000	$1,670	$51,200 x 0.15 = $7,680	$69,150 x 0.25 = $17,288	$71,800 x 0.28 = $20,104	$164,100 x 0.33 = $54,153	($1,000,000− 372,950) x 0.35 = $219,468	$320,362 (A + B + C + D + E + F)

(Note: These calculations assume no capital gains income.)

The effective tax rate (the actual percentage of their entire taxable income that each family pays in taxes) is 12.22 percent for the family that makes $30,000, 14.83 percent for the family that makes $75,000, and 32.04 percent for the family that makes $1 million. The increasing percentage with the increase in income is why it is called *progressive* taxation.

capital gains tax   a tax levied on the returns that people earn from capital investments, like the profits from the sale of stocks or a home

income than it is of the wealthy person's. Furthermore, poor people spend a higher portion of their incomes on consumables that are subject to the sales tax; the wealthy, in contrast, spend a significant portion of their income on investments, stocks, or elite education for their children, which are not subject to sales taxes.

Other regressive taxes include excise taxes and Social Security taxes. Like sales tax, everyone pays the same percentage in excise tax when they buy alcohol, cigarettes, or gasoline. Social Security taxes are also regressive because, as we discussed in Chapter 17, people pay taxes only on the first $106,800 of their incomes (in 2010). A person who makes $1 million a year then contributes a smaller share of his or her salary to Social Security than would someone who makes $80,000. Because of the regressiveness of the Social Security tax, some observers—mostly Democrats—have called for an increase in the salary cap.

The congressional parties' different points of view on the Social Security cap clearly illustrate their contrasting approaches to tax policy, particularly on the issue of the progressivity of taxes—who should bear the brunt of the tax burden and whose tax loads should be relieved. In general, Democrats focus on easing the tax burden on lower-income groups in the name of fairness and equity. As a matter of fiscal policy, they tend to want to put money into the hands of workers and the working poor on the assumption that this will translate quickly into consumer spending, which increases demand and stimulates the whole economy. This is the "trickle-up" strategy. Give benefits to those with less and let the effects percolate upward, throughout the economic system. In contrast, Republicans focus more on lowering the high rates of taxation on those with larger incomes. Their sentiments are motivated by a different view of fairness; those who make more money should have the freedom to keep it. Republicans argue that the wealthy are more likely to save or invest their extra income (from a tax break), thus providing businesses with the capital they need to expand—an argument similar to supply side economics discussed earlier. Not only do they believe that the rate of taxation on the top tax brackets should be reduced, but they argue for a reduction in the **capital gains tax**, the tax levied on the returns that people earn from capital investments, like the profits from the sale of stocks or a home. The notion here is that if wealthy people are taxed at lower rates, they will invest and spend more, the economy will prosper, and the benefits will "trickle down" to the rest of the members of society. The debate between trickle-up and trickle-down theories of taxation represents one of the major partisan battles in Congress, and not only reveals deep ideological divisions between the parties but also demonstrates the very real differences in the constituencies they respond to.

President Bush's Tax Relief Act, implemented in 2001, demonstrates these divisions between the two major political parties on fiscal policy. President Bush supported this tax cut to fulfill campaign promises made in the 2000 election, and Congress argued that the legislation was in response to slowing economic growth in the United States. The act provided for an immediate tax "rebate" based on the benefit from the cut a taxpayer was estimated to receive from his or her 2001 tax return. Additionally, it provided for a gradual decrease in each level of the tax bracket structure (although the levels did not decrease equally) and the gradual repeal of the *estate tax*, or taxes on an estate left to beneficiaries after someone's death. Republicans supported the tax cut and, as we just saw in our discussion of the 2010 midterm elections, want to make it permanent, citing the benefits to middle-class families who would retain more of their income under the new tax structure. However, the reduction in taxes also substantially benefited the wealthiest 1 percent of taxpayers in the United States (one analyst estimates 37 percent of the tax cut went to this group).[26] Democrats' preference is to repeal the Tax Relief Act for the wealthiest 2 percent of taxpayers (defined as those making over $250,000 per year), returning about a trillion dollars to federal coffers.

Reforming the Tax Code

As all tax-paying Americans know, the system of tax regulations—known as the tax code—is extremely complex. It comprises more than 2.8 million words and is roughly six thousand pages long.[27] Because of the tax code's length and complexity, many people turn to professional help to navigate the rules and to be sure they are taking advantage of every loophole they can; Americans spend close to $125 billion on accountants each year to file their taxes.[28]

The complexity stems in part from the fact that you don't pay tax on your entire salary. Many expenses are deductible, that is, they can be subtracted from your salary before calculating the tax that is owed. To minimize your tax bill, you need to be aware of all the deductions you can take. If you are traveling on business, for instance, the money you spend on the trip may be deductible from your overall salary.

> **flat tax** a tax system in which all people pay the same percentage of their income
>
> **consumption tax** a plan in which people are taxed not on what they earn but on what they spend

> **value-added tax (VAT)** a consumption tax levied at each stage of production, based on the value added to the product at that stage

If you take a job in another state, you may write off some of the moving expenses. If you donate money to a charity, again, you can deduct that money on your taxes. If you have bought a home, you can deduct the interest you pay on your mortgage. Furthermore, the government often gives tax benefits to promote certain behaviors. Businesses might receive tax credits if they buy environmentally friendly equipment. Likewise, first-time homeowners get tax relief when they buy a house. Farmers may be able to write off the expenses of a new tractor. Knowing which deductions you are entitled to can save you hundreds or thousands of dollars at tax time. It is not just the number of potential deductions or credits that makes filing taxes so difficult. All of your income needs to be reported, and taxes paid on it. If in addition to your salary you receive money from, say, winning the lottery or gambling or investing in the stock market, that becomes part of your income, too. These examples provide just a tiny glimpse of the intricacies of the tax code, which is only getting more complex as additional provisions and loopholes are added.[29]

The tax code is so frustrating to so many taxpayers that politicians periodically propose reforms to make filing taxes easier and, they argue, fairer. Perhaps the most common change proposed by tax reform groups is the institution of a **flat tax**. Under a flat tax, all people would pay the same percentage of their incomes in taxes, regardless of how much money they make or what their expenses are. According to advocates, the plan would vastly simplify the tax code and almost everyone would be able to file their taxes on their own.

However, much more is at stake here than just making it easier to file taxes; there are ideological reasons for a flat tax as well. Recall that we said earlier that progressive taxes are redistributive policies. As a result, wealthier people pay a greater percentage of their salary in taxes (as we saw in Table 18.1). Not only do conservatives argue against this redistribution on grounds of fairness, but advocates of lower, flatter taxes, such as Grover Norquist's Americans for Tax Reform, usually align with the conservative notion of limited government. In their eyes, government is providing too many unnecessary services—cutting taxes would force the government to shrink for lack of resources.

Another option that is proposed occasionally is a national sales tax—otherwise known as a **consumption tax**. Currently all but five states have their own sales tax, but a national tax would apply in addition to these sales taxes. Under such a plan, the national income tax would be abolished and people would be taxed not on what they earn but on what they spend. Again, one of the advantages proponents argue is that a consumption tax would simplify the tax code. European countries have a version of a consumption tax called a **value-added tax (VAT)**. Unlike the consumption tax proposed in the United States, where the tax is implemented at the point of sale, the VAT is levied at each stage of production based on the value added to the product at that stage.

The most recent version of the consumption tax, called the "FairTax," is being advocated by an organization called "Americans for Fair Taxation" and would replace all income taxes with a 23 percent sales tax on all consumable goods sold.[30] Proponents argue that over a fifth of the price of goods we already buy represents hidden corporate, income, and payroll taxes, and that the sales tax would generate more revenue, more equitably, with less tax avoidance.[31] Opponents argue that such a tax would be regressive—thus penalizing lower income earners, but the FairTax proposal includes a "prebate" to those in poverty to offset the sales tax paid. Bills have been introduced in Congress for the FairTax, and in both 2008 and 2010 it became a minor issue in some congressional campaigns.

The adoption of either a flat income tax or a consumption tax would dramatically simplify tax-paying for Americans, but there is significant resistance to implementing these reforms. Some opponents argue that the taxes are unfair to the less well off because they are regressive. While under a flat tax, for instance, everyone would pay the same percentage in taxes, the relative burden would be greater on those who make less money. Let's say we have a flat tax of 10 percent and two people, one who earns $1 million a year and one who earns $10,000 a year. The person who earns $1 million per year would pay $100,000, and the person who makes $10,000 would pay only $1,000. But the loss of $1,000 will have a bigger impact on the poorer person's ability to obtain life's necessities. That person is more dependent on each dollar than is the person who is well off. A consumption tax is also regressive, as we explained earlier. Those who support consumption taxes claim that the wealthy will buy more expensive goods and therefore will pay a greater share of the taxes.

Other opponents of reforming the current tax code fear that such reforms will seriously reduce donations to charitable organizations. Under the current tax code, citizens have an incentive to give to charity because they can write off their

▶ Who, What, How, and WHEN: Taxation

They say that only death and taxes are certain in this life. But taxes in the United States are anything but certain; what Uncle Sam collects from his people has varied a lot over time. So how did we evolve from throwing tea in tax protest to sending off our tax returns on April 15? Below are a few of the big points in the development of U.S. tax policy:

1773 — Boston Tea Party

Protests over taxes in the colonies had occurred before; the Stamp Act, a tax on paper, had been repealed due to the colonists' outrage in 1766. Problems with tea started when colonists smuggled it to avoid paying high prices on British tea. The Tea Act made British tea cheaper, ruining business for smugglers and infuriating colonists. In response, colonists threw the cargo of a tea ship into Boston Harbor. The British reaction to the Tea Party was a catalyst toward revolution.

1861 — First Income Tax

Though the federal government had collected other kinds of taxes before, it never had an income tax until 1861, when it needed to pay for the Civil War. The tax was initially 3 percent on the amount of income over $800 a year. Payment for the Civil War also came from excise taxes on items like feathers, playing cards, yachts, and whiskey.

1913 — Sixteenth Amendment

Until 1913, income taxes weren't permanent policies. The U.S. government raised money from excise taxes and tariffs instead. People protested these types of taxes because they disproportionately hurt the poor, but the Supreme Court had ruled a permanent income tax was not constitutional unless it was apportioned by state. The Sixteenth Amendment changed this by giving Congress the ability to levy an income tax on individuals. The initial tax ranged from 1 percent to 7 percent of a person's income.

---

donations. Under a true flat or consumption tax system, there would be no write-offs at all and thus no financial incentive for people to give to charity (other incentives to charitable giving, like moral or religious imperatives, of course, would still exist).

Although many Americans would like to see the tax code made less complex, few can agree on how to make this happen. No one really wants to give up the advantages he or she has under the current system. Homeowners, organized under the American Homeowners Association, do not want their mortgage interest deductions eliminated; businesses, including those represented in the U.S. Chamber of Commerce, the National Association of Manufacturers, and the National Retail Federation, do not want to lose their tax incentives; individuals are reluctant to do away with write-offs for business expenses or charitable donations; and charities, organized under the group Independent Sector, are no less anxious to keep those deductions in place. And, of course, accountants have a stake as well—having no desire to relinquish the complexities that make their services necessary to the tax-paying public. When it comes to tax policy, all kinds of groups want to organize to defend their interests. This helps to explain how the tax code became so unwieldy in the first place.

Thinking Outside the Box

What would a just tax code look like?

1935   **Federal Insurance Contributions Act (FICA)**

Though the United States had booms and busts throughout the nineteenth century, the economic problems of the Great Depression led the government to look for a way to redistribute income to the unemployed and elderly. FICA set up a payroll tax to provide this money, with one-half of the tax coming from employees' checks and the other half paid by employers.

1941   **Gasoline Tax**

Though the Revenue Act of 1932 put a 1 cent per gallon tax on gas, this tax was temporary (though continuously renewed) until 1941. In 1941 the tax became permanent at 1.5 cents per gallon. Over the years the tax has risen steadily, to 18.4 cents per gallon, mostly through acts to pay for interstate construction and repair. States also levy gas taxes, ranging from 8 cents per gallon in Alaska to 45.5 cents in California.

1981   **Economic Recovery Tax Act**

In response to inflation in the 1970s, Congress passed a major reform of tax law, the Economic Recovery Tax Act, in 1981. The act made two major changes: it reduced the percentage of income paid in taxes for each tax bracket (and reduced the number of brackets), and it gave tax incentives to businesses to invest in expansion. The 1981 act is most important because major tax reductions following this act (the 1986 Tax Reform Act, for instance) continued to lower tax brackets and offer new incentives, such as the Per Child Tax Credit in 1997.

Who What How

We all have a stake in a smoothly functioning economy. As citizens, we want to be protected from the vagaries of the economic market while enjoying a prosperous life. We are sometimes tempted, however, to take a short-term economic windfall in the form of tax cuts or expensive government programs rather than enduring the fiscal discipline that can be necessary for long-term economic growth and stability. We are protected from such temptations by the fact that monetary policy is taken out of the electoral arena and placed in the far more independent hands of the Fed.

The president, and members of Congress, torn between the twin goals of lawmaking and representation, battle over fiscal policy. While they want to create a stable and prosperous economy, they are tempted by the tools of taxing and spending to ensure their reelection by giving constituents what they want, or at least what they think they want. They too are saved from themselves by the Fed, which can make many hard, and potentially unpopular, economic decisions without wondering what effect such decisions will have on the job security of its members.

Economic Regulatory Policy

Managing behavior to protect rights and guarantee safety

Whereas fiscal policies tend to be redistributive in nature, most economic policy, including monetary policy, is regulatory. As we discussed in Chapter 17, a regulatory policy is designed to restrict or change the behavior of certain groups or

deregulation the elimination of regulations in order to improve economic efficiency

Signing Off

Lehman Brothers, a 158-year-old investment bank, was one of several major financial institutions that crumbled beneath the weight of the credit crisis and falling real estate values in 2008. Mergers, bankruptcies, sell-offs, and layoffs became the norm as the U.S. economic sector took blow after blow. A sign of the times, here, Steve Goldstein, a former employee of Lehman Brothers laid off in 1993, signs artwork with the likeness of the firm's CEO Richard Fuld Jr. in front of company headquarters in New York.

individuals. We have already seen, in Chapter 9, that government can regulate business in the interests of consumer safety, for instance, and in Chapter 17 that government can intervene to impose environmental standards and to limit the impact industry might have on the environment. When it comes to the American system of regulated capitalism, economic regulatory policy aims to protect economic rights and make procedural guarantees. So far we have been discussing government's role in regulating the markets to even out the highs and lows and encourage the growth of prosperity. Government can also intervene for other purposes as well.

Economic regulation can be an extremely controversial issue in a capitalist economy. Those who favor such regulation argue that the market, left to its own devices, can be unfair and unpredictable, causing havoc in individual lives and having the potential for systemwide disaster. They point to problems such as the subprime mortgage crisis in 2008 that we discussed in *What's at Stake?*, in which thousands of loans were made to high-risk home buyers without adequate background checks. When the economy soured, foreclosures soared as buyers could not make their home payments. The crisis extended to legions of other homeowners facing declining property values and to failing mortgage companies

and the collapse of some of the largest financial corporations on Wall Street.[32] Opponents of regulation argue that when industries face more regulation, it increases their costs of production, which in turn makes prices rise and limits consumer choice. However, in the mortgage crisis, even the industry agreed that corrective steps needed to be taken. Ironically, in the wake of an unregulated period like the years leading to the 2008 crash, even more regulation may be needed to try to restore health to the system.

Both sides often cite the classic example of the airline industry to make their point. In 1938 the government began to make laws determining how the airline industry would run, on the grounds that it was a new industry in need of regulation and a public utility. The Civil Aeronautics Board was established to set prices, determine routes, and set up schedules while ensuring the airlines earned a fair rate of return. By the 1970s the system was bogged down in bureaucratic rules. Flying was not easily accessible to many Americans; airfares were expensive because competition was limited, parts of the country had no easy air service, and consumers were unhappy. Under President Jimmy Carter, the process of **deregulation**—the removal of excessive regulations in order to improve economic efficiency—began, to be completed by Congress in 1978. Under deregulation, airfares dropped, new routes opened, low-cost airlines started up, and scheduling became more flexible.

Proponents of deregulation insist that the increased efficiency is reason enough to reduce regulation. At the same time, opponents point to the costs of deregulation—bankruptcies that left many airline workers unemployed and without pensions, and continuing labor problems as the remaining airlines struggle to stay in business.[33] In general, because it helps some groups and hurts others, the issue of regulation remains controversial in American politics. Both political parties tend to support making business more efficient by removing excessive regulations, but Republicans, with their closer ties to business, tend to push for more deregulation, while Democrats, with a traditional alliance with labor, push for less.

In this section we look at three general categories of regulatory policy—regulation to ensure fair business competition, regulation to guarantee fair labor practices, and regulation to protect U.S. interests in international trade.

Regulating Business

Certainly governments have an incentive to support policies that help businesses prosper. If companies are doing well, then GDP is up and unemployment and prices are likely down. As a result, constituents are happy and politicians get reelected. But sometimes businesses have externalities that affect constituents adversely, and even if they didn't favor regulation beforehand, voters often demand it when the economy falters, when jobs are lost, or when prices go up.

Regulating Competition

For example, if one company is doing so well that it eliminates its competition, trouble ensues. As we just saw in the airline deregulation example, competition helps keep prices low. Consider what would happen if there were only one automobile manufacturer. It could charge high prices for cars because consumers would have no one else to buy from. If a second automobile manufacturer gets into the game, consumers would likely buy from the company whose cars were cheapest, causing the manufacturer of the more expensive cars to drop its prices. When a single producer dominates a market and there is no competition, it is called a *monopoly*. Where there are monopolies, prices are greatly inflated. The monopolistic businesses can rake in the profits, but consumers are deeply unhappy. While Americans are generally strong supporters of capitalism, they are also suspicious of business, especially when one business has too much control over a commodity. Americans have long supported government action to eliminate monopolies.

Government regulations that try to keep monopolies from emerging are known as *antitrust policies*. The first national antitrust policies were the Interstate Commerce Act and the Sherman Antitrust Act, both of which Congress passed in the late 1800s. The Interstate Commerce Act created the Interstate Commerce Commission, whose job it was to control the monopolistic practices of the railroads. The Sherman Antitrust Act was more encompassing and was designed to protect trade and commerce against unlawful restraints and monopolies. According to two well-known scholars of American history, "No statute ever enacted by Congress reflected more accurately and overwhelmingly popular demand" than the Sherman Act.[34] The problem with the act was that it was rarely enforced until the election of Theodore Roosevelt, a progressive who was deeply concerned with eliminating corruption.[35] In 1914 President Woodrow Wilson further opposed monopolies by signing the Clayton Act, which, among other things, allowed private parties to obtain damages in antitrust cases won by the government.

Antitrust legislation continues to break up monopolies today as major U.S. companies have come under scrutiny from the Justice Department. In 1984 American Telephone and Telegraph (AT&T), also known as "Ma Bell," was forced to split into eight separate companies because of its dominance of the telephone industry. AT&T's assets fell from $150 billion (in 1984 dollars) before the breakup to $34 billion afterward.[36] In 1998 Microsoft, another U.S. mega company, came under fire from the government. The Justice Department and twenty states indicted Microsoft when the company began requiring that computers run by its Windows 98 operating system be preloaded with an icon for Internet Explorer, Microsoft's web browser. According to the government, this action was an attempt to cripple Microsoft's main browser competitor, Netscape Navigator. In 2001 Microsoft came to a settlement with the Bush administration that required the company to disclose portions of its Windows code to allow competing companies' software to operate more smoothly and give computer-makers more leeway to place rivals' software on the desktop. The settlement was opposed by nine states and the District of Columbia, all of which wanted stricter sanctions placed on the company. In 2002 a federal judge upheld the agreement between Microsoft and the federal government.[37]

Government agencies try to regulate monopolies to preserve the competitive health of the economy. Consumer advocacy groups, representing consumers in general, also push for enforcement of antitrust legislation to ensure competition and drive down prices. As one advocate says, "It is critical for policymakers to understand that vigorous, head-to-head competition, which is promoted by antitrust laws, is the key to ensuring not only that consumers receive quality products at the lowest economic cost but also that new and innovative products flow freely into the market."[38] Even businesses themselves sometimes push for antitrust policies. Massive corporations like AT&T or Microsoft might not like the laws, but their competitors have a great deal at stake in keeping these companies from becoming too powerful. In the Microsoft antitrust case, for example, it was Netscape Communications Corporation that pushed the Justice Department to file suit against Microsoft after Netscape's revenues began to plummet.[39]

Regulating the Bank

Government has focused its regulatory efforts not only on competition, but also on internal business practices, particularly those of banks since the security of savings and the granting of credit has such a decided influence on the rest of the economy. As the run on the banks that launched the Great Depression made clear, if people could not trust the repository of their funds, the economy could not function. In 1933 Congress passed the Glass-Steagall Act, which, among other banking reforms, created the Federal Deposit Insurance Corporation (FDIC) that insured the money people deposited in banks, and created a division between Wall Street investment banks and the savings and loans. Banks are where people deposit money. Parts of the 1933 Glass-Steagall Act were repealed in 1999, amid the deregulatory fervor of the last quarter of the last century. Some observers blame that repeal for setting up the conditions that allowed Wall Street to trade in mortgage-backed securities, leading to the subprime mortgage debacle that caused the economic crisis of 2008.

Responding to calls for reregulation, Congress passed, and President Barack Obama signed, another financial reform bill in 2010. Called the Dodd-Frank bank reform bill, it establishes a consumer protection agency, sets in place some banking reform, and increases federal oversight and control over derivatives trading, the financial instrument that allowed mortgage speculation and that brought down such financial giants as insurance giant American International Group (AIG).[40] The bill's so-called "Volcker rule" prevents banks from speculating with their own money. The bill was criticized by the left for not going far enough to control the excesses on Wall Street and by the right for going too far and inhibiting the free play of capital. That it was passed at all under the partisan conditions of 2010 politics in America is notable itself. It was filibustered for a week in the Senate before Republicans allowed debate to go forward and, in the end, not one Republican on the conference committee that reconciled the House and Senate bills ended up voting to pass the bill out of committee.

The Dodd-Frank bill is not a dramatic change in the way banks do business. As the *Wall Street Journal* wrote after the bill passed, "From the beginning, lawmakers opted against a dramatic reshaping of the country's financial architecture. Instead, they moved to create new layers of regulation to prevent companies from taking on too much risk."[41]

Regulating Labor

In an unregulated market, labor is subject to the laws of supply and demand, like anything else. If workers are in short

> **collective bargaining** the ability of unions to determine wages, hours, and working conditions in conjunction with the employer

supply, they can command high wages; if they are plentiful, their wages are low. But always they are at the mercy of factors beyond their control. An unregulated market gives them no protection.

As they did everywhere in the early days of industrialization, eighteenth- and nineteenth-century American workers struggled with their employers over poor wages, long hours, and unsuitable working conditions. It was not until 1938, during Franklin Roosevelt's New Deal, that the federal government took a major step in protecting the rights of workers with the passage of the Fair Labor Standards Act. The passage of the act was a significant victory for labor reformers as it established a minimum wage, limited the work week to forty hours, provided time and a half for working overtime, and prohibited the interstate commerce of any goods manufactured by children under the age of sixteen.

While legislation like the Fair Labor Standards Act improved working conditions and wages, laborers pushed for formal union representation. Business owners, concerned that unionization would give them less control over their companies, fought the organization of labor unions by requiring such things as yellow-dog contracts, which forced employees to agree that they would not join a union if they were given a job. During the 1930s, a Democratic-controlled Congress again took a major step in protecting workers when it passed the Norris-La Guardia Act, which eliminated the use of yellow-dog contracts, and the Wagner Act, which allowed for the unionization of employees. The Wagner Act also established the National Labor Relations Board to oversee labor laws and investigate complaints. One of the most important aspects of this law was that it allowed unions to engage in *collective bargaining*—the ability to determine with the employer wages, hours, and working conditions. The passage of these acts was controversial in the business community—especially the steel industry—but the growing power of the labor movement during the early 1930s and a government that was receptive to the needs of workers in the midst of the Great Depression was enough to overcome business's opposition.[42]

Conservatives became concerned that too much power was being given to workers at the expense of employers. As a result, in 1947 a Republican-led Congress overrode Democratic president Harry Truman's veto and passed the Taft-Hartley Act, which was designed to limit the power of labor unions. For instance, the act outlaws closed shops—companies with a labor agreement that requires that employees be

Figure 18.5

Percentage of Employed Workers Who Are Union Members, 1973–2008

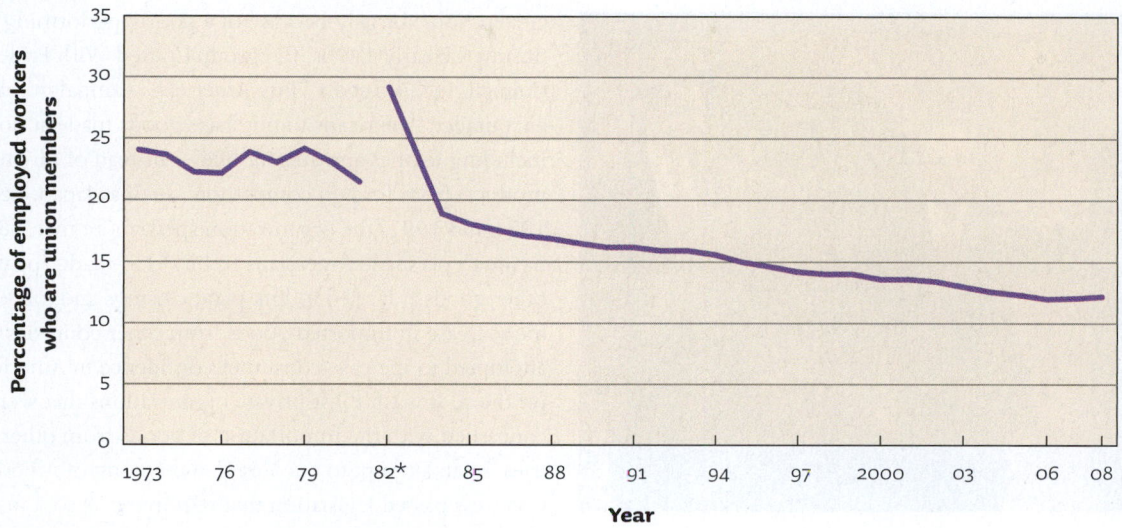

Source: Union Membership and Coverage Database, www.unionstats.com; Statistical Abstract of the United States, 2010, Table 648.

Note: Data not available for 1982.

members of a union in order to be hired and makes it an unfair labor practice for unions to refuse to bargain with employers. In addition, the act prohibits federal workers from striking and allows the firing of workers who do strike. Although it is rare for federal employees to go on strike, in 1981 President Reagan fired more than 12,000 striking federal air traffic controllers. The air traffic controllers were striking over wages and working conditions, but Reagan argued that they did not have the right to strike under the Taft-Hartley Act. The inability of federal workers to strike severely limits their collective bargaining power.

With the Republican takeover in Congress after the 1994 elections, unions were again under assault. The Republican-led Congress challenged the Fair Labor Standards Act's limits on overtime work and pay, and passed a bill that would allow companies to create "employment involvement committees." Unions opposed this latter measure because they believed that it would create company unions, which would limit the negotiating power of the independent unions. President Clinton vetoed the bill.[43]

After September 11, controversy between the Republican Party and some union leaders emerged again. As a response to the attacks, Congress and President Bush created a new Department of Homeland Security. While Democrats in Congress and President Bush were in agreement over the

creation of the department, bipartisanship disappeared quickly when issues of worker rights emerged. The president received criticism from many on the left when he tried to limit the collective bargaining power of department employees. Bush argued that protecting the collective bargaining rights of department workers was not as important as protecting the country from another terrorist attack. Ultimately, Bush and Democratic congressional leaders reached a compromise under which the president is able to exempt unionized workers from collective bargaining agreements in the name of national security, but he must renew the collective bargaining exemption every four years. The compromise also gave union leaders more influence over the creation of new personnel rules than the administration had initially planned.[44]

Legislation like Taft-Hartley and actions by some government officials has limited the power of unions. A further concern to union supporters is that union membership has been continually declining (see Figure 18.5), and the ability of unions to gain more at the bargaining table in terms of wages and benefits has waned.[45] There are several explanations for these occurrences, including a decrease in jobs in heavily unionized industries, an inability to aggressively push unionization in developing industries, and employers who are increasingly antiunion.[46] The situation

A NAFTA Balancing Act
From left, Canadian prime minister Stephen Harper, Mexican president Felipe Calderon, and U.S. president Barack Obama meet in Guadalajara in 2009 for a NAFTA summit in which they discussed common issues like the economic recession. While campaigning for the presidency, Obama vowed to add labor and environmental protections to NAFTA, but in 2009 a U.S. trade representative announced that the administration had no current plans to reopen negotiations. The act has received mixed reviews since its 1993 passage.

has led some labor scholars to write that "U.S. unions are in a crisis."[47] Still, unions continue to give large campaign contributions to candidates, mostly to Democrats (in 2004 union PACS gave close to $54 million to federal candidates, 86 percent of which went to Democrats),[48] and members regularly show up at the polls to support pro-union candidates.[49]

Regulating Trade

People usually think of trade policy as more of a foreign policy than an economic policy. That is because trade policy requires the United States to work and negotiate with other countries. We explore trade policy further in Chapter 19, but a few words must be said here as well because trade policy has a clear impact on the health of the U.S. economy.

In general, trade policy is driven by one of two stances: protectionism or free trade. **Protectionism** is the view that laws should limit the sale of foreign imports in order to protect producers at home. A reliance on imported goods, such as televisions or cars, costs U.S. businesses money and American

citizens jobs. Largely because of a poorly performing economy during the early 1990s, the group Crafted With Pride in USA Council, Inc., waged a "Buy American" campaign that encouraged Americans to purchase goods made at home—including textiles and automobiles—instead of buying products from foreign competitors, such as Japan. Between 1984 and 1992, the organization spent more than $80 million trying to persuade Americans to buy U.S.-made apparel and other goods.[50] It tried to link plant closings and job losses to the increase in imported goods from other countries and also attempted to increase consumer confidence in American-made products. It wasn't just private organizations that were concerned with the importation of goods from other countries. In an attempt to encourage the buying of American cars, Congress passed legislation that required cars sold in the United States to have labels indicating what percentage of the vehicle's parts were made in the United States.[51]

The government can implement protectionist policies in several ways. It can place quotas—or caps—on the number of foreign imports that the United States can receive and it can levy tariffs—government taxes on foreign goods. Also, it can create nontariff barriers, which are more covert measures to protect the domestic economy. For example, Congress could pass health and safety regulations that prohibit the sale of "substandard" imports.

Not everyone is convinced that protectionism is the best policy or, for that matter, that it has a positive effect on a country's economy. **Free trade policies** eliminate measures such as quotas, tariffs, or nontariff barriers, and encourage open borders between trading partners. Proponents of free trade, such as the World Trade Organization (WTO), an international organization that deals with the rules of trade between nations, argue that the long-term economic interests of all countries are advanced when restrictions on trade are kept to a minimum. According to free traders, prices of goods are higher under protectionist policies because of large tariffs and less competition. If only two or three companies in a country produce a good, they are likely to be able to sell that good for a higher price than if they have to compete with a wide range of international companies as well. Also, supporters of free trade policies argue that protectionist policies could lead to retaliatory protectionist policies from other countries, creating a trade war no one can win. The WTO has even argued that free trade policies actually help promote peace around the world. According to the organization, "Sales people are usually reluctant to fight their customers."[52]

Debates over trade policy and its effect on economic growth have been around since the country's birth, right along with questions such as whether the United States should have a national bank and what role the United States should play in world affairs. Alexander Hamilton was a strong proponent of protectionist trade policy. In his influential *Report on Manufactures,* Hamilton encouraged Congress to implement tariffs on foreign goods to help the United States' "infant industries" to prosper.[53]

Hamilton's view guided American trade policy until the 1930s. In the midst of the stock market crash of 1929, President Herbert Hoover backed the Hawley-Smoot Tariff Act of 1930. The act was designed to help the United States' agricultural and manufacturing industries by increasing tariffs to their highest levels in the country's history. However, the act was a resounding failure. It did little to help the U.S. economy, and it infuriated trade partners who responded with increased tariffs of their own. As a result, American trade suffered and people began to rethink trade policy.

In 1934, American trade policy changed substantially with the passage of the Reciprocal Trade Agreement, which allocated the duty of creating trade agreements to the executive branch. With that act, the United States began steps to pursue a more open trade policy. In 1947 the United States, along with twenty-three other countries, entered into the General Agreement on Tariffs and Trade (GATT). GATT greatly reduced tariffs on imported goods and provided an agreement regarding trade policy that members would follow. GATT evolved into the WTO.

American trade policy continues to be hotly debated, especially with the growth of the trade deficit since the mid-1980s. The **trade deficit** is the difference between the value of the goods a country imports and what it exports. While the United States generally maintained a balance of trade between imports and exports after World War II, that began to change in the 1980s. As Figure 18.6 indicates, from 1980 to 1989, the trade deficit rose from $19.5 billion to $109.4 billion. The trade deficit then dropped slightly in the early 1990s, but it has since grown enormously. In 2008 the U.S. trade deficit stood at $840 billion, the largest in the country's history.

A large trade deficit can negatively affect the U.S. economy because it means that Americans are buying more foreign-made goods than people from other countries are buying American-made products. The deficit hurts American businesses, which could mean fewer jobs and higher unemployment. As a result, unions are more likely to support protectionist trade policies, which would narrow the trade deficit.

The debate between protectionists and free traders came to a head over the passage of the **North American Free Trade Agreement (NAFTA)** in 1993. NAFTA removed most of the barriers to trade and investment that existed among the United States, Mexico, and Canada. Supporters of NAFTA, including American corporations and several economists, claimed that the program would actually *create* new jobs and raise living conditions in the three countries. USA*NAFTA, a group of corporations in support of the measure, tried to sway public opinion by running television commercials that featured business icons Bill Gates, the head of Microsoft, and Lee Iacocca, the retired chair of Chrysler Corporation, talking about how NAFTA would generate job growth. Opponents of the legislation—including labor unions; environmental groups such as Greenpeace USA, Friends of the Earth, and Environmental Action; and those concerned about the effects of globalization in general—claimed just the opposite. They argued that NAFTA would eliminate jobs, lower wages, and threaten the environment and food safety standards. The politics surrounding NAFTA were interesting, as they crossed traditional partisan alliances. Republican president George H. W. Bush originally pushed NAFTA and then Democrat Bill Clinton backed the bill after his election in 1992. Many Democrats in Congress opposed NAFTA, including then–majority leader Richard Gephardt, a strong ally of labor.

Different people are likely to give very different assessments of the success of NAFTA. According to the Department of Agriculture, exports of food and agricultural products from the United States to Canada and Mexico have grown.[54] Others aren't so sure of NAFTA's benefits. According to Public Citizen, NAFTA has increased trade deficits with Mexico and Canada and has cost the United States hundreds of thousands of jobs and job opportunities.[55] The nonpartisan Congressional Budget Office splits the difference, acknowledging gains in overall trade but dislocations for specific sectors in all of the member countries.[56] The debate over trade policy is not likely to subside any time soon. As long as the trade deficit continues to increase (and at this point there is no indication that it will not) free traders and protectionists will continue to argue their positions and push for policies that support their interests.

Figure 18.6

U.S. Trade Deficit, 1980–2008

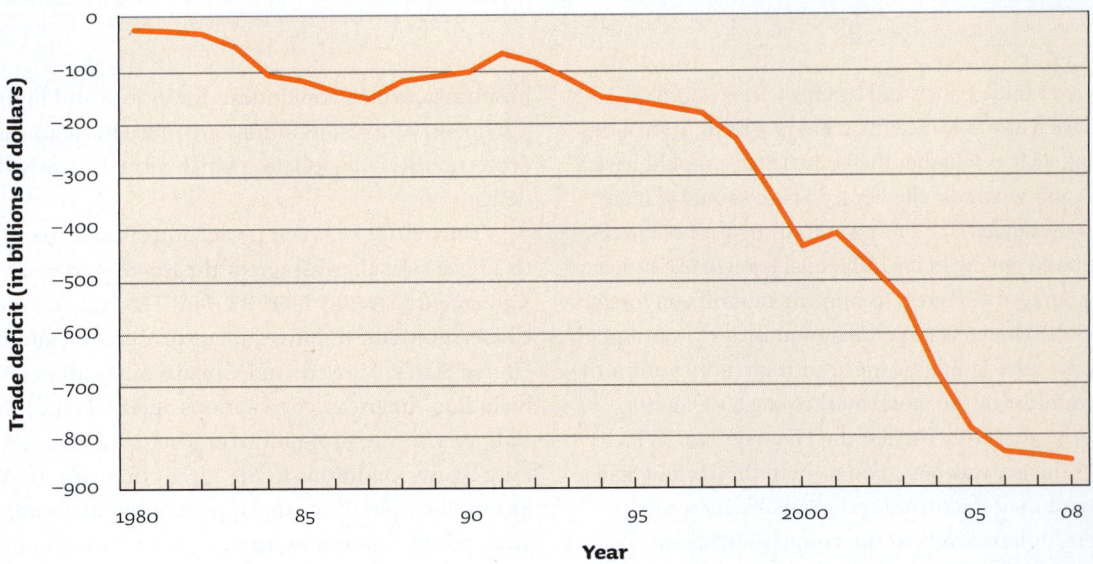

Source: Statistical Abstract of the United States, 2008 (Table 1271) and 2010 (Table 1251).

Businesses, unions, and consumers all have something at stake when the government regulates the economy. Businesses want government to keep regulations to a minimum to create efficient production of goods and to maximize profits. They also want government to restrict union power. Union members want the government to back policies that defend workers, such as improving working conditions, making it easier to engage in collective bargaining with employers, and passing protectionist trade policies. Consumers want government's protection from the negative impact of unregulated businesses and inflated prices caused by monopolies or restrictive trade policies.

In all instances, these groups try to get government to adopt economic regulatory policies that benefit them, often at the expense of another group. They do so by donating money to political candidates, lobbying government officials, and increasingly, carrying out public relations campaigns to get the public on their side.

Who What How

Thinking Outside the Box

Would there be any benefits to allowing the market to remain unregulated?

The Citizens and Economic Policy
Keeping the process removed from politics

In Chapter 17, we discussed how well the pluralist theory of competing interest group influence explains domestic policy making. Whereas domestic policymaking tends to be more pluralistic or participatory, economic policy is more likely to be elite driven. Certainly, antitax groups like the Howard Jarvis Taxpayers Association play a big role in lobbying for tax cuts. Likewise, if the economy is not performing well or people aren't happy with a skyrocketing budget deficit, they may vote elected officials out of office. But much of economic policy is shielded from the public, and decisions are made entirely by elected and—in many cases—unelected officials with little input from the public. Clearly, monetary policy is the product of a closely guarded elite policymaking process that could not be less democratic at its core. It is designed specifically to protect the economy from the forces of democracy— from the short-term preferences of the citizenry, and the eagerness of elected representatives to give them what they want. In the end, the fact that economic policy is elite driven may not be a bad thing. As we've discussed throughout this book, the founding fathers were extremely concerned with controlling the whims of the public, especially in a case like the economy, where so much self-interest is at stake.

▶ What's at Stake Revisited

We began this chapter with a look at the financial crisis that hit the United States in mid-September 2008 and spread rapidly across the globe. It began as an excess of risky subprime home mortgages in the late 1990s and into the first few years of the new century, often given to would-be homeowners with little or no consideration of their ability to pay back the loan. When the housing bubble that had promised limitless prosperity for so many burst in 2005–2006, as bubbles are wont to do, at first it was the individual homeowners who bore the consequences, losing their homes and finding their credit in tatters.

But by 2008 the crisis was not just affecting those who had borrowed more than they could pay and the people who had lent them the money. When, in September, we witnessed failing investment banks and plunging stock prices, it was clear something even grimmer was going on. What *was* at stake in a lifestyle based on borrowing money today contingent on tomorrow's ability to pay it back?

What happened to the mortgage industry is complex, and the very fact that few understood it helped it stay undetected until it was too late. Essentially some of the bad loans that mortgage lenders were making so freely were sold to other investors, creating a thriving market in mortgage-backed securities. Everyone wanted a piece of it, spurring on more bad-loan-making and banking on the continued increase in home values to help them make a bundle.

But as the housing market lost value, those loans became worthless. As banks lost money, those who had invested in the mortgage-backed securities became worried and tried to pull out their money—causing what amounted to an electronic run on the banks. On September 15 the investment bank Lehman Brothers declared bankruptcy, Merrill Lynch was merged with Bank of America, and AIG hovered on the brink of disaster and required bailing out by the federal government that thought AIG was too big to allow it to fail.

With the investment banks going under, other businesses were unable to obtain the short-term loans they depended on to carry out their regular activities. With no money to borrow, business started to dry up and people lost their jobs. Families tightened their belts and quit spending money, which worsened the downward spiral. Treasury Secretary Hank Paulsen worried that, if the government did nothing, the entire economy would fail, and he urged Congress to pass a $700 billion bailout program so that he could cover the bad debts when they were endangering financial institutions.

How bad the crisis will be and how long it will last are questions we can't answer yet. With a new Democratic administration in Washington, a stimulus bill was passed to try to get the economy going and financial regulation was passed to try to ensure that such a collapse could not happen again. But political constraints meant that both the stimulus and the reform bill were weaker than President Obama had called for—critics on the left said they did not go far enough; critics on the right said they went too far. One lesson that seems pretty clear, however, is that Americans will have to begin to live more within their means. As credit becomes harder to acquire, the happy-go-lucky days of living on borrowed funds, which got us into this fix in the first place, will be over.

To Sum Up

Key terms, chapter summaries, practice quizzes, Internet links, and other study aids are available on the companion web site at http://republic.cqpress.com.

Define | Understand | Practice | Read | Click | Watch

antitrust policies (p. 699)
balanced budget (p. 682)
business cycle (p. 678)
capital gains tax (p. 694)
collective bargaining (p. 700)
consumption tax (p. 695)
deficits (p. 682)
depression (p. 681)
deregulation (p. 698)
economic boom (p. 678)
economic bust (p. 678)
economic policy (p. 676)
excise taxes (p. 691)
Federal Reserve System (p. 684)
fiscal policy (p. 682)
flat tax (p. 695)
free trade policies (p. 702)
gross domestic product (GDP) (p. 678)

inflation (p. 678)
interest rates (p. 683)
Keynesianism (p. 682)
laws of supply and demand (p. 678)
monetary policy (p. 683)
monopoly (p. 699)
national debt (p. 689)
North American Free Trade Agreement (NAFTA) (p. 703)
progressive taxes (p. 691)
protectionism (p. 702)
recession (p. 678)
regressive taxes (p. 692)
self-regulating market (p. 681)
supply side economics (p. 688)
surpluses (p. 682)
trade deficit (p. 703)
value-added tax (VAT) (p. 695)

Define | **Understand** | Practice | Read | Click | Watch

- Economic policy addresses the problem of economic security not for some particular group or segment of society but for society as a whole. For much of our history, policymakers believed that government should not play much of a role in regulating the economy, instead letting the market take care of itself. Since the Great Depression, government has played a more active role in regulating the economy.
- The capitalist market operates according to the laws of supply and demand. These laws influence a country's gross domestic product, or GDP. Because supply and demand may increase or decrease, the economy is not stagnant. It can enter periods of booms, when GDP rises, or busts, when GDP drops.
- Economic policy has two principal subsets: fiscal and monetary. Fiscal policy, created by Congress and the president, uses change in government spending or taxation to produce desired changes in discretionary income, employment rates, or productivity. The Federal Reserve directs monetary policy by changing the supply of money in circulation in order to alter credit markets, employment, and the rate of inflation.

- The politics of monetary and fiscal policies are quite different. Because the Fed sets monetary policy, it is insulated from political pressures. Fiscal policy is extremely political as politicians try to balance the competing goals of providing goods and services to constituents and keeping taxes low.
- Since the 1930s, government has been more involved in economic regulation, specifically regarding business, unions, and trade. Government has tried to limit the power and possible corruption of business by passing antitrust policies and placing regulations on companies. It has protected workers by allowing them to unionize and to engage in collective bargaining, and it has limited the strength of unions with legislation like Taft-Hartley. Finally, the government has long debated whether it should take a protectionist stance toward trade policy by implementing things such as tariffs, or whether it should promote more open, free trade policies.
- Economic policy making is generally made by elites, with limited input from the public. Still, interest groups and public opinion can influence economic policy making.

Define | Understand | **Practice** | Read | Click | Watch

1. A(n) _____ is a decline in GDP for two consecutive quarters.
   a. recession
   b. depression
   c. economic bust
   d. economic boom
   e. inflationary period

2. **Members of Congress do not have the power to make monetary policy because**
   a. it is too complicated for policy generalists to understand.
   b. they generally don't have any political interest in the effects of monetary policy.
   c. monetary policy often requires unpopular decisions that members might not be willing to make.
   d. it is the president's job to make monetary policy.
   e. individual states can best manage their own monetary policies.

3. **In the United States, which of the following is NOT a regressive tax?**
   a. Social Security tax
   b. Consumption tax
   c. Excise tax
   d. Income tax
   e. Flat tax

4. **_____ policies encourage open borders among trading partners by eliminating measures such as quotas, tariffs, and nontariff barriers.**
   a. Protectionist
   b. Redistributive
   c. Free trade
   d. Trade deficit
   e. Monopolistic

5. **The _____ theory of democracy best reflects how economic policy making in the United States works.**
   a. pluralist
   b. participatory
   c. direct
   d. elite
   e. indirect

Define | Understand | Practice | **Read** | Click | Watch

Cooper, George. 2009. *The Origin of Financial Crises: Central Banks, Credit Bubbles and the Efficient Market Fallacy.* Hampshire, U.K.: Harriman House. This timely analysis of the recent U.S. financial crisis received high marks from The Economist magazine and is sure to be an interesting (albeit somewhat technical) read for those seeking to learn more about U.S. financial and monetary policy.

Freeman, Richard B. 2007. *America Works: Critical Thoughts on the Exceptional U.S. Labor Market.* New York: Russell Sage Foundation. This book offers a comprehensive look at the U.S. labor market and examines the effects of globalization, immigration, and unionization on the U.S. labor market and economy.

Gosling, James J. 2005. *Budgetary Politics in American Governments,* 4th ed. New York: Routledge. An excellent resource for questions about the budgetary process and politics at the federal, state, and local levels.

Greider, William. 1989. *Secrets of the Temple: How the Federal Reserve Runs the Country.* New York: Simon & Schuster. A book on the Fed may not seem exciting, but this one is. Greider provides an exceptional overview of the most important agency for determining economic policy.

Kuttner, Robert. 1997. *Everything for Sale: The Virtues and Limits of Markets.* New York: Knopf. Offering a different spin on the pros and cons of free enterprise and free markets, Kuttner argues that, in some cases, free markets fail those who they are supposed to serve.

Schick, Allen. 2007. *The Federal Budget: Politics, Policy, Process,* 3rd ed. Washington, D.C.: Brookings Institution Press. An in-depth look at the ins and outs of the federal budget process.

Teller-Elsberg, Jonathan, Nancy Folbre, James Heintz, and the Center for Popular Economics. 2007. *Field Guide to the U.S. Economy: A Compact and Irreverent Guide to Economic Life in America.* New York: New Press. The title of this book speaks for itself! Written by progressive economists, this book includes interesting facts on the U.S. economy and economic policy.

Weisman, Steven R. 2002. *The Great Tax Wars: Lincoln to Wilson: the Fierce Battles Over Money and Power That Transformed the Nation.* New York: Simon & Schuster. A historical account of the battle to pass a permanent income tax.

Wiggin, Addison, and Kate Incontrera. 2009. *I.O.U.S.A.: One Nation. Under Stress. In Debt.* Hoboken: Wiley. An engaging (and opinionated) analysis of four U.S. deficits: the personal savings deficit, the budget deficit, the trade deficit, and the leadership deficit.

Define **Understand** **Practice** **Read** **Click** **Watch**

The Board of Governors of the Federal Reserve *www.federalreserve.gov.* Home page of the Federal Reserve Board, which includes current information on monetary policy, data, and recent publications.

DanielDrezner.com *www.danieldrezner.com/blog.* Visit the blog of political science professor Daniel Drezner for timely, incisive, and entertaining analyses of U.S. economic policy.

Department of Commerce *www.doc.gov.* A comprehensive and informative site with the latest news about the Commerce Department, as well as up-to-date information about the various economic indicators.

The Economist Online *www.economist.com/world/unitedstates/.* The Economist *offers timely and highly informative analyses of key issues facing the U.S. and global economy.*

Office of Management and Budget *www.whitehouse.gov/omb.* An exceptional site with much information on the budget.

red equities.

Energy prices continued their long mo

Tough times

Chapter 19

Foreign Policy

▶ What's at Stake?

Was it a gaffe, as critics claimed, or a reflection of good judgment? In a 2008 debate among contenders for the Democratic presidential nomination, Senator Barack Obama indicated that he would be willing to sit down with America's enemies and attempt to find common ground. His Democratic opponents pounced, and once Republican senator John McCain had locked up the nomination, he jumped on the remark, as well, calling it reckless policy.[1] McCain claimed that the idea that progress can be made by talking to grave enemies is naive and that such negotiations only embolden the enemy. Obama, on the other hand, continued to contend that "strong countries and strong presidents talk to their adversaries."[2]

The dilemma is a familiar one to most of us. Did you ever get so mad at someone that you simply refused to talk to him until he apologized to you or changed his ways? If so, you know what a mixed-bag this strategy can be. You use the silent treatment as a way to get your friend to change his attitude, but if he decides to keep on doing whatever got you mad in the first place, you have very little leverage since you're not talking to him anymore. Even reaching out through a third person to keep the lines of communication open can be complicated and confusing. And having adjusted to life without talking to you, your friend may have decided he's just fine that way. Of course, some transgressions are so serious that silence may be the best and permanent solution, but short of that, how do you decide when "going silent" is the wisest move?

The U.S. government confronts this dilemma regularly and from time to time has decided that another country's behavior is so contrary to American interests that we should not even talk to its leaders, at least not directly. For example, after Fidel Castro took power in the Cuban Revolution of 1959, his government cracked down on political opposition and became allies with the Soviet Union. In response, the United States cut off relations with the island nation.

The tactic of not talking to enemy countries became standard practice, however, in the George W. Bush administration. In his address to a joint session of Congress, after the attacks of September 11, 2001, President Bush announced a

Keep Your Enemies Closer?

During a 2008 debate, presidential candidate Barack Obama announced that he'd be willing to talk with America's enemies. Obama's critics jumped on the statement, calling it reckless, but American presidents have often alternated between policies of engagement and alienation with enemies such as Iran, led now by president Mahmoud Ahmedinejad (pictured) and identified by President George W. Bush as part of an "axis of evil." The United States hasn't had formal relations with Iran since the Iranian Revolution of 1979 that overthrew the U.S.-favored leader and installed an Islamic republic hostile to the United States of America.

key element of the emerging war on terrorism:

> Every nation, in every region, now has a decision to make. Either you are with us, or you are with the terrorists. From this day forward, any nation that continues to harbor or support terrorism will be regarded by the United States as a hostile regime.[3]

The administration decided that Iran and North Korea were indeed "against us" due to their support of terrorism and pursuit of nuclear weapons, and President Bush refused to talk one-on-one with leaders from either of these countries, which he labeled (along with Iraq) as members of the "axis of evil." Although the Bush administration remained open to talks with these countries as long as other states were also at the table, it believed that to have "bilateral" talks with either nation would make the United States look weak. Before we would meet with them alone, they had to change their behavior.

Barack Obama, of course, defeated John McCain and won the White House in the November 2008 election. In his inaugural address he signaled to friends and enemies, and to governments and to people around the world, his vision of using diplomacy and negotiations as part of America's foreign policy toolbox:

> For we know that our patchwork heritage is a strength, not a weakness. We are a nation of Christians and Muslims, Jews and Hindus, and non-believers. We are shaped by every language and culture, drawn from every end of this Earth; and because we have tasted the bitter swill of civil war and segregation, and emerged from that dark chapter stronger and more united, we cannot help but believe that the old hatreds shall someday pass; that the lines of tribe shall soon dissolve; that as the world grows smaller, our common humanity shall reveal itself; and that America must play its role in ushering in a new era of peace.
>
> To the Muslim world, we seek a new way forward, based on mutual interest and mutual respect. To those leaders around the globe who seek to sow conflict, or blame their society's ills on the West, know that your people will judge you on what you can build, not what you destroy.
>
> To those who cling to power through corruption and deceit and the silencing of dissent, know that you are on the wrong side of history, but that we will extend a hand if you are willing to unclench your fist.
>
> To the people of poor nations, we pledge to work alongside you to make your farms flourish and let clean waters flow; to nourish starved bodies and feed hungry minds. And to those nations like ours that enjoy relative plenty, we say we can no longer afford indifference to the suffering outside our borders, nor can we consume the world's resources without regard to effect. For the world has changed, and we must change with it.[4]

How are we as citizens to evaluate this foreign policy approach? Obama's view of talking to our enemies is not unique or new. In fact, many presidents have agreed that diplomacy can be a crucial tool of American foreign policy. Nixon talked to Vietnam's leaders during the Vietnam War, after all, and Reagan talked to the Soviets during the Cold War. (Of course, it's also true that at the same time Reagan refused to talk to Cuba.) Sometimes our "interests" might dictate that we talk to someone, because we have things in common, even though we have other vast differences, but our "values" might suggest we shouldn't talk, because our enemy's actions are so repugnant to the basic tenets of democracy and freedom. This is not just a theoretical question; it's one that our national leaders must answer as they steer the ship of state. What are advantages of talking, and the merits of refusing to meet? What is really at stake in deciding whether to talk with our enemies? We return to these questions after we learn more about how U.S. foreign policy is made. ∎

[O]ur foreign policy is crucial to our domestic tranquility, . . . without a strong and effective foreign policy, our security as a rich and peaceful country could be blown away in a heartbeat.

foreign policy a country's official positions, practices, and procedures for dealing with actors outside its borders

isolationism a foreign policy view that nations should stay out of international political alliances and activities, and focus on domestic matters

internationalism a foreign policy view that the United States should actively engage in world affairs in order to try to shape events in accordance with U.S. interests

Foreign policy, even in the wake of the attacks of September 11, 2001, still fails to capture most Americans' attention. Only about 10 percent of Americans today say that the wars in Iraq and Afghanistan or terrorism are the nation's top problem. By contrast, nearly 55 percent pick the economy, unemployment, and jobs; 5 percent say the price of gas; 7 percent say immigration; and lots of other issues like health care and disaster relief get votes as well.[5] After all, foreign policy is so, well, *foreign*. Despite witnessing how vulnerable we can be, Americans tend to see the rest of the world as a place that doesn't much affect us. And if we aren't particularly attentive to policy issues within our own borders, why would we pay much attention to things that happen outside those borders?

In this chapter we discuss *foreign policy*—official U.S. policy designed to solve problems that take place between us and actors outside our borders. We will see that our foreign policy is crucial to our domestic tranquility, that without a strong and effective foreign policy, our security as a rich and peaceful country could be blown away in a heartbeat. Our foreign policy is almost always carried out for the good of American citizens or in the interest of national security. Even foreign aid, which may seem like giving away American taxpayers' hard-earned money to people who have done nothing to deserve it, is part of a foreign policy to stabilize the world, to help strengthen international partnerships and alliances, and to keep Americans safe. Similarly, humanitarian intervention, like the NATO (North Atlantic Treaty Organization) military action in Kosovo in 1999, is ultimately conducted to support our values and the quality of life we think other nations ought to provide for their citizens.

Many politicians have tried to encourage Americans to turn their backs on the rest of the world, promoting a foreign policy called *isolationism*, which holds that Americans should put themselves and their problems first and not interfere in global concerns. This sentiment has been increasing among the public in recent years; a 2008 survey found that 35 percent of the American public holds the view that we should stay out of world affairs—up about 10 points since 1982 and the highest number since the poll was first taken in 1947.[6] The United States has tried to pursue an isolationist policy before, perhaps most notably after World War I, but this experiment was largely seen as a failure.

Most recently, the events of September 11 have put to rest the fiction that what happens "over there" is unrelated to what is happening "over here." In opposition to isolationism, *internationalism* holds that to keep the republic safe, we must be actively engaged in shaping the global environment and participating in world events and international institutions (like the United Nations). Those who hold the internationalist view, which is shared by over 60 percent of the American public and the vast majority of foreign policy makers, might differ on the extent to which we should intervene militarily in global affairs. However, the belief that American leadership is a necessary and positive force in global events is common both to those who prefer diplomacy and to those who are more willing to use force. Indeed, the history of U.S. foreign policy is mostly one of international activism.

Foreign policy exists to support American interests, but determining what American interests are can be very difficult. In crisis situations, as we will see, foreign policy decisions are often made in secret. At the beginning, only a handful of people knew about the Cuban missile crisis that President John Kennedy faced, even though the consequences of that crisis could have sent us into a nuclear war. Similarly, part of the current war on terrorism takes place outside of public sight—although much of the war in Iraq and Afghanistan is in full view. In secret decision-making situations, American interests are whatever elite policymakers decide they are. When situations are not critical, however, foreign policy decisions are made in the usual hubbub of American politics. Here, as we know, many actors with competing interests struggle to make their voices heard and influence policy to their own benefit. Foreign policy, just like domestic policy, is about who

intergovernmental organizations   bodies, such as the United Nations, whose members are countries

nongovernmental organizations (NGOs)   organizations comprising individuals or interest groups from around the world focused on a special issue

multinational corporations   large companies that do business in multiple countries

gets what, and how they get it. The difference is that in foreign policy the stakes can be a matter of life and death, and we have far less control over the other actors involved.

In this chapter we look at American foreign policy in far more depth than most Americans ever do. Specifically, you will learn about

- **the nature of foreign policy**
- **who makes foreign policy**
- **the international and domestic contexts of foreign policy**
- **the strategies and instruments of foreign policy**
- **American foreign policy in the new century**
- **the challenges faced by democratic citizens in a policymaking context where secrecy is often necessary**

Understanding Foreign Policy

Seeking to solve problems occurring outside national borders

Foreign policy focuses on U.S. governmental goals and actions directed toward actors outside our borders. This outward focus separates foreign policy from domestic policy, although sometimes the distinction between *foreign* and *domestic* policy is not so clear. Consider, for example, how environmental policy in America can have foreign repercussions. American industries located on the border with Canada have been the source of some tensions between the two countries because pollution from U.S. factories is carried into Canada by prevailing winds. This pollution can damage forest growth and increase the acidity of lakes, killing fish and harming other wildlife. Environmental regulations are largely a domestic matter, but because pollution is not confined to the geography of the United States, the issue takes on unintended international importance. Or by not seriously reducing the emission of "greenhouse" gases in the United States, because many think doing so would be bad for business, the whole world is less capable of addressing global climate change, which has led to some anti-U.S. sentiment. In this chapter we focus our discussion of foreign

policy on actions that are intentionally directed at external actors and the forces that shape these actions. External actors include the following:

- *Other countries*—sovereign bodies with governments and territories, like Mexico or the Republic of Ireland.

- ***Intergovernmental organizations***—bodies that have countries as members, such as the United Nations, which has 192 member countries; NATO, which has 28 members from North America and Europe; the Organization of Petroleum Exporting Countries (OPEC), which has 12 member countries from Africa, Asia, the Middle East, and Latin America; and the European Union (EU), which has 27 members from across Europe and 4 more waiting to join.

- ***Nongovernmental organizations (NGOs)***—organizations that focus on specific issues and whose members are private individuals or groups from around the world. Greenpeace (environmental), Amnesty International (human rights), International Committee of the Red Cross (humanitarian relief), and Doctors Without Borders (medical care) are NGOs.

- ***Multinational corporations***—large companies that do business in multiple countries and that often wield tremendous economic power, like Nike or Microsoft.

- *Other nonstate actors*—groups that do not fit the other categories, including those that have a "government" but no territory, like the Palestinians, and groups that have no national ties, such as terrorist groups like al Qaeda.

The Post–Cold War Setting of American Foreign Policy

Before we can hope to have a clear understanding of contemporary American foreign policy, a historical note is in order. At the end of World War II, when the common purpose of fighting Adolf Hitler and ending German fascism no longer held the United States and the Soviet Union in an awkward alliance, the tensions that existed between the two largest and strongest superpowers in global politics began to bubble to the surface. Nearly all of Europe was divided between allies of the Soviets and allies of the United States, a division seen most graphically in the splitting of postwar Germany into a communist East and a capitalist West. On March 5, 1946, former British prime minister Winston Churchill, who led his country during the war, gave a famous speech at Westminster College in Fulton, Missouri, in which he warned of this new divided world: "From Stettin in the Baltic to Trieste in the Adriatic an Iron Curtain has descended across the continent." Churchill's words were not meant just as a description but as a call to action.

For nearly fifty years following World War II the tension between the two superpowers shaped U.S. foreign policy and gave it a predictable order. The **Cold War** was waged between the United States and the Soviet Union from 1947 to 1989, a war of bitter global competition between democracy and authoritarianism, capitalism and communism. Although the tensions of the Cold War never erupted into an actual "hot" war of military action directly between the two countries, each side spent tremendous sums of money on nuclear weapons to make sure it had the ability to wipe out the other side, and a number of so-called proxy wars between allies of each superpower did break out in places like the Middle East, Asia, and Africa. In this era, American foreign policy makers pursued a policy of **containment**, in which the United States tried to prevent the Soviet Union from expanding its influence, especially in Europe. As we will see later in the chapter, a key part of this strategy of containment was to deter potential Soviet aggression against the United States or our allies with the threat of a massive nuclear response that would erase any gains the Soviets might make.

But as dangerous as the world was during the Cold War, it—and the threat posed by nuclear deterrence—seemed easy to understand, casting complicated issues into simple choices of black or white. Countries were either with us or against us: they were free societies or closed ones, capitalist or communist economies, good or bad. Relations among nations might put us in treacherous waters, but we had a well-marked map. As late as the 1980s, President Ronald Reagan referred to the Soviet Union as the "Evil Empire," an allusion to the popular *Star Wars* world, in which good and evil were defined clearly. Though the world was hardly this simple, it certainly seemed that way to many, and much of the complexity of world politics was glossed over—or perhaps bottled up, only to explode at the end of the Cold War in 1989.[7]

Perhaps the most dramatic image of the collapse of the Soviet Union and its iron curtain was the eager tearing down of the Berlin Wall by the citizens it had divided into two separate cities—capitalism and democracy on one side of the wall, communism and totalitarianism on the other. The countries in Eastern Europe that had been Soviet satellite countries broke away as the power holding the Soviet Union together dissolved. In some countries, like Germany, the end came more or less peacefully; in others, like Romania, the break was more violent.

In 1991 the Soviet Union finally fell apart, to be replaced by more than a dozen independent states (see "*Consider the Source: Don't Be Fooled by Maps*"). While most Westerners have hailed the fall of the Soviet Union as an end to the tension that kept the Cold War alive, Russia (one of the states of the former Soviet Union) still holds the Soviet nuclear arsenal, and a majority of its citizens still hold a negative view of the leaders of the United States (although, it should be pointed out, a majority of Russians have a positive view of the American people). U.S.-Russian relations have also been complicated because the Western military alliance NATO has enlarged by absorbing members of the former Soviet alliance, the Warsaw Treaty Organization, or Warsaw Pact. The United States has also been moving forward with a missile defense system that has components in countries that were former members of the Soviet alliance, seen by many in Russia as a potential threat.

This "new world order," or post–Cold War era, has eluded easy description in terms of global organization and threats to the United States, especially in the days since September 11, 2001.[8] Who is likely to be our most dangerous adversary? What threats must we prepare for? How much should we spend on military preparedness? Are we the world's policeofficer, a global banker, or a humanitarian protector? We have experimented with all these roles in the past decade.[9] In September 2002, President George W. Bush opened the door to a new foreign policy role when he asserted that the United States' role is to maintain its military supremacy and take preemptive action against hostile and threatening states. He also said that the United States would make no distinction between terrorist groups that threaten or attack the United States and countries that harbor those groups. In identifying an "axis of evil" of Iran, Iraq, and North Korea, President Bush set out a vision of American foreign policy rooted in taking active steps to promote democracy and to use force, alone if necessary, to eliminate perceived threats before they can develop more fully. This **Bush Doctrine** joins a long list of presidential foreign policy

The next time you happen to be in Asia, take a look at a map of the world. Guess what? The United States is not in the center; in fact, it's squished over to one side. Asia is in the center. Can it be that Asian mapmakers are just poorly trained or out of touch? Of course not. The Asia-centric maps used by schoolchildren in Korea, China, and Japan reveal an important feature of mapmaking—it is political. The national boundaries that we see on a map are not etched into the earth; they are made by humans and are constantly being rearranged as the peoples of the earth rearrange themselves. For instance, mapmakers had their hands full in 1991, when the Soviet Union fell. As we can see in the map here, a giant republic had broken down into many small countries—as if the United States were all at once fifty separate nations. The lines of Eastern Europe had to be redrawn, and redrawn again, as the ethnic and national rivalries suppressed by Soviet domination began to work themselves out politically and militarily (see the map inset on Yugoslavia). The political nature of mapmaking means that we need to ask ourselves some important questions about the maps—in the media, in books, in classrooms—that purport to tell us what the world looks like.

1. **What type of information is being conveyed by the map?** Maps are not just graphic illustrations of national boundaries. They can also reveal topography (mountains, hills, oceans, rivers, and lakes), population density, weather patterns, economic resources, transportation, and a host of other characteristics. The map on page 87 for instance, shows how the various colonies voted on the Constitution. Maps can also show regional patterns of colonization, immigration, industrialization, and technological development.

2. **Who drew the map?** This information can explain not only why Asia is at the center of a world map, but more overtly political questions as well. Palestinians and Israelis, for instance, might draw very different maps of contested territories. Mapmaking can be not only a precise way of delineating national borders, but also a way of staking a claim.

3. **When was the map drawn?** A map of today's Europe would look very different from a map of Europe in 1810, when the continent was dominated by the Napoleonic, Austrian, and Ottoman Empires; the Confederation of the Rhine; and at least three separate kingdoms in what is now Italy. The map of Europe continued to change throughout the nineteenth and twentieth centuries until it reflected the Cold War division between the East and West from the mid-1900s on. The map at right shows how the end of the Cold War again changed the map of Europe. Not only do boundaries change over time, but even the names of countries can be different. The countries once known as Siam, the Congo, and Rhodesia have changed their names to Thailand, Zaire, and Zimbabwe, respectively. Name changes often reflect a country's attempt to emphasize a particular part of its heritage, or to disavow foreign influences.

---

doctrines that have tried to define and protect U.S. interests in the world (see *Who, What, How, and WHEN* timeline). It remains to be seen how closely President Obama will follow this course, though he has gone to great lengths to strike a different tone in U.S. relations with the rest of the world.

Types of Foreign Policy

Foreign policy is a term that includes a huge domain; understanding the dynamics that shape American foreign policy might be easier if we break it down into three specific types:[10]

- *Crisis policy* deals with emergency threats to our national interests or values. Such situations often come as a surprise, and the use of force is one way to respond.[11] This is the kind of policy people often have in mind when they use the term *foreign policy*. Iraq's invasion of Kuwait in 1990 provoked a crisis for the United States, as did the attacks on New York and Washington, D.C., in 2001.

- *Strategic policy* lays out the basic U.S. stance toward another country or a particular problem. Containment, for example, was the key strategy for dealing with the Soviets during the Cold War—the plan was to prevent communism from spreading to other countries.

- *Structural defense policy* focuses largely on the policies and programs that deal with defense spending and military bases. These policies usually focus on, for example, buying new aircraft for the air force and

THE BREAKUP OF YUGOSLAVIA

SLOVENIA

CROATIA

BOSNIA AND HERZEGOVINA · SERBIA

MONTE-NEGRO

MACEDONIA

U.S. troops join NATO peacekeeping forces, Dec. 1995

Communist regimes overthrown since 1989
- Rise of Solidarity in Poland, 1980
- Czechoslovakia broken into Czech Republic and Slovakia in 1993

Soviet Union, dissolved in 1991 and replaced by Commonwealth of Independent States

Yugoslavia, dissolved in civil war, 1991–1992

Gorbachev assumes power, 1985; Moscow coup fails, Boris Yeltsin declared President of Russia, 1990; USSR dissolved, 1991

Fall of Berlin Wall, 1989; Germany unified, 1990

Chechnya declares independence, 1991; Russia attacks, 1994

See inset

SWEDEN, FINLAND, NORWAY, ESTONIA, LATVIA, LITHUANIA, DENMARK, UNITED KINGDOM, IRELAND, NETH., GERMANY, BELG., POLAND, BELARUS, CZECH REP., SLOVAKIA, UKRAINE, AUSTRIA, SWITZ., HUNGARY, MOLDOVA, FRANCE, ITALY, ROMANIA, ATLANTIC OCEAN, PORTUGAL, SPAIN, ALBANIA, BULGARIA, GREECE, RUSSIA, MOSCOW, KAZAKHSTAN, GEORGIA, ARMENIA, AZERBAIJAN, UZBEKISTAN, KYRGYZSTAN, TURKMENISTAN, TAJIKISTAN, TURKEY, CHINA, TUNISIA, CYPRUS, LEBANON, SYRIA, ISRAEL, IRAQ, IRAN, AFGHANISTAN, MOROCCO, JORDAN, PAKISTAN, INDIA, ALGERIA, LIBYA, EGYPT, SAUDI ARABIA

Baltic Sea, North Sea, Black Sea, Aral Sea, Caspian Sea, Mediterranean Sea, Red Sea, Persian Gulf, Arabian Sea, Berlin

0 250 500 mi
0 250 500 km

Source: Thomas Bailey, David M. Kennedy, and Lizabeth Cohen, *The American Pageant*, 11th ed. (Boston: Houghton Mifflin, 1998). Copyright © 1998 by Houghton Mifflin Company. Reprinted with permission.

navy, or deciding what military bases to consolidate or close down.

We come back to these distinctions in the next section, when we discuss what kinds of actors are involved in making each of these types of policies. They provide important insights into who is involved in different types of American foreign policy.

Americans also seek to define a role for themselves in world affairs since the Cold War and since 9/11. So far there has been no definitive answer to what role the world's only remaining superpower will play.

Who What How

In foreign policy, official government actors seek to solve problems that occur outside our borders. They do this by constructing crisis, strategic, and structural defense policies.

Does being the world's sole remaining superpower carry any special obligations?

Thinking Outside the Box

crisis policy foreign policy, usually made quickly and secretly, that responds to an emergency threat

strategic policy foreign policy that lays out a country's basic stance toward international actors or problems

structural defense policy foreign policy dealing with defense spending, military bases, and weapons procurement

Truman Doctrine policy of the United States starting in 1947 that the United States would aid free peoples to maintain their freedom in the face of aggressive communist movements

And the Wall Came Tumbling Down

In November 1989 an East German official announced that East Germans would be allowed to move freely between East and West Berlin. Almost immediately, people flocked to the wall that had kept them separated from their fellow Berliners for twenty-eight years, a wall that had symbolized the division not only of a city, but of ideals and political systems—capitalism and democracy on one side and totalitarianism on the other.

Who Makes American Foreign Policy?

Competition and cooperation between the executive and legislative branches

Consider the following headlines: "U.S. Opens Relations With China" and "U.S. Attacks al Qaeda Base in Afghanistan." These headlines make it sound as if a single actor—the United States—makes foreign policy. Even as a figure of speech,

this is misleading in two important ways. First, the image of the United States as a single actor suggests that the country acts with a single, united mind, diverting our attention from the political reality of conflict, bargaining, and cooperation that takes place *within* the government over foreign policy.[12] Second, it implies that all foreign policies are essentially the same—having the same goals and made by the same actors and processes. Our earlier description of the three different policy types indicates that this is not so; and in fact, as we will see, each type of policy is made by different actors in different political contexts.

The political dynamics behind crisis policy, for instance, are dominated by the president and the small group of advisers around the Oval Office. Congress tends not to be much engaged in crisis policy, but rather, often watches with the rest of the public (and the world) as presidents and their advisers decide how to respond to international crises. The choice of going to war in Iraq in 2003, for example, was made by President Bush and a number of key government policymakers around him.

Strategic policy tends to be formulated in the executive branch, but usually deep in the bureaucracy rather than at the top levels. This gives interest groups and concerned members of Congress opportunities to lobby for certain policies. The public usually learns about these policies (and responds to and evaluates them) once they are announced by the president. The U.S. policy of containment of communism in the 1940s, for example, was developed largely in the State Department and was then approved by President Harry Truman. The *Truman Doctrine* said that the United States would use its power to help free people maintain their freedom in the face of aggressive movements, which is to say the United States would try to contain Soviet influence by helping make sure that no new countries fell to communism.[13]

Finally, structural defense policy, which often starts in the executive branch, is crafted largely in Congress, whose members tend to have their fingers on the pulses of their constituents, with much input from the bureaucracy and interest groups. When a plan to build and deploy a new fighter jet is developed, for example, it is made with coordination between Congress and the Defense Department—usually with members of Congress keeping a close eye on how their states and districts will fare from the projects.

Clearly a variety of actors are involved in making different types of foreign policy. What they all have in common is that they are officially acting on behalf of the federal government. It is not official U.S. foreign policy when New York City and San Francisco impose economic sanctions on Burma, or when private citizens like former president Jimmy Carter or the Reverend Jesse Jackson attempt to help resolve conflicts in Africa or Serbia.[14] Understanding why a particular foreign policy is developed means understanding what actors are involved in what processes.

The President

As we saw in Chapter 8, the president has come to be seen as the chief foreign policy maker. Presidents are more likely to set the foreign policy agenda than are other actors in American politics because of the informal powers that come from their high-profile job and their opportunities to communicate directly with the public. Understanding the power that comes with agenda control is a key part of understanding presidential power. But the president's foreign policy authority also derives from the Constitution, which gives him specific roles to play. Recall from Chapter 8 that the president is the head of state, the chief executive, the commander-in-chief, and the country's chief diplomat. For a president, making foreign policy is a bit like walking a tightrope. On the one hand, presidents get a lot of power to make foreign policy from the Constitution, from their "implied powers," and, sometimes,

Working as a Team

As chief executive, the president relies on a host of agencies and individuals to assist him in crafting U.S. foreign policy. Here, President Barack Obama speaks to the media about the New START Treaty in March 2010 as members of his team look on. From left are Press Secretary Robert Gibbs, Joint Chiefs of Staff Chairman Admiral Mike Mullen, Secretary of State Hillary Clinton, and Defense Secretary Robert Gates. Though opponents of the treaty—which would further nuclear arms reduction with Russia—tried to block it in the Senate, the Obama administration succeeded in getting it ratified in December 2010.

from Congress. On the other hand, the president is confronted with many obstacles to making foreign policy in the form of domestic issues (particularly if he is trying to get reelected) and other foreign policy makers, especially Congress and the bureaucracy, as well as the media and public opinion.

The Executive Branch

The president sits at the top of a large pyramid of executive agencies and departments that assist him in making foreign policy. If he does not take time to manage the agencies, other individuals may seize the opportunity to interpret foreign policy in terms of their own interests and goals. It is largely up to the president to sort out conflicting goals in the executive branch. In a sense, the president provides a check on the power of the executive agencies, and without his leadership, foreign policy can drift. During his administration, President Reagan didn't pay a lot of attention to foreign affairs and so

To Serve and Protect

Politicians and the U.S. military share an edict to protect the lives and rights of Americans, at home or abroad, and to defend democracy worldwide. Here, a U.S. Marine spends time with two Afghan babies during a village medical outreach in November 2010.

▶ Who, What, How, and WHEN: Presidential Foreign Policy Doctrine

In response to world events, presidents often publicly define U.S. foreign policy interests and state what the U.S. **role in protecting those interests will be. Watch some of these doctrines change and develop over time:**

1823 — Monroe Doctrine

In the wake of discussion among France, Britain, Spain, and Russia about expansion of trading colonies in South America, Monroe wished to limit European influence in North and South America to protect U.S. security and options for what became manifest destiny. He declared the Western Hemisphere off limits to further European colonization.

1904 — Roosevelt Corollary to the Monroe Doctrine

To keep Germany from intervening in Venezuela's economic and political affairs, Teddy Roosevelt declared that the United States would act as a police power in Caribbean and Central American nations if they could not pay their debts, to keep European powers from controlling these countries.

1947 — Truman Doctrine

In response to the Soviet Union and its control of the Iron Curtain in Eastern Europe, Truman declared the United States would support foreign governments facing internal or external subversion from communist movements.

1957 — Eisenhower Doctrine

When the Soviet Union attempted to gain control of the Suez Canal and Egypt, Eisenhower declared that the Middle East was a vital region to the United States, and that the United States would support the region with aid and respond to threats against the United States pertaining to the region.

---

staff members in the National Security Council began to make foreign policy themselves. The result was the Iran-contra affair in the mid-1980s, in which profits from selling arms to Iran (technically illegal in U.S. law but done in an effort to get Iran's help to release western hostages) were used to help fund the Nicaraguan contra rebels, aid for whom Congress had refused to approve.

Within the president's inner circle (in the Executive Office of the President, or EOP) is the **National Security Council (NSC)**, a body created in 1947 by the National Security Act to advise the president on matters of foreign policy. By law its members include the president, vice president, secretary of state, and secretary of defense. The Director of National Intelligence and the Chair of the Joint Chiefs of Staff (the head of the commanders of the military

services) sit as advisers to the NSC. Beyond this, though, the president has wide discretion to decide what the NSC will look like and how he will use it by appointing other members and deciding how the council will function. The national security adviser, the president's chief adviser on foreign policy and national security matters, coordinates the NSC and its staff.

In addition to the NSC, several executive departments and agencies play a critical role in foreign policy making. The **Department of State** is charged with managing foreign affairs. It is often considered to be "first among equals" in its position relative to the other departments because it was the first department established by the Constitution in 1789. The State Department is headed by the secretary of state, who is part of the president's cabinet and fulfills a variety of foreign

MONROE DOCTRINE PROCLAIMED · 1823

1969 — **Nixon Doctrine**

As unrest over involvement in the Vietnam War continued to grow, Nixon declared that the United States would continue to provide help such as monetary aid to its allies but would expect these allies, such as South Vietnam, to start defending themselves.

1980 — **Carter Doctrine**

After the Soviet Union invaded Afghanistan in 1979, Carter declared the United States would repel any attempt by an outside force to gain control of the Persian Gulf region using any means necessary, including military force.

1985 — **Reagan Doctrine**

As Cold War tension with the Soviet Union resurged in the mid-1980s, Reagan declared the United States would provide aid to any country fighting communism by way of insurgents, or "freedom fighters," particularly in Africa, Latin America, and Asia.

2001 — **Bush Doctrine**

After the September 11 attacks, Bush stated the United States would consider any country that harbored terrorists to be a threat to the United States; later, the doctrine was expanded to defend attacks by the United States in an effort to preempt state-sponsored terrorism.

2009 — **An Obama Doctrine?**

Not yet fully in focus, the Obama foreign policy emphasizes reengagement with allies and international organizations, an openness to negotiate with opponents, a willingness to use military force when necessary, and a sense that the United States must hold itself to a higher standard in order to try to lead a complex global system.

policy roles. The first of these roles is maintaining diplomatic and consular posts around the world. These diplomatic posts are designed to facilitate communication between the United States and foreign countries, provide assistance for U.S. travelers, and grant visas or political asylum to foreign nationals seeking to enter the United States. A second function of the State Department is to send delegates and missions (groups of government officials) to a variety of international organization meetings. A third function of the State Department is to negotiate treaties and executive agreements with other countries. Among the best-known employees of the State Department are the foreign service officers, the most senior of whom are U.S. ambassadors. Foreign service officers play a key role in diplomacy as they represent the United States abroad, report back on events

overseas, help manage ongoing negotiations, and assist U.S. citizens traveling abroad.

The second major department involved in foreign policy is the ***Department of Defense***, headquartered in the Pentagon—the distinctive five-sided building in Arlington, Virginia. The main job of the department is to manage American soldiers and their equipment to protect the United States. The Defense Department is headed by the secretary of defense, whose job in part is to advise the president on defense matters and who, it is important to note, is a civilian. The idea that the military should be under the authority of civilians is an important check in U.S. politics.

The ***Joint Chiefs of Staff*** is part of the Defense Department. It consists, at the top, of the senior military officers of the armed forces: the army and air force chiefs of staff, the

National Security Council (NSC) organization within the Executive Office of the President that provides foreign policy advice to the president

Department of State the executive department charged with managing foreign affairs

Department of Defense the executive department charged with managing the country's military personnel, equipment, and operations

Joint Chiefs of Staff the senior military officers from four branches of the U.S. armed forces

intelligence community the agencies and bureaus responsible for obtaining and interpreting information for the government

Central Intelligence Agency (CIA) the government organization that oversees foreign intelligence gathering and related classified activities

director of national intelligence overseer and coordinator of the activities of the many agencies involved in the production and dissemination of intelligence information in the U.S. government, as well as the president's main intelligence adviser

Department of Homeland Security the executive department meant to provide a unifying force in the government's efforts to prevent attacks on the United States and to respond to such attacks through law enforcement and emergency relief should they occur

chief of naval operations, and the commandant of the marine corps. The chair is selected by the president. The Joint Chiefs of Staff advises the secretary of defense, and the chair is the primary military adviser to the president and the secretary of defense.

Another executive actor in foreign policy making is the group of agencies and bureaus that make up the *intelligence community* (see Figure 19.1). This community's job is the collection, organization, and analysis of information. That information can be gathered in a number of ways, from the mundane, such as reading foreign newspapers, to the more clandestine, like spying by human beings and by more high-tech means such as surveillance satellites. This community of more than a dozen separate agencies, many housed inside the Defense Department, was until recently coordinated by the director of central intelligence, who was also the head of the *Central Intelligence Agency (CIA)*. The CIA oversees intelligence gathering and classified activities abroad. In addition to the CIA, there are intelligence components in each of the four branches of the armed forces, as well as intelligence groups within the Departments of State, Defense, Energy, and Treasury, and within the Federal Bureau of Investigation (FBI). The intelligence community also includes certain specialized agencies such as the National Security Agency (NSA), which is responsible for cryptology (code breaking) and monitoring communications with sophisticated satellites that can see and listen to much of the planet.

At the end of 2004, in the wake of many studies and hearings about the events leading up to September 11, as well as current security concerns, President Bush signed legislation that altered how the intelligence community is managed. The job of the director of central intelligence was limited to directing the CIA. The job of coordinating the entire network of agencies now falls to the *director of national intelligence*. Although this person does not have direct authority over all members of the community, or budgetary authority over the network, the director does have the ear of the president, meeting with him each day. This arrangement, in concert with

some other changes, is intended to clarify who runs the intelligence community. The National Counterterrorism Center was also created, which serves as a central hub for intelligence and the development of plans to counter terrorism.

Because of the secrecy surrounding its activities, the exact size of the intelligence community, its budget, and its activities are not very clear. The 2008 budget for the intelligence community was reported to be $75 billion, although what that money was spent on will never be known publicly because much of what these agencies do is classified as top-secret.

Another major change after September 11 was the establishment of the *Department of Homeland Security*, a new cabinet-level agency to better coordinate the steps taken by the government to keep us safe at home. Agencies that were spread throughout the government but that all had some role in protecting the homeland were pulled together under this new umbrella. Immigration services, the U.S. Secret Service, the Federal Emergency Management Agency (FEMA), and the Coast Guard, to name a few, now all share a common home.

In addition to the State Department, the Defense Department, the Department of Homeland Security, and the intelligence community, a variety of other departments also play a role in foreign policy. These include the Treasury Department, the Commerce Department, and the office of the U.S. Trade Representative, all of which are concerned with American foreign economic policy—for example, with the export of American goods abroad. The Department of Agriculture is interested in promoting American agricultural products abroad and gets involved when the United States ships food overseas as part of a humanitarian mission, for example, to help refugees in the aftermath of a civil war. Finally, the Department of Labor is involved with labor issues around the world, such as studying the impact of the North American Free Trade Agreement (NAFTA) on American jobs.

Figure 19.1

Key Foreign Policy Agencies

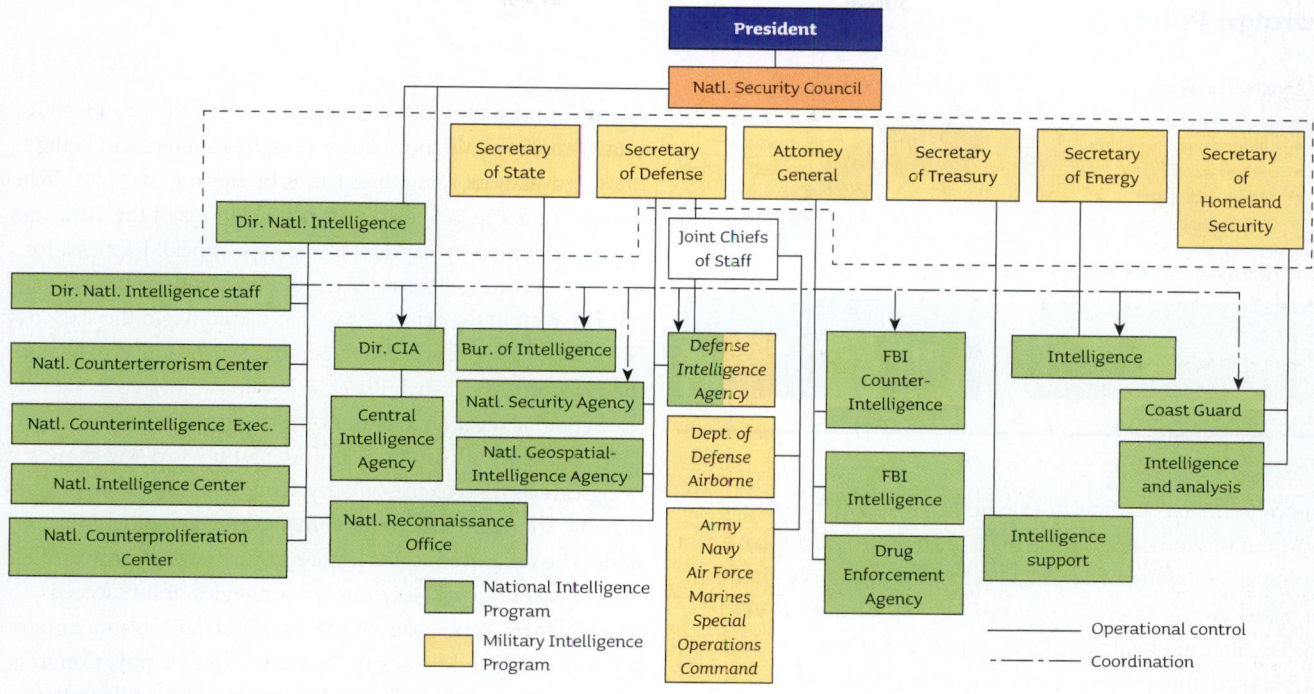

Source: Mark Lowenthal, *Intelligence*, 4th ed. (Washington, D.C.: CQ Press, 2009).

Congress

As we saw in Chapter 7, Congress has a variety of constitutional roles in making foreign policy, including the power to make treaties, to declare war, and to appropriate money. But Congress also faces obstacles in its efforts to play an active foreign policy role. For most of the twentieth century until the 1970s, the president took the lead on foreign policy, prompting one scholar to refer to an "imperial" presidency.[15] George W. Bush revived that role in fighting the war on terrorism. Even when Congress wants to play a role, it is limited in what it can do. One reason is that Congress is more oriented toward domestic than foreign affairs, given the constant imperative of reelection. Congressional organization can also hamper the congressional role in foreign policy. The fragmentation of Congress, the slow speed of deliberation, and the complex nature of many foreign issues can make it difficult for Congress to play a big role—particularly in fast-moving foreign events.

Presidential-Congressional Power Struggles

The relationship between the executive and legislative branches in the foreign policy realm has been called an "invitation to struggle" because the Constitution has given both bodies some power to act in foreign policy.[16] The jurisdictions of each, however, are not established clearly by the Constitution and, in keeping with the principles of checks and balances, the powers are to some extent shared. In this inherent tension, the president and Congress both maneuver for the top position (see Figure 19.2). Presidents, for example, try to get around the need for Senate approval of treaties by using executive agreements instead, or they try to circumvent the Senate's confirmation power by making appointments while Congress is in recess. Such strategies have real costs, however, since the Senate does not take kindly to being bypassed and the president needs the cooperation of Congress to accomplish his agenda. The Senate was so angry when President Bill Clinton made one appointment while it was on break that one senator vowed to block Clinton's future nominations. Clinton eventually promised to make no more such appointments without notifying Senate leaders, and Senate leaders withdrew the block on Clinton's other nominations.

The foreign policy tension between the president and Congress is exacerbated further by the complex issues surrounding the use of military force. The president is in charge of the armed forces, but only Congress can declare war. Presidents try to get around the power of Congress by committing

Figure 19.2

Executive/Legislative "Struggle" Over Foreign Policy

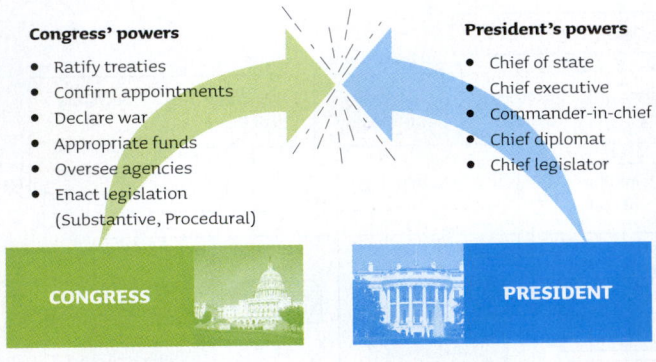

Congress' powers
- Ratify treaties
- Confirm appointments
- Declare war
- Appropriate funds
- Oversee agencies
- Enact legislation (Substantive, Procedural)

President's powers
- Chief of state
- Chief executive
- Commander-in-chief
- Chief diplomat
- Chief legislator

CONGRESS

PRESIDENT

troops to military actions that do not have the official status of war, but this too can infuriate the legislators. Presidents have sent troops abroad without a formal declaration of war on a number of occasions, for example, in Korea (1950), Vietnam (1965), the Dominican Republic (1965), Lebanon (1982), Grenada (1983), Panama (1989), the Persian Gulf (1990), Afghanistan (2001), and Iraq (2003)—among others. As the Vietnam War became a bigger issue, Congress became increasingly unhappy with the president's role but did not take steps to try to challenge him until the early 1970s, when public opinion against the war became too much for Congress to resist. Then Congress turned on the commander-in-chief, passing the War Powers Act of 1973 over President Richard Nixon's veto. The act makes the following provisions:

1. The president must inform Congress of the introduction of forces into hostilities or situations where imminent involvement in hostilities is clearly indicated by the circumstances.

2. Troop commitments by the president cannot extend past sixty days without specific congressional authorization (though another thirty days is permitted for the withdrawal of the troops).

3. Any time American forces become engaged in hostilities without a declaration of war or specific congressional authorization, Congress can direct the president to disengage such troops by a concurrent resolution of the two houses of Congress.

The War Powers Act has not stopped presidents from using force abroad, however. Chief executives have largely sidestepped the act through a simple loophole: they don't make their reports to Congress exactly as the act requires, and therefore they never trigger the sixty-day clock. They generally report "consistent with but not pursuant to" the act, a technicality that allows them to satisfy Congress's interest in being informed without tying their hands by starting the clock. When President George W. Bush informed Congress of the campaign against terrorism in response to the September 11 attacks, for instance, he did so "consistent with the War Powers Act" but not pursuant to the act in a way that would begin the sixty-day clock. Nor have the courts stepped in to help Congress here, as they typically avoid such issues as "political questions" rather than genuine legal or constitutional cases.

Despite its difficulties in enforcing the War Powers Act, Congress has tried to play a fairly active role in foreign policy making, sometimes working with a president, sometimes at odds. The calculation for Congress is fairly straightforward: let the president pursue risky military strategies. If he succeeds, take credit for staying out of his way; if he fails, blame him for not consulting and for being "imperial." Either way, Congress wins, or at least it doesn't lose by seeming to meddle in the affairs that many people see as the president's domain.[17] Even after the Democrats took control of Congress after the 2006 elections, they were unable to alter Bush's war policy in Iraq, due to these kinds of barriers, and because the president's potential veto meant that they needed a supermajority in both houses, not just their own simple majority of votes.

American foreign policy making is just as crowded an arena as any other aspect of American politics. Actors vie with each other to realize their goals and manipulate the rules to get their way. The primary direct actors in the process are the president, the various executive bodies with foreign policy authority, and Congress. To maximize their power and influence, these actors use their constitutional powers where they can, the laws on the books, and their power to create new laws. We have seen this most graphically in the power struggle between the president and Congress, illustrated by the politics surrounding the War Powers Act.

Who What How

Are there enough checks and balances in the foreign policy process? Are there too many?

Thinking Outside the Box

How Do We Define a Foreign Policy Problem?

A distinctive style forged by international and domestic pressures

The actors we have just discussed work in a distinctive political environment that helps them decide when a foreign situation constitutes a problem, and when and how it should be acted on. Most foreign policy is either action to correct something we don't like in the world or reaction to world events. How do policymakers in Washington, members of the media, or average citizens on the street decide what is sufficiently important to Americans and American interests that a foreign policy should be made? What makes the United States act or react?

The answer is complex. First, over the years a distinctive American approach to foreign policy has developed that reflects our view of our global role, our values, and our political goals. Because of inherent tensions among these roles, values, and goals, our approach to foreign policy is not always entirely consistent. Foreign policy is also shaped by politics, plain and simple. The political context in which American foreign policy is forged involves the actors we have just met, in combination with pressures both global and domestic. In this section we explore our distinctive approach to foreign policy and then examine the variety of global and domestic pressures that help to define American foreign policy problems.

The American Style of Foreign Policy

American foreign policy goals have consistently included the promotion of democracy, capitalism, and free trade. At the same time, the record of American foreign policy is full of inconsistencies. We change allies and friends from time to time. For example, Japan and Germany were enemies of the United States during World War II, while the Soviet Union was an ally. After World War II, those positions switched: Japan and Germany became our friends, whereas until the 1990s the Soviet Union was our enemy. After 1950 the United States supported Taiwan as the true China, then switched in 1979 and recognized the People's Republic and the government in Beijing. In 1979 Iranian revolutionaries held fifty-four Americans hostage in the U.S. embassy for over one year; less than a decade later, the United States sold arms

to Iran. Likewise, the United States sold weapons to Iraq in the 1980s, and then went to war against it in 1990 and again in 2003. These inconsistencies in American foreign policy are partly due to the fact that international and domestic pressures are not static; they change over time, sometimes presenting challenges to the United States and sometimes opportunities, sometimes forcing action, sometimes preventing action. But the inconsistencies in American foreign policy also result from three underlying tensions in Americans' ideas about the world: global activism, moral values, and conflicting goals. These tensions help create a distinctive "American" approach to foreign policy.

Global Activism

The first tension concerns the way Americans see their global role.[18] An American military presence hovers over many areas of the globe, we are a major exporter of goods and services, and American culture has spread throughout the world. In fact the United States is so involved and so powerful that it is often called a **hegemon**, or the dominant actor in world politics. Much of this involvement is a matter of choice. As we discussed earlier, since World War II, American leaders and the public have believed that it is important for the United States to play an active role in global affairs, a philosophy known as internationalism. Internationalism is still the predominant foreign policy view in this country.

Critics of internationalism argue that when the United States gets involved in other countries' affairs, it often ends up with worse results than if it did nothing. The covert operation against Salvador Allende in Chile in the early 1970s is an example: in attempting to keep a constitutionally elected left-wing Marxist government from taking control, the United States helped a right-wing repressive regime come to power. Many other critics think that we have enough troubles at home that we should focus our efforts here, rather than focusing on foreign problems. As we mentioned before, this isolationist impulse has perhaps been on the rise in recent years.[19]

Both courses of action have benefits and costs. The main benefit of internationalism is that the United States can steer the courses of others in ways it likes; the primary cost is that it drains attention and resources from domestic policy. The primary benefit of isolationism is that it keeps the United States from being bogged down in someone else's problems; the primary cost is that their problems could become quickly ours, and the opportunity to shape the global environment

> **hegemon** the dominant actor in world politics

will be ceded to someone else. American policymakers have responded to this dilemma by being inconsistent; at times they support internationalism, and at times they support isolationism.

Moral Values

A second tension that makes American foreign policy seem inconsistent is the dispute over whether it should be guided more by practical or by moral considerations. Moral statements try to define particular actions as right or wrong. For example, although many people believe that going to war is the moral thing to do under certain circumstances—for example, to defend America from foreign invasion or to stop human rights violations in another country—most people also consider it wrong to attack innocent civilians while fighting a war. An important question for Americans is whether foreign policy should be constrained by moral guidelines and, if so, to what extent the government should be bound by those essentially self-imposed restrictions.

Just as Americans and their foreign policy leaders have fluctuated between internationalism and isolationism over time, so too have we flip-flopped between emphasizing morality and practicality in foreign policy.[20] For example, under President Carter the moral component of American foreign policy found its way into policies reducing the number of arms America exported abroad, promoting human rights, improving our relations with the Soviets, and pulling back our support of repressive regimes, even though we might have supported them in the past for being anticommunist.[21] Congress was also very assertive in this period, cutting military and economic aid to countries that did not support human rights. When President Reagan, much more of a pragmatist, came to power, he reversed much of what President Carter had done. For instance, in El Salvador, where Carter had tried to get tough on a repressive regime, Reagan put the fight against communism first and so backed the existing regime—death squads and all—rather than push for human rights and risk "losing" part of Central America to communism.

Conflicting Goals

A final tension affecting the American approach to foreign policy concerns three basic goals the United States tries to pursue: defending the homeland (security), encouraging the growth of our economy (economic), and supporting democracy in the world (political).[22] Sometimes these goals cannot be attained simultaneously and we have to prioritize them.

One of the key flash points has been between the protection of political goals (particularly human rights) and security goals (containment). Despite its preference for taking the moral high ground, the United States in practice has been largely willing to work with any anticommunist leader and country, regardless of its domestic policies on human rights. This led us into strategic alliances with some countries that were not only not democratic but in fact quite repressive, the Philippines being one such example. And, indeed, the United States has forged links with nondemocratic regimes, such as Pakistan and Saudi Arabia, as part of the war against terrorism.

The current war on terrorism is emblematic of the tension between conflicting U.S. goals. When President Bush talked of the important role of the United States in promoting democratic change and extending human liberty around the globe, he drew on very "idealistic" principles often associated with President Woodrow Wilson after World War I. At the same time, though, his administration's willingness to use torture against suspected terrorists cut at the very heart of the U.S. commitment to human rights and dignity.[23] Finding the right balance between safety and security, liberty and freedom is a constant challenge to democratic governments.

Global Pressures

In addition to being influenced by the distinctive culture of American foreign policy, policy problems are defined by the combination of global and domestic pressures we spoke of earlier. Global pressure is exerted by external forces, events that take place outside America. Although the United States is an independent sovereign nation and a global superpower, it is also just one state in a larger system of states. All the states, plus other actors such as the United Nations and global terrorist groups, together comprise the international system. The nature of the international system has an impact on what sorts of things are defined as problems requiring action or reaction from America.[24] Here we discuss briefly some characteristics of that system.

Anarchy and Power

The international political system is characterized by two concepts we discussed in Chapter 1: anarchy and power. Anarchy is a theory of politics that holds that there should be no laws at all. In the international context, this means that there is no central authority that individual nations must obey. International laws are effective only to the degree that nations agree to be bound by them. Since they cannot be

free trade economic system by which countries exchange goods without imposing excessive tariffs and taxes

protectionism the imposition of trade barriers, especially tariffs, to make trading conditions favorable to domestic producers

International Monetary Fund (IMF) economic institution that makes short-term, relatively small loans to countries to help balance their currency flows

Promoting Peace

U.S. president Barack Obama greets Israeli prime minister Benjamin Netanyahu, left, and Palestinian president Mahmoud Abbas, right, during a 2009 meeting. Though Obama's 2009 Cairo speech raised hopes in the Middle East, his meeting with Israeli and Palestinian leaders later that year to restart the peace process failed to reap results. Domestic political pressure within governments of both sides are making resolution of the conflict hard to reach.

enforced, except by military might, they are more like conventions than laws. When nations get into conflicts with each other, there is no organization that can authoritatively resolve the conflicts without the cooperation of those nations themselves. Even though there is a world court—the International Court of Justice, which is part of the U.S. justice system—the impact of its rulings and those of other world judicial bodies depends on the willingness of countries to abide by them.

The condition of anarchy has special implications for what Americans define as foreign policy problems. First, because power is what ultimately counts, the United States has taken care to build on its natural advantages to become a very powerful country, rather than counting on other states to defend it should the need arise, as smaller, less wealthy nations sometimes have to do. Although we are involved in international organizations like NATO, we also have the capacity to act on our own, without the cooperation or consent of our allies if need be. Second, American foreign policy has tended to focus on the behavior and actions of other nations, rather than international organizations, since that is where the competing areas of power are. It is other states that pose a military threat, and so other states are most likely to be at the center of our foreign policy problems (although in recent years nonstate actors like international terrorists have also become a focus of American foreign policy, especially as they are increasingly able to obtain weapons of mass destruction). Finally, since power has traditionally been defined first and foremost in military terms, we tend to put a priority on threats to our security.[25] Security issues often become the primary focus of our foreign policy.

Economic Interdependence

Even though the nations of the world are technically sovereign and independent actors, more and more they are economically interdependent—that is, most of the national economies of the world are linked together through the trade of goods and services and currencies. As the global stock market panic following the collapse of the U.S. credit market in the fall of 2008 makes painfully clear, ups and downs in one economy tend to be felt throughout the global economy, which has a hand in shaping our foreign policy.[26] The United States sells some of the goods it makes to actors outside the country, and individuals and companies inside the United

States buy other products from abroad. Between domestic production and foreign trade, our economy often prospers, but we are increasingly dependent on what other countries do, and we are vulnerable to the effects of the economic crises they might encounter.

The United States played a pivotal role in setting up the current world economic system in 1944, in a meeting that took place in Bretton Woods, New Hampshire. The meeting brought together forty-four countries (notably *not* including the Soviet Union), under the leadership of the United States, to design a system that would regulate international trade and the international money system, and help restore war-ravaged Europe. The participating countries agreed to found a global economic system based on the principles of capitalism at home and free trade among states. **Free trade** means that countries exchange goods across their borders without imposing taxes and tariffs that make goods from another country more expensive than those made at home. Because such measures protect their home producers at the expense of the global market, the imposition of such restrictions is known as **protectionism**.

The Bretton Woods system, an example of a strategic economic policy, set up three key economic institutions that continue to play a central role in the global economy:

- The **International Monetary Fund (IMF)** was created to make relatively small and short-term loans to help

World Bank economic institution that makes large, low-cost loans with long repayment terms to countries, primarily for infrastructure construction or repairs

General Agreement on Tariffs and Trade (GATT) a series of agreements on international trading terms; now known as the World Trade Organization (WTO)

most favored nation the status afforded to WTO trading partners; a country gives the same "deal" to member nations that it offers to its "most favored" friend

balance the flow of currency in and out of countries. Originally the IMF focused on making loans to address balance-of-payments deficits. It still does so, but increasingly the IMF and World Bank work together on massive loans for economic restructuring.

- The **World Bank**, or International Bank for Reconstruction and Development, was created to make large loans with long repayment terms and better interest rates than those available from banks. It addresses the needs of building and rebuilding economic infrastructure in countries—roads, dams, ports, bridges, and so on.

- The **General Agreement on Tariffs and Trade (GATT)** was an agreement about the terms on which member countries would trade with one another. At the heart of GATT was the principle of **most favored nation**, which meant that a country gives the same "deal" to all other GATT members as it gives to its "most favored" friend. The idea was to develop a multilateral trade organization that would work over time to move toward freer and freer trade among member nations. The GATT has now evolved into the World Trade Organization (WTO).

By the 1970s, however, it was becoming increasingly difficult to manage the world economy. First, other countries such as Japan were becoming more powerful economically. Second, some less-developed countries felt that free trade gave countries like the United States and those in Europe an advantage, and they wanted to protect their markets. Finally, the U.S. leadership role was weakening. The United States was beginning to pay larger costs to maintain the system, and its own economy was losing strength.[27]

The world economy affects the definition of foreign policy problems in several ways. First, Americans seek to preserve the capitalist free trade system, partly for ideological reasons and partly because of its benefits. Inevitably the United States gets into conflicts with states that want some limits on free trade. For example, when Japan put up protectionist barriers that made it harder for American companies to sell their products in Japan, American foreign policy aimed to get Japan to remove or at least reduce these barriers. One should note that the United States also uses

protectionist measures to insulate the U.S. economy from foreign competition. For example, "domestic content" rules on automobiles require that a certain percentage of a car's components be built or assembled in the United States.

And the public can have strong views about the role of U.S. foreign policy in promoting economic interests. In 2008, 80 percent of those surveyed in the general public thought it was a "very important" goal of U.S. foreign policy to protect American jobs and workers, while 73 percent thought it was a "very important" goal to stop the spread of nuclear weapons.[28] Only 41 percent of the nation's "leaders" in the survey thought it was the purpose of foreign policy to protect jobs and workers, however, and 87 percent thought we ought to stop the spread of nuclear weapons.[29] The public is clearly more worried than their leaders about the outsourcing of jobs abroad, in which generally high-wage jobs that had been held at home by Americans are shipped overseas, where wages are lower. Some studies predict that by 2015 as many as three million jobs could be lost to workers overseas.[30] Although not everyone agrees with this prediction, it certainly is the case that the complexity of globalization and the imperatives of international economic competition can run secondary to the public's sense that their jobs are being taken and that it is the role of foreign policy to do something about it. This creates tough conflicts for policymakers.

Clearly, much of foreign policy is also economic policy. Domestic policy efforts to stimulate the American economy and to revise financial regulations are also joined by U.S. efforts to work in concert with other countries as they address their own economic struggles. One way this happens is with the "G-20," a group comprising the twenty largest global economies—including the United States, Brazil, Germany, China, and Russia. The G-20 meets regularly to work on economic issues, such as at its summer 2010 meeting in Canada.

Domestic Pressures

Global pressures are not the only ones that shape what is defined as a foreign policy problem. Three important forces within America can have an influence on government policymakers: public opinion, the media, and interest groups.

Pressure in Numbers?

Several thousand antiwar demonstrators fill Waterfront Park in downtown Portland, Oregon, in mid-March 2003, to protest a possible war with Iraq. Although their voices did not prevent the war, public opinion of the protracted conflict grew increasingly critical over the next couple of years and forced the Bush administration to defend its policies.

Public Opinion

Public opinion influences foreign policy in a number of ways. First, since broad-based public beliefs are relatively stable, public opinion can limit drastic changes in foreign policy because decision makers believe the public will not stand for a radical new policy direction.[31] This is the case particularly when it comes to taking risks that can lead to U.S. casualties— Americans might quickly reject a policy if the costs in human lives are high. Second, public opinion matters in foreign policy because, on occasion, changes in public opinion actually help bring about changes in foreign policy. For example, people supported the idea of recognizing the People's Republic of China long before President Carter changed our strategic policy toward China and decided to recognize it; the public became vocally dissatisfied with Vietnam policy before U.S. leaders did; and popular support for a nuclear freeze preceded President Reagan's resumption of nuclear arms control negotiations with the Soviet Union.[32] Third, public opinion

may be used as a bargaining chip in diplomacy. Here the idea is that a leader negotiating policies with other countries' leaders can use public opinion to set limits on what positions are acceptable. Diplomacy is often referred to as a "two-level game" because a leader is simultaneously negotiating with a foreign government and also gauging what is acceptable at home.[33]

The Media

The media also exert domestic pressure on the definition of American foreign policy problems. All media sources cover foreign policy, but their role is limited for three reasons: the media must also pay attention to domestic issues; the media are effective only to the point that people actually pay attention to what they say; and the government can limit the media's coverage of certain sensitive stories, as it did during the Persian Gulf War in 1990–1991, and in the ongoing wars in Afghanistan and Iraq. Generally, foreign news is shrinking as a percentage of the news. For example, ABC's nightly news foreign coverage dropped from 3,733 minutes in 1989 to 1,838 minutes in 1996—and ABC offers the most foreign coverage of the three major networks.[34] Some of this drop in coverage has been picked up by the Internet and twenty-four-hour news networks. The aftermath of the September 2001 attacks made some foreign coverage more relevant to Americans, although much of the coverage focused on domestic issues or American concerns overseas. In recent years, coverage of foreign affairs has declined to pre-9/11 levels.

The relationship between the media and the government in foreign policy is a two-way street. First, the media can influence the government by providing policymakers with pertinent information. Policymakers learn much in their daily talks with journalists. This appears to have been the case during the operations in Somalia and Haiti, when the military commanders learned a lot about what was going on around them from reporters and CNN.[35] Second, the media can stimulate changes in elite attitudes, which are then dispersed throughout society. The coverage of the famine in Somalia in 1991, for example, appears to have had an impact on President George H. W. Bush, who decided that the United States must do something to help. He then sold this policy to the American public.[36] Third, the media can create foreign policy issues that the government must deal with. By focusing the public's attention on a problem, such as pictures of a dead American soldier being dragged through the streets in Somalia in October 1993, the media can in a sense create a problem to which policymakers must respond quickly.

However, the government can also influence the media. Government officials can give cues to the media as to what the government leaders think is important and should be told to the public—they can leak stories or put a certain spin or interpretation on a story. Since CNN and other networks carry live news briefings, the administration can speak for hours directly to the public. The government can also restrict access to information as it has done during the war on terrorism. The media rely heavily on official sources for information on foreign affairs. Recent revelations that some reporters were secretly on the government payroll to promote administration policies, and the recognition that especially in matters of foreign affairs the government sometimes gives false news to confuse our enemies (but also potentially confusing us), shows how blurry the line between the media and the

government can get. On the other hand, as the media communicate even faster with the public, leaders in Washington feel the pressure to act equally quickly, which can make for hasty and less effective foreign policy.[37]

Interest Groups

The final source of domestic pressure that helps define foreign policy problems comes from interest groups. Some groups are issue focused, like Human Rights Watch, which monitors and advocates human rights policy, and USA*Engage, which generally opposes U.S. economic sanctions and supports free trade. Many groups are organized around *diaspora*, or ethnic groups in the United States, with a common ethnic or religious background or homeland. These groups lobby for foreign policies related to their countries of origin. Such groups have become increasingly active in recent years. For example, Cuban Americans lobby about U.S. policy toward Cuba, and both Jewish Americans and Arab Americans lobby for policies that affect the Middle East. Iraqi exiles also worked hard to promote the policy of "regime change" to oust Saddam Hussein from power.[38]

Organized interest groups representing the interests of big businesses that compete for defense contracts tend to be especially powerful. The interesting thing about policymaking in this area is that here the president and the Pentagon on the one hand, and members of Congress on the other hand, tend to share an interest in increased defense spending. Policy therefore tends to be made in fairly nonconfrontational ways. This mutual interest among defense groups and contractors, Congress, and the Pentagon is an example of the iron triangle policy relationship we noted in other chapters. This metaphor might be too strong, but it illustrates the roles that interest groups can play in foreign policy.[39]

Defining foreign policy problems is the business of the foreign policy actors who are influenced by interests and pressures from both inside the United States and abroad. Their goal is to focus on problems that are supported by the prevailing American ideology about our role in the world and are consistent with American values and goals. To some extent, they must work within a distinctive culture of American foreign policy. At the same time, they are buffeted by global and domestic political pressures that help to determine which foreign situations can be defined as solvable policy problems, and which cannot.

Who What How

deterrence maintaining military might so as to discourage another actor from taking a certain action

compellence using foreign policy strategies to persuade, or force, an actor to take a certain action

coercive diplomacy the calibrated use of threats of the use of force aimed to make another actor stop or undo an aggressive action

preemption action that strikes and eliminates an enemy before it has a chance to strike you

preventive war to use force without direct provocation in order to assure that a chain of events does not unfold that could put you at immediate risk at some later date

How Do We Solve Foreign Policy Problems?
Crafting solutions from strategy, diplomacy, and force

Most U.S. foreign policies are designed to influence other actors in the world to act in a manner consistent with American goals.[40] Once foreign policy makers have defined a situation as a problem, they have to make key decisions about how best to approach it and what sort of instrument to use: political, economic, or military. We explore each of these in turn, after we examine the different approaches open to policymakers.

Strategies: Deterrence, Compellence, and Preemption

Traditionally, foreign policy makers could use two accepted strategies to influence other political actors: deterrence and compellence. The goal of **deterrence** is to prevent another actor from doing something it might be expected to do.[41] Earlier in this chapter we saw that the United States spent a great deal of money on military weapons from the end of World War II until about 1989 to *deter* the Soviet Union from attacking Western Europe. The cost of the nuclear program alone from 1940 to 1996 was $5.5 trillion.[42] This is an example of deterrence because the United States employed threats to prevent the Soviets from doing something that the United States did not want them to do.

The goal of **compellence**, on the other hand, is to get another actor to do something that it might otherwise not do, such as starting a new policy or stopping an existing one.[43] For example, after the war in the Persian Gulf between Iraq and a U.S.-led multinational coalition of states, the United States wanted Iraq to stop producing weapons of mass destruction (biological, chemical, and nuclear), and to destroy the weapons it had already stockpiled. The United Nations imposed strict economic sanctions on Iraq, prohibiting other countries from trading with Iraq until compliance with the international demands was verified. When, in December 1998, the United States had reason to believe that Iraq's Saddam Hussein had resumed production of weapons of mass destruction, it began bombing raids to destroy Iraq's weapons-producing capacity.

Both economic sanctions and military strikes were foreign policies of compellence, designed to force Iraq to disarm, to increase global security, and perhaps to overthrow Saddam, thereby making democratic reform possible.

Foreign policies can deter or compel in positive or negative ways. We often refer to foreign policies as "carrots" or "sticks." A *carrot*, or positive foreign policy, is a reward or a promise to do something nice for another country, or to lift a punishment or sanction. Good examples of positive foreign policy are economic or foreign aid and increased opportunities for trade and commerce. A *stick*, or negative foreign policy, is a punishment or a threat to enact a punishment, or the withdrawal of an existing reward. The U.S. government frequently cuts off or diminishes foreign aid to countries as a form of punishment. The careful manipulation of threats of the use of force as a form of negotiation, while hoping to avoid war, is often called **coercive diplomacy**.[44]

In 2002 President George W. Bush added a third foreign policy to the mix—one that seemed to break with previous practice and with the way international law had generally been understood to that point, the so-called Bush Doctrine that we mentioned earlier. The new strategy was one of **preemption**, striking an enemy and removing it from action before it has the chance to strike you. The administration used the word *preemption*, indicating the need to act now to stop an *immediate* and imminent threat, but the strategy may be better thought of as waging **preventive war**, waging war now so as to prevent a sequence of events that *could* pose a threat later. Bush's strategy was based on the idea that some enemies cannot be deterred or compelled to act appropriately because they are motivated by implacable hate for the United States. If we know that such an enemy, either a hostile state or a stateless entity like a terrorist network, has the means to attack the United States or U.S. interests and to do horrible damage—using weapons of mass destruction such as chemical or biological weapons, for example—then there is no point in waiting for them to strike first. In fact, Bush's position was that the United States had a duty to act first in such a situation, lest America and the world suffer the consequences of inaction. Bush asserted that he was willing to act preemptively and unilaterally, if necessary, to prevent such first strikes.

The new strategy was announced shortly after Bush had asked the United Nations to pass a resolution allowing force

Assisting in Recovery

Former presidents Bill Clinton and George W. Bush are taken by Haitian president Rene Preval, center, on a tour of Port-au-Prince, Haiti, after the nation suffered a devastating earthquake on January 12, 2010. The U.S. government mobilized aid to Haiti within hours of the earthquake's strike, and President Obama pledged $100 million in aid. Such assistance is not entirely altruistic, as it can help promote a positive image of the United States and encourage political stability, which is especially important in a nation situated in such close proximity to the United States.

to be used to remove Saddam from power in Iraq, again for his failure to allow weapons inspections and, it was thought, for continuing to develop those weapons. In a 2002 document titled "The National Security Strategy of the United States of America," Bush made it clear, however, that he would act alone if the United Nations failed to approve the action. The policy was immediately controversial, as critics both at home and abroad pointed out that it set a dangerous precedent and argued that Bush should not ignore his allies. Many critics of the plan worried that it put tremendous pressure on the government to "get it right" when it comes to intelligence, and to get it right early—since there's no time to wait. Others were concerned that it could lead to a dangerous new reality in international relations, in which "shooting first and asking questions later" becomes the new norm. Nevertheless, Bush was resolved to act, and the new policy of preemption was put into effect in Iraq in 2003, although it turned out, in retrospect, that Saddam had not in fact begun his nuclear, biological, and chemical weapons programs again as had been feared.

propaganda the promotion of information, which may or may not be correct, designed to influence the beliefs and attitudes of a foreign audience

diplomacy the formal system of communication and negotiation between countries

Foreign Policy Instruments

Once leaders in Washington decide to make a foreign policy, they can take a wide range of actions.[45] That is, once the president or Congress has decided to deter, compel, or preempt a country and has decided to use a positive or negative action, a menu of practical options is open to them. These actions can be grouped into three main categories: political, economic, and military. Preemptive action is likely to be exclusively military. Each category contains several instruments.

Political Instruments

Political instruments include propaganda, diplomacy, and covert operations. **Propaganda** is the promotion of information designed to influence the beliefs and attitudes of a foreign audience. The hope behind American propaganda is that the people of the targeted foreign country will view America more favorably or will apply pressure on their government to act more democratically. Propaganda is a form of communication that can be conducted via the media—radio broadcasts, television, film, pamphlets—or through scholarly exchanges, such as speaking tours of Americans abroad or tours given to foreign officials visiting the United States. American efforts at what is sometimes called "public diplomacy" are relatively new. The Voice of America began broadcasting in 1942, Radio Free Europe (to Eastern Europe) in 1951, and Radio Liberty (to the Soviet Union) in 1953. Much of U.S. propaganda is the responsibility of the United States Information Agency (USIA), also established in 1953.[46] More recent additions to American propaganda efforts are Radio Marti and TV Marti, directed toward Cuba, and now, Radio Free Afghanistan.

Diplomacy, formal communication and negotiation between countries, is a second political tool—perhaps the oldest political tool of the United States. The State Department is primarily responsible for American diplomatic activities.[47] Diplomats perform a variety of functions. They represent America at ceremonies abroad, gather information about what is going on in foreign countries, and conduct negotiations with foreign countries. Diplomats can often be recognized in media accounts by titles like "ambassador," "special envoy," and "special representative."

Diplomacy is a tricky business in many ways, including the decision of whether or not to talk to those nations we view as enemies, as we discussed in the *What's at Stake?* at the

> *covert operations* undercover actions in which the prime mover country appears to have had no role

> *foreign aid* assistance given by one country to another in the form of grants or loans

beginning of this chapter. But even when we know we want to open communications, spreading Washington's message abroad and correctly interpreting other countries' messages can be difficult. A recent example may be seen in the June 2009 speech that President Obama gave at Cairo University in Egypt, designed to give a fresh start to relations between the United States and the world's 1.5 billion Muslims. Obama said there is no inherent competition between America and Islam; many in the Muslim world welcomed his speech, even if some saw it as unconvincing.[48] The importance of diplomacy has been lessened today by two important developments: the technological revolution in communications and transportation, and increasing scrutiny by the media. Faster communications mean that if an American president wants to talk to the French prime minister, the German chancellor, or the Russian president, all he needs to do is pick up the phone. Indeed, following the attacks of September 11, Russian president Vladimir Putin was the first to call President Bush to offer his sympathies and support. Faster transportation means that the secretary of state or the secretary of defense or the president can fly anywhere at any time when negotiations or meetings need to take place within hours. These technological developments have made *shuttle diplomacy* possible as heads of state or their personal envoys travel back and forth to deal directly with one another and have to some extent taken the professional diplomats out of the loop.

Broader publicity as a result of greater media attention has also diminished the effectiveness of diplomacy. Sometimes diplomacy needs to be started, if not undertaken completely, in secret. Secrecy allows the diplomats to explore various bargaining positions without initially having to worry about whether those positions are politically feasible and publicly supported back home. Today, that secrecy is much harder to obtain. For instance, the constant publicity around the peace process in the Middle East provides leaders with opportunities to score points with their constituencies rather than buckle down and hammer out an agreement.

A final type of political tool, one with potential military implications, *covert operations* are undercover actions in which the United States is a primary mover, although it does not appear to have had any role at all. The main ingredients in a covert operation are secrecy (the covert part) and the appearance that the U.S. government has nothing to do with the action. The CIA is the American agency primarily charged with conducting covert operations, although in recent years the Defense Department has become more engaged in this

area as well. Covert operations can take several forms.[49] Efforts to assassinate foreign leaders are one example. Perhaps the leader most often on the receiving end of such efforts is Fidel Castro, who came to power in Cuba in 1959. However, the United States and many other countries view such actions as ineffective, with the added disincentive of seeming to invite retaliation on their own chief executives. President Gerald Ford banned such efforts by executive order in 1976. As a result, despite calls to assassinate Saddam Hussein, such an attempt was never implemented.

Covert operations also involve efforts to change the governments of countries the United States does not like, by facilitating a coup d'état—an internal takeover of power by political or military leaders—against the ruling government. Examples include the overthrows of the Iranian prime minister Mohammad Mosaddeq in 1953 and of Chilean president Salvador Allende in the early 1970s. A final example of covert political operations is meddling in foreign countries' elections, for example, by giving money to a political party for the purpose of helping U.S.-preferred candidates to win and keeping others out of power. In recent years we have seen more examples of what might be called "overt covert operations," that is, policies designed to force political change inside another country that in the past would have been secret, or covert, but that now are carried out very publicly. Efforts to aid dissidents in Iran or in Cuba, for example, are now well-known by Americans and the governments that are the targets of the programs.

The secrecy of covert operations is worth touching on because, more than any other instrument of foreign policy available to U.S. policymakers, this policy instrument seems to be at odds with democratic principles—aside from the fact that covert operations often involve illegal or unethical undertakings. Only beginning in the 1970s did the media and Congress begin to seek out information on covert operations. In 1980 President Carter signed into law the Intelligence Oversight Act, which was intended to keep Congress informed. If anything, the bits of information that do surface have contributed to the increasing public opinion that conspiracies abound in American politics.

Economic Instruments

We have already touched briefly on the two basic economic instruments available to foreign policy makers: foreign aid and economic sanctions (see Figure 19.3). **Foreign aid** is economic aid or military assistance from the United States (or other

> **Marshall Plan** America's massive economic recovery program for Western Europe following World War II

Figure 19.3

U.S. Foreign Policy Economic Instruments

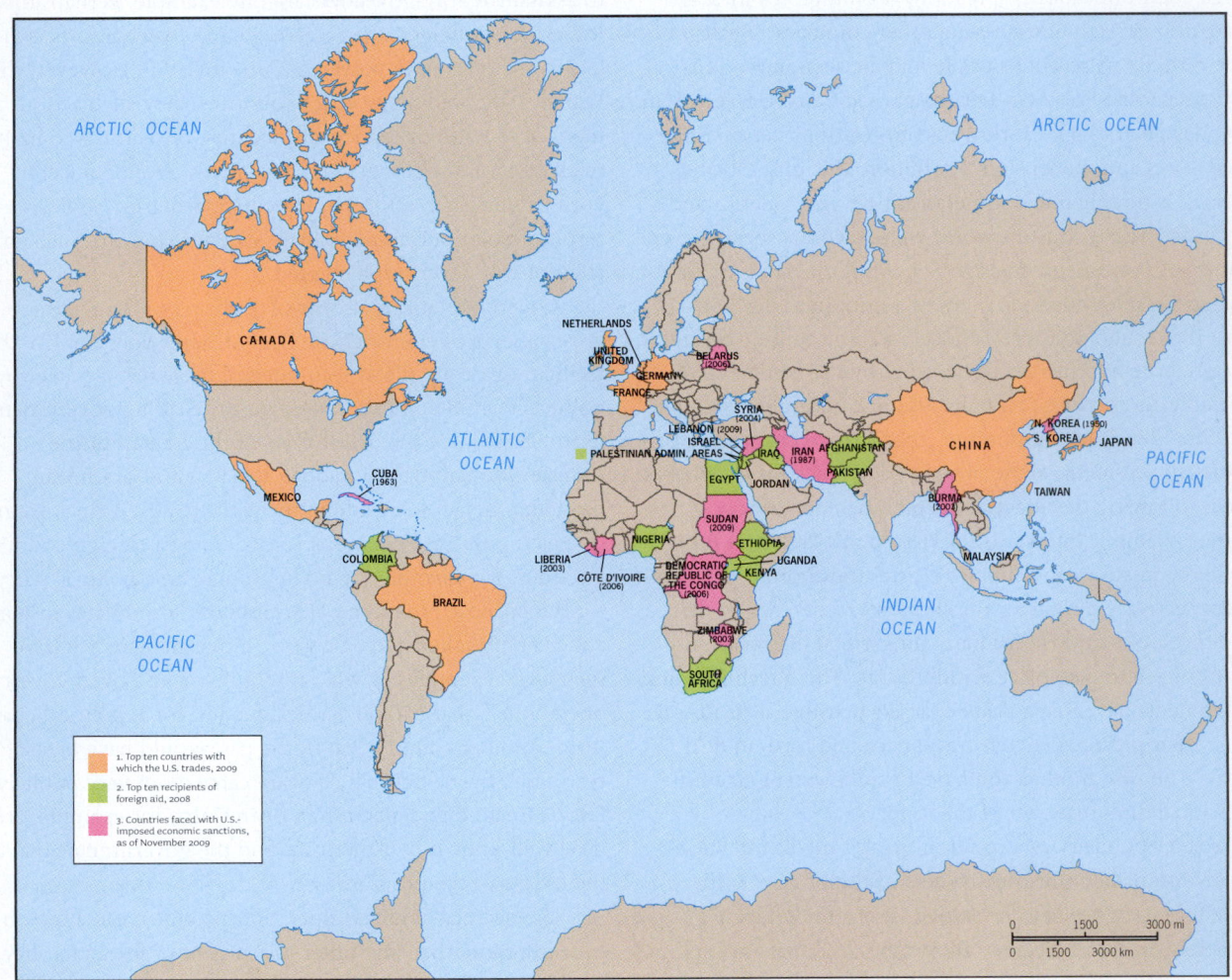

1. Top ten countries with which the U.S. trades, 2009
2. Top ten recipients of foreign aid, 2008
3. Countries faced with U.S.-imposed economic sanctions, as of November 2009

Source: Steven W. Hook, *U.S. Foreign Policy*, 3rd ed. (Washington, D.C.: CQ Press, 2011).

countries) to poorer states; here we focus primarily on economic aid. Foreign aid became a major part of U.S. foreign policy after World War II when the United States instituted the **Marshall Plan**. The war had devastated the economies of Western Europe, and with the consolidation of power by the Soviet Union in Eastern Europe, leaders in Washington worried that economic instability would contribute to political instability and open the door to communism in the West as well. Economic aid would bolster the European economies and thus prevent the spread of communism. The Marshall Plan announced by Secretary of State George Marshall in June 1947 was the first major economic aid package designed to help the ruined economies of Europe recover. While the plan was extended to the Soviets, the United

States knew the Soviet Union, with its communist economy, would not accept the capitalist recovery plan. Indeed, the Soviets rejected the plan and forced their newly acquired Eastern European satellites to join them. Thus the Marshall Plan covered only Western Europe, and the Cold War division of Europe was made even more distinct.

Since the Marshall Plan days, the United States has given money and assistance to many countries around the world. Economic aid comes in three forms: grants, loans, and technical assistance. Grants are gifts of aid. Loans are monies that must be paid back (at least in theory) to the United States, though usually at very good interest rates (much lower than you get on your Visa card). Technical assistance is the sending

> **economic sanctions** restrictions on trade imposed on one country by another state or group of states, usually as a form of punishment or protest

> **embargo** the refusal by one country to trade with another in order to force changes in its behavior or to weaken it

of knowledgeable people to help with economic projects (such as construction, agriculture, and technology).

The United States gives foreign aid to strengthen foreign countries; to pursue development goals—such as improving a nation's health care system, education system, or agricultural output; to promote international stability; and for humanitarian reasons. Note, however, that there is a good deal of self-interest behind foreign aid even though we sometimes think of the giving of foreign aid as an altruistic act.[50] For example, the United States has been a major donor to Pakistan following the terrible floods that hit that country in summer 2010. Much of that aid is aimed at addressing the risk of disease that follows such a tragedy among the survivors. This aid is not only about helping Pakistanis hit hard by a natural disaster—a worthwhile goal and altruistic act. It is also about trying to make sure that Pakistan (which has a nuclear arsenal and is a key ally for U.S. efforts in Afghanistan and is also locked in a long dispute with India over Kashmir) is able to get back on its feet and not to allow conditions to emerge that might help fuel radical elements in the country that are trying to destabilize the government. Many Americans believe we give too much aid. However, this is in part because many Americans think that the U.S. government gives much more aid than it actually does. For instance, in one study, Americans thought aid constituted as much as 15 percent of the federal budget, whereas in reality it is less than one percent of government spending, and U.S. spending on foreign aid as a portion of gross domestic product (GDP) puts it near the bottom of a list of major countries that give aid.[51] Furthermore, much of what we give in foreign aid comes back home because we often grant aid to countries with the provision that they buy goods and services from the United States.[52]

The second type of foreign economic instrument is **economic sanctions**. We discussed economic sanctions earlier, in our consideration of compellence policy toward Iraq. In common parlance, economic sanctions are thought of as negative sanctions—that is, as a punishment imposed on a nation, such as the economic sanctions enacted by the United States against Cuba in 1960 in an effort to destabilize the Castro regime. During the period 1914–1990, the United States enacted seventy-seven sanctions on various countries, or about one per year.[53] Economic sanctions have become a major foreign policy tool since the end of the Cold War. Government estimates identified sixty-one American economic sanctions between 1993 and 1996,[54] and the use of sanctions has increased in recent years.[55] The rise in sanctions may be the result of the decreasing utility of both political

tools (as noted earlier) and the increased stakes and decreased public popularity involved with the use of military force. The removal of sanctions can serve as a *carrot*, as well.

One of the most serious forms of economic sanctions is an **embargo**, or the refusal by one country to trade with another in order to force changes in the other country's behavior or to weaken it. In rare circumstances, all trade is forbidden except shipments of a purely humanitarian nature, such as medicine. This means that the country can neither export nor import goods. A classic example is the U.S. policy toward Cuba. Since Fidel Castro came to power in Cuba's 1959 revolution, the United States has imposed heavy sanctions on the communist island so close to the Florida coast. The United States currently has severe restrictions on the right of its citizens to travel to the island and allows the sale of food and medicine from U.S. firms only under special circumstances. The Bush administration tightened the sanctions policy that had been in place since Eisenhower and Kennedy were in office; the Obama administration eased some of those restrictions, but the embargo remains.

This use of embargoes and other economic sanctions raises a number of problems, however. First, for such a sanction to have real teeth, most nations must go along. If some countries refuse to observe the embargo, the targeted nation may do just fine without trading with the United States. Second, the goal of economic sanctions is to hurt the government so that it changes its policies. But negative sanctions often hurt ordinary citizens, such as Iraqis who couldn't get food and other imported items while sanctions were in effect. Third, sanctions can alienate allies. For example, U.S. efforts to enact a strong embargo against Cuba have hurt American relations with countries that trade with Cuba, such as Canada. Finally, economic sanctions, because they prohibit exports to a particular country, may deprive U.S. companies of billions of dollars of export earnings. Overall, it may be more effective to use positive sanctions as a tool of foreign policy, but giving rewards to change behavior may be politically unpalatable. For instance, many Americans cringe over our open trade relations with China, believing it rewards that country for its many human rights violations.

Military Instruments

The final instrument of foreign policy available to policymakers in Washington is military power. With the Cold War over, the United States has emerged as the most powerful military state in the world, possessing a wide range of technologically sophisticated weapons systems and developing new

> **nuclear triad** the military strategy of having a three-pronged nuclear capability, from land, sea, or air

technologies for the battlefields of the future. This military might has not been inexpensive to build and maintain. Every year the United States spends hundreds of billions of dollars on defense: defense spending for 2010 will exceed $700 billion, when you add to the baseline budget the cost of operations in Afghanistan and Iraq (which is budgeted separately) and the cost of defense programs that are in other parts of the federal budget. This is almost as much as the rest of the world spends on defense combined.[56]

Military power can be used for its threat value, to deter or compel an adversary, or to strike preemptively or in retaliation for an attack on us. The United States has used its military in a variety of interventions, from small-scale conflicts such as bombing Libya in 1986 to all-out war in Iraq in 2003. Every postwar president has sent U.S. troops to fight abroad (see Table 19.1). These troops have been called into service most recently in Afghanistan and Iraq.

Interestingly, the commitment to such a large military is a relatively new phenomenon in American history. The United States has always been distrustful of a large standing peacetime military. British occupation in the American colonies fed the American conviction that there should not be an army during peacetime. Thus Americans mobilized large armies when needed, as at the outset of the two world wars, and demobilized the troops after those wars ended. President Truman was one of the first to believe that America should stay active in world affairs after World War II, and to argue for a large and permanent military. Nevertheless, skepticism continued, prompting President Dwight Eisenhower to warn about the growing influence of a *military-industrial complex* in his presidential farewell address in January 1961.

In addition to a huge army, the United States also possesses the most sophisticated weapons of war. The United States was the first, and currently is the largest, nuclear power in the world. America developed atomic weapons during World War II and dropped two of the bombs on Japan, at Hiroshima and Nagasaki, in August 1945, bringing an end to the war in the Pacific. American scientists quickly developed an even more powerful successor: the hydrogen bomb, also known as a nuclear bomb.

The U.S. arsenal today still revolves around the notion of the **nuclear triad**. Like three legs of a stool, some nuclear weapons are based on land (on intercontinental ballistic missiles), some at sea (on missiles on board submarines), and some in the air (to be dropped by aircraft like the B-2 Stealth bomber). In addition, nuclear warheads can be attached to cruise missiles that can be launched from the ground, sea, or air. The idea is that even if one of these legs were destroyed or disabled by an enemy, the others would still be able to retaliate against attack. This swift and assured retaliation is meant to deter an attack on the United States from ever happening in the first place.

U.S. nuclear weapons, the backbone of a policy of mutual assured destruction, or MAD—may actually have helped keep the peace between the Americans and Soviets after World War II, because the Soviets believed we would use these weapons if provoked.[57] Even though President George W. Bush and Russian president Vladimir Putin agreed in May 2002 to reduce each country's arsenal from about six thousand nuclear weapons to about two thousand (each state is likely to store many of these weapons rather than destroy them, however), and recently President Barack Obama and Russian president Dmitry Medvedev have agreed to more cuts, each country's goal remains deterrence.

Nuclear weapons, which can seem awesome because of their incredible destructive power, are relatively cheap compared to more *conventional* weapons. War on a battlefield, like the war in Iraq begun in 2003, requires more expensive elements: tanks, guns, planes, ships, and troops. The Navy, for example, is currently exploring a new combat ship that can cruise coastlines; the ship design selected will likely cost more than $450 million per ship. Each new Joint Strike Fighter costs more than $110 million, and Predator drones, armed, unmanned aircraft that have increasingly been used to strike at targets in Afghanistan and even inside Pakistan, cost $4.5 million a piece.

These weapons of war can be used to deter attacks on the United States, as well as to compel other actors to comply with American objectives.[58] Sending troops to ports of call in other countries is one way to show the world that the United States has an interest in what goes on in that country. For example, when the Chinese fired missiles into the water near Taiwan on the eve of Taiwan's 1996 presidential election, the United States sent naval ships, including an aircraft carrier, to the region to bolster Taiwan and symbolically warn the Chinese not to intervene. A second type of military compellence is sending troops or weapons to another country to demonstrate that the United States has a commitment to that country. U.S. troops in South Korea contribute to the security of that state by making North Korea think twice about an invasion, although our presence is not always foolproof against that volatile country's own internal politics.

Table 19.1

Presidential Uses of Force Since 1981

President	Year	Place	Action	U.S. Deaths
Reagan	1981	Libya	Shot down Libyan warplanes over Gulf of Sidra	0
Reagan	1982	Egypt	Deployed troops to the Sinai buffer zone between Egypt and Israel	0
Reagan	1982	Lebanon	Deployed Marines to assist the withdrawal of Palestinian Liberation Organization forces	0
Reagan	1982	Lebanon	Deployed forces as part of multinational peacekeeping force	273
Reagan	1983	Egypt	Deployed AWACS radar planes after Libya bombed a city in Sudan and invaded northern Chad	0
Reagan	1983	Grenada	Invaded in order to topple leftist government and to protect American students	19
Reagan	1986	Libya	Engaged Libyan ships and missiles in clash over extent of Libya's territorial waters	0
Reagan	1986	Libya	Used air strikes to retaliate for terrorist activity	2
Reagan	1987	Persian Gulf	Engaged Iranian naval vessels	0
Reagan	1987	Persian Gulf	Attacked Iranian (armed) oil-drilling platform	0
Reagan	1988	Persian Gulf	Attacked Iranian (armed) oil-drilling platforms and naval vessels	0
Reagan	1988	Persian Gulf	Engaged Iranian naval craft and (mistakenly) shot down Iranian commercial jetliner	0
Reagan	1988	Persian Gulf	Engaged Iranian naval vessels	0
Bush	1989	Philippines	Provided air support to suppress rebellion	0
Bush	1989	Panama	Invaded to topple and arrest Manuel Noriega	23
Bush	1990	Saudi Arabia	Deployed troops in Operation Desert Shield	84
Bush	1991	Kuwait	Launched Operation Desert Storm to force Iraqi forces to withdraw from Kuwait	299
Bush	1992	Somalia	Started Operation Restore Hope to provide relief	43
Clinton	1993	Balkans	Authorized U.S. participation in enforcing no-fly zone over Bosnia-Herzegovina	0
Clinton	1993	Macedonia	Sent ground troops to join UN forces	0
Clinton	1993	Iraq	Attacked Baghdad with cruise missiles in retaliation for alleged Iraqi plot to assassinate George H. W. Bush	0
Clinton	1993	Haiti	Enforced UN blockade of Haiti with naval forces	4
Clinton	1995	Bosnia	Participated in air operations, then "IFOR," a NATO-led multinational force	1
Clinton	1998	Iraq	Launched air strikes (continuing)	0
Clinton	1999	Kosovo	Launched air strikes	0
Bush	2001	Afghanistan	Launched Operation Enduring Freedom	1,398
Bush	2003	Iraq	Launched Operation Iraqi Freedom	4,427

Source: Adapted from John T. Rourke, Ralph G. Carter, and Mark A. Boyer, *Making American Foreign Policy*, 2d ed. Copyright © 1996 by Times Mirror Higher Education Group, Inc. Reprinted by permission of Dushkin/McGraw-Hill, a division of the McGraw-Hill Companies, Inc. Updated by the authors.

peace dividend the expectation that reduced defense spending would result in additional funds for other programs

terrorism an act of violence that targets civilians for the purpose of provoking widespread fear that will force government to change its policies

Much of the violence that U.S. policymakers must contend with does not fit the model of armies squaring off on a battlefield with defined limits between combatants and noncombatants. Civil wars inside countries like the former Yugoslavia in the mid-1990s and situations where a government faces ongoing violent resistance from organized groups inside its borders, like Colombia in 2002, are just two examples of complicated challenges that U.S. policymakers face. Carrying on a counterinsurgency campaign in Afghanistan is another obvious example of the complexity of current military operations. The use of force in these settings tends to revolve around *unconventional* means, like sniper attacks against a larger military force, or bombing runs on a force's supply depots.

The United States has often tried to stay out of these situations, in part because our military structure is not as well suited to this kind of activity as it is to conventional warfare. The case of Somalia, where a peacekeeping mission led to gruesome U.S. casualties (the subject of the 2001 film *Blackhawk Down*), serves to underscore these difficulties.

Special Operations Command in the Pentagon centralizes control over the various units in the armed forces—such as the Army Rangers, the Navy SEALS, and groups that focus on *psychological operations*—that prepare to fight in these unconventional environments. Indeed, the Pentagon has paid increasing attention to the means of unconventional warfare and has employed many of those means recently, notably in Afghanistan. The use of remotely piloted, unmanned drone aircraft, for example, in both reconnaissance missions and to attack targets in dangerous areas, has increased dramatically in recent years both in Afghanistan and in Pakistan.

Many observers believed that the end of the Cold War would bring about a *peace dividend*, a surplus of money formerly spent on defense that could be shifted into social issues. Early efforts to shrink the military and redefine its role in the post–Cold War world proved contentious, however. Many people are dependent on the military for jobs, and whole communities and local economies are founded on nearby military bases. And who was to say that no new threats would arise, only to find a complacent America disarmed and unready?

The attacks of September 11 appear to have closed this debate for the moment; the defense budget seems certain to continue to rise in order to fund an ongoing war against terrorism, to replenish materiel used or damaged in the wars in Afghanistan and Iraq, and to bring into the arsenal a new generation of sophisticated weapons. Nevertheless, even Defense Secretary Robert Gates has recently argued that the defense budget is getting too big and needs to be pared down. Policymakers, scholars, and commentators alike still ask, What should the military look like in the twenty-first century? How big should it be? What sorts of conflicts should it be prepared to wage, with what types of weapons? We discuss in the next section these and other questions that will play a large role in determining what U.S. foreign policy will look like in the future.

Who What How

American foreign policy makers have many options when it comes to creating solid, effective policies. They may choose to use strategies of deterrence, compellence, or preemption, and they may lure with a carrot or brandish a stick. The foreign policy instruments open to them are political (propaganda, diplomacy, and covert operations), economic (foreign aid and sanctions), and military (potential and actual use of force).

American Foreign Policy Today
Evolving threats and challenges

The threat environment that faces the United States today has changed dramatically since the end of the Cold War. The attacks of September 11, 2001 showed how much the kinds of threats we face had changed in just a decade, and they have continued to change since then. There is no single threat on the scale of the old Soviet nuclear today, but a variety of critical foreign policy issues and dangers still face the United States.

Terrorism

As we learned painfully on September 11, 2001, even superpowers are vulnerable to external threats. A chief foreign policy issue today is dealing with the threat of terrorism. *Terrorism* is typically defined as an act of violence that specifically targets innocent civilians for the purpose of provoking widespread fear that will force government to change its policies. Increasingly those who use terror as a tactic are not states, but rather individuals or groups (though they may

weapons of mass destruction nuclear, biological, or chemical weapons that can kill huge numbers of people at one time

superterrorism the potential use of weapons of mass destruction in a terrorist attack

rogue states countries that break international norms and produce, sell, or use weapons of mass destruction

antiterrorism measures to protect and defend U.S. citizens and interests from terrorist attacks

counterterrorism activities to stop terrorists from using force and responding when they do

have state support) who face an opponent much more powerful than they are. The U.S. government keeps a list of foreign terrorist organizations, such as al Qaeda, and a list of states that support terrorism, such as Iran and Syria.

The attacks of September 11 and al Qaeda's campaign against the United States and U.S. interests abroad provide a classic case of the new face of terrorism. The goals of these attacks were not so much to force U.S. policy change (although bin Laden's group would like to drive the United States from Arab and Muslim lands) as to provoke U.S. reaction and fuel a rebellion against our Middle Eastern allies, many of which deny their own citizens basic rights. Sometimes, however, states can use terrorist tactics against their own people as a way to quash dissent. Iraq's use of chemical warfare against minorities in that country is but one example.

Weapons of Terrorism

Terrorists have used weapons as simple as box cutters and as elaborate as bombs to kill citizens by striking undefended targets like office buildings and shopping malls. The attacks of September 11 were essentially low tech, taking advantage of security weaknesses in our open society rather than relying on advanced weaponry. There is, however, some concern that terrorists in the future may gain access to more sophisticated and dangerous **weapons of mass destruction**, including chemical, biological, and even nuclear weapons that can kill huge numbers of people in one blow. We have witnessed a biological weapons attack in the form of the anthrax spores put into the U.S. mail in 2001, and we have also seen other isolated cases of biological and chemical attacks, such as the sarin nerve gas attack on the Tokyo subway in 1995. The potential use of weapons of mass destruction in terrorist attacks has come to be called **superterrorism**[59] because of the extremely high number of casualties that would surely follow such an attack on a populated area. Approximately two dozen countries possess these kinds of weapons, and there is growing concern that some of these weapons could be bought or stolen by a terrorist group. Of particular concern to the United States are **rogue states**—countries like Iran, Syria, and a handful of others[60] that break international norms and might produce, sell, or use these destructive weapons. Some of these rogue nations have known or suspected links to terrorist organizations. A strong effort to stop the proliferation of weapons of mass destruction will likely be a hallmark of U.S. foreign policy for decades to come.

Fighting Terrorism

U.S. policy toward terrorism focuses on two fronts: anti-terror and counterterror efforts. **Antiterrorism** measures are designed to protect and defend U.S. citizens and interests from terrorist attacks. Metal detectors and other screening devices at airports and concrete barricades in front of government buildings to prevent car bombings are examples. **Counterterrorism** measures include a range of activities to stop terrorists from using force and responding when they do. Examples include using electronic means to track communications of terrorists, trying to cut off the flow of money to terrorist groups by freezing bank accounts, bombing terrorist training sites, arresting those conspiring to carry out such attacks, and arresting or bombing those who have in fact carried out terrorist attacks. In the wake of September 11, all of these kinds of steps have been taken, though the most prominent step has been the military campaign in Afghanistan against al Qaeda and the Taliban ruling forces that harbored al Qaeda and its leader, Osama bin Laden.

Fighting terrorism is complicated. When a state attacks you, you know who did it, and you have targets to hit in retaliation. And because states own targets of value, you can try to deter aggression by having your own weapons aimed at them, saying, essentially, "Don't attack me, or I'll attack you right back." Terrorists, on the other hand, usually do not provide good targets and are often willing to die for their cause. Further complicating matters is the fact that terrorist organizations, like al Qaeda, are often transnational—they exist across several states, and they can move across borders with little notice. And they often find refuge in "failed states," places where either no central government exists or the central government is powerless to control them. Much of Afghanistan was like this in the 1990s; Somalia is now, as are parts of Pakistan. It is not clear whom to threaten or attack in response to a terrorist attack waged by a stateless entity, making them very hard to deter.

In the war on terrorism, the Bush administration tried to translate the strategies of a state-based world where U.S. military could be brought to bear onto the nonstate-based world of global terrorism. By linking al Qaeda to the Taliban in Afghanistan, the Bush administration was able to respond to the September 11 attacks by taking aim against identifiable targets: not just known al Qaeda camps but also the Taliban forces and government. They tried to make a similar link to Iraq as part of the lead-up to the invasion.

Petals for Profit

For centuries Afghan farmers have grown poppies for their opium, which is then exported worldwide to fuel the international drug trade. A large percentage of the profits earned has been used to support terrorist activities in the country and globally. For this reason, the Afghan government and the U.S. military destroy the poppy fields before the flowers can be harvested. Here, Mohammed Agha has started his harvest early to try and avoid the government destroying his crop.

The Obama administration has so far continued the war in Iraq, which Obama strongly opposed as a candidate for the U.S. Senate, but with a timeline to dramatically reduce the American presence there from the 170,000 troops present during the "surge" to about 50,000 after the summer of 2010. Meanwhile, Obama has ordered an increase in troop strength in Afghanistan, which he thinks should be the focal point of the war, with about 100,000 Americans joining other NATO forces to comprise a presence of about 150,000. Obama has also ordered a change in the strategy in Afghanistan that he hopes will allow the United States to begin drawing down forces in July 2011. The increased numbers of troops are meant to target al Qaeda and the Taliban and try to provide better security for civilians in Afghanistan. Obama has also sharply increased the use of drone aircraft in Afghanistan and even inside Pakistan to target insurgents and terrorists, already launching more drone strikes in Pakistan than were launched in the entire Bush administration.[61]

Defending Ourselves at Home

Another important component of the war on terrorism is organizational and bureaucratic in nature: how do we organize our government's efforts to fight terrorism and prevent future attacks and future intelligence failures? President Bush created the Office of Homeland Security in October 2001 and appointed Pennsylvania governor Tom Ridge as its head. After initially resisting the notion, Bush proposed that the office be converted to a cabinet-level department in 2002, and, as we mentioned earlier, in March 2003 the Department of Homeland Security (DHS) was born. This new department brought together twenty-two agencies and bureaus that had been scattered across the landscape of the federal government but that all have something to do with defending the homeland and responding to emergencies. The Coast Guard was moved from the Transportation Department; the Secret Service was moved from Treasury; and FEMA, which had been an independent agency, was moved into DHS. The Immigration and Naturalization Service was moved from the Department of Justice and the Customs Service was moved from the Treasury Department; the two were reorganized to form the new offices of Citizenship and Immigration Services and also Immigration and Customs Enforcement (ICE) inside DHS. The total DHS budget for 2010 will be about $43 billion.

The purpose of DHS is to coordinate the efforts of the government's many agencies as they focus on preventing future terrorist attacks on the United States and mitigating the impact of natural disasters, as well as working with state and local governments and agencies that deal with these issues. This is a difficult task, since a variety of fairly independent agencies are involved in the process, including the intelligence community, as we discussed earlier. Traditional divisions of labor complicate the issue. For example, the CIA is not permitted to spy on domestic targets and does not typically share its information with the FBI, which is permitted to engage in such activities. The FBI, for its part, has historically tried to solve crimes after they have happened and to bring criminals to justice. It has not traditionally been involved in preventing crimes, like terrorist attacks, before they happen. To try to coordinate policymaking that deals with so many different agencies, President Bush created a Homeland Security Council built on the same principles as its older cousin, the National Security Council, as a vehicle for bringing together key officials in agencies across the government who focus at least in part on keeping the homeland safe. Because of concerns that these two security councils were too duplicative, President Obama in 2009 merged the staffs into a single unit.

The relationship between federal government agencies and state and local officials is a complicated one. Every state in the Union has some kind of office that coordinates security and emergency management, and there are now *Fusion Centers* around the country where federal, state, and local law enforcement and intelligence officials come together to share information. The FBI runs Joint Terrorism Task Forces (JTTFs) around the country that include state and local law enforcement members as well. These JTTFs have made the news recently with the arrests of several people around the country charged with aiding terrorist organizations. Still, the botched bombing at Times Square in spring 2010 by Faisal Shahzad and the failed attempt by Najibullah Zazi to detonate a bomb on a Northwest Airlines flight in Detroit on Christmas Day 2009 show how difficult it is to coordinate this system to prevent all terrorist attacks. Thankfully, and luckily, neither of these attacks worked as planned.[62] The job of providing

security at home poses a number of difficult trade-offs, not only between intelligence gathering and law enforcement but also, as we indicated in earlier chapters, between national security and civil liberties. Resolving these trade-offs in ways that keep us both safe and free is one of the primary challenges of the future. (See the box "International and Homegrown Terrorism.")

Conflicts and Alliances

Now that the Cold War is over, the East-West split no longer defines world politics, and old alliances are not necessarily relevant to the new world order. The **North Atlantic Treaty Organization (NATO)**, formed in 1949 and dominated by the United States, was designed to defend Europe from the Soviets and was a quintessential part of our containment policy. The Soviets initiated their own military alliance—the Warsaw Treaty Organization (or Warsaw Pact) to counter NATO. Since the end of the Cold War, the Warsaw Pact is gone, but NATO lives on—so much so, in fact, that in 1999 it admitted to membership the Czech Republic, Hungary, and Poland, all former Warsaw Pact members. In 2004 more countries from the old "other side" joined NATO: Bulgaria, Estonia, Latvia, Lithuania, Romania, Slovakia, and Slovenia; in 2008 Croatia and Albania joined, bringing the total to twenty-eight members. NATO's expansion and recent missions in Bosnia, Kosovo, and Afghanistan show that it is trying to add to its original defensive mission to include an ability to create order beyond the borders of Western Europe.[63] Still, the 2008 crisis between Georgia and Russia over the status of Ossetia, as well as the controversy over adding Ukraine to NATO, underscores that old tensions between the West and Russia have not disappeared entirely. Although no new Cold War is in the offing, the potential for deep disagreements between the United States and NATO on the one hand, and a stronger, oil-rich Russia on the other, can still be dangerous.

Today the world is focused on other regional conflicts that were once dwarfed or silenced by Cold War politics but that now clearly have consequences for all nations. These include conflicts in the Middle East, Kashmir, Darfur and other parts of Africa, Korea, the former Yugoslavia, and Chechnya.[64] It is difficult to predict where these conflicts might arise in the future, let alone predict in which ones we might become involved, but it is a safe bet that events like those in Bosnia, Somalia, Rwanda, and Kosovo will recur. Although it is not in the power of the United States to solve all of the world's

▶ International and Homegrown Terrorism

There was a time, not that long ago, when it was easier to know who your enemy was when it came to terrorists. Both in political science and in everyday use, we used to distinguish between *international terrorism* on the one hand, and *domestic* or *homegrown* terrorism on the other. A classic definition of terrorism is that it is actions taken by people who intend to create fear in others as a way of influencing policy change. International terrorism that targeted U.S. interests was usually motivated by a perceived grievance and carried out overseas. For instance, in the 1980s the Abu Nidal Organization (ANO) carried out attacks in Europe and the Middle East, including a simultaneous assault on the Israeli airline El Al's counters at the Rome and Vienna airports in 1985 that killed nineteen people, among them several Americans.[1] ANO targeted Italy and Austria because of their support for both the state of Israel and the Palestine Liberation Organization, an ANO rival for representation of the Palestinian cause.

Because of the United States' strong influence around the world, American casualties, be it in citizens or symbols, have often been a goal for terrorist groups based overseas. A more recent example is Osama bin Laden's founding of the international terrorist group al Qaeda in the late 1980s. Chief among the group's goals is to drive the West, particularly the United States, from Arab and Muslim lands.[2] At al Qaeda's peak, with the attacks of September 11, 2001 that killed nearly three thousand people, it was a relatively tightly controlled organization run out of Afghanistan by Osama bin Laden and Ayman al-Zawahiri. The 9/11 attacks were the first time an overseas terrorist group hit the United States on its own shores.

Domestic or homegrown terrorism has been driven by people born and raised right here, motivated by domestic concerns to create policy change inside the United States. The Ku Klux Klan, for example, in the late nineteenth century used acts of terror against African Americans to induce them not to engage in rights to which the Constitution and U.S. policy entitled them, such as voting. Other domestic extremists feel violence is justified to overthrow what they perceive to be an illegitimate government. Timothy McVeigh bombed the Alfred P. Murrah Federal Building in Oklahoma City, Oklahoma, in 1995, killing 168 people and injuring hundreds more, because of his belief that the federal government was violating the U.S. Constitution. In other cases, doctors who perform abortions have been killed or threatened with violence as a way to intimidate physicians out of providing abortions. As you can see from these examples, the people considered to be international terrorists and domestic terrorists have been very different kinds of actors with very different motivations.

This classic distinction may no longer be valid, however.[3] By most accounts, after nearly ten years of military, paramilitary, economic, and diplomatic pressure by the United States and many other countries, al Qaeda is not the organization it once was. While Osama bin Laden hides out in a remote location, likely in Afghanistan or Pakistan, terrorism watchers argue that a second version of al Qaeda has emerged. This new incarnation, instead of masterminding and carrying out attacks, aims to inspire others to mount their own assaults against the United States and the West, including small-scale attacks within the United States. Instead of running training camps in Afghanistan, al Qaeda now relies on the Internet to reach a wider audience

problems, many observers would argue that the United States is in a unique position to be able to bring disputing parties to the table for negotiation and, it is hoped, to reach a peaceful settlement. Especially in a conflict like that between India and Pakistan, where both parties have nuclear weapons, the costs of standing by while countries go to war can be very high.

It is not clear what will trigger future U.S. involvement— whether preventing violence against regional inhabitants will be enough to cause the United States to intervene, or whether the violence must threaten some important U.S. goals or allies in order to push us to act.[65] Our need for help from allies in dealing with Iraq, Afghanistan, Iran, and North Korea, for instance, creates constraints on other choices an administration might wish to make concerning states like Syria, Pakistan, Turkey, and other Persian Gulf states like Qatar, as well as our European allies. The way we try to cultivate allies in the Middle

East to deal with Iraq and Afghanistan can also have implications for the politics of the Israeli-Palestinian conflict, since not all of these potential allies are partners with us in the peace process. It is too soon to know how the new partnerships formed to wage war on terrorism will affect the calculus used by U.S. policymakers in determining when and how to intervene with diplomacy as well as force. As an example of how complicated this can get, perhaps no other partner is more central to the U.S. mission in Afghanistan than Pakistan, yet Pakistan is locked in a struggle with India over Kashmir, and India—as a democracy in the region—is also an important friend of the United States. Most U.S. policymakers see Afghanistan as more important to our interests than Kashmir, but Pakistan probably sees it the other way around. And both India and Pakistan have a nuclear arsenal. Balancing these interests and commitments is the age-old challenge of statecraft.

and provide basic training, such as in basic bomb-making, to those wishing to take up its cause. The Internet truly has a global reach, and al Qaeda supporters today are as likely to be in the United States as anywhere else in the world.[4]

In 2009, as many as twenty-four men living in the United States were charged with terrorism-related activities, including Najibullah Zazi, an Afghan immigrant driver in Denver; David Coleman Headley, a Pakistani American from Chicago; and five men from Virginia who are accused of having sought training in Pakistan to fight U.S. soldiers in Afghanistan.[5] One of the most violent recent incidents of domestic terrorism is the case of Army major Nidal Malik Hasan, a Palestinian American medical officer and a rigidly observant Muslim who made no secret of his opposition to the U.S. wars in Iraq and Afghanistan. Hasan went on a shooting spree at the army base at Fort Hood, Texas, on November 5, 2009, killing thirteen.[6] In another example, Kevin Lamar James, radicalized in California's Folsom prison, set about to recruit others to help him assemble plans for terrorist strikes in the United States. Michael C. Finton was arrested in 2009 for trying to blow up a federal building in Springfield, Illinois. And Paul Rockwood, a former National Weather Service employee in King Salmon, Alaska, and his wife, were charged recently with terrorism-related activities.[7] Many of the people in these examples were inspired to action as a result of exposure to exhortations from terrorist groups overseas. The line between international and domestic terrorists in the twenty-first century has become decidedly blurry.

While the threat to people and property from these homegrown terrorists is one problem, to be sure, another problem is what the government ought to do—or even can do—about it. For instance, thousands of people travel to Pakistan from the United States every year for perfectly legitimate reasons. Should U.S. officials track everyone who goes to Pakistan just in case they join up with a terror group or receive terrorist training while they are there? Even if the United States cracks down on people traveling to places with known terrorist activity, what do we do about the very real likelihood that the terrorists-in-training will avoid direct travel to suspect locales, making it difficult for U.S. officials to know their end destinations until, perhaps, it's too late. Exacerbating the threat is the fact that would-be homegrown terrorists don't have to travel anywhere, because the Internet can provide training for them here at home. The reality is that we can't "LoJack" everyone. So how do we keep the republic safe against this new evolving threat?

1. U.S. Department of State, *2008 Country Reports on Terrorism, Foreign Terrorist Organizations*, www.state.gov/s/ct/rls/crt/2008/122449.htm.
2. See, e.g., Jayshree Bajoria and Greg Bruno, "Backgrounder: al-Qaeda," December 30, 2009, Council on Foreign Relations, www.cfr.org.
3. See Raleigh Wilson, "U.S. Counterterrorism and Islamic Jihad." Working Briefing from Self-Designed Senior Capstone, Department of Political Science, Miami University, April 2010.
4. Peter Bergen and Katherine Tiedemann, "The Almanac of Al Qaeda: FP's Definitive Guide of What's Left of the Terrorist Group," *Foreign Policy*, May/June 2010, www.foreignpolicy.com/articles/2010/04/26/the_almanac_of_al_qaeda.
5. Andrea Elliot, "The Jihadist Next Door," *New York Times Sunday Magazine*, January 31, 2010, www.nytimes.com/2010/01/31/magazine/31Jihadist-t.html?ref=magazine&pagewanted=print.
6. Ibid; Bergen and Tiedemann.
7. Kim Murphy, "Terrorism Case Baffled Remote Alaska Town," *Los Angeles Times*, July 23, 2010, http://articles.latimes.com/2010/jul/23/nation/la-na-adv-alaska-terrorists-20100723–1.

Free Trade Versus Protectionism

The global economic crisis reminds us that economics stands alongside security issues at the heart of day-to-day foreign policy. The central economic issues for the United States are the global competitiveness of the U.S. economy, which is strengthened through both domestic and foreign economic policy, and the price of oil, which has huge implications for the strength of the U.S. economy. How the United States reacts to trade pressures, for example, is critical. Every country wants to maximize its exports while minimizing its imports. Exports make money; imports cost money. The United States has a number of ways to try to cajole foreign countries to sell more American goods abroad, and it could also take steps to try to limit imports at home. However, such protectionist measures can spark other countries to behave likewise, ultimately hurting trade for everyone.

Another critical issue is how we deal with regional trading blocs. The United States has to compete with a trade bloc in Europe—the European Union, twenty-seven nations that have agreed to merge their economies and use a single currency—and a series of competitive economies in Asia. So as not to be at a relative disadvantage, the United States set up NAFTA with Canada and Mexico. Establishing a North American trade group seemed to make sense not only for domestic economics but for foreign economic policy as well.[66] But good economics does not always make good politics. NAFTA is very controversial at home because loosening trade barriers with Canada and Mexico has made it easier for American jobs to go south, where labor costs are cheaper, and many critics worry that NAFTA has accelerated environmental degradation (see Chapter 18).

This movement toward free trade is not without its detractors, especially now that the global capitalist system has been rocked by crisis. Meetings to promote more free trade, such as the 2001 Summit on a Free Trade Area of the Americas in Quebec City and the 1999 meeting of the WTO in Seattle, met with fervent and even violent protests; the 2010 meeting of the G-20 in Toronto was also the target of significant protests. Those who oppose more free trade come from a variety of perspectives. Some are concerned about the impact of global capitalism on local development around the world, some about the impact on the environment, and some about workers' rights. And some simply protest the loss of local control over local affairs that seems to come with globalization. Since these summits are often held behind closed doors, many people protest the lack of democracy involved in the process of moving toward more free trade. The latest global round of talks to extend the free trading system of the WTO is currently bogged down; the global financial system has been uprooted in crisis; the move toward more and more free trade, which seemed like a sure bet not that long ago, is certainly being put to the test. This controversy promises to be with us for the foreseeable future. Plus, as we discussed earlier, a world with fewer trade barriers is a world where goods and services—and jobs—can move across borders more easily and cheaply. Many Americans are against this move toward increasing free trade because of its implications for *outsourcing* jobs and thus making American workers—already under siege in a lengthy recession—less secure.

Problems Without Borders

Additional challenges facing the United States in the post–Cold War era have taken on larger prominence as the old security issues have changed. These global issues are those that do not stop conveniently at national borders: the environment, international narcotics trafficking, and transnational organized crime. Environmental problems are most notable in this respect. Problems such as global climate change affect everyone, not just Americans.[67] While the United States can take some actions to help the environment worldwide, such as trying to cut so-called greenhouse gases (emissions that promote global warming), one country acting alone cannot

Heads in the Sand
As a UN summit on climate change convened nearby in Cancun, Mexico, in December 2010, members of the Sierra Club demonstrate against the nations they feel are refusing to face the consequences of their energy policies. Environmental problems such as climate change extend beyond national borders and affect everyone, making them foreign policy issues that need to be addressed.

save the world's environment. Every country has to pitch in. This means that dealing with the issue must be a multilateral affair, involving most countries, and on the home front it must involve a combination of political and economic tools. The United States has displayed a reluctance to push the environment as a foreign policy issue. In 2001, for instance, the Bush administration refused to ratify the Kyoto Protocol, a treaty requiring the United States and other nations to reduce emissions of greenhouse gases. The administration did not like the targets that were set on how much greenhouse gases states can emit; claimed that restrictions on the United States were unfair, compared with those on developing states like India and China; and disagreed with some of the science of global warming on which the treaty was premised. The 2009 global climate conference in Copenhagen, which was supposed to develop a follow-up plan after Kyoto, ended without agreement; even steps inside the United States to deal with carbon emissions and to move toward a "greener" economy are largely stuck in Congress, the victim of partisan differences.

International narcotics dealers and organized crime, ranging from Mexican drug rings to drug producers in Afghanistan to the Russian mafia, also affect the United States. Perhaps the key question is whether fighting drugs and organized crime should be foreign or domestic policy, or both. Where should the United States meet the threat? Until recently the drug problem has been regarded as a domestic issue, and the strategy has been to treat Americans with drug addictions and to fund police and Drug Enforcement Agency efforts to stem the distribution of drugs. During the administration of George H. W. Bush, the United States got more interested in stopping drugs *before* they entered the country through interdiction, using intelligence monitoring and force to stop the flow of drugs, either by arresting the smugglers or by destroying the cargo. President Bush, for example, gave military assistance to Bolivia, Colombia, and Peru to try to compel those states to fight drugs more vigorously in their countries. Bush also authorized the invasion of Panama in 1989, in part because of President Manuel Noriega's links to the drug trade. Noriega was a longtime ally of the United States who fell out of favor because of the new emphasis on a drug war. After serving a lengthy sentence in a Florida prison, Noriega was extradited to France, where he was convicted of laundering drug money and sentenced to more time in prison. The worldwide leader in producing poppies, which are processed into heroin, is Afghanistan once again. But shutting down the poppy fields is difficult, and doing so takes away Afghanistan's major cash crop. How to balance the drug war and the war on terrorism is

another example of how complicated these issues can get. Violence by Mexican drug cartels has rocked parts of Mexico, including fancy tourist resort towns, and appears to be moving into Central America; this problem right at our border also brings these tensions quickly to the forefront.

Extending the Reach of Democracy

Finally, although much of our foreign policy is focused on issues like national and economic security, pollution, and international crime, the United States also takes an active role in promoting its ideology around the globe. Over the past few decades, the number of democracies in the world has increased dramatically as a percentage of total countries.[68] The number of democracies has, according to ratings kept by the group Freedom House, increased from fewer than 70 countries in 1986 to over 116 today, or from about 40 percent of the world's countries to about 60 percent.[69] In the last handful of years, interestingly, the number has actually declined a bit. The United States would like to see even more countries become democratic and thus has a policy of promoting democracy whenever and wherever possible. But this policy has created a number of problems for the United States. First, the United States has long believed that building a strong capitalist economy is a key step toward democracy, but encouraging capitalism often involves infusing large amounts of money into an economy. The United States doesn't seem to be as willing to provide that money as it was in 1947. President George W. Bush tried to increase foreign aid spending, but even these increases only restored levels to just above where they were at the beginning of the Clinton administration. President Obama would like to double foreign assistance spending by 2012, to about $50 billion, but in the midst of an economic downturn, that is politically as well as economically difficult.

A second problem associated with increased democratization is that countries that are moving toward greater democracy require support, such as impartial election monitors, advice on how to set up democratic institutions, and occasionally troops to fend off those who would push the country in a nondemocratic direction. A third problem arises from the fact that the United States promotes capitalism and open markets abroad as well as democracy, and some countries with capitalist economies are not particularly democratic, like China. This puts the United States in the position of having to decide whether to place a priority on capitalism or democracy.[70]

Human rights is another critical political issue facing the United States today in its support of democracy.[71] As noted

▶ Profiles in Citizenship: Joe Biden

"I've been here for eight presidents, and I'm an optimist because I know the history of the story of American progress. I mean the American people have never ever, never shied away when you've given them a vision, a challenge . . ."

In January 2011, Vice President Joe Biden visited Afghanistan to assess progress toward the transition to Afghan-led security beginning in 2011, and to demonstrate the United States' commitment to a long-term partnership with Afghanistan. (Pictured: Vice President Joe Biden and General David Petraeus tour Forward Operating Base Airborne in Wardak Province, Afghanistan, January 11, 2011). *Official White House Photo by David Lienemann.*

In the cold December that followed the 2010 midterm elections—with the 111th Congress in the waning days of its lame-duck session before the members headed home for their holiday break—the Obama administration still had a long Christmas wish list. Senate ratification of the New START Treaty with Russia was on its agenda, as were extending the tax cuts for those making under $250,000 a year and getting unemployment insurance extended for those especially hard hit by the recession. The administration wanted to repeal the "don't ask, don't tell" policy in the military and get the DREAM Act passed, which would allow kids brought to this country by parents who entered illegally to find a path to citizenship through education or military service. After what President Obama described as the "shellacking" the Democrats took in the midterm elections, no one thought he had a chance of getting any of those things done, but his administration was scrambling to end the year on a positive note.

Our interview with Vice President Joe Biden took place in the thick of the administration's negotiations with congressional Republicans over extending the tax cuts, and Biden was the negotiator-in-chief. We were slotted in for an appointment in his White House office between cabinet members who wanted to discuss the implications of agreeing to extend the Bush tax cuts for the country's wealthiest citizens, and Nancy Pelosi, then the Speaker of the House, and Harry Reid, the Senate majority leader, who were adamantly opposed to extending the tax cuts for the wealthy. The air in his White House office fizzed with power and excitement as Biden waited for a call from Senate minority leader Mitch McConnell to cement a deal that would, he argued, "save the economy from a double dip recession, make a compromise where the working poor continue to get their tax cuts even though we have to give temporarily on the upper end, where you see an increase in the stimulus that you'll end up with a million and a half more jobs than you would've next year, and where in the process we get the arms control treaty ratified and the trade deal."

Though the call didn't come while we were there, by late afternoon it would be announced that, due in large part to Biden's bargaining, the White House had gotten much of what it wanted in the tax cut deal. The repeal of "don't ask, don't tell" followed days later, as did ratification of the New START Treaty and passage of several other key pieces of legislation. While the administration didn't get everything it wanted that December—the tax cuts were extended for the wealthiest Americans as well as for those in the middle class and the DREAM Act did not pass—no one argued when President Obama hailed the lame-duck session as the most productive in decades.

That day in early December, the vice president clearly relished his role in brokering the deal that would make it possible for the rest to follow, and he was eloquent and hopeful about the possibilities of using power to good purpose. It's a great time to be in service, he said, what he called "the single greatest opportunity" in his forty years of public life. "We are in one of those inflection points in history," he says, "I don't think it's occurred in American history but three times, where . . . if we do nothing, the momentum is going to drag us in the direction that makes it increasingly more difficult to correct the course." He discusses some of the biggest challenges we face—global warming, inequalities in education, our changing economy, and our standing in the world. "So you are at one of those moments where if we get it right, this can be a truly transformational moment where you look back twenty years from now and say, we had set the course of the nation, we put it on a trajectory that puts us in the position to be able to lead the world in the twenty-first century or not."

Being a key actor in a transformational moment is a pretty heady place to be for someone who started life, as Biden often reminds people, as a working-class kid from Scranton, Pennsylvania. How he got from there to here is an unlikely story but in some ways a quintessentially American one. Biden was born to a large Irish Catholic family that moved, in time, to Delaware, but it was in his "Grandpop" Finnegan's kitchen in Scranton that he learned the first principles of politics: that no one and no group is above any other and that politics was a matter of personal honor.[1] Those themes have guided Biden's career, through his college years, law school, a stint on the New Castle County Council, and a long-shot candidacy for the U.S. Senate when he was only twenty-nine years old that launched his thirty-six years

in that institution before he joined the Obama ticket and ascended to the vice presidency in 2009.

You can tell by his face, as he talks about his career, that it has been fun. He's been thrilled at the experiences it has brought his family (a granddaughter, for instance, plays basketball with the President and his daughters), and he has the satisfaction of knowing that what he does on a daily basis makes a difference in people's lives. He says, "My dad used to have an expression, he'd say it's a lucky person that gets up in the morning, puts both feet on the floor, knows what they are about to do, and thinks it still matters."

Today, at the pivotal moment in which he serves, he is enormously hopeful that the things he will help do will matter immensely both domestically and globally. He has more power than the traditional vice presidential office that John Nance Garner (vice president to Franklin Roosevelt) once said wasn't worth a pitcher of warm spit. He is an essential liaison with Congress for the Obama administration (witness his work with McConnell on the tax cut extension) and a key adviser to the president on foreign policy and issues facing the middle class. Asked whether he can stay optimistic in the face of partisan battles at home and dire challenges abroad, he lights up. "Absolutely, I am absolutely optimistic," he says. "I've been here for eight presidents, and I'm an optimist because I know the history of the story of American progress. I mean the American people have never ever, never shied away when you've given them a vision, a challenge and you know where you want to take it. They've never let the

country down, never. That's not American exceptionalism. I would argue, as a student of history, that that's literally true, literally true; we rise to the occasion."

And the boy from Scranton is right in the middle of it. Here are some other words of advice from the Vice President:

On the importance of confidence:

Look, . . . there are a lot of advantages, people don't all show up on the playing field with the same equipment, and I'm not talking intellect. The great advantage I had is that I don't ever remember a time my parents not drilling into me—"You're a man of your word, without your word you're not a man. Joey, nobody is better than you in the whole world, you're no better but nobody is better than you." My mother gave me absolute confidence. It was a gigantic, gigantic, asset.

On keeping the republic:

I'd tell [students] to be engaged. . . . [Y]ou know that old quote from Plato, the penalty good men pay for not being engaged in politics is being governed by men worse than themselves. [Students] have nobody to blame but themselves, zero. My dad used to say never complain and never explain, and . . . that's exactly what I'd tell them . . . stop whining, get engaged. Number two, the political system is so wide open you can drive a Mack truck through it, so the idea that "Oh, God, I have to come from influence and money to have an impact?" Simply not true.

1. Joe Biden, *Promises to Keep*. (New York: Random House, 2007), xv. ■

earlier, a number of countries have ongoing civil conflicts, which invariably produce millions of refugees, as well as casualties, starvation, and disease. Aid for such human rights refugees is expensive, and Americans increasingly view this involvement with little enthusiasm.[72] Furthermore, some of the governments of countries with which the United States has close relationships are human rights violators. As we have indicated, this tension between morality and pragmatism in American foreign policy is not new and is not likely to fade. It is complicated further by the United States' own ethically controversial behavior with respect to the torture of some individuals detained during the war on terrorism. Our need for allies in the Middle East, for example, has caused us to turn a blind eye to civil rights violations in countries such as Saudi Arabia and Egypt. In the case of China, too, issues of democracy and human rights have been edged aside by economic and security issues. The genocide in Darfur is another example of how complicated these tragedies can be, because the only country with much leverage over the government of Sudan is China, and no one seems to have much leverage over it right now. On the other hand, the United States and NATO did use force in Kosovo in 1999, maintaining that Slobodan Milosevic's campaign of ethnic cleansing was a horrific violation of human rights demanding immediate and drastic action. The debate over whether to be actively engaged around the world or to pursue a more minimalist or even isolationist approach has been reopened, but no consensus exists on the proper course of American action. Witness the reactions to the use of force in Kosovo: many pundits and citizens did not see sufficient national interest to warrant the spending of American money and the risking of American lives.

The dawn of the twenty-first century finds the United States facing an array of unprecedented foreign policy issues. International terrorism, globalization, global climate change, international crime, humanitarian and environmental catastrophes, and expanding democracy pose challenges for U.S. foreign policy makers that cannot be solved with the old Cold War paradigm. U.S. policymakers must resolve inherent tensions between valued but conflicting resources in order to deal with problems and issues that transcend national borders, and they must craft solutions that reflect the new world order.

Who
What
How

The Citizens and Foreign Policy

A complex process outside the public eye

As we have seen throughout this chapter, the terrain of foreign policy is complex, dangerous, and confusing in the post–Cold War and post–September 11 era. But a related complexity is that, in the United States, policy—including foreign policy—is supposed to be made in a democratic fashion. The story of foreign policy making that we have examined here shows it to be largely an elite activity, even though elites may take public opinion into account. Much of foreign policy, at least since World War II, has been dominated by the president and the executive agencies with foreign policy authority—perhaps the least democratic and least accountable actors in American politics. The shroud of secrecy surrounding foreign policy, especially during the Cold War, has made it hard for citizens to know not only what policymakers know but even what they do in the name of the United States. It is thus difficult for citizens to evaluate their elected representatives and the important unelected actors in the bureaucracy, and to hold them accountable for their actions. This secrecy seemed necessary during the Cold War because of the obvious dangers of the nuclear age, but we should recognize that clear trade-offs were made between steps taken in the name of security (secrecy) and processes required by democracy (openness and accountability). Some of this secrecy was lifted in the wake of the Cold War, only to find new restrictions emerge in the wake of September 11, with few members of Congress even privy to the plans of the Bush administration.

The tension between foreign policy and democracy is perhaps unavoidable. *Crisis policy* is by its very nature made quickly, often out of sight, by the president and a small group of advisers. Presidents take the likely reaction of the public into account when they make crisis policy, but citizens have little input and often little information about what happened.[73] *Strategic policy* is typically made in the bureaucracy of the executive branch. While interest groups and Congress may have some voice in the process and anticipated public reaction is probably taken into account, this kind of policy too is made with little citizen input. And even *structural defense policy*, which is crafted largely in Congress with heavy input from interest groups, defense contractors, and the military, is made without a large degree of public scrutiny. So the dual challenge of keeping the republic comes into sharp focus: foreign policy must keep the republic safe, but it must also meet some meaningful democratic standard. Sometimes it is hard to know which challenge is greater.

Unfortunately, meeting a democratic standard in foreign policy making is even harder than we think. As we saw earlier in this chapter, a large part of the American public does not pay much attention to foreign policy issues and knows little about them. This makes it even more difficult to hold policymakers like the president accountable in the arena of foreign policy. Just as it would be hard for you to hold someone accountable for the job he or she is doing when you know little about how that job works, so too is it hard to hold policymakers accountable for their foreign policy acts if you have little or no information about them. The old question—Who guards the guardians?—is nowhere so complex as in the foreign policy and national security realm.

The end of the Cold War presented an opportunity to open up the foreign policy process, to cut through the shroud of secrecy that has cloaked America's foreign and security policy. The "excuse" that information could leak that might trigger World War III or lead to the global triumph of the Soviet Union was no longer plausible. The CIA and the rest of the intelligence community especially come under fire in this new era for their perceived failures. For example, despite the attention they lavished on the Soviet Union, Americans watched it crumble live on CNN with no warning from the CIA.[74] A book by former senator Daniel Patrick Moynihan, D-N.Y., makes an intriguing observation about the pernicious effects of secrecy, one worth considering here.[75] Moynihan argues that we should see secrecy as a form of government regulation—part of the list of rules and procedures for how the government works. We are in a position now when people from both political parties argue that government is too big, that it has too many rules

and regulations; it must be redesigned to have less red tape; it must be more effective and more efficient. Moynihan proposes that as we scale back other rules, we also rethink these secrecy regulations. Designed to protect the United States, over time the regulations have tended to endanger the republic more than protect it because they shut down the process of discussion and evaluation that is so important to developing wise policy. Moynihan argues that regulations be eliminated not just so that foreign policy can be more open and accountable to the public but also so that it can be made better in the future. Yet while so many people across both parties want smaller government, we have actually increased the size of government in recent years and returned to the wholesale classification of information. Legislation like the USA Patriot Act passed after the attacks of September 11 are meant to help law enforcement work better to track terrorists, but many of its provisions, and the continued heavy use of classification, can make it easier for the government to track any of us and harder for us to know what the government is doing. The 2010 release of a reported quarter-million documents on U.S. diplomatic relations, leaked to the web site WikiLeaks,[76] reminds us, if nothing else, that the government classifies tons of information that probably doesn't need to be kept secret, and that many citizens are willing to go to great lengths to combat this secrecy. Balancing security and liberty, safety and freedom, is the never-ending challenge of keeping the republic.

Thinking Outside the Box

How much should foreign policy reflect the will of the people?

▶ What's at Stake Revisited

We began this chapter by asking what is at stake when U.S. leaders decide whether or not to talk to the country's enemies. Many people argue that national leaders have to deal with the world as it is, and that includes talking to our enemies. It might be nice to ignore them, but to think that we could do so is folly, as a practical matter, and potentially dangerous.[77] Others argue that negotiating with our enemies is the more dangerous course of action, giving them a strategic asset that they would not otherwise have, and thus an advantage over us.[78] President Obama's views, and the position of his administration, are generally in line with the first position, that we need to talk, even with our enemies.

The stakes involved in this question might be the highest imaginable. If talking prevents Iran from developing nuclear weapons, then we think it was a wise thing to do. But what if we start negotiating with Raul Castro in Cuba and our negotiations serve to strengthen his antidemocratic control over Cuba, setting back the cause of democratic reform on the island? Getting the answer right on issues like this is more serious than negotiating a trade deal; it could make the difference between war and peace, life and death.

As we discussed in this chapter, the Bush administration was very opposed to negotiating with enemies like North Korea (even though toward the end of the Bush presidency we did enter into negotiations with that country). The Obama administration, on the other hand, has tried to use diplomacy and negotiations—including with our enemies—and so the president and his advisers have had the difficult task of deciding just how far they want to go down the road of direct talks with those who do not wish us well. Although Obama might wish to break with the Bush's foreign policy in critical respects, it is also true that he inherits the policies and problems of the previous administration. However much Obama might want to just "start over" on a foreign policy problem, the real world doesn't work that way.

So what have been the results of Obama's new foreign policy approach? At two years into his administration, the verdict is mixed. One measure of its effects can be seen in opinion polls of people around the world. Recent polling has suggested that the view of the United States has been more positive in many countries, including China, Germany, France, and Russia, since Obama took office; but the perception of the United States in the Arab and Muslim world remains very negative.[79] Another marker is "results." Although it is early still, some notable achievements have been made. A few examples help highlight how complicated these issues are. The United States and Russia entered into a sweeping new nuclear weapons reduction treaty, and in September 2010 a new round of peace talks began between Israel and the Palestinians. The Obama administration has begun an extensive round of negotiations with China across a range of areas, including economic issues. The removal of U.S. combat troops from Iraq is proceeding on schedule. And the renewed effort of engaged diplomacy has led to some success in moving Russia to be more helpful at confronting Iran over its nuclear program.

But in other cases the Obama approach has not borne fruit, often because of political conditions in these countries that are largely outside of our control. Obama's approach to Iran, however, has not been more successful than Bush's hard-line approach, in part because domestic politics in Iran have given its leaders an incentive to reject our advances. Similarly, the now-nuclear-armed North Korea, which is perhaps in a leadership transition from Kim Jung-Il to one of his sons, remains a big problem. Still, Obama has had some success persuading Russia and China to put pressure on both Iran and North Korea; his success is partly the result of the improved relationship between the United States and those two important countries that has followed Obama into office. Obama's hopes to restart the Middle East peace process have largely been dashed as well, partly because the current government in Israel seems to have little interest in moving forward and partly because of troubles on the Palestinian side. If anything, Afghanistan appears to be a bigger mess than we thought it was two years ago. The debate now is over whether we ought to be negotiating with part of the Taliban—our former enemy—in Afghanistan as a way to isolate the remnants of al Qaeda there and to hasten U.S. withdrawal from the country.

None of this is a ringing endorsement of the policy of talking to our enemies, but it also shows that the policy, where the Obama administration has applied it, has done no harm. On the contrary, the good will garnered by the approach may help to make coalition building among countries that were formerly our enemies a tool of our foreign policy. If that is the case, then the benefits yielded may be less a question of bringing dramatic change and more a matter of using small and incremental steps to change the environment in which our foreign policy takes place.

To Sum Up

Key terms, chapter summaries, practice quizzes, Internet links, and other study aids are available on the companion web site at http://republic.cqpress.com.

Define   Understand   Practice   Read   Click   Watch

antiterrorism (p. 739)

Bush Doctrine (p. 715)

Central Intelligence Agency (CIA) (p. 722)

coercive diplomacy (p. 731)

Cold War (p. 715)

compellence (p. 731)

containment (p. 715)

counterterrorism (p. 739)

covert operations (p. 733)

crisis policy (p. 716)

Department of Defense (p. 721)

Department of Homeland Security (p. 722)

Department of State (p. 720)

deterrence (p. 731)

diplomacy (p. 732)

director of national intelligence (p. 722)

economic sanctions (p. 735)

embargo (p. 735)

foreign aid (p. 733)

foreign policy (p. 713)

free trade (p. 727)

General Agreement on Tariffs and Trade (GATT) (p. 728)

hegemon (p. 725)

intelligence community (p. 722)

intergovernmental organizations (p. 714)

internationalism (p. 713)

International Monetary Fund (IMF) (p. 727)

isolationism (p. 713)

Joint Chiefs of Staff (p. 721)

Marshall Plan (p. 734)

most favored nation (p. 728)

multinational corporations (p. 714)

National Security Council (NSC) (p. 720)

nongovernmental organizations (NGOs) (p. 714)

North Atlantic Treaty Organization (NATO) (p. 741)

nuclear triad (p. 736)

peace dividend (p. 738)

preemption (p. 731)

preventive war (p. 731)

propaganda (p. 732)

protectionism (p. 727)

rogue states (p. 739)

strategic policy (p. 716)

structural defense policy (p. 716)

superterrorism (p. 739)

terrorism (p. 738)

Truman Doctrine (p. 718)

weapons of mass destruction (p. 739)

World Bank (p. 728)

Define   Understand   Practice   Read   Click   Watch

- Foreign policy refers to a government's goals and actions toward actors outside the borders of its territory. These foreign actors may include other countries, multinational corporations, intergovernmental organizations, nongovernmental organizations, and groups that fall outside these categories.

- Strained relations rather than actual battles marked the Cold War, waged from 1947 to 1989 between the United States and the Soviet Union. The American foreign policy of containment sought to halt the development of communism in all parts of the world. Having achieved that goal, American leaders still struggle to develop a foreign policy for the post–Cold War era and to combat global terrorism.

- There are three types of American foreign policy, each dominated by different actors. Crisis policy requires immediate decision making and is controlled by the president and his national security advisers. Strategic policy (long range) tends to be formulated within the executive branch. Structural defense policy, which deals primarily with defense spending and military bases, is most often crafted by the Defense Department and Congress, which has the ultimate authority when it comes to spending.

- The American public and its leaders since World War II have largely embraced internationalism, the active role of a country in global affairs. Internationalists endorse free trade and favor involvement in the United Nations and the World Trade Organization. Other actors, whose focus is mostly domestic, advocate both economic protectionism and isolationism from foreign affairs.
- The United States has three basic foreign policy goals: security of the homeland, economic growth, and support of democracy in the world. However, when these goals are in conflict, support for democracy has often lost out. The anarchical international system and increasing global economic interdependence ensure that security and economic problems will be top priorities.
- American foreign policy makers use many strategies and tools to create effective policy, including deterrence and compellence strategies, as well as economic tools, such as foreign aid and sanctions; political tools, such as diplomacy, coercive diplomacy, and covert operations; and, when these options fail, military action.
- Ongoing foreign policy challenges include dealing with the war on terrorism, ongoing operations in Iraq and Afghanistan, forming alliances in a post–Cold War world, protecting American interests in a global economy, managing problems without borders (like global climate change and the drug trade), and balancing pragmatic security concerns with the desire to extend democracy throughout the world.
- Tension may be unavoidable between foreign policy and democracy. Secrecy may be essential for successful foreign policy; crisis policy in particular requires both surprise and quick decision making. Democracy, on the other hand, demands openness and accountability on the part of public officials.

Define   Understand   **Practice**   Read   Click   Watch

1. **The three major types of foreign policy are**
   a. crisis policy, war policy, and peace policy.
   b. war policy, peace policy, and Cold War policy.
   c. strategic policy, nonstrategic policy, and tactical policy.
   d. crisis policy, strategic policy, and structural defense policy.
   e. defense policy, spending policy, and terrorism policy.

2. **The executive department charged with managing diplomacy and foreign affairs is the**
   a. State Department.
   b. National Security Council.
   c. Defense Department.
   d. Foreign Relations Council.
   e. Homeland Security Council.

3. **Restricting the sale of arms to countries that violate human rights would be an example of**
   a. a policy driven by economic goals.
   b. a policy based on moral concerns.
   c. policy decisions designed to reduce international conflict.
   d. a return to isolationism.
   e. disarmament.

4. **The doctrine of protectionism is defined as**
   a. the imposition of trade barriers such as tariffs to make trading conditions favorable to domestic producers.
   b. the formation of organizations such as NATO to ensure protection from military threats.
   c. civil defense policies that protect populations from attack.
   d. the policy of trying to guarantee human rights to minorities around the world.
   e. the use of military force to achieve foreign policy goals.

5. **An example of a transnational challenge to the United States is**
   a. the Arab League.
   b. the European Union.
   c. al Qaeda.
   d. Serbian nationalism.
   e. the Cold War.

Define   **Understand**   **Practice**   **Read**   **Click**   **Watch**

Allison, Graham, and Philip Zelikow. 1999. *Essence of Decision: Explaining the Cuban Missile Crisis*, 2nd ed. New York: Longman. The classic study of decision making by President Kennedy and his advisers during the Cuban missile crisis; this revised edition reflects much of the new scholarship on the crisis that has emerged since the Cold War ended.

Alter, Jonathan. 2010. *The Promise: President Obama, Year One*. New York: Simon and Schuster. One of the first assessments of the start of the Obama administration, from an insightful journalist.

Bergen, Peter L. 2011. *The Longest War: A History of the War on Terror and the Battles With al Qaeda Since 9/11*. New York: Simon and Schuster. A definitive history of Osama bin Laden's terrorist network and America's response to it by one of the journalists who has actually interviewed bin Laden.

Carter, Ralph G., and James M. Scott. 2009. *Choosing to Lead: Understanding Congressional Foreign Policy Entrepreneurs*. Durham, N.C.: Duke University Press. An excellent overview of the literature on Congress and foreign policy with some great data on the activism of both chambers and also of individual members.

Chandrasekaran, Rajiv. 2006. *Imperial Life in the Emerald City: Inside Iraq's Green Zone*. New York: Knopf. Award-winning book by a Washington Post reporter about the steps, and missteps, at the start of the U.S. occupation of Iraq. Inspired the 2010 film The Green Zone.

Clarke, Richard. 2004. *Against All Enemies: Inside America's War on Terror*. New York: Free Press. A veteran counter-terrorism expert from the Clinton and Bush years, Clarke provides a memoir that is gripping and, at times, depressing.

Crawford, John. 2005. *The Last True Story I'll Ever Tell: An Accidental Soldier's Account of the War in Iraq*. New York: Penguin. An eyewitness account of one soldier's war in Iraq, and the journey home again.

Fried, Amy. 1997. *Muffled Echoes: Oliver North and the Politics of Public Opinion*. New York: Columbia University Press. An interesting study of the relationships among policymakers, the public, and the media, seen through the lens of Oliver North and the Iran-contra scandal.

Gelb, Leslie H., and Richard K. Betts. 1979. *The Irony of Vietnam: The System Worked*. Washington, D.C.: Brookings Institution. A classic study of the roots of U.S. policy in Vietnam. Gelb and Betts reject the popular idea that Vietnam was a "quagmire" in which we got caught; rather, they argue, U.S. involvement was the predictable result of a calculated policy to "not lose this year."

Gelman, Barton. 2008. *Angler: The Cheney Vice Presidency*. New York: Penguin. Excellent book about the rise of the powerful vice presidency under Cheney, and the mechanisms of power in the area of foreign policy and the war on terrorism that Cheney cultivated.

Janis, Irving L. 1989. *Crucial Decisions: Leadership in Policymaking and Crisis Management*. New York: Free Press. An incisive study of how presidents lead and manage advisers in foreign policy—sometimes well and sometimes poorly.

Johnson, Loch K. 1989. *America's Secret Power: The CIA in a Democratic Society*. New York: Oxford University Press.

A classic presentation of the roles and tensions of the secret organization at the heart of our open society's intelligence community.

Kolko, Gabriel. 1969. *The Roots of American Foreign Policy: An Analysis of Power and Purpose*. Boston: Beacon Press. A different view: a Marxist analysis of the roots of American foreign policy, emphasizing the economic interests at the heart of U.S. policy.

McDougall, Walter. 1985. . . . *the Heavens and the Earth: A Political History of the Space Age*. New York: Basic Books. An outstanding overview of the race for space by the United States; it won the Pulitzer Prize in 1986.

Schulzinger, Robert D. 2007. *U.S. Diplomacy Since 1900*, 6th ed. New York: Oxford University Press. An excellent history of U.S. foreign relations, with especially insightful chapters about the path of American foreign policy before our rise to global preeminence.

Sheehan, Neil. 1988. *A Bright Shining Lie: John Paul Vann and America in Vietnam*. New York: Random House. A fascinating look into America's war in Vietnam through the eyes of controversial war hero Vann, by one of the journalists who covered the war.

Strobel, Warren P. 1997. *Late-Breaking Foreign Policy: The News Media's Influence on Peace Operations*. Washington, D.C.: U.S. Institute of Peace Press. A good discussion of the effects of the modern media on U.S. foreign policy making, highlighting recent case studies such as Somalia, Haiti, and others.

Suskind, Ron. 2006. *The One Percent Doctrine: Deep Inside America's Pursuit of its Enemies Since 9/11*. New York: Simon and Schuster. A penetrating journey through the Bush administration's policies for the war on terrorism.

Define · **Understand** · **Practice** · **Read** · **Click** · **Watch**

Council on Foreign Relations *www.cfr.org. The Council on Foreign Relations is a nonpartisan organization that promotes understanding of foreign policy and America's role in the world. It also publishes the journal Foreign Affairs, which for decades has been perhaps the most significant publication of its kind.*

Foreign Policy Association *www.fpa.org. The Foreign Policy Association (FPA) is a national, nonprofit, nonpartisan educational organization founded in 1918 to inform Americans about significant*

world issues that have an important impact on their lives. The FPA web site provides historical background on important foreign policy decisions, monthly news analysis of major foreign policy issues, and an opportunity for readers to voice their opinions.

Foreign Policy Magazine *www.foreignpolicy.com. Not just a web portal for the magazine, the web site includes lots of news and analysis and blogs by experts on topics ranging from general foreign affairs reporting to military analysis and coverage of terrorism.*

Define · **Understand** · **Practice** · **Read** · **Click** · **Watch**

Charlie Wilson's War *2007. Starring Tom Hanks, this movie is based on the real-life efforts of former Texas representative Charlie Wilson to increase support for the Afghan rebels fighting the Soviets in the Carter and Reagan years.*

Dr. Strangelove or: How I Learned to Stop Worrying and Love the Bomb *1964. A comedy-thriller satirizing Cold War madness and featuring manic performances from George C. Scott and Peter Sellers (who plays three separate*

roles, including the title part). It's so good, I'm watching it as I write this.

The Hurt Locker *2008. Award-winning nail-biter about a bomb squad operating in Iraq.*

Seven Days in May *1964. Outstanding "conspiracy theory" movie based on the novel by the same name about a military coup attempt against the U.S. government. It delves into Cold War politics and civilian-military relationships.*

Appendix Material

Appendix 1

Articles of Confederation

To all to whom these Presents shall come, we the under-signed Delegates of the States affixed to our Names send greeting.

Articles of Confederation and perpetual Union between the states of New Hampshire, Massachusetts-bay Rhode Island and Providence Plantations, Connecticut, New York, New Jersey, Pennsylvania, Delaware, Maryland, Virginia, North Carolina, South Carolina and Georgia.

ARTICLE I

The Stile of this Confederacy shall be "The United States of America".

ARTICLE II

Each state retains its sovereignty, freedom, and independence, and every power, jurisdiction, and right, which is not by this Confederation expressly delegated to the United States, in Congress assembled.

ARTICLE III

The said States hereby severally enter into a firm league of friendship with each other, for their common defense, the security of their liberties, and their mutual and general welfare, binding themselves to assist each other, against all force offered to, or attacks made upon them, or any of them, on account of religion, sovereignty, trade, or any other pretense whatever.

ARTICLE IV

The better to secure and perpetuate mutual friendship and intercourse among the people of the different States in this Union, the free inhabitants of each of these States, paupers, vagabonds, and fugitives from justice excepted, shall be entitled to all privileges and immunities of free citizens in the several States; and the people of each State shall free ingress and regress to and from any other State, and shall enjoy therein all the privileges of trade and commerce, subject to the same duties, impositions, and restrictions as the inhabitants thereof respectively, provided that such restrictions shall not extend so far as to prevent the removal of property imported into any State, to any other State, of which the owner is an inhabitant; provided also that no imposition, duties or restriction shall be laid by any State, on the property of the United States, or either of them.

If any person guilty of, or charged with, treason, felony, or other high misdemeanor in any State, shall flee from justice, and be found in any of the United States, he shall, upon demand of the Governor or executive power of the State from which he fled, be delivered up and removed to the State having jurisdiction of his offense.

Full faith and credit shall be given in each of these States to the records, acts, and judicial proceedings of the courts and magistrates of every other State.

ARTICLE V

For the most convenient management of the general interests of the United States, delegates shall be annually appointed in such manner as the legislatures of each State shall direct, to meet in Congress on the first Monday in November, in every year, with a power reserved to each State to recall its delegates, or any of them, at any time within the year, and to send others in their stead for the remainder of the year.

No State shall be represented in Congress by less than two, nor more than seven members; and no person shall be capable of being a delegate for more than three years in any term of six years; nor shall any person, being a delegate, be capable of holding any office under the United States, for which he, or another for his benefit, receives any salary, fees or emolument of any kind.

Each State shall maintain its own delegates in a meeting of the States, and while they act as members of the committee of the States.

In determining questions in the United States in Congress assembled, each State shall have one vote.

Freedom of speech and debate in Congress shall not be impeached or questioned in any court or place out of Congress, and the members of Congress shall be protected in their persons from arrests or imprisonments, during the time of their going to and from, and attendence on Congress, except for treason, felony, or breach of the peace.

ARTICLE VI

No State, without the consent of the United States in Congress assembled, shall send any embassy to, or receive any embassy from, or enter into any conference, agreement, alliance or treaty with any King, Prince or State; nor shall any person holding any office of profit or trust under the United States, or any of them, accept any present, emolument, office or title of any kind whatever from any King, Prince or foreign State; nor shall the United States in Congress assembled, or any of them, grant any title of nobility.

No two or more States shall enter into any treaty, confederation or alliance whatever between them, without the consent of the United States in Congress assembled, specifying accurately the purposes for which the same is to be entered into, and how long it shall continue.

No State shall lay any imposts or duties, which may interfere with any stipulations in treaties, entered into by the United States in Congress assembled, with any King, Prince or State, in pursuance of any treaties already proposed by Congress, to the courts of France and Spain.

No vessel of war shall be kept up in time of peace by any State, except such number only, as shall be deemed necessary by the United States in Congress assembled, for the defense of such State, or its trade; nor shall any body of forces be kept up by any State in time of peace, except such number only, as in the judgement of the United States in Congress assembled, shall be deemed requisite to garrison the forts necessary for the defense of such State; but every State shall always keep up a well-regulated and disciplined militia, sufficiently armed and accoutered, and shall provide and constantly have ready for use, in public stores, a due number of filed pieces and tents, and a proper quantity of arms, ammunition and camp equipage.

No State shall engage in any war without the consent of the United States in Congress assembled, unless such State be actually invaded by enemies, or shall have received certain advice of a resolution being formed by some nation of Indians to invade such State, and the danger is so imminent as not to admit of a delay till the United States in Congress assembled can be consulted; nor shall any State grant commissions to any ships or vessels of war, nor letters of marque or reprisal, except it be after a declaration of war by the United States in Congress assembled, and then only against the Kingdom or State and the subjects thereof, against which war has been so declared, and under such regulations as shall be established by the United States in Congress assembled, unless such State be infested by pirates, in which case vessels of war may be fitted out for that occasion, and kept so long as the danger shall continue, or until the United States in Congress assembled shall determine otherwise.

ARTICLE VII

When land forces are raised by any State for the common defense, all officers of or under the rank of colonel, shall be appointed by the legislature of each State respectively, by whom such forces shall be raised, or in such manner as such State shall direct, and all vacancies shall be filled up by the State which first made the appointment.

ARTICLE VIII

All charges of war, and all other expenses that shall be incurred for the common defense or general welfare, and allowed by the United States in Congress assembled, shall be defrayed out of a common treasury, which shall be supplied by the several States in proportion to the value of all land within each State, granted or surveyed for any person, as such land and the buildings and improvements thereon shall be estimated according to such mode as the United States in Congress assembled, shall from time to time direct and appoint.

The taxes for paying that proportion shall be laid and levied by the authority and direction of the legislatures of the several States within the time agreed upon by the United States in Congress assembled.

ARTICLE IX

The United States in Congress assembled, shall have the sole and exclusive right and power of determining on peace and war, except in the cases mentioned in the sixth article— of sending and receiving ambassadors—entering into treaties and alliances, provided that no treaty of commerce shall be made whereby the legislative power of the respective States shall be restrained from imposing such imposts and duties on foreigners, as their own people are subjected to, or from prohibiting the exportation or importation of any species of goods or commodities whatsoever—of establishing rules for deciding in all cases, what captures on land or water shall be legal, and in what manner prizes taken by land or naval forces in the service of the United States shall be divided or appropriated—of granting letters of marque and reprisal in times of peace—appointing courts for the trial of piracies and felonies commited on the high seas and establishing courts for receiving and determining finally appeals in all cases of captures, provided that no member of Congress shall be appointed a judge of any of the said courts.

The United States in Congress assembled shall also be the last resort on appeal in all disputes and differences now subsisting or that hereafter may arise between two or more States concerning boundary, jurisdiction or any other causes whatever; which authority shall always be exercised in the manner following. Whenever the legislative or executive authority or lawful agent of any State in controversy with another shall present a petition to Congress stating the matter in question and praying for a hearing, notice thereof shall be given by order of Congress to the legislative or executive authority of the other State in controversy, and a day assigned for the appearance of the parties by their lawful agents, who shall then be directed to appoint by joint consent, commissioners or judges to constitute a court for hearing and determining the matter in question: but if they cannot agree, Congress shall name three persons out of each of the United States, and from the list of such persons each party shall alternately strike out one, the petitioners beginning, until the number shall be reduced to thirteen; and from that number not less than seven, nor more than nine names as Congress shall direct, shall in the presence of Congress be drawn out by lot, and the persons whose names shall be so drawn or any five of them, shall be commissioners or judges, to hear and finally determine the controversy, so always as a major part of the judges who shall hear the cause shall agree in the determination: and if either party shall neglect to attend at the day appointed, without showing reasons, which Congress shall judge sufficient, or being present shall refuse to strike, the Congress shall proceed to nominate three persons out of each State, and the secretary of Congress shall strike in behalf of such party absent or refusing; and the judgement and sentence of the court to be appointed, in the manner before prescribed, shall be final and conclusive; and if any of the parties shall refuse to submit to the authority of such court, or to appear or defend their claim or cause, the court shall nevertheless proceed to pronounce sentence, or judgement, which shall in like manner be final and decisive, the judgement or sentence and other proceedings being in either case transmitted to Congress, and lodged among the acts of Congress for the security of the parties concerned: provided that every commissioner, before he sits in judgement, shall take an oath to be administered by one of the judges of the supreme or superior court of the State, where the cause shall be tried, 'well and truly to hear and determine the matter in question, according to the best of his judgement, without favor, affection or hope of reward': provided also, that no State shall be deprived of territory for the benefit of the United States.

All controversies concerning the private right of soil claimed under different grants of two or more States, whose jurisdictions as they may respect such lands, and the States which passed such grants are adjusted, the said grants or either of them being at the same time claimed to have originated antecedent to such settlement of jurisdiction, shall on the petition of either party to the Congress of the United States, be finally determined as near as may be in the same manner as is before presecribed for deciding disputes respecting territorial jurisdiction between different States.

The United States in Congress assembled shall also have the sole and exclusive right and power of regulating the alloy and value of coin struck by their own authority, or by that of the respective States—fixing the standards of weights and measures throughout the United States—regulating the trade and managing all affairs with the Indians, not members of any of the States, provided that the legislative right of any State within its own limits be not infringed or violated—establishing or regulating post offices from one State to another, throughout all the United States, and exacting such postage on the papers passing through the same as may be requisite to defray the expenses of the said office—appointing all officers of the land forces, in the service of the United States, excepting regimental officers—appointing all the officers of the naval forces, and commissioning all officers whatever in the service of the United States—making rules for the government and regulation of the said land and naval forces, and directing their operations.

The United States in Congress assembled shall have authority to appoint a committee, to sit in the recess of Congress, to be denominated 'A Committee of the States', and to consist of one delegate from each State; and to appoint such other committees and civil officers as may be necessary for managing the general affairs of the United States under their direction—to appoint one of their members to preside, provided that no person be allowed to serve in the office of president more than one year in any term of three years; to ascertain the necessary sums of money to be raised for the service of the United States, and to appropriate and apply the same for defraying the public expenses—to borrow money, or emit bills on the credit of the United States, transmitting every half-year to the respective States an account of the sums of money so borrowed or emitted—to build and equip a navy—to agree upon the number of land forces, and to make requisitions from each State for its quota, in proportion to the number of white inhabitants in such State; which requisition shall be binding, and thereupon the legislature of each State shall appoint the regimental officers, raise the men and cloath, arm and equip them in a solid-like manner, at the expense of the United States; and the officers and men so cloathed, armed and equipped shall march to the place appointed, and within the time agreed on by the United States in Congress assembled. But if the United States in Congress assembled shall, on consideration of circumstances judge proper that any State should not raise men, or should raise a smaller number of men than the quota thereof, such extra number shall be raised, officered, cloathed, armed and equipped in the same manner as the quota of each State, unless the legislature of such State shall judge that such extra number cannot be safely spread out in the same, in which case they shall raise, officer, cloath, arm and equip as many of such extra number as they judge can be safely spared. And the officers and men so cloathed, armed, and equipped, shall march to the place appointed, and within the time agreed on by the United States in Congress assembled.

The United States in Congress assembled shall never engage in a war, nor grant letters of marque or reprisal in time of peace, nor enter into any treaties or alliances, nor coin money, nor regulate the value thereof, nor ascertain the sums and expenses necessary for the defense and welfare of the United States, or any of them, nor emit bills, nor borrow money on the credit of the United States, nor appropriate money, nor agree upon the number of vessels of war, to be built or purchased, or the number of land or sea forces to be raised, nor appoint a commander in chief of the army or navy, unless nine States assent to the same: nor shall a question on any other point, except for adjourning from day to day be determined, unless by the votes of the majority of the United States in Congress assembled.

The Congress of the United States shall have power to adjourn to any time within the year, and to any place within the United States, so that no period of adjournment be for a longer duration than the space of six months, and shall publish the journal of their proceedings monthly, except such parts thereof relating to treaties, alliances or military operations, as in their judgement require secrecy; and the yeas and nays of the delegates of each State on any question shall be entered on the journal, when it is desired by any delegates of a State, or any of them, at his or their request shall be furnished with a transcript of the said journal, except such parts as are above excepted, to lay before the legislatures of the several States.

ARTICLE X

The Committee of the States, or any nine of them, shall be authorized to execute, in the recess of Congress, such of the powers of Congress as the United States in Congress assembled, by the consent of the nine States, shall from time to time think expedient to vest them with; provided that no power be delegated to the said Committee, for the exercise of which, by the Articles of Confederation, the voice of nine States in the Congress of the United States assembled be requisite.

ARTICLE XI

Canada acceding to this confederation, and adjoining in the measures of the United States, shall be admitted into, and entitled to all the advantages of this Union; but no other colony shall be admitted into the same, unless such admission be agreed to by nine States.

ARTICLE XII

All bills of credit emitted, monies borrowed, and debts contracted by, or under the authority of Congress, before the assembling of the United States, in pursuance of the present confederation, shall be deemed and considered as a charge against the United States, for payment and satisfaction whereof the said United States, and the public faith are hereby solemnly pledged.

ARTICLE XIII

Every State shall abide by the determination of the United States in Congress assembled, on all questions which by this confederation are submitted to them. And the Articles of this Confederation shall be inviolably observed by every State, and the Union shall be perpetual; nor shall any alteration at any time hereafter be made in any of them; unless such alteration be agreed to in a Congress of the United States, and be afterwards confirmed by the legislatures of every State.

And Whereas it hath pleased the Great Governor of the World to incline the hearts of the legislatures we respectively represent in Congress, to approve of, and to authorize us to ratify the said Articles of Confederation and perpetual Union. Know Ye that we the undersigned delegates, by virtue of the power and authority to us given for that purpose, do by these presents, in the name and in behalf of our respective constituents, fully and entirely ratify and confirm each and every of the said Articles of Confederation and perpetual Union, and all and singular the matters and things therein contained: And we do further solemnly plight and engage the faith of our respective constituents, that they shall abide by the determinations of the United States in Congress assembled, on all questions, which by the said Confederation are submitted to them. And that the Articles thereof shall be inviolably observed by the States we respectively represent, and that the Union shall be perpetual.

In Witness whereof we have hereunto set our hands in Congress. Done at Philadelphia in the State of Pennsylvania the ninth day of July in the Year of our Lord One Thousand Seven Hundred and Seventy-Eight, and in the Third Year of the independence of America.

Agreed to by Congress 15 November 1777
In force after ratification by Maryland, 1 March 1781

Appendix 2

Declaration of Independence

On June 11, 1776, the responsibility to "prepare a declaration" of independence was assigned by the Continental Congress, meeting in Philadelphia, to five members: John Adams, Benjamin Franklin, Thomas Jefferson, Robert Livingston, and Roger Sherman. Impressed by his talents as a writer, the committee asked Jefferson to compose a draft. After modifying Jefferson's draft the committee turned it over to Congress on June 28. On July 2 Congress voted to declare independence; on the evening of July 4, it approved the Declaration of Independence.

In Congress, July 4, 1776.
The unanimous Declaration of the thirteen United States of America,

When in the Course of human events, it becomes necessary for one people to dissolve the political bands which have connected them with another, and to assume among the Powers of the earth, the separate and equal station to which the Laws of Nature and of Nature's God entitle them, a decent respect to the opinions of mankind requires that they should declare the causes which impel them to the separation.

We hold these truths to be self-evident, that all men are created equal, that they are endowed by their Creator with certain unalienable Rights, that among these are Life, Liberty and the pursuit of Happiness. That to secure these rights, Governments are instituted among Men, deriving their just powers from the consent of the governed. That whenever any form of Government becomes destructive of these ends, it is the Right of the People to alter or to abolish it, and to institute new Government, laying its foundation on such principles and organizing its powers in such form, as to them shall seem most likely to effect their Safety and Happiness. Prudence, indeed, will dictate that Government long established should not be changed for light and transient causes; and accordingly all experience hath shown, that mankind are more disposed to suffer, while evils are sufferable, than to right themselves by abolishing the forms to which they are accustomed. But when a long train of abuses and usurpations, pursuing invariably the same Object evinces a design to reduce them under absolute Despotism, it is their right, it is their duty, to throw off such Government, and to provide new Guards for their future security. Such has been the patient sufferance of these Colonies; and such is now the necessity which constrains them to alter their former Systems of Government. The history of the present King of Great Britain is a history of repeated injuries and usurpations, all having in direct object the establishment of an absolute Tyranny over these States. To prove this, let Facts be submitted to a candid world.

He has refused his Assent to Laws, the most wholesome and necessary for the public good.

He has forbidden his Governors to pass Laws of immediate and pressing importance, unless suspended in their operation till his Assent should be obtained; and when so suspended, he has utterly neglected to attend to them.

He has refused to pass other Laws for the accommodation of large districts of people, unless those people would relinquish the right of Representation in the Legislature, a right inestimable to them and formidable to tyrants only.

He has called together legislative bodies at places unusual, uncomfortable, and distant from the depository of their Public Records, for the sole purpose of fatiguing them into compliance with his measures.

He has dissolved Representative Houses repeatedly, for opposing with manly firmness his invasions on the rights of the people.

He has refused for a long time, after such dissolutions, to cause others to be elected; whereby the Legislative Powers, incapable of Annihilation, have returned to the People at large for their exercise; the State remaining in the mean time exposed to all the dangers of invasion from without, and convulsions within.

He has endeavored to prevent the population of these States; for that purpose obstructing the Laws of Naturalization of Foreigners; refusing to pass others to encourage their migration hither, and raising the conditions of new Appropriations of Lands.

He has obstructed the Administration of Justice, by refusing his Assent to Laws for establishing Judiciary Powers.

He has made Judges dependent on his Will alone, for the tenure of their offices, and the amount and payment of their salaries.

He has erected a multitude of New Offices, and sent hither swarms of Officers to harass our People, and eat out their substance.

He has kept among us, in times of peace, Standing Armies without the Consent of our legislature.

He has affected to render the Military independent of and superior to the Civil Power.

He has combined with others to subject us to a jurisdiction foreign to our constitution, and unacknowledged by our laws; giving his Assent to their acts of pretended legislation:

For quartering large bodies of armed troops among us:

For protecting them, by a mock Trial, from Punishment for any Murders which they should commit on the Inhabitants of these States:

For cutting off our Trade with all parts of the world:

For imposing taxes on us without our Consent:

For depriving us in many cases, of the benefits of Trial by Jury:

For transporting us beyond Seas to be tried for pretended offences:

For abolishing the free System of English Laws in a neighbouring Province, establishing therein an Arbitrary government, and enlarging its Boundaries so as to render it at once an example and fit instrument for introducing the same absolute rule into these Colonies:

For taking away our Charters, abolishing our most valuable Laws, and altering fundamentally the Forms of our Governments:

For suspending our own Legislature, and declaring themselves invested with Power to legislate for us in all cases whatsoever.

He has abdicated Government here, by declaring us out of his Protection and waging War against us.

He has plundered our seas, ravaged our Coasts, burnt our towns, and destroyed the lives of our people.

He is at this time transporting large armies of foreign mercenaries to compleat the works of death, desolation and tyranny, already begun with circumstances of Cruelty & perfidy scarcely parallel in the most barbarous ages, and totally unworthy the Head of a civilized nation.

He has constrained our fellow Citizens taken Captive on the high Seas to bear Arms against their Country, to become the executioners of their friends and Brethren, or to fall themselves by their Hands.

He has excited domestic insurrections amongst us, and has endeavoured to bring on the inhabitants of our frontiers, the merciless Indian Savages, whose known rule of warfare, is an undistinguished destruction of all ages, sexes and conditions.

In every stage of these Oppressions We have Petitioned for Redress in the most humble terms: Our repeated Petitions have been answered only by repeated injury. A Prince, whose character is thus marked by every act which may define a Tyrant, is unfit to be the ruler of a free People.

Nor have We been wanting in attention to our British brethren. We have warned them from time to time of attempts by their legislature to extend an unwarrantable jurisdiction over us. We have reminded them of the circumstances of our emigration and settlement here. We have appealed to their native justice and magnanimity, and we have conjured them by the ties of our common kindred to disavow these usurpations, which would inevitably interrupt our connections and correspondence. They too have been deaf to the voice of justice and of consanguinity. We must, therefore, acquiesce in the necessity, which denounces our Separation, and hold them, as we hold the rest of mankind, Enemies in War, in Peace Friends.

We, therefore, the Representatives of the United States of America, in General Congress, Assembled, appealing to the Supreme Judge of the world for the rectitude of our intentions, do, in the Name, and by Authority of the good People of these Colonies, solemnly publish and declare, That these United Colonies are, and of Right ought to be Free and Independent States; that they are Absolved from all Allegiance to the British Crown, and that all political connection between them and the State of Great Britain, is and ought to be totally dissolved; and that as Free and Independent States, they have full Power to levy War, conclude Peace, contract Alliances, establish Commerce, and to do all other Acts and Things which Independent States may of right do. And for the support of this Declaration, with a firm reliance on the Protection of Divine Providence, we mutually pledge to each other our Lives, our Fortunes and our sacred Honor.

John Hancock

New Hampshire:
Josiah Bartlett,
William Whipple,
Matthew Thornton.

Massachusetts-Bay:
Samuel Adams,
John Adams,
Robert Treat Paine,
Elbridge Gerry.

Rhode Island:
Stephen Hopkins,
William Ellery.

Connecticut:
Roger Sherman,
Samuel Huntington,
William Williams,
Oliver Wolcott.

New York:
William Floyd,
Philip Livingston,
Francis Lewis,
Lewis Morris.

Pennsylvania:
Robert Morris,
Benjamin Harris,
Benjamin Franklin,
John Morton,
George Clymer,
James Smith,
George Taylor,
James Wilson,
George Ross.

Delaware:
Caesar Rodney,

George Read,
Thomas McKean.

Georgia:
Button Gwinnett,
Lyman Hall,
George Walton.

Maryland:
Samuel Chase,
William Paca,
Thomas Stone,
Charles Carroll of Carrollton.

Virginia:
George Wythe,
Richard Henry Lee,
Thomas Jefferson,
Benjamin Harrison,
Thomas Nelson Jr.,

Francis Lightfoot Lee,
Carter Braxton.

North Carolina:
William Hooper,
Joseph Hewes,
John Penn.

South Carolina:
Edward Rutledge,
Thomas Heyward Jr.,
Thomas Lynch Jr.,
Arthur Middleton.

New Jersey:
Richard Stockton,
John Witherspoon,
Francis Hopkinson,
John Hart,
Abraham Clark.

Appendix 3

Constitution of the United States

The United States Constitution was written at a convention that Congress called on February 21, 1787, for the purpose of recommending amendments to the Articles of Confederation. Every state but Rhode Island sent delegates to Philadelphia, where the convention met that summer. The delegates decided to write an entirely new constitution, completing their labors on September 17. Nine states (the number the Constitution itself stipulated as sufficient) ratified by June 21, 1788.

The framers of the Constitution included only six paragraphs on the Supreme Court. Article III, Section 1, created the Supreme Court and the federal system of courts. It provided that "[t]he judicial power of the United States, shall be vested in one supreme Court," and whatever inferior courts Congress "from time to time" saw fit to establish. Article III, Section 2, delineated the types of cases and controversies that should be considered by a federal—rather than a state—court. But beyond this, the Constitution left many of the particulars of the Supreme Court and the federal court system for Congress to decide in later years in judiciary acts.

We the People of the United States, in Order to form a more perfect Union, establish Justice, insure domestic Tranquility, provide for the common defence, promote the general Welfare, and secure the Blessings of Liberty to ourselves and our Posterity, do ordain and establish this Constitution for the United States of America.

ARTICLE I

Section 1. All legislative Powers herein granted shall be vested in a Congress of the United States, which shall consist of a Senate and House of Representatives.

Section 2. The House of Representatives shall be composed of Members chosen every second Year by the People of the several States, and the Electors in each State shall have the Qualifications requisite for Electors of the most numerous Branch of the State Legislature.

No Person shall be a Representative who shall not have attained to the age of twenty five Years, and been seven Years a Citizen of the United States, and who shall not, when elected, be an Inhabitant of that State in which he shall be chosen.

[Representatives and direct Taxes shall be apportioned among the several States which may be included within this Union, according to their respective Numbers, which shall be determined by adding to the whole Number of free Persons, including those bound to Service for a Term of Years, and excluding Indians not taxed, three fifths of all other Persons.][1] The actual Enumeration shall be made within three Years after the first Meeting of the Congress of the United States, and within every subsequent Term of ten Years, in such Manner as they shall by Law direct. The Number of Representatives shall not exceed one for every thirty Thousand, but each State shall have at Least one Representative; and until such enumeration shall be made, the State of New Hampshire shall be entitled to chuse three, Massachusetts eight, Rhode-Island and Providence Plantations one, Connecticut five, New-York six, New Jersey four, Pennsylvania eight, Delaware one, Maryland six, Virginia ten, North Carolina five, South Carolina five, and Georgia three.

When vacancies happen in the Representation from any State, the Executive Authority thereof shall issue Writs of Election to fill such Vacancies.

The House of Representatives shall chuse their Speaker and other Officers; and shall have the sole Power of Impeachment.

Section 3. The Senate of the United States shall be composed of two Senators from each State, [chosen by the Legislature thereof,][2] for six Years; and each Senator shall have one Vote.

Immediately after they shall be assembled in Consequence of the first Election, they shall be divided as equally as may be into three Classes. The Seats of the Senators of the first Class shall be vacated at the Expiration of the second Year, of the second Class at the Expiration of the fourth Year, and of the third Class at the Expiration of the sixth Year, so that one third may be chosen every second Year; [and if Vacancies happen by Resignation, or otherwise, during the Recess of the Legislature of any State, the Executive thereof may make temporary Appointments until the next Meeting of the Legislature, which shall then fill such Vacancies.][3]

No Person shall be a Senator who shall not have attained to the Age of thirty Years, and been nine Years a Citizen of the United States, and who shall not, when elected, be an Inhabitant of that State for which he shall be chosen.

The Vice President of the United States shall be President of the Senate, but shall have no Vote, unless they be equally divided.

The Senate shall chuse their other Officers, and also a President pro tempore, in the Absence of the Vice President, or when he shall exercise the Office of President of the United States.

The Senate shall have the sole Power to try all Impeachments. When sitting for that Purpose, they shall be on Oath or Affirmation. When the President of the United States is tried, the Chief Justice shall preside: And no Person shall be convicted without the Concurrence of two thirds of the Members present.

Judgment in Cases of Impeachment shall not extend further than to removal from Office, and disqualification to hold and enjoy any Office of honor, Trust or Profit under the United States: but the Party convicted shall nevertheless be liable and subject to Indictment, Trial, Judgment and Punishment, according to Law.

Section 4. The Times, Places and Manner of holding Elections for Senators and Representatives, shall be prescribed in each State by the Legislature thereof; but the Congress may at any time by Law make or alter such Regulations, except as to the Places of chusing Senators.

The Congress shall assemble at least once in every Year, and such Meeting shall [be on the first Monday in December],[4] unless they shall by Law appoint a different Day.

Section 5. Each House shall be the Judge of the Elections, Returns and Qualifications of its own Members, and a Majority of each shall constitute a Quorum to do Business; but a smaller Number may adjourn from day to day, and may be authorized to compel the Attendance of absent Members, in such Manner, and under such Penalties as each House may provide.

Each House may determine the Rules of its Proceedings, punish its Members for disorderly Behaviour, and, with the Concurrence of two thirds, expel a Member.

Each House shall keep a Journal of its Proceedings, and from time to time publish the same, excepting such Parts as may in their Judgment require Secrecy; and the Yeas and Nays of the Members of either House on any question shall, at the Desire of one fifth of those Present, be entered on the Journal.

Neither House, during the Session of Congress, shall, without the Consent of the other, adjourn for more than three days, nor to any other Place than that in which the two Houses shall be sitting.

Section 6. The Senators and Representatives shall receive a Compensation for their Services, to be ascertained by Law, and paid out of the Treasury of the United States. They shall in all Cases, except Treason, Felony and Breach of the Peace, be privileged from Arrest during their

Attendance at the Session of their respective Houses, and in going to and returning from the same; and for any Speech or Debate in either House, they shall not be questioned in any other Place.

No Senator or Representative shall, during the Time for which he was elected, be appointed to any civil Office under the Authority of the United States, which shall have been created, or the Emoluments whereof shall have been encreased during such time; and no Person holding any Office under the United States, shall be a Member of either House during his Continuance in Office.

Section 7. All Bills for raising Revenue shall originate in the House of Representatives; but the Senate may propose or concur with Amendments as on other Bills.

Every Bill which shall have passed the House of Representatives and the Senate, shall, before it become a Law, be presented to the President of the United States; If he approve he shall sign it, but if not he shall return it, with his Objections to that House in which it shall have originated, who shall enter the Objections at large on their Journal, and proceed to reconsider it. If after such Reconsideration two thirds of that House shall agree to pass the Bill, it shall be sent, together with the Objections, to the other House, by which it shall likewise be reconsidered, and if approved by two thirds of that House, it shall become a Law. But in all such Cases the Votes of both Houses shall be determined by yeas and Nays, and the Names of the Persons voting for and against the Bill shall be entered on the Journal of each House respectively. If any Bill shall not be returned by the President within ten Days (Sundays excepted) after it shall have been presented to him, the Same shall be a Law, in like Manner as if he had signed it, unless the Congress by their Adjournment prevent its Return, in which Case it shall not be a Law.

Every Order, Resolution, or Vote to which the Concurrence of the Senate and House of Representatives may be necessary (except on a question of Adjournment) shall be presented to the President of the United States; and before the Same shall take Effect, shall be approved by him, or being disapproved by him, shall be repassed by two thirds of the Senate and House of Representatives, according to the Rules and Limitations prescribed in the Case of a Bill.

Section 8. The Congress shall have Power To lay and collect Taxes, Duties, Imposts and Excises, to pay the Debts and provide for the common Defence and general Welfare of the United States; but all Duties, Imposts and Excises shall be uniform throughout the United States;

To borrow Money on the credit of the United States;

To regulate Commerce with foreign Nations, and among the several States, and with the Indian Tribes;

To establish an uniform Rule of Naturalization, and uniform Laws on the subject of Bankruptcies throughout the United States;

To coin Money, regulate the Value thereof, and of foreign Coin, and fix the Standard of Weights and Measures;

To provide for the Punishment of counterfeiting the Securities and current Coin of the United States;

To establish Post Offices and post Roads;

To promote the Progress of Science and useful Arts, by securing for limited Times to Authors and Inventors the exclusive Right to their respective Writings and Discoveries;

To constitute Tribunals inferior to the supreme Court;

To define and punish Piracies and Felonies committed on the high Seas, and Offences against the Law of Nations;

To declare War, grant Letters of Marque and Reprisal, and make Rules concerning Captures on Land and Water;

To raise and support Armies, but no Appropriation of Money to that Use shall be for a longer Term than two Years;

To provide and maintain a Navy;

To make Rules for the Government and Regulation of the land and naval Forces;

To provide for calling forth the Militia to execute the Laws of the Union, suppress Insurrections and repel Invasions;

To provide for organizing, arming, and disciplining, the Militia, and for governing such Part of them as may be employed in the Service of the United States, reserving to the States respectively, the Appointment of the Officers, and the Authority of training the Militia according to the discipline prescribed by Congress;

To exercise exclusive Legislation in all Cases whatsoever, over such District (not exceeding ten Miles square) as may, by Cession of particular States, and the Acceptance of Congress, become the Seat of the Government of the United States, and to exercise like Authority over all Places purchased by the Consent of the Legislature of the State in which the Same shall be, for the Erection of Forts, Magazines, Arsenals, dock-Yards, and other needful Buildings;—And

To make all Laws which shall be necessary and proper for carrying into Execution the foregoing Powers, and all other Powers vested by this Constitution in the Government of the United States, or in any Department or Officer thereof.

Section 9. The Migration or Importation of such Persons as any of the States now existing shall think proper to admit, shall not be prohibited by the Congress prior to the Year one thousand eight hundred and eight, but a Tax or duty may be imposed on such Importation, not exceeding ten dollars for each Person.

The Privilege of the Writ of Habeas Corpus shall not be suspended, unless when in Cases of Rebellion or Invasion the public Safety may require it.

No Bill of Attainder or ex post facto Law shall be passed.

No Capitation, or other direct, Tax shall be laid, unless in Proportion to the Census or Enumeration herein before directed to be taken.[5]

No Tax or Duty shall be laid on Articles exported from any State.

No Preference shall be given by any Regulation of Commerce or Revenue to the Ports of one State over those of another; nor shall Vessels bound to, or from, one State, be obliged to enter, clear, or pay Duties in another.

No Money shall be drawn from the Treasury, but in Consequence of Appropriations made by Law; and a regular Statement and Account of the Receipts and Expenditures of all public Money shall be published from time to time.

No Title of Nobility shall be granted by the United States: And no Person holding any Office of Profit or Trust under them, shall, without the Consent of the Congress, accept of any present, Emolument, Office, or Title, of any kind whatever, from any King, Prince, or foreign State.

Section 10. No State shall enter into any Treaty, Alliance, or Confederation; grant Letters of Marque and Reprisal; coin Money; emit Bills of Credit; make any Thing but gold and silver Coin a Tender in Payment of Debts; pass any Bill of Attainder, ex post facto Law, or Law impairing the Obligation of Contracts, or grant any Title of Nobility.

No State shall, without the Consent of the Congress, lay any Imposts or Duties on Imports or Exports, except what may be absolutely necessary for executing its inspection Laws: and the net Produce of all Duties and Imposts, laid by any State on Imports or Exports, shall be for the Use of the Treasury of the United States; and all such Laws shall be subject to the Revision and Controul of the Congress.

No State shall, without the Consent of Congress, lay any Duty of Tonnage, keep Troops, or Ships of War in time of Peace, enter into any Agreement or Compact with another State, or with a foreign Power, or engage in War, unless actually invaded, or in such imminent Danger as will not admit of delay.

ARTICLE II

Section 1. The executive Power shall be vested in a President of the United States of America. He shall hold his Office during the Term of four Years, and, together with the Vice President, chosen for the same Term, be elected, as follows:

Each State shall appoint, in such Manner as the Legislature thereof may direct, a Number of Electors, equal to the whole Number of Senators and Representatives to which the State may be entitled in the Congress: but no Senator or Representative, or Person holding an Office of Trust or Profit under the United States, shall be appointed an Elector.

[The Electors shall meet in their respective States, and vote by Ballot for two Persons, of whom one at least shall not be an Inhabitant of the same State with themselves. And they shall make a List of all the Persons voted for, and of the Number of Votes for each; which List they shall sign and certify, and transmit sealed to the Seat of the Government of the United States, directed to the President of the Senate. The President of the Senate shall, in the Presence of the Senate and House of Representatives, open all the Certificates, and the Votes shall then be counted. The Person having the greatest Number of Votes shall be the President, if such Number be a Majority of the whole Number of Electors appointed; and if there be more than one who have such Majority, and have an equal Number of Votes, then the House of Representatives shall immediately chuse by Ballot one of them for President; and if no Person have a Majority, then from the five highest on the list the said House shall in like Manner chuse the President. But in chusing the President, the Votes shall be taken by States, the Representation from each State having one Vote; A quorum for this Purpose shall consist of a Member or Members from two thirds of the States, and a Majority of all the States shall be necessary to a Choice. In every Case, after the Choice of the President, the Person having the greatest Number of Votes of the Electors shall be the Vice President. But if there should remain two or more who have equal Votes, the Senate shall chuse from them by Ballot the Vice President.][6]

The Congress may determine the Time of chusing the Electors, and the Day on which they shall give their Votes; which Day shall be the same throughout the United States.

No Person except a natural born Citizen, or a Citizen of the United States, at the time of the Adoption of this Constitution, shall be eligible to the Office of President; neither shall any Person be eligible to that Office who shall not have attained to the Age of thirty five Years, and been fourteen Years a Resident within the United States.

In Case of the Removal of the President from Office, or of his Death, Resignation, or Inability to discharge the Powers and Duties of the said Office,[7] the Same shall devolve on the Vice President, and the Congress may by Law provide for the Case of Removal, Death, Resignation or Inability, both of the President and Vice President, declaring what Officer shall then act as President, and such Officer shall act accordingly, until the Disability be removed, or a President shall be elected.

The President shall, at stated Times, receive for his Services, a Compensation, which shall neither be encreased nor diminished during the Period for which he shall have been elected, and he shall not receive within that Period any other Emolument from the United States, or any of them.

Before he enter on the Execution of his Office, he shall take the following Oath or Affirmation:—"I do solemnly swear (or affirm) that I will faithfully execute the Office of President of the United States, and will to the best of my Ability, preserve, protect and defend the Constitution of the United States."

Section 2. The President shall be Commander in Chief of the Army and Navy of the United States, and of the Militia of the several States, when called into the actual Service of the United States; he may require the Opinion, in writing, of the principal Officer in each of the executive Departments, upon any Subject relating to the Duties of their respective Offices, and he shall have Power to grant Reprieves and Pardons for Offences against the United States, except in Cases of Impeachment.

He shall have Power, by and with the Advice and Consent of the Senate, to make Treaties, provided two thirds of the Senators present concur; and he shall nominate, and by and with the Advice and Consent of the Senate, shall appoint Ambassadors, other public Ministers and Consuls, Judges of the supreme Court, and all other Officers of the United States, whose Appointments are not herein otherwise provided for, and which shall be established by Law: but the Congress may by Law vest the Appointment of such inferior Officers, as they think proper, in the President alone, in the Courts of Law, or in the Heads of Departments.

The President shall have Power to fill up all Vacancies that may happen during the Recess of the Senate, by granting Commissions which shall expire at the End of their next Session.

Section 3. He shall from time to time give to the Congress Information of the State of the Union, and recommend to their Consideration such Measures as he shall judge necessary and expedient; he may, on extraordinary Occasions, convene both Houses, or either of them, and in Case of Disagreement between them, with Respect to the Time of Adjournment, he may adjourn them to such Time as he shall think proper; he shall receive Ambassadors and other public Ministers; he shall take Care that the Laws be faithfully executed, and shall Commission all the Officers of the United States.

Section 4. The President, Vice President and all civil Officers of the United States, shall be removed from Office on Impeachment for, and Conviction of, Treason, Bribery, or other high Crimes and Misdemeanors.

ARTICLE III

Section 1. The judicial Power of the United States, shall be vested in one supreme Court, and in such inferior Courts as the Congress may from time to time ordain and establish. The Judges, both of the supreme and inferior Courts, shall hold their Offices during good Behaviour, and shall, at stated Times, receive for their Services, a Compensation, which shall not be diminished during their Continuance in Office.

Section 2. The judicial Power shall extend to all Cases, in Law and Equity, arising under this Constitution, the Laws of the United States, and Treaties made, or which shall be made, under their Authority; —to all Cases affecting Ambassadors, other public Ministers and Consuls; —to all Cases of admiralty and maritime Jurisdiction; —to Controversies to which the United States shall be a Party; —to Controversies between two or more States; —between a State and Citizens of another State;[8] —between Citizens of different States; —between Citizens of the same State claiming Lands under Grants of different States, and between a State, or the Citizens thereof, and foreign States, Citizens or Subjects.[8]

In all Cases affecting Ambassadors, other public Ministers and Consuls, and those in which a State shall be Party, the supreme Court shall have original Jurisdiction. In all the other Cases before mentioned, the supreme Court shall have appellate Jurisdiction, both as to Law and Fact, with such Exceptions, and under such Regulations as the Congress shall make.

The Trial of all Crimes, except in Cases of Impeachment, shall be by Jury; and such Trial shall be held in the State where the said Crimes shall have been committed; but when not committed within any State, the Trial shall be at such Place or Places as the Congress may by Law have directed.

Section 3. Treason against the United States, shall consist only in levying War against them, or in adhering to their Enemies, giving them Aid and

Comfort. No Person shall be convicted of Treason unless on the Testimony of two Witnesses to the same overt Act, or on Confession in open Court.

The Congress shall have Power to declare the Punishment of Treason, but no Attainder of Treason shall work Corruption of Blood, or Forfeiture except during the Life of the Person attainted.

ARTICLE IV

Section 1. Full Faith and Credit shall be given in each State to the public Acts, Records, and judicial Proceedings of every other State. And the Congress may by general Laws prescribe the Manner in which such Acts, Records and Proceedings shall be proved, and the Effect thereof.

Section 2. The Citizens of each State shall be entitled to all Privileges and Immunities of Citizens in the several States.

A Person charged in any State with Treason, Felony, or other Crime, who shall flee from Justice, and be found in another State, shall on Demand of the executive Authority of the State from which he fled, be delivered up, to be removed to the State having Jurisdiction of the Crime.

[No Person held to Service or Labour in one State, under the Laws thereof, escaping into another, shall, in Consequence of any Law or Regulation therein, be discharged from such Service or Labour, but shall be delivered up on Claim of the Party to whom such Service or Labour may be due.]⁹

Section 3. New States may be admitted by the Congress into this Union; but no new State shall be formed or erected within the Jurisdiction of any other State; nor any State be formed by the Junction of two or more States, or Parts of States, without the Consent of the Legislatures of the States concerned as well as of the Congress.

The Congress shall have Power to dispose of and make all needful Rules and Regulations respecting the Territory or other Property belonging to the United States; and nothing in this Constitution shall be so construed as to Prejudice any Claims of the United States, or of any particular State.

Section 4. The United States shall guarantee to every State in this Union a Republican Form of Government, and shall protect each of them against Invasion; and on Application of the Legislature, or of the Executive (when the Legislature cannot be convened) against domestic Violence.

ARTICLE V

The Congress, whenever two thirds of both Houses shall deem it necessary, shall propose Amendments to this Constitution, or, on the Application of the Legislatures of two thirds of the several States, shall call a Convention for proposing Amendments, which, in either Case, shall be valid to all Intents and Purposes, as Part of this Constitution, when ratified by the Legislatures of three fourths of the several States, or by Conventions in three fourths thereof, as the one or the other Mode of Ratification may be proposed by the Congress; Provided [that no Amendment which may be made prior to the Year One thousand eight hundred and eight shall in any Manner affect the first and fourth Clauses in the Ninth Section of the first Article; and]¹⁰ that no State, without its Consent, shall be deprived of its equal Suffrage in the Senate.

ARTICLE VI

All Debts contracted and Engagements entered into, before the Adoption of this Constitution, shall be as valid against the United States under this Constitution, as under the Confederation.

This Constitution, and the Laws of the United States which shall be made in Pursuance thereof; and all Treaties made, or which shall be made, under the Authority of the United States, shall be the supreme Law of the Land; and the Judges in every State shall be bound thereby, any Thing in the Constitution or Laws of any State to the Contrary notwithstanding.

The Senators and Representatives before mentioned, and the Members of the several State Legislatures, and all executive and judicial Officers, both of the United States and of the several States, shall be bound by Oath or Affirmation, to support this Constitution; but no religious Test shall ever be required as a Qualification to any Office or public Trust under the United States.

ARTICLE VII

The Ratification of the Conventions of nine States, shall be sufficient for the Establishment of this Constitution between the States so ratifying the Same.

Done in Convention by the Unanimous Consent of the States present the Seventeenth Day of September in the Year of our Lord one thousand seven hundred and Eighty seven and of the Independence of the United States of America the Twelfth. IN WITNESS whereof We have hereunto subscribed our Names,

> *George Washington, President and*
> *deputy from Virginia, and*
> *thirty-eight other delegates.*

[The language of the original Constitution, not including the Amendments, was adopted by a convention of the states on September 17, 1787, and was subsequently ratified by the states on the following dates: Delaware, December 7, 1787; Pennsylvania, December 12, 1787; New Jersey, December 18, 1787; Georgia, January 2, 1788; Connecticut, January 9, 1788; Massachusetts, February 6, 1788; Maryland, April 28, 1788; South Carolina, May 23, 1788; New Hampshire, June 21, 1788.

Ratification was completed on June 21, 1788.

The Constitution subsequently was ratified by Virginia, June 25, 1788; New York, July 26, 1788; North Carolina, November 21, 1789; Rhode Island, May 29, 1790; and Vermont, January 10, 1791.]

Amendments

AMENDMENT I
(First ten amendments ratified December 15, 1791.)

Congress shall make no law respecting an establishment of religion, or prohibiting the free exercise thereof; or abridging the freedom of speech, or of the press; or the right of the people peaceably to assemble, and to petition the Government for a redress of grievances.

AMENDMENT II
A well regulated Militia, being necessary to the security of a free State, the right of the people to keep and bear Arms, shall not be infringed.

AMENDMENT III
No Soldier shall, in time of peace be quartered in any house, without the consent of the Owner, nor in time of war, but in a manner to be prescribed by law.

AMENDMENT IV
The right of the people to be secure in their persons, houses, papers, and effects, against unreasonable searches and seizures, shall not be violated, and no Warrants shall issue, but upon probable cause, supported by Oath or affirmation, and particularly describing the place to be searched, and the persons or things to be seized.

AMENDMENT V
No person shall be held to answer for a capital, or otherwise infamous crime, unless on a presentment or indictment of a Grand Jury, except in cases arising in the land or naval forces, or in the Militia, when in actual service in time of War or public danger; nor shall any person be subject for the same offence to be twice put in jeopardy of life or limb; nor shall

be compelled in any criminal case to be a witness against himself, nor be deprived of life, liberty, or property, without due process of law; nor shall private property be taken for public use, without just compensation.

AMENDMENT VI

In all criminal prosecutions, the accused shall enjoy the right to a speedy and public trial, by an impartial jury of the State and district wherein the crime shall have been committed, which district shall have been previously ascertained by law, and to be informed of the nature and cause of the accusation; to be confronted with the witnesses against him; to have compulsory process for obtaining witnesses in his favor, and to have the Assistance of Counsel for his defence.

AMENDMENT VII

In Suits at common law, where the value in controversy shall exceed twenty dollars, the right of trial by jury shall be preserved, and no fact tried by a jury, shall be otherwise re-examined in any Court of the United States, than according to the rules of the common law.

AMENDMENT VIII

Excessive bail shall not be required, nor excessive fines imposed, nor cruel and unusual punishments inflicted.

AMENDMENT IX

The enumeration in the Constitution, of certain rights, shall not be construed to deny or disparage others retained by the people.

AMENDMENT X

The powers not delegated to the United States by the Constitution, nor prohibited by it to the States, are reserved to the States respectively, or to the people.

AMENDMENT XI *(Ratified February 7, 1795)*

The Judicial power of the United States shall not be construed to extend to any suit in law or equity, commenced or prosecuted against one of the United States by Citizens of another State, or by Citizens or Subjects of any Foreign State.

AMENDMENT XII *(Ratified June 15, 1804)*

The Electors shall meet in their respective states and vote by ballot for President and Vice-President, one of whom, at least, shall not be an inhabitant of the same state with themselves; they shall name in their ballots the person voted for as President, and in distinct ballots the person voted for as Vice-President, and they shall make distinct lists of all persons voted for as President, and of all persons voted for as Vice-President, and of the number of votes for each, which lists they shall sign and certify, and transmit sealed to the seat of the government of the United States, directed to the President of the Senate; — The President of the Senate shall, in the presence of the Senate and House of Representatives, open all the certificates and the votes shall then be counted; — The person having the greatest number of votes for President, shall be the President, if such number be a majority of the whole number of Electors appointed; and if no person have such majority, then from the persons having the highest numbers not exceeding three on the list of those voted for as President, the House of Representatives shall choose immediately, by ballot, the President. But in choosing the President, the votes shall be taken by states, the representation from each state having one vote; a quorum for this purpose shall consist of a member or members from two-thirds of the states, and a majority of all the states shall be necessary to a choice. [And if the House of Representatives shall not choose a President whenever the right of choice shall devolve upon them, before the fourth day of March next following, then the Vice-President shall act as President, as in the case of the death or other constitutional disability of the President. —][11] The person having the greatest number of votes as Vice-President, shall be

the Vice-President, if such number be a majority of the whole number of Electors appointed, and if no person have a majority, then from the two highest numbers on the list, the Senate shall choose the Vice-President; a quorum for the purpose shall consist of two-thirds of the whole number of Senators, and a majority of the whole number shall be necessary to a choice. But no person constitutionally ineligible to the office of President shall be eligible to that of Vice-President of the United States.

AMENDMENT XIII *(Ratified December 6, 1865)*

Section 1. Neither slavery nor involuntary servitude, except as a punishment for crime whereof the party shall have been duly convicted, shall exist within the United States, or any place subject to their jurisdiction.

Section 2. Congress shall have power to enforce this article by appropriate legislation.

AMENDMENT XIV *(Ratified July 9, 1868)*

Section 1. All persons born or naturalized in the United States, and subject to the jurisdiction thereof, are citizens of the United States and of the State wherein they reside. No State shall make or enforce any law which shall abridge the privileges or immunities of citizens of the United States; nor shall any State deprive any person of life, liberty, or property, without due process of law; nor deny to any person within its jurisdiction the equal protection of the laws.

Section 2. Representatives shall be apportioned among the several States according to their respective numbers, counting the whole number of persons in each State, excluding Indians not taxed. But when the right to vote at any election for the choice of electors for President and Vice President of the United States, Representatives in Congress, the Executive and Judicial officers of a State, or the members of the Legislature thereof, is denied to any of the male inhabitants of such State, being twenty-one years of age,[12] and citizens of the United States, or in any way abridged, except for participation in rebellion, or other crime, the basis of representation therein shall be reduced in the proportion which the number of such male citizens shall bear to the whole number of male citizens twenty-one years of age in such State.

Section 3. No person shall be a Senator or Representative in Congress, or elector of President and Vice President, or hold any Office, civil or military, under the United States, or under any State, who, having previously taken an oath, as a member of Congress, or as an officer of the United States, or as a member of any State legislature, or as an executive or judicial officer of any State, to support the Constitution of the United States, shall have engaged in insurrection or rebellion against the same, or given aid or comfort to the enemies thereof. But Congress may by a vote of two-thirds of each House, remove such disability.

Section 4. The validity of the public debt of the United States, authorized by law, including debts incurred for payment of pensions and bounties for services in suppressing insurrection or rebellion, shall not be questioned. But neither the United States nor any State shall assume or pay any debt or obligation incurred in aid of insurrection or rebellion against the United States, or any claim for the loss or emancipation of any slave; but all such debts, obligations and claims shall be held illegal and void.

Section 5. The Congress shall have power to enforce, by appropriate legislation, the provisions of this article.

AMENDMENT XV *(Ratified February 3, 1870)*

Section 1. The right of citizens of the United States to vote shall not be denied or abridged by the United States or by any State on account of race, color, or previous condition of servitude.

Section 2. The Congress shall have power to enforce this article by appropriate legislation.

AMENDMENT XVI *(Ratified February 3, 1913)*

The Congress shall have power to lay and collect taxes on incomes, from whatever source derived, without apportionment among the several States, and without regard to any census or enumeration.

AMENDMENT XVII *(Ratified April 8, 1913)*

The Senate of the United States shall be composed of two Senators from each State, elected by the people thereof, for six years; and each Senator shall have one vote. The electors in each State shall have the qualifications requisite for electors of the most numerous branch of the State legislatures.

When vacancies happen in the representation of any State in the Senate, the executive authority of such State shall issue writs of election to fill such vacancies: Provided, That the legislature of any State may empower the executive thereof to make temporary appointments until the people fill the vacancies by election as the legislature may direct.

This amendment shall not be so construed as to affect the election or term of any Senator chosen before it becomes valid as part of the Constitution.

AMENDMENT XVIII *(Ratified January 16, 1919)*

Section 1. After one year from the ratification of this article the manufacture, sale, or transportation of intoxicating liquors within, the importation thereof into, or the exportation thereof from the United States and all territory subject to the jurisdiction thereof for beverage purposes is hereby prohibited.

Section 2. The Congress and the several States shall have concurrent power to enforce this article by appropriate legislation.

Section 3. This article shall be inoperative unless it shall have been ratified as an amendment to the Constitution by the legislatures of the several States, as provided in the Constitution, within seven years from the date of the submission hereof to the States by the Congress.[13]

AMENDMENT XIX *(Ratified August 18, 1920)*

The right of citizens of the United States to vote shall not be denied or abridged by the United States or by any State on account of sex.

Congress shall have power to enforce this article by appropriate legislation.

AMENDMENT XX *(Ratified January 23, 1933)*

Section 1. The terms of the President and Vice President shall end at noon on the 20th day of January, and the terms of Senators and Representatives at noon on the 3d day of January, of the years in which such terms would have ended if this article had not been ratified; and the terms of their successors shall then begin.

Section 2. The Congress shall assemble at least once in every year, and such meeting shall begin at noon on the 3d day of January, unless they shall by law appoint a different day.

Section 3.[14] If, at the time fixed for the beginning of the term of the President, the President elect shall have died, the Vice President elect shall become President. If a President shall not have been chosen before the time fixed for the beginning of his term, or if the President elect shall have failed to qualify, then the Vice President elect shall act as President until a President shall have qualified; and the Congress may by law provide for the case wherein neither a President elect nor a Vice President elect shall have qualified, declaring who shall then act as President, or the manner in which one who is to act shall be selected, and such person shall act accordingly until a President or Vice President shall have qualified.

Section 4. The Congress may by law provide for the case of the death of any of the persons from whom the House of Representatives may choose a President whenever the right of choice shall have devolved upon them, and for the case of the death of any of the persons from whom the Senate may choose a Vice President whenever the right of choice shall have devolved upon them.

Section 5. Sections 1 and 2 shall take effect on the 15th day of October following the ratification of this article.

Section 6. This article shall be inoperative unless it shall have been ratified as an amendment to the Constitution by the legislatures of three-fourths of the several States within seven years from the date of its submission.

AMENDMENT XXI *(Ratified December 5, 1933)*

Section 1. The eighteenth article of amendment to the Constitution of the United States is hereby repealed.

Section 2. The transportation or importation into any State, Territory, or possession of the United States for delivery or use therein of intoxicating liquors, in violation of the laws thereof, is hereby prohibited.

Section 3. This article shall be inoperative unless it shall have been ratified as an amendment to the Constitution by conventions in the several States, as provided in the Constitution, within seven years from the date of the submission hereof to the States by the Congress.

AMENDMENT XXII *(Ratified February 27, 1951)*

Section 1. No person shall be elected to the office of the President more than twice, and no person who has held the office of President, or acted as President, for more than two years of a term to which some other person was elected President shall be elected to the office of the President more than once. But this Article shall not apply to any person holding the office of President when this Article was proposed by the Congress, and shall not prevent any person who may be holding the office of President, or acting as President, during the term within which this Article becomes operative from holding the office of President or acting as President during the remainder of such term.

Section 2. This article shall be inoperative unless it shall have been ratified as an amendment to the Constitution by the legislatures of three-fourths of the several States within seven years from the date of its submission to the States by the Congress.

AMENDMENT XXIII *(Ratified March 29, 1961)*

Section 1. The District constituting the seat of Government of the United States shall appoint in such manner as the Congress may direct:

A number of electors of President and Vice President equal to the whole number of Senators and Representatives in Congress to which the District would be entitled if it were a State, but in no event more than the least populous State; they shall be in addition to those appointed by the States, but they shall be considered, for the purposes of the election of President and Vice President, to be electors appointed by a State; and they shall meet in the District and perform such duties as provided by the twelfth article of amendment.

Section 2. The Congress shall have power to enforce this article by appropriate legislation.

AMENDMENT XXIV *(Ratified January 23, 1964)*

Section 1. The right of citizens of the United States to vote in any primary or other election for President or Vice President, for electors for President or Vice President, or for Senator or Representative in Congress, shall not be denied or abridged by the United States or any State by reason of failure to pay any poll tax or other tax.

Section 2. The Congress shall have power to enforce this article by appropriate legislation.

AMENDMENT XXV *(Ratified February 10, 1967)*

Section 1. In case of the removal of the President from office or of his death or resignation, the Vice President shall become President.

Section 2. Whenever there is a vacancy in the offie of the Vice President, the President shall nominate a Vice President who shall take office upon confirmation by a majority vote of both Houses of Congress.

Section 3. Whenever the President transmits to the President pro tempore of the Senate and the Speaker of the House of Representatives his written declaration that he is unable to discharge the powers and duties of his office, and until he transmits to them a written declaration to the contrary, such powers and duties shall be discharged by the Vice President as Acting President.

Section 4. Whenever the Vice President and a majority of either the principal officers of the executive departments or of such other body as Congress may by law provide, transmit to the President pro tempore of the Senate and the Speaker of the House of Representatives their written declaration that the President is unable to discharge the powers and duties of his office, the Vice President shall immediately assume the powers and duties of the office as Acting President.

Thereafter, when the President transmits to the President pro tempore of the Senate and the Speaker of the House of Representatives his written declaration that no inability exists, he shall resume the powers and duties of his office unless the Vice President and a majority of either the principal officers of the executive departments or of such other body as Congress may by law provide, transmit within four days to the President pro tempore of the Senate and the Speaker of the House of Representatives their written declaration that the President is unable to discharge the powers and duties of his office. Thereupon Congress shall decide the issue, assembling within forty-eight hours for that purpose if not in session. If the Congress, within twenty-one days after receipt of the latter written declaration, or, if Congress is not in session, within twenty-one days after Congress is required to assemble, determines by two-thirds vote of both Houses that the President is unable to discharge

the powers and duties of his office, the Vice President shall continue to discharge the same as Acting President; otherwise, the President shall resume the powers and duties of his office.

AMENDMENT XXVI *(Ratified July 1, 1971)*

Section 1. The right of citizens of the United States, who are eighteen years of age or older, to vote shall not be denied or abridged by the United States or by any State on account of age.

Section 2. The Congress shall have power to enforce this article by appropriate legislation.

AMENDMENT XXVII *(Ratified May 7, 1992)*

No law varying the compensation for the services of the Senators and Representatives shall take effect, until an election of Representatives shall have intervened.

Source: U.S. Congress, House, Committee on the Judiciary, The Constitution of the United States of America, as Amended, 100th Cong., 1st sess., 1987, H Doc 100–94.

Notes:
1. The part in brackets was changed by section 2 of the Fourteenth Amendment.
2. The part in brackets was changed by the first paragraph of the Seventeenth Amendment.
3. The part in brackets was changed by the second paragraph of the Seventeenth Amendment.
4. The part in brackets was changed by section 2 of the Twentieth Amendment.
5. The Sixteenth Amendment gave Congress the power to tax incomes.
6. The material in brackets was superseded by the Twelfth Amendment.
7. This provision was affected by the Twenty-fifth Amendment.
8. These clauses were affected by the Eleventh Amendment.
9. This paragraph was superseded by the Thirteenth Amendment.
10. Obsolete.
11. The part in brackets was superseded by section 3 of the Twentieth Amendment.
12. See the Nineteenth and Twenty-sixth Amendments.
13. This amendment was repealed by section 1 of the Twenty-first Amendment.
14. See the Twenty-fifth Amendment.

Appendix 4

Federalist No. 10

The Same Subject Continued: The Union as a Safeguard Against Domestic Faction and Insurrection.

From the New York Packet
Friday, November 23, 1787.
Author: James Madison

To the People of the State of New York:

AMONG the numerous advantages promised by a well constructed Union, none deserves to be more accurately developed than its tendency to break and control the violence of faction. The friend of popular governments never finds himself so much alarmed for their character and fate, as when he contemplates their propensity to this dangerous vice. He will not fail, therefore, to set a due value on any plan which, without violating the principles to which he is attached, provides a proper cure for it. The instability, injustice, and confusion introduced into the public councils, have, in truth, been the mortal diseases under which popular governments have everywhere perished; as they continue to be the favorite and fruitful topics from which the adversaries to liberty derive their most specious declamations. The valuable improvements made by the American constitutions on the popular models, both ancient and modern, cannot certainly be too much admired; but it would be an unwarrantable partiality, to contend that they have as effectually obviated the danger on this side, as was wished and expected. Complaints are everywhere heard from our most considerate and virtuous citizens, equally the friends of public and private faith, and of public and personal liberty, that our governments are too unstable, that the public good is disregarded in the conflicts of rival parties, and that measures are too often decided, not according to the rules of justice and the rights of the minor party, but by the superior force of an interested and overbearing majority. However anxiously we may wish that these complaints had no foundation, the evidence, of known facts will not permit us to deny that they are in some degree true. It will be found, indeed, on a candid review of our situation, that some of the distresses under which we labor have been erroneously charged on the operation of our governments; but it will be found, at the same time, that other causes will not alone account for many of our heaviest misfortunes; and, particularly, for that prevailing and increasing distrust of public engagements, and alarm for private rights, which are echoed from one end of the continent to the other. These must be chiefly, if not wholly, effects of the unsteadiness and injustice with which a factious spirit has tainted our public administrations.

By a faction, I understand a number of citizens, whether amounting to a majority or a minority of the whole, who are united and actuated by some common impulse of passion, or of interest, adversed to the rights of other citizens, or to the permanent and aggregate interests of the community.

There are two methods of curing the mischiefs of faction: the one, by removing its causes; the other, by controlling its effects.

There are again two methods of removing the causes of faction: the one, by destroying the liberty which is essential to its existence; the other, by giving to every citizen the same opinions, the same passions, and the same interests.

It could never be more truly said than of the first remedy, that it was worse than the disease. Liberty is to faction what air is to fire, an aliment without which it instantly expires. But it could not be less folly to abolish liberty, which is essential to political life, because it nourishes faction, than it would be to wish the annihilation of air, which is essential to animal life, because it imparts to fire its destructive agency.

The second expedient is as impracticable as the first would be unwise. As long as the reason of man continues fallible, and he is at liberty to exercise it, different opinions will be formed. As long as the connection subsists between his reason and his self-love, his opinions and his passions will have a reciprocal influence on each other; and the former will be objects to which the latter will attach themselves. The diversity in the faculties of men, from which the rights of property originate, is not less an insuperable obstacle to a uniformity of interests. The protection of these faculties is the first object of government. From the protection of different and unequal faculties of acquiring property, the possession of different degrees and kinds of property immediately results; and from the influence of these on the sentiments and views of the respective proprietors, ensues a division of the society into different interests and parties.

The latent causes of faction are thus sown in the nature of man; and we see them everywhere brought into different degrees of activity, according to the different circumstances of civil society. A zeal for different opinions concerning religion, concerning government, and many other points, as well of speculation as of practice; an attachment to different leaders ambitiously contending for pre-eminence and power; or to persons of other descriptions whose fortunes have been interesting to the human passions, have, in turn, divided mankind into parties, inflamed them with mutual animosity, and rendered them much more disposed to vex and oppress each other than to co-operate for their common good. So strong is this propensity of mankind to fall into mutual animosities, that where no substantial occasion presents itself, the most frivolous and fanciful distinctions have been suffIcient to kindle their unfriendly passions and excite their most violent conflicts. But the most common and durable source of factions has been the various and unequal distribution of property. Those who hold and those who are without property have ever formed distinct interests in society. Those who are creditors, and those who are debtors, fall under a like discrimination. A landed interest, a manufacturing interest, a mercantile interest, a moneyed interest, with many lesser interests, grow up of necessity in civilized nations, and divide them into different classes, actuated by different sentiments and views. The regulation of these various and interfering interests forms the principal task of modern legislation, and involves the spirit of party and faction in the necessary and ordinary operations of the government.

No man is allowed to be a judge in his own cause, because his interest would certainly bias his judgment, and, not improbably, corrupt his integrity. With equal, nay with greater reason, a body of men are unfit to be both judges and parties at the same time; yet what are many of the most important acts of legislation, but so many judicial determinations, not indeed concerning the rights of single persons, but concerning the rights of large bodies of citizens? And what are the different classes of legislators but advocates and parties to the causes which they determine? Is a law proposed concerning private debts? It is a question to which the creditors are parties on one side and the debtors on the other. Justice ought to hold the balance between them. Yet the parties are, and must be, themselves the judges; and the most numerous party, or, in other words, the most powerful faction must be expected to prevail. Shall domestic manufactures be encouraged, and in what degree, by restrictions on foreign manufactures? are questions which would be differently decided by the landed and the manufacturing classes, and probably by neither with a sole regard to justice and the public good. The apportionment of taxes on the various descriptions of property is an act which seems to require the most exact impartiality; yet there is, perhaps, no legislative act in which greater opportunity and temptation are given to a predominant party to trample on the rules of justice. Every shilling with which they overburden the inferior number, is a shilling saved to their own pockets.

It is in vain to say that enlightened statesmen will be able to adjust these clashing interests, and render them all subservient to the public good. Enlightened statesmen will not always be at the helm. Nor, in many cases, can such an adjustment be made at all without taking into view indirect and remote considerations, which will rarely prevail over the immediate interest which one party may find in disregarding the rights of another or the good of the whole.

The inference to which we are brought is, that the CAUSES of faction cannot be removed, and that relief is only to be sought in the means of controlling its EFFECTS.

If a faction consists of less than a majority, relief is supplied by the republican principle, which enables the majority to defeat its sinister views by regular vote. It may clog the administration, it may convulse the society; but it will be unable to execute and mask its violence under the forms of the Constitution. When a majority is included in a faction, the form of popular government, on the other hand, enables it to sacrifice to its ruling passion or interest both the public good and the rights of other citizens. To secure the public good and private rights against the danger of such a faction, and at the same time to preserve the spirit and the form of popular government, is then the great object to which our inquiries are directed. Let me add that it is the great desideratum by which this form of government can be rescued from the opprobrium under which it has so long labored, and be recommended to the esteem and adoption of mankind.

By what means is this object attainable? Evidently by one of two only. Either the existence of the same passion or interest in a majority at the same time must be prevented, or the majority, having such coexistent passion or interest, must be rendered, by their number and local situation, unable to concert and carry into effect schemes of oppression. If the impulse and the opportunity be suffered to coincide, we well know that neither moral nor religious motives can be relied on as an adequate control. They are not found to be such on the injustice and violence of individuals, and lose their efficacy in proportion to the number combined together, that is, in proportion as their efficacy becomes needful.

From this view of the subject it may be concluded that a pure democracy, by which I mean a society consisting of a small number of citizens, who assemble and administer the government in person, can admit of no cure for the mischiefs of faction. A common passion or interest will, in almost every case, be felt by a majority of the whole; a communication and concert result from the form of government itself; and there is nothing to check the inducements to sacrifice the weaker party or an obnoxious individual. Hence it is that such democracies have ever been spectacles of turbulence and contention; have ever been found incompatible with personal security or the rights of property; and have in general been as short in their lives as they have been violent in their deaths. Theoretic politicians, who have patronized this species of government, have erroneously supposed that by reducing mankind to a perfect equality in their political rights, they would, at the same time, be perfectly equalized and assimilated in their possessions, their opinions, and their passions.

A republic, by which I mean a government in which the scheme of representation takes place, opens a different prospect, and promises the cure for which we are seeking. Let us examine the points in which it varies from pure democracy, and we shall comprehend both the nature of the cure and the efficacy which it must derive from the Union.

The two great points of difference between a democracy and a republic are: first, the delegation of the government, in the latter, to a small number of citizens elected by the rest; secondly, the greater number of citizens, and greater sphere of country, over which the latter may be extended.

The effect of the first difference is, on the one hand, to refine and enlarge the public views, by passing them through the medium of a chosen body of citizens, whose wisdom may best discern the true interest of their country, and whose patriotism and love of justice will be least likely to sacrifice it to temporary or partial considerations. Under such a regulation, it may well happen that the public voice, pronounced by the representatives of the people, will be more consonant to the public good than if pronounced by the people themselves, convened for the purpose. On the other hand, the effect may be inverted. Men of factious tempers, of local prejudices, or of sinister designs, may, by intrigue, by corruption, or by other means, first obtain the suffrages, and then betray the interests, of the people. The question resulting is, whether small or extensive republics are more favorable to the election of proper guardians of the public weal; and it is clearly decided in favor of the latter by two obvious considerations:

In the first place, it is to be remarked that, however small the republic may be, the representatives must be raised to a certain number, in order to guard against the cabals of a few; and that, however large it may be, they must be limited to a certain number, in order to guard against the confusion of a multitude. Hence, the number of representatives in the two cases not being in proportion to that of the two constituents, and being proportionally greater in the small republic, it follows that, if the proportion of fit characters be not less in the large than in the small republic, the former will present a greater option, and consequently a greater probability of a fit choice.

In the next place, as each representative will be chosen by a greater number of citizens in the large than in the small republic, it will be more difficult for unworthy candidates to practice with success the vicious arts by which elections are too often carried; and the suffrages of the people being more free, will be more likely to centre in men who possess the most attractive merit and the most diffusive and established characters.

It must be confessed that in this, as in most other cases, there is a mean, on both sides of which inconveniences will be found to lie. By enlarging too much the number of electors, you render the representatives too little acquainted with all their local circumstances and lesser interests; as by reducing it too much, you render him unduly attached to these, and too little fit to comprehend and pursue great and national objects. The federal Constitution forms a happy combination in this respect; the great and aggregate interests being referred to the national, the local and particular to the State legislatures.

The other point of difference is, the greater number of citizens and extent of territory which may be brought within the compass of republican than of democratic government; and it is this circumstance principally which renders factious combinations less to be dreaded in the former than in the latter. The smaller the society, the fewer probably will be the distinct parties and interests composing it; the fewer the distinct parties and interests, the more frequently will a majority be found of the same party; and the smaller the number of individuals composing a majority, and the smaller the compass within which they are placed, the more easily will they concert and execute their plans of oppression. Extend the sphere, and you take in a greater variety of parties and interests; you make it less probable that a majority of the whole will have a common motive to invade the rights of other citizens; or if such a common motive exists, it will be more difficult for all who feel it to discover their own strength, and to act in unison with each other. Besides other impediments, it may be remarked that, where there is a consciousness of unjust or dishonorable purposes, communication is always checked by distrust in proportion to the number whose concurrence is necessary.

Hence, it clearly appears, that the same advantage which a republic has over a democracy, in controlling the effects of faction, is enjoyed by a large over a small republic,—is enjoyed by the Union over the States composing it. Does the advantage consist in the substitution of representatives whose enlightened views and virtuous sentiments render them superior to local prejudices and schemes of injustice? It will not be denied that the representation of the Union will be most likely to possess these requisite endowments. Does it consist in the greater security afforded by a greater variety of parties, against the event of any one party being able to outnumber and oppress the rest? In an equal degree does the increased variety of parties comprised within the Union, increase this security. Does it, in fine, consist in the greater obstacles opposed to the concert and accomplishment of the secret wishes of an unjust and interested majority? Here, again, the extent of the Union gives it the most palpable advantage.

The influence of factious leaders may kindle a flame within their particular States, but will be unable to spread a general conflagration through the other States. A religious sect may degenerate into a political faction in a part of the Confederacy; but the variety of sects dispersed over the entire face of it must secure the national councils against any danger from that source. A rage for paper money, for an abolition of debts, for an equal division of property, or for any other improper or wicked project, will be less apt to pervade the whole body of the Union than a particular member of it; in the same proportion as such a malady is more likely to taint a particular county or district, than an entire State.

In the extent and proper structure of the Union, therefore, we behold a republican remedy for the diseases most incident to republican government. And according to the degree of pleasure and pride we feel in being republicans, ought to be our zeal in cherishing the spirit and supporting the character of Federalists.

PUBLIUS.

Appendix 5

Federalist No. 51

The Structure of the Government Must Furnish the Proper Checks and Balances Between the Different Departments.

From the New York Packet.
Friday, February 8, 1788.
Author: James Madison

To the People of the State of New York:

TO WHAT expedient, then, shall we finally resort, for maintaining in practice the necessary partition of power among the several departments, as laid down in the Constitution? The only answer that can be given is, that as all these exterior provisions are found to be inadequate, the defect must be supplied, by so contriving the interior structure of the government as that its several constituent parts may, by their mutual relations, be the means of keeping each other in their proper places. Without presuming to undertake a full development of this important idea, I will hazard a few general observations, which may perhaps place it in a clearer light, and enable us to form a more correct judgment of the principles and structure of the government planned by the convention.

In order to lay a due foundation for that separate and distinct exercise of the different powers of government, which to a certain extent is admitted on all hands to be essential to the preservation of liberty, it is evident that each department should have a will of its own; and consequently should be so constituted that the members of each should have as little agency as possible in the appointment of the members of the others. Were this principle rigorously adhered to, it would require that all the appointments for the supreme executive, legislative, and judiciary magistracies should be drawn from the same fountain of authority, the people, through channels having no communication whatever with one another. Perhaps such a plan of constructing the several departments would be less difficult in practice than it may in contemplation appear. Some difficulties, however, and some additional expense would attend the execution of it. Some deviations, therefore, from the principle must be admitted. In the constitution of the judiciary department in particular, it might be inexpedient to insist rigorously on the principle: first, because peculiar qualifications being essential in the members, the primary consideration ought to be to select that mode of choice which best secures these qualifications; secondly, because the permanent tenure by which the appointments are held in that department, must soon destroy all sense of dependence on the authority conferring them.

It is equally evident, that the members of each department should be as little dependent as possible on those of the others, for the emoluments annexed to their offices. Were the executive magistrate, or the judges, not independent of the legislature in this particular, their independence in every other would be merely nominal. But the great security against a gradual concentration of the several powers in the same department, consists in giving to those who administer each department the necessary constitutional means and personal motives to resist encroachments of the others. The provision for defense must in this, as in all other cases, be made commensurate to the danger of attack. Ambition must be made to counteract ambition. The interest of the man must be connected with the constitutional rights of the place. It may be a reflection on human nature, that such devices should be necessary to control the abuses of government. But what is government itself, but the greatest of all reflections on human nature? If men were angels, no government would be necessary. If angels were to govern men, neither external nor internal controls on government would be necessary. In framing a government which is to be administered by men over men, the great difficulty lies in this: you must first enable the government to control the governed; and in the next place oblige it to control itself.

A dependence on the people is, no doubt, the primary control on the government; but experience has taught mankind the necessity of auxiliary precautions. This policy of supplying, by opposite and rival interests, the defect of better motives, might be traced through the whole system of human affairs, private as well as public. We see it particularly displayed in all the subordinate distributions of power, where the constant aim is to divide and arrange the several offices in such a manner as that each may be a check on the other that the private interest of every individual may be a sentinel over the public rights. These inventions of prudence cannot be less requisite in the distribution of the supreme powers of the State. But it is not possible to give to each department an equal power of self-defense. In republican government, the legislative authority necessarily predominates. The remedy for this inconveniency is to divide the legislature into different branches; and to render them, by different modes of election and different principles of action, as little connected with each other as the nature of their common functions and their common dependence on the society will admit. It may even be necessary to guard against dangerous encroachments by still further precautions. As the weight of the legislative authority requires that it should be thus divided, the weakness of the executive may require, on the other hand, that it should be fortified.

An absolute negative on the legislature appears, at first view, to be the natural defense with which the executive magistrate should be armed. But perhaps it would be neither altogether safe nor alone sufficient. On ordinary occasions it might not be exerted with the requisite firmness, and on extraordinary occasions it might be perfidiously abused. May not this defect of an absolute negative be supplied by some qualified connection between this weaker department and the weaker branch of the stronger department, by which the latter may be led to support the constitutional rights of the former, without being too much detached from the rights of its own department? If the principles on which these observations are founded be just, as I persuade myself they are, and they be applied as a criterion to the several State constitutions, and to the federal Constitution it will be found that if the latter does not perfectly correspond with them, the former are infinitely less able to bear such a test.

There are, moreover, two considerations particularly applicable to the federal system of America, which place that system in a very interesting point of view. First. In a single republic, all the power surrendered by the people is submitted to the administration of a single government; and the usurpations are guarded against by a division of the government into distinct and separate departments. In the compound republic of America, the power surrendered by the people is first divided between two distinct governments, and then the portion allotted to each subdivided among distinct and separate departments. Hence a double security arises to the rights of the people. The different governments will control each other, at the same time that each will be controlled by itself. Second. It is of great importance in a republic not only to guard the society against the oppression of its rulers, but to guard one part of the society against the injustice of the other part. Different interests necessarily exist in different classes of citizens. If a majority be united by a common interest, the rights of the minority will be insecure.

There are but two methods of providing against this evil: the one by creating a will in the community independent of the majority that is, of the society itself; the other, by comprehending in the society so many separate descriptions of citizens as will render an unjust combination of a majority of the whole very improbable, if not impracticable. The first method prevails in all governments possessing an hereditary or self-appointed authority. This, at best, is but a precarious security; because a power independent of the society may as well espouse the unjust views of the major, as the rightful interests of the minor party, and may possibly be turned against both parties. The second method will be exemplified in the federal republic of the United States. Whilst all authority in it will be derived from and dependent on the society, the society itself will be broken into so many parts, interests, and classes of citizens, that the rights of individuals, or of the minority, will be in little danger from interested combinations of the majority.

In a free government the security for civil rights must be the same as that for religious rights. It consists in the one case in the multiplicity of interests, and in the other in the multiplicity of sects. The degree of security in both cases will depend on the number of interests and sects; and this may be presumed to depend on the extent of country and number of people comprehended under the same government. This view of the subject must particularly recommend a proper federal system to all the sincere and considerate friends of republican government, since it shows that in exact proportion as the territory of the Union may be formed into more circumscribed Confederacies, or States oppressive combinations of a majority will be facilitated: the best security, under the republican forms, for the rights of every class of citizens, will be diminished: and consequently the stability and independence of some member of the government, the only other security, must be proportionately increased. Justice is the end of government. It is the end of civil society. It ever has been and ever will be pursued until it be obtained, or until liberty be lost in the pursuit. In a society under the forms of which the stronger faction can readily unite and oppress the weaker, anarchy may as truly be said to reign as in a state of nature, where the weaker individual is not secured against the violence of the stronger; and as, in the latter state, even the stronger individuals are prompted, by the uncertainty of their condition, to submit to a government which may protect the weak as well as themselves; so, in the former state, will the more powerful factions or parties be gradually induced, by a like motive, to wish for a government which will protect all parties, the weaker as well as the more powerful.

It can be little doubted that if the State of Rhode Island was separated from the Confederacy and left to itself, the insecurity of rights under the popular form of government within such narrow limits would be displayed by such reiterated oppressions of factious majorities that some power altogether independent of the people would soon be called for by the voice of the very factions whose misrule had proved the necessity of it. In the extended republic of the United States, and among the great variety of interests, parties, and sects which it embraces, a coalition of a majority of the whole society could seldom take place on any other principles than those of justice and the general good; whilst there being thus less danger to a minor from the will of a major party, there must be less pretext, also, to provide for the security of the former, by introducing into the government a will not dependent on the latter, or, in other words, a will independent of the society itself. It is no less certain than it is important, notwithstanding the contrary opinions which have been entertained, that the larger the society, provided it lie within a practical sphere, the more duly capable it will be of self-government. And happily for the REPUBLICAN CAUSE, the practicable sphere may be carried to a very great extent, by a judicious modification and mixture of the FEDERAL PRINCIPLE.

PUBLIUS.

Appendix 6

Presidents, Vice Presidents, Speakers, and Chief Justices, 1789–2011

PRESIDENT/VICE PRESIDENT	TERM	CONGRESS	SPEAKER OF THE HOUSE	CHIEF JUSTICE OF THE UNITED STATES
George Washington[1] John Adams	(1789–1797)	1st 2nd 3rd 4th	Frederick A.C. Muhlenberg, Pa. Jonathan Trumbull, F-Conn. Muhlenberg Jonathan Dayton, F-N.J.	John Jay (1789–1795) John Rutledge (1795) Oliver Ellsworth (1796–1800)
John Adams, F Thomas Jefferson, D-R	(1797–1801)	5th 6th	Dayton Theodore Sedgwick, F-Mass.	Ellsworth John Marshall (1801–1835)
Thomas Jefferson, D-R Aaron Burr (1801–1805) George Clinton (1805–1809)	(1801–1809)	7th 8th 9th 10th	Nathaniel Macon, D-N.C. Macon Macon Joseph B. Varnum, Mass.	Marshall
James Madison, D-R George Clinton[2] (1809–1812) Elbridge Gerry[2] (1813–1814)	(1809–1817)	11th 12th 13th 14th	Varnum Henry Clay, R-Ky. Clay/Langdon Cheves, D-S.C. Clay	Marshall
James Monroe, D-R Daniel D. Tompkins	(1817–1825)	15th 16th 17th 18th	Clay Clay/John W. Taylor, D-N.Y. Philip P. Barbour, D-Va. Clay	Marshall
John Quincy Adams, D-R John C. Calhoun	(1825–1829)	19th 20th	Taylor Andrew Stevenson, D-Va.	Marshall
Andrew Jackson, D John C. Calhoun[3] (1829–1832) Martin Van Buren (1833–1837)	(1829–1837)	21st 22nd 23rd 24th	Stevenson Stevenson Stevenson/John Bell, W-Tenn. James K. Polk, D-Tenn.	Marshall Roger B. Taney (1836–1864)
Martin Van Buren, D Richard M. Johnson	(1837–1841)	25th 26th	Polk Robert M.T. Hunter, D-Va.	Taney
William Henry Harrison,[2] W John Tyler	(1841)			Taney
John Tyler, W	(1841–1845)	27th 28th	John White, W-Ky. John W. Jones, D-Va.	Taney
James K. Polk, D George M. Dallas	(1845–1849)	29th 30th	John W. Davis, D-Ind. Robert C. Winthrop, W-Mass.	Taney
Zachary Taylor,[2] W Millard Fillmore	(1849–1850)	31st	Howell Cobb, D-Ga.	Taney
Millard Fillmore, W	(1850–1853)	31st 32nd	Cobb Linn Boyd, D-Ky.	Taney
Franklin Pierce, D William R. King[2] (1853)	(1853–1857)	33rd 34th	Boyd Nathaniel P. Banks, R-Mass.	Taney
James Buchanan, D John C. Breckinridge	(1857–1861)	35th 36th	James L. Orr, D-S.C. William Pennington, R-N.J.	Taney

(Continued)

PRESIDENT/VICE PRESIDENT	TERM	CONGRESS	SPEAKER OF THE HOUSE	CHIEF JUSTICE OF THE UNITED STATES

Abraham Lincoln,[2] R
    Hannibal Hamlin (1861–1865)
    Andrew Johnson,[4] D (1865)
	(1861–1865)	37th
		38th
			Galusha A. Grow, R-Pa.
			Schuyler Colfax, R-Ind.
				Taney
				Salmon P. Chase (1864–1873)

Andrew Johnson, D	(1865–1869)	39th 40th	Colfax Colfax/Theodore M. Pomeroy, R-N.Y.	Chase

Ulysses S. Grant, R
    Schuyler Colfax (1869–1873)
    Henry Wilson[2] (1873–1875)
	(1869–1877)	41st
		42nd
		43rd
		44th
			James G. Blaine, R-Maine
			Blaine
			Blaine
			Michael C. Kerr, D-Ind./
			    Samuel J. Randall, D-Pa.
				Chase
				Morrison R. Waite (1874–1888)

Rutherford B. Hayes, R William A. Wheeler	(1877–1881)	45th 46th	Randall Randall	Waite
James A. Garfield,[2] R Chester A. Arthur	(1881)			Waite
Chester A. Arthur, R	(1881–1885)	47th 48th	Joseph Warren Keifer, R-Ohio John G. Carlisle, D-Ky.	Waite
Grover Cleveland, D Thomas A. Hendricks[2] (1885)	(1885–1889)	49th 50th	Carlisle Carlisle	Waite Melville W. Fuller (1888–1910)
Benjamin Harrison, R Levi P. Morton	(1889–1893)	51st 52nd	Thomas Brackett Reed, R-Maine Charles F. Crisp, D-Ga.	Fuller
Grover Cleveland, D Adlai E. Stevenson	(1893–1897)	53rd 54th	Crisp Reed	Fuller

William McKinley,[2] R
    Garret A. Hobart[2] (1897–1899)
    Theodore Roosevelt (1901)
	(1897–1901)	55th
		56th
			Reed
			David B. Henderson, R-Iowa
				Fuller

Theodore Roosevelt, R
    Charles W. Fairbanks
    (1905–1909)
	(1901–1909)	57th
		58th
		59th
		60th
			Henderson
			Joseph G. Cannon, R-Ill.
			Cannon
			Cannon
				Fuller

William Howard Taft, R
    James S. Sherman[2]
    (1909–1912)
	(1909–1913)	61st
		62nd
			Cannon
			James B. "Champ" Clark, D-Mo.
				Fuller
				Edward D. White (1910–1921)

Woodrow Wilson, D Thomas R. Marshall	(1913–1921)	63rd 64th 65th 66th	Clark Clark Clark Frederick H. Gillett, R-Mass.	White
Warren G. Harding,[2] R Calvin Coolidge	(1921–1923)	67th	Gillett	William Howard Taft (1921–1930)

Calvin Coolidge, R
    Charles G. Dawes
    (1925–1929)
	(1923–1929)	68th
		69th
		70th
			Gillett
			Nicholas Longworth, R-Ohio
			Longworth
				Taft

Herbert C. Hoover, R Charles Curtis	(1929–1933)	71st 72nd	Longworth John Nance Garner, D-Texas	Taft Charles Evans Hughes (1930–1941)

Franklin D. Roosevelt,[2] D
    John Nance Garner
    (1933–1941)
	(1933–1945)	73rd
		74th
			Henry T. Rainey, D-Ill.
			Joseph W. Byrns, D-Tenn./
			    William B. Bankhead, D-Ala.
				Hughes
				Harlan F. Stone (1941–1946)

PRESIDENT/VICE PRESIDENT	TERM	CONGRESS	SPEAKER OF THE HOUSE	CHIEF JUSTICE OF THE UNITED STATES
Franklin D. Roosevelt (continued) Henry A. Wallace (1941–1945) Harry S. Truman (1945)		75th 76th 77th 78th 79th	Bankhead Bankhead/Sam Rayburn, D-Texas Rayburn Rayburn Rayburn	Stone
Harry S. Truman, D Alben W. Barkley (1949–1953)	(1945–1953)	79th 80th 81st 82nd	Rayburn Joseph W. Martin Jr., R-Mass. Rayburn Rayburn	Stone Frederick M. Vinson (1946–1953)
Dwight D. Eisenhower, R Richard Nixon	(1953–1961)	83rd 84th 85th 86th	Martin Rayburn Rayburn Rayburn	Vinson Earl Warren (1953–1969)
John F. Kennedy,[2] D Lyndon B. Johnson	(1961–1963)	87th 88th	Rayburn/John W. McCormack, D-Mass. McCormack	Warren
Lyndon B. Johnson, D Hubert H. Humphrey (1965–1969)	(1963–1969)	88th 89th 90th	McCormack McCormack McCormack	Warren
Richard Nixon,[3] R Spiro T. Agnew[3] (1969–1973) Gerald R. Ford[5] (1973–1974)	(1969–1974)	91st 92nd 93rd	McCormack Carl Albert, D-Okla. Albert	Warren Warren E. Burger (1969–1986)
Gerald R. Ford, R Nelson A. Rockefeller[5]	(1974–1977)	93rd 94th	Albert Albert	Burger
Jimmy Carter, D Walter F. Mondale	(1977–1981)	95th 96th	Thomas P. O'Neill Jr., D-Mass. O'Neill	Burger
Ronald Reagan, R George Bush	(1981–1989)	97th 98th 99th 100th	O'Neill O'Neill O'Neill Jim Wright, D-Texas	Burger William Rehnquist (1986–2005)
George H. W. Bush, R Dan Quayle	(1989–1993)	101st 102nd	Wright/Thomas S. Foley, D-Wash. Foley	Rehnquist
Bill Clinton, D Al Gore	(1993–2001)	103rd 104th 105th 106th	Foley Newt Gingrich, R-Ga. Gingrich J. Dennis Hastert, R-Ill.	Rehnquist
George W. Bush, R Richard B. Cheney	(2001–2009)	107th 108th 109th 110th	J. Dennis Hastert, R-Ill. Nancy D. Pelosi, D-Calif.	Rehnquist John Roberts (2005–)
Barack H. Obama, D Joseph R. Biden	(2009–)	111th 112th	Pelosi John Boehner, R-Ohio	Roberts

Notes: The vice president's term or party is noted when it differs from that of the president. Key to abbreviations: D—Democrat; D-R—Democratic-Republican; F—Federalist; R—Republican; W—Whig.

1. Washington belonged to no formal party.
2. Died in office.
3. Resigned from office.
4. Democrat Johnson and Republican Lincoln ran under the Union Party banner in 1864.
5. Appointed to office.

Appendix 7

Political Party Affiliations in Congress and the Presidency, 1789–2011

| YEAR | CONGRESS | HOUSE | | SENATE | | PRESIDENT |
		MAJORITY PARTY	PRINCIPAL MINORITY PARTY	MAJORITY PARTY	PRINCIPAL MINORITY PARTY	
1789–1791	1st	AD-38	Op-26	AD-17	Op-9	F (Washington)
1791–1793	2nd	F-37	DR-33	F-16	DR-13	F (Washington)
1793–1795	3rd	DR-57	F-48	F-17	DR-13	F (Washington)
1795–1797	4th	F-54	DR-52	F-19	DR-13	F (Washington)
1797–1799	5th	F-58	DR-48	F-20	DR-12	F (John Adams)
1799–1801	6th	F-64	DR-42	F-19	DR-13	F (John Adams)
1801–1803	7th	DR-69	F-36	DR-18	F-13	DR (Jefferson)
1803–1805	8th	DR-102	F-39	DR-25	F-9	DR (Jefferson)
1805–1807	9th	DR-116	F-25	DR-27	F-7	DR (Jefferson)
1807–1809	10th	DR-118	F-24	DR-28	F-6	DR (Jefferson)
1809–1811	11th	DR-94	F-48	DR-28	F-6	DR (Madison)
1811–1813	12th	DR-108	F-36	DR-30	F-6	DR (Madison)
1813–1815	13th	DR-112	F-68	DR-27	F-9	DR (Madison)
1815–1817	14th	DR-117	F-65	DR-25	F-11	DR (Madison)
1817–1819	15th	DR-141	F-42	DR-34	F-10	DR (Monroe)
1819–1821	16th	DR-156	F-27	DR-35	F-7	DR (Monroe)
1821–1823	17th	DR-158	F-25	DR-44	F-4	DR (Monroe)
1823–1825	18th	DR-187	F-26	DR-44	F-4	DR (Monroe)
1825–1827	19th	AD-105	J-97	AD-26	J-20	DR (John Q. Adams)
1827–1829	20th	J-119	AD-94	J-28	AD-20	DR (John Q. Adams)
1829–1831	21st	D-139	NR-74	D-26	NR-22	DR (Jackson)
1831–1833	22nd	D-141	NR-58	D-25	NR-21	D (Jackson)
1833–1835	23rd	D-147	AM-53	D-20	NR-20	D (Jackson)
1835–1837	24th	D-145	W-98	D-27	W-25	D (Jackson)
1837–1839	25th	D-108	W-107	D-30	W-18	D (Van Buren)

YEAR	CONGRESS	HOUSE		SENATE		PRESIDENT
		MAJORITY PARTY	PRINCIPAL MINORITY PARTY	MAJORITY PARTY	PRINCIPAL MINORITY PARTY	
1839–1841	26th	D-124	W-118	D-28	W-22	D (Van Buren)
1841–1843	27th	W-133	D-102	W-28	D-22	W (W. Harrison) W (Tyler)
1843–1845	28th	D-142	W-79	W-28	D-25	W (Tyler)
1845–1847	29th	D-143	W-77	D-31	W-25	D (Polk)
1847–1849	30th	W-115	D-108	D-36	W-21	D (Polk)
1849–1851	31st	D-112	W-109	D-35	W-25	W (Taylor) W (Fillmore)
1851–1853	32nd	D–140	W–88	D–35	W24	W (Fillmore)
1853–1855	33rd	D-159	W-71	D-38	W-22	D (Pierce)
1855–1857	34th	R-108	D-83	D-42	R-15	D (Pierce)
1857–1859	35th	D-131	R-92	D-35	R-20	D (Buchanan)
1859–1861	36th	R-113	D-101	D-38	R-26	D (Buchanan)
1861–1863	37th	R-106	D-42	R-31	D-11	R (Lincoln)
1863–1865	38th	R-103	D-80	R-39	D-12	R (Lincoln)
1865–1867	39th	U-145	D-46	U-42	D-10	U (Lincoln)[1] U (A. Johnson)[1]
1867–1869	40th	R-143	D-49	R-42	D-11	R (A. Johnson)
1869–1871	41st	R-170	D-73	R-61	D-11	R (Grant)
1871–1873	42nd	R-139	D-104	R-57	D-17	R (Grant)
1873–1875	43rd	R-203	D-88	R-54	D-19	R (Grant)
1875–1877	44th	D-181	R-107	R-46	D-29	R (Grant)
1877–1879	45th	D-156	R-137	R-39	D-36	R (Hayes)
1879–1881	46th	D-150	R-128	D-43	R-33	R (Hayes)
1881–1883	47th	R-152	D-130	R-37	D-37	R (Garfield) R (Arthur)
1883–1885	48th	D-200	R-119	R-40	D-36	R (Arthur)
1885–1887	49th	D-182	R-140	R-41	D-34	D (Cleveland)
1887–1889	50th	D-170	R-151	R-39	D-37	D (Cleveland)
1889–1891	51st	R-173	D-159	R-37	D-37	R (B. Harrison)

(Continued)

YEAR	CONGRESS	HOUSE		SENATE		PRESIDENT
		MAJORITY PARTY	PRINCIPAL MINORITY PARTY	MAJORITY PARTY	PRINCIPAL MINORITY PARTY	
1891–1893	52nd	D-231	R-88	R-47	D-39	R (B. Harrison)
1893–1895	53rd	D-220	R-126	D-44	R-38	D (Cleveland)
1895–1897	54th	R-246	D-104	R-43	D-39	D (Cleveland)
1897–1899	55th	R-206	D-134	R-46	D-34	R (McKinley)
1899–1901	56th	R-185	D-163	R-53	D-26	R (McKinley)
1901–1903	57th	R-198	D-153	R-56	D-29	R (McKinley) R (T. Roosevelt)
1903–1905	58th	R-207	D-178	R-58	D-32	R (T. Roosevelt)
1905–1907	59th	R-250	D-136	R-58	D-32	R (T. Roosevelt)
1907–1909	60th	R-222	D-164	R-61	D-29	R (T. Roosevelt)
1909–1911	61st	R-219	D-172	R-59	D-32	R (Taft)
1911–1913	62nd	D-228	R-162	R-49	D-42	R (Taft)
1913–1915	63rd	D-290	R-127	D-51	R-44	D (Wilson)
1915–1917	64th	D-231	R-193	D-56	R-39	D (Wilson)
1917–1919	65th	D-216	R-210	D-53	R-42	D (Wilson)
1919–1921	66th	R-237	D-191	R-48	D-47	D (Wilson)
1921–1923	67th	R-300	D-132	R-59	D-37	R (Harding)
1923–1925	68th	R-225	D-207	R-51	D-43	R (Coolidge)
1925–1927	69th	R-247	D-183	R-54	D-40	R (Coolidge)
1927–1929	70th	R-237	D-195	R-48	D-47	R (Coolidge)
1929–1931	71st	R-267	D-163	R-56	D-39	R (Hoover)
1931–1933	72nd	D-216	R-218	R-48	D-47	R (Hoover)
1933–1935	73rd	D-313	R-117	D-59	R-36	D (F. Roosevelt)
1935–1937	74th	D-322	R-103	D-69	R-25	D (F. Roosevelt)
1937–1939	75th	D-333	R-89	D-75	R-17	D (F. Roosevelt)
1939–1941	76th	D-262	R-169	D-69	R-23	D (F. Roosevelt)
1941–1943	77th	D-267	R-162	D-66	R-28	D (F. Roosevelt)
1943–1945	78th	D-222	R-209	D-57	R-38	D (F. Roosevelt)
1945–1947	79th	D-243	R-190	D-56	R-38	D (F. Roosevelt) D (Truman)

YEAR	CONGRESS	HOUSE		SENATE		PRESIDENT
		MAJORITY PARTY	PRINCIPAL MINORITY PARTY	MAJORITY PARTY	PRINCIPAL MINORITY PARTY	
1947–1949	80th	R-246	D-188	R-51	D-45	D (Truman)
1949–1951	81st	D-263	R-171	D-54	R-42	D (Truman)
1951–1953	82nd	D-234	R-199	D-48	R-47	D (Truman)
1953–1955	83rd	R-221	D-213	R-48	D-46	R (Eisenhower)
1955–1957	84th	D-234	R-201	D-48	R-47	R (Eisenhower)
1957–1959	85th	D-233	R-200	D-49	R-47	R (Eisenhower)
1959–1961	86th	D-283	R-153	D-64	R-34	R (Eisenhower)
1961–1963	87th	D-262	R-175	D-64	R-36	D (Kennedy)
1963–1965	88th	D-258	R-176	D-67	R-33	D (Kennedy) D (L. Johnson)
1965–1967	89th	D-295	R-140	D-68	R-32	D (L. Johnson)
1967–1969	90th	D-248	R-187	D-64	R-36	D (L. Johnson)
1969–1971	91st	D-243	R-192	D-58	R-42	R (Nixon)
1971–1973	92nd	D-255	R-180	D-54	R-44	R (Nixon)
1973–1975	93rd	D-242	R-192	D-56	R-42	R (Nixon) R (Ford)
1975–1977	94th	D-291	R-144	D-60	R-37	R (Ford)
1977–1979	95th	D-292	R-143	D-61	R-38	D (Carter)
1979–1981	96th	D-277	R-158	D-58	R-41	D (Carter)
1981–1983	97th	D-242	R-192	R-53	D-46	R (Reagan)
1983–1985	98th	D-269	R-166	R-54	D-46	R (Reagan)
1985–1987	99th	D-253	R-182	R-53	D-47	R (Reagan)
1987–1989	100th	D-258	R-177	D-55	R-45	R (Reagan)
1989–1991	101st	D-260	R-175	D-55	R-45	R (G.H.W. Bush)
1991–1993	102nd	D-267	R-167	D-56	R-44	R (G.H.W. Bush)
1993–1995	103rd	D-258	R-176	D-57	R-43	D (Clinton)
1995–1997	104th	R-230	D-204	R-52	D-48	D (Clinton)
1997–1999	105th	R-226	D-207	R-55	D-45	D (Clinton)
1999–2001	106th	R-223	D-211	R-55	D-45	D (Clinton)

(Continued)

YEAR	CONGRESS	HOUSE		SENATE		PRESIDENT
		MAJORITY PARTY	PRINCIPAL MINORITY PARTY	MAJORITY PARTY	PRINCIPAL MINORITY PARTY	
2001–2003	107th	R-221	D-212	D-50	R-50	R (G.W. Bush)
2003–2005	108th	R-229	D-204	D-48	R-51	R (G. W. Bush)
2005–2007	109th	R-232	D-202	D-44	R-55	R (G. W. Bush)
2007–2009	110th	D-233	R-202	D-49	R-49	R (G. W. Bush)
2009–2011	111th	D-254	R-175	D-57	R-40	D (Obama)
2011–2013	112th	R-242	D-193	D-51	R-47	D (Obama)

Sources: For data through the 33rd Congress, see U.S. Bureau of the Census, *Historical Statistics of the United States, Colonial Times to 1970* (Washington, D.C.: Government Printing Office, 1975), 1083–1084; for data after the 33rd Congress, see U.S. Congress, *Joint Committee on Printing, Official Congressional Directory* (Washington, D.C.: Government Printing Office, 2008), 553–554. For House data and Senate data, see CQ Politics Election 2008 web site, www.cqpolitics.com/wmspage.cfm?parm1=2. See also http://innovation.cq.com/election_night08?tab2=f.

Notes: Figures are for the beginning of the first session of each Congress. Key to abbreviations: AD—Administration; AM—Anti-Masonic; D—Democratic; DR—Democratic-Republican; F—Federalist; J—Jacksonian; NR—National Republican; Op—Opposition; R—Republican; U—Unionist; W—Whig.

1. The Republican Party ran under the Union Party banner in 1864.

Appendix 8

Summary of Presidential Elections, 1789–2008

YEAR	NUMBER OF STATES	CANDIDATES		ELECTORAL VOTE		POPULAR VOTE	
1789[a]	10	Fed. George Washington		Fed. 69		——[b]	
1792[a]	15	Fed. George Washington		Fed. 132		——[b]	
1796[a]	16	Dem.-Rep. Thomas Jefferson	Fed. John Adams	Dem.-Rep. 68	Fed. 71	——[b]	
1800[a]	16	Dem.-Rep. Thomas Jefferson Aaron Burr	Fed. John Adams Charles Cotesworth Pinckney	Dem.-Rep 73	Fed. 65	——[b]	
1804	17	Dem.-Rep. Thomas Jefferson George Clinton	Fed. Charles Cotesworth Pinckney Rufus King	Dem.-Rep 162	Fed. 14	——[b]	
1808	17	Dem.-Rep. James Madison George Clinton	Fed. Charles Cotesworth Pinckney Rufus King	Dem.-Rep 122	Fed. 47	——[b]	
1812	18	Dem.-Rep. James Madison Elbridge Gerry	Fed. George Clinton Jared Ingersoll	Dem.-Rep 128	Fed. 89	——[b]	
1816	19	Dem.-Rep. James Monroe Daniel D. Tompkins	Fed. Rufus King John Howard	Dem.-Rep 183	Fed. 34	——[b]	
1820	24	Dem.-Rep James Monroe Daniel D. Tompkins	——[c]	Dem.-Rep 231	——[c]	——[b]	
1824[d]	24	Dem.-Rep Andrew Jackson John C. Calhoun	Dem.-Rep John Q. Adams Nathan Sanford	Dem.-Rep 99	Dem.-Rep. 84	Dem.-Rep 151,271 41.3%	Dem.-Rep 113,122 30.9%
1828	24	Dem.-Rep. Andrew Jackson John C. Calhoun	Nat.-Rep. John Q. Adams Richard Rush	Dem.-Rep. 178	Nat.-Rep. 83	Dem.-Rep. 642,553 56.0%	Nat.-Rep. 500,897 43.6%
1832[e]	24	Dem. Andrew Jackson Martin Van Buren	Nat.-Rep. Henry Clay John Sergeant	Dem. 219	Nat.-Rep. 49 54.2%	Dem. 701,780	Nat.-Rep. 484,205 37.4%
1836[f]	26	Dem. Martin Van Buren Richard M. Johnson	Whig William H. Harrison Francis Granger	Dem. 170	Whig 73	Dem. 764,176 50.8%	Whig 550,816 36.6%

(Continued)

YEAR	NUMBER OF STATES	CANDIDATES		ELECTORAL VOTE		POPULAR VOTE	
1840	26	Dem. Martin Van Buren Richard M. Johnson	Whig William H. Harrison John Tyler	Dem. 60	Whig 234	Dem. 1,128,854 46.8%	Whig 1,275,390 52.9%
1844	26	Dem. James Polk George M. Dallas	Whig Henry Clay Theodore Frelinghuysen	Dem. 170	Whig 105	Dem. 1,339,494 49.5%	Whig 1,300,004 48.1%
1848	30	Dem. Lewis Cass William O. Butler	Whig Zachary Taylor Millard Fillmore	Dem. 127	Whig 163	Dem. 1,233,460 42.5%	Whig 1,361,393 47.3%
1852	31	Dem. Franklin Pierce William R. King	Whig Winfield Scott William A. Graham	Dem. 254	Whig 42	Dem. 1,607,510 50.8%	Whig 1,386,942 43.9%

YEAR	NUMBER OF STATES	CANDIDATES		ELECTORAL VOTE		POPULAR VOTE	
		DEM.	REP.	DEM.	REP.	DEM.	REP.
1856 [g]	31	James Buchanan John C. Breckinridge	John C. Fremont William L. Dayton	174	114	1,836,072 45.3%	1,342,345 33.1%
1860 [h]	33	Stephen A. Douglas Herschel V. Johnson	Abraham Lincoln Hannibal Hamlin	12	180	1,380,202 29.5%	1,865,908 39.8%
1864 [i]	36	George B. McClellan George H. Pendleton	Abraham Lincoln Andrew Johnson	21	212	1,812,807 45.0%	2,218,388 55.0%
1868 [j]	37	Horatio Seymour Francis P. Blair Jr.	Ulysses S. Grant Schuyler Colfax	80	214	2,708,744 47.3%	3,013,650 52.7%
1872 [k]	37	Horace Greeley Benjamin Gratz Brown	Ulysses S. Grant Henry Wilson		286	2,834,761 43.8%	3,598,235 55.6%
1876	38	Samuel J. Tilden Thomas A. Hendricks	Rutherford B. Hayes William A. Wheeler	184	185	4,288,546 51.0%	4,034,311 47.9%
1880	38	Winfield S. Hancock William H. English	James A. Garfield Chester A. Arthur	155	214	4,444,260 48.2%	4,446,158 48.3%
1884	38	Grover Cleveland Thomas A. Hendricks	James G. Blaine John A. Logan	219	182	4,874,621 48.5%	4,848,936 48.2%
1888	38	Grover Cleveland Allen G. Thurman	Benjamin Harrison Levi P. Morton	168	233	5,534,488 48.6%	5,443,892 47.8%
1892 [l]	44	Grover Cleveland Adlai E. Stevenson	Benjamin Harrison Whitelaw Reid	277	145	5,551,883 46.1%	5,179,244 43.0%
1896	45	William J. Bryan Arthur Sewall	William McKinley Garret A. Hobart	176	271	6,511,495 46.7%	7,108,480 51.0%
1900	45	William J. Bryan Adlai E. Stevenson	William McKinley Theodore Roosevelt	155	292	6,358,345 45.5%	7,218,039 51.7%
1904	45	Alton B. Parker Henry G. Davis	Theodore Roosevelt Charles W. Fairbanks	140	336	5,028,898 37.6%	7,626,593 56.4%
1908	46	William J. Bryan John W. Kern	William H. Taft James S. Sherman	162	321	6,406,801 43.0%	7,676,258 51.6%

YEAR	NUMBER OF STATES	CANDIDATES		ELECTORAL VOTE		POPULAR VOTE	
		DEM.	REP.	DEM.	REP.	DEM.	REP.
1912[m]	48	Woodrow Wilson Thomas R. Marshall	William H. Taft James S. Sherman	435	8	6,293,152 41.8%	3,486,333 23.2%
1916	48	Woodrow Wilson Thomas R. Marshall	Charles E. Hughes Charles W. Fairbanks	277	254	9,126,300 49.2%	8,546,789 46.1%
1920	48	James M. Cox Franklin D. Roosevelt	Warren G. Harding Calvin Coolidge	127	404	9,140,884 34.2%	16,133,314 60.3%
1924[n]	48	John W. Davis Charles W. Bryant	Calvin Coolidge Charles G. Dawes	136	382	8,386,169 28.8%	15,717,553 54.1%
1928	48	Alfred E. Smith Joseph T. Robinson	Herbert C. Hoover Charles Curtis	87	444	15,000,185 40.8%	21,411,991 58.2%
1932	48	Franklin D. Roosevelt John N. Garner	Herbert C. Hoover Charles Curtis	472	59	22,825,016 57.4%	15,758,397 39.6%
1936	48	Franklin D. Roosevelt John N. Garner	Alfred M. Landon Frank Knox	523	8	27,747,636 60.8%	16,679,543 36.5%
1940	48	Franklin D. Roosevelt Henry A. Wallace	Wendell L. Willkie Charles L. McNary	449	82	27,263,448 54.7%	22,336,260 44.8%
1944	48	Franklin D. Roosevelt Harry S. Truman	Thomas E. Dewey John W. Bricker	432	99	25,611,936 53.4%	22,013,372 45.9%
1948[o]	48	Harry S. Truman Alben W. Barkley	Thomas E. Dewey Earl Warren	303	189	24,105,587 49.5%	21,970,017 45.1%
1952	48	Adlai E. Stevenson II John J. Sparkman	Dwight D. Eisenhower Richard M. Nixon	89	442	27,314,649 44.4%	33,936,137 55.1%
1956[p]	48	Adlai E. Stevenson II Estes Kefauver	Dwight D. Eisenhower Richard M. Nixon	73	457	26,030,172 42.0%	35,585,245 57.4%
1960[q]	50	John F. Kennedy Lyndon B. Johnson	Richard M. Nixon Henry Cabot Lodge	303	219	34,221,344 49.7%	34,106,671 49.5%
1964	50*	Lyndon B. Johnson Hubert H. Humphrey	Barry Goldwater William E. Miller	486	52	43,126,584 61.1%	27,177,838 38.5%
1968[r]	50*	Hubert H. Humphrey Edmund S. Muskie	Richard M. Nixon Spiro T. Agnew	191	301	31,274,503 42.7%	31,785,148 43.4%
1972[s]	50*	George McGovern Sargent Shriver	Richard M. Nixon Spiro T. Agnew	17	520	29,171,791 37.5%	47,170,179 60.7%
1976[t]	50*	Jimmy Carter Walter F. Mondale	Gerald R. Ford Robert Dole	297	240	40,830,763 50.1%	39,147,793 48.0%
1980	50*	Jimmy Carter Walter F. Mondale	Ronald Reagan George H. W. Bush	49	489	35,483,883 41.0%	43,904,153 50.7%
1984	50*	Walter F. Mondale Geraldine Ferraro	Ronald Reagan George H. W. Bush	13	525	37,577,185 40.6%	54,455,075 58.8%

(Continued)

YEAR	NUMBER OF STATES	CANDIDATES		ELECTORAL VOTE		POPULAR VOTE	
		DEM.	REP.	DEM.	REP.	DEM.	REP.
1988[u]	50*	Michael S. Dukakis Lloyd Bentsen	George H. W. Bush Dan Quayle	111	426	41,809,074 45.6%	48,886,097 53.4%
1992	50*	William J. Clinton Albert Gore	George H. W. Bush Dan Quayle	370	168	44,909,326 43.0%	39,103,882 37.4%
1996	50*	William J. Clinton Albert Gore	Robert J. Dole Jack F. Kemp	379	159	47,402,357 49.2%	39,198,755 40.7%
2000	50*	Albert Gore Joseph I. Lieberman	George W. Bush Richard B. Cheney	266	271	50,992,335 48.4%	50,455,156 47.9%
2004	50*	John Kerry John Edwards	George W. Bush Richard B. Cheney	252	286	59,026,013 47.3%	62,025,554 50.7%
2008	50*	Barack Obama Joseph Biden	John McCain Sarah Palin	365	173	69,498,459 52.9%	59,948,283 45.6%

Sources: Harold W. Stanley and Richard G. Niemi, *Vital Statistics on American Politics, 2007–2008* (Washington, D.C.: CQ Press, 2008), 26–30; *CQ Press Guide to U.S. Elections*, 5th ed. (Washington, D.C.: CQ Press, 2006), 715–719. For presidential race electoral vote data, see CQ Politics Election 2008 website, http://innovation .cq.com/election_night08?tab2=f. For presidential race popular vote data, see the *New York Times*'s Presidential Big Board—http://elections.nytimes.com/2008/ results/president/votes.html.

Notes: Dem.-Rep.—Democratic-Republican; Fed.—Federalist; Nat.-Rep.—National-Republican; Dem.—Democratic; Rep.—Republican.

a.   Elections from 1789 through 1800 were held under rules that did not allow separate voting for president and vice president.

b.   Popular vote returns are not shown before 1824 because consistent, reliable data are not available.

c.   1820: One electoral vote was cast for John Adams and Richard Stockton, who were not candidates.

d.   1824: All four candidates represented Democratic-Republican factions. William H. Crawford received 41 electoral votes and Henry Clay received 37 votes. Because no candidate received a majority, the election was decided (in Adams's favor) by the House of Representatives.

e.   1832: Two electoral votes were not cast.

f.   1836: Other Whig candidates receiving electoral votes were Hugh L. White, who received 26 votes, and Daniel Webster, who received 14 votes.

g.   1856: Millard Fillmore, Whig-American, received 8 electoral votes.

h.   1860: John C. Breckinridge, southern Democrat, received 72 electoral votes. John Bell, Constitutional Union, received 39 electoral votes.

i.   1864: Eighty-one electoral votes were not cast.

j.   1868: Twenty-three electoral votes were not cast.

k.   1872: Horace Greeley, Democrat, died after the election. In the Electoral College, Democratic electoral votes went to Thomas Hendricks, 42 votes; Benjamin Gratz Brown, 18 votes; Charles J. Jenkins, 2 votes; and David Davis, 1 vote. Seventeen electoral votes were not cast.

l.   1892: James B. Weaver, People's Party, received 22 electoral votes.

m.   1912: Theodore Roosevelt, Progressive Party, received 88 electoral votes.

n.   1924: Robert M. La Follette, Progressive Party, received 13 electoral votes.

o.   1948: J. Strom Thurmond, States' Rights Party, received 39 electoral votes.

p.   1956: Walter B. Jones, Democrat, received 1 electoral vote.

q.   1960: Harry Flood Byrd, Democrat, received 15 electoral votes.

r.   1968: George C. Wallace, American Independent Party, received 46 electoral votes.

s.   1972: John Hospers, Libertarian Party, received 1 electoral vote.

t.   1976: Ronald Reagan, Republican, received 1 electoral vote.

u.   1988: Lloyd Bentsen, the Democratic vice presidential nominee, received 1 electoral vote for president.

*Fifty states plus the District of Columbia.

Appendix 9

The American Economy

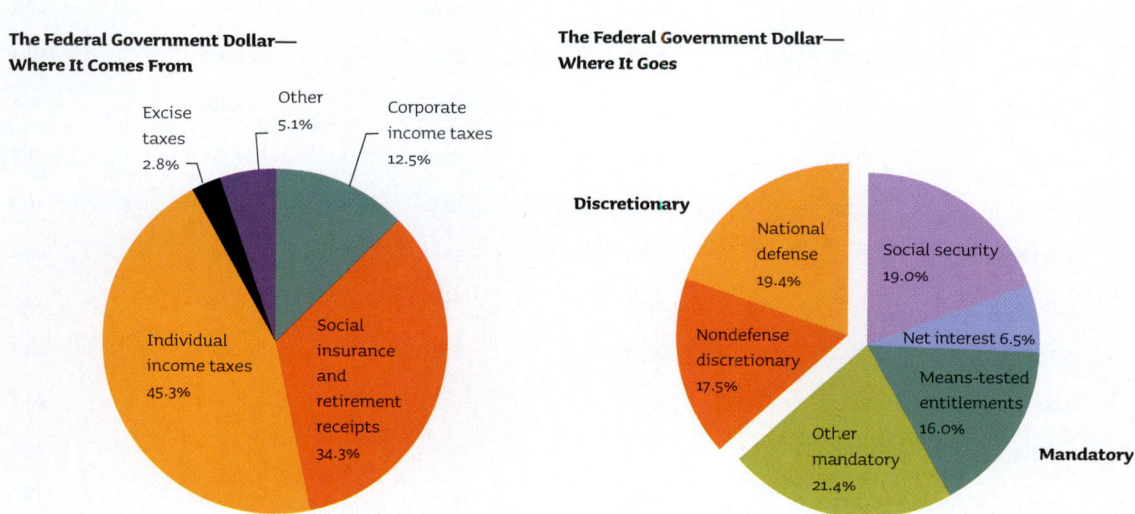

2012 Estimated Budget

The Federal Government Dollar—Where It Comes From

- Excise taxes 2.8%
- Other 5.1%
- Corporate income taxes 12.5%
- Individual income taxes 45.3%
- Social insurance and retirement receipts 34.3%

The Federal Government Dollar—Where It Goes

Discretionary
- National defense 19.4%
- Social security 19.0%
- Nondefense discretionary 17.5%
- Net interest 6.5%
- Means-tested entitlements 16.0%
- Other mandatory 21.4%

Mandatory

Source: Office of Management and Budget, Budget of the United States Government, Fiscal Year 2011 (Washington, D.C.: U.S. Government Printing Office, 2010).

YEAR	GDP (IN CONSTANT 2005 DOLLARS)	FEDERAL GOVERNMENT SPENDING (BILLIONS) (IN CONSTANT 2005 DOLLARS)			NATIONAL DEBT (CURRENT DOLLARS)	
		NATIONAL DEFENSE	NONDEFENSE	TOTAL	DEBT HELD BY THE PUBLIC (MILLIONS)	AS A PERCENTAGE OF GDP
1940	1,166.9	$24.4	$93.4	$117.8	42,772	44.2
1941	1,366.1	77.3	86.0	163.3	48,223	42.3
1942	1,618.2	250.1	125.4	375.4	67,753	47.0
1943	1,883.1	596.6	169.1	765.6	127,766	70.9
1944	2,035.2	790.6	171.8	962.1	184,796	88.4
1945	2,012.4	907.7	117.0	1,024.4	235,182	106.3
1946	1,792.2	492.9	117.0	609.6	241,861	108.6
1947	1,776.1	141.1	204.0	345.0	224,339	95.6
1948	1,854.2	108.8	172.4	281.3	216,270	84.3
1949	1,844.7	156.9	222.4	379.2	214,322	78.9
1950	2,006.0	164.8	235.0	400.0	219,023	80.1
1951	2,161.1	267.5	167.0	434.7	214,326	66.8

(Continued)

YEAR	GDP (IN CONSTANT 2005 DOLLARS)	FEDERAL GOVERNMENT SPENDING (BILLIONS) (IN CONSTANT 2005 DOLLARS)			NATIONAL DEBT (CURRENT DOLLARS)	
		NATIONAL DEFENSE	NONDEFENSE	TOTAL	DEBT HELD BY THE PUBLIC (MILLIONS)	AS A PERCENTAGE OF GDP
1952	2,243.9	497.7	152.0	650.2	214,758	61.6
1953	2,347.2	515.1	161.8	677.1	218,383	58.5
1954	2,332.4	472.8	136.7	609.2	224,499	59.4
1955	2,500.3	396.0	172.7	568.9	226,616	57.3
1956	2,549.7	369.4	189.7	559.3	222,156	51.9
1957	2,601.1	375.5	201.6	577.1	219,320	48.7
1958	2,577.6	370.7	216.0	586.5	226,336	49.1
1959	2,762.5	365.0	265.6	630.8	234,701	47.7
1960	2,830.9	369.4	259.3	628.9	236,840	45.6
1961	2,896.9	370.7	277.8	648.5	238,357	44.8
1962	3,072.4	388.3	318.4	707.0	248,010	43.6
1963	3,206.7	379.0	326.1	705.0	253,978	42.4
1964	3,392.3	387.0	354.1	741.3	256,849	40.1
1965	3,610.1	360.8	368.8	729.8	260,778	37.9
1966	3,845.3	399.1	412.2	811.4	263,714	35.0
1967	3,942.5	473.6	452.9	926.3	266,626	32.8
1968	4,133.4	518.2	491.4	1,009.3	289,545	33.3
1969	4,261.8	492.8	483.7	976.3	278,108	29.3
1970	4,269.9	463.9	518.7	982.7	283,198	28.0
1971	4,413.3	422.9	562.6	985.3	303,037	28.0
1972	4,647.7	385.5	625.0	1,010.4	322,377	27.3
1973	4,917.0	346.5	672.3	1,018.7	340,910	26.1
1974	4,889.9	332.7	695.0	1,027.7	343,699	23.8
1975	4,879.5	326.8	823.5	1,150.3	394,700	25.3
1976	5,141.3	314.3	878.5	1,192.8	477,404	27.5
TQ[1]	n/a	76.2	222.9	299.1	495,509	27.1
1977	5,377.7	311.4	902.7	1,213.9	549,104	27.8
1978	5,677.6	311.8	966.8	1,278.6	607,126	27.4
1979	5,855.0	318.7	972.9	1,291.7	640,306	25.6
1980	5,839.0	330.1	1,038.5	1,368.6	711,923	26.1
1981	5,987.2	348.2	1,068.2	1,416.2	789,410	25.8
1982	5,870.9	378.0	1,074.0	1,452.0	924,575	28.6
1983	6,136.2	405.8	1,093.1	1,498.9	1,137,268	33.1
1984	6,577.1	407.5	1,093.5	1,501.0	1,306,975	34.0

YEAR	GDP (IN CONSTANT 2005 DOLLARS)	FEDERAL GOVERNMENT SPENDING (BILLIONS) (IN CONSTANT 2005 DOLLARS)			NATIONAL DEBT (CURRENT DOLLARS)	
		NATIONAL DEFENSE	NONDEFENSE	TOTAL	DEBT HELD BY THE PUBLIC (MILLIONS)	AS A PERCENTAGE OF GDP
1985	6,849.3	433.1	1,179.6	1,612.7	1,507,260	36.4
1986	7,086.5	460.9	1,184.2	1,645.2	1,740,623	39.4
1987	7,313.3	467.1	1,149.7	1,616.8	1,889,753	40.7
1988	7,613.9	475.5	1,188.3	1,663.7	2,051,616	41.0
1989	7,885.9	481.6	1,242.3	1,724.1	2,190,716	40.6
1990	8,033.9	461.2	1,370.6	1,831.9	2,411,558	42.0
1991	8,015.1	399.4	1,449.4	1,849.0	2,688,999	45.3
1992	8,287.1	428.5	1,429.4	1,857.9	2,999,737	48.1
1993	8,523.4	413.4	1,432.1	1,845.5	3,248,396	49.4
1994	8,870.7	394.6	1,484.4	1,878.9	3,433,065	49.3
1995	9,093.7	375.6	1,521.0	1,896.6	3,604,378	49.2
1996	9,433.9	355.0	1,551.9	1,906.8	3,734,073	48.5
1997	9,854.3	354.6	1,561.4	1,916.1	3,772,344	46.1
1998	10,283.5	346.1	1,612.8	1,958.8	3,721,099	43.1
1999	10,779.8	347.6	1,641.8	1,989.5	3,632,363	39.8
2000	11,226.0	361.3	1,679.3	2,040.6	3,409,804	35.1
2001	11,347.2	363.1	1,709.5	2,072.7	3,319,615	33.0
2002	11,553.0	401.7	1,799.6	2,201.3	3,540,427	34.1
2003	11,840.7	444.6	1,859.3	2,303.9	3,913,443	36.1
2004	12,263.8	480.3	1,897.4	2,377.5	4,295,544	37.2
2005	12,638.4	495.3	1,976.7	2,472.0	4,592,212	37.5
2006	12,976.2	499.3	2,064.5	2,563.8	4,828,972	37.1
2007	13,228.9	509.2	2,055.7	2,565.1	5,035,129	36.8
2008	13,228.8	548.6	2,155.7	2,704.3	5,803,050	40.2
2009	12,880.6	580.2	2,606.2	3,186.3	7,544,707	53.0
2010 est.	n/a	626.2	2,688.8	3,315.2	9,297,653	63.6
2011 est.	n/a	644.3	2,724.5	3,368.9	10,498,325	68.6
2012 est.	n/a	576.8	2,667.0	3,243.9	11,472,112	70.8
2013 est.	n/a	549.3	2,772.0	3,321.3	12,325,653	71.7
2014 est.	n/a	547.7	2,915.3	3,463.1	13,139,347	72.2

Sources: Office of Management and Budget, *Budget of the United States Government, Fiscal Year 2011*, Historical Tables, Table 6.1: Composition of Outlays: 1940–2015; Table 7.1: Federal Debt at the End of the Year, 1940–2015 (Washington, D.C.: U.S. Government Printing Office, 2010); U.S. Department of Commerce Bureau of Economic Analysis, *National Economic Accounts*, National Income and Product Tables, Table 1.1.6: Real Gross Domestic Product, Chained Dollars, revised November 23, 2010.

1. Transitional quarter when fiscal year start was shifted from July 1 to October 1.

Notes

Chapter 1

1. Frank Rich, "It Still Felt Good the Morning After," *New York Times*, November 9, 2008.
2. Emily Hoban Kirby and Kei Kawashima-Ginsberg, "The Youth Vote in 2008," www.civicyouth.org/PopUps/FactSheets/FS_youth_Voting_2008_updated_6.22.pdf.
3. Center for Information & Research on Civic Learning and Engagement, "Youth Turnout Rate Rises to at Least 52%," November 7, 2008, www.civicyouth.org/?p=323#comments.
4. E. J. Dionne, *Why Americans Hate Politics* (New York: Simon & Schuster, 1991), 354, 355.
5. Harold D. Lasswell, *Politics: Who Gets What, When, How* (New York: McGraw-Hill, 1938).
6. Joseph A. Schumpeter, *Capitalism, Socialism, and Democracy*, 3rd ed. (New York: Harper Colophon Books, 1950), 269–296.
7. A. Dahl, *Pluralist Democracy in the United States* (Chicago: Rand McNally, 1967).
8. Carole Pateman, *Participation and Democratic Theory* (New York: Cambridge University Press, 1970).
9. For an explanation of this view, see, for example, Russell L. Hanson, *The Democratic Imagination in America: Conversation With Our Past* (Princeton: Princeton University Press, 1985), 55–91; and Gordon Wood, *The Creation of the American Republic, 1776–1787* (New York: Norton, 1969).
10. Bruce E. Johansen, *Forgotten Founders: Benjamin Franklin, the Iroquois and the Rationale for the American Revolution* (Ipswich, Mass.: Gambit, 1982).
11. Dionne, 354, 355.
12. Daniel M. Shea, Director of Allegheny College's Center for Political Participation in Meadville, Pa., cited in Bryan Bender, "Turnout Was Strong, But Maintaining Interest Is Key," *Boston Globe*, November 5, 2004, A6.
13. Mark Carreau, "America Responds," *Houston Chronicle*, September 22, 2001, A26; Bronwen Maddox, "America Feels the Draft," *Times* (London), October 4, 2001; Chuck Haga, "Rules for Draft Changed Since Vietnam," *Minneapolis Star Tribune*, September 19, 2001, 11A.
14. "GOP Warns Rock the Vote About 'Malicious' Draft-Themed Campaign," *Chicago Sun-Times*, November 4, 2004, 50.

Chapter 2

1. *Graham v. Richardson*, 403 U.S. 532 (1971).
2. See, for instance, Nicole Cusano, "Amherst Mulls Giving Non-Citizens Right to Vote," *Boston Globe*, October 26, 1998, B1; "Casual Citizenship?" Editorial, *Boston Globe*, October 31, 1998, A18.
3. David M. Kennedy et al., *The American Pageant*, 12th ed. (Boston: Houghton Mifflin, 2002), 731.
4. Randal C. Archibold, "Arizona Enacts Stringent Law on Immigration," *New York Times*, April 23, 2010, www.nytimes.com/2010/04/24/us/politics/24immig.html.
5. Kate Zernike and Megan Thee-Brenan, "Poll Finds Tea Party Backers Wealthier and More Educated," *New York Times*, April 14, 2010.
6. Benjamin R. Barber, "Foreword," in Grant Reeher and Joseph Cammarano, eds., *Education for Citizenship: Ideas and Innovations in Political Learning* (New York: Rowman & Littlefield, 1997), ix.
7. Rasmussen Reports, June 2, 2008, www.rasmussenreports.com.

Chapter 3

1. David Barstow, "Tea Party Lights Fuse for Rebellion on Right," *New York Times*, February 15, 2010, www.nytimes.com/2010/02/16/us/politics/16teaparty.html?emc=eta1.
2. Richard A. Serrano, "Uneasy in Oklahoma: Fifteen Years After the McVeigh Bombing, Anger at Washington and Talk of a State Militia," *Los Angeles Times*, April 18, 2010.
3. Toni Lucy, "Anti-Government Forces Still Struggle to Recover From Oklahoma City Fallout," *USA Today*, May 9, 2000, 9A; Evan Thomas and Eve Conant, "Hate: Antigovernment Extremists Are on the Rise—and On the March," *Newsweek*, April 19, 2010.
4. Mark Guarino, "Hutaree Militia Arrests Point to Tripling of Militias Since 2008," *Christian Science Monitor*, March 29, 2010, www.csmonitor.com/USA/Justice/2010/0329/Hutaree-militia-arrests-point-to-tripling-of-militias-since-2008.
5. There are many good illustrations of this point of view. See, for example, Gordon Wood, *The Creation of the American Republic, 1776–1787* (New York: Norton, 1969); Lawrence Henry Gipson, *The Coming of the Revolution, 1763–1775* (New York: Harper Torchbooks, 1962); Bernard Bailyn, *The Ideological Origins of the American Revolution* (Cambridge, Mass.: Belknap, 1967); and Jack P. Greene, ed., *The Reinterpretation of the American Revolution, 1763–1789* (New York: Harper & Row, 1968).
6. Robert Darcy, Susan Welch, and Janet Clark, *Women, Elections, and Representation* (Lincoln: University of Nebraska Press, 1994), 5–6.
7. Donald R. Wright, *African Americans in the Colonial Era* (Arlington Heights, Ill.: Harlan Davidson, 1990), 52.
8. Ibid., 56.
9. Ibid., 57–58.
10. Lawrence Henry Gipson, "The American Revolution as an Aftermath of the Great War for the Empire, 1754–1765," in Edmund S. Morgan, ed., *The American Revolution* (Englewood Cliffs, N.J.: Prentice Hall, 1965), 160.
11. Bailyn, 160–229.
12. Gipson, "The American Revolution," 163.
13. Thomas Paine, *Common Sense and Other Political Writings* (Indianapolis, Ind.: Bobbs-Merrill, 1953).
14. Cited in John L. Moore, *Speaking of Washington* (Washington, D.C.: Congressional Quarterly, 1993), 102–103.
15. John Locke, *Second Treatise of Government*, C. B. Macpherson, ed. (Indianapolis: Hackett, 1980), 31.
16. Garry Wills, *Inventing America* (New York: Doubleday, 1978), 377.
17. Wright, 122.
18. Ibid., 152.
19. Mary Beth Norton et al., *A People and a Nation* (Boston: Houghton Mifflin, 1994), 159.
20. Darcy, Welch, and Clark, 8.
21. See, for example, Sally Smith Booth, *The Women of '76* (New York: Hastings House, 1973); and Charles E. Claghorn, *Women Patriots of the American Revolution: A Biographical Dictionary* (Metuchen, N.J.: Scarecrow Press, 1991).
22. Carl Holliday, *Woman's Life in Colonial Days* (Boston: Cornhill, 1922), 143.
23. Wood, 398–399.
24. Ibid., 404.
25. Alexander Hamilton, James Madison, and John Jay, *The Federalist Papers*, Clinton Rossiter, ed. (New York: New American Library, 1961), 84.

26. Adrienne Koch, "Introduction," in James Madison, *Notes of Debates in the Federal Convention of 1787* (New York: Norton, 1969), xiii.

27. Moore, 9.

28. James Madison, *Notes of Debates in the Federal Convention of 1787 Reported by James Madison*, reissue ed. (New York: Norton, 1987).

29. There are many collections of Anti-Federalist writings. See, for example, W. B. Allen and Gordon Lloyd, eds., *The Essential Antifederalist* (Lanham, Md.: University Press of America, 1985); Cecilia Kenyon, ed., *The Antifederalists* (Indianapolis, Ind.: Bobbs Merrill, 1966); and Ralph Ketcham, *The Anti-Federalist Papers and the Constitutional Convention Debates* (New York: New American Library, 1986).

30. Hamilton, Madison, and Jay, 322.

31. Ketcham, 14.

32. James H. Kettner, *The Development of American Citizenship, 1608–1870* (Chapel Hill: University of North Carolina Press, 1978).

33. Carl Hulse, "Recalling 1995 Bombing, Clinton Sees Parallels," *New York Times*, April 16, 2010.

Chapter 4

1. Stephanie Armour, "Employers Grapple With Medical Marijuana Use: Ethical, Liability Issues Rise as More States Make It Legal," *USA Today*, April 17, 2007, 1B.

2. *Gonzales v. Raich*, 545 U.S. 1 (2005).

3. Jerry Seper, "DEA Raids Medical Marijuana Centers," *Washington Times*, January 19, 2007, A9.

4. Carrie Johnson, "U.S. Eases Stance on Medical Marijuana," *Washington Post*, October 20, 2009.

5. Alexander Hamilton, James Madison, and John Jay, *The Federalist Papers*, Clinton Rossiter, ed. (New York: New American Library, 1961), 82.

6. James Madison, *Notes of Debates in the Federal Convention of 1787*, reissue ed. (New York: Norton, 1987), 86.

7. David M. Olson, *The Legislative Process* (Cambridge, Mass.: Harper & Row, 1980), 21–23.

8. Richard F. Fenno Jr., *The United States Senate: A Bicameral Perspective* (Washington, D.C.: American Enterprise Institute for Public Policy Research, 1982), 5.

9. Madison, 136, 158.

10. Hamilton, Madison, and Jay, 465.

11. Lawrence S. Graham et al., *Politics and Government: A Brief Introduction*, 3rd ed. (Chatham, N.J.: Chatham House Publishers, 1994), 172–173.

12. Baron de Montesquieu, *The Spirit of the Laws*, Thomas Nugent, trans. (New York: Hafner Press, 1949), 152.

13. Hamilton, Madison, and Jay, 322.

14. Ibid., 84.

15. Ibid., 322.

16. Ibid., 321–322.

17. James C. McKinley Jr., "Agreement on Tougher Drunken-Driving Standard," *New York Times*, May 10, 2001, B5.

18. For a full explanation of the bakery metaphors, see Morton Grodzins, *The American System* (Chicago: Rand McNally, 1966). A more updated discussion of federalism can be found in Joseph Zimmerman, *Contemporary American Federalism: The Growth of National Power* (New York: Praeger, 1992).

19. Paul E. Peterson, *City Limits* (Chicago: University of Chicago Press, 1981).

20. Charles Mahtesian, "Romancing the Smokestack," *Governing* (November 1994): 36–40.

21. Harold Wolman, "Local Economic Development Policy: What Explains the Divergence Between Policy Analysis and Political Behavior?" *Journal of Urban Affairs* 10 (1988): 19–28; Martin Saiz and Susan Clarke, "Economic Development and Infrastructure Policy," in Virginia Gray and Russell Hanson, eds., *Politics in the American States*, 8th ed. (Washington, D.C.: CQ Press, 2004).

22. Christopher Swope, "Mississippi Signs on the Assembly Line," *Governing* (January 2001): 62; Jonathan Walters, "Gone With the Windfall," *Governing* (January 2004): 12.

23. Kierstan Gordan, "Scholars, Dollars and Sense," *Governing* (May 2000): 44.

24. The National Organization for the Reform of Marijuana Laws, "State By State Laws," February 22, 2005, www.norml.org/index .cfm?Group_ID=4516.

25. James Dao, "Red, Blue and Angry All Over," *New York Times*, January 16, 2005.

26. *McCulloch v. Maryland*, 4 Wheat. 316 (1819).

27. *Gibbons v. Ogden*, 9 Wheat. 1 (1824).

28. *Cooley v. Board of Wardens of Port of Philadelphia*, 53 U.S. (12 How.) 299 (1851).

29. *Dred Scott v. Sanford*, 60 U.S. 393 (1857).

30. *Pollock v. Farmer's Loan and Trust Company*, 1157 U.S. 429 (1895).

31. *Lochner v. New York*, 198 U.S. 45 (1905).

32. *Hammer v. Dagenhart*, 247 U.S. 251 (1918).

33. John Kincaid, "State-Federal Relations: Dueling Policies," in *The Book of the States 2008* (Lexington, Ky.: The Council of State Governments, 2008), 19.

34. Ibid.

35. Morris Fiorina, *Congress: Keystone of the Washington Establishment*, 2nd ed. (New Haven: Yale University Press, 1989); John E. Chubb, "Federalism and the Bias for Centralization," in John E. Chubb and Paul E. Peterson, eds., *The New Directions in American Politics* (Washington, D.C.: Brookings Institution, 1985), 273–306.

36. *Statistical Abstract of the United States, 2010* (Washington, D.C.: U.S. Census Bureau), Table 419.

37. David Walker, *The Rebirth of Federalism* (Chatham, N.J.: Chatham House, 1995), 139, 224.

38. Quote from Rochelle L. Stanfield, "Holding the Bag," *National Journal*, September 9, 1995, 2206.

39. Walker, 232–234; Kincaid, "State-Federal Relations: Dueling Policies."

40. Priscilla M. Regan, "Opposition to REAL ID Act at the State Level: Privacy, Immigration or Unfunded Mandates," prepared for delivery at the annual meeting of the American Political Science Association, Boston, August 28–31, 2008; U.S. Department of Homeland Security, "REAL ID Final Rule," www.dhs.gov/files/ laws/gc_1172765386179.shtm.

41. Martha Derthick, "Madison's Middle Ground in the 1980s," *Public Administration Review* (January–February 1987): 66–74.

42. Advisory Commission on Intergovernmental Relations, *Federal Mandate Relief for State, Local, and Tribal Governments* (Washington, D.C.: U.S. Government Printing Office, January 1995), 18.

43. Donald F. Kettl, "Mandates Forever," *Governing* (August 2003): 12; Tom Diemer, "Unfunded Mandate Bill Working Well," *Cleveland Plain Dealer*, February 8, 1998, 20A; Jonathan Walters, "The Accidental Tyranny of Congress," *Governing* (April 1997): 14.

44. Hamilton, Madison, and Jay, 278.

45. Jacob Sullum, "The Power to Regulate Anything," *Los Angeles Times*, April 22, 2008.

46. Warren Richey, "Showdown Over Medical Marijuana," *Christian Science Monitor*, November 29, 2004.

Chapter 5

1. "Mr. Cuccinelli's Witch Hunt: Virginia's Attorney General Declares War on Academic Freedom and Climate Reality," *Washington Post*, Editorial, May 7, 2010, www.washingtonpost.com/ wp-dyn/content/article/2010/05/06/ AR2010050605936.html.

2. Lawrence Biemiller, "U. of Virginia Asks Court to Halt Attorney General's Demand for Documents," *Chronicle of Higher Education*, May 27, 2010, http://chronicle

.com/article/U-of-Virginia-Asks-Court-to/65721/?sid=at&utm_source=at&utm_medium=en; "Mr. Cuccinelli's Witch Hunt."

3. "Petition to Set Aside Civil Investigative Demands Issued to the University of Virginia," May 27, 2010, www.virginia.edu/uvatoday/newsRelease.php?id=12022.

4. Rosalind S. Helderman, "U-Va Urged to Fight Cuccinelli Subpoena in Probe of Scientist; Climate Researchers Are Victims of Political Assault, Many Say," *Washington Post*, May 9, 2010.

5. Darren K. Carlson, "Far Enough? Public Wary of Restricted Liberties," *Gallup Poll*, January 20, 2004.

6. *West Virginia Board of Education v. Barnette*, 319 U.S. 624 (1943).

7. *Hamdi v. Rumsfeld*, 124 S. Ct. 2633 (2004); *Rasul v. Bush*, 124 S. Ct. 2686 (2004).

8. *Hamdan v. Rumsfeld*, 548 U.S. 557 (2007).

9. *Korematsu v. United States*, 323 U.S. 214 (1944).

10. Associated Press, *The Cold War at Home and Abroad 1945–1953* (New York: Grollier, 1995), 145.

11. Robert Frederick Burk, *The Eisenhower Administration and Black Civil Rights* (Knoxville: University of Tennessee Press, 1984), 204.

12. Ben Conery, "Administration Seeks Patriot Act Extensions; Defies Liberties Groups," *Washington Times*, September 16, 2009, 1.

13. Jack N. Rakove, "James Madison and the Bill of Rights," in *This Constitution: From Ratification to the Bill of Rights*, American Political Science Association and American Historical Association (Washington, D.C.: Congressional Quarterly, 1988), 165.

14. David M. O'Brien, *Constitutional Law and Politics*, vol. 2 (New York: Norton, 1995), 300.

15. Ann Bowman and Richard Kearney, *State and Local Government*, 3rd ed. (Boston: Houghton Mifflin, 1996), 39.

16. *Barron v. The Mayor and City Council of Baltimore*, 7 Peters 243 (1833).

17. *Chicago, Burlington & Quincy Railroad Co. v. Chicago*, 166 U.S. 226 (1897).

18. *Gitlow v. New York* 268 U.S. 652 (1920), cited in David M. O'Brien, *Constitutional Law and Politics*, vol. 2 (New York: Norton, 1995), 304.

19. Peter Irons, *Brennan vs. Rehnquist: The Battle for the Constitution* (New York: Knopf, 1994), 116.

20. O'Brien, 646.

21. Ibid., 647.

22. Ibid., 645; Henry J. Abraham and Barbara A. Perry, *Freedom and the Court* (New York: Oxford University Press, 1994), 223.

23. Ibid., 648.

24. Irons, 137.

25. *Abington School District v. Schempp*, 374 U.S. 203, 83 S. Ct. 1560 (1963).

26. Ibid.; *Murray v. Curlett*, 374 U.S. 203 (1963).

27. *Engel v. Vitale*, 370 U.S. 421, 82 S. Ct. 1261 (1962).

28. *Epperson v. Arkansas*, 393 U.S. 97 (1968).

29. *Lemon v. Kurtzman*, 403 U.S. 602, 91 S. Ct. 2105 (1971).

30. *O'Brien*, 661.

31. *Lynch v. Donnelly*, 465 U.S. 668 (1984).

32. *Wallace v. Jaffree*, 472 U.S. 38 (1985).

33. *Edwards v. Aguillard*, 482 U.S. 578 (1987).

34. *Board of Education of Westside Community Schools v. Mergens*, 496 U.S. 226 (1990).

35. *Lee v. Weisman*, 112 S. Ct. 2649 (1992).

36. *Santa Fe Independent School District v. Doe*, 530 U.S. 290 (2000).

37. *Locke v. Davey*, 124 S. Ct. 1307 (2004).

38. *Cantwell v. Connecticut*, 310 U.S. 296 (1940).

39. *Minersville School District v. Gobitis*, 310 U.S. 586 (1940).

40. *West Virginia State Board of Education v. Barnette*, 319 U.S. 624 (1943).

41. *McGowan v. Maryland*, 36 U.S. 420; *Two Guys From Harrison-Allentown, Inc., v. McGinley*, 366 U.S. 582; *Gallagher v. Crown Kosher Super Market of Massachusetts*, 366 U.S. 617; *Braunfield v. Brown*, 366 U.S. 599 (1961).

42. *Sherbert v. Verner*, 374 U.S. 398 (1963).

43. *Employment Division, Department of Human Resources v. Smith*, 494 U.S. 872 (1990).

44. *City of Boerne v. Flores*, 521 U.S. 507, 1997.

45. *Gonzales v. O Centro Espirata Beneficente Uniao do Vegetal*, 546 U.S. 418 (2006).

46. *Reynolds v. U.S.*, 98 U.S. 145 (1878).

47. *Welsh v. United States*, 398 U.S. 333 (1970).

48. John L. Sullivan, James Piereson, and George Marcus, *Political Tolerance and American Democracy* (Chicago: University of Chicago Press, 1982), 203.

49. *O'Brien*, 373; Samuel Walker, *In Defense of American Liberties: A History of the ACLU* (New York: Oxford University Press, 1990), 29.

50. Cited in Walker, 14.

51. *Schenck v. United States*, 249 U.S. 47 (1919); *Debs v. United States*, 249 U.S. 211 (1919); *Frowerk v. United States*, 249 U.S. 204 (1919); *Abrams v. United States*, 250 U.S. 616 (1919).

52. *Whitney v. California*, 274 U.S. 357 (1927).

53. *Brandenburg v. Ohio*, 395 U.S. 444 (1969).

54. *United States v. O'Brien*, 391 U.S. 367 (1968).

55. *Tinker v. Des Moines*, 393 U.S. 503 (1969).

56. *Street v. New York*, 394 U.S. 576 (1969).

57. *Texas v. Johnson*, 491 U.S. 397 (1989).

58. *United States v. Eichman*, 110 S. Ct. 2404 (1990).

59. *Virginia v. Black*, 538 U.S. 343 (2003).

60. *National Association for the Advancement of Colored People v. Alabama*, 357 U.S. 449 (1958).

61. *Sheldon v. Tucker*, 364 U.S. 516 (1960).

62. *Heart of Atlanta Motel v. United States*, 379 U.S. 241 (1964).

63. *Roberts v. United States Jaycees*, 468 U.S. 609 (1984).

64. *Jacobellis v. Ohio*, 378 U.S. 476 (1964).

65. *Miller v. California*, 413 U.S. 15 (1973).

66. *Cohen v. California*, 403 U.S. 15 (1971).

67. *Chaplinsky v. New Hampshire*, 315 U.S. 568 (1942).

68. *Terminello v. Chicago*, 337 U.S. 1 (1949).

69. *Cohen v. California*, 403 U.S. 15 (1971).

70. *Doe v. University of Michigan*, 721 F. Supp. 852 (E. D. Mich. 1989); *UMW Post v. Board of Regents of the University of Wisconsin*, 774 F. Supp. 1163, 1167, 1179 (E. D. Wis. 1991).

71. *R.A.V. v. City of St. Paul*, 60 LW 4667 (1992).

72. *Near v. Minnesota*, 283 U.S. 697 (1930).

73. *New York Times Company v. United States*, 403 U.S. 670 (1971).

74. Anthony Lewis, *Make No Law: The Sullivan Case and the First Amendment* (New York: Vintage Books/Random House, 1991).

75. *New York Times v. Sullivan*, 376 U.S. 254 (1964).

76. *Sheppard v. Maxwell*, 385 U.S. 333 (1966).

77. *Nebraska Press Association v. Stuart*, 427 U.S. 539 (1976).

78. *Reno v. ACLU*, 521 U.S. 1113 (1997).

79. *Ashcroft v. ACLU*, 124 S. Ct. 2783 (2004).

80. *United States v. American Library Association, Inc.*, 539 U.S. 194 (2003).

81. Pamela LiCalzi O'Connell, "Compressed Data: Law Newsletter Has to Sneak Past Filters," *New York Times*, April 2, 2001, C4.

82. Jeffery Seligno, "Student Writers Try to Duck the Censors by Going On-line," *New York Times*, June 7, 2001, G6.

83. *United States v. Lopez*, 514 U.S. 549 (1995); *Printz v. United States*, 521 U.S. 898 (1997).

84. Robert J. Spitzer, *The Politics of Gun Control* (Chatham, N.J.: Chatham House, 1995), 49.

85. Ibid., 47.

86. *United States v. Cruikshank*, 92 U.S. 542 (1876); *Presser v. Illinois*, 116 U.S. 252 (1886); *Miller v. Texas*, 153 U.S. 535 (1894); *United States v. Miller*, 307 U.S. 174 (1939).

87. *Printz v. United States*, 521 U.S. 898 (1997).

88. Warren Richey, "Supreme Court Asserts Broad Gun Rights," *Christian Science Monitor*, June 27, 2008.

89. Robert Barnes and Dan Eggen, "Supreme Court Affirms Fundamental Right to Bear Arms," *Washington Post*, June 29, 2010, www.washingtonpost.com/wp-dyn/content/article/2010/06/28/AR2010062802134.html.

90. *Olmstead v. United States*, 277 U.S. 438 (1928).

91. *Katz v. United States*, 389 U.S. 347 (1967).

92. *Berger v. State of New York*, 388 U.S. 41 (1967).

93. *Skinner v. Railway Labor Executive Association*, 489 U.S. 602 (1989).

94. *Veronia School District v. Acton*, 515 U.S. 646 (1995).

95. *Weeks v. United States*, 232 U.S. 383 (1914).

96. *Wolf v. Colorado*, 338 U.S. 25 (1949).

97. *Mapp v. Ohio*, 367 U.S. 643 (1961).

98. *United States v. Calandra*, 414 U.S. 338 (1974).

99. *United States v. Janis*, 428 U.S. 433 (1976).

100. *Massachusetts v. Sheppard*, 468 U.S. 981 (1984); *United States v. Leon*, 468 U.S. 897 (1984); *Illinois v. Krull*, 480 U.S. 340 (1987).

101. *Herring v. United States*, No. 07-513. Argued October 7, 2008—Decided January 14, 2009.

102. *Miranda v. Arizona*, 382 U.S. 925 (1965); *Dickerson v. United States*, 530 U.S. 428, 120 S. Ct. 2326; 2000 U.S. LEXIS 4305.

103. *Johnson v. Zerbst*, 304 U.S. 458 (1938).

104. *Gideon v. Wainwright*, 372 U.S. 335 (1963).

105. *Ross v. Mofitt*, 417 U.S. 600 (1974); *Murray v. Giarratano*, 492 U.S. 1 (1989).

106. Henry Weinstein, "Many Denied Right to Counsel, Group Says," *Los Angeles Times*, July 13, 2004, A10.

107. *In re Kemmler*, 136 U.S. 436 (1890).

108. *Atkins v. Virginia*, 536 U.S. 304 (2002).

109. *Roper v. Simmons*, 543 U.S. 551 (2005).

110. *Kennedy .v. Louisiana*, No. 07-343. Argued April 16, 2008—Decided June 25, 2008; modified October 1, 2008.

111. *Furman v. Georgia, Jackson v. Georgia, Branch v. Texas*, 408 U.S. 238 (1972).

112. *Gregg v. Georgia*, 428 U.S. 153 (1976); *Woodson v. North Carolina*, 428 U.S. 280 (1976); *Roberts v. Louisiana*, 428 U.S. 325 (1976).

113. *McClesky v. Kemp*, 481 U.S. 279 (1987).

114. *McClesky v. Zant*, 111 S. Ct. 1454 (1991).

115. *Baze v. Rees*, 553 U.S. 35 (2008).

116. Jack Hitt, "The Moratorium Gambit," *New York Times Magazine*, December 9, 2001, 82.

117. Keith Richburg, "New Jersey Approves Abolition of Death Penalty," *Washington Post*, December 14, 2007, A3.

118. Frank Newport, "In U.S., Two-Thirds Continue to Support Death Penalty," October, 13, 2009, www.gallup.com/poll/123638/In-U.S.-Two-Thirds-Continue-Support-Death-Penalty.aspx.

119. Samuel D. Warren and Louis D. Brandeis, "The Right to Privacy," *Harvard Law Review* 4 (1890).

120. *Griswold v. Connecticut*, 391 U.S. 145 (1965).

121. *Eisenstadt v. Baird*, 405 U.S. 438 (1972).

122. *Roe v. Wade*, 410 U.S. 113 (1973).

123. *Harris v. McRae*, 448 U.S. 297 (1980).

124. See, for example, *Webster v. Reproductive Health Services*, 492 U.S. 4090 (1989) and *Rust v. Sullivan*, 111 S. Ct. 1759 (1991).

125. *Gonzales v. Carhart*, 550 U.S. 124 (2007).

126. Lydia Saad, "U.S. Abortion Attitudes Closely Divided," August 4, 2009, www.gallup.com/poll/122033/U.S.-Abortion-Attitudes-Closely-Divided.aspx.

127. *Bowers v. Hardwick*, 478 U.S. 186 (1986).

128. *Commonwealth of Kentucky v. Wasson*, 842 S.W.2d 487 (1992).

129. *Lawrence v. Texas*, 539 U.S. 558 (2003).

130. *Romer v. Evans*, 517 U.S. 620 (1996).

131. *Cruzan v. Director, Missouri Department of Health*, 497 U.S. 261 (1990).

132. Frank Newport, "The Terri Schiavo Case in Review: Support for Her Being Allowed to Die Consistent," April 1, 2005, www.gallup.com.

133. *Washington v. Glucksberg*, 521 U.S. 702 (1997); *Vacco v. Quill*, 521 U.S. 793 (1997).

134. Stephen Adler and Wade Lambert, "Just About Everyone Violates Some Laws, Even Model Citizens," *Wall Street Journal*, March 12, 1993, 1.

135. Thomas Janoski, *Citizenship and Civil Society: A Framework of Rights and Obligations in Liberal, Traditional and Social Democratic Regimes* (Cambridge, U.K.: Cambridge University Press, 1998), 53–54.

136. "Mr. Cuccinelli's Witch Hunt."

137. See the American Association of University Professors, "1940 Statement of Principles on Academic Freedom and Tenure," www.aaup.org/AAUP/pubsres/policydocs/contents/1940statement.htm.

138. Kelly Simmons, "Students Fight Alleged Political Prejudice," *Atlanta Journal-Constitution*, March 24, 2004, 1B.

139. Ibid.

Chapter 6

1. Patrick Healy and Jeff Zeleny, "Obama and Clinton Tangle at Debate," *New York Times*, January 22, 2008, www.nytimes.com/2008/01/22/us/politics/22dems.html?partner=rssnyt&emc=rss.

2. Mark Mellman, "Can a Woman or a Black Man Win?" *Los Angeles Times*, February 3, 2008, www.latimes.com/news/opinion/commentary/la-op-mellman3feb03,0,2099860.story.

3. Katharine Q. Seelye and Julie Bosman, "Media Charged With Sexism in Clinton Coverage," *New York Times*, June 13, 2008, www.nytimes.com/2008/06/13/us/politics/13women.html?partner=rssnyt.

4. Andy Barr, "Davis Apologizes for Calling Obama 'Boy,'" *The Hill*, April 14, 2008, http://thehill.com/leading-the-news/davis-apologizes-for-calling-obama-boy-2008-04-14.html.

5. Eugene Robinson, "An Inarticulate Kickoff," *Washington Post*, February 2, 2007, A15.

6. Jake Tapper, "Bubba: Obama Is Just Like Jesse Jackson," *Political Punch*, January 26, 2008, http://blogs.abcnews.com/politicalpunch.

7. Kathy Kiely and Jill Lawrence, "Clinton Makes Case for Wide Appeal," *USA Today*, May 8, 2008, www.usatoday.com/news/politics/election2008/2008–05–07-clintoninterview_N.htm.

8. Sean Wilentz, "Race Man," *New Republic*, February 27, 2008.

9. Kathy Kiely, "These Are America's Governors. No Blacks. No Hispanics," *USA Today*, January 21, 2002, 1A.

10. David O'Brien, *Constitutional Law and Politics*, vol. 2 (New York: Norton, 1991), 1265.

11. American Civil Liberties Union, "Felon Enfranchisement and the Right to Vote," www.aclu.org/votingrights/exoffenders/index.html.

12. *Dred Scott v. Sanford*, 19 How. (60 U.S.) 393 (1857).

13. Scholars are divided about Lincoln's motives in issuing the Emancipation Proclamation; whether he genuinely desired to end slavery or merely used political means to shorten the war is hard to tell at this distance. Donald G. Nieman, *Promises to Keep: African-Americans and the Constitutional Order, 1776 to the Present* (New York: Oxford University Press, 1991), 55.

14. Bernard A. Weisberger, *Many Papers, One Nation* (Boston: Houghton Mifflin Company, 1987), 200.

15. Nieman, 107.

16. *The Civil Rights Cases*, 109 U.S. 3 (1883).

17. *Plessy v. Ferguson*, 163 U.S. 537 (1896).

18. Weisberger, 205–206.

19. *Guinn v. United States*, 238 U.S. 347 (1915).

20. *Missouri ex rel Gaines v. Canada*, 305 U.S. 337 (1938).

21. *Sweatt v. Painter*, 339 U.S. 629 (1950).

22. *Korematsu v. United States*, 323 U.S. 214 (1944).

23. *Brown v. Board of Education of Topeka (I)*, 347 U.S. 483 (1954).

24. *Brown v. Board of Education of Topeka (II)*, 349 U.S. 294 (1955).

25. *Gayle v. Browder*, 352 U.S. 903 (1956).

26. *Heart of Atlanta Motel, Inc. v. United States*, 379 U.S. 241 (1964); *Katzenbach v. McClung*, 379 U.S. 294 (1964); *Harper v. Virginia Board of Elections*, 383 U.S. 663 (1966).

27. Nieman, 179.

28. Ibid., 180.

29. *Swann v. Charlotte-Mecklenberg Board of Education*, 402 U.S. 1 (1971).

30. *Milliken v. Bradley*, 418 U.S. 717 (1974).

31. "*Brown v. Board*'s Goals Unrealized," *Atlanta Journal-Constitution*, May 16, 2004, 6C; Gary Orfield and Chungmei Lee, "*Brown* at 50: King's Dream or *Plessy*'s Nightmare?" Report conducted by the Harvard Civil Rights Project, 2004, www.civilrightsproject.harvard.edu/research/reseg04/brown50.pdf.

32. *Regents of the University of California v. Bakke*, 438 U.S. 265 (1978).

33. See, for example, *United Steelworkers of America v. Weber*, 443 U.S. 193 (1979); *Fullilove v. Klutznick*, 448 U.S. 448 (1980); *Firefighters Local Union No. 1784 v. Stotts*, 467 U.S. 561 (1984); and *Wygant v. Jackson Board of Education*, 476 U.S. 267 (1986).

34. *Patterson v. McLean Credit Union*, 491 U.S. 164 (1989).

35. *Wards Cove Packing, Inc. v. Atonio*, 490 U.S. 642 (1989).

36. *City of Richmond v. J. A. Croson*, 488 U.S. 469 (1989).

37. Darryl Fears, "A Diverse—and Divided—Black Community," *Washington Post*, February 24, 2002, A1.

38. Carmen DeNavas-Walt, Bernadette D. Proctor, and Jessica C. Smith, "Income, Poverty, and Health Insurance Coverage in the United States, 2008," www.census.gov/prod/2009pubs/p60–236.pdf; "African Americans by the Numbers," 2009, www.infoplease.com/spot/bhmcensus1.html.

39. Jonathan D. Glater, "Racial Gap in Pay Gets a Degree Sharper, a Study Finds," *Washington Post*, November 2, 1995, 13.

40. Joel Dresang, "Black Professional Men Paid Less Than White Peers," *Milwaukee Journal Sentinel*, August 16, 2001, 1D.

41. Ford Fessenden, "Examining the Vote: The Patterns," *New York Times*, November 12, 2001, A17.

42. National Conference of Black Mayors, "About Us," www.ncbm.org/aboutncbm/index.html.

43. CNNPolitics.com, "Poll: 76 Percent Say U.S. Ready for Black President," April 4, 2008, http://edition.cnn.com/2008/POLITICS/04/03/poll.black.president/index.html.

44. U.S. Census Bureau, "Voter Turnout Increases by 5 Million in 2008 Presidential Election U.S. Census Reports," July 20, 2009, www.census.gov/Press-Release/www/releases/archives/voting/013995.html.

45. Pew Research Center for the People and the Press, "Blacks Upbeat About Black Progress, Prospects," January 12, 2010, www.people-press.org/reports/576.

46. Kathy Kiely, "National Elite Political Circles Lack Minorities," *USA Today Online*, January 21, 2002.

47. Pew Research Center for the People and the Press, "Public Backs Affirmative Action but Not Minority Preferences," June 2, 2009, http://pewresearch.org/pubs/1240/sotomayor-supreme-court-affirmative-action-minority-preferences.

48. Jodi Wilgoren, "U.S. Court Bars Race as Factor in School Entry," *New York Times*, March 28, 2001, A1.

49. Jacques Steinberg, "Redefining Diversity," *New York Times*, August 29, 2001, A14.

50. *Gratz v. Bollinger*, 539 U.S. 244 (2003).

51. *Grutter v. Bollinger*, 539 U.S. 306 (2003).

52. Ward Connerly, "Up From Affirmative Action," *New York Times*, April 29, 1996.

53. David K. Shipler, "My Equal Opportunity, Your Free Lunch," *New York Times*, March 5, 1995.

54. *Cherokee Nation v. Georgia*, 30 U.S. (5 Pet.) 1, 20 (1831).

55. Vine Delori Jr. and Clifford M. Lytle, *The Nations Within: The Past and Future of American Indian Sovereignty* (New York: Pantheon, 1984), 17.

56. J. Bretting and B. Morris, "Fry-Bread Federalism Revisited: A Model of American Indian Intergovernmental Relations," paper presented at the 2005 annual meeting of the Western Political Science Association, Oakland, Calif.

57. *Lyng v. Northwest Indian Cemetery Protective Association*, 485 U.S. 439 (1988).

58. *Employment Division v. Oregon*, 494 U.S. 872 (1990).

59. U.S. Census Bureau, "Income Climbs, Poverty Stabilizes, Uninsured Rate Increases," August 29, 2007, www.census.gov/Press-Release/www/releases/archives/income_wealth/007419.html.

60. William Roller, "Groups Aim to Boost Native American Graduation Rate," *Yuma Sun*, January 12, 2009, www.yumasun.com/news/evidenced-47067-crisis-says.html.

61. "Despite Prayers, a Navajo-Mormon Culture Clash," *New York Times*, July 24, 1996, A8.

62. *Seminole Tribe of Florida v. Butterworth*, 658 F.2d 310 (1981); cert. denied, 455 U.S. 1020 (1982); *State of California v. Cabazon Band of Mission Indians*, 480 U.S. 202 (1987).

63. National Indiana Gaming Commission web site, www.nigc.gov/Default.aspx?tabid=67.

64. Adrian Sainz, "Indian Gambling Revenues Up in 2006, But Growth Slows," *North County Times*, June 28, 2007; National Indian Gaming Commission, "Tribal Gaming Revenues (in thousands) by Region Fiscal Year 2003 and 2002," n.d., www.nigc.gov/nigc/tribes/tribaldata2003/gamerevenue.jsp.

65. Pew Hispanic Center, *Statistical Portrait of Hispanics in the United States, 2008*, Table 1, http://pewhispanic.org/factsheets/factsheet.php?FactsheetID=58.

66. Pew Hispanic Center, *Latinos by Country of Origin*, http://pewhispanic.org.

67. Mark Falcoff, "Our Language Needs No Law," *New York Times*, August 5, 1996.

68. Rene Sanchez, "Both Parties Courting Latinos Vigorously," *Washington Post Online*, October 26, 1998, 2.

69. Douglas R. Hess and Jody Herman, "Representational Bias in the 2008 Electorate," November 2009, www.projectvote.org.

70. "Hawaii: ACS Demographic and Housing Estimates: 2006–2008," American Survey Community, U.S. Census Bureau; "California: ACS Demographic and Housing Estimates: 2006–2008," American Survey Community, U.S. Census Bureau.

71. Christine Nifong, "Hispanics and Asians Change the Face of the South," *Christian Science Monitor*, August 6, 1996.

72. Ronald Takaki, *Strangers From a Different Shore* (Boston: Little, Brown, 1989), 363–364.

73. *Hirabayashi v. United States*, 320 U.S. 81 (1943); *Korematsu v. United States*, 323 U.S. 214 (1944).

74. DeNavas-Walt, Proctor, and Smith, "Income, Poverty, and Health Insurance Coverage in the United States, 2008."

75. Data from harvard.edu, stanford.edu, mit.edu, and berkeley.edu.

76. Ibid., 479.

77. Norimitsu Onishi, "Affirmative Action: Choosing Sides," *New York Times* Education Life Supplement, March 31, 1996, 27.

78. Lena H. Sun, "Getting Out the Ethnic Vote," *Washington Post*, October 7, 1996, B5; K. Connie Kang, "Asian Americans Slow to Flex Their Political Muscle," *Los Angeles Times*, October 31, 1996, A18.

79. Sun, B5; Kang, A18.

80. William Booth, "California Race Could Signal New Cohesion for Asian Voters," *Washington Post*, November 3, 1998, 1.

81. "Asian Americans' Political Mark," *Los Angeles Times*, November 25, 1996, B4.

82. CNN.com, national exit polls, November 10, 2004, www.cnn.com/election/2004/pages/results/states/us/p/00/epolls.0.html. See polls for each state.

83. Sun, B5.

84. Paul Van Slambrouck, "Asian-Americans' Politics Evolving," *Christian Science Monitor*, September 8, 1998, 2.

85. Eleanor Flexner, *Century of Struggle: The Woman's Rights Movement in the United States* (New York: Atheneum, 1973), 148–149.

86. Nancy E. McGlen and Karen O'Connor, *Women's Rights: The Struggle for Equality in the 19th and 20th Centuries* (New York: Praeger, 1983), 272–273.

87. *Bradwell v. Illinois*, 16 Wall. 130 (1873).

88. Quoted in Flexner, 178.

89. Flexner, 296.

90. McGlen and O'Connor, 83.

91. Jane Mansbridge, *Why We Lost the ERA* (Chicago: Chicago University Press, 1986), 13.

92. *Reed v. Reed*, 404 U.S. 71 (1971); *Craig v. Boren*, 429 U.S. 190 (1976).

93. *Weinberger v. Wiesenfeld*, 420 U.S. 636 (1975); *Califano v. Goldfarb*, 430 U.S. 199 (1977); *Califano v. Westcott*, 443 U.S. 76 (1979); *Orr v. Orr*, 440 U.S. 268 (1979).

94. Shelley Donald Coolidge, "Flat Tire on the Road to Pay Equity," *Christian Science Monitor*, April 11, 1997, 9; National Committee on Pay Equity, "The Wage Gap Over Time; In Real Dollars, Women See a Continuing Decline," www.pay-equity.org/info-time.html.

95. *Ledbetter v. Goodyear Tire & Rubber Co.*, 550 U.S. 618 (2007).

96. *Johnson v. Transportation Agency, Santa Clara, California*, 480 U.S. 616 (1987).

97. Barbara Noble, "At Work: And Now the Sticky Floor," *New York Times*, November 22, 1992, 23.

98. Kenneth Gray, "The Gender Gap in Yearly Earnings: Can Vocational Education Help?" Office of Special Populations' Brief, vol. 5, no. 2. National Center for Research in Vocational Education, University of California, Berkeley, Office of Special Populations, University of California, Berkeley.

99. Stephanie Armour, "Pregnant Workers Report Growing Discrimination," *USA Today*, February 16, 2005.

100. Binnie Fisher, "Gender Equity Laws: A Push for Fair Prices for the Fair Sex," *Christian Science Monitor*, March 7, 1996.

101. Ibid.

102. Center for American Women and Politics, "Women in Elective Office 2010," www.cawp.rutgers.edu/fast_facts/index.php; "Women Mayors in U.S. Cities 2009," www.cawp.rutgers.edu/fast_facts/levels_of_office/Local-WomenMayors.php.

103. Barbara Burrell, "Campaign Finance: Women's Experience in the Modern Era," in Sue Thomas and Clyde Wilcox, eds., *Women and Elective Office: Past, Present, and Future* (New York: Oxford University Press, 1998), 27.

104. Gary F. Moncrief, Peverill Squire, and Malcolm E. Jewell, *Who Runs for the Legislature?* (Upper Saddle River, N.J.: Prentice Hall, 2001), 98–99.

105. Siena Research Institute, "Do you think the United States is ready for a woman president in 2008?" February 22, 2005, www.siena.edu/sri/firstwomanpresident/fwp_release_final_sans.pdf.

106. Moncrief, Squire, and Jewell, 98–99.

107. Center for Women and Politics, "Women Candidates for Governor 1970–2006," www.cawp.rutgers.edu/Facts3.html#history.

108. Kristin Eliasberg, "Making a Case for the Right to Be Different," *New York Times*, June 16, 2001, B11.

109. *Bowers v. Hardwick*, 478 U.S. 186 (1986).

110. *John J. Hurley, and South Boston Allied War Veterans Council v. Irish-American Gay, Lesbian, and Bisexual Group of Boston*, 115 S. Ct. 714 (1995).

111. *Romer v. Evans*, 115 S. Ct. 1092 (1996).

112. Linda Greenhouse, "The Supreme Court: The New Jersey Case; Supreme Court Backs Boy Scouts in Ban of Gays From Membership," *New York Times*, June 29, 2000, A1.

113. *Lawrence v. Texas*, 539 U.S. 558 (2003).

114. *Goodridge v. Dept. of Pub. Health*, 440 Mass. 309 (2003).

115. David W. Dunlap, "Gay Survey Raises a New Question," *New York Times*, October 18, 1994, B8.

116. National Gay and Lesbian Task Force, "The Gay, Lesbian, and Bisexual Vote: As Much as 5% of Presidential and Congressional Voters," 2004, www. thetaskforce.org/theissues/issue.cfm?issueID=32.

117. OpenSecrets.org, *Human Rights Campaign: Summary 2008*, www.opensecrets.org/orgs/all_summary.php?id=D000000158&nid=1276.

118. "Military Misguidance," *Chicago Sun Times*, November 20, 2002, 51.

119. Nathaniel Frank, "What the Changes to DADT Mean: The Good, the Bad and the Politically Dangerous," *Huffington Post*, March 25, 2010, www.huffingtonpost.com/nathaniel-frank/what-the-changes-to-dadt_b_513665.html

120. Pew Research Center for the People and the Press, "Less Opposition to Gay Marriage, Adoption, and Military Service," Survey Reports, March 22, 2006, http://people-press.org/report/273/less-opposition-to-gay-marriage-adoption-and-military-service.

121. Pew Forum on Religion and Public Life, "Public Opinion on Gay Marriage: Opponents Consistently Outnumber Supporters," July 9, 2009, http://pewforum.org/gay-marriage-and-homosexuality/public-opinion-on-gay-marriage-opponents-consistently-outnumber-supporters.aspx#3.

122. *Massachusetts Board of Retirement v. Murgia*, 427 U.S. 307 (1976).

123. *Massachusetts Board of Retirement v. Murgia; Vance v. Bradley*, 440 U.S. 93 (1979); *Gregory v. Ashcroft*, 501 U.S. 452 (1991).

124. *Alabama v. Garrett*, 531 U.S. 356 (2001).

125. *Graham v. Richardson*, 403 U.S. 365 (1971).

126. *Pyler v. Doe*, 457 U.S. 202 (1982).

127. Robert J. Samuelson, "Immigration and Poverty," *Newsweek*, July 15, 1996, 43.

128. Sanford J. Ungar, "Enough of the Immigrant Bashing," *USA Today*, October 11, 1995, 11A.

129. Theda Skocpol, "Advocates Without Members: The Recent Transformation of American Civil Life," in Theda Skocpol and Morris P. Fiorina, eds., *Civic Engagement in American Democracy* (Washington, D.C., and New York: Brookings Institution and the Russell Sage Foundation, 1999), 470–472.

130. Hillary Clinton, "Hillary's Remarks in Washington, DC," June 7, 2008. www.hillaryclinton.com.

131. Eugene Robinson, "What He Overcame," *Washington Post*, June 6, 2008, A19.

132. MLDB, "Just a Second, Obama Is Speaking," *Daily Kos*, July 25, 2008, www.dailykos.com/storyonly/2008/7/25/93510/1800/555/556771.

Chapter 7

1. Katherine Seelye, "Fighting Health Care Overhaul, and Proud of It," *New York Times*, August 30, 2009, www.nytimes.com/2009/08/31/us/politics/31demint.htm?scp=4&sq=Obama%20Waterloo%20DeMint&st=cse.

2. Ryan Grim, "Pelosi: End the Filibuster," *Huffington Post*, July 1, 2010, www.huffingtonpost.com/2010/07/01/pelosi-end-the-filibuster_n_632851.html.

3. David Herszenhorn, "How the Filibuster Became the Rule," *New York Times*, December 3, 2007, www.nytimes.com/2007/12/02/weekinreview/02herszenhorn.html?scp=1&sq=McConnell%20umpteenth&st=cse.

4. John R. Hibbing and Elizabeth Theiss-Morse, *Congress as Public Enemy* (New York: Cambridge University Press, 1995), chs. 2, 3.

5. Glenn R. Parker and Roger H. Davidson, "Why Do Americans Love Their Congressmen So Much More Than Their Congress?" *Legislative Studies Quarterly* (February 1979): 52–61.

6. Heinz Eulau and Paul D. Karps, "The Puzzle of Representation: Specifying Components of Responsiveness," *Legislative Studies Quarterly* 2 (1977): 233–254.

7. Richard Fenno, *Homestyle* (Boston: Little, Brown, 1978), ch. 3.

8. Gary Jacobson, *The Politics of Congressional Elections*, 4th ed. (New York: Longman, 1997), ch. 8.

9. Ross K. Baker, *House and Senate* (New York: Norton, 1989).

10. D. C. W. Parker and M. Dull, "Divided We Quarrel: The Politics of Congressional Investigations, 1947–2004," *Legislative Studies Quarterly* 34 (2009): 319–345.

11. Lyle Denniston, "GAO Sues for Access to Cheney Records," *Boston Globe*, February 23, 2002, A1; Adam Cohen, "Bush v. Congress: The Looming Battle of Executive Privilege," *New York Times*, April 10, 2007, 20; Bruce Fein, "Restoring Congressional Oversight," *Washington Times*, November 28, 2006; Sheryl Gay Stolberg, "Bush Moves Toward Showdown With Congress on Executive Privilege," *New York Times*, June 29, 2007, 23.

12. Parker and Dull.

13. Neil A. Lewis, "Justice Dept. Nominee Avoids Confrontation at Hearing," *New York Times*, February 26, 2009, 23; Charlie Savage, "Long After Nomination, An Obama Choice Withdraws," *New York Times*, April 10, 2010, 16.

14. Gail Russell Chaddock, "Congress Girds Up for Return to Oversight," *Christian Science Monitor*, April 9, 2007, 1; Elizabeth Williamson, "Revival of Oversight Role Sought; Congress Hires More Investigators, Plans Subpoenas," *Washington Post*, April 25, 2007, A1.

15. Charles Cameron, Albert Cover, and Jeffrey Segal, "Senate Voting on Supreme Court Nominations," *American Political Science Review* 84 (1990): 525–534.

16. David Mayhew, *Congress: The Electoral Connection* (New Haven: Yale University Press, 1974).

17. *Baker v. Carr*, 396 U.S. 186 (1962); *Westberry v. Sanders*, 376 U.S. 1 (1964).

18. Karen Mills, *Census 2000 Brief: Congressional Apportionment* (Washington, D.C.: U.S. Census Bureau, 2001), www.census.gov/ prod/2001pubs/c2kbr 01–7.pdf.

19. Roger H. Davidson and Walter J. Oleszek, *Congress and Its Members*, 9th ed. (Washington, D.C.: CQ Press, 2004), 48.

20. Charles Cameron, David Epstein, and Sharyn O'Halloran, "Do Majority-Minority Districts Maximize Substantive Black Representation in Congress?" *American Political Science Review* 90 (December 1996): 794–812; Kevin Hill, "Does the Creation of Majority Black Districts Aid Republicans? An Analysis of the 1992 Congressional Election in Eight Southern States," *Journal of Politics* 57 (May 1995): 384–401; D. Lublin, "Racial Redistricting and African-American Representation: A Critique of 'Do Majority-Minority Districts Maximize Substantive Black Representation in Congress?'" *American Political Science Review* 93 (1999): 183–186.

21. Holly Idelson, "Court Takes a Hard Line on Minority Voting Blocs," *CQ Weekly*, July 1, 1995, 4, 5.

22. *Shaw v. Reno*, 509 U.S. 630 (1993); *Miller v. Johnson*, 115 S. Ct. 2475 (1995).

23. *Shaw v. Hunt*, 116 S. Ct. 1894 (1996); *Bush v. Vera*, 116 S. Ct. 1941 (1996); *Hunt v. Cromartie et al.*, 532 U.S. 534 (2001).

24. Peter Urban, "Congress Gets Lavish Benefits," *Connecticut Post*, January 16, 2005; Debra J. Saunders, "Perks of Office" Editorial, *San Francisco Chronicle*, November 19, 2000, 9.

25. Commission on the Executive, Legislative and Judicial Salaries, *Fairness for Public Servants* (Washington, D.C.: U.S. Government Printing Office, 1988), 23.

26. Eric Uslaner, *The Decline of Comity in Congress* (Ann Arbor: University of Michigan Press, 1993).

27. Gary Jacobson, *The Politics of Congressional Elections*, 3rd ed. (New York: HarperCollins, 1992); Peverill Squire, "Challengers in Senate Elections," *Legislative Studies Quarterly* 14 (1989): 531–547; David Cannon, *Actors, Athletes and Astronauts: Political Amateurs in the United States Congress* (Chicago: University of Chicago Press, 1990).

28. Norman J. Ornstein, Thomas E. Mann, and Michael J. Malbin, *Vital Statistics on Congress, 2001–2002* (Washington, D.C.: AEI Press, 2002), 69; Davidson and Oleszek, 60; Peter E. Harrell, "A Slightly Redder Hue," *CQ Weekly*, November 6, 2004, 2621–2625; *Vital Statistics on American Politics Online Edition*, "Table 1-15: Mean Turnover in the House of Representatives from Various Causes, by Decade and by Party System, 1789–2008," CQ Press Electronic Library. Originally published in Harold W. Stanley and Richard G. Niemi, *Vital Statistics on American Politics, 2007–2008* (Washington, D.C.: CQ Press, 2008).

29. Calculated by the authors from *Vital Statistics on American Politics* Online Edition, "Table 1-19: Incumbent Reelection Rates, Representatives, Senators, and Governors, General Elections, 1960–2008," CQ Press Electronic Library.

30. Calculated by the authors from the Campaign Finance Institute data table, "Expenditures of House Incumbents and Challengers, by Election Outcome, 1974–2008," www.cfinst.org/pdf/vital/ VitalStats_t3.pdf.

31. *Vital Statistics on American Politics* Online Edition, "Table 1-19: Incumbent Reelection Rates, Representatives, Senators, and Governors, General Elections, 1960–2008."

32. Harold Stanley and Richard Niemi, *Vital Statistics on American Politics*,

5th ed. (Washington, D.C.: CQ Press, 1995).

33. Edward R. Tufte, *Political Control of the Economy* (Princeton: Princeton University Press, 1978); Robert S. Erikson, "The Puzzle of the Midterm Loss," *Journal of Politics* 50 (November 1988): 1011–1029; Robert S. Erikson and Gerald C. Wright, "Voters, Candidates, and Issues in Congressional Elections," in Lawrence Dodd and Bruce Oppenheimer, eds., *Congress Reconsidered*, 9th ed. (Washington, D.C.: CQ Press, 2005), 13271–14096.

34. John Adams, "Thoughts on Government," cited in Gordon S. Wood, *The Creation of the American Republic, 1776–1787* (New York: Norton, 1969), 165.

35. Davidson and Oleszek; Jennifer E. Manning, "Membership in the 111th Congress: A Profile," Congressional Research Service, www.senate.gov/CRSReports/crs-publish .cfm?pid=%26oBL%29PL%3B%3D%oA.

36. Manning.

37. Alexander Bolton and Tom Sullivan, "Not All Lawmakers Are Millionaires—Shock! More Than 1 in 4 in House Have 7-Figure Assets," *The Hill*, June 17, 2004, 1.

38. Kathleen Dolan, "Voting for Women in the 'Year of the Woman,'" *American Journal of Political Science* 42 (1998): 272–293.

39. Jennifer Lawless and Richard Fox, *It Takes a Candidate: Why Women Don't Run for Office* (New York: Cambridge University Press, 2005).

40. Richard E. Cohen, "Is It an Earthquake, or Only a Tremor?" *National Journal*, July 8, 1995, 1786; K. Tate, *Black Faces in the Mirror: African Americans and Their Representatives in the U.S. Congress* (Princeton: Princeton University Press, 2003); K. J. Whitby, *The Color of Representation: Congressional Behavior and Black Interests* (Ann Arbor: University of Michigan Press, 1997); D. Lublin, *The Paradox of Representation: Racial Gerrymandering and Minority Interests in Congress* (Princeton: Princeton University Press, 1997).

41. Arian Campo-Flores, "Will Arizona's Tough Immigration Law Fuel Hispanic Turnout for Democrats?" *Newsweek*, May 20, 2010, www.newsweek.com/authors/arian-campo-flores.html; Michael Gerson, "The GOP's Harsh Immigration Stance Will Cost It," *Washington Post*, May 14, 2010.

42. Kay Lehman Schlozman, Sidney Verba, and Henry E. Brady, "Civic Participation and the Inequality Problem," in Theda Skocpol and Morris Fiorina, eds., *Civic Engagement in American Democracy* (New York: Russell Sage, 1999), ch. 12; Martin Gilens, "Inequality and Democratic Responsiveness," *Public Opinion Quarterly*

69 (2005): 778–796; Larry Bartels, *Unequal Democracy: The Political Economy of the New Gilded Age* (New York: Russell Sage, 2008), ch. 9.

43. Claudine Gay, "The Effect of Black Congressional Representation on Political Participation," *American Political Science Review* 95 (2001): 589–602; Cindy Simon Rosenthal, "The Role of Gender in Descriptive Representation," *Political Research Quarterly* 48 (1995): 599–611; Jennifer L. Lawless, "Politics of Presence? Congresswomen and Symbolic Representation," *Political Research Quarterly* 57 (2004): 81–99.

44. Michele Swers, *The Difference Women Make: The Policy Impact of Women in Congress* (Chicago: University of Chicago Press, 2002).

45. Tate; Whitby; Lublin.

46. David Canon, *Race, Redistricting, and Representation: The Unintended Consequences of Black Majority Districts* (Chicago: University of Chicago Press, 1999); Lublin.

47. Jane Mansbridge, "Should Blacks Represent Blacks and Women Represent Women? A Contingent 'Yes,'" *Journal of Politics* 61 (1999): 628–657.

48. Glenn Parker, *Characteristics of Congress: Patterns in Congressional Behavior* (Englewood Cliffs, N.J.: Prentice Hall, 1989), 17–18, ch. 9.

49. Davidson and Oleszek, 155–156.

50. Leroy Rieselbach, *Congressional Reform in the Seventies* (Morristown, N.J.: General Learning Press, 1977); Leroy Rieselbach, *Congressional Reform* (Washington, D.C.: CQ Press, 1986).

51. Ed Gillespie and Bob Schellhas, eds., *Contract With America: The Bold Plan by Rep. Newt Gingrich, Rep. Dick Armey and the House Republicans to Change the Nation* (New York: Random House, 1994); James G. Gimpel, *Legislating the Revolution* (Boston: Allyn & Bacon, 1996).

52. Perry Bacon Jr., "Don't Mess With Nancy Pelosi," *Time*, August 27, 2006.

53. Edward Epstein, "Her Key to the House," *CQ Weekly*, October 29, 2007, 3158.

54. Edward Epstein, "Pelosi's Action Plan for Party Unity," *CQ Weekly*, March 30, 2009, 706.

55. Ronald Peters, coauthor of *Speaker Nancy Pelosi and the New American Politics*, quoted in Edward Epstein, "Pelosi Gets Good Marks in Two New Books," *CQ Weekly*, May 10, 2010, 1128.

56. Alex Wayne, "Senate Passes Sweeping Health Overhaul," *CQ Weekly*, December 28, 2009, 2944.

57. Michael D. Shear, "Obama's Future Plans Rely on Reid's Survival," *Washington Post*, July 9, 2010, www.washingtonpost.com/wp-dyn/content/article/2010/07/09/AR2010070903678.html.

58. Kathleen Hunter, "Betting It All on His Own Winning Way," *CQ Weekly*, October 26, 2009, 2434.

59. Davidson and Oleszek, 193.

60. Matthew McCubbins and Thomas Schwartz, "Congressional Oversight Overlooked: Police Patrols Versus Fire Alarms," *American Journal of Political Science* (February 1984): 165–179.

61. Barbara Sinclair, "Party Leaders and the New Legislative Process," in Lawrence Dodd and Bruce Oppenheimer, eds., *Congress Reconsidered*, 6th ed. (Washington, D.C.: CQ Press, 1997), 229–245.

62. Jonathan Cohn, "Dems 'Almost Certain' to Bypass Conference," *New Republic*, January 3, 2010, www.tnr.com/blog/the-treatment/exclusive-dems-almost-certain-bypass-conference.

63. Richard Fenno, *Congressmen in Committees* (Boston: Little, Brown, 1973); Glenn R. Parker, *Characteristics of Congress* (Englewood Cliffs, N.J.: Prentice Hall, 1989).

64. Davidson and Oleszek, 204.

65. Steven Smith and Eric Lawrence, "Party Control of Committees in the Republican Congress," in Lawrence Dodd and Bruce Oppenheimer, eds., *Congress Reconsidered*, 6th ed. (Washington, D.C.: CQ Press, 1997), 163–192.

66. Davidson and Oleszek, 219–220.

67. Copies of these and hundreds of other GAO reports are available online at www.gao.gov.

68. Barbara Sinclair, *The Transformation of the U.S. Senate* (Baltimore: Johns Hopkins University Press, 1989).

69. Roger H. Davidson, Walter J. Oleszek, and Frances E. Lee, eds., *Congress and Its Members*, 11th ed. (Washington, D.C.: CQ Press, 2008), 276.

70. John Stewart, "A Chronology of the Civil Rights Act of 1964," in Robert Loevy, ed., *The Civil Rights Act of 1964: The Passage of the Law That Ended Racial Segregation* (Albany: SUNY Press, 1997), 358.

71. Ibid., 358–360.

72. Barbara Sinclair, "The New World of U.S. Senators," in Lawrence C. Dodd and Bruce I. Oppenheimer, eds., *Congress Reconsidered*, 8th ed. (Washington, D.C.: CQ Press, 2005), 11; Richard Beth and Stanley Bach, "Filibusters and Cloture in the Senate," Congressional Research Service, March 28, 2003, www.senate.gov/reference/resources/pdf/RL30360.pdf.

73. Emily Pierce, "Cloture, Filibusters Spur Furious Debate," *Roll Call*, March 5, 2008; U.S. Senate Virtual Reference Desk, "Cloture Motions—110th Congress," www.senate.gov/pagelayout/reference/cloture.motions/110.htm.

74. Donald R. Matthews and James A. Stimson, *Yeas and Nays* (New York: Wiley, 1975).

75. Richard Smith, "Interest Group Influence in the U.S. Congress," *Legislative Studies Quarterly* 20 (February 1995): 89–140.

76. Richard S. Dunham, "Power to the President—Courtesy of the GOP," *Business Week*, October 20, 1997, 51.

77. Stephen C. Craig, *The Malevolent Leaders: Popular Discontent in America* (Boulder: Westview Press, 1993); David Easton, "A Reassessment of the Concept of Political Support," *British Journal of Political Science* 5 (1975): 435–457; Glenn Parker, "Some Themes in Congressional Unpopularity," *American Journal of Political Science* 21 (1977): 93–110; E. J. Dionne Jr., *Why Americans Hate Politics* (New York: Simon & Schuster, 1991).

78. Seymour M. Lipset and William Schneider, *The Confidence Gap: Business, Labor, and Government in the Public Mind* (Baltimore: Johns Hopkins University Press, 1987).

79. Parker and Davidson; Richard F. Fenno Jr., "If, as Ralph Nader Says, Congress Is 'the Broken Branch,' How Come We Love Our Congressmen So Much?" in Norman J. Ornstein, ed., *Congress in Change* (New York: Praeger, 1975), 277–287.

80. Grim.

81. Herszenhorn.

82. Ibid.

Chapter 8

1. Charlie Savage, "Bush Shuns Patriot Act," *Boston Globe*, March 24, 2006, A1.

2. Ibid.

3. Ibid.

4. Charlie Savage, "Bush Challenges Hundreds of Laws," *Boston Globe*, April 30, 2006, www.boston.com.

5. Philip Cooper, cited in ibid.

6. Jack Goldsmith, cited in ibid.

7. Bruce Miroff, "Monopolizing the Public Space: The President as a Problem for Democratic Politics," in Bruce Miroff, Raymond Seidelman, and Todd Swanstrom, eds., *Debating Democracy* (Boston: Houghton Mifflin, 1997), 294–303.

8. Max Farrand, *The Framing of the Constitution of the United States* (New Haven: Yale University Press, 1913), 163.

9. Skip Thurman, "One Man's Impeachment Crusade," *Christian Science Monitor*, November 18, 1997, 4.

10. Brian Montopoli, "Seven Republicans All For Special Prosecutor in Sestak Case," CBS

News *Political Hotsheet*, May 26, 2010, www.cbsnews.com/8301–503544-162–20006072–503544.html; Jeffrey T. Kuhner, "Impeach the President?" *Washington Times*, March 19, 2010, www.washington times.com/news/2010/mar/19/impeach-the-president/.

11. Robert DiClerico, *The American President*, 4th ed. (Englewood Cliffs, N.J.: Prentice Hall, 1995), 374; Susan Milligan, "Democrats Scuttle Proposal to Impeach Bush: Move Avoids House Debate," *Boston Globe*, June 12, 2008, A5.

12. Joseph A. Pika and John Anthony Maltese, *The Politics of the Modern Presidency*, 6th ed. (Washington, D.C.: CQ Press, 2004), 3; Jeffrey K. Tulis, "The Two Constitutional Presidencies," in Michael Nelson, ed., *The Presidency and the Political System* (Washington, D.C.: CQ Press, 1994), 91–123.

13. Loch Johnson and James M. McCormick, "The Making of International Agreements: a Reappraisal of Congressional Involvement," *Journal of Politics* 40 (1978): 468–478.

14. Pika and Maltese, 374; and author calculations from Library of Congress, http://thomas.loc.gov/home/treaties/treaties.html.

15. Lawrence Margolis, *Executive Agreements and Presidential Power in Foreign Policy* (New York: Praeger, 1985).

16. D. Roderick Kiewiet and Mathew D. McCubbins, "Presidential Influence on Congressional Appropriations Decisions," *American Political Science Review* 32 (1988): 713–736.

17. Joseph J. Schatz, "With a Deft and Light Touch, Bush Finds Ways to Win," *CQ Weekly*, December 11, 2004, 2900–2904.

18. Peter Baker, "A Veto From Obama Does Not Stop Presses," *The Caucus*, December 20, 2009, http://thecaucus.blogs.nytimes.com/2009/12/30/a-veto-from-obama-does-not-stop-presses/.

19. Peter Baker, "Obama Making Plans to Use Executive Power," *New York Times*, February 12, 2010, www.nytimes.com/2010/02/13/us/politics/13obama.html.

20. Kenneth R. Mayer, *With the Stroke of a Pen: Executive Orders and Presidential Power* (Princeton: Princeton University Press, 2002), 88–89.

21. Adam L. Warber, *Executive Orders and the Modern Presidency: Legislating From the Oval Office* (Boulder, Colo.: Lynne Rienner Publishers, 2006); William G. Howell, *Power Without Persuasion: The Politics of Direct Presidential Action* (Princeton: Princeton University Press, 2003).

22. Robert A. Carp, Ronald Stidham, and Kenneth L. Manning, *Judicial Process in America*, 6th ed. (Washington, D.C.: CQ Press, 2004), 168.

23. Amy Goldstein, "Civil Rights Organizations Question Nominee Elena Kagan's Record on Race," *Washington Post*, June 27, 2010.

24. Charlie Savage, "Obama Backers Fear Opportunities to Reshape Judiciary Are Slipping Away," *New York Times*, November 14, 2009, www.nytimes.com/2009/11/15/us/politics/15judicial.html?scp=3&sq=Obama%20judicial%20appointments&st=cse.

25. Quoted in Henry Abramson, *Justices and Presidents: A Political History of Appointments to the Supreme Court*, 2nd ed. (New York: Oxford University Press, 1985), 263.

26. Gerald Boyd, "White House Hunts for a Justice, Hoping to Tip Ideological Scales," *New York Times*, June 30, 1987; Alan I. Abramowitz and Jeffrey A. Segal, *Senate Elections* (Ann Arbor: University of Michigan Press, 1992), 1–6.

27. David Plotz, "Advise and Consent (Also, Obstruct, Delay, and Stymie): What's Still Wrong With the Appointments Process," *Slate Magazine*, March 19, 1999, www.slate.com/StrangeBedfellow/99–03–19/StrangeBedfellow.asp.

28. Ibid.

29. "Clinton Knows Better Than to Lean on a Judge," [Greensboro, N.C.] *News and Record*, March 25, 1996, A6.

30. Rebecca Mae Salokar, *The Solicitor General: The Politics of Law* (Philadelphia: Temple University Press, 1992), 29.

31. Bob Woodward, *Shadow: Five Presidents and the Legacy of Watergate* (New York: Simon & Schuster, 1999), 212–217.

32. Cited in David O'Brien, *Constitutional Law and Politics* (New York: Norton, 1991), vol. 1, 218.

33. *In re Neagle*, 135 U.S. 546 (1890); *In re Debs*, 158 U.S. 564 (1895); *United States v. Curtiss-Wright Export Corp.*, 299 U.S. 304, 57 S. Ct. 216 (1936); *Youngstown Sheet & Tube v. Sawyer*, 343 U.S. 579 (1952).

34. Lyn Ragsdale, *Presidential Politics* (Boston: Houghton Mifflin, 1993), 55.

35. *Historical Statistics of the United States: Colonial Times to 1970* (Washington, D.C.: U.S. Government Printing Office, 1975).

36. *Inaugural Addresses of the United States* (Washington, D.C.: U.S. Government Printing Office, 1982), quoted in Ragsdale, 71.

37. Suzanne Bilyeu, "FDR: How He Changed America—and Still Affects Your Life Today," *New York Times Upfront*, January 14, 2008.

38. *United States v. Curtiss-Wright Export Corp.*, 299 U.S. 304, 57 S. Ct. 216 (1936).

39. *Youngstown Sheet & Tube v. Sawyer*, 343 U.S. 579 (1952).

40. Arthur M. Schlesinger Jr., *The Imperial Presidency* (Boston: Mariner Books, 2004).

41. Richard Nixon interview with David Frost, May 20, 1877, cited in Charles Savage, *Takeover: The Return of the Imperial Presidency and the Subversion of American Democracy* (New York: Little, Brown, 2007), 21.

42. Roger H. Davidson and Walter J. Oleszek, *Congress and Its Members*, 9th ed. (Washington, D.C.: CQ Press, 2004), 407.

43. *Clinton v. Jones*, 520 U.S. 681 (1997).

44. Dana Milbank, "Cheney Refuses Records' Release; Energy Showdown With GAO Looms," *Washington Post*, January 28, 2002, A1.

45. Vikki Gordon, "The Law: Unilaterally Shaping U.S. National Security Policy: The Role of the National Security Directives," *Presidential Studies Quarterly* (June 2008): 368–370; Christopher S. Kelley, "The Law: Contextualizing the Signing Statement," *Presidential Studies Quarterly* (December 2007): 737–749; Louis Fisher, "Invoking Inherent Powers: A Primer," *Presidential Studies Quarterly* (March 2007): 1–22; Charlie Savage, "Candidates on Executive Power: A Full Spectrum," *Boston Globe*, December 22, 2007.

46. See, for example, Peter Jamison, "Obama 'Even Worse' Than Bush on Secret Wiretapping Case, Says S.F. Lawyer," *The Snitch*, April 1, 2010, http://blogs.sfweekly.com/thesnitch/2010/04/obama_wiretap_ruling.php; Editorial, "We Can't Tell You," *New York Times*, April 3, 2010, www.nytimes.com/2010/04/04/opinion/04sun1.html.

47. Peter M. Shane, "The Ambivalent Presidency? Executive Power Under the Obama Administration," *Executive Watch*, May 5, 2009, http://executivewatch.net/2009/05/05/the-ambivalent-adminstration-executive-power-under-the-obama-administration/; Charlie Savage, "Obama's Use of a Bush Tactic Riles Congress," *New York Times*, August 8, 2009, www.nytimes.com/2009/08/09/us/politics/09signing.html?_r=1&hpw.

48. Jeffrey Tulis, *The Rhetorical Presidency* (Princeton: Princeton University Press, 1987).

49. Richard E. Neustadt, *Presidential Power and the Modern Presidents* (New York: Free Press, 1990), 10.

50. Ibid.

51. George Edwards III, *The Strategic President: Persuasion and Opportunity in Presidential Leadership* (Princeton: Princeton University Press, 2009).

52. Samuel Kernell, *Going Public: New Strategies of Presidential Leadership*, 2nd ed. (Washington, D.C.: CQ Press, 1996).

53. Barbara Hinckley, *The Symbolic Presidency* (London: Routledge, 1990), ch. 2.

54. See Hedrick Smith, *The Power Game: How Washington Works* (New York: Random House, 1988), 405–406, for similar reports on the Nixon and Reagan administrations.

55. Lee Sigelman, "Gauging the Public Response to Presidential Leadership," *Presidential Studies Quarterly* 10 (Summer 1980): 427–433; James A. Stimson, "Public Support for American Presidents: A Cyclical Model," *Public Opinion Quarterly* 40 (Spring 1976): 1–21; Michael MacKuen, "Political Drama, Economic Conditions, and the Dynamics of Presidential Popularity," *American Journal of Political Science* 27 (February 1983): 165–192.

56. Gerald Pomper, "The Presidential Election," in Gerald Pomper, ed., *The Election of 1992* (Chatham, N.J.: Chatham House, 1993), 144–150; Richard L. Berke, "Poll Finds Most Give Clinton Credit for Strong Economy," *New York Times*, September 6, 1996, A1.

57. John R. Hibbing and Elizabeth Theiss-Morse, *Stealth Democracy: Americans' Beliefs About How Government Should Work* (New York: Cambridge University Press, 2002).

58. Paul Brace and Barbara Hinckley, *Follow the Leader: Opinion Polls and the Modern Presidents* (New York: Basic Books, 1992), ch. 5.

59. Ibid., ch. 6.

60. Neustadt, 50–72.

61. Mark A. Peterson, *Legislating Together: The White House and Capitol Hill From Eisenhower to Reagan* (Cambridge, Mass.: Harvard University Press, 1990); George Edwards, *At the Margins: Presidential Leadership of Congress* (New Haven: Yale University Press, 1989), ch. 9.

62. James L. Sundquist, "Needed: A Political Theory for a New Era of Coalition Government in the United States," *Political Science Quarterly* 103 (Winter 1988–1989): 613–635.

63. *Congressional Quarterly Weekly Report*, December 21, 1996, 3455.

64. Shawn Zeller, "Historic Success, at No Small Cost," *CQ Weekly*, January 11, 2010, 112.

65. David Mayhew, *Divided We Govern: Party Control, Lawmaking, and Investigations, 1946–1990* (New Haven: Yale University Press, 1991).

66. Ragsdale, 1–4.

67. Terry Moe, "Presidents, Institutions, and Theory," in George C. Edwards III, John H. Kessel, and Bert A. Rockman, eds., *Researching the Presidency: Vital Questions, New Approaches* (Pittsburgh: University of Pittsburgh Press, 1993), 370.

68. Ibid.

69. The President's Committee on Administrative Management, *Report of the Committee* (Washington, D.C.: U.S. Government Printing Office, 1937).

70. Jane Meyer and Doyle MacManus, *Landslide: The Unmaking of the President, 1984–1988* (Boston: Houghton Mifflin, 1988).

71. Tom Hamburger and Christi Parsons, "President Obama's czar system concerns some," *Los Angeles Times*, March 5, 2009; Zachary Coile, "Obama's big task: Managing the best, brightest," *San Francisco Chronicle*, January 11, 2009.

72. White House, "2010 Annual Report to Congress on White House Staff," www.whitehouse.gov/briefing-room/disclosures/annual-records/2010.

73. James P. Pfiffner, *The Modern Presidency*, 2nd ed. (New York: St. Martin's, 1998), 91.

74. Harold Relyea, "Growth and Development of the President's Office," in David Kozak and Kenneth Ciboski, eds., *The American Presidency* (Chicago: Nelson Hall, 1985), 135; Pfiffner, 122.

75. Sid Frank and Arden Davis Melick, *The Presidents: Tidbits and Trivia* (Maplewood, N.J.: Hammond, 1986), 103.

76. Timothy Walch, ed., *At the President's Side: The Vice-Presidency in the Twentieth Century* (Columbia: University of Missouri Press, 1997), 45.

77. Ann Devroy and Stephen Barr, "Reinventing the Vice Presidency: Defying History, Al Gore Has Emerged as Bill Clinton's Closest Political Advisor," *Washington Post National Weekly Edition*, February 27–March 5, 1995, 6–7.

78. See, for example, Stephen F. Hayes, *Cheney: The Untold Story of America's Most Powerful and Controversial Vice President* (New York: HarperCollins, 2007); Bruce Kluger, David Slavin, and Tim Foley, *Young Dick Cheney: Great American* (San Francisco: AlterNet Books, 2008); John Nichols, *Dick: The Man Who Is President* (New York: The New Press, 2004); Lou Dubose and Jake Bernstein, *Vice: Dick Cheney and the Hijacking of the American Presidency* (New York: Random House, 2006).

79. Evan Thomas, "Inconvenient Truth Teller; From Health-Care Reform to Afghanistan, Joe Biden Has Bucked Obama—as Only a Good Veep Can," *Newsweek*, October 19, 2009, 30+; Howard Kurtz, "Finding Virtue in Vice; Despite Gaffes, Biden Has Blossomed as Obama's Most Recent Prime Spokesman," *Washington Post*, June 10, 2010, C01.

80. Michelle Obama, "As Barack's First Lady, I Would Work to Help Working Families and Military Families," *U.S. News & World Report*, October 1, 2008.

81. Robert K. Murray and Tim H. Blessing, "The Presidential Performance Study: A Progress Report," *Journal of American History* 70 (December 1983): 535–555.

82. Jon R. Bond and Richard Fleisher, *The President in the Legislative Arena* (Chicago: University of Chicago Press, 1990); George C. Edwards III, *Presidential Influence in Congress* (San Francisco: Freeman, 1980).

83. James David Barber, *The Presidential Character*, 4th ed. (Englewood Cliffs, N.J.: Prentice Hall, 1992).

84. See Michael Nelson, "James David Barber and the Psychological Presidency," in David Pederson, ed., *The "Barberian" Presidency: Theoretical and Empirical Readings* (New York: Peter Lang, 1989), 93–110; Alexander George, "Assessing Presidential Character," *World Politics* (January 1974): 234–283; Jeffrey Tulis, "On Presidential Character," in Jeffrey Tulis and Joseph Bessette, eds., *Presidency and the Constitutional Order* (Baton Rouge: Louisiana State University Press, 1981).

85. Joseph Califano, *A Presidential Nation* (New York: Norton, 1975), 184–188.

86. Joel Achenbach, "In a Heated Race, Obama's Cool Won the Day," *Washington Post*, November 6, 2008, A47.

87. Gallup poll, December 19, 1998, http://institution.gallup.com/documents/topics.aspx.

88. Savage, "Bush Shuns Patriot Act."

89. Jonathan Weisman, "'Signing Statements' Study Finds Administration Has Ignored Laws," *Washington Post*, June 19, 2007, A4.

90. Savage, "Obama's Embrace of a Bush Tactic Riles Congress."

91. Quoted in Savage, "Bush Shuns Patriot Act."

Chapter 9

1. Organic Trade Association, "U.S. Organic Product Sales Reach $26.6 Billion in 2009," press release, April 22, 2010, www.organicnewsroom.com/2010/04/us_organic_product_sales_reach_1.html.

2. Dann Denny, "Defining 'Organic,'" *Bloomington Herald Times*, April 16, 1998, D1.

3. Marian Burros, "Eating Well: U.S. Proposal on Organic Food Gets a Grass-Roots Review," *New York Times*, March 25, 1998, F10.

4. Gene Kahn, "National Organic Standard Will Aid Consumers," *Frozen Food Age* 47 (September 1998): 18.

5. Burros, "Eating Well," F10.

6. H. H. Gerth and C. Wright Mills, eds., *From Max Weber* (New York: Oxford University Press, 1946), 196–199.

7. Herbert Kaufman, "Emerging Conflicts in the Doctrines of Public Administration,"

American Political Science Review 50 (December 1956): 1057–1073.

8. Morris P. Fiorina, *Congress: Keystone of the Washington Establishment* (New Haven: Yale University Press, 1977).

9. Herbert Kaufman, *Red Tape, Its Origins, Uses, and Abuses* (Washington, D.C.: Brookings Institution, 1977).

10. Bureau of Labor Statistics, *Career Guide to Industries, 2010–2011 Edition*, www.bls.gov/oco/cg/cgs041.htm.

11. Kenneth J. Meier, *Politics and the Bureaucracy*, 4th ed. (Fort Worth, Texas: Harcourt-Brace, 2000), 17.

12. Ibid., 18–19.

13. U.S. National Debt Clock, accessed July 29, 2010, www.brillig.com/debt_clock.

14. White House, "The Cabinet," www.whitehouse.gov/administration/cabinet.

15. William G. Howell and David E. Lewis, "Agencies by Presidential Design," *Journal of Politics* 64: 1095–1114.

16. Dennis D. Riley, *Controlling the Federal Bureaucracy* (Philadelphia: Temple University Press, 1987), 139–142.

17. Kenneth J. Meier, *Politics and the Bureaucracy*, 5th ed. (Fort Worth, Texas: Harcourt-Brace, 2007), 72–78.

18. *U.S. News and World Report*, February 11, 1980, 64.

19. David E. Lewis, "The Adverse Consequences of the Politics of Agency Design for Presidential Management in the United States: The Relative Durability of Insulated Agencies," *British Journal of Political Science* 34 (2004): 377–404.

20. John B. Judis, "The Quiet Revolution: Obama Has Reinvented the State in More Ways Than You Can Imagine," *New Republic*, February 1, 2010, www.tnr.com/article/politics/the-quiet-revolution.

21. Robert Pear, "Health Insurance Companies Try to Shape Rules," *New York Times*, May 15, 2010.

22. U.S. Office of Personnel Management, *Federal Civilian Workforce Statistics: The Fact Book, 2007 Edition*, www.opm.gov/feddata/factbook/2007/2007FACTBOOK.pdf.

23. Meier, 4th ed., 177–181.

24. Quoted in Donald F. Kettl, *System Under Stress: Homeland Security and American Politics* (Washington, D.C.: CQ Press, 2004), 48.

25. "The 9/11 Commission Report: Final Report of the National Commission on Terrorist Attacks Upon the United States, Executive Summary," www.c-span.org/pdf/911finalreportexecsum.pdf.

26. Quoted in Kettl, 53.

27. Catherine Rampell, "Whistle-blowers Tell of Cost of Conscience," *USA Today*, November 24, 2006, 13A; Peter Eisler,

"Whistle-blowers' Rights Get Second Look; Bills to Strengthen Protections Now Have Better Chance to Pass, Backers Say," *USA Today*, March 15, 2010, 6A.

28. David E. Lewis, "Staffing Alone: Unilateral Action and the Politicization of the Executive Office of the President, 1988–2004," *Presidential Studies Quarterly* 35 (2005): 496–514.

29. Dana Milbank, "Bush Seeks to Rule the Bureaucracy; Appointments Aim at White House Control," *Washington Post*, November 22, 2004, A4.

30. Terry Moe, "The President's Cabinet," in James Pfiffer and Roger J. Davidson, eds., *Understanding the Presidency*, 3rd ed. (New York: Longman, 2003), 208.

31. Office of Personnel Management, *Federal Workforce Statistics: The Fact Book 2003 Edition* (Washington, D.C.: OPM, 2003), 10, www.opm.gov/feddata/03factbk.pdf.

32. Francis E. Rourke, *Bureaucracy, Politics and Public Policy*, 3rd ed. (Boston: Little, Brown, 1984), 106.

33. Albert B. Crenshaw, "Cash Flow," *Washington Post*, June 28, 1998, H1.

34. Anthony E. Brown, *The Politics of Airline Regulation* (Knoxville: University of Tennessee Press, 1987).

35. Lewis, 496–514.

36. Charlie Savage, "Bush Aide Admits Hiring Boasts; Says He Broke No Rules Giving Jobs to Conservatives," *Boston Globe*, June 6, 2007, A9; Charlie Savage, "Scandal Puts Spotlight on Christian Law School; Grads Influential in Justice Dept.," *Boston Globe*, April 8, 2007, A1; Eric Lipton, "Colleagues Cite Partisan Focus by Justice Officials," *New York Times*, May 12, 2007, A1.

37. Walter Pincus, "CIA Director Cuts Meetings on Terrorism; Coordinating Sessions Reduced to 3 a Week," *Washington Post*, January 10, 2005, A15; Walter Pincus, "Changing of the Guard at the CIA; Goss's Shake-Ups Leave Some Questioning Agency's Role," *Washington Post*, January 6, 2005, A3.

38. John B. Judis, "The Quiet Revolution: Obama has Reinvented the State in More Ways Than You Can Imagine," *New Republic*, February 1, 2010.

39. Riley, ch. 2.

40. Harold Seidman and Robert Gilmour, *Politics, Position, and Power: From the Positive to the Regulatory State*, 4th ed. (New York: Oxford University Press, 1986), 3.

41. Quoted in Riley, 43.

42. Edmund L. Andrews, "Blowing the Whistle on Big Oil," *New York Times*, December 3, 2006.

43. Quoted in Jason DeParle, "Minerals Service Had a Mandate to Produce Results," *New York Times*, August 7, 2010.

44. Center for Responsive Politics, "Oil and Gas," www.opensecrets.org/industries/indus.php?ind=e01.

45. Hugh Heclo, "Issue Networks and the Executive Establishment," in Anthony King, ed., *The New American Political System* (Washington, D.C.: American Enterprise Institute, 1978), 87–124.

46. Deborah Zabarenko, "Environmental Group to Sue U.S. Over Oil Permits," Reuters, May 14, 2010, www.reuters.com/article/idUSTRE64D64320100515.

47. Matthew McCubbins and Thomas Schwartz, "Congressional Oversight Overlooked: Police Patrols Versus Fire Alarms," *American Journal of Political Science* 28 (1984): 16–79.

48. Thomas E. Mann, Molly Reynolds, and Peter Hoey, "Is Congress on the Mend?" *New York Times*, April 28, 2007.

49. Kenneth Shepsle and Barry Weingast, "The Institutional Foundations of Committee Power," *American Political Science Review* 81 (1987): 85–104.

50. Felicity Barringer, "Limits on Logging are Reinstated," *The New York Times*, July 16, 2009, www.nytimes.com/2009/07/17/science/earth/17forest.html?_r=1&ref=earth.

51. Matthew Crenson and Francis E. Rourke, "By Way of Conclusion: American Bureaucracy Since World War II," in Louis Galambois, ed., *The New American State: Bureaucracies and Policies Since World War II* (Baltimore: Johns Hopkins University Press, 1987), 137–177.

52. Charles Lane, "High Court Rejects Detainee Tribunals: 5 to 3 Ruling Curbs President's Claim of Wartime Power," *Washington Post*, June 30, 2006, A1; Robert Barnes, "Justices Say Detainees Can Seek Release," *Washington Post*, June 13, 2008, A1.

53. Martha Derthick, *Policymaking for Social Security* (Washington, D.C.: Brookings Institution, 1979), reprinted in "The Art of Cooptation: Advisory Councils in Social Security," in Francis E. Rourke, ed., *Bureaucratic Power in National Policy Making*, 3rd ed. (Boston: Little, Brown, 1986), 109.

54. Charles T. Goodsell, *The Case for Bureaucracy* (Chatham, N.J.: Chatham House, 1993), ch. 3; Robert L. Kahn, Barbara A. Gutek, Eugenia Barton, and Daniel Katz, "Americans Love Their Bureaucrats," in Francis E. Rourke, ed., *Bureaucracy, Politics, and Public Policy*, 4th ed. (Boston: Little, Brown, 1988).

55. Meier, 210–211.

Chapter 10

1. This list is based loosely on the discussion of the functions of law in James V. Calvi and Susan Coleman, *American Law and Legal Systems* (Upper Saddle River, N.J.: Prentice Hall, 1997), 2–4; Steven Vago, *Law and Society* (Upper Saddle River, N.J.: Prentice Hall, 1997), 16–20; and Lawrence Baum, *American Courts: Process and Policy*, 4th ed. (Boston: Houghton Mifflin, 1998), 4–5.

2. Christopher E. Smith, *Courts, Politics, and the Judicial Process* (Chicago: Nelson-Hall, 1993), 179.

3. Henry Abraham, *The Judicial Process* (New York: Oxford University Press, 1993), 97.

4. Ibid., 96–97.

5. Smith, 329.

6. Jethro K. Lieberman, *The Litigious Society* (New York: Basic Books, 1981), 6.

7. Smith, 324.

8. Ibid., 324, 327.

9. Lieberman, 168–190.

10. Lawrence Friedman, *Total Justice: What Americans Want From the Legal System and Why* (Boston: Beacon Press, 1985), 31–32, cited in Smith, 323.

11. "Prison Suits," *Reader's Digest*, August 1994, 96.

12. Alexander Hamilton, James Madison, and John Jay, *The Federalist Papers*, ed. Clinton Rossiter (New York: New American Library, 1961).

13. Robert A. Carp and Ronald Stidham, *The Federal Courts* (Washington, D.C.: CQ Press, 1991), 4.

14. Lawrence Baum, *The Supreme Court*, 5th ed. (Washington, D.C.: CQ Press, 1995), 13.

15. *Marbury v. Madison*, 5 U.S. (1 Cranch) 137 (1803).

16. *Dred Scott v. Sanford*, 60 U.S. (19 How.) 393.

17. Lawrence Baum, *The Supreme Court*, 8th ed. (Washington, D.C.: CQ Press, 2004), 170, 173.

18. Baum, *The Supreme Court*, 5th ed., 1995, 22–24.

19. Matthew J. Streb, "Just Like Any Other Election? The Politics of Judicial Elections," in Matthew J. Streb, ed., *Law and Election Politics: The Rules of the Game* (Boulder: Lynne Rienner, 2005).

20. Joan Biskupic, "Making a Mark on the Bench," *Washington Post National Weekly Edition*, December 2–8, 1996, 31.

21. Sheldon Goldman, Sara Schiavoni, and Elliot Slotnick, "George W. Bush's Judicial Philosophy: Mission Accomplished," *Judicature* 92 (May/June 2009): 276.

22. Current data are available at www.fjc.gov.

23. Biskupic.

24. Ibid.

25. Goldman, Schiavoni, and Slotnick, 283.

26. David G. Savage, "Conservative Courts Likely Bush Legacy," *Los Angeles Times*, January 2, 2008, A11.

27. Doug Kendall, "The Bench in Purgatory: The New Republican Obstructionism on Obama's Judicial Nominees," *Slate*, October 26, 2009, www.slate.com/id/2233309/.

28. David M. O'Brien, "Ironies and Disappointments: Bush and Federal Judgeships," in Colin Campbell and Bert Rockman, eds., *The George W. Bush Presidency* (Washington, D.C.: CQ Press, 2004), 139–143.

29. Manu Raju, Republicans Warn Obama on Judges, *Politico*, March 2, 2009, www.politico.com/news/stories/0309/19526.html.

30. Greg Gordon, "Federal Courts, Winner Will Make a Mark on the Bench," *Minneapolis Star Tribune*, September 27, 2004, 1A.

31. The Gallup Organization, *Polls, Topics & Trends: Trust in Government*, various dates through 2004, www.gallup.com/poll/content/?ci=5392&pg=1; Linda Greenhouse, "The Nation: Vote Count Omits a Verdict on the Court," *New York Times*, November 18, 2001, sec. 4, 4.

32. Cited in Robert Marquand, "Why America Puts Its Supreme Court on a Lofty Pedestal," *Christian Science Monitor*, June 25, 1997, 14.

33. Although the president has no official "list" of criteria, scholars are mostly agreed on these factors. See, for instance, Henry J. Abraham, *The Judiciary* (New York: New York University Press, 1996), 65–69; Lawrence Baum, *American Courts: Process and Policy*, 4th ed. (Boston: Houghton Mifflin, 1998), 105–106; Philip Cooper and Howard Ball, *The United States Supreme Court: From the Inside Out* (Upper Saddle River, N.J.: Prentice Hall, 1996), 49–60; and Thomas G. Walker and Lee Epstein, *The Supreme Court of the United States* (New York: St. Martin's Press, 1993), 34–40.

34. Baum, *American Courts*, 4th ed., 105.

35. From the filmstrip *This Honorable Court* (Washington, D.C.: Greater Washington Educational Telecommunications Association, 1988), program 1.

36. Ibid.

37. Peter Baker, "Kagan Nomination Leaves Longing on the Left," *New York Times*, May 10, 2010, www.nytimes.com/2010/05/11/us/politics/11nominees.html?scp=1&sq=Elena%20Kagan%201iberal&st=cse.

38. Baum, *American Courts*, 4th ed., 105.

39. Walker and Epstein, 40.

40. Sonia Sotomayor, "A Latina Judge's Voice," address at U.C. Berkeley, October 26, 2001, www.berkeley.edu/news/media/releases/2009/05/26_sotomayor.shtml.

41. Baum, *The Supreme Court*, 8th ed., 103.

42. U.S. Supreme Court, "2009 Year-End Report on the Federal Judiciary," www.supremecourt.gov/publicinfo/year-end/2009year-endreport.pdf.

43. Philip Cooper and Howard Ball, *The United States Supreme Court: From the Inside Out* (Upper Saddle River, N.J.: Prentice Hall, 1996), 104.

44. Ibid., 134.

45. Walker and Epstein, 90.

46. Ibid., 91–92.

47. David O'Brien, *Storm Center* (New York: Norton, 1990), 272.

48. Walker and Epstein, 129–130.

49. Adam Cohen, "Psst . . . Justice Scalia . . . You Know, You're an Activist Too," *New York Times*, April 19, 2005, web version.

50. Walker and Epstein, 126–130.

51. What follows is drawn from the excellent discussion in ibid., 131–139.

52. Baum, *The Supreme Court*, 9th ed., 79.

53. *Gratz v. Bollinger*, 539 U.S. 244 (2003); *Grutter v. Bollinger*, 539 U.S. 306 (2003).

54. Max Lerner, *Nine Scorpions in a Bottle: Great Judges and Cases of the Supreme Court* (New York: Arcade Publishing, 1994).

55. Philip J. Cooper, *Battles on the Bench: Conflict Inside the Supreme Court* (Lawrence: University Press of Kansas, 1995), 42–46.

56. For a provocative argument that the Court does not, in fact, successfully produce significant social reform and actually damaged the civil rights struggles in this country, see Gerald N. Rosenberg, *The Hollow Hope: Can Courts Bring About Social Change?* (Chicago: University of Chicago Press, 1991).

57. *Marbury v. Madison*, 1 Cr. 137 (1803).

58. *Martin v. Hunter's Lessee*, 14 U.S. 304 (1816).

59. *McCulloch v. Maryland*, 4 Wheat. 316 (1819).

60. *Gibbons v. Ogden*, 9 Wheat. 1 (1824).

61. *Lochner v. New York*, 198 U.S. 45 (1905).

62. *Hammer v. Dagenhart*, 247 U.S. 251 (1918).

63. *Adkins v. Children's Hospital*, 261 U.S. 525 (1923).

64. *Dred Scott v. Sanford*, 19 How. 393 (1857).

65. *Plessy v. Ferguson*, 163 U.S. 537 (1896).

66. *Brown v. Board of Education*, 347 U.S. 483 (1954).

67. For example, *Mapp v. Ohio*, 367 U.S. 643 (1961); *Gideon v. Wainwright*, 372 U.S. 335 (1963); and *Miranda v. Arizona*, 382 U.S. 925 (1965).

68. *Baker v. Carr*, 396 U.S. 186 (1962).

69. *Roe v. Wade*, 410 U.S. 113 (1973).

70. *Citizens United v. Federal Election Commission*, 558 U.S. _____ (2010).

71. Maria Puente, "Poll: Blacks' Confidence in Police Plummets," *USA Today*, March 21, 1995, 3A.

72. Michael Tonry, "Racial Politics, Racial Disparities, and the War on Crime," *Crime and Delinquency* (1994): 475–494.

73. John H. Langbein, "Money Talks, Clients Walk," *Newsweek*, April 17, 1995, 32.

74. Legal Services Corporation, "Fact Sheet: What Is LSC?" www.lsc.gov/about/factsheet_whatislsc.php.

75. Consortium on Legal Services and the Public, *Agenda for Success: The American People and Civil Justice* (Chicago: American Bar Association, 1996); see also Legal Services Corporation, "Serving the Civil Legal Needs of Low-Income Americans," April 30, 2000, www.lsc.gov/pressr/exsum.pdf.

76. Linda Greenhouse, "*Bush v. Gore:* A Special Report," *New York Times*, February 20, 2001.

Chapter 11

1. Mike Gravel, "Philadelphia II: National Initiatives," *Campaigns and Elections* (December 1995/January 1996): 2.

2. According to a September 1994 Roper poll, 76 percent favor a national referendum.

3. Survey by Fox News and Opinion Dynamics, May 24–May 25, 2000, iPOLL database, Roper Center for Public Opinion Research, University of Connecticut, www.ropercenter.uconn.edu/ipoll.html.

4. "Exchange With Reporters in Waco, Texas, August 7, 2001," Public Papers of the Presidents: George W. Bush—2001, vol. 2, 945; U.S. Government Printing Office via GPO Access.

5. Joshua Green, "The Other War Room," *Washington Monthly*, April 2002, 16.

6. Sam Stein, "Obama Mocks Polls But Spends More on Them ($4.4M) Than Bush," *Huffington Post*, July 29, 2010, www.huffingtonpost.com/2010/07/29/obama-mocks-polls-but-spe_n_663553.html.

7. V. O. Key Jr., *Public Opinion and American Democracy* (New York: Knopf, 1961), 7.

8. John Kingdon, *Congressmen's Voting Decisions*, 2nd ed. (New York: Harper & Row, 1981), ch. 2.

9. Gary C. Jacobson, "The War, the President, and the 2006 Midterm Congressional Elections," paper presented at the annual meeting of the Midwest Political Science Association, Chicago, April 12–15, 2007.

10. Many works repeat this theme of the uninformed and ignorant citizen. See, for example, Bernard Berelson, Paul F. Lazarsfeld, and William N. McPhee, *Voting: A Study of Opinion Formation in a Presidential Campaign* (Chicago: University of Chicago Press, 1954); Angus Campbell, Philip E. Converse, Warren E. Miller, and Donald E. Stokes, *The American Voter* (New York: Wiley, 1960); W. Russell Neuman, *The Paradox of Mass Politics* (Cambridge: Harvard University Press, 1986); and Michael X. Delli Carpini and Scott Keeter, *What Americans Know About Politics and Why It Matters* (New Haven: Yale University Press, 1996).

11. These data come from Delli Carpini and Keeter, 70–75.

12. Calculated by the authors from the 2004 American National Election Studies survey.

13. 2008 American National Election Studies, www.electionstudies.org.

14. John Marzulli and Michael Saul, "A Disturbing Wave of Hatred: Anti-Muslim, Anti-Arab Incidents in City, Nation," *New York Daily News*, September 19, 2001.

15. Herbert McClosky and Alida Brill, *Dimensions of Tolerance* (New York: Russell Sage Foundation, 1983), 50.

16. Ibid., 250.

17. Robert S. Erikson and Kent Tedin, *American Public Opinion*, 5th ed. (Boston: Allyn & Bacon, 1995), 127–128.

18. M. Kent Jennings and Richard G. Niemi, *The Political Character of Adolescence* (Princeton: Princeton University Press, 1974); Robert C. Luskin, John P. McIver, and Edward Carmines, "Issues and the Transmission of Partisanship," *American Journal of Political Science* 33 (May 1989): 440–458; Christopher H. Achen, "Parental Socialization and Rational Party Identification," *Political Behavior* 24 (June 2002): 151–170.

19. Shirley Engle and Anna Ochoa, *Education for Democratic Citizenship: Decision Making in the Social Studies* (New York: Teachers College of Columbia University, 1988).

20. Robert D. Hess and Judith V. Torney, *The Development of Political Attitudes in Children* (Chicago: Aldine, 1967).

21. Kenneth D. Wald, Dennis E. Owen, and Samuel S. Jill Jr., "Political Cohesion in Churches," *Journal of Politics* 52 (1990): 197–215; Robert Huckfeldt, Paul Allen Beck, Russell J. Dalton, and Jeffrey Levine, "Political Environments, Cohesive Social Groups, and the Communication of Public Opinion," *American Journal of Political Science* 39 (1995): 1025–1054; David C. Leege, Kenneth D. Wald, Brian S. Krueger, and Paul D. Mueller, *The Politics of Cultural Differences: Social Change and Voter Mobilization in the Post–New Deal Period* (Princeton: Princeton University Press, 2002).

22. Elisabeth Noelle-Neumann, *The Spiral of Silence: Public Opinion, Our Social Skin* (Chicago: University of Chicago Press, 1984).

23. Paul R. Abramson and Ada W. Finifter, "On the Meaning of Political Trust: New Evidence From Items Introduced in 1978," *American Journal of Political Science* 25 (May 1981): 295–306; Arthur H. Miller, "Is Confidence Rebounding?" *Public Opinion* (June/July 1983); Robert S. Erikson and Kent L. Tedin, *American Public Opinion*, 7th ed. (New York: Pearson-Longman, 2005), 162–166.

24. Angus Campbell, Philip E. Converse, Donald E. Stokes, and Warren E. Miller, *The American Voter* (New York: Wiley, 1960); Donald P. Green, Bradley Palmquist, and Eric Schickler, *Partisan Hearts and Minds: Political Parties and the Social Identities of Voters* (New Haven: Yale University Press, 2002).

25. Larry M. Bartels, "Beyond the Running Tally: Partisan Bias in Political Perceptions," *Political Behavior* 24 (June 2002).

26. CBS News poll, February 2–4, 2009. Telephone survey of 864 respondents. Calculated by the authors from data obtained from the Roper Center.

27. M. J. Hetherington, "Resurgent Mass Partisanship: The Role of Elite Polarization," *American Political Science Review* 95 (2001): 619–631; Alan Abramowitz, *The Disappearing Center: Engaged Citizens, Polarization and American Democracy* (New Haven: Yale University Press, 2010).

28. Norman H. Nie, Jane Junn, and Kenneth Stehlik-Barry, *Education and Democratic Citizenship in America* (Chicago: University of Chicago Press, 1996).

29. For more on the effects of education, see Delli Carpini and Keeter, 188–189; Erikson and Tedin, 7th ed., 152–159; and Herbert H. Hyman, Charles R. Wright, and John Shelton Reed, *The Enduring Effects of Education* (Chicago: University of Chicago Press, 1975). But for a dissenting view that formal education is just a mask for intelligence and native cognitive ability, see Robert Luskin, "Explaining Political Sophistication," *Political Behavior* 12 (1990): 3298–3409.

30. Christine L. Day, *What Older Americans Think: Interest Groups and Aging Policy* (Princeton: Princeton University Press, 1990).

31. Scott Helman, "Obama Strikes Chord With Generation Next: Campaign Targets Youth Vote in Ind," *Boston Globe*, May 3, 2008; Cynthia Burton and Joseph A. Gambardello,

"Turnout for N.J. Primary Highest in Half a Century," *Philadelphia Inquirer*, February 7, 2008.

32. Warren E. Miller and J. Merrill Shanks, *The New American Voter* (Cambridge: Harvard University Press, 1996), ch. 7.

33. Figure calculated by the authors from National Election Studies data.

34. Erikson and Tedin, 5th ed., 208–212.

35. Based on the authors' analysis of the 1996 and 2000 Voter News Service Election Day exit polls.

36. Lee Sigelman and Susan Welch, *Black Americans' Views of Racial Equality—The Dream Deferred* (Cambridge: Cambridge University Press, 1991).

37. Katherine Tate, "Black Political Participation in the 1984 and 1988 Presidential Elections," *American Political Science Review* 85 (December 1991): 1159–1176.

38. Frank Newport, "Mormons Most Conservative Major Religious Group in U.S.," www.gallup.com/poll/125021/mormons-conservative-major-religious-group.aspx.

39. Robert S. Erikson, Gerald C. Wright, and John P. McIver, *Statehouse Democracy* (New York: Cambridge University Press, 1993), 18.

40. Susan Herbst, *Numbered Voices: How Opinion Polling Has Shaped American Politics* (Chicago: University of Chicago Press, 1993), ch. 4.

41. William Safire, *Safire's New Political Dictionary: The Definitive Guide to the New Language of Politics* (New York: Random House, 1993), 764.

42. Robert S. Erikson and Kent Tedin, *American Public Opinion*, 5th ed. (Boston: Allyn & Bacon, 1995), 29–31.

43. Richard Morin, "Don't Ask Me: As Fewer Cooperate on Polls, Criticism and Questions Mount," *Washington Post*, October 28, 2004, C1.

44. Pew Research Center for the People and the Press, "Opinion Poll Experiment Reveals Conservative Opinions Not Underestimated, But Racial Hostility Missed," March 27, 1998, www.people-press.org/content.htm; Andrew Rosenthal, "The 1989 Elections: Predicting the Outcome; Broad Disparities in Votes and Polls Raising Questions," *New York Times*, November 9, 1989, A1; Adam Clymer, "Election Day Shows What the Opinion Polls Can't Do," *New York Times*, November 12, 1989, sec. 4, 4; George Flemming and Kimberly Parker, "Race and Reluctant Respondents: Possible Consequences of Non-Response for Pre-Election Survey," May 16, 1998, www.people-press.org/content.htm.

45. George F. Bishop et al., "Pseudo-Opinions on Public Affairs," *Public Opinion Quarterly* 44 (Summer 1980): 198–209.

46. Howard Schuman and Stanley Presser, *Questions and Answers in Attitude Surveys* (New York: Academic Press, 1981), 148–160.

47. This was a Roper Starch Worldwide poll conducted in November 1992 for the American Jewish Committee, and it was reported in conjunction with the dedication of the Holocaust Memorial Museum.

48. Debra J. Saunders, "Poll Shows Americans in Deep Dumbo," *San Francisco Chronicle*, April 23, 1993, A30; Leonard Larsen, "What's on Americans' Mind? Not Much, History Poll Finds," *Sacramento Bee*, June 2, 1993, B7, cited in David W. Moore and Frank Newport, "Misreading the Public: The Case of the Holocaust Poll," *Public Perspective* (March–April 1994).

49. Moore and Newport, 29.

50. John Zaller, *The Nature and Origins of Mass Opinion* (New York: Cambridge University Press, 1992).

51. See, for example, abcnews.go.com/US/PollVault/, www.cbsnews.com/sections/opinion/polls/main500160.shtml, www.washingtonpost.com/wp-dyn/politics/polls, www.nytimes.com/pages/politics/index.html (click on "Poll Watch" to see recent polls), www.latimes.com/news/custom/timespoll, www.people-press.org, and www.gallup.com/poll/; for an excellent roundup of political polls, see www.pollingreport.com.

52. Two recent additions to the large-scale surveys are the National Annenberg Elections Surveys, which launched large, complex, in-person surveys of voter attitudes and decision making in the 2000, 2004, and 2008 elections (www.annenbergpublicpolicycenter.org/ProjectDetails.aspx?myId=1) and the recurring (since 2006) Cooperative Congressional Elections studies, which are Internet-based surveys. Each carries questions by teams of scholars from dozens of universities exploring a wide variety of questions about political behavior; see web.mit.edu/polisci/portl/cces/index.html.

53. Most of the exit poll reporting is based on surveys done by Edison Media Research and Mitofsky International for the National Election Pool. This is a consortium of ABC News, Associated Press, CBS News, CNN, Fox News, and NBC News. Each of the media organizations has its own analysts who then highlight different aspects of the exit poll data.

54. Adam Lisberg, "Exit Polls Out of Whack: Early Numbers Told Wrong Story," New York *Daily News*, November 4, 2002, 11; "Evaluation of Edison/ Mitofsky Election System 2004," prepared by Edison Media Research and Mitofsky International for the National Election Pool (NEP), January 19, 2005.

55. Quoted in "Planting Lies With 'Push Polls,'" *St. Petersburg Times*, June 7, 1995, 10A.

56. Quoted in Betsy Rothstein, "Push Polls Utilized in Final Weeks," *The Hill*, October 28, 1998, 3.

57. "Pollsters Seek AAPC Action," *Campaigns and Elections* (July 1996): 55.

58. Paul Sniderman and Thomas Piazza, *The Scar of Race* (Cambridge: Harvard University Press, 1995).

59. TESS Time-Sharing Experiments for the Social Sciences, http://tess.experimentcentral.org/.

60. William Saletan, "Phoning It In," *Slate*, December 7, 2007, www.slate.com/iod/2179395/.

61. SurveyUSA home page, www.surveyusa.com.

62. David Sanders, Harold D. Clarke, Marianne C. Stewart, and Paul Whiteley, "Does Mode Matter for Modeling Political Choice? Evidence From the 2005 British Election Study," *Political Analysis* 15 (2007): 257–285; Robert P. Berrens, Alok K. Bohara, Hank Jenkins-Smith, Carol Silva, and David L. Weimer, "The Advent of Internet Surveys for Political Research: A Comparison of Telephone and Internet Samples," *Political Analysis* 11 (2003): 1–22; Taylor Humphrey, "The Case for Publishing (Some) Online Polls," *Polling Report*, January 15, 2007; Linchiat Chang and Jon A. Krosnick, "National Surveys via RDD Telephone Interviewing Versus the Internet," *Public Opinion Quarterly* 2009 (73): 641–678.

63. J. Michael Brick, Pat D. Brick, Sarah Dipko, Stanley Presser, Clyde Tucker, and Yangyang Yuan, "Cell Phone Survey Feasibility in the U.S.: Sampling and Calling Cell Numbers Versus Landline Numbers," *Public Opinion Quarterly* 71 (Spring 2007): 23–39. See the special issue of *Public Opinion Quarterly* (Winter 2007) for perspectives on the challenge of cell phones for surveys.

64. Erikson and Tedin, 5th ed., 42–47.

65. Research suggests that use of information shortcuts does allow the electorate to make decisions that are more in line with their values than if they did not have such shortcuts; see Samuel Popkin, *The Reasoning Voter* (Chicago: University of Chicago Press, 1991); and Paul Sniderman,

Richard Brody, and Philip Tetlock, *Reasoning and Choice: Exploration in Political Psychology* (New York: Cambridge University Press, 1991). However, this is not the same as saying that, if fully informed, everyone would make the same decision as they do without information. Indeed, information really does count; see Larry Bartels, "Uninformed Votes: Information Effects in Presidential Elections," *American Journal of Political Science* 40 (February 1996): 194–230; and Scott Althaus, "Information Effects in Collective Preferences," *American Political Science Review* 92 (September 1998): 545–558.

66. Milton Lodge, Kathleen McGraw, and Patrick Stroh, "An Impression-Driven Model of Candidate Evaluation," *American Political Science Review* 82 (June 1989): 399–419.

67. Berelson, Lazarsfeld, and McPhee, 109–115.

68. Larry M. Bartels, "Uninformed Votes: Information Effects in Presidential Elections," *American Journal of Political Science* 40, no. 1 (1996): 194–230.

69. Gerald C. Wright, "Level of Analysis Effects on Explanations of Voting," *British Journal of Political Science* 18 (July 1989): 381–398; Samuel Popkin, *The Reasoning Voter* (Chicago: University of Chicago Press, 1991); Benjamin Page and Robert Shapiro, *The Rational Public* (Chicago: University of Chicago Press, 1993).

70. Erikson, Wright, and McIver.

71. Michael B. MacKuen, Robert S. Erikson, and James A. Stimson, "Macropartisanship," *American Political Science Review* 89 (December 1989): 1125–1142.

72. Larry Bartels, *Unequal Democracy: The Political Economy of the New Gilded Age* (Princeton: Princeton University Press, 2008), ch. 9; Martin Gilens, "Inequality and Democratic Responsiveness," *Public Opinion Quarterly* 69 (2005): 778–896.

73. Jean Bethke Elshtain, "A Parody of True Democracy," *Christian Science Monitor*, August 13, 1992, 18.

Chapter 12

1. Jennifer Steinhauer, "Nevada Challenger Lifted by Tea Party Ardor," *New York Times*, June 9, 2010, www.nytimes.com/2010/06/10/us/politics/10nevada.html?scp=1&sq=sharron%20angle%20primary&st=cse.

2. Ibid.; Brian Stelter, "Reid and Angle Campaigns Fight Over Web Site," *The Caucus*, July 6, 2010, http://thecaucus.blogs.nytimes.com/2010/07/06/reid-and-angle-campaigns-fight-over-web-site/?scp=1&sq=sharron%20angle%20website&st=cse; Adam Weinstein, "Nevada Tea Partiers' Memory Hole," *Mother Jones*, June 9, 2010, http://motherjones.com/mojo/2010/06/nevada-tea-partier-memory-hole-website-sharron-angle-harry-reid-senate.

3. Stelter.

4. Jessica Taylor, "Mason-Dixon Poll: Reid Rises Again," *Politico*, July 16, 2010, www.politico.com/news/stories/0710/39842.html.

5. Jonathan Allen and Jake Sherman, "GOP Leery of Tea Party Caucus," *Politico*, July 20, 2010, http://dyn.politico.com/members/forums/thread.cfm?catid=1&subcatid=1&threadid=42805501; Paul Kane, "Lieberman Savoring Life on Both Sides of the Aisle: Democrats Want Him in Caucus Despite His Backing of McCain," *Washington Post*, June 6, 2008, A17.

6. See, for example, James Bryce, *The American Commonwealth* (Chicago: Sergel, 1891), vol. 2, pt. 3.

7. E. E. Schattschneider, *Party Government* (New York: Holt, Rinehart, and Winston, 1942), 1.

8. This division and the following discussion are based on Frank Sorauf, *Party Politics in America* (Boston: Little, Brown, 1964), ch. 1; and V. O. Key Jr., *Politics, Parties, and Pressure Groups*, 5th ed. (New York: Corwell, 1964).

9. Richard G. Niemi and M. Kent Jennings, "Issues of Inheritance in the Formation of Party Identification," *American Journal of Political Science* 35 (1991): 970–988.

10. The discussion of the responsible party model is based on Austin Ranney, *The Doctrine of the Responsible Party Government* (Urbana: University of Illinois Press, 1962), chs. 1, 2.

11. Morris P. Fiorina, "The Decline of Collective Responsibility in American Politics," *Daedalus* 109 (Summer 1980): 25–45; John H. Aldrich, *Why Parties? The Origin and Transformation of Party Politics in America* (Chicago: University of Chicago Press, 1995), 3.

12. American Political Science Association, "Toward a More Responsible Two-Party System: A Report of the Committee on Political Parties of the American Political Science Association," *American Political Science Review* 44 (1950; 3, pt. 2): 1–99.

13. Alan I. Abramowitz, "Exploring the Bases of Partisanship in the American Electorate: Social Identity vs. Ideology," *Political Research Quarterly* 59 (2006): 175–187.

14. Alan I. Abramowitz and Kyle L. Saunders, "Ideological Realignment in the U.S. Electorate," *Journal of Politics* 60 (1998): 634–652; Geoffrey C. Layman and Thomas M. Carsey, "Party Polarization and 'Conflict Extension' in the American Electorate," *American Journal of Political Science* 46 (2002): 786–802; Geoffrey C. Layman et al., "Activists and Conflict Extension in American Party Politics," *American Political Science Review* 104 (2010): 324–346.

15. Calculated by the authors using data from the CBS News/*New York Times* national surveys; Abramowitz and Saunders report the same basic pattern in their analysis of white party identifiers using data from the American National Election Studies, Abramowitz and Saunders, "Ideological Realignment of the U.S. Electorate," 186.

16. Edward G. Carmines and Geoffrey C. Layman, "Issue Evolution in Postwar American Politics: Old Certainties and Fresh Tensions," in Byron E. Shafer, ed., *Present Discontents: American Politics in the Very Late Twentieth Century* (Chatham, N.J.: Chatham House, 1997), 89–134.

17. John H. Aldrich, "A Downsian Spatial Model With Party Activism," *American Political Science Review* 77 (1983): 974–990; David W. Brady, Hahrie Han, and Jeremy C. Pope, "Primary Elections and Candidate Ideology: Out of Step With the Primary Electorate?" *Legislative Studies Quarterly* 27 (2007): 79–105; Layman et al.; James L. Gibson and Susan E. Scarrow, "State Organizations in American Politics," in Eric M. Uslaner, ed., *American Political Parties: A Reader* (Itasca, Ill.: F. E. Peacock, 1993), 234.

18. James Q. Wilson, *The Amateur Democrat: Club Politics in Three Cities* (Chicago: University of Chicago Press, 1965).

19. Walter J. Stone and Alan I. Abramowitz, "Winning May Not Be Everything, but It's More Than We Thought: Presidential Party Activists in 1980," *American Political Science Review* 77 (1983): 945–956.

20. Joseph A. Aistrup, *The Southern Strategy Revisited: Republican Top-Down Advancement in the South* (Lexington: University of Kentucky Press, 1996), 148–151; Robert S. Erikson, Gerald C. Wright, and John P. McIver, *Statehouse Democracy: Public Opinion and Policy in the American States* (Cambridge: Cambridge University Press, 1993), ch. 5.

21. Gerald C. Wright and Michael B. Berkman, "Candidates and Policy in U.S. Senatorial Elections," *American Political Science Review* 80 (1986): 576–590.

22. Anthony Downs, *An Economic Theory of Democracy* (New York: Harper & Row, 1957).

23. Keith T. Poole and Howard Rosenthal, "The Polarization of American Politics," *Journal of Politics* 46 (1984): 1061–1079; Alan Abramowitz, *The Disappearing Center: Engaged Citizens, Polarization,*

and American Democracy (New Haven: Yale University Press, 2010).

24. Aldrich, *Why Parties?*

25. Ibid., 5.

26. This discussion of the Jacksonian Democrats and machine politics and patronage is based on Aldrich, *Why Parties?* ch. 4; Leon D. Epstein, *Political Parties in the American Mold* (Madison: University of Wisconsin Press, 1986), 134–143; and Frank J. Sorauf and Paul Allen Beck, *Party Politics in America*, 6th ed. (Glenview, Ill.: Scott, Foresman, 1988), 83–91.

27. Gerald C. Wright, John P. McIver, Robert S. Erikson, and David B. Holian, "Stability and Change in State Electorates, Carter Through Clinton," paper presented at the Midwest Political Science Association Meetings, Chicago, 2000; Larry Bartels, "Partisanship and Voting Behavior, 1952–1996," *American Journal of Political Science* 44 (2000): 35–50.

28. Gary C. Jacobson, *The Electoral Origins of Divided Government* (Boulder: Westview Press, 1990), and *The Politics of Congressional Elections*, 6th ed. (New York: Longman, 2003).

29. Xandra Kayden and Eddie Mahe Jr., "Back From the Depths: Party Resurgence," in Uslaner, 192, 196; Aistrup, ch. 4.

30. Sarah McCally Morehouse and Malcolm E. Jewell, *State Politics, Parties, & Policy,* 2nd ed. (Lanham, Md.: Rowman & Littlefield, 2003), 127–133.

31. Alec MacGillis and Peter Slevin, "Did Rush Limbaugh Tilt Result in Indiana? Conservative Host Urged 'Chaos' Votes," *Washington Post*, May 8, 2008, A01.

32. David E. Price, *Bring Back the Parties* (Washington, D.C.: Congressional Quarterly, 1984), 130–132.

33. Sorauf and Beck, 218–233.

34. Jill Serjeant, "John McCain Speech Draws Record TV Ratings," September 5, 2008, www.washingtonpost.com.

35. Benjamin Ginsberg, *Consequences of Consent* (New York: Random House, 1982), 128–133.

36. Michael Luo and Mike McIntyre, "McCain to Rely on Party Money Against Obama," *New York Times*, May 19, 2008.

37. C. P. Cotter, J. L. Gibson, J. F. Bibby, and R. J. Huckshorn, *Party Organizations in American Politics* (New York: Praeger, 1984); John J. Coleman, "Resurgent or Just Busy? Party Organizations in Contemporary America," in John Green and Daniel Shea, eds., *The State of the Parties* (Lanham, Md.: Rowman & Littlefield, 1996), ch. 22.

38. Jill Abramson, "Democrats and Republicans Step Up Pursuit of 'Soft Money,'" *New York Times*, May 13, 1998, 2;

Jill Abramson, "Cost of '96 Campaign Sets Record at $2.2 Billion," *New York Times*, November 25, 1997, 1.

39. Marjorie Randon Hershey, *Party Politics in America*, 13th ed. (New York: Pearson Longman, 2008), ch. 12.

40. Aistrup, 76; Paul S. Herrnson, *Congressional Elections: Campaigning at Home and in Washington*, 2nd ed. (Washington, D.C.: CQ Press, 1998), ch. 4.

41. Sorauf and Beck.

42. Gerald Pomper with Susan Lederman, *Elections in America* (New York: Longman, 1980), 145–150, 167–173.

43. Samuel Huntington, "The Visions of the Democratic Party," *Public Interest* (Spring 1985): 64; Layman and Carsey.

44. This section is based on Alan Ware, *Political Parties and Party Systems* (New York: Oxford University Press, 1996).

45. L. Sandy Maisel, *Parties and Elections in America*, 2nd ed. (New York: McGraw-Hill, 1993), ch. 10; Epstein; Price, 284.

46. Nelson Polsby, *The Consequences to Party Reform* (New York: Oxford University Press, 1983), 83.

47. Michael Powell, "Seared but Unwilted: Democrats See Red but Green Party Faithful Say They Made Their Point," *Washington Post*, December 27, 2000, C1.

48. David Leonhardt, "The Election: Was Buchanan the Real Nader?" *New York Times*, December 10, 2000, sec. 4, 4.

49. Gerald C. Wright, "Charles Adrian and the Study of Nonpartisan Elections," *Political Research Quarterly* 61 (2008): 13–16.

50. Joseph Cooper and David W. Brady, "Institutional Context and Leadership Style: The House From Cannon to Rayburn," *American Political Science Review* 75 (1981): 411–425; John H. Aldrich and David W. Rohde, "The Logic of Conditional Party Government: Revisiting the Electoral Connection," in Lawrence Dodd and Bruce Oppenheimer, eds., *Congress Reconsidered*, 7th ed. (Washington, D.C.: CQ Press, 2001).

51. Michelle Cottle, "House Broker," *New Republic*, June 11, 2008, www.tnr.com.

52. Aldrich and Rohde.

53. Morris Fiorina, *Divided Government* (New York: Macmillan, 1992).

54. See, for example, ibid.; and John R. Hibbing and Elizabeth Theiss-Morse, *Congress as Public Enemy: Public Attitudes Toward American Political Institutions* (Cambridge: Cambridge University Press, 1995).

55. Ibid., 157.

Chapter 13

1. PBS, "Obama's Deal," Part I, *Frontline*, www.pbs.org/wgbh/pages/frontline/obamasdeal/.

2. Alexis de Tocqueville, *Democracy in America*, Richard D. Heffner, ed. (New York: New American Library, 1956), 198.

3. James Madison, "*Federalist No. 10*," in Roy P. Fairfield, ed., *The Federalist Papers*, 2nd ed. (Baltimore: Johns Hopkins University Press, 1981), 16.

4. This definition is based on Jeffrey M. Berry, *The Interest Group Society*, 3rd ed. (New York: Longman, 1997); and David Truman, *The Governmental Process: Political Interest and Public Opinion*, 2nd ed. (New York: Knopf, 1971).

5. Berry; Truman; Allan J. Cigler and Burdett A. Loomis, eds., *Interest Group Politics*, 6th ed. (Washington, D.C.: CQ Press, 2002).

6. Burdett A. Loomis and Allan J. Cigler, "Introduction: The Changing Nature of Interest Group Politics," in Cigler and Loomis, *Interest Group Politics*, 6th ed., 2–5, 21–22.

7. Jonathan Rauch, *Demosclerosis: The Silent Killer of American Government* (New York: Crown, 1994), 39.

8. Michael Luo, "Money Talks Louder Than Ever in Midterms," *New York Times*, October 7, 2010, www.nytimes.com/2010/10/08/us/politics/08donate.html?scp=1&sq=Luo%20Money%20talks%20louder&st=cse.

9. Marian Currinder, Joanne Connor Green, and M. Margaret Conway, "Interest Group Money in Elections," in Allan J. Cigler and Burdett A. Loomis, eds., *Interest Group Politics*, 7th ed. (Washington, D.C.: CQ Press, 2007), 187.

10. On this last point, see Rauch.

11. Berry, 6–8; John W. Kingdon, *Agendas, Alternatives, and Public Policy* (Boston: Little, Brown, 1984).

12. Kingdon.

13. Children's Defense Fund, 2005, www.childrensdefense.org.

14. Truman, 66–108.

15. Berry, 66.

16. Jeffrey Berry, Kent E. Portney, and Ken Thomson, *The Rebirth of Urban Democracy* (Washington, D.C.: Brookings Institution, 1993).

17. Robert Salisbury, "An Exchange Theory of Interest Groups," *Midwest Journal of Political Science* 13 (1969): 1–32.

18. For a full description of these incentives, see Peter B. Clark and James Q. Wilson, "Incentive Systems: A Theory of Organizations," *Administrative Science Quarterly* 6 (1961): 129–166.

19. Mancur Olson Jr., *The Logic of Collective Action* (New York: Schocken, 1971).

20. The idea of selective incentives is Olson's (1971, 51). This discussion comes from the work of Clark and Wilson (1961), 129–166, as interpreted in Salisbury. Clark and

Wilson use the terms *material, solidary, and purposive* benefits, while Salisbury prefers *material, solidary,* and *expressive.* We follow Salisbury's interpretation and usage here.

21. John P. Heinz et al., *The Hollow Core* (Cambridge: Harvard University Press, 1993), 1–3.

22. Ronald G. Shaiko, "Making the Connection: Organized Interests, Political Representation, and the Changing Rules of the Game in Washington Politics," in Paul S. Herrnson, Ronald G. Shaiko, and Clyde Wilcox, eds., *The Interest Group Connection* (Washington, D.C.: CQ Press, 2005), 6.

23. Foundation for Public Affairs, *Public Interest Group Profiles, 2004–2005* (Washington, D.C.: CQ Press, 2004), 486–488.

24. Ibid., 674–676.

25. Dan Eggen, "Chamber and Democrats Battle Over the Midterms and Election Spending," *Washington Post*, October 8, 2010, www.coalition4healthcare.org/about/members/?_c=z6sxqglfdc1vuk.

26. Ibid.

27. AFL-CIO: America's Union Movement, "About Us," www.aflcio.org/aboutus/index.cfm.

28. "Labor Pains," *Houston Chronicle*, July 28, 2005, B10; Amanda Paulson, "Union Split: Sign of Decline or Revival," *Christian Science Monitor*, July 27, 2005, 2.

29. International Brotherhood of Teamsters, 2008, www.teamsters.org; United Auto Workers, 2008, www.uaw.org; United Mine Workers at Answers.com, 2005, www.answers.com/topic/united-mine-workers.

30. Steve Lohr, "Bush's Next Target: Malpractice Lawyers," *New York Times*, February 27, 2005, sec. 3, 1.

31. American Farm Bureau, "We Are Farm Bureau," 2005, www.fb.org/about/thisis/wearefarmbureau.pdf; American Agriculture Movement, 2005, www.aaminc.org; National Farmers Union, 2005, www.nfu.org.

32. AARP, 2008, "AARP History," www.aarp.org/about_aarp/aarp_overview/a2003-01-13-aarphistory.html.

33. Children's Defense Fund, 2005, www.childrensdefense.org.

34. Foundation for Public Affairs, 483–485; NAACP, 2008, www.naacp.org.

35. League of United Latin American Citizens, 2008, www.lulac.org.

36. Foundation for Public Affairs, 460–462.

37. American Indian Movement, 2008, www.aimovement.org.

38. Southeast Asia Resource Action Center, 2008, www.searac.org.

39. Foundation for Public Affairs, 545–547.

40. Eagle Forum, 2008, www.eagleforum.org.

41. American Coalition for Fathers and Children, 2005, www.acfc.org; National Congress for Fathers and Children, 2005, www.ncfc.net.

42. Log Cabin Republicans, "About Log Cabin," 2008, http://online.logcabin.org/about/.

43. Allan J. Cigler and Anthony J. Nowns, "Public Interest Entrepreneurs and Group Patrons," in Allan J. Cigler and Burdett A. Loomis, eds., *Interest Group Politics*, 4th ed. (Washington, D.C.: CQ Press, 1995), 77–78.

44. Christopher J. Bosso, "The Color of Money," in Cigler and Loomis, *Interest Group Politics*, 4th ed., 104.

45. Ben Smith, "NRA: Obama Most Anti-Gun Candidate Ever; Will Ban Guns," *Politico*, August 6, 2008, www.politico.com/blogs/bensmith/0808/NRA_Obama_most_antigun_candidate_ever_will_ban_guns.html.

46. William Booth, "Logging Protester Killed by Falling Redwood Tree," *Washington Post*, September 19, 1998, A2; Ed Henry, "Earth First! Activists Invade Riggs's California Office. In Aftermath, Congressman Considers Bill to Strengthen Penalty for Assaulting Congressional Staffers," *Roll Call*, October 27, 1997.

47. For a discussion of coalition politics involving Ralph Nader, see Loree Bykerk and Ardith Maney, "Consumer Groups and Coalition Politics on Capitol Hill," in Cigler and Loomis, *Interest Group Politics*, 4th ed., 259–279.

48. Consumers Union, 2005, www.consumersunion.org.

49. Foundation for Public Affairs, 197–199.

50. See James Guth et al., "Onward Christian Soldiers: Religious Activist Groups in American Politics," in Cigler and Loomis, *Interest Group Politics*, 4th ed., 55–75; Guth et al., "A Distant Thunder?" in Cigler and Loomis, *Interest Group Politics*, 6th ed., 162–165.

51. Joseph A. Aistrup, *Southern Strategy Revisited* (Lexington: University Press of Kentucky, 1996), 56–61.

52. Adam Clymer, "Decision in the Senate: The Overview; Crime Bill Approved 61–38, but Senate Is Going Home Without Acting on Health Care," *New York Times*, August 26, 1994, 1.

53. Sheryl Gay Stolberg, "Effort to Renew Weapons Ban Falters on Hill," *New York Times*, September 9, 2004, A1; Edward Epstein, "Supporters of Gun Ban Lament Its Expiration," *San Francisco Chronicle*, September 10, 2004, A1.

54. Jon Jeter, "Jury Says Abortion Opponents Are Liable; Efforts to Close Clinics Violate Racketeering Law," *Washington Post*, April 21, 1998, A1; "Operation Rescue Founder Files for Bankruptcy Due to Lawsuits," *Washington Post*, November 8, 1998, A29.

55. American Civil Liberties Union, "About Us," 2005, www.aclu.org/about/aboutmain.cfm.

56. Foundation for Public Affairs, 76–78; Amnesty International, "Current Campaigns," 2005, www.amnesty.org/campaign.

57. Loomis and Cigler, 22–23; People for the Ethical Treatment of Animals, 2005, www.peta.org.

58. Animal Rights Law Project, 2005, www.animal-law.org; Animal Liberation Front, 2005, http://animalliberationfront.us; "Deaths of More Baby Rats on Shuttle Prompt Protests," *Los Angeles Times*, April 29, 1998, A14; Daniel B. Wood, "Animal Activists vs. Furriers: Now It's All in the Label," *Christian Science Monitor*, November 27, 1998, 2; Brad Knickerbocker, "Activists Step Up War to 'Liberate' Nature," *Christian Science Monitor*, January 20, 1999, 4.

59. Ronald J. Hrebenar and Clive S. Thomas, "The Japanese Lobby in Washington: How Different Is It?" in Cigler and Loomis, 1995, 349–368.

60. Judy Sarasohn, "For Lobbyists, the $65 Million List," *Washington Post*, March 17, 2005, A23; *Congressional Quarterly Weekly Report*, December 12, 1992, 3792; Allison Mitchell, "A New Form of Lobbying Puts Public Face on Private Interests," *New York Times*, September 30, 1998, web version.

61. Beverly A. Cigler, "Not Just Another Special Interest: Intergovernmental Representation," in Cigler and Loomis, 1995, 134–135.

62. William Safire, *Safire's New Political Dictionary* (New York: Random House, 1993), 417–418.

63. Jeffrey H. Birnbaum, "The Road to Riches Is Called K Street," *Washington Post*, June 22, 2005, A1; Matt Kelley, "Pull of Lobbyists' Revolving Door: Salary vs. Service," *USA Today*, December 25, 2008, www.usatoday.com/news/washington/2008-12-25-revolvingdoor-inside_N.htm.

64. Jeffrey H. Birnbaum, "When Candidates Decry Lobbying, Ex-Lawmakers Embrace It," *Washington Post*, January 8, 2008, A17.

65. Matt Kelley, "Third of Top Aides Become Lobbyists," *USA Today*, December 26, 2008, www.usatoday.com/news/washington/2008-12-25-revolving-door_N.htm.

66. Bart Jansen, "Lobbying Bill Signed Into Law," *CQ Today*, CQPolitics.com, September 14, 2007; see also www.commoncause.org.

67. Dan Eggen and R. Jeffrey Smith, "Lobbying Rules Surpass Those of Previous

Administrations, Experts Say," *Washington Post*, January 22, 2009, www.washington post.com/wp-dyn/content/article/2009/01/21/AR2009012103472.html.

68. See Diana M. Evans, "Lobbying the Committee: Interest Groups and the House Public Works and Transportation Committee," in Allan J. Cigler and Burdett A. Loomis, eds., *Interest Group Politics*, 3rd ed. (Washington, D.C.: CQ Press, 1991), 264–265. For a graphic example of this practice, see Michael Weisskopf and David Maraniss, "Forging an Alliance for Deregulation; Rep. DeLay Makes Companies Full Partners in the Movement," *Washington Post*, March 12, 1995, A1.

69. Carl Hulse, "Tough Going as Negotiators Hammer Out Energy Bill," *New York Times*, September 30, 2003, A20.

70. Ibid.

71. Mike Soraghan, "Measure Stresses Drilling in Rockies; Energy Bill Gets OK, May Go to House Today," *Denver Post*, November 18, 2003, A1.

72. Coalition for Advanced Health Care Reform, "Who Are We," www.coalition4healthcare.org/about/?_c=z6sxqglfdc1vuk.

73. Adam Clymer, "Congress Passes Bill to Disclose Lobbyists' Roles," *New York Times*, November 30, 1995, 1.

74. Adam Clymer, "Senate, 98–0, Sets Tough Restriction on Lobbyist Gifts," *New York Times*, July 29, 1995, 1; "House Approves Rule to Prohibit Lobbyists' Gifts," *New York Times*, November 17, 1995, 1.

75. Jeff Zeleny and David D. Kirkpatrick, "House, 411–8, Passes a Vast Ethics Overhaul," *New York Times*, August 1, 2007, www.nytimes.com.

76. Jeffrey H. Birnbaum, "Seeing the Ethics Rules, and Raising an Exception," *Washington Post*, October 23, 2007, A17.

77. Ibid.

78. Jeffrey H. Birnbaum, *The Lobbyists: How Influence Peddlers Work Their Way in Washington* (New York: Random House, 1992), vi, viii.

79. Kenneth P. Vogel, "President Obama's Lobbying Reforms Praised by Congressional Research Service," *Politico*, December 3, 2009, www.politico.com/news/stories/1209/30185.html; Peter Baker, "Obama's Pledge to Reform Ethics Faces an Early Test," *New York Times*, February 2, 2009, www.nytimes.com/2009/02/03/world/americas/03iht-03lobby.19884903.html?scp=3&sq=Obama%27s%20Pledge%20to%20Reform%20Ethics&st=cse.

80. See Douglas Yates, *Bureaucratic Democracy* (Cambridge: Harvard University Press, 1982), ch. 4.

81. Cindy Skrzcki, "OSHA Set to Propose Ergonomics Standards; Long-Studied Rules Repeatedly Blocked," *Washington Post*, February 19, 1999.

82. Samuel Kernell, *Going Public: New Strategies of Presidential Leadership* (Washington, D.C.: CQ Press, 1986), 34.

83. Berry, 121–122.

84. The Tax Foundation, "America Celebrates Tax Freedom Day," 2010, www.taxfoundation.org/taxfreedomday.html.

85. Luo; *Citizens United v. Federal Election Commission*, 558 U.S. 50 (2010).

86. Diana Dwyre, "527s: The New Bad Guys of Campaign Finance," in Cigler and Loomis, *Interest Group Politics*, 7th ed., 212–232.

87. John Green, "John Green Discusses Differences Between 527 Groups and Political Action Committees" (interview), *All Things Considered*, National Public Radio, August 19, 2004.

88. William B. Browne, "Organized Interests, Grassroots Confidants, and Congress," in Cigler and Loomis, *Interest Group Politics*, 4th ed., 288; John W. Kingdon, *Congressmen's Voting Decisions*, 2nd ed. (New York: Harper & Row, 1981).

89. Evans, 269.

90. *Censure and Move On* (news release), October 15, 1998, www.moveon.org.

91. MediaMatters, "Report: 'Fair and Balanced' Fox News Aggressively Promotes 'Tea Party' Protests," MediaMatters For America, April 8, 2009, http://mediamatters.org/reports/200904080025.

92. Colleen O'Connor, "Prayer War: Civil Disobedience Is an Increasingly Popular Cross to Bear," *Denver Post*, December 23, 2004, F1; Anna Badkhen, "Protesters Drawn to Schiavo's Hospice; Christian Conservatives Sponsor Some, Others Say They're Following Their Hearts," *San Francisco Chronicle*, March 24, 2005, A1; Dennis Mahoney, "Christian Group Plans Rallies, Protests; Gay Rights, Abortion Focus of Weeklong Visit to Columbus," *Columbus Dispatch*, June 7, 2004, 5D.

93. Chris Good, "The Tea Party Movement: Who's In Charge?" *The Atlantic*, April 13, 2009, www.theatlantic.com/politics/archive/2009/04/the-tea-party-movement-whos-in-charge/13041/.

94. Mark Brunswick, "Prescription Politics; Drug Lobby Intensifies Fight on Price Controls and Imports," *Minneapolis Star Tribune*, November 16, 2003, 1A; Jim VandeHei and Juliet Eilperin, "Drug Firms Gain Church Group's Aid; Claim About Import Measure Stirs Anger," *Washington Post*, July 23, 2003, A1.

95. John Stauber, director of the Center for Media & Democracy, quoted in J. A. Savage, "Astroturf Lobbying Replaces Grassroots Organizing: Corporations Mask Their Interests by Supporting Supposed Grassroots Organizations," *Business and Society Review*, September 22, 1995, 8.

96. Mike Murphy in Mitchell, A1.

97. Bill McAllister, "Rainmakers Making a Splash," *Washington Post*, December 4, 1997, A21.

98. Federal Election Commission, "Growth in PAC Financial Activity Slows," April 24, 2009, http://fec.gov/press/press2009/20090415PAC/20090424PAC.shtml.

99. Federal Election Commission, "PAC's Grouped by Total Spent," April 13, 2005, www.fec.gov/press/press2005/20050412pac/groupbyspending2004.pdf; Richard L. Hall and Frank W. Wayman, "Buying Time: Money Interests and the Mobilization of Bias in Congressional Committees," *American Political Science Review* 84 (1990): 797–820.

100. Luo; *Citizens United v. Federal Election Commission*.

101. Jeffrey H. Birnbaum, "To Predict Losers in a Power Shift, Follow the Money," *Washington Post*, October 16, 2006, D1.

102. Andrew Bard Schmookler, "When Money Talks, Is It Free Speech?" *Christian Science Monitor*, November 11, 1997, 15; Nelson W. Polsby, "Money Gains Access. So What?" *New York Times*, August 13, 1997, A19.

103. "Senators Supporting Public Option Received Half as Much Money From Health Insurers," October 9, 2009, http://maplight.org/senators-supporting-public-option-got-half-as-much-money-from-health-insurers.

104. See John R. Wright, *Interest Groups and Congress* (Boston: Allyn & Bacon, 1996), 136–145; "Contributions, Lobbying, and Committee Voting in the U.S. House of Representatives," *American Political Science Review* 84 (1990): 417–438; Richard L. Hall and Frank W. Wayman, "Buying Time: Money Interests and the Mobilization of Bias in Congressional Committees," *American Political Science Review* 84 (1990): 797–820.

105. Theda Skocpol, *Diminished Democracy: From Membership to Management in American Civic Life* (Norman: University of Oklahoma Press, 2003); Theda Skocpol, "Advocates Without Members: The Recent Transformation of American Civic Life," in Theda Skocpol and Morris Fiorina, eds., *Civic Engagement in American Democracy* (Washington, D.C.: Brookings Institution, 1999).

106. Kelly D. Patterson and Matthew M. Singer, "The National Rifle Association in the Face of the Clinton Challenge," in Cigler and Loomis, *Interest Group Politics*, 6th ed., 62–63.

107. A. Lee Fritscheler and James M. Hoefler, *Smoking and Politics*, 5th ed. (Upper Saddle River, N.J.: Prentice Hall, 1996), 20–35.

108. Truman, 519.

109. See C. Wright Mills, *The Power Elite* (New York: Oxford University Press, 1956); G. William Domhoff, *The Powers That Be* (New York: Vintage, 1979).

110. David S. Hilzenrath, "Health Care Factions Clashing on Medicare Battlefield," *Washington Post*, July 19, 1997, C1; Ruth Marcus, "Some Swat Home Runs, Others Strike Out on Budget Deal," *Washington Post*, August 3, 1997, A1; Jennifer Mattos, "Clinton Proposes Medicare Cuts," *Time Daily*, January 14, 1997.

111. The problem is that there are a relatively small number of groups with large memberships. Labor unions, some environmental groups like the Sierra Club, some social movements revolving around abortion and women's rights, and the NRA currently have large memberships spread across a number of congressional districts.

112. Linda Greenhouse, "Justices to Rule on Tobacco," *New York Times*, May 2, 1999, sec. 4, 2; David E. Rosenbaum, "The Tobacco Bill: The Overview," *New York Times*, June 18, 1999, 1.

113. Katie Hafner, "Screen Grab: Mobilizing on Line for Gun Control," *New York Times*, May 20, 1999, G5; Francis X. Clines, "Guns and Schools: In Congress—Sketchbook," *New York Times*, June 17, 1999, 30.

114. PBS, "Obama's Deal," Part I.

115. PBS, "Obama's Deal," Part II, *Frontline*, www.pbs.org/wgbh/pages/frontline/obamasdeal/.

116. David Frum, "Waterloo," *FrumForum*, March 21, 2010, www.frumforum.com/waterloo.

117. Jane Hamsher, "We Want the Public Option," *The Guardian*, September 9, 2009, www.guardian.co.uk/commentisfree/cifamerica/2009/sep/08/healthcare-public-option-barack-obama; David Dayen, "The Deal With the Hospital Industry to Kill the Public Option," October 5, 2010, http://news.firedoglake.com/2010/10/05/the-deal-with-the-hospital-industry-to-kill-the-public-option/.

118. Jonathan Cohn, "How They Did It, Part Four," *New Republic*, May 25, 2010, www.tnr.com/article/politics/75147/ow-they-did-it-part-four.

Chapter 14

1. Adam Liptak, "Justices, 5–4, Reject Corporate Spending Limit," *New York Times*, January 21, 2010, www.nytimes.com/2010/01/22/us/politics/22scotus.html?scp=1&sq=Citizens%20United&st=cse.

2. Linda Greenhouse, "Justice Alito's Reaction," *New York Times Online*, January 27, 2010, http://opinionator.blogs.nytimes.com/2010/01/27/justice-alitos-reaction/?scp=2&sq=Obama%20Citizens%20United&st=cse.

3. Gerald Pomper, *Elections in America* (New York: Dodd, Mead, 1970), 1.

4. John Stuart Mill, *Considerations on Representative Government* (New York: Liberal Arts Press, 1958), 114.

5. David W. Brady, *Critical Elections and Congressional Policy Making* (Palo Alto, Calif.: Stanford University Press, 1988); Barbara Sinclair, "Party Realignment and the Transformation of the Political Agenda: The House of Representatives, 1925–1938," *American Political Science Review* 71 (September 1977): 940–954.

6. Robert S. Erikson, Gerald C. Wright, and John P. McIver, *Statehouse Democracy* (New York: Cambridge University Press, 1993).

7. Robert Erikson and Gerald Wright, "Voters, Candidates, and Issues in Congressional Elections," in Lawrence Dodd and Bruce Oppenheimer, *Congress Reconsidered*, 6th ed. (Washington, D.C.: CQ Press, 1997); Gerald C. Wright and Michael Berkman, "Candidates and Policy Position in U.S. Senate Elections," *American Political Science Review* 80 (June 1986): 576–590; Robert S. Erikson, Michael MacKuen, and James A. Stimson, *The Macro Polity* (New York: Cambridge University Press, 2002).

8. Gerald Pomper with Susan Lederman, *Elections in America*, 2nd ed. (New York: Longman, 1980), chs. 7 and 8; Benjamin Ginsberg, *The Consequences of Consent* (Reading, Mass.: Addison Wesley Longman, 1982); Ian Budge and Richard I. Hofferbert, "Mandates and Policy Outputs: U.S. Party Platforms and Federal Expenditures, 1950–1985," *American Political Science Review* 84 (March 1990): 248–261.

9. Robert S. Erikson, Michael MacKuen, and James A. Stimson, *The Macro Polity* (New York: Cambridge University Press, 2002).

10. Carole Pateman, *Participation and Democratic Theory* (Cambridge: Cambridge University Press, 1970).

11. Sidney Verba and Norman H. Nie, *Participation in America* (New York: Harper, 1972).

12. Robert S. Erikson, Costas Panagopoulos, and Christopher Wlezien, "The Crystallization of Voter Preferences During the 2008 Presidential Campaign," *Presidential Studies Quarterly* 40 (2010): 482–496; Robert Andersen, James Tilley, and Anthony F. Heath, "Political Knowledge and Enlightened Preferences: Party Choice Through the Electoral Cycle," *British Journal of Political Science* 35 (2005): 285–302; Steven F. Finkel, "Reexamining the 'Minimal Effects' Model in Recent Presidential Elections," *Journal of Politics* 55 (February 1993): 1–21.

13. Ginsberg.

14. Roper Center for Public Opinion Research, Community Consensus Survey, February 12–14, 1999.

15. Steven J. Rosenstone and John Mark Hansen, *Mobilization, Participation, and Democracy in America* (New York: Macmillan, 1993); Ruy A. Teixeira, *The Disappearing American Voter* (Washington, D.C.: Brookings Institution, 1992); Raymond E. Wolfinger and Steven J. Rosenstone, *Who Votes?* (New Haven: Yale University Press, 1980); Richard J. Timpone, "Structure, Behavior, and Voter Turnout in the United States," *American Political Science Review* 92 (March 1998): 145–158.

16. Michael MacDonald, "2008 Current Population Survey Voting and Registration Supplement," United States Elections Project, http://elections.gmu.edu/CPS_2008.html.

17. U.S. Bureau of the Census, Current Population Survey Report, "Voting and Registration in the Election of November 2008—Detailed Tables," Table 1, www.census.gov/hhes/www/socdemo/voting/publications/p20/2008/tables.html.

18. Ibid., Table 8.

19. Current Population Reports, "Voting and Registration in the Election of November 2008," www.census.gov/prod/2010pubs/p20–562.pdf.

20. Calculated by the authors from U.S. Census Bureau, "Voting and Registration in the Election of November 2008—Detailed Tables," www.census.gov/hhes/www/socdemo/voting/publications/p20/2008/tables.html.

21. Sidney Verba, Kay Lehman Schlozman, and Henry E. Brady, *Voice and Equality: Civic Voluntarism in American Politics* (Cambridge: Harvard University Press, 1995).

22. Kay Lehman Schlozman, Sidney Verba, and Henry E. Brady, "Civic Participation and the Inequality Problem," in *Civic Engagement in American Democracy,* Theda Skocpol and Morris P. Fiorina, eds. (New York, Russell Sage, 1999); Henry E. Brady, Kay Lehman Schlozman, and Sidney Verba,

"Prospecting for Participants: Rational Expectations and the Recruitment of Political Activists," *American Political Science Review* 93 (1999): 153–168.

23. Richard Brody, "The Puzzle of Political Participation in America," in Anthony King, ed., *The New American Political System* (Washington, D.C.: American Enterprise Institute, 1978), 287–324.

24. Stephen Knack, "Drivers Wanted: Motor Voter and the Election of 1996," *PS: Political Science & Politics* (June 1999): 237–243.

25. International Institute for Democracy and Electoral Assistance, "Turnout in the World, Country by Country Performance," 2005, www.idea.int/vt/survey/voter_turnout_pop2.cfm.

26. Benjamin Highton, "Voter Registration and Turnout in the United States," *Perspectives on Politics* 2 (2004): 507–515.

27. Linda Greenhouse, "In a 6-to-3 Vote, Justices Uphold a Voter ID Law," *New York Times*, April 29, 2008; Jeffrey Milyo, "The Effects of Photographic Identification on Voter Turnout in Indiana: A Count-Level Analysis," Report 10-2007, Institute for Public Policy, Harry S. Truman School of Public Affairs, http://web.missouri.edu/%7Emilyoj/files/Indiana% 20Photo%20ID.pdf.

28. Teixeira, ch. 2; Paul R. Abramson, John H. Aldrich, and David W. Rohde, *Change and Continuity in the 1996 and 1998 Elections* (Washington, D.C.: CQ Press, 1999).

29. Rosenstone and Hansen.

30. Alan S. Gerber and Donald P. Green, "The Effects of Canvassing, Direct Mail, and Telephone Contact on Voter Turnout: A Field Experiment," *American Political Science Review* 94 (2000): 653–663.

31. Stephen Ansolabehere and Shanto Iyengar, *Going Negative: How Political Ads Shrink and Polarize the Electorate* (New York: Free Press, 1995).

32. Jeff Mapes, "National Parties Try Personal Touch," *Oregonian*, December 23, 2003, A1; Sharon Schmickle and Greg Gordon, "Vying for Voters," Minneapolis *Star Tribune*, October 31, 2004, 13A; Thomas B. Edsall, "Labor Targets Nonunion Voters; $20 Million Turnout Effort Expands Effort to Regain Influence," *Washington Post*, February 27, 2003, A4.

33. Gerald Pomper, "The Presidential Election: The Ills of American Politics After 9/11," in Michael Nelson, ed., *The Elections of 2004* (Washington, D.C.: CQ Press, 2005), 46.

34. Teixeira, 36–50; Robert Putnam, *Bowling Alone: The Collapse and Revival of American Community* (New York: Simon & Schuster, 2000), 31–47.

35. Warren E. Miller and Merrill J. Shanks, *The New American Voter* (Cambridge: Harvard University Press, 1996); Kevin Chen, *Political Alienation and Voting Turnout in the United States, 1969–1988* (Pittsburgh: Mellon Research University Press, 1992).

36. Anthony Downs, *An Economic Theory of Democracy* (New York: Harper & Row, 1957), 260–276.

37. John Petrocik, "Voter Turnout and Electoral Preference: The Anomalous Reagan Elections," in Kay Lehman Schlozman, ed., *Elections in America* (Boston: Allen & Unwin, 1987), 239–260.

38. Jack Citrin, Eric Schickler, and John Sides, "What If Everyone Voted? Simulating the Impact of Increased Turnout in Senate Elections," *American Journal of Political Science* 47 (January 2003): 75–90.

39. Petrocik, 243–251; Stephen Earl Bennett and David Resnick, "The Implications of Nonvoting for Democracy in the United States," *American Journal of Political Science* 34 (August 1990): 795.

40. Calculated by the authors from the 2004 and 2008 Pre- and Post-American National Election Studies.

41. V. O. Key Jr., *The Responsible Electorate: Rationality in Presidential Voting, 1936–1960* (Cambridge: Harvard University Press, 1966); Miller and Shanks.

42. CNN Election Center 2008, www.cnn.com/election/2008/results/polls/#uspoop1.

43. Angus Campbell, Phillip Converse, Warren Miller, and Donald Stokes, *The American Voter* (New York: Wiley, 1960); Donald Green, Bradley Palmquist, and Eric Schickler, *Partisan Hearts and Minds* (New Haven: Yale University Press, 2002); Larry M. Bartels, "Beyond the Running Tally: Partisan Bias in Political Perceptions," *Political Behavior* 24 (2002): 117–150.

44. M. Margaret Conway, Gertrude A. Steuernagel, and David W. Ahern, *Women and Political Participation: Cultural Change in the Political Arena*, 2nd ed. (Washington, D.C.: CQ Press, 2005).

45. Eric Plutzer and John Zipp, "Identity Politics, Partisanship and Voting for Women Candidates," *Public Opinion Quarterly* 60 (1996): 30–57.

46. Center for American Women and Politics, "Proportions of Women and Men Who Voted for Hillary Clinton in the Super Tuesday Races of February 5, 2008," www.cawp.rutgers.edu/fast_facts/voters/documents/SuperTuesday_Clinton.pdf.

47. Calculated from Harold W. Stanley and Richard G. Niemi, *Vital Statistics on American Politics, 2007–2008* (Washington, D.C.: CQ Press, 2008), 127.

48. These figures are taken from media exit polls for the 2004 and 2008 presidential elections.

49. Wendy K. Tam, "Asians—A Monolithic Voting Bloc?" *Political Behavior* 17 (1995): 223–249; Pie-Te Lein, M. Margaret Conway, and Janelle Wong, *The Politics of Asian-Americans: Diversity and Community* (New York: Routledge, 2004); Atiya Kai Stokes, "Latino Group Consciousness and Political Participation," *American Politics Research* 41 (2003): 361–378; Benjamin Highton and Arthur L. Burris, "New Perspectives on Latino Voter Turnout in the United States," *American Politics Research* 30 (2002): 285–306.

50. Pei-Te Lien, Christian Collet, Janelle Wong, and S. Karthick Ramakrishnan, "Asian Pacific American Public Opinion and Participation," *PS: Political Science and Politics* 34 (2001): 628; David L. Leal, Matt A. Barreto, Jongho Lee, and Rodolofo O. De la Graza, "The Latino Vote in the 2004 Election," *PS: Political Science and Politics* 38 (2005): 41–49.

51. Downs.

52. Edward Carmines and James Stimson, "Two Faces of Issue Voting," *American Political Science Review* 74 (March 1980): 78–91.

53. James Fallows, "Why Americans Hate the Media," *Atlantic Monthly*, February 1996, 45–64.

54. Morris P. Fiorina, *Retrospective Voting in American National Elections* (New Haven: Yale University Press, 1981).

55. "The Candidates' Confrontation: Excerpts From the Debate," *Washington Post*, October 30, 1980, A14.

56. Fiorina; Benjamin I. Page, *Choice and Echoes in Presidential Elections* (Chicago: University of Chicago Press, 1978).

57. CNN/Opinion Research Corporation poll, October 17–19, 2008; national poll of likely voters and ABC News/*Washington Post* poll, October 16–18, 2008. Both polls accessed via http://pollingreport.com/who08.htm.

58. Linda Feldmann, "Before Any Votes: A 'Money Primary,'" *Christian Science Monitor*, February 26, 2007, 1; Craig Gilbert, "'Invisible Primary' Already Begun: Some Think Presidential Field Narrowing Too Soon," *Milwaukee Journal Sentinel*, March 5, 2007; Chris Cillizza and Michael A. Fletcher, "Candidates Woo Bush Donors for 'Invisible Primary,'" *Washington Post*, December 10, 2006, A01.

59. Jill Abramson, "Unregulated Cash Flows Into Hands of P.A.C.s for 2000," *New York Times*, November 29, 1998, web version.

60. Leslie Wayne and Jeff Zeleny, "Enlisting New Donors, Obama Reaped $32 Million in

January," *New York Times*, February 1, 2008, A18.

61. Thomas R. Marshall, "Turnout and Representation: Caucuses Versus Primaries," *American Journal of Political Science* 22 (1978): 169–182; Gerald C. Wright, "Rules and the Ideological Character of Primary Electorates," in Steven S. Smith and Melanie J. Springer, eds., *Reforming the Presidential Nomination Process* (Washington, D.C.: Brookings Institution, 2009).

62. Barry Burden, "The Nominations: Technology, Money, and Transferable Momentum," in Nelson, 21–22.

63. Max Follmer, "Everything You've Ever Wanted to Know About Delegates and Superdelegates," *Huffington Post*, February 13, 2008, www.huffingtonpost.com/2008/02/13/everything-youve-ever-wa_n_86335.html.

64. Burden, 21.

65. Jack Germond and Jules W. Witcover, "Front-Loading Folly: A Dash to Decision, at a Cost in Deliberation," *Baltimore Sun*, March 22, 1996.

66. Calculated by the authors from the *Washington Post* Campaign Tracker, http://projects.washingtonpost.com/2008-presidential-candidates/tracker/.

67. Sholomo Slonim, "The Electoral College at Philadelphia," *Journal of American History* 73 (June 1986): 35.

68. Brian C. Mooney, "Technology Aids Obama's Outreach Drive: Volunteers Answer Call on Social Networking Site," *Boston Globe*, February 24, 2008, A1.

69. Robin Kolodny and Angela Logan, "Political Consultants and the Extension of Party Goals," *PS: Political Science & Politics* (June 1998): 155–159.

70. Patrick Sellers, "Strategy and Background in Congressional Campaigns," *American Political Science Review* 92 (March 1998): 159–172.

71. Ruth Shalit, "The Oppo Boom," *New Republic*, January 3, 1994, 16–21; Adam Nagourney, "Researching the Enemy: An Old Political Tool Resurfaces in a New Election," *New York Times*, April 3, 1996, D20.

72. John Petrocik, "Issue Ownership in Presidential Elections, With a 1980 Case Study," *American Journal of Political Science* 40 (August 1996): 825–850.

73. American Museum of the Moving Image, "The Living Room Candidate: Presidential Campaign Commercials 1952–2004," 2005, http://livingroomcandidate.movingimage.us/index.php.

74. Darrell M. West, *Air Wars: Television Advertising in Election Campaigns, 1952–2004* (Washington, D.C.: CQ Press, 2005).

75. Kathleen Hall Jamieson, "Shooting to Win; Do Attack Ads Work? You Bet—and That's Not All Bad," *Washington Post*, September 26, 2004, B1.

76. Wisconsin Advertising Project, press release, through October 8, 2008, http://wiscadproject.wisc.edu/wiscads_release.100808.pdf.

77. Shanto Iyengar and Donald Kinder, *News That Matters: Television and American Opinion* (Chicago: University of Chicago Press, 1987); James N. Druckman, "Priming the Vote: Campaign Effects in a U.S. Senate Election," *Political Psychology* 25, no. 4 (2004): 577–594.

78. Thomas Patterson, *Out of Order* (New York: Knopf, 1993); Fallows, 45–64.

79. Elihu Katz and Jacob Feldman, "The Debates in Light of Research," in Sidney Kraus, ed., *The Great Debates* (Bloomington: Indiana University Press, 1962), 173–223.

80. Thomas Holbrook, "Campaigns, National Conditions, and U.S. Presidential Elections," *American Journal of Political Science* 38 (November 1994): 986–992; John Geer, "The Effects of Presidential Debates on the Electorate's Preferences for Candidates," *American Politics Quarterly* 16 (1988): 486–501; David Lanoue, "The 'Turning Point': Viewers' Reactions to the Second 1988 Presidential Debate," *American Politics Quarterly* 19 (1991): 80–89.

81. David Lanoue, "One That Made a Difference: Cognitive Consistency, Political Knowledge, and the 1980 Presidential Debate," *Public Opinion Quarterly* 56 (Summer 1992): 168–184; Carol Winkler and Catherine Black, "Assessing the 1992 Presidential and Vice Presidential Debates: The Public Rationale," *Argumentation and Advocacy* 30 (Fall 1993): 77–87; Lori McKinnon, John Tedesco, and Lynda Kaid, "The Third 1992 Presidential Debate: Channel and Commentary Effects," *Argumentation and Advocacy* 30 (Fall 1993): 106–118; Mike Yawn, Kevin Ellsworth, and Kim Fridkin Kahn, "How a Presidential Primary Debate Changed Attitudes of Audience Members," *Political Behavior* 20 (July 1998): 155–164; Annenberg Public Policy Center, "Voters Learned Positions on Issues Since Presidential Debates," NAES04 National Annenberg Election Survey, 2005, www.naes04.org.

82. OpenSecrets.org, "Banking on Becoming President" and "U.S. Election Will Cost $5.3 Billion, Center for Responsive Politics Predicts," www.opensecrets.org/pres08/index. php.

83. Federal Election Commission, "Chapter Two: Presidential Public Funding," 2005, www.fec.gov/info/arch2.htm.

84. Federal Election Commission, "Contribution Limits Chart 2007–08," www.fec.gov/pages/brochures/contriblimits.shtml.

85. Susan Glasser, "Court's Ruling in Colorado Case May Reshape Campaign Finance; Limits on Political Parties' 'Hard Money' Spending Nullified," *Washington Post*, March 28, 1999, A6; *FEC v. Colorado Republican Federal Campaign Committee*, 121 S. Ct. 2351, 2371 (2001).

86. 558 U.S. 50 (2010).

87. "How Corporate Money Will Reshape Politics: Restoring Free Speech in Elections," *New York Times*, January 21, 2010, http://roomfordebate.blogs.nytimes.com/2010/01/21/how-corporate-money-will-reshape-politics.

88. "The Court's Blow to Democracy," *New York Times*, January 21, 2010; Warren Richey, "Supreme Court: Campaign-Finance Limits Violate Free Speech," *Christian Science Monitor*, January 21, 2010; John Samples and Ilya Shapiro, "Supreme Court: Free Speech for All," *Washington Examiner*, January 21, 2010.

89. Dan Balz and David S. Broder, "Close Election Turns on Voter Turnout," *Washington Post*, November 1, 2002, A1.

90. Steven J. Rosenstone and John Mark Hansen, *Mobilization, Participation, and Democracy in America* (New York, Macmillan, 1993).

91. Adam Nagourney, "The '08 Campaign: A Sea Change for Politics as We Know It," *New York Times*, November 4, 2008, A1.

92. Les Blumenthal, "Down to the Wire; Canvassers Set a Frenetic Pace to Get Out the Vote," *Sacramento Bee*, October 25, 2004, A1.

93. Sam Roberts, "2008 Surge in Black Voters Nearly Erased Racial Gap," *New York Times*, July 21, 2009, 14.

94. Craig Gilbert, "Personal Touch in Political Race; Bush, Kerry Sides Try to Rally Support Like Never Before," Milwaukee *Journal Sentinel*, June 28, 2004, 1A.

95. Blumenthal.

96. Pew Research Center for the People and the Press Survey Reports, "Voters Liked Campaign 2004, But Too Much 'Mud-Slinging,'" November 11, 2004, http://people-press.org/reports/display.php3?ReportID=233.

97. Blumenthal.

98. Lawrence J. Grossback, David A. M. Peterson, and James A. Stimson, "Comparing Competing Theories on the Causes of Mandate Perceptions," *American Journal of Political Science* 49 (2005): 406–419.

99. Marjorie Hershey, "The Constructed Explanation: Interpreting Election Results in the 1984 Presidential Race," *Journal of Politics* 54 (November 1992): 943–976.

100. Bernard Berelson, Paul Lazarsfeld, and William N. McPhee, *Voting* (Chicago: University of Chicago Press, 1954), ch. 10.

101. Sidney Verba, Kay Lehman Schlozman, Henry Brady, and Norman H. Nie, "Race, Ethnicity and Political Resources: Participation in the United States," *British Journal of Political Science* 23 (1993): 453–497.

102. Erikson, MacKuen, and Stimson; James A. Stimson, Michael B. MacKuen, and Robert S. Erikson, "Dynamic Representation," *American Political Science Review* 89 (September 1995): 543.

103. Erikson, Wright, and McIver.

104. Paul Burstein, "The Impact of Public Opinion on Public Policy: A Review and an Agenda," *Political Research Quarterly* 56 (2003): 29–40; David Jones and Monika McDermott, *Americans, Congress, and Democratic Responsiveness: Public Evaluations of Congress and Electoral Consequences* (Ann Arbor: University of Michigan Press, 2009); Stephen Ansolabehere and Phillip Edward Jones, "Constituents' Responses to Congressional Roll Call Voting," *American Journal of Political Science* 54 (2010): 58–97.

105. Katrina vanden Heuvel, "*Citizens United* Aftershocks," *Washington Post*, August 25, 2010, www.washingtonpost.com/wp-dyn/content/article/2010/08/24/AR20100 82405642.html?hpid=opinionsbox1.

106. Chris Good, "*Citizens United* Decision: Republicans Like it, Liberals Don't," *Atlantic*, January 21, 2010, www.the atlantic.com/politics/archive/2010/01/citizens-united-decision-republicans-like-it-liberals-dont/33935/.

Chapter 15

1. Frank Ahrens, "The Accelerating Decline of Newspapers," *Washington Post*, October 27, 2009, www.washingtonpost.com/wp-dyn/content/article/2009/10/26/AR2009102603272.html.

2. Richard Perez-Pena, "U.S. Newspaper Circulation Falls 10%," *New York Times*, October 26, 2009, www.nytimes.com/2009/10/27/business/media/27audit.html?scp=1&sq=Audit%20Bureau%20of%20Circulations&st=cse.

3. Newspaper Death Watch, http://newspaperdeathwatch.com.

4. T. J. Sullivan, "Newspapers Don't Matter," *LA Observed*, December 15, 2008, www.laobserved.com/intell/2008/12/newspapers_dont_matter.php.

5. David Lieberman, "Extra! Extra! Are Newspapers Dying?" *USA Today*, March 18, 2009, www.usatoday.com/printedition/money/20090318/newspapers18_cv.art.htm.

6. Thomas Jefferson to Edward Carrington, 1787, ME 6:57, Thomas Jefferson on Politics and Government, http://etext.virginia.edu/jefferson/quotations/jeff1600.htm.

7. Pew Research Center for the People and the Press, "Audience Segments in a Changing News Environment: Key News Audiences Now Blend Online and Traditional Sources," Pew Research Center Biennial News Consumption Survey, August 17, 2008, 31, http://people-press.org/reports/pdf/444.pdf.

8. Ibid., 7, 21.

9. Ibid., 3–5.

10. Pew Research Center for the People and the Press, "The Times Mirror News Interest Index: 1989–1995," www.people-press.org.

11. Pew Research Center for the People and the Press, "Audience Segments in a Changing News Environment," 44.

12. Ben H. Bagdikian, *The Media Monopoly*, 5th ed. (Boston: Beacon Press, 1997), 203.

13. Philip Weiss, "A Guy Named Craig: How a Schlumpy IBM Refugee Found You Your Apartment, Your Boyfriend, Your New Couch, Your Afternoon Sex Partner— and Now Finds Himself Killing Your Newspaper," *New York Magazine*, January 8, 2006, http://nymag.com/nymetro/news/media/internet/15500/.

14. Richard Davis, *The Press and American Politics: The New Mediator* (Upper Saddle River, N.J.: Prentice Hall, 1996), 60.

15. Ibid., 63.

16. Ibid., 67.

17. Harold W. Stanley and Richard G. Niemi, *Vital Statistics on American Politics* (Washington, D.C.: CQ Press, 1998), 47.

18. "U.S. Homes Receive a Record 118.6 TV Channels on Average," Marketcharts.com, June 13, 2008, www.marketingcharts.com/television/us-homes-receive-a-record-1186-tv-channels-on-average-4929/.

19. Nielsen Media, "Nielsen Reports Television Tuning Remains at Record Levels," press release, October 17, 2007, www.nielsen media.com/nc/portal/site/Public/.

20. "U.S. Homes Receive a Record 118.6 TV Channels on Average."

21. For an in-depth study of the negative effects of this sort of advertising on national community, see Joseph Turow, *Breaking Up America: Advertisers and the New Media World* (Chicago: University of Chicago Press, 1997).

22. See, for example, Dana Davis Rehm, "Why Can't NPR Staff Go to 'Rally to Restore Sanity' or 'March to Keep Fear Alive?'" October 13, 2010, www.npr.org/blogs/thisisnpr/2010/10/13/130549777/why-can-t-npr-staff-go-to-stewart-s-rally-to-restore-sanity-or-colbert-s-march-to-keep-fear-alive.

23. Pew Internet, "Home Broadband 2010," August 11, 2010, www.pewinternet.org/Press-Releases/2010/Home-Broadband-2010.aspx; "Mobile Access 2010," July 7, 2010, www.pewinternet.org/Press-Releases/2010/Mobile-Access-2010.aspx.

24. Pew Research Center for the People and the Press, "The New News Landscape: Rise of the Internet," March 1, 2010, http://pewresearch.org/pubs/1508/internet-cell-phone-users-news-social-experience.

25. Robert Marquand, "Hate Groups Market to the Mainstream," *Christian Science Monitor*, March 6, 1998, 4.

26. Davis, 27.

27. Michael Emery and Edwin Emery, *The Press and America* (Upper Saddle River, N.J.: Prentice Hall, 1988), 115.

28. David Broder, *Behind the Front Page* (New York: Simon & Schuster, 1987), 134–135.

29. Bagdikian, xv.

30. Bagdikian, ix.

31. Robert Entman, *Democracy Without Citizens* (New York: Oxford University Press, 1989), 110–111.

32. Walter Goodman, "Where's Edward R. Murrow When You Need Him?" *New York Times*, December 30, 1997, E2.

33. Mark Crispin Miller, "Free the Media," *Nation*, June 3, 1996, 9.

34. Bagdikian, xxii.

35. Neil King Jr. and Louise Radnofsky, "News Corp. Gives $1 Million to GOP," *Wall Street Journal*, August 18, 2010, http://online.wsj.com/article/SB20001424052748703824304575435922310302654.html.

36. Bagdikian, 217.

37. Miller, 2.

38. David Armstrong, "Alternative, Inc.," *In These Times*, August 21, 1995, 14–18.

39. Jeff Gremillion, "Showdown at Generation Gap," *Columbia Journalism Review* (July–August 1995): 34–38.

40. Pew Research Center for the People and the Press, "Audience Segments in a Changing News Environment," 26.

41. Ibid., 61–62.

42. Doris Graber, *Mass Media and American Politics*, 5th ed. (Washington, D.C.: CQ Press, 1997), 62.

43. Federal Trade Commission, "Broadband and Connectivity Competition Policy," June 2007, www.ftc.gov/reports/broadband/v070000report.pdf.

44. "Democracy and the Web," Editorial, *New York Times*, May 19, 2008, www.nytimes.com.

45. David H. Weaver and G. Cleveland Wilhoit, *The American Journalist in the 1990s* (Mahwah, N.J.: Erlbaum Associates, 1996), 133–141.

46. Cited in Broder, 138.

47. Graber, 95–96.

48. William Schneider and I. A. Lewis, "Views on the News," *Public Opinion* (August–September 1985): 6.

49. Data in Weaver and Wilhoit, 15–19.

50. Dave D'Alessio and Mike Allen, "Media Bias in Presidential Elections: A Meta-Analysis," *Journal of Communication* (Autumn 2000): 133–156.

51. Mark Hertsgaard, *On Bended Knee: The Press and the Reagan Presidency* (New York: Farrar, Straus & Giroux, 1988), 3.

52. Greg Mitchell and Dexter Hill, "Final Friday Tally of Newspaper Endorsements— Obama in Landslide, at 287 to 159," *Editor and Publisher*, November 7, 2008, www.editorandpublisher.com.

53. William P. Eveland Jr. and Dhavan V. Shah, "The Impact of Individual and Inter-personal Factors on Perceived News Media Bias," *Political Psychology* (2003): 101.

54. Pew Research Center for the People and the Press, "Audience Segments in a Changing News Environment," 56.

55. Kathleen Hall Jamieson and Joseph N. Cappella, "Preface," in *Echo Chamber: Rush Limbaugh and the Conservative Media Elite* (New York: Oxford University Press, 2008).

56. Michael Calderone, "How Dems Grew to Hate the Liberal Media," August 24, 2008, www.politico.com.

57. Jamieson and Cappella, "Preface."

58. Broder, 126.

59. Ibid., 148.

60. Dom Bonafede, "Crossing Over," *National Journal*, January 14, 1989, 102; Michael Kelly, "David Gergen, Master of the Game," *New York Times Magazine*, October 31, 1993, 64ff; Jonathan Alter, "Lost in the Big Blur," *Newsweek*, June 9, 1997, 43.

61. Shanto Iyengar, *Is Anyone Responsible?* (Chicago: University of Chicago Press, 1991), 2.

62. Shanto Iyengar and Donald R. Kinder, *News That Matters* (Chicago: University of Chicago Press, 1987).

63. Stephen Hess, *News and Newsmaking* (Washington, D.C.: Brookings Institution, 1996), 91–92.

64. Iyengar and Kinder, 72.

65. Benjamin I. Page, Robert Y. Shapiro, and Glenn R. Dempsey, "What Moves Public Opinion?" *American Political Science Review* (March 1987): 23–43. The term *professional communicator* is used by Benjamin Page, *Who Deliberates? Mass Media in Modern Democracy* (Chicago: University of Chicago Press, 1996), 106–109.

66. Iyengar and Kinder, 93.

67. W. Russell Neuman, Marion R. Just, and Ann N. Crigler, *Common Knowledge: News and the Construction of Political Meaning* (Chicago: University of Chicago Press, 1996), 106–119.

68. Steven Kull, "Misperceptions, the Media, and the Iraq War," the PIPA/Knowledge Networks poll, Program on International Policy Attitudes, October 2, 2003, 13–16, www.pipa.org/OnlineReports/Iraq/Media_10_02_03_Report.pdf.

69. James Fallows, "Why Americans Hate the Media," *Atlantic Monthly*, February 1996, 16.

70. Ibid., 5–6.

71. Center for Media and Democracy, "Sound Bites Get Shorter," O'Dwyer's PR Newsletter, November 11, 2000, www.prwatch.org/node/384.

72. Thomas E. Patterson, *Out of Order* (New York: Vintage Books, 1994), 74.

73. Goodman, E2.

74. Larry J. Sabato, *Feeding Frenzy: How Attack Journalism Has Transformed American Politics* (New York: Free Press, 1991), 6.

75. Patterson, 243.

76. Ibid., 245.

77. Ibid., 23.

78. Judith Valente, "Do You Believe What Newspeople Tell You?" *Parade Magazine*, March 2, 1997, 4.

79. Joseph N. Cappella and Kathleen Hall Jamieson, *Spiral of Cynicism: The Press and the Public Good* (New York: Oxford University Press, 1997), 9–10.

80. S. Robert Lichter and Richard E. Noyes, *Good Intentions Make Bad News: Why Americans Hate Campaign Journalism* (Lanham, Md.: Rowman & Littlefield, 1995), xix.

81. Walter Cronkite, "Reporting Political Campaigns: A Reporter's View," in Doris Graber, Denis McQuail, and Pippa Norris, eds., *The Politics of News, The News of Politics* (Washington, D.C.: CQ Press, 1998), 57–69.

82. Joe Klein, "The Perils of the Permanent Campaign," *Time*, October 30, 2005.

83. Scott McClellan, *What Happened: Inside the Bush White House and Washington's Culture of Deception* (New York: Public Affairs, 2008).

84. Kelly, 7.

85. Ibid., 7–10.

86. Kenneth T. Walsh, *Feeding the Beast: The White House Versus the Press* (New York: Random House, 1996).

87. Hess, 68–90.

88. Hertsgaard, 6.

89. Anne Kornblut, "Administration Is Warned About Its Publicity Videos," *New York Times*, February 19, 2005, 11.

90. David Barstow and Robin Stein, "Under Bush, a New Age of Prepackaged News," *New York Times*, March 13, 2005, 1.

91. Johanna Neuman, "An Identity Crisis Unfolds in a Not-So-Elite Press Corps," *Los Angeles Times*, February 25, 2005, 18.

92. Jack Shafer, "The Propaganda President: George W. Bush Does His Best Kim Jong-il," *Slate*, February 3, 2005, www.slate.msn.com/id/2113052.

93. Michael Kinsley, "Filter Tips," October 16, 2003, http://slate.msn.com/id/2089915.

94. Jeff Zeleny, "Robert Gibbs," *New York Times*, November 6, 2008.

95. Stephen Ansolabehere, Roy Beyr, and Shanto Iyengar, *The Media Game: American Politics in the Television Age* (New York: Macmillan, 1993); Iyengar, *Is Anyone Responsible?*

96. Clay Shirky, "Newspapers and Thinking the Unthinkable," March 13, 2009, www.shirky.com/weblog/2009/03/newspapers-and-thinking-the-unthinkable/.

97. Ibid.

98. Dan Gillmor, *We the Media: Grassroots Journalism by the People, for the People* (Sebastopol, Calif.: O'Reilly Media, 2008).

99. Andrew Sullivan, "A Blogger Manifesto: Why Online Weblogs Are One Future for Journalism," *The Sunday Times of London*, February 24, 2002.

100. Andrew Sullivan, "Happy 4th," *The Daily Dish*, July 4, 2010, http://andrewsullivan.theatlantic.com/the_daily_dish/2010/07/happy-4th.html.

101. Shirky.

Chapter 16

1. Jonathan J. Cooper, "Arizona Immigration Conflict Heats Up," AP News, April 26, 2010, www.talkingpointsmemo.com/news/2010/04/arizona_immigration_conflict_heats_up.php?ref=fpblg.

2. David G. Savage, "High Court Ruling on Arizona Act Could Shape Immigration Law," *Los Angeles Times*, December 6, 2010, www.latimes.com/news/nationworld/nation/la-na-court-immigration-20101206,0,901485.story.

3. CBS/AP, "Arizona Immigration Law Faces Legal Challenges," April 26, 2010, www.cbsnews.com/stories/2010/04/27/national/main6436027.shtml.

4. Ibid.

5. Daniel Elazar, *American Federalism: A View From the States*, 3rd ed. (New York: Harper & Row, 1984).

6. Ira Sharkansky, "The Utility of Elazar's Political Culture: A Research Note," *Polity* (Fall 1969): 66–83; Timothy D. Schlitz and R. Lee Rainey, "The Geographic Distribution of Elazar's Political Subcultures Among the Mass Population: A Research Note," *Western Political Quarterly* (September 1978): 410–415.

7. John G. Peters and Susan Welch, "Politics, Corruption and Political Culture: A View

From the State Legislatures," *American Politics Quarterly* (July 1978): 345–356; David C. Nice, "Political Corruption in the American States," *American Politics Quarterly* (October 1983): 507–517.

8. Robert S. Erikson, Gerald C. Wright, and John P. McIver, *Statehouse Democracy* (New York: Cambridge University Press, 1993), ch. 7.

9. Jody L. Fitzpatrick and Rodney E. Hero, "Political Culture and Political Characteristics of the American States," *Western Political Quarterly* (March 1988): 145–153.

10. Steven Koven and Christopher Mausolff, "The Influence of Political Culture on State Budgets: Another Look at Elazar's Formulation," *American Review of Public Administration* 32 (2002): 66–77; James A. Gardner, *Interpreting State Constitutions: A Jurisprudence of Function in a Federal System* (Chicago: University of Chicago Press, 2005).

11. Erikson, Wright, and McIver, ch. 3.

12. "USA Today's 2006 College Tuition and Fees Survey," *USA Today*, September 5, 2006, www.usatoday.com/news/education/2006-08-30-tuition-survey_x.htm.

13. Advisory Commission on Intergovernmental Relations, *State Constitutions in the Federal System* (Washington, D.C.: U.S. Government Printing Office, 1989), 7.

14. Daniel J. Elazar, "The Principles and Traditions Underlying State Constitutions," *Publius* (Winter 1982): 11–25.

15. Ibid.

16. John Kincaid, "State Constitutions in the Federal System," *Annals* (March 1988): 13–14; Robert S. Lorch, *State and Local Politics: The Great Entanglement*, 6th ed. (Englewood Cliffs, N.J.: Prentice Hall, 2001), 13.

17. Christopher W. Hammons, "Was James Madison Wrong? Rethinking the American Preference for Short, Framework-Oriented Constitutions," *American Political Science Review* (December 1999): 840.

18. For more information, see National Conference of State Legislators, "Ballot Measures Database," 2003, www.ncsl.org/programs/legman/elect/statevote2003.htm#BalMe.

19. David Broder, "In California, Elected Officials Get Relegated to the Sidelines," *Bloomington Herald-Times*, August 17, 1997, A8.

20. California Secretary of State, "Ballot Pamphlets and Voter Information Guides," www.ss.ca.gov/elections/elections_bp.htm#bp.

21. U.S. Term Limits, www.termlimits.org/Current_Info/current_info.html.

22. Quoted in Daniel A. Smith, "Unmasking the Tax Crusaders," in Bruce Stinebrickner, ed., *Annual Editions: State and Local Government*, 9th ed. (Guilford, Conn.: Dushkin/McGraw-Hill, 1998), 84.

23. Ibid.

24. Daniel A. Smith, *Tax Crusaders and the Politics of Direct Democracy* (New York: Routledge, 1998).

25. Raymond E. Wolfinger and Fred I. Greenstein, "The Repeal of Fair Housing in California: An Analysis of Referendum Voting," *American Political Science Review* (September 1968): 753–769; David Magleby, "Taking the Initiative: Direct Legislation and Direct Democracy in the 1980s," *PS: Political Science & Politics* (Summer 1988): 603.

26. Bruce E. Cain and Kenneth P. Miller, "The Populist Legacy: Initiatives and the Undermining of Representative Government," in Larry J. Sabato, Howard Ernst, and Bruce A. Larson, eds., *Dangerous Democracy? The Battle Over Ballot Initiatives in America* (Lanham, Md.: Rowman & Littlefield, 2001); Barbara S. Gamble, "Putting Civil Rights to a Popular Vote," *American Journal of Political Science* (January 1997): 245–269; Rodney Hero and Caroline Tolbert, "A Racial/Ethnic Diversity Interpretation of Politics and Policy in the States of the U.S.," *American Journal of Political Science* (August 1996): 851–871.

27. Tiffany Sharples, "Ballot Initiatives: NO to Gay Marriage, Anti-Abortion Measures," *Time*, November 5, 2008, www.time.com/time/politics/article/0,8599,1856820,00.html; Glenn Adams and David Crary, "Maine Voters Reject Gay-Marriage Law," *The Guardian*, November 4, 2009, www.guardian.co.uk/world/feedarticle/8789627.

28. Belle Zeller, ed., *American State Legislatures: Report of the Committee on American Legislatures of the American Political Science Association* (New York: Crowell, 1954); John Burns, *The Sometimes Governments: A Critical Study of the 50 American Legislatures* (New York: Bantam Books, 1971); Larry Sabato, *Goodbye to Good-time Charlie: The American Governor Transformed*, 2nd ed. (Washington, D.C.: Congressional Quarterly Press, 1983).

29. Garry Wills, "The War Between the States . . . and Washington," *New York Times Sunday Magazine*, July 5, 1998, 3.

30. Stephen Ansolabehere and James Snyder Jr., *The End of Inequality* (New York: Norton, 2008).

31. National Conference of State Legislatures, "Full- and Part-time Legislatures," June 2004, www.ncsl.org/programs/press/2004/backgrounder_fullandpart.htm.

32. National Conference of State Legislatures, "Legislator Demographics," www.ncsl.org/default.aspx?tabid=14850.

33. Thad Kousser, *Term Limits and the Dismantling of State Legislative Professionalism* (Cambridge: Cambridge University Press, 2005).

34. Alan Greenblatt, "Term Limits Aren't Working," *Governing*, April 2005, 13.

35. Karl T. Kurtz, Bruce Cain, and Richard G. Niemi, *Institutional Change in American Politics: The Case of Term Limits* (Ann Arbor: University of Michigan Press, 2007).

36. Bruce E. Cain and Thad Kousser, *Adapting to Term Limits: Recent Experiences and New Directions* (San Francisco: Public Policy Institute of California, 2004), www.ppic.org/main/publication.asp?i=347; Marjorie Sarbaugh-Thompson, Lyke Thompson, Charles D. Elder, John Strate, and Richard C. Elling, *The Political and Institutional Effects of Term Limits* (New York: Palgrave MacMillan, 2004).

37. Greenblatt.

38. Robert S. Lorch, *State and Local Politics: The Great Entanglement* (Englewood Cliffs, N.J.: Prentice Hall, 1995), 158–160.

39. Erikson, Wright, and McIver, ch. 4.

40. Paul Brace, Kellie Sims-Butler, Kevin Arceneaux, and Martin Johnson, "Public Opinion in the American States: New Perspectives Using National Survey Data," *American Journal of Political Science* (January 2002): 173–189; Barbara Norrander, "Measuring State Public Opinion With the Senate National Election Study," *State Politics and Policy Quarterly* (March 2001): 111–125.

41. Gary F. Moncrief, Peverill Squire, and Malcolm E. Jewell, *Who Runs for the Legislature?* (Upper Saddle River, N.J.: Prentice Hall, 2001), ch. 2.

42. Christina Fastnow and Peverill Squire, "Comparing Gubernatorial and Senatorial Elections," *Political Research Quarterly* (September 1994): 705–720.

43. Sabato.

44. R. Allen, *Our Sovereign State* (New York: Vanguard, 1949), xi.

45. Sabato.

46. F. Ted Herbert, Jeffrey L. Brudney, and Deil S. Wright, "Gubernatorial Influence and State Bureaucracy," *American Politics Quarterly* (April 1983): 243–264.

47. Thomas Dye, *Politics in States and Communities*, 8th ed. (Englewood Cliffs, N.J.: Prentice Hall, 1994), 207.

48. Charles Barrilleaux and Michael Berkman, "Do Governors Matter? Budgeting Rules and the Politics of State Policymaking," *Political Research Quarterly* (December 2003): 409–417.

49. Quoted in Thad Beyle, "Governors: The Middlemen and Women in Our Political System," in Virginia Gray and Herbert Jacob, eds., *Politics in the American States: A Comparative Analysis*, 6th ed. (Washington, DC: CQ Press, 1996), 207.

50. National Institute for Money in State Politics, *www.followthemoney.org*.

51. Gerald C. Wright, *Electoral Choice in America* (Chapel Hill, N.C.: Institute for Research in Social Science, 1974); Fastnow and Squire.

52. Jeffrey Cohen, "Gubernatorial Popularity in Nine States," *American Politics Quarterly* (April 1983): 194–207; Susan Kone and Richard Winters, "Taxes and Voting: Electoral Retribution in the American States," *Journal of Politics* (February 1993): 22–40.

53. Randall Partin, "Economic Conditions and Gubernatorial Elections," *American Politics Quarterly* (January 1995): 81–95; Kevin M. Leyden and Stephen A. Borrelli, "The Effect of State Economic Conditions on Gubernatorial Elections: Does Unified Government Make a Difference?" *Political Research Quarterly* (June 1995): 275–290.

54. Kevin B. Smith, Alan Greenblatt, and John Buntin, *Governing States and Localities* (Washington D.C.: CQ Press, 2005).

55. Thomas M. Carsey and Gerald C. Wright, "State and National Forces in Gubernatorial and Senatorial Elections," and "Rejoinder," *American Journal of Political Science* (July 1998): 944–1002, 1008–1011.

56. Thomas M. Carsey, *Campaign Dynamics: The Race for Governor* (Ann Arbor: University of Michigan Press, 2000).

57. John J. Harrigan, *Politics and Policy in State and Communities*, 5th ed. (New York: HarperCollins, 1994), 310–311.

58. Todd Donovan, Caroline Tolbert, Daniel Smith, and Janine Parry, "Did Gay Marriage Elect George W. Bush?" Paper presented at the Fourth Annual State Politics and Policy Conference, East Lansing, Michigan, May 13, 2005, http://polisci.msu.edu/sppc2005/papers/fripm/dtsp_sppc05.pdf.

59. Henry R. Glick, "The Politics of Court Reform: In a Nutshell," *Policy Studies Journal* (June 1982): 688.

60. Matthew Mosk, "Study Shows Money Flooding Into Campaigns for State Judgeships," ABC News, March 17, 2010, http://abcnews.go.com/Blotter/study-shows-money-flooding-campaigns-state-judgeships/story?id=10120048; Melinda Gann Hall, "Competition as Accountability in State Supreme Court Elections," in Matthew J. Streb, ed., *Running for Judge: The Rising Political, Financial, and Legal Stakes of Judicial Elections* (New York: New York University Press, 2007).

61. Robert Barnes, "Ruth Bader Ginsburg Says She Would Forbid State Judicial Elections," *Washington Post*, March 12, 2010.

62. Paul Brace and Melinda Gann Hall, "Studying Courts Comparatively: The View From the American States," *Political Research Quarterly* (March 1995): 5–29.

63. Jess Bravin and Kris Maher, "Justices Set New Standard for Recusals," *Wall Street Journal*, June 9, 2010.

64. James N. G. Cauthen, "Expanding Rights Under State Constitutions: A Quantitative Appraisal," *Albany Law Review* (June 2000), web version.

65. Elder Witt, "State Supreme Courts: Tilting the Balance Toward Change," *Governing*, August 1989, 30–38; Stanley Mosk, "The Emerging Agenda of State Constitutional Rights Law," *Annals of the American Academy of Political and Social Sciences* (March 1988): 54–64.

66. *Serrano v. Priest*, 487 P. 2d 1241 (Cal. 1971).

67. Mosk.

68. *Bowers v. Hardwick*, 478 U.S. 186 (1986).

69. *Baker v. State* (98–032), December 20, 1999.

70. G. Alan Tarr, "The New Judicial Federalism in Perspective," *Notre Dame Law Review* 72 (1997): 1097; *Goodridge v. Dept. of Public Health*, 798 N.E.2d 941 (Mass.2003).

71. Albert Karnig and Susan Welch, "Electoral Structure and Black Representation on City Councils," *Social Science Quarterly* (March 1982): 99–114. Some evidence suggests that the bias of at-large systems against African Americans is less today than it was twenty or thirty years ago; see Susan Welch, "The Impact of At-Large Representation of Blacks and Hispanics," *Journal of Politics* (November 1990): 1050–1076.

72. U.S. Bureau of the Census, *2002 Census of Governments*, http://ftp2.census.gov/govs/cog/2002COGprelim_report.pdf.

73. Peter Miezkowski and Edwin S. Mills, "The Causes of Metropolitan Suburbanization," *Journal of Economic Perspectives* 7 (1993): 135–147.

74. Richard Child Hill, "Separate and Unequal: Government Inequality in the Metropolis," *American Political Science Review* (December 1974): 1557–1568.

75. John Harrigan, *Political Change in the Metropolis* (Boston: Little, Brown, 1985).

76. Vincent L. Marando and Carl Whitley, "City-County Consolidation: An Overview of Voter Response," *Urban Affairs Quarterly* (December 1972): 181–203.

77. David Rusk, *Cities Without Suburbs*, 2nd ed. (Baltimore: Johns Hopkins University Press, 1995); and *Inside Game/Outside Game: Winning Strategies for Saving Urban America* (Washington, D.C.: Brookings Institution Press, 1999).

78. Advisory Commission on Intergovernmental Relations, *State Mandating of Local Expenditures* (Washington, D.C.: U.S. Government Printing Office, 1978); and *Mandates: Cases in State-Local Relations* (Washington, D.C.: U.S. Government Printing Office, September 1990); Russell L. Hanson, *Governing Partners: State-Local Relations in the United States* (Boulder, Colo.: Westview Press, 1998).

79. John Maggs, "Hizzoner, the Pizza Man," *National Journal*, November 21, 1998, 2796–2798.

80. Kevin Sack, "More Retirees Discover Small-Town South" *New York Times*, May 24, 1997, 1; "Over the Hill and Off to a Town in Mississippi," *Wall Street Journal*, February 6, 1996, A1; Hattiesburg retirement web site, www.retirementamerica.com/hattiesb.htm.

81. "Over the Hill and Off to a Town in Mississippi."

82. Paul Peterson, *The Price of Federalism* (Washington, D.C.: Brookings Institution Press, 1995); Paul Peterson and Mark Rom, *Welfare Magnets* (Washington, D.C.: Brookings Institution Press, 1990).

83. Christoper Z. Mooney, "Modeling Regional Effects on State Policy Diffusion," *Political Research Quarterly* (March 2001): 103–124; Craig Volden, "The Politics of Competitive Federalism: A Race to the Bottom in Welfare Benefits?" *American Journal of Political Science* (April 2002): 352–363; Jack L. Walker, "The Diffusion of Innovations Among the American States," *American Political Science Review* 63 (1969): 880–899; Virginia Gray, "Innovation in the States: A Diffusion Study," *American Political Science Review* (December 1973): 1174–1185.

84. National Governors Association, "Governors Offer Bipartisan Plan to Reform, Improve Medicaid," press release, June 15, 2005, www.nga.org.

85. Linda Feldmann, "America's Governors Emerge as 'Third House of Congress,'" *Christian Science Monitor*, February 8, 1996, 1, 4.

86. Edgar Ruiz, "Regional Cooperation: The Border Legislative Conference," *Spectrum: The Journal of State Government* (Fall 2004): 20–21.

87. Savage.

88. Randal C. Archibold, "Arizona Enacts Stringent Law on Immigration," *New York Times*, April 23, 2010, www.nytimes.com/2010/04/24/us/politics/24immig.html?scp=1&sq=Arizona%20Enacts%20Stringent%20Law%20on%20Immigration&st=cse.

89. Nicholas Riccardi and Anna Gorman, "Federal Judge Blocks Key Parts of Arizona Immigration Law," *Los Angeles Times*, July 28, 2010, http://articles.latimes.com/2010/jul/28/nation/la-na-arizona-immigration-20100729.

90. "Obama Signs Border Security Bill, With No Comment," *USA Today*, August 13, 2010, www.usatoday.com/communities/theoval/post/2010/08/obama-signs-border-security-bill/1.

91. Dan Nowicki, "Border Security, Immigration Reform Continue to Vex U.S.," *Arizona Republic*, December 12, 2010, www.azcentral.com/arizonarepublic/news/articles/2010/12/10/20101210global-immigration-us.html.

Chapter 17

1. Barbara Hagenbaugh, "Oil Drilling Up, But Impact May Be Slight," *USA Today*, May 31, 2005, 4B.

2. Energy Information Administration, "Data on US Field Production and Imports January and February 2008," http://tonto.eia.doe.gov/dnav/pet/pet_sum_crdsnd_adc_mbbl_m.htm; Mark Clayton, "Can Hybrids Save US From Foreign Oil?" *Christian Science Monitor*, May 19, 2005, www.csmonitor.com/2005/0519/p14s01-sten.html.

3. "Vote on Arctic Drilling Heads in Wrong Direction," *San Antonio Express-News*, March 18, 2005, 6B.

4. Jeffrey M. Jones, "Americans Divided on Increased Coastal Oil Drilling," Gallup.com, May 28, 2010, www.gallup.com/poll/137885/americans-divided-increased-coastal-oil-drilling.aspx.

5. The Pew Research Center for the People and the Press, "As Gas Prices Pinch, Support for Energy Exploration Rises," July 1, 2008, http://people-press.org/report/433/gas-prices.

6. Courtney Mabeus, "Boiling Oil: The Money Behind the Debate Over Drilling in the Arctic National Wildlife Refuge," *Capital Eye*, March 17, 2005, www.capitaleye.org/inside.asp?ID=160.

7. Peter Bachrach and Morton S. Baratz, "The Two Faces of Power," *American Political Science Review* 56 (December 1962): 948.

8. This definition of public policy is based on the one offered by James E. Anderson, *Public Policymaking: An Introduction* (Boston: Houghton Mifflin, 1997), 9.

9. Theodore Lowi, "American Business, Public Policy Case Studies, and Political Theory," *World Politics* (July 1964): 677–715.

10. For a discussion of the effect of lawsuits on air emissions standards, see Robert Percival, Alan Miller, Christopher Schroeder, and James Leape, *Environmental Regulation: Law, Science and Policy*, 2nd ed. (Boston: Little, Brown, 1996).

11. Alison Mitchell and Frank Bruni, "House Vote Deals a Stinging Defeat to Gun Control," *New York Times*, June 18, 1999, A1.

12. See John W. Kingdon, *Agendas, Alternatives and Public Policies* (Boston: Little, Brown, 1984), for a discussion of factors that put policies on the congressional agenda.

13. "Pro-life Senator With Stem Cells, Specter Is on the Side of Humanity," *Pittsburgh Post-Gazette*, May 31, 2005, B6.

14. Murray Light, "Politics Had a Big Role in Creation of Department," *Buffalo News*, December 8, 2002, H5.

15. "Bush Signs Into Law Bankruptcy Overhaul," *Wall Street Journal*, April 21, 2005, A4.

16. "Bracing for Worst," *Rocky Mountain News*, April 2, 2005, 29A.

17. Roni Rabin, "Pyramid Power: A New Version of Dietary Guides Places More Emphasis on Exercise and a Personal Eating Plan," *Newsday*, April 20, 2005, A5.

18. Charles Lane, "Kennedy Reversal Swings Court Against Juvenile Death Penalty," *Washington Post*, March 7, 2005, A17.

19. See, for example, Martha Derthick, *New Towns In-Town* (Washington, D.C.: Urban Institute, 1972); Jeffrey L. Pressman and Aaron Wildavsky, *Implementation* (Berkeley: University of California Press, 1971); and Eugene Bardach, *The Implementation Game: What Happens After a Bill Becomes Law* (Cambridge: MIT Press, 1977).

20. Paul A. Sabatier and Daniel Mazmanian, "Policy Implementation: A Framework for Analysis," *Policy Studies Journal* (1980): 538–560.

21. Michael Lipsky, *Street-Level Bureaucracy: Dilemmas of the Individual in Public Service* (New York: Russell Sage, 1980).

22. Servicemembers Legal Defense Network, "Tenth Annual Report on Don't Ask, Don't Tell, Don't Pursue," 2004, http://dont.stanford.edu/commentary/sldn.10.pdf.

23. For a full discussion of the challenges of intergovernmental policy implementation, see Malcolm L. Goggin, Ann O. Bowman, James P. Lester, and Laurence O'Toole, *Implementation Theory and Practice: Toward a Third Generation* (Glenview, Ill.: Scott Foresman, 1990). For a discussion of how intergovernmental implementation occurs in environmental policy, see Denise Scheberle, *Federalism and Environmental Policy: Trust and the Politics of Implementation* (Washington, D.C.: Georgetown University Press, 1997).

24. For a discussion of policy analysts and the techniques they use to evaluate policies, see Robert A. Heineman, William T. Bluhm, Steven A. Peterson, and Edward N. Kearny, *The World of the Policy Analyst: Rationality, Values and Politics* (Chatham, N.J.: Chatham House, 1990).

25. James M. McElfish, *Environmental Regulation of Coal Minings: SMCRA's Second Decade* (Washington, D.C.: Environmental Law Institute, 1990).

26. Office of Family Assistance, "Temporary Assistance for Needy Families (TANF): Sixth Annual Report to Congress," www.acf.hhs.gov/programs/ofa/annualreport6/ar6index.htm.

27. Public Citizen, "The Ten Year Track Record of the North American Free Trade Agreement: U.S. Workers' Jobs, Wages, and Economic Security," www.citizen.org/documents/NAFTA_10_jobs.pdf.

28. U.S. Department of Health and Human Services, "2009/2010 Federal Poverty Threshold," *Federal Register*, 74, no. 14, http://aspe.hhs.gov/poverty/09fedreg.shtml.

29. U.S. Census Bureau, "Income, Poverty and Health Insurance in the United States: 2008—Highlights," www.census.gov/hhes/www/poverty/data/incpovhlth/2008/highlights.html.

30. Ibid.

31. U.S. Census Bureau, 2008 American Community Survey, Table S1702: Poverty in Past 12 Months of Families, http://factfinder.census.gov/servlet/STSelectServlet?_lang=en&_ts=298161944607.

32. Social Security Administration, Statistical Tables, www.ssa.gov/OACT/STATS/index.html.

33. Calculate this for yourself at www.ssa.gov/OACT/quickcalc.

34. Social Security Administration, "Fast Facts and Figures About Social Security," www.ssa.gov/policy/docs/chartbooks/fast_facts/2009/fast_facts09.pdf

35. Congressional Research Service Report for Congress, "Social Security: Brief Facts and Statistics," updated May 1, 1998 (Washington, D.C.: Library of Congress).

36. The Concord Coalition, "Demographics Is Destiny," www.concordcoalition.org/issues/fedbudget/old-doc/charts/charttalk%204087.pdf.

37. Social Security Administration, "A Summary of the 2005 Annual Reports," www.ssa.gov/OACT/TRSUM/trsummary.html.

38. U.S. Census Bureau, *Statistical Abstract of the United States*, calculated from federal outlays tables, www.census.gov/compendia/statab/cats/federal_govt_finances_employment/federal_budgetreceipts_outlays_and_debt.html.

39. U.S. Census Bureau, "Table No. 465: Federal Outlays by Detailed Function: 1990–2004," in *Statistical Abstracts of the United States*, 2005 (Washington, D.C.: U.S. Census Bureau).

40. Jonathan Weisman, "Domestic Issues on the Front Burner; Bush's Legacy May Depend on Policies," *Washington Post*, November 7, 2004, A8.

41. Peter Wallsten and Joel Havemann, "Bush Shifts Pension Stance," *Los Angeles Times*, February 17, 2005, A1.

42. Robert J. Shiller, "American Casino: The Promise and Perils of Bush's 'Ownership Society,'" *Atlantic Monthly*, March 2005, 33–34; "Insuring America," *New Republic*, February 28, 2005, 9; Joel Havemann, "One Person's Fix Is Another's Flaw," *Los Angeles Times*, May 1, 2005, A22; "The Risks in Personal Accounts," *Washington Post*, February 20, 2005, B6.

43. Peter G. Gosselin, "Bush Plan Aids Poor, Squeezes the Rest," *Los Angeles Times*, April 30, 2005, A1.

44. Susan Jones, "Obama's Social Security Plan: Some Will Pay More," http://CNSNews.com, May 19, 2008.

45. Social Security Administration, "The History of Social Security," www.ssa.gov/history.

46. U.S. Census Bureau, *Statistical Brief: Mothers Who Receive AFDC Payments: Fertility and Socioeconomic Characteristics* (Washington, D.C.: U.S. Department of Commerce, Economics and Statistics Administration, March 1995).

47. *1996 Green Book*, Ways and Means Committee Print WMCP: 104–114, Section 8. Aid to Families With Dependent Children and Related Programs (Title IV-A). U.S. Government Printing Office Online via GPO Access.

48. U.S. Department of Labor, Bureau of Labor Statistics, "A Profile of the Working Poor, 2000," www.bls.gov/cps/cpswp2000.htm.

49. Office of Family Assistance.

50. Peter Edelman, "The True Purpose of Welfare Reform," *New York Times*, May 29, 2002, A21.

51. Jason DeParle, "Slumping Economy Tests System Tied to Jobs," *New York Times*, May 1, 2009, www.nytimes.com/2009/06/01/us/politics/01poverty.html.

52. Jason DeParle, "As Welfare Rolls Shrink, Burden on Relatives Grows," *New York Times*, February 21, 1999, www.nytimes.com.

53. Nina Bernstein, "Side Effect of Welfare Law: The No-Parent Family," *New York Times*, July 29, 2002, A1.

54. Nina Bernstein, "Strict Limits on Welfare Benefits Discourage Marriage, Studies Say," *New York Times*, June 3, 2002, A1.

55. Center for Law and Social Policy, *Implementing the TANF Changes in the Deficit Reduction Act*, 2nd ed., www.cbpp.org/2-9-07tanf.htm.

56. U.S. Department of Agriculture, "The Food Assistance Landscape," 2006, www.ers.usda.gov/publications/eib6–2/eib6–2.pdf.

57. U.S. Department of Agriculture, "Food Assistance Landscape, FY 2009 Annual Report," www.ers.usda.gov/publications/eib6–7/eib6–7.pdf.

58. Ibid.

59. U.S. Department of Agriculture, "Supplemental Nutrition Assistance Program Eligibility Requirements," 2010, www.fns.usda.gov/snap/applicant_recipients/eligibility.htm#income.

60. Sarah Glazer, "Head Start: Does the Much-Touted Preschool Program Really Deliver?" *CQ Researcher*, April 9, 1993, 296.

61. U.S. Department of Health and Human Services, "Head Start Impact Study Final Report," www.acf.hhs.gov/programs/opre/hs/impact_study/reports/impact_study/executive_summary_final.pdf.

62. U.S. Department of Health and Human Services, Head Start Bureau, "Head Start Program Facts," 2009, www.acf.hhs.gov/programs/ohs/about/fy2010.html.

63. Glazer, 292.

64. Kathleen Sebelius, "Obama Administration Has Plans for Head Start Improvement," *USA Today*, July 20, 2010, www.usatoday.com/news/opinion/letters/2010–07–20-letters20_ST1_N.htm.

65. Organization for Economic Cooperation and Development, "OECD Health Data, 2010," www.oecd.org.

66. Robert Pear, "Health Costs Will Keep Rising, U.S. Says, Along With Government Share of Paying Them," *New York Times*, February 24, 2005, A20.

67. Carmen DeNavas-Walt, Bernadette D. Proctor, and Jessica C. Smith, "Income, Poverty, and Health Insurance Coverage in the United States: 2008," U.S. Census Bureau, www.census.gov/prod/2009pubs/p60–236.pdf.

68. Leif Wellington Haase, "The Debate Over Medicare Costs: A Primer," September 24, 2004, www.tcf.org/4L/4LMain.asp?SubjectID=1&TopicID=0&ArticleID=489.

69. Centers for Medicare and Medicaid Services, "Medicare Enrollment Report: National Trends, 1966–2008," www.cms.gov/MedicareEnRpts/Downloads/HISMI08.pdf.

70. Kaiser Family Foundation, "Medicare Fact Sheet: Medicare at a Glance," January 2010, www.kff.org/medicare/upload/1066–12.pdf.

71. Centers for Medicare and Medicaid Services, "2005 Annual Report of the Boards of Trustees of the Hospital Insurance and Supplementary Medical Insurance Trust Funds," www.cms.hhs.gov/publications/trusteesreport/default.asp?

72. Murray Light, "Medicare Reform Being Neglected," *Buffalo News*, March 6, 2005, H3.

73. Joel Havemann and Maura Reynolds, "Bush Budget Plan Focuses on Tax Cuts and Defense," *Los Angeles Times*, February 8, 2005, http://articles.latimes.com/2005/feb/08/nation/na-budget8/3.

74. CBS News, "Transcript: Obama's Health Care Speech," September 9, 2009, www.cbsnews.com/stories/2009/09/09/politics/main5299229.shtml.

75. Open Congress Blog, "What Is the Public Option?" August 20, 2009, www.opencongress.org/articles/view/1174--What-is-the-Public-Option-.

76. Kaiser Family Foundation, "Focus on Health Reform: Summary of New Health Reform Law," March 26, 2010, www.kff.org/healthreform/upload/8061.pdf.

77. Huffington Post/Pollster, "Health Care Plan: Favor/Oppose," October 1, 2010, http://www.pollster.com/polls/us/healthplan.php.

78. Michael Crowley, "Will Health Reform be a Key Factor in Midterms?" *Time Magazine*, August 20, 2010, www.time.com/time/politics/article/0,8599,2011907,00.html.

79. Andrew Mollison, "Interest Rates on Student Loans to Drop," *Atlanta Journal-Constitution*, June 5, 2001, 12A.

80. Peter Baker and David M. Herszenhorn, "Obama Signs Overhaul of Student Loan Program," *New York Times*, March 30, 2010, www.nytimes.com/2010/03/31/us/politics/31obama.html.

81. Internal Revenue Service, "Education Credits," www.irs.gov/individuals/article/0,,id=121452,00.html.

82. Congressional Budget Office, "An Overview of Federal Support for Housing," November 3, 2009, www.cbo.gov/ftpdocs/105xx/doc10525/HousingPrograms.1.1.shtml.

83. Robert McIntyre, "Your Federal Tax Dollars at Work," *American Prospect*, May 20, 2002.

84. Environmental Working Group, "Farm Subsidy Database," http://farm.ewg.org/summary.php.

85. For a discussion of environmental policy in the 1980s, see Walter A. Rosenbaum, *Environmental Politics and Policy*, 4th ed. (Washington, D.C.: CQ Press, 2004).

86. Robert D. Bullard, *Dumping in Dixie: Race, Class and Environmental Quality*, 2nd ed. (Boulder: Westview Press, 1994).

87. U.S. Environmental Protection Agency, "EPA Needs to Consistently Implement the Intent of the Executive Order on Environmental Justice," Report No. 2004-P-0007, March 1, 2004, www.epa.gov/oig/reports/2004/20040301-2004-P-00007.pdf; Brentin Mock, "Will Environmental Justice Finally Get its Due?" *The American Prospect*, December 22, 2008, www.prospect.org/cs/articles?article=will_environmental_justice_finally_get_its_due; PolitiFact.com, "Barack Obama Campaign Promise No. 257: Strengthen Federal Environmental Justice Programs," December 21, 2009, www.politifact.com/truth-o-meter/promises/promise/267/strengthen-federal-environmental-justice-programs/; Jim Erikson, "MLK: Environmental Justice Advocate Says Obama Brings Optimism," The University Record Online, University of Michigan, January 11, 2010, www.ur.umich.edu/0910/Jan11_10/419-mlk-environmental-justice-advocate-says-obama-brings-optimism.

88. "President Bush Delivers State of the Union Address," January 31, 2006, www.whitehouse.gov/stateoftheunion/2006/.

89. Andrew Sullivan, "The Case for a War Tax—on Gas," *Time*, April 19, 2004, 104.

90. Peter Katel, "Oil Jitters," *CQ Researcher*, Vol. 18, No. 1 (2008): 1–24.

91. Steven Mufson, "Vehicle Emission Rules to Tighten," *Washington Post*, May 19, 2009, www.washingtonpost.com/wp-dyn/content/article/2009/05/18/AR2009051801848.html.

92. Mary Cooper, "Energy and the Environment," *CQ Outlook*, April 22, 2000.

93. Jad Mouawad, "Hybrid Cars Won't Save Much Oil," *New York Times* Green Blog, January 11, 2010, http://green.blogs.nytimes.com/2010/01/11/hybrid-cars-wont-save-much-oil/.

94. Department of Energy, "The Energy Act of 2005: What It Means to You," www.doe.gov/taxbreaks.htm.

95. "For Hybrid Car Buyers, the End of a Sales Tax," *New York Times*, October 3, 2004, 14CN, 2.

96. Union of Concerned Scientists, HybridCenter.org.

97. Sheryl Gay Stolberg, "Senate Votes to Allow Drilling in Arctic Reserve," *New York Times*, March 17, 2005, www.nytimes.com/2005/03/17/politics/17arctic.html.

98. John M. Broder, "House Passes Bill to Address Threat of Climate Change," *New York Times*, June 26, 2009, www.nytimes.com.

99. John M. Broder, "Environmental Advocates Are Cooling on Obama," *New York Times*, February 18, 2010, www.nytimes.com.

100. Robert S. Erikson, Gerald C. Wright, and John P. McIver, *Statehouse Democracy* (New York: Cambridge University Press, 1993).

101. Michael B. MacKuen, Robert S. Erikson, and James A. Stimson, "Macropartisanship," *American Political Science Review* (December 1989): 1125–1142.

102. Carl Hulse and Steven Lee Myers, "Congress Votes to Stop Stockpiling Oil," *New York Times*, May 14, 2008, www.nytimes.com.

103. The city of Kaktovik's web page, www.kaktovik.com.

104. Leslie Kaufman, "Arctic Drilling Poses Untold Risks, Study Concludes," *New York Times* Green Blog, November 11, 2010, http://green.blogs.nytimes.com/2010/11/11/arctic-drilling-poses-untold-risks-study-concludes/?scp=5&sq=offshore%20drilling&st=cse.

105. Julie Cart and Ralph Vartabedian, "Refuge Has Long Been a Major Environmental Battleground," *Los Angeles Times*, March 17, 2005.

106. Michael T. Klare, "Arctic Drilling Is No Energy Answer," *Los Angeles Times*, April 3, 2005, M5.

107. Cart and Vartabedian.

108. Paul Mirengoff, "Trading Places: Have Republicans Replaced Democrats as the Party of Pragmatism?" *Daily Standard*, March 21, 2005.

109. Jonah Goldberg, "Ugh, Wilderness!" *National Review Online*, March 18, 2005.

Chapter 18

1. "CSI: Credit Crunch," *The Economist*, October 17, 2007, www.economist.com/specialreports/displaystory.cfm?story_id=9972489.

2. "CSI: Credit Crunch."

3. "U.S. Foreclosure Activity Increases 75 Percent in 2007," Realty Trac, June 29, 2008, www.realtytrac.com/ContentManagement/pressrelease.aspx?ChannelID=9&ItemID=3988&accnt=64847.

4. Adam Smith, *The Wealth of Nations* (London: W. Strahan & T. Cadell, 1776).

5. Central Intelligence Agency, "The World Factbook," www.cia.gov/library/publications/the-world-factbook/.

6. Haynes Johnson, *Sleepwalking Through History: America in the Reagan Years* (New York: Anchor Books, 1991).

7. Barbara Hagenbaugh, "Economist Fears 'Nasty' Recession Headed Our Way This Year; His Panel Calls It When It Happens," *USA Today*, January 9, 2008, 4B; Patrice Hill, "Recession Inevitable, Economists Predict; Housing, Credit Crunches Cited," *Washington Times*, December 25, 2007, A01; Robert Gavin, "Are We or Aren't We in a Recession?" *Boston Globe*, January 23, 2008, C11.

8. Phil Izzo, "Recession Over in June 2009," *Wall Street Journal*, September 20, 2010, http://blogs.wsj.com/economics/2010/09/20/nber-recession-ended-in-june-2009/.

9. William A. Link and Arthur S. Link, *A History of the United States Since 1900, Volume 1: War, Reform, and Society, 1900–1945*, 7th ed. (New York: McGraw Hill, 1993).

10. James Thurber, "Centralization, Devolution, and Turf Protection in the Congressional Budget Process," in Lawrence C. Dodd and Bruce I. Oppenheimer, eds., *Congress Reconsidered*, 6th ed. (Washington, D.C.: CQ Press, 1997), 331. Thurber credits James Saturno of the Congressional Research Service for this observation.

11. Office of Management and Budget, Historical Tables, "Table 6.1: Composition of Outlays: 1940–2015," www.whitehouse.gov/omb/budget/Historicals.

12. Daniel Wirls, "Busted: Government and Elections in the Era of Deficit Politics," in Benjamin Ginsberg and Alan Stone, eds., *Do Elections Matter?* 3rd ed. (Armonk, N.Y.: M. E. Sharpe, 1996), 65–85.

13. Barbara Sinclair, "Party Leaders and the New Legislative Process," in Dodd and Oppenheimer, 229–245.

14. George Hager, "End of Deficit Era Marks Beginning of Battle Over Surpluses," *Washington Post*, September 30, 1998, C10.

15. Catherine Rudder, "The Politics of Taxing and Spending in Congress: Ideas, Strategy, and Policy" in Lawrence Dodd and Bruce Oppenheimer, eds., *Congress Reconsidered*, 8th ed. (Washington, D.C.: CQ Press, 2005), 319–342.

16. CBS News, "2008 U.S. Budget Deficit Bleeding Red Ink; First 4 Months of Budget Year at Nearly $88B, Double Amount Recorded for Same 2007 Period," February 12, 2008, www.cbsnews.com/stories/2008/02/12/national/main3822385.shtml.

17. Tobin Harshaw, "Will TARP Turn to Gold?" *New York Times*, October 1, 2010.

18. Paul Krugman, "That 30's Show," *New York Times*, July 2, 2009, www.nytimes.com/2009/07/03/opinion/03krugman.html.

19. Lori Montgomery, "Report Gives Stimulus Package High Marks," *Washington Post*, October 1, 2010.

20. Ibid.

21. David Leonhart, "Imagining a Deficit Plan From Republicans," *New York Times*, September 28, 2010, www.nytimes

.com/2010/09/29/business/economy/ 291eonhardt.html?scp=1&sq=R Epublican%20pledge&st=cse.

22. Al Hunt, "Democrats Relish Battle Over High-Income Tax Cuts," Bloomberg News, August 1, 2010, www.bloomberg.com/ news/2010-08-01/democrats-relish-fight-over-big-income-tax-cuts-commentary-by-albert-hunt.html.

23. Pew Research Center for the People and the Press, "Deficit Concerns Rise, But Solutions Are Elusive," March 10, 2010, http://pewresearch.org/pubs/1519/ deficit-concerns-rise-little-support-for-spending-cuts.

24. Office of Management and Budget, *Budget of the United States Government, Fiscal Year 2010*, Historical Tables, Table 1.1, www .gpoaccess.gov/usbudget/fy10/hist.html.

25. U.S. Census Bureau, *Statistical Abstracts of the United States, 2010*, "Table No. 463: Federal Receipts by Sources: 1990 to 2009," www.census.gov/compendia/statab/2010/ tables/10s0463.pdf.

26. Laura Tyson, "Bush's Tax Cut: Nickels and Dimes for the Working Poor," *Business Week*, July 2, 2001, www.businessweek.com/ magazine/content/01_27/b3739133.htm.

27. U.S. Tax Code Online, www.fourmilab.ch/ ustax/ustax.html.

28. Connie Mack and John Breaux, "Tax Reform Panel Invites Testimony in Tampa," *Tampa Tribune*, March 8, 2005, 11.

29. Ibid.

30. FairTax.org, www.fairtax.org/site/Page Server.

31. Leo Linbeck, "FairTax Facts," *Wall Street Journal*, December 26, 2007, http://online .wsj.com/article/SB119863013677849835 .html.

32. David Leonhardt, "Can't Grasp Credit Crisis? Join the Club," *New York Times*, March 19, 2008, A1; Robert Gavin, "Frank Urges Overhaul of Business Regulations," *Boston Globe*, March 21, 2008, C3; Paul Davidson, "Mortgage Brokers Fall on Tough Times; Many Now Victims of a Crisis They May Have Played Role In," *USA Today*, August 31, 2007, 1B; Joe Nocera, "On Wall St., A Problem of Denial," *New York Times*, September 15, 2008, www.nytimes.com.

33. Michael Maynard, "Navigating Turbulent Skies," *New York Times*, October 10, 2004, sec. 5, 4; Matthew L. Wald, "Advances in Airplanes Are Mostly Invisible," *New York Times*, May 18, 2003, sec. 5, 3; Agis Salpukas, "Future of Airline Deregulation," *New York Times*, May 8, 1982, sec. 2, 29; Leslie Wayne, "The Airlines Stacked Up in Red Ink," *New York Times*, February 14, 1982, sec. 3, 1.

34. Link and Link.

35. Thomas Bailey and David M. Kennedy, *The American Pageant: A History of the Republic*, 6th ed. (Lexington, Mass.: D. C. Heath, 1979).

36. Karen W. Arenson, "AT&T Heads for the Unknown," *New York Times*, December 4, 1983, sec. 3, 1.

37. Amy Harmon, "Judge Backs Terms of U.S. Settlement in Microsoft Case," *New York Times*, November 2, 2002, A1.

38. Mark Cooper, "Vigorous Antitrust Enforcement the Key to Consumer Protection in the New Economy," January 15, 2001, www.consumerfed.org/pdfs/ microsoftoverview.pdf.

39. Elizabeth Corcoran, "Netscape Stock Plunges After Forecast of Losses," *Washington Post*, January, 6, 1998, D1.

40. Andrew Leonard, "The Dodd-Frank Bank Reform Bill: A Deeply Flawed Success," *Salon*, June 25, 2010, www.salon.com/ technology/how_the_world_works/2010/ 06/25/the_dodd_frank_bank_reform_bill.

41. Damian Paletta, "U.S. Lawmakers Reach Accord on New Finance Rules," *Wall Street Journal*, June 25, 2010, http://online.wsj .com/article/SB1000142405274870361510457 5328020013164184.html?mod=djemalert NEWS.

42. Link and Link.

43. Marick F. Masters, *Unions at the Crossroads: Strategic Membership, Financial, and Political Perspectives* (Westport, Conn.: Quorum Books, 1997).

44. David Firestone, "Lawmakers Move Toward Compromise Curbing Worker Rights in New Department," *New York Times*, November 12, 2002, A15.

45. Masters, 1.

46. Herbert B. Asher, Eric S. Heberlig, Randall B. Ripley, and Karen Snyder, *American Labor Unions in the Electoral Arena* (Lanham, Md.: Rowman & Littlefield, 2001).

47. George Strauss, Daniel G. Gallagher, and Jack Fiorito, *The State of the Unions* (Madison, Wis.: Industrial Relations Research Association, 1991), v.

48. Center for Responsive Politics, "PAC Contributions to Federal Candidates, 2003–2004," www.opensecrets.org/pacs/ sector.asp?txt=P01&cycle=2004.

49. Asher, Heberlig, Ripley, and Snyder.

50. Paula L. Green, "Buy American Message Sells in Slow Economy," *Journal of Commerce*, April 9, 1992, 1A.

51. Yoshikuni Sugiyama, "U.S. Congress Passes Car Content Bill," *Daily Yomiuri*, October 3, 1992, 17.

52. World Trade Organization, "Ten Benefits of the WTO Trading System," www.wto.org/english/thewto_e/ whatis_e/10ben_e/10b00_e.htm.

53. Irwin Unger, *These United States, Volume I: To 1877*, 5th ed. (Englewood Cliffs, N.J.: Prentice Hall, 1992), 172.

54. A. Ellen Terpstra, *Statement Before the Senate Foreign Relations Committee, Subcommittee on International Economic Policy, Export and Trade Promotion*, April 20, 2004, www.fas.usda.gov/info/speeches/ ct042004.htm.

55. Public Citizen, "The Ten Year Track Record of the North American Free Trade Agreement: U.S. Workers' Jobs, Wages, and Economic Security," www.citizen.org/ documents/NAFTA_10_jobs.pdf.

56. Congressional Budget Office, *A CBO Paper: The Effects of NAFTA on U.S.-Mexican Trade and GDP*, May 2003, www.cbo.gov/ ftpdocs/42xx/doc4247/Report.pdf.

Chapter 19

1. Caren Bohan, "Analysis: Obama, McCain Spar Over Talking to Enemies," May 20, 2008, www.reuters.com.

2. "CSI: Credit Crunch," *The Economist*, October 17, 2007, www.economist.com/ specialreports/displaystory.cfm?story_ id=9972489.

3. George W. Bush, "Address to a Joint Session of Congress and the American People," September 20, 2001, http:// georgewbush-whitehouse.archives.gov/ news/releases/2001/09/20010920-8.html.

4. Barack Obama, "Inaugural Address," www .whitehouse.gov/blog/inaugural-address/.

5. Gallup poll, July 8–11, 2010, www.gallup .com.

6. Chicago Council on Global Affairs, *Global Views 2008*, www.ccfr.org.

7. See John Lewis Gaddis, *Strategies of Containment* (New York: Oxford University Press, 1982).

8. John Lewis Gaddis, *The United States and the End of the Cold War* (New York: Oxford University Press, 1992); Richard Ned Lebow and Thomas Risse-Kappen, eds., *International Relations Theory and the End of the Cold War* (New York: Columbia University Press, 1995); Richard N. Haass, *The Reluctant Sheriff: The United States After the Cold War* (New York: Council on Foreign Relations, 1997).

9. See, for example, Haass.

10. Randall B. Ripley and Grace A. Franklin, *Congress, the Bureaucracy, and Public Policy*, 5th ed. (Belmont, Calif.: Wadsworth, 1991).

11. See Charles F. Hermann, *Crises in Foreign Policy* (Indianapolis, Ind.: Bobbs-Merrill, 1969); Michael Brecher, "A Theoretical Approach to International Crisis Behavior," *Jerusalem Journal of International Relations* 3 (2–3): 5–24.

12. See Graham Allison, *Essence of Decision* (New York: HarperCollins, 1971); Helen V. Milner, *Interest, Institutions, and Information: Domestic Politics and International Relations* (Princeton: Princeton University Press, 1997).

13. See X (George F. Kennan), "The Sources of Soviet Conduct," *Foreign Affairs*, July 25, 1947, 566–582.

14. See, for example, Michael H. Shuman, "Dateline Main Street: Local Foreign Policies," *Foreign Policy* 65 (winter 1986/87): 154–174.

15. Arthur M. Schlesinger Jr., *The Imperial Presidency* (Boston: Houghton Mifflin, 1973); Ralph G. Carter and James M. Scott, *Choosing to Lead: Understanding Congressional Foreign Policy Entrepreneurs* (Durham, NC: Duke University Press, 2009).

16. Edward Corwin, cited in Cecil Crabb and Pat Holt, *Invitation to Struggle: Congress, the President, and Foreign Policy,* 4th ed. (Washington, D.C.: Congressional Quarterly, 1992).

17. Louis Fisher, *Congressional Abdication on War and Spending* (College Station: Texas A&M Press, 2000); Gordon Silverstein, *Imbalance of Powers: Constitutional Interpretation and the Making of American Foreign Policy* (New York: Oxford University Press, 1997).

18. See, for example, Ole R. Holsti and James N. Rosenau, "The Political Foundations of Elites' Domestic and Foreign-Policy Beliefs," in Eugene R. Wittkopf and James M. McCormick, eds., *The Domestic Sources of American Foreign Policy: Insights and Evidence* (Lanham, Md.: Rowman & Littlefield, 1999).

19. Sidney Blumenthal, "The Return of the Repressed: Anti-Internationalism and the American Right," *World Policy Journal* 12 (fall 1995).

20. John Stoessinger, *Crusaders and Pragmatists*, 2nd ed. (New York: Norton, 1985).

21. See, for example, Gaddis Smith, *Morality, Reason, and Power: American Diplomacy in the Carter Years* (New York: Hill & Wang, 1986).

22. "National Security Strategy for a New Century," *Foreign Policy Bulletin* (July–August 1997): 27–64.

23. Jane Mayer, "Outsourcing Torture: the Secret History of America's 'Extraordinary Rendition' Program," *New Yorker*, February 14 & 21, 2005, 106–123.

24. Kenneth N. Waltz, *Man, the State, and War* (New York: Columbia University Press, 1959).

25. Hans J. Morgenthau, *Politics Among Nations*, 3rd ed. (New York: Knopf, 1963).

26. Robert O. Keohane and Joseph S. Nye, *Power and Interdependence*, 2nd ed. (Glenview, Ill.: Scott Foresman, 1989).

27. See Joan Edelman Spero and Jeffrey A. Hart, *The Politics of International Economic Relations*, 5th ed. (New York: St. Martin's, 1997).

28. Chicago Council on Global Affairs, *Global Views 2008*, www.ccfr.org.

29. Chicago Council on Global Affairs, *Global Views 2004*, www.ccfr.org.

30. McKinsey Global Institute, *Offshoring: Is It a Win-Win Game?* August 2003, www.crimsonventures.com/pdf/offshoring_win_win_game.pdf; see also Daniel W. Drezner, "The Outsourcing Bogeyman," *Foreign Affairs* (May/June 2004).

31. For a discussion of how presidents view the public, see Douglas C. Foyle, *Counting the Public In: Presidents, Public Opinion, and Foreign Policy* (New York: Columbia University Press, 1999); see also Paul Brace and Barbara Hinckley, *Follow the Leader: Opinion Polls and the Modern Presidents* (New York: Basic Books, 1992).

32. Eugene Wittkopf, Charles W. Kegley Jr., and James M. Scott, *American Foreign Policy,* 6th ed. (Belmont, Calif.: Wadsworth, 2003): 273–274.

33. Robert D. Putnam, "Diplomacy and Domestic Politics: The Logic of Two-Level Games," *International Organization* 42 (summer 1988): 427–460.

34. Garrick Utley, "The Shrinking of Foreign News," *Foreign Affairs* (March–April 1997): 2–10.

35. Warren Strobel, *Late-Breaking Foreign Policy: The News Media's Influence on Peace Operations* (Washington, D.C.: U.S. Institute of Peace Press, 1997).

36. Maryann K. Cusimano, *Operation Restore Hope: The Bush Administration's Decision to Intervene in Somalia* (Washington, D.C.: Institute for the Study of Diplomacy, 1995).

37. Strobel.

38. See Patrick J. Haney and Walt Vanderbush, *The Cuban Embargo: The Domestic Politics of an American Foreign Policy* (Pittsburgh: University of Pittsburgh Press, 2005); Paul Glastris, "Multicultural Foreign Policy in Washington," *U.S. News and World Report*, July 21, 1997, 30–35; Yossi Shain, "Multicultural Foreign Policy," *Foreign Policy* (fall 1995): 69–87; and *Marketing the American Creed Abroad: Diasporas in the U.S. and Their Homelands* (New York: Cambridge University Press, 1999).

39. Donald M. Snow, *United States Foreign Policy: Politics Beyond the Water's Edge* (Belmont, Calif.: Wadsworth, 2004).

40. Some U.S. foreign policies, such as sailing naval vessels into ports of foreign countries, are symbolic and are designed to show other countries that we have the capability to influence world affairs or to demonstrate an American commitment to particular countries or policies. Keeping U.S. ships in the Persian Gulf is thus a reminder to allies and potential enemies in the region that the United States intends to play a role in that part of the world.

41. Two general treatments of the concept are Patrick Morgan, *Deterrence*, 2nd ed. (Beverly Hills, Calif.: Sage, 1983); and John Mearsheimer, *Conventional Deterrence* (Ithaca, N.Y.: Cornell University Press, 1993). See also David Baldwin, *Economic Statecraft* (Princeton: Princeton University Press, 1985).

42. Stephen I. Schwartz, *Atomic Audit: The Costs and Consequences of U.S. Nuclear Weapons Since 1940* (Washington, D.C.: Brookings Institution, 1998).

43. See Thomas Shelling, *Arms and Influence* (New Haven: Yale University Press, 1966) and *Strategy of Conflict* (Cambridge: Harvard University Press, 1980).

44. Alexander George, *Forceful Persuasion: Coercive Diplomacy as an Alternative to War* (Washington, D.C.: U.S. Institute of Peace, 1991).

45. Gordon Craig and Alexander George, *Force and Statecraft,* 3rd ed. (New York: Oxford University Press, 1995).

46. Originally, propaganda efforts were housed in the State Department. However, President Eisenhower, with the establishment of the USIA, moved control over propaganda into a separate institution. In 1999 the USIA was moved back into the State Department. For a discussion of the creation of the USIA, see Shawn Parry-Giles, "The Eisenhower Administration's Conceptualization of the USIA: The Development of Overt and Covert Propaganda Strategies," *Presidential Studies Quarterly* (spring 1994): 263–276.

47. For a general treatment of diplomacy, see David Newsom, *Diplomacy and the American Democracy* (Bloomington: Indiana University Press, 1988).

48. "The President's Speech in Cairo: A New Beginning," White House blog, www.whitehouse.gov/blog/NewBeginning/.

49. See Harry Ransom, "Covert Intervention," in Peter J. Schraeder, ed., *Intervention Into the 1990s: U.S. Foreign Policy in the Third World*, 2nd ed. (Boulder: Lynne Rienner, 1992), 113–129; and Gregory Treverton, *Covert Action* (New York: Basic Books, 1987).

50. David H. Lumsdaine, *Moral Vision in International Politics: The Foreign Aid Regime, 1949–1989* (Princeton: Princeton University Press, 1993).

51. Steven Krull, "Americans and Foreign Aid, 1995," in David Skidmore and Thomas Larson, eds., *International Political Economy: The Struggle for Power and Wealth*, 2nd ed. (New York: Harcourt Brace, 1997), 275.

52. Associated Press, "Businesses Say Foreign Aid Helps U.S. Economy," June 25, 1996.

53. Kimberly Elliot, "Economic Sanctions," in Schraeder, 97–112. See also Carroll Doherty, "Proliferation of Sanctions Creates a Tangle of Good Intentions," *Congressional Quarterly Weekly Report*, September 13, 1997, 2113–2120; Jesse Helms, "What Sanctions Epidemic?" *Foreign Affairs* (January–February 1999): 2–8.

54. "The Many-Handed Mr. Eizenstat," *The Economist*, January 24, 1998, 30.

55. Michael P. Malloy, *Study of New U.S. Unilateral Sanctions: 1997–2006*, USA* Engage, 2006.

56. See World Military Spending, http://www .globalissues.org/article/75/world-military-spending#InContextUSMilitarySpending VersusRestoftheWorld.

57. Charles W. Kegley Jr., ed., *The Long Postwar Peace* (New York: HarperCollins, 1991).

58. See Alexander L. George, *Forceful Persuasion* (Washington, D.C.: U.S. Institute of Peace Press, 1991); Barry Blechman and Stephen Kaplan, *Force Without War* (Washington, D.C.: Brookings Institution, 1978); and Robert J. Art and Patrick M. Cronin, *The United States and Coercive Diplomacy* (Washington, D.C.: U.S. Institute of Peace Press, 2003).

59. Ehud Sprinzak, "The Great Superterrorism Scare," *Foreign Policy* (fall 1998).

60. Michael Klare, *Rogue States and Nuclear Outlaws: America's Search for a New Foreign Policy* (New York: Hill & Wang, 1995); Michael Mandelbaum, "Lessons of the Next Nuclear War," *Foreign Affairs*

(March–April 1995): 22–37; Richard K. Betts, "The New Threat of Mass Destruction," *Foreign Affairs* (January–February 1998): 26–41.

61. Peter Bergen and Katherine Tiedemann, "The Year of the Drone: An Analysis of U.S. Drone Strikes in Pakistan, 2004–2010," April 26, 2010, www.foreignpolicy.com/ articles/2010/04/26/the_year_of_the_ drone.

62. Peter Grier, "Times Square Bomber Joins the Growing List of Inept Terrorists." *Christian Science Monitor*, May 4, 2010, www.csmonitor.com/USA/2010/0504/ Times-Square-bomber-joins-the-growing-list-of-inept-terrorists.

63. David S. Yost, *NATO Transformed* (Washington, D.C.: U.S. Institute of Peace Press, 1998).

64. For an overview, see Donald M. Snow, *National Security for a New Era: Globalization and Geopolitics* (New York: Longman, 2004).

65. Donald C. F. Daniel and Bradd C. Hayes, with Chantal de Jonge Oudraat, *Coercive Inducement and the Containment of International Crises* (Washington, D.C.: U.S. Institute of Peace Press, 1996).

66. See William A. Orme Jr., *Understanding NAFTA* (Austin: University of Texas Press, 1996); and Richard S. Belous and Jonathan Lemco, eds., *NAFTA as a Model of Development* (Albany: State University of New York Press, 1995); for a different viewpoint, see Ralph Nader et al., *The Case Against Free Trade: GATT, NAFTA, and the Globalization of Corporate Power* (San Francisco: Earth Island Press, 1993).

67. See Jessica Tuchman Mathews, "Redefining Security," *Foreign Affairs* (spring 1989); Stephen Hopgood, *American Foreign Environmental Policy and the Power of the State* (New York: Oxford University Press, 1998).

68. See, for example, the Freedom House web site for more information and data, www .freedomhouse.org; and Bruce Russett, *Controlling the Sword* (Cambridge: Harvard University Press, 1990).

69. Freedom House, "Freedom in the World 2010," www.freedomhouse.org/template .cfm?page=363&year=2010.

70. See Morton H. Halperin, "Guaranteeing Democracy," *Foreign Policy* (summer 1993): 105–123.

71. Michael Posner, "Rally Round Human Rights," *Foreign Policy* (winter 1994–1995): 133–139.

72. John E. Reilly, "Americans and the World: A Survey at Century's End," *Foreign Policy* 114 (spring 1999): 97–114.

73. For an example of how what happened in a crisis often is more complicated than it at first appears, see Seymour M. Hersh, "The Missiles of August," *New Yorker*, October 12, 1998, 34–41.

74. See, for example, Melvin A. Goodman, "Ending the CIA's Cold War Legacy," *Foreign Policy* 106 (spring 1997); and Roger Hilsman, "Does the CIA Still Have a Role?" *Foreign Affairs* (September–October 1995).

75. Daniel Patrick Moynihan, *Secrecy: The American Experience* (New Haven: Yale University Press, 1998).

76. "WikiLeaks Archive: A Selection From the Cache of Diplomatic Dispatches," retrieved from www.nytimes.com/interactive/2010/ 11/28/world/20101128-cables-viewer.html.

77. See, for example, Fred Kaplan, *Daydream Believers: How a Few Grand Ideas Wrecked American Power* (New York: Wiley, 2008).

78. See, for example, "Q&A: John Bolton," *National Journal*, May 23, 2008, www .nationaljournal.com/njonline/no+2008 0523-5434.php.

79. See, for example, Pew Research Center, "Pew Global Attitudes Project," http:// pewglobal.org/.

Glossary

accommodationists supporters of government nonpreferential accommodation of religion (5)

accountability the principle that bureaucratic employees should be answerable for their performance to supervisors, all the way up the chain of command (9)

administrative law law established by the bureaucracy, on behalf of Congress (10)

advanced industrial democracy a system in which a democratic government allows citizens a considerable amount of personal freedom and maintains a free-market (though still usually regulated) economy (1)

adversarial system trial procedures designed to resolve conflict through the clash of opposing sides, moderated by a neutral, passive judge who applies the law (10)

affirmative action a policy of creating opportunities for members of certain groups as a substantive remedy for past discrimination (6)

agency capture process whereby regulatory agencies come to be protective of and influenced by the industries they were established to regulate (9)

allocative representation congressional work to secure projects, services, and funds for the represented district (7)

amendability the provision for the Constitution to be changed, so as to adapt to new circumstances (4)

amicus curiae briefs "friend of the court" documents filed by interested parties to encourage the court to grant or deny certiorari or to urge it to decide a case in a particular way (10)

analysis understanding how something works by breaking it down into its component parts (1)

anarchy the absence of government and laws (1)

Anti-Federalists advocates of states' rights who opposed the Constitution (3)

antiterrorism measures to protect and defend U.S. citizens and interests from terrorist attacks (19)

antitrust policies government regulations that try to keep monopolies from emerging (18)

appeal a rehearing of a case because the losing party in the original trial argues that a point of law was not applied properly (10)

appellate jurisdiction the authority of a court to review decisions made by lower courts (10)

Articles of Confederation the first constitution of the United States (1777) creating an association of states with weak central government (3)

astroturf lobbying indirect lobbying efforts that manipulate or create public sentiment, "astroturf" being artificial grassroots (13)

asylum protection or sanctuary, especially from political persecution (2)

authoritarian capitalism a system in which the state allows people economic freedom but maintains stringent social regulations to limit noneconomic behavior (1)

authoritarian governments systems in which the state holds all power over the social order (1)

authority power that is recognized as legitimate (1)

bad tendency test rule used by the courts that allows speech to be punished if it leads to punishable actions (5)

balanced budget a budget in which expenditures equal revenues (18)

benchmark poll initial poll on a candidate and issues on which campaign strategy is based and against which later polls are compared (11)

bicameral legislature legislature with two chambers (4, 7)

Bill of Rights a summary of citizen rights guaranteed and protected by a government; added to the Constitution as its first ten amendments in order to achieve ratification (3)

bills of attainder laws under which specific persons or groups are detained and sentenced without trial (5)

black codes a series of laws in the post–Civil War South designed to restrict the rights of former slaves before the passage of the Fourteenth and Fifteenth Amendments (6)

block grant federal funds provided for a broad purpose, unrestricted by detailed requirements and regulations (4, 16)

blogs web logs, or online journals, that can cover any topic, including political analysis (15)

boycott refusal to buy certain goods or services as a way to protest policy or force political reform (6)

Brown v. Board of Education of Topeka Supreme Court case that rejected the idea that separate could be equal in education; catalyst for civil rights movement (6)

bureaucracy an organization characterized by hierarchical structure, worker specialization, explicit rules, and advancement by merit (9)

bureaucratese the often unintelligible language used by bureaucrats to avoid controversy and lend weight to their words (9)

bureaucratic culture the accepted values and procedures of an organization (9)

bureaucratic discretion bureaucrats' use of their own judgment in interpreting and carrying out the laws of Congress (9)

Bush Doctrine policy that supports preemptive attacks as a legitimate tactic in the U.S. war on state-sponsored terrorism (19)

business cycle the peaks and valleys of the economy between boom and bust (18)

busing achieving racial balance by transporting students to schools across neighborhood boundaries (6)

cabinet a presidential advisory group selected by the president, made up of the vice president, the heads of the federal executive departments, and other high officials to whom the president elects to give cabinet status (8)

capital gains tax a tax levied on the returns that people earn from capital investments, like the profits from the sale of stocks or a home (18)

capitalist economy an economic system in which the market determines production, distribution, and price decisions, and property is privately owned (1)

casework legislative work on behalf of individual constituents to solve their problems with government agencies and programs (7)

categorical grant federal funds provided for a specific purpose, restricted by detailed instructions, regulations, and compliance standards (4, 16)

Central Intelligence Agency (CIA) the government organization that oversees foreign intelligence-gathering and related classified activities (19)

checks and balances the principle that allows each branch of government to exercise some form of control over the others (4)

chief administrator the president's executive role as the head of federal agencies and the person responsible for the implementation of national policy (8)

chief foreign policy maker the president's executive role as the primary shaper of relations with other nations (8)

chief of staff the person who oversees the operations of all White House staff and controls access to the president (8)

citizen advisory council a citizen group that considers the policy decisions of an agency; a way to make the bureaucracy responsive to the general public (9)

citizen legislators part-time state legislators, who also hold other jobs in their community while serving in the statehouse (16)

citizens members of a political community having both rights and responsibilities (1)

civic journalism a movement among journalists to be responsive to citizen input in determining what news stories to cover (15)

civil laws laws regulating interactions between individuals; violation of a civil law is called a tort (10)

civil law tradition a legal system based on a detailed comprehensive legal code, usually created by the legislature (10)

civil liberties individual freedoms guaranteed to the people primarily by the Bill of Rights (5)

civil rights citizenship rights guaranteed to the people (primarily in the Thirteenth, Fourteenth, Fifteenth, Nineteenth, and Twenty-sixth Amendments) and protected by the government (5, 6)

civil service nonmilitary employees of the government who are appointed through the merit system (9)

Clean Air Act legislation that set emission standards for companies (17)

clear and present danger test rule used by the courts that allows language to be regulated only if it presents an immediate and urgent danger (5)

clientele groups groups of citizens whose interests are affected by an agency or department and who work to influence its policies (9)

closed primaries primary elections in which only registered party members may vote (12, 14)

cloture a vote to end a Senate filibuster; requires a three-fifths majority, or sixty votes (7)

coattail effect the added votes received by congressional candidates of a winning presidential party (7)

coercive diplomacy the calibrated use of threats of the use of force aimed to make another actor stop or undo an aggressive action (19)

Cold War the half-century of competition and conflict after World War II between the United States and the Soviet Union (and their allies) (19)

collective bargaining the ability of unions to determine wages, hours, and working conditions in conjunction with the employer (18)

collective good a good or service that, by its very nature, cannot be denied to anyone who wants to consume it (13)

commander-in-chief the president's role as the top officer of the country's military establishment (8)

commercial bias the tendency of the media to make coverage and programming decisions based on what will attract a large audience and maximize profits (15)

commission the basic component of the county form of government; combines executive and legislative functions over a narrow area of responsibility (16)

common law tradition a legal system based on the accumulated rulings of judges over time, applied uniformly—judge-made law (10)

Common Sense 1776 pamphlet by Thomas Paine that persuaded many Americans to support the Revolutionary cause (3)

communist democracy a utopian system in which property is communally owned and all decisions are made democratically (1)

communitarians those who favor a strong, substantive government role in the economy and the social order in order to realize their vision of a community of equals (2)

compellence using foreign policy strategies to persuade, or force, an actor to take a certain action (19)

compelling state interest a fundamental state purpose, which must be shown before the law can limit some freedoms or treat some groups of people differently (5)

concurrent powers powers that are shared by both the federal and state governments (4)

concurring opinions documents written by justices expressing agreement with the majority ruling but describing different or additional reasons for the ruling (10)

confederal systems governments in which local units hold all the power (4)

confederation a government in which independent states unite for common purpose but retain their own sovereignty (3)

conference committees temporary committees formed to reconcile differences in House and Senate versions of a bill (7)

congressional oversight a committee's investigation of the executive and of government agencies to ensure they are acting as Congress intends (7); efforts by Congress, especially through committees, to monitor agency rule making, enforcement, and implementation of congressional policies (9)

conservatives people who generally favor limited government and are cautious about change (2)

constituency the voters in a state or district (7)

constitution the rules that establish a government (3)

Constitutional Convention the assembly of fifty-five delegates in the summer of 1787 to recast the Articles of Confederation; the result was the U.S. Constitution (3)

constitutional law law stated in the Constitution or in the body of judicial decisions about the meaning of the Constitution handed down in the courts (10)

consumption tax a plan in which people are taxed not on what they earn but on what they spend (18)

containment the U.S. Cold War policy of preventing the spread of communism (19)

cooperative federalism the federal system under which the national and state governments share responsibilities for most domestic policy areas (4, 16)

cost-benefit analysis an evaluation method in which the costs of the program are compared to the benefits of the policy (17)

council-manager government form of local government in which a professional city or town manager is appointed by elected councilors (16)

Council of Economic Advisers organization within the EOP that advises the president on economic matters (8)

counterterrorism activities to stop terrorists from using force and responding when they do (19)

courts institutions that sit as neutral third parties to resolve conflicts according to the law (10)

covert operations undercover actions in which the prime mover country appears to have had no role (19)

criminal laws laws prohibiting behavior the government has determined to be harmful to society; violation of a criminal law is called a crime (10)

crisis policy foreign policy, usually made quickly and secretly, that responds to an emergency threat (19)

critical election an election signaling a significant change in popular allegiance from one party to another (12)

critical thinking analysis and evaluation of ideas and arguments based on reason and evidence (1)

cycle effect the predictable rise and fall of a president's popularity at different stages of a term in office (8)

dealignment a trend among voters to identify themselves as independents rather than as members of a major party (12)

Declaration of Independence the political document that dissolved the colonial ties between the United States and Britain (3)

de facto discrimination discrimination that is the result not of law but rather of tradition and habit (6)

deficits shortfalls in the budget due to the government spending more in a year than it takes in (18)

de jure discrimination discrimination arising from or supported by the law (6)

democracy government that vests power in the people (1)

department one of the major subdivisions of the federal government, represented in the president's cabinet (9)

Department of Defense the executive department charged with managing the country's military personnel, equipment, and operations (19)

Department of Homeland Security the executive department meant to provide a unifying force in the efforts of the government to prevent attacks on the United States and to respond to such attacks through law enforcement and emergency relief should they occur (19)

Department of State the executive department charged with managing foreign affairs (19)

depression a sharp reduction in a nation's GDP for more than a year accompanied by high unemployment (18)

deregulation the elimination of regulations in order to improve economic efficiency (18)

descriptive representation the idea that an elected body should mirror demographically the population it represents (7)

deterrence maintaining military might so as to discourage another actor from taking a certain action (19)

devolution the transfer of powers and responsibilities from the federal government to the states (4, 16)

diplomacy the formal system of communication and negotiation between countries (19)

direct lobbying direct interaction with public officials for the purpose of influencing policy decisions (13)

director of national intelligence overseer and coordinator of the activities of the many agencies involved in the production and dissemination of intelligence information in the U.S. government, as well as the president's main intelligence adviser (19)

dissenting opinions documents written by justices expressing disagreement with the majority ruling (10)

distributive policies policies funded by the whole taxpayer base that address the needs of particular groups (17)

divided government political rule split between two parties: one controlling the White House and the other controlling one or both houses of Congress (8)

divine right of kings the principle that earthly rulers receive their authority from God (1)

dual federalism the federal system under which the national and state governments are responsible for separate policy areas (4, 16)

due process of law guarantee that laws will be fair and reasonable and that citizens suspected of breaking the law will be treated fairly (5)

economic boom a period of fast economic growth in GDP, signaling prosperity (18)

economic bust a period of steep decline in GDP, signaling recession (18)

economic conservatives those who favor a strictly procedural government role in the economy and the social order (2)

economic interest groups groups that organize to influence government policy for the economic benefit of their members (13)

economic liberals those who favor an expanded government role in the economy but a limited role in the social order (2)

economic policy all the different strategies that government officials employ to solve economic problems (18)

economics production and distribution of a society's material resources and services (1)

economic sanctions restrictions on trade imposed on one country by another state or group of states, usually as a form of punishment or protest (19)

electioneering the process of getting a person elected to public office (12)

Electoral College an intermediary body that elects the president (4)

electoral mandate the perception that an election victory signals broad support for the winner's proposed policies (14)

elite democracy a theory of democracy that limits the citizens' role to choosing among competing leaders (1)

embargo the refusal by one country to trade with another in order to force changes in its behavior or to weaken it (19)

English-only movements efforts to make English the official language of the United States (6)

Enlightenment a philosophical movement (1600s–1700s) that emphasized human reason, scientific examination, and industrial progress (1)

entitlement program a federal program that guarantees benefits to qualified recipients (17)

enumerated powers of Congress congressional powers specifically named in the Constitution (Article I, Section 8) (4)

environmental policy distributive, redistributive, and regulatory policy that seeks to improve the quality of the physical world in which we live (17)

equal opportunity interest groups groups that organize to promote the civil and economic rights of underrepresented or disadvantaged groups (13)

Equal Rights Amendment constitutional amendment passed by Congress but never ratified that would have banned discrimination on the basis of gender (6)

establishment clause the First Amendment guarantee that the government will not create and support an official state church (5)

evaluation assessing how well something works or performs according to a particular standard or yardstick (1)

excise taxes consumer taxes levied on specific merchandise, such as cigarettes or alcohol (18)

exclusionary rule rule created by the Supreme Court that evidence illegally seized may not be used to obtain a conviction (5)

executive the branch of government responsible for putting laws into effect (4)

executive agreements presidential arrangements with another country that create foreign policy without the need for Senate approval (8)

Executive Office of the President collection of nine organizations that help the president with policy and political objectives (8)

executive orders clarifications of congressional policy issued by the president and having the full force of law (8, 10)

exit polls election-related questions asked of voters right after they vote (11)

ex post facto laws laws that criminalize an action after it occurs (5)

expressive benefits selective incentives that derive from the opportunity to express values and beliefs and to be committed to a greater cause (13)

factions groups of citizens united by some common passion or interest and opposed to the rights of other citizens or to the interests of the whole community (3, 13)

federalism a political system in which power is divided between the central and regional units (3)

The Federalist Papers a series of essays written in support of the Constitution to build support for its ratification (3)

Federalists supporters of the Constitution who favored a strong central government (3)

Federal Register publication containing all federal regulations and notifications of regulatory agency hearings (9)

Federal Reserve System independent commission that controls the money supply through a system of twelve federal banks (18)

feeding frenzy excessive press coverage of an embarrassing or scandalous subject (15)

feudalism a social system based on a rigid social and political hierarchy based on the ownership of land (3)

fighting words speech intended to incite violence (5)

filibuster a practice of unlimited debate in the Senate in order to prevent or delay a vote on a bill (7)

fiscal policy economic policy in which government regulates the economy through its powers to tax and spend (18)

527 groups groups that mobilize voters with issue advocacy advertisements on television and radio but may not directly advocate the election or defeat of a particular candidate (13)

flat tax a tax system in which all people pay the same percentage of their income (18)

foreign aid assistance given by one country to another in the form of grants or loans (19)

foreign policy a country's official positions, practices, and procedures for dealing with actors outside its borders (19)

framing process through which the media emphasize particular aspects of a news story, thereby influencing the public's perception of the story (15)

franking the privilege of free mail service provided to members of Congress (7)

freedom of assembly the right of the people to gather peacefully and to petition government (5)

Freedom of Information Act (FOIA) 1966 law that allows citizens to obtain copies of most public records (9)

free exercise clause the First Amendment guarantee that citizens may freely engage in the religious activities of their choice (5)

free rider problem the difficulty groups face in recruiting when potential members can gain the benefits of the group's actions whether they join or not (13)

free trade economic system by which countries exchange goods without imposing excessive tariffs and taxes (19)

free trade policies policies that encourage open borders between trading partners by eliminating protectionist policies (18)

French and Indian War a war fought between France and England, and allied Indians, from 1754 to 1763; resulted in France's expulsion from the New World (3)

front-loading the process of scheduling presidential primaries early in the primary season (14)

front-runner the leading candidate and expected winner of a nomination or an election (14)

fusion of powers an alternative to separation of powers, combining or blending branches of government (4)

gatekeepers journalists and media elite who determine which news stories are covered and which are not (15)

gender gap the tendency of men and women to differ in their political views on some issues (11)

General Agreement on Tariffs and Trade (GATT) a series of agreements on international trading terms; now known as the World Trade Organization (WTO) (19)

gerrymandering redistricting to benefit a particular group (7)

get-out-the-vote (GOTV) drives efforts by political parties, interest groups, and the candidate's staff to maximize voter turnout among supporters (14)

Gibbons v. Ogden Supreme Court ruling (1824) establishing national authority over interstate business (4)

going public a president's strategy of appealing to the public on an issue, expecting that public pressure will be brought to bear on other political actors (8)

governing activities directed toward controlling the distribution of political resources by providing executive and legislative leadership, enacting agendas, mobilizing support, and building coalitions (12)

government a system or organization for exercising authority over a body of people (1)

government corporations companies created by Congress to provide to the public a good or service that private enterprise cannot or will not profitably provide (9)

government matching funds money given by the federal government to qualified presidential candidates in the primary and general election campaigns (14)

grandfather clauses provisions exempting from voting restrictions the descendants of those able to vote in 1867 (6)

grassroots lobbying indirect lobbying efforts that spring from widespread public concern (13)

Great Compromise the constitutional solution to congressional representation: equal votes in the Senate, votes by population in the House (3)

gross domestic product (GDP) total market value of all goods and services produced by everyone in a particular country during a given year (18)

habeas corpus the right of an accused person to be brought before a judge and informed of the charges and evidence against him or her (5)

hard money campaign funds donated directly to candidates; amounts are limited by federal election laws (14)

Hatch Act 1939 law limiting the political involvement of civil servants in order to protect them from political pressure and keep politics out of the bureaucracy (9)

head of government the political role of the president as leader of a political party and chief arbiter of who gets what resources (8)

head of state the apolitical, unifying role of the president as symbolic representative of the whole country (8)

hegemon the dominant actor in world politics (19)

honeymoon period the time following an election when a president's popularity is high and congressional relations are likely to be productive (8)

horse-race journalism the media's focus on the competitive aspects of politics rather than on actual policy proposals and political decisions (15)

House Rules Committee the committee that determines how and when debate on a bill will take place (7)

ideologies sets of beliefs about politics and society that help people make sense of their world (2)

immigrants citizens or subjects of one country who move to another country to live or work (2)

imminent lawless action test rule used by the courts that restricts speech only if it is aimed at producing or is likely to produce imminent lawless action (5)

incorporation Supreme Court action making the protections of the Bill of Rights applicable to the states (5)

incumbency advantage the electoral edge afforded to those already in office (7)

independent agencies government organizations independent of the departments but with a narrower policy focus (9)

independent regulatory boards and commissions government organizations that regulate various businesses, industries, or economic sectors (9)

indirect lobbying attempts to influence government policymakers by encouraging the general public to put pressure on them (13)

individualism belief that what is good for society is based on what is good for individuals (2)

individualistic political culture a political culture that distrusts government, expects corruption, downplays citizen participation, and stresses individual economic prosperity; mid-Atlantic region, lower Midwest, West Coast (16)

inflation an increase in the price of goods (18)

inherent powers presidential powers implied but not explicitly stated in the Constitution (8)

initiative citizen petitions to place a proposal or constitutional amendment on the ballot, to be adopted or rejected by majority vote, bypassing the legislature (4, 16)

inquisitorial systems trial procedures designed to determine the truth through the intervention of an active judge who seeks evidence and questions witnesses (10)

institutions organizations in which governmental power is exercised (1)

intelligence community the agencies and bureaus responsible for obtaining and interpreting information for the government (19)

interest group an organization of individuals who share a common political goal and unite for the purpose of influencing government decisions (13)

interest group entrepreneurs effective group leaders who are likely to have organized the group and can effectively promote its interests among members and the public (13)

interest rates the cost of borrowing money calculated as a percentage of the money borrowed (18)

intergovernmental organizations bodies, such as the United Nations, whose members are countries (19)

intermediate standard of review standard of review used by the Court to evaluate laws that make a quasisuspect classification (6)

internationalism a foreign policy based on taking an active role in global affairs; the predominant foreign policy view in the United States today (19)

International Monetary Fund (IMF) economic institution that makes short-term, relatively small loans to countries to help balance their currency flows (19)

interstate compacts agreements between two or more states, frequently formed to manage a common resource (16)

invisible primary early attempts to raise money, line up campaign consultants, generate media attention, and get commitments for support even before candidates announce they are running (14)

iron triangles the phenomenon of a clientele group, congressional committee, and bureaucratic agency cooperating to make mutually beneficial policy (9)

isolationism a foreign policy view that nations should stay out of international political alliances and activities, and focus on domestic matters (19)

issue advocacy ads advertisements that support issues or candidates without telling constituents how to vote (13, 14)

issue networks complex systems of relationships between groups that influence policy, including elected leaders, interest groups, specialists, consultants, and research institutes (9)

issue ownership the tendency of one party to be seen as more competent in a specific policy area (14)

Jim Crow laws southern laws designed to circumvent the Thirteenth, Fourteenth, and Fifteenth Amendments and to deny blacks rights on bases other than race (6)

Joint Chiefs of Staff the senior military officers from four branches of the U.S. armed forces (19)

joint committees combined House-Senate committees formed to coordinate activities and expedite legislation in a certain area (7)

judicial activism view that the courts should be lawmaking, policy-making bodies (10)

judicial interpretivism a judicial approach holding that the Constitution is a living document and that judges should interpret it according to changing times and values (10)

judicial power the power to interpret laws and judge whether a law has been broken (4)

judicial restraint view that the courts should reject any active lawmaking functions and stick to judicial interpretations of the past (10)

judicial review power of the Supreme Court to rule on the constitutionality of laws (4, 10)

jurisdiction a court's authority to hear certain cases (10)

Keynesianism an economic theory that government could stimulate a lagging economy by putting more money into it or cool off an inflationary economy by taking money out (18)

laissez-faire capitalism an economic system in which the market makes all decisions and the government plays no role (1)

laws of supply and demand basic principles that regulate the economic market and influence the price of a good (18)

leaks confidential information secretly revealed to the press (15)

legislative agenda the slate of proposals and issues that representatives think it worthwhile to consider and act on (7)

legislative liaison executive personnel who work with members of Congress to secure their support in getting a president's legislation passed (8)

legislative supremacy an alternative to judicial review, the acceptance of legislative acts as the final law of the land (4)

legislature the body of government that makes laws (4)

legitimate accepted as "right" or proper (1)

Lemon test three-pronged rule used by the courts to determine whether the establishment clause is violated (5)

libel written defamation of character (5)

liberals people who generally favor government action and view change as progress (2)

libertarians those who favor a minimal government role in any sphere (2)

literacy tests tests requiring reading or comprehension skills as a qualification for voting (6)

lobbying interest group activities aimed at persuading policymakers to support the group's positions (13)

majority party the party with the most seats in a house of Congress (7)

Marbury v. Madison the landmark case that established the U.S. Supreme Court's power of judicial review (10)

marriage gap the tendency for married people to hold political opinions that differ from those of people who have never married (11)

Marshall Plan America's massive economic recovery program for Western Europe following World War II (19)

mass media means of conveying information to large public audiences cheaply and efficiently (15)

material benefits selective incentives in the form of tangible rewards (13)

mayoral government form of local government in which a mayor is elected in a partisan election (16)

McCulloch v. Maryland Supreme Court ruling (1819) confirming the supremacy of national over state government (4)

means-tested programs social programs whose beneficiaries qualify by demonstrating need (17)

Medicaid a federally sponsored program that provides medical care to the poor (17)

Medicare the federal government's health insurance program for the elderly and disabled (17)

merit system of judicial selection the attempt to remove politics—either through elections or appointments— from the process of selecting judges (16)

metropolitan-wide government a single government that controls and administers public policy in a central city and its surrounding suburbs (16)

midterm loss the tendency for the presidential party to lose congressional seats in off-year elections (7)

Miller test rule used by the courts in which the definition of obscenity must be based on local standards (5)

minimum rationality test standard of review used by the Court to evaluate laws that make a nonsuspect classification (6)

momentum the widely held public perception that a candidate is gaining electoral strength (14)

monetary policy economic policy in which government regulates the economy by manipulating interest rates to control the money supply (18)

monopoly a situation in which a single producer dominates a market and there is no competition (18)

moralistic political culture a political culture that expects government to promote the public interest and the common good, sees government growth as positive, and encourages citizen participation; New England, upper Midwest, and Pacific Northwest (16)

most favored nation the status afforded to WTO trading partners; a country gives the same "deal" to member nations that it offers to its "most favored" friend (19)

Motor Voter Bill legislation allowing citizens to register to vote at the same time they apply for a driver's license or other state benefit (14)

muckrakers investigative reporters who search for and expose misconduct in corporate activity or public officials (15)

multinational corporations large companies that do business in multiple countries (19)

narrowcasting the targeting of specialized audiences by the media (15)

National Association for the Advancement of Colored People (NAACP) an interest group founded in 1910 to promote civil rights for African Americans (6)

national debt the total of the nation's unpaid deficits, or simply the sum total of what the national government owes (18)

national lawmaking the creation of policy to address the problems and needs of the entire nation (7)

National Security Council (NSC) organization within the executive office of the president that provides foreign policy advice to the president (8, 19)

naturalization the legal process of acquiring citizenship for someone who has not acquired it by birth (2)

necessary and proper clause constitutional authorization for Congress to make any law required to carry out its powers (4)

negative advertising campaign advertising that emphasizes the negative characteristics of opponents rather than one's own strengths (14)

neutral competence the principle that bureaucracy should be depoliticized by making it more professional (9)

New Jersey Plan a proposal at the Constitutional Convention that congressional representation be equal, thus favoring the small states (3)

new media high-tech outlets that have sprung up to compete with traditional newspapers, magazines, and network news (15)

news management the efforts of a politician's staff to control news about the politician (15)

nominating convention formal party gathering to choose candidates (12)

nongovernmental organizations organizations comprising individuals or interest groups from around the world focused on a special issue (19)

normative describes beliefs or values about how things should be or what people ought to do rather than what actually is (2)

norms informal rules that govern behavior in Congress (7)

North American Free Trade Agreement (NAFTA) trade agreement that removed most of the barriers to trade and investment that existed among the United States, Mexico, and Canada (18)

North Atlantic Treaty Organization (NATO) multinational organization formed in 1949 to promote the Cold War defense of Europe from the communist bloc (19)

nuclear triad the military strategy of having a three-pronged nuclear capability, from land, sea, or air (19)

nullification declaration by a state that a federal law is void within its borders (4)

Office of Management and Budget organization within the EOP that oversees the budgets of departments and agencies (8)

on-line processing the ability to receive and evaluate information as events happen, allowing us to remember our evaluation even if we have forgotten the specific events that caused it (11)

open primaries primary elections in which eligible voters do not need to be registered party members (12, 14)

opinion the written decision of the court that states the judgment of the majority (10)

opinion leaders people who know more about certain topics than we do and whose advice we trust, seek out, and follow (11)

oppo research investigation of an opponent's background for the purpose of exploiting weaknesses or undermining credibility (14)

original jurisdiction the authority of a court to hear a case first (10)

pardoning power a president's authority to release or excuse a person from the legal penalties of a crime (8)

parliamentary system government in which the executive is chosen by the legislature from among its members and the two branches are merged (4)

participatory democracy a theory of democracy that holds that citizens should actively and directly control all aspects of their lives (1)

partisanship loyalty to a political cause or party (12)

party activists the "party faithful"; the rank-and-file members who actually carry out the party's electioneering efforts (12)

party base members of a political party who consistently vote for that party's candidates (12)

party bosses party leaders, usually in an urban district, who exercised tight control over electioneering and patronage (12)

party caucus local gathering of party members to choose convention delegates (14)

party discipline ability of party leaders to bring party members in the legislature into line with the party program (12)

party eras extended periods of relative political stability in which one party tends to control both the presidency and Congress (12)

party identification voter affiliation with a political party (12)

party-in-government members of the party who have been elected to serve in government (12)

party-in-the-electorate ordinary citizens who identify with the party (12)

party machines mass-based party systems in which parties provided services and resources to voters in exchange for votes (12)

party organization the official structure that conducts the political business of parties (12)

party platform list of policy positions a party endorses and pledges its elected officials to enact (12)

party polarization greater ideological (liberal versus conservative) differences between the parties and increased ideological consensus within the parties (7)

party primary nomination of party candidates by registered party members rather than party bosses (12)

patronage system in which successful party candidates reward supporters with jobs or favors (9, 12)

peace dividend the expectation that reduced defense spending would result in additional funds for other programs (19)

Pendleton Act 1883 civil service reform that required the hiring and promoting of civil servants to be based on merit, not patronage (9)

permanent campaign the idea that governing requires a continual effort to convince the public to sign onto the program, requiring a reliance on consultants and an emphasis on politics over policy (15)

Plessy v. Ferguson Supreme Court case that established the constitutionality of the principle "separate but equal" (6)

pluralist democracy a theory of democracy that holds that citizen membership in groups is the key to political power (1)

pocket veto presidential authority to kill a bill submitted within ten days of the end of a legislative session by not signing it (7)

police power the ability of the government to protect its citizens and maintain social order (5)

policy entrepreneurship practice of legislators becoming experts and taking leadership roles in specific policy areas (7)

policy representation congressional work to advance the issues and ideological preferences of constituents (7)

political accountability the democratic principle that political leaders must answer to the public for their actions (15)

political action committees (PACs) the fundraising arms of interest groups (13)

political correctness the idea that language shapes behavior and therefore should be regulated to control its social effects (5)

political culture the broad pattern of ideas, beliefs, and values about citizens and government held by a population (2)

political efficacy citizens' feelings of effectiveness in political affairs (14)

political generations groups of citizens whose political views have been shaped by the common events of their youth (11)

political gridlock the stalemate that occurs when political rivals, especially parties, refuse to budge from their positions to achieve a compromise in the public interest (12)

political party a group of citizens united by ideology and seeking control of government in order to promote their ideas and policies (12)

political socialization the process by which we learn our political orientations and allegiances (11)

politics who gets what, when, and how; a process of determining how power and resources are distributed in a society without recourse to violence (1)

poll taxes taxes levied as a qualification for voting (6)

popular sovereignty the concept that the citizens are the ultimate source of political power (1, 3)

popular tyranny the unrestrained power of the people (3)

pork barrel public works projects and grants for specific districts paid for by general revenues (7)

position issues issues on which the parties differ in their perspectives and proposed solutions (14)

poverty threshold the income level below which a family is considered to be "poor" (17)

power the ability to get other people to do what you want (1)

power to persuade a president's ability to convince Congress, other political actors, and the public to cooperate with the administration's agenda (8)

precedent a previous decision or ruling that, in common law tradition, is binding on subsequent decisions (10)

preemption action that strikes and eliminates an enemy before it has a chance to strike you (19)

presidential primary an election by which voters choose convention delegates committed to voting for a certain candidate (14)

presidential style image projected by the president that represents how he would like to be perceived at home and abroad (8)

presidential system government in which the executive is chosen independently of the legislature and the two branches are separate (4)

presidential veto a president's authority to reject a bill passed by Congress; may be overridden only by a two-thirds majority in each house (8)

preventive war to use force without direct provocation in order to ensure that a chain of events does not unfold that could put you at immediate risk at some later date (19)

priming the way in which the media's emphasis on particular characteristics of people, events, or issues influences the public's perception of those people, events, or issues (15)

prior restraint censorship of or punishment for the expression of ideas before the ideas are printed or spoken (5)

Privacy Act of 1974 a law that gives citizens access to the government's files on them (9)

procedural due process procedural laws that protect the rights of individuals who must deal with the legal system (10)

procedural guarantees government assurance that the rules will work smoothly and treat everyone fairly, with no promise of particular outcomes (1, 2)

procedural laws laws that establish how laws are applied and enforced—how legal proceedings take place (10)

progressive taxes taxes whose rates increase with income (18)

propaganda the promotion of information, which may or may not be correct, designed to influence the beliefs and attitudes of a foreign audience (19)

prospective voting basing voting decisions on well-informed opinions and consideration of the future consequences of a given vote (14)

protectionism the imposition of trade barriers, especially tariffs, to make trading conditions favorable to domestic producers (18, 19)

Protestant Reformation the break from the Roman Catholic Church in the 1500s by those who believed in direct access to God and salvation by faith (1)

public interest groups groups that organize to influence government to produce collective goods or services that benefit the general public (13)

public opinion the collective attitudes and beliefs of individuals on one or more issues (11)

public opinion polls scientific efforts to estimate what an entire group thinks about an issue by asking a smaller sample of the group for its opinion (11)

public policy a government plan of action to solve a problem (17)

pundit a professional observer and commentator on politics (15)

push polls polls that ask for reactions to hypothetical, often false, information in order to manipulate public opinion (11)

racial gerrymandering redistricting to enhance or reduce the chances that a racial or ethnic group will elect members to the legislature (7)

racism institutionalized power inequalities in society based on the perception of racial differences (6)

random samples samples chosen in such a way that any member of the population being polled has an equal chance of being selected (11)

ratification the process through which a proposal is formally approved and adopted by vote (3)

rational ignorance the state of being uninformed about politics because of the cost in time and energy (11)

realignment substantial and long-term shift in party allegiance by individuals and groups, usually resulting in a change in policy direction (12)

reapportionment a reallocation of congressional seats among the states every ten years, following the census (7)

recall elections votes to remove elected officials from office (4, 16)

recession a decline in GDP for two consecutive quarters (18)

Reconstruction the period following the Civil War during which the federal government took action to rebuild the South (6)

redistributive policies policies that shift resources from the "haves" to the "have-nots" (17)

redistricting process of dividing states into legislative districts (7)

red tape the complex procedures and regulations surrounding bureaucratic activity (9)

referendum an election in which a bill passed by the state legislature is submitted to voters for approval (4, 16)

refugees individuals who flee an area or country because of persecution on the basis of race, nationality, religion, group membership, or political opinion (2)

regressive taxes taxes that require poor people to pay a higher proportion of their income than do the well off (18)

regulated capitalism a market system in which the government intervenes to protect rights and make procedural guarantees (1)

regulations limitations or restrictions on the activities of a business or individual (9)

regulatory policies policies designed to restrict or change the behavior of certain groups or individuals (17)

representation the efforts of elected officials to look out for the interests of those who elect them (7)

republic a government in which decisions are made through representatives of the people (1, 4)

responsible party model party government when four conditions are met: clear choice of ideologies, candidates pledged to implement ideas, party held accountable by voters, and party control over members (12)

retrospective voting basing voting decisions on reactions to past performance; approving the status quo or signaling a desire for change (14)

revolving door the tendency of public officials, journalists, and lobbyists to move between public and private sector (media, lobbying) jobs (13, 15)

rogue states countries that break international norms and produce, sell, or use weapons of mass destruction (19)

roll call votes publicly recorded votes on bills and amendments on the floor of the House or Senate (7)

Rule of Four the unwritten requirement that four Supreme Court justices must agree to grant a case certiorari in order for the case to be heard (10)

rules directives that specify how resources will be distributed or what procedures govern collective activity (1)

sample the portion of the population that is selected to participate in a poll (11)

sample bias the effect of having a sample that does not represent all segments of the population (11)

sampling error a number that indicates within what range the results of a poll are accurate (11)

sedition speech that criticizes the government (5)

segregation the practice and policy of separating races (6)

select committee a committee appointed to deal with an issue or problem not suited to a standing committee (7)

selective incentives benefits that are available only to group members as an inducement to get them to join (13)

selective incorporation incorporation of rights on a case-by-case basis (5)

selective perception the phenomenon of filtering incoming information through personal values and interests (15)

self-regulating market an ideal market that corrects itself when it moves in an inflationary or recessionary direction (18)

senatorial courtesy tradition of granting senior senators of the president's party considerable power over federal judicial appointments in their home states (8, 10)

seniority system the accumulation of power and authority in conjunction with the length of time spent in office (7)

separationists supporters of a "wall of separation" between church and state (5)

separation of powers the institutional arrangement that assigns judicial, executive, and legislative powers to different persons or groups, thereby limiting the powers of each (4)

sexual harassment unwelcome sexual speech or behavior that creates a hostile work environment (6)

Shays's Rebellion a grassroots uprising (1787) by armed Massachusetts farmers protesting foreclosures (3)

slavery the ownership, for forced labor, of one people by another (3)

social connectedness citizens' involvement in groups and their relationships to their communities and families (14)

social conservatives those who endorse limited government control of the economy but considerable government intervention to realize a traditional social order; based on religious values and hierarchy rather than equality (2)

social contract the notion that society is based on an agreement between government and the governed in which people agree to give up some rights in exchange for the protection of others (1)

social democracy a hybrid system combining a capitalist economy and a government that supports equality (1)

social insurance programs programs that offer benefits in exchange for contributions (17)

socialist economy an economic system in which the state determines production, distribution, and price decisions and property is government owned (1)

social liberals those who favor greater control of the economy and the social order to bring about greater equality and to regulate the effects of progress (2)

social order the way we organize and live our collective lives (1)

social policies distributive and redistributive policies that seek to improve the quality of citizens' lives (17)

social protest public activities designed to bring attention to political causes, usually generated by those without access to conventional means of expressing their views (13)

Social Security a social insurance program under which individuals make contributions during working years and collect benefits in retirement (17)

Social Security Act the New Deal Act that created AFDC, Social Security, and unemployment insurance (17)

social welfare policies public policies that seek to meet the basic needs of people who are unable to provide for themselves (17)

soft money unregulated campaign contributions by individuals, groups, or parties that promote general election activities but do not directly support individual candidates (12, 14)

solicitor general Justice Department officer who argues the government's cases before the Supreme Court (8, 10)

solidary benefits selective incentives related to the interaction and bonding among group members (13)

sound bite a brief, snappy excerpt from a public figure's speech that is easy to repeat on the news (15)

Speaker of the House the leader of the majority party who serves as the presiding officer of the House of Representatives (7)

spin an interpretation of a politician's words or actions, designed to present a favorable image (15)

spiral of silence the process by which a majority opinion becomes exaggerated because minorities do not feel comfortable speaking out in opposition (11)

spoils system the nineteenth-century practice of rewarding political supporters with public office (9)

standing committees permanent committees responsible for legislation in particular policy areas (7)

State of the Union address a speech given annually by the president to a joint session of Congress and to the nation announcing the president's agenda (8)

statutory laws laws passed by a state or the federal legislature (10)

strategic policy foreign policy that lays out a country's basic stance toward international actors or problems (19)

strategic politicians office-seekers who base the decision to run on a rational calculation that they will be successful (7)

straw polls polls that attempt to determine who is ahead in a political race (11)

strict constructionism a judicial approach holding that the Constitution should be read literally, with the framers' intentions uppermost in mind (10)

strict scrutiny a heightened standard of review used by the Supreme Court to assess the constitutionality of laws that limit some freedoms or that make a suspect classification (6)

structural defense policy foreign policy dealing with defense spending, military bases, and weapons procurement (19)

subjects individuals who are obliged to submit to a government authority against which they have no rights (1)

subsidy financial incentive given by the government to corporations, individuals, or other governments (17)

substantive guarantees government assurance of particular outcomes or results (1)

substantive laws laws whose content, or substance, defines what we can or cannot do (10)

sunshine laws legislation opening the process of bureaucratic policymaking to the public (9)

Superfund legislation designed to oversee the cleanup of toxic waste disposal sites (17)

super legislation the process of amending state constitutions to include interest groups' policy preferences (16)

superterrorism the potential use of weapons of mass destruction in a terrorist attack (19)

Supplemental Nutrition Assistance Program (SNAP) a federal program that provides food stamps to the poor to help them buy food (17)

supply side economics President Ronald Reagan's economic plan, by which tax cuts would ultimately generate more, not less, government revenues by allowing for increased investments and productivity (18)

supremacy clause constitutional declaration (Article VI) that the Constitution and laws made under its provisions are the supreme law of the land (4)

surpluses the extra funds available because government revenues are greater than its expenditures (18)

suspect classification classification, such as race, for which any discriminatory law must be justified by a compelling state interest (6)

swing voters the approximately one-third of the electorate who are undecided at the start of a campaign (14)

symbolic representation efforts of members of Congress to stand for American ideals or identify with common constituency values (7)

Temporary Assistance to Needy Families (TANF) a welfare program of block grants to states that encourages recipients to work in exchange for time-limited benefits (17)

terrorism an act of violence that targets civilians for the purpose of provoking widespread fear that will force government to change its policies (19)

Three-fifths Compromise the formula for counting five slaves as three people for purposes of representation that reconciled northern and southern factions at the Constitutional Convention (3)

totalitarian a system in which absolute power is exercised over every aspect of life (1)

tracking polls ongoing series of surveys that follow changes in public opinion over time (11)

trade deficit the difference between the value of the goods a country imports and what it exports (18)

traditionalistic political culture a political culture that expects government to maintain existing power structures and sees citizenship as stratified, with politicians coming from the social elite; South and Southwest (16)

treaties formal agreements with other countries; negotiated by the president and requiring approval by two-thirds of the Senate (8)

trial balloon an official leak of a proposal to determine public reaction to it without risk (15)

triggering event an external event that puts an issue onto the policy agenda (17)

Truman Doctrine policy of the United States starting in 1947 that the United States would aid free peoples to maintain their freedom in the face of aggressive communist movements (19)

two-step flow of information the process by which citizens take their political cues from more well-informed opinion leaders (11)

unfunded mandate a federal order mandating that states operate and pay for a program created at the national level (4, 16)

unicameral legislature a legislature with one chamber (4)

unified state court systems court systems organized and managed by a state supreme court (16)

unitary system government in which all power is centralized (4)

valence issues issues on which most voters and candidates share the same position (14)

value-added tax (VAT) a consumption tax levied at each stage of production, based on the value added to the product at that stage (18)

values central ideas, principles, or standards that most people agree are important (2)

veto override reversal of a presidential veto by a two-thirds vote in both houses of Congress (7)

Virginia Plan a proposal at the Constitutional Convention that congressional representation be based on population, thus favoring the large states (3)

voter mobilization a party's efforts to inform potential voters about issues and candidates and persuade them to vote (14)

weapons of mass destruction nuclear, biological, or chemical weapons that can kill huge numbers of people at one time (19)

wedge issue a controversial issue that one party uses to split the voters in the other party (14)

weighting adjustments to surveys during analysis so that selected demographic groups reflect their values in the population, usually as measured by the census (11)

whistleblowers individuals who publicize instances of fraud, corruption, or other wrongdoing in the bureaucracy (9)

White House Office the approximately four hundred employees within the EOP who work most closely and directly with the president (8)

World Bank economic institution that makes large, low-cost loans with long repayment terms to countries, primarily for infrastructure construction or repairs (19)

writs of certiorari formal requests by the U.S. Supreme Court to call up the lower court case it decides to hear on appeal (10)

Index

References in bold typeface denote defined terms. References ending with "f" or "t" denote figures and tables. References in italic typeface denote illustrations and photographs. Alphabetization is letter-by-letter (e.g., Socialist Party precedes Social networking).

B

C

S

Profile and Timeline Sources

Profiles in Citizenship

Chapter 1: Meagan Szydlowski spoke with Christine Barbour in July 2010.

Chapter 2: Esmeralda Santiago spoke with Christine Barbour and Gerald Wright on March 25, 2005.

Chapter 3: Newt Gingrich spoke with Christine Barbour on March 21, 2005.

Chapter 4: Mitch Daniels spoke with Christine Barbour and Gerald Wright on April 12, 2005.

Chapter 5: Bill Maher spoke with Christine Barbour and Gerald Wright on May 9, 2005.

Chapter 6: Ward Connerly spoke with Christine Barbour and Gerald Wright on April 1, 2005.

Chapter 7: Senator Jon Tester spoke with Christine Barbour and Gerald Wright on July 27, 2010.

Chapter 8: Rahm Emanuel spoke with Christine Barbour and Gerald Wright on May 17, 2005.

Chapter 9: Coleen Rowley spoke with Christine Barbour on March 28, 2005.

Chapter 10: Sandra Day O'Connor talked with Christine Barbour on March 3, 2005.

Chapter 11: Nate Silver spoke with Christine Barbour in July 2010.

Chapter 12: David Frum spoke with Christine Barbour and Gerald Wright on September 17, 2010.

Chapter 13: Wayne Pacelle talked with Christine Barbour on March 10, 2005.

Chapter 14: James Carville spoke with Christine Barbour and Gerald Wright June 21, 2005.

Chapter 15: Andrew Sullivan talked with Christine Barbour in August 2010.

Chapter 16: Bill Richardson spoke with Christine Barbour and Gerald Wright on July 22, 2008.

Chapter 17: Christine Todd Whitman spoke with Christine Barbour and Gerald Wright on April 22, 2005.

Chapter 18: Peter Orszag spoke with Christine Barbour and Gerald Wright on December 3, 2010.

Chapter 19: Joe Biden talked with Christine Barbour, Gerald Wright, and Patrick Haney on December 6, 2010.

Timelines

Chapter 2

Sources: http://memory.loc.gov/learn/features/immig/ irish2.html; www1.cuny.edu/portal_ur/content/nationofimmigrants/milestones.php, www.ourdocuments.gov/doc.php?flash= true&doc=47, and www.archives .gov/locations/finding-aids/chinese-immigration.html; http://lcweb2 .10c.gov/learn/features/immig/italian8.html, http://lcweb2.10c.gov/ learn/features/immig/italian6.html, and http://lcweb2.10c.gov/learn/ features/immig/italian3.html; www.usimmigrationsupport.org/cuba immigration.html; http://lcweb2.10c.gov/learn/features/immig/ mexican6. html, http://lcweb2.10c.gov/learn/features/immig/mexican8. html, and www.pbs.org/kpbs/theborder/history/timeline/17.html.

Chapter 3

Source: Kesselman, Mark, ed. *Introduction to Comparative Politics*, 4th ed. (Boston: Houghton Mifflin, 2007).

Chapter 4

Sources: www.yale.edu/lawweb/avalon/medieval/hammenu.htm; www .wsu.edu/~dee/ANCJAPAN/ANCJAPAN.HTM; Lutz, Donald. 1998. "The Iroquois Confederation Constitution: An Analysis." *Publius* 28, no. 2: 99–127.

Chapter 5

Sources: www.tsa.gov/index.shtm; http://topics.nytimes.com/top/news/ national/usstates territoriesandpossessions/guantanamobaynavalbase cuba/index.html?scp=1&sq=Guantanamo%20Bay&st=cse and www.nytimes .com/2008/06/13/washington/13gitmo.html; www.dhs.gov/index.shtm; www.nytimes.com/2008/07/10/washington/10fisa.html?_r=1&oref=login and http://topics.nytimes.com/top/reference/timestopics/subjects/f/ foreign_intelligence_surveillance_act_fisa/index.html?scp=1-spot&sq= FISA&st=cse; http://topics.nytimes.com/top/reference/timestopics/ subjects/t/torture/waterboarding/index.html?scp=1-spot&sq=water boarding&st=cse and www.nytimes.com/2007/10/04/washington/ 04interrogate.html.

Chapter 6

Sources: www.nps.gov/nr/travel/civilrights/a14.htm; http://clnet.ucla .edu/research/chavez/bio and www.ufw.org/_page.php?inc=history/07 .html&menu=research; www.nps.gov/history/museum/exhibits/alca/ indian.html and www.pbs.org/itvs/alcatrazisnotanisland/activism.html; Carter, David, *Stonewall: The Riots that Sparked the Gay Revolution* (New York: Macmillan, 2005).

Chapter 7

Sources: www.ed.gov/pubs/TitleIX/part3.html; Dorothy Stetson *Women's Rights in the USA* (New York: Routledge, 2004); http://nwlc.org/ pdf/whatsatstake.pdf; http://chronicle.com/free/v48/i41/41a03801.htm; http://nwlc.org/pdf/whatsatstake.pdf.

Chapter 8

Source: The White House Historical Association, www. whitehouse history.org; David Stewart, *Summer of 1787: The Men Who Invented the Constitution* (New York: Simon and Schuster, 2007).

Chapter 11

Sources: Dennis Jamison, "Political Polls in the Early 1900s: Early History of Political Polls in Presidential Elections," http://modern-us-history.suite101.com/article.cfm/political_polls_in_the_early1900s; Philip Pollock, *The Essentials of Political Analysis* (Washington, D.C.: CQ Press, 2005), 96–97; Anthony G. Greenwald, Department of Psychology, University of Washington, http://faculty.washington.edu/agg/Bradley_&_Reverse_Bradley.6Feb08.pdf.

Chapter 13

Sources: www.wctu.org/earlyhistory.html; Clift, Eleanor, *Founding Sisters and the 19th Amendment* (New York: Wiley and Sons, 2003); www.now.org/history/index.html; www.eagleforum.org/misc/descript.html; www.equalrightsamendment.org/era.htm; Stetson, Dorothy, *Women's Rights in the USA*, 3e (New York: Routledge, 2003); and www.catwinternational.org/about/index.php#history.

Chapter 14

Source: Mosk, Matthew. "As Campaigns Chafe at Limits, Donors Might Be in Diapers." Washington Post 10/24/2007: A06; The Campaign Legal Center, www.campaignfinanceguide.org/guide-17.html; The Federal Election Commission, www.fec.gov/ans/answers_general.shtml.

Chapter 15

Sources: www.museum.tv/exhibitionssection.php?page=79; www.museum.tv/archives/etv/K/htmlK/kennedy-nixon/kennedy-nixon.htm.

Chapter 16

Source: www.cbsnews.com/stories/2003/10/23/60minutes/main579696.shtml.

Chapter 17

Sources: www.servintfree.net/~aidmn-ejournal/publications/2001–11/PublicEducationInTheUnitedStates.html; www.ssa.gov/history/briefhistory3.html; www.fns.usda.gov/FSP/rules/Legislation/about_fsp.htm; www.thehistoryof.net/history-of-student-loans.html; www.cms.hhs.gov/home/schip.asp.

Chapter 18

Sources: www.treasury.gov/education/fact-sheets/taxes/ustax.shtml; www.treasury.gov/education/fact-sheets/taxes/ustax.shtml; www.fhwa.dot.gov/infrastructure/gastax.cfm; www.taxfoundation.org/research/show/245.html; www.treasury.gov/education/fact-sheets/taxes/ustax.shtml.

Illustration Credits

Front matter

vii   Official White House Photo by David Lienemann

Chapter 1

2   iStockPhoto

4   AP Images

7   Getty Images

9   Reuters

10   Mary Marin/iStockphoto

14   AP Images

15   Courtesy of Christine Barbour

19   AP Images

24   Chip Bok Editorial Cartoon used with the permission of Chip Bok and Creators Syndicate. All rights reserved.

Chapter 2

30   Corbis

32   AP Images

35   Steve Kelley Editorial Cartoon ©Steve Kelley. Used with the permission of Creators Syndicate. All rights reserved.

37   AP Images

38   Photo by Frank Cantor

43   By permission of Mike Luckovich and Creators Syndicate, Inc.

51   AP Images

Chapter 3

64   Getty Images/Brendan Smialowski

66   AP Images

69   For Better or For Worse © 1998 Lynn Johnston Productions. Dist. By Universal Uclick. Reprinted with permission. All rights reserved.

72   The Granger Collection, New York

73   The Granger Collection, New York

77   By permission of Michael Ramirez and Creators Syndicate, Inc.

78   The Granger Collection, New York

82   The Granger Collection, New York

88   Getty Images/Chip Somodevilla

90   © Sidney Harris

Chapter 4

96   Library of Congress

98   AP Images

99   Calvin and Hobbes © 1990 Watterson. Dist. By Universal Uclick. Reprinted with permission. All rights reserved.

102   AP Images

105   AP Images

106   © Tribune Media Services, Inc. All Rights Reserved. Reprinted with permission.

115   © 2008 Paresh Nath, The *National Herald*, India, and PoliticalCartoons.com

120   The Granger Collection, New York

123   AP Images

128   AP Images

130   David Ulmer/Stock Boston

Chapter 5

136   Vespasian/Alamy Images

138   Clay Jones, The *Freelance Star*

141   AP Images

143   The Granger Collection, New York

145   © 2007 RJ Matson, The *St. Louis Post Dispatch*, and PoliticalCartoons.com

152   Doug Potter/*Austin Chronicle*

156   ©Mark Godfrey / The Image Works

158   Photo by Darla Khazei/Wenn/Landov

162   Corbis

168   Getty Images

169   Reuters

170   AP Images

172   The Collection of the Supreme Court of the United States

178   Reuters

Chapter 6

186   Getty Images

188   Chip Somodevilla/Getty Images

195   Corbis

197   (left) Corbis; (right) Will Counts Collections, Indiana University Archives

201   AP Images

205   Library of Congress

208   AP Images

212   © Kevin Fleming/Corbis

213   Robyn Beck/AFP/Getty Images

224   © From the collection of Christine Barbour

225   AP Images

229   Reuters

Chapter 7

238   iStockphoto

240   © CinemaPhoto/Corbis

250   Library of Congress

252   Eric Miller/Reuters/Corbis

254   Tom Williams/*Roll Call*/Getty Images

257   Saul Loeb/AFP/Getty Images

265   LBJ Library

279   Ann Telnaes Editorial Cartoon used with the permission of Ann Telnaes, Women's eNews and the Cartoonist Group. All rights reserved.

280   The Boondocks © 2002 Aaron McGruder. Dist. By Universal Uclick. Reprinted with permission. All rights reserved.

Chapter 8

286   iStockphoto

288   Reuters